ALSO BY SIMON SCHAMA

Patriots and Liberators: Revolution in the Netherlands 1780 – 1813

Two Rothschilds and the Land of Israel

The Embarrassment of Riches:
An Interpretation of Dutch Culture in the Golden Age

ITIZENS

A Chronicle of the French Revolution

Simon Schama

VIKING

VIKING

Published by the Penguin Group
27 Wrights Lane, London W8 5TZ, England
Viking Penguin Inc., 40 West 23rd Street, New York, New York 10010, USA
Penguin Books Australia Ltd, Ringwood, Victoria, Australia
Penguin Books Canada Ltd, 2801 John Street, Markham, Ontario, Canada L3R 1B4
Penguin Books (NZ) Ltd, 182-190 Wairau Road, Auckland 10, New Zealand
Penguin Books Ltd, Registered Offices: Harmondsworth, Middlesex, England

First published in the USA by Alfred A. Knopf, Inc., New York 1989
First published in Great Britain by Viking 1989
1 3 5 7 9 10 8 6 4 2

Copyright © Simon Schama, 1989
Maps © Jean Paul Tremblay, 1989

Printed in the United States of America
A CIP catalogue record for this book is available from the British Library
ISBN 0-670-81012-6

FOR JACK PLUMB

J'avais rêvé une république que tout le monde eût adorée. Je n'ai pu croire que les hommes fussent si féroces et si injustes.

—CAMILLE DESMOULINS
to his wife from prison
April 4, 1794

. . . 'Twas in truth an hour
Of universal ferment; mildest men
Were agitated; and commotions, strife
Of passion and opinion fill'd the walls
Of peaceful houses with unquiet sounds.
The soil of common life was at that time
Too hot to tread upon; oft said I then,
And not then only, 'what a mockery this
Of history; the past and that to come!
Now do I feel how I have been deceived,
Reading of Nations and their works, in faith,
Faith given to vanity and emptiness;
Oh! laughter for the Page that would reflect
To future times the face of what now is!'

—WILLIAM WORDSWORTH
The Prelude (1805 text)
Book IX 164–77

L'histoire accueille et renouvelle ces gloires déshéritées; elle donne nouvelle vie à ces morts, les ressuscite. Sa justice associe ainsi ceux qui n'ont pas vécu en même temps, fait réparation à plusieurs qui n'avaient paru qu'un moment pour disparaître. Ils vivent maintenant avec nous qui nous sentons leurs parents, leurs amis. Ainsi se fait une famille, une cité commune entre les vivants et les morts.

—JULES MICHELET
Preface to *Histoire
du XIXe Siécle,* Vol. II

Contents

Contents

ix

Contents

Contents

ENGLAND

DUTCH
REPUBLIC

Calais

Boulogne
BOULONNAIS

FLANDERS

AUSTRIAN
NETHERLANDS

Lille

ARTOIS AND

Abbeville

Arras

HAINAULT

ENGLISH CHANNEL

Cherbourg

Dunkirk

Amiens

PICARDY

Le Havre

Forges-
les-Eaux

Sedan

METZ AND VERDUN

Rouen

ILE-DE-FRANCE

Reims

Verdun

Metz

Seine

Paris

Marne

LORRAINE

Nancy

Quimper

BRITTANY

NORMANDY

CHAMPAGNE

ALSACE

Rhine

Rennes

MAINE

Strasbourg

Le Mans

ORLÉANAIS

Troyes

ANJOU

Orléans

Angers

Nantes

Tours

Loire

Saumur

TOURAINE

Bourges

NIVERNAIS

Dijon

FRANCHE-

SAUMUROIS

BERRY

Nevers

Besançon

BURGUNDY

COMTÉ

POITOU

Poitiers

Moulins

SWITZERLAND

La Rochelle

AUNIS

BOURBONNAIS

Guéret

Saintes

Angoulême

MARCHE

Clermont-
Ferrand

LYONNAIS

SAVOY

ATLANTIC

SAINTONGE

ANGOUMOIS

Limoges

Lyon

OCEAN

LIMOUSIN

AUVERGNE

Seine

Grenoble

Bordeaux

Dordogne

DAUPHINÉ

PIEDMONT

Garonne

GUIENNE AND GASCONY

Rhône

COMTAT
VENAISSIN

Avignon

Pau

Toulouse

PROVENCE

NAVARRE AND
BÉARN

LANGUEDOC

Aix

Marseille

Foix

FOIX

Perpignan

SPAIN

ROUSSILLON

Bastia

CORSICA

Ancien-Régime France:
Provinces, Major Cities and Towns

0   100 Miles
0   100 Kilometers

MEDITERRANEAN SEA

Preface

ASKED WHAT he thought was the significance of the French Revolution, the Chinese Premier Zhou En-lai is reported to have answered, "It's too soon to tell." Two hundred years may still be too soon (or, possibly, too late) to tell.

Historians have been overconfident about the wisdom to be gained by distance, believing it somehow confers objectivity, one of those unattainable values in which they have placed so much faith. Perhaps there is something to be said for proximity. Lord Acton, who delivered the first, famous lectures on the French Revolution at Cambridge in the 1870s, was still able to hear firsthand, from a member of the Orléans dynasty, the man's recollection of "Dumouriez gibbering on the streets of London when hearing the news of Waterloo."

Suspicion that blind partisanship fatally damaged the great Romantic narratives of the first half of the nineteenth century dominated scholarly reaction during the second half. As historians institutionalized themselves into an academic profession, they came to believe conscientious research in the archives could confer dispassion: the prerequisite for winkling out the mysterious truths of cause and effect. The desired effect was to be scientific rather than poetic, impersonal rather than impassioned. And while, for some time, historical narratives remained preoccupied by the life cycle of the European nation-states—wars, treaties and dethronements—the magnetic pull of social science was such that "structures," both social and political, seemed to become the principal objects of inquiry.

In the case of the French Revolution this meant transferring attention away from the events and personalities that had dominated the epic chronicles of the 1830s and 1840s. De Tocqueville's luminous account, *The Old Regime and the Revolution,* the product of his own archival research, provided cool reason where before there had been the burning quarrels of partisanship. The Olympian quality of his insights reinforced (albeit from a liberal point of view) the Marxist-scientific claim that the significance of the Revolution was to be sought in some great change in the balance of social power. In both these views, the utterances of orators were little more than vaporous claptrap, unsuccessfully disguising their helplessness at the hands of impersonal historical forces. Likewise, the ebb and flow of events could only be made intelligible by being displayed to reveal the *essential*, primarily social, truths of the Revolution. At the core of those truths was an axiom, shared by liberals, socialists and for that matter nostalgic Christian royalists alike, that the Revolution had indeed been the crucible of modernity: the vessel in which all the characteristics of the modern social world, for good or ill, had been distilled.

By the same token, if the whole event was of this epochal significance, then the causes that generated it had necessarily to be of an equivalent magnitude. A phenomenon of such uncontrollable power that it apparently swept away an entire universe of traditional customs, mentalities and institutions could only have been produced by contradictions that lay embedded deep within the fabric of the "old regime." Accordingly, weighty volumes appeared, between the centennial of 1889 and the Second World War, documenting every aspect of those structural faults. Biographies of Danton and Mirabeau disappeared, at least from respectable scholarly presses, and were replaced by studies of price fluctuations in the grain market. At a later stage still, discrete social groups placed in articulated opposition to each other—the "bourgeoisie," "sans-culottes,"—were defined and anatomized and their dialectical dance routines were made the exclusive choreography of revolutionary politics.

In the fifty years since the sesquicentennial, there has been a serious loss of confidence in this approach. The drastic social changes imputed to the Revolution seem less clear-cut or actually not apparent at all. The "bourgeoisie" said in the classic Marxist accounts to have been the authors and beneficiaries of the event have become social zombies, the product of historiographical obsessions rather than historical realities. Other alterations in the modernization of French society and institutions seem to have been anticipated by the reform of the "old regime." Continuities seem as marked as discontinuities.

Nor does the Revolution seem any longer to conform to a grand historical design, preordained by inexorable forces of social change. Instead it seems a thing of contingencies and unforeseen consequences (not least the summoning of the Estates-General itself). An abundance of fine provincial studies has shown that instead of a single Revolution imposed by Paris on the rest of a homogeneous France, it was as often determined by local passions and interests. Along with the revival of place as a conditioner have come people. For as the imperatives of "structure" have weakened, those of individual agency, and especially of revolutionary utterance, have become correspondingly more important.

Citizens is an attempt to synthesize much of this reappraisal and to push the argument a stage further. I have pressed one of the essential elements in de Tocqueville's argument—his understanding of the destabilizing effects of modernization *before* the Revolution—further than his account allows it to go. Relieved of the revolutionary coinage "old regime," with its heavy semantic freight of obsolescence, it may be possible to see French culture and society in the reign of Louis XVI as troubled more by its addiction to change than by resistance to it. Conversely, it seems to me that much of the anger firing revolutionary violence arose from hostility towards that modernization, rather than from impatience with the speed of its progress.

The account given in the pages that follow, then, emphasizes, possibly excessively, the dynamic aspects of prerevolutionary France without turning a blind eye to the genuinely obstructive and archaic. Important to its argument is the claim that a patriotic culture of citizenship was created in the decades after the Seven Years' War, and that it was thus a cause rather than a product of the French Revolution.

Three themes are developed in the course of this argument. The first concerns the problematic relationship between patriotism and liberty, which, in the Revolution, turns into a brutal competition between the power of the state and the effervescence of politics. The second theme turns on the eighteenth-century belief that citizenship was, in part, the public expression of an idealized family. The stereotyping of moral relations between the sexes, parents and children, and brothers, turns out, perhaps unexpectedly, to be a significant clue to revolutionary behavior. Finally, the book attempts to confront directly the painful problem of revolutionary violence. Anxious lest they give way to sensationalism or be confused with counter-revolutionary prosecutors, historians have erred on the side of squeamishness in dealing with this issue. I have returned it to the center of the story since it seems to me that it was not merely an unfortunate by-product of politics, or the disagreeable instrument by which other more virtuous ends were accomplished or vicious ones were thwarted. In some depressingly unavoidable sense, violence *was* the Revolution itself.

I have chosen to present these arguments in the form of a narrative. If, in fact, the Revolution was a much more haphazard and chaotic event and much more the product of human agency than structural conditioning, chronology seems indispensable in making its complicated twists and turns intelligible. So *Citizens* returns, then, to the form of the nineteenth-century chronicles, allowing different issues and interests to shape the flow of the story as they arise, year after year, month after month. I have also, perhaps perversely, deliberately eschewed the conventional "survey" format by which various aspects of the society of the old regime are canvassed before attempting political description. Placing those imposing chapters on "the economy," "the peasantry," "the nobility" and the like at the front of books automatically, it seems to me, privileges their explanatory force. I have not, I hope, ignored any of these social groups, but have tried to introduce them at the points in the narrative where they affect the course of events. This, in turn, has dictated an unfashionable "top down" rather than "bottom up" approach.

Narratives have been described, by Hayden White among others, as a kind of fictional device used by the historian to impose a reassuring order on randomly arriving bits of information about the dead. There is a certain truth to this alarming insight, but my own point of departure was provided by a richly suggestive article by David Carr in *History and Theory* (1986), in which he argued a quite different and ingenious case for the validity of the narrative. As artificial as written narratives might be, they often correspond to ways in which historical actors construct events. That is to say, many, if not most, public men see their conduct as in part situated between role models from an heroic past and expectations of the judgment of posterity. If ever this was true, it was surely so for the revolutionary generation in France. Cato, Cicero and Junius Brutus stood at the shoulders of Mirabeau, Vergniaud and Robespierre, but very often they beckoned their devotees towards conduct that would be judged by the generations of the future.

Finally, the narrative, as will be obvious, weaves between the private and public lives of the citizens who appear on its pages. This is done not only in an attempt to understand their motivation more deeply than pure public utterance allows, but also because so many of them, often to their ruin, saw their own lives as a seamless whole, their calendar of birth, love, ambition and death imprinted on the almanac of great events. This necessary interconnection between personal and public histories was self-evident in many of the nineteenth-century narratives and, to the extent that I have followed their precedent, what I have to offer, too, runs the risk of being seen as a mischievously old-fashioned piece of storytelling. It differs from the pre-Tocquevillian narratives in being offered more as witness than judgment. But like those earlier accounts it tries to listen attentively to the voice of the citizens whose lives it describes, even when those voices are at their most cacophonous. In this sense too it opts for chaotic authenticity over the commanding neatness of historical convention.

I T W A S Richard Cobb who first preached the "Biographical Approach" to the history of the Revolution twenty years ago, though he mostly had in mind the unsung victims of revolutionary turmoil rather than those who had been responsible for it. I hope, then, he won't take amiss my own declaration of allegiance to that approach. From his unforgettable seminar in Balliol College in the late 1960s, I learned to try to see the Revolution not as a march of abstractions and ideologies but as a human event of complicated and often tragic outcomes. Other members of that seminar—Colin Lucas; Olwen Hufton, now my colleague at Harvard University; and Marianne Elliott—have over the years been an enormous source of enlightenment and scholarly friendship, for which this book is a rather blundering gesture of gratitude.

One of my greatest debts is to another of my colleagues, Patrice Higonnet, who has been kind enough to read the manuscript and save me from many (though I fear not all) errors and muddles. Much of what I have to say, especially concerning the group I call the "citizen-nobility," owes its point of departure to his important and original work *Class, Ideology and the Rights of Nobles During the French Revolution* (Oxford, 1981). Other friends—John Brewer, John Clive and David Harris Sacks—also read parts of the work and were, as always, generous with their comments and helpful with their criticisms.

My preoccupation with reexamining the oratory of the Revolution, and with the self-consciousness of the political elite, originates with a paper given to the Consortium on Revolutionary Europe at Charleston, South Carolina, in 1979. I am most grateful to Owen Connelly for inviting me to participate in a memorable panel that also included Elisabeth Eisenstein and George V. Taylor. It was at Charleston that long conversations with Lynn Hunt helped stimulate my interest in the force of revolutionary language and I am grateful to her and to Tom Laqueur for their interest and encouragement since. Robert Darnton, whose first book on Mesmerism and the late Enlightenment set me thinking many years ago about the sources of revolutionary truculence, on far more occasions than he deserves has had to hear me out. He has always offered helpful advice and gentle correction and has been a constant source of inspiration.

The book could not have been written without the posthumous help of one of Harvard's most extraordinary scholars: Archibald Cary Coolidge, University Librarian in the 1920s. By buying the entire library of Alphonse Aulard, the first professor of the history of the Revolution at the Sorbonne, Coolidge created a priceless resource for scholars working in this field: a collection as rich in newspapers and pamphlets as it is in extremely rare and obscure works of local history. I am most grateful, as always, to the splendid staff of the Houghton Library, without whose patience and efficiency hard-pressed professors would find it impossible to do research in a busy teaching year. Susan Reinstein Rogers and her colleagues at the Kress Library of the Harvard Business School have been helpful as always and provided superb photographs from their spectacular editions of the *Description des Arts et Métiers*.

I am also most grateful to Philippe Bordes of the Musée de la Révolution Française at Vizille for help in tracking material connected with the Day of Tiles. Mrs. Perry Rathbone was kind enough to allow me to include an illustration of her Hubert Robert drawing of Desmoulins. Emma Whitelaw reminded me of the importance of Mme de La Tour du Pin's memoirs.

Many colleagues and students contributed generously with time, patience and friendship to making this book possible when it seemed impossible, in particular Judith Coffin, Roy Mottahedeh and Margaret Talbot. I am also grateful to Philip Katz for allowing me to read his remarkable undergraduate dissertation on the iconology of Benjamin Franklin. Friends at the Center for European Studies, especially Abby Collins, Guido Goldman, Stanley Hoffmann and Charles Maier, have all kept me on the rails at the many moments when I have threatened to go careening off them and have restrained their incredulity at this whole enterprise in the most collegial way.

At Alfred A. Knopf, I owe a great debt of gratitude to my editor Carol Janeway for spurring me on to finish the book and for keeping the faith that it would, indeed, get done. Robin Swados has been a pillar of strength in every possible way, and I am also most grateful to Nancy Clements and Iris Weinstein for seeing the work through to its final version. Peter Matson in New York and Michael Sissons in London have, as usual, been enormously supportive at all times and have both demonstrated that fine literary agents also make good friends.

Fiona Grigg did virtually everything for this book except write it. Her help with picture research, proofreading, museum diplomacy and soothing ragged nerves with generous helpings of intelligence and goodwill made the whole work possible. I can never thank her enough for her collaboration.

Throughout the writing of the book my children, Chloë and Gabriel, and my wife, Ginny, endured far more in the way of uneven temper, eccentric hours and generally impossible behavior than they had any right to expect. In return I received from them love and tolerance in helpings more generous than I deserved. Ginny has throughout offered her infallible judgments on all kinds of questions about the book, from its argument to its design. If there is any one reader to whom all my writing is addressed, it is to her.

Peter Carson of Penguin Books first suggested to me the idea of writing a history of the French Revolution, and when I responded by mooting the idea of a full-blooded narrative along what were already eccentric lines, he never flinched. I am most grateful to him for all his support and encouragement over the years, though I fear the end result is not exactly what he originally had in mind.

The idea that I might tackle this subject, however, came from my old friend and teacher Jack Plumb. I believe he urged me to do it in the vain hope that, at last, I might be capable of writing a short book. I am sorry to disappoint him in so overwhelming a way, but I hope he will see in this book's expansiveness some of his own concern that history should be synthesis as well as analysis, chronicle as well as text. He also encouraged me to ignore conventional barriers that have grown up like intellectual barbed wire about the subdivisions of our discipline, and I hope he enjoys this attempt to tear those fences down. Most of all he taught me that to write history without the play of imagination is to dig in an intellectual graveyard, so that in *Citizens* I have tried to bring a world to life rather than entomb it in erudite discourse. Since whatever virtues there may be in the book owe so much to his teaching, it is dedicated to him with great affection and friendship.

Lexington, Massachusetts
1988

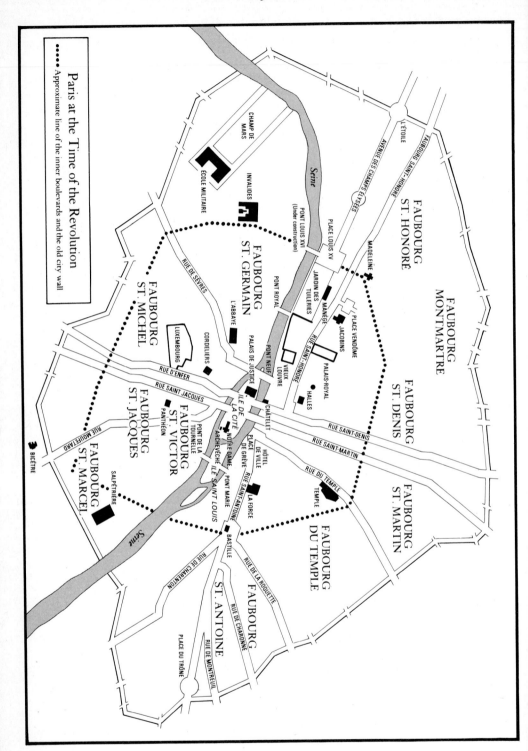

Paris at the Time of the Revolution

••••• Approximate line of the inner boulevards and the old city wall

CITIZENS

1. Jean-Antoine Alavoine, watercolor drawing for the project of the elephant
in the place de la Bastille

Powers of Recall—
Forty Years Later

ETWEEN 1814 and 1846 a plaster elephant stood on the site of the Bastille. For much of this time it presented a sorry spectacle. Pilgrims in search of revolutionary inspiration were brought up short at the sight of it, massive and lugubrious, at the southeast end of the square. By 1830, when revolution revisited Paris, the elephant was in an advanced state of decomposition. One tusk had dropped off, and the other was reduced to a powdery stump. Its body was black from rain and soot and its eyes had sunk, beyond all natural resemblance, into the furrows and pockmarks of its large, eroded head.

This was not what Napoleon had intended. Concerned with obliterating the revolutionary memory, he had first thought of siting a grand triumphal arch on the empty space vacated by the demolished fortress. But eastern Paris was unfashionable, and the decision was taken to move the arch to the west of the city instead. Rummaging around in the fancies of antiquity, Napoleon came up with another idea that would signify, just as decisively, he believed, the superiority of imperial conquest over chaotic insurrection. Never mind that elephants belonged to the defeated party in the Punic Wars. For the grab-bag Emperor they suggested Alexander as much as Hannibal, the trophies of Egypt, the tricolor flying from Acre to Lisbon. The elephant would be cast in bronze taken from enemy cannon in Spain and would be large enough so that visitors could ascend by an interior staircase to the tower it would carry on its back. Water would splash from its trunk. It would be heroic and delightful and all who beheld it would forget the 1789, forget the Bastille and immerse themselves instead in imperial self-congratulation.

But 1789, the beginning of the French Revolution, has always remained more memorable than 1799, when Bonaparte proclaimed its end. The Bastille and its conquerors have been commemorated, while the elephant has been forgotten. In fact, from its very beginning, it was doomed to suffer hubris. Counsels among those delegated with the unenviable commission were divided, and by the time that some consensus was reached, the fortunes of empire had changed. Victories in Spain were dearly bought and they were followed by slaughters so expensive that they were indistinguishable from defeats. By 1813, when the elephant was to have been erected, cannon could not be spared and neither could hard cash. So instead of a bronze monolith, a plaster model went up on the place de la Bastille pending final plans for a grand remodeling of the site.

Initially it must have been hard to ignore. Standing as high as a three-story house, the Elephant of Revolutionary Oblivion stood sentinel over the seditious memories of angry crowds, popular demolitions, royal humiliations. So when the Empire collapsed for good after Waterloo, the Bourbon governments of the Restoration, with their fear of revolutionary memories, had good use for the distraction it provided. But it was now to be sculpted in peaceful marble rather than warlike bronze, and to be surrounded with other more conventional allegorical monuments: representations of Paris, of the seasons, of useful arts and sciences such as surgery, history and dance. Ministers who dreamed of new empires in North Africa may even have found elephantine allusions to Carthage timely. But if the late Empire had been hard up, the Restoration (and especially Louis XVIII) was skinflint. All that they could afford was the eight hundred francs paid to a watchman named Levasseur who survived denunciation as a Bonapartist and took up residence with the rats in one moldering leg of the creature.

The *concierge* of the elephant might stand guard against vandals or against surreptitious celebrations of the memory of 1789. But he could not fight off the revenge of time. The place de la Bastille was an urban wilderness: a mudhole in winter, a dustbowl in summer. Excavations for the Canal d'Ourcq and repeated efforts to level the space had left the elephant steadily sinking into a boggy depression as though gradually subsiding with age and exhaustion. Nature then added its own indignities. As the plaster hulk crumbled, its plinth became overgrown by dandelions and thistles. Great cavities opened in the torso, beckoning rodents, stray cats and overnight vagrants. The rat problem became so serious that local residents found their own houses colonized by raiding parties sent out from the elephant. From the late 1820s they regularly but unsuccessfully petitioned for its demolition. The authorities of the Restoration remained in a quandary. Perhaps it could be repainted and reinstalled somewhere more innocuous like the Invalides or even the Tuileries. But nervousness prevailed. The elephant or what was left of it stayed.

Only in 1832, after the revolutionary memory had been taken to the streets in the uprising that replaced the Bourbons with the "Citizen King" Louis-Philippe, was the elephant joined, at the other end of the square, by a tall column (still there) memorializing not 1789 but the fallen dead of the 1830 July Revolution. It was not until 1846 that the coup de grâce finally put the disintegrating hulk out of its misery. And as if memory had been freed from this prison, a new revolution and a new republic followed swiftly on.

The Elephant of Deliberate Forgetfulness was, then, no match for the Persistence of Revolutionary Memory. But refreshed recollection is at least as difficult as historical amnesia. The French Revolution was, after all, a great demolition, and repeated attempts to monumentalize it have been doomed by the contradiction in terms. Yet attempts there have been, starting with the Jacobin "Fountain of Regeneration" erected in 1793: a plaster version of the Goddess Isis from whose breasts spouted (on ceremonial occasions) the milk of Liberty. At the "Festival of Unity" that commemorated the fall of the monarchy, the President of the Convention, Hérault de Séchelles, drank this republican libation from a custom-designed goblet which he raised to the assembled crowd in salutation. Eight years later, the fountain collapsed into rubble and was taken away in carts. Other projects—a new town hall, a people's theater, a legislative assembly—were all mooted and all discarded. Instead, there remained a gaping space at the precise frontier between patrician Paris and artisan Paris: a no-man's-land of the historical memory.

Commemoration has been easiest when least monumental. Annual pyrotechnics and dancing on the fourteenth of July have served better than grandiose architectural projects. But it was the feat of the first generation of Romantic historians to celebrate the Revolution by lighting bonfires in their prose. Even as the elephant was slowly turning to dust and rubble, Jules Michelet's triumphal narrative made of the Revolution a kind of spectacular performance, at once scripture, drama and invocation. Other chronicles followed—by Lamartine, Victor Hugo—none of them quite drowning out the mighty tympanum of Michelet's epic. The culmination was history as mimesis: Lamartine addressing the crowds in yet a third revolution: that of 1848.

The apotheosis of Romantic history was also its death-wish. In 1850, as the Second Republic's own rhetorical vapor disappeared before the hard, inexorable realities of money, power and state violence, a great historical cooling-down occurred. In 1848, throughout Europe, but especially bloodily in Paris, revolutionary rhetoric had been vanquished at the barricades by counter-revolutionary calculation; passion had been mastered by dispassion, artisans by artillery. Unsurprisingly, then, written history turned from lyric engagement to scientific analysis, from unblushing subjectivity to cool objectivity. Where once the success of revolution had seemed to turn on spontaneous embrace, it now seemed to depend on lucid understanding. Beginning with Alexis de Tocqueville and Karl Marx (albeit in very different ways), historians endeavored to give their accounts scientific rigor. For the first time they turned away from the bewitching drama of events—the surface brilliance of the historical record—to probe deeper into archival sources or general laws of social behavior. The causes of the French Revolution were depersonalized, cut loose from the speech and conduct of Great Men and instead located deep within the structure of the society that preceded it. Class rather than utterance, bread rather than belief, was taken to be the determinant of allegiance. Scientific—or at least sociological—history had arrived and with it, the demotion of chronicle to anecdotal unimportance. So for a long time now, cloaked in the mantle of rigorous objectivity, historians have busied themselves with structure; with cause and effect; with probabilities and contingencies; with pie charts and bar-graphs; with semiotics and anthropologies; with microhistories of *départements*, districts, cantons, villages, hamlets.

What follows (I need hardly say) is not science. It has no pretensions to dispassion. Though in no sense fiction (for there is no deliberate invention), it may well strike the reader as story rather than history. It is an exercise in animated description, a negotiation with a two-hundred-year memory without any pretense of definitive closure. And both the form of its telling and its chosen subject matter represent a deliberate turning away from analytical history towards Events and Persons, both long forbidden, or dismissed as mere froth on the great waves of history. It is a narrative not by default but by choice: a beginning, middle and end that tries to resonate with its protagonists' own overdeveloped sense of past, present and posterity. For it is not in the least fortuitous that the creation of the modern political world coincided precisely with the birth of the modern novel.

M o s t revolutionary histories present themselves as linear: a passage in time from oldness to newness. But they can hardly avoid circularity. In its early usage, *revolution* was a metaphor drawn from astronomy, signifying the periodic turning of the spheres. It implied predictability, not unpredictability. "The World Turned Upside Down," as the popular anthem of the American Revolution was called, paradoxically implied an adjustment to its becoming right side up. Correspondingly, the men of 1776 (and still more the framers of the Constitution) were more concerned with preserving order than with perpetuating change. Some of the same nervousness was apparent in France in the way the men of 1789 used the word. But in their case, its transformative rhetoric overwhelmed any apprehensive second thoughts. Curiously, those who hoped for *limited* change in 1789 were the most given to the hyperbole of the irreversible. And from that time on *revolution* would be a word of inauguration, not repetition.

It was in 1830 that the "French Revolution" became a transferable entity. It was no longer a finite series of events, anchored to a particular historical mooring (say, 1789–94). Instead, the memory (primarily written, but also sung, engraved, spoken) constructed political reality. All along, there had been a strain of Romantic recollection which had coped with the actual obliteration of much of the French Revolution by proclaiming its immortality in patriotic memory. Attempting to galvanize a country already under occupation in 1815, Napoleon, who had been the Revolution's most enthusiastic gravedigger, tried to wake it from the tomb. Wrapping himself in revolutionary slogans and emblems, he tried to invoke the fear and comradeship of 1792: *la patrie en danger.* But Waterloo was to finish off what the Battle of Valmy had begun.

Returned to the throne by foreign invasion, the Bourbons appreciated that all hope of their legitimacy turned on an act of prudential forgetting. Their first king, Louis XVIII, with his supremely bourgeois appetites for money and gourmandizing, was good at political forgetfulness. He scarcely balked at appointing ministers who had served the Revolution and the Empire and avoided altogether a formal coronation. But his brother Charles X was himself the captive of a much more restless memory. As he went out of his way to affront the revolutionary past—by having himself crowned with all the traditional ritual in Reims Cathedral—so he stirred revolutionary ghosts from their tomb of memory. Although he was haunted by those memories, his behavior guaranteed their reappearance. His last, most recalcitrant minister was a Polignac from perhaps the most universally hated aristocratic clan of the 1780s. In 1830, arbitrary decrees recalled those of 1788, and to confront them, the bundle of emotive rallying cries, costumes, flags and songs that had been handed like an historical parcel across the generations reconstituted itself at the barricades.

There was much to provoke popular anger in 1830. A trade depression with its automatic high bread prices and unemployment had caused groups of angry artisans to assemble in the faubourg Saint-Antoine to listen to journalists and orators denounce the government. But what triggered their emotions and fired their determination was the exposure of revolutionary mementos like holy relics: the tricolor that was flown again from Notre Dame; bodies bayoneted by royal troops, paraded in their bloodied winding sheets through the streets as an incitement to revolt. Once more the Hôtel de Ville was besieged by cabinetmakers, hatters and glove makers from the faubourg Saint-Antoine, this time impeded on their march west by nothing more than the scabby rump of a plaster elephant. The "Marseillaise" sounded again, the red hats of liberty (no more anachronistic in 1830 than they had been in 1789) were thrust onto unwigged heads and rusty ten-pound cannon were again hauled over the cobbles. A Duc d'Orléans once again plotted (this time successfully) to be the beneficiary of the demise of a Bourbon king. Even Maréchal Marmont, charged with the defense of Paris, seemed imprisoned in this historical reverie. On seeing the allegiance of the military disintegrate he could find nothing better to say to his king than to repeat, verbatim, the words of the Duc de La Rochefoucauld-Liancourt to Louis XVI on July 15, 1789: "Sire, this is not a riot, it is a revolution." But while Louis had completely failed to grasp the significance of transformed political vocabulary, Charles X knew precisely what these words portended. He had read the script. He had read the histories. Even his fate was preordained to repeat not Louis' but his own conduct in 1789, for he had been quick to depart then, and he was even quicker now.

If the lines were the same, the lead players had aged badly. The advanced years of many of the principals of the July Revolution of 1830 were an embarrassment. "Bliss was it in that dawn to be alive, but to be old was to be level-headed" would not do. Veterans were playing the leads that should have gone to promising juveniles. Revolutions are the empire of the young. Michelet, who had been born four years after the Terror, lectured on rejuvenation to classrooms packed with doting students. In his fiery narrative, the youths of 1789 had taken green sprigs for favors in the garden of the Palais-Royal on July 12 as a signal of the springtime of a new France. The old men of the Bastille were cast only as villains or victims: the Invalides guards who manned the towers; the Comte de Solages (detained by his own family), whose usefully poignant white beard, shrunken form and immemorial wrinkles seemed to indict, by mere appearance, the longevity of despotism. By the lights of the mentor of revolution, Rousseau, to be young was to be innocent and unstained, so that the proper object of revolution should be to liberate the child of nature trapped in the carapace of maturity. Rousseau's most ardent young disciples in the Revolution had consumed themselves with Virtue and then killed each other before suffering the disenchantment of long memories. The Terror even beatified the dead, but deathless, young. The immortal Bara, aged thirteen, was shot rather than surrender horses to rebels he called "brigands"; the Young Darruder saw his father fall on the battlefield, picked up his drum and led the charge. Camille Desmoulins was already a revolutionary veteran at twenty-eight when he perished at the hands of Saint-Just, who was himself guillotined at twenty-six.

Superannuated revolutionaries were hard to take seriously. They ran the risk of ridicule, from which no revolution can properly recover. The men who made 1830 possible—students from the Polytechnique, journeymen-printers and national guardsmen—were certainly a new generation. And if the journalists and liberal politicians who committed themselves to a violent change of regime were not in their first bloom of youth, neither were they dodderers. But the major actors of the July days (and to a greater extent the "Notables" who composed the new elite of the constitutional monarchy—bankers, bureaucrats and lawyers) were conspicuously long in the tooth. Daumier's scathing caricatures of bald pates and pinched cheeks, of paunches and withered hams, were dangerously closer to the reality than Delacroix's athletic Liberty at the barricades. Throughout 1830 and for the next two decades, the old were frightened by the young, the cerebral intimidated by the visceral. The Revolution and the Restoration it deposed were historical curiosities, exhumed from the past, costumed afresh for their encounter but with old bones rattling inside the fancy dress. The ostentatiously pious King, Charles X, was a feeble reincarnation of his notorious old persona, the Comte d'Artois, who had been the most dashing of the Versailles bloods: a notorious rakehell at the hunt and in the ballroom and in bed. He had spat in the eye of the revolution of '89, had trampled cockades underfoot and made *"O Richard mon roi"* the anthem of the counter-revolution. The incoming Prince, Louis-Philippe, a flabby facsimile of his regicide father "Philippe Egalité," circulated his memoirs in an effort to present himself as the young citizen-soldier of the revolutionary armies at Jemappes in 1792, but to little avail. And he created the Gallery of Battles at Versailles with painting after painting by Horace Vernet designed to identify him with the virility of French arms. But to the wider public, who chuckled at the caricatures of Philipon and Daumier, the protecting sword of France—*la Joyeuse*—was comically transmogrified into Louis-Philippe's ubiquitous umbrella. Even worse, the figure of majesty had resolved itself into the lethally absurd shape of a pear.

While it was a misfortune to be old in 1830, age alone did not dictate comportment. For two particular septuagenarian walking histories, the call of revolutionary memory meant very different things. To Gilbert de Lafayette, Hero of the Two Worlds, a boyish and spry seventy-three, it meant delusions of youth, passion rekindled and the pumping of the pulse. To

2. Charles Philipon, "Les Poires," from *Charivari*

physiognomists, it must have seemed that his complexion suggested a temper designed for ignition. And Lafayette complemented his perennially ruddy glow with a wiry reddish wig, which together announced that the fire of revolutionary action was still smoldering within.

In contrast to Lafayette's revolutionary sanguine, Maurice de Talleyrand, Prince de Bénévent, presented to the world an exterior of imperturbable phlegm. At seventy-five he was two years Lafayette's senior and at least as rich in revolutionary memories. This latest crisis seemed tiresomely déjà vu, but nonetheless an occasion for careful maneuver and the avoidance of anything impulsive. While one old man heard the cock crowing over France reborn, the other heard the "Marseillaise" as cacophony, disturbing his calm twilight. For Lafayette the moment sang of celebrity, for Talleyrand it murmured a low profile. And while Lafayette rode towards Paris to appear before the adoring throng, Talleyrand removed the bronze nameplate from the front of his town house to avoid recognition.

Lafayette took his memory seriously and he knew how to use it as a weapon. Suitably edited to exclude the embarrassments, which were as many as his triumphs, his revolutionary recall was a last summons by posterity. "Rest assured," he promised the crowds in 1830, "my conduct at the age of 73 will be the same as it was at the age of 32." "The Restoration took as its motto 'Unite and Forget,' " he told a legion of the National Guard; "I will take as mine, 'Unite and Remember.' " And remember he did. In Grenoble, at one of the many banquets that marked his triumphal progress across France, he responded to a toast by reminding the citizenry of their "Day of Tiles" in 1787, when they had confronted royal troops. It was because he had been commander of the National Guard in 1789 that the nervous leaders of the opposition thought his resumption of the office would be a prudent move. Lafayette duly donned his old uniform and with disingenuous modesty announced in public that "a veteran may be of some service in our present grave crisis." When he arrived at the Hôtel de Ville amidst a riotous crowd as commander of the National Guard, a well-meaning officer attempted to show him the route. "I know my way," he replied with heavy emphasis, "I have been here before."

Most of all he remembered how to greet the revolutionary muse: with a fraternal embrace. And so Lafayette kissed the tricolor; he kissed his Guard officers; he kissed the Duc d'Orléans as he gave him his benediction.

3. Charles de Larivière, Lafayette greeting Louis-Philippe at the Hôtel de Ville

He kissed the new age with so much ardor that his kissing became notorious and men giggled about him as the incorrigible "Père Biseur." But how many have three apotheoses in a single lifetime? Accustomed to occupy center stage, Lafayette understood instinctively the call of political theater: of gestures, and body language, of physical as well as verbal rhetoric enacted at crucial moments. In America on a last triumphal progress just five years before, he had become the first creation of populist politics, transformed into "Marcus D. Lafayette," reveling in the applause and rose petals that rained down on him from Maine to Virginia; tirelessly pressing flesh, shaking hands till his were raw; and with transparent sincerity repeating over and over again before ecstatic crowds: "Zo appy; zo appy." Before the swarm of people at the Hôtel de Ville, many of them seeing in the old Marshal their chance for a republic, he draped Louis-Philippe in the tricolor as though it were the toga of his constitutionalism and shoved him unceremoniously to the balcony. In that one vaudeville gesture Lafayette stole the show and drew the teeth of republicanism. He undoubtedly remembered the dismay of Louis XVI when a mere cockade was stuck on his hat in the aftermath of the fall of the Bastille. For a king who would survive, nothing less than a great tricolor winding sheet was necessary.

Lafayette was the Great Reminder. In 1815, when, even after the disaster at Waterloo, there was an attempt to preserve the Napoleonic Empire, he delivered a devastating speech that summoned as witnesses for the prosecution the ghosts of millions of soldiers left to die by the Great Man in Egypt, Russia and Germany. In America he always sought to reinforce, by constant reminders of fraternal liberties, a friendship that had badly eroded since 1783. It was for that reason that he presented a key from the Bastille to George Washington. For Lafayette, memory was the spur to action, and revolution was itself part of the process of perpetual renewal, a way in which France could recover its *élan vital*.

Talleyrand was not interested in the birdsong of political springtimes. He had become comfortably reconciled to political winter. His own memories left him exhausted rather than elated, and Romantic dash had always been out of the question. His lame foot had hobbled him since he was a baby and he had long learned to cultivate a kind of studied languor that irritated the second-rate. All his life, he had been anathema to any apostle of Rousseau, for he placed his trust in disguise rather than candor, civility rather than spontaneity, reflection rather than impulse, diplomacy rather than aggression, negotiation behind closed doors rather than orations to public meetings. Forever being written off as a political fossil, an archaic survival of the *ancien régime*, he knew better than most that all these arts were required as much by the political future as by the past.

4. Jean-Baptiste Belliard, portrait of Talleyrand

In 1830 he yearned for nothing better, for himself and for France, than a quiet life. At Valençay, his stunningly beautiful Renaissance château, he played the provincial squire, installed as mayor and experimenting with new varieties of escarole and carrot and tending his nursery of Scotch pines. At Rochecotte, the house of his much younger companion Dorothée de Dino, he enjoyed even simpler pleasures, sampling peaches from his own grafts, which he ate with Brie, the "King of Cheeses" ("the only King to whom he has been loyal," said one of his many detractors). In Paris he rarely stirred from the great *hôtel* on the rue Saint-Florentin where he sat propped up on thicknesses of pillows (even in bed, for he was much afraid of falling at night and concussing himself), nibbling on a biscuit, sipping his Madeira and reading, without the help of spectacles, from his immense and spectacular private library. For Talleyrand was still fastidious, his thick hair powdered and teased into white ringlets, his wattles crammed into a high Directory collar, his famous retroussée nose (which he could still cock like a deadly weapon) subject to a peculiar rinsing operation at the end of the one meal he allowed himself each day.

To Ary Scheffer, who painted him in 1828, he seems to have looked like death in black silk. But like some immensely aged and formidable tortoise, Talleyrand was able to make the most of life by treating it with deliberateness and caution. This is why the purblind stupidity of Charles X so exasperated him. For in his reckless determination to confront all but the most reactionary bigots he had condemned France to yet another period of "anarchy, a revolutionary war, and all the other evils from which France had been rescued with so much difficulty in 1815." If revolution came to Lafayette as an onrush of feeling, an elixir of youth, for Talleyrand, the tocsin sounded an alarm in his intelligence. For Lafayette 1830 had to be the harbinger of Freedom and Democracy, not just for France but for the whole world (and especially Poland). For Talleyrand the only point to a change of regime was damage control.

If Lafayette's brilliantly histrionic business with the tricolor flag and his benediction before the crowds—"*Voilà la meilleure des républiques*" (Behold the best of republics)—had been, in effect, Louis-Philippe's popular coronation, Talleyrand (who had been present at all three coronations of Louis XVI, Napoleon and Charles X) supplied the nominee. So that while Lafayette was at center stage, it was Talleyrand who in every sense controlled the action behind the scenes. The two men had always occupied this curiously symbiotic relationship, actor and producer, performer and puppeteer, and they had always disagreed wherein lay the reality of revolutionary power. For Lafayette utterances, forms, costumes, symbols and a missionary belief in Just Causes constituted the only historical epic worth remembering. For Talleyrand these same symbolic constructions were history's mummeries, potions for the credulous, the secular mumbo-jumbo that had replaced that of relics and miracles. Such performances were circus antics, simultaneously indispensable and spurious. He had seen Lafayette on a white horse before: when, as commander of the National Guard, he was the focal point of 400,000 revolutionary enthusiasts as he took the oath to the Nation on the Champ de Mars on the fourteenth of July 1790. But it was Talleyrand, the Citizen-Bishop of Autun, who had written the Mass that gave this ceremony its benediction and Talleyrand who went on calculating. For while Lafayette bathed in the radiance of revolutionary celebrity, Talleyrand broke the bank at the card tables.

While once more Lafayette played to the gallery, Talleyrand played the stock exchange ("*Jouez à la baisse,*" he recommended to friends three days before the street fighting in Paris). Equally, their mopping-up operations were in striking, but related, contrast. Lafayette compensated for his desertion of the republican cause in 1830 by proclaiming messianic revolutionary internationalism and the immediate liberation of Poland. Talleyrand took up his last official post in 1830 as French ambassador to London, where he went about putting out the fires that Lafayette had so freely kindled and promising his old doppelgänger from Vienna, the Duke of Wellington, that Louis-Philippe's most dangerous weapon was a furled umbrella. *Tout va bien.*

In their own persons, Lafayette and Talleyrand embodied the split personality of the French Revolution. For while it is commonplace to recognize that the Revolution gave birth to a new kind of political world, it is less often understood that that world was the product of two irreconcilable interests—the creation of a potent state and the creation of a community of free citizens. The fiction of the Revolution was to imagine that each might be served without damaging the other and its history amounts to the realization of that impossibility.

It would be the worst possible mistake, though, to assume at the outset an unduly ironic tone towards the more idealistic of these goals. Talleyrand, who was wont to do just that, was by a sublime irony the indirect grandfather of the most enduring of all the images of revolutionary exaltation: Eugène Delacroix's *Liberty Leading the People.* Standing on the rubble of a barricade, his bare-breasted Marianne of the People, wearing the red hat of the sans-culottes, urges workers and students towards the indeterminate destination of revolutionary arcadia. Notre Dame de la Liberté is framed against the background of Notre Dame de Paris, already conquered for Freedom, the tricolor flying from its towers.

And Talleyrand? What had he to do with this thunderbolt in oils, so

5. Eugène Delacroix, *Liberty Leading the People*, 1830

viscerally stirring that Louis-Philippe took fright and bought Delacroix's painting so that he could hide it away from public view for a generation? Talleyrand had not brought this imperishable revolutionary embarrassment into the world but he had, it seems, created Eugène Delacroix. In the revolutionary year VI (1798), as the first revolution was quietly being put to sleep by its corrupt custodians in Paris and kicked to death by its generalissimi in the field, Talleyrand had been more than usually mischievous. Replacing the Republic's Minister for Foreign Affairs, Charles Delacroix (who had been exiled to the unenviable dreariness of the French Embassy at The Hague), Talleyrand also replaced him in the bed of Mme Delacroix. She was, we may assume, receptive to his advances, for her husband had been for some time incapacitated by a monstrous goiter that extended from his belly to his groin. Its successful excision by the most brilliant surgeons in Paris was a medical *cause célèbre* and the deformity of M. Delacroix a widely publicized historical event. Talleyrand's own deformity, his limping broken foot dragging along its specially designed shoe, had never been an obstacle to his success as a lover. He believed that power and intelligence were the perfume of courtship and he wielded them with deadly charm. Mme Delacroix duly succumbed. Their progeny was the prodigy Eugène, the greatest Romantic of the new age sired by the most formidable skeptic of the old.

Blood of revolutionary passion then issued from flesh of revolutionary intelligence. Those two tempers—rhetorical and rational, visceral and cerebral, sentimental and brutal—shall not be separated in this history. Indeed, it was from their imperfect union that a new politics was born.

Part One

ALTERATIONS
THE FRANCE OF LOUIS XVI

6. Anonymous portrait of Talleyrand at age 16

CHAPTER ONE
New Men

i FATHERS AND SONS

N THE brilliant spring of 1778, Talleyrand went to pay his respects to Voltaire. Even in a society where the worldliness of the clergy was notorious, this was a little unseemly. The ink had hardly dried on his theology degree from the Sorbonne before the young priest, already the holder of a benefice in Rheims, and a delegate to the Assembly of the Clergy, hastened to do homage to the most notorious scourge of the Church. The visit had a flavor of filial impiety to it since Talleyrand was undoubtedly in search of a father figure more satisfactory than his natural parents. It was they who had placed him in the hands of a nurse and she who had let him drop from a cabinet, crushing a bone in his foot that would never mend. Disgraced as a cripple, the young Talleyrand was, in effect, also disinherited. For a boy who could neither fence nor dance could never hope to succeed either at court or in the army, the only two callings proper for a scion of the line of Périgord. Only one course was possible: a career in the Church, where he might rise in wealth and eminence, but for which, it was plain early on, he had the deepest aversion. At the Collège d'Harcourt, where he was sent at the age of seven, he was commanded to obey and to believe, whereas all his instincts and his intelligence urged him to disobey and to question. At the seminary of Saint-Sulpice he was further required to respect authority. Instead he began collecting a library of works by the most skeptical Enlightenment philosophers as well as fruity pornography, prominently featuring the libidos of priests and nuns. Destined by his misfortunes and his intellectual inclinations to be an outsider, he was drawn to other outsiders. On a wet night in 1771, after Mass, he offered his umbrella to a young actress of Jewish origins, Dorothée Dorinville, known on the stage of the Comédie-Française as Luzy. It was the first in a long line of *amours* and possibly the most tender: the heretical seminarian limping along in his black soutane with the pious convert, to what he called her "sanctuary" in the rue Férou.

For Talleyrand, the meeting with Voltaire was a kind of paternal benediction: a laying of gnarled hands on long, perfumed blond hair. Sixty years separated antigodfather from acolyte, the twenty-three-year-old from the eighty-four-year-old. While the worldly young cleric was seeking the courage of his convictions, the old philosopher was drawing a veil over his. Exiled from France for twenty-seven years, Voltaire had returned in February 1778 to a noisy and public apotheosis. He was ancient and unwell, and the long trip from Ferney over the Swiss border had not helped his infirmities. Periodically, in the town house of the Marquis de Villette, where he stayed, there would be a coughing fit of sputum and blood. Dr. Tronchin, the famous Swiss physician who had moved to France partly to attend his famous patients (the other being Rousseau), would be summoned. Expressions of anxiety would be made in the press. But Voltaire was determined to survive long enough to enjoy the adoration of young disciples who flocked to see him, and the embarrassment of older, fair-weather friends who now came to him for comfort and absolution. Yet whatever his own mixed feelings, he showed only his most gracious aspect to the admirers who lined up to be ushered into his presence. "I may be suffocated," he mock-complained, "but it will be beneath a shower of roses."

When the weather and his own health improved enough for him to venture out he appeared at the Théâtre-Français to direct rehearsals for his tragedy *Irène.* At the opening on March 16 all the royal family, except the King himself, was present to greet the author. And at the end of the sixth performance, on March 30, a specially commissioned portrait bust by Caffieri was placed on stage and was crowned with laurel by the actors. All the audience rose in standing ovation while the old man drank in the applause. He made no secret of enjoying this preliminary immortalization. Even his deathbed at the end of May was turned into a semipublic event, with *le tout Paris* watching to see if he would succumb to the wiles of the confessor who, to the very last, attempted an orthodox rite of absolution, rather than the artfully noncommittal formula Voltaire had devised—"I die in the Catholic religion into which I was born." Even his reputed last words refusing to deny the Devil ("Is this a time to make enemies?") were strictly apocryphal, the actual parting rebuff to the dogged priest being almost as good: "Leave me to die in peace."

So there was something slightly worshipful about Talleyrand's visit. Some accounts even have him kneeling before Voltaire in sacrilegious

7. Charles-Etienne Gaucher (after Moreau le Jeune), *The Crowning of Voltaire at the Théâtre-Français*, 1778

veneration. And there is no doubt that the worldly young priest idolized the wicked old deist whose battle cry had been *"Écrasez l'infâme"* (crush the infamous—meaning the Church). He was brought to the Hôtel de la Villette in the rue de Beaune by his school friend the Chevalier de Chamfort. Talleyrand was led into a small room, almost completely darkened except for one shutter, strategically opened to permit a single ray of sunlight to play on the cracked, puckish features of Voltaire: the Enlightenment illuminated. For a moment, the young man's fastidiousness was disconcerted, even repelled, by the spectacle of spindly legs and bony feet protruding from a loose dressing gown. Somewhere in the gloom Voltaire's niece, Mme Denis, no longer, if she had ever been, *belle et bonne*, busied herself with the chocolate, and wisps of sweet vapor curled about the room as the philosopher politely and admiringly inquired about the family in Périgord. From this banal beginning, Voltaire gathered conversational momentum, so that it seemed to his impressionable young admirer that the famous *esprit* took wing. Words "flew from him, so rapid, so neat, yet so distinct and so clear. . . . He spoke quickly and nervously with a play of features I have never seen in any man except him. . . . His eye kindled with vivid fire, almost dazzling." Everything was as anticipated: the brilliantly animated cranium talked and talked at his silent and devoted disciple. It was one of the decisive moments of Talleyrand's life. "Every line of that remarkable countenance is engraved in my memory," he remembered in his own old age. "I see it now before me—the small fiery eyes staring from shrunken sockets not unlike those of a chameleon." And although in the time it took to get to the Palais-Royal after the audience, Talleyrand forgot exactly *what* it was that Voltaire had said to him, he never forgot the manner in which it was addressed nor the peculiar gentleness of his leave-taking. It was, he said, a paternal farewell.

F OR TALLEYRAND, the Revolution may have begun with this consecration of unbelief in the rue de Beaune. For Lafayette it began with an act of faith. For France, without any question, the Revolution began in America.

While Talleyrand was kneeling at the feet of his intellectual patron, Lafayette was shivering at Valley Forge, Pennsylvania. There, among the "little shanties, scarcely gayer than dungeon cells," that housed the pathetic remnant of the Continental Army, the twenty-year-old Marquis had found his surrogate father in the imposing shape of George Washington. His first account of the General written to his wife Adrienne after meeting with Washington in Philadelphia the previous July described him as "a quiet reserved gentleman old enough to be my father" though easily distinguished "by the majesty of his face and figure." And it was during what Lafayette called "the great conversation" of October 14, 1777—perhaps to compensate for being unable to give the Marquis the division for which he hungered—that Washington remarked that he would be pleased to have his confidence "as a friend and a father." However casually the Virginian may have let slip this gentle compliment, it was Lafayette's moment of epiphany. Henceforth he was the adopted son, devoted, almost to the point of slavishness, to the cause of his new father, the *patrie* and the *pater* now tied tightly together in an emotional knot.

If Talleyrand had thought himself a virtual orphan, "the only man of distinguished birth and belonging to a numerous family . . . who never enjoyed for a week of his life the joy of living beneath the paternal roof," Lafayette felt his own loss with a keener pang. When Lafayette was two his father, a colonel in the Grenadiers de la France, had been killed in the Battle of Minden. His uncle had likewise been killed at the siege of Milan in 1733 during the War of Polish Succession. So that young Gilbert was

brought up on the Auvergne estate of Chavaniac, his head swimming with
dreams of martial glory. Near to the château were some fields known to the
peasants as the "champs de bataille" and there Lafayette communed with
the shades of Vercingetorix armed for the fray. But if his head was filled
with historical romance, his heart was bent on dynastic vindication. Much
later he would discover the identity of, and seek out, the Major Philips who
had commanded the battery that had mown down his papa's regiment. But
as an adolescent it was enough for him to respond to the American cause
as a perfect opportunity for revenge: both for the humiliations suffered by
France in the Seven Years' War and for his family's particular share in those
losses. In October 1777 he wrote to the French Foreign Minister, Vergennes,
who was as yet proceeding in a pro-American policy with the utmost
circumspection:

> firmly persuaded that to harm England is to serve (dare I say
> revenge) my country I believe in the idea of putting to work all
> the resources of every individual who has the honor to be French.

Pater and *patrie* were collapsed into one passion burning in the sentimental breast of the orphaned Marquis (for his mother had died in 1770
when he was just thirteen). And the same martial restlessness affected many
of his contemporaries. "We were tired of the *longueur* of the peace that had
lasted ten years," wrote Lafayette's fellow volunteer the Comte de Ségur,
"and each of us burned with a desire to repair the affronts of the last wars,
to fight the English and to fly to help the American cause." Experience of
Louis XV's court at Versailles, where Lafayette's wealth and connections
(including his marriage at fourteen into the great clan of the Noailles)
dictated an appearance, did nothing to quench these emotional dissatisfac-
tions. While not crippled like Talleyrand, Lafayette was so ungainly on the
dance floor that he might as well have been. Acutely aware of his provincial
lack of polish, he already felt that his raw qualities were as much assets as
handicaps in that they had preserved for him the qualities of natural manli-
ness. "The awkwardness of my manner while not out of place during great
events," he later wrote in his memoirs, "did not enable me to stoop to the
graces of the Court."

It was the same inability to live with the trappings, rather than the
substance, of military life that spurred him on further to some sort of *action
d'éclat.* By 1775 he had had enough of the horseplay that passed for boldness
among his circle of rich, aristocratic friends at their favored inn, the Epée
de Bois. Among this "Company of the Wooden Sword" were to be found
a number of young men—La Rochefoucauld, Noailles, Ségur—who were

not only to embrace the cause of the American "Insurgents" but who were to be among the most conspicuous citizen-nobles of 1789. And it was while Lafayette was serving with another military noble of advanced ideas, the Duc de Broglie, that he determined to use his enormous fortune (120,000 livres a year, inherited from his maternal grandfather) to transform un-formed stirrings into concrete action. Ironically, de Broglie had under-taken, as the comrade of Lafayette's father, to keep an eye on the restless young man and to deter him from anything so foolhardy that it might jeopardize what remained of the male line of the family. But following an eloquent advocacy of the American cause by none other than George III's own brother the Duke of Gloucester, Lafayette's commitment was such that, after attempting to reason with him, de Broglie resigned himself to accepting (or at least not physically preventing) some sort of American adventure. Indeed so far from detaining Lafayette, de Broglie actually decided, with Ségur and Noailles, to follow in his train.

The causes of personal, family and patriotic vindication, allied to a pre-Romantic thirst for glory, were paramount in motivating Lafayette to fit out the *Victoire* and sail for America in the autumn of 1777. But there was another, scarcely less vital element in his decision, and that was his deeply felt allegiance to the cause of "Liberty." By his own account, this came early and it came naturally. Indeed it is the Romantic vein of his autobiography, which depicts the young Marquis as a child of nature empathizing with the free and untamed, that gives the best clue to his subsequent political infatua-tions. The craggy, forested uplands of the Auvergne where he grew up were about as far from the urbane civilities of Parisian society as could be imagined, and in that setting Lafayette's Romantic imagination was left to run happily wild. In 1765, when he was eight, a beast known as the "hyena of the Gévaudan," described in warning notices as "of the size of a young bull," was not only slaughtering livestock but reputedly "attacking by preference women and children and drinking their blood." Bands of peas-ants were sent in pursuit of this "monster," but the boy Lafayette identified with the fugitive carnivore and together with a friend roamed the woods in the hope of a chance encounter. "Even at the age of eight," he wrote, "my heart beat in sympathy with the hyena." Years later, when attending the ex-Jesuit Collège du Plessis in Paris, he was asked to write an essay describing the perfect horse. In response, Lafayette eulogized an animal that bucked, reared and unseated his rider as soon as he sensed the whip—a piece of impertinence for which he himself was duly flogged.

Lafayette's creative insubordination at the Collège is of more than anec-dotal importance. Since the days of the great riding instructor Pluvinel in the reign of Henri IV, the mastery of equitation had been both metaphor

8. The hyena of the Gévaudan, 1764–65

and a literal preparation for the exercise of public power. From Richelieu onwards a succession of rulers had learned through the didactic parallel between horsemanship and statesmanship the importance of self-control, the breaking of the spirit and the display of authority. But during the 1760s, the growing cult of Sensibility, with its dramatic emphasis on the natural rather than the tutored, and on freedom rather than discipline, had supplied an alternative model for social and even political conduct. And what began with childish acts of sympathy for recalcitrant animals would not long after flower in a generalized preference for liberty over authority, spontaneity over calculation, candor over artifice, friendship over hierarchy, heart over head and nature over culture. That was the making of a revolutionary temper. "You will admit, my heart," Lafayette wrote to Adrienne as he was about to embark on the *Victoire*,

> that the business and life for which I am bound, are very different from those for which I was destined in that futile Italian journey [a Grand Tour of cultural sights]. Defender of that liberty which I worship, utterly free in my own person and going as a friend to offer my services to the most interesting of Republics, bringing to the service only my candor and goodwill without ambition or ulterior motive. Working for my own glory will become working for their happiness.

For many of Lafayette's contemporaries in the French nobility, America corresponded precisely to their ideal vision of a society happily separated from the cynicism and decrepitude of the Old World. Its landscape, lovingly described by Abbé Delaporte, even its savages, hopelessly idealized on the Paris stage in plays like Billardon de Sauvigny's *Hirza ou les Illinois*, and its settlers all represented to greater and lesser degrees the admired qualities of innocence, rugged directness and freedom. On arriving in Charleston in the summer of 1777, Lafayette claimed already to see this unspoiled fraternity in the local inhabitants. (The fact of a strong Huguenot presence probably reinforced the impression.) "They are as friendly as my enthusiasm had made me picture them," he reported back to Adrienne. "Simplicity of manners, willingness to oblige, love of country and of liberty and an easy equality prevail here. The richest and the poorest are on the same level and although there are immense fortunes, I defy anyone to find the least difference in their bearing toward each other."

In George Washington, all these qualities were writ large, and added to them in Lafayette's eyes were the virtues of the heroes of antiquity: stoicism, fortitude in adversity, personal bravery and self-sacrifice; incorruptibility; lack of personal ambition; contempt for faction and intrigue; loftiness of soul; even the taciturn reserve that rebuked the insincere loquacity of Old World manners. Indeed a great part of Lafayette's decision to remain in America, despite the disappointment of not receiving his coveted division, and when many of his French companions were preparing to return home, stemmed from his burning determination to prove himself in the eyes of his father figure. Blooded in combat at Brandywine Creek, he shared the rigors of Valley Forge and agreed to lead a manifestly futile expedition north to Canada through the winter snows. Adhesive in his attachment to Washington, he took it upon himself to defend the General from the captious attacks of rivals and critics in the Continental Army. He waxed indignant at anyone presuming to compare General Gates with Washington, and if anything, the naive passion of his defense gained from the fractured English in which it was expressed.

> Which marches, which movements, what has he done to compare him to that hero who at the head of sixteen hundred peasants pursued last winter a strong disciplined army through an open and vast country—to that great general who is born for the salavation of his country and the admiration of the universe? Yes, Sir, that very same campaign of last winter would do one of the finest part of the life of Caesar, Condé, Turenne, and those men whose any soldier cannot pronounce the name without an entousiastik adoration.

Reflected in the doting gaze of the adopted son, Washington became the paragon of all virtues: martial, personal and political. To a striking degree he resembled the perfect leader because he also appeared to be the perfect father: simultaneously strong and compassionate, just and solicitous; the Citizen-General who cared paternally for his men, and by extension for the new nation. And although Washington was initially disconcerted by the ardor of Lafayette's puppylike devotion, he accustomed himself, and not without some pleasure, to the role of surrogate father. When Lafayette was wounded, he made sure that he saw his own personal physician. He took a direct and active interest in Lafayette's wife and family and sincerely commiserated with him at the death of his daughter in France. In return Adrienne Lafayette embroidered a Masonic apron for the General (for this was another bond the two men shared, the Marquis having joined, aptly enough, the lodge Saint-Jean de la Candeur in 1775). And Washington wore this apron when he presided over the supremely Masonic act of laying the foundation stone of the Capitol. Not surprisingly, Lafayette named his first son (born in 1780) George Washington "as a tribute of love and respect for my dear friend." (A daughter was named Virginia.) And later George Junior would be sent to Mount Vernon to be tutored by his namesake when Lafayette's paternal responsibilities were constrained by an Austrian prison. At times, indeed, the lines of paternity became complicated. One possibly not apocryphal anecdote claims that when a young American officer was due to return home from France, he called on Mme Lafayette to see if he could bring her husband any messages. And their small son is supposed to have responded, *"Faites mon amour à mon papa Fayette et à mon papa Washington."*

ii HEROES FOR THE TIMES

Had Washington's aura of paternal authority only influenced Lafayette, it would still be of more than purely biographical importance, for it gave the rich and impressionable boy an heroic role-model that would affect his own public persona at crucial moments in French history, not least in 1789 and 1830. Yet the American general's reputation had far wider and more potent celebrity as the embodiment of a new kind of citizen-soldier: the reincarnation of Roman republican heroes. And there was an additional important element in his extraordinary appeal in France (as well as elsewhere in Europe). The secular religion of Sensibility, in part imported from England, with its emphasis on emotional truth, candor and naturalness, had received its definitive form in Rousseau's sentimental writings in the early 1760s. One of the many important consequences of this revolution in moral taste was the purification of egotism. With the ascendancy of Romanticism, sentimental personality cults became possible. Paradoxically, the more apparently self-effacing and modest the subject, the more potent his celebrity. And in this formula patriotism and parenthood were inextricably mixed.

The Asgill episode is a case in point. Captain Asgill was a British soldier, taken prisoner at Yorktown and condemned to be executed in reprisal for the summary hanging of the American captain Joshua Huddy by the Loyalists. Washington was unhappy with the sentence and took action to stay the execution, but as commander initially felt unable to overturn it. It was only after Asgill's mother had gone to see Vergennes to implore him to intervene, and when the French Minister in turn had shown the grieving mother's letter to the King and Queen, that Washington finally acted to commute the sentence. Needless to say, the Asgill story became a minor phenomenon in France, transformed into a sentimental novel, poems and a curious play by Billardon de Sauvigny (subsequently the author, during the Revolution, of *Vashington*) in which the scene was shifted to a mythical Tartary and Washington appeared in the light disguise of "Wazirkan." However flimsy this disguise, "Wazirkan's" lines *"Je commande aux soldats et j'obéis aux lois"* (I command soldiers and I [must] obey the law) announced the supreme quandary of the contemporary hero: how to order public and private values; how to reconcile justice with emotion.

This was the standard subject matter of many of the "Moral Tales" performed on the Paris stage in the 1760s and 1770s, and the bias given to renewed productions of the classical tragic repertoire of Racine and Corneille. It also supplied narrative power in some of the most outrageously grandstanding paintings of Greuze, such as *The Wicked Son Punished*. Jacques-Louis David's *Belisarius,* shown in 1779, the painting that prompted Diderot to remark that the young artist showed he had "soul," had at its heart the contention between good and evil surrogate fathers. For its subject was the recognition by a young soldier of the general Belisarius, reduced to the condition of a blind beggar by the ingratitude and cruelty of the Emperor Justinian. The conflict between family feeling and patriotic duty surfaced again in the same artist's masterpiece *The Oath of the Horatii,* which appeared in the biennial exhibit of paintings in Paris known as the Salon at the same time that Billardon de Sauvigny's Asgill play was performed at the Théâtre-Français. And both *The Death of Socrates,* where the teacher's students grieve over their master's patriotic suicide, and more specifically *Brutus Receiving the Bodies of His Sons from the Lictors,* where an implacably righteous father has sacrificed his own children to the Res Publica, recapitulated this theme in the most unsparing way. But while the official line taken by the revolutionary Jacobins would subordinate personal and family feeling to public and patriotic calling, the power of Washing-

9. Jacques-Louis David, *Belisarius*, 1781

ton's appeal was precisely that he (and more improbably, Vergennes) had succumbed to the tears of a stricken mother. Mrs. Asgill to Marie-Antoinette, mother to mother; Louis to "Vashington," father to father—the sentimental effect was irresistible.

From father to Fatherland was but a short step. Washington's embodiment of both in France owed its appeal to some deeper and more general desire for a new generation of patriotic heroes. Some young aristocrats became politicized precisely because they failed to see in the person of the court and the monarchy (especially in the last years of Louis XV) the virtues proper to patriotic severity. Indeed they sometimes accused the court of besmirching the reputation of patriots for reasons of base expediency and self-exculpation. The young Lally-Tollendal, for example, was set on course to become a revolutionary aristocrat by his crusade to vindicate the reputation of his father, who had been tried and executed as the scapegoat for French military failure in India. So awful was this disgrace that the boy was brought up in absolute ignorance of his father. Even his surname was altered to Trophime, his given name, as a way of sparing him the taint. At the age of fifteen, however, he inadvertently discovered the truth from an old comrade of his father's and, as he later wrote, he "ran to the judicial records"

> to give him [my father] my first homage and my eternal adieu; to let him at least hear the voice of his son amidst the jeers of his executioners and to embrace him on the scaffold where he perished.

After a ten-year, dogged campaign to reverse the injustice, the new reign took heed. In 1778, following discussion in thirty-two sessions, Louis XVI's royal council annulled the proceedings against Lally Senior, though the case still had to be referred to the Parlement of Rouen for formal overturning. When the news of the council's decision was announced, Lally went to see Voltaire, who had been enlisted in the cause, and the old warrior, on his deathbed, placed his hands on the head of the young noble as a last act of paternal blessing.

It was a story good enough for the Romans, to whom the victims of imperial injustice were constantly being compared. (The analogy between Lally's fate and Belisarius's repudiation by Justinian was often made.) Young men of Lafayette and Lally's generation had been saturated at school with the virtues of the Roman Republic, set out in the histories of Plutarch, Livy and Tacitus. But their concept of the *exemplum virtutis* was not confined exclusively to the models presented in antiquity. In his *Histoire du Patriotisme Français,* published in 1769, the lawyer Rossel claimed that patriotic sentiments "are livelier and more generous in the French citizen than in the most patriotic Roman." Following the defeats of the Seven Years' War, there were distinct signs of a fresh, if selective search, amidst the annals of French history, for heroes who represented its happier moments. Saint-Louis was a perennial favorite, but something close to a cult of Henri IV grew up among the younger courtiers at Versailles. Louis XII was expressly celebrated for having been proclaimed, at the Estates-General of 1506, the "Father of the People." Equally consolatory was the renewed interest in William the Conqueror, idealized in Lépicié's massive history painting—some twenty-six feet long—by far the largest in the Salon of 1769.

The publication of an historical anthology, the *Portraits des Grands Hommes Illustres de la France,* was an important event in the creation of a new, exclusively French pantheon of heroes, not least because it drew so many of them from medieval history, preferring figures who were unequivocally of the *patrie* to more remote exemplars from Roman antiquity. The Bourbons, with the exception of Henri IV, were missing, so that while Turenne and Condé were present, Louis XIV was not. And the *Hommes Illustres* broadened its criteria for worthies to include events and figures from civilian life like Chancellor d'Aguesseau, commemorated for "saving France from famine" at the beginning of the eighteenth century, and the philosopher Fontenelle "contemplating the plurality of worlds." More modern heroes were often, like François de Chevert, the hero of the retreat from Prague in the War of Austrian Succession, praised for the modesty of their origins, their commendable closeness to the common soldier and a career which depended "on merit rather than either flattery or intrigue." De Chevert's epitaph in the Church of Saint-Eustache in Paris, quoted in the book, began, "Without noble ancestors, without fortune, without powerful support, an orphan since infancy, he entered the service at the age of eleven. . . ." Women were included for their exemplary patriotism, especially when it was directed, as in the case of Jeanne d'Arc, at the British. Moreover, the most extravagant eulogies were perhaps reserved for those who had died in battle against the hated foe, none more sublimely than the Marquis de Montcalm on the heights of Abraham in Quebec. The overall tone of the work was optimistic if not triumphal, heralding a new age of patriotism in which the heroes

CHEVERT INSPIRE L'INTRÉPIDITÉ.
10. "François de Chevert," from *Portraits des Grands Hommes Illustres*

would be marked out in opposition to the vanities of court life by their simplicity, sobriety and stoicism. Standing at the head of the gallery with no hint of ironic incongruousness was Louis XVI himself, celebrated as the benefactor of American independence in company with Franklin, "Waginston" (George) and the personification of America, shown holding aloft the hat of liberty and trampling a British imperial beast more leopard than lion.

In this campaign to create a modern patriotic canon, no one labored harder to replace classical with French historical paragons than the dramatist Pierre de Belloy. In the preface of his play *The Siege of Calais* (dedicated to Louis XV in the somewhat improbable guise of *"Père de la Patrie"*), de Belloy specifically stated his project of reforming the subject matter of historical tragedy to include French history. As an educational task alone he thought this urgent.

> We know exactly everything that Caesar, Titus and Scipio did, but we are in perfect ignorance of the most famous deeds of Charlemagne, Henri IV and the Grand Condé. Ask a child leaving school who was the victorious general at Marathon . . . and he will tell you right away; ask him which King or which French general won the Battle of Bouvines, the battle of Ivry . . . and he will remain silent. . . .
>
> It is by stimulating the veneration of France for the great men that she has produced, that one may be able to inspire the Nation with the esteem and self-respect by which alone she may return to what she once was. The soul is led by admiration to imitate the virtues . . . [it should be] that one no longer always says, on leaving the theater, "the great men that I have just seen represented were Romans and since I was not born in that country I can not resemble them." Rather it should be said, at least sometimes, "I have just seen a French Hero; I can be a Hero like him."

And in another passage de Belloy went further by attacking Anglomania:

> Should one suppose that by imitating, good or bad, their carriages, their card games, their promenades, their theater and even their supposed independence we should merit the esteem of the English? No, love and serve our *Patrie* as they love theirs. . . .

INDÉPENDANCE DES ÉTATS-UNIS.

11. *The Independence of America.* The inscription on the pedestal reads "America
and the Seas acknowledge you, O Louis, as their Liberator."
From *Portraits des Grands Hommes Illustres.*

De Belloy did his best to promote this program through his own drama, writing a series of historical melodramas which, on publication, he supported with (what was for the time) an impressive set of historical notes. He was, as his more merciless critics like La Harpe, the ferocious editor of the *Journal Littéraire et Politique,* pointed out, handicapped by an insuperable mediocrity as a dramatist, especially when it came to the development of character. In *Gaston et Bayard,* loosely based on the stormy friendship of Gaston de Foix (the Duc de Nemours) and the Chevalier Bayard (the flower of French Renaissance chivalry), La Harpe reasonably complained that de Belloy had given the young Gaston all the characteristics of stern middle age and the older Bayard those of impetuous youth. But the distinctly second-rate quality of the plays did not preclude their popular success.

It was undoubtedly *The Siege of Calais* that meant most to de Belloy as an exercise in patriotic instruction, not least because it was a drama taken from the history of his native town. When the play was published it was his peculiar pride to print beneath his name (and above the designation of his membership in the Académie Française) that he was *CITIZEN OF CALAIS.* The drama—which takes some liberties with history, omitting the famous intercession of Queen Philippa with Edward III for the lives of the burghers—is something of a tract on patriotic citizenship, transplanted from ancient Rome to medieval France. It was not of incidental significance, of course, that the villain of the piece was the nearly implacable Plantagenet Edward III, nor that the heroes were Eustache de Saint-Pierre, the simple mayor, and his five burgher-citizens, who offer to sacrifice their lives to deflect the wrath of the English King from the rest of their townsmen. And once again, the father-son relationship was at the center of the drama, since the Philippa scene was replaced by a tear-jerking passage in which Saint-Pierre's own son (called, implausibly, Aurelius/Aurèle) implored the intractable King that he might go to the stake first and out of the sight of his bereaved father. And it is at this moment, of course, that Edward relents, struck with awe at the selflessness and courage of the patriotic martyrs.

De Belloy's play was a stunning success. In 1765, at the Comédie-Française, it was given a free performance that attracted an audience drawn from all walks of Paris society, including artisans and shopkeepers. Nineteen thousand people saw the play during its first run, which would undoubtedly have been record-breaking had it not been interrupted by a serious quarrel among the actors—one of the habitual problems of the eighteenth-century theater. In that same year, *The Siege of Calais* was the first French play to be published in French America, where the Comte d'Estaing, the Governor of Saint-Domingue (present-day Haiti), ordered a special print-

PIERRE LAURENT BUIRETTE DE BELLOY
DE L'ACADEMIE FRANÇOISE.
Citoyen de Calais
Né à Saint Flour le 17 9bre 1727 Mort à Paris le 5 Mars 1775

12. Frontispiece from Pierre de Belloy's *Works*.
Below his portrait are his honorific titles,
Academician and Citizen of Calais.

ing to be distributed gratis to the population and to the local garrison. Its
first performance in the French West Indies, on the seventh of July, moreover, was timed with an assembly of militia to whom it was obviously
addressed. And in case the point was missed, the illuminations that evening
prominently featured especially appropriate verses from the drama.

"He revealed to the French the secret of their love for the State and
taught them that patriotism did not belong to Republics alone," said de
Belloy's eulogist after his death in 1775. This was a large undertaking and
it seems very unlikely that the hack dramatist accomplished a great deal, but
at the very least, his preoccupations, and his casual use of terms like *patrie*,
patriotique, la Nation and *citoyen*, looked directly forward to the stock
vocabulary of revolutionary exhortation. In de Belloy's plodding meter,
moreover, may be found that soupily vague equation of "Liberty" and

"Patriotism" that spurred devotion to the American cause in the young liberal nobility.

During the course of the war there were opportunities to move from the realm of historical melodrama to contemporary heroics. The most spectacular (but by no means solitary) example of the new patriotic mythology was the case of the naval hero the Chevalier du Couëdic. The Sieur du Couëdic de Kergoaler, to give him the full magnificence of his Breton name, was a career officer who had served on board since the age of sixteen. During the Seven Years' War he had been a prisoner of the British—always a sharp spur to personal and patriotic vindication. Later, he had joined his fellow Breton Kerguéulen on one of the voyages of circumnavigation to Australia, which restored to the French a sense that they were in every sense Britain's peers in the pioneering of imperial geography. On the morning of November 5, 1779, du Couëdic sailed his sloop *La Surveillante* out of Brest and ran straight into a British frigate, the *Quebec,* reconnoitering the coast. Instead of both vessels beating a swift retreat or maneuvering fruitlessly around in the wind for marginal advantage, the ships engaged in a six-and-a-half-hour,

13. Engraving of the battle between *La Surveillante* and the *Quebec*

14. The coiffure "Belle-Poule"

side-by-side cannonade of horrifying relentlessness. At about half past four in the afternoon what was left of the *Quebec* blew up, leaving the *Surveillante* the Pyrrhic victor. Dismasted, its timbers almost shot to pieces, the *Surveillante* was towed back to Brest carrying with it forty-three British seamen who had been saved from drowning. The master of the ship, still dressed in his buckled shoes and silk stockings, was so badly wounded that he had to be carried ashore. The crowds waiting at the harbor, who had been expecting to cheer their heroes, were instead horrified at the gory mess to which the crew and ship had been reduced by the savage battle.

Du Couëdic duly died of his wounds three months later, but not before he had become a symbol of the reborn patriotic fortitude of France. There had been important and widely publicized naval victories before, most famously the success of the *Belle-Poule* at holding off the *Arethusa* in 1778—the contest that launched the coiffure "Belle-Poule": fashionable women dressed their hair with miniature ships bobbing on waves of powdered curls. But the very grimness of the story of the *Surveillante* gave it tragic authority. At a time when the promised invasion of Britain was being frustrated, the saga provided the French with a paragon of heroic endurance: a *chevalier* ancient and modern, courageous and compassionate. In the funeral eulogy given in the Estates of Brittany the qualities most admired by the devotees of *sensibilité* were emphasized. Thus du Couëdic was described as a "benevolent citizen" *(citoyen bienfaisant);* a "generous friend"; a "good master to his servants who adored him; a most tender father, who when he was at Quimperlé spent the greater part of every morning playing with his children who adored him." And for its part the French government responded in the same vein of family goodwill, announcing that the widow Couëdic would receive a pension of two thousand livres, and each of her children five hundred in recognition of their father's unique contribution to the *patrie*. On the orders of the King, who was passionately interested in naval matters, a great mausoleum was to be built in the Church of Saint-Louis at Brest with a special inscription designed for the edification of the local cadets: "Young pupils of the Marine, admire and imitate the example of the brave Couëdic." And when Sartine, the Minister of the Navy, proposed a whole program of paintings celebrating the victories of the American war, du Couëdic's battle was designed as the centerpiece.

The appeal of du Couëdic as a kind of latter-day waterborne knight-errant is important. For it is at the top, rather than in any imaginary middle of French society, that the cultural roots of the Revolution should be sought. While any search for a conspicuously disaffected bourgeoisie is going to be fruitless, the presence of a disaffected, or at the very least disappointed, young "patriot" aristocracy is dramatically apparent from the history of French involvement with the American Revolution. That revolution did not, as is sometimes supposed, create French patriotism; rather, it gave that patriotism the opportunity to define itself in terms of "liberty," and to prove itself with spectacular military success. It was among the Noailles and Ségurs—even in the heart of the court itself—that passions became most inflamed in the 1770s. Lafayette's ecstatic welcome on his return from America in 1779 is symptomatic of this. From an amusingly impulsive provincial youth he had become transformed, in the eyes of *les Grands,* into a paragon of contemporary French chivalry. The fact that he was placed under a token form of "house arrest" for a whole week in Paris at the town house of his wife's family, for his temerity in going to America despite the King's disapproval, only served to distinguish the brand of new patriotism from stuffy tradition. Besides, now that France had formally concluded a treaty with Congress, he had the best possible vindication, and he wrote to the King in a vein of modest but determined self-exoneration, "My love for my country, my desire to witness the humiliation of her enemies, a political instinct which the recent treaty would seem to justify . . . are, Sire, the reasons which determined the part I took in the American cause."

15. Portrait of Couëdic

Louis signaled his favor by inviting Lafayette to join him at the hunt, and Marie-Antoinette, who had not long before dismissed Lafayette as a conceited bumpkin, now could not do enough to advance him in status. It was on her intervention that he was granted a dramatic rise in rank to become commander-in-chief (at the age of twenty-one) of the King's Dragoons. Lafayette's own fame extended beyond the court to the wider Parisian public, eager for young heroes to celebrate. Mme Campan, the Queen's lady-in-waiting, wrote that some verses in de Belloy's *Gaston et Bayard* were taken by the theater public as a eulogy to their knight-errant.

J'admire sa prudence et j'aime son courage
Avec ces deux vertus un guerrier n'a point d'âge.

"These verses," Mme Campan wrote, "were applauded and asked for again and again at the Théâtre-Français . . . there was no place where the help given by the French government to the cause of American independence was not ecstatically applauded."

Lafayette's celebrity is an important moment in the coining of a new patriotism, in that it nativized and modernized a genre that had previously been confined to classical ideals. It also gave that patriotism a distinct ideological color, however faintly tinted. It would be naive to imagine that popularity alone could have pushed France down the road to a more aggressive intervention in the American war, had not Vergennes and Maurepas, the King's ministers, decided upon that course for reasons wholly unconnected with "Liberty" or other fancy modern notions. But, as we shall later see, already in the France of Louis XVI, the security of ministerial tenure, and the policies associated with the ministers themselves, were to some extent governed by a favor that extended well beyond Versailles. At the very least, the orchestrated campaign of huzzahs that greeted Lafayette's return and the sensational nature of his exploits in America did no harm at all to those within the government determined to press foreign policy towards a full war with the British Empire.

It was not, of course, Lafayette himself who did the orchestration. For his own fame and that of the distant "god-like Hero" Washington were both the more brilliantly illuminated by the phenomenal electricity generated by Benjamin Franklin. It was Franklin, for example, who turned into a major promotional opportunity Congress's instruction to award Lafayette a ceremonial sword for his services. He had the finest Parisian craftsmen work on the sword, which had Lafayette's unintentionally apt motto "*Cur Non*" (Why not?) engraved on the handle. But he also added the image of the rising moon and the motto "*Crescam ut Prosim*" (Let me wax to benefit mankind), a device that axiomatically associated America's cause with the happiness of humanity, a prominent theme in Franklin's diplomatic propaganda. On the scabbard were allegorical medallions representing France crushing the British lion and America handing laurels to Lafayette, together with scenes from the Marquis' military engagements. The sword was presented to Lafayette on behalf of Congress by Franklin's grandson at the encampment at Le Havre that was meant to be the expeditionary force destined to invade England. And Lafayette did his part in rising to the opportunity, expressing the hope that he might carry the sword "into the very heart of England"—a hope that was to be denied to him by the incompetence of the French fleet and the unpredictable violence of the cross-Channel weather. Naturally, the whole episode, charged as it was with such heavy symbolic eloquence, was widely reported in the French press, and both the sword itself and the engravings on which its designs were based were reproduced for popular consumption.

Franklin's own popularity was so widespread that it does not seem exaggerated to call it a mania. Mobbed wherever he went, and especially whenever he set foot outside his house in Passy, he was probably better known by sight than the King, and his likeness could be found on engraved glass, painted porcelain, printed cottons, snuffboxes and inkwells, as well as the more predictable productions of popular prints issuing from the rue Saint-Jacques in Paris. In June 1779 he wrote to his daughter that all these likenesses "have made your father's face as well known as that of the moon . . . from the number of *dolls* now made of him he may be truly said to be i-doll-ized in this country." On one famous occasion, his fame even goaded the King into a solitary act of wit, for, in an attempt to make Diane de Polignac desist from her daily eulogies of the Great Man he had a Sèvres chamber pot painted with Franklin's image on the inside.

Franklin was, of course, the designer of his own particular celebrity, and by extension, the Patriot cause, on both sides of the Atlantic. Aware that the French idealized America as a place of natural innocence, candor and freedom, he milked that stereotype for all it was worth. Not the most typical Quaker, he also exploited that group's half-understood reputation for probity and simplicity to commend himself further to French polite opinion. And Franklin knew that this image of the incorruptible, virtuous old fellow went down so well precisely because it threw into unflattering relief the more sybaritically rococo aspects of court style—which, in fact, were already on their way out under the altogether more sober style of the new King and Queen. Hence his occasional adoption of the peculiar beaver cap—used in many of his promotional portrait prints—and derived directly from earlier images of Jean-Jacques Rousseau. Franklin's undressed hanks of white hair and his ostentatiously unostentatious brown coat, deliberately worn at court audiences, were expressly affected with public sensation in mind and they succeeded brilliantly. Mme Campan naively described him appearing at court "in the dress of an American farmer" but emphasized how that contrasted invidiously with "the laced and embroidered coats, the powdered and perfumed hair of the courtiers at Versailles." The hack eulogist and chronicler Hilliard d'Auberteuil went even further, virtually turning him into a figment of Rousseau's imagination or one of the "good old men" of a Greuze melodrama: "Everything in him announced the simplicity and innocence of primitive morals. . . . He showed to the astonished multitude a head worthy of the brush of Guido [Reni] on an erect and vigorous body clad in the simplest garments . . . he spoke little. He knew how to be impolite without being rude and his pride seemed to be that of nature. Such a person was made to excite the curiosity of Paris. People gathered around as he passed and said: 'Who is this old farmer who has such a noble air?' "

Dubbed the "Electrical Ambassador," Franklin was also acutely aware of the rage for scientific learning that gripped the French elite, and how to exploit it. "It is universally believed in France," wrote John Adams, not without a certain sourness, "that his electric wand has accomplished all this revolution." And Franklin's science became a vital feature of his appeal because it seemed to be as much the work of the heart as the head: it was wisdom moralized. Hence his *Poor Richard's Almanack* was translated as *La Science du Bonhomme Richard* and as such became a best-seller in 1778. Paris society at this time was, in any case, hungry for scientific learning and there was no shortage of both amateur and professional scientists, from the most implausible frauds to the most rigorous empiricists, willing to popularize their findings. Virtually every issue of the daily *Journal de Paris* was packed with reports of experiments from the provinces as well as the capital and advertisements for series of public lectures to be given by the best-known luminaries, like Fourcroy and Pilâtre de Rozier. So the image of Franklin, who could tap the heavens for the celestial fire of electricity, became woven into the celebration of his other "American" virtues, most especially that of liberty. Turgot may have coined the famous epigram *Eripuit Coelo Fulmen, Sceptrumque Tyrannis* (He seized fire from the heavens and the sceptre from tyrants) as an innocuous play on words, but it very rapidly became a kind of byword for Franklin's role as the harbinger of liberty. Popularized first on a medallion bearing his likeness, then on a number of engravings, the theme with its standard iconography of lightning bolts and stricken British lions became a standard subject for painted porcelain and printed fabrics, even those displayed at Versailles. Made

16. Marguerite Gérard (after Fragonard), "Au Génie de Franklin." The obligatory lightning bolt is on the right.

casually respectable, the link between the fall of tyrants and celestial fire had ominous implications in absolutist France. For it inescapably suggested, in a Romantic vein, that liberty was a natural and hence ultimately irresistible force, and contributed further to a growing polarity between things natural on the one hand ("Humanity"; "Freedom"; "Patriotism") and things artificial on the other ("Privilege"; "Despotism"; the court). Not surprisingly this equation of liberty and lightning was eagerly endorsed in the Revolution, so that in Jacques-Louis David's pictorial account of the Tennis Court Oath, for example, a bolt of electrically charged freedom cracks over Versailles as a great gust of wind blows fresh air through the crowd-filled window spaces.

To some extent, the infatuation of fashionable society with the American cause was a facile matter: the latest novelty to come along after English novels and Italian opera. It is hard to judge whether the beautiful textile designs manufactured by Jean-Baptiste Huet at Joüy in 1784, celebrating "American Liberty" and "America Independent" in allegorical devices and portraits of Washington and Franklin, are evidence of the seriousness with which the revolution was taken, or of a consumer fad. When Mme Campan describes the most ravishing of three hundred court ladies selected to adorn Franklin's venerable pate with a crown of laurel, the craze for the "Insurgents" seems reduced to the level of a beauty contest. Yet there are other indications of a more serious engagement with the American cause spreading well beyond *le monde* of the court and fashionable society. In March 1783, for example, the *Journal de Paris* advertised a complete set of engrav-

17. Jacques-Louis David drawing, *The Tennis Court Oath*, 1791.
Detail of bolt of lightning striking the Chapel-Royal.

ings, with textual commentaries, of the battles of the American war for just one livre: a high price for an artisan to pay but well within the range of the broader reading public of the petty professions and trades. In Marseille, the unlucky associations of the number 13 were stood on their head by a group of citizens who expressed their solidarity with the insurgent colonies by fetishizing their number. In this group of thirteen, each wore an emblem of one of the colonies and they went on picnics on the thirteenth of the month at which thirteen toasts to the Americans were drunk. At another festive performance on the thirteenth of December 1778, Pidanzat de Mairobert sat through an heroic poem of thirteen stanzas, the thirteenth of which was reserved for praise of Lafayette.

The consequences of French involvement in the revolutionary war were, in fact, profoundly subversive and irreversible. The American historian Forrest Macdonald attempted to show a high degree of correspondence between returning French veterans of the war and the outbreak of rural violence in 1789. Recently, this has been shown by more careful research to be suspect, although there remain striking cases of returning soldiers who show up in the chronicle of the Revolution, most famously Lieutenant Elie and Louis La Reynie, both "conquerors" of the Bastille on July 14. But the case for an "American" cause of the French Revolution does not have to rest on this kind of geographical literalism. A more qualitative approach can hardly fail to register the extraordinary importance of the flirtation with armed freedom to a section of the aristocracy that was rich, powerful and influential. On their own they could not conceivably have constituted any kind of independent "revolutionary" opposition to the crown. But once the money crisis of the monarchy was transformed into a political argument, the vocabulary of "liberty" was apt to take on a life of its own—and become available to those who were prepared to play politics for very high stakes. Ségur, who was to be just such a participant, wrote to his wife in 1782, before he embarked with the French army, that "arbitrary power weighs heavily on me. The freedom for which I am going to fight, inspires in me the liveliest enthusiasm and I would like my own country to enjoy such a liberty that would be compatible with our monarchy, our position and our manners." The fact that Ségur, on the highest rung of the nobility, could blithely assume that such a transformation *would* be compatible with the monarchy may well suggest a myopic naiveté, but it also explains how many of his peers could take the exemplary nature of America seriously without ever dreaming it would lead directly to a Dictatorship of Virtue.

In the euphoria that greeted a great military triumph and a brilliant peace in 1783, few commentators were wont to pour cold water on the elation. More commonly, writers like the Abbé Gentil saw the American example as contributing in some warm and woolly way to the "regeneration" of France or even, more generally, the whole world. "It is in the heart of this new-born republic," he wrote, "that the true treasures that will enrich the world will lie." And in 1784, a literary and debating academy at Toulouse set as its prize essay question the importance of the American Revolution. The winner was a captain in a Breton army regiment, evidently an ardent disciple of Rousseau who saw it as the beacon of virtue and happiness and a model to emulate in France. And much of the reporting of the war, especially by commentators who had not been eyewitnesses, emphasized aspects that presented the Americans as harbingers of a kind of new golden age of almost childlike love and harmony. The Abbé Robin (a leading Freemason), for example, who had written extensively on the American landscape and inhabitants, noticed that when encamped the Americans played music.

> Then, officers, soldiers, American men and women, all join and dance together. It is the Festival of Equality. . . . These people are still in the happy time when distinctions of birth and rank are ignored and can see, with the same eye, the common soldier and the officer.

There were, however, some pessimists, who made up in their intelligent prescience what they lacked in numbers. The Queen was said to have harbored distinctly mixed feelings about the enthusiasm with which elite and commons alike rejoiced over the humiliation of a monarchy. And more to the point, the most intelligent of all Louis XVI's ministers, Turgot, had argued bitterly against active intervention in America, predicting that its costs would be so overwhelming that they would postpone, perhaps forever, any attempt at necessary reform. He even went so far as to suggest that the fate of the monarchy might hinge on this fateful decision. But he lost the argument to the immensely powerful Foreign Minister, Vergennes, for whom the embarrassment of the British crown in America was simply an opportunity so golden that it could not possibly be squandered. Vergennes was no warmonger. A lifetime professional diplomat, he was, in fact, a loyal adherent of the standard eighteenth-century concept of the "balance of power." But following the disastrously one-sided Seven Years' War he came to the not unreasonable conclusion that it was Britain that was the insatiably aggressive imperial power, and merely to hold the British at the line set out in the Treaty of Paris in 1763 required some kind of salutary chastisement. In alliance with the "family crown" of the Spanish Bourbons, and with the Dutch Republic, Vergennes crafted a foreign policy designed to present Britain as the aggressor, and the Coalition as intervening only to preserve the justly claimed independence of the Americans. The reasons for which Vergennes took France across the Atlantic/Rubicon were, then, wholly pragmatic, and, as he supposed, ideologically risk-free. Nothing could have been further from his mind than the promotion of some vaguely defined message of "liberty." In 1782, after all, he intervened militarily on the side of reaction in the affairs of the strategically important Republic of Geneva, where the ruling patriciate had been overthrown by a coalition of democratically minded citizens and artisans. And, as he explained, his reasoning in both the Genevan and the American cases was pragmatically the same:

> The insurgents whom I am driving from Geneva are agents of England while the American insurgents are friends for years to come. I have dealt with both of them, not by reason of their political systems but by reason of their attitudes towards France. Such are my reasons of state.

And, in truth, in 1778, when the crucial decisions were taken to enter into treaty relations with America, or even in 1783, when the Treaty of Fontainebleau was signed, Vergennes' sunny view of the war seemed to have been vindicated. For all the red ink on the government's account books, no one seriously dared to suggest that the American policy had been, for either fiscal or political reasons, a terrible mistake. France was a great power and had done, quite brilliantly, what great powers do to sustain their preeminence in the world and fend off the competition. It seemed likely that the British treasury was suffering quite as severely as the French and that their politics might even be in greater disorder. The French West Indies were pouring money from the sugar economy back into the mother country and the successes of Suffren's fleet in south India suggested that even there the prospects for economic recovery were brighter. As the Vicomtesse de Fars-Fausselandry put it, "The American cause seemed our own; we were proud of their victories, we cried at their defeats, we tore down bulletins and read them in all our houses. None of us reflected on the danger that the New World could give to the old." Or, as another of the French "Insurgents," the Comte de Ségur, commented, in the rueful aftermath of the American Revolution, "we stepped out gaily on a carpet of flowers, little imagining the abyss beneath."

LOUIS   SEIZE,
ROI DE FRANCE   *ET DE NAVARRE.*
Né à Versailles, le   *23. Aoust. 1754.*
Sacré à Reims   *le 11. Juin 1775.*

18. Louis XVI, from *Portraits des Grands Hommes Illustres*

CHAPTER TWO
Blue Horizons, Red Ink

i *LES BEAUX JOURS*

IKE ALL his generation, Louis XVI was brought up
to worry about happiness. His grandfather, Louis XV, had redesigned
Versailles around its pursuit and had a natural aptitude for its indulgence.
But for his young successor, happiness was hard work, and being king of
France put it virtually out of reach. Gradually enveloped by anxiety, he
would later recall just two occasions when the business of being king
actually made him happy. The first was his coronation in June 1775; the
second, his visit to Cherbourg in June 1786. On the first occasion he wrapped
himself in the mantle of arcane royal mystery; on the second he revealed
himself as modern man: scientist, sailor and engineer. To onlookers on both
occasions, the paradoxes of the royal personality were cause for comment,
perhaps even for concern. But it was part of Louis' innocence that he never
perceived a problem. If his authority owed everything to the past, his
overdeveloped sense of duty pointed him firmly towards the future. The
Revolution would represent this Janus-like quality as duplicitous rather
than undecided. But it was only its equation of past-future with treason-
patriotism that put the King in the dilemma that would end his reign and
his life. He began, in 1774, with the highest expectations, echoed throughout
France, that the future would be blessed with a renewal of the Golden Age.

The symbol of those hopes was the sun. At the coronation in Reims, when
Louis was twenty, the sun's rays, rays most obviously recalling the apogee of
the monarchy under Louis XIV, decorated every column and triumphal
arch erected for the ceremony. And the theme of renewal was echoed on the
pedestal of a statue representing Justice by an inscription proclaiming the
dawn of *les beaux jours.* However, the coronation was not unmixed rapture.

For tension between past and future played on concerns about the present, especially since, while the ceremonies were being planned, France was in the throes of the most serious grain riots seen for years. In the circumstances, the Controller-General, Turgot, urged Louis to exemplary modesty: a simplification of the rites and their celebration in Paris rather than Reims. Privately, he expressed the view that "of all the useless expenses the most useless and the most ridiculous was the *sacre.*" But if there had to be a coronation, he argued, better that it should be in the presence of the Parisians, whose monarchist sentiments could well use some cultivation. Foreigners would be impressed and the crowds diverted. And the bill would come in well under the seven million livres estimated for Reims.

But Louis was adamant. Perhaps influenced by the zeal of the court confessor, the Abbé de Beauvais, and by the Archbishop of Paris, who himself was eager to have the ceremonies not at Notre Dame but at Reims, the King insisted on traditional forms, even the oath "to extirpate heretics," which seemed gratuitously offensive to the tolerant sensibilities of the 1770s. It was symptomatic of Louis' split personality that having duly taken that oath he would go on to support the emancipation of the Protestants and lend his personal authority to its enactment in 1787.

It would be mistaken to suppose that it was reactionary piety or dynastic self-indulgence that led Louis to embrace the full medieval panoply of his coronation with such ardor. It was much more likely that, at least intuitively, he shared the rather advanced view of a young Lorraine lawyer and pamphleteer, Martin de Morizot, who supported the *sacre* as a form of "national election": a signification of the marriage alliance between the Prince and his people. In this view the spectacle was meant to approximate more closely the marriage of Venice and the sea administered by the Doge every year and symbolizing the public good, rather than a rite or ornate reaction. And there were certain ritual gestures—the liberation of prisoners through royal clemency; the peculiar ceremony of touching the scrofulous to commemorate the thaumaturgical healing power of the royal hands— that could bear witness to these good intentions. Nevertheless, as on many occasions in the future, Louis allowed others less attuned to public opinion than himself to intervene, with unfortunate results for his reputation. In this case, the clergy responsible for orchestrating the orders of the ceremony significantly altered exactly the item that could best be construed as symbolizing the relationship between prince and people. Before the Bourbons, there had been a moment when, following the first oath, the people had been invited to indicate their assent by the acclamation *Oui.* Since the time of Henri IV that had been replaced by a more perfunctory "tacit consent," but in Louis XVI's coronation the formal appeal to the people was omitted altogether. This tactless gesture did not go unnoticed, least of all by the underground press, who claimed that it had caused great "indignation" amongst true patriots.

So the great occasion that was meant as a placebo for the flour and grain riots ended up by pleasing very few indeed. Local artisans were upset because Parisian carpenters and decorators had been imported to do the work on the triumphal arches and the long arcaded gallery that led to the cathedral porch. There was much grumbling about the apartment that had to be erected for the Queen's special use and which featured English water closets. Peasant families of the region were particularly angry that their menfolk were conscripted to rebuild the city gate at Soissons, so that the coronation coach might pass through, at a time when their labor was urgently needed in the fields. Tradesmen were unhappy as few foreigners came to spend freely and to be impressed. Indeed, beds in the inns around Rheims were embarrassingly available since even the gentry of northern and eastern France, who were expected to show in numbers, had been deterred by the extortionate tariff demanded by local innkeepers.

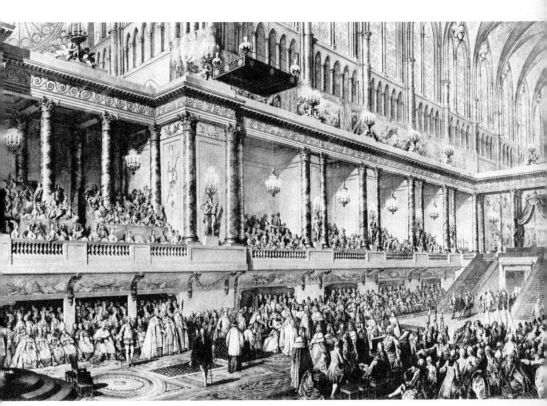

19. Moreau le Jeune, Louis XVI's coronation oath, 1775

For reformers like Turgot the event was a costly and badly managed entertainment that pandered to ludicrous anachronisms like the sacred ampoule of oil, allegedly supplied to King Clovis by a divinely dispatched dove. For traditionalists like the Duc de Croÿ the entire affair was somewhat vulgar. The applause that rained down on the King and Queen, he commented, was the result of the new and undesirable habit of greeting them at public theatrical performances. The whole event had been turned into opera. But as opera it was not without a certain power to move those spectators who were there. The young Talleyrand, watching his father preen himself in his great black-plumed hat, observed how vanity and passion could come together to generate irrational ardor. When the populace were admitted in a great throng to the cathedral and the Te Deums sounded, he saw tears of joy trickle down the cheeks of the boy-king while the young Queen, overcome, made for the exit.

If Louis had begun his reign with a great fanfare of archaic celebration, he was to continue it in the opposite vein of sober conscientiousness. Nothing gave him more pleasure than mechanics and as much as possible he chose to live in a world of numbers rather than words, lists rather than utterances. Everything he valued was compulsively enumerated: the 128 horses he had ridden; the 852 trips he had taken between 1756 and 1769. (This was less of a nomadic existence than the list suggests, for the majority of these *"voyages"* consisted of royal commuting within a narrowly circumscribed area in the Ile de France, where most of the châteaux and hunting lodges were located. But Louis faithfully transcribed each dull journey from Versailles to Marly [six times], Versailles to Fontainebleau [six] and on and on.) Even the pastime into which he flung himself with the greatest enthusiasm—hunting—was reduced in writing to lists of the daily bag. So that in July 1789—the month his monarchy collapsed—we know more about his daily kill than we do of his thoughts on the political events in Paris.

Yet, as François Bluche has pointed out, there was nothing trivial in Louis XVI's addiction to the hunt. It was the one theater in which he indisputably excelled and in which he fitted the role of equestrian king: *chevalier et imperator,* the warrior in the forest. On horseback he was courageous and even graceful: a quality by which the eighteenth century set great store, and which contemporaries found dramatically lacking in his other public appearances. But there was another world in which this physically awkward man came into his own. That was his private study filled with mathematical instruments, hand-colored maps and nautical charts, telescopes, sextants and the locks which the King himself designed and made. The struggle to make the perfect lock was a symbol of sublime aptness for the monarch who repeatedly failed to make things turn as he wished. But in his *appartements privés* he moved silently in his plain frock coat amidst polished lenses, armillary spheres, burnished brass and orreries with all the freedom and power of a magus.

It was in the nautical world that all these talents could come together. Like his father and grandfather Louis had played with toy galleons and barques on the pool known as *"la petite Venise"* at Versailles. His personal tutor, Nicolas-Marie Ozanne, had taught naval drawing to the cadets at Brest and imparted to his eager student both knowledge and zeal for the sea. So Louis became a passionate and compendiously knowledgeable expert on everything naval: from ship designs to nautical artillery, marine maladies and their cures, rigging and the movement of the tides, ballast and cargo calculations, military maneuvers and the language of flag signals. He even insisted on and helped design new uniforms that would abolish the old distinction between gentlemen and commoner officers. The antipodean voyage of La Pérouse was personally planned by the King together with the explorer, and he plotted its progress on special charts until the painful realization that it had come to grief somewhere in the Australian Pacific. He needed no one to point out to him that the way to recover the colonial power lost by his grandfather in the Seven Years' War was to embark on a radical program of naval construction. So he took care to confide the direction of the Marine to only the most gifted and able men: at first Turgot himself; then the brilliant Sartine, who more than any other transformed the navy into the equal of the British fleet; and after his fall, de Castries, scarcely less visionary (but perhaps less fiscally responsible) than his predecessor. For the King as for his ministers the future of imperial France *was* the navy: the azure horizon of a great Atlantic and perhaps even oriental Empire.

It should come as no surprise, then, to discover that after the coronation, the event of his reign which Louis recalled with most satisfaction was his visit to the new military port of Cherbourg on the Normandy peninsula of the Cotentin. Pointing directly toward the south coast of England, a new harbor and fortifications at Cherbourg would be of major significance for French patriotic amour-propre as well as practical strategy. In 1759 the port had been subjected to a British naval raid and occupation led by Captain William Bligh which, together with a secret treaty clause prohibiting French naval works at Dunkirk (and even providing for on-site British inspection), rankled as a bitter humiliation. Committed to a policy of challenging the British in America, Vergennes had evicted the British presence from Dunkirk, an occasion which was described as producing "great national joy." But the vulnerability of the Channel ports still played a part in the ambitious French invasion plans, thwarted in 1779 (as so often before and after) by persistent bad weather. A new and powerfully protected port would provide exactly the shelter needed by beleaguered French fleets without the need to abandon expeditions entirely. Not for nothing, then, was the news of Cherbourg's transformation received with considerable anxiety and irritation in Westminster. With favorable winds it was just three to four hours from Portsmouth.

When Louis began his reign in 1774 Cherbourg was not much more than a bedraggled fishing village of some six thousand souls who lived in wind-beaten monotony around the debris of masonry destroyed by the Royal Navy. By the time of the Revolution its population had nearly doubled, but more important, it had become home to a formidable concentration of capital, labor and applied engineering. The new Cherbourg was, at least for the King and his chief engineer, M. de Cessart, the symbol of a France reborn in the light of applied science and maritime vigor. The project to create a harbor was monumental in conception and execution. At a time when paintings and engravings of the colossi of antiquity were fashionable, it must have seemed a project that was at once antique in grandeur and futuristic in imagination. The more modest of the two engineers, de Bretonnière proposed building a great sea wall or containing dike behind which the harbor could be created. But it was the more spectacular and improbable scheme of de Cessart that appealed to the newly appointed commandant of Cherbourg, a career officer named Charles-François Dumouriez, fresh from the conquest of Corsica. It also struck the roving imaginations of the King and his navy minister de Castries.

De Cessart's plan was for immense, hollow chests of oak, each formed in the shape of a truncated cone and stabilized by a ballast of rock, to constitute a kind of barrier chain across the roadsteads. The space thus enclosed would then form the harbor. Each cone was a hundred and forty-two feet in diameter at its base and rose sixty feet from the waterline to its flat top. It required 20,000 cubic feet of wood for construction and, when filled, weighed 48,000 tons. Manipulating these monsters was tricky. They had to be towed from the shore to their anchorage, filled with only as much ballast as was needed to prevent them from capsizing. Once in place, they were then filled with the remaining rock through thirty openings in the sides of the cone. When sufficiently heavy to submerge properly, they would be cemented shut so that the top could constitute a kind of platform. De Cessart's original plan called for no less than ninety-one of these extraordinary objects. It was a scheme sufficiently lunatic to appeal to a culture besotted with the wilder claims of science. After Franklin's electricity—the patriotic lightning bolt—anything was possible. Men already ascended into the skies over Versailles in gas-filled balloons; others sat in copper tubs to

20. Cherbourg cone being towed out to the harbor, 1786

experience the therapeutic power of animal magnetism. In this climate of scientific delirium, de Cessart's underwater mountain ranges must have seemed almost modest.

The first cone was successfully submerged in June 1784 in the presence of Naval Minister de Castries. Encouraged by the progress of the project, the King sent his youngest brother, Artois, to watch the submersion of the eighth cone in May 1786, and it was his excited report that decided the King to make a unique expedition to Cherbourg to inspect the works at first hand. This was an extraordinary departure. Since the early reign of Louis XIV the Bourbons had abandoned any kind of "progresses" around France and had made the monarchy sedentary within the huge court-barracks of Versailles. France, or the part of it that "mattered," came to the King, not vice versa. So, as Napoleon drily noted later, when Louis announced his intention of going to Normandy "it was a great event."

On the twenty-first of June, then, with what counted as a modest retinue of fifty-six, the King and Queen set off from Versailles for the west Normandy coast. Louis had had a scarlet coat embroidered with gold fleurs-de-lis specially made for the occasion but evidently he was concerned about presenting himself to the people in a familiar rather than regal manner: the *bon père du peuple* that Louis XII had been dubbed. At the Château d'Harcourt, where he stayed overnight with the governor of Normandy, he pardoned six deserters from the navy who had been condemned to death by the tribunal at Caen. And at Caen itself the streets were packed with cheering crowds as the mayor presented the keys of the city beneath flower-bedecked triumphal arches. On the twenty-third Louis arrived at Cherbourg. Impatient to see the harbor works, the King said mass at three a.m. and was taken out in a barge, rowed by twenty oarsmen in scarlet and white, to the location of the ninth cone. At the same time, the cone was towed to its assigned place and two hours later it was successfully stabilized. Once it was in place the hatches were opened, and rocks were fed in until the King could command its submersion. This took exactly twenty-eight minutes (recorded of course, in Louis' journal). At the moment of sinking, an abruptly tightened cable leading from one of the casks stabilizing the cone threw three men into the water, drowning one of them instantly. Amidst the cheering and naval salutes that greeted the submersion, their cries went unheard. But Louis, who was watching the event with a telescope from the platform of the next cone, saw it only too clearly. Dismayed by the accident he subsequently offered a pension to the widow.

It took more than an accidental death to dampen the enthusiasm of the occasion. Amidst continuing applause, the court party sat down to a cold collation that had been prepared for them beneath a tent pitched on the top of one of the cones. Never had magnificence and absurdity been so closely allied.

The rest of the visit was taken up with reviewing the fleet, watching the maneuvers that only in his reign had become a standard naval practice, and dining aboard the significantly named *Patriote.* When he spoke with officers and men, Louis addressed them with easy familiarity, very much in the manner of twentieth-century British royalty, dutifully expert in technological detail. But this was clearly as much pleasure as duty for the King, and the normally scurrilously critical *Mémoires Secrets* reported that on this trip

> the King is perfectly instructed in everything concerning the navy and seems familiar with both construction and equipment as well as the manœuvres of the ships. Even the terminology of this barbarous tongue is clearly nothing new to him and he speaks it like a sailor.

Indeed the King's notoriously coarse sense of humor, which horrified the court and the Parisian *monde* (he particularly enjoyed turning on the Versailles fountains to douse unsuspecting strollers), was perfectly suited to the

Cherbourg salts. When his entourage threw up on the deck of the *Patriote* as harbor waves tossed the boat about, he guffawed with unsympathetic laughter. During another rough crossing of the Seine estuary from Honfleur to Le Havre on the return journey, the captain of the ferry boat swore out loud when he mistimed a maneuver, checked himself and apologized profusely to the King. "Nothing to apologize for," replied Louis. "It's your trade language and I should have said at least as much myself."

The visit was, for all concerned except perhaps the seasick courtiers, a brilliant success. Popular prints and engravings and the usual torrent of ecstatic verse proclaimed the triumph. But the crowds who had the rare opportunity of seeing the King seemed genuinely affectionate and Louis responded with natural affability, a quality that would altogether desert him in the critical days of 1789. To the shouts of "*Vive le roi*" in the streets of Cherbourg he replied, without any prompting, "*Vive mon peuple.*" In 1786 it sounded, as indeed it was, benign and spontaneous. In 1789 it would sound, as indeed it was, forced and defensive.

There is, moreover, an important footnote to the history of the *beaux jours* on the Côtentin. For if they showed the monarchy in the best possible light—familiar, endearing, energetic, patriotic: a monarch for citizens rather than subjects—this splendid impression came at a price. For the great harbor project of Cherbourg was, in reality, an expensive fantasy, even perhaps a ruinous fiasco. The expense of the cones mounted alarmingly as it became apparent that neither time nor money could be spent indefinitely on their construction and immersion. From ninety the total number projected dropped to sixty-four. The distance between them correspondingly widened and as a result chains often came awry; the cones collapsed into each other and the sea smashed the oak chests. The surviving chests were attacked by voraciously hungry teredinid seaworms which honeycombed the cones so badly that some resembled huge wooden colanders with rocks pouring through the gaping holes. Moreover, as it became evident that the cones could only be successfully stationed during two or three months of the year, it was soon calculated that it would take eighteen years before the work was completed.

Not without regret, then, in 1788 the effort to place more cones was abandoned and a year later the project was suspended, and replaced by the original plans to build the more modest sea dike. Between 1784, when the first cone had been sunk, and December 1789, when the project was called off, it had consumed no less than twenty-eight million livres, a phenomenal sum. It was, in every respect, the "high-profile strategic defense initiative" of its day and it was a costly and ludicrous failure. When in 1800, with an eye to the still inhospitable Channel, the engineers of the First Consul came to look over Cherbourg harbor they found just one cone still lurching about

21. Woodcut of the royal barge in Cherbourg harbor. The figures in the foreground are "young men" said to be swimming alongside to express their loyal enthusiasm.

in the waves. It was the ninth, the royal cone. By seven years it had survived the nautical King who had lifted a glass of red wine by its side to drink to its long life.

ii OCEANS OF DEBT

On a warm morning in 1783, in the Atlantic harbor of Brest, René de Chateaubriand had a vision. By his own account already a young Romantic, he was nonetheless unprepared for the kind of exaltation he was to feel at the sight of Louis XVI's navy returning to port.

> One day, I directed my walk to the far end of the port, on the sea side. It was hot and I stretched out on the shore and slept. Suddenly I was awoken by a magnificent sound; I opened my eyes like Augustus when he saw the triremes appear in the Sicilian roadsteads after the victory of Sextus Pompey. Cannon fire sounded over and again; the harbor was crowded with ships: the great French fleet had returned after the signature of the peace [of Versailles]. The vessels manœuvred under full sail; blazing in fire and light; decorated with flags; presenting prows, poops and sides; stopping and casting anchor in the midst of their course or continuing to ride on the waves. Nothing has ever given me a higher idea of the human spirit. . . .

For many of Chateaubriand's contemporaries the success of the French arms in both the Atlantic and the Indian oceans (for Suffren was the greatest hero of all) was indeed thrilling. In 1785, for example, the Estates of Brittany (which had not enjoyed the best of relations with the Bourbons) voted to erect a statue of Louis XVI in glorification of his role in restoring the prowess of the navy. And it was decided to place the image beside the hill of the Château de Brest so that it would be seen, like the Colossus of Rhodes, by all ships entering the great harbor.

But the pleasures of witnessing British imperial disarray and the belated satisfaction for the defeats of the Seven Years' War carried an expensive price tag. In a single year—1781, the year of Yorktown—227 million livres were spent on the American campaign, of which 147 million were for the navy alone. That was nearly *five times* the amount customarily allotted for the peacetime navy, even at the rebuilt strength of Louis XVI's standards. This force was being asked to perform four equally arduous tasks. Its first job was to convey troops to America and keep them supplied. Second, it had to thwart any attempt at British reinforcement, if necessary by aggressively seeking engagements. Third, it had to guard the major naval installations at home (a lesson of the previous global war); and finally, Vergennes and his naval ministers hoped to shorten the war by either threatening or actually carrying out a seaborne invasion of Britain in 1779. It was the distinctly imperfect success that the French fleets enjoyed in carrying out all these assignments that added to the length and hence the cost of the war. After the disastrous Battle of the Saints, there was a hasty appeal for a "patriotic subscription" to refit the fleet and, as in 1762, various public and private bodies stepped into the breach. Among others, the Chamber of Commerce at Marseille contributed over a million livres toward the construction of a formidable seventy-four-gun ship of the line that was named, in gratitude, *Le Commerce de Marseille*. Such was the patriotic ardor of the aldermen and bourgeois of the Midi port that they added another 312,414 livres to support families of seamen who had perished. Other institutions followed, like the Estates of Burgundy and Brittany, and even the much reviled private tax company of the Farmers-General, whose ship was called, unblushingly, *La Ferme*. But it was no more possible to wage war by patriotic donation in the 1780s than at any other time before or since. And it was to the much less altruistic loan market that Louis XVI's Controllers-General had to go to support their military obligations. For while the previous naval war had been funded partly from loans but partly from new, temporarily imposed direct taxes, levied on all classes of the population, 91 percent of the monies needed for the American war came from loans.

The best estimates of the costs of the American alliance in both its surreptitious and openly military forms—from 1776 to 1783—come to 1.3 billion livres, exclusive of interest payments on the new debts incurred by the government as a result. So that, without much exaggeration, it can be said that the costs of Vergennes' global strategy policy brought on the terminal crisis of the French monarchy. For the pursuit of a "forward" policy in the Atlantic and Indian oceans was not meant to be at the expense of France's traditional role of sustaining the balance of power in dynastic Europe. To support that "old" diplomacy still required an army of at least 150,000. No other European power attempted to support both a major continental army and a transcontinental navy at the same time. (And, arguably, none ever has without long-term costs debilitating its financial stability.) More than any inequity in a society based on privilege, or the violent cycles of famine that visited France in the 1780s, the Revolution was occasioned by these decisions of state.

If the causes of the French Revolution are complex, the causes of the downfall of the monarchy are not. The two phenomena are not identical, since the end of absolutism in France did not of itself entail a revolution of such transformative power as actually came to pass in France. But the end of the old regime was the necessary condition of the beginning of a new, and that was brought about, in the first instance, by a cash-flow crisis. It was the politicization of the money crisis that dictated the calling of the Estates-General.

To do them justice, the ministers of Louis XVI were painfully impaled on the horns of a dilemma. It was quite reasonable for them to wish to restore France's position in the Atlantic since they correctly saw that it was in the sugar islands of the Caribbean and the potential markets of the Anglophone colonies that the greatest fortunes were being made. In this sense, prudent economic strategy demanded a policy of intervention on the side of the Americans. Both during the war and after the peace of 1783 official statements defended that intervention as designed not to annex imperial possessions but rather to secure freedom of commerce. And it was in that guise—as the protector of free navigation—that Louis XVI appears on most celebratory engravings. There can be no doubt that in the short run these aims were accomplished, for Atlantic trade from Nantes and Bordeaux to the French West Indies reached an unprecedented height of prosperity in the decade before the Revolution. In this sense, military investment in the spoils of empire had paid off handsomely.

The financial consequences of that same policy, however, made it a pyrrhic victory. For the ballooning of the deficit so weakened the *nerfs*— the sinews—of state that by 1787, its foreign policy was robbed of real freedom of action. For in that year sheer financial exigency prevented

France from intervening decisively in the civil war in the Dutch Republic to support its own partisans, themselves going by the name of "Patriots." Paradoxically, then, the war that had been intended to restore the imperial power of France ended up compromising it so badly that king and *patrie* seemed to be two different, and before long irreconcilable, entities. It was not much longer before this process was taken even further, so that the court itself seemed a foreign parasite feeding off the body of the "true" Nation.

It needs to be stressed that it was policies—fiscal and political as well as military—that brought the monarchy to its knees. Excessively influenced by the obsolescence implied by the nomenclature of the *ancien régime* (a term not used until 1790 and then, in Mirabeau's letter to the King, meaning "previous" not "archaic"), historians have been accustomed to tracing the sources of France's financial predicament to the structure of its institutions, rather than to particular decisions taken by its governments. Heavy emphasis on both institutional and social history at the expense of politics has reinforced the impression of administrations hopelessly trapped inside a system that, some day or other, would be doomed to collapse under the strain of its own contradictions.

As we shall see, nothing of the sort was true. What, seen from the vantage point of the Revolution, might look incorrigibly inflexible was in fact open to a number of approaches in coping with French financial problems. The trouble lay rather in the political difficulties in sustaining those policy decisions to the point where they might have paid off, and in the repeated retreats of the King to what he judged was the temporarily least painful political alternative. If anything, as de Tocqueville pointed out, it was not an aversion to reform but an obsession with it that made consistent financial management difficult if not impossible. Where de Tocqueville erred, though, was in supposing that French institutions were themselves intrinsically incapable of solving the regime's fiscal problems. In this view, there were no short-term problems, only deep-seated structural ones that could not be changed—*even by the Revolution*—for he thought he saw the same ills of centralization and the heavy hand of bureaucratic despotism recurring endlessly and hopelessly through French history.

How grave was France's financial predicament after the American war? It had, it is true, run up an imposing debt, but one that was no worse than comparable debts incurred in fighting the other wars deemed equally essential to sustain the nation's position as a great power. Those quick to condemn the ministers of Louis XVI for their hopeless prodigality might pause to reflect that no state with imperial pretensions has, in fact, ever subordinated what it takes to be irreducible military interests to the considerations of a balanced budget. And like apologists for powerful military force in twentieth-century America and the Soviet Union, advocates of similar "indispensable" resources in eighteenth-century France pointed to the country's vast demographic and economic reserves and a flourishing economy to sustain the burden. Indeed the prospering of that economy was, they claimed, contingent on such military expenditure, both directly in naval bases like Brest and Toulon, and indirectly in the protection it gave to the most rapidly expanding sector of the economy.

Moreover, on each occasion following the wars of the eighteenth century, there had been a period of painful but necessary adjustment to allow the finances of the realm to be brought into manageable order once more. The wretched end to Louis XIV's wars, for example, saw simultaneously the specter of bankruptcy, the virtual disintegration of the French army in the field, tax revolts and mass famine. And by 1714 the debt was calculated at around 2.6 billion livres *tournois* or, in a population of twenty-three million, 113 livres—about two-thirds the annual income of a master carpenter or tailor—for each subject of the Sun King. In the sobering aftermath, there was an attempt to learn from the "victorious" Anglo-Dutch side by importing their banking principles into French public finance. An enterprising Scotsman, John Law, was given the opportunity to manage and eventually liquidate the French debt in return for exclusive license to a newly created Bank of France. Unhappily, Law used the capital subscribed to the Bank to speculate in phantom American land companies and when the inflated bubble burst, so did the principle of a Bank-managed national deficit. In fact, Law's speculations were no more outrageous or indeed reprehensible than identical gambling by the South Sea Company in Britain. But the principle of a public Bank survived the debacle better there because such financial institutions were transferred more strictly to parliamentary control. In France, there was no comparable institution that could act as a dependable watchdog and so reassure future depositors and creditors of the government. It has been well said by Michel Morineau that the difference between the two debts is that the French deficit was burdened by being broadly conceived by the public as "royal" while the British debt was held to be "national."

Short of a Bank-managed loan system, there were still financial strategies open to French governments to keep their debt at a manageable level. Controllers-General of the period of the Regency following Louis XIV's death indulged in a drastic writing-down of the scale of debt and intervened radically in redemption schedules. This was, to be sure, a kind of bankruptcy by installments but, perhaps surprisingly, it did not seriously impair the future credit of the French crown. As long as there was capital, both within and outside the country, looking for yields that were even marginally higher than other kinds of domestic investment, France did not lack for lenders. By 1726 the French budget was more or less in balance, and with the help of inflation reducing the real value of the debt, the nation's finances even survived the War of Polish Partition in the 1730s without excessive new burdens.

It was quite otherwise, however, with the two major wars that then followed: the War of Austrian Succession from 1740 to 1748 and, still more spectacularly, the Seven Years' War from 1756 to 1763. The first conflict, essentially on land, cost around 1 billion livres and the second, both a naval and land war, 1.8 billion. By 1753 the principal of the deficit had shot up to 1.2 billion and annual interest to 85 million livres, already 20 percent of current revenue. Yet the postwar Controller-General Machault d'Arnouville projected that the deficit might be paid off within fifty to sixty years, assuming no further wars. That was, of course, like assuming there would be no France or, more seriously, no Britain. After the next war, in 1764, the deficit was up to 2.324 billion livres in principal with debt service alone taking something like 60 percent of the budget, or twice the proportion of the 1750s. In thirteen years the debt had grown by 1 billion livres.

While this makes grim (if familiar) reading for accountants, it did not of itself set France on a trajectory to revolution. The mid-eighteenth century had witnessed an enormous expansion, both quantitative and qualitative, in the scale and sophistication of warfare, which had taken a heavy toll of all major belligerent powers. Hohenzollern Prussia, which we are accustomed to think of as a success story of bureaucratic militarism, was in a desperate plight at the end of the Seven Years' War even though it had been kept afloat by British subsidies. Its remedy for ills was in fact to import the *French* system of tax management: the *régie,* which actually returned it to some degree of fiscal soundness. Not even neutrals escaped, for the Dutch Republic, which itself had been busy funding any and all customers, went into serious depression in 1763–64. And Britain, held up as the other major example of fiscal competence, went into debt (as it would during the American war) on precisely the same scale and magnitude as its archenemy. Not only do we now know that the British per capita tax burden was *three times* heavier than in France, but by 1782, the percentage of public revenue consumed to service Britain's debt—on the order of 70 percent—was also considerably greater than the French equivalent.

So in absolute terms, even after the immense fiscal havoc wrought by the American war, there are few grounds for seeing the scale of the French deficit as *necessarily* leading to catastrophe. But it was the domestic perception of financial problems, not their reality, that propelled successive

French governments from anxiety to alarm to outright panic. The determining elements in the money crisis of the French state, then, were all political and psychological, not institutional or fiscal. On each occasion—after the expensive midcentury wars, for example—there were serious debates about debt management and the relative desirability of new taxes as against different loan possibilities. These led to apparently minor technical alterations of financial strategy that were, as James Riley has argued in a brilliant history of the problem, disproportionately damaging. One such change was the growing concern with the schedule of amortization. Eagerness to capture that most elusive of all will-o'-the-wisps—redemption of principal—persuaded French governments to shift loan offers from so-called "perpetual annuities" (which could be passed on beyond the term of a single life) to "life annuities" terminating with the holder. While this might have seemed a good idea to redemption-minded managers, it meant in practice that the crown was now paying 10 percent to its creditors rather than 5 percent on the perpetual loans. This added immensely to the real burden of service for the future.

Second, it was in the aftermath of both the Austrian and the Seven Years' wars that Controllers-General who attempted to perpetuate temporary wartime direct taxes ran headlong into powerful and articulate political resistance. The reason for all that indignation in the name of French "liberties" was that these taxes were levied on all sections of the population, irrespective of social rank. It may seem odd to us that the French "public" (for there was already such a thing called "public opinion") did not see this opposition as motivated by the selfish protection of privileged tax exemptions. But in the 1750s and the 1760s, when these attacks on "ministerial despotism" were launched, that political "public" consisted, for the most part, either of people already within the system of privilege or those who had a good chance of entering it. And in these circumstances, "privilege" became synonymous with "liberties." A "modern" position by which the crown might have appealed over the heads of the privileged groups for public support of its no-exemption taxes was not yet conceivable. Even in 1789, it did so with the utmost reluctance. Twenty years before, it was quite out of the question. Controller-General Silhouette, for example, in 1759, had proposed a tax on luxury items like gold and silver plate, jewelry, carriages—as well as on celibacy—and was drummed out of office for his temerity, amidst a chorus of execration. In his last, uncharacteristically determined years, Louis XV was prepared to push through unpopular financial measures by the royal *fiat* of the *lit de justice*. But since his grandson was more sensitive to the issue of popularity, Louis XVI's ministers tried to avoid anything that suggested arbitrary rule. "No bankruptcies, no taxes, no loans" was the optimistic formula by which Turgot announced his policies in 1775. And Jacques Necker, the Genevan Director-General of Finance, determined to finance the American war overwhelmingly by loans rather than taxes. The real difference between the British and French predicaments following that war was that William Pitt could raise revenue from new taxes without threatening a major political crisis, an option that was not open to his French counterparts.

For a long time now, historians have argued that what ministers of the French crown did or didn't do about the debt is of minor importance. For it was the nature of the old-regime monarchy itself that was the real problem. Hamstrung by privilege, how could a government consisting of men who bought or inherited their offices hope for even a modicum of bureaucratic efficiency? Even with the best will in the world, and with able public servants (neither of which could be counted on), French government was a vacuum presiding over a chaos. Add to this its monstrous deficit, and the wonder is not that it ended badly, but that it survived as long as it did.

But is this argument valid? It assumes, to begin with, that to work adequately, the eighteenth-century state should have approximated some early version of "civil service" government. This might be defined as a polity in which public functions are the monopoly of salaried officials, trained for the bureaucracy, hired by merit, disentangled from any private interest in the jurisdiction they serve and accountable to some sort of disinterested sovereign body. It is true enough that the outlines of such a bureaucratic mechanism were articulated in the eighteenth-century "science" of "cameral government" and that, for the first time, professors of such *Kameral-und-polizeiwissenschaft*—what we would call government and finance—were occupying specially created chairs at universities, especially in the German-speaking world. But it takes no more than a glance at the reality of eighteenth-century government throughout Europe to see that these principles were most honored in the breach. The celebrated Prussian bureaucracy, for example, was riddled with corruption, was the creature of dynasties of nobles who settled in swarms on its offices. And in that state, local government officers were appointed not for their separation from, but adhesion to the local society of landowners. By comparison the French *intendants* were models of integrity and objectivity. Even in Britain, Hanoverian government was notorious for sinecures created to generate chains of political loyalty. I don't mean to suggest that bureaucratic competence was not possible within such a system, but the same holds true for French government as much as any other.

It is in the forests of privilege which grew so luxuriantly in France that it is said the purposes of government most seriously lost their way. Privilege, after all, was defined by tax exemption. And the immunity of the nobility and clergy to direct taxes most obviously denied the royal Treasury desperately needed funds. But it is misleading to see the privileged classes *en bloc* removed altogether from the revenue base of the state. Nobles were subject to the *capitation* poll tax, and the several direct property taxes like the *"vingtième,"* levied at 5 percent of their property. In some cases they were even subject to the *taille:* the major direct tax of the old regime. For while in some areas the *taille* fell on persons, in others it fell on property. So that if, for example, a young nobleman came into possession of a property as part of a dowry from a family that had in origin been bourgeois, he and his heirs would have to pay the *taille* on the estate. And since a very fluid pattern of property inheritance and exchange between different social groups was becoming more and more common in France, the number of nobles qualifying to pay the *taille* in all likelihood was rising too.

Fiscal immunity as a feature of privilege was, then, being steadily broken down, to the point that well before the Revolution leading aristocratic writers could cheerfully propose its abolition altogether. But by the same token, had the privileged been brought fully within the taxable classes much earlier, it is very unlikely that the additional revenue would have made much difference to the problems of the deficit. The most that can be said is that the principle of exemption at the top of society filtered down as the necessity of evasion at the bottom. So that many in France—as the petitions of complaint before the Revolution were to testify so eloquently—perceived their relationship to the state as a kind of fiscal zero-sum game. For the impoverished peasant, this meant moving one's few sticks of property— a bed, a few pans and a half-starved goat—to a village other than one's own parish to avoid assessment. For the parish was the unit of the *taille.* This kind of desperation tactic was hardly conducive to building up "the cultivator's rural capital" as the economic theorists of the time fantasized. At the level of the urban bourgeois it meant accumulating enough money to buy one of the many thousands of petty municipal offices that would confer tax exemption. So that in every major town and especially in Paris, there were wardens of the oyster sellers' guild and gaugers of cheese and curds and inspectors of tripe who gloried in their small dignities and enjoyed their exemptions.

Linked to privilege, but not synonymous with it, venality was perhaps a greater plague, and certainly a greater impediment to stanching the hemorrhage of the crown. For the sale and purchase of office was more deeply and broadly rooted in France than in any other major power in Europe. It had begun as a medieval practice but in 1604 Henri IV had institutionalized the sale of office as a way of raising revenue for the crown. In effect the purchaser lent the government a capital sum (the purchase price), for which he received as a return certain monies and perquisites (the *gages*) from the office. He also received status (including tax exemption) and it was if anything the nonpecuniary aspects of venal office that made Frenchmen so determined to resist its abolition.

Under Louis XVI several ministers made spirited efforts to reduce the crown's dependence on this kind of revenue, but after the fall of Necker, it seemed still an irresistible expedient at a time of fiscal crisis. The effective rate paid by the monarchy on old offices or the creation of new ones was, after all, between 1 percent and 3 percent—much less than on other kinds of loans. According to David D. Bien, from the American to the French Revolution something like 45 million livres were raised from the sale of offices—not a large sum spread over these years, but at least indicative of the obstacles to radical reform. So that at the same time that the long-term purpose of the government was to try to *extend* control over its finances and functions, short-term wants were making that harder, rather than easier to achieve.

The problem was also a matter of attitude. Just because privileges were so widely available and no longer at all synonymous with birth or class, those who stood to lose status as well as cash constituted an ever-broadening coalition. And even among reforming writers who could wax indignant at every other kind of abuse and anachronism, there was little enthusiasm for some sort of nonvenal, bureaucratic state. Voltaire and d'Alembert, for example, were as eager as anyone else to obtain a position such as that of *secrétaire du roi* as the first step to grander things. Louis XVI's reforming ministers were only too aware of the problem, but were nervous about any wholesale attack. Only Necker, who was notoriously impervious to most peccadillos, was prepared to take on the recalcitrant officeholders. And even then it was among the court—always a popular target—that he found the most flagrantly useless offices to prune. But as long as offices were treated as simply another kind of private property no one could imagine their expropriation without adequate compensation. It has been calculated that there were on the order of fifty-one thousand such venal offices in France on the eve of the Revolution, representing a capital of between 600 and 700 million livres. To redeem them all at once would have cost the state approximately the equivalent of one year's revenue. This would have been tantamount to shutting down France for a year, until, as it were, the burden could be shifted to the public sector.

The notion of government office as a form of private property strikes modern sensibilities as, by definition, irreconcilable with the public interest. Indeed, the most chronically "ancient" feature of the *ancien régime* seems to be that it was unable to distinguish adequately between the public and the private realms in matters as vital as its own finances. But even here, some perspective is needed to judge the failings of the French monarchy by its own standards rather than those of modern administrative theory. All European warrior states in this period—and for a long time to come—drew their revenue from three sources: direct taxes usually (as in France) collected by state officials; loans from groups, institutions and individuals all of whom certainly aligned their private interest with the interest of the state; and finally indirect taxes which in some places were administered by bureaucrats and in some places leased out to private individuals who would advance the state a sum of money in return for the right to collect taxes themselves. The difference between what they had lent and what they collected supplied both their profit and operational costs. The Napoleonic state, which is sometimes taken as a bureaucratic state *par excellence*, in fact used all three just as the old regime had, and even then only kept its finances in order by the crudest forms of military extortion, coercively extracting gigantic sums of money from countries "liberated" by the French army.

So just how serious were the results of the eighteenth-century monarchy's combination of business and bureaucracy in managing its own finances? For a long time it has been said that the messiness of these arrangements, for example, delayed the appearance of a systematic budget until Necker tried to provide his own published one in 1781. But as Michel Morineau, in a superlative study of these issues, has shown, while there was no public record, there certainly were *arrangements* that enabled Controllers-General both to apportion expenses among departments of state and to see with fairly reliable accuracy how much money was actually disbursed to those departments. And historians have been equally certain that had the monarchy had the courage to assume directly the business of administering and collecting indirect taxes, it would have saved the admittedly enormous profits going to the commercial "middlemen" who did the taxing on its behalf. On the other hand, however, it would have been saddled with those extra costs of administration, which might well have offset the gains, not to mention the odium which inescapably went with the collection of taxes on basic commodities. It has been estimated that the "overheads" of French revenue collection amounted to 13 percent of the total, compared with 10 percent in the case of Britain, where a centralized bureaucracy did indeed run the customs and excises. If this is really all that was at stake, no wonder Controllers-General were reluctant to upset their habitual regime for some sort of theoretical sovereignty over public business.

It was the policies of the old regime rather than its operational structure that brought it close to bankruptcy and political disaster. Compared with the consequences that flowed from the great decisions of foreign policy, privilege, venality and indirect administration of revenue were of much less significance. At the root of its problems was the cost of armaments when coupled with political resistance to new taxes and a growing willingness of governments to accept high interest-bearing obligations from both domestic and, increasingly, foreign creditors. No doubt it was reckless of French governments in the 1780s to lay up so much trouble for themselves. But it takes a very superior form of hindsight on the part of an American in the 1980s to write them off as hopelessly obtuse.

iii MONEY FARMS AND SALT WARS

The old regime may have been more efficient at supplying itself with revenue, and even at managing it, than is usually acknowledged. But for the peasant on the run from the parish tax collector this hardly mattered. In fact if there is one aspect of the traditional picture of the monarchy that remains emphatically unrevised by recent research, it is the eloquent hatred among nearly all sections of society (but becoming more savagely desperate at the bottom) of the tax-collecting apparatus of state and *seigneur* alike. As the petitions of grievance (*cahiers de doléances*) that accompanied elections to the Estates-General testified, those who taxed in the King's name were the enemies of the people. At the simplest level of society, this execration fell on the head of the unfortunate individual who had been saddled with the job of parish collector of the *taille*. Should he fail to produce the portion allotted to his assessment by the bureau of the intendant, his own property and even his freedom might stand brutal forfeit. But if he was too efficient at his work, an even worse fate might befall him, meted out by his fellow villagers in the dead of night.

At the summit of society, a similar kind of hostility was aimed at the plutocratic money merchants, the *gens de finance*. In Darigrand's polemic *L'Anti-Financier*, published in 1763, the engraved frontispiece showed France on her knees before Louis XV, who was being thanked (somewhat prematurely) for instituting a single property tax and so robbing the finance contractors of their raison d'être. Justice with her sword aloft obliges the *financier* to disgorge his ill-gotten gains at the feet of the poor cultivator. In the same tract, the *financiers* were characterized as "blood-suckers [*sang-sues*] fattening themselves off the substance of the people." A play by the satirist Lesage created the grotesque character Turcaret: low-born; crude, grasping and vindictive; a petty baron of the world of money whose infamy

22. Frontispiece to Darigrand, *L'Anti-Financier*

was only made bearable by his comic vulgarity. Many of the themes of what might be called Romantic patriotism crystallized in hostility towards the *financiers:* the town devouring the substance of the innocent countryside; luxury sustaining itself by perpetuating poverty; corruption and brutality in league against rustic simplicity. And it was in the guise, above all, of patriotic citizens that polemicists like Darigrand attacked the *gens de finance* for their selfishness, rehearsing precisely what the revolutionary Jacobins would mean when they stigmatized capitalists as *riches égoïstes.*

While any of the conspicuous creditors of the crown came in for this kind of treatment, much of the harshest invective was reserved for the Farmers-General. Their power, after all, lay at the heart of the system, and they were responsible for perhaps as much as one third of all revenues in France. Every six years, the crown contracted with a syndicate of these men for a *bail*, or lease, by which they agreed to advance a specific sum to the Treasury in return for the right to "farm" certain indirect taxes. These were, principally, and most notoriously, the salt and tobacco taxes (*gabelle*, *tabac*), as well as a number of other minor duties on commodities like leather, ironware and soap, known collectively as the *aides*. (Other indirect taxes were taken in the form of customs—the *octrois*—imposed most significantly on wine as it moved from one customs zone to another, or in and out of cities.)

The Farmers attracted a disproportionate share of detestation not because they were the most reactionary element in the fiscal machine of the state but because they were the most brutally efficient. It was in the tax farms that the gap between what people paid and what the royal Treasury received was said to be most glaring. The fact that their profit—or the difference between what they collected and what they paid to the crown—remained a commercial secret did not help soften this stereotype of a gang of rapacious, royally licensed brigands. If there was one symbol of the callous unaccountability of the old regime to the basic wants of the people, the Farmers-General embodied it in their collective and individual persons.

Not surprisingly they would be singled out for attention by the Revolution. In 1782, the popular writer and journalist Louis-Sébastien Mercier wrote that he could never walk past the Hôtel des Fermes on the rue Grenelle-Saint-Honoré without being consumed by the desire "to reverse this immense and infernal machine which seizes each citizen by the throat and pumps out his blood." One of the earliest and most spectacular acts of the great uprising in Paris in July 1789 would be to tear down the Farmers' customs wall erected to thwart smugglers. In person they would fare even worse than their property. Pursued by their reputation as economic vampires, they were also widely rumored to have secreted away three to four hundred million livres of their booty. "Tremble, you who have sucked the blood of poor unhappy wretches," warned Marat, and in November 1793 Léonard Bourdon demanded that "these public bloodsuckers" (by now an instantly recognizable synonym for the Farmers) either give an account of their larceny and restore to the Nation what they had stolen or else "be delivered to the blade of the law." In May 1794, amidst one of the more spectacular mass executions, a group of them including the great chemist Lavoisier was guillotined.

The Farmers-General were not, however, just speculators in crown debt and gougers of the people. They were a state within a state. Half a business and finance corporation, half a government, with personnel that ran to at least thirty thousand, they were the largest employer in France after the King's army and navy. Of that number, twenty-one thousand made up a paramilitary force, uniformed and armed not only with weapons, but with the right to enter, search and seize any property or household they deemed suspicious. For fiscal purposes they commanded their own map of France, divided into multiple and separate jurisdictions (*la grande gabelle, pays de quart bouillon,* etc.) for each of the commodities they farmed. Nor were they merely tax collectors and excise enforcers. In the major commodities with which they were concerned—especially salt and tobacco—they were producers, manufacturers, refiners, warehouse keepers, wholesalers, price regulators and monopoly retailers as well.

To appreciate how the business of the Farmers-General insinuated itself into the daily life of every French household one need do no more than follow the tortuous progress of a sack of salt from the marshes of Brittany to the kitchen. At every stage it was watched over, checked, registered, guarded, rechecked, reregistered and, above all, taxed before it got into the hands of the consumer. From the beginning to the end of the process the commodity was a captive of the Farmers' right to exercise iron-clad regulation. Everything hinged on their control over pricing. In 1760, for example, the producers of salt from the marshes west of Nantes were required to sell their product to the Farmers at prices fixed after one-sided negotiation. From there the salt was shipped to coastal depots at the mouths of rivers, and packed into registered and sealed sacks. Each of these depots had been allotted the task of supplying a batch of further depots in the interior, to which they shipped the salt by barge. This second group of depots was located at the navigable limits of the rivers, and from there to yet another set of warehouses the salt went by wagon, inspected at each stage of the journey. Finally it ended up at the major *greniers à sel*—the central warehouses rented by the Farmers. These were large buildings staffed by a considerable number of clerks and guards with a chief who was responsible for selling salt, duly taxed of course, to the consumer. Every sale had to be accompanied by an invoice and receipt made out in duplicate. For those who were too far from the *grenier* to buy, there were small village concessions licensed to sell to the local population but at a slightly higher price than the Farmers' official tariff.

Even had the Farmers not had the right to set the price of salt, the sheer bureaucratic weight of its official distribution would have enormously increased its price. Few households could have conceived of doing without this most basic commodity, but they were not even given the possibility of forgoing it, since they were legally required to buy a minimum annual amount, determined by individual assessment. Captive to this astonishing system of control and taxation, the hard-pressed consumer had one way out, albeit an illegal one: smuggling. And here the sheer elaborateness of the Farmers' fiscal map worked against their own security. Since salt could be had across the border of the *pays de grande gabelle* at almost ten times less than the Farmers' price, smuggling naturally thrived along the straggling customs frontiers. This applied with even greater force to the tobacco regimes, close to the Spanish border in the west and Savoy in the east. But

Elevation

GRENIER   A SEL

Le Doux Architecte du Roi.

Echelle de

23. Architectural drawing, by C. N. Ledoux, for a gate in the Paris customs wall

salt smuggling achieved the almost epic status of an all-out war between the army of the Farmers-General and gangs of smugglers especially concentrated in the west. In an effort to deter smugglers the state had provided draconian sentences: whipping, branding, the galleys or (in the case of assaulting the guards) death by breaking on the wheel. Yet hundreds and perhaps even thousands of people—men, women, children and even trained dogs—collaborated in the dangerous but lucrative trade throughout western France. Necker—who was in the habit of giving suspiciously round numbers to everything—estimated that as many as 60,000 people were involved in salt smuggling. This was certainly an exaggeration, but between 1780 and 1783 some 2,342 men, 896 women and 201 children were convicted in the one region of Angers along the border with Brittany. And for every conviction there may have been five arrests with too little evidence to proceed.

To their own, the Farmers were much kinder. While guards and clerks were badly paid, their jobs were fairly secure and supplemented by improbable fringe benefits. In 1768, the Farm seems to have invented the first contributory pension plan made up by wage deductions to which the company added its own matching sum. (By 1774 this pension fund was already worth some 260,000 livres). After twenty years of employment a guard could retire on a life pension the amount of which was based on his rank and seniority.

The Farm was a compressed version of old-regime government, rich in both its virtues and its vices. At the local level it provided an extraordinary mixture of corporate paternalism and no-holds-barred commercialism, regulation and enterprise, efficient administration and ponderous bureaucracy, elaborate procedure and haphazard military brutality. At the center of its affairs in Paris, it presented quite another face: polished, urbane, technocratic and, above all, overpoweringly rich. However much public abuse they were subjected to on the stage and in pamphlets, the Farmers knew that they were the cynosure of all eyes. Their houses were the most splendid, their salons packed with stunning art, much of it the result of an adventurous taste for Dutch cabinet paintings as well as French genre and still life. Their daughters, coveted as prize catches, often married into the cream of the old nobility, especially the legal aristocracy, whose orators were denouncing the Farm even as they calculated the size of the prospective brides' dowries.

The Farmers were far from being the knuckle-cracking, clodhopping, parvenu philistines that the stage caricature of Turcaret suggested. Helvétius, the *philosophe,* was not atypical in combining intellectual speculation of a daring kind with financial speculation of a prudent kind. When he died in 1771, he left a vast fortune to his widow, the Comtesse de Ligniville d'Autricourt, who ran the most brilliant salon in Paris, surrounded by a vast troop of Angora cats, each answering to a different name and dressed in silk ribbon. Equally remarkable was the Laborde dynasty, in origin West Indian sugar merchants from Bordeaux. Jean-Benjamin, the third Farmer-General in the line, apart from sustaining the family acumen for finance and commerce, was a prolific composer, scientist and writer on medical, geological and archaeological topics of enormous diversity. But much the most extraordinary of all these men was Antoine Lavoisier, widely celebrated as France's greatest chemist.

Lavoisier was a phenomenon, but the fact that he could apply his scientific inventiveness to something so apparently archaic and repressive as the great customs barrier the Farmers were building around Paris says much about the contradictions of Louis XVI's France. Like so many in the culture of that time, Lavoisier was at once pioneering and arcane, intellectually free and institutionally captive, public-spirited but employed by the most notoriously self-interested private corporation. Yet there is no doubt that

Lavoisier believed his science to be compatible with (indeed crucial to) his profession and that by administering the Farm to the best of his abilities he was serving France in the true spirit of patriotic citizenship.

Certainly his work routine was hardly that of the stereotypically languid old-regime aristocrat living for pleasure and attended by swarms of obsequious servants. Rising at dawn he worked either on Farm papers or in his private laboratory from six to nine. Until late afternoon, at his office in the Hôtel des Fermes, he attended one or more of the five committees to which he was assigned (including the administration of the royal saltpeter and gunpowder works). After dining rather frugally he returned to his laboratory, where he worked again from seven to ten in the evening. Twice a week he gathered friends and colleagues in the sciences and philosophy to hear papers read and informally discuss current projects. And his family life was no less outgoing and productive. His wife was a fine artist in her own right, and Jacques-Louis David's brilliant and animated double portrait shows husband and wife very much as professional partners as well as conjugal friends.

Like other senior officials of the Farm, Lavoisier was not satisfied with supervising its work from afar. Periodically he went on a *tournée* of inspection to the provincial bureaux and warehouses. Although he traveled in some style, with a retinue of eighteen (including uniformed armed guards) and a battery of clerks and accountants, these journeys were long and grueling, sometimes lasting several months. We know that on a similar *tournée* in 1745–46, a Farmer named M. Caze visited no fewer than thirty-two salt warehouses, thirty-five custom houses, twenty-two tobacco stores; settled disputes among local officials of the Farm; and saw as many posts of the military guards as he could manage. Lavoisier was unlikely to have been less thorough.

Although the quality and breadth of Lavoisier's virtuosity mark him out as something of a prodigy, it was not all that unusual in the France of Louis XVI for public men to be simultaneously intellectuals, administrators and businessmen. In all three roles, such men ran certain risks. As a scientist Lavoisier could rise and fall with the fickle ebb and flow of scientific fashion, which in the 1780s was much the most important feature of cultural life in France. His financial security was not immune from unpredictable changes in government policy. For although the *financiers* were polemically depicted as risk-free speculators, they were vulnerable as bond holders to sudden and unforeseen partial repudiations of the kind that had been used in the 1720s and in 1770 to bring the scale of the deficit under control. There were at least as many bankrupt *financiers* as there were millionaires.

Lavoisier was typical of the majority of Farmers in that he had not

24. Jacques-Louis David, *Lavoisier and His Wife*

financed from his own funds the very large deposit needed to install himself but had borrowed as well as having taken on sleeping partners (the so-called *croupiers,* from the word *croupe,* meaning the exposed rump of the horse available for an additional rider). They supplied a share of his working capital and he repaid them with a share of his salary and business proceeds. This meant, in effect, that he was trading on the margin and that under unpredictably adverse conditions was not entirely master of his own destiny. If the government decided to alter or abrogate the terms of a contract, there would immediately be a run on the *billets de ferme*—the negotiable notes that the Farmers were allowed to issue on their own personal security. This actually happened in 1783 when Controller-General d'Ormesson attempted to abrogate the "Lease Salzard" (each lease being titled after its principal contractor). But the Farmers refused to honor their paper, arguing that the government had incurred the responsibility by interfering with the lease. Faced with the popular fury, the government retreated and reinstated the old lease.

This crisis was symptomatic of the deterioration of the mutual interest which had bound the monarchy and the Farmers-General together. On the one hand, the crown needed, more desperately than ever, the kind of up-front revenue that the Farmers so obligingly provided, and it had little inclination to take on the huge enterprise of collecting indirect taxes itself. On the other hand, the more courageous souls in the administration were coming to realize that the price for repeated transfusions of short-term funds was increasing dependence on whatever asking price the Farmers— and other creditors, some of them Dutch or Genevan—demanded. For the Farmers, that price was jacked-up profit levels with no questions asked; for the creditors, it was jacked-up interest rates, running at levels so high that by 1788 debt service was consuming almost 50 percent of all current revenues. And it was at that stage that the government, as we shall see, had no alternative but to abandon fiscal fine-tuning, and turn instead to drastic political solutions for its problems. Those solutions turned out to be revolutionary.

iv LAST BEST HOPES:
THE COACHMAN

Public bankruptcies are a state of mind. The exact point at which a government decides that it has exhausted resources so completely that it can no longer fulfill its most basic function, the protection of its sovereignty, is quite arbitrary. For great powers never go into receivership. However dreadful a financial situation they may get into, there generally will always be moneymen lurking in the wings prepared to set them on their feet—at a price. Only recently has that price been some sort of partial abdication of sovereignty—to the decrees of the International Monetary Fund, for example, or in the age of Victorian imperialism, the international debt commissions that the British and their partners imposed over the fiscally prostrate corpses of the Egyptians and the Chinese. For the French monarchy in the late 1780s, the moment of truth seemed to occur when it ran out of "anticipations" of future revenue to secure new loans. And those loans were needed to service past ones. At this point the technical apparatus of refunding seemed to have broken down. While there was no international financial agency waiting in the wings to shoulder the debt and dictate terms of repayment, the return of Jacques Necker, associated with the international money market, was the closest thing to such an agency. But only a more popular form of domestic political authority would gain the public confidence necessary to secure government credit. Financial rescue, then, was contingent on political change.

This had been apparent to a succession of Louis XVI's ministries, each of which was clearly exercised by the need to reform the way in which the crown obtained its income. Indeed, even under Louis XV this had been the most pressing priority of Controllers-General, but during the 1750s and still more in the 1760s, the political arm that they had flexed to institute tax reform had been that of absolutism. Time and again in the 1760s Louis XV had called a *lit de justice* to utter the most emphatic command in the royal vocabulary: "*Le roi le veult*" (The King so wishes it). Against that command there was no appeal.

Louis XVI, however, as befitted his incoherently amiable character, came to the throne wanting to be loved. This pathetic passion survived even the grim flour wars that disturbed the early years of his reign when rioters were turned back from the gates of the royal palace at Versailles (the court having prudently evacuated). So he got rid of those ministers identified with the muscular absolutism of his grandfather and replaced them with reformers who would somehow conjure up changes that might be both politically liberal and fiscally copious. The trouble was that no two ministries had identical ideas about which strategies of change to pursue. Not only were their policies not consistent, but each virtually defined its government as the complete reversal of the preceding one, both in men and measures. Needless to say, this did not make for positive results.

There had been three classic ways in which Controllers-General had dealt with the growing burden of French government finance: disguised bankruptcies, loans from domestic and foreign syndicates and new taxes. Louis XV's last controller, the Abbé Terray, had used all three. Louis XVI's first controller, Turgot, repudiated all three. Instead, he proposed the lessons of liberal economic theory, in particular that of Physiocracy, whose very name proclaimed it to be the "Law of Nature" and thus irrefutable.

The "sect" of the physiocrats argued that it was corporatism, regulation and protection—the heavy hand of the state—that was stifling productivity and enterprise in France. Internal customs barriers; restrictions on the movement of grain and other basic commodities; elaborate tariffs of tolls and excises: all had to go so that the economy could breathe the pure and heady air of market exchange. The crazy-quilt pattern of indirect impositions and property levies in some but not other parts of France should be swept away and replaced with a single property tax—the *impôt unique.* That would make it possible for cultivators—the only true producers of wealth—to calculate precisely their costs and aim at supplying the market, where in the natural course of things higher prices would buoy up rural incomes and create capital accumulation on the land. Those savings and profits would then be plowed back into technical improvements, thus further improving productivity and creating disposable income that would be spent on the manufactured goods produced in towns. Hence the urban and rural sectors would co-exist in charmed reciprocity and France would swarm with contented, rational rustics all plowing, producing, saving and spending to the deep rhythm of the market.

That, at any rate, was the theory. Its most famous authors were the court physician Quesnay and his temperamental opposite, the fulminating Marquis de Mirabeau (the father of the revolutionary orator). Oddly enough, Mirabeau had made his name denouncing the inroads that capitalism and individualism had made in what he fondly imagined to be the paternalistic virtues of seigneurial feudalism. It was in a long personal interview which Mirabeau later described as "the cracking of the skull of Goliath" that he became converted to *laissez-faire.* So, for better or worse, did a number of Louis XV's Controllers-General who proceeded in the 1760s to remove all restrictions from both the internal and external transshipment of grain, as well as regulations on place of sale and price. The result was immediate dearth and riot. Granaries were pillaged, barges halted before they could depart, merchants forced to sell at the tariff deemed "just" by the crowds. In 1770, Terray restored most of the restrictions, obliging merchants once again to be officially licensed and sell their product only in designated markets. Calm was restored.

All of Terray's actions, however, some of them eminently sensible, were badly compromised by the way he and his colleague Maupeou had elected to execute them: through the absolute writ of royal decree. When Turgot came into office as Controller-General in 1774, having served briefly as minister for the navy, it was not just as an economic but as a political liberal. Only if he could depend on support from the noble Parlements could he deliver policies that avoided the most arbitrary excesses of the previous reign in respect of bankruptcies, loans and taxes. So, with the King's warm endorsement, he rescued the Parlements from the limbo into which Chancellor Maupeou had sent them. His mistaken assumption was that they would back his reforms out of a combination of gratitude and rationality. But nothing was quite that simple in Louis XVI's France.

It followed from Turgot's sympathy with physiocratic ideas that the liberalization of the French economy would, of itself, generate the kind of prosperity that would solve the financial problems of the government. This would happen in two ways. Public confidence, that most alchemical of economic quantities, would revive, disposing of the need for additional new loans since the old ones, duly honored, would suffice. Trade and manufactures would flourish to such an extent that they too, from increased turnover, would yield enough revenues to repair the damage. All this was, of course, the direct ancestor of supply-side public finance, and had just about as much chance of success as its version two hundred years later in a different but similarly fiscally overstretched empire.

Lest this account sound too sardonic it should be said immediately that Turgot was no ministerial Pangloss. A rather somber, self-questioning man whose principal recreation was his work, he had an excessively dim view of human nature but an excessively cheerful view of the possibilities of its improvement. He was, in short, typical of the later years of the Enlightenment. Born into a family long distinguished for public service, Turgot *père* had been *prévôt des marchands* in Paris and had crowned his career as town planning expert there by designing and constructing a great sewer for the right bank of the Seine. His son Anne-Robert came to the Contrôle having spent many years as a brilliant and exceptionally hard-working *intendant* in the impoverished province of the Limousin in southwest France. There he had labored industriously to do good, building roads and persuading the peasants to plant and consume potatoes, a crop previously thought unfit even for animals and certainly less nourishing than the boiled chestnut and buckwheat gruel that had been the standard Limousin fare.

Unfortunately the region of the Limousin was peculiarly unsuited to the application of his most cherished ideas, especially those he had published on capital accumulation, for it was difficult to accumulate any capital while subsisting on boiled chestnuts, or, for that matter, on potatoes. It was only when Turgot became Controller-General that the opportunity arose to

25. Joseph Drouais, portrait of Turgot

apply them on a national scale. Far more than the pragmatic succession of Controllers-General who came into office with nothing much on their minds except personal and national survival, Turgot, as Carlyle put it, "came into the Council of the King with a whole peaceful revolution in his head." A memorandum sent to the King in 1775 revealed just how sweeping was his vision of a France transformed by economic and political liberty. "In ten years," he claimed, "the nation would be unrecognizable . . . in enlightenment, morals, zeal for your service and for the *patrie*, France would surpass all other people who exist and who ever have existed."

Turgot's basic operational method was to dismantle all obstacles to the flow of free trade, free labor and free market pricing, while giving some active encouragement to what he believed to be the enterprises of the future. The encouragement took the form of education and direct subsidy. Serious men in tricorn hats were sent off to study the British coal industry, while grants were given out in the manner of a superior Chamber of Commerce for mechanical silk looms in Lyon, lead-rolling machines in Rouen and—predictably—porcelain manufactures at Limoges. His learned friends Condorcet and d'Alembert were recruited to serve on a committee to study river navigation and pollution, and in the spirit of his father's Grand Designs the Controller-General began construction of the "*machine*

Turgot," which was supposed to break ice floes at the mouth of the Marne and the Seine. Instead, the machine broke itself after incurring considerable expense. More happily, the foundation of a new system of mail and passenger transport, the *messageries royales,* based on light-sprung coaches known as "Turgotines," cut travel time in half between French cities and made the dream of a national market slightly less absurd.

Turgot's principal line of attack, though, was directed against the barriers that were in the way of realizing the free economy. First to go had to be the local tolls on grain (except for Paris and Marseille) and with them went all monopolies of chandlers, merchants and porters. While this represented the dismantling of Terray's system of regulated supply, Turgot wisely continued the prohibition on export abroad. Yet he still chose the worst possible time for the reform. The year 1774 saw the return of bad harvests, and with them the resumption of dearth, high prices and anger directed at engrossers accused of hoarding to profit from price rises. The natural consequence of this by the spring of 1775 was a resumption of the riot patterns of the mid-1760s: barges stopped at river stations, attacks on granaries and millers and compulsory sales at prices demanded by the crowds. In Paris the militia of the *gardes françaises* failed to prevent a crowd from pillaging the Abbaye Saint-Victor because it was busy having its regimental banners blessed in Notre Dame.

Turgot's response to this impertinent interruption of free trade was to call out twenty-five thousand troops and institute summary tribunals and exemplary hangings. The commander of the royal guards at Versailles, the Prince de Poix, who had hastily promised flour at two sous a pound to a crowd of five thousand on the point of storming the palace at Versailles, was reprimanded for his temerity. As they had done in the last round of free grain trade, local police and magistrates widely ignored Turgot's edicts in favor of immediate public peace, and it was this as well as a better harvest, rather than martial law, that restored a measure of calm by the summer of 1775. Stung by violent pamphlet polemics against his policy, Turgot believed (as do many sympathetic historians to this day) that the "flour war" was all an elaborate conspiracy, and that people were pretending to be hungry in order to embarrass his ministry.

Turgot was equally determined to deregulate the meat trade. And in this case he did not stop at the gates of Paris but abolished outright the large number of officeholders and officials of the so-called Bourse de Sceaux et Poissy who held the right to set the price at which drovers could sell their stock to butchers. Under old regulations, suet and tallow (essential for candle lighting) could not be collected by butchers after slaughter but had to be taken by special guilds that enjoyed the monopoly of their sale. They too went under Turgot's axe. This happened at a time least auspicious for success, for 1775 saw a visitation of cattle murrain that devastated the country's herds, and in trying to establish a *cordon sanitaire* within which peasants were required to destroy infected stock and bury the carcasses in lime, Turgot's well-meaning *intendants* ran straight into local resistance. Especially in the southwest the meadows and woods were populated by eerie nocturnal processions of peasants attempting to smuggle cows across the sanitary border.

It was with the *Six Edicts* that Turgot's policies came most seriously unstuck. The principal elements of this bundle of reforms concerned the abolition of the trade guilds, which had confined labor, production and sale of commodities to licensed corporations with their own internal monopoly of training, goods and services. The guild system was directly at odds with Turgot's vision of the market determining wages, demand and supply of all these economic elements. His reform would have done away with most of the guilds except barbers, wig makers and bathhouse keepers, whose officeholders would have required special reimbursement. Also exempt were goldsmiths, pharmacists and printers but on the very different grounds that it was in the public interest for their respective trades (wealth, health and wisdom) to remain under some sort of license. More ominously, the edicts strictly prohibited any kind of assembly of masters or journeymen for the purposes of wage negotiations, or anything else: a principle that the Revolution would uphold in 1791.

The other major proposal was the abolition of the forced labor service, the *corvée,* which commoners owed to the state and from which much of its road building program had been manned. Turgot was quite right to suppose that the *corvée* was generally loathed in the French countryside for abducting a precious (indeed often the only) source of manpower from a tiny family farm precisely at the time when it was most needed for crucial labor, such as plowing or harvest. The *corvée* could be commuted by the payment of a sum of money, but that presupposed that the peasant belonged to the kind of cash economy where this was feasible, and for the vast majority of the French peasantry nothing of the sort was true. The most courageous and controversial element in the reform, however, was the proposal to put in place of the *corvée* a property tax, payable by *all sections of the population.* With the revenue thus gathered the state would have the roads built by contractors with the terms of the contract published to show the relationship between the cost of local works and revenues taken to finance them. This measure would thus have redistributed the burden of funding roads and canals to the whole population and would have been in effect the withdrawal of another privilege from the exempt classes.

Predictably, then, the abolition of forced labor service was greeted with intense and vocal hostility by the nobles through their collective voice in the Parlements. Apart from the dilution of privilege, the abolition also threatened, by example, the right of the nobles to demand comparable services from their own peasants on their estates, an effect that Turgot probably had in mind. Defending his reform he was drawn into an extraordinary but telling exchange of views with Miromesnil, the Keeper of the Seals (in effect the Minister of Justice), over the legitimacy of privilege. Privileges, Miromesnil claimed, were grounded in the exemptions granted to the warrior caste in return for their blood service to the crown. "Take away from the nobility its distinctions, you destroy the national character, and the nation ceasing to be warlike will soon be the prey of neighboring nations." The silliness of this claim provoked Turgot to remind his opponent of the obvious truism that "the nations in which the nobility pays taxes as do the rest of the people are not less martial than ours . . . and in the provinces of the *taille réelle* where the nobles and commoners are treated the same . . . the nobles are no less brave nor less attached to the crown." For that matter, he argued, he was unable to recall any society where the idea of exempting nobles from taxes "has been regarded as otherwise than an antiquated pretension abandoned by all intelligent men, even in the order of the nobility."

Other equally selfish vested interests were responsible for similar opposition to the abolition of the guilds. Turgot defended the measure in the high-flown philosophical rhetoric of economic natural rights. "God, by giving to man certain needs and making them dependent on the resource of labor, has made the right of labor the property of all men and that property is primary, the most sacred and imprescriptible of all." But for its opponents the measure destroyed rather than protected property, for a number of the masters of such guilds were far from being horny-handed sons of toil laboring in leather aprons. They were in fact the aristocratic purchasers of municipal sinecures and dignities which they did not care to see disappear in the name of some theoretically determined version of the general good. Nor for that matter did more genuine artisans who had sunk precious capital, not to mention years of apprenticeship, in a system that guaranteed them both skilled labor and remunerative prices. Compared with those securities Turgot's brave new world of economic liberty was a very uncertain prospect.

Yet it was less the substance of Turgot's reforms that played into the hands of this opposition than the manner in which he attempted to carry them out. For once it became apparent that his restored Parlements were not, in fact, going to be the tame creatures of royal reform, Turgot collapsed back onto precisely the same absolutist legal enforcement that he had found so repugnant in Maupeou and Terray. He did not go so far as to abolish the remonstrating courts, but he did urge Louis XVI, who was himself extremely reluctant to play the absolutist, not to shrink from a *lit de justice,* should that become necessary. This classically high-handed way of proceeding looked particularly bad since Turgot had encouraged the *dévolution* of power to provincial assemblies and had set up two such bodies in the provinces of Berri and Haute-Guienne in 1774. Viewing himself as the most liberal of Controllers-General he was in fact the one who most freely used the arbitrary arrest granted in the *lettres de cachet,* and a number of opponents of his policies ended up smartly in the Bastille.

This was the undoing of the Minister, for it ensured that, in addition to his many personal enemies at court, Turgot could no longer rely on figures within the ministry who had previously been his allies. By the spring of 1776 he was complaining to the King about the open factions that were appearing in the council and demanded that Louis throw the full weight of his authority behind the reforms. His way of putting this was not tactful.

> You are too young to judge men and you have yourself said,
> Sire, that you lack experience and need a guide. Who is that
> Guide to be? . . . Some people think that you are weak, Sire,
> and indeed on occasions I have been afraid that your character
> has this defect. On the other hand on more difficult occasions I
> have seen you show real courage.

This schoolmasterly approach did not pay off. Thirteen days later Turgot was dismissed amidst the usual hurrahs of despotism laid low. With him went some of his men and many of his measures. The guilds were restored, though in an attenuated form; and local parishes were given the choice of whether to supply the *corvée* or comply with a tax.

This was a long way from the peaceful revolution that Turgot had hoped to accomplish. Almost by definition, his macroeconomic approach to solving both the economic and financial troubles of France required time if it was to have any chance at all of working. His most easygoing and worldly colleague, Maurepas, who in his seventy years had seen ministries come and go with the seasons, counseled him to spread his reforms over a number of years rather than take them at a hectic rush. But Turgot had been in a frantic hurry. Mortality was pressing in: "In our family we die at fifty," he replied to Maurepas. A more urgent mortality, he felt, was that of the regime. Without drastic action, he told the King, "the first gunshot [of a new war] will drive the state to bankruptcy."

v LAST BEST HOPES:
THE BANKER

The physiocrats, Turgot included, had always been strong on ends, weak on means. For all their powerful intellectual exertions they failed to see a contradiction in their commanding liberalism to come into being through the instruments of absolutism. They even took some pride in calling an absolutist policy the "legal despotism" required to bring about the promised land of free labor, free trade and free markets. They also made no allowance for the kind of short-term dislocations—such as riots and wars—that constituted everyday reality in an eighteenth-century state. It was understandable—especially given Turgot's bleak warnings on the calamities that would ensue if ever another war was entertained—that once such a war did indeed beckon across the Atlantic, the monarchy turned to quite a different kind of answer.

It would be well to suppose that the promotion of Jacques Necker, following a brief period of business as usual under Controller-General Clugny, represented a turn from theory to pragmatism. And in the sense in which he was as eager to turn to loan finance coupled with administrative reform as Turgot had been to eschew them, this was indeed the case. But in fact the real authority that Necker brought to his office as Director-General (for as a Protestant he was forbidden the office of controller) was magical. For one kind of mystique—that of the intellectual—was substituted another: that of the Protestant Bank. As an outsider he was doubly charmed. Blameless for the ills that afflicted Catholic France, he was thought to embody the contrary set of virtues crudely associated with Protestant capitalism: probity, frugality and rock-solid credit. But also by virtue of his being an outsider he had precious links with the international loan market, which was increasingly seen as an alternative to the extortion of the *gens de finance*.

Public opinion saw Necker as a banking wizard: someone who could pull rabbits out of hats and money out of thin air. He was invested with the sort of miraculous powers associated with the electrical Franklin, Dr. Mesmer's magnetic tubs, or Montgolfier's balloons. His overwhelming personal ordinariness only excited the flattery of those who wanted to contrast him even further with the sybaritic *financiers* or the pretentious physiocrats. He appeared, in fact, to be the perfect solid citizen, happily nested in a marriage so overflowing with conjugal joys that it might have been invented by

26. Joseph-Siffrein Duplessis, portrait of Necker

Jean-Jacques Rousseau. His wife Suzanne presided over the most influential salon in Paris and spread a little Protestant seriousness among the *monde* by doing charity work with the poor and sick. When she burst into tears during one of the *philosophes'* more candid discussions of atheism, Grimm only found the spectacle even more deliciously innocent. Diderot, whose "bourgeois dramas" were currently moistening the Paris theater, followed suit and professed to Mme Necker, "It is really too bad that I never got to know you sooner. You would certainly have inspired me with a taste for purity and delicacy which would have passed into my books."

Mme Necker's vivacity and zeal found a little echo in her daughter, Germaine—the future Mme de Staël. And the brilliance of the feminine side of the family only threw the sterling virtues of stout, solid Jacques into bolder relief. He would have had to be a saint not to have had his head turned by the flattery that followed the publication of his *Elogy of Colbert* in 1773. And he was not. He was even somewhat puffed up by his own sense of certainty, as one extraordinary sentence in the *Elogy* suggests: "If men are made in the image of God, then the minister of finance, next to the king, must be the man who most closely approximates to that image."

In the apprehensive climate of an impending war, Necker's indomitable self-belief was reassuring, especially since the best that the preceding

Controller-General, Clugny, could come up with was a lottery. While Turgot had come from the ethos of government service and philosophical speculation, Necker came from the business world. He had come to Paris from Geneva at the age of eighteen to join the family bank of Thélusson et Cie and on the death of its senior partner had succeeded to the direction of the firm. It had been handed the poisoned chalice of the French India Company to manage but somehow survived the debacle of French imperialism in the subcontinent, and had helped the government with grain provisioning during the difficult period of the 1760s. It was this experience that led Necker to publish his own treatise on the grain trade during Turgot's renewal of deregulation, a timing that clearly stung the Minister, and he wrote telling Necker as much. Genuinely surprised by Turgot's angry tone, Necker reiterated that he stood squarely behind the general principles of a free grain trade. But it was his reservations—namely that in periods of dearth crisis, the government should assume responsibilities for pricing and provisioning—that struck his reading public at a time when the countryside around Paris was fired with riot.

Most important for a ministry now dominated by the foreign affairs minister, Vergennes, Necker promised to fund the American policy without incurring all the dire consequences predicted by Turgot. The question that has raged around Necker's reputation ever since is whether he lived up to these promises. Until fairly recently the consensus has been overwhelmingly negative. Necker's publication of his famous *Compte Rendu*— the first budget made available for wide publication—has been treated as a piece of disingenuous and self-serving propaganda. And it has been characterized as exactly the kind of spurious good cheer that led the French monarchy down the primrose path to perdition.

Necker's fall from grace was the inevitable product of unrealistic expectations that circulated about his abilities. Lately, however, a much more balanced, sympathetic and in the end wholly convincing view of his management has emerged from more careful research, notably from the Necker papers in the Château de Coppet in Switzerland. From these sources emerges Necker the prudent but determined reformer, rather than Necker the fraudulent prestidigitator. Although no less than Turgot he saw the fundamental prosperity of the crown as being contingent on a freely developed economy, he was not prepared to sacrifice to long-term economic planning the immediate priority of restoring royal credit. What counted for Necker were immediate, measurable savings in rationalized administration and the maximizing of revenue.

Knowing it was out of the question to abolish all venal offices at one blow, he concentrated on those areas where waste was most conspicuous and where venal offices most obviously deprived the crown of income. So he abolished the 48 offices of Receivers-General, each with its own exchequer for receiving direct taxes, replacing them with twelve officials directly accountable to his own ministry. Likewise the 6 *intendants* of finance who uselessly duplicated the Ministry's own bureaucracy; the 304 receivers of income from the "Waters and Forests"; and not least, 27 Treasurers-General and Controllers-General of the military departments were similarly dispatched. Thus was created the first phalanx of Necker's powerful enemies.

To this hecatomb of defunct offices Necker then added a number from the royal household, where he saw special opportunities for economy. No fewer than 406 offices in the bloated regime of the *bouche du roi,* the King's kitchen, disappeared. No one at Versailles went hungry as a result, or for that matter was even kept waiting for dinner, for all 406 of the offices were ceremonial appointments that allowed courtiers to dress up on special occasions and display their particular place in the by now rather self-conscious pecking order that passed for court ritual. Away went the 13 chefs and 5 assistants of the Grand Pantry; away went the 20 royal cup bearers (not to be confused with the 4 carriers of the royal wine), the 16 "hasteners" of the royal roast, platoons of tasters, battalions of candle snuffers, brigades of salt passers and (most regrettably) the 10 *aides spéciaux* for the *fruits de Provence.* In all some 506 venal offices were abolished with a saving of about 2.5 million livres a year. Necker's critics complained that this was hardly worth all the effort, especially since the Director was committed to reimbursing all the officeholders to the tune of a capital sum of 8 million livres over five years. But this meant that after four years the reform would pay for itself and thereafter would be a net saving. Perhaps more importantly it represented the return to strict government control of a huge empire of patronage that had simply become the personal plaything of courtiers. Louis XVI seemed delighted. "I wish to put order and economy in every part of my household," he told one of those courtiers, the Duc de Coigny, "and those who have anything to say against it I will crush like this glass." At this point, the King threw a goblet to the floor for dramatic emphasis, prompting the satisfactory response from the Duc that "It is perhaps better to be nibbled than smashed."

Necker was even prepared to take on the Farmers-General, comparing them unflatteringly with a kind of weed that flourished in a swamp. It seems likely that, ideally, he would have wanted to abolish the contract system altogether and have repatriated to the state the responsibility of collecting indirect taxes. But understandably (and especially in wartime) he flinched at the administrative costs that would suddenly have been entailed, not to mention the immediate disappearance of advances on revenue. But he was determined to take for the state a greater share of the profits accruing to the Farm, and after the expiration of the "Lease David" in 1780, he transferred a number of taxes, in particular duties on wine and spirits, to the more direct method of the *régie*. In that form, the tax was still collected by a third party, but instead of collaring all of the proceeds, whatever they amounted to, the collectors were only entitled to a percentage of the revenue over and above a prior stipulated sum. Even in the Farm that remained for the salt tax, Necker made it clear that, should revenues surpass the money advanced for the lease by a certain sum, the crown would then be entitled to a portion of that profit. This was a brilliant stroke, for it got to the heart of the matter of French finance: not that the farming system was itself depriving the crown of income, but that the Farmers, rather than the state, were collecting the benefits of a rapidly rising gross national product. For it was by then obvious that indirect, not direct, taxes were the true growth area of revenue.

The principle of fiscal profit sharing at low administrative cost was extended to other obviously lucrative areas. The *messageries royales* post and transport system that Turgot had farmed out under contract was converted instead into a *régie*, and it was in the 1780s that it began to prosper spectacularly. A *régie* was also applied to the management of the royal domains and forests, where timber was taken for the enormous expansion of urban building that was proceeding in Louis XVI's reign, making that asset immensely profitable.

All of these savings were designed by Necker for one end: to balance the *ordinary* revenues and expenditures of the crown. And it was that balance which was reflected in his *Compte Rendu*. Its publication in 1781 was itself an event. The royal printers and the greatest editor-publisher in Paris, Panckoucke, decided to print what by contemporary standards was a huge, virtually unprecedented run of twenty thousand copies (from several presses), and the weighty document was sold out within a few weeks. It was also rapidly translated into Dutch, German, Danish, Italian and English, the Duke of Richmond alone buying six thousand copies. It produced, said the Protestant pastor Rabaut Saint-Etienne, "the effect of sudden light in the midst of darkness." Marmont, who was to become one of Napoleon's marshals, even claimed that he had been taught to read from the *Compte*. Yet although it was a runaway best seller, its popularity never survived Necker's fall. After 1781 there were no new editions and it became a kind of scapegoat for subsequent Controllers-General, in particular Calonne, who characterized it as an absurd fraud, a pretense that all was well when in fact all was very much ill.

The center of their accusation was that Necker had deliberately constructed a flimsy and artificial balance that bore no reality to the new burden of debt service. But Necker never made any pretense of covering up the cost of war debts. The intention of the *Compte Rendu* was quite different. It was meant to show that as long as, in peacetime, the fixed obligations of the crown could be met from current income, loans taken out for "extraordinary" purposes such as war might be financed on more advantageous terms than had generally been the case in the second half of the century. To his sound Swiss mind, everything depended on public confidence and credit. With that elusive quantity present, there was no reason not to seek funding for foreign and military purposes that were deemed essential by both the government and public opinion. And given the climate of ecstatic support for the American war, there could hardly be any argument with that.

The fiscal exhaustion that Calonne related to Louis XVI in 1786 as an emergency, and which in effect precipitated the French Revolution, was directly attributable not to Necker's wartime funding of 530 million livres but to the *peacetime* loans of his successors, and to their wholesale abandonment of his economies. His retrenchment had created a host of enemies among deprived officeholders. And within the government were ministers, including Vergennes, who became increasingly alienated by both the manner and substance of his policies. In May 1781 Necker met the challenge aggressively by asking the King to bring him into the royal council notwithstanding his Protestantism and title of Director-General. Both Maurepas and Vergennes replied that they would resign if this was done. On May 19 Necker resigned.

Joly de Fleury, who followed him into office, immediately restored most of Necker's abolished receivers and treasurers; and Calonne actually embarked on a deliberate and flagrant spending spree on behalf of the monarchy, buying Rambouillet and Saint-Cloud and promoting ambitious military works like the naval yards at Toulon and the great harbor project at Cherbourg. Calonne was also an administrative prodigal, abandoning the careful accounting requirements that had caused so much pain in the army and navy (especially on their procurement side) and in the royal household. As R. D. Harris rightly points out, only when the last *vingtième* tax imposed as a wartime measure was due to expire in 1786 did Calonne suddenly discover that the relation between ordinary income and expenditure was not a surplus as indicated in Necker's document but a deficit of 112 million livres. This was indeed an emergency but it had been made not by Necker but by those who followed him, and none more culpably than Calonne.

Later Necker was to sigh over lost opportunities:

Ah! What might have been accomplished in other circumstances. The heart aches to think about it. I labored to keep the
ship afloat during the tempest . . . the days of peace belonged to
others.

But as with Turgot it had, in part, been his own determination to secure
increasingly exclusive control over finance that cost him friends at court.
In particular and perhaps not unreasonably, he had insisted on full membership in the royal council, rather than assuming the outsider role that his
anachronistic post of Director-General implied. This was not just a matter
of amour-propre. He had been losing ground within the government to the
expansionist military policies of de Castries and Ségur and had rashly
attempted a mediation to end the American war before it ended the monarchy. This lost him Vergennes' support. His attack on office and the Farmers-
General had made him many powerful enemies, but it was over a specific
issue that Necker insisted he be admitted to the council.

He had always argued that broad political support was indispensable to
the success of any serious reform program. And to a greater extent than
Turgot and other predecessors, Necker as an outsider was prepared to go
beyond the circumscribed political realm of court and Parlements to get it.
He had established elected provincial assemblies in the Berri and Haute-
Guienne to which tasks formerly entrusted to the *intendants* had been
transferred. These were some way from being the top-to-bottom overhaul
of institutions advocated by Turgot (who proposed a chain of elected
bodies from village assemblies all the way to a national representation), and
while the members of Necker's assemblies met in the traditional three
orders of the Estates, the representatives of the Third Estate—the commoners—were, for the first time, present in "double numbers" to equal the
number of deputies of the clergy and the nobility. It was when he met not
just resistance but total disregard from the Intendant of the Bourbonnais
in his proposal to establish a third assembly at Moulins that Necker made
his demand of the King. In fact, such was his position that he had to ask
one of his enemies, Miromesnil, to forward the proposal to the King in
council, something the Minister declined to do.

While Necker had often affronted the stalwarts of the old-regime traditions, no offense was more rank than the central principle of his *Compte
Rendu:* public scrutiny. One of his critics claimed that the essence of royal
government had been its secrecy and that "It will be a long time before
Your Majesty heals this wound inflicted on the dignity of the throne." But
establishing some sort of accountability in French government was, for
Necker, the heart of the matter. Handled by men of integrity and compe-

tence like his own loyal assistant Bertrand Dufresne, such publicity was not a handicap but actually the working condition of financial success. It was the essence of credit. As much as anything, the *Compte Rendu* was an exercise in public education. Its deliberately simple language, and its effort to make a financial account readable by the common man, testifies to its attempt to form an engaged citizenry.

So the issue was much more than a matter of fiscal management style. It arose from a deep and passionate theme in late eighteenth-century French culture, one that flowed over from personal public morality and which was to make the two inseparable in the discourse and conduct of the Revolution. That was the opposition of transparency and opacity, of candor against dissimulation, of public-spiritedness against self-interest, of directness against disguise. The Revolution would make the manners of the *ancien régime,* with their emphasis on polite insincerities, a form of treason. But already, in the shape of court intrigue, they were enough to dissuade the King from standing by his most successful reformer.

For Necker, the preservation of secrecy was, in effect, the rescue of despotism. This was not only immoral, it was imprudent. The real difference between British and French credit, he thought, was the ability of the former to use representative institutions like Parliament (however imperfect) to symbolize the relationship of trust and consent between governors and governed. "The strong bond between citizens and the state, the influence of the nation on government," he wrote, "the guarantees of civil liberty to the individual, the patriotic support which the people always give to the government in crisis all contribute to make English citizens unique in the world."

But if it was foolish to try to provide a simulacrum of English constitutional history in France, at least there should be some concerted attempt to go in that direction. The worst result of his dismissal, he believed, was that it struck down this union between fiscal retrenchment and political liberalization before it had time to begin. Should there ever be another opportunity when Necker and reform would once again seem a solution, indeed the only solution, it would likely be in circumstances of traumatic upheaval. Others evidently feared the worst. Grimm reported that when the news of Necker's dismissal spread

One would have thought there was a public calamity . . . people looked at each other in silent dismay and sadly pressed each other's hand as they passed.

CHAPTER THREE
Absolutism Attacked

i THE ADVENTURES OF M. GUILLAUME

ONE MORNING in August 1776, a rather shabbily dressed, stout gentleman stood on the dockside at Rotterdam. Puffing on a pipe, his tricorn hat planted carelessly over a perruque that had seen better days, he watched intently the slow progress of timber barges as they sailed down the canal in the direction of Dordrecht. This perfectly ordinary scene struck him as astonishing. In his journal he described it as "one of the most singular spectacles that I have seen in my whole life: a whole floating town on which was nailed a fine house made of planks of wood." Moved by curiosity, he asked, when the barge next stopped, if he might visit the floating cabin and was welcomed aboard by a woman *d'une certaine âge* who, to his further amazement, turned out to be the owner of the whole fleet. She received him, he wrote, "most honestly, purely in my capacity as traveller."

This traveler, known on his many journeys simply as "M. Guillaume," was probably the best-loved man in France. He was Chrétien-Guillaume de Lamoignon de Malesherbes, who three months before had been a colleague of Turgot's and Master of the Royal Household. For Malesherbes, this vision of floating bounty, directed by a formidable bargewoman, was about as far from old-regime France as he could come. Like the whole of the Dutch Republic it proclaimed wealth, freedom of goods and persons and the homely dignities that stood in damning contrast to the court at Versailles from which he had come. The Netherlands suited "M. Guillaume" very well. Miraculously, he thought, as did a whole caravan of distinguished French visitors who included Diderot, Montesquieu and d'Argenson, it had preserved simplicity of manners even at the height of its powers. Moreover, it was a nation of pipe smokers, and in society in France only snuff was permitted with its enameled boxes, lace handkerchiefs and fussy business with thumb and forefinger. Nor did anyone there seem to attach much store to appearance, which was as well since Malesherbes had been notorious for lumbering about, even at court, in his grimy brown coat and black hose, looking for all the world like a small-town apothecary rather than a minister of the King.

He was a passionate traveler, and regular dismissals from office (the penalty paid for his independent mind) had provided him with time to indulge himself in his real vocation: botany. Hardly had he submitted his letter of resignation to Louis XVI, following Turgot's "disgrace," than he was off on a walking trip to southwest France to look at viticulture and the sandy pine woods of the Landes southwest of Bordeaux. His real mission in life, he claimed, was to succeed in refuting the naturalist theories of Buffon, whom he denounced as a scoundrel as well as a fool, and to rehabilitate the work of his own intellectual master, Linnaeus. Forty volumes of his *Herbier,* as well as the most extensive scientific garden in France, were to accomplish this great enterprise. For Malesherbes, his château was simply a kind of glorified potting shed with a botanical reference library of a thousand works attached. In his great collection were Virginian dogwoods, Pennsylvanian junipers, Canadian spruce, as well as tropical gum trees and Brazilian nut woods. He even had an entire stand of English elms shipped from Dover on a specially commissioned packet

27. Malesherbes

and transplanted. To him, the most painful sight in the world—after the state of the Paris prisons—was a burned-over forest such as the one he found on his long ramble through Provence in 1767. In Holland his encyclopedic mind raced. Entranced with a culture where natural disaster was compensated for by natural ingenuity, he observed everything. Colonies of rabbits threatened the dunes but the Dutch replied by discovering a kind of shallow-rooted tree that fixed the sand. Even seaweed could be used to strengthen the dikes. Lying in a clean bed on a warm August morning at the tip of the north Holland peninsula, looking from his window at the ocean, Malesherbes felt, at last, cleansed of the dirt of court politics.

He had never really been happy in office. In Switzerland, two years later, a Protestant pastor had tried to offer the anonymous, learned disputant a vacant curacy. When Malesherbes attempted to extricate himself, the pastor assumed he was questioning his right to make the appointment, adding, reassuringly, "*Mais moi, ministre.*" To which his companion replied, temporarily discarding his incognito, "*Et moi, ex-ministre.*" In fact he reveled in this repudiation of official authority. He had turned down his friend Turgot on the first occasion the Controller-General had tried to persuade him to take office in 1774. And shortly after his departure from the ministry he found himself in an inn where two men were lamenting the removal of the fine M. de Malesherbes. "M. Guillaume" hotly disputed the ex-minister's fitness for office, insisting that Malesherbes was simply not cut out for the job.

There was, of course, an element of inverted self-congratulation in all this. An admirer, indeed a correspondent of Rousseau's, Malesherbes consciously struck the attitude of the *honnête homme*. Continuing to wear down-at-heel clothes as the Master of the Royal Household was not a matter of absent-minded slovenliness but a deliberate defiance of Versailles etiquette that prescribed court dress for ministers. If economy was to be the order of the day, let it start with him. He scored even more points from the story (probably true) that the famous dancing master Marcel, hired to instruct him as a youth, had despaired of the task and warned Malesherbes *père* that with such miserable deportment his son could never hope to succeed in any career of public or political distinction. Unlike that other quintessential *honnête homme*, Benjamin Franklin, Malesherbes was virtually incapable of insincerity or social calculation. And he had enough personal disasters and unhappinesses to endear him to a generation that believed sorrow to be a badge of nobility. In 1771, Malesherbes had found the body of his wife Marie-Françoise, the daughter of Farmer-General Grimod de La Reynière, in the woods near his house. With careful expertise she had tied a rifled musket to a tree, wound a blue silk ribbon to the trigger, propped the muzzle against her breast and pulled. Rousseau had written in condolence the best praise he knew: that "she knew neither how to feign nor to deceive. That must at least be some consolation in the affliction that all sensitive hearts must feel."

Within Malesherbes there dwelled all the political contradictions of the old-regime nobility. Since he was temperamentally unsuited to court, Turgot put him in charge of the royal household. There he pretended not to notice the creatures of the *grands appartements* snickering behind their hands at this owl come among peacocks. And he used his unimpeachable reputation to prepare the way for Necker's wholesale onslaught on court office. Despite his appearance and manners, Malesherbes had nothing to apologize for in his pedigree. His family was one of the most distinguished noble dynasties in France. As little covetous as he was, he had married into one of the richest. While the family had risen to prominence under Cardinal Mazarin as a great clan of the *robe*—the judicial nobility—it had, like many others, served both in royal office and in the sovereign courts that had become an unofficial opposition to absolutism. Malesherbes' father had been chancellor and his cousin Lamoignon was to be Louis XVI's most determined Keeper of the Seals.

When Malesherbes had taken office under Louis XV, it was in such a way as to constrain rather than enforce the authority of absolutism. He had begun his career at the age of twenty in Parlement. Between 1750 and 1775 he had occupied two positions crucial to the defense of what Malesherbes, in common with many of the elite, saw as fundamental liberties. The first of these was the freedom to read. From 1750 to 1763 he occupied the post of *directeur de la librairie*: the official who decided whether or not a book might be published. It need hardly be said that his attitude was one of creative complaisance. Virtually everything short of outright atheism, tracts preaching regicide and pornography got published under his regime. Most important, both Rousseau and the editors of the *Encyclopédie*, Diderot and d'Alembert, received the protection they needed to produce their great work. In 1752 the royal council, angered by articles in the second volume attacking the Jesuits, demanded its suppression and provided heavy fines for anyone caught printing or distributing it. Worse, Malesherbes was ordered to seize all the relevant manuscripts, plates and unbound and bound copies. Instead, he not only tipped off Diderot before the police arrived but actually persuaded him to hide the offending copy in his own house, assuming correctly that it was the last place they might look for incriminating material.

In his other office, as president of the Cour des Aides, Malesherbes proved himself to be no less willing to use high position to defend the citizen (for the word was commonly used) against the agents of absolutism. Most of the business of the Cour des Aides was to hear appeals against decisions given by the administrative tribunals of the tax and finance authorities: customs officers, excise men and the commissioners of the Farmers-General. This made it one of the more popular institutions of the old regime, and its sympathetic reputation was probably enhanced by the fact that most of its advocates and magistrates came from a lower social stratum of the nobility than the *grands* of the Parlements.

The President could be terrierlike in his tenacity when he became convinced an injustice had been committed. For example, an itinerant hawker from the Limousin named Monnerat had been arrested on suspicion of smuggling and thrown in the underground cells of the Bicêtre prison for twenty months without being given a hearing. On release he attempted through the Cour des Aides to win damages against the Farmers-General. This resulted in his being rearrested, at which point Malesherbes countered by apprehending the officer of the Farm. A head-on collision then ensued between the Cour des Aides and the Controller-General, Terray, that only ended when the latter dissolved the Court. But if the crown temporarily had the upper hand, the episode ensured that when the Court was reinstated under Louis XVI, its standing as a protector of the subject against arbitrary administrative justice would never be higher.

The Court had a second, no less important function. Like the thirteen high courts of Parlement, it retained the right to "register" any royal edict. Only with that ratification could edict become law, although the crown could override a prolonged refusal to register by holding a *lit de justice* and commanding it into execution. Also in common with the Parlements the Court had a power of "remonstrance." At the height of royal ascendancy in the seventeenth century this power had lapsed, but following the death of Louis XIV in 1715, the Regent had restored it and with this one stroke rejuvenated the political authority of the courts. Remonstrances were, in effect, critical admonitions or protests—often in the form of lengthy lectures—against policies considered violations of the "fundamental laws" of the realm. Just what that body of fundamental law comprised was, as we shall see, a matter of serious dispute. But as the fiscal policies of Louis XV became more aggressive following each of his major wars, so remonstrances against them became correspondingly more frequent and combative.

Most of the remonstrances issuing from Parlement concerned the breach of privilege implied by taxes like the *vingtième*, even though Parlement claimed to be reacting to assaults on "liberties." But those coming from the Cour des Aides from 1759 onwards had a much more radical character. For Malesherbes used his presidency to attack the entire system of taxation, especially the inequities of assessment and collection. In the first place, he argued, following Montesquieu, that under the medieval French monarchy, taxes had never been levied without the consent of the people assembled in the Estates-General. Second, it was axiomatic that the total amount of taxes ought never to exceed the proven needs of state. And for the correct relationship between revenue and necessary expenditures to be restored, some form of public accountability had to be introduced. Third, the inequities of taxation had to be addressed—between different classes of citizens and between different regions of the country.

In 1771 he would go even further. Exasperated by Parlementaire obstruction, Chancellor Maupeou had persuaded Louis XV to take drastic action. The sovereign courts were done away with altogether in favor of appointed bodies of magistrates who would do the crown's bidding. In February 1771 Malesherbes issued a remonstrance on behalf of the Court that guaranteed its own dissolution shortly thereafter. But not before he had attacked the crown for violating fundamental rights of property by depriving the members of Parlement of their offices. This was no more than following the acceptable Parlementaire line. But the remonstrance had a sting in its tail. For in closing, Malesherbes argued that since the "nation" had been deprived of "intermediary bodies" that might defend its "fundamental laws" there was now no alternative to despotism except to summon an assembly of the nation, presumably the Estates-General. "The incorruptible witness of its representatives will at least show you if it is true whether, as your ministers ceaselessly claim, the magistrates violate the law, or whether the cause we defend today is not that of the People *by whom you reign and for whom you reign.*"

The conditional, even contractual basis of this sovereignty was a long way from the absolutism proclaimed in Louis XV's formal utterance in the *lit de justice* that "we hold our Crown from God alone." And in March, the King duly summoned the recalcitrant President to Versailles to witness the mortifying ceremony in which he would personally annul the Court's remonstrance. But en route to this ritualized humiliation, an extraordinary event occurred. When Malesherbes arrived at the doors to the royal apartments, the wall of ornamental popinjays, who made a great point of condescending to the black-garbed magistrates, parted down the middle to allow the grubby little fat man undisputed access to the King. A colleague of Malesherbes' later recalled this act of unexpected deference as "astonishing" and described the "respect and consideration . . . all the more striking because the men of the robe . . . sometimes have difficulty in entering [the apartments] even when the King has requested their presence."

Malesherbes' hope for the new reign was that Louis XVI might be rescued from his court. So he very reluctantly joined Turgot's ministry on the understanding that he would not be co-opted into the world of *les petits maîtres*, as he contemptuously called the courtiers. And lest he still be misunderstood, before taking office he published a final remonstrance that was a massive indictment of both the spirit and the letter of French government. The bulk of the long and powerfully argued treatise was taken up with an attack on the abuses of the Farmers-General and their officers, the inequities of the *taille* and the need to replace the cherished "secrecy" of administration with public scrutiny and accountability. But Malesherbes also took it on himself to reiterate that this necessarily meant breaking down the bureaucratic power of *intendants* and substituting the elected authority of local and provincial assemblies. Only when the crown could depend on a loyal national representation would government be treated as a trust rather than a despotic imposition by those it presumed to rule.

Needless to say Louis XVI missed the point. Instead of seeing the remonstrance as an appeal to alter in its fundamentals the nature of government, he saw it as a long-winded advocacy of specific piecemeal measures to which he was not especially opposed. Likewise, in the same year, Turgot's *Memoir on Municipalities,* which proposed an even more drastic decentralization of government, starting with local village assemblies and reaching all the way to a national representation, failed to make much of an impression on the King. Much of Malesherbes' urging that the King should give public demonstrations of a new candor and public-spiritedness fell on deaf ears, or was defeated by the claims of traditional decorum advanced by Maurepas. So that while Louis was content that Malesherbes personally visit the Bicêtre prison and the Bastille (from which he emerged aghast at conditions in the worst cells), he refused the Minister's entreaties to accompany him. Nor would he abolish, as Malesherbes strongly recommended, *lettres de cachet* (the instrument by which the crown could command the arrest and detention of prisoners without a hearing). Nothing much more than lip service was paid to the Minister's cherished proposals for public toleration of Protestantism.

All the great hopes placed in Louis XVI at the time of his coronation, then, were rapidly petering out. But coming as they did from two of the most powerful men in France, the remonstrance and Turgot's *mémoire* constituted a blueprint for an alternative monarchy in France: local rather than centralized, elected rather than bureaucratic, public rather than clandestine and legal rather than arbitrary.

Before long Malesherbes ran afoul of the Queen when he balked at granting an embassy to one of her more notorious favorites. But once his friend Turgot fell from power, he was able to depart with a clean conscience: he had not compromised his independence with the taint of office. He went back to his château, poring over seedlings and his immense manuscript late into the night, dressed in a gray flannel gown and white nightcap. Nor had he altogether despaired of the monarchy. The year 1775 had also witnessed his triumphal reception into the Académie Française, where he had made an inaugural address that rang with brilliant optimism for the destiny of France. His own fate and that of his king were, in fact, more closely united than he could have imagined. He would once more play the lawyer, and his unhappy client would be Louis XVI.

ii SOVEREIGNTY REDEFINED: THE CHALLENGE OF THE PARLEMENTS

As time would show, Malesherbes was no revolutionary. The sharp tone of his onslaught on "despotism" and "ministerial tyranny" would have been unthinkable had it not been sanctioned by long use in the polemics of the Parlements. Since the 1750s, the tone of Parlementaire resistance to royal policy had been irate vehemence. The more desperately the crown sought remedies for its financial plight in taxes imposed on privileged and unprivileged alike, the more infuriated the Parlements became. And their belligerence was much more than a fit of collective bad temper. It represented a concerted effort to replace the unconfined absolutism of Louis XIV with a more "constitutional" monarchy. In that new regime they were to be the arbiters of legitimate power, the virtual representatives of the "Nation" patrolling any and every excess of governmental authority.

In this process of mutation from an absolute to a "mixed" monarchy, the Parlements were assisted by a change of emphasis in the self-definition of government. In keeping with the eighteenth century's invention of a theory of administration (principally, but not exclusively, in Germany), officers of the crown had become accustomed to expressing their loyalty not to the person of the King but the impersonal entity of the State. *Intendants,* who were referred to as the *commissaires départis* of the central government, thought of themselves essentially as the administrative organs of the royal council rather than as emanations of the dynastic power. This alteration was noticed by Turgot's friend the Abbé Veri. "The commonplaces of my youth," he remarked, "[like] 'serve the King' are no longer on the lips of Frenchmen. . . . Dare one say that for 'serve the King' we have substituted 'serve the State,' a word which, since the time of Louis XIV, has been blasphemy?"

This subtle but important distinction cannot be blamed on any indecisiveness on the part of Louis XV. As the disputes with the Parlements over religious and tax policies at the end of his reign became more acrimonious, so the King became more adamantly absolutist. The premature death of the Dauphin in 1765 created a distinct possibility of another period of political uncertainty while Louis' grandson grew to maturity. In these circumstances it may have seemed especially important to reiterate unequivocally the irreducible principles on which the monarchy rested. In a rebuttal to the Parlement of Rouen's claim that on his coronation he had taken an oath to the *nation*, Louis interrupted the reading of their remonstrance to affirm, with some indignation, that he had taken an oath only to God. In the document written for him by Gilbert de Voisins early in 1766 and used as the instrument of mortification against the Paris Parlement on the third of March, he developed the traditional view of absolutism with uncompromising clarity. "In my person alone resides the sovereign power," he insisted,

> and it is from me alone that the courts [the Parlements] hold
> their existence and their authority. That . . . authority can only
> be exercised in my name . . . and can never be turned against me.
> For it is to me exclusively that the legislative power belongs
> without any qualification or partition [*partage*]. The whole public
> order emanates from me since I am its supreme guardian. My
> people and my person are one and the same, and the rights and
> the interests of the nation that some presume to make a body
> separate from the monarch are necessarily united with my own
> and can only rest in my hands.

Louis XV's utterance radiated cool infuriation with the pretensions of Parlementaire ideology. But the defensiveness of his counterclaims concerning the indivisibility of the legislative power was an implicit recognition that this axiom was indeed threatened. For at least fifteen years it had been the Parlements that had taken the initiative in developing something like a constitutional theory of government that all but replaced absolutism with a much more constrained and divided version of monarchy.

What were the institutions responsible for this transformation? The Parlements were not, as their name might suggest, French counterparts of the British Houses of Parliament. They were thirteen sovereign courts of law, sitting in Paris and provincial centers, each comprising a body of noble judges that, in different Parlements, numbered from 50 to 130. The area of their jurisdiction varied dramatically with some in the more remote regions like the Béarn in the southwest and Metz on the eastern frontier acting as regional courts. The Parlement of Paris, on the other hand, exercised jurisdiction over an enormous area of central and northern France stretching from northern Burgundy through the Ile-de-France and the Orléannais up to Picardy on the Channel coast. The scope of their office was equally broad, hearing both appellate cases and a wide variety of first-instance cases—the *cas royaux*—ranging from charges of *lèse-majesté*, sedition and highway robbery to unlawful use of the royal seal, debasement of currency to other kinds of forgery and tampering with documents (in a society where bureaucratic writ was all-important), a capital crime. In addition they exercised jurisdiction over most criminal and civil cases concerning the privileged orders; acted as censors of theater and literature, and as guardians of social and moral propriety. But what made their power especially difficult to circumscribe was that they also shared with the King's bureaucrats—the *intendants* and the governors—administrative responsibility for provisioning cities, setting prices in times of dearth and policing markets and fairs.

The Parlements, then, were both an institution and an ethos. In the more dynamic commercial centers of France—like Bordeaux—they represented the means through which raw wealth became translated into legal status and political dignity. In sleepier provincial towns like Dijon, Grenoble and Besançon, the whole economy and society of the region revolved round their presence—regiments of scribes, amanuenses, petty advocates and pleaders, booksellers, not to mention the ancillary trades that supported their aristocratic style of life: coach makers, tailors, wig makers, *traiteurs*, cabinetmakers, dancing masters and liveried domestics. And this sense of social solidarity between the *robins*—the judicial nobility of the "robe"— and their co-citizens was played out every November in the elaborate spectacles that greeted their return to sessions from country vacation. For this "red Mass" they would don scarlet robes in place of their habitual black; parade through the streets of the city attended by militia and music; receive the benediction of the clergy for their new year; and only after more grave mummery, shuffling to and fro in the stylized mutual obeisances (often known as the "dance of the Presidents"), would they finally take up their seats.

In many of the Parlementaire residences, the building that housed their court was known as a *palais de justice*. But it was in Paris that the additional title of the residence, Capitole de la France, most aptly symbolized their senatorial pretensions. Cheek by jowl with Notre Dame and the Tuileries, the immense pile housed what contemporaries described as virtually a miniature city in itself. Its courtyard was a bazaar echoing with the din of criers and hawkers, swarming with trades of every kind—ribbon sellers and lemonade vendors as well as booksellers. Many of its stall holders specialized in the cheap prints and satires, very often directed against the government, that were protected from the police in this inner sanctum of justice. It was a place where rich and muddy currents of gossip, rumor and scandal converged to make a thick river of suggestion issuing out of the Palais towards the islands of journalists and libel-mongers waiting on the banks of the Seine for their news of the day.

Within the chambers of the Palais, the presidents and councillors of the court asserted their status in the realm by all manner of symbolic expressions. The mere appearance of the great "gilded chamber" was designed to intimidate, dripping with crested ceiling bosses and finials, emblazoned with arms, and the walls adorned with royal portraits and history paintings representing the majesty of judgment. The *robins* sat on the fleur-de-lis benches which were expressly denied to mere dukes and other members of the peerage of "the sword" (the military nobility) and "the blood" (the royal dynasty and its cadets) entering the court. Since 1681, when Président Potier de Novion had the audacity and sang-froid to keep his hat on in the presence of dukes of the blood royal, they had preserved this right, a matter that may seem picayune to us, but which in the eighteenth century proclaimed aloud that deference was due *to* them *from* the nobility of the sword and not the other way about. Even the nature of their headgear, the black mortarboard, beribboned in gold tassels, was suggestive of a direct, unmediated relationship with the crown since it was held, by the Parlements' antiquaries, to be the mark of the *coiffe royale* specially granted by Philip the Fair to his sovereign courts.

Not surprisingly, then, the *robins* were intensely self-conscious of their collective dignity and jealous of any attempts to encroach on their local authority. Inescapably, the Parlements became a forum for political statements articulated through their remonstrances, entered when royal edicts required registration in the Parlements before becoming enforceable. It was in this requirement that their ideologues saw the principle of assent that they claimed made the monarchy conditional rather than absolute. The basis of that argument was historical. For although the truth of the matter was that the Parlements only went back to the thirteenth century they proposed a much more hoary pedigree. Already in 1740 the Abbé Laboureur in his *History of the Peerage* had asserted that "the Parlement represents the French nation in its ancient state," and a whole phalanx of earnest antiquarians combed antique charters and capitularies to prove that it was directly descended from the Frankish assemblies of the early Middle Ages. Their ancestry was, then, not only contemporary with, but possibly anterior to the founding of the Frankish monarchy. As with so many other usable pasts invented by constitutional theorists in the seventeenth and eighteenth centuries, French antiquarians located the birth of liberty in the Teutonic forest where the Frankish hosts had assembled, with spear and horse, in primitive gatherings. It was these tribal assemblies which delegated power to the chiefs who became the "Kings of the First Race"—the Merovingians.

What this all meant was that in their view the Parlements had never been a dependent creation of the monarchy (as Louis XV claimed). As a condition of its foundation, and throughout the Middle Ages, the crown had acknowledged that its power was limited by legal accountability. The watchdogs of that accountability were the Parlements and they alone were the arbiters of when and whether creeping despotism threatened to overrun legitimate royal authority. This was not an esoteric view confined to antiquarian quibbles. Drawing on previous historical work Montesquieu's *Esprit des Lois*, first published in 1748, lent it enormous political respectability and wide currency. Montesquieu was himself a president of the Parlement of Bordeaux, and at a time when Parlements were claiming to protect the "liberties of Frenchmen" from the tax policy of the crown, the book became an overnight best-seller, going through twelve editions in six months. In April 1750 the Chevalier de Solar congratulated Montesquieu on what he said was the twenty-second edition of that work. "Since the creation of the sun," a *bel esprit* of Baillon wrote, "this work will do most to illuminate the world."

In 1762 the ultimate accolade was bestowed on the work when Alexandre Deleyre produced a handbook of edited extracts, the *Génie de Montesquieu*, designed for polemical use. Well before this the kind of historical arguments embedded in it had become not just theory but the ammunition in political crossfire. When their remonstrances were overruled and the monarchy sought to enforce an edict by command, the magistrates responded with a judicial strike. In return they were threatened with exile if they refused the crown's bidding. Bludgeoned in this way, the presidents of the Parlements of Aix and Dijon both invoked Montesquieu's assertion that the magistracy formed an intermediate body between the King and his people that was not removable without bringing down the constitution of France itself. In 1760, the remonstrance of the Parlement of Toulouse warned still more dramatically:

> Woe betide the power established on the ruin of the laws . . .
> the Prince will be forced to reign over his state as he would over
> a conquered land.

Nor were the partisans of this view confined to the *robins*. One of the most committed of their allies among the nobility of the sword was the Prince de Conti, the King's own cousin and a powerful and articulate spokesman. It was his archivist, Le Paige, who was the most resourceful and uncompromising of all the Parlementaire propagandists. At the other end of the spectrum of aristocratic fashion, deep in the backwaters of rural Poitou, a retired cavalry officer, the Baron de Lezardière (after some initial misgivings), encouraged his seventeen-year-old daughter Pauline in her ambitions to become a medieval historian and political theorist. From long hours spent with dusty charters and annals, she eventually constructed an immense multivolume account of the founding of the Frankish monarchy and its relationship with the early medieval assemblies. This was more than chronicle. In its completed version it presented itself as a worked-up theory of the legitimacy of French political institutions. But by the time Mlle de Lezardière put the finishing touches to her work, its authority had been overwhelmed by the Revolution and her family scattered to their several tragic resting places: in British exile, in a royalist army and among the bloody cadavers of the Paris prison massacres.

Compared with what was to come, the issues that provoked this intense conflict over the nature of the monarchy seem arcane or wildly paradoxical. The government was first stigmatized as "despotic" in the 1750s when it tried to enforce the Papal Bull *Unigenitus* denying the sacraments of baptism, marriage and last rites to anyone not able to prove impeccable orthodoxy. This was a measure designed to root out the Catholic heresy of Jansenism, which took a much more austere view of salvation than the acceptable norm, and which had adherents at high levels of the Parlements, especially in Paris. But when it came to the practical matter of priests actually refusing sacraments to persons who had lived apparently exemplary lives, the Parlements were able to go on the offensive in the name of both "the people" and the "nation." Jesuits, they said, were determined to capture the national "Gallican" church for international Romish designs and in so doing turn the monarchy into a foreign despotism. And they were successful enough to force the government into a complete reversal of position that culminated in the liquidation of the Jesuit order in France in 1762. Similarly, it was when taxes threatened to affect the privileged classes, for example, that the Parlements posed as the protectors of the nation's "liberties"—an irony not lost on Voltaire, who thought them hypocrites.

It was in the last years of the reign of Louis XV that this bitter dispute boiled over. In 1770 Chancellor Maupeou decided to short-circuit Parlementaire resistance by doing away with the entitling offices that allowed the magistrates their jurisdiction, and at the same time he created new tribunals directly responsible to the crown. Resisting Parlements were exiled. This did not mean some sort of *ancien régime* Siberia. In most cases the magistrates were packed off to a well-upholstered rural retreat where (their banqueting inventories suggest) they did not go short of the twelve-course amenities of life. In some cases, though, their leaders did suffer the real discomforts of imprisonment through *lettres de cachet.* Even before the *crise Maupeou*, the most eloquent of all Parlementaire spokesmen, the Breton La Chalotais, had suffered without due process an imprisonment that would endure nine years before his release.

The initial response to the Maupeou coup was a storm of polemical fury describing these policies as the introduction of "oriental despotism" into France. In 1771, no fewer than 207 pamphlets violently attacking the Chancellor and the Ministry were published, and the *philosophe* Denis Diderot wrote to a friend in Russia that the crisis "had made the constitution teeter on the brink. . . . It will not finish with remonstrances this time . . . this fire will spread by degrees until it has consumed the kingdom."

He was wrong. For all the apparent unanimity of their outrage, the judicial nobility was in fact deeply divided in their conduct. They had much to lose: their offices, status, titles and some not inconsiderable perquisites that went with them. Not surprisingly, then, as the volume of opposition polemics abated in 1772 and 1773, many of them quietly signed up for the new tame "Maupeou" courts and risked the ostracism of their former colleagues. It was only the sudden death of the King in 1774 that brought an abrupt end to the experiment in unimpeded bureaucratic government.

The prospect of their emasculation, however, had forced the Parlements into even more radical defense of their constitutional position. In particular it generated a solidarity by which, in the work of their most formidable propagandist, Le Paige, they claimed to reflect an historical unity. The thirteen Parlements, he argued, were the arbitrarily divided descendants of the one body that exercised legal constraints on the monarchy. And their right of remonstrance became progressively converted into something like a right of representation. In 1771, the Parlement of Rennes in Brittany was the first to call explicitly for the convening of the Estates-General as the only possible check on the overweening ambitions of ministerial despotism, an appeal repeated by Malesherbes.

Even in this heated political climate it was possible for oppositional rhetoric to overreach its own boundary of prudence. In 1775, after the Parlements had been restored by Louis XVI, a young lawyer, Martin de Marivaux, seeking to ingratiate himself with the Paris court, addressed copies of his tract *L'Ami des Lois* to the magistrates. With the memory of their crisis still brutally recent he could have expected to be encouraged in his commonplaces about ministerial despotism. But the grounds on which he criticized arbitrary power were dangerously novel: not those of historical precedent or the "fundamental laws" of the constitution, but of natural equality:

Man is born free. No man has any natural authority over his peer; force alone confers no such right; the legislative power belongs to the people and can belong only to the people. . . .

The Parlement immediately recognized what was a thinly disguised version of Rousseau's *Social Contract,* drew the logical conclusions and instead of congratulating the young zealot, ordered his book to be burned by the public executioner.

There were other risks involved in taking on the crown—risks not of incurring official retaliation but rather of unleashing a dangerous popular outburst. At the height of the Maupeou crisis, popular placards appeared threatening some sort of general insurrection. The most notorious was *"Paris à louer; Chancelier à rouer; Parlement à rappeler ou Paris à brûler"* (Paris to let; Chancellor to break on the wheel; Parlement to recall or Paris to burn). But there were others of an even more ominous character directly connecting anger with hunger, politics with subsistence:

Bread at 2 sous; [bring back] the Parlement; death to the Chancellor or revolt.

There were, then, serious limits to the ability of the Parlements to act as the vanguard of a general rebellion against the crown. If they were oppositional orators, they were also hanging (and burning and torturing) judges: the upholders of civic peace and the scourge of sedition. Lest it be imagined they lived up to their self-designation as apostles of liberty, it should be recalled that it was in a Parlement that a sentence of burning at the stake was handed down to a young nobleman convicted of sacrilege and there that other similar judicial atrocities were committed which received less glaring publicity. This was precisely Voltaire's objection. He wrote a stinging parody of their remonstrances which upheld " 'fundamental laws,' the fundamental laws of venal office . . . the fundamental law which allows them to ruin the province and turns over to lawyers the property of widows and orphans."

On their return in 1775 the Parlements were bound to object to the modest abridgments that Turgot placed on their ability to hold up royal legislation. But for the most part they avoided the all-out collisions with the crown that in 1771 had forced them to choose between rebellion and extinction. Instead, the ceremonies that marked their return were demonstrations of the myths of harmony—between crown and magistrates and between magistrates and people. Sometimes these celebrations were implausibly inclusive. In Metz, for example, the Jewish community (which had to endure much from the local nobility) gave a special *fête,* in which the major illumination was a Hebrew device from the book of Isaiah: "He will restore your Judges, your Magistrates as they were before and your City will be called City of Justice and Faithful Town." In Bordeaux the returning nobles of the robe received delegations of gratitude from tradesmen, including the city's fishwives, among whom the President moved with condescending graciousness.

At the Pyrenean city of Pau (where the *robins* had been most bitterly divided in their loyalties) there was the most extraordinary demonstration of all. For in addition to the conventional speeches, congratulatory odes and bouquets, the cradle of King Henri IV, who was born in the town, was carried aloft in a procession through the streets. The local governor, in conjunction with the Parlement, did his best to make the procession as innocuous as possible but it very rapidly turned into an occasion for acts of spontaneous popular piety. As the procession bearing the cradle passed by, people dropped to their knees in reverent silence, and it was carried to a specially constructed dais beneath a portico at the city gates. There the commissioners of the crown listened as homage was paid to the memory of Henri IV and gallant efforts were made to connect the memory of the best loved of the Bourbons with their latest incarnation.

The Parlements went into the critical years of the mid-1780s with a mixed inheritance. On the one hand, their position as an indispensable constitutional constraint on arbitrary royal power had become unchallengeable. Radicalized by the years of the Maupeou crisis, their propagandists and historians had to all intents and purposes succeeded in persuading the political reading public of the basic justice of their cause. If they acted more politely towards Louis XVI and his ministers than they had to his grandfather, it was because greater pains were taken to avoid their displeasure. When that was broached, they could show themselves to be dangerous, as their part in the fall of Turgot amply demonstrated. But if they had inflicted irreversible damage on the credibility of absolutism, their own ascendancy was not invulnerable or risk-free. The excessive zeal of some of their hack writers, the violence of the polemical language that they now embraced and the occasionally visceral forms in which popular enthusiasm for their cause was expressed suggested a narrowing room for maneuver. Their eagerness to present themselves as a quasi-representative body left some questions hanging dangerously in the air. If there was to be some sort of national representation, how was that to be constituted? And for how long would they be able to defend privilege and liberty as interchangeable? It was on these awkward issues (and specifically on the composition and procedure of the Estates-General) that the unity of noble opposition to crown policy broke apart in 1788 and 1789, so that colleagues who had stood shoulder to shoulder in a campaign against "despotism" suddenly found themselves divided by a choice of unprecedented painfulness: be a traditionalist or be a revolutionary. Among the black-robed orators of the Paris Parlement this would send their presidents like d'Aligre and Joly de Fleury to an early emigration, their most outspoken firebrands like Adrien Duport to a revolutionary career and constitutionalists like d'Eprémesnil to the guillotine.

iii NOBLESSE OBLIGE?

In the morning Président Hénault was a magistrate. In the evening he was an aristocrat. In the morning he would clothe himself in somber black robes and denounce the evils of ministerial tyranny. Faced with despotism, neither he nor his colleagues would flinch from their duty to protect the "fundamental laws" of the Nation. Well before sunset he would await one of his twelve coaches and return to the stupendous *hôtel* in the rue Saint-Honoré where he held court. He would be amply fed by what was commonly acknowledged to be Paris's best kitchen and would eat from Sèvres porcelain laid on a green marble table. Since his dining room was furnished with twenty-eight chairs and ten *fauteuils*, he was generally in a position to receive company and often did. It would be entertained beneath a vast Bohemian crystal chandelier and overlooked by a dazzling collection of art in which Italian history paintings shared the walls with Watteau and ter Borch.

To the revolutionary sensibility the discrepancy between political utterance and social habitat would be a kind of moral crime. To the modern reader it may seem at least incongruous that *les Grands* and the nobility more generally could have remained unchallenged as the natural leaders of a political opposition until the very eve of the Revolution. More concretely it may seem odd that a monarchy so consistently frustrated in its will by the collective opposition of the judicial nobility should not have exploited their social vulnerability more decisively.

This was, in fact, exactly what its most far-sighted ministers recommended. As far back as 1739, the most visionary and forceful of all Louis XV's public servants, René-Louis de Voyer, the Marquis d'Argenson, wrote a treatise outlining what he himself called a "royal democracy." Known in court circles (which, like Malesherbes, he detested) as "the Beast," d'Argenson was not the average government minister. An aficionado of English novels, he was the admiring reviewer of Fielding's

Tom Jones; but he was also the friend of Voltaire, an avid reader of the seventeenth-century British regicide Algernon Sidney and an advocate of a French air force aloft in hot-air balloons. His proposals for reform in the *Considerations on the Government of France* were so radical that they could only be published in 1764, thirty years after they had been written, and in Amsterdam. The real author, many surmised, must have been Jean-Jacques Rousseau.

But it was d'Argenson, the son of Louis XIV's Keeper of the Seals and the descendant of one of the most ancient Parlementaire families in France, who proclaimed the hereditary nobility as the source of all the evils in French government and society. It was their irresponsibility that allowed the provinces to fester and rot; it was they who treated public offices like casually acquired private property and who frustrated even the best intentions of conscientious *intendants.* The only way to overcome their obstruction, in his view, was for the monarchy to embrace democracy, for "democracy is as much a friend to monarchy as the aristocracy is an enemy." If the Parlements purport to represent the "people," he argued, their bluff should be called by instituting elected provincial assemblies. A national representation might even be elected indirectly and be accountable to the electors every two years. Upon this base the King—who would be rescued from the corruptions of the court by governing from the Tuileries, not Versailles—would preside over a true republic of citizens, rather than a subdued body of subjects. "What a beautiful idea," d'Argenson exclaimed, ". . . a republic protected by a King."

Within this realm, the separate orders would remain but heredity would be abolished. Nobility would be conferred strictly according to service and merit and would have only honorific status. Among a community of equals, each would have the same rights and obligations. Governed by an honest corps of public servants who held office by appointment rather than by purchase, citizens would relinquish only the taxes needed for their protection and would do so gladly since they were in effect surrendering a portion of their private property to a pool of the public domain that they could claim was equally theirs. Even military service would seem more like an honor than a burden since from this transformation would undoubtedly come a rejuvenated sense of the *patrie.*

D'Argenson's new France uncannily anticipated the revolutionary prescriptions of 1789 and 1791, especially in its emphasis on the embrace between citizens and king and the obliteration of any intermediate jurisdictions that could come between them. This is not to suggest that d'Argenson's utopia would have been a mere aggregate of atomized individuals bouncing against each other like beans in a bottle. His understanding was that "royal democracy" would be more than the sum of its parts: a purified *patrie* in which the individual interests of citizens would become harmonized into a new kind of collective community.

It was not beyond the remotest possibility that such a fantasy could become reality in the late eighteenth century. Marie-Antoinette's brother, the Habsburg Emperor Joseph II, imagined himself to be just such an enlightened despot and *pater patriae*. Though he dispensed with any thought of local or national representation, in the name of an uninterrupted relationship between sovereign and citizens, he launched a violent and uncompromising assault on his own hereditary aristocracy. As edict after edict tumbled from his inexhaustible pen, commoners and aristocrats were designated to share the same schools, the same graveyards, the same taxes. Nobles who balked before the draconian scheme of state service, which alone was to justify their status, would be sent to perform useful work like sweeping the streets of Vienna.

The wages of audacity were not much more gratifying than those of reticence, for Joseph's reign ended, like Louis XVI's, in wholesale insurrection in 1790. One major reason for the debacle was the chronic inadequacy of bureaucratic resources that the monarchy could put into the field to enforce its will over and against the local nobility. And while the Bourbons were not faced with having to administer an empire that stretched discontinuously from the Scheldt to the Danube, their dependence on local elites for effective provincial administration was no less serious. The model of central government (one largely reiterated in de Tocqueville's famous account), inherited from Colbert and Louis XIV, was of the *commissaires départis*—the *intendants*—faithfully carrying out instructions from the royal council, if necessary against the obstruction of local magistrates and corporations. And the history of Louis XV's reign was plagued by direct confrontations between *intendants* and provincial military governors on the one hand, and recalcitrant Parlements on the other. But at least as often, the story was one of local collaboration. The *intendant*, after all, whatever his inclinations, had little choice. The personnel of his bureaux, responsible for everything from troop movements to the containment of epidemics, from highways, bridges and canals to institutions of public relief and the suppression of brigandage, was paltry. In 1787, for example, Bertrand de Moleville, the Intendant of Brittany, had just ten clerks he could call on in his central office. He was, it is true, supported by sixty-three local assistants—the *subdélégués*—but they were either hopelessly underpaid or often not paid at all and not always reliable. In the Dauphiné, Bove de La Caze claimed that of his sixty-five *subdélégués* he thought only twenty really capable of fulfilling their duties.

In these circumstances there was no option for the *intendant* but to rely as much as he could on the collaboration of the local notables, whether of magistrates and aldermen in the towns or the local tribunals in the country-side. In many cases this was the natural thing to do, for officers of the royal administration and those of the Parlements were, after all, not so alien to each other as their respective ideologies often suggested. They were all from the same service nobility, connected by education and often even by family ties of marriage or blood. The famous clans of the Lamoignon and Joly de Fleury, for example, supplied members to high positions in both royal government and the Parlements. The Maupeou family, which is most often remembered for providing the Chancellor, who was the most deter-mined scourge of the Parlements, had, for a long time, sent members to the sovereign courts. The same is true for the Séguiers and many other similar dynasties. Moreover, Louis XVI's government recognized the need to har-monize as much as possible the interests of government and local elites by departing from the earlier policy of never sending *intendants* to provinces where they had personal or family ties.

There was another reason why the Bourbons were unlikely to follow d'Argenson's recommendation that they establish their power on the tomb of the hereditary nobility. Both Louis XV and his grandson prided them-selves on being "the first gentleman of France." And in this familiar title there lay an entire set of assumptions about royal legitimacy that wholly precluded the oxymoron of a revolutionary monarchy. The phrase meant, in particular, that the crown existed to protect the elaborate bundle of corporate entities, each invested with something like a "little sovereignty," that to-gether made up the kingdom. Responding to the Turgot edicts in March 1776, the Advocate-General of the Paris Parlement, Séguier, compared this system with a great chain binding together the different links—the three estates, or orders; guilds and corporations; universities and academies; com-mercial and financial associations; courts and tribunals. At the center was the crown itself holding the chain together, and without the guarantee of its good faith in this matter all these delicate reciprocities would fall asunder and with them all social peace.

At different times, of course, Louis XVI toyed with the possibility of modifying this constraining concept of his sovereignty as a presidency of privilege. His support of Turgot's reforms and later of Necker's abolition of venal offices went in this direction. But in both these cases, experiment was followed by ignominious withdrawal and the restoration of what had been annulled. In fact the crown's own position with regard to privilege was deeply ambiguous. On the one hand, it remained in the crown's inter-est, if for no other than fiscal reasons, to extend its paternal authority over recalcitrant areas of society. It was Necker's ambition, as we have seen, to try to replace venal intermediaries in the financial bureaucracy with directly accountable bureaucrats. But on the other hand, the crown was equally busy not just tolerating but *extending* privilege, even in those self-same areas of finance. This was in part from a deep reluctance to abandon a system of sale of offices which brought the hard-pressed Treasury something like four million livres a year. But it was also because in each creation of office it was hoped new lines of clientage and allegiance might be created that would strengthen rather than weaken the monarchy's political hand.

Superficially this might seem hopelessly short-sighted. If the crown truly wished to mobilize its authority, it should surely, by modern lights, have been busy suppressing, rather than extending, the world of corporate privilege and association. But this modern view is so clouded by the normative vocabulary of the Revolution itself that it is bound to misunderstand the real nature of privilege in late eighteenth-century France. Privilege could function as successfully as it did precisely because it was *not* what subsequent revolutionary polemics made it seem to be: an ossified, archaic system of exclusion that by definition denied access to the qualified aspirant and which, cumulatively, made any kind of social and economic progress impossible.

To begin with, privilege was not a monopoly of the nobility. Tens of thousands of commoners had been brought within its fold, either by virtue of the offices they held in municipal corporations and guilds, or by marrying into privileged families. Conversely, as we have already seen, privilege and especially nobility did not always carry with them the rights of exemption from taxes. But most important of all, in the second half of the eighteenth century access to the privileged orders became easier and easier to gain. To protest against nobility on the grounds of exclusion was to beat against an open door. Which is why the historian seeks in vain for some putative revolutionary class—let us call them the bourgeoisie—thwarted in upward social mobility, and bent on the destruction of the privileged orders. In 1789 there would indeed be such a group but their most significant and powerful members would come not from outside but from the inside of the nobility and the clergy. And they were not the product of an "aristocratic reaction" but its exact opposite: an aristocratic modernization.

Never had the avenues to nobility been broader or more welcoming than under Louis XVI. In a brilliant history of the society and culture of this nobility, Guy Chaussinand-Nogaret sees this process of social assimilation as so effortless that "a noble was nothing more than a successful bourgeois." To take the Parlements—those bastions of aristocratic values—as an example, a full two thirds of all the magistrates of the Parlements of Metz and

Perpignan were newly ennobled commoners. In Bordeaux, Pau and Douai the figure was one half and in Rouen and Dijon one third. Paris was the great exception but primarily because the magistrates there promoted from within the legal order according to stricter rules of professional seniority. And inside that body the escalator of status moved with reassuring predictability. Fully one quarter of the entire French nobility—some six thousand families—were ennobled during the eighteenth century and *two thirds* during the seventeenth and eighteenth centuries. This was, as Chaussinand-Nogaret insists, a young social class. Indeed if Lawrence Stone is correct, and the British aristocracy was not an open but a relatively closed elite, the stereotypes of France and England should be completely reversed. It was in Britain that a landed aristocracy resisted newcomers to form a kind of unbreakable crust on the top of politics and society, whereas in France, the elite was fluid and heterogeneous, constantly groping for sources of human and economic replenishment.

Ennoblement in France could come in one of many different ways. It was possible to receive it directly from the crown by "letters patent" as a mark of particular service. Military men, engineers, *intendants* and, to an increasing degree, artists, architects and men of letters were recognized in this way. If one had the funds it was possible to buy an entitling office, like the *secrétaire du roi*. No less than fifteen hundred nobles joined the order through the Paris Chamber in this way. Then again local notables—mayors, aldermen, *prévôts des marchands* (the officers responsible for patrolling markets and tradesmen), judges, even town clerks—all had some entitlement to nobility if they served continuously over a specified period, often no more than two years. Then a whole battery of bigwigs who had organized some grand reception for the King or a member of the royal family might well receive a formal mark of *reconnaissance* (recognition) that would elevate him to the second order.

Chaussinand-Nogaret also emphasizes an important change in the stated criteria for ennoblement in the second half of the century. Instead of lineage being mentioned, the reasons for promotion become, almost invariably, those of service, talent and merit. So that, as he argues, where in the previous century the ennobled bourgeois was required to divorce himself entirely from his background and immerse himself totally in a new and alien culture of honor, in the later eighteenth century the process of social integration worked the opposite way about. The nobility had become colonized by what modern historians think of as "bourgeois" values: money, public service and talent. This change represented a fundamental caesura in the continuity of French history. For it takes back to the eighteenth century the birth date of the class of "Notables" that dominated

French society and government until at least the First World War. We can now see that that elite was not a creation of the Revolution and the Empire but of the last decades of the Bourbon monarchy, and that it marched into the nineteenth century not as a consequence of the French Revolution, but in spite of it. In the circumstances the designation *old regime* seems more of a misnomer than ever.

If the French nobility was open to new blood it was also open to new ideas and occupations. One of the prevailing clichés of old-régime history is that privilege was inimical to commercial enterprise. But even a cursory examination of the eighteenth-century French economy (itself far more dynamic and abundant than the stereotype allows) reveals the nobility deeply involved in finance, business and industry—certainly as much as their British counterparts. The monied nobility drew their income from a wide variety of sources which included rents and profits from landed estates, government bonds and debt notes and urban real estate. That portfolio is familiar. Less well known, however, is the extent to which they were important participants in banking, maritime trade, especially in the booming Atlantic economy, and in industrial enterprise of the most innovative kind. At the very heart of the French elite, then, was a capitalist nobility of immense significance to the future of the national economy.

This would not have surprised the Abbé Coyer. In 1757 he published his *Development and Defense of the System of a Commercial Nobility*, which was meant to overcome lingering prejudices that the nobility might harbor about the dishonorable nature of business—as well as to resist what he took to be the sentimental neofeudalism of his protagonist the Chevalier d'Arcq. The Chevalier's mission was to turn the aristocracy away from the morally poisoned world of money and back to the simple virtues of patriotic, preferably military, service. Both doctrines were to influence the revolutionary generation, that of the crusading Chevalier perhaps more than that of the businessman Abbé. But there is little doubt that any reluctance on the part of the well-to-do to seek the most lucrative investments for their capital had disappeared. And in 1765 a royal edict officially removed the last formal obstacles to the nobility (other than the magistrature) directly participating in trade and industry.

And participate they did. Pooling their capital, nobles founded a wide variety of commercial concerns, from a horse-importing business to a company set up to convert spoiled wine into vinegar. Another syndicate manufactured the lighting oil and acquired the monopoly to illuminate the streets of Paris and provincial cities. The nobles were especially well placed to exploit opportunities linked to foreign policy, so that it is not surprising to discover great families in the shipbuilding and armaments trade, especially in Brittany. But it was colonial trade with its high risks but even higher rates of return that attracted them like flies to a honey pot, and substantial fortunes were made and lost in the West Indies.

Many of the investors in these businesses (as in the banks and finance companies managing the royal debts) were silent partners. But there was an impressive number of nobles actively engaged in what were the formative industrial enterprises in France. For example, the King's youngest brother, the Comte d'Artois, may have been the frivolous hunting and cards-addicted ne'er-do-well that the popular journalists satirized. But he was also an owner of factories that made both porcelain and iron. In the latter case he took personal care to draw up contracts specifying details of the furnaces and heavy equipment. Prominent coal-mine owners included the Rastignacs of Périgord, the ducs de Praslin of Normandy, the Duc d'Aumont in the Boulonnais and the ducs de Lévis in the Roussillon. The Advocate-General of the Parlement of Dijon in Burgundy, Guyton de Morveau, was the first entrepreneur at Chalon-sur-Saône to experiment with coke, from which he supplied fuel to his own glassworks. The Duc d'Orléans had glassworks at Cotteret, textile plants at Montargis and Orléans; the Vicomte de Lauget had paper mills; the Duc de La Rochefoucauld-Liancourt a linen manufacture—examples that could be multiplied indefinitely. The most advanced industry of all—metallurgy—was wholly dominated by the nobility. The great de Wendel dynasty, which built the massive works at Le Creusot, is for some inexplicable reason often thought of as bourgeois but in fact it had been ennobled since 1720—at least as long as many of the prominent Parlementaires—and in company with two aristocratic Treasurers-General, Saint-James and Sérilly, the concern grew to be the most formidable industrial concentration of both workers and capital in western Europe. Equally it was aristocratic capitalists who provided the entrepreneurial assets—both monetary and human—to begin building steam engines, start the mechanical exploitation of coal mines and introduce cotton machinery from Britain into factories in the north and east of the country.

The French nobility, then, did not hold their noses while raking in the cash. They positively wallowed in plutocracy. The marriages made between overmortgaged young nobles and monied bourgeois heiresses that proliferated over the course of the century were not, as Chaussinand-Nogaret emphasizes, thought of as *mésalliances* but as golden opportunities. This was at least because the education and life-style of the opulent bourgeois and the grandiose noble were, to all intents and purposes, indistinguishable. A greater or lesser degree of splendor was a function of wealth, not of legal status.

Not all the nobility was in this fortunate position. For every noble entrepreneur inspecting coke furnaces or spinning jennies in his powdered perruque and silk breeches, there were ten who vegetated on their country estates in a condition of genteel shabbiness. No less than 60 percent of the nobility—some sixteen thousand families—lived in conditions that ranged from modest dilapidation to outright indigence. At the very bottom there were those (perhaps five thousand families) who were too poor to possess the minimal accoutrements of nobility—a sword, a dog and a horse. If they were lucky they sold trout from a stream or thrushes from the woods they nominally owned. Many lived in conditions indistinguishable from the peasants who surrounded them, and not necessarily the better-off peasants. In the countryside around Angoulême one Antoine de Romainville, for example, plowed the stony fields with his ox just as his neighbors did. At his death he left his son nothing other than some straw chairs and his debts. Others more indebted still landed in prison or were reduced to begging for alms from the Church.

At an only slightly superior level were impoverished country gentry, living off their farms and a little rent. For this class—perhaps 40 percent of the total—there could be no question of any kind of urban life. Often they depended crucially on placing their children in the Church or the military to keep their small property intact. These were the *hobereaux* whom Arthur Young saw in the Bordelais—squires whose wardrobe was so thin that they had to stay in bed while their breeches were repaired.

The Abbé Coyer's recipe for these distressed noblemen—that they should in effect leave the land and join the marketplace as productive members of a bustling commonwealth—was bound to fall on deaf ears. Insofar as they read at all (itself unlikely) they were much more likely to respond to the Chevalier d'Arcq's call for a renewal of patriotic duty. And by the same token it was the poorest among the nobility who clung to their privileges with the greatest tenacity. Privilege was, in many cases, all that they had and in many others, their seigneurial dues were the difference between squalor and destitution. It was with some consciousness of their plight that the notorious *loi Ségur* was passed in 1781 confining commissions in the army to noble families that could trace their lineage back at least four generations. Often mistaken as evidence of the "aristocratic reaction," the *loi Ségur* was in fact testimony to the feeling that there was an increasingly desperate need to protect at least some portion of the public realm from the invasiveness of money, the ubiquitous *softness* of social distinctions.

At the other end of the scale, *les Grands* could afford to dispense with many of their privileges altogether. When they defended them it was not for pecuniary value so much as from a belief in the propriety of corporate

institutions. In 1788 and 1789 they would in fact divide along lines of generation and conviction rather than of social status or economic position as to
whether to retain or discard traditional legal distinctions. Among the poorer
nobility, opinion seems to have been more unanimous in opposing the
abolition of their prerogatives. Ironically, it was the electoral process which,
for the first time, eliminated the immense distance between the mighty and
the midgets among the nobility, so that the poor and the many could actually
dictate to the few and the sophisticated what the collective position of the
noble estate should be. A similar process of polarization within the First
Estate—the clergy—produced, as we shall see, the opposite result, with poor
curés pressing democracy on a rich and recalcitrant episcopacy. But in both
cases, the disintegration of the old order occurred not when outsiders
exasperated with their exclusion from privilege determined to destroy it by
force. It came instead from insiders, enamored of d'Argenson's vision of
aristocrats-become-citizens, pulling down the walls of their own temple and
proclaiming the advent of a democratic monarchy on its debris.

By 1788, Montesquieu, the paragon of noble constitutionalism, was being
attacked by noble radicals. The young Parlementaire lawyer Mounier accused him of conveniently defending everything that he found to be established. Another commentator, Grouvelle, reproached him even more
directly:

> O Montesquieu, you were a Magistrate, a Gentleman, a rich
> man; you found it congenial . . . to demonstrate the advantages of
> a government in which you occupied an advantageous place.

The Comte d'Antraigues went even further in the first and most famous
of all the aristocratic pronouncements of self-liquidation. Moving significantly from historical precedent and immemorial laws to the much more
radical vocabulary of natural rights, he claimed that legitimacy rested alone
with the Third Estate, for that

> is the people and the People is the foundation of the State; indeed
> it is the State itself; the other orders are merely political divisions
> while by the immutable laws of nature the people are by law
> everything . . . it is in the people that all national power resides
> and it is for them every state exists and for them alone.

The People so apostrophized, though, would not behave themselves in
quite the manner ordained by aristocratic radicalism. If the Comte d'Antraigues began as revolutionary he would end as counter-revolutionary.

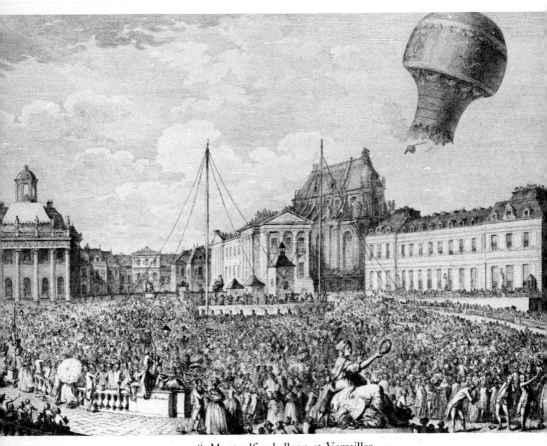

28. Montgolfier balloon at Versailles

CHAPTER FOUR

The Cultural Construction of a Citizen

i COLLECTING AN AUDIENCE

ON SEPTEMBER 19, 1783, at around one in the afternoon, to the sound of a drum roll, an enormous taffeta spheroid wobbled its way unsteadily into the sky over the royal palace at Versailles. Sixty feet high, it was painted azure blue and decorated with golden fleurs-de-lis. In a basket-cage suspended from its neck were a sheep named Montauciel (Climb-to-the-sky), a duck and a rooster. When a violent gust of wind made a tear near the top of the balloon, there were some fears for the safety of the barnyard aeronauts. All, however, survived the eight-minute flight reasonably well. Once it landed in the woods of Vaucresson a few miles beyond the château, the sheep was discovered nibbling imperturbably on straw while the cock and the duck cowered in a corner. But the story was too much like a La Fontaine fable to suppress speculation. Some reports insisted that the rooster's neck had been broken in the descent; others that its right wing had merely been grazed by a kick from the sheep. Later consensus was benign. "It was judged that they had not suffered," ran one press comment, "but they were, to say the least, much astonished."

Astonishment was not confined to the passengers. As many as 130,000 spectators were said by one account to have witnessed the event, and most reports put the number at 100,000. These estimates are numerically meaningless but it is certain that an immense crowd congregated on, and in front of, the palace courtyard where a special octagonal platform had been erected for the occasion. Most of the throng had traveled from Paris, where Etienne Montgolfier had already become a celebrity. The previous August he had sent aloft a small balloon, powered by inflammable gas (rather than the hot air with which he had pioneered the experiments). Six thousand had braved a steady downpour and had paid for special viewing seats on the Champ de Mars while a far bigger crowd observed standing. Expectations of a more spectacular flight that would receive the official royal blessing ran high.

Thus by ten in the morning all the avenues and highways leading to Versailles were choked with carriage traffic. Armies of pedestrians and sedan chairs then struggled to make their way by foot towards the *cour des ministres.* Like pilgrims drawn to a hearsay miracle they were determined not to miss what was generally agreed to be an epochal event. "One might say with Ovid," caroled one account, invoking the prophet of the Golden Age, "that many things will now be done that hitherto have been regarded as absolutely impossible." "At last," wrote Rivarol, another enthusiast, "we have discovered the secret for which the centuries have sighed: man will now fly and so appropriate for himself all the power of the animal kingdom; master of the earth, the waters and the air." There were other, more sardonic remarks on this balloonomania. The author of the *Correspondance Secret* (probably Louis Petit de Bachaumont) commented drily that "the invention of M. de Montgolfier has given such a shock to the French that it has restored vigor to the aged, imagination to the peasants and constancy to our women."

The *globes airostatiques* were epochal in other ways too, for they helped reorder the nature of public spectacle in France. In doing so they generated an audience that was hard to contain within the old regime's sense of decorum.

The ascent at Versailles was itself a major breach of court protocol. The palace had been built around the ceremonial control of spectacle through which the mystique of absolutism was preserved and managed. At its center, both symbolically and architecturally, was the closeted monarch. Access to his person was minutely prescribed by court etiquette, and proximity or distance, audience or dismissal, defined the pecking order of the nobility permitted to attend him. The palace exterior facing the town expressed this calculated measurement of space and time by confronting the approaching visitor with a succession of progressively narrowing enclosures. From the stables and the Grand Commun housing the kitchens, where space was at a premium, to the "marble court" at the center of which the King's bedroom was housed, the visiting ambassador would negotiate a series of pierced barriers or grilles, each one admitting a further measure of access.

All this graduated etiquette had been swept unceremoniously aside by rioting crowds in the first year of Louis XVI's reign when they had marched on the palace to demand the restoration of fixed prices for flour and bread. In October 1789 the palace would again become engulfed by the hunger and anger of a revolutionary march from Paris. But six years earlier, the apparently innocent spectacle of Montgolfier's balloon disposed of the elaborate protection of court procedure with almost as much brusqueness. The event, after all, was staged not behind the palace in the park, where it could have been more carefully patrolled by the household corps of Swiss guards, but in the unconfined space of the ministers' courtyard. While cordons of soldiers were placed so as to protect the balloon itself and Montgolfier, no serious attempt was made to restrain numbers or to order them in the neat, ordained spaces generally required by old regime regulations. Nor was it possible, beyond giving special places to the immediate royal family, to preserve the hierarchies of court seniority in the huge pell-mell throng. Instead of being an object of privileged vision—the speciality of Versailles—the balloon was necessarily the visual property of everyone in the crowd. On the ground it was still, to some extent, an aristocratic spectacle; in the air it became democratic.

The official and enclosed science of the Royal Academy made way for the theatrical science of public experiment. And although the balloons generally bore some form of the royal crest, this formal deference could not hide the fact that the King was no longer the cynosure of all eyes. He had been displaced by a more potent magus: the inventor. The Montgolfier brothers were paper manufacturers from the Vivarais in southeast France. But like tens of thousands of literate Frenchmen they were also amateur scientists. Thunderously applauded by the crowd, congratulated by the King and Queen, lionized by the Academy, compared incessantly with Christopher Columbus, they approximated more to a new type of citizen-hero: Franklins of the stratosphere. A typical contemporary description of Etienne Montgolfier paints him as the epitome of sober virtues—at once classical-Roman and French-modern: in clothes and manner, the antithesis of the foppish, ornamental courtier.

> He was dressed in black and throughout the course of
> the experiment gave his orders with the greatest *sang-froid*.
> The severity of his countenance and its tranquillity seemed
> to announce the certainty that this able physician had of the
> success of the experiment. There is no-one more modest
> than M. Montgolfier.

And along with this reputation for Virtue and Usefulness went a certain streak of independence, even insubordination. Montgolfier's principal scientific collaborator was M. Charles, a professor of physics who had been the first to propose the gas produced by vitriol instead of the burning, dampened straw and wood that he had used in earlier flights. Charles himself was also eager to ascend but had run into a firm veto from the King, who from the earliest reports had been observing the progress of the flights with keen attentiveness. Anxious about the perils of a maiden flight, the King had then proposed that two criminals be sent up in a basket, at which Charles and his colleagues became indignant. "The King might be sovereign master of my life but he is not keeper of my honor" was one reported response. And it was quickly appreciated by both critics and enthusiasts that manned flight had serious implications for the preservation of the status quo. Smuggling was an immediate concern since contraband carried by balloon would make customs posts and excise walls redundant. Perhaps there might even be war in the skies. Rivarol mocked the more hysterical of these fears when he claimed that religion had just lost its grip since, to future generations, the Assumption of the Virgin would no longer seem miraculous. Furthermore:

> Everything seemed turned upside down—the civil, political and moral world. They saw already armies slaughtering each other in the air and blood raining down on the earth. Lovers and thieves might descend by chimney and carry away to distant places both our treasures and our daughters.

The most self-consciously independent of the aviators was, characteristically, also the youngest: Pilâtre de Rozier, a twenty-six-year-old physician. Together with an army officer, the Marquis d'Arlandes, he succeeded in launching the first manned ascent on the twenty-first of November 1783. The combination of scientist and military man—technical knowledge and physical audacity—that was to be the standard format of aviation and space exploration was already established. But Pilâtre de Rozier, more than many other scientists, had always had an eye for the public. A native of Metz in Alsace, he had been one of the most conspicuous of the many who gave afternoon lectures on scientific topics in Paris for a public eager for novelty. In 1781 he had opened a Musée des Sciences on the rue Sainte-Avoie specifically designed to cater to constituencies excluded by the Royal Academy. It housed a collection of instruments, books and experimental equipment, and amateurs could rub shoulders with the learned and engage in public and private discussion. Women might be admitted—though only if recommended by three members of the Musée. Over seven hundred subscribers signed on from all ranks and conditions and heard Pilâtre himself lecture on the art of swimming as well as demonstrate a watertight robe by emerging dry from a bath filled to a depth of six feet. Among other inventions on display at the Musée was a hat with a built-in light for nocturnal rescues, and Pilâtre offered readings of his book *Electricity and Loving,* which presumably made the most of the new cult of animal magnetism.

Pilâtre de Rozier completed his credentials as citizen-balloonist by becoming a "martyr to science" at the age of twenty-eight. As he attempted to cross the English Channel from Boulogne in June 1785, his balloon exploded, "enveloped by a violet flame." Watched by another enormous crowd at the coast, Pilâtre and his companion fell fifteen hundred feet onto rocks opposite Croy, just outside the port. Horrified reports were grimly detailed. Pilâtre's body was shattered, a foot separated from the leg; the young hero "swam in his own blood." The country treated him like a dead warrior: "It is said that perhaps he loved glory too much," wrote one eulogist. "Ah! how could one be French and not love it." From England, Jean-Paul Marat mourned that "all hearts are stricken with grief." Joint funerals of great pomp were held in Boulogne and in his native town of Metz; the King ordered a medal struck, busts commissioned and a special pension provided for his family. To complete a scenario that might have

29. The wreck of Pilâtre de Rozier's balloon

30. François Pilâtre de Rozier, *The Scientist as Hero*

been written by Rousseau or one of the dramatists of the sentimental stage, Pilâtre's fiancée herself died just eight days later, possibly by her own hand.

The sentiment that ballooning was an aspect of the Sublime and that its practitioners were Romantic demigods was infectious. One of the most tireless of the aeronauts was François Blanchard, who four months before Pilâtre's accident had been the first to cross the Channel from Dover, with a British colleague, Dr. Jeffries. On his third voyage from Rouen he came down in a field, where the dumbfounded peasants greeted him as if he were extraterrestrial. Only when he undressed and allowed them to poke him in several decisive zones of his body were they satisfied. But the local elite was as curious in its way as the peasantry. Blanchard descended into a storm of excitement and competition as to who would have the honor of entertaining him overnight while the balloon was being inflated. Women were especially excited by the prospect and often more courageous than the men in following up their well-informed scientific curiosity. On this same flight, for example, the Marquise de Brossard, the Comtesse de Bouban and Mme Déjean all insisted that they be allowed some sort of test flight. Blanchard sent them up eighty feet—while attaching the balloon with light cords as they took careful measurements of their speed and altitude. "They showed," he wrote admiringly in the press account, "not the slightest sign of anxiety even at the greatest elevation."

Similar spectacles were enacted throughout the country from Lyon to Picardy, from Besançon to the Luxembourg Gardens in Paris. Patrons of rival cafés in the Palais-Royal, the Caveau and the National, adopted competing balloon teams almost as if they were favorite racehorses. Miniature portraits and ballads celebrating their exploits went on sale in Paris. Books were published that gave detailed advice on how to construct one's own balloon or a miniature replica. The most expensive of these could be made up for six livres, the cheapest for forty sous (the price of five large loaves of bread). A bladder membrane from ox innards was advised for the thirty-inch model, held together with the best fish glue. Amateurs were warned about the perils of using methane and connoisseurs inspired to build little balloons in the shape and color of fruit so that at whimsical moments in an evening's entertainments they might rise into the air suspended over the claret decanter.

But ballooning was much more than a fashionable amusement. Its public was enormous, elated and unconstrained, and spoke not with accents of polite society but with the emotional vocabulary of Rousseau's sublimity.

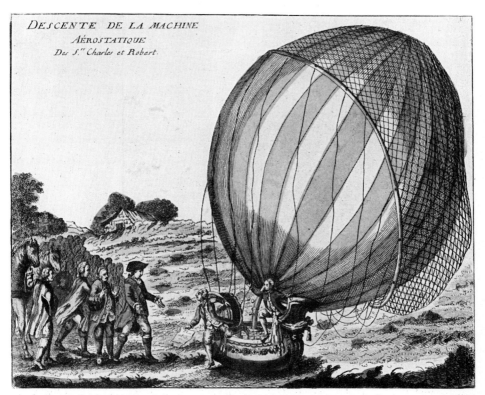

31. Descent of the balloon of MM. Charles and Robert on December 1, 1783. The Duc de Chartres, shortly to be the Duc d'Orléans, is seen greeting the aviators after their ninety-minute flight from the Tuileries gardens.

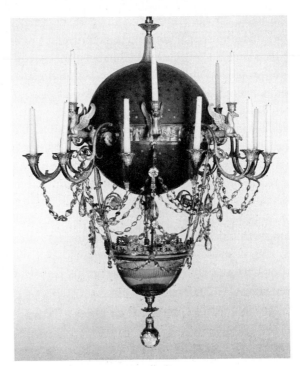

32. André Galle, chandelier in the shape of a
Montgolfier balloon

In this poetic mode, terror and joy were invariably yoked together and feelings were often eloquently expressed in body language. When the balloon of MM. Charles and Robert went up over Saint-Cloud in July 1784, "men and women," a spectator wrote, "great and humble, fell to their knees, completing the most extraordinary tableau ever seen." More dramatically, an enormous, and suddenly horrified crowd on the plaine des Broteaux beside the Rhone near Lyon saw the soon-to-be-doomed Pilâtre de Rozier, Montgolfier and six passengers, including the son of the Prince de Ligne, descend vertically amidst smoke and flames. Their response *en masse* was to "hold up their arms and hands by an involuntary movement as if to support the balloon in its fall." When it was seen that they had survived the wreckage of the enormous three-hundred-foot globe, their carriages were unharnessed and they were borne aloft on the shoulders of a surging tide of celebrants. "Covered in sweat and smoke [they were] constantly stopped on their progress by those who wanted to see them up close and to embrace them." At a performance of Gluck's *Iphigénie en Aulide* at the Opéra that same night they were showered with more wild huzzahs. The singer playing Agamemnon produced a crown of laurels which, characteristically, Montgolfier placed on his wife's head, while Pilâtre (competing in modesty) placed his on Montgolfier's.

In other words, Montgolfier, Pilâtre de Rozier and Blanchard succeeded in establishing a direct and unmediated relationship of comradeship with enormous multitudes of people. The crowds of spectators who ran the gamut of unconfined emotions while watching them behaved exactly as crowds were not supposed to in the old regime. In Lyon, for example, as in other provincial towns—and especially those with Parlements—crowd events were regulated through religious or civic processions. The coherence and structure of these occasions was prescribed by the order of participants, the costume they wore or the attributes they carried. Preceded by priests or dignitaries, their ceremonies expressed the corporate and hierarchical world in which they had been brought up.

Charismatic physics altered all that. As a spectacle it was unpredictable; its crowds were incoherent, spontaneous and viscerally roused. Yet they were neither a mob (*un attroupement*) nor a random aggregate. The sense that they were witnessing a liberating event—an augury of a free-floating future—gave them a kind of temporary fellowship in the open air, under the Parisian summer drizzle or the snowflakes of a Lyonnais January. Though it was less grimly calisthenic than the neo-Spartan gymnastics recommended by Rousseau (and later ordained by the Jacobins), it exemplified the philosopher's vision of a festival of freedom: uplifting glimpses of the Sublime in which the experience, not the audience, was noble.

B A L L O O N S were not the only spectacle to attract the kind of crowds in which the formal distinctions of rank were swallowed up by shared enthusiasms. The closing decades of the old regime were remarkable for the number of cultural phenomena in which popular and elite tastes converged. The size and diversity of the public for boulevard theater, popular song and even the biennial Salon exhibition was such that it engulfed the traditional distinctions of social and legal order preserved in official forms of art licensed by the monarchy. The vivid description given by the popular journalist Pidanzat de Mairobert of the Salon public at the end of the 1770s emphasizes this uninhibited mixing of social types within a confined space. Bodies, voices and aromas were so pressed and jostled that together they made up, in the august surroundings of the Salon Carré of the Louvre, a huge boiling soup of humanity. Forced up a staircase always packed with people, the visitor was plunged into a "chasm of heat and a whirlwind of dust and noise." There "in a poisonous atmosphere,

33. Gabriel de Saint-Aubin, *The Salon of 1753*

impregnated with the breath of unhealthy persons . . . deafened by a din like the crashing of waves at sea," one nonetheless beheld a "mixture of all orders of the State, all ranks of society, every age and sex" . . .

> the disdainful fop or the [*vaporeuse*] woman; the Savoyard odd-job man rubs shoulders with the *"cordon bleu"* [grandee]; the market woman trades scents with the woman of quality, making the latter pinch her nose to escape the powerful smell of brandy sent her way; the rough artisan, guided by instinct alone, throws out a just comment which, because of his comical accent, prompts the foolish *bel esprit* to mirth while the Artist hidden in the crowd disentangles meaning from it all and turns it to his profit. There too, schoolboys give instruction to their teachers . . . for it is these young pupils spread amidst this immense gathering who almost always provide the most telling judgments.

In its origins the Salon had been the temple of academic and institutional hierarchy. The Academy, under whose auspices the show was organized, was itself divided into three rigidly structured classes. And on the walls of the exhibition, the formal hierarchy of genres—with history painting at the top and genre and still life at the bottom—was carefully preserved. But these formalities became superfluous in the chaotic ebb and flow of public excitement. In the 1760s and 1770s the paintings which attracted crowds and excited comment in the press were not pompous histories by official artists like Brenet and Lagrenée but the sentimental genre dramas of Greuze.

A similar process of breaking boundaries was occurring in the theater. This is all the more surprising since, on the face of it, Paris theater was divided into two sharply contrasting worlds. The drama of high taste and official respectability was housed in licensed companies like the Comédie-Française and the Opéra. Fronted by colonnaded porticos, the grand theaters offered a steady diet of classical tragedies and acceptably literary comedies by Molière. Actors declaimed their Alexandrine couplets according to time-honored conventions of elocution and cadence. Nothing could be further from the raucous and earthy world of the boulevard theaters in which bawdy farces rich in slang and gutter humor competed for attention with freak shows, high-wire acts and balladeers.

Historians have often portrayed the eighteenth century as the period when popular culture was finally subdued by dour guardians of official moral taste. From occupying a central place in the life of the people, they argue, it became marginal, yielding to campaigns of Improvement and Edification. Something of this sort would indeed be attempted by the revolutionary Jacobins. But thanks to the research of Michele Root-Bernstein and Robert Isherwood we now know that during the last decades of the old regime, something like the opposite process was at work. It was the official theater that was losing its vitality, and to some extent, its audience. And it was the popular theater that was becoming the main attraction. Even more striking was the phenomenon, widely noticed by contemporaries, that the two worlds were not so much pulling apart as coming together. A single public was in the process of forming, hungry for entertainment and stretching from the royal family and the court all the way down to the artisans, shopkeepers, tradesmen and soldiers. They flocked to see *The Marriage of Figaro* at the Comédie-Française, where they could stand in the rowdy *parterre* in front of the stage. Or they might, for a mere twelve or twenty-four sous, patronize Nicolet's Grands Danseurs on the boulevard du Temple, with its winning mixture of acrobatics, burlesque, pantomime, mime acts, song and sentimental drama. (For a while its star attraction was a monkey named Turcot who mimicked the great "serious" actor Molé.)

There are countless examples of this cultural fusion at work. The *Journal de Paris* gave daily information on the "high" theater of the Opéra, the Comédie-Française and the Comédie Italienne, but it also listed current attractions at the Variétés and the Ambigu Comique. Crossovers from one world to the other abounded. The founder of the Ambigu Comique, Audinot, had himself been a singer (and the son of a singer) at the Opéra Comique and had staged spectacles at Versailles before founding his thriving theater on the boulevard. The great hit of the 1770s, Dorvigny's *Les Battus* (The Beaten) featured a hapless servant, Janot, who, having had a chamber pot emptied on him, attempts to find legal redress and instead finds himself in jail. By 1780 *Les Battus* had been performed a thousand times, had made its principal actor, Volange, a Parisian celebrity and had been performed in private before the King and Queen at Versailles.

Indeed, the royal family was as much engaged in this stage culture as anyone else. Artois, for example, is known to have composed verses for the unsparingly satirical and often obscene popular songs that ballad-mongers hawked on the Pont Neuf. And though the King frowned on Marie-Antoinette frequenting the Paris theater as a breach of decorum, she often did so and created, through audience reaction to her presence, a barometer of public popularity. This was obviously enjoyable so long as the plaudits lasted, but by the mid-1780s the frosty silences or worse reinforced her own sense of alienation from public favor. But the Queen remained interested enough in the earthy patois of the markets—*poissard* (named for "pitch")— to have members of the Montansier troupe come to the Trianon to instruct her own group of court actors (including Artois) in its gritty slang. Among that troupe was the Grammont family, who in their own persons exemplified the inclusiveness of the dramatic world. At home on the boulevards, where they had started out with Nicolet's troupe of tightrope artists and clowns, but accustomed to performances at Versailles, the Grammonts would go on to become officers in the *armées révolutionnaires,* the Parisian shock troops commissioned to enforce revolutionary laws and weed out traitors for the guillotine.

It was the Duc de Chartres, though, who did most to institutionalize this cultural melting pot by turning the Palais-Royal into the most spectacular habitat for pleasure and politics in Europe. In 1776 he was given this prime site, once the gardens of Cardinal Richelieu and bordering on the Louvre and the Tuileries, by his father the Duc d'Orléans. And the combination of his prodigal life-style and entrepreneurial initiative led him to dream up an extravagant plan to turn the gardens into an arcaded resort that would combine cafés, theaters, shops and places of more doubtful recreation. The architect Victor Louis, who had created the magnificent theater at Bordeaux, was hired to create the interior space, but needless to say ambition ran ahead of funds and not until 1784 was anything resembling the full plan beginning to be realized. In the meantime a wooden gallery had been erected running along the Palais; known as the *camp des tartares,* it rapidly became notorious as a haunt of prostitutes and pickpockets. Inside, for a few

34. Philibert-Louis Debucourt, the gallery of the Palais-Royal

sous one could marvel at the girth of the four-hundred-pound German Paul Butterbrodt or (for a few sous more) inspect the credentials of a naked (wax) "belle Zulima" allegedly dead for two hundred years and in a marvelous state of preservation.

By 1785, when the old Duc d'Orléans died, leaving his son with funds to complete the work, the Palais-Royal had nonetheless succeeded in bringing the raw and Rabelaisian popular culture right into the heart of royal and aristocratic Paris. A decade earlier it had still been possible to see central Paris as the exclusive preserve of official art, with "lower" forms relegated to the boulevards and the fairs of Saint-Germain and Saint-Laurent. The enclosure of these unofficial forms within these great paddocks of pleasure even gave the police a sense that mischief was at least confined to predictable zones and if respectable citizens chose to frequent them it was at their own risk. The elite theaters might look askance at the growing popularity and enviable prosperity of their rivals, but at least they had the satisfaction of seeing them housed in poky back rooms well outside the fashionable quarters.

The arrival of the Palais-Royal as a quotidian carnival of the appetites drastically altered all that. As the private domain of Orléans it was virtually safe from patrol by the police and it exploited this freedom to the utmost. "This enchanted place," wrote Mercier, "is a small luxurious city enclosed in a large one." Eagerly welcomed by Chartres/Orléans, the Théâtre

Beaujolais (named for Chartres' brother) opened with three-foot-tall marionettes and continued with child actors, and at the Variétés Amusantes, the farces and melodramas of the boulevards moved in alongside, both playing to packed houses. Cafés of every kind flourished, from the more staid Foy to the risqué Grotte Flamande. One could visit wig makers and lace makers; sip lemonade from the stalls; play chess or checkers at the Café Chartres (now the Grand Vefour); listen to a strolling guitar-playing abbé (presumably defrocked) who specialized in bawdy songs; peruse the political satires (often vicious) written and distributed by a team of hacks working for the Duc; ogle the magic-lantern or shadow-light shows; play billiards or gather around the miniature cannon that went off precisely at noon when struck by the rays of the sun.

Inside the confined spaces of the boulevard theater it had been difficult if not impossible to maintain any kind of formal distinctions of rank. Nicolet's theater held four hundred people crammed into a space not much more than forty feet by thirty-six. The tallow candles barely gave enough light to allow for much in the way of social display and Nicolet's dirt-cheap prices meant that people of drastically different social worlds were pressed together like sardines. But even in the avenues and arcades of the Palais-Royal, where promenading (not to say soliciting), gazing and inspecting were a major pastime, conditions and classes were indiscriminately jumbled together. In the melee it was easy to mistake a flashily dressed courtesan sporting imitation brilliants for a countess decorated with the real thing. Young soldiers dressed to impress girls with their uniforms (a relatively recent innovation in the army), on which insignia of rank were either unmarked or indeterminate. In their black robes noble magistrates from the Parlement were dressed in much the same fashion as humble barristers and clerks. And it is evident that contemporaries relished this social potpourri. Louis-Sébastien Mercier, who had railed against the boulevards for encouraging feeble-minded dissipation among "honest citizens," adored the Palais-Royal, where he witnessed "the confusion of estates, the mixture, the throng." And Mayeur de Saint-Paul, who wrote even more lyrically, insisted that "all the orders of citizens are joined together, from the lady of rank to the dissolute, from the soldier of distinction to the humblest official in the Farms."

Within the dignified halls of the Comedie-Française or the Opéra, of course, the social order was far more pronounced. But the governing condition of conspicuousness (as throughout the old regime) was not birth or estate but money. Moreover, even in the "serious" theater, there is some evidence of an increasing infusion of middle-class and even lower-middle-class audiences: shopkeepers and master artisans from the "honest" trades like cabinetmaking and watchmaking. On special occasions, like the birthday of the Dauphin in 1781, free performances would be given and the theater would be packed with this more modest kind of spectator. But even during the regular season, the relatively modest price of the *parterre* made it accessible to habitués like students and law clerks. Very often the eager theatergoer could pay for his place by signing on with one of the organized *claques,* paid to cheer or jeer at actors and plays, depending on the commission. And because of the license expected in the *parterre,* it was here that the tone could be set on first night for the success or failure of the play. The playwright Marmontel, who was no friend of the *parterre,* when much cheered by the success of his *Belisarius* was forced to concede that "amidst the mass of uncultivated men there are certainly some who are very enlightened."

Were *les enfants du paradis* closely related, then, to *les enfants de la patrie?* It is hard to know whether the social commingling apparent in theater audiences and amidst the strollers in the pleasure gardens may be taken as an accurate indicator of the collapse of rank in old-regime France. We are, after all, dealing here with metropolitan Paris at its most relaxed. But against the teeming backdrop of a great melee of citizens it did turn isolated incidents of hostility between great and small, privileged and citizen, into an exemplary type of social and political drama: that of anachronism. So in this sense there were indeed rehearsals for the great theater of the Estates-General at work in the Paris audiences.

A case in point was the famous war of the theater seat that reached the courts of the Paris Parlement itself. The dispute came to symbolize the transfer to the auditorium of one of the stock dramas performed on stage: that of virtuous citizenship bullied by aristocratic arrogance. On April 9, 1782, an argument broke out in the balcony of the Comédie-Française. The disputants were one Pernot-Duplessis, a proctor of the Parlement, and the Comte de Moreton-Chabrillant, captain of the guard of the Comte de Provence—the King's younger brother. In the court case that ensued, it was stressed that the plaintiff was "an honest man in all respects, known by the mildness of his manner and the graciousness of his disposition"; that he was dressed in sober black and wore no wig that evening. The officer, on the other hand, arrived late in a rose-colored coat and was wearing a sword and plumed hat—in other words, the essence of a military courtier. According to the court record this is what followed:

CHABRILLANT: What are you doing here?
DUPLESSIS: I am at my seat.
CHABRILLANT: Withdraw, I say.

DUPLESSIS: I have a right to be here for my money . . . I have
paid for my seat and I am not going to withdraw. I shall remain.
CHABRILLANT: A f— *robin* dares insult me [at which point he
shoved the plaintiff]. I am M. le comte de Chabrillant, captain of
the guard of Monsieur the King's brother. I have right of command here. It is by order of the King. Into prison scamp, into
prison. . . .
DUPLESSIS: No matter who you are a man like you cannot make a
man like me spend the night in prison without cause.

The battle of the balcony was won by the abusive aristocrat, but the war
by the righteous advocate. Chabrillant did indeed summon the guard, who
forced Duplessis downstairs by the hair and locked him up for four and a
half hours—until well after the performance was over. But it was, to say
the least, imprudent to humiliate a member of the sovereign court, even if,
as the defense claimed, the Comte did not believe anyone so "rude" could
possibly be a magistrate. Duplessis' attorney, Blondel, made a meal of the
contrast between the haughty officer-courtier, contemptuous of basic legal
rights and quick to use arbitrary force, and the quietly determined, modestly dressed man of the law. It was, he stated in court, "in the general
interest of the Public to defend the individual *whose simple status as Citizen
should have warded off any kind of insult in a place where money alone put
commoners and nobles on the same footing*" (emphasis added). Needless to say,
the court found for Duplessis and ordered the Comte to pay six thousand
livres in damages—a considerable sum—as well as to avow in court that the
man he had insulted was "a man of honor and probity."

There were other, similar cases where the theater was turned into a
battlefield of contested rights. In Bordeaux in 1784, for example, the mayor
and his municipal councillors were denied entrance to the theater on orders
of the military governor and were even imprisoned when they persisted in
attempting to enter. The governor then tried to have the mayor (a noble)
tried by military tribunal. In so doing, he pitted his military force against
the civic claims of the mayor to exercise authority in the theater in the name
of his co-citizens.

Politics, then, could affect the theater, but equally the theater was itself
capable of creating political drama. The most spectacular of all these cases
was of course that of Beaumarchais and *The Marriage of Figaro*. Invariably
the trying circumstances in which this play was performed are taken to
represent a way station on the road to the collapse of the old regime.
Beaumarchais is duly cast as a warrior for freedom of expression and the
King as a frightened and petulant martinet. But this simple scenario is
considerably complicated by the fact that, by the time *Figaro* came to be

written and performed, Beaumarchais was himself no oppressed Figaro but an ennobled magistrate of considerable wealth and formidable influence. The significance of the diatribe against the settled order that he put into the mouth of Figaro in Act 5 was not that it came from one of the literary underclass but from one of the favored sons of the establishment.

With these reservations it would be equally mistaken to deromanticize Beaumarchais so completely as to mistake him for merely another aristocrat playing at radical chic. His remarkable life was stained with the social ambiguities of late eighteenth-century France. He had been magistrate and prisoner, courtier and rebel, diplomat and spy, businessman and bankrupt, publisher and publicist, insider and outsider. Nor had the trajectory of his career been one of uninterrupted upward progression from modest artisan to swaggering nobleman. At many stages it had been marked by spectacular leaps in fame and fortune crushed by equally spectacular rejections and disappointments. If he cultivated paradox assiduously, it came to him naturally. In one of his many court appearances as defendant against libel, he donned the apparel of the "honest man"—black coat and breeches (and made his face up to look especially pale)—but could not resist sporting at the same time the huge diamond ring given to him by the Austrian Empress, Maria Theresa. In 1787 he would hire the fashionable architect Lemoyne to build him a spectacular mansion boasting two hundred windows and costing nearly a million livres. But he would site it in the very unfashionable faubourg Saint-Antoine: the heart of artisan Paris, and the fulcrum of sans-culotte radicalism in the Revolution.

To understand the unprecedented appeal of *The Marriage of Figaro* and why it became used as a stick to beat over the head of the more obdurate elements of the old regime, it is necessary to see just how its author cast himself in the part of injured *honnête homme* and citizen. Like Rousseau, Beaumarchais was the son of a Protestant watchmaker, but unlike the philosopher he extended his knowledge of that craft to become a brilliant and prodigious inventor in his own right. Robbed by his master of the credit for inventing the double-action escarpment, Beaumarchais unmasked the usurper and became, in very short order, famous and well off. Presented to Louis XV at the age of twenty-two, he was appointed watchmaker to the court. Association with the rich *financier* Paris-Duverney opened up the path to nobility and he duly bought his way in, in 1761. At the age of twenty-nine, then, he ceased to be Pierre-Augustin Caron and was entitled to use the name of his estate, Beaumarchais. And since nobility, new-style, presupposed service, he also became a presiding judge in the court that dealt with offenses against the game laws—a particularly harrowing tribunal in which he showed no special tenderness to the multitudes of pathetic poachers, professional and amateur, dragged before his bench.

35. Jean-Marc Nattier, portrait of Beaumarchais

It was of course *The Barber of Seville* that made his name as a playwright, though he followed it with a succession of rather feeble dramas featuring all the correct expressions of elevated sensibility: friendship, thwarted love, honored posterity and the like. And as he became a celebrated figure so he also became a target for jealous husbands and opportunistic hack writers. His own taste for pleasures of all sorts only attracted further attacks. But for all his notoriety (some richly deserved), the Chevalier Beaumarchais co-existed with Citizen Beaumarchais. The rake and the boaster was also the startlingly aggressive and enterprising propagandist for the Americans, who fitted out an entire private navy and armaments for the rebels and whose own pocket made up the difference between the escalating cost of French assistance and secret royal disbursements. Another project of almost comparable significance brought him even greater ruin. For he decided to take on the publication of the complete works and manuscripts of Voltaire when the great Paris publisher and bookseller Panckoucke had despaired of the enterprise. Beaumarchais edited the colossal work, tangled with affronted parties on all sides (including Frederick the Great of Prussia) who did not care to have their correspondence made public, established his own printing press in Lorraine, bought type in England and attempted to break even by finding thirty thousand advance subscribers. Predictably, all he got was a paltry two thousand. Starved of pay, printers vandalized his machinery, and a cashier absconded with some receipts. Running to seventy-two volumes in quarto, the entire business was a commercial fiasco of titanic proportions. But it was also a cultural glory, perhaps the finest thing Beaumarchais ever did.

It was Beaumarchais' unquestionable ability to play Everyman that lent *The Marriage of Figaro* its universal voice. It broke rank and it mixed genres. It brought the mordant satire of the popular theater into the august hall of the Comédie-Française. And it gave instant renown to skilled actors like Louise Contat (Suzanne) and d'Azincourt (Figaro) who were capable of playing their parts with spontaneity and freshness. While there had been plenty of boulevard comedies assailing the pretensions of seigneurial power, none had done so with such stinging hilarity. It was closer to the kind of "people's drama" that Mercier had called for in 1773 than anything yet seen in the century. Those who know only the operatic version by Mozart and da Ponte know only a *Figaro* from which much of the raw mischief has been edited out. As the author of the *Correspondance Secret* commented, Beaumarchais' predecessors

> had always had the intention of making the great laugh at the
> expense of the small; here, the lowly could laugh at the expense

of the great and the number of those ordinary people being so considerable one should not be astonished at the huge throng of spectators from every walk of life summoned by Figaro.

There can be no doubt that Beaumarchais would have liked the play to be produced without any official interventions. But once they were clumsily offered he seized the opportunity to publicize them as a battle between overbearing despotism and citizens' liberties. Typically, he was able to pose in this guise because among the citizens eager to see the play were Marie-Antoinette and most of the court. Beaumarchais had given the manuscript to Chamfort (Talleyrand's friend) and he in turn had placed it in the hands of the Queen's favorite Vaudreuil. A private reading had been organized and the more outrageous the denunciations of the established order, the better the Queen liked it. The King was less amused. In the middle of Figaro's notorious monologue in Act 5 he rose from his chair and, in a rare fit of eloquence and prescience, declared that it was "detestable. It will never be played; the Bastille would have to be destroyed if the performance of the play is not to have dangerous consequences."

Though the project was officially proscribed, Beaumarchais used every means to keep it alive. He had astutely incorporated into the play a popular song, *"Marlborough S'en Va-t-en Guerre." "Va-t-en guerre"* was an ironic slight, meaning war by fanfare (rather than deed), and the song had been composed during Louis XIV's campaigns, when a false rumor had circulated that his nemesis, the Duke of Marlborough, had been killed in battle. Revived in the 1780s it was sung to jeer at British humiliation in America and in the Indian Ocean, where Admiral Suffren was embarrassing the Royal Navy. Beaumarchais adopted the song as if his own battle were the dramatic equivalent of a military campaign, and the joking banter of the song as if his enemy were soon to be laid low. In a street and salon culture where the *double-entendre* was virtually an official language, the innuendo did not go unnoticed.

As usual, though, it was the eagerness of a section of the fashionable nobility to humiliate the court that undermined the latter's authority. Manuscripts of the play were copied and privately circulated among all the great houses of the liberal (and not so liberal) nobility. Some of these had their own private theaters where the writ of the police could not run. It was the threat that these private performances might go ahead and, what was even more embarrassing, the threat of a premiere sponsored by the Grand Duke of Russia in St. Petersburg that produced an informal agreement whereby the play might be performed in Paris on the Queen's property of the Salle des Menus Plaisirs, used for rehearsals by the Opéra. On June 13, 1783, thousands packed the streets outside the theater defiantly singing "Marl-brouck." Half an hour before the curtain was due to rise the King sent his chamberlain armed with *lettres de cachet* to order that the production be abandoned "on pain of His Majesty's indignation," which clearly meant a spell in prison. Beaumarchais' response was Figaro-like in its menace. "*Eh bien Messieurs,* there may be no performance here, very well, I swear to you that it shall be performed, perhaps in the very choir of Notre-Dame."

This showdown between citizen and sovereign was, for the moment, inconclusive. Beaumarchais consented to make some emendations—all of which turned out to be wholly inconsequential—and the King relented, making no secret that he expected the play to be a great flop. He was bitterly disappointed. On April 21, 1784, it opened at the new neoclassical Théâtre-Français (now the Odéon). The perceptive young aristocrat Baronne-d'Oberkirch witnessed the fistfights that broke out in the gigantic crowd that had gathered in front of the theater to try to grab the few remaining seats. No radical, she was swept off her feet by the performance, specifically taking to task the critics who thought it succeeded only by playing to the gallery in the crudest way. She wrote in her memoirs in 1789 that, on the contrary,

> *The Marriage of Figaro* is perhaps the cleverest thing that has ever been written excepting perhaps the works of M. Voltaire. It is dazzling, a true piece of fireworks. The rules of art are overturned from one end to the other and this is why in four hours of performance there is not one moment of boredom.

But she also had the acumen to notice a peculiar obtuseness on the part of aristocrats in the audience who guffawed when Figaro turned his wrath on Count Almaviva:

> Because you are a *grand seigneur* you think yourself a great genius . . . nobility, wealth, rank, offices! all this makes you so high and mighty! What have you done to have so much? You've hardly given yourself the trouble to be born and that's about it: for the rest you're an ordinary person while I, damn it, lost in the anonymous crowd, have had to use all my science and craft just to survive.

Joining the bursts of applause that invariably greeted the speech, Baronne-d' Oberkirch observed, the *grands seigneurs* in the audience "smacked them-selves across their own cheeks [*ils se sont donnés un soufflet sur leur propre joue*]; they laughed at their own expense and what is even worse they made others laugh too . . . strange blindness!"

There are signs, though, that the "bravos" and "bis" died on the lips of the nobility as they began to grasp the significance of a polemic that was directed not at the monarchy or ministers but at themselves. Once *Figaro* had been taken out of the Théâtre-Français run in January 1785, they began to orchestrate a campaign of counterattack. First the Archbishop of Paris denounced the atrocity from the pulpit; then the writer Suard, posing as a priest, followed him with a stinging and sarcastic criticism. Responding in the *Journal de Paris*, Beaumarchais used withering scorn. After fighting off the onslaught of "lions and tigers," he said, he was not going to demean himself by continuing to reply to little parasites, for that would put him in the position of "Dutch housemaids who have to beat the mattress each morning to shake out the filthy little bed-bugs."

On March 6 the article was brought to the King's attention and, presumably still smarting from his wishes being thwarted, he took the reference to wild (rather than verminous) creatures as a personal attack. It was enough to put Beaumarchais in prison. And Louis, full of silly pique, decided that the most crushing reproof he could give to an ironist would be comic humiliation. That evening, while at the card table, he scribbled on the back of the seven of spades that Beaumarchais should be confined not in the Bastille (the usual detention for insubordinate writers) but in Saint-Lazare, the correction center for delinquent boys. In the short term, this facetious humiliation took the wind out of Beaumarchais' sails. Refusing to emerge from the prison, knowing he was the butt of jokes, he never quite regained the breezy confidence which had sustained him through many misfortunes. In the very last years of the old regime he himself became the whipping boy of radicals and reactionaries alike.

His stay in Saint-Lazare may have turned Beaumarchais permanently from the offensive to the defensive, but it did not do the same for *Figaro*. The play continued to be overwhelmingly the most popular and durable success of the Paris "legitimate" theater. Beaumarchais had many enemies who rejoiced at his comeuppance and who believed that his self-appointment as the champion of liberty was hypocritical posturing. But he also had many friends in the "anonymous crowd" listening attentively to Figaro's self-description as an "honest man" obliged to cringe and grovel at the feet of a disdainful aristocracy and whose talent and wit chafed at the arbitrary barriers of rank. For if it is a myth that among the revolutionary clubs and crowds there were legions of Figaros impatient to inflict revenge on their Almavivas, it is a reality that former playwrights, pamphleteers, actors and theater managers were among the most enthusiastic devotees of the guillotine.

ii CASTING ROLES:
CHILDREN OF NATURE

A year before his chastening stay in Saint-Lazare, Beaumarchais had an inspired promotional idea. He proposed to donate the proceeds from *The Marriage of Figaro* to a worthy cause: the encouragement of maternal breast-feeding. An Institute of Maternal Welfare was to be established in Paris that would provide subsidies to mothers who would otherwise have to send their infants out to village wet nurses in order to be able to work.

In Paris the lieutenant of police, Lenoir, thought that perhaps only one thirtieth of mothers of the twenty thousand babies born each year nursed their own babies. And these were almost exclusively from better-off families who followed Rousseau's passionate advocacy of domestic breast-feeding. Others who could afford it had wet nurses come to their homes or sent their infants to the *faubourgs*. But the vast majority of modest and poor homes

36. Engraving, Figaro as the benefactor of nursing mothers, 1785

used an official bureau and its traveling agents—the *meneurs*—to find village wet nurses in the countryside around the capital. The poorest abandoned their children on church steps for the Foundling Hospital, and they too were farmed out to country wet nurses. For every one in two babies sent away in this manner, village wet nursing was a death warrant: urban poverty succored by rural destitution. Desperate for the pittance that they received for nursing, the women sometimes deceived the *meneur* about their lactating ability and fed the infant animal milk or a *bouillie*-pap, made of water and boiled (and often moldy) bread. Sometimes their mouths would be crammed with rotting rags. Infants sat in animal and human filth, were suspended on a hook in unchanged swaddling bands or were slung from the rafters in an improvised hammock. Dysenteric fevers put them out of their misery by the tens of thousands, and often the *meneur* responsible for informing the parents (or the Foundling Hospital) about the child's progress would conceal its death and pocket the money.

Affected by reports of this cottage industry of death, Beaumarchais mobilized Figaro to come to the rescue of the nursing mother. A topical engraving celebrating his scheme shows Figaro distributing charity to generously endowed and contentedly nursing mothers while others behind him greet their liberator from a "prison for nurses." A standing Philosopher shows this happy scene to "Welfare" while above them "Humanity" holds up a tablet inscribed "Succor for Nursing Mothers."

Beaumarchais' success at the theater was already galling enough for his enemies in Paris. They were certainly not prepared to have his halo shine even more brightly through philanthropy. But the Archbishop of Lyon got wind of the idea and welcomed the 85,000 livres donation that established an "Institute" in that city. By all accounts it was a success, reporting a marked decline in infant mortality. It was astute of Beaumarchais, who was constantly on the defense against charges of libertinism, to associate himself with such a high-minded philanthropy. Against critics who dismissed his play as a comic trifle, full of witticisms but empty of substance, the scheme highlighted its underlying moral themes: the defense of nuptial innocence against aristocratic lust and force. Figaro is himself a foundling whose rediscovery of his mother is one of the means by which Almaviva's strategies are thwarted. As much as in any of the "bourgeois dramas" of Sensibility of the 1750s, the triumph of virtue over vice (as well as intelligence over rank) is the clinching dénouement of *The Marriage of Figaro*.

Breast-feeding, moreover, was not just a concern of public health. It is true that its advocates did often emphasize how its reduction of infant deaths would enable France to escape the threat of depopulation (always on the official mind). But this rhetorical opposition between vitality and mortality, natural and social practice, drew its persuasiveness from the moral politics of the bosom. Resistance to breast-feeding, it had been argued, arose from the ascendancy of sensual self-indulgence over domestic duty. It was assumed that lactation and sexual activity were mutually exclusive for fear of tainting the milk or provoking the disgust of men. Thus male writers including Rousseau and his physician friend Dr. Tronchin often ascribed the decrease in maternal nursing to feminine wantonness or the anxiety against offending husbands. Marie-Angélique Le Rebours, however, who in 1767 published her *Advice to Mothers Who Wish to Nurse Their Children,* more reasonably blamed male resentment of the interruption of their sexual habits and criticized men who became violently jealous or incensed against the presence of crying babies. At stake was a contested view of the bosom as either a sensual enticement, half exhibited in fashionable décolletage, or as a natural gift offered in candid abundance from mother to child. In a play written to advertise the virtues of breast-feeding, *The True Mother* (of seven months) smartly rebukes her husband for treating her as an object of sexual gratification. "Are your senses so gross as to look on these breasts—the respectable treasures of nature—as merely an embellishment, destined to ornament the chest of women?"

Eroticism and maternity could, occasionally, become connected in irregular ways, at least in the experience of Rousseau, who was more influential than anyone in the campaign for home breast-feeding. In the *Confessions* he admitted (amongst other things) to being aroused by the glimpse of a swelling breast pressing against a muslin décolletage. Equally it was the discovery of an inverted nipple on the breast of a Venetian prostitute that for him transformed the girl from a creature of transcendent beauty into a repulsive and lubricious monster. The relationship which shaped his entire life was with his protectress, Mme de Warens (only twelve years older than he), whom, well after they had become lovers, he continued to address as "Mama." Equally, Jean-Baptiste Greuze, the painter who more than any other artist made the idylls and dramas of domestic life a matter of public attention, and who was repeatedly congratulated by Denis Diderot for the morality of his subjects, was quite capable of a disingenuous manipulation of voluptuousness and innocence, as his *White Hat* of around 1780 more than adequately suggests.

For most of the public who read Rousseau, listened to Diderot's "bourgeois dramas" at the Comédie-Française and saw Greuze's paintings of domestic bliss and sorrow in the Salon, matters were much more simple. What was being proclaimed was the antithesis of rococo court culture with its wasteful indulgence in decoration, its insistence on wit and man-

37. Adélaide Labille-Guiard, portrait of Madame Mitoire and her children:
the first modern French painting of breast-feeding, exhibited in the Salon of 1783

ner, graciousness and style. In place of these amoral formal effects, esteem was to be transferred to the realm of virtue. In this new world, heart was to be preferred to head; emotion to reason; nature to culture; spontaneity to calculation; simplicity to the ornate; innocence to experience; soul to intellect; the domestic to the fashionable; Shakespeare and Richardson to Molière and Corneille; English landscape gardening to French-Italian formal parks. It generated a new literary vocabulary, saturated with emotive associations that drowned out not only the light repartee of rococo wit, but even the hallowed sonorities of classicism. Lavish use of words like *tendresse* (tenderness) and *âme* (soul) conferred immediate membership in the community of Sensibility; and words that had been used more casually, like *amitié* (friendship), were invested with feelings of intense intimacy. Verbs like *s'enivrer* (to become drunk) when coupled with *plaisir* or *passion* became attributes of a noble rather than a depraved character. The key word was *sensibilité:* the intuitive capacity for intense feeling. To possess *un coeur sensible* (a feeling heart) was the precondition for morality.

Outward expressions of inner sentiments began, in this period, to be acceptable. Cameo pendants bearing the likeness of the beloved or lockets containing locks of hair from spouses or children became commonplace

38. Jean-Baptiste Greuze, *The White Hat*

39. Virtue fleeing from décolletage, engraving by
Moreau le Jeune for Rousseau's *La Nouvelle Héloïse*

badges of the feeling heart. When the locks belonged to loved ones who
had departed this world, the significance became even more poignant, and
by the 1780s, uninhibited expressions of grief had already replaced stoical
fatalism as the expected response to the death of a child. Love letters
borrowed ecstatic hyperbole from Rousseau's *Nouvelle Héloïse* and then
piled declarations of passion on top of that. In a not untypical example of
her 180 love letters, Julie de Lespinasse, heroine of the *Nouvelle Héloïse*,
gasped: "*Mon ami*, I love you as one must love, with excess, madness,
rapture and despair."

In this remade world of utterance and expression, tears were especially
prized as evidence not of weakness but sublimity. They were cherished
precisely because (it was assumed) they were unstoppable: the soul directly
irrigating the countenance. Tears were the enemy of cosmetics and the
saboteur of polite disguise. Most important, a good fit of crying indicated
that the child had been miraculously preserved within the man or woman.
So Rousseau's heroes and heroines, beginning with himself, sob, weep and

blubber at the slightest provocation; but so did reviewers of opera on hearing Gluck and Salon critics on beholding Greuze. On seeing the second version of the painter's *Girl Weeping over Her Dead Canary* in the Salon of 1765, Charles Mathon de La Cour placed the girl's age (around eleven) as exactly at the stage where "Nature begins to soften the heart to receive the sweetest impressions," with the result that her tears were both childish and pre-adult. He then went on to examine in great detail the painterly treatment of this damp sorrow:

> One sees that she has been crying for a long time and that she
> has finally given herself over to the prostration of a profound
> grief. Her eyelashes are wet, her eyelids red, her mouth still in the
> contraction that brings on tears; looking at her chest one can also
> feel the shudder of her sobs.

"Connoisseurs, women, fops, pedants, wits, the ignorant and the foolish," he claimed, were "all of one mind about this painting," for in it "one sees nature, one shares the grief of the girl and one wishes above all to console her. Several times I have passed whole hours in attentive contemplation so that I became drunk with a sweet and tender sadness."

40. Jean-Baptiste Greuze,
Girl Weeping over Her Dead Canary

41. "Dear and Precious Tears!" Weeping as
an expression of sincerity, engraving by
Barbier the Elder from the 1783 edition of
La Nouvelle Héloïse

It was his ability to engage the viewer directly in the world of displayed
emotions (while at the same time, as Michael Fried has argued, presenting
the fiction of their obliviousness to the beholder) that accounts for the
persuasive power of Greuze's domestic operas. "Move me, astonish me,
unnerve me, make me tremble, weep, shudder and rage," demanded Diderot, and there is no doubt, at any rate, that in his most ambitious paintings—
for example, *The Village Bride* of 1761—Greuze did just that to a great many
spectators. Many contemporaries report the onrush of feeling that struck
the crowds who swarmed around the works so densely that, as Diderot tells
us, one could barely fight one's way through to see them. Of the drawings
for the pair *The Wicked Son* and *The Wicked Son Punished*, which represented a young man deserting his family to join the military and his belated
return to discover his father dead, Mathon de La Cour commented that he
didn't know whether he could advise Greuze to complete them as paintings, as "one suffers too much to see them [as it is]. They poison the soul
with a sentiment so terrible and so profound that one has to avert one's
eyes."

The drastic cultural alteration represented by this first hot eruption of the Romantic sensibility is of more than literary importance. It meant the creation of a spoken and written manner that would become the standard voice of the Revolution, shared by both its victims and its most implacable prosecutors. The speeches of Mirabeau and Robespierre as well as the letters of Desmoulins and Mme Roland and the orchestrated festivals of the Republic broadcast appeals to the soul, to tender humanity, Truth, Virtue, Nature and the idyll of family life. The virtues proclaimed in Greuze's paintings formed the moral basis of what the Revolution was to understand as Virtue. "It is virtue that divines with the speed of instinct what will be conducive to the general advantage," wrote Mercier in 1787. "Reason with its insidious language can paint the most equivocal enterprise in captivating colors but the virtuous heart will never forget the interests of the humblest citizen. Let us place the virtuous statesman before the clever politician." This was exactly the view of Robespierre, for whom, as he often said, politics was nothing more than public morality. Motherhood; a contented conjugality in which casual lust was vanquished by conscientious lactation; respect for the old; gentleness to the young: all these values were held to be a school for citizenship. In this scheme of values there could be no

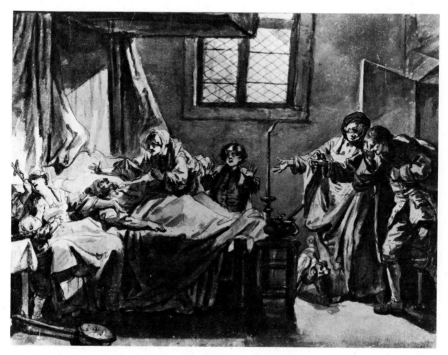

42. Jean-Baptiste Greuze, drawing, *The Wicked Son Punished*

43. Jean-Baptiste Greuze, *The Well-Beloved Mother*

distinction between the private and the public realm. Indeed, wholesome domesticity was officially considered a necessary attribute of patriotism. Its painterly apotheosis might be *The Well-Beloved Mother*, commissioned by the Farmer-General and prolific writer Laborde to display himself and his family in a state of exemplary domestic bliss. Shown at the Salon it was praised by Diderot as "excellent on two counts: as a work of art and as an example of the good life. It preaches population and depicts with great feeling the inestimable happiness and value of domestic felicity."

The revolutionary generation grew up attuned to this overwrought manner of expression. Greuze stumbled badly in 1769 when he attempted to translate his father-son confrontation into the genre of history painting with a *Severus and Caracalla*, in which the Roman emperor accuses his son of conspiracy. Instead of promoting Greuze to the senior hierarchy of the Academy it produced the crushing public humiliation of an admission "in his capacity as genre painter." But although his reputation faded somewhat in the 1770s before the newer more austere manner of Roman history painting, the domestic dramas of the 1750s and 1760s maintained their grip on the public's imagination and even extended their reach through engraved versions by Jean-Georges Wille and others.

Though Greuze's paintings, like Diderot's plays and Rousseau's novel, are sometimes classified as "bourgeois," it is crucial to appreciate that their devotees began at the very top of French society. If the old regime was subverted by the cult of Sensibility, then much of the damage (as in so many other respects) was self-inflicted. *The Marriage Contract*, which actually represented a Protestant ceremony with a notary standing in for a priest, and which stood as the exact antithesis of grandiose dynastic marriages at Versailles, was bought by Louis XV's Minister for the Arts, the Marquis de Marigny. His sister was the King's mistress Madame de Pompadour and it was she who organized the first performance of Rousseau's opera *The Village Soothsayer* at Fontainebleau in 1752. Its composer took great care to dress down for the occasion "with a rough-combed beard and ill-dressed wig." In the simplicity of its rustic setting, story and music, the opera exemplified the victory of childlike Nature over the products of urban and court culture. The *Mercure de France* praised it precisely for the "truth and rare naivety of expression in the music."

With the accession of Louis XVI, this infatuation did not go away. Indeed the King's father, the Dauphin, was said to have been so moved by Rousseau's praise for simple artisanal crafts that it was he who provided the

44. Jean-Baptiste Greuze, *The Marriage Contract*

education of a locksmith for his son. Guided by her dressmaker Rose Bertin, Marie-Antoinette made no secret of favoring the relatively simple costumes, much strewn with fresh flowers and bucolic affectations, that the cult required. Her friend Elisabeth Vigée-Lebrun obliged further by painting her portrait in this startlingly informal manner, complete with straw baskets and bonnets. The creation at the Petit Trianon of the "Rustic Village" (*Hameau Rustique*) for the Queen by the landscape architect Mique, complete with beribboned cows, Alpine sheep and water mill, was a sincere if disastrously misjudged attempt to cultivate the innocence of rural life amidst the pomposity of court protocol. In 1789 it would seem an obscene parody for Marie-Antoinette to be playing shepherdess and boiling fresh eggs for her breakfast while scarecrow peasants begged on the roads of the Ile-de-France.

More astonishingly still, it was Marie-Antoinette who, in 1782, visited Rousseau's grave at Ermenonville, twenty-five miles outside Paris. For if Sensibility was the unofficial religion of budding citizens, Ermenonville was their most hallowed shrine. It was there that the Marquis de Girardin, a wealthy cavalry officer and Farmer-General, had provided a last "hermitage" where Rousseau could work and walk in the near-solitude he recom-

45. Botanical virtue as exemplary lesson, engraving by Moreau le Jeune for Rousseau's *Emile*

mended for himself and others. Childlike to the last, Rousseau had insisted on adopting Girardin and his wife as his latest and last "Mama and Papa." He died at the beginning of July 1778, and was hardly cold before stories circulated in the capital speculating on his parting words to his wife Thérèse: expressions of remorse for having abandoned all five of their infant children to the Foundling Hospital, and the whereabouts of the "memoirs" or "confessions" that were said to be unprecedented in their candor and which certain famous persons—Diderot and Madame d'Epinay—were eager to see suppressed. Before long, curious sightseers began to arrive on the Girardin estate, beginning with the editors of the *Journal de Paris,* who had known Rousseau quite well and who were impatient to get their hands on any remaining literary fragments. By the middle of 1779, Rousseau, who had been shunned by so many during his life, was already acquiring the halo of immortality. A statue had been erected in Geneva, a bust modeled by Houdon in Paris; a semi-official *Necrology* of celebrated Frenchmen had included his portrait and eulogy along with those of Voltaire, Turenne and King Henri IV; and a revival of *The Village Soothsayer* was being performed to large audiences in Paris. In 1781 a collection of melodies by Rousseau called *Consolations for the Sorrows of My Life* was published and proceeds donated in the name of his widow to the Foundling Hospital. Among the subscribers were the Queen and Benjamin Franklin.

As early as 1780, so the author of the *Mémoires Secrets* claimed, "half of France has transported itself to Ermenonville to visit the little island consecrated to him where the friends of his morals and his doctrine each year renew their little philosophical journey." Luc-Vincent Thiéry included Ermenonville in his sightseeing guide of the country around Paris. But it was the estate-owner, the Marquis de Girardin, who thoughtfully provided the fullest walking itinerary for the pilgrim. His *Promenade* was a tour of the mental as well as topographical landscape of Rousseau's sensibility. Girardin made it clear that his park was not to be regarded as a seigneurial estate but as a kind of free gift for all devotees. "There is no need for permission from the master to enter this park," he emphasized, though he would be only too delighted to provide a personal guide for any "celebrated foreigners or artists."

"It is to you, friends of Rousseau that I address myself," wrote Girardin with the appropriate expression of sincerity, and his guide was written as if a friendly hand was leading the disciple through the scenery of virtue. It presupposed not only an intimate knowledge of Rousseau's works and life ("here you can see his cabin"; there is where Saint-Preux brooded on his thwarted passion) but a shared taste in nature. The three- to four-hour walk began with a little hamlet, which according to Thiéry "seems inhab-

46. The entrance to the park, anonymous engraving in Girardin, *Promenade*

ited by faithful lovers," and proceeded to "a forest where the immense silence and solitude seizes one so that one advances with terror into the depths of the wood." Surprised by the sudden appearance of a little temple consecrated to Nature, one emerged onto a plain where another monument to Philosophy stood, and thence to a "wilderness" planted only with pines, cedars and junipers, with craggy outcrops and cascades. From there one could walk to a lake beside which was a stone engraved with verses from both Petrarch and Julie of the *Nouvelle Héloïse*. After that might come some suggestion of the presence of man, but only at his most artisanally virtuous: the water mill and the wine press. A pre-ruined Gothic tower, streams full of fat fish, and a "Dutch" meadow stocked with fat cattle gave on to a space which on special days Girardin would fill with rustics, trained to look jolly, disporting themselves in innocent pastimes and musical games.

The Holy Grail of the pilgrimage was of course Rousseau's tomb, set on the Isle of Poplars in the middle of the lake. There on a bench expressly provided for mothers to nurse their infants while other children played contentedly, they could contemplate the modest monument erected by Girardin. Its epitaph read

Among these poplars, beneath their peaceful shade
Rests Jean-Jacques Rousseau
Mothers, old men, children, true hearts and feeling souls
Your friend sleeps in this tomb

At this point, crying was obligatory. "Let your tears flow freely," wrote Girardin, an authorial arm about the shoulder of the pilgrim. "Never will you have spilled such delicious or such well-merited teardrops."

Some of the most ardent disciples went even further in search of the ghost of the solitary genius. Louis-Sébastien Mercier traveled through Switzerland with his friend the Genevan Etienne Clavière, visiting places and people of importance in Rousseau's life. Manon Philipon, who as a girl had identified passionately with Julie, took her husband, the future Girondin Minister Roland, on a similar tour and managed to track down the mayor who had witnessed Rousseau's marriage to Thérèse. Not content with her own private obsession she cast her husband in the role of Wolmar, the older, rather austere but devoted figure whom Julie dutifully marries in preference to the besotted young tutor Saint-Preux. Writing to Roland,

47. The Isle of Poplars, anonymous
engraving in Girardin, *Promenade*

she made this identification quite plain: "I have just devoured *Julie* as if it were not the fourth or fifth time . . . it seems to me that we would have lived very well with all those personages and that they would have found us as much to their taste as they are to ours."

The publication of the *Confessions* in 1782, with its introductory promise to "display a portrait in every way true to nature," only reinforced the intensely personal bond that Rousseau's countless disciples felt with him. In his lifetime, as Robert Darnton has shown, they wrote to his publisher Marc-Michel Rey in Amsterdam inquiring after his personal welfare and health as though he were an intimate friend. Nothing in the *Confessions*— not the bald admission of the abandonment of his children, of his various addictions to masturbation and masochism, his share in a *ménage à trois* with Mme de Warens and her herbalist—nothing could shake their faith in his essential moral purity. The breathtaking candor of his admissions of vice as well as virtue strengthened their view that he was the greatest *honnête homme* of their century. Rousseau's paranoid conviction that he was persecuted by jealous *philosophes* such as his erstwhile friend Diderot as well

48. The grave of Rousseau at Ermenonville,
anonymous engraving in Girardin,
Promenade

as Voltaire and Melchior Grimm, fed the alienation felt by many writers who believed themselves unappreciated by the literary establishment in Paris. They too attributed this lack of recognition to a conspiracy of the mediocre. They also shared much of Rousseau's ambivalence about the necessary dependence on aristocratic patrons and his scorn for corrupt fashion and the atrophied rule of Reason.

Rousseau, then, became the Divinity (apostrophized as such) of the literary underclass. Spurned, mistreated and nomadic, he was at once their consolation and their prophet. And they took as their gospel his commitments to Nature, Virtue and Truth.

Historians have long been concerned to judge Rousseau's influence on the revolutionary generation by gauging that generation's familiarity or unfamiliarity with the formal works of political theory, in particular *The Social Contract.* While there is growing evidence that this work was in fact read and understood before the Revolution, it is undoubtedly true that it never reached the huge and adoring readership of his educational "biography" *Emile* and the *Nouvelle Héloïse.* But to assume that those works had little influence on political allegiance is to adopt a much too narrow definition of the word *political.* As much as his writings dealing with sovereignty and the rights of man, Rousseau's works dealing with personal virtue and the morality of social relations sharpened distaste for the status quo and defined a new allegiance. He created, in fact, a community of young believers. Their faith was in the possibility of a collective moral and political rebirth in which the innocence of childhood might be preserved into adulthood and through which virtue and freedom would be mutually sustained.

Just how this was to be accomplished was, in all of Rousseau's writings, notoriously obscure. In his lifetime he had shown himself circumspect about, if not downright hostile to, any suggestion of revolt. What he invented was not a road map to revolution, but the idiom in which its discontents would be voiced and its goals articulated. And most of all he provided a way in which the torments of the ego—an increasingly popular pastime in the late eighteenth century—could be assuaged by membership in a society of friends. In place of an irreconcilable opposition between the individual, with his freedom intact, and a government eager to abridge it, Rousseau substituted a sovereignty in which liberty was not alienated but, as it were, placed in trust. The surrender of individual rights to the General Will was itself conditional on that entity preserving them, so that the citizen could truly claim (so the theory ran) that for the first time he governed himself.

The impossibly paradoxical nature of this bargain was to be revealed all too brutally during the Revolution itself. But for Rousseau's acolytes in the 1780s, visions opened up of possible societies that might be capable of integrating the imperious "I" within the comradely "We." That, at least, was the comforting vision offered by a two-act spectacle, *The Assembly on the Elysian Fields,* which represented Rousseau's reception among the immortals. In attendance were, naturally, Julie with her afflicted lover Saint-Preux holding a bunch of roses; Emile attacked in the deep woods by a Monster of Fanaticism and rescued by Truth; and a scene where a nursing mother, a suckling child and a wet nurse extolled the virtues of the maternal breast. One feature of the spectacle, however, remained incongruous. Throughout the action Rousseau himself remained uncharacteristically silent, detached from his own creations. But it was only when his sentiments broadcast themselves through the power of public eloquence that they became the speech of revolution.

iii PROJECTING THE VOICE: THE ECHO OF ANTIQUITY

On an August afternoon in 1785 a correspondent for the *Journal de Paris* saw a young man in his mid-twenties addressing a crowd on a platform in front of the Châtelet. As a newly appointed advocate-general of the Parlement, Hérault de Séchelles was for the first time exercising his right to speak in this manner and he warmed to his subject. It was one calculated to wring the hearts of *les coeurs sensibles.* A self-made man who came from a poor family, it seems, had wished to express his gratitude for his good fortune by making a donation to the poor of the parish of Saint-Sulpice. Inadvertently, he had departed from the prescribed official forms in which such donations could be made and the tribunal of the Châtelet as a result had declared them invalid. Hérault had taken on the task of pressing the donor's claims and harangued the crowd on the absurdity of the annulment. But the subject of his speech was less important than its spoken form. For it was apparent to the journalist, as to the crowd, that this was an exhibition of public oratory in which the young speaker was testing his powers to affect a spontaneously gathered audience.

According to this same account, published in the newspaper, Hérault's debut as a public speaker was a triumph, all the more impressive for avoiding the flashy excesses of the stage (though in fact this future Jacobin was already taking lessons from the actress Mlle Clairon):

The speech of the young Magistrate had no pretensions to eloquence; his style was calm and tranquil like that of the law itself: he had something of the control of the passions so necessary to the intelligence if it is to discover the truth. Conviction and enlightenment emerged gently and by degrees from his words . . . with none of those syllogisms that have nothing to do with reason . . . all those who heard this young Magistrate speak could appreciate the wisdom with which the tone of his speech advanced the nature of his cause.

Even if Hérault's chosen manner was that of the grave man of the law, the entire performance was no less theatrically calculated for that. When he had finished, loud applause broke out among the crowd, to which he responded with self-deprecation, waving the acclaim on to the senior magistrates who had preceded him. This was stagecraft of a very high order and for which Hérault would become justly famous in the Convention and even, at last, on the scaffold before his beheading with his comrade Danton. In 1785 he seemed, even to the hard-boiled reporter from the *Journal,* to ooze sincerity. "Never has talent shown so much graciousness as when he [Hérault] effaced himself so as to turn his own renown to other[s'] talents." One thinks of Pilâtre in the theater of Lyon, taking the laurels from his brow and placing them on the crown of Montgolfier: the new, Roman heroics.

After austerity and modesty came Sensibility. Descending from the dais, Hérault was embraced by his senior colleagues of the robe, including the famous orator Gerbier, whom he publicly addressed as his professional "Father." "Never," said the writer, had his soul "been so moved as by this scene."

Although he shrewdly affected the air of a novice in the art of legal oratory, Hérault was, at the age of twenty-six, already something of a master. With so many of the most eloquent and ambitious radicals of this period he shared an aristocratic background. Like Lafayette he was an orphan of the Battle of Minden, where his father, a cavalry colonel, had charged the British lines in the futile gesture that had cut down the flower of the French military aristocracy, then died of his wounds at Cassel, in the year of Hérault's birth. His grandfather had been a schoolfellow of Voltaire's and a lieutenant of police in Paris, where he endeavored to suppress public bull-baiting and organize ordure removal from the city's filthy streets. From this tradition of patriotism and public service the young Hérault de Séchelles, blessed with precocious talent, decided, self-consciously, "to embrace the toga rather than the sword." Educated by the Oratorians and promoted by his relatives he was appointed *avocat du roi* in the Parlement at the astonishing age of nineteen. Learning perhaps from one of the new standard works on legal rhetoric—Pierre-Louis Gin's *The Eloquence of the Bar* (1768), for example— he made a reputation by specializing in the defense of those who could plausibly be represented as "victims of oppression." His cases, for example, included the defense of a wife, separated from her husband, whom the Parlement of Rennes had condemned to the cloister at the husband's request, and that of an illegitimate girl whose father wanted to seize property bequeathed by her mother.

In 1779 Hérault extended his rhetorical range by writing for a competition of the Academy, a eulogy of the Abbé Suger, the great twelfth-century creator of Saint-Denis. Still in his early twenties, in his intellectual enthusiasm he rebounded from Rousseau (predictably) and, less predictably, the natural historian Buffon. In 1783 he embarked on a journey of homage to Zurich with his aristocratic friend Michel Lepeletier (from another of the great Parlementaire clans) to see the great man. Sources close to Buffon insist that, stricken with acute pain from gallstones, the scientist was unable to see Hérault and Lepeletier. But this did not prevent the former from putting about, indeed publishing, a detailed account of their meeting. In this version Buffon was cast as the venerable sage, in whom the simplicity of nature had been preserved, conferring his benediction on the ardent young acolyte. Dressed in a yellow robe with white stripes and blue flowers:

> He came to greet me majestically, opening his two arms . . . and said, "I regard you as an old friend since you have desired to see me." I looked upon a fine countenance, noble and calm. Despite his seventy-eight years, one would have said he was but sixty and what was more singular was that, having just endured sixteen nights without shutting his eyes and in unconscionable suffering which still persisted, he was still fresh as a child and tranquil as though in perfect health.

Skilled at self-promotion, Hérault was a powerful (and strikingly handsome) young orator, and his reputation as such reached the Queen. He was, after all, officially one of the "King's men" (appointed by the government) in the Parlement. She received him at court and was evidently so smitten by his dashing self-confidence that she had a scarf especially embroidered as a present. Hérault relished showing off this favor and was said to wear it throughout his years as a militant Jacobin right up to the day when the guillotine struck off his own head. In 1786, a year after the performance at the Châtelet, he was given the honor of opening the so-called "harangues" following the Parlement of Paris's return for the new session. This was a great public occasion, and in the *Gazette des Tribuneaux* a fellow lawyer reported that "his speech was awaited with great impatience by the numerous audience. It was filled with the forms and the beauty that distinguished the orators of the ancient Republics . . . he was interrupted by frequent bursts of applause and it was noticeable that the advocates especially were seized with the enthusiasm that can arouse men and through which they discover their own strengths and the secret of their power."

Hérault's spectacular early career, then, may have been helped on its way by birth, education and connections. But it was largely made by the systematic exploitation of eloquence, as his *Reflections on Declamation* acknowledged. He was able to use his oratorical skills to climb within the career ladder of the old regime and yet strike out as a public figure with a reputation for integrity and independence. The idea of using the bar as a kind of generalized public tribune, though, had limits, which when severely tested could expel, rather than absorb, the radical. Much depended on the line taken by the orator. Hérault and his colleague Target, who would become a revolutionary and one of the authors of the constitution of 1791, could be depended on to take the side of the Parlements in most disputes with the crown. It was not until late 1788 that they parted company with the court over the form and composition of the Estates-General. But the man who in the 1760s had done more than anyone else to invent the concept and practice of a bar designed to appeal directly to the public—Simon Linguet—had done so as part of a campaign *against* the Parlements.

Linguet was nothing short of a phenomenon in the public life of the old regime. A thorn in the side of virtually all its governing institutions, he developed a manner of speech and writing that exactly anticipated the revolutionary manner of waspish incrimination and passionate anger. Until fairly recently Linguet has been written off as, at best, an eccentric curiosity, too quirky to have had any serious influence on the direction of old-regime politics. A splendid biography by Darline Gay Levy has done the most to rescue him from this obscurity and it is becoming rapidly apparent that there were almost no corners of the political world of France in this period that were untouched by his talent and reputation. As a precocious trial lawyer in the 1760s he won fame and notoriety for embracing a series of spectacular *causes célèbres*, including the case of the Chevalier de La Barre, accused of mutilating a crucifix and condemned to have his tongue cut out, head struck off and body and head burned separately at the stake. Disbarred for systematically using the bar to wage war against the courts and magistrates, Linguet turned to journalism, where his gifts for stinging and powerful attack were quite as impressive as in his speech. Two aspects of his writing, however, anticipated revolutionary discourse more directly than anything else: his concern with confronting the rhetoric of "Liberty" with issues of hunger, property and subsistence; and the angry *Memoirs of the Bastille*, written in 1783 after a two-year sentence that resulted from a *lettre de cachet*. In huge demand, Linguet's *Memoirs* did more than anything to create a mythic symbol of old-regime despotism that concentrated in itself all the rage, spleen and desperation accumulating in the late 1780s.

Linguet was really the inventor of the lawyer as public advocate, and so it was he who made it possible for a subsequent generation to slide easily from courtroom harangues to political debates. His *History of . . . the Century of Alexander*, published in 1762, had already looked back to ancient Greece for the ideal of the lawyer-orator able to articulate for the public "the springs of the human heart." By contrast, modern states had deprived the public tribune of any important role in judicial proceedings, enclosing them either in secrecy or trapping them within formalistic legal conventions. It was for the gifted orator to uncloak these mystifications by exposing them directly to the censure of the people.

And Linguet proceeded in his trial cases to do just that, using the crowds of spectators who came to hear him speak in the Grand' Chambre of the Parlement exactly like a theater audience, rousing them to applaud, cheer and whistle, cry and stamp their feet. He made sure that he had cases (few of which he won) that would connect directly with issues of Sensibility. In the La Barre case he pulled out all the emotional stops, creating an aural tableau worthy of Greuze. Criticizing the confessional testimony of a young companion of La Barre's as the product of brutal intimidation, he painted a word portrait of "this unfortunate child, prostrate at the feet of the judge. . . ." In addition to the La Barre case, he defended the Protestant wife of the Vicomte de Bombelles, who had been deserted by her husband for a Catholic woman and whose children had been removed to Catholic custody. Linguet lost the case but won public acclaim. His tactics of playing to the gallery were deeply shocking to the magistracy. A royal judge instructed young lawyers not to "take him [Linguet] for a model . . . whether it be his dangerous art of covering everything with sarcasm . . . or . . . in the unbridled audacity of formulating independent apostrophes to the public and the attempt to use them as a rampart to force the judges' vote."

Even this disruptive public style might have been acceptable had Linguet been more politically compliant. But instead of expressing solidarity with the courts in their conflicts with the crown, his *Theory of Civil Laws* actually *endorsed* "Oriental Despotism" as the best of all systems since it alone could guarantee the protection of the people from material deprivation. Staking out a position so wildly reactionary that it became, in effect, radical, he defended slavery as a social system more likely to guarantee the reciprocities of obligation and subsistence than would the "freedoms" of a market in labor. Moreover, Linguet attacked the personal credentials and competence of judges (many of whose legal education left much to be desired since they had bought their offices) to decide on important cases. In the name of royal justice and the protection of the poor, then, Linguet mounted a direct attack on the entire system of legal nobility. Since, at the same time, he had launched an equally violent attack on the *philosophes* as another self-perpetuating elite, he managed to assemble a formidable coalition of enemies. In 1775 he became his own client in a disbarral proceeding which he lost, but only after five hundred of his supporters from the gallery rushed the Grand' Chambre waving sticks and knives. "I can succumb as Socrates," announced the tribune, defeated but unbowed, in what by all accounts was a reedy, piping alto, "but I do not want my Anituses to rest unpunished. You allege that you are judging me. I agree to all this but I will place between you and me this Supreme Judge to which the most absolute tribunals are subordinated: *public opinion.*"

Self-consciously casting himself as the Rousseau of the courts— persecuted, isolated and ostracized, unable to suppress the truths that the heart dictated to the lips—Linguet became an improbable hero to a whole generation of young writers and lawyers eager to recast themselves in the role of Greco-Roman Tribune. He was the first person sought out by Jacques-Pierre Brissot when the latter arrived in Paris from the provinces. Brissot would also attempt to use a legal career to make audible what had been written argument. And like his role-model, he too became impatient with the byzantine processes by which he could penetrate the order of barristers. Wearying of his apprenticeship he campaigned for a reborn version of what he imagined was the Roman republican bar. In such a new order of lawyers, advocates would be able to plead directly at a public tribune before the assembled people, be free of all hierarchical guild restrictions, unbridled by any kind of censorship of opinions; and judges would be appointed by the state purely on the basis of unimpeachable integrity and eloquence. Brissot's mythical vision of virtuous advocacy was drawn directly from Linguet's nostalgia for an antiquity where there had been "inconceivable assemblies of the entire nation where a single man could harangue twenty thousand. . . ."

Linguet and his admirers privileged the spoken over the printed word because they believed it somehow to be less capable of alienation. The voice, in this sense, was held to be "indivisible" from the man, whereas the pamphlet or the treatise could be more easily censored, suppressed or amended by authority. Supposedly more spontaneous in its expression, the oratorical voice more faithfully announced the particular qualities of the individual and so was less open to the sophistries, concealments and artifices that could be brought to the printed page. When he went to England in the 1770s, Linguet was dismayed to discover how ponderous, formulaic and uninspired speeches in Parliament were, and he distinguished them sharply from the kind of neo-Roman declamation that would be the preaching voice of public virtue.

And it was this superior virtue that came to be prized so highly by the revolutionaries. Indeed, public utterance in different forums—the revolutionary club, the convention, even the military camp—would assume a strategic importance. At several critical moments, the ability to sway audiences, large or confined, made the difference between life and death, triumph and disaster. The great cascades of rhetoric pouring from the mouths of revolutionary orators so appealed to the Romantic historians of the nineteenth century, who admired its theatrical flamboyance, that they tried to reproduce these speeches as set pieces of their narratives. And that in turn has led modern accounts, until quite recently, to downplay somewhat the effect of spoken rhetoric on allegiance. But Mirabeau's famous retorts to royal intervention in the Estates-General; Desmoulins' inflammatory speech atop a table in the Palais-Royal on July 12, 1789; Saint-Just's rousing rhetoric before the Army of the Sambre-et-Meuse all played a vital part in replacing an inchoate wash of fear and anger with a sense of brotherly solidarity. In this sense it does not seem too much to say that it was oratory that created "The People," not vice versa. Conversely, failure to be heard could be a death sentence. Robespierre made sure that Danton's booming baritone would not sabotage his trial by isolating him from a big public audience. But it was the collapse of Robespierre's own eloquence before the Convention that drowned out his speech and ensured his own overthrow on the ninth of Thermidor.

Public diction, then, was public power. And there were sources of speech training, other than the bar, to enrich its elocution. Hérault, for example, went to the theater to polish his timing and inflection. Tutored by Mlle Clairon, he tried to imitate a specific style in the classical theater: that of the actors Molé and de Larive, famous for their grave portrayal of patriarchal heroes. A striking number of other revolutionaries had direct and professional connections with the theater—Collot d'Herbois, Camille Desmoulins, the Chénier brothers, the sans-culotte militant Ronsin and many others. Philippe Fabre from the little Pyrenean town of Limoux turned into the more grandiosely named "Fabre d'Eglantine" after being awarded the golden briar rose (eglantine) as a prize in eloquence by the Academy of Toulouse. And it was this that launched him on his nomadic career as a playwright, poet, songwriter, guitar player and traveling actor who ended up in Paris on the eve of the Revolution with a string of spectacular flops.

The pulpit sermon was another important form of rehearsal. In the later part of the eighteenth century the Church attempted to arrest the progress of secularization by launching evangelical preaching missions in both Paris and the provinces. They met with a good deal of success, and a number of the most forceful orators of the Revolution came from this ecclesiastical background. Claude Fauchet, the Bishop of Caen who preached the gospel of social equality at his "Social Circle" meetings in Notre Dame, was one such figure; the Abbé Grégoire, advancing the principles of toleration and equal rights for Jews, was another.

In the lay world there were many opportunities for public declamation outside the realm of politics. Academies required eulogies of both recently deceased luminaries and long-dead figures they wished to praise. Speeches of reception for members newly welcomed to the ranks performed the same function. And some notables in the Paris elite became famous for their rhetoric. Talleyrand's friend Chamfort, for example, had won a prize in eloquence in 1769 from the Academy and was elected a member in 1781 largely on the strength of his rhetorical polish. Classical drama provided one model for the grave elocution favored in these performances, but a more likely source was the schoolroom Latin in which virtually all aspirants to public eloquence would have been steeped.

As the report on Hérault's 1786 speech suggests, there was no higher praise for orators than to be compared with the figures from antiquity whom they sought to emulate. The French Revolution was obsessed with the model of the Roman Republic in particular, and it was Cicero's speeches as well as oratory reported in the histories of Sallust, Livy and Plutarch to which it looked for inspiration. Camille Desmoulins, for example, quoted from Cicero no less than forty-three times during his relatively brief periods in the revolutionary assemblies, and Brissot quoted him by way of Plutarch ten times. The Abbé Boisgelin, who was to be a deputy of the clergy in 1789 and who published a work on antique eloquence ten years earlier, summed up the reputation of this paragon by claiming that "when Cicero spoke in the Senate, he was the father of his country [*père de la patrie*]." Boisgelin went on to complain of the absence of comparably serious rhetoric in his own time, because "there are no longer great subjects to treat." Before very long this was to be remedied. But already those who consciously sought to revive the antique tradition of political oratory associated it (in Athens as well as republican Rome) with the practice of freedom. The "bar" thus became the "bar of the people," or the "tribune," as it came to be called in the revolutionary assemblies at which the voice of those seeking to persuade the representatives of the people could be fairly judged.

It was the active citizenship that was believed to have existed in certain periods of antiquity that the revolutionary generation sought to revive through the power of oratory. In all likelihood they had first encountered it at school, where it was the staple diet of curricula in many colleges. This was the case, for example, at the Collège Louis-le-Grand, where Robespierre was one of many scholarship boys—some of whom came from even more modest backgrounds in trade, shopkeeping and the skilled artisanal crafts. Camille Desmoulins recollected that at the same school teachers like the Abbé Royau told their pupils to admire the simplicity, frugality, austerity, courage and patriotism of the heroes of the Roman Republic. And it was in college that students were required to model speeches on Cicero's precise construction using, successively, exordium, narration, confirmation, refutation and peroration. There too they would have been introduced to the ornaments of the rhetoric: metaphor, trope, exclamation and interrogation—all of which were much on exhibition in revolutionary utterance.

There was no doubt that in the heroes of republican antiquity, the revolutionary generation found stirring role-models—and at the same time, that admiration sharpened their view that the stereotypes of the age in which they lived corresponded to the worst excesses of gilded corruption decried in the Roman histories. They read, for example, in Sallust's *Conspiracy of the Catilines* that after the defeat of Carthage "virtue began to lose its lustre . . . as the result of riches, luxury and greed." By contrast, in the golden age of the Republic

> good morals were cultivated at home and in the field, . . . justice and probity prevailed among them thanks not so much to laws as to nature. Quarrels, discord and strife were reserved for their enemies; citizens contended with each other only in merit. They were lavish in offerings to the gods, frugal at home and loyal to their friends. . . .

That this view of an exemplary relationship between private morals and public virtues sounded like Rousseau did nothing to discourage it as a model. Equally, Cicero's designation of *homines novi*—new men—as those who rose by virtue of their sound civism and eloquence provided the generation of the 1780s with their own collective badge of merit.

The result was to create a powerful bond of identification between ancient and modern republicans. When she was nine, Manon Philipon carried a copy of Plutarch to church with her, and recalled that "it was from that moment that I date the impressions and ideas that were to make me a republican." Reading the history "inspired in me a veritable enthusiasm for public virtues and for liberty." Some indeed were so carried away that they found it difficult if not impossible to be reconciled to the present. Mercier, who had taught at college in his twenties, was another idolater of the ancients and after wallowing in the majesty of the Republic found it "painful to leave Rome and find oneself still a commoner of the rue Noyer."

"Roman" patriotism (for it was much more rarely Athenian) shared some of the virtues of the cult of Sensibility, but in other respects it was differently accented. For one thing, it was less inclined to marinate in the lachrymose, but instead exalted stoical self-possession over emotional outpouring. It was, quite self-consciously, a "virile" or masculine culture: austere, muscular and inflexible, rather than tender, sensitive and compassionate. As a style of architecture and interior decoration neoclassicism worked with stripped-down and severe forms: capitals that were plain Doric rather than elaborately Corinthian or delicately Ionic. And the publication of Roman wall painting (by the future ultra-Jacobin Sylvain Maréchal among others) from Pompeii and Herculaneum popularized a relieflike formalism.

Some enthusiasts of antiquity managed to travel to its most famous sites to commune directly with its ghosts. Some even went as far afield as the Peloponnese, a few more to Sicily, Naples and the Campania. But French visitors tended to be fewer than their English counterparts on the Grand Tour. Mostly, it was the establishment of the Prix de Rome by the Royal Academy of Painting, and its school in the same city, that made it possible for aspiring French painters to drink at the fountainhead of classical culture. Louis XVI's new director of arts (officially the Surintendant des Bâtiments), d'Angiviller, was particularly concerned to use the scholarships available in a more austerely meritocratic fashion than had been the case under his predecessor Marigny. And in the late 1770s he also launched a program to encourage a new generation of history painting expressly designed to inculcate the public virtues associated with republican Rome: patriotism, fortitude, integrity and frugality.

So the heroes that embodied these values were paraded in large format at the Salons: Junius Brutus, who had executed his own sons when they were convicted of involvement in a royalist plot; Mucius Scaevola, who held his hand in the fire to demonstrate his patriotic inflexibility; Horatio Cocles, who had defended the bridge single-handed against the Etruscans;

Gaius Fabricius and Scipio, whose imperviousness to corruption had been eulogized in the histories. Added to them were exemplary deathbed scenes in which philosophers of unbending integrity—Socrates, Seneca and Cato—died by their own hand rather than truckle to dictators.

Many of these worthies were already a familiar feature of the official self-advertisement of other republican cultures. Brutus, Gaius and Scipio, for example, were all prominently featured in the sculpted and painted decorations of the Amsterdam Town Hall in the mid-seventeenth century. But as they appeared in the Salons of the late 1770s and 1780s—and especially in the paintings of Jacques-Louis David—they registered a new message with disturbing eloquence: the painted equivalent to the rhetoric of Linguet.

The most spectacular of all such painted manifestos was David's *Oath of the Horatii*, which appeared—late, and oversize—in the Salon of 1785. A great deal has been written about this extraordinary painting, and the debate over its political implications or lack of them is by no means yet exhausted. That it was aggressively unorthodox and self-consciously broke with academic conventions (even those hallowed by neoclassicists like Poussin) is indisputable. That it used a deliberately purified and somber color language and disregarded the obligatory "pyramid" composition for a relieflike arrangement within a shallow box, with groups of figures abruptly separated into three disconnected arrangements, is also self-evident. What remains contentious is whether these dramatic alterations of form constituted in themselves some sort of radical vocabulary and were recognized as such by contemporaries. David painted his subject, after all, as a royal commission sponsored by d'Angiviller, and his entire career had been typical of the escalator of talent that moved him easily upwards to renown and fortune in the 1780s. Official organs like the *Mercure de France* as much as unofficial reviews like Métra's *Correspondance Secret* were agreed on the genius of the work. But as we have seen in the case of Beaumarchais and even Rousseau, it was quite possible for the court as well as the grandest of *les Grands* to endorse what in hindsight appear to be the most subversive messages.

What is not in doubt is that *The Oath of the Horatii* triggered an unprecedented uproar in the Salon itself and in critical circles in Paris. The *Mercure* rhapsodized that "the composition is the work of a new genius; it announces a brilliant and courageous imagination. . . ." Part of its fame at least was due to the intense narrative interest of the story. Attacked by the Curiatii, the three sons of Horace had challenged three of their young counterparts in the enemy camp to mortal combat so as to spare their respective populations the devastation of general war. But the story is complicated by the fact that while one of the Horatii was married to a sister

49. Jacques-Louis David, *The Oath of the Horatii*, 1785

of the Curiatii, their own sister, Camilla, was betrothed to one of their enemies. The combat turned out to be so lethal that only one of the Roman brothers survives and when he returns to find his sister in mourning for her fiancé kills her in a patriotic rage.

The story of the Horatii, then, married the moral themes of domestic virtues exhibited in the Sensibility paintings of the 1760s and 1770s to the martial and patriotic epics of the next generation. And David had imagined a scene not anticipated in any of the predictable sources, including the most familiar one—Corneille's tragedy *Les Horaces.* For the moment when the father swore his sons to patriotic sacrifice was one where the emotional sword was sharply double-edged. The stern masculine determination of the patriotism on the left and center of the painting is set off against the tender genre group on the right with grief-stricken women and innocently rendered children already shadowed by the impending tragedy. It was this stunning articulation between the heroic and the tragic that so roused many of the painting's admirers, who didn't hesitate to place it not only in the context of neoclassical rhetoric but also in that of Rousseau's emotional candor. The report in the *Journal de Paris* was typical:

One must absolutely see [this painting] to understand how
it merits so much admiration. I observed . . . a correct design
. . . a style that is noble without being forced [*clinquant*], true
and harmonious color . . . an effect that is sharp and clear and a
composition full of energy, supporting an expression strong and
terrible [i.e., on the faces of the central group] that contrasts with
the prostration reigning in the group of women. In the end if I
am to judge from the feeling of others as well as my own, one
feels in seeing this painting a sentiment that exalts the soul and
which, to use an expression of J.J. Rousseau, has something
poignant about it that attracts one; all the attributes are so well
observed that one believes oneself transported to the earliest days
of the Roman Republic.

It would be premature to see in the painting (even if some critics did)
an unequivocal prophecy of David's later Jacobinism. Even if the doyens
of the Academy (in particular the official First Painter to the King, Pierre)
were made nervous by the unorthodoxy of the picture, there is no evidence
that it lost David favor with d'Angiviller or even with the court, which
offered him more commissions. If the outstretched arm of the Horatii was
to become the standard manner of taking a revolutionary oath—and recorded in David's later unfinished painting of the Tennis Court Oath of
1789—it would be because the gesture had been appropriated by the Revolution. But it would be equally myopic not to notice that all the required
ingredients for revolutionary rhetoric were spectacularly announced in this
painting: patriotism, fraternity and martyrdom. And where, for an earlier
generation of Salon-goers, public virtue had been born and nursed in the
bosom of a tender family, it had now been weaned to an attitude of brutal
defiance.

iv SPREADING THE WORD

Suppose a courtier had a hankering for banned publications: the juicy
gossip sheet *English Spy* put out by Pidanzat de Mairobert from London;
Rousseau's *Confessions;* Linguet's *Memoirs of the Bastille;* the Abbé Raynal's
incendiary attack on European colonization, the *History . . . of the Two
Indies.* Where would he go to find them? Not far, for just at the foot of the
ramp from the terrace of the palace at Versailles was a bookstall belonging
to M. Lefèvre where, at the right time and for the right sum, a choice

selection of all these items could be acquired. With a direct line to one of the most prolific printers of forbidden books, Robert Machuel of Rouen, and a wife from the bookselling dynasty of the Mérigot, Lefèvre seemed assured in his position as tolerated hawker on the very doorstep of royal power. But in 1777 he overstepped the mark by actually dealing in pornographic pamphlets that libeled the Queen—perhaps the famous *Anandria*, in which she was depicted in lesbian love triangles. He was duly arrested and on release from the Bastille ended his career in the safer profession of toy-shop owner.

Startling as it may seem, the court and the high nobility were prime customers for the works that did most to damage their own authority. The town of Versailles had a number of shops where the most professional hawkers *(colporteurs)* unloaded their stock. Delorme, for example, who used Dunkirk as a port of entry for his books, had his own outlet at Versailles and he was by no means alone. The appetite of the court for daring literature—both political and erotic—may be gauged from the fact that similar outlets were located at towns to which the court seasonally moved, in particular Compiègne, Fontainebleau and Saint-Cloud. In an only slightly less direct manner, the immunity of the great aristocratic families from search and seizure meant that the *colporteurs* used them shamelessly to smuggle their goods. The coachman of the Duc de Praslin was a virtual *colporteur* in his own right and in 1767 six bales of clandestine books were discovered in a wagon bearing the arms of the Maréchal de Noailles. Even the King's youngest brother, Artois (who as Charles X was to take such a censorious line with seditious literature), was said to be protecting hawkers of libels.

These stories seem to vindicate de Tocqueville's view that the old regime brought about its own undoing by irresponsibly flirting with ideas it only half understood, but which it found diverting: the literary equivalent of the Figaro syndrome. To counter-revolutionary writers, looking back on the disaster of 1789, the proliferation of seditious and libelous material seemed even more sinister, evidence of a conspiracy hatched between godless followers of Voltaire and Rousseau, Freemasons, and the Duc d'Orléans. Was not the Palais-Royal after all one of the most notorious dens of iniquity, where even the police were forbidden from pouncing on peddlers of literary trash?

Understandably, modern historians have steered clear of anything that could be construed as subscribing to the literary conspiracy theory of the French Revolution. Having failed to discover in libraries of the time the work officially canonized by the Revolution—Rousseau's *Social Contract*—they have largely set aside the concept of the upheaval as the product of dangerous reading habits. Robert Darnton's discovery of a rich seam of literary muck—an indiscriminate jumble of pornographic libels, vitriolic satire and radical political theory—has reinstated the corrosive importance of risky publications. But while it is quite true that the producers of much of this material directed their most withering fire at the grandees of the literary and political establishment, it would be misleading to see them altogether as "outsiders." On the contrary, it was from within the well-fortified camp of aristocratic radicalism—the Palais-Royal or the courtyard of the Palais de Justice—that their broadsides took aim. And it was not the disconnection, but the connection between the world of monied patronage and fiery polemics which made the damage to the dignities of the old regime so serious.

In its initial euphoria, the Revolution abandoned all forms of censorship and control over publication. The explosion of printed information that resulted was so phenomenal that, by contrast, the old regime is bound to seem deprived. In fact, the last decade of the monarchy witnessed a proliferation of ephemeral literature of all kinds—newspapers, literary journals, brochures and pamphlets, printed ballads and poems. This transformation of the press must have done much to create the news-hungry and politically receptive public whose allegiance revolutionary journalists fought to acquire and hold.

Before the mid-1770s, political news could only be had from abroad. Inside France two journals were officially licensed: the *Gazette de France* and the *Mercure de France*, a descendant of the literary journal founded in the 1630s. The *Gazette* produced a largely mythical view of the monarchy, proceeding through undisturbed ceremonies and uncontentious administration; the *Mercure* was filled with harmless essays from the polite world of the academies and belles-lettres. The major source of reliable foreign news was the Dutch gazettes, of which much the most important was the biweekly *Gazette de Leyde* (The Leiden Gazette). Similar newspapers were published in other Dutch towns like Amsterdam and Utrecht, in the papal enclave of Avignon and just over the frontiers in Geneva or Cologne. Packed with reports of military and political events in virtually every major state in Europe and in North America, they represented themselves as both topical and reliable, avoiding the casually gathered anecdote or hearsay. More important, as Jeremy Popkin has pointed out, they published in full the great manifestos of "opposition politics" in France: the remonstrances of the Parlements and the Cour des Aides. By giving these prominence, the Luzac family (like so many other publishers, a branch of the Huguenot dispersion), who edited the *Gazette de Leyde*, made no secret of their support for an antiabsolutist view of the French constitution. Despite this, not only were the gazettes tacitly tolerated in France, but they were allowed openly to advertise their places of sale throughout France, solicit subscriptions and use the royal mail to distribute the papers. The best estimate of the circulation of the *Gazette de Leyde* puts it at about four thousand, by eighteenth-century standards a considerable number.

The man who did most to turn the newspaper business from a minor branch of polite letters into a modern commercial enterprise was the formidable publisher Charles-Joseph Panckoucke. Brought up in Lille by his father, who was an author and a bookseller in his own right, Panckoucke turned to writing and translation before moving to Paris in 1760. There he bought two substantial bookselling and publishing houses, and got a further entree into the literary world by marrying the sister of one of its perennial nonentities, Suard. In no time at all Panckoucke became the great mogul of the Paris book trade. Taking unheard-of pains with his authors, traveling to see Voltaire at Ferney and Buffon at Montbard, he pampered their egos and, at a time notorious for fraud and piracy, tried to assure them a decent income, in some cases even producing advances.

As a newspaper operator Panckoucke was equally bold. He put out two powerful and important papers, the *Journal de Genève* and the *Journal de Bruxelles,* and in 1774 hired Linguet to edit the latter. Predictably, in response to Linguet's habit of throwing acid in the faces of all the intellectual and political luminaries of the day, the circulation shot up, reaching some six thousand. But Panckoucke, always torn between commercial acumen and a yearning for respectability, found Linguet's deadly sniping at some of his own favored authors too much to take, and got rid of him after two years, replacing him with one of Linguet's favorite targets, La Harpe. From London, Linguet then began his own paper, the *Annales Politiques et Littéraires,* which set new standards in sardonic vituperation, but which was also full of lively pieces on the arts and science. Equipped, rather surprisingly, with the *permission tacite* that protected it from prosecution while not openly giving it respectability, no less than seventy-one issues of the *Annales* were published between 1777 and Linguet's incarceration in the Bastille in 1780. All of them were distributed in Paris by a wealthy cloth merchant, Lequesne. Linguet's biographer thinks that the circulation may have risen as high as twenty thousand.

Not satisfied with his foothold, Panckoucke created the first daily paper, the *Journal de Paris,* essentially a listing of daily events together with short reviews and dispatches, making his brother-in-law Suard editor and co-owner. The *Mercure de France* was next, in 1778, and it was in this paper that the drastically altered aspect of the press was most apparent. From being a dull and starchy journal, the *Mercure* expanded to forty-eight pages, and boasted a great miscellany of items: standard news reports from European and American capitals and digests of the gazettes, but also popular songs (music and verses printed), puzzles and riddles, reviews of music, theater and literature. In the May 8, 1784, number *The Marriage of Figaro* was given sixteen pages of review all to itself. It was a winning formula, and the circulation of the *Mercure* rose to some twenty thousand on the eve of the Revolution. If a contemporary's own estimates of the ratio of circulation to readership is correct, then it seems possible that Panckoucke's paper had a readership of over a hundred and twenty thousand at the time it was reporting in grim detail the final debacle of Louis XVI's government. "This review," observed one commentator, "has spread everywhere, to the commoner as well as the noble, in the salons of the aristocracy as well as the modest household of the bourgeois, delighting equally both court and Town." Nor was this just a Parisian phenomenon, since over half the copies of the *Mercure* were sold in the provinces.

There were other forms of publicity to cater to the eager literary appetites of the French. Muckraking reviews like the *Correspondance Secret* (ascribed to Métra) and the *Mémoires Secrets* circulated in manuscript form and dwelt lingeringly on the sexual politics of the court or scandals involving money and, if at all possible, the clergy. And while it is impossible to gauge their circulation, the printed *English Spy* (or *The Correspondence of Milord All-Ear with Milord All-Eye*), exported from London, repeated many of the same stories and achieved wide currency in the sensational climate of the 1780s.

It is hard to avoid the impression that the world of "low" literature in the reign of Louis XVI was like an empire of ants: columns of energetic and determined couriers bearing precious objects to their several destinations. Certainly France swarmed with these purveyors of gossip and ideology, packing, bribing and hurrying as they traveled on well-established routes and networks. Canals and rivers were crucial to their transport. Some began by using storage depots in the more out-of-the-way ports like Agde on the Mediterranean and Saint-Malo on the Breton coast, and then carefully made their way upstream in prudent stages. Smuggling out of Avignon, surrounded by French territory, was trickier, but fishing boats on the Rhone were used to take bales of books and papers downstream to Tarascon and Arles. Another route connected with the royal canal at Toulouse, from which the transports could go west towards Bordeaux. Others worked the eastern frontiers from Strasbourg to Dunkirk, trying to avoid the big customs posts at Sainte-Menehould, at the entrance to the Champagne, and Peronne, at the gate to Picardy.

In any event one may assume that the *colporteurs* did their job well enough, for Lyon, Rouen, Marseille, Bordeaux and most of the major cities were all well stocked with ostensibly "forbidden" works. In Paris, they could be had not only in the Palais-Royal but from stands on the Pont Neuf and the quais—the ancestors of the modern *bouquinistes.* Though expressly prohibited, vendors hawked books in the lobbies of theaters and at the Opéra, and did the rounds of cafés and fairs with parcels under their arms. Others used the simplest possible forms of display—spreading out their wares on a cloth in full public view on the street. Some of the vendors became well known, even powerful, like Kolman, Prudent de Roncours, and Pardeloup, and some of the most formidable were women, notably *la Grande Javotte*, who sold from a stall on the quai des Augustins, and her partner the Widow Allaneau, still going strong well into her seventies.

There was an extraordinary degree of complicity on the part of the authorities in all this trafficking. Girardin, for example, the vendor who specialized in violent libels against the Queen, operated with impunity from the cul-de-sac de l'Orangerie at the heart of the Tuileries. The courtyard of the Hôtel de Soubise (now the National Archives) was another semipublic place crowded with subversive literature, and before the Jacobins and the Cordeliers were revolutionary clubs they were religious houses with a difference since they too entertained the ubiquitous *colporteurs.* Linguet's *Annales*, with their no-holds-barred attacks on courtiers, academicians, Panckoucke, and Farmers-General, were subject to just one censor: the lieutenant-général of police in Paris, Lenoir. And he proved to be a largely complaisant critic.

Why? Lenoir may well have enjoyed the spectacle of professed reformers and critics of the monarchy themselves undergoing a good dousing at the hands of Linguet (who still represented himself as a devoted albeit cranky royalist). But there is also reason to believe that he thought it useful to know what was going on in the wilder fringes of opinion, rather than drive it underground. In other words, in common with many other levels of official authority he had come to accept the *fact* of public opinion, and rather than be its helpless target, preferred, as much as he could, to be its manipulator. Others like the Duc d'Orléans and his son the Duc de Chartres may have been still bolder in seeing opinion, gossip and libel as a weapon useful in embarrassing their immediate opponents. Short-term tactical advantage, then, obscured completely the long-term dangers posed by the cultivation of this fickle world of opinion. As they jockeyed for position in public esteem, the patrons of innuendo and scandal still assumed their own position rested on the bedrock, whereas in fact it was slipping into quicksand. It was impossible to sustain the general principle of unquestioned deference while it was being sabotaged daily, in the particulars of personal attacks on the court, the ministry, the Church, the academies and the law.

Nor were those who toyed with Pandora's box aware of how broad the constituency for polemics and propaganda had become. From within the drawing room of a *grand seigneur* who was unwrapping pink-ribboned parcels of forbidden books, the traffic of opinion must have seemed safely circumscribed: a matter of Paris fashions, here today, gone tomorrow. But the retaining walls of polite opinion were rapidly weakening. "Paris reads ten times more than a century ago," reported Mercier, and the change was a function of the number of readers as well as the volume and variety of matter. From studying signatures of wills Daniel Roche has discovered astonishing figures for adult literacy in the capital at the end of the old regime. In Montmartre, for example, where 40 percent of the testators belonged to the artisan or salaried classes, 74 percent of men and 64 percent of women could sign their names. In the rue Saint-Honoré—a fashionable street, but one where a third of the residents belonged to the common people—literacy rates stood at 93 percent. In the artisanal rue Saint-Denis, 86 percent of men and 73 percent of women made out and signed their own contracts of marriage.

In other words, literacy rates in late eighteenth-century France were much higher than in the late twentieth-century United States. It was only in the pools of unskilled, day-wage labor—market porters, construction workers, stevedores, chimney sweeps and coachmen, many of them immigrant workers from the provinces—that illiteracy predominated. By contrast domestic servants, who also came from the countryside, were virtually all literate, able to read their contracts of employment. The "little schools" promoted by the Catholic missions of the seventeenth and eighteenth centuries had evidently done their work well. Around 1780, according to Roche, 35 percent of all wills made by the popular classes contained some books as did 40 percent of those in the shopkeeping and petty trades.

What this population read, of course, did not necessarily connect them with the fast tides of public opinion. There is no doubt that religious and devotional literature remained most widespread, followed by the fantasies and fairy stories called the "Blue Library" and cheaply available from the Pont Neuf stalls and the fairs of Saint-Laurent and Saint-Germain. But if they were not drinking directly at the well of Rousseau, there were many examples of popular literature that imparted the same messages: of innocence corrupted, the wickedness of urban money and the brutality of power. There is no doubt, for example, that Restif de Bretonne, who laced with detailed sexual adventures his own stories of country boys and girls going down the urban drain, was a huge success among simple as well as sophisticated readers.

And it was unbound literature—almanacs and the posting of notices and placards—that would have increasingly connected the common people of the French towns with the world of public events. Every morning in Paris forty bill stickers would paste the city with news of battles won or lost; edicts of the King and the government; public festivities to mark some auspicious event; timely indications about the transport of ordure or the removal of graves. At moments of crisis they would be defaced or (illegally) supplanted by notices parodying government orders or pillorying ministers. And the exuberance of their visual broadcasting system was matched by the flamboyance of the oral world of the Parisian, tuned as it was to a whole universe of songs. The subsequent importance of the "Marseillaise" or the "Carmagnole" as revolutionary anthems can only be understood if the universal passion for songs in Louis XVI's France is appreciated. Songs were sold by strolling vendors on the boulevards, bridges and quais and were sung at the cafés, their themes spanning a whole universe from the predictable airs of songs of courtship, seduction and rejection, to others that caroled the sons of Liberty in America, the profligacy of the court, the impotence of the King and the naughtiness of the Queen.

The empire of words—spoken, read, declaimed or sung—at the end of the old regime stretched out to very far-flung boundaries. While it was at its most excited in Paris, it was by no means an exclusively metropolitan phenomenon. There may have been nothing quite like the Palais-Royal in the provinces, but traveling hawkers, adventurous booksellers and eager customers all ensured that both the newspaper press and the market for clandestine works were as lively in Bordeaux, Lyon, Rennes, and Marseille as in the capital. There too could be found the other communities of discussion: Masonic lodges, literary and scientific academies, the *sociétés de pensée* and *musées* on which local elites prided themselves. And if some took care to retain distinctions of rank that corresponded to formal social divisions, they almost invariably opened themselves to the corresponding members, whose sense of being simultaneously included and rejected in these intellectual fraternities sharpened their public conscience.

And in realms beyond words—in open-air spectacles; in Rousseau's little opera, still playing in the 1780s; in the tear-soaked canvases of Greuze—the phalanxes of citizens were lining up. Indeed their individual and collective personalities were, by the mid-1780s, already constructed. They were devotees of Nature, tender-hearted, contemptuous of fashion, scornful of the ostentation of the mighty, passionate in their patriotism and enraged at the abuses of despotism. Above all they were apostles of public virtue who saw a France on the verge of being reborn as a republic of friends. And it was with their arms linked, their pens busily scratching letters and their lungs rehearsing speeches and songs, that this army of young citizens watched as their government fell apart.

CHAPTER FIVE
The Costs of Modernity

i HOW NEW WAS THE
OLD REGIME?

I N H E R winning memoirs, Mme de Genlis remembers dressing up with her sister-in-law as peasant girls. Thus disguised, they collected all the milk they could from farms on their estate and carried it home on the backs of donkeys. It was then dumped into their bath—a locally famous tub that could comfortably accommodate four—where the girls wallowed for two hours in a milky pool strewn with rose petals.

This is probably the sort of thing Talleyrand had in mind when he mourned the disappeared *douceur de vivre* of the old regime. And these social frivolities, sketched in pastel by Fragonard, costumed by Diana Vreeland, lit by a crepuscular glow and perfumed with summer flowers, still linger as a pleasant historical myth. Inevitably, there is about them something insubstantial and self-deceiving, like the King playing locksmith and the Queen minding her sheep. And beyond this dreamy, toyland France, historians are quick to remind us, lay Reality: armies of emaciated beggars dying on the roads; Paris streets slopping with ordure and butchers' offal; relentless *feudistes* screwing the last sou out of peasants barely subsisting on chestnut gruel; prisoners rotting in the hulks for stealing a loaf of sugar or smuggling a box of salt; horse and hound laying waste to standing crops in the name of the lord's *droit de chasse;* filthy bundles of rags deposited every morning on the steps of Paris churches containing newborn babies with pathetic notes claiming baptism; four to a bed in the Hôtel-Dieu, expiring in companionable dysentery.

To many of those who became revolutionaries, these opposites not only co-existed; they made each other possible. Great opulence and folly were fed by great wretchedness and despair. In his futuristic fantasy, *The Year 2440,*

Louis-Sébastien Mercier imagined a France miraculously freed from despotism and poverty and ruled by an amiable Citizen-King. In a gallery filled
with allegorical paintings, that representing the eighteenth century took the
form of a gaudily dressed whore, with painted cheeks and mouth, holding
two rose-colored ribbons that concealed iron chains. At ground level

> her robe was in tatters and covered with dirt. Her naked feet
> were plunged in a kind of bog and her lower extremities were as
> hideous as her head was brilliant. . . . Behind her [were] a number
> of children with meager livid aspects who cried to their mother
> while they devoured a morsel of black bread.

The impression conveyed by these images is one of enduring hopeless-
ness, a world that needed to be blown up if it was ever to be substantially
changed. Virtually as soon as the term was coined, "old regime" was
semantically freighted with associations of both traditionalism and senes-
cence. It conjured up a society so encrusted with anachronisms that only
a shock of great violence could free the living organism within. Institutionally torpid, economically immobile, culturally atrophied and socially strati-
fied, this "old regime" was incapable of self-modernization. The Revolution
needed to smash it to pieces before acting as a Great Accelerator on the
highway to the nineteenth century. Beforehand, all was inertia; afterwards,
all was energy; beforehand, there was corporatism and *Gemeinschaft*; afterwards, individualism and *Gesellschaft*. The Revolution, in short, was the
permitting condition of modernity.

It could be argued, though, that the French Revolution was as much the
interruption, as the catalyst, of modernity. Not in all respects, since in its
most militant phase, the Revolution did indeed invent a new kind of politics, an institutional transference of Rousseau's sovereignty of the General
Will that abolished private space and time, and created a form of patriotic
militarism more all-embracing than anything that had yet been seen in
Europe. For one year, it invented and practiced representative democracy;
for two years, it imposed coercive egalitarianism (though even this is a
simplification). But for two decades its enduring product was a new kind
of militarized state.

But this is not what most historians mean when they write of the Revolution ushering in a modernity inimical to the "old regime." What they
usually have in mind is a world in which capital replaces custom as the
arbiter of social values, where professionals rather than amateurs run institutions of law and government, and where commerce and industry rather
than land lead economic growth. In virtually all these respects, though, the

great period of change was not the Revolution but the late eighteenth century. In fact it might even be argued that the Revolution drew much of its power from the (ultimately hopeless) attempt to *arrest*, rather than hasten, the process of modernization. And in many respects it was all too successful. In 1795, the total value of France's trade was less than half what it had been in 1789; by 1815 it was still at about 60 percent. The momentum of economic and social change in France only picked up as the Revolution and the military state it created in its wake disappeared.

The abolition of privilege did, of course, mean a sweeping away of legal distinctions that are correctly seen as premodern. But since the general availability of titles was coming to be a matter of money and merit, not birth, eighteenth-century privileges seem to have more in common with the honorific distinctions and forms common to all modern societies in the nineteenth and, in many cases, the twentieth centuries. They were certainly not incompatible with the creation of either a modern economy or a modern state. Equally, if the Revolution abolished old forms of social dues on seigneurial estates, many of these dues had already been commuted into money and were simply converted into rent in the "new regime."

The "old regime," then, was not a society doddering its way to the grave. Far from appearing moribund, signs of dynamism and energy may be found wherever the historian looks. From the King downward, the elite were less obsessed with tradition than with novelty, and less preoccupied with feudalism than with science. In the great pile of the Louvre were housed not just the Académie Française and academies of painting and inscriptions and medals, but those of science and the latest royal foundation, the Academy of Medicine. Moreover it was a royal initiative in 1785 that expanded the sections of the Academy of Science to include mineralogy, natural history and agriculture. If gifted prodigies in the arts like Jacques-Louis David could be lodged in an apartment in the Louvre, so could paragons of the new mathematics like Lagrange, lured back to France from Berlin. Certified geniuses were promoted early and showered with status and honor. Fourcroy, the most inventive chemist of the age, was a professor at twenty-nine in the Jardin du Roi and one of the luminaries of the Academy; Gaspard Monge, the son of a peddler and the founder of modern descriptive geometry, had a chair at twenty-five. Others were placed in positions of honor and public esteem, like Lalande the astronomer, Haüy the mineralogist and especially the mathematician Laplace, who was given a special post at the Ecole Militaire.

Nor was this official enthusiasm for science purely a matter of speculative theory. Wherever possible, the crown and government endeavored to apply new data to practical purposes. Military technology produced the Gribeauval cannon and the musket which, together with the tactical changes introduced by the great reformer Guibert, created the ascendancy of French arms over the next quarter of a century. On the outskirts of Paris, at Vanves, Charenton and Javel, were a number of workshops all devoted to developing chemical processes helpful to industry: vitriols for bleaches, lead-whites for paints, inflammable gases.

The partnership of government and the academies subscribed to the late Enlightenment view—especially cherished by its exemplary figure the Marquis de Condorcet—that the empirical gathering of data was the first step towards a society that could progressively free itself from poverty, ignorance and pain. A rain of paper, designed to elicit the information on which action might then be taken, descended from Paris on the provinces. No sooner had it been set up, for example, than the Academy of Medicine distributed to 150 physicians a circular on the ecology of local sickness: its seasonal incidence; the contribution of contaminated water, filthy streets, malnutrition and the like. Out from the Louvre issued instructions to the Normandy cider makers on how to avoid barrel tainting, and to the peasants of Sologne to stop eating the blighted rye that gave them ergotism (with the attendant side-effects of gangrene and decomposing feet). Traveling lecture tours were arranged for the formidable Dame de Coudray, along with her mechanical uterus capable of contracting at different rates, to offer courses in basic obstetrics to provincial midwives. M. Parmentier's propaganda for the potato as the miracle crop that would save France from famine received official support to the point where the Queen replaced her usual corsage with potato flowers as a misplaced gesture of public-spiritedness.

Wherever government could busy itself with the public good, it did. After fifteen memoranda dealing with the gruesome problem of slaughterhouse waste, it attempted to move some of the butchers out from the quartier Saint-Jacques. It tried to limit the casual dumping of ordure by creating great cesspits at Montfaucon and in the name of public hygiene even disturbed the repose of the dead (whose noxious vapors were thought to poison the atmosphere), exhuming remains from Paris churches and carting them out to the newly created cemetery of Père Lachaise. In the land of the (barely) living, torture was abolished in 1787, Turgot's project to emancipate Protestants was finally realized in the same year and the bewildering array of internal customs duties replaced by a single duty.

This is by no means an exhaustive list. The extraordinary outbreak of official activism it catalogues may be read—in the manner of de Tocqueville—as further evidence of the deadening effect of bureaucratic intervention. But much of what was done made a measurable and most often a positive difference to lives touched by conscientious government. Even the much vilified *intendants* were capable of altering conditions in their region for lasting good. Raymond de Saint-Sauveur found the southwestern generality of the Roussillon, and especially its capital Perpignan, in a state of dilapidated penury when he arrived. The city had food stocks for one month and the road to Catalonia that might import further supplies was collapsed. Torrential rains had washed away most of the province's few usable bridges. Within a few weeks he had reopened the mountain passes using gangs of laborers (some of them hired from Barcelona). Before the year was out he had repaired the bridges and constructed rows of gravel dikes as a crude but effective defense against further flooding in low-lying

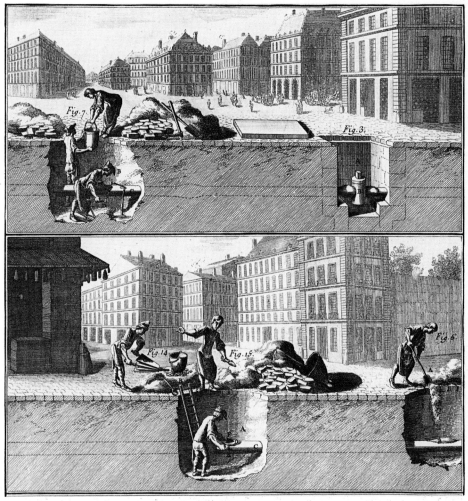

50. Urban sanitation revolutionized by lead pipes, engraving
from *Description des Arts et Métiers*

areas. Over the next three years he built new wells to provide Perpignan with a clean water supply, available from seven public fountains or (at a price) delivered in pipes to the houses of the well-to-do. A fire corps of twelve paid and permanent men was introduced, and a system of street cleaning during the summer months. Public baths, street lighting, a night watch, an *atelier de charité* to train poor children in "useful arts" (wool carding, spinning and weaving). A father of nine children, Saint-Sauveur was taken aback by the ignorance of basic obstetrics that he found during his two lengthy mule-back tours of inspection in the mountainous interior and established a course of midwifery in Perpignan to which each village in the province could send one woman free of cost. A mineral water spa was established in the hills, available for the therapy of poor as well as well-off patients.

The *intendant* had grander dreams of turning Roussillon into the hub of a thriving regional economy that would stretch from Languedoc to Catalonia unimpeded by boundaries of state or language. Agricultural societies were established with royal subsidies, new strains of sheep introduced on model farms. At the same time he eased off on the ferocity of the war against the salt smugglers, publicly blaming high duties and appreciating that brutal policing would only be met by counter-brutality from the smuggling gangs. Many of Saint-Sauveur's more ambitious plans were unrealized, but he managed to fund his program of public works with the help of direct government subsidies and without imposing further taxes on the local population. None of this necessarily made him liked. In common with many other efficient and honest *intendants,* he had to flee from his post in 1790, pursued by a revolutionary crowd. But his accomplishments were substantial nonetheless and in miniature they speak eloquently to the energy and practicality that were the hallmarks of government at the end of the old regime.

At the symbolic center of all these public endeavors was Louis XVI. For all his addiction to the hunt, his inarticulate reticence in council, his increasing tolerance of the excesses of his wife and brothers, there is ample evidence of his engaged and lively concern in much of this public business. The day following Christmas 1786, for example, he attended an event that gave him even more satisfaction than the outing to Cherbourg. At a special school for blind children—the first of its kind in the world—run by Valentin Haüy, the younger brother of the great mineralogist, the King witnessed the miracles of Enlightenment, benevolence and skill. Twenty pupils, all of them blind since either birth or infancy, read out loud from books specially printed in raised relief-print, identified places and features on maps, sang and played musical instruments in his honor. The older children were also able to set type, spin yarn and knit hose. Especially impressive was an eleven-year-old boy, Le Sueur, who had been the first of Haüy's pupils, discovered pathetically begging for himself and his seven brothers and sisters, and who now was the prodigy of the class, almost a teacher in his own right. A few months earlier the Academy of Music had the first of a number of benefit concerts for this "Philanthropic School" and the King was moved and impressed enough to endow it with special funds and scholarships. A similar institution run by the Abbé L'Epée cared for deaf-mutes and had invented the first lip-reading system, which enabled his charges to lead a normal and evidently happy life.

The Terror was to wreck these institutions as infamous relics of absolutist charity and clerical superstition, and return the children to the goodwill of the citizenry at large (in other words, to beggary and persecution). But in the 1780s, public knowledge that the blind and the deaf, traditionally treated as cursed pariahs, could be revealed as happy, working men and women was sign enough that a better time was at hand.

Until the calamitous harvests and industrial slump of the late 1780s, there was some reason for optimism about the prospects of the French economy. Here too, despite obstinately backward agricultural production, the pattern was one of growth and modernization disastrously disrupted by the Revolution. The best estimates of that growth put it at around 1.9 percent a year. Only during the Empire, when military power simultaneously sealed France off from British competition and expanded material supplies and captive markets in "Greater France," was industry able to progress at a rate comparable to that of the old regime.

By 1780, goods, mail and passengers were on the move around France at a rate, volume and frequency that had altered dramatically from only twenty years before. By the fast and reliable (if rather jolting) *diligence*, it took eight days to reach Toulouse from Paris instead of the fifteen it had taken in the 1760s, five to Bordeaux instead of fourteen, three to Nancy instead of a week and just a day to Amiens instead of two. Every day at noon the Rouen coach would leave Paris and reach its destination at nine the following morning. Even though the business had been farmed out to a private company, the state retained control over fare prices for both passengers and goods. An inside seat on the Lyon coach, for example, was 114 francs, inclusive of food and board. At the other end, a place atop the *impériale* was just 50 francs without food. Each traveler could take one bag free provided it did not exceed ten pounds.

Better communications—by a network of canals as well as roads—meant the expansion of markets. If France was still a long way from the kind of nationally unified market virtually in place in Britain, it was emerging from its extreme parochialism. By the end of Louis XVI's reign, 30 percent of all agricultural goods (the most sluggish of all commodities to reach a market economy) were being sold and consumed at places other than their point of production. Even if this meant no more than cartloads of eggs, milk and vegetables moving from a farm or village to a small town, it represented a change of enormous significance in the rural economy and the alteration of a subsistence peasant into a cash farmer. The progressive—and then very sudden—removal of internal tariff barriers must also have made a substantial difference to longer-distance trade, especially if one considers that a cargo of timber traveling from Lorraine to the Mediterranean would have had to encounter thirty-four different duties at twenty-one halts.

French international trade, on the eve of the Revolution, was likewise at an all-time high, estimated at a billion livres in value, much of it concentrated in the thriving ports of the Atlantic economy. Buoyed up by the colonial trade with the French Caribbean, Bordeaux had undergone a spectacular expansion from 60,000 inhabitants in 1760 to 110,000 by 1788. Of the enormous quantity and value of goods landed there, 87 percent of the sugar, 95 percent of the coffee and 76 percent of the indigo was immediately reexported at a substantial profit. Other ports like Nantes in Brittany shared in the booming trade—in slaves as well as consumer goods—and a whole string of ports profited from the important ancillary trades and services: mast- and sail-making, ship repairs, naval artillery stores and the like. On the Mediterranean, Marseille was in an almost equally enviable position, trading primarily with the Levant, but also exporting woollen goods manufactured by the thriving industries of Languedoc.

Even French industry, always in the shadow of the spectacular expansion taking place in Britain, was growing at the end of the old regime. France was indisputably the most important industrial power on the Continent, and though its production in absolute figures paled beside the British, its rate of growth in some sectors was actually superior. In both manufactured cotton and coal mining, for example, output was growing by 3.8 percent *per year*. At the great Anzin mines alone, production increased 700 percent during the second half of the century and at Mulhouse, the number of cotton manufactures increased 1,800 percent. In the metallurgical industries, too, French growth between 1720 and 1790 was on the order of 500 percent compared with Britain's 100 percent. Other data put the comparison in perspective. While 25 percent of what historians estimate to be the British gross national product was industrial in 1790, the equivalent figure for France was 20 percent (of which almost half, it is true, came from textiles). It would be idle to pretend that France was going through the same kind of explosive industrialization as Britain, but it is equally indisputable that on the eve of the Revolution the trajectory was pointing sharply upwards.

This was not just a matter of output data, impressive though these are. The entrepreneurial ethos and technical sophistication that are often assumed to have been missing from France were in fact to be found. Beginning in the 1760s, for instance, the Académie des Sciences commissioned a spectacular series of volumes constituting a Dictionary of Arts and Crafts. Using copious engravings of great technical precision and beauty, these volumes were a primer not just on traditional industrial techniques but on the newest machinery. And while they began with volumes on the luxury crafts—porcelain, glass and furniture—they rapidly expanded to include much more industrial processes in iron, coal, textile dyeing, mechanical silk production

51. The romance of technology has here been grafted onto an old pictorial tradition by which women spinning and weaving denoted virtue. Engraving, silk manu-facture from *Description des Arts et Métiers*

and sugar refining. The volumes on the mechanical production of cotton, for example, were written by Roland de La Platière, the inspector-general of manufactures for the province of Picardy in the northeast.

New enterprises involving mechanization seemed to spring up almost every month in the 1780s, connecting capital to technology. In some cases they brought new investment to older concerns that languished for want of capital. In 1786, much encouraged by the Royal School of Mines, which had been opened in 1783, a new company was set up, heavily capitalized, to reopen the copper mines of Bigorre in the French Pyrenees. The partners who signed the contract of incorporation were a typical mix of aristocrats from the world of high finance (Saint-James and Pache de Montguyon), business-minded Parlementaires (François-Jean Rumel) and bankers like Thélusson et Cie. Another spectacular success was the syndicate formed around the Pereire brothers to operate a great mechanical pumping engine at Chaillot designed to provide Paris with a decent water supply for the first time.

It is often said, even by the more optimistic historians of this time, that there were in reality two Frances. One was the modernizing, expanding France of the periphery and the Paris basin, with booming Atlantic and Mediterranean commerce; textiles in the northeast but more especially in the Champagne and eastern regions; coal in the Pas-de-Calais; metallurgical furnaces and foundries in Lorraine. This was a France of concentrated capital and labor, innovative technology (even if at the beginning some of it was thieved from the British), adventurous investment, good communications, a France market-driven. But it co-existed with another France of the center: somnolent and lethargic, locked into old and local traditions of supply and demand, unperturbed by any powerful demographic impulses, where towns dominated by the law, clergy and government presided over a rural hinterland comprising for the most part subsistence peasant cultivators. So that for every Mulhouse, Hayange or Bordeaux, there were many more places like Tours, where in 1783 the *intendant* complained that the inhabitants "preferred the indolence in which they were brought up to the cares and hard work that are required by major enterprises and bold investments."

There is a great deal of truth in this contrast, but it disguises some other important processes which were, if anything, tending to prod the sleepier France awake, and which made the spread of industrial and commercial enterprise much more even. The most significant was the huge proliferation of rural cottage industries on the outskirts of older centers. Freed from guild restrictions, entrepreneurs were increasingly placing raw materials with village spinners and weavers (sometimes supplying their basic equipment)

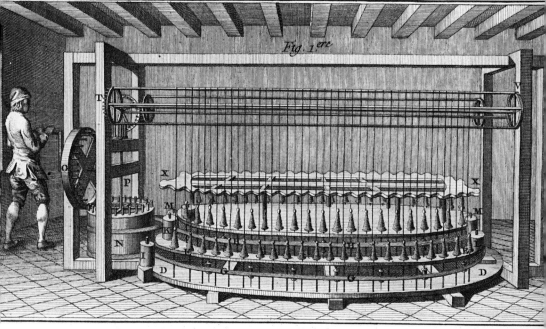

52. Engraving, cotton manufacture from *Description des Arts et Métiers*

and taking delivery of the finished goods for precontracted prices. So that beyond the apparently torpid economy of medium-size and small towns there lay a wholesale commercialization of the countryside. For some time this was thought to be a retarding factor in the process of industrialization, but wherever it took place (in much of the Rhineland, for example, as well as in France) it can clearly be seen as complementary rather than inimical to the modernization of manufactures. Some processes—such as weaving—remained cottage industries, while spinning became quickly concentrated in mechanized factories. This was the case in French Flanders, for instance, where Lille's losses were the making of Roubaix-Tourcoing.

In some areas this semimanufacturing, semidomestic industrial partnership shook up the local economy. In the case of the Parlement city of Grenoble, more than six thousand men and women within the city's walls and on its outskirts worked for some sixty master glovers, cutting, dressing and scenting hides and then stitching and embroidering the finished products. Some of the larger shops housed as many as twenty workers, but far more common was a pattern of four or five artisans sharing domestic space.

Other medium-size towns, like Rouen in Normandy, that saw their traditional staple trade—textiles—dwindle in the early part of the century, had a complicated evolution. A few capitalists revitalized production by importing British factory equipment and creating modern spinning factories, but others still used rural labor. The city itself diversified its trades, exported far more to the Paris region and elsewhere in Normandy, made goods for local rural artisans who in fair times could afford to buy them and provided a market for commercially produced and processed market produce. Rouen may have had the unenviable reputation as the most malodorous and unhealthy town in northern France, but economically it was certainly one of the most robust. By the end of the old regime it was turning out (in addition to manufactured cottons) woollen hose, hats, porcelain, paper, refined sugar, glass, and soap, linen bleached with the new Berthollet chloride process, copper products and sulfuric acid.

It was the spectacle of these little urban beehives buzzing with commercial activity that gladdened the heart of optimists like the Marquis de Condorcet. Though he was impatient to see the empire of science and reason brush aside the last institutional impediments to its ascendancy, he believed there was no reason why this should not happen in a reforming monarchy as enlightened as that of Louis XVI.

ii VISIONS OF THE FUTURE

The old-regime version of benevolent capitalism never expressed its evolutionary cheerfulness so eccentrically as in the extraordinary *Testament of M. Fortuné Ricard*. Published as a supplement to the universally popular French edition of Franklin's *Poor Richard's Almanack*, the *Testament* was written by Charles Mathon de La Cour, a Lyonnais man of letters and art critic. In the text, the fictitious M. Ricard remembers his own grandfather, who had taught him reading, arithmetic and the principles of compound interest whilst Ricard was still a lad. " 'My child,' he had said drawing 24 livres from his pocket, 'remember that with economy and careful calculation, nothing is impossible for a man. Invested and left untouched, at your death you will have enough to do good works for the repose of your soul and mine.' "

At the age of seventy-one Ricard had accumulated 500 livres from this original sum. Though this was no great fortune, he had great plans for it. Dividing it into five sums of 100 livres each, he proposed leaving the first for one hundred years, the second for two hundred and so on. Each would thus generate sums from which a progressively ambitious program could be funded. The first sum, after a century, would yield a mere 13,100 livres, from which a prize would be awarded for the best theological essay proving the compatibility of commerce and religion. A hundred years later the second sum (1.7 million) would expand this prize program into eighty annual awards for the best work in science, mathematics, literature, agriculture ("proven through the best harvests") and a special category for "virtuous deeds." The third sum (three hundred years on) would amount to more than 226 million, enough to establish throughout France five hundred "patriotic funds" for the relief of poverty and for investment in industry and agriculture, administered by "the most honest and zealous citizens." A remaining sum would endow twelve *musées* in Paris and the major towns of France, each to house forty superior intellectuals in all fields. Lodged in comfort but not opulence, they would have a concert hall, theater, laboratories of chemistry and physics, natural history shops, libraries and experimental parks and menageries. The libraries and art collections would be open every day free to the public and members of the *musées* would give public lectures in their respective fields. Members would be admitted "only after having submitted proof, not of nobility, but of morals" and would take an oath "to prefer virtue, truth, and justice over everything."

This is heady stuff but it is nothing compared with what was to follow in the fourth and fifth centuries of the Ricard will. The fourth sum (30 billion livres) would suffice, he thought, to build "in the most pleasant sites one could find in France" a hundred new towns each of forty thousand people, planned on ideal lines of beauty, salubriousness and community. With the final sum (3.9 trillion livres) it would be possible to solve pretty much all that remained of the world's problems. Six billion would be enough to pay off the French national debt (even at the rate the Bourbons were spending); 12 billion as a gesture of magnanimity and the opening of *entente cordiale* would do the same for the British. The remainder would go into a general fund to be distributed among all the powers of the world *on condition they never went to war with each other.* In such an eventuality, the aggressor would forfeit his bonanza, which would be transferred to the victim of the attack. And from a special sum earmarked for France, all kinds of perplexing problems would be cleared up: venal offices would be bought out all at once; the state would establish a system of salaried midwives and curates; half a million uncultivated lots would be cleared and given to peasants in need of land. Schools would cover the country as well as "Hospices of the Angels" intended for seven-year-old girls. There they would be brought up to a life and instruction of useful domesticity and provided with a dowry at eighteen when they graduated. Finally, towns would be provided with parks, squares and fountains, and sources of contagion eliminated—swamps drained, cesspools dried, cemeteries removed to remote and pleasing valleys.

This comprehensive utopia—a hybrid of Rousseau's and Condorcet's visions of the perfect republic—would come about not by revolution or violence but by the simple and gradual operation of compound interest. It was the ultimate fantasy of a painlessly modernized France transformed by collective wisdom and husbanded capital into the benefactor not only of itself, but of the entire world. Mathon de Lacour's vision of the future embraced modernity without much sense of apprehension. Indeed its castle in the clouds was built on what he saw as the unfolding and potentially limitless achievements of enlightened government. Its telling stipulation that members of its intellectual elite prove "not their nobility but their morality" was not a tract against, but in keeping with, the times.

For others, however, modernity was increasingly judged not a blessing but a curse. The same concentrations of capital and technology, of urban manpower and rural commerce that exhilarated "modernists" like Condorcet, colored other commentators with gloom and foreboding. Most of all, modernity filled many of them with the kind of righteous indignation that turned them into revolutionaries.

Many of these pessimists were recanted optimists. Simon Linguet—whom we find everywhere as the voice of prerevolutionary alienation—had published his first memorandum on economic concerns in 1764. He had then proposed the dredging of the Somme and the cutting of a new canal through Picardy to connect the city of Amiens with the sea. He knew that this would be met with opposition from the privileged textile masters of Abbeville, a town just a few miles from the mouth of the river. But his vision was for the kind of investment that might reconcile the two urban interests and in place of their mutual suspicion create a common economic energy. His model was Holland where, he (quite wrongly) supposed, the commonwealth lent its support to such projects and eschewed worthless vanities like monumental buildings and patrician town houses. The project, though eloquently argued, was tinged with realistic pessimism about the prospects for agreement. (In fact, in the 1780s it was revived on a much larger scale and would probably have been built but for the Revolution.)

However disappointed, the Linguet of the 1760s did at least embrace the culture of commercial modernity. Ten years later he had changed his mind and, during Turgot's ministry, directed on the free grain trade policy an attack so devastating that it was ordered suppressed. In the course of arguing against the physiocrats obsession with long-term benefits and their disregard of present wants, Linguet painted a grim view of the horrors of industrial society. Returning to Abbeville, with its masters tyrannizing the labor of their hands and taking or jettisoning it as business cycles dictated, he stood on its head the physiocratic/Condorcet equation of capital and technology with prosperity and happiness. In any two cities "you can be sure that the one where the most human beings are at the point of dying of hunger is the one where the most hands are employed in working the shuttle. No city in France has more looms than Lyon and Lyon is consequently the city of France with the largest number of poor who lack bread." In such a heartless place there could be a brand-new hospital but it could never be big enough to shelter "all those who having toiled fifty years over silk . . . come there groaning to die on straw mats." Industrial capitalism, he thought, promised heaven and delivered hell. It created a new lord of the entrepreneur and made subhuman troglodytes of his urban peons. They were doomed to live in "dwellings,"

> regular burrows like the ones beavers build; dark holes where
> herds of laborious animals hide out, breathing only a fetid air,
> poisoning one another with the contaminations unavoidable in that
> crowd, inhaling at every moment the seeds of death while toiling
> without respite to earn enough to protract their wretched lives.

Linguet's rhetoric was apocalyptic, his solutions (such as they were) peculiar but not without sense. His answer to the perennial bread crisis, for example, was to wean the French from their obsession with grain and towards a diet of potatoes, fish, maize, vegetables and rice. He was even prepared to try to persuade them that chestnuts (regarded as worse than starvation), properly prepared, might be both palatable and nutritious.

There were others, too, whose revolutionary fire was ignited by their rejection of commercialism and the modern city. Their hatred of the old regime paradoxically was directed not against what it preserved, but what it had destroyed. They idealized a whole parade of imaginary and exemplary human types: the independent craft artisan (*vide* the watchmaker, whose children they so often were) who had been ruined by machines, turned into a nomadic knife grinder or chimney sweep left to degrade himself as a huckster in the urban jungle; the cultivator who had been ruined by the greed of *seigneurs* who fleeced him to pay for their grandiose town houses, or who, in the name of absolute property rights, annexed the common fields on which he grazed his cows and goats or refused him access to the woods where he gathered his fuel. The polemics were applied Rousseau, but in 1789 they would have a distinctive appeal for large numbers of people who had indeed been disadvantaged in exactly the ways described. For those people, the onrush of a modernizing monarchy had aggravated, not alleviated, their condition. And what they wanted was not social en-lightenment or public works but primitive justice.

No work expressed this sense of rage against a world divided into luxury and destitution better than Mercier's twelve-volume *Tableau de Paris*. Like Linguet he too was a reformed optimist, though his optimism had always been a weaker force than his skepticism. In *The Year 2440* France had been transformed into a paradise of Rousseauean virtue, rising over the ruins of Versailles and the rubble of the Bastille and governed by a modest and conscientious king. Meritorious citizens wore hats with their names on them but the hereditary nobility had disappeared. All this seemed to have happened by political magic. "It only needed a powerful voice to rouse the multitude from its sleep. . . . Liberty and happiness belong to those who dare to seize them," the visitor to the future was told. Yet there did not appear to have been that apocalyptic convulsion of violence that Mercier very soon saw as inevitable.

Fascinated both by the geology that suggested the regularity of great upheavals in primordial history and the archaeology that implied its coun-terpart in earlier civilizations, Mercier became something of a connoisseur of catastrophe. From the perspective of his exile in Switzerland he surveyed a France, and especially a Paris, rushing along the tracks prepared by science and commerce towards their own doom. This he positively wel-comed as a catharsis, terrible but necessary to cleanse the metropolis of the excesses of both riches and poverty. "Will war, a plague, famine, an earth-quake or flood, a fire or a political revolution annihilate this superb city? Perhaps rather a combination of these causes together will bring about a colossal destruction."

Paris was, at one and the same time for Mercier, a rotting, oozing place of ordure, blood, cosmetics and death, and a kind of irrepressible, omnivo-rous organism. It sweated with meaty animal pleasure and buried itself under a sickly shroud of misery and destitution. It was the fair of the Palais-Royal that Mercier loved and the horror of the huge open pit of bodies at Clamart. It was the parades and farces of the boulevards and the spectacle at Bicêtre of condemned prisoners smashed with iron bars against the wheel; whores in gilded carriages; gourmands so crammed with delica-cies that their palates had jaded; stench rising from the open sewers and gutters; suicides throwing themselves from the Seine bridges.

On this vast metropolitan empire of money and death, Louis-Sébastien Mercier, the apostle of Rousseau writing of the urban inferno from his view of Mont Blanc, declared war. His Romantic imagination, working at a vision of the sublime and the terrible, imagined a vast, cosmic convul-sion. In such a second Lisbon earthquake, the ground would tremble and open, and "in two minutes the work of centuries would be overturned. Palaces and houses destroyed, churches overturned, their vaults torn asunder. . . ." It would be the reckoning of justice with materialism, and only from some such day of judgment could a true republic of citizens be born.

Part Two

EXPECTATIONS

53. The queen's diamond necklace

CHAPTER SIX
Body Politics

i UTERINE FURIES AND DYNASTIC OBSTRUCTIONS

HERE WAS a type of oversize necklace, briefly in vogue in the 1780s, that was known as a *rivière*. As the name implies, it looped about the neck and fell generously over the bodice towards the waist. At a time when fashion was becoming much simpler, the *rivière* was a loud item, much associated with actresses in the Palais-Royal, who might not blush to show off the generosity of their benefactors. One evening at the theater two young friends saw just such a river pouring over the décolletage of a conspicuous courtesan. "Look at that," one of them remarked, "a *rivière* that flows very low." "That's because it's returning to its source," replied his companion.

Jokes about sex and jewelry were nothing new. But in 1787, readers of the gossipy *Moving Tableau of Paris,* where the gibe was published, would have recognized more than a smutty double entendre. For two years, the reputation of the Queen had been mired in scandal, the centerpiece of which was a diamond necklace of 647 brilliants and 2,800 carats. It had been made with Mme Du Barry in mind by the court jewelers Böhmer and Bassenge but Louis XV had died before they could deliver it. At 1.6 million livres it was a ruinous item of back inventory, and at first, Marie-Antoinette seemed a likely customer. She had already bought from the same firm a pair of "chandelier" earrings, a spray and a bracelet. When funds ran low she repeatedly went to the King, who usually indulged her. As a young woman she indulged a weakness for diamonds that was reported by a disapproving Austrian ambassador and earned her a smart rap over the knuckles from her imperial mother. "A Queen can only degrade herself," wrote Maria Theresa, "by this sort of heedless extravagance in difficult times."

By the 1780s, Marie-Antoinette seemed to have taken this lesson to heart, since she had become more conscious of avoiding conspicuous luxuries. At any rate she repeatedly declined to acquire the necklace. Driven to distraction (and perhaps knowing Marie-Antoinette's weakness for tear-sodden *drames bourgeois*) the jeweler Böhmer had made a scene at court, sobbing his eyes out, yelling, swooning and threatening to do away with himself unless the Queen took the necklace off his hands. This tremendous performance was of no avail. Even had she been inclined to ignore official pleas for economy, the monstrosity was not to the Queen's taste. It was altogether too much—the kind of blowsy vulgarity she associated with the Du Barry circle. Hoisting the wailing jeweler off his knees she counseled him to break up the necklace and get what he could for the separate stones.

This dinosaur of rococo jewelry would indeed be cut down to size, but not by its creator. In fact its public history had barely begun. For it became the prize in a confidence trick of breathtaking audacity. The Diamond Necklace Affair—as it became capitalized—is often treated as a scandalous sideshow to the "real" drama of empty coffers, famished peasants and

54. Portraits of the Cardinal de Rohan, Jeanne de La Motte, Nicole Le Guay and other principals in the Diamond Necklace Affair

55. *"Ma Constitution"*: A later, graphic example of body politics, probably dating from 1790. Lafayette has his hand on the *"Res Publica"* of the Queen.

growling artisans that heralded the end of the French monarchy. The cast of characters who were paraded before the French reading public as the bizarre plot unraveled in the summer of 1785 seemed perfect symbols of a regime worm-eaten with corruption: a dissolute, gullible, aristocratic cardinal; a scheming adventuress claiming descent from the Valois kings of France; a Neapolitan charlatan who said he had been born in Arabia and could tap the healing arts of the occult; an ash-blond *grisette* picked up in the Palais-Royal to impersonate the Queen; hapless creditors wringing their hands and cracking their knuckles; sundry jewelers from the Paris *quais,* from Piccadilly and Bond Street, on whose counters had fallen black velvet bags packed with diamonds the size of thrushes' eggs. But at the very center of it all, unavoidably, was Marie-Antoinette. It was her transformation in public opinion from innocent victim to vindictive harpy, from Queen of France to the "Austrian whore" (*putain autrichienne*), that damaged the legitimacy of the monarchy to an incalculable degree.

There was nothing inevitable about this. Until the affair came to light, the Queen had been an oblivious bystander to the intrigue. But the phobic hysterias gathering about her, even before the plot was hatched, meant that she would be suspected of collusion, of luring others to their doom in the service of her insatiable appetite for *luxure*: a term that usefully compressed together opulence and libido.

In all kinds of ways, however unwittingly, Marie-Antoinette designed her own downfall. It was precisely her reputation for unaffected girlish sentimentality that made Louis, the Cardinal de Rohan, believe that he could restore his position at court through her favors, rather than by di-

56. Allegorical satire of Marie-Antoinette
as orgiast. The King slumps on his throne
while a monster Queen seizes the scepter.
"A people is without honor and deserves
its chains / When it stoops beneath the
scepter of queens" read the inscription
that accompanied the print.

rectly approaching the King. Too rich for their own good, with a long
history of conspiracy, and boasting the most spectacular *hôtel* in the Marais,
the de Rohans were kept at arm's length by the Bourbons. De Rohan's
period as ambassador to Vienna had been equally disastrous, alienating
Marie-Antoinette's mother, the Empress Maria Theresa.

De Rohan's well-known craving to be accepted at Versailles was exactly
the windfall Jeanne de La Motte had been looking for. Born into abject and
obscure rural penury, she claimed descent from one of the last Valois kings,
Henri II, and it was with this tattered pedigree that she too staged fainting
fits in the path of Mme Elisabeth, the King's sister, until she got a chance
to tell her story of downtrodden gentility. Smitten by her apparent sincerity, Mme Elisabeth then set her up modestly at Versailles, from which she
proceeded to persuade de Rohan that she was an intimate of the Queen's.
Should he do her bidding now and again, there was a fine prospect that he
might indeed one day bathe in the radiance of Marie-Antoinette's smile. De
Rohan rose like a moth to the flame, supplying Jeanne periodically with

sums of money that were supposed to go to favored acts of charity but in fact usually went to her dressmaker.

The clinching act in this comedy of persuasion was drawn straight out of *The Marriage of Figaro*. On the tenth of August 1784, a blond milliner (later described, not altogether fairly, as a common prostitute) Nicole Le Guay was dressed by Jeanne de la Moite in the Queen's favored white muslin gown and ushered into the Grove of Venus in the gardens of Versailles at eleven o'clock at night. There she found the Cardinal waiting anxiously and pressed into his hand a single rose. She had one line to speak (though de Rohan later fantasized that she had uttered two)—"You know what this means"—before hurrying back into the obscurity from which she had come. Dizzy with joy at this long-awaited sign of favor, de Rohan became putty in Jeanne de La Motte's hands. Larger and larger sums passed from the one to the other.

Display bought credibility, and in November she had the (now desperate) jewelers bring her the necklace while de Rohan was away. When he returned she convinced him that the Queen wished to acquire it and pay in four installments. A forged letter commissioning the Cardinal to act on her behalf apparently confirmed this. As an ambassador, de Rohan should have noticed that this letter was signed incorrectly "Marie-Antoinette de France," but attentiveness had never been his strong suit. On January 29, 1785, the necklace was brought to the Palais du Cardinal and almost immediately transferred to the supposed courier of the Queen (Jeanne's lover, de Réteaux). He broke it up and began the tricky business of fencing it around Paris. When suspicions became aroused, her complicit husband took it to London, where he sold the stones, partly for cash, partly for articles that included ruby brooches, enamel snuffboxes and a pair of silver asparagus tongs.

Surprisingly, success went to Jeanne's head. She became imprudent. At last able to bring her property into line with her pretensions she affected the title "Baronne de La Motte de Valois" and bought a substantial estate at Bar-sur-l'Aube to which no less than forty-two cartloads of elegant loot—Adam furniture, works of art, d'Aubusson tapestries—made their way in the spring of 1785. In the meantime the Cardinal waited for the Queen to sport her new bauble and give him some sign, any sign, of grace. He was disappointed. Candlemas (for which the Queen, by letter, had said she wished to wear the necklace) came and went. Weeks and months passed. More seriously, none of the money had materialized from which de Rohan was supposed to pay the first 400,000-livre installment on the first of August. Böhmer, the histrionic jeweler, was still in blissful ignorance of these difficulties. On July 12 he thrust a note into the Queen's hands that referred to "the most beautiful diamonds in the world adorning the greatest and best of queens." Marie-Antoinette assumed he was off his head again and burned the note.

On the eve of the day the first payment was due, Jeanne informed de Rohan there was no money available until October. He attempted to calm the jewelers, who were themselves being pressed by creditors. Oddly resigned to the unraveling of the plot, Jeanne de La Motte then directly informed the jewelers that they had been cheated by a forged letter. They in turn went to see Mme Campan, the Queen's lady-in-waiting, on August 5. It took no time at all for the appalling truth to emerge, and on the fifteenth de Rohan was summoned to the King's presence. He admitted being taken in by a woman claiming to act for the Queen and implored the King to conceal the scandal for the sake of his family. But Louis, understandably, was in the grip of a white rage and had the Cardinal arrested and taken to the Bastille.

While de Rohan was to be colorfully depicted by his lawyer Target as languishing in "irons" in the Bastille, he actually moved into a specially furnished apartment outside the prison towers where he spent nine months entertaining an unending stream of distinguished visitors. Oysters and champagne were laid on as a collation for guests, and the Cardinal had choice works from his library and a retinue of servants to help him overcome the hardships of incarceration.

Nonetheless, the very word *Bastille* (especially following the phenomenal success of Linguet's *Memoirs,* which dwelled on its torments) was enough to guarantee de Rohan popular martyrdom. A great flood of pamphlets and broadsides represented him as the pathetic victim of absolutist oppression. At his trial before the Parlement of Paris, Target brilliantly played on another sympathetic motif of the late Enlightenment by claiming that the Cardinal had been brought down only by his "excess of candor" (*"crédule par excès de franchise"*), his simplicity of nature, his trusting good humor, his chivalrous urge to serve the Queen and so on. The defense was further helped by the fact that at least some of this was true. He was, in fact, a callow simpleton with a poor record of private morals. But that was not enough to merit the full force of royal prosecution, and the result was (though by a slender margin) his acquittal. The chorus of popular hallelujahs was so loud and so riotous that de Rohan headed straight back to the Bastille for the night until things had calmed down enough for him to make a safe exit.

The briefs for the accused, their so-called *mémoires,* were published in large batches and made widely available to the public, as were engravings of the principal defendants, so that the proceedings became a kind of public theater in which the preposterous drama was played out before a large audience. And before very long it became rapidly apparent that what was on trial was not de Rohan, de La Motte and her co-conspirators so much as the old regime itself. Even though the chances of acquittal for some of the defendants were, to say the least, slim, some of the most powerful and eloquent of the Parlement's lawyers rushed to take on the case because of the flattering glare of publicity. And reading the briefs, the historian can readily see that they did a brilliant job, varying their appeal depending on the particular qualities of the client, but in each case appealing to one or another of the key *idées fixes* of the 1780s.

How to defend Nicole Le Guay, the "Baronne d'Oliva," as Jeanne de La Motte had generously ennobled her? The prosecution called her a common whore, but the defense represented her as a vulnerable girl, orphaned at an early age, lodged in a little room on the rue du Jour near Saint-Eustache (rather too convenient to the Palais-Royal) and working as a milliner to make ends meet, devoted to her lover and lured by de La Motte's promise of fifteen thousand livres for impersonating the Queen. In other words she was a vulnerable child of nature, a three-dimensional painting by Greuze, recruited for a stratagem of which she had only the barest glimmer of understanding. The news that she had delivered an illegitimate baby in the Bastille only helped reinforce this impression of pathos. And so did her inability to answer any questions in court through her sobbing. It was clear, as her lawyer Blondel claimed, that the girl had *de l'âme* (soul). She was acquitted. Cagliostro, the infamous charlatan, had become the Cardinal's personal prophet by claiming to commune with the deities of the Nile and the Euphrates. He had exploited his influence to convince de Rohan that he was indeed in favor with the Queen. Accused of boasting that he was thousands of years old and and other absurdities, he adopted the unlikely role of Enlightenment skeptic, and immediately announced he was thirty-seven—though he exploited the taste for Orientalism by continuing to claim that he had been born and raised in Medina and Mecca and had traveled the Levant acquiring his "art." He and his wife had also been locked up in the Bastille, and Cagliostro moved the court with heart-rending appeals to their sense of desolation at seeing such an exemplary pair of spouses separated. "The most amiable and virtuous of all women has been dragged into the same abyss; its thick walls and many bolts separating her from me . . . she groans and I cannot hear" and much more in this coloratura vein.

Even Jeanne de La Motte had found a usable tactic. She appealed to history, to the memory of the Valois from whom she said she was descended, and brandished elaborate genealogical charts to prove the relationship. Indeed, it may not actually have been wholly spurious. There was, in the 1780s, a growing cult of distressed chivalry, one that linked itself with the Romantic hatred of the New, of a world dominated by cash and corruption. And it was exactly that world that was Jeanne de La Motte's natural element. She managed to represent herself as an orphan of an older France, a heroine from the sticks, an innocent gone astray like so many of the cautionary fallen girls of Restif de Bretonne's novels. Staggering though it may seem, she pitted her own invented reputation against that of the Queen, claiming that Marie-Antoinette had indeed wanted the necklace, that she had written many letters to say so and that they were all genuine, not forged. (In his misplaced zeal to save the Queen embarrassment, de Rohan had burned all the letters he had seen, so that there was no counter-evidence with which to challenge this claim.)

In the short term this did her no good. Her husband was condemned in absentia to the galleys for life. She was convicted and sent to La Salpêtrière indefinitely, but was also condemned to a public flogging, a hanging rope about her neck, and to be branded with the letter *V* (for *voleuse*—thief). At the moment of this terrible mortification, and in the presence of a huge throng, the executioner's hand slipped from the shoulder where the letter was to scorch her and burned instead a great mark on the underside of her breast. No one who saw that would forget it. When, two years later, Jeanne escaped from prison to London, where she launched a diatribe of phenomenal venom against the Queen, she found a ready-made audience.

The real casualty of the whole affair was its principal victim: Marie-Antoinette (though the King's meanness in going through with the case was invidiously contrasted with the hapless Cardinal's sense of misplaced honor). Mysteriously, it was the Queen who emerged from the business portrayed as a spendthrift and a vindictive slut who would stop at nothing to satisfy her appetites. She had deliberately set out to destroy de Rohan, it was said, because he would not respond to her indecent advances (an amazing scenario) and had spitefully manipulated de La Motte to bring him down. The more imaginative of the *libelles* that circulated at the time had her engaged in lesbian acts with Jeanne, whom she discarded when other sexual favorites seemed more appetizing. "What rapture," she is made to confess of this scene. "I thought that I saw Olympus open and that I entered, for my ecstasies were not of a mortal kind."

None of this would have been possible had there not already been a rich and unsavory vein of court pornography to tap. Though the genre was very old (owing something to Suetonius and later to Aretino) it evolved into a particularly ripe phase during the last years of Louis XV, when "histories" of his private brothel at Versailles, the Parc aux Cerfs (the Stag Park), were in vogue, outsold only by the innumerable versions of the anecdotes of Mme Du Barry, the prototype written by Pidanzat de Mairobert. Her support for the infamous "triumvirate" of Terray, Maupeou and d'Aiguillon made it possible for anti-Maupeou satirists to connect sex and tyranny. The standard tales of buggery, adultery, incest and promiscuity thus became a kind of metaphor for a diseased constitution. When Louis XV died rather suddenly of smallpox, it was rumored that the carrier had been a girl procured for him by Mme Du Barry.

The political constitution of France and the physical constitution of the monarch were, to the popular imagination, one and the same. The King's body had always been a public realm, one or another of its regions privileged as the peculiar location of authority. In the flowing locks of the long-haired Merovingian Frankish kings had lain their sacred mystique. Even when the Carolingian "mayors of the palace" had stripped them of power, the Merovingians were preserved as holy totems, complete with waist-length tresses, and driven about in oxcarts to legitimate their successors. Court ritual at Versailles fetishized the royal body so that hierarchies were established according to who might pass the King's slipper or hand the Queen her chemise. Louis XIV's body—in reality an exceptionally impressive frame—was projected to his subjects as being invested with superhuman power. The King's phenomenal appetite was said to be the consequence of a stomach cavity many times normal size (for unlike Louis XVI he never really grew stout) and its godlike dimensions duly reported to the public after a postmortem.

For a dynastic regime, by far the most important region of the King's body lay below the waistline. In contrast with many of their counterparts elsewhere, the Bourbons were a remarkable success at reproducing themselves. Disastrous rates of mortality among dauphins were offset by their ability to produce male heirs before dying off. Louis XV thus was Louis XIV's great-grandson, and Louis XVI the grandson of his predecessor. Given the questionable circumstances of the old King's death, much was made of Louis XVI's decision to be inoculated. As pustules erupted on the royal trunk, bulletins announced their satisfactory progress to the world outside. Marie-Antoinette communicated the same to her mother the Empress (who was wholeheartedly in favor of the procedure), commenting on the particularly impressive pustules that had appeared on the royal nose. But while this was an admirable example to his subjects, their most pressing expectations were centered elsewhere. At the level of common consensus the King-as-Father-of-the-*Patrie* had three basic duties: to see that his people had bread, that his realm was victorious in battle and that it was supplied with heirs. In the years following his succession there were already doubts on the first two scores but it was in the last matter that his failure provoked most comment.

Though their first daughter was born in 1778, it was only when a dauphin was produced three years later that dynastic expectations were satisfied. A grand ball was given at the Hôtel de Ville; fireworks and feasting were celebrated in the streets of Paris; and a delegation of market women actually came to congratulate the Queen. (They would return eighteen years later in an unfriendlier mood.) The rejoicing was general just because the Queen's ability to bear children had been a topic of caustic popular comment for some years. The real problem, however, lay with her partner. For some years (it is uncertain exactly how many), sexual relations between Louis and Marie-Antoinette were complicated, if not actually precluded, by the King's phymosis. This is a condition in which the foreskin is deprived of its elasticity, making erections painful. Intercourse, from both the conjugal and dynastic view, was thus perfunctory and unsatisfactory. The Queen was bewildered and unhappy; the King pursued the boar and stag with all the ardor denied to him in bed. Both of the partners seem to have confided to Joseph II when he visited his sister in 1777, since he wrote a characteristically clinical report of the problem back to his brother Leopold.

> [Louis] has strong, well-conditioned erections, introduces the member, stays there without moving for perhaps two minutes and withdraws without ejaculating but still erect and says goodnight; this is incomprehensible because he sometimes has nightly emissions but once in place and going at it, never—he says plainly he does it from a sense of duty.

Brotherly intervention in this delicate affair seems to have produced the minor surgery necessary to correct the abnormality. And in August— two months after Joseph's letter—Marie-Antoinette wrote rapturously to her mother, making it plain that their marriage was now "perfectly consummated."

The failure of a royal pregnancy to materialize for the first seven years of the marriage was enough, however, to start tongues wagging and to end the grace period that Marie-Antoinette had enjoyed on coming to France. It was her own attitude to her position, though, that caused the most serious damage. She had grown up in a Habsburg court where the excesses of traditional ceremony and protocol were being discarded in favor of a simpler, more engaged style of government. Her mother had herself come to the throne as a young girl at a catastrophic moment in the history of the Empire—the loss of Silesia to Frederick the Great—and had learned enlightened absolutism the hard way. Her brother, Joseph, was a notorious iconoclast when it came to the polite rituals of court. Yet both understood that in an age when monarchs were supposed to be "servants of the state" it was especially important to present an image of devoted self-sacrifice to their subjects.

But it was precisely this rather grave demeanor that Marie-Antoinette shrugged off when she arrived at Versailles. A bride at fifteen and a queen at nineteen, like all adolescent girls of her generation she drank deep at the well of sentimental literature. Her library was full of Richardson, Rousseau, Mercier and even Restif de Bretonne. A passion for flowers, a rather merry candor and a dislike of stolid formality were, after all, the virtues in vogue. But they were supposed to be hidden behind the mask of royalty.

Almost from the outset, the Queen made no concessions to her public role. She giggled at the pecking wars of ladies-in-waiting, yawned or sighed ostentatiously at the admittedly interminable ceremonies that left her stark naked in the cold of her Versailles apartment while they went through the business of passing the royal shift or selecting the royal ribbons. Worst of all, she began to rebel against wearing stays and corsets at all. The King's sisters were tiresome, his brothers' wives aggressively unsympathetic and, even worse, they were pregnant. Gradually they came to understand that Marie-Antoinette was not prepared to resign herself to the customary role played by Bourbon queens and princesses: the production of heirs in meek invisibility, leaving the King to disport himself as he chose. If anything, the roles were reversed, Louis remaining awkward, secluded and retiring as his wife became more brazenly outgoing. Her brother was shocked by this impolitic defiance of convention. "She has no etiquette," he wrote to his brother Leopold, "goes out and runs around alone or with a few people without the outward signs of her position. She looks a little improper and while this would be all right for a private person she is not doing her job. . . ."

Joseph saw clearly that his sister wanted the privileges and indulgences of monarchy while being free to pretend that she was really a private individual. This, he predicted, was to court unpopularity, even to under-mine her legitimacy. But Marie-Antoinette remained determined to design her own identity. Repudiating her officially assigned councillor, the Princesse de Noailles, she selected her own friends. The first in this galère was the Princesse de Lamballe, whose husband had died of syphilis, leaving her a widow at nineteen. She was supplemented by the Princesse de Guéménée and, finally and most disastrously, the indisputably ravishing but dim-witted Yolande de Polignac. None of this would have mattered a great deal except for the fact that the Queen used her authority to shower gifts, offices and money on her chosen favorites. Much to the horror of the economizing Malesherbes the Queen revived the redundant office of Superintendent of the Queen's Household, carrying a stipend of 150,000 livres a year, specifi-cally for the Princesse de Lamballe. And along with each of the favorites came a large clan of relatives and cronies who clung to the sides of the royal ship of state with the tenacity of barnacles. There were impecunious aunts, profligate brothers, scapegrace grandpas, broken-down baronies and mortgaged plantations in the Antilles, all to be satisfied and made good. So that what to the Queen seemed innocent enough—putting favors in the way of her friends—to less partial judgment looked like a gigantic network of sinecure and graft; the empire of "Madame Deficit," as her brother-in-law Provence called her.

The more the Queen struck out for independence, the greater seemed the impropriety. Dismayed as she was by Louis' loutish humor and his brother Provence's total devotion to the joys of the table, the youngest brother, Artois, must have seemed a paragon of elegance, charm and conceivably even intelligence (though this is stretching credibility). But, undoubtedly, Artois did make *her* feel clever, graceful and—with her large eyes, protruding lower lip and shade of the Habsburg chin—even beautiful. They spent a good deal of time together at the theater, the gaming table and the *concerts spirituels* that were Paris's nightly musical entertainments. They both were fanatical partisans of the composer Gluck against his foe Piccini; and both, mirabile dictu, were staunch champions of Beaumarchais. Together they created the amateur court theater at the Trianon, where they acted out Rousseau's *The Village Soothsayer* and *The Barber of Seville.*

There were other *chevaliers servants* on hand to keep the Queen flattered and amused: Arthur Dillon, the Duc de Lauzun, Axel von Fersen, the Baron de Besenval, the Prince de Ligne and especially the Comte de Vaudreuil. Other than Lauzun—who flirted so outrageously with the Queen at one outing to the racetrack at the Plaine des Sablons that he was banished—none of them were from conventional noble backgrounds. For uncharitable gossips they were all conspicuous by their foreign ancestry or affiliation: the Dillons were Irish-Jacobite, Fersen was a Swedish soldier-courtier, and the Prince de Ligne came from the Habsburg Netherlands. It seems obvious that the Queen felt more comfortable with these foreigners and parvenus than with the established court hierarchy, but her favoritism courted its alienation. The whispering campaigns that dogged her reign began in the palace itself. Vaudreuil was a particular target. He came from a West Indian planter family and had made a splash in Paris society by spending his sugar fortune as freely as he could. His mistress was the Queen's favorite, Yolande de Polignac, and that in turn opened for him not just the blessings of the Queen's presence but a cornucopia of offices—some very lucrative, all of them high-status. In 1780 alone he was made grand falconer of France, governor of Lille and *maréchal de camp.* In turn, Vaudreuil looked after his own. He saw to it that Elisabeth Vigée-Lebrun, who

57. Elisabeth Vigée-Lebrun,
Le Comte de Vaudreuil

in 1784 painted a portrait of the Comte weighed down with decorations, became the most important artist at court (no more than she deserved), that her brother joined the company of the *secrétaires du roi,* thus ennobling him, and that her dealer-husband received a constant stream of high-born and well-heeled customers. He himself reveled in being the clotheshorse of the old regime, and its best amateur actor (by general consent an inspired Almaviva). Trailing enormous debts, scrabbling for offices to pay for them and never quite succeeding, Vaudreuil was everything the revolutionaries had in mind when they characterized the court as a playpen of spoiled and greedy children.

It seems improbable that any of these men (other, perhaps, than Fersen and that, much later) were anything more than companionable flatterers for the Queen. But the informal manner she promoted and the visibility she courted at all three of Paris's major theaters—the Comédie-Française, the Opéra and the Comédie Italienne (against the express wishes of the King)— were bound to play into the hands of the scandal-mongers and pornographers. Marie-Antoinette was hopelessly unprepared for the kind of criticism to which she opened herself by redesigning the royal identity. *Nature* was the word in vogue by the 1780s and she blithely assumed that by acting "naturally" she would be taken for the innocent she mostly was. But what seemed spontaneous to her appeared as shockingly licentious to many of her subjects. And there was, in their angry, visceral response, more than an element of psychosexual anxiety. Marie-Antoinette—though she could hardly have dreamed of it—represented a threat to the settled system of gender relations. If the King was supposed to be the emblematic head of a patriarchal order, by the same token his wife was supposed to show a face of especial obedience, humility and submission. This had not always been the case in French history, of course, and it is not surprising to find a sudden crop of "histories" appearing in the 1780s of other wayward (that is, head-strong and independent) queens—especially Anne of Austria (the widow of Louis XIII) and even more infamously Catherine de Medici—each with thinly veiled analogies to the present incumbent.

Most important is the directness with which the Queen represented her own femininity. What had been permissible, even expected, in a *mistress* of the monarch was somehow intolerable in a queen. It made matters even worse that this femininity was candidly presented and designed, more or less exclusively, by other women. Rose Bertin, the Queen's dressmaker, became one of the most influential women in France, and it was she who encouraged Marie-Antoinette to abandon the stiffness (both material and figurative) of formal court dress for the loose, simple gowns of white lawn, cotton and muslin that she came to favor. Formal appearances, complete with hooped *panier* dresses and piled coiffeur, were restricted to "Sunday courts" and even then, as Mme de la Tour Du Pin recalled, it had become fashionable to complain of the dreariness of the routine. Certainly, it was the more unconventional face of the monarchy, displayed in the paintings of the Queen's other most important friend, Elisabeth Vigée-Lebrun, that provoked further comment.

Though much of her work is of manifestly spectacular quality, Vigée-Lebrun has, until quite recently, been written off as just another light entertainer of the *ancien régime*: a lady-in-waiting with brush and palette. And she has suffered as much from sentimental nostalgia for the old regime as from dismissive neoclassicism. But in her time she was correctly recognized as a phenomenon, exhibiting no less than forty paintings at the biennial Salons. In 1783, the year she became one of two women admitted to the Royal Academy (the other being her rival Adelaide Labille-Guiard), the *Mémoires Secrets* testified to her influence and renown:

> When someone announces that he has just come from the
> Salon, the first thing he is asked is: have you seen Mme Le Brun?
> What do you think of Mme Le Brun? And immediately the

answer suggested is: Mme Le Brun—is she not astonishing? . . .
the works of the modern Minerva are the first to attract the eyes
of the spectator, call him back repeatedly, take hold of him,
possess him, elicit from him exclamations of pleasure and
admiration . . . the paintings in question are also the most highly
praised, talked about topics of conversation in Paris.

Part of Elisabeth Vigée-Lebrun's appeal lay in the person as much as the
art. The daughter of a minor portraitist and a hairdresser mother from
peasant stock, she was largely self-trained following her father's death when
she was twelve. Using models from her own family but presenting them
in a bold, expressive manner in which the brilliance of her color matched
the flamboyance of poses and composition, she made a reputation as a
prodigy. At nineteen she was already enrolled in the painters' academy of
Saint-Luc. Marrying her mother's landlord, the dealer Lebrun, propelled
her into Paris society and gave her a ready-made showcase for her talent
in the galleries and soirées held at their town house. She was clever, articulate and strikingly beautiful: a winning combination in the Paris of the
1780s. And she succeeded in differentiating herself from the mass of dull
academicians or pseudo-Bouchers by promoting, in her social life as well
as her art, the cult of the unaffected. Her soirées served nothing other than
fish, fowl and salad. At the famous *souper au grec* she stripped Lebrun of
his pretensions by "wiping off his powder, undoing his side curls and
putting a wreath of laurel about his head" as honey cake with Corinth
raisins was served together with a Cypriot wine.

The painter carried these airs of ostentatious simplicity right into the
court. In her (doubtless idealized) memoirs Elisabeth recalled improvised
Grétry song duets with the Queen. On another occasion she looked on
admiringly as Marie-Antoinette obliged her six-year-old princess to dine
with (indeed to wait on) a peasant girl of her own age. Hair powder,
elaborately structured coiffures, stays and hoop petticoats were all banished
except for formal ceremonies. Instead hair was encouraged to fall in natural
curls over the shoulders; flowers and grasses were used for ornament on
straw bonnets and wide-brimmed rustic hats. The natural line of the body
was exposed beneath diaphanous, shiftlike dresses of white or ivory-colored
cotton lawn gathered below the breast, and fastened loosely with a ribbon.
The Duchesse de Polignac, who was, by any standard, strikingly comely,
was painted in this new uniform looking like some freshly harvested and
luscious fruit. Even when sitters were reluctant to go the whole way
towards informality, Vigée-Lebrun found ways of making their attitudes
less monumental.

58. Elisabeth Vigée-Lebrun, self-portrait

59. Elisabeth Vigée-Lebrun,
Duchesse de Polignac

60. Elisabeth Vigée-Lebrun,
Bacchante

61. Elisabeth Vigée-Lebrun,
Mme Grand

As I despised the costume then worn by women I tried in every way to make it more picturesque and I was delighted when I obtained the confidence of my sitters, who allowed me to drape them as I pleased. Shawls were not yet the fashion but I made use of large scarves lightly woven about the body and over the arms with which I attempted to imitate the beautiful style of Raphael and Domenichino.

This was all presented as the costume of natural innocence, but like some of the poses of the Greuze girls, of whom it was reminiscent, it had unmistakable erotic power. In Vigée-Lebrun's *Bacchante,* painted in the year of the Diamond Necklace scandal, this was explicit, but some of the elements in this sexually charged design were transferred to portraiture: the highlighted teeth of an open-mouthed smile or the upward-rolled pupils in the painting of the "maintained" actress Catherine Grand, later Talleyrand's wife. The Grand painting, though, is an exception in presenting a woman as a kind of sexual property. For the most part the great series of female portraits done by Vigée-Lebrun in the 1780s are strikingly free from rococo voyeurism. Instead of having their heads turned from the beholder and bodies exposed, the women depicted here—not least the artist—stare directly back in expressions of challenging independence. They are often seen in groups of friends or with their children in uninhibited poses of affection and embrace. It was this refusal to ingratiate that contemporaries found simultaneously exciting and alarming.

When it came to representing the Queen, of course, some special concerns intervened between Vigée-Lebrun's "natural" manner and the commission. First summoned to court in 1778, when she was just twenty-three years old, she dutifully turned out a wholly traditional image, face seen in three-quarters profile, decorated with feathers and costumed in an enormous tanklike *robe à panier.* By 1783, a transformation had taken place and the portrait of the Queen that appeared in the Salon showed her in a simple muslin dress, holding a rose. Others in the same vein followed, many of them copied for French embassies abroad and for private clients.

None of this helped arrest the deterioration of the Queen's reputation. In fact it might have hastened it by appearing to confirm an image of casual disregard for propriety. At any rate, by the Salon of 1785 there was concern as to how Marie-Antoinette ought to be represented before the public. The painting displayed that year was by the Swedish court artist Wertmuller and showed her walking in the park at Versailles with her children. It was presumably expected to appeal to the vogue for sentimental family groups. But it was so awkwardly rendered and stiff as to reinforce the uncharitable view that domestic propaganda concealed private libertinism. The painting was removed and a replacement commissioned from Vigée-Lebrun, who exploited sympathy for the Queen's loss of a child by having her seated with her surviving children in front of a significantly empty crib. Spectacular though the work was, it too suffered from an ideological defensiveness that sat uneasily with the painting's domestic platitudes. For if there was an effort to show Marie-Antoinette as Mother, placing her nursery immediately in front of the Hall of Mirrors at Versailles and enveloping her in a formal velour dress was bound to signal that she also remained Queen. Exhibited in the Salon of 1787, it met with a mixed reception.

By the time that this grand portrait went on view, the Salon was the only place that the Queen could be seen outside court. Wounded by the barrage of violent pornography—of which she was certainly aware—she shrank from the public gaze. On the few occasions she ventured to the theater she was greeted with frosty silence or even hisses. In contrast with this silence were the cheerfully insulting songs that could be heard around the Paris cafés and on the Pont Neuf:

Notre lubrique reine	Our lascivious Queen
D'Artois le débauché	With Artois the debauched
Tous deux sans moindre peine	Together with no trouble
Font ce joli péché	Commit the sweet sin
Eh! mais oui-da	But what of it
Comment peut-on trouver du	How could one find harm in that?
mal à ça?	

Cette belle alliance	This fine pair
Nous a bien convaincu	Have certainly convinced us
Que le grand Roi de France	That the great King of France
Est un parfait cocu	Is a perfect cuckold
Eh! mais oui-da	But what of it
Comment peut-on trouver du	How could one find harm in that?
mal à ça?	

Others speculated on the size of the King's equipment and/or its potency, or the number of the Queen's lovers of either sex and the chronology of their favors. A coin was actually minted at Strasbourg showing the King's profile with an unmistakable pair of cuckold's horns attached to his head. The gutter literature was even more brazen. One popular item, *Les Amours de Charlot* [Artois] *et Toinette*, began with Marie-Antoinette masturbating and proceeding to the usual orgy.

62. Elisabeth Vigée-Lebrun, Marie-Antoinette *en gaulle*

63. Elisabeth Vigée-Lebrun, Marie-Antoinette and her children

The prototype for many of these productions was the *Essai Historique sur la Vie de Marie-Antoinette,* first published in 1781, again in 1783 and then with annual revisions to keep up with events right through to her execution in 1793. Five hundred and thirty-four copies were burned by the public hangman at the Bastille in 1783 but it was still a favorite item of the clandestine book smugglers and widely distributed in Paris. Its form was that of autobiographical confession, which at times seemed to anticipate precisely the most vitriolic revolutionary indictments:

Catherine de Medici, Cleopatra, Agrippina, Messalina, my deeds have surpassed yours, and if the memory of your infamies still provokes a shudder, if its frightful detail makes the hair stand on end and tears pour from the eyes, what sentiments will issue from knowledge of the cruel and lascivious life of Marie-Antoinette . . . barbaric Queen, adulterous wife, woman without morals, soiled

64. Print from the pornographic satire
*Essai Historique sur la Vie de
Marie-Antoinette*

with crime and debauchery, these are the titles that are my
decorations.

The "life" that follows is that, as she herself confesses, of "a despicable
prostitute": spending the night before the coronation in 1775 on the Porte
Neuve at Reims, an "islet of love," dressed as a Bacchante, copulating for
three hours with a selected "Hercules"; learning new positions from Artois
at the Trianon; experimenting at will with her ladies of the household, and
especially with the Polignac. The three most featured vices of this literature
were masturbation, lesbianism and insatiable nymphomania. This was not
accidental, since each of these also figured prominently in the medical
literature of the 1780s, written up in both the scientific genre and the more
predictable vulgarized versions: titillation masquerading as edification. The
confessional account of Marie-Antoinette's sexual appetite in the *libelles*
featured exactly the sort of symptoms readers of Bienville's very popular
Nymphomania, or a Treatise on the Uterine Fury were told to recognize in
the compulsive nymphomaniac. "At the mere sight of a handsome man or
beautiful woman, my body became restless, an expression of pleasurable
possession spread over my face; I could scarcely conceal the violence of my
desires."

The Marie-Antoinette of the *libelles* was a sexual monster, infected with
disease from sleeping with a dissolute cardinal, and since lesbianism was
known as "the German vice," an alien presence in the body politic. Her
sexual perversions, then, were often treated as political stratagems.

In 1785 a crisis blew up when her brother the Austrian Emperor Joseph II attempted to force open the estuary of the river Scheldt so that he
could expand freedom of navigation from the Austrian Netherlands ports
of Ostend and Antwerp. This was in violation of treaty commitments
France had made with the Dutch Republic, which stood to lose from the
change, and since the two powers had been allies in the American war, the
logical move would have been to resist the Austrian maneuver, if necessary
with threats of war. Distressed by this possibility the Queen actively intervened and persuaded the King to moderate the French position. Though
the crisis defused itself, the interference was taken by those hostile to the
Queen as another instance of her colonizing the court in the interests of a
foreign power. She became, more than ever, Marie-Antoinette of *Austria*.

All of these sexual demonologies—of the spy-whore, the King's domina-
trix, the infector of the constitution—were stirred up into a richly poisonous polemic and undoubtedly contributed to the phenomenally rapid
erosion of royal authority in the late 1780s. Early on in the Revolution, when
the Queen took a more aggressive part in politics and was widely suspected

65. "Harpy discovered at Santa Fe, Peru"   66. Marie-Antoinette as harpy

of fomenting military plots against the National Assembly, her critics invoked yet another source of monstrosity to graft on to the already repulsive image. In the mid-1780s, stories circulated of a "harpy"—a winged creature of savage appetites and brutal talons—said to have been discovered at Santa Fe in Peru. The engravers of popular prints, always looking for novelties, made much of it, and predictably in 1791 the Queen duly appeared in the guise of the fabled horror, clutching "The Rights of Man" in her claws.

The deconstruction of her image was a pathetic thing. She had stripped herself of the mask of royalty in the interests of Nature and Humanity (as well as her own predilections) only to end up represented as, of all women, unnatural and inhuman. When, finally, the "Widow Capet" was arraigned before the revolutionary tribunal, the conflation of sexual and political crime was made explicit. Insulted very much in the language of the *libelles* as "immoral in every respect, a new Agrippina"; accused of being in league with the Emperor and (before the Revolution) secretly smuggling two hundred million livres to him, she was finally accused by the editor of the newspaper *Le Père Duchesne* and the President of the Paris revolutionary Commune, René Hébert, of sexually abusing her own son, the wretched ex-Dauphin, then about eleven years old. She and Mme Elisabeth, her sister-in-law, were said (on the boy's confession) to have made him sleep between them "in which situation he had been accustomed to the most abominable indulgences." They had taught him to masturbate but not, Hébert thought, simply for their own pleasure but for even more sinister political purposes. Drawing on the grim prognosis of the effects of masturbation set out in Dr. Tissot's *Onania,* the accusation was that they meant to "enervate the constitution of the child in order that they might acquire an ascendancy over his mind."

Harassed into making a response to those charges, Marie-Antoinette replied, "I remain silent on that subject because nature holds all such crimes in abhorrence." But her final retort was in the manner of the Vigée-Lebrun painting of a maternal queen: "I appeal to all mothers who are present in this room—is such a crime possible?"

ii CALONNE'S PORTRAIT

On the fourteenth of February 1787 Talleyrand was summoned to Versailles by the Controller-General, Calonne. By his own account he went with mixed feelings. On one hand he was flattered by the attention. Calonne had persuaded the King to convene an Assembly of Notables that was supposed to consider measures necessary to rescue French public finance from bankruptcy. Though the Assembly was intended to be strictly consultative, its opening (twice postponed but now set for February 22) was already hailed as the beginning of a new era in French history. In his letter to Talleyrand, Calonne asked him to help draft memoranda that would be set before the Notables as the basis for their deliberations. Aware that this might be a special opportunity to advance his reputation, Talleyrand could hardly decline a commission of such importance.

On the other hand he was not overeager to leave the creature comforts of Paris for the tedium of Versailles, especially in the dark rains of winter. Life had been good to the man his friends sardonically called called "l'Abbé de Périgord." At thirty-three, he had even created the sort of domestic nest he had never known as a child—though in a characteristically unorthodox version. His mistress, the Comtesse de Flahaut (herself the illegitimate daughter of a Farmer-General), had been married at eighteen to a fifty-four-year-old officer. Her brother-in-law, the Comte d'Angiviller, was superintendent of the King's buildings (that is, the majordomo of official culture) and obligingly provided the young Countess with a private apartment at the Louvre. There she established a salon of tame artists and intellectuals, but also a happy *ménage* with Talleyrand, who, in 1785, became the father of a lively infant son. For all his reputation for aloofness, those select few admitted to this family circle describe an atmosphere of gentle intimacy quite at odds with the Abbé's public persona. Gouverneur Morris, the American commercial agent, who was seriously enamored of Adelaide de Flahaut, upset himself further by witnessing their apparently unshakable contentment.

Talleyrand supped often with his mistress and son, but he breakfasted late with friends in his house on the rue de Bellechasse. With his usual perspicacity he had understood that Paris society was a galaxy comprising many little planetary constellations, all revolving in their own orbits, sometimes crossing the path of others and sometimes colliding. The essential thing was to be recognized as the center of one such constellation, and this he had achieved by the time he was thirty. The satellites who revolved around him were all conspicuously luminous: Choiseul-Gouffier, whose travels in Greece had earned him the reputation of expertise and a seat in the Academy; the Comte de Narbonne (the brightest of Louis XV's many bastards), articulate, amoral and well connected; the young physiocrat writer Du Pont de Nemours; the Duc de Lauzun, American hero-warrior whose banishment from the presence of the Queen had enhanced rather than sullied his reputation; the obligatory physician-scientist, Dr. Barthès of Montpellier, and the equally obligatory Swiss banker, Panchaud, a fierce enemy of Jacques Necker's.

It was as though Talleyrand had constructed this company like a rich but well-balanced meal, the intellectual astringency of Panchaud and Du Pont de Nemours setting off the rich confectionery of Lauzun and Narbonne. They discussed serious matters but they did so without undue solemnity. And it was probably this manner of making light work of hard business that recommended Talleyrand in particular to Calonne, whose modus operandi was much the same. They were close neighbors and were each to be found at the other's social occasions. But a graceful style would not, however, have been enough had not Calonne seen something else much more important in Talleyrand: an appreciation of the power of data. After his ordination in 1779, he had been given a benefice in Reims that was enough to support a comfortable life, but Talleyrand was much more ambitious. He directed himself to the only area of the ecclesiastical world he found supportable: business management. And in that area, as agent-general with an eye on the immense property of the episcopacies, he was in his element. Applied greed was a natural talent and he exercised it conscientiously in his own behalf as well as that of his order.

His other major talent was bureaucratic, and as agent-general he undertook a massive survey of all the economic concerns of the Church, ranging from the salaries of village curates to the hospitals and poorhouses maintained by the Church throughout the country. While on one tour of inspection he even found himself straying into affairs that were not part of any conventional brief but which his eye for public business saw required attention. In Brittany, for example, he was so struck by the numbers of women whose husbands had failed to return from the sea, but could not be officially declared dead, that he sought to allow them to remarry after a number of years had elapsed. At the General Assembly of the Clergy in 1785 the suggestion was thought deeply improper and rejected, but many more were impressed by Talleyrand's grasp of an immense portfolio of numbers and information relating to the Church. His huge report, commented the Archbishop of Bordeaux, was "a monument of talent and zeal" and the Assembly duly recompensed his services with a special award of twenty-four thousand livres.

With this reputation for hard-headed business and political savoir faire, Talleyrand was employed by Calonne to serve as an unofficial agent and assistant. His most conspicuous and difficult recruit was Honoré-Gabriel Mirabeau, the impetuous son of a tyrannical father who had had him imprisoned many times for various acts of defiance. Though six years older than Talleyrand, Mirabeau began by throwing bouquets of gushing admiration at his feet. A mission at the court of Frederick the Great in Berlin was found, but its unofficial status irked Mirabeau and before very long he was turning on his mentor. "He would gladly sell his soul for money," he complained of Talleyrand, "and he would be getting the better of the deal for it would be an exchange of shit for gold." At the beginning of 1787, though, the two men shared a sense of the importance of the impending Assembly of Notables. Mirabeau wrote to Talleyrand that he saw "a new order of things which can regenerate the monarchy. I would think myself a thousand times honored to be the least secretary of that assembly, the idea of which [he took good care to add] it was my good fortune to have first. . . ." And he begged Talleyrand to release him from his Prussian exile so that he could participate in this momentous rebirth.

It was with these kinds of fanfares blowing in his ears that Talleyrand responded to Calonne's summons. Inflated expectations of a new epoch, of finances restored to health, public trust flowering with the snowdrops, made him distinctly uneasy. But he did certainly expect Calonne, whom he genuinely admired, to have a firm grasp on the matter at hand. He was to be abruptly disillusioned.

On entering Calonne's private study, Talleyrand saw there an oddly assorted group. It included Pierre Gerbier, a senior magistrate in the Parlement of Paris, a famous orator and one of the few *robins* to have been forgiven for taking office with Maupeou's court. Perhaps it was this past history that recommended him to Calonne as a useful pragmatist. With him was an immensely aged fossil from three reigns, the Marquis de La Galaizière, who had started out on his long career as an *intendant* under the Regency. Du Pont de Nemours was there from Talleyrand's own set, together with two other of Calonne's assistants who had been working on projects to be presented to the Notables. Once seated, each of the men was presented with great sheaves of documents tied up with ribbon, which

Calonne announced were the raw materials from which they were supposed to construct a reform program that would be credible to the Assembly—or which at the very least would persuade it to forego obstruction. Talleyrand, who was given the project of restoring a free grain trade, was taken aback. Like everybody else, he knew that Calonne had been seriously ill (his friends said with bloody coughing fits; his enemies said with the punishment of debauchery), and that this had delayed both the preparation of the reform projects and the opening of the Assembly (originally announced for January 29). But he had not expected that he would have a mere week to get raw information into sufficiently persuasive shape to disarm the skepticism that everyone was expecting from the Notables.

He suddenly saw that the Controller-General, whom he had admired for years as a shrewd judge of public business, had made a colossal political blunder. For he had completely failed to grasp the open-ended consequences of his initiative. Only that could possibly explain the apparent casualness of his preparations. It was plain to Talleyrand that Calonne saw the Assembly as an obedient rubber stamp for the land tax that he was about to propose.

The sudden revelation of Calonne as an impulsive gambler was all the more alarming to Talleyrand because he had shared the general view of the Controller-General as a skilled manager of unforeseen contingencies. Calonne had been appointed to the office in 1783 in the wake of a panic brought on by his predecessor d'Ormesson's attempts at financial reform. All that d'Ormesson had done was to revive Necker's plans to hive off part of the General Farm to a state-run *régie*. And he had tried to give the Caisse d'Escompte—founded in 1776 as an undercapitalized imitation of the Bank of England—some effectiveness by requiring the circulation of its paper currency. It was not much, but in the jittery state of the Paris money market it was enough to start a run on the Farm's own bills of exchange, which were widely used to make commercial payments. Calonne smoothed ruffled feathers by restoring the full terms of the General Farm contract for taxes and making it clear that he would work within rather than against the current financial conventions. Rather than bulldoze the paper of the Caisse, he preferred to raise confidence in the Bank by permitting the use of its money in settling taxes and by extending its franchise. Most important he believed its viability would be linked to demonstrated commercial success, so that from 1785 dividends were to be linked to actual profits of preceding terms (rather than short-term speculations).

Calonne has been much reproached (and was, at the time, by Necker in particular) for this supine capitulation to vested interests. He had, the critics said, traded short-term calm for long-term disaster. And since he then proceeded, over the next three years, to borrow over five hundred million more livres to keep the government afloat, it is hard to argue with this negative verdict on his stewardship.

But Calonne was not just an empty head presiding over an empty purse. His regime did follow a principled policy of sorts, even if in the end that turned out to be disastrously unsound. It was, in any case, dominated by one major consideration that Necker, Calonne's most persistent critic, failed to take into account: the costs of peace were almost as heavy as the costs of war. Necker's calculations turned on the assumption that following the end of the American war, the French government could adhere to a significantly more modest level of military spending. But Vergennes, who was still the dominant figure in the government until his death in February 1787, knew otherwise. To benefit from the opportunities opened up by the peace of 1783, he believed, it was essential that the equipment and readiness of the French navy and army remain at a high level. And in this view he was sustained by de Castries and Saint-Germain, respectively the ministers for the navy and the army and both aggressive, reforming, modern military managers. Following Suffren's victories in the Indian Ocean there was even an opportunity to ally with the growing power of the Sultan of Mysore to restore French influence in the Carnatic region of the subcontinent. To neglect these matters, Vergennes argued, was to invite another drubbing on the order of the Seven Years' War. It was this requirement, rather than any prodigal spending by the court, that governed Calonne's unfortunate borrowing pattern. Even though it was probably imprudent for the Controller-General to buy the palaces of Rambouillet and Saint-Cloud for the crown, expenditure on all court items—including the households of the King's extravagant brothers—never varied above forty million livres from a total budget of around six hundred million, or 6 to 7 percent. To put this in perspective, it was about half the proportion of the British budget spent on the monarchy.

Given this demand, what could Calonne do to make it supportable? He did not just stagger from contingency to contingency with wholly improvised expedients. On the contrary, if anything it was under his Contrôle that the government had the nearest thing to a concerted economic policy since Turgot. With little background in economics and finance himself, he depended on three resources for advice. The first was Isaac Panchaud, the Genevan whose work on public credit had appeared in 1781 and who had won a formidable reputation among all those who were put off by Necker's self-righteousness. (Paris offered, as well as everything else, a choice of Swiss bankers.) Panchaud's basic advice to Calonne was to avoid structural damage to the financial machinery in place and, rather, make its operation less disabling by creating new lines of credit at better terms. Specifically this meant avoiding direct attacks on the Farmers-General but allowing competition from banks in Amsterdam, where annuities could be floated at 5 percent. In the 1780s, Dutch loans as well as Swiss suddenly became important, giving the administration more flexibility in its schedules and terms of repayment.

The breathing space secured by this new credit was to be used not just for sitting still but for concerted efforts to improve French economic infrastructure and performance. And it was here that Calonne's other two sets of advisers came into play: the second generation of physiocrats, and the ablest of the royal officials trained to oversee economic enterprises. Among Calonne's stable of young bureaucrats were Mollien, Gaudin, the Abbé Louis, Maret—all of whom were to be at the center of the Napoleonic government and some of whom (like Louis) were to be almost permanent fixtures of early nineteenth-century French financial management. Only if one supposes that such an "old regime" was destined to disappear from the face of the earth should one be surprised to find these walking data-processors part of the future rather than the past. Together with physiocrats like Du Pont de Nemours they hammered out an economic policy that was a calculated compromise between free enterprise and state paternalism. A number of these measures were strikingly radical and they required careful preparation. The fact that they were presented as part of the tax package to the Notables should not, however, obscure their independent importance.

In the "Single Duty Project," for example, the myriad internal customs barriers were to be done away with and a single tariff to be imposed instead. This was less a gesture of pure laissez-faire faith than of economic nationalism (again anticipating Napoleonic policy) since freedom of trade *within* France was to be complemented by imposing higher barriers on its frontiers. The same careful distinction was observed in restoring free circulation to the grain trade. For while the domestic trade was liberated, export outside the country (a source of bitter grievance in the past) was tied to the index of current prices. Should it rise above a certain platform, prohibitions on exports would be resumed. Above all, the economic relationship with Britain was governed by what might be called state opportunism. Engineers had been brought to northern France to install spinning jennies and Crompton's mechanical mule, and at the end of 1786 hopes were raised of spiriting away the famous Matthew Boulton and James Watt from the British Midlands. They did indeed visit Paris but only for consultations over the steam engines to be used in new pumping machines at Marly.

While joint-stock companies did grow in this period, finance originating with the state became newly significant in funding concerns needing venture capital to innovate with new plants. Yet what Calonne's government gave with one hand it seemed to take away with the other, since the capstone of the new policies was a trade agreement with Britain, signed in 1786, that opened both markets to each other's goods. It need hardly be said that while French wine and silk prospered under this arrangement, other textiles and ironwares suffered an onslaught of cheap competition from the much more advanced British manufactures. But the view of Calonne and his advisers seems to have been that, in the long term, this was all healthy competition that would stimulate French producers to emulate their British counterparts.

A bald list of these economic initiatives, honorable though most were, misses the point. Calonne's government all along assumed (like Turgot's before him) that his plans were to be imposed on, rather than proposed to, France. That is probably why so many of his protégés made such good Napoleonic bureaucrats. He had been brought up in the absolutist tradition of crown service as an *intendant,* first of his native Flanders and then of Metz in the generality of the "Three Bishoprics." Both were very important areas of economic enterprise, especially in textiles, and Calonne had a conscientious record in their encouragement. But he was the epitome of de Tocqueville's centralizing official—handing out subsidies here and there, giving prizes for inspiring essays in mechanical wool-carding like a schoolmaster rewarding diligent pupils.

As Controller-General, he was no better at public relations. Calonne did show some interest in writers like Mirabeau and Brissot, but only as spies in the literary underground or serviceable hacks who could be hired to pump out propaganda pieces in the service of the official line. (Mirabeau turned out to be incapable of this kind of unflagging loyalism.) For the most part, though, he went along with Vergennes' determination to muzzle the vituperation of the opposition press, block their smuggling routes and dry up the sources of hostile opinion. Those publishers like Panckoucke who would be prepared to settle for moderate opinion (in the relatively anodyne *Mercure de France*) might be domesticated through co-optation.

This policy of stifling the opposition was not without some success, especially in the early years of Calonne's administration. At the height of his powers, in 1784 he sat for Mme Vigée-Lebrun wearing, to judge by the finished portrait, an expression of creamy self-satisfaction. But the painter took good care to give her subject an air of alert intelligence in his eyes and through the attributes of office scattered on the desk. Calonne's portrait proclaims high status secured through conscientious duty. It would only be later that the unintended ironies of the representation would be painfully revealed. For while Calonne holds a letter conspicuously addressed to *his*

67. Elisabeth Vigée-Lebrun, Calonne

only master, the King, the most prominent document on his desk is the charter for the Caisse d'Amortissement—the "Sinking Fund" supposed to husband resources that could be devoted to reducing the principal of the immense national debt. But it was Calonne, not the debt, that would be sunk by 1787.

And when Calonne's reputation for prodigality and opulence became impossible to shake off, his portrait would read like a glorified tailor's account. There are the lace cuffs *à la valencienne* and the Florentine taffeta coat, all from Vanzut and Dosogne, the sharpest and most expensive clothiers in Paris. There are the grandiose inkwells from the Queen's jeweler, Granchez on the quai de Conti, where Calonne had bought a bamboo cane topped with an elaborate gold pommel that was the talk of the Palais-Royal. The painting almost smells of the lavender water that he was known to favor. The Controller-General made no attempt to disguise his taste for costly luxuries. He dressed his many servants in full livery and provided fur-lined seats not just for the interior of his coaches but to keep his coachmen warm in winter. Apart from the Contrôle itself, which he redecorated from top to bottom, he could choose to reside in one of two châteaux or in the house on the rue Saint-Dominique, where his spectacular collection of paintings—Watteau, Rembrandt, Titian, Giorgione, Boucher, Fragonard and Teniers—was housed.

His kitchen was equally famous or notorious, depending on whether one was on the regular guest list. The head chef, Olivier, presided like a baron over a huge *équipe* of *sauciers, pâtissiers* and other specialists of the table. There were three servants alone to look after the roasted meats, with their own assigned kitchen boy called Tintin. Calonne had a weakness for truffles, which he had sent in baskets from Périgord, for fresh crayfish, young partridge and, more surprisingly, "macarony de Naples" eaten with Parmesan or Gruyère, a dish which one would have thought incompatible with lace cuffs. When he went from his own unofficial palace to the official one at Versailles, Calonne was sure to reproduce its splendors on a suitably regal scale. Under his regime the last balls of Versailles were thrown with an elegant abandon that for generations of nostalgic admirers to come would create the vision of the old monarchy forever moving at the pace of a minuet, while marble fountains threw perfumed water into scalloped bowls.

This was all very well as long as loans continued to be funded and the economic climate remained fair. But the outlook in all these matters darkened considerably from 1785. In Amsterdam, the prospect of further loans at low rates of interest had been complicated by a political crisis that threatened to become a revolution. A bad drought that summer had produced the worst harvest for some time. That in turn seemed likely to deplete the purchasing power of French consumers and worsen a market which had already been seriously damaged by the inflow of British manufactures following the commercial treaty.

When all this bad news was coupled with the Diamond Necklace Affair, a punishingly critical gloss could be put on Calonne's stewardship of the nation's affairs. For all the strenuous efforts of the police to stanch the flow, the demand for scurrilous pamphlets and libels was too great and the supply too forthcoming to gag opposition. In their view, Calonne's financial prodigality somehow became associated with the extravagances of the court, with conspiracy, mendacity and self-indulgence. It was at this time that the story of his delivering to Mme Vigée-Lebrun a box of pastilles, each wrapped in a three-hundred-livre note, first circulated. He was, in fact, rumored to be her lover, a story she later attributed to his actual mistress the Comtesse de Cerès borrowing her carriage for the theater and deliberately leaving it outside Calonne's residence all night for the gossips to identify.

Many of Calonne's most conspicuous initiatives could, with little effort, be made to look like conspiracies against the public interest. In 1785, on the advice of a broker, Modinier, he decided to remint the currency, adjusting its gold-silver ration in line with market rates. Anticipating some confusion, the Controller-General provided for a year of grace before the new coin definitively replaced the old. But to shopkeepers or country millers with boxes under the bedstead, the scheme was a thinly disguised act of extortion that would replace "good" money with "bad." Similarly the new customs wall for the Farmers-General (since Paris was not to enjoy the freedom from internal duties allowed to the rest of the country) aroused deep suspicions. Commissioned by Lavoisier, the visionary neoclassical architect Ledoux had designed stunning propylaea with antique figures and motifs to adorn the several barrier-gateways, but this did nothing to disarm those suspicions (indeed the strangeness of the plan may even have reinforced them). The new wall, it was popularly said, would trap Parisians within an atmospherically foul prison by depriving them of the country air needed to ventilate their urban staleness, the source of contagions and epidemics. Someone even calculated the exact cubic amount of fresh air loss that would result from the new wall. No wonder, as the saying went, "le mur murant Paris rend Paris murmurant."

There were other similar charges of self-interest. Pretending to be a statesman, Calonne, it was said, was nothing more than a jumped-up speculator. His new Company of the Indies (launched to try to capitalize on the new opportunities opening up in south India) was a spurious enterprise designed to extract capital from the gullible with no prospect of foreseeable returns. Other choice contracts and companies, like the syndicate established to steam-pump a fresh water supply for Paris, were rigged to give favorable advance terms to inside investors. Piece by piece, then, a portrait of Calonne was being put together that was much less flattering than Mme Vigée-Lebrun's. He was the man who would gag the press, stifle the lungs, fleece the pockets, debase the currency, squander the national fortune and dance attendance on the court.

With his reputation in such difficulties, why would Calonne have embarked on so dangerous and radical a step as the Assembly of the Notables, where his entire authority was going to be opened to public scrutiny? The conventional answer is that he had no alternative, and that indeed is the view that he put to the King in August 1786 when he first broached the subject. The deficit on the current year he estimated at 80 million livres (and was subsequently discovered to be 112 million). It was thus consuming nearly 20 percent of current revenue. But a much larger proportion had to be assigned to interest payments on back loans. Worse still, the relatively rapid redemption schedule accepted by Necker during the American war meant that substantial payments fell due in the following year. Yet more loans were not inconceivable, but as Calonne had discovered in December 1785 when he had attempted to float the latest round, they could no longer be secured on advances from current or future revenues. That meant that he had to do what he had all along wished to avoid: impose new taxes, less for their actual value than for collateral in public credit.

The King's response on being told of the plan to summon an Assembly of Notables that would legitimate the new tax was to retort, "Why, that is pure Necker that you are giving me." And it was indeed the sense of Necker breathing down his neck that surely spurred Calonne to his dramatic proposal. In 1784 the old Director-General had published his *Views on the Administration of the Finance of France* and in the course of it had attacked Calonne's stewardship, especially for his addiction to new loans in peacetime. In the following year, when the Diamond Necklace scandal was at its height, he returned from his Swiss exile to an enthusiastic welcome in Paris. Part of Calonne's decision to make public the gruesome truth of the deficit, and to present it as a near bankruptcy, was to refute the optimism of the *Compte Rendu* of 1781 with its cheerful view of surpluses between "ordinary" income and expenditure. Specifically, he said that in place of Necker's surplus he had actually found a deficit of some 40 million for that year.

Despite evidence of mounting public hostility, Calonne decided to play Necker's own game of appealing for public support. It was not just a cynical gambit as Talleyrand suspected. Egged on by survivors of the Turgot regime like Du Pont de Nemours, the Controller-General was reaching back to the politics of a popular monarchy, outlined by d'Argenson in the 1740s, that would somehow vault over the heads of vested interests and Parlementaire obstruction to achieve a new freedom of action with the blessings of the people.

The Assembly of the Notables was thus designed as an exercise in what might be called popular absolutism. But, as Talleyrand saw, even before its first session had convened, it would, inevitably, become an apprenticeship in national representation.

iii NOTABLE EXCEPTIONS

The Assembly of the Notables finally got under way in the Salle des Menus Plaisirs at Versailles on February 22, 1787. The many delays between the King's official announcement on the last day of the old year and the eventual meeting had given Calonne's many enemies an opportunity to mount a campaign of opposition. They were helped by the obvious fact that at its critical juncture, the government was falling apart, both physically and politically. Vergennes was gravely ill and died on February 13, leaving the Controller-General without his most powerful supporter. The Keeper of the Seals, Miromesnil, was angry at having been excluded from early discussions and openly critical. After being taken aback by Calonne's unpredictable transformation from sunny optimist to seer of the apocalypse, Louis XVI had promised his full support. Having signed the decree authorizing the Assembly he wrote to Calonne: "I couldn't sleep last night but it was only from pleasure." His insomnia, though, gradually turned to the anxious variety. As the opening approached he became more, rather than less nervous about the experiment that lay ahead. And the loss of Vergennes, whom he had constantly looked to for fatherly advice, left him badly shaken. He was undoubtedly aware of the Comte de Ségur's comment on hearing of the proclamation: "The King has just resigned."

The response of public opinion to Calonne's initiative—after initial enthusiasm—had become equally guarded. There were widespread suspicions that the Controller-General had enjoyed a three-year spree and was now about to send the people the bill. Grandiose rhetoric about the national crisis was, it was said in the pamphlets, a fancy way of covering his tracks. Worst of all, satire was aiming its weapons at the event. The most famous popular print had a monkey addressing a barnyard of poultry: "My dear creatures, I have assembled you here to deliberate on the sauce in which you will be served." More significantly, there seem to have been many

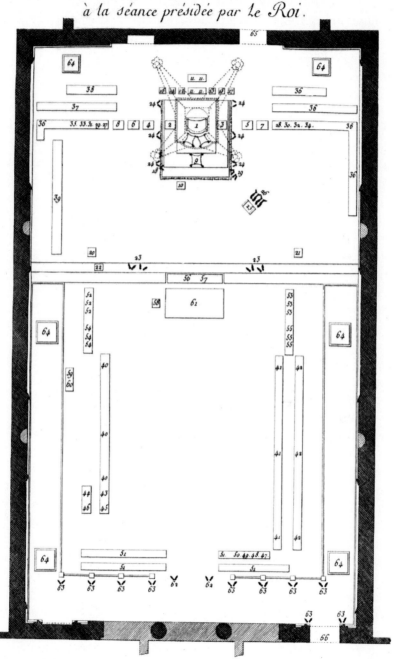

68. The Assembly of Notables; floor plan from the *Procès Verbal*. Outlines of feet indicate correct ceremonial seating or standing positions.

variations on the same theme appearing in a very brief span of time. Another group of animals was told that it was to be slaughtered without right of appeal but that it would have the luxury of deciding exactly how it might be cooked. On the doors of the Contrôle was discovered a parody playbill advertising a "new troop of comedians to perform at Versailles on the 29th," opening their program with *Les Fausses Confidences* and *Les Consentements Forcés.*

Calonne had anticipated this opposition. Indeed it was to avoid the past fate of royal tax reforms—Parlementaire resistance—that he had decided on an Assembly of Notables, a consultative form last used in 1626. Incorporating a proposal on elected provincial assemblies into the plan, he hoped, would defuse the growing demand for an Estates-General. And such an assembly also offered the advantage of a strictly controlled membership that could lay no claims to representation. The social composition of its 144 members seemed to confirm Calonne's caution. The seven princes of the blood—the King's two brothers plus the ducs de Bourbon, Orléans, Condé, Penthièvre and Conti—were to preside over seven separate deliberative bureaux. Immediately below them were seven leading archbishops, including Champion de Cice, the liberal and strongly Neckerite Archbishop of Bordeaux, as well as another foe of Calonne's, Loménie de Brienne, the Archbishop of Toulouse. These were followed by seven hereditary dukes, eight marshals of France, six marquis, nine counts, a single baron, presidents of the Parlements and high officials including the *prévôt de Paris* and the *prévôt des marchands.* The most surprising inclusion of all was Lafayette, whose budding radicalism greatly displeased the King and Queen, but who was included at the behest of his kinsman Noailles.

On the face of it, this did not look like a club of revolutionaries. But as soon as the sessions opened, it was apparent that the intensely aristocratic character of the Assembly did not at all preclude political radicalism. Nor did it incline the members to be the obedient instrument of Calonne's program. Insubordination started at the very top since, of all the princes of the blood, only Artois was prepared to offer wholehearted support to the government. His elder brother, "Monsieur," was particularly scathing about the procedure and others, like Orléans and Conti, who were notoriously disaffected from the court, naturally followed in trenchant criticism.

Yet the Controller-General was by no means resigned to personal defeat. After the King's formal opening remarks, in which he alluded not just to the need for revenues but to the principle of more equal distribution of the tax burden, Calonne took the floor with a long speech of great intellectual power and eloquence. His distinctive quality had always been an articulate tongue allied to the kind of applied classicism he had used in his administra-

69. Satirical print of the Assembly of Notables

70. Jean-Louis Prieur, engraving, The Assembly of Notables

tive career. The King himself had had a sample of this the previous August when Calonne had produced his memorandum divided into the headings

1. the present situation
2. what to do about it?
3. how to do it?

This kind of starkly enumerated clarity was perfect for the locksmith monarch, but something more complex was needed for the captious Notables, and assisted by Du Pont de Nemours, Calonne gave it to them. His speech began badly, with an aggressive revision of Necker and an equally self-serving review of his administration. No less than 1,250 million livres had been borrowed since 1776, he said, much of it to fight the "national war" and create a powerful navy. But this way of proceeding had finally become self-defeating and mired in "abuses," by which he meant the excessive confusion of private and public finance and unjustifiable exemptions in the name of privilege. The answer to this sorry situation was threefold. First came fiscal justice. Instead of a mess of complicated direct taxes, the new land tax would be imposed on all subjects and would take into account the conditions of the cultivator and even his fortunes from season to season. Second was political consultation: local assemblies—parish, district and provincial—would be elected to participate in the assessment, distribution and administration of the tax. Third and last was economic liberty. The *corvée* (public works conscription), which robbed the peasant of his labor just when it was most needed, would be replaced with a money tax. More important, the adoption of the single duty would end the dreadful smuggling wars and create a new era of commercial markets in the nation. *Ex tenebris lux*, from the very edge of disaster, the nation would recover its destiny. And he ended with a fine peroration:

> Others may recall the maxim of our monarchy: *"si veut le roi; si veut la loi"* [as the King wishes it, so be the law]. The maxim of His Majesty [now] is *"si veut le bonheur du peuple; si veut le roi"* [as the happiness of the people commands, so the King desires].

Much of Calonne's program was recycled Turgot. Indeed, the proposal on local assemblies drafted by Du Pont de Nemours was based on the earlier memorandum that he had written for Turgot over a decade earlier. (He was not pleased to discover that Mirabeau had pirated a version and circulated it under his own name.) But the fact of the reforms' earlier history did not weaken their genuine radicalism. And on the precedent of Parlementaire confrontations, Calonne must have expected resistance as a result of the breaches of privilege contained in the lack of exemptions for nobility and clergy in the land tax. He was not altogether disappointed, for in some of the bureaux there were indeed murmurings that the proposals attacked privilege and questions as to the constitutionality of the local assemblies.

Yet what was truly astonishing about the debates of the Assembly is that they were marked by a conspicuous *acceptance* of principles like fiscal equality that even a few years before would have been unthinkable. Vivian Gruder has shown how the social personality of the Notables—as landown-ers and agrarian businessmen—gave them a strong sense of the redundancy of privilege. In this sense, like so much else, they were already part of a "new" rather than an "old regime" and had merely been waiting for an opportunity to institutionalize their characteristically new concerns. There was, for example, no opposition to eliminate exemption from tolls paid in transporting produce from estates to markets. Some bureaux proposed that all exemptions from the *taille* be eliminated, others that ennoblement be (what everyone knew it was) essentially a matter of status and no longer confer any kind of tax exemptions.

In other words, they matched Calonne's radicalism, step for step, and in many cases even advanced well beyond him. He had assumed that the new tax paid in lieu of labor service *corvée* would only be paid by the previously *corvéable*. But three bureaux insisted it be a proper public works tax paid by all subjects. Others argued that the new property tax should not just be restricted to land but fall on other kinds of property such as urban real estate (in which *les Grands* had a special interest). Others again demanded that the tax be based on a comprehensive land register that would be periodically revised to ensure fair assessment. Further proposals concentrated on lower-ing taxes for those too poor to pay and especially all day laborers.

Where disagreement occurred, it was not because Calonne had shocked the Notables with his announcement of a new fiscal and political world; it was either because he had not gone far enough or because they disliked the operational methods built into the program. The debates over the land tax do not at all suggest a group of rich landowners (for that is indeed what they were) digging in their heels at the threatened onslaught on their privileges. They bore a much closer resemblance to the lengthy sessions of a provincial academy, convened to discuss the effects of alternative versions of fiscal equity on agrarian production. Du Pont de Nemours reported himself amazed by the familiarity with current theory shown in the discus-sions. When Calonne proposed that the tax be based on a percentage of gross product in any given year (the rate to vary slightly depending on the quality of the land), the Notables argued instead for a levy on the *net* product once costs of seed, labor and equipment were deducted. They also preferred a fixed sum to be partitioned down from the parish level rather than one which rose each year with levels of individual production. The latter, they claimed with the true voice of the new economics, would penalize productivity. Moreover, while Calonne thought the tax should be in kind, they believed that the difficulties of assessment dictated that it be in cash.

While historians have been inclined to write off the Notables as an ephemeral episode in the jockeying for power that preceded the onset of the Revolution, the merest glance at the debates confirms that something extremely serious was in the offing. (The land tax, as amended by the Notables, would be adopted by the Revolution and, little changed, would persist in France until the First World War.) Taxation was discussed in light of its relation to other economic activities and for the first time there was no disagreement that its acceptance was strictly conditional on some form of representation. Indeed, it was dissatisfaction with the limits of the intended provincial assemblies' authority that was most vocally expressed. Lafayette, as might be expected, wanted to transfer virtually all the powers of the *intendant*—over all forms of taxation (not just the land tax): public works, administration of billeting and the like—to these local authorities. Many more Notables hewed to the Parlementaire line that the body to deliberate on any new form of imposition had to be the Estates-General. And while Calonne had played safe by stipulating a six-hundred-livre income as the qualification for voting in parish assemblies, the majority of the bureaux actually supported lowering this threshold. This was still a long way from democracy, but there was a genuine sense that elected bodies ought to be a broad representation of "interests" in the nation.

This scenario in which the elite of France competed with each other for prizes in public-spiritedness was clearly not what Calonne had anticipated. It was rather as if he had set out to drive an obstinate mule with a very heavy wagon, only to find that the mule was a racehorse and had galloped into the distance, leaving the rider in the ditch. Vivian Gruder stresses, quite reasonably, that it was the social identity of the group as landed proprietors that made them so apparently complaisant about ditching privileges and anachronisms to which their caste had long been attached. But while the economic modernization of the group undoubtedly played a part in the realism with which they approached the reforms, it was also their shared sense of the historical moment that prompted their display of patriotic altruism. Allotted the role of a dumb chorus, they suddenly found that, individually and collectively, they had a powerful voice—and that France was paying attention. This abrupt self-discovery of politics was intoxicating and there are signs that though they are usually dismissed as the tail end of the old regime, with respect to political self-consciousness the Notables were the first revolutionaries.

And so far from needing the Controller-General to complete the process of reform, they very rapidly made it plain that his removal was the condition of success. His reputation was by now too thoroughly mired in scandal and suspicions of double-dealing to sustain the Assembly's credibility. In March, details of real-estate transactions in which Calonne had persuaded the King to part with some scattered properties in return for the less valuable county of Sancerre emerged in an unflattering light. Calonne and friends of his, it appeared, had been among the first and most advantaged buyers of the lots. On the Bourse, questions were asked about the Company of the Indies and about the floating of the syndicate contracted to provide Paris with its water supply. Mirabeau, who was still supposed to be at least a lukewarm supporter, dramatically altered course by publishing a *dénonciation* of these speculations in which Calonne was particularly compromised. And as a member of the most loyalist of the seven bureaux, that of Artois, Lafayette broke ranks with a public pronouncement attacking the "monster speculation." A full criminal inquiry, he insisted, should be mounted to reveal those involved in enriching themselves at the expense of the "sweat, tears and even blood" of the people.

Harassed on all sides, the Controller-General struck back for the last time, using the same techniques of public polemic that had been leveled against him. It was a measure of how the language of debate had so significantly changed that his *avertissement* (notice) to the public had at its center the accusation that it was the privileged classes who were misrepresenting his plans the better to conspire against the people. Sounding like a revolutionary orator in 1789 or even a Jacobin denouncing the "rich egoists," Calonne answered the question on everyone's mind: "More will be paid? To be sure. But by whom? Only by those who have not paid enough. The privileged will be sacrificed, yes—when justice requires it and need demands it. Would it be better to tax yet again the unprivileged, the People?"

Appealing in so direct and candid a way to public opinion did not save Calonne. In fact, it may even have made his position worse. He had become so unpopular that this last sally was greeted as a disingenuous ploy to conceal his own culpability in private and public misdeeds. More seriously, he was rapidly losing favor at court. The King had been dismayed, even enraged, to discover the true extent of the deficit, 32 million in excess of Calonne's estimate. The exact figure was, by this time, somewhat academic, but it was the trust that the King had placed in the Minister that was the main casualty. Not for the last time he began to repent of his political boldness and scrambled for the least painful exit. Not for the last time the Queen appeared to provide one. As Calonne's star descended, so she began to list the occasions when he had declined to honor her wishes (which usually meant money and office for her favorites). She listened carefully, then, when Breteuil represented to her that Calonne's departure was indispensable for the survival of the reform program. Increasingly vexed by the position Calonne had placed him in, Louis gave the Minister an earnest of his intentions by permitting the responses to his *avertissement* to be published.

Calonne attempted to extract what credit he could from an increasingly difficult situation. He offered to resign on condition that the program was assented to, but he was hardly bargaining from strength. Like Turgot and Necker before him, he was maneuvered into an ultimatum that would be impossible to meet, demanding the removal of his most powerful adversaries. It seemed, at first, that the King would meet him halfway by getting rid of Miromesnil, but this proved to be only the prelude to an act of Solomonic authority. Calonne was dismissed on April 8.

More than just a resignation was involved. The term given to his dismissal, like Turgot's, was *disgrâce*. And in this case, the King took care to launder his own authority by fouling Calonne's. "Everyone is happy," reported one observer at court. The Queen was pleased to be rid of a bad apple and to have the chance of inserting a minister of her own choosing. All the princes of the blood were delighted to see the jumped-up *intendant* disappear back into obscurity. Public opinion roared its pleasure at the demise of the arch-speculator and burned Calonne in effigy on the Pont Neuf. Louis XVI himself lost no opportunity to express his own pleasure in acts of petty vindictiveness. The Minister was stripped of the blue riband of the Order of Saint-Esprit, which he had enjoyed showing off so conspicuously, and he was forced to surrender his estate at Hannonville as a kind of bail against further proceedings. On his way to exile, Calonne's carriage was often surrounded by sullen or jeering crowds who stopped just short of actual violence against his person.

Calonne was the first in a long line of French politicians who were to be the casualties of their own adventurism. But it would be a crass mistake to dismiss him as merely a lightweight, recklessly exploiting the financial crisis for short-term advantage. He was, in fact, the first public man to understand its political consequences, and the picture he drew for the Notables of a great caesura in French history was, for all his disingenuousness, absolutely correct. The language he spoke and his vision of what lay ahead were, in other words, more important than the issue of his motives for the exposure. After Calonne, anything was possible.

Typically, he continued to hedge his bets. On the incorrect assumption that his exile would not be long-lived (in fact it was but the prelude to a further exile from France), Calonne made some provisions for a return to Paris society. On the very day of his disgrace he asked a monastery situated on the rue Saint-Dominique near his house if it would rent him enough space to keep a thousand bottles of wine. He would never get to sample its riches.

CHAPTER SEVEN

Suicides
1787–1788

i THE REVOLUTION NEXT DOOR

I N T H E summer of 1787 it was possible to travel two days northeast from Paris and arrive in the midst of a revolution. The setting for this turmoil was deceptive: the gabled squares and placid canals of the Dutch Republic that had long been a byword for political stability. And the element of spontaneous and, later, managed violence that would be the distinctive sign of the French Revolution was largely absent in Holland. There would be no cartloads of condemned aristocrats nor baskets of severed heads in Amsterdam. But the turmoil of Dutch politics in the 1780s was no less revolutionary for that. Utrecht, Leiden and Haarlem were patrolled by regiments of armed citizens' militia: the Free Corps. Parading and drilling beneath banners extolling "Liberty or Death" they engaged in ceremonies of oath-taking by day and patriotic bonfires by night. At a great assembly in Leiden in 1785 thousands of these Patriot militiamen came together to swear an "act of federation" that bound them in common defense.

To what were they committed? In the principal square of Utrecht, a "Temple of Liberty" had been erected to proclaim the defeat of dynasticism and aristocracy and the victory of representation. And it was in the same town that the Free Corps had used their muscle to mobilize crowds against the sitting patrician regime of the Town Hall. In its place were installed "people's representatives" elected directly, as were the officers of the militia themselves. A radical manifesto published in Leiden in 1785, and strongly reminiscent of both the American Declaration of Independence and the Bordeaux lawyer Saige's *Catechism of the Citizen,* made the same point even more forcefully. "Liberty," it insisted, "is an inalienable right of all citizens

71. Reinier Vinkeles, engraved portrait of Otto
Dirk Gordon, captain of the Utrecht Free Corps, 1786

of the commonwealth. No power on earth much less any power derived truly from the people . . . can challenge or obstruct the enjoyment of this liberty when it is so desired." Likewise, "the Sovereign is none other than the vote of the people."

Within five years, politics in Holland had exploded from the realm of a politely circumscribed elite to a chaotic and impulsive mass activity. An uncensored, radical press was directed at a readership among shopkeepers and the petty professions. The two most popular weeklies, the *Post van Neder Rijn* and the *Politieke Kruijer*, both reached at least five thousand readers with each issue. Their pages denounced Prince William V of Orange as a drunken imbecile and his Prussian wife as a haughty termagant. And before long the targeted enemies extended to recalcitrant "aristocrats" (the traditional "regent" classes of the towns) attempting to preserve systems of nepotism and oligarchy in local government. Efforts to muffle the outspokenness of the Patriot press only resulted in its editors and publishers becoming overnight popular heroes. Hespe, the editor of the *Kruijer* in

Amsterdam, cultivated his celebrity as a political prisoner by having visiting cards printed with broken fetters as his personal emblem. Invective flowed from the printed page to the world of images: caricatures pillorying Orangists and "aristocrats" and counter-caricatures against the Patriots circulated in coffeehouses and taverns. Rival establishments decorated their premises and signs with appropriate emblems: the Orange tree and ribbons for the supporters of the Stadtholder, the black cockade and the Patriot *keeshond* for their opponents. The tone of these polemics could be aggressively vulgar. One Patriot print showed the *keeshond* with its leg up against the Orange tree. Even domestic life retreated before the onslaught of sloganizing. Snuffboxes, engraved goblets, beer tankards, porcelain dishes were all covered in partisan mottoes. Even baking boards and pudding basins were carved so that loaves and puddings could emerge bearing the appropriate devices of the family line.

This saturation of daily life by political contention directly anticipated the climate of the French Revolution. There were many other similarities: the transfer of patriotic sentiment from Prince to Citizens, the imputation of sinister foreign motives to the Prince's consort, the creation of clubs to "educate" people in their rights and an emphasis on public ceremonies and parades to dramatize the "armed freedom." And although the conflict had begun as a protest against the power of the Stadtholder's government in controlling local appointments, the radical means used to press those claims had themselves generated new ends. From attacking the House of Orange, the journalists and Free Corps leaders had turned sharply against the entire traditional system of officeholding in the Netherlands by which "regents" were installed for life and replaced by co-opted members of the same clique. Against this "aristocracy," described in the polemical literature as a "Gothic monstrosity" and a "tyranny," a democratic system of direct and frequent elections was supposed to purify Dutch politics and re-create the Republic in the imagined vigor of its origins.

Though Dutch Patriot rhetoric was mostly expressed in the standard late eighteenth-century idiom of universal rights, there would have been much about this miniature revolution that would have seemed bewilderingly parochial to the French visitor. In the appeals to the memory of dead heroes like Admiral de Ruyter and Johan de Witt he would have found echoes of the past rather than auguries of the future. It would have seemed more like a quarrel of factions than a war between "aristocracy" and "democracy." Yet although the Patriot tumults were never treated by French governments with anything like the seriousness given to American affairs, there were complicated ways in which the fate of each of the two countries was tangled up with that of the other.

72. Teapot with Patriot revolutionary emblems

73. Dutch breadboard with caricature
of William V

Since the American war the Dutch Republic had been an ally and an important if rather hapless element of the anti-British coalition put together by Vergennes. Increasingly, too, the Amsterdam money market had become a vital source of short-term loans and annuities, much of it supplied through syndicates that were themselves Patriot rather than Orangist in their sympathies. Money and "American" Patriot politics seemed to march in step. Since the House of Orange was traditionally pro-British, the more acute its embarrassment, the better the chances of establishing a Francophile Patriot regime in its stead. But this golden opportunity was by no means risk-free. The confrontation in the Dutch Republic was rapidly turning into an all-out civil war. As street tactics became rougher, the level of alarm at Versailles rose correspondingly. A French envoy from Holland reported that "the ferment here has made terrifying progress and if it is not stopped it is to be feared that it may cause an explosion which will have incalculable consequences."

The militarization of the conflict, however, intensified during the spring of 1787. In May the first pitched battle took place, albeit on a small scale, near Utrecht, with the Patriots getting the better of the action. At the end of June, Princess Wilhelmina was apprehended by Patriot guards while attempting to travel from the Orangist stronghold of Gelderland to The

Hague to rally supporters. Inside the eastern border of the province of Holland she was held in close and undignified arrest. Her brother the King of Prussia, Frederick William, took umbrage at this humiliation and, egged on by the British Ambassador, prepared an invasion.

What was France to do about this crisis? Louis XVI had made no secret of his distaste for the conduct of the Dutch Patriots and was disinclined to intervene on their behalf. Before his death in February, Vergennes had made it clear that the satisfaction to be derived from dislodging British influence was not to be taken as an endorsement of insurrection. But despite these reservations the impression had undoubtedly been given in Holland that France would use its own military power to offset and deter the threat of an Anglo-Prussian intervention. And there were voices in France itself, some of them famous and eloquent, that proclaimed the cause of freedom to be indivisible—as apparent in Amsterdam and Utrecht as it had been in Boston and Philadelphia. Mirabeau (with the blessing of his latest patron, the Duc d'Orléans) had published an appeal, *To the Batavians,* denouncing Stadtholderian infamy. And Lafayette actually rode hard to the Dutch border expecting to be named to the command of the Patriot troops, only to find (to his disgust) that it had been given to an incompetent mercenary, the Rhinegrave of Salm.

The dilemma for French policy was acute. If nothing was done to forestall a Prussian invasion, the credibility of French power and authority would suffer a disastrous humiliation virtually on France's doorstep. A token military presence, together with rumors of mobilization, might be enough to have a deterrent effect, but if the bluff was called the choice between war and capitulation would be even more galling. But war in behalf of a cause repudiated by the King seemed equally foolhardy. In the event, the deciding factor was money. Though the ministers of the army and navy, Ségur and de Castries, thought it unseemly to put a price on the honor and integrity of France, they were overruled by the new chief minister, Loménie de Brienne. Reviving Turgot's predictions about the costs of the American war, and reinforced by the bleak lessons of hindsight, Brienne warned that any kind of military action would immediately drive the state into bankruptcy. "*Pas un sou*" was the grim message relayed from Versailles to the French Ambassador at The Hague.

It did not take long for the British and the Prussians to discover that the rumors of an encampment of thirty thousand French soldiers on the southern border of the Republic were a sham. For all the posturing of citizens' militias, armed Patriot resistance melted before the Prussian troops and within a month the Duke of Brunswick's Prussian grenadiers had reached Amsterdam and The Hague. Thousands of embittered Patriots fled to

France, where they added to the burden of the French debt by demanding (and receiving) pensions as honorable refugees. Lafayette grieved in public for the tarnished honor of France, raised high in America and brought low in Holland.

What the Dutch crisis had done was to expose the loss of credibility of French power in the most brutally naked way. Things had come to such a pass, it seemed, that until drastic action was taken France could not afford a foreign policy befitting a great power. Brienne's exclusion of the military option was a somber recognition that the monarchy was already a hostage to the deficit. It also meant that the monarchy would never regain its freedom of action through any kind of palliatives. Pushing the argument a little further, it was apparent that from this painful moment, traditional absolutism was dead. There were but two alternatives left, neither of which could possibly restore to the French crown the plenitude of power enjoyed by Louis XIV. The first was reform from above, sufficiently dramatic to galvanize popular support and through which the crown might at least preserve the initiative in the reshaping of the constitution. The second, more ominous option, was a kind of self-imposed abdication in which the authority of the state would be transferred from the crown alone to some sort of quasi-parliamentary regime vested in the Estates-General. Some observers in 1787 believed this had already happened. Reporting on one particularly captious meeting of the Notables, Du Pont de Nemours commented that

> on the 1st of May France was still a monarchy and the first
> in Europe. On the 9th of May . . . France became a Republic
> in which there remains a magistrate decorated with the title and
> honors of royalty but forever obliged to assemble his people to ask
> them to supply his wants, for which the public revenue without
> this new national consent would be forever inadequate. The King
> of France became a king of England.

Not everyone, though, was prepared to accept that the old regime had in fact perished from inanition. The entire history of its last, remarkable government, that of Loménie de Brienne, amounted to a stubborn defense of the possibilities of enlightened absolutism. And its eventual defeat was an acknowledgment that representation was the condition of reform, not the other way round.

ii THE LAST GOVERNMENT
OF THE OLD REGIME

To survive, the French monarchy needed both determined reform and artful politics. From the government of Loménie de Brienne it got a full measure of the former and absolutely none of the latter. This was all the more surprising since Brienne was a figure from the opposition recruited to legitimize the reforms he had criticized in the Assembly of the Notables. But once this outsider had become an insider, he too fell victim to the traditional assumption that government and politics were mutually incompatible. From the standpoint of the government, politics had come to mean opposition and opposition a synonym for obstruction. Reform, then, had to be pushed through in the teeth of that obstruction, rather than implemented through cooperation.

Brienne was not, in fact, adamantly hostile to government through representation, not even to the Estates-General. In the autumn of 1788 he committed the government to convening that body, promising that it should be in place by 1792 at the latest. But given the manifestly catastrophic condition of French finance, he was unwilling to wait on the Estates-General for deliverance. Money first, elections later, were his priorities to

74. Loménie de Brienne

deal with what he perceived (not unreasonably) as a national emergency. (After 1789, the governments of the Revolution would come to much the same conclusion.)

Many of his difficulties arose from disappointed public expectations. Brienne had come to power as the beneficiary of Calonne's disgrace. There had been a brief interregnum in which the aged Bouvard de Fourqueux had been appointed Controller-General but it was precisely because he was seen as Calonne's hanger-on that he remained repugnant to the Notables. Brienne, on the contrary, seemed acceptable to everyone. The Queen (somewhat improbably in view of the Minister's swift attack on sinecures and court expenses) pressed his claims enthusiastically to her husband. The clergy, who had become extremely nervous about Calonne's plans to attack their fiscal exemptions, were delighted to see an archbishop of Toulouse in high office. And public opinion assumed that he would henceforth avoid any kind of arbitrary proceeding, implementing reforms through consultation and representation. When the King addressed the Notables on April 23 he essentially recited Brienne's own positions on a number of important issues. "Never did a King of England speak more popular truths or a more national language" was the verdict of the Archbishop of Aix.

Not all of these assumptions were confounded. In office, Brienne amended Calonne's land tax in exactly the manner he had recommended as a Notable. Instead of a proportionate tax collected in kind, expanding along with production, Brienne redefined the tax as a specific amount of money to be determined by revenue needs each year. That amount would then be partitioned by quota, giving the taxable a clear idea of their liability from year to year. This immediately removed what had been publicized as the sinister, indefinitely expanding character of the imposition. He also adopted the Notables' willingness to extend to all sections of the population (not just those who had previously been *corvéable*) the tax that was to replace the state labor conscription of the *corvée*. Other items on Calonne's agenda, such as the reestablishment of the free trade in grain and the institution of a customs union, were uncontentious and passed into the new government's program.

Once the Notables were able to inspect the government books, the bleak situation advertised by Calonne was no longer seen as a self-serving act of publicity. It was grim reality—to the tune of a current deficit of 140 million livres (later revised upward to 161 million). The magnitude of this crisis gave Brienne confidence that, unlike his predecessor, he could call on a kind of patriotic consensus to swallow stringent fiscal medicine. Moreover, the administration he gathered around him to make good his commitments to retrenchment as well as revenue was of high quality in terms of sheer intellectual and administrative abilities. It was, it is true, a strikingly close-knit group of friends and even relatives. Malesherbes' cousin Lamoignon was persuaded by Brienne to abandon his botany for the public good and become Keeper of the Seals. Malesherbes' nephew La Luzerne became the Minister for the Navy after de Castries resigned over the Dutch crisis, and Brienne's own brother was his counterpart in the war office.

Yet at the outset the government was not accused of being a family cabal. In part, this was due to the high reputation of individuals within the government for integrity as well as intelligence. Chrétien-François de Lamoignon had been one of the most generally admired and respected of the presidents of the Parlement of Paris and thus, it was assumed, a help-ful liaison with the notoriously recalcitrant magistracy. Malesherbes re-mained something of a popular hero and as soon as he joined the govern-ment in the summer of 1788 he resumed the retrenchment of the royal household he had begun under Turgot. Superfluous châteaux and lodges were sold off, saving five million. Malesherbes even presumed to trespass on the court's most sacred domain, the hunt, dooming whole packs of falconers, wolf hunters and boar stickers. By merging the greater with the lesser royal stables, he saved two to four million livres, though in so doing he much provoked the Queen, who saw her favorite, the Duc de Coigny, made redundant. Offices in the postal service that had been created as sinecures for the Polignac clan were abolished outright, and pensions to the under-seventy-fives (a notorious source of abuse) substantially reduced.

All this helped the plausibility of the government's claim that it would rule sternly for the general good. And Brienne himself had established his own reputation for independence through his forthright criticisms as a Notable. He came from the circle of impressively well-read prelates (like Dillon of Narbonne and Boisgelin of Aix) who combined worldly charm and sophistication with considerable intellectual toughness. Though he suffered from a disfiguring skin disease that often left his face a mass of peeling scabs and tissue, Loménie de Brienne was thought of as a personable and congenial man: as clever as Calonne but without his vanity or devious-ness. Only the playwright Marmontel, who served on a commission to draft a plan of national education, thought "his gaiety too disturbing and his countenance too calculating to trust."

Brienne did not want to be seen merely as an engineer of fiscal rescue—crucial though that was. The legitimacy of his government he thought depended on it being seen as a reforming administration that would reach out to many different areas of French life. At the urging of Malesherbes (who in turn was being pressed by his friend the pastor Rabaut Saint-

Etienne), the civil emancipation of Protestants was undertaken, no mean accomplishment in the government of an archbishop of the Gallican Church. Rabaut had hoped for a full emancipation, meaning the public right of Protestants to practice their confession, including open worship in chapels. He also urged that public office henceforth be open to Protestants. This was to push Louis XVI (who had taken a coronation oath to "extirpate the heretic") further than he was prepared to go. Portable, folding pulpits were to remain standard equipment for pastors-on-the-run a little while longer. But the measure passed did decriminalize the "heresy" and make it possible for marriages, births and deaths to be officially notarized and for members of the Reformed Church to practice trades and professions. A century after the revocation of the Edict of Nantes, the Huguenots had at last become civil persons once again.

In the same spirit of judicial liberalism, the remaining procedure by which torture was used to extract information about accomplices was abolished. The crushing boot, thumbscrews and waterpipes thus joined the general bonfire of anachronisms that blazed merrily in the very last year of the old monarchy. A committee presided over by the Parlementaire (and future revolutionary) Target also recommended a mandatory delay of execution of all death sentences, allowing for possible royal review and commutation—though the measure was ultimately unacceptable to Target's own Parlement. And the administration of prisons—accommodation and clothing—was also made the subject of reforming inquiry.

The most formidable of all Brienne's colleagues was not a minister at all but a figure in whom political power and intellectual authority were nonetheless concentrated to an almost alarming degree. This was Jacques, Comte de Guibert: drama critic, laureate of the French Academy and, until Clausewitz, the most influential military writer in Europe. At forty-three he was one of the great prodigies of French intellectual life. Sometimes gripped by black fits of dour Romantic melancholy, Guibert shone in public, disconcerting gatherings with his encyclopedic grasp of science, philosophy and literature. "His conversation," wrote Necker's daughter, Germaine de Staël (who was not easily impressed), "was the most far-ranging, spirited and fertile I have ever known."

Guibert's reputation had been established sixteen years earlier with the *Essay on Tactics.* That prophetic and forbidding document had foreseen with chilling prescience a time when war would no longer be the genteel sport of dynasts nor armies obligingly lined up in neat rows of infantry in the rational manner of Frederick the Great. Instead he predicted massive deployment of conscript armies, embroiled in wars of national ideology where distinctions between civilians and soldiers became blurred and where the theater of conflict expanded brutally to fill not just delineated zones of battle but entire regions and countries. Accordingly he remodeled logistics, field artillery and military engineering, stressing mobility, irregularity, adaptability: all cardinal sins in the old rule books. In March 1788, he regrouped regiments of cavalry and infantry into combined brigades that were then trained together intensively for battle-readiness. Not surprisingly, then, it was Guibert, a figure cut from the cloth of the "old regime" who was (as Napoleon would freely acknowledge) the real architect of French military ascendancy in the years to come.

"Only suppose," he wrote in a passage much quoted both at the time and since,

> the appearance in Europe of a people who should join to austere virtues and a citizen army a fixed plan of aggression, who should stick to it—understanding how to conduct war economically and to live at the enemy's expense . . . such a people would subdue its neighbors and overthrow our feeble constitution like a gale bends the reeds.

Officially Guibert was subordinate to the Minister of the Army, the Comte de Brienne (Loménie's younger brother), who succeeded Ségur when the latter resigned over the Dutch crisis. But in reality it was Guibert who immediately exerted control through the institution of a new war council of nine that combined serving officers with administrators and strategists: an embryonic general staff. Believing he could actually save money while making the army more efficient, Guibert closed the Ecole Militaire in Paris, which he had long suspected was more of an aristocratic finishing school than a serious training ground. So it was duly replaced by twelve provincial schools, lavishly endowed with scholarships to help the sons of country gentlemen. Bonaparte was a scholar of just one such institution, aptly enough at Brienne. The King's own military household, another decorative institution, was likewise cut back and the honorific colonelcy-generals, reserved for the royal family, made to lapse on the death of each incumbent. Guibert also cut back sharply on the total number of the French officer corps, believing that its inflation had devalued the meaning of rank and eroded the chain of command. Most significantly, the notoriously corrupt business of military procurement was taken out of the hands of private contractors and placed under the direct administration of the state— yet another of the innovations sustained during the Revolution.

With all these and other reforms, Guibert saved something on the order of thirty million livres. With those savings he raised the pay of the common soldier from the penury into which it had fallen. But it would be misleading to represent Guibert as the Enlightenment in Arms. His darker side was fully in evidence at the same time. If anything, he made the disciplinary provisions of the army code more rather than less savage, if much less arbitrary. And neither was he any kind of social egalitarian. On the contrary, while he was prepared to see bright young men from the middle classes and professions man posts in the artillery and engineers, he believed the bulk of the officer corps had to come from the nobility. Paradoxically, this was not inconsistent with his vision of a reborn citizens' army. What he wanted to expel from the army was the ethos of money and replace it instead with a neo-Roman ideal of patriotic sacrifice and physical courage. Those values he associated with a transformed nobility: one not defined by privilege and certainly not by wealth so much as an unbending profession of devotion to the service of the state.

Very little of this program was calculated to endear Guibert to the professional soldiers, either officers or men. The former did not care for his abrupt juggling with the independence of their regiments and even less for his puritanical attitude towards promotion. For private soldiers, the pleasure of improved pay was offset by the severe punishments codified in the new handbooks. Nor did strategists of the old school think much of Guibert's wild notions of uninhibited warfare and demonic destruction visited on an enfeebled foe. The overall effect of his reforms was unsettling, perhaps even demoralizing in the short term. His was a truly revolutionary temperament still trapped in the body of royal government.

The more visionary the reforms of the Brienne government, the less the public liked them. The emancipation of the Protestants was deeply unpopular and provoked street demonstrations in the more pious areas of France in the west and southeast. (It was to continue to be one of the great divides during the Revolution.) The provincial assemblies which Brienne had preserved from Calonne's proposals and which were brought into existence during the course of 1787 and 1788 had been designed as an exercise in devolution. But in much of France (though by no means all of it) they were stigmatized as the playthings of the government: tools of its tax policies.

Neither the seriousness of the financial crisis in the late spring of 1787 nor the acknowledged excellence of the government's reforms was enough to disarm what had become insuperable political objections to traditional government procedure. The Assembly of the Notables that had been designed by Calonne to obviate opposition had, by taking itself seriously, turned conventional priorities on their heads. Representation and consent were now required not as the auxiliary of government but as its working condition. And by taking his case to the public—literally to the pulpits of the clergy—Calonne had made politics a matter of national attention. Once

Pandora's box had been opened in this way, it proved impossible to close the lid and Brienne's administration foundered on the same contentions that had undone its predecessor. While the Notables were prepared to authorize loans to rescue the government from immediate bankruptcy and to assent to economic reforms, on the matter of the land tax and the stamp tax that supplemented it, they were adamant. Only the Estates-General had the authority to make such measures lawful. Faced with this recalcitrance, Brienne dissolved the body on May 25.

His alternatives were now starkly obvious. He could transform the monarchy into a representative regime by directly convening the Estates-General and assuming that this would generate the public confidence—and hence the public funds—needed to sustain the government. Or he could try to prevail over the anticipated opposition of the Parlements to the new tax policy by a judicious mixture of incentives and threats. The dangers of both policies were apparent, and it was unclear in the summer of 1787 by which course of action the vital matter of credit would be helped rather than hurt. And at a time when the King himself might have been expected to offer some leadership, he had collapsed into a world of compulsive alternation between hunting and eating, killing and gorging. On one occasion he was discovered weeping and bemoaning the loss of Vergennes. But through this neurotic helplessness it was apparent to Brienne that Louis was not ready to accept the kind of constitutional regime that could produce reform through consent.

This left only the path of confrontation.

iii THE SWAN SONG OF THE PARLEMENTS

The Assembly of the Notables was a remarkable instance of a group hand-picked for compliance discovering instead the excitement of opposition. The more vocal their complaints, the more enthusiastically they were applauded in pamphlets and broadsides. The lapdogs of the government had turned into the terriers of the people. Many of the provincial magistrates, municipal councillors and bishops who had come to Versailles at least neutral towards the cause of tax reform found that by sheer obstruction they could exert more power than they had ever imagined. Their entry into political life was thus defined as opposition rather than co-optation. And even after the Notables had been dismissed, this approach of creative truculence persisted.

The immediate stumbling block for the government's program was the Parlement of Paris. When Brienne's administration presented its proposals to that court in May and June 1787, the Parlement sat in its augmented form as the Court of Peers. This expansion included a number of lay peers of the realm, many of whom had been Notables—as indeed had prominent magistrates themselves. The intensity of Parlementaire opposition was not preordained, since the court (as well as the supplementary peerage) was beginning to divide within itself on the political costs of opposition. Président d'Aligre, who represented the older and professionally senior magistrates, had in fact suggested to Brienne that he could expect a degree of cooperation from the court on registering loans and some of the major items left over from the agenda of the Notables, in particular the customs union and the reestablishment of freedom of the grain trade. And so indeed it proved at the outset. Even the provincial assemblies, which were regarded with deep suspicion as dependencies of the government rather than truly free deliberative bodies, failed to rouse united opposition among the provincial Parlements. But d'Aligre and his governmentally inclined colleagues like Séguier were confronted with two other groups within the court who used sheer rhetorical force to seize the political initiative and to stigmatize collaboration with the government as a betrayal of Parlementaire tradition.

What made matters worse was that the more formidable of these two groups came from the highest ranks of the magistracy. It was led by Jean-Jacques d'Eprémesnil, a squat figure whose peppery eloquence more than compensated for his lack of inches. D'Eprémesnil's position was conservative, even reactionary. But that did not compromise its popularity. On the contrary it probably strengthened it, since so much of what was to be revolutionary feeling drew its force from wounded reaction rather than high-minded progressivism. D'Eprémesnil's rhetoric was a throwback to the resistance against Chancellor Maupeou and the Controllers-General of Louis XV. He reiterated their standard view that the Parlements had the responsibility to guard the "fundamental laws" of France against ministerial designs on the "liberties of the people." But he had more ambitious plans for constitutional reconstruction, summarily stated as "de-Bourbonizing France." He meant to take the argument beyond the boundary of resistance to unlawful edicts and to press instead for a positive share in the making of legislation: in effect, a redefinition of sovereignty. In 1777 he had already made it clear that this was not the role of the Parlements. Rather their opposition had to act as midwife to the Estates-General, with which such responsibility for the creation of new law truly lay. This was his position ten years later. Brienne must have supposed that the gravity of the financial crisis would persuade orators like d'Eprémesnil to suspend this doctrine at least until the emergency had passed. But the lions of the Parlement were disinclined to political mercy. On the contrary, it was precisely the plight of the government that they saw as offering a supreme opportunity to force the end of absolutism. It would indeed be a revolution but one made not in blood but law: a French edition of the Glorious Revolution of 1688.

The trouble with this prognosis was that belief in it was not shared by all those who, for the time being, rallied to d'Eprémesnil's opposition. A younger and more aggressively radical group of advocates in the Parlements (including Hérault de Séchelles and his friend Lepeletier de Saint-Fargeau) saw the Estates-General not as an end but a beginning of a new France. This group, led by the twenty-eight-year-old Adrien Duport de Prelaville, was a minority within the senior magistrates of the Grand' Chambre, but it commanded a much larger and noisier following among the barristers and trial lawyers of the junior courts, the *maîtres d'enquêtes*. Duport had himself become a councillor in the Chambre at the tender age of nineteen, was a friend of Lafayette's and made his house on the rue du Grand Chantier a center of discussion about the political future of France. Chez Duport (he dropped the aristocratic "de Prelaville" to identify with the Third Estate in 1788), the talk was not of traditional privileges and the old Estates so much as a sovereignty vested in the citizenry. Many of these radical arguments had been set out in Saige's *Catechism of the Citizen,* a widely read work that had a new edition in 1788. For Duport's group, this new sovereignty was to be embodied in a *national* representation, and by "national" they necessarily meant antithetical to privilege, differentiation and the separation of social orders.

As long as it was the Parlement itself that seemed to be the focus of resistance and thus the target of government force, the two groups would come together in a show of solidarity. Both had an interest in denying the government any possibility of carrying out its programs without paying the price of constitutional devolution. But as soon as that price had been conceded, and the issue of representation came to the fore, the differences would emerge with sudden and brutal clarity. In the end it would distinguish citizens from nobles, revolutionaries from conservatives. The British Ambassador in Paris saw that, one way or another, the current campaign would be ultimately self-defeating. Either the Parlementaires would provoke the government into drastic repression or the Parlements would yield to more genuinely representative institutions. In any event it was "the last gasp of the Sovereign Courts." And not all of the magistrates were themselves oblivious to what was in store. Etienne Pasquier, who was to end up a chancellor of the Napoleonic Empire but who in 1788 was an impressionable young lawyer, recalled in his memoirs that the sober heads of the Grand' Chambre were troubled at the prospect. I could never forget what one of those old judges said to me as he passed behind my bench and saw how enthused I was. "Young man, a similar idea was brought forward in your grandfather's time." This is what he said then: "Messieurs, this is not a game for children; the first time that France sees the Estates-General she will also see a terrible revolution."

Any such reservations were drowned out by the inspirational power of d'Eprémesnil's rhetoric. Brienne's scheme to supplement the revenues of the land tax with a stamp duty played straight into d'Eprémesnil's hands. Not only was it an immediate reminder of the tax that had triggered the "sacred cause" of liberty in America, but the Parlementaire orator was able to represent it as an imposition that would strike the great and humble alike, festooning tradesmen, booksellers, shopkeepers and guildsmen in reams of paper, and which would furnish yet another pretext for the heavy hand of government to press on the shoulder of defenseless citizens. On the subject of the fines to be meted out to those discovered leaving their papers unstamped, d'Eprémesnil produced a cascade of oratorical melodrama:

> It is cruel to imagine the lonely citizen living in the most profound solitude, the tranquil merchant working to increase the national commerce . . . the wise practitioner consecrating his labors to the repose of families—all face the appalling prospect of finding themselves linked together by a common chain and subject at the moment they least thought themselves vulnerable . . . to fines whose weight would swallow up . . . the innocent along with the guilty. . . .

Relishing its role as defender of the weak and puny, Parlement rejected the stamp duty outright on July 2. Two weeks later the amended land tax met the same fate. It was apparent to the government by now that the majority of the Parlement was bent on thwarting *any* measures that would recover freedom of action for the state. So a collision became inevitable. On the sixth of August, the King convened a *lit de justice* at the Parlement. The Grand' Chambre was jammed with hundreds of magistrates and peers sweating into their robes in the broiling summer heat. Despite the drama of the occasion Louis XVI took the presence of the ceremonial "bed" too literally by falling asleep early in the proceedings, forcing Lamoignon to raise his voice above the powerful royal snoring coming from beneath the corner canopy. He was gratified, he said, that the Parlement accepted the principles set out by the Notables (for it had indeed registered edicts on the grain trade, the *corvée* tax and the customs union). The tax laws were then to be registered, in the traditional form, since *le roi le veult*.

A day later, d'Eprémesnil declared the enforcement of the edicts to be illegal and thus null and void, a view which was formalized in a grand remonstrance. "The constitutional principle of the French monarchy," it flatly stated, "was that taxes should be consented to by those who had to bear them." And on August 10 the Parlement took the counter-attack further by instigating criminal proceedings against Calonne (who, by this time, was safely in England). Duport took the opportunity to launch a ferocious attack on the discredited Minister. He was declared to be the fountainhead of infamy and corruption—pecuniary, political and sexual. Indeed, he was said to be so obnoxious that merely to refrain from proscription constituted a kind of tacit endorsement. Duport's vituperation, which drew on violent polemics then circulating written by the publicists Bergasse and Carra, was an important moment in the history of revolutionary rhetoric. It was the first time that the prosecution of a particular politician was worked into a general indictment of the sitting administration, even if that administration had no part in his conduct. This incrimination by association was to be a standard tool of opposition groups exploiting the public need for villains on whom whatever disaster was in the offing could be blamed. During the Revolution these campaigns would produce not just scoundrels but traitors, and they would be not merely disgraced but guillotined.

As the Parlement rode high on foamy waves of oratory, it was carried along by powerful and noisy public support. Beyond the Grand' Chambre itself, the *basoche* of the law—scribes, pleaders, sedan-chair carriers, printers and *colporteurs:* the entire commonwealth of the Palais de Justice—constituted a perpetual and noisy claque cheering their heroes, booing villains (like the Comte d'Artois) and urging the magistrates on to greater shows of defiance. In their turn they took this theater outside to the Pont Neuf, the Palais-Royal and the cafés, and to a pamphlet press that was growing daily more uninhibited in its denunciations of government "despotism." Government *affiches* were torn down as soon as they were posted; effigies of Lamoignon were burned in the streets. And as resistance became more daring, so Brienne and Lamoignon collapsed back onto the stereotypes prepared for them by acting as counter-revolutionaries. There was a kind of surgical deliberateness on their part that uncannily anticipated the systematic counter-revolutionary tactics of the nineteenth century. First they acted to close the "theater" and deport the actors—Parlement was exiled to Troyes on August 15. On the seventeenth the Palais de Justice was itself invested by Swiss guards who sealed off the entrance and exits of the chambers to prevent the physical disruption of the enforced edicts. This was followed by a mopping-up campaign to silence the opposition. Printers were raided, journals closed down and, most strikingly, any club or assembly that might be suspected of fomenting opposition was closed down. This included those notorious nests of subversives, chess clubs.

The exile at Troyes together with the sudden and heavy use of force did little to silence the uproar in the streets. But it undoubtedly sobered the magistrates themselves. It did, at any rate, dispose some of the less courageous among them to listen to the prudent counsels offered by the older magistrates like d'Aligre and Séguier. At the same time, during August, an interesting transformation was taking place. Provincial assemblies were being inaugurated with a great patriotic fanfare by the *intendants,* who ostentatiously declared them to be a transfer of power from the King's servant to the People. Since the assemblies were recruited from the lower levels of the legal profession, from functionaries and physicians as well as from the loyal nobility—in other words, from the reading classes—they were deliberately designed to undercut the claims of the Parlements to represent the Nation, especially in matters of taxation. The formal adieux of the *intendants* emphasized this peaceful revolution. "The Nation has summoned you," declared Bertier de Sauvigny, opening the assembly of the Ile-de-France on the eleventh of August; ". . . enlightened by your own interest and excited by the spirit of patriotism you will show no less zeal than I in establishing a just proportion for taxes . . . you will be moved to tears by the enormous burden of the taxable."

De La Galaizière, at Alsace, in a remarkable speech on the twentieth of August, was even more self-conscious about the significance of the moment. It was, he told the assembly,

> a memorable epoch in the history of our century and nation.
> . . . Time, the progress of knowledge, the change of manners and
> opinions have brought about and necessitated revolutions [his
> word exactly] in the political system of governments. Over thirty
> years we have seen patriotic ideas sow themselves invisibly in
> every head. Every citizen today desires to be called to support the
> general good. This disposition cannot be too much encouraged.
> The King wishes above all the happiness of his subjects.

Elsewhere, *intendants* competed with each other in expressions of zeal for the common good. At Caen, for example, Cordier de Launay compared Louis XVI with Solon and Lycurgus and claimed that his own heart was "burning with new patriotism."

The authorized encouragement of this kind of language clearly represented an attempt by the government to come between the Parlements and people. By stressing the social equity of the work of tax assessment and by co-opting personnel who might otherwise have been expected to belong to the Parlementaire camp, the government was trying to show that the reforms were popular rather than bureaucratic. And its efforts were by no means wasted. During the autumn all the evidence suggests that the provincial assemblies did in fact begin their work in earnest and that Parlementaire protests became desultory and ineffective. And this development may well have prompted a more conciliatory attitude in the Court of Peers in Paris.

At the same time, more moderate voices in the government itself were trying to work out a compromise that would enable revenue to be collected without political confrontation. The addition of Malesherbes in August was especially significant since no one knew better than he to take remonstrances seriously. He reminded his colleagues that, whether they liked it or not, "the Parlement of Paris is at this moment the echo of the public of Paris . . . and that of Paris is the echo of the entire Nation. . . . So we are dealing with the entire Nation and it is to the Nation that the king responds when he answers the Parlement." Malesherbes was also unafraid of the prospect of the Estates-General. In fact he envisioned it as a way for the authority of the monarchy to be enhanced rather than diminished.

There was, then, some room for negotiation on both sides. But in the compromise that emerged in September, it was Brienne who appeared to have gone more than halfway. The new land tax that all along had been at the heart of the reform program and on which a major reconstruction of public finance depended was rescinded. With it went the unlamented stamp duty. In their place, Brienne asked for exactly the kind of palliative he and Calonne had hoped to avoid: a second, traditional *vingtième* tax (imposed, like past *vingtièmes,* on all sections of the population). This was to be collected for five years, by the end of which the Estates-General would be summoned. The edict of suspension on the Parlements was also withdrawn. By abandoning confrontation, the government hoped to buy five years of political peace during which the finances of the state could be repaired. There would not only be light at the end of the tunnel but a blaze of royal sunshine. To the Cour des Pairs on the nineteenth of November Lamoignon held out the alluring prospect of 1792:

> His Majesty in the midst of his Estates, surrounded by his
> faithful subjects, confidently presenting to them the comforting
> picture of order restored to finances, of agriculture and com-
> merce mutually encouraged under the auspices of freedom, of a

formidable navy, the army regenerated by a more economical
and military constitution, of abuses eliminated, a new port built on
the English Channel to insure the glory of the French flag
[Cherbourg!], of laws reformed, public education perfected . . .

Though the more radically minded among the magistracy were reluctant
to accept anything the government had to offer, opinion was divided on the
degree of obstruction the court should place in its way. As a result, the
outcome of the proceedings of November 19 was uncertain. The government still lacked tact. Anxious about the intimidation of the moderate
magistrates, it had again invested the Palais de Justice with guards. Under
this military presence tempers frayed. D'Eprémesnil and the Comte d'Artois nearly came to blows over the serious issue of parking for their respective carriages in the courtyard. But the form the assembly took was meant
to be reassuring: a *séance royale* in which opinions of all sorts were permitted
to be aired, and the King sat on a dais rather than beneath the ominous
canopy that betokened the compulsion of the *lit de justice.*

After a long day of rambling speeches it seemed likely that the Parlement
would in fact register the new edicts. But a completely unpremeditated turn
of events shattered the grudging consensus. The King himself, perhaps
irritated by repeated calls for the Estates-General to be summoned earlier
than 1792, was determined to avoid a vote and ordered the registration of
the edicts. He had, in effect, impulsively converted the more informal *séance
royale* into a coerced *lit de justice.* The response to this brusque proceeding
was an appalled silence, finally broken from the unlikeliest quarter. The
King's cousin Philippe, Duc d'Orléans, got to his feet. This was, to say the
least, unexpected. The entire royal family—Bourbon, Condé, Orléans—
(the Conti excepted) were famous for their conspicuous inability to articulate anything in public that was not prescribed by ceremony. Artois, who
could fulminate impressively in private, several times struggled to defend
the royal will in the Cour des Pairs but invariably collapsed either into
stuttering incoherence or sulky silence. Orléans, the great proprietor-
patron of the Palais-Royal, liked to surround himself with wits and intel-
lects. The teams of literary drones (including Mirabeau and Choderlos de
Laclos) who all produced polemics on his behalf gave Orléans an un-
deserved reputation for political outspokenness. But his intervention on
November 19 was nonetheless an immense shock to detractors and admirers
alike. Turning directly to the King he remarked, "Sire, I beg Your Majesty
to allow me to place at your feet and in the heart of this court [the view]
that I consider this registration illegal."

It was one of those theatrical moments that, frozen in time and embellished in his son's memoirs, would be represented as the first revolutionary *tableau*. The King's response unerringly struck the worst possible note—petulance followed by facetiousness. "The registration is legal because I have heard the opinions of everyone." He then followed this strange non sequitur with an offhand, bantering jest at Orléans: "Oh well, I don't care, you're the master, of course." The effect of this peculiar performance could not have been more damaging: despotism that failed to have the courage of its convictions.

At that point Louis and his brothers left the Parlement; Orléans remained to recite a text that had obviously been prepared for him confirming the illegality of the proceedings. His strategy to turn himself into a popular hero was further gratified by arrest and exile to his estate at Villers-Cotterêts, where he reveled in the reputation of a martyr for the cause of liberty. His château even began to take on the character of an alternative court. Two other Parlementaires, deemed to have spoken insolently, were also arrested.

Orléans' intervention proved to be another turning point in the sabotage of any kind of collaborative reform between government and Parlements. Resigned to a more systematic show of force, Brienne decided he had little to lose by pressing the tax issue further than his September agreement with the Parlements had suggested. The *vingtième* was deemed not to be an open-ended tax but one which was required to meet a specific revenue figure of the government. Any shortfall was to be made up by so-called *abonnements*—in effect, supplements levied through the provincial assemblies. This looked suspiciously like the abandoned land tax promulgated by stealth.

As a result of this maneuver, the plausibility of the provincial assemblies as bulwarks of the people's welfare was fatally damaged. Their members either began to resist the *intendants* or else abandon cooperation with the government and offer expressions of support instead to the Parlements. In January 1788, Lafayette reported to Washington his own pleasure in the assembly of the Auvergne at Riom, where he succeeded in obstructing attempts to collect additional revenue. "I had the good fortune," he wrote, rather smugly, "to please the people and the misfortune to displease the government to a very high degree." Moreover, the doctrine allowing that the thirteen Parlements were in reality one unified body vested with the protection of French liberties had made such headway that the Parlement of Paris spent the spring of 1788 issuing a series of pronunciamentos, in effect declaring this to the King. On April 11 the Parlement of Paris told the King that "the will of the King alone is not enough [to make] law"; on the twenty-ninth of April it formally refused to endorse any further collection of revenues and on May 3 it insisted that the Estates-General was a precondition of future taxation and that *lettres de cachet* and other arbitrary arrests were unlawful.

For its part, the government was now disinclined to sit still. On the seventeenth of April, in a speech written for the King, Lamoignon had represented royal authority as a shield against sectional interests. If the courts could coerce the royal will, "the monarchy would be nothing but an aristocracy of magistrates, as contrary to the rights and interests of the nation as to those of the sovereign." But this tactic of "popular absolutism" was not confined to rhetorical rebuttals. Its most powerful weapon was a set of judicial reforms of breathtaking sweep and boldness. They were plainly intended to destroy the oppositional power of the Parlements once and for all. But the stripping exercise was meant as a precondition for a wholly new system of justice that could plausibly bid for public support. Once again the government shrewdly targeted lawyers lower down in the legal hierarchy (and blocked from advancement by the high magistracy) for co-optation. The minor courts of the provinces were suddenly to be exalted to the status of *grands bailliages* and it was these courts which would henceforth deal with the vast majority of criminal and civil cases. The Parlements would be restricted to cases concerning the nobility and civil actions over twenty thousand livres. They would, in effect, be reduced to an intra-elite arbitration bureau. They were also to be stripped of their political power to register edicts before they became enforceable. This power would belong instead to one central "plenary court" appointed by the government. With this drastically reduced volume of business, many of the offices currently required by the Parlement ceased to serve any purpose and would be eliminated. And the deliberately antiaristocratic bias of the reforms was further emphasized by abolishing the "seigneurial courts" through which the nobility administered personal justice to their peasant dependents.

Together with its new provisions concerning prisons and procedure in capital sentences, Lamoignon's revolutionary program was intended to create "enlightened justice": swift, impartial, accessible to the majority of Frenchmen and free from the clutches of the venal aristocracy. In keeping with many other reforms of the period, it was a direct *attack* on corporate institutions and the most dramatic example of the *ancien régime* slain by its own government. It was for this reason that many members of the liberal intellectual elite, like the Marquis de Condorcet, found it hard to deny the value of the reforms. In a similar spirit Lally-Tollendal believed that the "plenary court" would be more likely than the Parlement to produce a "Magna Carta" for France.

Any rational appraisal of the reforms was, however, drowned out by the howl of rage against the way they were introduced. They also had geopolitical implications that provoked more opposition than assent. The demotion of the old Parlementaire centers meant the loss of their monopoly over justice to neighboring towns of the province, and stirred up a hornet's nest of local jealousies. In Brittany, for example, Rennes would see its privileges devolved to rival centers like Nantes and Quimper. Throughout France there were countless small-town competitions to be new administrative and legal centers—organized by precisely the professional classes who stood to gain from the transfer of authority. And these battles of provincial clerks continued with a vengeance—sometimes literally—throughout the Revolution.

In the pamphlet campaign against Lamoignon, he was commonly said to have been possessed by the spirit of Chancellor Maupeou, who had engineered the last assault on the Parlements. The more extreme of these polemics featured Brienne and Lamoignon in compact with an even more formidable power of darkness—the Devil—to destroy the liberties of France. In the *Dialogue Between M. the Archbishop . . . and M. the Keeper of the Seals,* Brienne confesses that the *grands bailliages* were meant to deceive the people into believing that justice would remain. But once the Parlements had gone, he would "deprive them [the new courts] of the slightest breath of life."

> LAMOIGNON: But justice will be very badly dispensed.
> BRIENNE: What does that matter . . . ? And if someone screams, the cries of individuals don't concern me at all. We have only to fear the Remonstrances of the Parlements . . . but soon (a delicious prospect) the Sovereign Courts will neither be able to write nor to speak. My genius will be able to proceed without finding my steps dogged by inconvenient nay-sayers. . . .

The sheer volume and audacity of the antigovernment polemics guaranteed that whatever concessions to the "public good" were embodied in Lamoignon's reforms, they would be preempted by their political repercussions. And the government could hardly have been confident about their reception since it determined to enact the program with swift and overwhelming force. On May 6, d'Eprémesnil and Goislard, the two leaders of the resistance in Paris, were arrested. Two days later Lamoignon himself braved the sullen but implacable hostility of the Parlement to enforce the edicts in a *lit de justice.* Throughout France, this scenario of military determination was repeated at the twelve other centers of the sovereign courts,

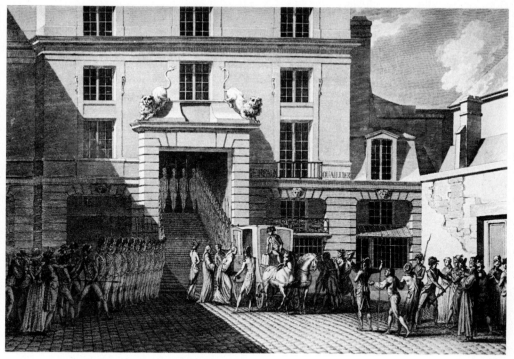

75. Niquet, engraving, the arrest of d'Eprémesnil and Goislard, May 6, 1788

where troops had been posted to persuade the magistrates to depart peacefully on their obligatory "vacation."

None of this worked. Neither the official publicity about the salutary effects of the reforms nor the military planning with which they were enacted could allay the immense outpouring of public wrath. It extended from the legal proletariat of sedan-chair carriers, wig makers, scribes and stall holders through the corps of working advocates and barristers all the way up to the high nobility and clergy. And the din was heard from one end of France to the other. What was especially ominous for the government was that resistance to the decrees actually appeared more intense in the provinces than in Paris. In Pau in the Pyrenees, a violent demonstration on June 19 broke open the doors of the Palais de Justice to demand the reinstatement of the Parlement. Unable to summon troops to so remote a province with the necessary speed, the royal governor had no alternative but to let the magistracy remain and calm the situation—openly contravening the orders of the Versailles government. In the Breton city of Rennes, the *intendant,* Bertrand de Moleville, barely escaped being stoned. In early

June, when the Parlementaires were required to leave by *lettres de cachet*, it was the *intendant*, not the magistrates, who beat a hasty retreat. It took an investment of some eight thousand troops in the city before the situation was calmed in July. In Besançon, Metz, Dijon, Toulouse and Rouen there was enough organized protest for the government to order the recalcitrant magistrates into exile. And in Bordeaux, Aix and Douai—as well as in the oddly subdued Paris Parlement—the courts remained in being, but declared the edicts to be the work of unrestrained despotism.

It seemed as though the Parlements had indeed become what they had always pretended to be: the tribunes of the people. Yet at the very moment of their triumph, they hesitated to enjoy it. The rowdy physicality of the popular support they had invited took many of the magistrates by surprise. And the surprise was not always agreeable. Impromptu invasions of the Palais de Justice or of the local town hall and the willingness of crowds in the street to confront troops opened up questions of public order, which, as the accustomed guardians of the civil peace, made the magistrates apprehensive. The Parlement of Pau, which had seen some of the most violent manifestations, duly protested against the May edicts but went on to justify its protest on the grounds that they had led to incessant tumult and the destruction of property against which, it was now apparent, "the regular police is impotent."

To those sensitive to such things, there were even more worrying signs that the crisis was rapidly ceasing to be a civil war among the elite. In Rennes, the British Ambassador was told, alarming auguries of the fall of the monarchy were circulating among the common people. On the equestrian statue of Louis XVI, it was said, the scepter held in his hand had begun to droop, perhaps by as much as six inches over a few months. By early July there was even worse news. A witness was putting it about that one hot midsummer night he had personally, definitely, seen the stone horse on which the King was seated sweat fat, viscous drops of blood.

iv THE DAY OF TILES

In Grenoble the sight of blood was not imaginary. On a day of riot, June 7, the five-year-old Henri Beyle (later to be known as Stendhal) watched from his parents' apartment as a wounded journeyman hatter, his arms about the shoulders of two mates, was dragged to safety. Stendhal claims to have always been fascinated by blood. His very first memory was of biting the cheek of a Mme Pison de Gallon, who had demanded to be kissed by the toothy infant in a field of marguerites. Two years later he pressed his face against the window to see blood issuing from a hole in the small of the hatter's back where it had received a bayonet thrust from a royal trooper. He continued to observe as the man's shirt and buff trousers stained more deeply crimson. Slowly and painfully, the hatter was taken into the house of a neighbor, a wealthy and liberal merchant named Périer. Suddenly realizing what their son was watching, his parents shook him away from the window and scolded him as though he were eavesdropping. Undeterred, Henri managed a little later to return to his observation post and saw the body dragged six flights up, framed in the broad rectangular windows of the house opposite. On the sixth landing, not surprisingly, the man expired. It was, wrote Stendhal in his autobiographical fragment *The Life of Henri Brulard*, "the first blood shed for the Revolution." That evening, his father, Cherubin Beyle, recited the story of the death of Pyrrhus to his family.

On the face of it, Grenoble was an unlikely place to be the "cradle of the Revolution," as it subsequently liked to call itself. Stendhal—who confused an intense hatred of his father with a hatred of his native town—did not remember it with any warmth. "Grenoble is for me," he later wrote, "like the recollection of a frightful attack of indigestion, not dangerous but horribly nauseating." This dyspepsia was brought on by what he characterized as the town's stifling provincial small-mindedness. But while Grenoble was no Bordeaux with swarming docks and money that was quickly come by and even more quickly spent, neither was it quite the stagnant pond of Stendhal's memory. The city had produced more than its share of Enlightenment *philosophes*, like the Abbé Mably and Condillac. And its spectacular site on the river Isère at the foot of the Savoyard Alps had put it on the pilgrims' route to Rousseau. Jean-Jacques had himself stayed there in 1768 while virtuously botanizing in the mountains. A year later Grenoble could boast its own *Almanach des Muses* modeled on the successful literary journal of the same name that first appeared in Paris in 1765. A little later *Les Affiches de Grenoble* appeared, a weekly newspaper selling for three sous and inviting "any citizen interested in taking part in observations on important matters" to submit articles for publication. In this same small but lively milieu, Stendhal's maternal grandfather, Dr. Gagnon, had established both a flourishing public library and a new Central School for promising students. Gagnon's published interests, which ranged from studies on urine retention to a history of volcanoes in the Auvergne, were typical of the encyclopedically minded and politically alert elite of the town. By the time that Antoine Barnave published his withering polemic against the Lamoignon reforms, *L'Esprit des Edits*, he could be assured of an attentive and indignant readership.

In many respects it was Grenoble's ordinariness that made it ripe for the first great urban insurrection of the Revolution. As the seat of the Parlement of Dauphiné it had the usual concentration of literate, poorly paid and easily excitable lawyers, pamphleteers, teachers and hack writers. Any threat to the sovereign court was a direct challenge to both their livelihood and their sense of prestige. But Grenoble was also a center of regional industry with four and a half thousand skilled artisans producing fine gloves that were exported throughout the country and as far away as Philadelphia and Moscow. Together with the hemp combers, who made up another important group in the work force, the artisans had gradually been pushed from the old center of the town to the rue Saint-Laurent on the opposite bank of the Isère and to the faubourg Très Cloître to the southeast. While years of prosperity had increased employment opportunities, the sudden disruption of the upward trade cycle in 1788, combined with abruptly steeper bread prices, had made these workers both angry and hungry. They were competing for supplementary jobs with a sizable community of regional immigrants from the surrounding regions of the Gévaudan and the Savoy who had settled in Grenoble as market porters, domestic servants and coachmen.

Given these tensions it was imprudent of the government to make its move on a market day: Saturday, June 7. The magistrates of the Parlement had taken to meeting at the house of their First President, Albert de Bérulle, and on May 20 had followed the lead of their colleagues in Paris and other provinces in declaring the enforcement of the May edicts illegal. Ten days later Brienne instructed the lieutenant-général of the Dauphiné, the Duc de Clermont-Tonnerre, to exile the magistrates from Grenoble and on the seventh the *lettres de cachet* were duly served. Two regiments of soldiers—the Marine-la-Royale and the Austrasie—were on hand to convince the Parlementaires to go quietly. And they might well have done so had it not been for the decisive intervention of the crowd. Typically, it was the *basoche* of the courts that began the day's action by haranguing people in the markets and distributing pamphlets and posters violently attacking Brienne and Lamoignon. The protest moved from speeches, shouted insults and songs to a strike. At around ten in the morning the stalls and shops all shut, and glove makers and hemp combers walked out of their workshops and poured into the center of the town, heading for the Palais de Justice and de Bérulle's house on the rue Voltaire. Their aim was to prevent the departure of the magistrates, by force if necessary, and they got as far as unbridling the coach horses that had been arranged for the President and taking them out of the courtyard. A second group shut the city gates to prevent reinforcements and a third organized itself to besiege the governor's own house.

At this point, Clermont-Tonnerre, as commander of the garrison, was faced with an unenviable decision. It was one that every officer, placed in a similar predicament, throughout the French Revolution—and through countless revolutions to come—would confront. Should he turn his soldiers into the streets to contain, deter or subdue the crowd? If so, should they be fully armed? If so, under what conditions might they fire? Which of these scenarios, if not all of them, might not risk making the situation worse, rather than better? And like many such officers placed in this quandary, he made a half-hearted response, only to find the decision taken out of his hands by the spontaneous brutality of events.

Soldiers were sent to the scenes of the riots in relatively small detachments, armed but with orders not to open fire. Their presence was just enough to enrage the crowds further but not concentrated enough to cow them. Many of the Grenoblois took to the roofs of their houses and began pelting the unprotected soldiers with tiles until a rain of them was clattering onto the cobbles below. As the troops began to take serious hits,

76. The Day of Tiles: Grenoble, June 10, 1788

the two regiments reacted differently. The soldiers of the Austrasie obeyed Lieutenant-Colonel Boissieux, who forbade them to shoot, even when he himself was struck directly in the face by a tile. The Marine-la-Royale was less stoical. At the place Grenette, directly in front of Stendhal's house, a small platoon from that regiment, goaded beyond endurance, opened fire and hit a twelve-year-old boy who later died of the blood lost from a shattered thigh. It was here too that the hatter was fatally struck. Blood-soaked clothes from the victims were paraded around the streets, and the tocsin bells were sounded from the cathedral, bringing in from the country-side more peasants, who had heard that their friends and family in Grenoble for the market were now under military attack.

By midafternoon, Clermont-Tonnerre and the *intendant* Caze de La Bove were desperately looking for some solution short of either bloody repression or capitulation. They made it known to the Parlementaires that they would withdraw troops from the streets in return for the magistrates' immediate departure. By this time the magistrates were probably eager to comply, but the decision had been preempted by the fury of the crowds. With no stomach for a slaughter, Clermont-Tonnerre evacuated his *hôtel* and the jubilant crowds took over the city. The governor's house was pillaged, beginning with his wine cellars and ending with his natural his-tory cabinet, from which a stuffed eagle was extracted as a trophy of the victory. Furniture was thrown into the streets and burned and mirrors smashed. Albert de Bérulle and his colleague-presidents of the court were hoisted onto the shoulders of a cheering throng and garlanded with the flowers of June. Thirty-two years old, handsome and rather vain, de Bérulle had courted this celebrity but now that he had it, he was not sure that he cared for it. Made to don their red robes trimmed with ermine and marched, ostensibly in triumph, to the Palais de Justice, where the windows were illuminated and a special session demanded by the crowds, the magistrates must have been uncertain as to who were the leaders and who the led. It was a moment of uncomfortable truth that was to recur over and over again in the years that followed.

Eventually, the wine was emptied to the lees; the last of the fireworks on the place Saint-André had fallen back to earth and the shouting against the Devil's twins, Brienne and Lamoignon, had died away. The senior Parlementaires, who had been more alarmed than elated by their victory, made haste to remove themselves from town before any further mayhem occurred. But the hardier and younger spirits among them—like the *juge royal* Jean-Joseph Mounier, and Antoine Barnave—saw the disorders and the naked helplessness of royal authority as an occasion to capitalize on its breakdown.

77. Anonymous, portrait of
Jean-Joseph Mounier

The Day of Tiles was, then, a threefold revolution. It signified the breakdown of royal authority and the helplessness of military force in the face of sustained urban disorder. It warned the elite beneficiaries of that disorder that there was an unpredictable price to be paid for their encouragement of riot and one that might very easily be turned against themselves. And most important of all, it delivered the initiative for further political action into the hands of a younger, more radical group who had no qualms at all about apostrophizing the People.

A week later, Mounier began to orchestrate opinion more systematically. His was the central organizing hand that turned the incoherent riot into a major political initiative. Not yet thirty, Mounier, the son of a draper, like so many others of the generation of 1789 was a product not of bourgeois frustration with the old regime, but of its effortless escalator to social promotion. He studied law at the local college, where his classmates nicknamed the somber, self-important young man Cato. Established as a barrister, in 1782 Mounier married the daughter of a well-placed *procureur du roi*. The following year, at twenty-five, Mounier became a noble, having bought the office of *juge royale* for twenty-three thousand livres. In other words, there was absolutely nothing in his social profile that would point him towards revolution except, that is, his own ardent belief in the rejuvenation of France as a nation of citizens loyal to a king who would honor their representation. And it may have been Stendhal's grandfather, Dr.

Gagnon, who set him on that course. For it was the ubiquitous small-town academician who lent the young Mounier the works of politics and philosophy in his library that began his intellectual formation. Twenty years later, in exile at Weimar, he would sorely try Goethe's patience in dismissing the importance of Immanuel Kant.

His objectives in the summer of 1788 went well beyond the conventionally conservative goal of restoring the Parlements. On June 14, in defiance of a ban by Clermont-Tonnerre, he organized a meeting at the Hôtel de Ville with over a hundred representatives of all three orders: clergy, nobility and the Third Estate. The last group was the most numerous and included, besides the three aldermen-"consuls" of Grenoble, Dr. Gagnon, Mounier's own father and a number of lawyers, notaries and physicians (as well as a few merchants): the typical personnel of the political Third Estate. The meeting addressed an appeal directly to the King to restore the Parlement and withdraw the new reforms. It also asked for the convening of the provincial Estates of Dauphiné and specified that there should be "free elections" to that body. In the Estates the numbers of the Third were to be equal to the other two combined, the first formal statement of the principle that was to become crucial to the Estates-General itself (for which the meeting also asked). While there was some hesitation before this principle, Mounier's eloquence swayed the meeting and it was finally adopted in a burst of "fraternal concord." It was this axiom which Barnave later identified as the foundation of a "democratic revolution."

From the Grenoble meeting there were other significant anticipations of what would become standard revolutionary themes. First was the identification of opposing forces as traitors. Those who dared to accept places in the Lamoignon courts, it was declared, should be "held to be traitors to the *patrie*" and dealt with accordingly. Second was the concern that a new political order should pay attention to the material grievances of the people who had empowered it. Nothing terribly radical was being proposed here: a subscription fund to assist unemployed or distressed artisans. But the fact that the tribunes were already mingling social with political issues was in itself a fateful development. Finally the assembly issued a ringing appeal to the towns and villages of the whole region of the Dauphiné to meet at Grenoble to prepare for their new representation.

Between this meeting and the second assembly, which was held not in Grenoble but at the Château de Vizille, which also belonged to the merchant Claude Périer, Grenoble was seized with a great onrush of patriotic emotion. Deputations and petitions were received daily by the councillors at the Hôtel de Ville, some of them from constituents who were being actively politicized for the first time. Schoolboys from the Collège-Royal-

Dauphin de Grenoble, for example, protested that though "we are still of tender years we will one day become citizens" and that required them to show expressions of virtuous solidarity with their elders. An even more extraordinary statement, a communication to the King signed by "the very humble but very intrepid subjects; all the women of your province of Dauphiné," reminded him that throughout the centuries women had always influenced "national sentiment . . . [and] that there is not one of us that does not burn with a patriotic fire, ready for the greatest sacrifices and the greatest efforts. . . ."

> You have tried to make us afraid by the marks of your power;
> by force and the bayonets of soldiers, guns, cannons and shells,
> but we will not retreat one step. We shall oppose them with our
> front of courage armed only with the lightest of clothes and a hel-
> met of gauze. But to our very last sigh, our wills and our hearts will
> demand the return of our magistrates, privileges and the reestab-
> lishment of the conditions which alone can make true laws. . . .

A whole year before the Revolution is usually thought to have started, public utterances like this were already saturated with Rousseau's rhetoric of virtue. Not only were there already citizens, but also citizenesses.

Part of Clermont-Tonnerre's difficulty was that he thought of himself as one of these citizens and was impossibly torn between duty to the King and his tender conscience. He was duly replaced by a much more formidable figure, the octogenarian veteran Maréchal de Vaux. And it was under his baleful gaze that a procession of "deputies" from each of the orders and from towns around the Dauphiné (though still very much dominated by the Grenoblois) set off on foot for Périer's château at Vizille on the twenty-first of July. Soldiers lined the route, but today, unlike the Day of Tiles, they seemed to some of the participants more friendly than ominous. The Maréchal de Vaux, who had seemed so threatening, had proved to be no firmer than his predecessors and faced with the inevitability of the assembly responded, "*Eh bien*, I will close my eyes." Of the 491 representatives at Vizille, there were 50 members of the clergy, no less than 165 from the nobility—a crucial contingent—and 276 from the Third Estate (of whom 187 were Grenoblois). The Comte de Morgues was elected president, and Mounier to the all-important post of secretary.

As at the earlier meeting at the Hôtel de Ville, Mounier had gone to some lengths to prepare the agenda for discussion. Though just a year later he was to protest bitterly against what he thought was the National Assembly's usurpation of royal power, in July 1788 Mounier himself undertook an exercise in political reconstitution. In doing this he was armed with absolutely no legal authority save what he declared to be some sort of mandate from "the laws and the people," a formula sufficiently elastic to apply to any contingency. And even though he could not have conceived of the assembly at Vizille as a rehearsal for the National Assembly, the euphoria generated among the three orders by working harmoniously together and wrapping themselves in the mantle of patriotic rhetoric was indeed a direct foreshadowing of the scene at Versailles one year later.

At Vizille, Mounier reemphasized his departure from traditional Parlementaire rhetoric with its borrowings from Montesquieu and emphasis on historically preserved rights. A little later he would even commit the heresy of rejecting the concept of an "immemorial" or "fundamental" constitution for France that the government was said to have violated. But even at Vizille his objections to its conduct were grounded instead on natural rights and the axiom that governments were founded to protect individual liberties—a completely new and obviously "American" concept in France. "The rights of man," he said "derive from nature alone and are independent of [historical] conventions." In the manifest absence of any constitution, he thought, one had to be created anew and by the Estates-General. At the assembly Mounier sounded the tocsin. "The welfare of the *patrie* is the concern of all when it is endangered . . . an assembly can never be considered illegal when it has no goal other than the safety of the State." His stigmatization of anyone accepting office from Brienne as a "traitor" was reiterated and he defined as a duty for all three orders the united defense of anyone persecuted by the ministry. Moreover, only true representatives of the people—with the Third doubled to equal the other orders—could assent to any kind of taxation.

All of these principles were given formal weight at the assembly. Barnave, who was one of the most lucid observers of events, saw that the importance of the meeting was to shake loose opposition rhetoric from the grip of Parlementaire conservatism. The judicial nobility had created enough of a crisis to thwart government reform but it had lost control of its politics. In the Dauphiné, issues of representation had been pushed to the fore even before the Estates-General had been announced. And the rhetoric of the *patrie* had swept the privileged along in supporting both the doubling of the Third Estate and common debates and votes—the great issues that would abruptly divide the political nation.

Despite the wholly unauthorized nature of the assembly, on the second of August Louis XVI agreed to convene the Estates of Dauphiné at Romans. By stages he was backing away from the firmness insisted on by his own government. Other spontaneously convened meetings, usually dominated by the nobility, had produced deputations sent to Versailles to ask either for the Estates of the province or the nation. One such delegation came from Brittany on July 12. The King refused to see it and as a result a meeting of all the great Breton nobles in Paris was held at the Hôtel d'Espagne. In response, twelve of its leaders were sent to the Bastille and others, including Lafayette (improbably identifying himself as a "Breton" through his mother's side), were summarily stripped of court favors. A second delegation from Rennes was similarly sent to prison. But Louis was not prepared to see this through. Where Louis XV's campaign against the Parlements had ended only with the King's death, his grandson committed the monarchy to suicide. Even in June, his eminently sensible sister, Mme Elisabeth, had noticed that

> The king is backing off. . . . He is always afraid of making
> a mistake. Once the first impulse is passed, he is no longer
> tormented by anything but the fear of having done an injustice
> . . . it seems to me that in government as in education one should
> not say "I will it" until one is sure of being right. But once
> having said it, never slack off from what you have ordered.

In this mood of nervous vacillation—which would last until the very end of his reign—Louis reversed his decision and admitted another Breton delegation, promising them the convening of their Estates. A week later, on August 8, this political swerve became irreversible when he made the announcement the whole nation was awaiting: the Estates-General would be convened at Versailles on May 1, 1789. Until the meeting Lamoignon's plenary court, which was to have been entrusted with the registration of new laws, would be in abeyance. In Grenoble, as throughout France, the proclamation was greeted with euphoria: more fireworks, illuminated windows, songs and torchlight parades expressing devotion to the King, though not to his ministers.

In the face of mounting evidence that their policies were unenforceable, Brienne and Lamoignon attempted to stay in power. Even by July their position was not wholly untenable. Outside of the Parlementaire centers, the new *grands bailliages* regional courts were in fact being established— notably at Lyon and Valence. They may even have been attractive to some elements in the Third Estate who were already beginning to separate themselves from aristocratic domination. Nor did Brienne concede that the calling of the Estates-General was itself the end of his government. He was quite correct to argue that he had always been in favor of the Estates and had differed with his critics only on the (not unimportant) matter of timing.

He took this process of "popularizing" the monarchy further by inviting the nation to make known its "views" on the form which the Estates-General should take. This was an astute attempt to exploit divisions that were already becoming apparent between the nobility and "Patriots" on the manner of representation and, by extension, just what sort of political nation should succeed the now moribund absolute monarchy.

But the monarchy's appeal to the people, used as a stick with which to beat its opponents, was seen—as Calonne's belated resort to public opinion had been seen and as similar appeals of the monarchy would be seen throughout the Revolution—as at best desperate and at worst disingenuous. It did not save Brienne. Indeed, as it became apparent that authority in France was speedily disintegrating, the removal of the Brienne administration began to seem a precondition for any kind of effective government. There was a short-term crisis of order, with the dispersion of available troops to different provincial centers as far away as Rennes and Aix opening up a dangerous vacuum at the center. But what really finished Brienne off was not so much his inability to enforce the May edicts as the sudden death of public credit.

In May, the Assembly of the Clergy, on which the government was depending for a substantial *don gratuit*—the traditional lump sum voted as its fiscal contribution—only came up with a derisory offering. Obviously its recalcitrance was a gesture of political solidarity with the Parlements. Much worse was to follow in August. At the beginning of the month Brienne was told by the chief of the Contrôle, Gojard, that there were just 400,000 livres remaining in the Treasury—or enough money for the government to function for an afternoon. After the initial shock his first reaction was (understandably) to wonder why Gojard had waited until the last extremity to let him know this not unimportant item of news. In retirement he came to what in all probability was the correct conclusion: In league with the growing number anxious to see Brienne off, Gojard had *deliberately* waited until the predicament was so appalling that the Minister could not possibly hope to extricate himself from the mess.

The ploy worked. Desperate measures were all that were left to Brienne if he was to protect military pay—without which what remained of internal order would have immediately collapsed. The immediate crisis was simple enough. The steep decline of government securities had made it virtually impossible for the Farmers-General, as well as the other financial syndicates on which the state relied to meet its medium-term obligations, to raise capital for their advance in the money market. In effect, the collateral against which that money could be lent had depreciated to the point at which it no longer represented a safe investment. Moreover, for the current deficit, the "anticipations" of future revenues had already been mortgaged too far ahead to alter that prudential calculation.

The bet was as much political as financial. Even in an apparently desperate situation, there was nothing about the intrinsic structure of the monarchy's institutions that led prospective lenders to write it off altogether. Rather, they were reminded that in Maupeou's day, repression went hand in hand with defaults (however finessed). The converse was that the Estates-General might prove a better guarantor of their investments than the crown.

It is not quite the whole truth, then, to describe the predicament of the French state in August 1788 as bankruptcy. It was Brienne's government, not France, that was bankrupt, as the speed with which his successor, Necker, raised loans of all kinds amply bore out. (Necker's personal ability to scrounge funds from colleagues on the Bourse and from the Corporations of Paris gave the government enough money to live on until the Valhalla of the Estates-General was finally realized.) But he was the beneficiary of a dramatic change of regime. In his last weeks Brienne had only a thinly disguised forced loan to fall back on for a modicum of fiscal relief. Issued on August 16 it took the form of Treasury bills bearing interest of 5 percent but with no fixed date of maturity. Payments of more than twelve hundred livres would be made, three fifths in cash and two fifths in these bills; those with lesser amounts would receive a slightly higher proportion of cash, and so on.

It was, in effect, an attempt to fob off bondholders with paper money, but it was seen as the financial equivalent of the Dutch crisis. In September 1787 France had abandoned a foreign policy until she could afford one. In August 1788 she was abandoning a financial policy until she could agree on one.

v END GAMES

An old motif in popular culture was the Death of Credit. Prints greeting this macabre dénouement bore images of grinning skeletons bearing worthless notes and empty purses. On August 16, 1788, Credit died in Paris and its demise threw the huge market in government paper into panic. Unlike Franklin Roosevelt's version of the statement in 1933, the royal edict's observation that "nothing is imperiled except through . . . fear" reassured no one. The Caisse d'Escompte was besieged with bondholders demanding redemption and had to close for fear of violence. The run lasted three days and nights before two further government announcements guaranteeing paper had a temporarily calming effect. But only a clean break was likely to restore the modicum of confidence needed to keep the government from disintegrating. In Brienne's council there had been some talk of attempting the impossible—bringing Necker into the ministry—but if France was to be resurrected by representative government, it could hardly do it through the most powerful exponent of absolutism. In any event, listening to the drumbeat of applause already sounding for his return, Necker had no intention of sharing his glory with the discredited Archbishop. On August 25, Brienne resigned. That same night ten thousand people filled the Palais-Royal cheering themselves hoarse and letting off firecrackers in celebration of the news.

In the week that followed, Paris was given over to an immense outpouring of hatred, fired by a steep increase in the price of bread. Straw dummies of Brienne and Lamoignon were burned night after night, and on the Pont Neuf anyone not bowing to that popular totem, the statue of Henri IV, was manhandled. An English eyewitness

walked out in the evening and saw the whole of the place Dauphine in a blaze from the burning of the Archbishop and the illumination of the windows; one huge sea of heads covered the whole Place and thousands and tens of thousands were wrapt in confusion, noise and violence.

On the twenty-ninth a mannequin dressed in Brienne's archepiscopal costume was given a mock trial by a parody of Lamoignon's *grands bailliages* courts and was sentenced to make "honorable amends" in front of the statue of Henri IV before being burned. There were so many of these bonfires that fuel became a problem for the celebrants. The stalls belonging to the women orange sellers of the Pont Neuf were seized, and when they had been burned, the sentry boxes on the bridge were snatched from their occupiers.

This did not please the *gardes françaises* militia or the troops who were gradually being mobilized for riot control. On the night of Brienne's resignation regular soldiers had been used to clear the place Dauphine, and in the days that followed mounted soldiers regularly charged civilians armed with clubs, canes and stones. On the twenty-ninth things got sufficiently out of hand for the officer in command to order a volley of fire in the air before the crowd retreated. Already, then, the ability of the authorities to preserve order in the capital was being seriously tested.

78. Riot in the place Dauphine, August 28, 1788

79. Forced obeisances to the statue of
Henry IV on the Pont Neuf

IN GRENOBLE, the funeral rites for absolutism were enacted with an uncanny literalness. On September 12 the ancient Maréchal de Vaux, who had come to Grenoble boasting that he had "ten thousand bolts to lock up the Palais de Justice," went to his own grave. His body was placed in the *chapelle ardente* of the cathedral in a black tomb surrounded by hundreds of candles. Little Henri Beyle breathed in the acrid fumes and gaped at the sarcophagus. The order of military obedience embodied in the old Marshal was expiring beside his corpse. The drummers assigned to beat the dead march for his cortège were complaining that their black muffling cloths thrown over the drum had been unjustly skimped. By rights, they said, they were entitled to enough to make a pair of trousers, and it was only the meanness of that rich skinflint, the Marshal's daughter, that had robbed them of their due.

Then came another death, much more disturbing. On October 8 the Bishop of Grenoble, Hay de Bonteville, was laid out in the cathedral as befitted a great prelate but with his face covered by a cloth that no one was permitted to lift. The reason was rapidly discovered. The previous evening he had withdrawn into his study in the Château d'Herbeys, burned all his papers, placed three bullets in a pistol, put the gun in his mouth, cocked the trigger and fired. Even while he had been professing support for the Grenoble Patriots, it seemed he had been secretly corresponding with Brienne and Lamoignon, offering support. He was one of the *infâmes* whom Mounier had wanted to excise from the body politic. At a prelimi-nary meeting of the Estates of Dauphiné at Romans, the Bishop, now bereft of his patrons in the government, had, it seemed, uttered some words of imprudence. In a string of letters to Mounier he had implored him (as secretary of the Estates) to erase them from the minutes. But Mounier's sense of correctness was inflexible. He failed to sense (what others saw) that Hay de Bonteville was deeply disturbed. "You drive me to despair," the Bishop wrote, and a few days later acted accordingly. It was the first victory of Revolutionary Virtue over human failing.

The punitive aspects of the Bishop's death did not go unremarked in Grenoble. It was, said local Patriot opinion, a fitting end for a scoundrel and a traitor. Indeed, as the old regime was in the process of doing away with itself, there was a quickening interest in the phenomenon of suicide. Malesherbes had found his own wife's body in the woods. And in the spring of 1789 his cousin Lamoignon, who had endeavored so much and had fallen in the endeavor, was himself discovered shot at his country estate. The likelihood was that this was a hunting accident, and old Malesherbes in his sorrow and anxiety was certainly inclined to accept the official verdict. In the political Nation, however, where Lamoignon had no friends, it was commonly said that he had done away with himself and that, after all, it had been the only decent thing to do.

Brienne's end was no happier. By resigning he had managed to avoid the full weight of odium that had befallen Calonne, but he was hardly a popular figure. During his ministry he had been promoted from the diocese of Toulouse to that of Sens, southeast of Paris. He returned there, attempting to ride out the storm. While, in England, Calonne was to become an active counter-revolutionary, Brienne did his best to abide by patriotic orthodoxy. In 1791, he was one of the few prelates of the old regime to swear the "civic oath" required by the revolutionary civil constitution. In a further gesture of patriotic good faith he even returned his cardinal's hat to Rome. But, inevitably, the Terror caught up with him and he was arrested in his house in February 1794. Kept under watch at home, he found enough privacy to swallow a lethal dose of the opium and stramonium (thorn apple) he used to soothe the torment of his skin disease.

He had, after all, watched the old regime commit suicide.

CHAPTER EIGHT

Grievances

Autumn 1788–Spring 1789

i 1788, NOT 1688

HE MONARCHY collapsed when the price of its financial rescue was measured not in profits or offices but in political concessions. In August 1788 it suffered a hemorrhage of confidence on the part of its creditors and prospective subscribers. Their reluctance to offer new funds against the usual "anticipations" of revenues signified a transfer of faith from a bureaucratic to a representative form of government. The reforms of the Brienne administration had been the last, strenuous effort to produce sufficient changes to shore up sovereignty without altering its basic premises. Its evident failure to prevail over resistance except through sustained military force was fatal. Henceforth, an alternative conviction was in the ascendant: that patriotic freedom would produce money where reforming absolutism had not.

There was nothing necessary or even logical about this connection. Other states at other times, including other French states like the Bonapartist empire, would draw exactly the opposite conclusion and return to the bureaucratic modernism and personnel of the 1780s. And the financiers of the great powers of the nineteenth century, especially the Rothschilds, generally preferred authoritarianism to liberalism as the guarantor of their loans. But there was an important anniversary in 1788: the centenary of the Glorious Revolution, a lodestar of liberal French historical writing since Voltaire and Montesquieu. And in that orderly transfer of power from an absolutist to a constitutional monarchy French commentators saw not merely a consummation of political virtue but the origins of British financial success. As the repository of public trust (and thus public money), the British Parliament, so the argument ran, had been a more solid bulwark than the ministerial agents of the crown. Whether this view was accurate or not hardly matters. What counted was the belief that liberty and solvency were natural partners. (A glance at the financial career of liberated America might have given these optimists some cause for skepticism, but no one, especially Lafayette, was concerned with such matters in 1788.) The day that Necker was appointed in place of Brienne, government funds rose by thirty points. All along, Necker had insisted that public accountability was the key to fiscal viability. So the mere prospect of the Estates-General, inaugurated by the Minister who had recommended it, was enough to produce subscribers for the loans necessary to keep the government of France working and the soldiers of France paid.

The transfer of the financial mandate was not, in the first instance, an act of pure political conviction. Investors in government funds—whether in Paris, Geneva, London or Amsterdam—calculated that a new regime was more likely to honor its obligations than the old one. This was especially true once it had become clear that the monarchy was not going to be allowed to introduce the reforms necessary to give it renewed freedom of action. But those who made such a decision in the salons of the faubourg Saint-Germain were, as social animals, members of the same class as the Parlementaires. Traditionally, even in extreme situations such as the Maupeou crisis of the 1770s, they had defined their interests not in automatic solidarity with the judicial nobility but in service to the crown. From that service they could expect, as Farmers-General or contractors of other loans, a tidy profit, and the perquisites and status of ennobling office. What had happened through the reign of Louis XVI, first under Turgot and Necker and then under Brienne, was that the rationale for that continued loyalty had been seriously strained by reforms. In other words, the monarchy's attempts to secure more direct access to revenue, and to tap the economic growth of France in this period more effectively, needed to have succeeded *completely* if they were to succeed at all. Partial success was the same as complete failure, for it meant running back to *financiers* whose interest in sustaining the monarchy was now moot.

From this point of view, a government instituted by the Estates-General would be a more dependable debtor. Broader consensus would remove the obstacles to new sources of revenue, and those in turn would be a firmer security for more loans. The benefits of liberalism would thus be self-replenishing. But this happy outcome assumed a French version of 1688 (annotated by Montesquieu) in which effective sovereignty would pass smoothly from the absolutist court to an assembly dominated by *les Grands*: the financial and judicial nobility. Concomitant with that momentous change would be some sort of French Bill of Rights, stripping absolutism of its arbitrary judicial powers—*lettres de cachet* and the like—and guaranteeing security of person and property. The freedom to publish and assemble peacefully would also be guaranteed. Ministers who purloined public monies for their own purposes (the Calonne fixation still ran strong) would be accountable to the representatives of the Nation. And that would be that. The crown would still have the indisputable right to appoint ministers, to propose and perhaps to veto legislation. But the legality of its government would henceforth be subject to public scrutiny.

This, then, was the vision of a constitutional reformation in which the grandees of France would have the senior role. It was what d'Eprémesnil and the other legal lions of the Parlement undoubtedly had in mind when they organized the systematic obstruction of the Brienne reforms. What they got instead was a revolution. And the engineers of the fall of the monarchy became not its successors but its first and most spectacular casualties.

How did this happen? The long-hallowed explanation is that, at the last minute, aristocratic expectations of succession were confounded by the sudden appearance of a new political class—the bourgeoisie. Thwarted in their efforts at upward social mobility and the possession of office, this Third Estate seized political leadership to destroy not just the monarchy but the entirety of the old "feudal" regime and installed themselves instead as the lords of the nineteenth century.

The wholly imaginary nature of this explanation hardly needs repeating here. The creation of a political alternative to aristocratic conservatism occurred not outside but inside the elite, and was by no means the invention even of relatively recently ennobled figures like Mounier. The man who first identified the true political Nation with the Third Estate was the arch-aristocratic Comte d'Antraigues. Such politicians ensured that the Estates-General could not be simply brandished in the face of the monarchy *without* the nature of its representation being addressed. It is as if the sponsors of King William III had included a powerful and articulate faction committed to the cause of parliamentary reform.

The effect of this early debate about representation on the cohesiveness of the putative "successor elite" was decisive, which meant that instead of a new political class rallying round their natural leaders (as had indeed been the case in England in 1688 or, for the most part, in America in 1776), deep cleavages opened up. Those on the radical side of that division were not only ready but eager to use popular force and the polarizing language of patriotism and treason to empower their ideology.

What was that ideology? In the first place its radicalism can be measured by what it was not. It repudiated historicity and the sanction of the past.

This itself was a shocking departure from the hallowed language of opposition to absolutism since the reign of Louis XV. It emphasized that a constitution was to be built *anew,* not simply rescued from atrophy. The criteria for this new construction were to be rational and patriotic. These were dangerously loose terms, and before very long differences among revolutionaries would make those priorities not so much complementary as opposed. "Rationalists"—exponents of modernity, of a popular monarchy, of a liberal economic and legal order—like Barnave, Talleyrand, the Marquis de Condorcet and the astronomer Sylvain Bailly were all products of the late Enlightenment. Believers in liberty, progress, science, capitalized property and just administration, they were heirs to the reforming ethos of Louis XVI's reign—and authentic predictors of the "new notability" to emerge after the Revolution had run its course. Their language was reasonable and their tempers cool. What they had in mind was a Nation vested, through its representatives, with the power to strip away the obstructions to modernity. Such a state (in all likelihood, a monarchy) would not wage war on the France of the 1780s but consummate its promise.

Rationality, however, did not have a monopoly of utterance in 1788 and 1789. The kind of eloquence needed to mobilize popular anger to the point at which it could be used as a lever of power was not cool but hot. And the stokers of revolutionary heat were not prepared to allow it to cool off for the benefit of moderate constitutional change. They were guided neither by rationality nor by modernity but by passion and virtue. For them the Enlightenment, like much of modern France, was at best a mixed blessing. "We have acquired enlightenment," wrote the lawyer Target,

> but it is patriotism, disinterestedness and virtue that are needed to seek and defend the interests of a great people. Each man must forget himself and see himself only as part of the whole of which he is a member, detach himself from his individual existence, renounce all *esprit de corps,* belong only to the great society and be a child of the fatherland [*un enfant de la patrie*].

A society that could be measured, informed, administered, capitalized and individualized was less important than one that would be simplified, moralized and made more innocent. The keystone of its government should not be rationality but justice, and for the arch of culture they proposed to substitute the dwelling of nature. This *patrie* would be a community of citizens, tender to its children and pitiless to its foes. A society of friends, it would, like Rousseau, its moral originator, be beset by enemies—some of the worst of them dressed up in the appearance of amity. One of the noblest tasks for a citizen would be to unmask those dangerous insincerities. From the beginning, then, revolutionary rhetoric was tuned to a taut pitch of elation and anger. Its tone was visceral rather than cerebral; idealistic rather than realistic; most powerful when it was dividing Frenchmen into Patriots and traitors, most stirring when it was most punitive.

The prospect of satisfaction—in the eighteenth-century sense of redress—was what pulled ordinary Frenchmen into politics for the first time. And it was their participation that turned a political crisis into a full-blooded revolution. Protecting the poor and punishing traitors were, after all, the tasks that the monarchy was traditionally supposed to perform. But as the handmaid of modernity, its government seemed to have abdicated that protective role. For example, instead of ensuring grain supplies at a just price, it had—most recently in 1787—committed itself to the modern principle of free trade. The result for many seemed catastrophically high prices and opportunities for speculative hoarding that went unpunished. In the name of some sort of incomprehensible principle it had done other unconscionable things that gave comfort to the very enemies it was supposed to pursue. Protestants had been emancipated who could now lord it over decent, poor Catholics in the south and southeast. British textiles had been let into France, robbing Norman and Flemish spinners and weavers of work. All this must have been the product of some sort of conspiracy against the People.

With considerable rhetorical skill, these grievances were fed into a great furnace of anger by the radical politicians of 1789. And from the other end issued a language of accusation, which was also a means of classifying enemies and friends, traitors and Patriots, aristocrats and the Nation. Surprisingly, it mattered little that those same politicians *endorsed* many of the reforms which so affronted the common people—freedom for internal trade and religious emancipation, for example. These contradictions were (for the time being) masked by the conviction that an assembly of the Nation would be the tribunal in which those grievances would be satisfied and those responsible for them, judged. Consequently, all those who declared themselves against such an assembly were, by definition, unpatriotic, and all those who advocated it, identified as the People's friends. The fact that the King himself had asked his people to submit their grievances at the same time they elected representatives to the Estates-General only reinforced these primitive convictions. For it appeared to be an invitation to assist him in distinguishing the false Patriots from the true.

The opportunity for constitutional reform was lost when the preservation of social distinctions—the orders of the old regime—became stigmatized as unpatriotic. (Virtually the opposite was true in Britain.) Worse still, those distinctions became identified with the causes of popular suffering. Once *aristocrat* became synonymous with *antinational,* it meant that anyone who wished to preserve distinctions of rank in the political bodies of the new order identified himself as incapable of citizenship. Such people were, in effect, outside the Nation, foreigners even before they had emigrated.

The possibility of reorganizing allegiances in this way turned on four matters, all of which, at this crucial juncture, pushed France away from evolution and towards revolution.

First, there had to be an aggressively dissenting group *within* the aristocratic and ecclesiastical elite determined to abandon their own status for the preferred role of citizen-leaders. Who could better distinguish amongst themselves the altruistic from the selfish, the patriotic from the treasonable? And by the same token that same group had to be prepared to provoke, mobilize and direct popular violence in the prosecution and punishment of uncitizens.

Secondly, those who defended a polity based on separate orders were without equivalent power to preserve their position. To dislodge royal absolutism, crowds had been brought onto the streets. But once there it was evident that they would not meekly return to passive obedience, especially when orators and pamphlets were urging them on to further action. Throughout the second half of 1788 and the spring of 1789 the Parlements attempted to act once more as the upholders of public order and to rely on royal troops for their police—an embarrassing predicament given their recent past.

Thirdly, the government made its position still more uncomfortable by leaving open the vital issue of the composition of the Estates-General. Brienne, of course, had fully intended this in July when he issued a general request for "advice" on the form the assembly should take. Meaning to exploit divisions he correctly detected amongst the magistracy, he made it possible for those advocating a truly "national" representation to claim that they, rather than the conservatives, reflected the true wish of the King.

Finally, the King's expressed wish that his people register their grievances at the same time they elected their representatives connected social distress with political change. That had not happened in Britain in 1688 nor for that matter in America in 1776, and it would prove the crucial difference. In this sense, at least, while social *structure* did not cause the French Revolution, social *issues* did.

Reflecting on the nature of patriotic rhetoric since Rousseau, one can see that this was bound to happen. For its sentimental panaceas were perfectly attuned to the resolution of social unhappinesses of all kinds: of the peasant trapped by usurious creditors; of soldiers ill-paid by martinet officers who had bought their commissions; of weavers put out of work by market forces they did not understand; of flower-seller guild-sisters unable to compete with itinerant hawkers; of impoverished curates who were confronted by the immense opulence of an aristocratic prelacy. Once all these people, and more, were told that a true national assembly would, by virtue of its higher moral quality—its common patriotism—provide satisfaction, they were given a direct stake in sweeping institutional change. This was exactly what happened in late 1788 and early 1789. The bringing together of political patriotism with social unrest—anger with hunger—was (to borrow the revolutionaries' favorite electrical metaphor) like the meeting of two live wires. At their touch a brilliant incandescence of light and heat occurred. Just what and who would be consumed in the illumination was hard to make out.

ii THE GREAT DIVIDE
August–December 1788

There was one more Indian summer left to Versailles. On August 10, 1788, the last great formal audience was held, for the ambassadors of the Sultan of Mysore, Tipu Sahib. A continent away in his palace at Seringapatam, faith in the imperial power of the French monarchy was undimmed. The fleur-de-lis still flew from naval bases in the Indian Ocean and the genius of French mechanics had produced a clockwork tiger for the Sultan, which when wound would proceed to devour a British grenadier in its mouth. Would not France help the Tiger of the Carnatic to rid India of the curse of British imperialism?

This was not a high priority for Brienne. The King gave the ambassadors polite reassurances of an even less substantial kind than had been given to the Dutch, and fitted them out with a carriage drawn by six white horses. At the Opéra, where they were given the best seats, Mme de La Tour du Pin admired their yellow slippers planted, orientally, on the edge of their box. Since they were almost on stage it was sometimes hard to tell where fantasy ended and reality began.

No such problem afflicted Malesherbes. An evening in the same summer found him, together with Lafayette, drinking in a *guinguette* just outside the customs walls that now girded Paris. These countrified taverns where tables and benches were set in the open air pleased Malesherbes. The famous watering holes at La Courtille and Les Porcherons were too crowded in the

80. The Indian ambassadors' carriage

warm months. But that still left a good number from the list proposed by Thiéry's *Guide*—La Nouvelle-France, La Petite Pologne, Le Gros-Caillou and Le Grand et Le Petit Gentilly—all to his taste and within easy distance of his daughter's house, where, these days, he liked to dine.

On this particular evening he had brought Lafayette along to help entertain two foreign visitors, a young Englishman, Samuel Romilly, and a Genevan, Etienne Dumont. Arriving from the Dover packet, they had reached Versailles in time to catch a glimpse of Tipu's turbaned ambassadors gliding through the state rooms. Romilly was a precocious young lawyer, the product of the network of "advanced" ideas that spread from the Scottish universities through the Dissenting academies and the Birmingham Lunar Society. His head was full of projects, and he had duly been taken up by the liberal wing of the Whigs that met at Lord Shelburne's mansion at Bowood. So Shelburne's many friends in France, including the Abbé Morellet and Malesherbes himself, became Romilly's and they talked together of "American" ideas of patriotism and liberty, linked together in comradely unity across the Channel.

Romilly was much taken with the "warmth and simplicity" he discovered in Malesherbes. His obvious pleasure in the joys of family life recommended him further. Romping with his grandchildren, the old man would toss his wig to the far side of the drawing room and lie on the rug so that small hands and feet could clamber merrily over his paunch. Informality towards adults and children alike was the coming thing in progressive Whig circles and would be celebrated in the family paintings of their most brilliant society artist, Thomas Lawrence. But it was often combined with a self-conscious modishness that jarred Romilly's earnest Huguenot temper. Dumont was cut from similar cloth: an exiled pastor from the democratic revolution in Geneva that had been squashed by Vergennes in 1782. As the champion of Protestant emancipation in 1787, Malesherbes was already much admired, and when he took them on his usual tour-for-reformers to the prisons of Bicêtre and Salpêtrière, they were even more struck by his seriousness of purpose. There were still other links which drew together the young and the old in a humanitarian league. Friend to the evangelical leader of the campaign against the slave trade, William Wilberforce, Romilly was already engaged in the antislavery movement to which much of his life would be dedicated, and his Paris friends were similarly involved in the Société des Amis des Noirs.

To his young admirers Malesherbes could plausibly appear as a "man of the people," for all his aristocratic rank and government service. With his bluff manner, shiny coat and snuff-bespattered cuffs he upstaged Lafayette and even Mirabeau in this guise. And in the tavern he planned a little joke turning on the discrepancy between nondescript appearance and democratic celebrity. "Have you by any chance heard of the Marquis de La-fayette?" he asked the innkeeper. The expected answer was "Of course, Monsieur, like all the world"—at which point he could reveal the identity of his redheaded drinking companion. But to still more merriment (except Lafayette's) the response was "Why no, Monsieur, I can't say I have. Pray, who is he?"

The relationship between leaders and led, tribunes and the People they so freely apostrophized, would be one of the great issues of the Revolution. But in the summer and autumn of 1788 it seemed unproblematic, at least to the circle in which Romilly and Dumont moved. Though Malesherbes' spirits had been dashed by seeing history repeat itself and well-intentioned reforms wrecked by absolutist politics, the prospect of the Estates-General had filled him with renewed zest and optimism. Moreover, he was one of the earliest spokesmen for a true "national assembly" that would have no qualms about departing radically from the old, prescribed form of 1614. In that version the Estates met, deliberated and voted in separate orders. The proceedings in the Dauphiné had already breached that precedent, and Mounier and his colleagues had determined that when their provincial Estates met it should be as a single body, voting as individual representatives. In July, before the decision to summon the Estates-General had been taken, Malesherbes had written to the King in characteristically blunt terms recommending a similarly courageous departure—one that would, he believed, lay the foundation for a truly popular monarchy.

What is this Estates-General that is being recommended to you? . . . It is a vestige of ancient barbarism, a battlefield where three factions of the same people come to fight each other; it is a collision of all interests with the general interest . . . a means of subversion, not a means of renovation. Take this old structure for what it is, a ruin. We are attached to it only by memory. Seize the popular imagination with an institution that will surprise and please them. . . . Let a King at the end of the eighteenth century not convoke the three orders of the fourteenth century; let him instead call together the proprietors of a great nation renewed by its civilization. A King who submits to a constitution feels degraded; a King who proposes a constitution obtains instead the highest glory among men and their liveliest and most enduring gratitude. . . .

It was this dramatic abandonment of historical precedent that marked the first great turning point of the Revolution. On September 25, two days after it was reinstated to general acclaim, the Parlement of Paris announced that the Estates-General should be convened exactly according to the forms of 1614. Overnight it forfeited all the immense popularity it had gained during the confrontation with Lamoignon. From being a hero of the crowds, d'Eprémesnil was spoken of with jeering contempt. Events in the Dauphiné, much publicized in Paris, had preempted this attempt to draw the line at a traditional Estates-General.

Moreover, the apparatus of legal repression had been largely dismantled in the summer at the specific behest of the Parlement's orators. Censorship, the Parlement's traditional weapon, was removed, permitting a torrent of political literature to come flooding onto the streets. By September, pamphlets were appearing at the rate of something like ten a day. Second, an articulate minority within the Parlement led by Adrien Duport, Hugues de Sémonville and Guy-Jean Target were themselves insisting on a new kind of Estates-General in which the Third Estate would have numbers at least equal to the other two and in which votes would be taken "by head" or individually, so that any attempt to obstruct popular decisions would be defeated by numbers. What was being proposed was, in effect, a new form of representation—not by corporate bodies but by citizenship. Any group wanting to isolate itself from that general body of citizens and demanding particular or disproportionate representation instantly isolated itself as somehow "outside the Nation."

Paradoxically, then, the "Third Estate" was an invention of the citizen-nobility. In November, a group calling itself first the Society of Thirty and later the Constitutional Club gathered at Duport's house twice a week, often for four hours or more, to debate the nature of the coming representation. It was not an exclusively radical group. D'Eprémesnil was among the group, as was a fellow "constitutionalist" from the Parlement, Sabatier de Cabre. They did their best to argue for the preservation of a separate noble order as a bulwark against the corrupting power of monied property that they claimed would overwhelm a general representation. The majority of Duport's club, however, were adamant that the Third Estate should have a representation at least equal to the other two combined and that the assembly should then deliberate and vote in common.

A striking number of the Society were men whose reputations had been made as "public men" and patriotic celebrities. Their self-image already presupposed a sympathetic rapport between leaders and citizens. The Parlementaire Target, for example, who broke most decisively with his conservative colleagues, was already the god of the *basoche*, huzzahed from the galleries. His first great trial oration had been a sentimental epic worthy of the most mawkish invention of Rousseau. It had involved the rights of the villagers of Salency in Picardy to choose their own annual "Rose Queen"— the *rosière*. The ritual had been adopted by the *bien-pensant* nobility as a bucolic idyll and Orléans' mistress Mme de Genlis had gone to Salency to play the harp at the crowning of the *rosière*. When the local *seigneur* had claimed that the right to select the *rosière* belonged to him, not the village elders, and had taken the case all the way to the Parlement of Paris, Target had represented it in court as a classic trial of strength between innocence and force. In 1788 he rehearsed many of the same themes, amplified to the scale of national politics.

Lafayette, his kinsman de Noailles, the Duc de La Rochefoucauld-Liancourt, the Duc de Luynes and the Duc de Lauzun were likewise citizens whose rhetoric was all the more influential because they hailed from the summit of the peerage. For many of them, moreover, this was merely the second stage of a crusade that had begun in America. They were courtiers against the court, aristocrats against privilege, officers who wanted to replace dynastic with national patriotism. Though he was committed to a national assembly, Lafayette was not without some anxieties about the consequences of popular politics. And in an attempt to bring him closer to their line the Parlement made the "Hero of the Two Worlds" an honorary councillor. This worried his fellow member of the Thirty, Condorcet, who knew Lafayette's weakness for adulation. To the American Philip Mazzei he wrote:

> If you go to Lafayette's house, try to exorcise the devil of
> aristocracy that will be there to tempt him in the guise of a
> councilor of Parlement or a Breton noble. For that purpose take

along in your pocket a little vial of Potomac water, and a sprinkler made from the wood of a Continental army rifle and make your prayers in the name of Liberty, Equality and Reason, which are but a single divinity in three persons.

Others among Duport's group included Talleyrand, already observing Lafayette with a leery eye; Mirabeau, whose boiling polemical radicalism was at this time compromised by scandals of every kind, sexual, monetary and diplomatic, collapsing about his ears; Genevan bankers like Clavière and Panchaud, both ex-allies of Calonne's and now reverting to their democratic principles of 1782; the Abbés Morellet and Sieyès; the Provençal pastor Rabaut Saint-Etienne and not least Louis-Sébastien Mercier, the prophet of the apocalypse. The "conspiracy of well-intentioned men," as they designated themselves, also included a number of those who had provided the brains for Calonne's reform program, among them Du Pont de Nemours and the Abbé Louis.

While they disagreed on many details, the majority of the Club all subscribed to some basic principles that marked a dramatic break with Parlementaire argument. They rejected outright the axiom that there had, all along, been some sort of "fundamental constitution" that the Parlements had been concerned to conserve. The only true "fundamental law," added Rabaut Saint-Etienne, was *salus populi lex est* (the welfare of the people is the supreme law). The mere fact, added Target, that antiquarians had to go rummaging around in the history of Charlemagne and the Carolingians was proof enough that France had no constitution and it was now necessary to create one from scratch.

Beyond Paris, there were provincial storm centers where urban champions of the Third Estate, following Mounier's example in the Dauphiné, were embattled with more conservative nobles over the structure of their provincial Estates—and by extension over national representation. The fiercest such combat took place in Brittany, where a young generation of lawyers in towns like Nantes and Rennes (schooled in street tactics by the battles for the Parlement) now used oratory and crowd pressure to press for a radical redefinition of representation. Arthur Young, the English agricultural writer who visited Nantes in September, found it "as *enflammé* in the cause of liberty as any town in France can be" and listened to conversations that "prove how great a change is effected in the midst of the French." The polemics issuing from the reading clubs and political committees that mushroomed in the Breton towns in 1788 made a point of ridiculing the sanction of antiquity, especially dear to the province's nobility. "What does it matter to us," wrote the lawyer Volney in his journal

The Sentinel of the People, "what our fathers have done or how and why they have done it . . . ? The essential rights of man, his natural relations to his fellows in the state of society—these are the eternal bases of every form of government." The *Patriotic Reflections* of the Rennes law professor Jean Lanjuinais were harsher in their parody of conservative obstruction:

> Negro slaves—you are reduced to the condition of brutes—but no innovations! Children of Asiatic kings—the custom is that the eldest of you strangle his brothers—but no innovations! People of Brittany you are badly off and the nobility is well off—but no innovations!

What is required, insisted Lanjuinais, is a constitution for the present, not the veneration of relics. "Would the garment of 1614 fit us any better than the garment of a child fits a man in the prime of life?" Likewise, the term *privilege*, which had been synonymous with *liberties* in the contest between crown and Parlements, was now deemed to be its antithesis. Political probity now required not that privileges be protected but obliterated.

Throughout much of France (and in some cases even in obstreperous Brittany) the nobility were ready to concede at least part of these demands made by their own radicals as well as bona fide spokesmen of the Third. As would be shown by the *cahiers*—statements of local complaints and expectations—a majority of the privileged class was prepared to abandon the most conspicuous feature of its status: exemption from taxation. So much of this exemption had been eroded that it was hardly a grand sacrifice, especially for the better-off nobles, who flourished it as a concession. But the command that they melt their order entirely into some more general union of the Nation was much more divisive, both between and within provinces. The repeated claim, that separate orders should persist simply because they had survived so long, increasingly fell on deaf ears.

At the end of 1788, then, the sanction of the past lost its power to persuade. The Parlementaire lawyer Pierre Lacretelle went so far as to regret that all monuments and ancient usages had not been consumed in a great fire (something the Revolution would symbolically enact in 1793). Instead, Condorcet and like-minded members of the Duport group argued, reason should guide the framers of a new constitution. "True principles, rationally determined," the Comte d'Antraigues agreed, would show that political liberty and civil equality before the law were the proper bases of such a new order. But d'Antraigues, a friend of Jean-Jacques Rousseau's, went on to make the much more radical case (typical of the citizen-nobility) that the state and the People were one and the same:

> The Third Estate is the People and the People is the
> foundation of the State; it is in fact the State itself; the other
> orders are merely political categories while by the *immutable laws
> of nature* the People is everything. Everything should be sub-
> ordinated to it [the People]; its safety should be the first law of the
> State. . . . It is in the People that all national power resides and it
> is for the People that all states exist. . . .

D'Antraigues' flirtation with popular sovereignty would not be long-lived. Elected a deputy to the Estates-General, he came to repent of his polemic and became as zealous a counter-revolutionary as he had been a proto-democrat. But his tract nonetheless went into fourteen editions and boiled down to the popular axiom "The Third Estate is not an order, it is the nation itself."

Once this revolutionary proposition became a common truism, the defense of separate orders took on the color of sectional interest, selfish, unpatriotic and heedless of the concerns of the common people. And because the King had asked to hear those concerns, such views could even be represented as antimonarchical. Necker's insistence on the strictly provisional nature of his administration and his abstention from declaring on the crucial issues of doubling the Third and voting by head opened up a political vacuum that was filled by arguments rather than solutions. On December 5 that space was made even wider when the Parlement of Paris backed away from its earlier intransigence. It now pronounced itself in agreement with Target that there was indeed no constitutional precedent for the Estates-General to follow. Instead, "reason, liberty and the general wish [*voeu général*]" would indicate the shape of the new institution!

Necker's interim solution had been to convene a second Assembly of the Notables to offer advice on the form of the Estates-General. But while its predecessor had been more radical than expected, the opposite was true of the second Assembly. Only a minority took up the "national" positions. Worse, the princes of the blood—with the important exceptions of Orléans and, more surprisingly, the King's brother Provence—declared, in a memorandum drawn up on December 5, that "the State is in peril" and that

> a revolution is being prepared in the principles of government,
> brought on by the agitation of minds. Institutions held sacred and
> by which the monarchy has prospered for so many centuries have
> now been converted into problematic questions or even decried as
> injustices.

81. Sergent, Necker takes the measure of
France: spring 1789.

To surrender to a majoritarian view of representation, they went on, was
to deliver France to extraordinary dangers. Should the Third Estate's "revolution in the constitution of the state" prevail, they foresaw kings coming
and going according to the caprice of public opinion dressed up as the
national will.

The Memorandum of the Princes was not unperceptive about the dangers of the course into which the monarchy was being swept in a state of
rudderless optimism. But to the pamphleteers of the Third Estate it was
taken as direct evidence of a conspiracy against the "popular monarchy"
in the process of being created. As the debate intensified the government
was even more reluctant to provide direction. On December 27 an exceptionally summary edict, without any kind of preamble, deepened this confusion. Against the advice of the Assembly of the Notables it proclaimed
that the Third Estate would indeed have double representation. But it
refrained from ordering deliberation in common and votes by head, a
decision that made a mockery of the generosity towards the Third.
Necker's view seems to have been that somehow the Estates-General would
make up its own mind without too much disorder.

All these fumbling initiatives, second thoughts and obfuscations were in
the strongest contrast to the Patriots of the Third Estate, whose view had

the virtue of clarity and decisiveness. Away with those who had for so long purported to represent the People but, when that representation was at hand, revealed themselves to be not its champions but its oppressors. Any current issue could be converted into the rhetoric of Patriots and Privileged. In his petition on behalf of *Citizens Domiciled in Paris,* Dr. Joseph-Ignace Guillotin (ex-Jesuit and physician) had argued for the doubling of the Third on the basis of exactly this distinction. His tract had been adopted by the Six Merchant Guilds of the city and six thousand copies had been distributed under their aegis. The Parlement attempted to suppress its circulation and on the eighth of December took steps against Guillotin himself. He was arraigned before the court but the crowd demonstration in his favor was so noisily intimidating that his triumphant acquittal was virtually a foregone conclusion.

There was one further feature of the Third Estate that in the bitter winter of 1788–89 would strengthen its claim to be the authentic embodiment of the reborn Nation: its labor. Many of the tracts that had designed the identity of the Third Estate had already drawn an invidious contrast between venally acquired privilege and the productivity of the *roturier,* a term that itself conjured up the emblem of the laboring shovel. A memorandum on the Estates-General drawn up by the municipal officers of Nantes was emphatic on this point:

> The third estate cultivates the fields, constructs and mans the vessels of commerce, sustains and directs manufactures, nourishes and vivifies the kingdom. . . . It is time that a great people count for something. . . .

The *cahier* of a village in the Vosges, Hareville-sous-Montfort, would make the same point more invidiously. The nobility that claimed it supported His Majesty, it explained, "only does so at the price of drawing fat pensions off the state," whereas it is "the Third Estate that pays all the time and which works night and day to cultivate the land which produces grain to feed all of the people."

The many prints that began to appear around this time, featuring the tiller of the soil bearing on his back the two privileged orders, made essentially the same point.

It was left to the Abbé Sieyès' *Qu'est-ce que le Tiers-Etat?*, the most incisive of all the pamphlets, to make the schism between the useful and the useless decisive. "What is necessary that a nation should prosper?" asked the first of his famous rhetorical questions. "Individual efforts and public functions" came the answer. And it was the Third Estate that supplied all

82. "Let's hope that the game finishes well." A
woman of the Third Estate carries the weight of the
other two orders.

of the former. The Third Estate, then, was not a mere "order." It was the
Nation itself. Those who claimed a special status outside the Nation were
thereby confessing their parasitism. By mischance and misappropriation the
Third Estate, which was everything, had been, politically, nothing. Only
when the fecklessness of the privileged had threatened the destruction of
the *patrie* could it seek to be, as Sieyès modestly put it, "something."

The Third Estate was an idea and an argument before it was a social
reality. And Sieyès' pamphlet was its most inspired invention: cogent,
lucid—apparently indisputable except by invoking the unfrightening phantom of historicity. It not only gave form and shape to the new national
polity, it pointed a threatening finger at those who separated themselves
from it. "It is impossible to say what place the nobility and clergy ought
to occupy in the social order," he warned. "This is equivalent to asking
what place should be assigned to a malignant disease which preys upon and
tortures the body of a sick man."

iii HUNGER AND ANGER

On July 13, 1788, a hailstorm burst over a great part of central France from Rouen in Normandy as far south as Toulouse. The Scottish gardener Thomas Blaikie, who witnessed it, wrote of stones so monstrous that they killed hares and partridge and ripped branches from elm trees. For many more the rain of icy white pellets was deadly enough not to need exaggeration. It wiped out budding vines in Alsace, Burgundy and the Loire; laid waste to wheat ripening in the fields of the Orléanais; pitted young apples in the Calvados; shriveled young olives and oranges in the Midi. In the western province of the Beauce, the cereal crops had already survived one hailstorm on May 29 but succumbed to the second blow in July. In the Ile-de-France south of Paris, where vegetable and fruit crops were wiped out as they were ripening, farmers wrote, "A countryside, erstwhile ravishing, has been reduced to an arid desert."

In much of France a drought followed. That, in turn, was succeeded by a winter of a severity the like of which had not been seen since 1709, when the red Bordeaux was said to have frozen in Louis XIV's goblet. The same stories of eighty years before recirculated with the gnawing cold. Birds were said to be frozen to their perches; wolves to come prowling from their lairs in the Cevennes down into the plains of Languedoc; poor men in wild places like the Tarn and the Ardèche to be reduced to boiling tree bark to make gruel. The verifiable reality was bad enough. Frozen rivers stopped water mills from turning what grain there was into flour, and prevented transportation of emergency supplies to the areas of greatest want. Deep snow lay on the ground as far south as the Haute-Garonne, west of Toulouse, where between February 26 and April 10 there were fresh falls almost every other day. In January Mirabeau described Provence as visited by the Exterminating Angel. "Every scourge has been unloosed. Everywhere I have found men dead of cold and hunger, and that in the midst of wheat for lack of flour, all the mills being frozen."

The thaw brought its own miseries. In mid-January, the frozen Loire melted suddenly, sending flood waters over fields and pasture and bursting through rudimentary retaining dikes into the streets of Blois and Tours.

Eighty years before, there had been unmistakable famine: roads littered with starved corpses. In 1789 there was famine's little sister, dearth—*la disette*—but that was bad enough. The cruelties of the weather followed a harvest in 1787 that was no better than mediocre. The four-pound loaf that formed the staple of three quarters of all French men and women and which, in normal times, consumed half their income, rose in price from eight sous in the summer of 1787 to twelve by October 1788 and fifteen by the first week of February. To feed a family of four required two of those loaves each day, while the average wage of a manual laborer was between twenty and thirty sous, of a journeyman mason at most forty. The doubling of bread prices—and of firewood—spelled destitution. Over the winter of 1788 some clergy estimated that as many as a fifth of the population of Paris, over 100,000 souls, were receiving some sort of relief. In grand gestures, magnates like the Duc d'Orléans sold paintings—it was said to succor the poor—but isolated acts of philanthropy could never produce enough food or firewood to make the winter bearable for the thousands of its victims.

The calamity touched different groups of the population in different ways, dragging each down to a level of subsistence from which it thought it had safely escaped. For the landless day laborers in the countryside, many of them migrant workers, the wreckage of the harvests robbed them of precious work. They had left their families, setting out on a familiar route for seasonal labor in vineyards, wheat fields or olive groves and hoping to return to sustain their own patch. Now they would probably never go back and would have to struggle to avoid perishing altogether. For the small holders—the *métayers*—who constituted the greater part of the rural population, it was the last turn of a tightening screw of debt and impoverishment. With too little land to feed their own family, they procured a little extra from the *seigneur,* together with seed, implements and draft animals in return for a share of the harvest. This burden precluded any kind of surplus, and the *métayers* were often obliged to buy additional food to make up their subsistence. They were, then, consumers as well as producers, and the punitive increases in the price of bread and firewood at the end of the eighties wiped out any chance they may have had of profiting from a gradual rise in value of their crop. With a season's harvest blackened by frost or hail, and taxes owed to the *seigneur* and the state, their creditors were likely to call in the debt. Eviction, and demotion to the class of the landless—and for the present, workless—was the result. In relatively prosperous areas like the countryside around Versailles, according to Georges Lefebvre, heads of households uprooted from their land constituted a third of the whole rural population. In lower Normandy the figure rose to as much as three quarters. So they too added to the rising tide of helpless humanity shuffling its way towards the churches for a handout of bread and milk, or towards the big towns.

Should they reach a city, their reception would be almost as bleak.

Migrant workers had filled the ranks of casual labor: market porters, coachmen, chimney sweeps, water sellers. But the crisis in the countryside swelled into a depression that spilled over into the rest of the economy. Reduced purchasing power shrank the market for manufactured items, already suffering from the competition of cheaper British goods that came flooding in as a result of the commercial treaty of 1786. Artisans were thrown out of work; piece jobs in cottage looms disappeared; building workers were laid off as the boom in urban construction in the great cities came to a sudden halt. Industrial towns like Lyon and Rouen had, respectively, twenty-five thousand and ten thousand unemployed. In Amiens, closer still to the entry point of British manufactures, the figure was as high as forty-six thousand.

Amidst evidence of general ruin, Necker did what he could to provide some relief. He forbade the export of grain, granted under the Brienne edicts of 1787, and embarked on a vigorous importing policy using nearly fifty million livres for both cereals and rice. But supplies were not easy to come by. The Russo-Turkish War in the Mediterranean had cut off Levantine sources for the south of the country, and another conflict in the Baltic had impeded more traditional sources from Poland and east Prussia. In the north, great ice floes packing the Seine estuary and harbor at ports like Le Havre made it impossible for ships to unload. Supplies that did reach France were, in any case, expensive since other countries, in much the same predicament, were competing for whatever grain was available. Frozen rivers and canals made transport by barge slow and difficult. And when Polish wheat and rye at last arrived in the north and northeast by way of Holland and the Austrian Netherlands, the grain had deteriorated so that it made a yellowish flour that smelled sickly-sour.

All in all, it was not, perhaps, the most auspicious moment to ask the people of France to air their grievances. Yet from the depths of their want and distress, the figure of the King-Father (addressed as such in many of the *cahiers de doléances*) assumed an almost saintly aspect, giving his subjects the opportunity of a kind of surrogate audience. So for all its horrors, the winter of 1788–89 should not be taken as an advance death sentence on the great political experiment then under way. But it did mean that in the popular mind, the business of a new constitution was somehow connected with the filling of empty bellies. This was to charge patriotism and representation with more than either could possibly deliver. Just as liberty was no magic answer to the problem of fiscal solvency, neither was equality an answer to the even more recalcitrant task of feeding the population in years of shortage.

Once brought to the attention of the populace, the interdependence of food and freedom would not go away. The illusion that new political institutions could provide sustenance where the old ones had not, rested on the belief that the parasitical agents of the old regime had deliberately used their power to engineer crises from which they might profit. In these *pactes de famine* periodic shortages had been the signal for speculators in grain to withhold supplies from the markets, driving prices upwards until the moment when they could be exploited for maximum profit. A policy of liberating the grain trade from regulations that required licensed sales at specified markets had only offered further opportunities for this extortion. These widely held beliefs needed people to blame: the *agioteurs* (speculators) and *accapareurs* (hoarders), for whom some rural *cahiers* demanded the death penalty, but just as often ministers in the government who were suspected of colluding in their conspiracy. At the beginning of the Revolution it was possible to pin responsibility for the prolongation of the food crisis on the intransigent aristocracy, said to be conspiring to starve the people into submission. But successive revolutionary administrations fell victim to the charge that it was their inadequate patriotism and punitive zeal that held the people hostage to the cycle of hunger. Only when harvests improved and soldiers fed, locustlike on the march in the countries they occupied, did the problem recede.

It was the connection of anger with hunger that made the Revolution possible. But it also programmed the Revolution to explode from overinflated expectations.

Those expectations began in earnest when the King called on his subjects to assemble in their parishes and bailiwicks to elect deputies and to write down a list of all their grievances and hopes for the future. In one sense, the exercise merely confirmed the traditional belief that the King would always come to the succor of his people in their distress. But it had never been confirmed in so direct and universal a way. The subsequent events of the Revolution are so dramatic that they distract attention from the magnitude of the experiment that took place across the whole of the country from February to April 1789. Nothing like it had ever been attempted, not in France or anywhere else—certainly not in that paragon of constitutional excellence, the Kingdom of Great Britain. Twenty-five thousand *cahiers* were drawn up in a simultaneous act of consultation and representation that was unprecedented in its completeness.

Not all of them, of course, echo with the unmuffled voice of the people. The machinery of election to the Estates-General set out in the royal convocation of January 24 ensured that while the nobility and clergy would elect their representatives directly, the process for producing the deputies of the Third would be both complicated and indirect. Local assemblies, under the medieval name *bailliages* (bailiwicks), were to be convened, roughly one for every hundred voters—those being liberally defined as all tax-paying residents of twenty-five or over. (Apparently in some local assemblies widows appeared, arguing optimistically that the royal edict had not specified sex.) The electorate thus created numbered some six million souls. With all its complications and practical difficulties, it was, up until that time, the most numerous experiment in political representation attempted anywhere in the world.

Most often convened at the village church, these primary assemblies drafted their *cahier* and elected deputies to represent the community at a further assembly. In some areas that "general assembly" then elected deputies but not infrequently it had to reduce itself by several stages before arriving at a final selection for the Estates at Versailles. The procedure also ensured that it would necessarily be the most eloquent, educated and politically adept who would survive the winnowing process. In practice that meant, overwhelmingly, lawyers and public officials—the stalwarts of local academies and *sociétés de pensée*—with a sprinkling of physicians, notaries and enlightened ex-abbés (like Sieyès) and the occasional businessman who made the grade.

On the other hand, the local assemblies were remarkably free from any kind of official intimidation. Necker honored his commitment to strict impartiality and total freedom from censorship during the elections. It was common, for example, for local government officials to preside over assemblies where the state and its servants, from *intendants* down to the agents of the tax farms, were roundly denounced for their many tyrannies, petty and grievous. Those denunciations were all incorporated into the final statement. So, for all the filtering out of beliefs and personalities, the *cahiers* offer an astonishingly complete account of what, in the late winter and early spring, was on the mind of the French people as their political nation was reborn.

The *cahiers* speak with two voices. A great number project the voice of patriotic unity, uttered in remarkable unison, often from all three Estates. Their statements were concerned primarily with political and legal matters and their voice was that of the educated urban world of modernizing France. From the countryside and from the artisans of the towns came a sharper tone, obediently repeating as a matter of form the pious clichés of Third Estate politics, but at heart concerned with quotidian matters of taxes, justice, the scourges (the word *fléau* may be the most commonly used term in all of the rural *cahiers*) of the militia and the game laws; in other words, with survival.

It is not so surprising that the first kind of language—that of political change—was so standardized. There were conscious efforts to reproduce a published "program" that would incorporate most of the principal issues rehearsed in the pamphlet literature of the autumn of 1788. Sieyès produced a primer for local assemblies that was printed up in thousands and distributed, with an endorsing note from the Duc d'Orléans, throughout the Ile-de-France. Curates were especially recommended to make use of the instructional pamphlet, which not only suggested (strongly) what might be said, but the order and manner in which it should be recorded in the *cahier*. Other *cahiers* became famous in their own right as model manifestos of the liberal future—none more so than the enormous document written by Du Pont de Nemours for the Third of Nemours.

The message was the same throughout. The Estates-General was the assembled body of the Nation and should be recalled, periodically, whenever the Nation's business demanded. Some documents proposed three-year sessions; bolder ones insisted it should sit until a new constitution was established. A number of *cahiers* specifically identified the legislative power with a national assembly and insisted, in the English manner, on the separation of powers. Virtually all required that it assent to any new taxation. Liberty of person, thought, utterance and publication was to be guaranteed, which meant the abolition of *lettres de cachet,* any forms of arbitrary justice (like the tribunals of the military) and virtually all censorship. Interference with mail was stated in innumerable *cahiers* as a direct assault on personal liberty.

On financial matters there was similar concord. The liabilities of the crown were to be consolidated as a national debt. There would be mandatory published budgets every year, with each department of state fully accounted for. Venal office was to be abolished (above all in finance) and no taxpayer was to be exempt from any obligations on account of rank or the claims of privilege. If nobility was to remain (said a number of the *cahiers* of the nobility) it should be merely an honorific matter, what Rabaut Saint-Etienne had called "the decorated part of the nation."

The *cahiers* of the liberal elite, whether in the first two orders or the Third, then translated the standard agenda of their debating academies into business of state. There should, many of them said, be a plan for national education. Lotteries, gaming houses and other frivolities that enticed the people from serious self-improvement should be banished. A substantial number also committed themselves to liberal economic principles: the abolition of the guilds and of all restraints on freedom and mobility of labor; the suppression of internal customs barriers and the end of all tax farming. In most of these respects it was, paradoxically, the *cahiers* of the nobility (that of Nemours excepted) that approximated most closely the "bourgeois" paradigm in their concern to match personal with economic liberty. Given the involvement of so many of their class with commerce, industry, finance and technology, this is perhaps less surprising than it may at first seem. But a large majority of the *cahiers* of the nobility pronounced themselves in favor of that basic "bourgeois" axiom, equality before the law.

It was a vision of France continuous with much of the modernizing ethos of the 1770s and 1780s. Rank would melt into citizenship; science and education, under the benign guidance of the elite, would do away with the brutish ignorance, poverty and sicknesses of the people. Enlightened self-interest would come to prevail on the land and create a prospering peasantry that, through rational methods of farming, could create sufficient surpluses to turn itself into customers for manufactured goods. That in turn would benefit a labor force that could be wooed away from defensive protection to entrepreneurial opportunity. Over this transformed realm an accountable administration, appointed for merit and competence, would govern with austerity and integrity. Patriotism and public service would be exemplary, starting with a monarch unsurpassed in popularity; the arts would blossom as never before and the new epoch would belong, simultaneously, to France and to all of humanity.

A surprisingly large number of the nobility shared these views. They were recorded in the *cahiers* of the major towns: in those of the four thousand nobility domiciled in Paris; in those of large towns like Bordeaux, and smaller provincial centers like Aix, Saumur, Grenoble, Blois, Orléans and Rouen. Even the members of some of the most distant gatherings, like that of the nobility of Moselle at Pont-à-Mousson, insisted in the name of "reason enlightened by philosophy" that all fiscal exemptions for its own class should be abolished, that all citizens should be treated alike in terms of their tax liability and that any kind of personal privilege whatsoever should be suppressed. And while the nobility assumed there would have to be some sort of reimbursement for the abolition of venal offices, it thought this could only be done very gradually in the interests of the state.

It was not a chorus of complete harmony. The paradoxical effect of the electoral machinery was to give representation to the much larger number of poorer backwoods nobles who had never been part of the culture of modernity and who had only their titles to cling to for esteem. In Brittany, they were the *épées de fer*, the steel swords, who took part in street brawls in Rennes during January 1789 with crowds supporting the Third Estate proposals to vote by head not order. Bested in both physical and political contests, they refused to elect deputies to the Estates at all. Elsewhere, groups of nobles who were less charmed by the idea of dissolving their inherited rank into a nation of citizens, took a stand on voting by order and elected deputies to the Estates who would support their view. In the Côtentin, for example, at Coutances, the deputies gloried in the illustrious names of Leclerc de Juigne, Achard de Bonvouloir, Beaudrap de Sotteville and Arthur de Villarnois. While endorsing in general terms a "concord of the orders," they made it clear that they should assemble, deliberate and vote, as "distinct, separate, equal and free" entities.

Between the Paris nobles who protested bitterly that the election regulations had *forced* them to separate from their co-citizens of the Third in the old "Commune," and the citizen-nobles of the Dauphiné, Provence and Languedoc on the one hand, and the bluebloods of Brittany, Burgundy, Franche-Comté and upper Normandy on the other, there was a large body of mixed opinion. In a number of noble assemblies the decision on voting by head or order was narrow: fifty-one to forty-three at Blois, for example. Many nobles whose social personalities were divided between an urban, modern existence and the management of a seigneurial estate argued that for items of national business—such as taxation and war and peace—they should debate and vote together in common; but for items of business concerning their respective orders they should retain a separate identity. Others still were prepared (as was Necker) to leave the decision to the Estates itself, so that if "the needs of the Nation demanded it" they would be prepared to vote in common after all. At Blois, when the votes were recast in exactly this way, the number determined to vote by order dropped dramatically to twenty-five and the number prepared to support a "mixed" compromise came to sixty-eight. If the *cahiers* of those assemblies prepared to vote by head in such circumstances and for "national business" are added to those already committed to voting by head on principle, then in fact a majority (approximately 60 percent) of the French nobility in 1789 came out in favor of a genuinely national assembly.

The "Third Estate," then, came into being as a joint political enterprise, initially designed by members of the liberal nobility and made possible by the deep divisions within their own elite. Within the clergy, there was a similar group of prelates prepared to endorse the bitter complaints of the village curates (abundantly represented in the assemblies of their order) against an overendowed ecclesiastical aristocracy. But there is no doubt that the process of the elections themselves gave the opportunity for new men—largely from the legal profession and public officialdom—to assert themselves as spokesmen for the Third. And within the clergy, an even more radical process occurred, whereby the country curates established themselves as an opposition to the diocesan hierarchy. In so doing, both groups emancipated themselves from their patrons, even to the point where they were emphatic that they should not be represented in the Estates-General by nobles, however well meaning.

The humiliating experience of Antoine Lavoisier was typical of this separation. Unpopular though he may have been as a Farmer-General—and worse, as the designer of the new customs wall encircling Paris—Lavoisier was also a pioneer of the new agriculture. Secretary of the Royal Committee on Agriculture, established at his urging, he had spent a considerable sum of his own in an experimental attempt to improve what was, arguably, the most wretched farming country in all of France: the Sologne. A boggy, badly drained, humid region south of the central Loire Valley, the Sologne had a dreadful climate that regularly blighted its rye harvest, obliging the peasantry to consume the grain even when it had been attacked by an ergotic fungus. At the least this led to the hallucinatory states associated with ergotism. More often it also included a form of arterial paralysis that ended with gangrene and a condition known to the many French physicians who examined it as "formication": the sensation of being eaten alive by ants.

In a long report presented by Lavoisier to the Committee in 1788 he described the results of ten years of hard labor on his model farm at Fréchines, where he spent three years attempting to create lucerne meadows before switching more successfully to clover and sainfoin, and introducing the potato and field beets. Rams and ewes were imported from Spain and Chanteloup cows crossbred with more local stock to produce hardier animals. At the end of the decade, he still concluded rather pessimistically that while all this had produced some gratifying results it was idle to expect the individual tenant farmer to do likewise since "at the end of a year (burdened with taxes) there remains virtually nothing for the cultivator who considers himself fortunate to survive, even to lead a miserable and sickly life."

To the small community of improving landlords in the Loire and the Ile-de-France, Lavoisier was a hero. And he evidently wanted very badly to identify himself as a Citizen-Patriot by achieving election as a deputy of the Third Estate. This was technically possible since the royal edict had specified that only two of the four initial electors had necessarily to be of the Third. But it was this very provision which caused a great deal of ill-feeling in their assemblies when well-meaning but patronizing members of the liberal nobility attempted to take advantage of it. Lavoisier apparently participated in at least one such meeting, since he signed the minutes of the assembly at La-Chapelle-Vendômoise, but at Villefrancoeur, his native parish, he was brusquely rejected by the Third Estate as socially disqualified from election.

While the view from the top down, then, was predominantly one of union and concord, that from the bottom up was just as often one of grievance and discord. If the statements of the elite were documents of Enlightenment optimism, those of the people were true *doléances*—laments. Their tone was a mixture of sorrow and anger and their appeal was less to the self-evident propositions of reason and nature than to a king-father who might redress their grievances. A local muse at Allainville, near Pithiviers, compared the "good heart" of the reforming King with a bee pollinating flowers. But he also implored him to rescue the villagers from the collectors of the *gabelle*, "those bloodsuckers of the Nation who quaff the tears of the unfortunate from their goblets of gold."

The curates, notaries or local lawyers who produced the written form of those grievances ensured that they included the standard catalogue of political reforms. Many of these small-town scribes traveled from village to village in the weeks of March helping the local population to organize their meetings and supplying a standard document, so that one finds virtually identical statements reproduced in the *cahiers* of neighboring hamlets. But there were also striking variations. Often the *cahier* would begin as though a personal messenger were giving the King a guided tour of the village and its terrain, and explaining how its ills were rooted in both local topography and the seigneurial baronies that had encamped on it. The village of Cabrerets, for example, in the mountainous southwest, cut by the river Lot, is today much visited by tourists on their way to sample the black wines of nearby Cahors. But in 1789 its villagers failed to appreciate the picturesque. The community, said their *cahier*, "is situated in the most frightful and abominable corner of the world and has no possessions at all other than rocky escarpments and virtually inaccessible mountains covered with scrub and other poor vegetation and with almost no pasture . . . it can be justly affirmed that the community of Cabrerets must be one of the poorest and most miserable in the Kingdom." The tracks which passed for its only communications were unfit even for horses or donkeys, so that it took six hours to walk to Cahors. Not surprisingly, the place had long been abandoned by a curate. Thus its overwhelming needs were simple and not at all revolutionary: a decent road and a church.

Elsewhere, the brutalities of geography or climate had been made worse by human depredations, and after reviewing their physical situation, village *cahiers* went on to catalogue a long list of licensed bullies who made the lives of the peasantry particularly difficult. Invariably, at the top of the list were the tax officers of both the state and the *seigneur*, bailiffs of all kinds, the *porteurs de contrainte* (enforcers), who at Combérouger in the Tarn were paid thirty sous a day to terrorize the local population into paying their taxes or seize what few belongings they had.

The *gabelous* of the salt tax were the worst. The tax was regarded as particularly regressive since, as one *cahier* put it, with pardonable exaggeration, "salt is often the only thing the poor have to put in their pot." The *cahier* of Kanfen, a village of seventy-four dwellings outside Thionville in the Ardennes (northeastern France), was especially eloquent on this. Most of its population, it explained, were forced to live as day laborers on farms, owing to the dearness of pasture, grain and wood. With their paltry wage— sometimes as little as five sous a day—they could not possibly afford salt at the high price it was taxed. So they were obliged to buy an eight-day supply of smuggled salt and "return trembling" to their house where, in all likelihood, the agents of the *gabelle* would be lurking, hidden behind a hedge. The malefactor would be attacked, arrested, forced to pay the tax and, if unable to do so, led away to prison without even notifying his family. "If it is a woman they are arresting,"

> having no shame they search everywhere and attack her with insults . . . if they enter a house they do so at the very break of day . . . not like honest men but like a band of robbers armed with sabres, hunting knives and steel-tipped sticks. If a woman is in bed, they search the bed, never noticing if she is sick and never ashamed of what they are doing, turn the bed upside down. We leave you to judge what happens if a gang like this comes into a house where a woman is pregnant. Often it ends with the death of the fruit of her womb.

There were many other undesirables classified by the farmers as "scourges": millers who defrauded them by taking indeterminate amounts of grain as their fee instead of a set money sum; gamekeepers who attacked them with dogs if they set traps for rabbits devouring their crops; "vagabonds" (usually the migrant workless scavenging for a barn to sleep in and a handout) whom they said were infesting the settled countryside. In Alsace, Lorraine and the Moselle, anti-Semitic complaints were commonplace, alleging that Jews were preying usuriously on peasant debts. In Brittany there were complaints about protected tobacco monopolists who held a captive clientele to ransom and then fobbed them off with moldy stock "more likely to poison than soothe the unfortunate." The same *cahier* from Boisse singled out horse rustlers as a particular breed of criminal, undeterred by a mere term in the galleys and meriting the death penalty. In the south and southeast there was harsh criticism of monastic orders living off the fat of the land while peasants starved. At Onzain, on the mid-Loire, the *cahier* went so far as to demand that all religious orders be abolished outright as worthless parasites. Officers and constables of the seigneurial courts were especially despised for their armed ignorance and brutality.

Attacks on these groups arose spontaneously, but they were urged on by propaganda campaigns directed by members of the very groups being attacked. Thus the most vehement statement against the wealth of the diocesan clergy and the abbeys was by the Augustinian canon Ducastelier. His *Gold in the Temple* urged that the Church be returned to its "primitive fortunes" so as to regain its "primitive sanctity." "Twenty million must subsist on half the wealth of France while the clergy and bloodsuckers devour the other half." Priests must be, quite simply, "citizens of the state." Likewise, it was an aristocratic magistrate from the Châtelet, André-Jean Boucher d'Argis, who compared seigneurial courts to "vampires pumping the last drop of blood from the bodies to which they have attached themselves."

The remedy for virtually all these ills was not so much freedom as protection. (Salt was the only exception.) A theme running through almost all the *cahiers* of the Third Estate was the need to turn the clock back and subordinate modern definitions of property rights to more traditional communal accountability. Where inheritance laws were mentioned, it was almost always to insist on the equal partition of land between heirs (even though it was precisely this customary practice that was producing unviable lots.) The grain trade should be regulated once more and only those licensed with official *brevets* be permitted to sell, and then only at officially designated markets. The parish of Nôtre-Dame-de-Franqueville in Normandy even wanted wheat prices to be pegged "to a rate that the poor can afford." Gleaning rights should be protected. Enclosures of common land where peasants had been accustomed to graze their animals should be discouraged or suppressed altogether, as should the drainage of ponds for conversion to fenced meadows, since that too was robbing the village of a watering place for their livestock.

Woodlands which had also traditionally been used for grazing as well as the customary collection of firewood were an even fiercer source of contention. In Burgundy, for example, three separate demands—for naval construction (notwithstanding its distance from the sea), the urban construction industry and most important of all the booming metallurgical industries, in which the nobility were so heavily invested—had all driven timber prices sky-high. Aggressive estate management of the kind favored from the 1760s onwards could not afford to be sentimental—or even traditional—about so valuable an investment. Private forest guards were resorted to in order to ensure that animals whose grazing destroyed saplings were kept out and malefactors pursued.

At Le Montat, near Cahors, the villagers were certain that change had been for the worse. The harvest was less plentiful than a hundred years before; clearances, enclosures and the cutting of forest had left them without pasture for their livestock and so without the manure to fertilize soil that had become exhausted. Taxes, rents and the price of basic commodities had doubled as conditions had worsened. The result was that the farmers of Montat "found themselves strangers amidst their own possessions and have been obliged to take to the life of wanderers and vagabonds. . . . Happiness, which is the base of all our hopes, sighs and labors, has fled from us . . . for several years we have been beset by calamities that have taken away our harvests; taxes without number accumulating on our heads and far greater than our strength. . . ." All they asked for was

> to have our own property from which we can subsist on a little
> bread moistened with our tears and our sweat, but for some time
> now we have not enjoyed even this happiness . . . the last crust of
> bread has been taken from us so that we are bereft even of our
> hopes for the future; despair and death being our only resource
> yet your [the King's] paternal voice has heard our hearts and has
> made us leap with joy.

Le Montat was buried deep in one of the most arid regions of the southwestern Massif Central. At the center of the *pays de petites cultures* it was a region where too many bodies scrambled for too little thin soil and where hundreds of thousands had given up sharecropping on their patch of hillside and had become nomadic landless laborers. But in the *pays de grandes cultures,* where lots were larger, cash crops for urban markets more common, communications better, land more fertile and crop yields more abundant, many of the complaints were the same. And just because, in these regions (like the Ile-de-France, the Beauce, the Loire Valley, French Flanders and Artois), the peasants were better off, with larger holdings and a smattering of education, they felt more acutely the threats posed to their new security by the developments of the second half of the century. Their resistance to enclosure of common land, pond drainage and woodland is perhaps better characterized as a struggle for capital resources with the agents of seigneurial estates than as blind conservatism. But it was based on collective principles and actions, not naked individualism. Well before 1789, resistance to landlords' appropriations had been mounted through village assemblies and local courts, where with increasing consistency the legal agents of the government as often as not took their side *against* the *seigneur.* As a result, by the time that the appeal for the *cahiers* went out, a local village leadership, usually in the hands of the better-off farmers, had already defined its grievances and tested its strength against the local nobility, assuming increasingly that the crown would be an ally in its campaign for communal rights.

Those same village "headmen" (in French Flanders they were literally called *hoofmannen*) were themselves not immune from criticism. Where, as in the Beauce and the Brie, they were profiting as individuals off the enclosure and partition of the common land, the *cahiers* produced a crop of bitter complaints from less well-off peasants on exactly that score. In many cases, as at Châtenay, Baillet, Marly and Servan-en-Brie, the wealthier *fermiers* were directly accused of impoverishing the many, and demands were made to limit the size of farms to land that could be cultivated with four plows. "It is time to put a brake on the ambitions of rich landowners," stated the *cahier* of Fosses, where they accused farmers of lending money to poorer cultivators on extortionate terms with the deliberate intention of using foreclosures to eat up their property. At Villeron, near Vincennes, there was an explicit request for a law that would "keep the land in small farms as they were in earlier times and when work could be provided for the inhabitants hereabout."

The rural *ancien régime* was thus caught in contradictions that it would pass on to the Revolution. On the one hand, through its agricultural societies, experimental farms (like the one where Lavoisier made his pioneering efforts in the wretchedly poor region of the Sologne) and free trade policies, the government was committed to a physiocratic vision of the future: cash markets, consolidated lots, capital accumulation, higher prices for produce, fodder crops—rationalized, "English" farming. But the here-and-now needs of taxes (more easily collected through communal institutions) and social peace pushed it in precisely the opposite direction, towards protection and intervention.

And it was also abundantly clear from the *cahiers* that much of France wanted more, not less, government in the countryside. Assembly after assembly asked for better policing against cattle and horse thieves, pilfering vagabonds, counterfeiters—even, at Cloyes in the Loiret, against an epidemic of traveling quacks and empirics, said to be infesting the region, doing harm to men and beasts alike. Villages—in both *grandes* and *petites cultures*—wanted curacies where they had none; better pay for those they had; schools, roads, bridges, asylums for the poor and infirm. The common theme was a desire to transfer social authority from private jurisdictions— be they the tax farmers, the seigneurial courts or the local abbey—to that of the government of the crown, and by extension the Nation. Thus royal (or National) justice alone should determine who had rights over watercourses or heathland, whether land could remain open or be fenced. The partnership envisaged was between a solicitous sovereign and an active, empowered, local community.

It also seemed axiomatic that a truly paternalist state of the kind set out in the rural *cahiers* was incompatible with the exploitation of what remained of anachronistic feudal rights. These had been fiercely attacked by writers like the Abbé Clerget and Turgot's colleague Boncerf, especially when they were used as a pretext for extorting money from local inhabitants, who would in return be freed from the obligation of performing some service. Clerget thought that one such claim—by a Franche-Comté *seigneur*—that he possessed the right to lead his vassals to the hunt in winter and "there make them open their bowels so he might warm his feet in their ordure" particularly bogus. In Burgundy and the Nivernais, oddities of this kind survived, like the obligation to surrender the tongue of every ox slaughtered for the delectation of the château. In the Vosges, a similar right required the presentation of bulls' testicles on the same occasion. More vexing was the remnant of *mainmorte* that required a lord's permission for a peasant to sell his land and which prohibited him from bequeathing it to anyone other than a direct relative who had shared his house. Yet these were but the rags and tatters of a feudalism that had disappeared in the rest of France.

More typically, privilege was converted by seigneurial managers into fees for alleged services rendered: milling, brewing, crossing a river, taking beasts to market—as well as the quitrents demanded each year for the mere privilege of farming on what was, in a titular sense, the lord's land. Such service and legal fees had been aggressively exacted as a new form of business practice, complete with the most up-to-date archival documentation (not an oxymoron in eighteenth-century France) and a new profession of researchers to make the claims stick, if contested in court (as they increasingly were).

From its outset, then, the Revolution was running fast in opposite directions. Its leaders wanted freedom, deregulation and mobility of labor; commercialization; rational economic activity. But the distress that would actually provoke men to commit acts of violence—licensed, as they supposed, by the King—arose from exactly the opposite needs. And this was as much true for urban artisans as it was for peasants. A striking number of *cahiers* both within towns themselves and especially from rural regions dependent on cottage weaving and spinning attacked mechanization and the amalgamation of industrial processes into factories. Still more were adamant in denouncing unskilled and unorganized retailing at fairs and markets. Hawkers and itinerant traders of all kinds were seen as interlopers, passing off shoddy goods at prices that undercut those who had to pay guild fees and go through years of apprenticeship for official licenses.

These views, it is true, were predictable, given that the primary assemblies of the Third Estate in towns were organized by guilds and corporations, so that one would expect the opinions of the master-craftsmen rather than journeymen to predominate, as indeed they did. But it would be equally naive to assume that masters and employees were *necessarily* divided about the threat of unregulated labor simply because other issues—principally the living wage—were a regular bone of contention. In most of the larger cities, hostility was of long standing between long-settled artisans in trades like tailoring and immigrant labor producing pieces for sale at improvised market stalls. Even in Paris, where the labor market was fluid, it is by no means clear that the *cahier* of the women florists and hat decorators did not represent workers as well as *patronnes* of the guild. They were particularly concerned that "these days anyone thinks they can compose a bouquet" and that "unprincipled women" were reducing "honest florists to the last extremes of poverty by their chaotic practices." It was not the guild baronesses but "mothers of families, having to pay out thirty sous a day for food," who were being driven to ruin by the free market. And they were particularly hostile to the practice of women from the outer *faubourgs* coming in at the break of day and offering flowers below agreed prices. No one, they demanded, should be allowed to sell before four A.M. between Easter and Saint Martin's Day (November 11) or earlier than six during the rest of the year.

In a smaller provincial town like the English Channel port of Le Havre, these animosities became even clearer. In the same *cahier* that complained about the inadequacy of pay, the guild of ship's carpenters objected strongly to the shipbuilders' practice of hiring casual labor on a day-by-day basis. Similarly, the coffee-lemonade-and-vinegar sellers took exception to unlicensed competition that filched supplies from unladen ships and set up cut-price stalls. And the hatters insisted that the twice-weekly Havre open market was actually destroying the community, since "the public was cheated by persons who without any knowledge insinuate themselves into the trade." The rise in theft, drunkenness and violent brawls in the town was due, they thought, to this floating, undisciplined element.

On the shifting frontiers between town and country, these conflicts were particularly sharp. The usual scenario was the difficulty townsmen had in enforcing regulations about the marketing of produce brought in from the suburban hinterland. But occasionally it could be the farmers of the villages "outside the walls" who felt themselves victimized by commercial exploitation. The *affaire des boues* (best translated as the "muck business") was *the* major concern for the many little communities to the south and west of Paris—now so many termini on the Métro—like Vanves, Ivry, Pantin and

La Villette. For a long time these bustling little hamlets had been held hostage by the Paris butchers' guild, which had been given the right to pasture its livestock in their fields. Under this monopoly, the radial zone around Paris had, in effect, been requisitioned to feed the great belly of the city. Local farmers were not permitted to raise animals or sell them to the city on their own account.

They were, however, allowed to grow cabbages and onions, carrots and beans. And in recognition of having surrendered their meadows to the Paris butchers, the villages had been given the right to collect street ordure, gratis, from the city: muck worth its weight in gold as market garden fertilizer. Since the late 1770s, the *cahiers* complained, barriers had been set up to charge their dung carts fees to freight the precious cargo out of the city, violating the quid pro quo. While exploited by this new business practice, they in their turn had not been allowed to charge the meat merchants anything at all for pasture. Redress, in their view, lay not in the liberal solution of allowing each party to charge the going rate for the service, but rather to restore the traditional terms of the agreement. If nothing was done they threatened to clear the butchers' stock in their own direct way.

Many other processes of economic modernization triggered angry responses. A syndicate formed by an entrepreneur, Defer de La Nouerre, to divert a tributary of the Seine, the Yvette, to a new canal provoked violent opposition from all the riverain parishes along its course. The plan would rob the faubourg Saint-Marcel of a major water supply, ruin the Gobelin tapestries and worst of all deprive sixteen water mills of their capability to produce flour. In February 1788 the Parlement of Paris banned the enterprise and ordered Defer to repair any damage he had done in the early works as well as restore the river to its original course. But both Brienne's and Necker's governments favored the project, and with its status uncertain, the *cahiers* of affected communities bristled with indignation lest the operation go ahead.

It was these kinds of highly specific, local grievances that could arouse mighty passions in the winter and spring of 1789. As cases before the Parlements, they had been isolated instances of the conflict between nascent capitalism and community rights. Woven into the texts of the *cahiers* and the procedure to elect deputies for the Estates-General, they contributed a great deal to the politicization of the Third Estate. In this sense at least, the politics of the Nation was composed as much of a myriad of local material complaints as it was of the high-sounding epithets of constitution-making. And as would be the case during the Revolution, the interests of center and locality, elite and rank-and-file did not always pull in the same direction.

While the *cahiers* of the liberal nobility offered an alluring picture of a briskly modernizing France that would consummate the great alterations of the 1770s and 1780s by shaking off restrictions like a butterfly emerging from a chrysalis, those of the Third Estate wanted, very often, to return to the cocoon. By implication they suggested a mythical France, governed by an all-seeing, just and benign monarch, cared for by a humble and responsible clergy. In that ideal commonwealth, administration would somehow manage to be both everywhere and nowhere, present in the local community when needed (as in the strengthened *maréchaussée* constabulary that many *cahiers* requested) but careful not to ride roughshod over local rights. Such a government would thus succeed in establishing just and reciprocal relations between citizens and between citizens and government.

Above all it was to be a France free of the corruptions of modern life. Innumerable *cahiers* of the Third urged the abolition of gaming houses, of lotteries—in some cases even of cafés—as places of ill repute that swallowed their young people in poverty and debauchery. For the scum of the gilded world—bankrupts, usurers, grain speculators—they reserved their fiercest punishments, like branding. Many of them urged the abolition of the *petits spectacles*—the boulevard theaters—with a fervor that would have warmed the heart of Jean-Jacques Rousseau. As if following the apocalyptic rhetoric of Mercier, they wished to lance the poisoned carbuncle of city life and clean it of its mess.

This was, of course, to ask for the impossible. But asking for the impossible is one good definition of a revolution.

iv DEAD RABBITS, TORN WALLPAPER
March–April 1789

The first heavy casualties of the French Revolution were rabbits. On March 10 and 11, 1789, the villagers of Neuville formed themselves into platoons, armed with clubs and sickles, and searched meadows and woods for their prolific little enemies. What dogs they had accompanied them, and the shout of "*Hou, hou*" signified to the rest of the hunting party a satisfactory kill. Where none were found, traps were laid in defiance of draconian game laws that had long terrified the peasantry into sullen obedience.

Throughout the Ile-de-France and elsewhere in northern France, from the estates of the Comte d'Oisy in Artois to those of the Prince de Conti at Pontoise, similar invasions took place. Disregarding the game laws that had protected birds and animals, and the brutal "captaincies" that enforced them, hobnail boots trampled through forbidden forests or climbed over fences and stone walls. Grass was mown in grain fields to reveal the nests of partridge and pheasant, snipe and woodcock; eggs were smashed or fledglings left to the dogs. Warrens were staved in, hares rooted out from behind rocks. In daring villages, pit traps were even set for the most prized game, which was also the most voracious consumer of green shoots: roe deer. The most spectacular assaults were on those châteaux in miniature: dovecots, from which the peasantry had seen aerial raiding parties launched against their seed, returning in absolute safety to their seigneurial compound. They were, said one *cahier,* "flying thieves." In one district of Lorraine, no less than nineteen *cahiers* called for their outright destruction, while another sixteen insisted that doves and pigeons should, at the very least, be firmly shut up for fifteen days after sowing.

It could hardly be called poaching since there was nothing furtive about the onslaught. In some cases, the slaughtered game was hung from poles like trophies and paraded about the village. Initially the gangs ran into mounted patrols serving the captaincies. But there were simply too many determined peasants who, with their winter crop destroyed by the climate, were not prepared to see their spring crop turn into rabbit fodder. In some places, like the estates of the Prince de Condé near Chantilly, villagers simply ignored the game laws and hunted at will. When they ran into gamekeepers, as on March 28, they shot them dead on the spot.

Faced with this kind of mass disobedience, systematic attempts at repression faltered, and before long authorities turned a blind eye to much of what was happening. At Oisy a united confederacy of villages overran the local count's game. At Herblay, where the onslaught had been particularly fierce, its ringleader, the aptly named Toussaint Boucher, was briefly apprehended, but later released. In defying the captaincies of game and in risking sentences of flogging, branding and banishment, the rabbit and bird killers obviously believed that they had Right—in the form of the King's will—on their side. One of the *cahiers* of the Ile-de-France had insisted that it was "the general will of the Nation that game should be destroyed since it carries off a third of the subsistence of citizens and this is the intention of our good King who watches over the common good of his people and who loves them."

To the desperate, there was something particularly satisfying about smashing in a dovecot. But when its mutilated contents were strewn over the lawn of a country estate, an unsubtle but eloquent message was being conveyed to the *seigneurs* of France. The game riots announced a movement from verbal complaint to violent action. It was as though the royal consultation of the people had produced the assumption that the King now licensed what had been unlawful; that his law, and by extension the will of the Nation, overrode the selfish appropriations of privilege. Killing game was not only an act of desperation, it was, by the lights of 1789, Patriotic.

Killing the game of the *seigneurs,* after all, was preferable to turning anger on their persons. And it is striking that throughout the rural insurrections of 1789 a succession of animal or inanimate targets was selected for the visceral discharge of hatred. Bloodshed through surrogate sacrifices, be they the mannequins burned on the Pont Neuf, prize white doves strangled in their cots or more inanimate targets like violently defaced coats of arms on carriages or church pews, all performed the same symbolic function: an oblation for freedom.

Attacks on grain transports, which broke out at about the same time, followed the same pattern. As in the "flour wars" of 1775, the rioters believed they were more faithfully carrying out the King's will than the authorities who had usurped his name. He had decreed, so it was rumored, that the price of a *setier* of wheat should be reduced from forty-two to twenty-four livres—as though there were a primitive justice performed in the transposition of the numbers. Bread was to be priced, justly, at two sous a pound instead of the market rate of nearly four. The King's enemies were the same as the People's: speculators, hoarders, fraudulent millers, profiteering bakers. The vacuum of power announced by the elections to the Estates-General reinforced this impression and made the leadership of the attacks on barges, wagons and flour stores more audacious. Conspicious in that leadership were women. At Viroflay it was women who set up a checkpoint on the road between Versailles and Paris, stopping convoys and searching them for grain or flour before permitting them to pass. At Joüy another *attroupement* of women demanded that grain be sold well below the market rate and the most substantial farmer of the neighborhood, a man named Bure, wisely let them have it at whatever price they asked. In a wide radius of countryside around Paris, from Bourg-la-Reine to Rambouillet, the story was the same.

In the early spring of 1789, the geography of popular intervention was much wider than it had been fourteen years earlier. Mid-March to mid-April saw attacks on bakeries and granaries throughout the Nord, from Cambrai and Valenciennes to Dunkirk and Lille. In Brittany, violence had never really died down since the street fighting of January in Rennes but had fanned out into smaller towns like Morlaix and Vannes. Between March 30 and April 3 a riot at Besançon led by women enforced maximum grain prices and went on to smash up the houses of recalcitrant Parlementaires.

The breadth and intensity of the disorders in the countryside required troops to contain the movement before it became a general insurrection. But the epidemic of disturbances in provincial towns spread available forces too thin. Increasingly, it was left to local communities to fend for themselves as best they could. As early as April 1788 Troyes had set an example by forming an urban militia responsible to local authorities rather than the officers of the crown. A year later, meetings convened for electoral purposes gave more momentum to this devolution under stress, and volunteer guards were armed in Marseille, Etampes, Orléans and Beaugency. It was a crucial moment in the collapse of royal authority. First came the recognition that the *père nourricier*—the King-as-Father-Provider—could not feed his subjects. Then followed the ample evidence that neither could he protect them.

It was in Paris, of course, that that anger and hunger were most dangerously joined. Collectively, the city was already indignant because it had been precluded from assembling on the model of the Dauphiné, as a united "Commune" (its medieval title). The twenty electoral assemblies of the nobility of Paris (as well as many of those of the clergy) all preceded their *cahier* with a formal complaint that they had thus been deprived of the blessings of patriotic fraternity. And whereas about one sixth of the citizens had been disfranchised by tax qualifications elsewhere in France, in Paris a higher tax qualification of six livres ensured that the proportion rose to one quarter. A typical pamphlet protesting this exclusion commented angrily that "our deputies are not going to be our deputies. Things have been so arranged that we can have no part in electing them, and the city of Paris, divided into sixty districts, will be, in every respect, like sixty flocks of sheep."

The Parisian worker was thus the first to experience, in short order, the euphoria of national representation followed by the sting of alienation. Aside from the industrial depression, the frozen Seine had taken livelihoods from the *gens de rivière*—dockers, bargemen, log floaters—and bitter conditions lasting into spring added to their number unemployed masons, house painters and carpenters. When the weather abated somewhat in April twelve thousand of the neediest were sent to dig at the *buttes* of Montmartre; others scraped the quais or dredged rivers and canals. But the scale of distress overwhelmed these modest work projects.

In the bakers' shops, the price of the all-important four-pound loaf fluctuated between twelve and fifteen sous. In February twenty-seven bakers were each fined fifty livres for exceeding the permitted ceiling of fourteen and a half sous. Their guild immediately protested that, given shortages and high wholesale prices, it was impossible for them to sell at this level without cheating on wheat or dangerously polluting the loaf with makeweight substitutes. Newspapers reported that men were exchanging their shirts for bread and, in one case, a woman removed her corset and gave it to the baker for a loaf. In such circumstances a *Cahier of the Poor* appeared arguing for a statutory minimum wage and guaranteed subsistence for all able-bodied working men and women. A similar *Cahier of the Fourth Order*, written by Dufourny de Villiers, urged a substantial tax on the rich to support the poor, since cupidity had created a society where "men are treated as though they are disposable."

At the end of April, a week after the Third Estate of Paris had held their much delayed primary assemblies, misery and suspicion boiled over in violence. The occasion was a rumor, circulating in the faubourg Saint-Antoine (immediately to the east of the Bastille), that the wallpaper manufacturer Réveillon had said he would cut his workers' wages to fifteen sous a day. Réveillon and his fellow victim the saltpeter manufacturer Henriot indignantly denied the story. He was, in fact, one of the more conscientious employers in Paris, paying on average between thirty-five and fifty sous a day and keeping much of his force on the books during the bitterest period of the winter when weather made their work impossible. But he was precisely the kind of capitalist entrepreneur guaranteed to provoke the wrath of both the independent craft artisans and journeymen who made up the majority of the population of the faubourg Saint-Antoine.

Réveillon's career was an exemplary story of the self-made businessman not uncommon at the end of the old regime. He had begun as a simple apprentice paperworker but had left the guild-controlled industry for the newer and freer line of wallpaper manufacture. Marrying well he had used the dowry to buy his own works. In 1789 it was located in the ground floor of a large house sold to Réveillon by a ruined *financier* whose furniture passed to the self-made man for his apartments in the upper stories. Instead of merely printing, gumming and finishing, Réveillon had acquired his own paper manufacture, thus controlling all the processes of production. As the history of the Montgolfiers had shown, there were close relations between papermakers and the world of science, and it was in Réveillon's workshop that Pilâtre de Rozier had made his first experiments in ballooning. Réveillon himself dabbled in chemistry enough to discover a new process for making vellum, which he turned out from his works in the Brie. By 1784 he employed four hundred workers, was commissioning designs from the best artists at the Gobelins and had received a special gold medal for excellence in manufacturing. He even managed to export his lines to England.

It was exactly the kind of modern enterprise that the artisans of the *faubourg* saw as a threat. Concentration of labor, the use of children outside the system of apprenticeship, integration of industrial processes were all enough to single Réveillon out as an enemy. Worse, his house, Titonville, stood out at the corner of the rue de Montreuil and the rue du faubourg Saint-Antoine, famous for its spectacular furniture, its immense library and, most important, its large and lovingly acquired two-thousand-bottle cellar.

Réveillon was the casualty of his own ill-digested reflections on modern economics. For what he had actually said at an electoral meeting in the district of Saint-Marguerite was that "since bread was the foundation of our national economy," its distribution should be deregulated, permitting lower prices. That in turn would allow lower wage costs, lower manufacturing prices and brisk consumption.

It was good Chamber of Commerce propaganda. But when taken together with similar comments by Henriot, it is not hard to see how it sounded like a threat to cut wages. But the first demonstrations seem to have been not in the faubourg Saint-Antoine, where Réveillon's workers lived (very few of them were implicated in the riots), but in the poorer faubourg Saint-Marcel across the river. This was a district dominated by brewery and

83. Réveillon riots, April 1789

tannery workers, whose industries had been badly interrupted by the freezing of the Bièvre River, on which both their manufacturing processes depended. A crowd of some hundreds, armed with sticks, made their way towards Saint-Antoine, shouting, "Death to the rich, death to the aristocrats." Armed with sticks they set off on a noisy demonstration to Réveillon's factory. The bookseller Siméon Hardy, the most valuable busybody in Paris, ran into one group of the demonstrators, now numbering around five hundred, carrying a mock gallows to which was attached the hanging effigy of Réveillon and a placard proclaiming "Edict of the Third Estate Which Judges and Condemns the Above Réveillon and Henriot to be Hanged and Burned in a Public Square." By the time they reached the place de Grève, the number had swelled again to three thousand, and there they attempted to stop traffic and set up their stake before proceeding on to Réveillon's house in the rue de Montreuil.

The assembly of electors from the sixty Paris voting districts had constituted itself into a virtual informal administration, sitting at the Archevêché. It sent three courageous volunteers, two of them textile manufacturers, to speak to the crowds. "Who are you and why do you want to stop us hanging Réveillon?" one of the crowd asked. With a grandiose magnanimity borrowed directly from the theater, the textile maker Charton replied, "I am the Father-Provider [*père nourricier*] of several of you [meaning their boss] and the brother of all of you." "Well then, since you are our brother, embrace us" (a proof of fraternity which many of the most zealous Jacobins at their apogee could not manage). "Willingly," replied Charton, "if you throw down your sticks." Explaining that Réveillon and Henriot were good patriots and friends of the people seemed to have the required calming effect, as the demonstrators disbanded.

Trouble had not gone away, however. Barred from reaching Réveillon's house by a company of fifty *gardes françaises,* the demonstrators did manage to reach Henriot's, which they tore apart from top to bottom, smashing furniture and burning the debris in the street.

On the following day, the twenty-eighth, things got worse. A crowd almost as large as the previous day's was harangued by a forty-year-old woman, Marie-Jeanne Trumeau, the pregnant wife of a day laborer from the faubourg Saint-Antoine. Together with the twenty-four-year-old Pierre-Jean Mary, listed in the trial records as a "writer," she incited the crowd to continue what had been begun the day before. As they made their way across the Seine, the reinforcements from Saint-Marcel had been enlarged by river people: unemployed stevedores and the *flotteurs* who pushed timber rafts. With the brewers and tanners and workers from Saint-Antoine they made up a formidable crowd of between five and ten thousand who faced a barrier of *gardes françaises* in front of Réveillon's house.

The riot threatened to do something much more serious than destroy property or overwhelm the policing of Paris; it threatened to interrupt horse racing at Vincennes. For whether they lived in *hôtels* in the Marais or in Saint-Germain, the society owners of fleet geldings and fillies, and the many more who bet on them, had to pass through Saint-Antoine to get to the racecourse. Riots were riots but traffic jams were really serious, not to mention the abuse and fist-brandishing at anyone in a fashionable carriage failing to show enthusiasm for the Third Estate. The Duc d'Orléans, hero of the crowd (and horse magnate), was the exception. Greeted as (yet another) "father of the people," the Duc alighted from his carriage, waved amiably and made a few noises to the effect that all his friends should calm down. When they retorted that that was all very well but the bastard bosses were about to cut their pay to fifteen sous a day, Orléans responded in the only way he knew—by scattering bags of money among the crowd, and exiting to appreciative applause.

Understandably, tension relaxed. But the crowd remained and so did the guards in front of Titonville. They stayed like that for some hours until the racegoers returned. Sensibly, most of the traffic had been diverted at the *barrière* of the Trône—all, that is, except the carriage of Orléans' own wife, who insisted on the direct route to the Palais-Royal. Fatally, the guards parted to let her through and thousands suddenly followed, pouring into Réveillon's factory. The manufacturer and his family barely managed to make their escape through the gardens, from which they ran to the Bastille for safety. In two hours there was nothing left of their house and factory except the vast array of bottles in the cellar, which even a crowd of thousands was unable to consume at once. Immense bonfires in the garden consumed paper, gum—a perfect inflammable—paint, furniture, paintings.

Belatedly, a military force of some hundreds—comprising detachments of the *gardes françaises*, the city watch (the Guêt) and regular troops armed with some cannon and with drums beating—made its way to the house. Showered with stones and tiles, they first shot into the air and when that had no effect, directly into the crowd. Even the normally cool Marquis de Ferrières, who happened to witness the scene, described this as a massacre, though tallies of the exact number of dead ranged from twenty-five to nine hundred. Certainly there were at least three hundred civilians injured, and it seems probable that there were as many fatalities.

In an attempt to show firmness, two men caught looting—a porter and a blanket worker—were convicted and hanged on the thirtieth. Three weeks later another group of seven were tried and one of them, the public letter writer Mary, was executed after being paraded through the streets with a sign declaring him "seditious." Five of his fellows, including a fifteen-year-old apprentice locksmith, were forced to witness Mary's death before they in their turn were branded "GAL" on each shoulder and sent to the galleys signified by that mark. Marie-Jeanne Trumeau was reprieved by personal intervention of Réveillon himself.

In all respects but one the Réveillon riots were an unmistakable sign of things to come. The exception was that the militia of the *gardes françaises,* many of them from the same classes as the rioters, had obeyed orders and had not detached themselves (as they would three months later) from the regular troops. But there are distinct signs that they too felt themselves abused by authority, especially when the sergeant who had given the order to let the Duchesse d'Orléans pass was demoted. They collected donations from among the men to make up his lost pay and at the same time repudiated the officer who had ordered them to fire on the crowd.

More blood was shed in the Réveillon riot than at any other *journée* of the Revolution until the great insurrection of 1792 that would bring down the monarchy. So it is not surprising that it came as a violent shock to the governance of the city. The received wisdom that Paris could be policed by its normal complement of six thousand or so assorted forces was no longer plausible. The army was needed, even though that prospect filled many of the elite with as much apprehension as reassurance. The riot also divided commentators further into citizen-nobles who were appalled by the bloodshed and others like a captain from the Strasbourg garrison of the Royal Cavalry whose dinner in the Marais had been interrupted by the noise and who went to watch the spectacle for himself. What he saw was not a tragedy but "fifteen or sixteen hundred of the excrement of the Nation, degraded by shameful vices . . . vomiting up brandy, presenting the most disgusting and revolting sight."

The officers observing the melee had been forced to beat a hasty retreat when it was noticed that two of them were wearing the military decoration of Saint-Louis on their uniforms, so attracting the wrath of the crowd. But what really offended the captain was their "insolence" in appropriating the respectable slogan of the Third Estate—"*Vive* Necker and the Third Estate"—for their battle cry. And the true significance of the Réveillon riot was that it suggested just how vulnerable the self-appointed leadership of the people would be if it was established on the shoulders of popular force. Since the artisans of the faubourgs Saint-Antoine and Saint-Marcel had been educated to believe that their plight was attributable to "aristocrats" and sundry other unpatriotic persons, the continuation of that plight presupposed that traitors were still in power. Starvation, in other words, was a plot. Its logic meant that unmasking the conspiracy and doing away with those responsible would be putting bread in the mouths of the hungry.

For their part, the shaken representatives of the Third of Paris suspected that the rioters had themselves been bribed by royalist spies to foment disorder and so embarrass their new authority. Réveillon, after all, was himself an elector—one of their own kind, a modern man, liberal in his politics, a model capitalist in his trade. But it was exactly this kind of self-satisfaction on which revolutionary violence would make war. Though the ringleaders of the crowd in April 1789 were hapless, inarticulate figures, there were others within the franchise who were ready to fashion this rhetoric of social incrimination. Pamphlets were already circulating on the streets of Paris that held politics to the accounting of the breadline. *What No One Has Yet Said* was one of the titles, the work not of a member of the "Fourth Estate" but a barrister of the Parlement, de La Haie. What *he* said was that bread should be the first object of the Estates-General and that the very first duty of all true citizens was to "tear from the jaws of death your co-citizens who groan at the very doors of your assemblies." The same writer described coming out of an electoral meeting the week before and encountering several citizens whose poverty had denied them entry:

> They had only one thing to say:
> "Are they concerned with us, Monsieur? Are they thinking of lowering the price of bread? We haven't eaten anything for two days."

There were two kinds of revolutionary temper in Paris in 1789. The first was that of modern man: Sylvain Bailly, astronomer, academician, resident of suburban Chaillot, for whom the electoral assembly was equivalent to a kind of political rebirth.

> When I found myself in the middle of the district assembly, I thought I could breathe fresh air. It was truly a phenomenon to be something in the political order and by virtue alone of one's capacity as a citizen . . . that assembly, an infinitely small fraction of the Nation, felt nonetheless part of the power and rights of the whole and it made no pretence that these rights and that power lent it a kind of authority.

It was precisely that authority that the *Four Cries of a Patriot of the Nation* challenged. To make that challenge real, the writer asserted, citizens must be armed, and immediately. To make it real, aristocrats must be banished so the Nation would be delivered from their "infernal machinations." What point was there "preaching peace and liberty to men dying of hunger? What use would a wise constitution be to a people of skeletons?"

That was the second voice of revolution. Through the first year of revolution, the two voices would harmonize as the chorus of the Third Estate, Citizens-and-Brothers. But before long, aristocrats would vanish or perish and hunger remain. At that point a more serious shouting match would begin.

CHAPTER NINE
Improvising a Nation

i TWO KINDS OF PATRIOT

The Marquis de Ferrières to Madame de Ferrières
20th April 1789

I have arrived at Orléans, *ma bonne amie*, so I am taking a
few minutes to chat with you. The journey hasn't tired me out
at all; the weather has been superb; we slept at Orléans, crossing
the river even though it was nearly eight o'clock; the collapse
of the bridge has created a great inconvenience for travelers. I
supped with a good appetite and slept very well. My travelling
companions are all good fellows. M. de Châtre is much more
agreeable than I was told; he reasons well though perhaps is a
little *outré* in his ideas. There has been a revolt at Sainte-Maure
that needed a hundred men of the regiment d'Anjou. Bread at
Tours cost 5 sous a pound; at Blois it costs five and a half; the
people are very worried and fear dying of hunger. . . . We bought
a cask of wine at Beaugency which we shall send on to Versailles.
It cost us 195 livres without counting duties and shipment but at
least we can be assured of decent and not adulterated wine.

You would do well to sell some wheat at market. One never
knows what may happen. Don't forget the poor and support
charity in proportion to its needs. . . .

We shall arrive tomorrow evening in Paris, lodging in the rue
Jacob, I'm not sure which hotel.

Adieu, *ma bonne amie*, banish all anxiety. I know your devotion
too well not to fear that you may easily alarm yourself. I feel well:

that's the essential thing; for the rest, it will go as God pleases but I will fulfill my duties without obstruction, neither for or against, according to what seems to me to be right.

Kiss my Séraphine and my Charlotte; tell them that I love them very much. Remember me to M. de La Messelière. I'll write Thursday.

SO CHARLES-ELIE DE FERRIÈRES-MARSAY, gentleman-farmer and *amateur des lettres,* middle-aged and even-tempered, began a correspondence of more than a hundred letters to his wife, Henriette. From the spring to the late fall she remained at their château in the Poitou to oversee the harvest and then rejoined her husband in Paris for the winter. For two years, Ferrières became engaged in the political life of his country. By the time he completed his term in the Constituent Assembly, France was utterly transformed. The King and Queen had been returned to Paris in ignominy after an abortive flight to the frontier; war with the Queen's brother the Emperor of Austria seemed a certainty; demonstrators demanding a republic had been shot down on the Champ de Mars. To his deep dismay, Ferrières' own brother had joined the emigration, and during the Terror, Ferrières prudently dispatched to the local Commune six sacks full of seigneurial titles, rents and other documents that the National Convention had ordered suppressed "so that they could be burned at the feet of the Tree of Liberty, according to the law."

That little expiation would take place in a dismal autumn of the revolutionary future. But in 1789, on his way to the Estates-General as a deputy for the nobility of Poitou, Ferrières was full of vernal optimism. The smoking scenery of disaster through which his carriage ambled did nothing to depress his boyish high spirits. Others, more attuned to the fashionable culture of melancholy, might have seen something more in the collapse of the bridge over the Loire than an inconvenience to travelers. At the height of the January thaw, just as the public coach from Saumur had begun to cross, the first arch caved in. Only the spontaneous action of the driver, who cut the reins of his first horse, sending it flying into the river, saved the lives of his passengers as the remaining arches crumbled one after the other.

The Pont de Tours had been a typical construction of *ancien régime* modernity: carefully engineered, designed to transform commercial and human communications. It had only been opened ten years before the disaster. And much of the ebullient optimism of that time was collapsing along Ferrières' route. Reaching Paris, he burbled excitedly to his wife of dinners, theater and his gilt buttons *à la mode.* Like so many provincials he was thrilled with the Palais-Royal, taking in the circus, bookshops and cafés packed with people listening to political orators. But he quickly recognized that if the moment was charged with excitement, it was also charged with danger. One evening he went to the Opéra to see Gluck's *Iphigénie en Aulide* but, as he recounted to Henriette, "while I was surrendering myself to the sweet emotions that stirred my soul, blood was flowing in the faubourg Saint-Antoine." To his horror, a family friend, the Abbé Roy, was accused of being one of the instigators of the Réveillon riot. Four days after he left Orléans there was an attack on a grain store and the pillage of a Carthusian convent, led by boatmen, masons and other artisans and their wives, armed with hatchets. As in Paris and many other cities around the country there were deaths, the intervention of troops, the formation of citizens' defense militia. "All this makes our poor Kingdom tremble—a tissue of horrors and abominations," wrote the shaken Marquis.

At Versailles, he recovered his nerve, for the great day was approaching on which so many impossible expectations rested. Ferrières thought of himself as a Man of the Enlightenment: reasonable, benevolent, public-spirited and, above all, cultured, in a gentlemanly way. A descendant of the poet du Bellay, he combined philosophical and scientific enquiry with literary expression. A first book, called *Theism* (misleadingly, since it was full of deism and in it a country priest made the unlikely comment "theology is but a science of words"), appeared in 1785, and a year later another work, *Woman in the Social and Natural Order.* A number of his fellow peers at their assembly at Saumur were like-minded members of the club of reason, so it is not surprising to find their *cahier* one of the more liberal of the order. In its preamble it already insisted on equality before the law for all citizens, worried about the overrepresentation not of the commons but the clergy, and as insistently as any *cahier* of the Third declared that no taxes could be raised until certain fundamental civil and political freedoms had been established.

In keeping with this patrician individualism, the assembly decided not to impose on its deputies binding instructions as to whether they should deliberate and vote by head or order. It would, somehow, be the "establishment of the constitution" that, magically, would lead them to do the right thing. Thus the Poitou nobility seems to have belonged to that "mixed" group in which it was left to political contingencies to determine their conduct.

At any rate, the issue did not weigh very heavily on Ferrières' mind as he preened himself for the ceremonial opening of the Estates. He had discovered among the nobility the virulent hostility against Necker as the instigator of their troubles and had been taken aback by it. And he saw, with misgivings, how easily some of his fellow deputies, like the Comte de Gallissonnière, could come under the sway of court reaction and behave quite differently than they had at Saumur. But in the days before the ceremonial opening he threw himself wholeheartedly into "the pleasant and almost ridiculous side" of the proceedings: its spectacle.

Ferrières poked gentle fun at himself as he strutted his finery before Henriette in a letter: "black silk coat . . . waistcoat of gold or silver cloth; lace cravat, plumed hat"; and for those in "grand mourning" (among whom he decided to count himself) the hat would, like the King's, be *à la Henri IV* with its brim turned up at the front. The Marquis grumbled that the hat would set him back at the very least 180 livres (or a third of the average stipend of the country curates who made up a majority of the order of the clergy). But, instinctively, he understood that the matter of dress, as well as other aspects of the protocol, was not at all trivial. It was an integral part of a spectacle designed to suspend disbelief. In the place of skepticism, there was to be awe and exhilaration on the part of both participants and beholders. Through enactment, they were meant to feel themselves incorporated into a ritual of France Renovated: past, present and future arrayed and harmonized like some Ovidian metamorphosis. It was to be a second rising of the sun that had labored so hard to climb over the horizon on coronation day fourteen years before.

For Ferrières the strategy certainly worked. Throughout the opening ceremonies he was beside himself with patriotic ardor. On the sixth of May

CLERGÉ   NOBLESSE   TIERS-ÉTAT

84. Costume of the three orders

85. Procession of the Estates-General

he wrote to Henriette in a tone of almost mystical devotion to the Idea of France—"France where I was born; where I spent the happiest days of my youth; where first was engendered my moral sensibility. . . ." Evidently he had not minded the excruciatingly drawn-out reception of the deputies by the King on May 2. Instead, his heart had risen like the lark to the fanfare of silver trumpets, blown by heralds, seated on white chargers and dressed in purple velvet embossed with the fleur-de-lis. On Monday the fourth of May, he had beheld Louis XVI, greeted by flutes and drums at the Church of Notre Dame, enthroned with his family and court as choirs sang the *Veni Creator.* Then he had walked in procession to the Church of Saint-Louis behind the Cent Suisses with their Renaissance coats, paneled with lozenges of scarlet and gold; behind the Royal Falconers, who rode with hooded birds attached to their wrists. His own order followed—a river of silk, lace and plumage flowing between banks of Gobelin tapestries that were draped over the houses lining the streets.

Even as he marched slowly along, hearing the occasional shout of "*Vive le Roi,*" the rational side of Ferrières began to assert itself, and his reflections grew suddenly more somber. "France here showed itself in all its glory. But I said to myself, Could saboteurs, the ambitious, wicked men engaged only in their selfish interests, succeed in disuniting everything great and honorable so that all this glory would vanish like smoke blown away with the wind?" But at the place Saint-Louis he surrendered himself again to the ceremonial magic.

> The beautiful windows decorated with the prettiest women, the variety of hats, feathers, gowns; the sympathetic gentleness expressed on everyone's face, the drunken joy that shone from all eyes; the clapping of hands; gestures expressive of the tenderest concern; the looks that greeted us and followed us even when we were lost from sight. Oh my dear France, amiable and good people, I have made an eternal alliance with you. Before this day I had no *patrie;* now I have one and it will always be dear to me.

As Ferrières uneasily sensed, though, the very means used to induce his flight of patriotic rapture worked *against* it being shared by the Third Estate. Historically, public ritual that supported the myth of a single community deliberately gave great prominence, in costume and banners, to precisely those groups that were, in reality, excluded from power. So in Renaissance Venice or seventeenth-century Amsterdam, on days of parade, confraternities and militiamen fully shared in the color and show of the festivity. Through this incorporation myth was much more than a pretext for fancy dress: it generated and bonded allegiance.

The exact opposite happened in the first week of May at Versailles. The opening of the Estates-General was treated not like a public occasion in which rank would be dissolved into patriotic duty, but as an extension of court ceremony. Instead of being inclusive, it was exclusive; instead of opening up space, it closed it off. Instead of reflecting the social reality of late eighteenth-century France in which station *was* actually eroded by property and culture, it asserted an anachronistic hierarchy. Necker may have feared this. Like Turgot in 1775 he wanted the ceremonies to be perfunctory and the occasion to be moved to Paris. When the King declined, he was captive to the expertise of masters of ceremonies and those who laid down the law about historical precedent. Much of this was spurious. The *chapeau à la mode de Henri IV* actually owed more to the Henri IV fashions of the 1780s than to serious antiquarian research into the costume of 1614. Tradition was being reinvented for the occasion just as coronations in the nineteenth and twentieth centuries in Britain would manufacture it to invest the monarchy with an imperial aura.

The consequence of all this was to ensure that the form of the Estates-General was at war with its substance. The more brilliantly the first two orders swaggered, the more they alienated the Third Estate and provoked it into exploding the institution altogether. From the beginning they were stung by gratuitous slights. While the King received the deputies of the privileged orders in the *cabinet du roi,* those of the Third were removed to another hall where they filed past him like a crocodile of sullen schoolboys. Their costume was as dowdy as that of the clergy and nobility was lustrous. In black from head to foot, they looked like crows amidst peacocks or like stage caricatures of the bourgeois: a convention of apothecaries. Some of them, however, taking a cue from Franklin's costume of the *honnête homme,* knew how to turn this humiliation to their own advantage. One old man from Rennes, Michel Gérard, had refused to wear the assigned black-and-white costume and took his seat in the Salle des Menus Plaisirs dressed in brown fustian. Instantly recognizable as "Père Gérard," he looked the very picture of rustic virtue, as though he had modeled for Moreau's engravings of Rousseau's works.

But there was another immensely commanding presence among the deputies of the Third that defied absorption into an undifferentiated throng. Sheer size singled out Mirabeau: a mountain of flesh and muscle crammed with difficulty into black coat and hose. His already remarkable height was extended by celebrated bolts of hair brushed back and piled up into a Gothic tower of fantastic cloudy forms. At the back, hanks of it fell into a black taffeta bag that swung about his shoulders. Some compared this shaggy brute with Samson, who drew his strength from his locks. Others, like the deputy Adrien Duquesnoy, thought he resembled a tiger whose expression was disfigured in a snarl when he sounded off. Fully conscious of this reputation as a wild man, Mirabeau made the most of it, throwing his head back as he walked, in an exaggerated gesture of unappeasable disdain. To everyone who saw him—and people craned their necks to do so—he was a force of nature: pagan, dangerous and uncontainable within clothes or custom. His huge face seemed to have been formed by some volcanic eruption that had cooled, possibly temporarily, into a crust of pumice: pitted with dark holes, scabs and craters. (Its remarkable surface was the result of his mother's misguided faith in an herbal healer who had smeared his smallpox pustules with a concoction from which it had never recovered.) Germaine de Staël, who had no reason to appreciate a man who publicly calumniated her father, Necker, for vanity and pusillanimity, confessed that it was impossible to take her eyes off this apparition once it had been beheld.

Honoré-Gabriel Riqueti, Comte de Mirabeau, but deputy for the Third Estate, had long understood how to trade on his appearance and, just as important, his history. His father, Victor, was already a practitioner of the

86. Mirabeau

paradoxes of nobility, styling himself the *Ami des Hommes* and, before he abruptly turned physiocrat, transposing his brand of Provençal feudal paternalism into a theory of social relations. "The Friend of Man," his son tartly remarked, "was friend to neither wife nor children." Mirabeau grew up in embattled defiance of his alarming father, hating him, yet in many ways doomed to resemble the person he hated. Mirabeau *père* fell for his wife's maid, installed her in the house and eventually turned his tormented wife out, as she complained in her suit against him, without a patch of clothing. Blaming his father but little loved by his mother—who at one point shot at him with a pistol and missed—Mirabeau *fils* embarked on a long, spectacular career of philandering. He became another Casanova but not in the sense in which Casanova is usually misread as the relentless discharger of libido, rather the true Casanova, who fell absurdly in love with virtually every pretty woman he beheld. Gabriel's stupendous ugliness, like Talleyrand's limp, was no handicap in these conquests. He used it as an instrument of desire and accompanied it with a booming baritone that might have been made for the ardent crescendi demanded by Romanticism. He was, in short, like his father: sublime and terrible.

In the army, Mirabeau served in the French invasion of Corsica in 1769, helping to extinguish its freedom in the year of Napoleon Bonaparte's birth. Forbidden a military career by Victor, he spent the rest of his young manhood leading a gypsy life: writing inflammatory tracts; eloping with heiresses, seducing wives; running up debts that amazed even the Provençal nobility; doing everything he possibly could to guarantee the rage of his father. But in old-regime France paternal rage could take the form of imprisonment, and Victor had Gabriel locked up for his delinquency, first on the Château d'If in the Midi; later, when he had run away with Sophie Monnier, but had been caught in Amsterdam and the lovers separated, in the Château de Vincennes. Though this latter detention lasted a full three years, from 1777 to 1781, it was not as much of an ordeal as Mirabeau made it sound, since he enjoyed private quarters, amiable companions and even a private garden in which (naturally) he could attempt the seduction of his jailor's wife.

It was a Dutch girl who finally succeeded, for a while, in taking Mirabeau off the boil. She too had complicated paternal relations, being the illegitimate daughter of a famous Dutch writer, Onno Zwier van Haren. In a disingenuous exercise that revealed more than it concealed, he had given her the surname "Nehra" as an anagram of his own. Over the course of their wanderings in Holland, London, Paris and Berlin, Henriette-Amélie ("Yet-Lie," Mirabeau called her, rather unfunnily), from the land of water, quenched Mirabeau's fire and made him, for the first time, a reflective man:

someone capable of self-knowledge. More than is usually appreciated Mira-beau's politics were the product of intelligent roving: a kind of magpie cosmopolitanism. From the Dutch he picked up the rhetoric of Patriot polemics and the history of heroic republicanism; from the English, an institutional model for representation; from the Genevan Swiss, journalistic practice. But his flair for temerity and the theatrical gift through which it was communicated was pure Riqueti.

In 1789 he broke with "Yet-Lie" but he finally exorcised the demon of paternal wrath by becoming, in the eyes of the Provençal population, their collective father: *le père de sa patrie,* as he was called in public. He returned to his native region in that exceptionally wintry January to seek election as a noble deputy to the Estates-General. Provence, being a *pays d'état,* was permitted election through its provincial Estates. Spontaneous resistance to this arrangement had already expressed itself at a "General Assembly" of the towns, convened by their mayors at Lambesc the previous May. And that resistance had been given greater momentum through inspirational example in the Dauphiné and the pamphlet campaign of the fall. In December a petition signed by over two hundred contradicted the right of the Estates to monopolize the representation of the province.

The reform movement was made possible precisely because it had allies within the nobility and clergy. The Estates had foolishly sustained the tradition of excluding all nobles without fiefs—manorial estates—from their order. Within the clergy, there was bitter resentment among impover-ished village curates at the enormous wealth of the bishops, all of them drawn predictably from the leading aristocratic dynasties, and they were supported in this hostility by a substantial population of Protestants in the region. Within the towns, the mayors and aldermanic "consuls" were equally drawn for the most part from the wealthier sector of the privileged and drew on themselves the antagonism of both journeymen and masters of the guilds.

Finally, but not least, Provence was going through an acute food crisis, and popular anger focused on the list of identifiable villains to blame for it. A new representation of citizens, it was believed—as it was believed throughout France—would provide the answer. Mirabeau was quick to pick up on the significance of all this and to cast himself as the noble champion of the People. He announced this role even in the procession of the Estates at Aix, where he carefully placed himself a distance apart from and behind the file of nobles and thus some distance ahead of the Third.

Inside the assembly Mirabeau attacked the legality of its constitution. Whom did it purport to represent? The nobility did not represent the many without fiefs; the clergy did not represent the humble pastors of the Church, and as for the Third, it was nothing but a bunch of mayors, many of them aristocrats themselves who were cravenly dependent on the privileged for their office. "Woe to the privileged orders, for privileges will cease, but the People are eternal" was the threatening prophecy of his peroration. Taken aback by the outburst, and alarmed by the wild acclaim which greeted it from the public galleries, the President of the assembly suspended the proceedings in an attempt to gag Mirabeau. It was of no avail. Within twenty-four hours he produced a fifty-six-page manifesto, *To the Provençal Nation,* distributed on the streets of Aix.

On the pretext that the credentials for his qualifying fief or estate were not in order, Mirabeau was then barred from the Estates, but this of course only added to his popularity. Everywhere he went, he was surrounded by jubilant crowds chanting his name, snaking about his sedan chair in Provençal dances, serenading him with shrieking fifes and jangling tambourines. At Marseille, palms were strewn blasphemously at his feet and laurels crowned his brow. Mothers offered the most famous debauchee in France their infants to cuddle and kiss. At Lambesc the church bells tolled in his honor and his considerable weight was borne aloft on strong shoulders. "My friends," he responded with a word for all occasions, "men were not made to carry a man, and you support too much already."

Drinking in this spontaneous adulation Mirabeau was cool enough to know how to exploit it. Together with the lawyer Brémont-Julien, who acted as the manager of his election campaign, he put together the features of a custom-designed public personality: the Tribune of the People. In Aix (where memories of Rome ran strong) he compared himself with Marius of the Gracchi, harried by the patricians. In Marseille he produced his own promotional pamphlet purporting to come from "A Citizen of Marseille to one of his Friends on MM. Mirabeau and Raynal." After a few obligatory comments on Raynal, the author of an immensely popular indictment of European colonization, Mirabeau proceeded with a shy description:

> This good citizen [is] the most eloquent man of his time; his voice dominates public meetings as the thunder overbears the roaring of the sea; his courage arouses yet more astonishment than his talent and there is no human power that could make him abandon a principle.

Mere bombast, though, would not have been enough to give Mirabeau credibility. His blood may have boiled, but his head was cool enough to retain full self-possession in crisis. Most crucially for revolutionary circumstances, he knew how to use his immense standing with the crowds of the cities and villages of Provence to contain riot. For by late March, much of the province had become ungovernable. The first target was the episcopacy. On the fourteenth, the Bishop of Sisteron had barely escaped stoning at Manosque. At Riez the Bishop had to ransom himself and his palace for fifty thousand livres, but his counterpart at Toulon was not given the option. His palace was torched as companies of sailors and troops declined to come to his rescue. Attacks on châteaux in the countryside became commonplace. "There is open war here on landowners and property," wrote the *intendant*, de La Tour. And all of it was being carried out in the name of the King's will and pleasure!

On the twenty-third, the town hall of Marseille and the headquarters of the *intendant* were wrecked and looted. Riding hard from Aix, Mirabeau took command from the unnerved military governor, de Caraman, and became, on the spot, a self-authorized provisional dictator, prohibiting the departure of a grain ship from the port, organizing a citizens' militia (the first of its kind in France), distributing red rosettes as the insignia of his revolutionary authority. The town was full of addresses, orders and exhortations all written by him, printed up and posted in marketplaces where once the edicts of the King had been attended to.

The tone of these *notices*, moreover, announced a new political language: that of conversational brotherhood. Their hero was no longer "the Count" but plain "Mirabeau," who spoke directly to "the People." His speech was not so much written as uttered, much as one might explain something in a company of drinking friends. It was the diction of transparency: of the *honnête homme* of Rousseau's ideal. Mastering its expression, Mirabeau was bold enough not only to try to calm the inflamed feeling of the Marseillais but even to justify taxation:

> My good friends, I have come to tell you what I think about
> the events of the past three days in your proud city. Listen to me,
> I want only to be helpful to you and not deceive you. Each one
> of you wants only what is good because you are all honest men;
> but not every one of you knows what needs doing. One often
> makes mistakes even about one's own interest. Let us first con-
> sider bread. . . . At the present time, dear friends, since wheat is
> expensive everywhere, how could it be cheap at Marseille? . . .
> The town of Marseille, like every other town, pays something
> toward the expenses of the kingdom and the support of our good
> king. Money is taken from this source and a little from that. . . .

Two days later, Aix followed Marseille in a riot, answered with troops' firing into the crowds. The Archbishop, a Breton, was terrified. "The common people in their hatred threaten nothing but death and speak of nothing but tearing our hearts out and eating them." Mirabeau was once again summoned as a pacifier, creating a citizen militia to provide an order that would be trusted by the people and distributing bread at regulated prices. Not surprisingly all these efforts paid off handsomely. He was elected by substantial margins for the Third Estate at both Aix and Marseille. After flattering orations to the citizens of Marseille to avoid giving offense, he finally decided that he would go to Versailles as the deputy for Aix.

By his own account Mirabeau was not just esteemed. He was loved. The black sheep of his family had become the white knight of the People. The man whose own reactionary brother hated and despised him had a whole province of brothers. The son who could never please his implacable father had become father to a country of adopted children. "I was obeyed like an adored father," he wrote of this time, "women and children bathed my hands, clothes, steps, with their tears."

ii *NOVUS RERUM NASCITUR ORDO*
May–June 1789

At this critical juncture, much was expected of a third kind of Patriot: the King. In village *cahiers* he had been cast as "the new Augustus" who "will renew the Age of Gold." Unlike the old Augustus, however, Louis became decreasingly godlike in his self-confidence. As the Estates-General approached, his apprehensions grew. Berated by his wife and Artois for accepting the detestable Necker, he was himself far from convinced of the Minister's capacity to defuse the crisis. Only hunting, eating and locksmithing worked to calm his ragged nerves. On one occasion he literally lost his grip. Because of repairs being done to the slates on the roof of the Marble Court, where Louis was walking, he was obliged to use a stepladder to reach the observatory. On the fifth rung the ladder began to slide. The drop was forty feet to the yard below and only the acrobatic reflex action of one of the workmen grabbing the King's arms and hauling him to safety spared him a sudden and terrible injury.

The grateful monarch duly settled a handsome pension of twelve hundred livres on the man who had saved his life. Royal gestures towards an heroic subject were simple to make compared with the acute problem of whether to preserve or depart from the strictures of protocol. His master of ceremonies, the twenty-three-year-old Marquis de Dreux-Brézé, was no help, and the court consensus was that all traditional observances should be carefully maintained to avoid the impression that the Estates-General could indeed make things up as it went along. So the King, for example, agreed to retain the custom, impolitic at best, of requiring any member of the Third Estate addressing the throne to do so on bended knee.

In the heat of the moment, however, even the most fastidiously planned staging could go badly awry. At the end of his speech on opening day in the Salle des Menus Plaisirs, Louis doffed his hat—an "Henri IV" production in beaver with white plumes and a brilliant diamond set in the center—in customary salute to the assembly. After the correct, royally casual wave, he replaced it on his head, followed by the nobility, who thus assumed their superiority over the unprivileged Third. Either unsure of what the form was, or led by calculating mischief-makers, the Third then committed a heinous breach of protocol by putting their hats on too. In great confusion, some kept them on; more took them off again and, seeing this, Louis felt he then had to remove his own. For Gouverneur Morris, the American agent, who watched with increasing mirth, it was a delicious moment. But for the Queen, white with rage, the ceremonial collapse boded badly for things to come.

The Great Hat Fiasco might not have mattered had the assembly been spellbound by what the King had had to say. But that was not exactly its response. His address had been brief to the point of being perfunctory, and a peculiar mixture of enthusiasm and vexation. While he referred to the "great day, so ardently desired," the King also made irritable references to the "much exaggerated desire for innovations." If he seemed thus to speak with two voices, it was because he had yet to find his own. No doubt there was a conflict of sentiment going on inside his own personality, tempted by the acclaim of the people but frightened of its meaning. But that conflict was as nothing compared with the battle being fought out in his ministry, principally between Necker's open-minded optimism and the more intransigent Keeper of the Seals, Barentin, who refused to consider anything but the traditional form of the separated Estates.

It was Barentin, in fact, whose speech followed the King's. He sustained the tone of grudging concession by offering debate on the issue of a free press but issuing headmasterly warnings against "dangerous innovations." Any damage that his speech might have done to the prospects of reconciliation was vitiated by its complete inaudibility. Necker, as usual, was better prepared to deal with the impossible accoustics in the 120-foot-long Salle des Menus Plaisirs. Since his own speech on finance lasted three hours it was just as well. He read the first half hour and then handed the text to the secretary of the Royal Committee on Agriculture, Broussonnet, whom he had hand-picked purely for the shrilly megaphonic quality of his vocal projection. The effect was catastrophically miscalculated. For hour after relentless hour, lugubrious financial data of the 280-million-livre deficit were screeched at an assembly that was waiting instead for some grand act of rhetoric. It wanted to hear Necker the fiscal messiah, not Necker the accountant. Even more serious was the mounting impression that the Minister considered the gathering more as an administrative auxiliary than a reinventor of sovereignty.

While Necker's address droned on, the King, as usual, fought a losing battle against the royal yawn. Deputies fidgeted, coughed, snoozed, sneezed and snored. Mme de La Tour Du Pin, seated on the benches of the noble spectators, suffered agonies of discomfort, having nothing but the knees of those behind her against which to rest her back. Germaine de Staël, for whom the occasion was supposed to be the apotheosis of Papa, became more and more downcast, her eyes, according to another close witness, visibly brimming with tears.

Despite this unpromising beginning, the King's personal popularity was still a huge asset for the government. Wherever it seemed at all credible (and there was not much room for maneuver), his speech was interrupted with bursts of loyal applause—and not merely from the privileged orders. For the paradoxical reason that acts of popular violence were being committed in his name, the Revolution was his to command.

This was precisely Mirabeau's hope, for if he was no longer an aristocrat, he would never be a democrat. Even in Provence, in the middle of his grandstanding, he made no secret of his royalism. What he sought, he insisted over and over again, was a new monarchy, one supported not by hierarchy and privilege, but by popular endorsement. Historians are inclined to dismiss this view as a disingenuously adopted pretext for self-advancement. And it would be idle to pretend that Mirabeau was not, in 1789, eaten up with ambition; that he saw himself as the first minister of such a monarchy. But it would be equally callow to see the concept of a popular monarchy as *intrinsically* foolish. It was, after all, exactly what d'Argenson had in mind nearly a half century before—an energetic king defining his sovereignty *against* rather than in behalf of privilege and aristocracy. And something like this plebiscitary patriot-royalism did, after all, come to pass in both the Bonapartist empires. It seems safe to say, however, that Mirabeau would have detested the despotism of the Bonapartes. Encouraged by the Shelburne-Whig view of monarchy, he believed its best warranty lay in governments that would be produced by, and remain accountable to, the legislature. And it was exactly the British flavor of this constitutional view that disqualified it in the eyes of his fellow citizens.

For if Mirabeau was much the most celebrated *personnage* among the deputies, he was not the only political talent. Most of the Society of Thirty that had met at Adrien Duport's house had won election, including Target, the two de Lameth brothers and the Abbé Sieyès. Lafayette sat for the nobility of the Auvergne and other citizen-aristocrats, like Lally-Tollendal and Clermont-Tonnerre, joined him in the second order. Among the clergy were to be found Talleyrand, who had at last been elevated to the bishopric of Autun and had celebrated his first and last Mass in the cathedral on his ordination, and the more aggressively liberal Archbishop of Bordeaux, Champion de Cicé. Other figures who had made important contributions to the transformation of the Estates-General into a national assembly were also among the deputies of the Third: Mounier and Barnave from the Dauphiné, Rabaut Saint-Etienne from Nîmes.

This core group was abundantly gifted in intellect and eloquence, but it also came to Versailles having already undergone an intensive political apprenticeship, first in the revolts of summer 1788, and then in the intensive pamphlet and electoral campaigns of the following fall and winter. Some of its members, like Mounier and Mirabeau, had had direct experience of angry crowds in the streets. Even the apparently unworldly astronomer-academician Bailly (whose speciality was the moons of Jupiter) could claim formidable political education by having presided over the Paris elections to the Third. In deliberate defiance of the royal apportionment, the sixty Paris districts had produced a college of 407 electors—far larger than the designated body—and in yet another demonstration of autonomy, this assembly had constituted itself an unofficial form of the Commune that the royal government had expressly overruled. At the Hôtel de Ville, Bailly presided over a committee that had already arrogated to itself effective power of government in Paris.

None of this meant that a consensus emerged in the Third Estate on the strategic issue of an eventual constitution for the reborn France. Mirabeau, in particular, was a disruptive force by gratuitously reiterating his insistence on a royal veto long before the matter required discussion. But on the tactical matter of how to treat their relationship with the other two orders, there was far more accord. Here, Mirabeau was more helpful, appreciating accurately the obstructive power of inertia. On the days following the opening, the deputies agreed not to verify their credentials or begin any kind of deliberations except as a common body, joined with the other two orders. This guaranteed deadlock, for it was soon evident that notwith-standing the presence of a famous and articulate minority of nobles (includ-ing the Duc d'Orléans, who had provoked the King's wrath by seating himself as a deputy), they were vastly outnumbered by a much larger majority who refused to budge from their separate convocation.

In fact, the position of the nobility seems to have actually hardened from the more fluid and moderate line taken in so many of their assemblies. While they were all prepared to surrender their tax exemptions, in the face of mounting violence in the countryside many of them were now *less* sure of doing away with local seigneurial dues than had been apparent from the *cahiers,* lest they give some sort of license to a general attack on property. Even fewer were prepared to melt their collective identity into a general assembly. The Comte d'Antraigues, for example, who had been the earliest and boldest voice identifying the Third as a synonym for the Nation, now became a stickler for form. He insisted that *until* a constituent assembly had been convened—which could do anything it wished—the deputies were necessarily bound by the preceding conventions of the Estates of 1614. That this alteration of the collective mood of the nobility should have occurred was perhaps a tribute to the bewitching powers of Versailles itself. In the midst of the Patriotic euphoria of the electoral assemblies, with each speaker outbidding the other in the magnanimity of his views, a greater number of the nobility had felt able to endorse a vision of a liberalized France. Collected together within the highly ritualized, pseudo-chivalric circumstances of the palace city, they fell under the sway of their own reinvented history. This was especially true of the most blue-blooded grandees, who had often been elected deputies out of sheer deference to their impressively congested armorial bearings. Their reaction to the fashionable "young colonels" of the Orléans set who were urging them to be "good Patriots and citizens" was to dig in their heels against metropolitan modishness. *They,* not some overdressed popinjay from the Palais-Royal, represented the blood and soil of France.

These sentiments of knightly fraternity—a Gothic version of the citizen variety—affected even champions of the up-to-date like Ferrières. Though indifferent about the issue of voting by head or order, he nonetheless confessed to his wife that he didn't have it in him to desert his brother-peers. Even Lafayette felt checked by the cluck-clucking noises coming from Mount Vernon, where Papa Washington was looking on disapprovingly at the antics of the impetuous and inconstant French.

Things stood quite otherwise, however, with the clergy. And that, in the end, was what broke the deadlock. Where small electorates often produced disproportionately archaic results in the second order, the opposite was true for the first. For it was in the Church, more than any other group in France, that the separation between rich and poor was most bitterly articulated. At stake was not some abstractly defined principle of social justice or natural rights—but the fate of the Christian mission itself. The Enlightenment cliché of a steadily secularizing France completely fails to take account of just how deeply rooted the hold of Christian belief was in very large areas of the country. (Of all the failures of the French Revolution, none would be so inevitable and so dismal as the campaign of "dechristianization.") It was not just that the Church in France was merely marking time. Rather it was going through one of its periodic upheavals in which the claims of the pastoral clergy to embody the true spirit of the primitive evangel—humble, property-less and teaching the Gospel through works of charity and education—were argued against the worldly reality of episcopal big business.

At its most extreme, the division was startling. The wealthiest bishops like Strasbourg enjoyed an income of fifty thousand livres a year. The very poorest—vicars on fixed incomes without supplemental property or reve-nues—like Bréauté of Rouen barely subsisted on three hundred, while the standard stipend for *curés congrués* was only seven hundred. According to the curé of Saint-Sulpice at Nevers, once he had paid for pastoral expenses and food and clothing for his one servant, he was left with five sous a day for himself—or one quarter of the daily wage of an unskilled laborer in Paris. "When a priest is fortunate enough," wrote the same Abbé Cassier, "after twenty years of work and so much misery to obtain a little living of four or five hundred livres he can consider his fortune made and, taking possession of his church, he can mark out in the churchyard, in his capacity as first pauper of the parish, the site of his grave."

Not all country priests were this desperate. At least half—the *curés bénéficiés*—supplemented their income from tithes and some small piece of revenue-yielding property that they might farm directly or rent. But this still made the country curates in the Estates-General much the most authen-tic representatives of the majority of Frenchmen. They were certainly much closer to the People so freely apostrophized by the Third Estate than the lawyers, functionaries and professional men who made up that body. In another important respect they could also claim to speak for their con-stituents, for the great majority (perhaps 70 percent) of the forty thousand rural priests were native to their parish district or region. This made a forcible contrast to the aristocratic clans who carved up the great bishoprics among them and dispatched their junior relatives off to this or that diocese without a thought of any but the most crudely proprietary relationship.

Since 1786, for example, Talleyrand had been waiting impatiently for one of the Archbishop of Bourges' many fits of apoplexy to finish him off so that he could mobilize friends and relations in a campaign for the succes-sion. But the old boy showed infuriating resilience, and by the time he did succumb, Talleyrand's patron, Calonne, had been replaced by the unsym-pathetic Brienne. He was forced to sit the matter out until another timely demise—at Lyon—produced the desired vacancy. The incumbent Bishop of Autun moved to Lyon, and at last Talleyrand found himself on his knees on January 16, 1789, with all the solemnity he could muster, vowing to obey the apostolic succession of Saint Peter and "preserve, defend, augment and promote the authority, honors, privileges and rights of the Holy Church." The next day he laid hands on the pallium of Autun, said to be made from the wool of blessed sheep that had grazed in the pastures of the first Christians of antiquity, and more to the point, on the twenty-two thousand livres of his episcopal income. Together with his old benefice of Saint-Rémy and a new one at Poitiers, this added up to a decent income of over fifty thousand livres a year. That evening the defender of Saint Peter had dinner as usual with his mistress, Adelaide de Flahaut, in the Louvre.

This immense transfer of property and power had been accomplished without Talleyrand going anywhere near Autun. It was the twelfth of March before he deigned to arrive for his official entry at the cathedral, where he vowed (again) to remain faithful to his "bride of Autun." Holy Week was impending, but it was the political, not the religious timetable that determined Talleyrand's appearance, for he was eager to be elected by the clergy of Autun to the Estates, and to this end he had fully prepared the *cahier* for the chapter and diocese. It was a typical document of his image of France: rational, liberal, constitutionalist—hardly concerned at all with the care of souls. To secure election on the second of April he went through the motions of being a Good Bishop—exhorting seminarians to prayer, attempting (unsuccessfully) to celebrate Mass without garbling the rubrics and, at his most bare-faced, preaching a homily—"The Influence of Morality on the Leaders of Peoples"—to the Oratorian college. Ten days after his election to the Estates, on the tenth of April, and less than a month after his arrival at Autun, he disappeared for good. It was Easter Sunday and he had, at all costs, to avoid saying Mass.

It is hard to imagine a greater distance between Talleyrand's concept of the Church and that of the country priests who composed almost two thirds of the order of the clergy at Versailles. It would be wrong to see the Bishop of Autun as wholly amoral. As he had already proved as agent-general of the clergy, his understanding of the Church was, as he supposed, "modern." Its clergy were spiritual functionaries of the state, vested with educational and social responsibilities, and supplying the kind of moral stewardship that would assuage the popular yearning for belief without presuming to adjudicate law or share in government. If this fell a good deal short of his episcopal oath, it was a view that would be institutionalized under the Directory, the Bonapartist state—and for much of the century that followed.

It was, however, remote from the kind of social evangel of Rousseau's *Savoyard Vicar,* in which simple souls were to abjure the corruptions of property and urbanity, the better to steer fellow children of nature to a morally pure existence. Many strands in French religious history led towards this austerely defined piety: Jansenism, "Richerism" and a form of Presbyterianism that was sometimes explicitly and sometimes only implicitly Protestant. It was also, however, embedded in much of what the angrier *cahiers* of the curates—both in town and country—had to say. Their enemies were wealth, whether monastic or episcopal, and aristocracy, lay or clerical. Their tocsin was rung for the poor and famished, the indebted and the vagrant, whom they fed and sheltered in the worst of circumstances.

Their strength of numbers in the electoral assemblies and the dovetailing of their gospel with Third Estate rhetoric emboldened the curates to confront the Lords of the Church directly. "Who are you, *Messieurs les Grands Vicaires?*" asked the curé of Charly, to puncture their pretensions. "Nothing. Me, I am a curé, and my title will never be effaced." At Béziers, the Bishop of Agde felt intimidated by the crowd of 260 curates in an assembly of 310. Often Bishops or their nominees failed to get elected at all. Others who were, made no secret of their dismay at having to sit on a deputation with a holy rabble. "It is not without repugnance that I accept this commission" was the gracious comment of the Bishop of Luçon on being elected along with five curés.

Against the purple and scarlet robes of the bishops and archbishops, the curates wore their black with the same self-conscious defiance as the deputies of the Third. Not surprisingly, enough of them shared the position of the Third for them to divide their order down the middle on the crucial matter of verification of credentials.

For a full month following the opening session on May 5, the proceedings of the Estates had been paralyzed (as Mirabeau and his colleagues fully intended they should be) over verification. Once the ceremonies were over, the deputies of the Third could have sat where they chose in the large Salle des Menus Plaisirs. But they carefully left the benches of the two orders vacant pending the day when they might return for common deliberation. On the eighteenth they issued a formal summons for common verification, arguing that all three orders were no more than arbitrary divisions of one body, and must proceed accordingly.

Ferrières was bored and exasperated. "Our Estates do nothing," he wrote to Henriette on the fifteenth. "Every day we gather at nine in the morning and leave at four in the afternoon, spending our time in useless gossip." Though he had come with liberal credentials, the more time elapsed the more impatient he became with the "intrigues" of the Third, whom he blamed for the impasse. He even dined with Artois, the Polignacs and Vaudreuil, who swept him off his feet with urbane charm. "The Count [Vaudreuil] and I have become friends," he warbled excitedly to Henriette.

Diane de Polignac threw him a compliment and he was hers to command. Commenting on its conversational freedom, he wrote that their house was *l'Hôtel de la Liberté.*

Mirabeau had a quite different notion of *Liberté.* As Ferrières was retreating from public opinion Mirabeau was busy shaping it. On the seventh of May he began publishing the *Journal of the Estates-General,* designed to communicate its proceedings—and editorialize on their import. Its banner bore the legend *Novus Rerum Nascitur Ordo*—A New Order of Things Is Born. The government immediately shut it down, thus guaranteeing a large readership for its successor, *The Letters of M. de Mirabeau to His Constituents.* The campaign of challenging the government through self-promotion was not casually adopted. His strategy seems to have turned on the eventual possibility of replacing Necker at the head of a ministry that could, simultaneously, command the confidence of the King and the assembly. For some weeks, all of his comments, public and private, on Necker were scathing. But in the last week of May, his friend Malouet—the ex-*intendant* of Saint-Domingue and the only high officer in the Third—discovered that for all the clash of personalities, the position of the two men on the assembly was not that far apart. Both wanted verification in common; both wanted to create a popular monarchy. But no sooner was this kite flown than it fell abruptly to earth. Mirabeau came to see Necker at his office. "Well, Monsieur," said the Minister without looking up from his papers, "M. Malouet tells me you have some propositions to put to me. What are they?" "My proposition is to wish you good day," retorted Mirabeau, who turned on his heel and departed, fuming.

Though "commissioners" were dispatched from the orders to conduct some sort of negotiations, they succeeded only in confirming the polarization of the second and third orders. On June 3, the deputies of Paris at last took their seats, with Sieyès the last on the list, considerably strengthening the radical forces in the assembly, which now habitually referred to itself as the "Commons." In particular, this radicalization meant sabotaging a compromise painfully worked out by Necker in which electoral disputes within each order were to be referred to a general commission of reconciliation composed of representatives from all three houses. On June 10, Mirabeau interrupted a reading of the agreement to allow Sieyès to present a motion. That statement dismissed compromise on the grounds of intransigence on the part of the nobles and proposed instead to send a final ultimatum to the other orders, before proceeding with the roll call. That would force either an admission of deadlock or a capitulation. In any event, it was an act of revolutionary self-authorization—though scarcely the first in a line of such departures that had begun in Grenoble a year earlier.

In a thoughtful recent study of Necker's role in the events of 1789,

R. D. Harris has made the point that it was this essentially unreasonable claim for the *ascendancy* of the Third over the other two orders that doomed any attempt at compromise and propelled France to revolution rather than peaceful change. He sees this as the ominous exercise of majoritarian rule over unprotected minorities. The alternative was a dispersed form of government, on something like the British model, with the aristocracy preserved in an upper house and the "Commons" making up a lower, representative body.

But this is to sigh for an option that had already become obsolete. Doubtless such an alternative was theoretically conceivable for Necker (whose Genevan version of a bicameral legislature had repeatedly collapsed), or for moderates like Malouet. But it utterly overlooks the entire history of the elections, the rhetoric of their assemblies and the *material* expectations that were riding on a much more ambitious political transformation. It was no longer merely a question of fine-tuning the modernizing monarchy, but of some sort of collective rebirth. Citizenship for many deputies of the Third, like Barnave from Grenoble and Robespierre from Arras, was, just as Rousseau had insisted, indivisible. It was the expression of a sublime reciprocity between the individual and the General Will: indeed the *only* way they could be reconciled and made whole. It was, to be sure, exactly the kind of "strange and unaccountable appeal . . . to ideal and visionary rights of nature" that Arthur Young found so objectionable, but it was the authentic voice of the Revolution.

Nor—for better or worse—had this moment been reached through sage deliberations on workable government in the manner of the American Constitutional Convention. To wish that it had is to mistake the process by which politics unfolded in France—a process that was always intensely theatrical and histrionic. That may have been deplorable, like the waves of applause from public spectators at the proceedings of the assembly, which Arthur Young could never accustom himself to and thought "grossly indecent." But it was only through such stage business, and the augmented reality of Romanticism, with its emotional swoop from euphoria to terror, that the advocates of change could mobilize their public. Reasoned debate was entirely beside the point. "The people of Paris," observed Etienne Dumont, "were filled with inflammable gas like a balloon."

Paradoxically, since he was the arch-manipulator of the charismatic moment, Mirabeau was sometimes embarrassed by this unruly spontaneity, "the spectacle of young schoolboys escaped from the rod and mad with joy because they are promised an extra day's vacation." To try to bring some semblance of order into the proceedings, he encouraged his Genevan friend Dumont to translate Romilly's account of British parliamentary rules—an initiative that brought down on him a storm of indignation for being enslaved to antique, foreign customs.

All of these considerations were swept aside on June 13. On that date, three curés responded to the roll call initiated by Sieyès. Since the first order had voted to verify separately only by the narrow margin of 133 votes to 114, the moment was decisive. The three were all from the Poitou—Ferrières' province—and their leader, Jallet, the curé of Cherigny, had become well known for his piety and patriotism. The son of a gardener on a seigneurial estate (more virtuous botany!), he had been for thirty years a model of saintly humility, administering to the sick and needy while subsisting in the most impoverished circumstances. He was so poor that initially he could not afford the journey to Versailles, which, along with his living expenses, was paid by subscription. Walking into the Salle des Menus Plaisirs and announcing his presence, he was greeted with a roar of acclaim, embraced by his colleagues over and over again and carried shoulder-high in triumph to a seat.

On the fourteenth, as the roll call proceeded inexorably, more priests, hailing from Brittany and Lorraine, appeared, including Grégoire, the curé of Embermémil and champion of the rights of Jews. By the nineteenth there were more than a hundred joining the assembly, which had by this time claimed a new name for itself. The debate on the subject of a title, begun

87. The Third Estate appeals for the support of the curés. "Take my hand, M. le Curé, I know that you'll be with us" read the inscription.

two days earlier, had quickly revealed different political personalities. Sieyès, still the most radical voice, had insisted that since the assembly represented "96 percent" of the nation, it should not delay any further the "common work of national restoration." His title for such a body, however, was not the stuff of inspirational manifestos: "The Known and Verifiable Representatives." Mounier had been even more cautious, proposing "the major part of the representation, convened in the absence of the minor part." Mirabeau, typically, had attempted to cut through these abysmally cumbersome nomenclatures by suggesting "Representatives of the People," a proposal criticized for its excessively plebeian connotations! Before the end of the proceedings at ten that night, the meeting had decided by a large majority to call itself "National Assembly" and—again on Mirabeau's motion—that all present taxes should be declared null and void unless authorized by that body.

It was a moment of self-definition. Ninety deputies had voted against the majority of four hundred and ninety. But their anxieties about this act of self-authorization were overwhelmed in the onrush of high patriotic passion. Arthur Young, normally all sobriety, was no more immune than the participants to this surge of political adrenaline.

> The spectacle of the representatives of twenty-five millions of people just emerging from the evils of two hundred years of arbitrary power and rising to the blessings of a freer constitution, assembled with open doors under the eye of the public, was framed to call into animated feelings every latent spark, every emotion of a liberal bosom; to banish whatever ideas might intrude of their being a people too often hostile to my own country and to dwell with pleasure on the glorious idea of happiness to a great nation, of felicity to millions yet unborn.

iii TABLEAUX VIVANTS
June 1789

On the fourth of June, the Dauphin died. He was seven years old and the second of the royal children to die in childhood. At his birth in 1781, fireworks had burst in the skies over Paris; the Hôtel de Ville had witnessed a spectacular banquet for privileged and commons alike. At his death France scarcely noticed and the Hôtel de Ville was the seat of what, in all but name, was a revolutionary municipal government. At a time when the eight-pound loaf was at an all-time high, 600,000 livres were reported to be assigned for his burial. "You see, *ma bonne amie,*" Ferrières reported drily to his wife as he prepared to go and sprinkle holy water on the body at Meudon, "the birth and death of princes is not an object of economy."

By all accounts he had been a bright and endearing boy, certainly the apple of his mother and father's eye. But he had not enjoyed good health. Lately it had become apparent that tuberculosis—"consumption"—had destroyed his right lung. He endured a long, wasting sickness in which he became so emaciated that his ribs and pelvis stuck out at irregular angles from his trunk. When he finally died, both parents were distraught, the more so because the political crisis hardly allowed for personal grief. Louis' spirits had, in any case, been downcast by the collapse of the conciliation committee, by which he had set much store and for which he had written a personal letter of commendation. The loss of his son and heir seemed a much worse blow. He withdrew from public business and after the week's formal lying-in-state removed himself altogether from Versailles to the country house at Marly-le-Roi prostrate with sorrow. A deputation from the Third duly arrived to offer condolences. But the *père de la patrie* wanted, simply, to be for a while the mourning *père de famille.* When told of their insistence on being admitted, he replied, "Is there no father among them?"

As he recovered himself, he did so by leaning on the support of his immediate family. It was not disinterested. News reached Marly of the self-authorization of the Third Estate as a National Assembly and of its declaration that current taxes were illegal. Both were direct challenges to the sovereign, and Artois and the Queen believed—not unrealistically—that if the monarchy was ever to recapture control of its own destiny it had to do so now. Supposing that some sort of stand was to be made, one of two courses of action was possible: direct military intervention, for which the crown did not have sufficient forces yet available, or an assertion of the King's legal authority, coupled with the promise of agreed reforms. Even in the latter option Necker, who recalled only too well the fate of the Brienne reforms, saw nothing but disaster. But he was brusquely shoved aside by Artois, who blamed him for the predicament of the crown and who made no secret of his determination to be rid of the Minister. On approaching the council chamber before the crucial meeting on June 19, he shouted that as a foreigner and an upstart Necker had no business being there.

Supported by three of his colleagues, Montmorin, Saint-Priest and La Luzerne, Necker laid out a list of proposals for reform that faithfully followed the consensus of much of the *cahiers.* Prominence would be given to gestures of "patriotic duty" like the abolition of tax exemptions for the

357

privileged. On what had become the most contentious issue, Necker's plan approximated the "mixed" vote solution, presumably hoping to detach the moderate nobility from the reactionary minority. Deputies were to be permitted to vote in common on "national" issues like the periodicity of the Estates but not on matters pertaining to the separate orders. Working on this program at the end of May, Necker had wanted the King to issue its substance in a grandiose "declaration" that would have preempted the radicalism of the leaders of the Third. But the opportunity had passed, and his compromise was now doomed to please no one. The preservation of a society of orders implicit in its provisions was wholly irreconcilable with the National Assembly of common citizens created on the seventeenth. So the plan was bound to be unacceptable to that body, reinforced as they were each day by a growing number of the clergy.

But it was much too radical for the reactionaries at court. Making no secret of their hatred for the man whom they blamed for the crown's predicament, Artois and the Queen did all they could to persuade the King of the necessity for his removal. As Louis seemed about to accept Necker's program, the Queen interrupted the council for a conversation with her husband. When he returned, to Necker's consternation, the King backed away from the plan, insisting that it had to be submitted to the enlarged council for further consideration. All that was agreed upon were the minatory elements of the plan, which reminded Necker all too vividly of the fate of the Brienne reforms. The King would confront the Estates in a grand plenary *séance royale*, simultaneously showing his paternal benevolence in reform and his august majesty in annulling the usurpations of June 17.

For so momentous an event, the ceremonial machine of Versailles had to be cranked up again. A dais had to be erected, the benches reorganized from their configuration for the Third to accommodate the entire assembly. But by virtue of what had happened on June 17, the Salle des Menus Plaisirs was no longer simply a piece of royal property to design at the King's pleasure. It had become, in effect, the first territory staked out by the Nation.

So when the Nation found itself locked out of its home without warning by workmen preparing the hall for the *séance royale,* it assumed that this had been intentional rather than inadvertent. Armed guards, after all, barred the entrance, at which were placards summarily announcing the *séance royale.* The letter from the master of ceremonies to Bailly had arrived only at the last minute and with no indication of an alternative meeting place. It seemed suspiciously like the first step in the dissolution of the Assembly. Chagrin turned to fury as the deputies stood about in heavy rain. The good Dr. Guillotin—the hero of the December petitioning campaign in Paris—

remembered a tennis court owned by a friend of his in the rue du Vieux Versailles. And it was to that address that six hundred wetly exhilarated representatives trooped, followed by a gathering crowd.

Though it was Real—that is, Royal—Tennis that was played there, the naked, echoing court was the perfect opposite of the profusely decorated palace from where they had come. There they had been in the realm of the monarchy, a place allowed to them. Here they were, as Rousseau intended, stripped down to elemental citizenship and brotherhood. There was nothing but their bodies, their voices bounding off the pitched interior roofs from which tennis balls usually rebounded. A simple pine table was requisitioned from a next-door tailor, which served for the desk of the President, Bailly. Spectators crammed into the lower galleries and thrust their heads through the gallery windows. Clearly a performance was at hand. But of what kind?

Sieyès argued that the deputies should remove themselves as a body to Paris and be done with the charade of Versailles once and for all. But it was Mounier, who needed no lessons on the improvisation of authority (but who was concerned to head off the most radical proposals), who produced an alternative. "Wounded in their rights and their dignities," he proclaimed, the members of the Assembly had been warned of attempts to push the King to a disastrous course of action. Against the threat of dissolution, they should instead swear an oath "to God and the *Patrie* never to be separated until we have formed a solid and equitable Constitution as our constituents have asked us to." It was a gesture of sheer genius, for it cut the Assembly loose from its mooring in a particular space. Until that moment, the ordering of sovereign institutions in France had been defined by the space they were given to occupy: palaces of justices, council rooms, courts. But Mounier's motion set the vessel of state off on a sea of abstraction. Wherever they were gathered was to be the National Assembly.

What kind of body language could possibly live up to the grandiloquence of the moment? With a sense that they had finally set themselves into a history worthy of the Romans, they joined in adopting the gesture given to the Horatii by Jacques-Louis David, and which they believed was the profession of patriot-martyrs. To give himself presidential prominence Bailly stood on the tailor's table, placed one hand on his heart—the gesture *par excellence* of Rousseauean sincerity—and raised the other in command. With right arms outstretched, fingers taut, six hundred deputies became new Romans, echoing the oath in a version polished by Barnave. Only one, Martin d'Auch of Castelnaudary—depicted in David's drawing of the scene as scowling, seated, his hands locked tight across his chest—declined. Arthur Young immediately recognized the revolutionary nature of the act. It

88. A B O V E : Detail of Jacques-Louis David, *The Oath of the Horatii,* 1785

89. B E L O W : Anonymous print, Tennis Court Oath (detail)

was "an assumption of all authority in the Kingdom. They have at one stroke converted themselves into the Long Parliament of Charles I."

On the following day, the augmented council met at Versailles, postponing by one day—till the twenty-third—the *séance royale* to allow more time for discussion (and, some feared, for military reinforcement). The effect of the Tennis Court Oath had been to aggravate even further the hostility to Necker on the part of the King's brothers. Artois in particular shouted abuse at him and made no secret of his determination to be rid of him. The following day was worse. Despite support from Necker's minister-colleagues, the princes were determined to reject any encroachment on the separate jurisdiction of the orders for any business whatever. In that view, it followed that there could be *no* business that could be declared "national" and so considered by the assembly as a whole. Any concessions on the part of the privileged orders as to their tax exemptions and the like would be purely for them to volunteer, not for general legislation. All this was to be upheld in the name of the inviolability of the "French constitution."

In its repudiation of the common purposes of the Nation, it was a breathtaking reaction that traveled backwards beyond the reform programs of the 1780s, beyond Turgot to some sort of fantastic France based on classical order and hierarchical obedience. It was a France that had never really existed save in the absolutist idyll of the Hall of Mirrors, where it was lit by the Sun King's five-foot silver candlesticks.

Would Louis XVI try to turn himself into Louis XIV? Before the last meeting on June 22 he asked Montmorin and Saint-Priest, the two ministers who supported Necker, for their views. Both were under no illusions that such a confrontational position would ever receive assent. It would have to be enforced. But there was no money in the Treasury to pay for the enforcers and, said Montmorin, a policy of reaction guaranteed that the Estates-General would never vote any further revenues. What was the alternative? Saint-Priest tried to make the King see that, however unfortunate unauthorized changes had been, it was "the weight of present circumstances" that had to govern his decision. "Shipwreck threatens the vessel of state," he wrote, hardly overstating the situation. And quite correctly he pointed out that, historically, there had been nothing immutable about the French constitution anyway. It was necessary to accept change when circumstances required it, for "nothing stays the same under the sun"—an unfortunate choice of cliché, since Louis' reign, after all, had begun with the emblem of a new sun rising over France.

All this was to no avail. Three councillors—Barentin, de La Galaizière and Vidéaud de La Tour, who wrote an alternative speech for the King—supported the hard line of Artois and Provence. The King then replaced

Necker's plan with theirs and braced himself for the inevitable collision of wills the following day.

Though it was a *séance royale*, not a *lit de justice*, the occasion had all the atmosphere of a traditional assertion of royal will. Soldiers surrounded the assembly hall. For the last time the Third Estate was gratuitously humiliated by being made to enter from a side door while the other two orders were seated. It was also forcibly separated from the deputies of the clergy, including now the liberal archbishops of Bordeaux and Vienne, who had rallied to its assembly. Necker was not present to listen to the formal defeat of all his attempts at conciliation. When the King spoke, it was with a perceptible nervousness that had not been apparent at the opening session on May 5. He was, he said, "the common father of all my subjects" and he owed it to them to end the unhappy divisions that had impeded the work of the Estates-General. Fifteen articles were then read for him, one after the other, making only too plain his intention to preserve the three orders and annul the "illegal" proceedings of the seventeenth and the "anticonstitutional" limits placed on deputies by the mandates of their constituents. There followed another set of personal remarks by the King, including the self-congratulatory comment "I can say, without illusion, that never has any King done so much for any nation."

It was a bitter pill to swallow. The thirty-five reform proposals that followed were intended to sweeten it, but they were covered with only the lightest powdering of sugar. The first item stated axiomatically that no taxes would be raised except by the assent of the representatives of the people—at the same time that that representation was itself being made moot. Similar reservations were scattered through the text. Liberty of press was granted provided it did not harm religion, morals or the "honor of citizens": virtually the status quo. *Lettres de cachet* were abolished *except* in cases of sedition or family delinquency. (Mirabeau must have had good cause for a sardonic smile at that point.) Tax exemptions could be ended, but only if the privileged agreed, and all seigneurial dues and rights were to be preserved and protected as an inviolable form of property.

At the end, the King issued an admonition. Should the assembly "abandon him" in his efforts, he would be forced "to proceed alone for the good of my people, and I will consider myself alone to be their true representative." If necessary, then, and with the utmost reluctance, he would turn himself into an Enlightened Despot. For now, "I command you, Messieurs, to adjourn directly and tomorrow assemble in your separate chambers to resume your sessions."

Nothing of the sort happened. On the twenty-second, while Necker's plan was being sabotaged in the royal council, the National Assembly had continued to meet, fortified now by over 150 of the clergy and a group of 47 nobles who had signified their clear intention to join their fellow citizens. In a display of childish petulance, Artois had actually rented the tennis court to prevent their meeting but, in the spirit of Mounier's motion, the Church of Saint-Louis did just as well. There they had determined to meet immediately following the *séance royale.*

Following the exit, in deathly silence, of the King and the court, carpenters entered to dismantle the dais and platforms used for the ceremony. The Third remained defiantly seated amidst the clatter and hammering and metamorphosed once again into the National Assembly. Under Bailly's presidency they stubbornly affirmed all their earlier decisions. Mirabeau, whose knowledge of summary arrest was unrivaled by anyone in the Assembly, in particular exhorted his colleagues to declare the personal inviolability of the deputies. Whatever good might have been contained in the reforms, he said, they had been imposed in the most offensive manner. It was not for "your mandatory" to impose laws but for the "mandatory" to receive laws from the "inviolable priesthood of the Nation." Any assault on that inviolability was to be, in a neologism he coined, *lèse-nation.*

At that point the young Marquis de Dreux-Brézé, the master of ceremonies, whom the King had specifically instructed to prepare the hall for the Third Estate, mustered up enough courage to reiterate the royal order to leave the hall forthwith. His remarks were addressed to Bailly, but it was Mirabeau whose shaggy head bore down on the preciously dressed boy, hat on head, condescending to give orders to the "unprivileged." Mirabeau was sick and enfeebled with hepatitis, and his voice may not have carried with its usual booming amplitude. Accounts differed as to whether the words that followed were actually as Mirabeau himself claimed: "Go tell those who have sent you that we are here by the will of the people and that we will not be dispersed except at the point of bayonets."

Accuracy of report is not the issue though. The French Revolution was to be made up of such *tableaux vivants,* crystallizing in theatrical form the intensity of emotion experienced by its participants. Only with this dramatic license could its message be communicated to the many millions who could thus share its euphoria, become engaged in its outcome and so bond themselves to its allegiance. It was, already, a new kind of religion.

Mirabeau's intervention was actually resented by Bailly as a gratuitous call to arms, but he repeated the Assembly's decisions to continue their proceedings. Dreux-Brézé withdrew, walking slowly backwards, hat on head, precisely as official etiquette prescribed: a suitable valediction for the ritual of absolutist Versailles. His was merely a retreat. Louis XVI's response, however, was surrender, no less complete for being so casually expressed. Told of the resolution of the Assembly, he shrugged his shoulders and remarked, "Oh well, let them stay."

As in the summer and autumn of 1787, the King did the worst possible thing by parading a show of royal authority but then shrinking from enforcing it. He was increasingly incapable of deciding whether he could indeed become some sort of King of the People as Mirabeau wanted or the anointed of Rheims, armed with the *oriflamme*. The question suddenly became urgent, since a popular riot seemed in the making in the center of Versailles in response to Necker's eloquent absence from the *séance royale*. In the late afternoon several hundred deputies were seen going to the Contrôle-Général in a gesture of solidarity, and they were rapidly joined by a crowd of five thousand, shouting *"Vive Necker."* Marie-Antoinette, who had been boldest in her defiance of the People, now was the first to be frightened by them as they poured into the courtyard of the château and then into its interior, unobstructed by the *gardes françaises* militia. Asking to see Necker, she implored him not to resign and in a separate interview the King followed suit.

Now that the hard-line policy was so evidently in ruins, Necker agreed to remain at his post on condition that the King implement his original program designed to reunite the three orders. Leaving the King he walked among deputies and rejoicing townspeople, characteristically attempting to sober their jubilation. "You are very strong now," he told the deputies, "but do not abuse your power." In contrast to this popular triumph, the King departed for Marly, his coachmen cutting through a surly and ominous crowd.

There were still fitful attempts to impose royal authority. On the day after the *séance royale* Bailly arrived at the hall to find it invested with troops who, as on the day before, had orders not to allow into the hall any deputies from the noble and clerical orders, nor any members of the public. But his indignation vanished when it became apparent that the officer charged with this duty had in effect gone over to the National Assembly and that his men were eagerly fraternizing with the deputies, insisting that "we, too, are citizens." The "patriotic clergy" was then taken through a back entrance into the Salle des Menus Plaisirs, where, led by the Archbishop of Vienne, they once again became part of the National Assembly. Later that day, the Archbishop of Paris, who had been mistakenly singled out as a prime enemy of the people, barely escaped stoning in his carriage.

The following day, June 25, brought another *tableau vivant* into the annals of the National Assembly when forty-seven of the liberal nobility finally joined the Assembly. They had been preceded by two nobles of the eight deputies from the Dauphiné, the remainder joining them *en*

90. "Better late than never"—the reunion of the
three orders within a sacred triangle inscribed
with the legend *Omnes Cives*: All Are Citizens

bonne compagnie, as they put it the next day. They were led by Stanislas
Clermont-Tonnerre and included many of the members of Duport's club
of the previous autumn: Lally-Tollendal the father-vindicator, the Duc
d'Aiguillon, the Duc de Luynes, La Rochefoucauld-Liancourt, Alexandre
de Lameth, Montmorency de Luxembourg and, not least, the King's own
cousin Philippe, Duc d'Orléans. These were not parvenus, but the very
highest cadre of the peerage: men whose forebears had died on the fields
of the Hundred Years' War; who had surrounded the young Sun King on
his military *promenade* through Franche-Comté and Flanders; who had
been marshals, constables, grand almoners of France. Now they were
citizens.

Missing was Lafayette. His absence was all the more remarkable since
he had been one of the party of liberal nobles who with their persons had
barred the way of a detachment of troops sent to intimidate the Third
following the *séance royale.* Lafayette belonged to a group of another seventy or so noble deputies that had previously voted for reunion but felt
bound by the wishes of their constituents to remain separate unless instructed otherwise by the King. There was a possibility of bringing over
a decisive number if the National Assembly was prepared to respect the
possibility of their retaining some sort of separate identity in matters concerning the nobility. But to ask this was in effect to ask the Assembly to

abandon the premise of its freshly invented identity: the indivisibility of citizenship. A "deputation" from the nobles was denied a hearing on the grounds that its reception would constitute an acknowledgment of those special claims.

On the twenty-seventh of June, the Estates-General finally died, given the coup de grâce by the King who had commanded it into existence. He wrote to the deputies of the two privileged orders, "engaging" them to unite "to achieve my paternal goals." By this he did not necessarily mean an unconditional capitulation to the acts of June 17 and 20—the obliteration of the orders within an indivisible sovereignty vested in the National Assembly. Even after the final reunion, at two o'clock in the afternoon, had been accomplished in an atmosphere of unhappy gravity rather than joyous reconciliation, some of the nobles and clergy continued to interpret the royal letter as meaning deliberation in common on matters of joint interest.

91. Necker leads Louis XVI to the three united orders
beneath medallions of Henry IV and his minister, Sully.

All these reservations were swept aside in a great surge of popular celebration out of doors. The streets of Versailles were illuminated; fire-crackers exploded in the afternoon air. Singing and dancing crowds packed the courtyards and streets leading to the palace, shouting *"Vive Necker"* and at least as often *"Vive le Roi."* Persuaded of the benign mood of the people, Louis and Marie-Antoinette made an impromptu appearance. They stood on the balcony of Louis XIV's bedroom, overlooking the Cour de Marbre, where Molière had acted and Lully conducted for the Sun King. They tried to look happy. Louis even made an attempt at a wave. But it was the Queen who was the cynosure of all eyes, not because of the magnificence of her appearance, but the humility. The sorrow of the death of her son had, it was said, noticeably grayed her hair, which she wore down over her shoulders like a citizeness. There were no jewels to be seen. She turned inward to the room and, fighting back tears, brought before the amazed crowd her two children. Together, *papa, maman, enfants* with blond curls tumbling to their shoulders stood quietly before people cheering themselves hoarse. It was the first of many such encounters to come, few of them this affable. For the moment, though, the sight of them gave fresh meaning to Bailly's remark earlier that afternoon: "Now the family is complete."

The Marquis de Ferrières to Madame de Médel, Sunday June 28:

> I will only say a word to you, my dear sister, since perhaps you have been worried about d'Iversay and me. We have come close to the bloodiest catastrophe, a renewal of the horrors of a Saint Bartholomew's Eve massacre. The weakness of the government seems to allow anything . . . The *séance royale* served only to bring about a triumph for the Third. On the same evening the King was made to change his declaration even though it had been accepted by us. . . . On Friday, fifty members of the nobility, at the head of which was the Duc d'Orléans, joined the Third even though most of their constituents expressly forbade them to vote by head. I would certainly have done the same with greater justification since my *cahier* did not say anything strict about voting by order or head and I am wholly indifferent to the manner of deliberation . . . but I did not think I could abandon my Order in the critical circumstances in which it found itself. People speak openly in the Palais-Royal of massacring us, our houses are marked out for this murder and my door was marked with a "P" in black [for *proscrit*—proscribed]. This butchery was

supposed to be carried out on the night of Friday or Saturday. To tell the truth all Versailles were accomplices.

The Court expected, at any minute, to see itself attacked by forty thousand armed brigands whom, it was said, were on their way from Paris. The *gardes françaises* refused to obey orders; whole companies deserted and went to the Palais-Royal where they were given drinks and ices and paraded in triumph. Fortunately the man in whose name this infernal plot was concocted [Orléans] is too cowardly to be a villain. So the nights of Friday and Saturday passed quietly and on Saturday the 27th the King wrote to us through our President, M. de Luxembourg, to join the Third. . . .

Everything now seems tranquil; however the *gardes françaises* no longer acknowledge their officers; the defection of troops is general and everything announces a great revolution. . . . The Estates-General of 1789 will be celebrated but by a banner of blood that will be carried to all parts of Europe. . . .

Adieu my dear, good sister; the state of affairs is not very comforting. If only there was one [dependable] man I would not regard things as desperate, but the ministers are so incapable.

Embrace Médel for me.

Your
Charles-Elie

CHAPTER TEN

Bastille

July 1789

i TWO KINDS OF PALACE

V E R S A I L L E S had been built against Paris. The first fountain to be seen in the park of the château on descending from the terrace tells the story. In a circular pool, Latona stands holding her infant boy Apollo. She has fled from the jealous wrath of Juno, whose husband Jupiter has been making advances to her. Stopping on her flight to drink some water, Latona is attacked by peasants, mobilized by the vindictive goddess. Seeing her plight, Jupiter intervenes and transforms the peasants into frogs. This is the moment at which the sculptor caught the story, with cat-sized amphibians squatting or jumping towards the nymph, croaking in their metamorphosis. Some still retain their human trunks while their heads have changed to popping eyes and broad, gaping mouths.

For the Sun King the story had direct personal significance. His mother, Anne of Austria, had been driven from Paris by the rebellion of the Fronde, carrying her infant Apollo as a fugitive. In his maturity, Louis XIV was determined never again to be held captive by the people and peers of Paris. Though the château at Versailles had begun as a hunting lodge and place of masque and revelry, the King rapidly made it the place in which he could redefine his absolutism. His minister Colbert spent enormous sums on the Louvre, hoping that Louis would make it his principal seat of government, but to no avail. To be the Sun King meant constructing a symbolic realm of stone and water, marble and mirrors, in which the monarch and the planet would traverse the course of the day serenely unoccluded by the havoc of city life. Court music would prevail over the croaking of the frogs.

For a century, the strategy worked. Paris and Versailles remained worlds apart. If the King's peace was disturbed at Versailles it was by local townsmen and peasants, for the six-hour walk from Paris was a deterrent against popular manifestations. Not only was such a journey daunting in time and distance, it was dangerous. The Bois de Boulogne, through which travelers would have to go to reach the western roads, was notoriously full of *bandes* of thieves and whores.

By carriage, however, the journey was two hours, three at the most. And in the reign of Louis XVI the center of gravity for the *grands* of the court shifted back from the château to the city. Their *hôtels* were in the faubourg Saint-Germain or expensively refurbished in the Marais, their places of recreation the Opéra, the city theaters and the *concerts spirituels,* beside which court entertainment seemed pallid and derivative. The best art was at the biennial Salon, the best talk in private dinners and "assemblies" like those to be found chez Duport or Necker. Most important, political initiative had gravitated from the corridors and apartments of Versailles to the Palais de Justice and the Palais-Royal. So the courtiers, whose status and identity had once been defined by the pecking order at the palace, gradually became absentees. "Even in the chains of despotism," commented Mirabeau, "Paris always preserved its intellectual independence which tyrants were forced to respect. Through the reign of arts and letters Paris prepared that of philosophy and through philosophy that of public morality."

Even before Paris came to fetch the King from Versailles, the Palais-Royal had conquered the Château de Versailles. In every respect it was its opposite; indeed its nemesis. At the core of the château was a pavilion block where the King's control over business was formalized by apartments enfilading off one another so that access at each stage could be barred or yielded as ritual and decorum required. North and south extended immense half-mile wings, dependencies in every sense, that housed the governmental and palatial services of the theoretically omnipotent monarch. The Palais-Royal was an open space, colonnaded at its perimeter: a Parisian equivalent of republican spaces like the Piazza San Marco in Venice. Its architecture gave no instructions. Rather it invited sauntering, watching, browsing, reading, buying, talking, flirting, pilfering, eating—all at random—in spontaneously improvised order or in no order at all. While Versailles was the most carefully patrolled place in France, the Palais-Royal, as the property of the Duc d'Orléans, prohibited the presence of any police whatsoever unless invited in by its proprietor. If institutional Versailles set great store by the hierarchy of rank, the frantic business of the Palais-Royal subversively jumbled it up. Versailles proclaimed corporate discipline; the Palais-Royal celebrated the public anarchy of the appetites.

At court, and even to some extent in council meetings, utterances were, in all senses, guarded. In the Palais-Royal, everything could be said, and the more extravagantly the better. At coffeehouses like the Café Foy, Arthur Young watched

> expectant crowds listening *à gorge déployée* to certain orators who from chairs or tables harangue their audience. The eagerness with which they are heard and the thunder of applause they receive for every sentiment of more than common hardiness or violence against the present government cannot easily be imagined.

He was just as shocked by the democratization of pyrotechnics. At Versailles, fireworks shows, since the days of Louis XIV, had been carefully constructed to pay tribute to majesty. In the Palais-Royal, courtesy of Orléans, twelve sous bought as many squibs, rockets and serpents as five livres would bring from regular sources of supply. On the night of June 27, in celebration of the reunion of the orders, the Paris sky exploded with noise and color while the heavens above Versailles remained mournfully silent.

That the Palais-Royal was the empire of liberty was no longer in doubt when mutinying companies of the *gardes françaises* went there on June 28 to announce that they would under no circumstances fire on the people. On the thirtieth, two of their number went to the National Assembly dressed in civilian clothes to denounce their commander, the Duc de Châtelet, and were arrested by hussars and sent, along with a dozen of their comrades, to the Abbaye prison. When word of the incarceration spread, they were released by a crowd of four hundred who then went on to treat the soldiers to a festive and public supper. The Duc d'Orléans opened the premises for all-night carousing, and guarded by their "citizen-brothers" the renegade grenadiers slept on the floor of the Variétés Amusantes music hall. The next day, baskets were suspended from their new accommodation in the Hôtel de Genève inside the Palais-Royal, so that well-wishers could make patriotic contributions to their heroes. Not wanting to endorse a complete defiance of authority, the electors at the Hôtel de Ville and the National Assembly concocted a face-saving compromise by which the guards agreed to return to the prison for one night, after which they would be pardoned and discharged.

In the climate of boozy, loquacious defiance that prevailed at the Palais-Royal, it was not surprising that the Paris revolution began there. But it was born less of festive revolt than desperation. By July, bread prices were reaching levels that were symptomatic not just of dearth but of famine. Conditions throughout urban France were rapidly approaching the level of a food war. In France's second city, Lyon, at the end of June, rioters had already enforced duty-exempt sales of grain in the mistaken belief that they were doing the King's bidding. In Paris, sporadic attacks on the customs *barrières* around the city were becoming so frequent that troops had to be posted both there and at the markets and accompany all convoys to protect grain and flour. Wednesdays and Saturdays, when the itinerant bakers sold their merchandise at Les Halles and other designated markets, were especially perilous occasions. The bakers were forbidden to remove from their stalls unsold loaves left at the end of the day, so it was at that time that hungry crowds congregated in the hope of bargains. And it was then that the danger of violence and the seizure of loaves was most acute.

Early July was also a crisis for the poor in another crucial respect. For at the end of its first week was the dreaded *terme:* the date for the settlement of all bills, including rent. As Richard Cobb so vividly describes, the July *terme* was the worst, since by the October *terme* the harvest would be in and bread cheaper, and in January more clemency and credit were often extended because of the bitter winter months. In July, prior to the harvest, bread prices were always at their highest and disposable income lowest. On the eve of the day of settlement, the seventh, whole families and colonies of families would decamp, sometimes taking with them the sheets they used to climb down from high windows. It was a time of fear, unsettlement and exodus.

So when the news that Necker had been summarily dismissed and sent into exile by the King reached the Palais-Royal on Sunday, the twelfth of July, it produced an instantaneous wave of panic and fury. For Necker had become not just a symbol of the victory of the Third Estate, but the latest *père nourricier.* In many of the countless prints celebrating his fame, he was shown as the bringer of cornucopias: the man who would make solvency from bankruptcy, create work where there was unemployment and bring bread where there was famine. It was his reputation for integrity that hovered over him like a halo, in direct contrast with aristocrats, who would stop at nothing, even engineering a famine, to dislodge him from power. (Not all this flattery was unmerited. Necker had put up his personal fortune as collateral for a grain shipment from the Amsterdam banking house Hope.)

The notion that famines were caused not by the climate but by conspiracy had a long pedigree in France. But it was never more widely shared nor more angrily expressed than in 1789. If bakers and millers who withheld their stock from the market to drive prices even higher were the immediate villains, behind them lay an even more sinister aristocratic cabal. Its immediate object was to discredit Necker and secure his dismissal. With him gone, so the pamphlets said, the people could be held hostage until the

National Assembly was itself safely dissolved. "Past centuries," said the author of one pamphlet, "can show no precedent for so foul a plot as that which this dying aristocracy has hatched against mankind."

Sometimes, conspiracy theories turn out to be correct. There was, of course, no plot to starve the people into submission, but there certainly was a design to remove Necker and dissolve the National Assembly. On July 9, for example, opinions about Necker were expressed in strikingly different ways at Versailles and at the Palais-Royal. As he was about to enter the royal council, Necker was greeted by Artois shaking his fist at him, abusing him as a "foreign traitor" and a "sorry bourgeois" who had no "place" in the council and who should go back to the "little city" where he belonged. In the meeting itself the Prince went so far as to tell the Minister he thought he should be hanged. On the same day at the Palais-Royal, a "woman of quality" was publicly spanked for allegedly spitting on a portrait of the hero-minister.

All these fears and suspicions seemed corroborated by the increasing numbers of troops in and around Paris. Estimates of their number exaggerated the threat, but there was no mistaking the conspicuous German and Swiss soldiers among them. (Even some of the native French regiments were German-speakers from Lorraine.) Foreign troops, in coalition with bands of "armed brigands," were commonly thought to be roaming the countryside and poised to invade towns as the avenging arm of despotism.

Systematic military concentration was not a figment of popular paranoia. Louis XVI had given the first of a succession of marching orders to frontier regiments on June 22, when he still expected the *séance royale* to abort the National Assembly. When that policy failed, he summoned more troops on

92. Woman spanked for spitting on Necker's portrait

the twenty-sixth. By the sixteenth of July, a series of reinforcements was to bring the complement of troops in the Paris and Versailles region to more than twenty thousand. A conspicuous number of the regiments—more than a third—were foreign, many of them German-speaking. The King claimed that troops were being mobilized to contain potential disorders in and around Paris. But for the Queen, Artois and the group of ministers led by Breteuil eager to see the back of Necker, the military show of force was to be the instrument by which the crown could recover its freedom of action.

That plan was to be frustrated by the anxiety of those entrusted with its enforcement, who feared that the chain of command was about to fall apart. There were some grounds for their fears. Throughout the 1780s the desertion rate in the French army had risen to three thousand a year. This was in spite of the savage punishment awarded to first offenders: ten runs through a gauntlet of fifty men armed with ramrods. On the second of July the British Ambassador reported that this same ordeal had been inflicted on two soldiers of the Swiss regiment of the Salis-Samade who had been colluding with mutinous *gardes françaises*. Two others were hanged.

The most serious problem was that disaffection was by no means confined to enlisted men but had seeped into the ranks of junior officers. If there was anywhere in the old regime where social reality corresponded to polemics about aristocratic monopolies and frustrated promotion, it was in the army. Guibert's reforms may have brought about some improvement in pay but they also brought with them Prussian discipline and no compromise in the reservation of commissions to the "old" nobility. Though the Ségur law was meant to offer protection for the older, poorer nobility, the most publicized grievance remained spoiled young sons of rich dynasties being presented with regimental commissions when barely out of college. That irked career officers and the noncommissioned, who saw all hope of rising into the officer caste blocked by the new law. It was for good reasons, then, that anti-aristocratic rhetoric made headway in the junior ranks.

Privates in the regular army may have been even more receptive to identifying themselves with the citizenry of the Third Estate. Over eighty percent of them, according to Samuel Scott, had practiced another trade at some time and a surprisingly high proportion came from an urban artisan background. The royal army of the line, then, was not a peasant force at all but closer to the workers of the *faubourgs* who had sacked Réveillon's works and would make up the majority of the "conquerors" of the Bastille. That improvised solidarity between troops and people was to be crucial on the fourteenth of July, when over fifty regular soldiers joined the people storming the fortress. But even before that date, reports of troops' reluctance to use force against grain seizures or forcible sales were becoming commonplace.

This instinctive fraternity was even more obvious among the *gardes françaises*. Until the monumental research of Jean Chagniot it was commonly thought that the guards were older, more settled among the Parisian population and often practicing trades to make up for their meager pay. We now have a quite different profile, but one which makes their vulnerability to revolutionary propaganda even more apparent. A great many of the guards were young, of provincial origins, especially from northern towns like Amiens, Caen and Lille, and far from settled. A series of reforms in the 1760s and 1770s had closed off the possibilities—open to their predecessors earlier in the century—of keeping shops or market stalls. Half of the men were married with families, and sometimes their wives supported them. But the rank-and-file of the military body on which the old regime most relied to supplement the fifteen hundred or so police was in fact rootless, impoverished and often insubordinate. Among the lower officers, especially the sergeants, there was, complained one older officer, a "sentiment of equality which unfortunately in the present century mixes together all stations and ranks." Jean-Joseph Cathol, the son of an Auvergnat notary and a sergeant in the guard, later said that it was in 1788 that he first started to read the papers "exposing the villainy of priests and nobles" and took his newfound political truculence into the ranks. Others who were less actively engaged in political argument were simply borne along by the atmosphere of opposition they found in the wine shops where they drank and the Palais-Royal where they promenaded. On the twelfth of July, for example, a cadet of the Reinach regiment at Versailles encountered two guards, in the company of women and evidently very drunk, who told him, "Come with us, money and advancement await you in Paris."

For whatever mixture of reasons, the Réveillon riots were, for the *gardes françaises*, a kind of traumatic turning point after which they became truculently disinclined to obey orders. Increasingly too, they began to live up to their name as native patriots. On the sixth of July at Versailles they almost came to blows with German-speaking hussars who had been mobilized to intimidate the townspeople. And on the eighth Jean-Claude Monnet, a lottery-ticket hawker, was arrested for distributing among soldiers seditious pamphlets, one of which was an appeal to grenadiers from "an old Comrade of the Gardes Françaises." "We are Citizens before Soldiers, Frenchmen before slaves" was its message.

Impressions became polarized very quickly. On one side appeared to be the Austrian Queen and her hangers-on at court, supported now by Hungarian hussars and German dragoons. Bivouacked on the Champ de

Mars at the Invalides, they were preparing, it was said, to mine the Palais-Royal. Another encampment, at Saint-Denis, was organized to bombard the city from the Buttes de Montmartre. Necker's principal opponent, Breteuil, had been reported as saying in council, "If we have to burn Paris, then Paris will burn," and now, it seemed, they had the men and the means to do so. Standing against this satanic conspiracy were native soldiers, led by the *gardes françaises*, but with other troops ready to follow should the people be seriously threatened. At Nangis, "near enough to Paris for the people to be politicians," on June 30, the *perruquier* who dressed Arthur Young told him to "be assured as we are that French soldiers will never fire on the people," adding, "but if they should, it is better to be shot than to starve."

Mirabeau shared this view. "French soldiers are not just automata . . . they will see in us their relatives, their friends and their families . . . they will never believe it is their duty to strike without asking who are the victims . . . ?" But he expressed it, on July 8, in a speech to the National Assembly that was dark with foreboding. In a speech of prophetic power, he painted a picture of impending civil war. Though he too exaggerated—at thirty-five thousand—the number of troops between Versailles and Paris, no one could be oblivious to the artillery rumbling over roads and bridges, and the batteries being dug in that he described. Worst of all was the transparent deceit being practiced—the incorrigible vice of the old regime confronted with New Men. Have those who embarked on these follies, he asked rhetorically, "foreseen the consequences they entail for the safety of the throne? Have they studied in the history of all peoples, how revolutions begin . . . ?"

He had touched a nerve in the Assembly. The deputies had watched, helpless and apprehensive, as tents went up, first in the Cour de Marbre, then in the great colonnaded Orangery built by Mansart on the model of a Roman circus. Pyramids of muskets stood propped up against the Doric columns. Mirabeau's eloquence gave voice to their gathering apprehension, and its peroration was greeted with waves of applause crashing over his sweaty head. When it subsided, an address was drafted to the King that spoke, only too correctly, of "danger . . . beyond all the calculations of human prudence. . . . The presence of troops [in Paris] will produce excitement and riot and . . . the first act of violence on the pretext of maintaining public order may begin a horrible sequence of evils." Louis was asked to withdraw his troops and defuse this explosive situation.

On July 10, two days later, the King responded. He attempted to calm the Assembly's anxieties by claiming that the troops had been summoned to contain violent disorders in Paris of the magnitude of the Réveillon riots, that they were for the "protection," not the intimidation, of the Assembly. All this was the classic preparatory language of the military coup d'état. The King even added a gratuitous suggestion of removing the Assembly to the Noyons or Soissons should "conditions" make its work untenable at Versailles!

Only the most gullible royalist could possibly have believed him. The truth of course was that on the same day as Mirabeau's address—and possibly provoked by it—Louis XVI had decided on a test of strength: his force against that claimed by the National Assembly. It was a more decisive act and a speedier one than those urging this confrontation on him—in particular the Queen and the princes—had dared to hope for. He had had, it seems, enough of being told what was good for him and for the monarchy. His exasperation with Necker's self-righteousness had grown into something close to detestation when he had been upstaged by the Minister on June 23. At some point in his pursuit of boar, bird and roebuck, which continued unabated, Louis XVI had decided to assert the honor of the Bourbons.

He first needed the assent of Breteuil, who was to be appointed Necker's successor in the ministry that would take on the National Assembly. When that was given, the King informed the princes on the tenth. Though their military planning called for all available troops to be in place on the sixteenth, no one was going to dampen the King's new ardor for self-assertion. The weekend, moreover, was ideal for the coup. The National Assembly would not meet on Sunday and Necker could be expedited out of the country before it had time to react.

On Saturday the eleventh, the Minister was about to begin a congenial dinner at the proper hour of three in the afternoon, when the Minister of the Navy, La Luzerne, arrived with a letter from the King. It was terse and to the point. It required Necker to remove himself *sans bruit*—in secret—from Versailles, indeed from France altogether, and return to Switzerland. Necker pocketed the note, spoke briefly to his wife and called for the carriage in which he usually took his evening drive. Around five o'clock a valise was slung into its interior; Mme Necker, still in her *tenue de soirée*, got in, followed by her husband. The coach should, by rights, have turned south towards the Mâconnais, Lyon and the Swiss frontier. Instead it traveled northeast towards Brussels, where the Neckers alighted the following day. From there he wrote a letter to the Dutch bankers Hope, assuring them that notwithstanding his dismissal the two million livres they had loaned as security for impending grain shipments to France remained good.

It was an act of an *honnête homme,* in dramatic contrast with the petulant insecurity of the monarch who had sacked him.

ii SPECTACLES: THE BATTLE
FOR PARIS
July 12–13, 1789

There had never been any doubt as to which attraction really pulled in the customers at M. Curtius' wax museum. *Le Grand Couvert* showed the royal family together with the Queen's brother, Joseph II, enjoying their dinner. It was the climax of a show which also featured celebrities and heroes like Voltaire and Vice Admiral d'Estaing. Each one was modeled and painted by Peter Creutz (for that was the German name he was born with), whose career was yet another of the showman-entrepreneur success stories in eighteenth-century France. Mayeur de Saint-Paul, whose book on the boulevard du Temple specialized in sneering at the low life and burlesque specialists to be discovered there, saw Curtius as a paragon of the self-made man: gifted, shrewd and, above all, industrious. Certainly he knew his market. At two sous a head Curtius was able to pack in nonstop lines of gaping visitors from every walk of life. When they had finished marveling at his skill and imagining themselves chuckling with Voltaire, sobbing with Rousseau or peeking at Marie-Antoinette preparing for bed, they could buy one of his little wax figures of "gallants" and "libertines" to provoke saucy giggles at home.

Emboldened by success and prosperity, Curtius did not hesitate when the Palais-Royal began to let commercial space in 1784. He took Salon Number 7 and filled it with the same successful mix of military and cultural heroes and court scenes that had served him so well on the boulevard and in the fairs of Saint-Germain and Saint-Laurent. To cater to a slightly grander clientele, he added a dividing balustrade that created a two-price admission: twelve sous for the front, two for the rear. There he had to compete with some powerful rival attractions like the four-hundred-pound Paul Butterbrodt and worse still the scoundrel who passed off a wax model as "the beautiful Zulima," dead for two hundred years but miraculously preserved and available for complete inspection for a few sous. But Curtius knew how to keep abreast of the competition. He installed a ventriloquist who gave performances daily from noon till two and five till nine. And he became topical, adding heroes of the hour—Lafayette, Mirabeau, Target and, of course, the Duc d'Orléans and M. Necker.

So when he saw a crowd of a thousand making for Salon Number 7 in a state of patriotic uproar around four o'clock on Sunday the twelfth of

June, he must have had a good idea who they were coming for. Surrendering the busts of Orléans and Necker, Curtius was able to deliver a little speech worthy of the best actors of the Théâtre-Français: "My friends," he declaimed, "he [Necker] is ever in my heart but if he were indeed there I would cut open my breast to give him to you. I have only his likeness. It is yours." A tremendous performance. The heads were marched off triumphantly by the cheering crowd.

All that day, the Palais-Royal had been a boiling pot of agitation. The King and his advisers had thought a Sunday the optimal time for news of Necker's exile to become public (as they realized, for all their secrecy, it must), since it precluded an immediate response by the National Assembly. But for the unofficial center of opposition—the Palais-Royal—Sunday was the perfect day for organized histrionics. It was packed with sightseers, *flaneurs,* orators, peasants from the villages *hors des murs,* artisans from the *faubourgs.* Around three o'clock a crowd of six thousand or so milled about a young man, pale-faced and dark-eyed, his hair spilling freely onto his shoulders, shouting excitedly from one of the tables in front of a café.

Camille Desmoulins was then twenty-six years old, the favored son of a large family from Guise in Picardy. His father, a lieutenant-colonel of the local *bailliage,* had scrimped and saved to send the precocious boy to Paris for his education. And his siblings contented themselves with careers as

93. Curtius' busts of Necker and the Duc d'Orléans taken by the crowd as heroic trophies, July 12, 1789 (Le Sueur, gouache from the series *Fifteen Scenes from the French Revolution*)

94. Martin, bust of Camille Desmoulins

junior officers in the army, modest marriages and, in the case of one sister, the inevitable nunnery. Desmoulins had gone to the Lycée Louis-le-Grand, where he encountered Maximilien Robespierre from Arras and a great mix of boys—some aristocratic, many bourgeois, some even from artisan backgrounds—who made up the student population of that extraordinary institution. Like them he had drunk deep of Cicero, Tacitus and Livy, had felt Roman stirrings in his blood.

Though his father hoped he would be destined for the law, Desmoulins tried to survive from occasional writings, producing, for his effort, an "Ode to the Estates-General." In June 1789 *La France Libérée* (France Liberated) was accepted by the publisher Momoro, who liked to style himself "The First Printer of Liberty." Though it was not published until a few days after the fall of the Bastille, Desmoulins' tract is a fine example of the breast-beating, sob-provoking declamation then in vogue at the Palais-Royal. From the first lines its manner assumes an audience rather than a readership:

Listen, listen to Paris and Lyon, Rouen and Bordeaux, Calais and Marseille. From one end of the country to the other the same, universal cry is heard . . . everyone wants to be free.

It was through the voice, rather than the eye, that the apostles of liberty would rally their troops. For while the eye seduced, the voice disciplined.

As a young habitué of the Palais-Royal, Desmoulins was particularly preoccupied with sexual temptation as a potent weapon of royal and aristocratic corruption. Monarchy, he wrote, tries its best to deprave us in order to "enervate the national character and bastardize us by surrounding our youth with places of seduction and debauchery and besieging us with prostitutes."

This Machiavellian design would be thwarted, for in the capital alone there were more than thirty thousand men ready to abandon their *délices* to unite themselves, "at the first signal, with the sacred cohorts of the *patrie.*" Already, they had taken command of the theater of eloquence. "Only Patriots now raise their voices. The enemies of the public good are silenced or, if they dare to speak . . . immediately mark themselves for the penalty of their felony and their treason."

Drawing on his schoolboy exercises in the classics, Desmoulins used in his peroration the same tone of Virtue Militant, but for extra effect added the patriotic martyrdom exemplified in neoclassical history paintings in the Salon and on the stage. Blood was important in these likenesses. Desmoulins compared himself with the fallen warrior Otyrhades, who wrote "Sparta has triumphed" in his own blood on a captured standard. "I who

95. Berthaut, Desmoulins' speech in the garden of the Palais-Royal

have been timid now feel myself to be a new man [so that] I could die with joy for so glorious a cause, and, pierced with blows, I too would write in my own blood 'France is free!' "

So Desmoulins had already scripted the performance he would give to such rousing effect before the crowd at the Café Foy on June 12. He wrote to his father that, on arriving at the Palais-Royal at about three, he joined with some fellows all urging citizens to take arms against the treachery that had removed Necker, "whom the Nation had asked to be preserved." A creature of impulse (obedient thus to Nature, not Culture), he jumped onto a table, his head "suffocating under a multitude of ideas" which he vocalized without any respect for order. Of Necker, he said a monument should be erected, not an exile decreed. "To arms, to arms and [plucking leaves from a chestnut tree] let us all take a green cockade, the color of hope." At that moment Desmoulins thought he saw police arrive—or so he claimed. The suspicion allowed him to pose as the imminent victim of tyranny. A new Saint Bartholomew's Eve massacre impended, he warned: a reference point that was already becoming an important cliché of Patriot rhetoric and which would be reinforced by the most popular play of 1789: Marie-Joseph Chénier's *Charles IX*. Pointing to his breast with one hand and waving a pistol in the other (another piece of stage business that would become standard in the Convention), Desmoulins defied the stooges of tyranny: "Yes, yes, it is I who call my brothers to freedom; I would die rather than submit to servitude."

The audience response was gratifying. Desmoulins was an instantaneous hero, surrounded by arms clasping him, shouts of "bravo," kisses, fiery oaths never to abandon his side. He was moved off amidst a great shouting and cheering throng that seized anything green that might be available— ribbon, leaves, whole branches: a small army in search of heroes and guns.

The heroes were missing in person: Necker at Brussels, Orléans playing in his own amateur theatricals at Saint-Leu. (Learning of the Paris revolt, one of his company, a painter named Giroux, rode posthaste still costumed as Polyphemus the Cyclops and was nearly roughed up by a crowd at the *barrière* who assumed his one eye to be the sinister mark of a police spy.) But Curtius could supply proxy *personnages* in wax. What they lacked in eloquence they more than made up for in portability and forbearance of conduct which their real personas might not have so wholeheartedly approved.

Theater had moved from its customary space onto the street. There, it was in deadly earnest and moved immediately to impose its serious drama on the world of mere *divertissement* (entertainment). Audiences were now required to give the Revolution their full attention. So a crowd of some three thousand invaded the Opéra, where Grétry's *Aspasie* was about to get under way, declaring the day one of mourning for the loss of Necker. Other theaters, especially those in the Palais-Royal and the boulevard du Temple, closed themselves without further invitation. *Agents* of the Bourse nearby announced the Exchange would remain shut on Monday, the following day, thus lending a fresh element of financial alarm to the accumulating sense of crisis. Like Desmoulins, many of the actors in this drama suddenly felt themselves to be framed within a brilliantly lit Historical Moment. Everything they did or said took on weight as though it were being chronicled by a new Tacitus even as it was being enacted. This self-conscious gravity became even more pronounced as the procession, now some six thousand strong, raised black banners and donned black coats and hats to signify the funereal seriousness of the occasion.

None of this might have mattered very much to the authorities had not the speeches, shouting and bells been accompanied by the demand for arms. It was apparent to the Baron de Besenval, who was now responsible for military command in Paris and the region, that the six thousand sundry units of police—the thousand guards; the Guêt constabulary; the crossbowmen and harquebusiers in their ceremonial pantaloons and the handful of *maréchaussées* (stationed outside the city limits)—could not possibly cope with the gathering tumult. Regular troops were stationed at Saint-Denis, Sèvres, Saint-Cloud and within the city at the Invalides, the Ecole Militaire, in the place Louis XV and on the Champs Elysées. On the Champ de Mars that same morning, before the news about Necker reached Paris, women had danced with Hungarian hussars of the Berzcheny regiment. Hours later the men were lined up in battle order. Four pieces of cannon had been moved to the Pont Louis XVI. But how and when to use this military force was as problematic in Paris in July 1789 as it had been in Grenoble a year before and in countless cities throughout France all through the spring.

At the place Vendôme, matters came to a head. The Prince de Lambesc, commanding a company of the Royal-Allemand stationed in the place Louis XV (shortly to be renamed the place de la Révolution and now the consensually bland space of the place de la Concorde), was ordered to clear the square. Standard procedure was for the cavalry to use the flat of their sabers, but the equally standard consequence was that the horses were surrounded to the point of immobility. Outnumbered, the dragoons retreated to the place Louis XV. From the place Vendôme the crowd ran into the Tuileries gardens. There they collided with troops, and the man who was carrying Curtius's bust of the Duc d'Orléans was dragged behind a horse back to the place Louis XV. As further cavalrymen struggled to get into the gardens, the crowd, shouting *"Au meurtre,"* moved to the balus-

96. Cavalry of the Prince de Lambesc
in the Tuileries

traded terrace, from where they heaved anything they could down onto the soldiers. Chairs, stones from a construction site, even parts of statues where they could be broken and moved rained down, panicking the horses and wounding the soldiers.

The skirmish went on long enough for word that "Germans and Swiss are massacring the people" to take wing around the city, and units of the *gardes françaises* arrived on the scene in battle order to confront Lambesc's troopers. It was the first moment that an organized armed force had faced the King's soldiers, determined to counter-attack. More astonishing still, the *gardes* were in sufficient force to push the cavalry troopers out of the Tuileries altogether. From that point, battle was joined for sovereignty over Paris.

For all the weeks of military planning and preparation, first by the Maréchal de Broglie, then by Besenval, it was not much of a battle. It was obvious that the beleaguered company on the place Louis XV needed help, but it was provided by the Swiss Salis-Samade regiment in the most laborious possible manner. As the sun was setting, troops were ferried across the Seine in just two boats, guns mounted in the bows to deter fire from the right bank, where the *gardes françaises* had strengthened their positions. After two hours of this miserable progress, they attempted to re-form in battle order under a night sky of inky darkness. Light came as they were fired on from *gardes françaises* positions on the boulevards. By one o'clock the commander of the Salis-Samade had decided that the position was untenable. When Besenval returned to the scene, he made the even more dramatic decision to evacuate the whole area, retreating westward to the Pont de Sèvres.

The retreat of royal troops from the center of the city delivered it over to haphazard violence. Gunsmiths and armorers were forced to hand over muskets, sabers, pistols and shoulder belts. One master gunsmith later reported to the National Assembly that his shop had been broken into thirty times and had lost 150 swords, 4 gross blades, 58 hunting knives, 10 brace of pistols and 8 muskets.

Armed with this assortment of weapons—as well as kitchen knives, daggers and clubs—crowds at the northern end of the city set about destroying the hated symbol of their confinement: the Farmers'-General wall and its fifty-four *barrières*. The *enceinte* had been Lavoisier's last technical masterpiece, ten feet high, eighteen miles in circumference, punctuated at intervals by Claude Ledoux's extraordinary customs posts. The crowd was

97. Sergent, engraving, the night of July 12–13 in Paris: the search for arms by torchlight. Sergent was an ardent revolutionary and friend of Danton and Desmoulins.

not interested in technology or in architecture. The wall meant high prices and brutal police: vexation and starvation. It was breached in several places, then haphazardly torn down, the stones serving as another kind of weapon to be used against troops. Forty of the customs posts were sacked, their doors and furniture burned together with papers and tax records. Among the attackers were fifteen who described themselves (in 1790) as smugglers who, in the euphoria of the moment, as Jacques Godechot has commented, failed to realize they were putting themselves out of business. The crowds were mostly from the northern *faubourgs* and included a number of masons, so that it is a reasonable bet that at least some of those who had helped construct the *enceinte* now joined in pulling it down.

The third target was, of course, bread or, at least, grain and flour. The monastery of Saint-Lazare (the scene of Beaumarchais' humiliation) was not only a prison but a commercial depot. Inevitably it attracted to itself the reputation of being a house full of corpulent monks sitting on immense piles of grain. Crowds, consisting of some of the poorest and hungriest

98. The pillaging of the monastery of Saint-Lazare

Parisians, put it to the sack and removed any kind of foodstuffs they could find. Large quantities of grain were taken, as were wine, vinegar, oil, twenty-five Gruyère cheeses and, more improbably, a dried ram's head.

During that single night of largely unobstructed riot and demolition, Paris was lost to the monarchy. Only if Besenval was prepared to use his troops the following day to occupy the city and deal brutally with disorder was there any hope of recapture. But the messy, chaotic nocturnal operation had, if anything, unsteadied his grip on command even further. Told by his own officers that their own soldiers, even the Swiss and Germans, could not be counted on, he was unwilling to take the offensive.

On Monday the thirteenth he was faced with a more serious threat than the kind of spontaneous havoc of the day before. At eleven the previous evening there had been a meeting of some of the electors at the Hôtel de Ville. They decided to summon emergency sessions at each of the sixty district headquarters at dawn the following day. The only way this could be announced was by the ringing of the recognized signal for times of peril—the tocsin—and reinforcing the message with cannon shots and the beating of drums. So it was with this thunderous cacophony—the clanging of church bells and the firing of guns—that citizens were summoned to their patriotic duty.

At the Hôtel de Ville the paramount concern was to take control of a situation that threatened to disintegrate into anarchy. The means, as in countless other cities in France, was to form a militia restricted to the electoral elements of the population: those, in other words, with something to lose. Units of eight hundred in each district were to be mobilized, making up in total a citizens' army of forty-eight thousand. Even when allowance had been made for its inevitable inexperience and the need to be guided and trained by the *gardes françaises,* it was an imposing force—substantial enough to perform its twin duties of facing down any further attempt at military repression and containing and, if necessary, punishing unlawful violence. Crucial to the transfer of authority represented in this act was the provision of identifiable insignia. Since uniforms could hardly be provided at short notice, cockades were to be worn on coats and hats. Green was ruled out when it was discovered to be the color not only of hope but the livery of the Comte d'Artois. As an alternative that signified more emphatically the passage of legitimacy, the colors of Paris, red and blue, became the colors of its citizen-soldiers. The official nature of this choice, however, did not preclude more romantic interpretations. In his capacity as poet-Patriot, Desmoulins described the colors of the uniform as red, representing the blood to be shed for freedom, and blue, representing the celestial constitution that would be its eventual blessing. And one of the first to wear the tricolor was Citizen Curtius, who volunteered his services to the militia on the first day of its duty.

Their first munitions did not do much for the dignity of the new militia, though these did provide yet more theatrical color. Ransacking the royal *garde-meuble* near the Tuileries, they extracted antique halberds and pikes, a sword said to have belonged to their folk hero Henri IV and a cannon inlaid with silver that had been presented to Louis XIV by the King of Siam. More serious equipment was harder to lay hands on. Powder had been moved from the Arsenal to the Bastille on Besenval's orders a few days earlier. When the royal *prévôt des marchands,* de Flesselles, was told to hand over weapons from the Hôtel de Ville he could come up with only three muskets. Alternative suggestions proposed by him—the Carthusian monastery by the Luxembourg and the gun factory at Charleville—turned out to be wild-goose chases, so that by the end of the day de Flesselles' own credibility was deeply compromised. He agreed to ask the commandant of the garrison at the Invalides, de Sombreuil, to hand over the thirty thousand muskets at his disposal, but he too procrastinated, replying that he had first to seek permission from Versailles.

Finally, thirty-five casks of powder were produced from a barge at the Port Saint-Nicolas and enough weapons and powder were distributed for patrols that night, the thirteenth. In contrast with the night before, bourgeois sympathizers with the Revolution felt safe enough to go on the streets as they saw the worker-sorties disarmed by the militia. There were even exemplary hangings of looters, and candles and oil lamps once again illuminated houses and streets.

It was early the next morning, with low clouds hanging over Paris, that the battle was won. Dissatisfied with the answer they had received the previous evening, an immense crowd, estimated by some to be eighty thousand strong, converged on the Invalides. Some days before, eighty of their comrades in the Invalides had already jumped the camp and the rest responded with a paralyzing slowdown action to de Sombreuil's order to sabotage the thirty thousand muskets in his barracks. The twenty *invalides* veterans assigned to this job may not have been in their prime but they could probably have done better than unscrewing twenty muskets in six hours had not patriotic enthusiasm caught up with them too. After some fruitless negotiation, weight of numbers forced an entrance and de Sombreuil barely escaped with his life. The garrison helped rather than hindered the invasion and, more seriously, there was no attempt to mobilize the troops nearby on the Champ de Mars. More than thirty thousand muskets were distributed, somewhat at random, as well as cannon (which had also been inadequately spiked).

It was not quite a conclusive victory. For despite the evidence of defection among some troops and the inertia of their commanders, there were still rumors that, before long, regiments would be on the march and cannon would sound from Montmartre. What use were muskets and cannon without powder? By now it was widely known where the powder was to be had that would make the citizens' army invincible in Paris: from the Bastille. It only remained to go and get it.

iii BURIED ALIVE? MYTHS AND REALITIES IN THE BASTILLE

The Bastille had an address. It was identified as No. 232, rue Saint-Antoine, as if it were some overgrown lodging house, full of *chambres garnies* and guests of different quality occupying rooms that varied according to their means and station. Its exterior court (except during the July rising) was open to the public, who could come and chat to the gatekeeper (who sat in the little lodge), lounge around the shops that crowded at its entrance or inspect the progress of the governor's vegetable garden.

But it was also a fortress. Eight round towers, each with walls five feet thick, rose above the Arsenal and the *faubourg*. Paintings that celebrated the fall and demolition of the Bastille invariably made it look taller than it really was. The highest of the irregularly built towers was no more than seventy-three feet, but Hubert Robert, a specialist in the grandeur of ruins, gave it Babylonian eminence. In his painting, those walls became monstrous cliff-like ramparts that could have been conquered only by the superhuman courage and will of the People.

Like so many others of its initial enthusiasts, Hubert Robert would himself end up a prisoner of the Revolution. But in 1789 he was already a devotee of Romantic aesthetics: the swooping emotions of the Sublime and the Terrible outlined in Edmund Burke's first great publication. His great visual mentor was Giambattista Piranesi, whom he followed in offering views of the masonry of antiquity fallen into picturesque decay. Perhaps, then, he also shared Piranesi's nightmare, the *carceri d'invenzione:* prisons of the mind in which the mechanical genius of the modern age was applied to the science of confinement and pain. Certainly the elevation of the Bastille in his painting, with tiny figures scampering jubilantly over its battlements, suggests an immense Gothic castle of darkness and secrecy, a place into which men would disappear without warning and never again see the light of day until their bones were disinterred by revolutionary excavators.

That was the legend of the Bastille. Its reality was far more prosaic.

99. Hubert Robert, demolition of the Bastille

Constructed at the end of the fourteenth century as a defense against the English, it had been converted into a state prison by Charles VI. It was Cardinal Richelieu, though, who gave it its sinister reputation as a place into which prisoners of state were spirited away. Throughout the reign of the Bourbons, most, though not all, of its prisoners were detained by *lettres de cachet* at the express warrant of the King and without any kind of judicial process. From the beginning, many of them were high-born: conspirators against the crown and its Ministers; others were religious prisoners, Protestants and, in the early eighteenth century, Catholic "convulsionaries" accused of fomenting heresy. There were two other important categories of detainees. The first were writers whose works were declared seditious and a danger either to public decency or order or both; the second were delinquents, usually young, whose families had petitioned the King for their incarceration.

Conditions varied widely. The infamous subterranean *cachots*, slimy with damp and overrun with vermin, were no longer in use by the reign of Louis XVI, but the *calottes* immediately below the roof were almost as bad, since they took in snow and rain in the winter and almost asphyxiated prisoners with heat in the summer. For the majority of prisoners, however, conditions were by no means as bad as in other prisons, in particular the horrors that prevailed at Bicêtre. (For that matter, compared with what twentieth-century tyrannies have provided, the Bastille was paradise.) Sums were allotted to the governor for the subsistence of different ranks: fifteen livres a day for *conseillers* of the Parlement, nine for *bourgeois* and three for commoners. Paradoxically, "men of letters," who created the myth of a fortress of atrocities, were allotted the highest sum of nineteen livres a day. Even granting that the governor and his *service* undoubtedly made a profit on these allowances, they were considerably above the level at which most of the population of France attempted to subsist.

Most prisoners were held in octagonal rooms, about sixteen feet in diameter, in middle levels of the five- to seven-storied towers. Under Louis XVI they each had a bed with green serge curtains, one or two tables and several chairs. All had a stove or chimney, and in many rooms prisoners were able to ascend to a triple-barred window by a three-stepped staircase against the wall. Many were permitted to bring in their own possessions and to keep dogs or cats to deal with the vermin. The Marquis de Sade, who was held there until the week before the Bastille fell, took full advantage of these privileges. He brought in (among other things) a desk, wardrobe, *nécessaire* for his dressing needs; a full complement of shirts, silk breeches, *frac* coats in camel-brown, dressing gowns, several pairs of boots and shoes; his favorite firedogs and tongs; four family portraits, tapestries to hang on the white plaster walls; velvet cushions and pillows, mattresses to make the bed more comfortable; a selection of hats; three fragrances—rose water, orange water and eau-de-cologne—with which to anoint himself and plenty of candles and oil night lamps. These were necessary since on admission in 1784 he also brought in a library of 133 volumes, including Hume's histories, the complete works of Fénelon, novels by Fielding and Smollett, the *Iliad*, the plays of Marmontel, travel literature about and by Cook and Bougainville in the South Seas as well as an *Histoire des Filles Célèbres* and the *Danger d'Aimer Etranger*.

If there ever was a justification for the Bastille, it was the Marquis de Sade. But if the crimes which put him there were unusually disgusting (by the standards of any century), his living conditions were not. He received visits from his long-suffering wife almost weekly and when his eyes deteriorated from both reading and writing, oculists came to see him on a regular basis. Like others in the "Liberty" tower, he could walk in the walled garden courtyard and on the towers. Only when he abused that right by shouting cheerful or indignant obscenities to passersby (which he did with increasing frequency in 1789) was it curtailed.

Food—that crucial event in the lives of prisoners—also varied according to social condition. The commoners detained in connection with the "flour war" riots of 1775 were probably fed gruels and soups, sometimes lined with a string of bacon or lardy ham. But even they had a decent provision of bread, wine and cheese. It was not necessary to be a noble, though, to enjoy a much better cuisine. The writer Marmontel drooled when he recalled "an excellent soup, a succulent side of beef, a thigh of boiled chicken oozing with grease [an eighteenth-century compliment]; a little dish of fried, marinaded artichokes or of spinach; really fine Cressane pears; fresh grapes, a bottle of old Burgundy and the best Moka coffee."

No one wanted to be in the Bastille. But once there, life for the more privileged could be made bearable. Alcohol and tobacco were allowed, and under Louis XVI card games were introduced for anyone sharing a cell as well as a billiard table for the Breton gentry who requested one. Some of the literary inmates even thought a spell in the Bastille established their credentials as a true foe of despotism. The Abbé Morellet, for example, wrote, "I saw literary glory illuminate the walls of my prison. Once persecuted I would be better known . . . and those six months of the Bastille would be an excellent recommendation and infallibly make my fortune."

Morellet's admission suggests that as the reality of the Bastille became more of an anachronism, its demonology became more and more important in defining opposition to state power. If the monarchy was to be depicted (not completely without justice) as arbitrary, obsessed with secrecy and vested with capricious powers over the life and death of its citizens, the Bastille was the perfect symbol of those vices. If it had not existed, it is safe to say, it would have had to be invented.

And in some senses it *was* reinvented by a succession of writings of prisoners who had indeed suffered within its walls but whose account of the institution transcended anything they could have experienced. So vivid and haunting were their accounts that they succeeded in creating a stark opposition around which critics of the regime could rally. The Manichean opposition between incarceration and liberty; secrecy and candor; torture and humanity; depersonalization and individuality; open-air and shut-in obscurity were all basic elements of the Romantic language in which the anti-Bastille literature expressed itself. The critique was so powerful that when the fortress was taken, the anticlimactic reality of liberating a mere seven prisoners (including two lunatics, four forgers and an aristocratic delinquent who had been committed with de Sade) was not allowed to intrude on mythic expectations. As we shall see, revolutionary propaganda remade the Bastille's history, in text, image and object, to conform more fully to the inspirational myth.

The 1780s were the great age of prison literature. Hardly a year went by without another contribution to the genre, usually bearing the title *The Bastille Revealed* (La Bastille Dévoilée) or some variation. It used the standard Gothic devices of provoking shudders of disgust and fear together with pulse-accelerating moments of hope. In particular, as Monique Cottret has pointed out, it drew on the fashionable terror of being buried alive. This was such a preoccupation in the late eighteenth century (and not only in France) that it was possible to join societies that would guarantee to send a member to one's burial to listen for signs and sounds of vitality and to insure against one of these living entombments.

In what was by far the greatest and deservedly the most popular of all the anti-Bastille books, Linguet's *Memoirs of the Bastille,* the prison was depicted as just such a living tomb. In some of its most powerful passages Linguet represented captivity as a death, all the worse for the officially extinguished person being fully conscious of his own obliteration.

Linguet's memoir burned with the heat of personal betrayal. He had, he said, been lured back to France in 1780 from England, where he had been publishing his *Annales Politiques,* on the express understanding that he would, in effect, be immune from prosecution. Almost as soon as he returned, he was whisked off to the Bastille because of his attack on the Maréchal Duras. His account of the physical conditions he endured is far more harrowing than anything experienced by Morellet, Marmontel or de Sade and is not altogether borne out by the Bastille archives. But there is no reason to assume he lied when he wrote of "two mattresses eaten by worms; a cane chair of which the seat had but a few strings holding it together, a folding table . . . two china pots, one to drink from, and two paving stones to hold a fire." (Some time later the warders brought him some fire irons and tongs—though not, he complained, brass dogs.) His worst moments came when the eggs of mites and moths hatched out and all his bed and personal linen was transformed into "clouds of butterflies."

However squalid these conditions, it was the mental rather than the physical ordeal of imprisonment that caused Linguet the most suffering and which he communicates with astonishing originality in his little book. The memoir is, in fact, the first account of prison psychology in Western culture and for the modern reader has a kind of prophetic power that still makes it disturbing reading. Michel Foucault was quite wrong in assuming that the categorization of prisoners was one of the techniques which was most repressive. For Linguet objected most strenuously to exactly the lack of such a categorization. "The Bastille, like death itself," he lamented, "equalizes all whom it engulfs: the sacrilegious who have meditated on the ruin of their *patrie* as well as the courageous man who is guilty only of having defended his rights with excessive ardor" [that is, himself]. Worst of all was having to share the same space with those confined for moral abominations.

Everything about the regime of the prison, even when it seemed, superficially, to take the edge off brutality, appeared part of a sinister design to strip the prisoner of his identity: the "I" which for Romantics was synonymous with life itself. On admission, for example, potentially dangerous objects—a category which included both scissors and money—were confiscated and inventoried, to be returned on release, exactly like modern procedure. The reasons for these confiscations were read out to the prisoner, a business which Linguet found deliberately humiliating: the systematic reduction of a rational adult to the dependency of a child. He found that condition reinforced by all manner of petty tyrannies, such as being obliged to have an escort while being exercised in the little high-walled yard.

Even worse was the inability to communicate, particularly galling for a writer and terrible in captivity of indeterminate length. Seized without warning—and usually at night—from the living world, the victim of this state abduction was then deprived of all means of communicating his existence to friends or family beyond the walls. For most prisoners this was not in fact a problem, but for some time Linguet was deprived of writing materials and it was this helplessness that most oppressed him. The massive thickness of the walls, which made it impossible to speak to, or hear, other prisoners or indeed even summon a doctor in case of sudden sickness, only added to the sense of live burial. The walls of the Bastille then became the frontier between being and nonexistence. When the prison barber was brought to him, Linguet made the grim quip that became famous: "*Hé,* Monsieur, you wield a razor? Why don't you raze the Bastille?"

iv THE MAN WHO LOVED RATS

If Linguet was the writer who enabled the thousands who read his book to feel, vicariously, the shutting out of light, another, quite different but equally popular book gave its readers the elation of escape. In this sense, the "Chevalier" Latude's autobiography was the perfect complement to Linguet's memoir.

"Latude" was in reality a soldier named Danry who found himself without means or prospects in Paris after the end of the War of Austrian Succession. Like countless petty adventurers, he attempted to use the machinery of court favoritism to advance himself but he did so with an unconventionally risky stratagem. In 1750 he wrote a personal letter to Mme de Pompadour—the object of countless personal plots—alerting her to a letter bomb that would shortly be sent her way. Danry/Latude could be confident of this because he himself was the author of just such a letter. The half-baked plan was very quickly unraveled, and instead of receiving a pension in gratitude for saving the life of the King's mistress, Latude found himself in the Bastille. Transferred after a few months to Vincennes, he made the first of what was to be a series of escapes.

Latude's account of his first moments of freedom, running through fields and vineyards, making for the highway, hiding away in a *chambre garnie* in Paris, has exhilarating credibility. But even more astonishing was his decision to extricate himself from the fear of discovery by writing again to Mme de Pompadour, explaining his folly and throwing himself on her mercy. Since he had become acquainted with no less an eminence than Dr. Quesnay, he entrusted him with this apologetic memorandum.

This was a serious mistake. Latude had been so naively confident of clemency that he had even indicated his address on the letter. Within a day or so he was back in the Bastille: a setback but not a defeat. The innocent was rapidly becoming accustomed to the cunning of the world. Within a few months he had devised a secret mailbox by working loose a brick in the prison chapel, and he with a cellmate, Alègre, spent six months constructing the rope ladder that would take him to freedom again. This extraordinary piece of work required considerable sacrifice since the rungs had to be made from the firewood given to the prisoners during the winter. Shirts and bed linen, torn apart, knotted and restitched with painstaking care, made up the length. A crude knife was fashioned from the iron crossbar of their trestle table. With his passion for giving sacred names to the instruments of freedom (also a precaution against discovery) Latude called the runged ladder "Jacob," the white rope his "dove." In his memoir he represents himself as the perfect artisan: frugal, industrious, ingenious and pure of heart—Jean-Jacques as convict.

On the night of the twenty-fifth of February the two prisoners climbed up the chimney of their cell, "almost suffocating from soot and nearly burned alive," then worked the iron grate apart to allow them onto the roof of one of the towers. From there they used the three-hundred-foot ladder to descend into one of the moats. It was here, said Latude, that he felt a pang of regret at having to abandon his tools and the ladder that had served him so well: "rare and precious monuments of human industry and the virtues

100. Antoine Vestier, portrait of Latude, 1789

that were the outcome of the love of liberty." The two men were still not free. The rain on which they had counted to remove the sentries had stopped and they were making their rounds as usual, armed with broad lanterns. The only way out was to work from below, removing the bricks of a wall, one by one, with a minimum of noise, to allow for an eventual exit. And when they finally had made a hole large enough to squeeze through, the two men, in the dark, fell headlong into an aqueduct and were nearly drowned.

After this ordeal they were hidden for a time in the Abbaye Saint-Germain by a tailor before going their separate ways through the Low Countries. In Antwerp, Latude encountered a Savoyard who, without blinking, recited to him the story of two men who had escaped from the Bastille. One of them, he said, had already been recaptured and the "exempts"—police who moved freely across borders—were out looking for the other. In Amsterdam they caught up with Latude and, tied into a dreadful leather harness "more humiliating than any slave's," he was taken back to the Bastille. His liberty had lasted just three months.

This time the jailbird's wings were clipped. Latude was placed in one of the appalling underground *cachots* to make escape quite impossible. And it was in this genuinely nightmarish confinement that he discovered new companions: the rats. Compared with the inhumanity Latude had endured, the rats seemed endearing. Using pieces of bread he trained them to eat off his plate and to allow him to scratch them around the neck and chin. They too were given names, and some, like the female "Rapino-hirondelle," would even beg like a dog or do jumping tricks for her pieces of bread. The scene of an idyll in hell was completed when Latude managed to make a primitive flute out of bits of his iron grille so that, from time to time, he could serenade his rodent friends with an air or a gavotte as they gnawed contentedly on his leavings. They were, as he wrote, his "little family," all twenty-six of them, and Latude studiously observed their life cycle—their matings and breedings, battles and games—with all the tender concern of Rousseau's guardian-tutor.

Years passed. Latude busied himself by preparing a project reforming the halberdiers and pikemen in the French army, which he was sure the Minister of War would want to see. Deprived of paper he used tablets of bread, moistened and flattened with his saliva and then dried, and for ink his own blood diluted with water. When he was hauled out of the *cachot,* he grieved to lose his rats but made a new family out of the pigeons, until in a vindictive fit they were killed on orders from the governor. Another escape was made in 1765, aborted again through Latude's incurable innocence when he presented himself at the Versailles office of a government minister whose reputation for benevolence he trusted. He was moved back to the Château de Vincennes, and it was only in the new reign that Malesherbes became acquainted with his plight and had him moved to Charenton, the asylum for the mentally disturbed. There he met up again with d'Alègre, his old companion in flight, whose years of incarceration had completely destroyed his sanity. Seeing Latude, d'Alègre thought he was God and covered him with tears and benedictions.

In 1777 Latude was finally released but immediately published his *Memoirs of Vengeance,* which guaranteed his rearrest, first in the Petit Châtelet and then in Bicêtre. From there he continued to write accounts of his many ordeals, one of which found its way to a poor vendor of pamphlets and magazines, Mme Legros. Campaigning for Latude at the doors of *les Grands* she finally found a willing audience in Mme Necker and even the Queen. In March 1784 Latude was finally released, and though he was formally "exiled" from Paris he was not only permitted to live there but was given a royal pension of four hundred livres a year. Unlike d'Alègre Latude had somehow come through twenty-eight years of prison with his wits very much intact, and he became an immediate celebrity. Lionized by the Academy Française, greeted by Jefferson, he became the beneficiary of a public fund.

Latude's story, published in many forms and editions before the Revolution, looked like the triumph of the *honnête homme* over the worst miseries that despotism could inflict. Together with Linguet's memoir and other writings like *The Bastille Revealed,* it contributed to a growing campaign, first to restrict *lettres de cachet* and summary imprisonment to those who genuinely threatened the public peace, and then to demolish the Bastille altogether. Such plans were in keeping with plans of urban embellishment that removed medieval walls and citadels to make room for public gardens, squares and promenades. In 1784, as an accompaniment to Breteuil's memorandum limiting the use of *lettres de cachet,* the architect Brogniard proposed an open, circular, colonnaded space and in June 1789 the project was revived by the Royal Academy of Architecture.

Just a few weeks before it fell to the citizens' army, then, the Bastille had already been demolished in official memoranda. In the broad open space to be created by its removal would be a column, perhaps in bronze, higher than the old prison. Its base was to be sheathed in rocks from which fountains would play, in keeping with the new Romantic aesthetic. A simple inscription would suffice to indicate to posterity the victory of benevolence over tyranny: "Louis XVI, Restorer of Public Freedom."

This peaceful victory was not to be. The attempt of the monarchy to impose its will by military force had ended any possibility of recasting its legitimacy as the benefactor of freedom. Instead, the towers of the Bastille, its cannon pointing from the embrasures, stood as the symbol of intransigence. So, although, as historians never tire of pointing out, the crowd of a thousand that gathered before its front court was after gunpowder rather than demolition, it was, without any question, also mobilized by the immense force of the Bastille's evil mystique.

The Marquis de Sade, for one, knew exactly how to exploit this. Briefed by his wife during her weekly visits on all the news from Versailles, he decided to join the roll of honorable martyrs of the Bastille. His periodically shouted addresses from the tower walks to passersby suddenly became political at the beginning of July. Deprived of those walks, he followed the tradition of artisanal ingenuity in the Bastille by adapting into an improvised megaphone the metal funnel used to deposit his urine and slops into the moat. From de Sade's window, at regular intervals, like news bulletins on the hour, came broadcast announcements to the effect that Governor de Launay planned a massacre of all the prisoners; that they were at this minute being massacred and that the People should deliver them before it was too late. Already in a state of jitters, de Launay had the troublemaker removed on about the fifth of July to Charenton, where he raged at the indignity of being shut up with so many epileptics and lunatics.

De Sade had become a revolutionary.

v THE FOURTEENTH OF JULY 1789

Bernard-René de Launay had been born in the Bastille, where his father had been governor, and he would die on the evening of the fourteenth of July in the shadow of its towers. The aristocratic revolutionary de Sade sneered at the "*soi-disant* marquis whose grandfather was a *valet-de-chambre.*" The truth was that the governor was a typical minor functionary of the old regime, reasonably conscientious if somewhat dour; certainly an improvement on martinets like Governor de Berryer, who had made Latude's life so wretched.

On the fourteenth of July he was, with good reason, apprehensive. By default the entire integrity of royal authority in Paris seemed to have devolved on him. The Baron de Besenval had virtually evacuated the center of the city. The commandant of the Invalides had sent him the huge consignment of 250 barrels of powder (about thirty thousand pounds), yet he had only a modest force with which to defend it. In response to an urgent request for reinforcements, he had been given, on July 7, a further thirty-two men from the Swiss Salis-Samade regiment to add to the eighty-two *invalides* pensioners stationed there. Well known in the *faubourg* as amiable layabouts, the *invalides* were unlikely to defend the fortress to the last man. Worst of all, in the event of siege, the Bastille had only a two-day supply of food and no internal supply of water at all. In the end, that was what probably decided its capitulation.

In front of the outer courtyard were gathered about nine hundred Parisians. They included a few men of standing and property like Santerre, a friend of Réveillon's who owned the famous Hortensia Brewery, which specialized in the English-style ales and stouts that were in great demand in the capital. There were also a sizable number of defecting soldiers and *gardes françaises*. But making up by far the largest number were local artisans living in the faubourg Saint-Antoine—joiners, cabinetmakers, hatters, locksmiths, cobblers, tailors and the like. There were also a good number—twenty-one according to the official list of the *vainqueurs de la Bastille*—of wine merchants, which is to say owners of the *cabarets* that served as well as sold wine and which were the headquarters of neighborhood gossip and politics. One of them, Claude Cholat, whose wine shop was in the rue Noyer, produced a justly famous "primitive" graphic rendering of the day's events. Of the six hundred of whom we have information, as many as four hundred in the crowd had immigrated to Paris from the provinces, and since July 14 saw the price of the four-pound loaf reach a record high, most of their families were undoubtedly hungry.

They were also prey to considerable fear. During the night rumors had circulated that troops were about to march or were already on their way from Sèvres and Saint-Denis to crush the Paris rising. And the Bastille seemed to be heavily munitioned, with fifteen eight-pounder cannon on the towers and a further three in the inner courtyard pointing at the gates. Twelve more guns on the ramparts could fire pound-and-a-half balls, and in his nervousness de Launay had even assembled a bizarre collection of siege missiles like paving stones and rusty ironmongery to drop on the assailants, should that be necessary.

The initial aim of the crowd was simply to neutralize the guns and to take possession of the powder. To this end, two delegates from the Hôtel de Ville asked to see the governor, and since it was around ten in the morning they were invited in for *déjeuner*. Even by the standards of the last day of the *ancien régime*, this seemed a lengthy entertainment. The crowd, from the beginning, had been suspicious when de Launay had refused entry to any but the two delegates and had demanded three "hostage" soldiers in exchange. The prolonged lunch combined with some indeterminate business around the rampart guns (in fact their withdrawal from the em-

101. The capture of the Bastille as seen by one of the combatants, the wine-shop keeper Claude Cholat. Typically for a popular print, all the events of the day are compressed into one image.

brasures) deepened those suspicions. A second deputy, Thuriot de La Ro-zière, was sent for from the district headquarters of Saint-Louis-la-Culture, and he too was admitted to see de Launay, this time armed with specific instructions. The guns, along with their powder, should be removed and delivered to the militia representing the city of Paris, and a unit of the militia should be admitted to the Bastille. This, de Launay replied, was impossible until he had received instructions from Versailles, but he took Thuriot up to the ramparts to inspect the withdrawal of the guns.

It was about half past twelve. Not much had been achieved on either side. None of the essential demands made by Thuriot had been granted, and although he had made efforts to persuade the *invalides* to come to some agreement with the people, de Launay's officers had insisted that it would be dishonorable to hand over the fortress without express orders from their seniors. Thuriot decided to report back to the electors at the Hôtel de Ville for further negotiating instructions. They were themselves reluctant to inflame the situation, and at half past one Thuriot was about to return to the Bastille with another elector, Ethis de Corny, equipped with bugle and loud-hailer by which the removal of the guns would be announced to the people, when the Hôtel de Ville shook to the sound of an explosion followed by the crackle of musket fire coming from the fort.

While he had been gone, the impatience of the crowd had finally burst its bounds. Shouts of "Give us the Bastille" were heard, and the nine hundred had pressed into the undefended outer courtyard, becoming angrier by the minute. A group, including an ex-soldier now carriage maker, had climbed onto the roof of a perfume shop abutting the gate to the inner courtyard and, failing to find the keys to the courtyard, had cut the drawbridge chains. They had crashed down without warning, killing one of the crowd who stood beneath, and over the bridge and his body poured hundreds of the besiegers. At this point the defending soldiers shouted to the people to withdraw or else they would fire, and this too was misinterpreted as encouragement to come further. The first shots were fired. Subsequently each side would claim the other fired first, but since no one among the melee knew that their own people had cut the drawbridge, it was assumed that they had been let into the inner courtyard in order to be mowed down in the confined space by the cannon.

It was of a piece with all the other assumptions of treachery and conspiracy—of the cordial greeting behind which was the plan of death and destruction. Artois and those responsible for Necker's removal; de Flesselles, who had sent the arms searchers on wild-goose chases; the Queen, who appeared tender-hearted yet plotted revenge were all among this cast of villains as far as the people were concerned. And now de Launay, the governor who let down the drawbridge to take better aim, joined their number. It was the fury unleashed by this "deceit" that made it impossible for subsequent delegations from the electors (of which there were many) to get past the fighting and organize some kind of cease-fire.

The battle became serious. At about half past three in the afternoon the crowd was reinforced by companies of *gardes françaises* and by defecting soldiers, including a number who were veterans of the American campaign. Two in particular, Second-Lieutenant Jacob Elie, the standard-bearer of the Infantry of the Queen, and Pierre-Augustin Hulin, the director of the Queen's laundry, were crucial in turning the incoherent assault into an organized siege. Like a number of key participants in the events of 1789, Hulin had been a Genevan revolutionary in 1782, and on encountering Mme de Staël the previous day had sworn to "avenge your father on those bastards who are trying to kill us," a promise she may or may not have found gratifying.

Hulin and Elie also brought an ample supply of arms taken from the Invalides that morning. With them were two cannon, one bronze and the other the Siamese gun inlaid with silver that had been seized from the royal storehouse the day before. It was Louis XIV's toy, then, that would end the old regime in Paris.

It was decided to aim the guns directly at the gate (since balls seemed to bounce harmlessly off the eight-foot-thick walls). Before that could be done, carts filled with burning dung and straw, which had been lit by Santerre to provide smoke cover for the movements of the besiegers, had to be removed from the approach to the gate. At some risk to himself Elie did this in company with a haberdasher familiarly known as "Vive l'Amour." The heavy guns were drawn back on gun carriages, charged and aimed.

A wooden gate now divided the cannon of the besiegers from those of the defenders—perhaps a hundred feet apart. Had they opened up at each other, dreadful carnage would have been guaranteed. But if the attackers could not see the defending guns, the defending troops were well aware of the peril they stood in. Faced with the increasing reluctance of the *invalides* to prolong the fighting, de Launay was himself demoralized. In any case, there was no food with which to withstand a prolonged siege, so that his main concern now was for a surrender that would preserve the honor and the lives of the garrison. He had one card—the powder. In his darkest moments he simply thought of exploding the entire store—and destroying a large part of the faubourg Saint-Antoine—rather than capitulating. Dissuaded from this act of desperation, he resolved to use the threat at least to secure an honorable evacuation.

With no white flag available, a handkerchief was flown from one of the towers and the Bastille's guns stopped firing. At around five, a note asking for such a capitulation, written by the governor—and threatening the explosion unless it was given—was stuck through a chink in through the drawbridge wall of the inner courtyard. A plank was laid down over the moat with men standing on one end to steady it. The first person on the plank fell into the moat but the second—whose identity thereafter was hotly disputed—retrieved it. The demand, however, was refused, and in response to the continued anger of the crowd Hulin was apparently preparing to fire the Siamese cannon when the drawbridge suddenly came down.

The *vainqueurs* rushed into the prison, liberated all seven of the prisoners, took possession of the gunpowder and disarmed the defending troops. The Swiss guards, who had prudently taken off their uniform coats, were initially mistaken for prisoners and unharmed. But some of the *invalides* were brutally dealt with. A soldier named Béquard, who had been one of those responsible for dissuading de Launay from detonating the gunpow-

102. Maillard takes de Launay's demand
for capitulation, from Janinet,
Gravures Historiques

der, had his hand severed almost as soon as he opened one of the gates of the fort. Under the impression that he was one of the prison warders, the crowd paraded the hand about the streets still gripping a key. Later that evening he was misidentified again, this time as one of the cannoneers who had first fired on the people, and was hanged in the place de Grève, along with one of his comrades, before the thirty Swiss guards lined up as an obligatory audience.

The battle itself had taken the lives of eighty-three of the citizens' army. Another fifteen were to die from wounds. Only one of the *invalides* had died in the fighting and three had been wounded. The imbalance was enough for the crowd to demand some sort of punitive sacrifice, and de Launay duly provided it. All of the hatred which to a large degree had been spared the garrison was concentrated on him. His attributes of command— a sword and baton—were wrenched away from him and he was marched towards the Hôtel de Ville through enormous crowds, all of whom were convinced he had been foiled in a diabolical plot to massacre the people. Hulin and Elie managed to prevent the crowd from killing him on the street, though more than once he was knocked down and badly beaten. Throughout the walk he was covered in abuse and spittle. Outside the Hôtel de Ville competing suggestions were offered as to how he should

103. The arrest of de Launay, from
Janinet, *Gravures Historiques*

meet his end, including a proposal to tie him to a horse's tail and drag him
over the cobbles. A pastry cook named Desnot said it would be better to
take him into the Hôtel de Ville—but at that point de Launay, who had
had enough of the ordeal, shouted "Let me die" and lashed out with his
boots, landing a direct hit in Desnot's groin. He was instantaneously covered with darting knives, swords and bayonets, rolled to the gutter and
finished off with a barrage of pistol shots.

The Revolution in Paris had begun with heads hoisted aloft over the
crowd. They had been the heads of heroes, made in wax, carried as proxy
commanders. It needed a symmetrical ending: more heads, this time serving
as trophies of battle. A sword was handed to Desnot, but he cast it aside
and used a pocketknife to saw through de Launay's neck. A little later, de
Flesselles, the *prévôt des marchands* who had also been accused of deliberately misleading the people about stores of arms, was shot as he emerged
from the Hôtel de Ville. The heads were stuck on pikes that bobbed and
dipped above cheering, laughing and singing crowds that filled the streets.

Nine days later there were two more heads to display: those of Bertier
de Sauvigny, the *intendant* of Paris, and Foulon, one of the ministers in the
government that was to have replaced Necker's. The latter was accused of
the famine plot, so the mouth of his severed head was crammed with grass,

104. Jean-Louis Prieur, engraving. Bertier de Sauvigny recognizes the severed head of Foulon.

straw and ordure to signify his particular crime. The young painter Girodet thought this popular symbolism so picturesque that he made a careful sketch as the heads passed before him.

More than the actual casualties of fighting (which, as we have seen, were very limited), it was this display of punitive sacrifice that constituted a kind of revolutionary sacrament. Some, who had celebrated the Revolution so long as it was expressed in abstractions like *Liberté,* gagged at the sight of blood thrust in their faces. Others whose nerves were tougher and stomachs less easily turned made the modern compact by which power could be secured through violence. The beneficiaries of this bargain deluded themselves into believing that they could turn it on and off like a faucet and direct its force with exacting selectivity. Barnave, the Grenoble politician who in 1789 was among the unreserved zealots of the National Assembly, was asked whether the deaths of Foulon and Bertier were really necessary to secure freedom. He gave the reply which, converted into an instrument of the revolutionary state, would be the entitlement to kill him on the guillotine:

"What, then, is their blood so pure?"

vi THE AFTERLIFE OF THE BASTILLE: PATRIOTE PALLOY AND THE NEW GOSPEL

The first number of the *Révolutions de Paris,* published on the seventeenth of July, was devoted to a lengthy—and rather muddled—account of the insurrection. Its climax around the Bastille was represented as a joyous family festival, with *gamins* scampering around the fighting:

Women did their utmost to back us up, and even children after every volley from the fortress ran hither and thither picking up bullets and shot then dodging back cheerfully to take shelter and give those missiles to our soldiers.

After the children came the grandpas. The liberation of the prison brought into the light of day patriarchs, men who had grown old, immured by the tyranny that had forgotten their incarceration. "The cells were thrown open to set free innocent victims and venerable old men who were amazed to behold the light of day." The reality was less dramatic. Of the seven prisoners, four were forgers who had been tried by regular process of law. The Comte de Solages, like de Sade, had been incarcerated at the request of his family for libertinism and was happy enough to be released. He was given free lodgings at the Hôtel de Rouen in the Oratoire district before disappearing into the city, much to the regret of his relatives. The remaining two prisoners were lunatics, and both returned in fairly short order to Charenton. One of them, however, "Major Whyte" (described in French sources as English and in English sources as Irish), was perfect for revolutionary propaganda, bearing as he did a waist-length beard. With his carpet of silvery whiskers and shrunken, bony form he seemed, to people expecting to see so many Latudes emerge from the dungeons, the incarnation of suffering and endurance. So Whyte was called the *major de l'immensité* and was borne around in triumph through the streets of Paris, amiably if weakly waving his hands in salutation, for in his bewildered condition he still assumed he was Julius Caesar.

Such was the symbolic power of the Bastille to gather to itself all the miseries for which "despotism" was now held accountable, that reality was enhanced by Gothic fantasies as the building was ransacked. Ancient pieces of armor were declared to be fiendish "iron corsets" applied to constrict the victim and a toothed machine that was part of a printing press was said to be a wheel of torture. Countless prints from the workshops of the rue Saint-Jacques, which had cranked up their production to service the acute hunger for news, supplied suitably horrible imagery, featuring standing skeletons, instruments of torture and men in iron masks.

A genuine encounter between legend and reality took place on the sixteenth when Latude came to survey the scene of his captivity. To his astonishment he was presented with the rope and rung ladder and the tools of his escape, all of which had been conscientiously preserved by the guards

105. "The first hour of liberty"—the prisoners from the Bastille paraded through the streets. Note the impressive length of beard and patriarchal appearance of the most conspicuous prisoner.

who had found them thirty-three years before. They were ceremoniously offered to the famous escapee as "property acquired by just title." In the Salon that autumn they were exhibited alongside a splendid portrait of Latude by Antoine Vestier in which the hero points to his escape route and shows off the ladder as the attribute of his revolutionary sainthood.

The Bastille, then, was much more important in its "afterlife" than it ever had been as a working institution of state. It gave a shape and an image to all the vices against which the Revolution defined itself. Transfigured from a nearly empty, thinly manned anachronism into the seat of the Beast Despotism, it incorporated all those rejoicing at its capture as members of the new community of the Nation. Participants, witnesses, celebrants, they were all friends of humanity, bringers of light into the citadel of darkness.

No one grasped the creative opportunities offered by the captured fortress better than Pierre-François Palloy. He was to be, simultaneously, both the entrepreneur and the impresario of the greatest demolition job in modern history. Though he used memoir writers and poets and graphic artists, it was Palloy's conception of the political usefulness of the cult of the Bastille that turned it into a national and international symbol of liberated humanity. Deconstructing the edifice, he reconstructed a myth which, packaged, marketed and distributed, was made available to audiences and customers throughout the length and breadth of the country.

Palloy also understood (and here he was not alone) that the Revolution had created a demand for a new kind of history: the epic of the common man. It had to be related in a new way, not at the leisurely tempo and with the sardonic detachment of a Gibbon or a Voltaire, but in passionately scissored cuts—*actualités*—in which history was made directly contemporary with the reader's life. Into that continuously unfolding present, the reader-participant could insert his own experience, even at second hand. This also called for a new style of presentation, full of breathless hyperbole and patriotic exclamation. Instead of contemplating the centuries in the manner of an armchair scholar, the new history had to be chopped up into the memory units of a working man—a single day or a week. Finally, to lend immediacy to those who were geographically distant from the event, its memories—*souvenirs*—had to take concrete form, if necessary mass-produced, so that by contemplating or touching them the citizen could share in the intensity of the great Revolutionary Day. Jean-François Janinet's *Gravures Historiques,* which appeared every Tuesday from November 1789 to March 1791, provided this newsreel-like presentation, offering, for just eight sous, an engraving of a famous event and eight pages of explanatory text. Such was the importance of the fourteenth of July that eight separate issues were devoted to that day alone.

Who was "Patriote Palloy"? He was yet another example of a self-made bourgeois who had prospered under the urban boom economy of the old regime and who certainly had no need of a revolution to make his fortune. Both his mother and father came from wine shop–owning families, but they managed nonetheless to send him to the Collège d'Harcourt, full of the sons of liberal aristocrats. Like them he took a commission in the army and at twenty, in what must have seemed a step backwards but which was actually a shrewd move, he became an apprentice mason. A year later he married his master's daughter and launched himself in the construction industry, which in the 1770s and early 1780s was the most spectacularly profitable line of business in Paris. Palloy worked on private houses in Saint-Germain, the Farmers'-General wall (which he later helped knock down), the new meat market at Sceaux and quickly moved from mason to foreman to entrepreneur. By 1789 he had accumulated an amazing fortune of half a million livres, possessed three houses, including one inherited from his father-in-

106. Hardener (after Klooger), the liberation of a prisoner turned into Gothic fantasy. Note the chained prisoners' decomposing skeletons, all figments of the engraver's imagination.

law, as well as a number of shops and parcels of as yet undeveloped real estate. He had all the trappings of worldly success—a carriage, fine furniture, a large and intelligently acquired library—and along with much of Paris liked to quote Roman histories as inspirational examples to the present generation. He was thirty-four years old.

Like so many other revolutionaries, Palloy was not a fuming failure, but a model success story of old-regime capitalism. This, however, did not preclude his immediate identification with the cause of the *patrie*. On the fourteenth of July he was commandant of his local district militia on the Ile Saint-Louis. Well within hearing range of the battle at the Bastille, he claimed that he had run to the scene and on arrival took a ball through his tricorn hat by the side of Lieutenant Elie. Though his name was misspelled as "Pallet" in the official list, there is no doubt that he did indeed acquire a *brevet de vainqueur* to certify that he had been one of the sacred nine hundred.

It took Palloy just one day to realize that as *vainqueur*, construction engineer and experienced boss of labor gangs he was in a position to acquire his most important piece of real estate to date. On the fifteenth he brought eight hundred men to the Bastille, ready to begin the work of demolition should the electors agree. Jumping the gun made him immediate enemies. Architects had plans that the Bastille might be preserved as a monument to fallen tyranny; some officers in the volunteer guard militia (soon to be the National Guard) thought they should have sole custody of the building. But Palloy's plans for demolition were expedited by the anxiety among the electors that royal troops might retake the citadel through underground passages that were rumored to extend all the way from the Château de Vincennes. The myths of the Bastille, then, exerted a hold even on tough-minded ex-prisoners like Mirabeau. For in response to reports by local residents that they had heard groans and conversations coming from deep within the ground, Mirabeau took a tour of the *cachots* and the underground vaults, knocking on walls and doors with the son of one of the ex-warders to see if there was not indeed some labyrinthine connection with Vincennes to the east.

Once he had set his mind at rest, Mirabeau mounted the towers for a less sinister ceremony. Waving to the crowds below, he swung a pick at the battlement and the first stone fell to great applause. Other notables like

107. Donchery, portrait of Patriote Palloy

108. Demachy, demolition of the Bastille in progress, 1789

Beaumarchais and the Marquis de Lusignan followed, after which there was a free-for-all. In the next few days, papers were scattered, burned or secreted as mementos, bonfires burned by day and fireworks exploded by night. Warders, now accepted as good Patriots, gave guided tours of the cells, embellishing their anecdotes to conform with the standard mythology of torture and chains. Women locked themselves in overnight so that they could claim in the morning to have slept with the rats, spiders and toads that had been the companions of Latude.

Through all these festivities, Palloy was planning his business. Inevitably, it was the Permanent Committee at the Hôtel de Ville, now established as a municipal executive, that licensed the work. Palloy was just one of five specialists appointed to see to the demolition, others being in charge of carpentry, joinery, ironwork and the like. But he very rapidly established himself as more than one of a board. Beside the work of demolishing the masonry, the rest was minor and Palloy's crew was by far the biggest, numbering almost a thousand workers at its height. He himself was paid 150 livres a month and in turn paid his men well: 45 sous a day for the foremen, 40 for the subforemen and 36 for the navvies. In the late summer of 1789, when work was exceptionally scarce and prices high, the job was a boon, especially to the local population in Saint-Antoine and the areas immediately north and south of the Seine from where much of the casual manual labor was recruited.

Palloy not only provided work and pay, he gave structure to the entire enterprise. All on-site men were required to carry identity cards, especially designed by Palloy himself and in the three patriotic colors: white for the entrepreneurs, blue for the site inspectors and red for the workers. Each showed a globe surmounted by the fleur-de-lis, the emblems of the three orders and the optimistic motto *Ex Unitate Libertas.* The cards themselves very soon became precious items for which collectors were said to offer as much as twelve livres each. On the site throughout the work, Palloy acted as boss-father, throwing parties for the workers, playing with the many children who took part and keeping them out of the falling debris. Wielding a cane and a clapper with which to call people to attention, he also was constable, judge and jury, fining malefactors who got into drunken fights or were caught pilfering. Two such culprits were even hanged, and at the end of the work Palloy summarized the casualties as "four insurrections; fifteen accidents; eight murders and two woundings"—which he evidently felt was about par for the course.

For all these interruptions, the work proceeded with startling speed. By the end of July the load-supporting vaults and beams were exposed, and throughout July, working downwards, floors were rapidly demolished. A clock tower that featured prisoners in chains striking the hours was melted down in a foundry, and in August the sculptor Dumont was paid four

109. Le Sueur, gouache, demolition of the Bastille

hundred livres for shattering the four stone figures of Saint Anthony, Charles V, Charles VI and Jeanne de Bourbon that had ornamented the Porte Saint-Antoine.

By the end of November, most of the Bastille was demolished. There was some anxiety among the workers that their zeal was now about to put them out of a job. Palloy was himself concerned that the commission should not end on the ruins of the fortress. Thus, while the physical work was completed, his own inspired version of the Bastille Business had only just begun.

Some of this involved new projects. The municipality took him up on a proposal to erect a platform on the Pont Neuf opposite the statue of Henri IV, where the cannon of the Bastille could be mounted. During the winter months a number of the original work gang cleared out the moats and ditches of the fort. But much more of Palloy's energies went into promoting the cult of the Bastille as a political tourist attraction, complete with guided tours, historical lectures and accounts from *vainqueurs* of the events of the fourteenth of July. Early in 1790, the son of a British physician, Millingen, was taken by his father to visit this famous attraction.

> Thousands crowded to behold the ruins of the Bastille, and my father led me to contemplate this fallen fortress of the tyrannic power. In the ruined dungeons close to the ditch and infested with water-rats, toads and other reptiles were still to be seen stones on which had reposed the unfortunate prisoners, doomed to expire in the *oubliettes,* forgotten by all the world, condemned to be buried alive, and the iron rings to which their chains had been fastened were still riveted in the flinty couch which bore impressions of aching limbs.

The important thing was to produce—in the theatrical sense—events which would recapitulate both the horrors of the Bastille and the euphoria of its fall so that successive waves of visiting Patriots could be recruited for revolutionary enthusiasm. Palloy's first such event was a ceremony he organized for the work crews themselves, who thus became *vainqueurs* of the masonry of the fort. On February 23 an "altar" (in the first among all the revolutionary festivals to follow), constructed entirely of iron balls, chains and manacles, was set up amidst the ruins. On the following day, after a religious ceremony at the Church of Saint-Louis, seven hundred workers all swore loyalty to the constitution, and through a mechanical contraption of great ingenuity, the punitive ironmongery self-destructed to reveal a huge array of flowers (artificial, given the season?). After this stage miracle, the seven hundred made their way in procession to the Hôtel de Ville carrying a model of the Bastille that they had fashioned from its stones.

The idea of a model of the Bastille was not Palloy's but that of one of his masons named Dax. Typically, however, Palloy took an ingenious artisanal idea and turned it into a major enterprise—claiming, as he did so, credit for the scheme. Other developments during the spring of 1790 helped him sustain interest in the Bastille. At the end of April bits and pièces of human skeletons were discovered in the substructure and were instantly described as the remains of prisoners who had died in captivity, manacled to the walls, forgotten even by their jailors. In all probability they were the bones of guards dating back to the Renaissance, but the opportunity for sensation was irresistible. They were exhumed with great solemnity and on June 1 taken in four separate coffins (though no one was certain which bones belonged to whom) to the cemetery of Saint-Paul, where they were reinterred. In his sermon the radical Bishop of Caen, Claude Fauchet, used the dry bones to cast himself as the revolutionary Ezekiel greeting a new "Day of Revelations, for the bones have risen to the voice of French liberty; through centuries of oppression and death they have come to prophesy the regeneration of nature and the life of Nations."

Palloy's own enterprises were, for a while, overshadowed by the monumental preparations for the Fête de la Fédération on the Champ de Mars, but its date—the fourteenth of July—helped sustain interest in the Bastille.

110. Dance and people's banquet given on the ruins of the Bastille, July 14, 1790

Prior to the first anniversary, plays reenacting the great day, a mass of prints and engravings, poems and songs were all grist for his mill. Not least were the hundreds of thousands of provincial National Guardsmen who had come to Paris for the great festival of patriotic unity and for whom a visit to the Bastille was an obligatory pilgrimage. For the guards Palloy threw a great ball on the ruins of the Bastille, with brilliant illuminations and fireworks, great tents decorated with the tricolor and an outsize sign that read *Ici l'on danse.*

That still left many millions of Frenchmen for whom the fall of the Bastille was a remote event. And it was to bring them within the patriotic fold that Palloy put together his traveling revolution kit. It was to be taken by specially commissioned and distinctively costumed "Apostles of Liberty" to all of the eighty-three departments into which France had been divided. Among them were to be Palloy's ten-year-old son; Fauchet; Dusaulx, the author of the popular *Work of Seven Days* (the re-creation of the world in July 1789) and another of Palloy's friends, Titon Bergeras, who would later deafen the Legislative Assembly with his baritone oratory. Whenever possible Latude himself was to accompany the apostles along with his rope ladder to give a personal account of his trials.

To supply his apostles, Palloy produced 246 chests of *souvenirs.* Prompted by Dax's idea, he had already gone into production, creating every conceivable kind of item from the debris of the Bastille that remained to him. Inkwells had been made from "fetters" and other items of ironwork; fans depicting the battle for the fortress made from its miscellaneous papers; paperweights from its stones in the shape of little Bastilles; snuffboxes; ceremonial daggers. The Dauphin even received a set of marble dominos shaped like Bastilles. These could be sold or provided gratis to provincial Patriots, but they were bonus items in the chests, whose makeup was strictly regulated by Palloy.

Each kit consisted of three chests. In the first was the *pièce de résistance,* a scale model of the Bastille, complete in virtually all details, with working doors, grilles and drawbridges. A miniature of Latude's ladder would be hooked to the appropriate turret and a little gibbet complete with dangling cord added to the courtyard for the right effect (though executions were never carried out in the Bastille). For the battle scenes there were miniature cannon, balls and a white flag. The clock was painted to read 5:30: the sacred moment of surrender. The second chest contained the wooden platform for the model and an engraved portrait of the King; the third, images concerning the "skeletons" and their reburial, portraits of revolutionary notables like Lafayette and Bailly, a ball and cuirass from the Bastille, Latude's biography, a plan of the fortress and poems on the various events custom-

111. Model of the Bastille made from its masonry

112. Medal in the shape of the
Bastille

113. Leather-bound box decorated with
the Bastille, guardsman and cannon

written by Palloy himself. A final item for the third box—also available to the public in Paris—was a "fragment of a crust, two to three inches thick, formed on the vaults of the cells by the breath, sweat and blood of the unfortunate prisoners."

An idea of their mission with the new gospel can be gleaned from the experience of one of the apostles: the actor François-Antoine Legros. Given traveling conditions and the burden of the thirty-three chests he was transporting, the scale of Legros' journey was little short of epic. He set out in November 1790 for Burgundy, traveling through Melun, Auxerre and Dijon, then heading south towards Provence. At Lyon he helped arrest conspirators against the *patrie*, but near Salons his mule train was attacked by brigands. Legros managed to kill one of them, but the pistol shot frightened his horse, which bolted, throwing him and breaking his leg. By the time he reached Toulon his money had run out (Palloy's allowance of nine livres a day being intermittently sent and in any case insufficient), and he was forced to rejoin a company in which he had once been a player. Though his performance in Voltaire's *Zaïre* did not, as he put it, "meet with the success I had expected," he seems to have earned enough to resume his mission, as he took ship for Bastia in Corsica, the last stage in his extraordinary trip. By the time he finished he had been ten months on the road, and had traveled nearly fifteen hundred miles.

If the apostles were exhausted by their efforts, Palloy himself was scarcely less so. Rather than his fortune having been made by the Revolution, he actually seems to have lost it in his tireless commitment to spreading the new gospel. There was a continuous demand for his *souvenirs,* one from as far away as "the Society of St. Tammany in New York" in 1792, and Palloy set up what he hoped would be a permanent "Museum of Liberty" near the Pont Neuf.

Politically, though, he was losing his grip. The myth of patriotic unity enshrined in the cult of the Bastille was being severely tested during 1792 and many of Palloy's pet heroes were becoming rapidly discredited. Mirabeau, whose bust he had made from a Bastille stone and presented at his funeral in April 1791, was unmasked as a royalist intriguer a year later; Lafayette, for whom he had a sword made from four bolts of the Bastille, decamped to the Austrians in the same year. Worst of all, the King, whose likeness had decorated all his chests, had been caught fleeing the country. Even in July 1792, a month before the final fall of the monarchy, Palloy was still hoping that the King would appear at a ceremony meant to launch the royal project of a column at the site of the Bastille.

In December 1793 he went to see his old friend Citizen Curtius, who was busy making a head of Louis XV's mistress Mme Du Barry for good

Patriots to abuse. Palloy knew another genius when he saw one. He marveled at the likeness, and Curtius told him in a businesslike sort of way that yes, he thought it especially good since he had been able to go to the cemetery of the Girondins and inspect the freshly severed real thing. Despite the cold, he had sat down then and there to achieve the best wax image he could to convey her expression at the coup de grâce.

Three weeks later Palloy found himself in the prison of La Force, notwithstanding calling himself the Republican Diogenes Palloy, the victim as he insisted of wrongful and treacherous conspiracy. On the eighth of February 1794, the man who had led France to believe that with the demolition of the Bastille prisons would never stain the face of freedom in France, wrote from what he called his *cachot,* protesting his innocence, his *patriotisme,* and still obligingly giving instructions for the dispatch of models of the Bastille to newly "liberated" departments. On the seventeenth of March he was freed, but although he turned his hand to assisting with republican festivities, he noted with unconcealed dismay in July that though "until now I have only utilized the ruins of the Bastille, sacred site of the beginnings of liberty, for allegorical feasts . . . citizens now want to see another genre of spectacle and have installed there the 'little window' of Guillotin."

vi PARIS, KING OF THE FRENCH

On July 14, 1789, Louis XVI's journal consisted of the one-word entry "Rien" (Nothing). Historians invariably find this a comic symptom of the King's hapless remoteness from political reality. But it was nothing of the sort. The journal was less a diary than one of his remorselessly enumerated lists of kills at the hunt. Since his favorite pastime had been more or less permanently interrupted, there could hardly have been a more negatively eloquent utterance on his predicament than "Rien."

To be sure, he was, in large part, the author of his plight. His personal popularity, especially outside Paris, was still immense. And even after the Tennis Court Oath he had had many opportunities to exploit it as both Mirabeau and Necker had wanted, and to create an authentic constitutional monarchy. They had all been squandered. Worse still, Louis had shown himself either feebly submissive—as in the immediate aftermath of the *séance royale*—or deviously reactionary, as in the military buildup to Necker's dismissal.

On the evening of the fourteenth, Lafayette's brother-in-law and fellow revolutionary enthusiast, the Vicomte de Noailles, reported the day's events in Paris to the National Assembly. In turn the Assembly decided to relay this information to the King, who preempted them by announcing that he had already determined to withdraw troops from the center of Paris to Sèvres and Saint-Cloud. He expressed sadness and disbelief that blood could possibly have been shed as the result of any orders given to the soldiers but did not offer, as the Assembly wanted, to restore Necker. Later that evening two of the Paris electors arrived confirming Noailles' reports, but it appears that the full gravity of the situation was not yet apparent to the King.

Later that night, around eleven, the Duc de La Rochefoucauld-Liancourt, yet another of the Lafayette circle, asked to see the King in his private apartments. A famous, anecdotal, version of the story has the citizen-noble informing Louis, for the first time, of the fall of the Bastille. The King reacts with the question "Is it a revolt?" and Liancourt replies, "No, Sire, it is a revolution." While Louis already knew of the rising from Noailles and the electors, it is entirely possible that this exchange took place and probable that it was Liancourt's apparently graphic account of the death of de Launay and de Flesselles that finally persuaded the King of the full enormity of the event. His military power in the capital had collapsed and with it any possible attempt to reverse the authority of the National Assembly by force.

In the Assembly the next morning, it was decided to send two deputies to see the King to demand the dismissal of the Breteuil ministry. As they were about to leave, Mirabeau made another of his famous interjections according to which the debauched lackeys of foreign powers were poised to trample underfoot the native rights of liberated France.

> Tell the·king that the foreign hordes by whom we are
> surrounded were visited by princes, princesses, favorites of both
> sexes who made much of them . . . all night long these foreign
> satellites gorged with gold and wine foretold in their impious
> songs the enslavement of France and the destruction of the
> Assembly; tell him that . . . courtiers danced to barbarous music
> and that a scene such as this preceded the Saint-Bartholomew's
> massacre. . . .

His speech had barely ended when Louis' arrival was announced. Mirabeau again asserted himself to silence the spontaneous applause, urging a more frosty reception, at least until the King's intentions were known. "The people's silence," he admonished, "is a lesson for kings." He need not have bothered, for the manner of the King's arrival was so astonishing, so disconcertingly naked, that it amounted to an abdication. He came on foot with no train or retinue, not even a single pantalooned and perruqued guard. At either side were his brothers, Provence and Artois, physically as well as ideologically to his left and right, respectively. To the Assembly he confirmed the withdrawal of the remaining troops from the Champ de Mars and expressly denied any design against the safety of its members.

Though the King stopped short of announcing the recall of Necker, the official confirmation of the end of a military threat was enough to earn a great wave of cheering inside the Assembly. It flowed into the crowd gathered outside and produced yet another of those demonstrations, half rapture, half threat, that required the presence of the royal family on the balcony of the palace. At two o'clock, an enormous cortège of eighty-eight deputies in forty carriages set out to report the good news to Paris. At their head was Lafayette, as vice-president of the Assembly. The last part of the journey, from the place Louis XV to the Hôtel de Ville, was made on foot and turned into a kind of triumphal march through the city. At the building where, forty-one years later, he would appear in a similar epiphany, Lafayette addressed the enormous crowd, which was covered in patriotic cockades. The King had been misled, he announced, but had now been returned to the full benevolence of his heart. In return the electors promised loyalty. And in what seems to have been an impromptu proposal (made by Lafayette's friend Brissot de Warville) and taken up by the crowd, the Marquis accepted command of the new Paris militia. Bailly, likewise, became the mayor of the city. A Te Deum in Notre Dame followed in which Lafayette vowed to defend liberty with his life.

With the King's penitential walk to the Assembly, the august court of the Bourbons had died. On the morning of the sixteenth of July the royal council met for the last time in its traditional form. It had serious things to discuss. Maréchal de Broglie made it quite clear that, given the disintegration of the army, any attempt at counter-attacking Paris was out of the question. What, then, could be salvaged? The Queen and Artois wanted the King to move to a provincial capital, the closer to a Prussian or an Austrian frontier the better—Metz, for example—and there to rally loyal troops. De Broglie, realistically, warned the King that with the chain of command disintegrating so quickly he could not possibly guarantee the King's safety in any long journey.

There was nothing left but surrender, with as good a grace as he could muster.

For the King's youngest brother and his set, the humiliation of the monarchy was insupportable. That same night, July 16, Artois, together with the princes de Conti and Condé, his friends the Polignacs and the

Abbé Vermond, the Queen's personal adviser since she had been a princess in Vienna, all departed Versailles for the frontier. The emigration vindicated everything revolutionary pamphlets said about the court: that it was a foreign enclave lodged at the expense of the nation. Now it would add to that odium the reputation of being a client of foreign armies on whom it depended to reassert its authority in France. Indeed, Artois made no secret of the fact that he expected some sort of alliance between loyal French regiments and as yet undetermined (but in all likelihood Austrian) forces to reverse the Revolution. He could hardly have expected, though, that it would take another fifteen years to accomplish the conquest.

The next day, the seventeenth, Louis XVI set out on his own road to Canossa. La Rochefoucauld-Liancourt had already urged him to show his personal goodwill by appearing in Paris, but it was only after the bitter realizations of the council on the sixteenth that he accepted the inevitable. His hand, in any case, had been forced over the matter of the government. Necker's recall and the dismissal of the Breteuil ministry had been announced to general rejoicing and troops had already begun to pack up on the Champ de Mars and retire to Sèvres, where another seventy-five of them immediately deserted.

Not for the last time, Louis mustered a dignity in helpless impotence that failed him in his fitful moments of self-assertion. Without showing any signs of panic, he made provision to continue royal government should he not return. He made his will and testament, and empowered Provence, who alone among the royal princes had decided to remain in France, with authority as lieutenant-general of the kingdom. The King prayed in the Chapel Royal with his family and then set off, dressed in a simple *frac* morning coat, without any of the usual appurtenances of majesty. Though his coach was drawn by eight black horses, it too was undecorated. Before it rode a small detachment of his personal bodyguard, who were outnumbered by a much larger escort of the Versailles militia in improvised, heavily cockaded uniforms. Behind them were a hundred deputies of the Assembly and a large, straggling retinue of Versailles townspeople, singing, shouting *"Vive le roi"* and *"Vive la nation"* and waving pikes, flintlocks and pruning hooks.

The weather, always described by contemporaries as though it were a revolutionary actor, was accomplice to the royal chagrin. For the sun that shone down resplendently on the procession to Paris announced the eclipse of the fantasy of the Sun King. Louis XIV had built Versailles as a retreat from the capital's constraints, a place in which he could indulge his Apollonian will in stone and water, ritual and icons. In 1775, at his coronation at Reims, Louis XVI was supposed to have begun a new age of solar enlightenment. Instead the sun had been brought down to earth.

What sort of king was he supposed to be now? Everywhere he went the answer was the same: not Louis XIV but Henri IV. The cult of the first Bourbon, who had ended the wars of religion and had been assassinated by a Catholic fanatic, had now reached epidemic proportions. In his person was supposed to have been combined every manner of benevolence, humanity and wisdom; he was the prototype of the citizen-King that the still overwhelmingly royalist people of France hoped to see reincarnated in Louis. Above all else, Henri was described, in popular songs and verses, as the ideal King-Father, who could no more have done harm to the people of France than he could have murdered his own children. That same concept had been expressed in a grandiose design for a new monument to Henri IV expressly meant to associate the patriotic martyr with his new incarnation, Louis. A vast rotunda was to be encircled by a double row of columns. At its center was to be a statue of the fallen King "in the attitude of a good father in the middle of his children . . . dressed in the simple costume that he loved." On the pedestal would be the inscription "To Henri IV from all humanity," and on a great festive day Louis XVI was to place a crown on his head and pronounce the words (as if in self-tutorial) "*Voilà le modèle des Souverains*" (Here is the model for sovereigns).

It was no surprise, then, that greeting Louis XVI at the Porte de Chaillot, Bailly alluded to this incessantly recommended ancestor and in particular to his entry into Paris in 1604. Offering the King the keys to the city—a custom associated with triumphal entries—the mayor even improved on the original scene. "These are the same keys," he said, "that were presented to Henri IV; he had conquered his people; now it is his people who have conquered their king." Louis may not have appreciated the reversal of form.

Other serious amendments to triumphal royal entries then followed. The Valois kings of the French Renaissance—François I, Henri II and Charles IX—had each been greeted by arches proclaiming his identity as the Gallic Hercules, the master (sometimes even the emperor, in the manner of Charlemagne) of *Gallia et Germania.* Louis XVI was greeted instead by Lafayette in civilian dress, wearing the blue and red cockade of the city (and, ominously, the colors of the House of Orléans), and taken through streets lined with armed citizen-guards to the place Louis XV. The rear of the procession was joined by market women, dressed in the white costume they kept for ceremonials, draped in red and blue ribbon and bearing flowers. At the Hôtel de Ville, above the archway of unsheathed swords formed for

114. J.-P. Houël, view of the Louvre at the moment of the King's arrival in Paris, July 17, 1789

him—as if both in homage and challenge—the King could read the official designation of his new identity:

LOUIS XVI, FATHER OF THE FRENCH, THE KING OF A FREE PEOPLE

Conceding this reinvention of kingship, Louis then accepted the cockade that Bailly offered him on the steps of the Hôtel de Ville and pinned it to his hat as trumpet and cannon shot accompanied bursts of cheering. After a brief and largely inaudible speech inside the Grand Salle, where the King attempted to express satisfaction with the appointments of Lafayette and Bailly—another legitimation of actions over which he had had no control—he showed himself again on the balcony, wearing the cockade.

At about ten that evening, Louis reached Versailles, exhausted and disoriented, though much relieved that the day had ended without bloodshed. He greeted his even more relieved wife and children affectionately. Their physical safety increasingly seemed his paramount concern. With his court virtually abolished and his royal ceremonial stripped from him, Louis XVI had become, at last, just another *père de famille.* And it was to protect them that he had consented to become at the same time the *"bon père de la France."* The idealists of a revolutionary monarchy were to claim that the second title was but an extension of the first. Pessimists (the minority in 1789) could see family quarrels ahead. And in the eventuality of such a conflict it was not yet clear, especially to Louis XVI, to which of the families he would devote the remainder of his life.

Part Three

CHOICES

CHAPTER ELEVEN

Reason and Unreason

July–November 1789

i PHANTOMS
July–August

I N JULY 1789, Mme de La Tour du Pin went to the spa of Forges-les-Eaux in Normandy to take the waters. Just nineteen years old, she had found the labor and birth of her second child to be particularly traumatic, and the family physician had insisted on a rest cure. Intelligent and good-natured, Henrietta-Lucy came from the Anglo-Irish Catholic clan of the Dillons, some of whom had exiled themselves to France on the ejection of King James II in 1688. By the time that she was born in 1770, they had become well established in the military nobility with regiments of their own and connections to the richest and most sophisticated families of the land. A child of the Enlightenment, like all her generation, she read deeply in Richardson and Rousseau and even the Whig Defoe. Spotting her cleverness, her worldly great-great-uncle, the Archbishop of Narbonne, had provided Chaptal (later Napoleon's minister of the interior) as a science tutor. Armed with expertise in chemistry, physics, geology and mineralogy, she was able to tour the Dillon coal and sulfur mines in the Cévennes as an informed visitor.

Received at court by the Queen, she was also launched into the fashionable society of the liberal nobility in Paris. Lally-Tollendal was a distant cousin; the even more militantly political de Lameth brothers were her relations through marriage to de La Tour du Pin. Throughout the last pleasures of the old regime in which, as she later wrote, "we laughed and drank our way to the precipice," Lucy remained warily sensible.

In the summer of 1789 the Revolution closed in around her family. Her distinguished father-in-law was being spoken of as Necker's minister of war (and was soon appointed to the post). Her husband was garrisoned forty miles away at Valenciennes but, increasingly anxious for her safety, left his regiment (belatedly securing leave) to join her in Normandy. Reunited, the family spent a last idyllic vacation of the kind sharply recalled by survivors of revolutions.

On the morning of July 28, she was about to go for her usual morning ride when she heard a great commotion in the street below her apartment. Crowds of villagers were standing about sobbing, wringing their hands, praying and wailing that "they were lost." At their center was a man in "a disreputable torn green coat," mounted on a gray horse that was still foaming at the mouth and bloodied on the flanks from being so hard ridden. "They will be here in three hours," he told his terrified audience; "at Gaillefontaine [about five miles away] they are pillaging everything, setting fire to the barns." Having delivered this helpful message, he then rode off to spread the good news at Neufchâtel.

"They" in this case meant Austrian troops said to have invaded France from the Netherlands. But in the panic-stricken weeks after the fall of the Bastille, "they" could as easily have been the British marines supposed to have landed at Brest and Saint-Malo, the regiment of Swedes led by the Comte d'Artois at the northeast frontier or the thirty thousand Spanish soldiers preparing to sack Bordeaux. Most commonly "they" were said to be "brigands," massed in armies and paid by Artois and the princes or the aristocracy in general to wreak a bloody revenge on the Third Estate for its temerity. This was a particularly gruesome prospect, since the brigands were supposed to relish atrocities like rape, dismemberment and the wholesale burning of crops, barns and cottages.

Since her husband had gone off by himself to the spa, Lucy was left alone to try to calm these agitated spirits. There was no war, she assured the villagers. Her husband, whose station was right on the frontier of the Austrian Netherlands, would certainly have known if their troops had been mobilized. But Forges was in the center of an area already made jittery by continuing food riots in Rouen, twenty-five miles to the northwest, and instructions given at Lille to sound the tocsin at the slightest sign of danger. Walking to the church, Lucy found the curé just about to pull the bell rope. Appreciating that with the first chime the panic would be irreversible, she seized the priest by the collar of his cassock and attempted to remonstrate with him while physically preventing him from sounding the alarm. The waters at Forges must have restored her powers, since when her husband returned he found the two still wrestling around the bell rope. Together, the de La Tour du Pins promised to go to Gaillefontaine, where the Austrians were supposed to be encamped, and then return to disabuse the village of its fears.

The day's excitement was not yet over. At Gaillefontaine they were confronted by peasants with rusty flintlocks demanding to know if the soldiers weren't at Forges. A gathering of the locals seemed persuaded by calming denials until one of them, looking intently at Lucy, identified her as the Queen. For a moment she was in danger; then a locksmith, braying with laughter, insisted that the real Queen was twice as old and twice as large as Mme de La Tour du Pin. Released, husband and wife returned to Forges, where the whole village had already assumed they had been taken prisoner by the Austrians and would never be heard from again.

Scenes like this were repeated throughout eastern France from Hainaut and Picardy in the north, down through Champagne and Alsace to Burgundy and the Franche-Comté. A western trail of what contemporaries called "the Fear" marked the Poitou and reached as far as the countryside around Versailles. Even in normal times, the four thousand *maréchaussée* provincial constabulary would have been inadequate to deal with mass hysteria on this scale. But now that the authority of the central government had virtually collapsed, the effect of such a panic was to shatter France into fragments of self-arming militias and self-authorizing municipal communes, all mobilized to scan the horizon for armies of brigands, Spaniards or Austrians.

Sometimes the panic lasted but a matter of hours. At the tiny hamlet of Vaux, near Creil, Marie-Victoire Monnet, the eldest of a family of fifteen children, hid in a hayloft with three of her sisters. Their mother had provided them with a loaf of bread and a quarter of a Brie, enough to sustain the siege of some days expected by the village. Brigands were already said to have slaughtered the menfolk in the immediately neighboring town. After sitting for three hours in the hot, dusty, dark barn and consuming all of the bread and cheese, the girls' terror had turned to boredom and boredom to disappointment. Marie, followed by her sisters, nervously clambered down, and with no sign of the guaranteed mayhem, returned to their house, where they found their mother and the rest of the children equally baffled by the nonappearance of the dreaded criminal element.

Elsewhere the consequences were more serious. In major cities like Lyon and Dijon (both, significantly, facing east), thousands of volunteer militiamen manned bridges and gates for weeks on end in the expectation that if they ever lowered their guard the brigands would be sure to materialize. At the same time, of course, they attempted to deal with violent attacks on grain stores, bakers' shops and the houses of royal officials within the city limits. It was the first instance of the *patrie en danger* syndrome: the patriotic emergencies that would empower ever more radically punitive regimes.

The seizure of local depots of munitions and the creation of enforcing militia, accountable to improvised revolutionary committees, led later generations of royalist historians to assume that the panic was itself a plot, designed by conspirators like the Duc d'Orléans to turn France into an armed camp, irrecoverable for traditional authority. At the same time, the court, and by extension the whole of the nobility, was stigmatized as, literally, an enemy camp: foreigners who had no qualms about planning the massacre of French men and women to recover their lost privileges.

It is indeed true that the paranoid state (in both senses) that was the most obvious feature of revolutionary politics was the creation not of the Terror but of 1789. But it is equally obvious that theories of consciously organized conspiracies are themselves imaginary. The Great Fear, as its historian Georges Lefebvre pointed out, bears all the signs of a spontaneous panic.

It had happened before. In 1703, when Louis XIV's armies appeared to be losing a war to resist the invasion of France and when famine had visited large parts of the country, the belief spread that King William III had instructed Protestant marauders to take indiscriminate revenge. Merely repeating the news that William had been dead for over a year had no effect on the hysteria. In 1789, the panic spread in the same way, by a rider abruptly appearing on a brutally ridden horse, announcing with obvious conviction that general slaughter was taking place in the next village. Very often such people were believed because they were types who were supposed to have special access to such information: innkeepers, letter carriers, soldiers. If they were men of quality their word was considered even more dependable. At Rochechouart near Limoges, on the twenty-ninth of July, for example, the Sieur Longeau de Bruyères galloped into town shouting, as he rode, that with his own eyes he had seen a massacre of old folk, women and little children. "It's horrible, frightful; fire and blood everywhere . . . save yourseves. . . . *Adieu adieu* perhaps for the last time. . . ."

What he had actually seen we shall never know, although his reference to "burning houses" might have indicated one of the many fires of manorial rolls and feudal titles that were lit that summer. But much less could set off a chain reaction in the hair-trigger atmosphere of late July. And as Lefebvre noted, at a time when the provincial hunger for news from Paris was inadequately and unpredictably supplied by the mail coaches, the credibility of self-appointed "couriers" and "witnesses" was disproportionately high. Moreover, official statements had confirmed that there were indeed "brigands," paid by the British, who were bent on sabotaging the new order with acts of random lawlessness.

So, near Angoulême, a dust storm was said to herald the arrival of the brigands. In Saint-Omer in the north and Beaucaire in the south, panic was started when a sunset seen reflected in the windows of the local château convinced people that the brigands had fired the property. In southern Champagne on the twenty-fourth, no less than three thousand men were fully mobilized to hunt down what had been reported to be a gang of brigands but which on closer inspection proved to be a large herd of cows.

The response was remarkably standard. As Mme de La Tour du Pin discovered, no one waited for further confirmation. The tocsin was rung, sending anyone in the fields running back to the village square. There a village militia would be assembled, armed with sickles and pitchforks if nothing more imposing was available. Women and children were evacuated or hidden, and the band was sent to warn the next hamlet and assist in its defense. Once on the road, however, *their* appearance as a motley, casually armed group would almost certainly be reported as evidence of the approach of the "brigands" they had mobilized against.

The phantom bandits were not conjured up fresh in 1789. The Great Fear was only an extremely concentrated form of general anxieties about drifters and vagrants—men without domicile who acknowledged no law—that was shared by villagers, townspeople and government officials alike in eighteenth-century France. Olwen Hufton has movingly reconstructed the great waves of migration that took the poorest rural laborers from their inadequate lots in mountainous and wooded regions down into the more densely settled plains for seasonal work at harvest time. Some provinces—among them the Auvergne in the center, the Limousin and the Pyrenées in the west and the Vosges, the Jura, the Morvan and Savoy, all in the east—lost the greater part of their male population to this wash of migration. The routes were well marked, and along them the migrants begged or often thieved fruit from orchards, eggs from unlocked henhouses, to make up their precarious subsistence. Sometimes they came with a complete family in tow, since children always made a better effect for serious beggars.

Some never came back, remaining settled with those of their own region in immigrant quarters of big cities like Marseille and Paris. But the depression of the late 1780s simultaneously reduced the demand for harvest work and cut short the possibilities of casual labor in the construction industries, and even in the markets. At the same time, steep inflation in the price of food (for none of these people could feed themselves from their own lot) and indebtedness had turned innumerable smallholders into a rural proletariat. Hufton has traced a two-way flow of indigents in this "make-shift economy": out from the towns back to the country in search of shrinking work, and from the villages towards the towns for the same thing.

When hardship turned into desperation, a number of those who had become accustomed to begging joined together. The line between begging and extortion became blurred, at least for the authorities who deemed *errants* (wanderers) to have become, successively, *errants-mendiants* (wandering beggars) and finally *vagabonds*. Criminal bands do seem to have been on the increase in the 1780s, and their occasionally spectacular exploits were widely reported and passed on by word of mouth. But it was the criminalization of poverty in official language which preyed on the general apprehensions of those only slightly superior to the destitute in the social hierarchy. What distinguished them from their imagined enemies was that, as villagers, they had stayed put to defend their patch of land or see in the harvest of 1789 (much better than that of the previous year). The local wars of July and August were, then, fought between those who had something to lose and those whom they imagined had nothing to lose.

In reality this was not the case. The violence which sparked the Great Fear was in most cases initiated not by the faceless, homeless hordes, but by settled countrymen like themselves. It was a continuation of the riots of the spring, directed against seigneurial game, the manorial rolls that recorded their obligations in kind and labor and other symbols of their subordination, like the lord's weather vane and the emblazoned pews in church. In some clearly defined areas of France—the Norman Bocage, Picardy, Burgundy, Franche-Comté and Alsace—the attacks on châteaux were ubiquitous. In some cases, as at the great château at Senozan near Mâcon that belonged to Talleyrand's brother, the house was literally razed. But there were remarkably few fatalities, and the attacking peasants were led by people who were recognizably from their own kind: some quite well-off farmers, even on many occasions the local village official, the *syndic*. In almost all cases, moreover, they claimed to be doing the King's work, just as they assumed he had not merely sanctioned, but actually encouraged, them to stop paying any kind of feudal taxes. In the Franche-Comté, where the seigneurial regime was unusually antiquated, a group of armed peasants on their way to set fire to a château attempted to reassure the Baron Tricornot that "we have the King's orders, they have been printed but don't worry; you are not on the list." In the Mâconnais, the curé of Péronne said that he had personally seen a paper written by hand in the name of the King that permitted peasants to enter châteaux and demand titles to seigneurial dues; if such documents were not forthcoming, they might then proceed to burn and plunder with impunity.

This distinction between violent and unlawful acts—that such violence was in fact more lawful than that of those who resisted it—had its counterpart in the urban food riots that continued to explode throughout France during the summer. In Cherbourg and Strasbourg, on the same day,

July 21, demands were made for bread at two sous a pound (instead of the market rate of nearly twice as much), again on the grounds that the King had ordered his citizen-subjects to be properly provisioned. In both town and country violent anger was then directed at those supposed to be thwarting his will: municipal officials who were said to have hoarded grain and flour to drive the price up, brigands and aristocrats who to starve the people had cut grain while it stood ripening in the fields. The result in both cases was incendiary. In the towns, the human targets not only had their houses ransacked (with the cellar always playing a prominent part) but sometimes, as at Saint-Denis, lost their lives too. In the countryside, human casualties were rarer but quite often stewards and bailiffs of seigneurial estates were badly beaten up before being driven off.

The result was a wholesale breakdown in the structure of local command, swiftly followed by the formation of new armed authorities, empowered to contain the unrest. But it was also these *real* outbreaks of disorder which, once reported, fed the expectations of an outbreak of brigandage. Town dwellers read reports of looting and burning in the countryside as evidence that the dreaded terror threatened by émigrés and aristocrats on the Third Estate was moving inexorably towards them. Country people heard accounts of riot and destruction in the towns and assumed that squadrons of *gens sans aveu*—men without calling—were fanning out from Paris and the other great cities towards their fields and cottages. Within the seriously crazy world of mutual misperceptions, individuals could appear in one guise in town and another in the country.

Frédéric Dietrich, for example, the talented scientist, ironmaster and businessman, exploited the hugely destructive riot of the twenty-first of July to eject the principal royal official of Strasbourg, Klinglin, from power. In his place Dietrich became the city's first mayor, supported by an armed citizens' militia. In the countryside, however, the hero of the Third Estate was also known as the Baron de Dietrich, lord of Rothau, whose *Schloss* was threatened with assault unless he abolished all his seigneurial rights. Even more vulnerable were his iron forges and the sawmills that provided them with their fuel. These were prime targets for the inflamed hatred of the peasantry, who had seen their customary rights to timber expropriated.

The real significance of the Great Fear was the vacuum of authority it exposed at the heart of the French government. Although it created, by default, a France of a myriad of communes, this armed decentralization was not at all what most people wanted. On the contrary, as the *cahiers* had shown over and over again, what was wanted was more, not less, policing. The repeated invocations of the King's august and beneficent name by people about to commit or threaten violence suggest how deep their fore-boding was of the emptiness opened up by the collapse of royal power. The same people who gleefully pelted the carriages of departing *intendants* with stones also yearned for the restoration of some great paternal authority that would feed them and shield them from the abuses of underlings. In this sense, the popular violence of 1789—at least outside Paris—was not meant to be in the service of innovation, but protection.

If the intention of the riots and mass arming was not revolutionary, its consequences certainly were. Peasants and townsmen alike were vividly aware that some sort of boundary had been crossed when they burned manorial titles or took their knives to the pigeon coop. They reassured them-selves that they were enacting a kind of primitive moral law authorized by the National Assembly and the King and which wholly superseded the institutions by which they had been held captive. But not far from the exhilaration of release was the apprehension of punishment. What if they had been led astray? Or what if the ministers who had separated the King from his loving people for so long should prevail again? In that case a terrible fate might yet befall them.

One response to this kind of graphically imagined fear of death, as René Girard has seen in the case of antiquity, is to externalize the terror and project it onto some third party on whom the fear of death may be sacrifi-cially concentrated. Put another way, individuals or groups held responsi-ble for the danger in which communities find themselves are first separated from the host in which they are said to have grown powerful and then destroyed in acts that are simultaneously defiance and propitiation. France in 1789 supplied all kinds of scapegoats in this way—some imaginary, some real. For villagers in the settled communities of the Mâconnais who had taken the torch to the feudal regime, their avenging nemesis might be the woodcutters and charcoal burners of the forests and mountains of the Morvan and the Jura. For the Alsatian peasantry the aliens to be expunged were emphatically the Jews, whose houses they pillaged and burned, and whose persons they injured in what can only be described as spontaneous pogroms. Peddlers whom had been known as more or less harmless itiner-ants hawking mole pelts, rabbit skins or quack remedies now took on the sinister aspect of poisoners. Galley slaves were another favorite group in the demonology of the Fear; their rumored imminent release by the aristocrats was said to be a prelude to terrible revenge. Some peasants even claimed to have met released galley slaves, identifying them by the branding mark of *GAL* on their backs or shoulders.

Most frightening of all were individuals now seen to be not properly French, not *citoyens de la patrie*, but foreigners, true aliens. By emigrating on July 16, Artois and Condé had revealed themselves to be the leaders of this foreign cabal. They had, it was commonly said, taken with them millions of livres' worth of French gold to pay for the foreign mercenaries who would be the instruments of their revenge. And worst of all, tavern talk said, was Marie-Antoinette, who had only remained behind to organize the destruction of the National Assembly at its heart. Traveling through Burgundy and Franche-Comté, Arthur Young found otherwise quite intelligent and educated persons at Dijon and Besançon insisting that the Queen was preparing to mine the National Assembly, poison the King and put Artois in his place. Even more common was the story that she had written to her brother the Emperor in Vienna, asking for an invasion force of fifty thousand.

The effect of this prolonged state of anxiety was to create the politics of paranoia that would eventually engulf the entire Revolution. The notion that, between 1789 and 1791, France basked in some sort of liberal pleasure garden before the erection of the guillotine is a complete fantasy. From the very beginning, the violence which made the Revolution possible in the first place created exactly the brutal distinctions between Patriots and Enemies, Citizens and Aristocrats, within which there could be no human shades of gray.

To his dismay and intense irritation, Arthur Young found himself having to deal with passport-obsessed petty officials far more obstructive and obtuse than anything he had experienced under the old regime. Harassed repeatedly, he wrote with understandable vexation that "these passports are new things from new men in new power and show that they do not bear new honors too meekly." As an Englishman traveling in France for no purpose local authorities could fathom (since agricultural and scientific research seemed a wildly unlikely reason to be riding on the roads of the Rhone and the Saône valleys), he came under intense suspicion. His frantic note-jotting was taken to be proof that he was a spy for the Queen, for Artois or, in the Vivarais, for the Comte d'Antraigues. Outside Besançon he was stopped for lacking a passport and then denied one on the grounds that he could prove no dependable acquaintances in the town. A hilarious encounter then followed in which the Suffolk farmer became increasingly more irate: "This is the first time I have had to deal with you Messieurs of the Third Estate and nothing gives me a very elevated idea of you gentlemen." The official shrugged his shoulders, responding: "*Monsieur, cela m'est fort égal*" (Monsieur, I don't give a hang). Thoroughly exasperated, Young finally flourished the writer's ultimate weapon: the promise to include the whole exchange in his next book. This terrible threat did not seem to reduce the official to jelly. "*Monsieur, je regarde tout cela avec la dernière indifférence"* (Monsieur, I regard that with the utmost indifference).

Young was repeatedly struck by the discrepancy between the expansive rhetoric of elite revolutionaries, especially in Paris, and the surly mistrust, political apathy and misinformation or chaotic violence he experienced in the provinces. As he watched a yelling mob sack the Hôtel de Ville in Strasbourg, he found it difficult to connect the scene with the grandiose sententiousness he was hearing from every side in the *soirées* of Paris and Versailles.

In fact, some of the most ardent disciples of change had been disturbed by matters getting out of hand. Lucy de La Tour du Pin's kinsman Lally-Tollendal, for example, may have been hastened in his growing conservatism by the events at the Château de Saulcy, which belonged to his friends. He described Mme de Listenay fleeing from the burning château with her daughters, the Chevalier d'Ambly dragged to a dunghill with his hair and eyebrows torn out, others of their companions suspended over a well while the crowd debated what to do with them. Stanislas Clermont-Tonnerre's family had been equally caught in the violent uprising at Vauvilliers that ended with twenty peasants either killed or seriously wounded by troops, and the Duchesse extracted from the hayloft where she had taken refuge.

It was a mixture of apprehension and demonstrative patriotism that swept up the noble and clerical deputies of the National Assembly on the night of the fourth of August. The seigneurial regime had long been eroding in France outside bastions of feudalism like Burgundy, Brittany and the Franche-Comté. In much of the country it had been converted into a form of commercial business practice, and there was no reason why the business should not continue after the formal apparatus of seigneurial power had been done away with. Typically the citizen-nobles who rose to their feet in the session of the fourth to propose and then to demand the extinction of their own customary society were from the upper crust: men like the Duc de Châtelet and the Duc d'Aiguillon, whose considerable wealth could easily withstand the subtraction of milling rights and labor levies. But those same aristocrats also had a consistent history of lending serious support to the cause of patriotic liberty that went back to their service to America in the 1770s. Thus one should not judge their famous intervention as a matter of feckless posturing or a cynical attempt to save something from the wreckage.

The outburst was unpredictable since the Assembly was ostensibly discussing the urgent need to maintain, rather than suspend, current taxes until new ones could be legislated. The Vicomte de Noailles, Lafayette's brother-in-law, then transformed a parochial debate into a set piece of revolutionary oratory. The kingdom, he said, "floated between the alternatives of a complete destruction of society and a government which would be admired and followed throughout Europe." To accomplish the latter it was necessary to calm the people by showing them that the Assembly was actively concerned with their happiness. With that in mind he proposed the formal obligation of all citizens to pay taxes according to their means, the abrogation of all feudal dues subject to their redemption and the outright abolition of any remnants of personal servitude like *mainmorte* and the *corvée.*

Noailles was seconded by his friend the Duc d'Aiguillon, one of the most heavily landed men in France, who specifically referred to "scenes of horror" in France and an insurrection which might be excused by the vexations endured by the people. Nothing would demonstrate better the Assembly's commitment to equality of rights than to remove the remnants of the "feudal barbarism" of which the people complained.

It was a moment of improvised self-discovery, though it had been prepared by the cultural revolution that had taken place in the heart of the nobility since the Peace of Paris. The vanguard of the liberal nobility had long professed to want to exchange their titular status and feudal "superstitions" for the new aristocratic dignity of "citizen." Now they had the opportunity to make good that claim. On the night of the fourth of August they took it. Following Noailles and d'Aiguillon, like nervous acolytes made giggly with the thrill of initiation, successive ducs, marquis, vicomtes, bishops and archbishops stripped themselves down to the happy nakedness of citizenship.

The Breton gentleman Le Guen de Kergall spoke of humiliating titles that "required men to be tied to the plow like draft animals" and that "forced men to spend whole nights beating swamps to prevent bullfrogs from disturbing the slumber of voluptuous seigneurs." The Duc de Châtelet (probably to the horror of many curés in the Assembly) proposed the abolition of tithes; the Bishop of Chartres and the Marquis de Saint-Fargeau proposed the extinction of all exclusive rights of game and the authorization of peasants to kill any animals interfering with their crops or merely for their own food. The Vicomte de Beauharnais spoke of the necessity for absolute equality of criminal sentencing and equal admission of all citizens to both civil and military office, only to find himself bested by the Marquis de Blacon, who boasted that the Estates of Dauphiné, that notoriously vanguard body, had already instituted such a regime. The Marquis de Saint-Fargeau, Hérault de Séchelles' colleague in the Parlement of Paris, not only proposed the abolition of all noble exemption from taxes but that the decree be made retrospective to the beginning of 1789.

Then followed a bonfire of particularisms. The same provincial privileges and special constitutions that had been so stubbornly defended against the reforms of the old regime as irreducible elements of the "French constitution" were now carelessly slung onto the heap of demolished anachronisms. Representatives of the old *pays d'états*—Burgundy, Artois, Languedoc, Dauphiné, Alsace, Franche-Comté, Normandy and the Limousin—all came forward to sacrifice their privileges; they were followed by deputies of privileged cities like Lyon, Bordeaux, Marseille and, not least, Paris. Venality and heredity of offices—other "liberties" for which Maupeou and Brienne had been condemned for threatening—were likewise jettisoned, as was any kind of plurality of benefices for the clergy. Gone were Talleyrand's portfolio of income-producing abbacies; gone were Lafayette's proprietary regiments. It was, said Ferrières, who was himself lost in admiration, "a moment of patriotic drunkenness."

After this tidal wave of revolutionary altruism, it was not surprising that the Archbishop of Paris proposed a Te Deum to celebrate the event. Others wanted a national feast to be held on the fourth of August each year and a special medal minted in commemoration. Through it all, Lally-Tollendal, one of the earliest and most passionate paladins of liberty, sat with an accumulating sense of unease. He was becoming educated in the callow quality of romantic inebriation and passed an urgent note to his friend the Duc de Liancourt, who was presiding. "They are not in their right minds," he wrote, "adjourn the session." But Liancourt was neither courageous nor foolhardy enough to try. Instead, the sunrise shone through the windows of the Salle des Menus Plaisirs as deputies wept, embraced, sang and surrendered themselves to the patriotic rhapsody. At least, thought Lally-Tollendal, the monarchy should gain some credit from the discharge of all this brotherly love.

So, last of all, he rose, and with some effort confessed himself, also, to be "drunk with joy." Stretching the truth a good deal, he asked the deputies to remember the king at whose invitation they had been convened, who had summoned them to the joyous reunion of minds and hearts. It was, after all, in the midst of his nation that the good King Louis XII was declared "Father of his People" and it should now be in the midst of the National Assembly that they should proclaim Louis XVI "Restorer of French Liberty."

The night of the fourth of August created a cult of self-dispossession. Giving something of one's own to the Nation became a demonstration of patriotic probity. Those who did not have feudal titles or abbacies to give away could contribute to the hard-pressed coffers of the government through other kinds of donation. On September 7, for example, a delegation

115. Anonymous, the night of August 4, 1789

of painters' wives, led by Mme Moitte and including Mmes David, Vestier, Vien, Vernet, Peyron and Fragonard, appeared before the Assembly to offer them their jewels as a patriotic contribution. It seems likely that (like the painters themselves) they had begun to live in the realm of neoclassical virtues, for the discarding of jewelry was highly reminiscent of the much-depicted story of Cornelia, the mother of the Gracchi, who, when asked by a visiting patrician where her jewels were, proudly presented her children. Mme Moitte and the other women were careful to dress themselves in white, hair simply coiffed as if they had stepped directly from a Roman history painting, and described the jewelry as baubles "they would blush to wear when patriotism commanded them to sacrifice." After hearing the official recognition and vote of gratitude, the women were given a torch-light procession to the Louvre with an honor guard from the students of the Academy of Painting, while a band played the familiar air "Where Better Could One Be Than in the Bosom of One's Family?"

Women then led the campaign for patriotic contributions. The nuns of the Priory of Belle-Chasse at Versailles sent their silver; the Marquise de Massolles her earrings; the Dame Pagès three thousand livres from her manufacturing business. The nine-year-old Lucile Arthur sent a gold chain, her savings of two louis d'or and a letter imploring the Assembly to receive them, since to decline would cause her "too much grief and pain." Even courtesans contributed something from their hearts of gold: Rabaut Saint-Etienne on September 22 read a letter from one of the "Magdalenes" announcing to the Assembly, "Messieurs, I have a heart made for love and I have accumulated some things through loving; now I place in your hands my homage to the *patrie*. May my example be imitated by my colleagues of all ranks."

While women undoubtedly set the tone, men too began to come forward and demonstrate their devotion to the common good. Camille Desmoulins' newspaper, *Les Révolutions de France et de Brabant*, carefully itemized the contributions as a way of expressing provincial solidarity with the patriotic cause. In Lyon a group of young people offered jewels and a poem dedicated to the "Fathers of the Patrie, august Senators"; eleven servants of an English milord sent 120 livres; the customers of the Café Procope (where Desmoulins himself drank with Danton and the printer Momoro) filled a tub with silver buckles from their shoes and made a chain of forty pairs that was then carried to the Assembly. Predictably an epidemic of silver-buckle removal then broke out in Paris and all the major provincial towns. To be caught with any on one's shoes was tantamount to self-incrimination.

The French Revolution, then, began with acts of giving as well as acts of taking. But its immediate future depended on what its first citizen, Louis XVI, could bring himself to offer up for the *patrie*. At one point when the needs of the Treasury were particularly pressing, and when taxes still required collection from his subjects, he sacrificed much of the royal table silver for the mint. Louis XIV had, after all, melted down the silver furniture in the Hall of Mirrors when the war chest called for it. But more was being asked of this King. The sacrifice he was called on to make was of his prerogatives rather than his ingots. And that seemed an altogether more painful dispossession.

ii POWERS OF PERSUASION
July–September

The August decrees were the first serious test of Louis XVI's credibility as a patriot-king. As usual he was of two minds. In a letter to the Archbishop of Arles he expressed satisfaction with "the noble and generous *démarche* of the first two orders of the state. They have made great sacrifices for the general reconciliation, for their *patrie* and for their king." On the other hand, as he made abundantly clear, even if the "sacrifice was fine [*beau*], I cannot admire it; I will never consent to the despoliation of my clergy and my nobility . . . I will never give my sanction to the decrees that despoil them, for then the French people one day could accuse me of injustice or weakness."

The letter has recently been charitably interpreted as indicating Louis' willingness to go along with much of the demolition job of the fourth of August. His principal concern, it is said, was with adequate compensation for the loss of both inherited offices and seigneurial dues that could be construed as originating with property rights rather than personal subjection. That much may be true, but the King's use, however inadvertent, of terms like "the first two orders" and the regal personal pronoun suggests the real difficulty he had in adjusting to the political world announced by the Declaration of the Rights of Man.

Though there were many differences of emphasis in the various drafts that came before the National Assembly, all were agreed on certain basic axioms around which the new constitution was to be constructed. The first was that sovereignty resided in the Nation, so that, in effect, the nation defined its monarch and not the other way about. Second, "all men are born free and equal." Stated flatly as a matter of incontrovertible natural law, this principle evidently precluded any sort of institutionalized distinctions of the kind presupposed in a society of orders. Third, the purpose of government lay exclusively in the furtherance of the happiness of the governed. Its fundamental duty in this respect was to safeguard the liberties that were an inalienable quality of citizenship.

Beyond these very general principles, however, there was remarkably little agreement, even among the relatively small group of politicians who dominated the constitutional committees set up in July. And nowhere were the divisions of opinion more obviously acute than over the role of the monarchy in the new France.

The bickering over first principles came as a severe disappointment to Lafayette, who had been the first to propose a draft Declaration of Rights to the Assembly on July 11. It goes without saying that he had something like the American model in mind, and he had assumed that such a statement could be sufficiently ecumenical to soften, rather than accentuate, differences and give French men and women a vivid sense of the community to which they now belonged. His father-mentor Washington, as the new President, seemed unavailable for detailed comment, either through pressure of business or through political discretion. But no such qualms bothered the Ambassador, Thomas Jefferson, who read all of Lafayette's several drafts through the summer and added some considerations of his own directly from American experience, especially a provision to have an amending constitutional convention at periodic intervals.

Lafayette's initial timing could not have been more unfortunate, since his proposal was laid before the Assembly the day before news of Necker's dismissal broke. And by the time that the Assembly returned to this matter, it was evident that the brief harmony that had prevailed in the aftermath of the reunion of the orders was a thing of the past. The division was fairly clear-cut. On one side stood a more pragmatic group, led by Mounier and including Lally-Tollendal, Clermont-Tonnerre, the Archbishop of Bordeaux Champion de Cicé and the ex-*intendant* of the navy Malouet. They feared that any Declaration of Rights would lead to expectations beyond those a practical working constitution would deliver. "Nothing is more dangerous," commented the Comte de La Blache, "than to give people ideas of an indeterminate liberty while leaving to one side an account of their obligations and duties." They appreciated, as Lafayette did not, that with the question of the monarchy out of the way, it had been much easier for the Americans than it would be for France to move from general principles to working institutions. "We should not forget," La Blache said on the ninth of July, somewhat tactlessly, "that the French are not a people who have just emerged from the depths of the woods to form an original association." Instead of seeking "natural" principles it would be better to create a constitution and a state with the materials at hand, not all of which were utterly disreputable. This meant accepting that the monarchy would remain the indispensable executive power, free to appoint ministers, control foreign policy and if necessary dissolve the legislature. For the monarchy to be at all a truly independent branch of the constitutional government it was also necessary to give the King the power to veto legislation as he saw fit.

Mounier, who developed his ideas more fully than the rest of his group, also insisted on a two-chamber legislature. At first he argued that an upper house should be appointed for life by the King but, in an attempt to secure some acceptance of the principle, was prepared to consider Lafayette's American alternative of a senate that would be elected for a six-year term. To this end he took good care to modify the statement on natural equality in the Declaration of Rights by allowing for subsequent distinctions, provided they were based exclusively on utility.

The British inspiration for much of the constitutional thinking of the *monarchiens* was readily conceded. Just a few years before, this might have been a recommendation. But in the heated patriotic climate of 1789, it was more likely to set their cause back than advance it, even when Mounier claimed it would be a British constitution with the imperfections ironed out.

Against this more conservative group was arrayed a broader and more diverse party that included Sieyès, Talleyrand, the de Lameth brothers, Barnave, Adrien Duport and the Breton Le Chapelier. Initially the Breton Club at Versailles had been organized to concert action prior to formal sessions of the Estates-General. It had included not only the more advanced spokesmen but those of Mounier's views as well. But by late July the differences had become too pronounced for the club to retain unity, and it became the principal center of organized opposition to the monarchists. Sieyès, in particular, turned Mounier's concern for a viable state upside down. Where the monarchists were concerned with stabilizing the constitution by clearly separating its three branches, he stressed unity. Where the danger for Mounier was from a dictatorial legislature and a feeble government, Sieyès put things the other way about.

At stake were not just picayune matters of institutional detail but a fault line that ran very deep in late eighteenth-century culture. Mounier and the "English" party were heirs to Montesquieu and, behind that, an Aristotelian tradition of seeing in diversity, divisions and balances a satisfying equilibrium. Their opponents, whether arguing from neoclassical rigor or from Rousseau-like consistency, were holists. For them, the *patrie* was indivisible, and they responded to charges that they were creating a new despotism of the many by retorting that the new, single sovereignty was a morally reborn animal that could have nothing in common with the impurities of the old. For Sieyès, whose debt to Rousseau's Social Contract was explicit, while the General Will was more than the sum of the wills that it comprised, it was, by definition, incapable of injuring the freedoms for which it was sovereign. Citizens were incapable, in this sense, of harming themselves.

For Mounier, such an assertion was either naive or disingenuous. The only sure protection against the tyranny of the many, and the only way to reconstruct an executive authority capable of governing France, was to give the King an "absolute" veto. To ignore the need for royal assent to reforms was, in his view, either to promulgate a Republic in all but name or else to invite civil war. But to give the King indefinite blocking power, many deputies pointed out, would be to jeopardize the constitution itself. Persuading Sieyès to abandon his opposition to any veto at all, they rallied around Necker's compromise of a "suspensive" veto. This would have the power to delay legislation through two full votes but could be overriden by a third.

The debate between the *monarchiens* and their opponents did not take place in discreet isolation at Versailles. It was avidly reported by the political press, overwhelmingly hostile to Mounier's position. Camille Desmoulins' *Révolutions de France et de Brabant,* in particular, stereotyped the supporters of the veto as "aristocrats" who were engaged in a rearguard action to preserve privilege and an overweening monarchy. The truth, of course, was that there were quite as many citizen-nobles among the Sieyès group as among Mounier's, the de Lameth brothers being hardly less aristocratic than Clermont-Tonnerre or Lally-Tollendal. But lacking organs of public opinion in Paris the *monarchiens* let themselves be depicted as somehow antipatriotic and quasi-English: men who mistrusted the People and who were quicker to condemn the People's occasional act of punishment than the guilty parties on whom it was visited.

All these issues boiled down to one great question: What is the relationship between violence and legitimacy? It was one that would dog the French Revolution through its entire history as successive regimes fell before their opponents' willingness to sanction punitive violence in the interests of patriotic righteousness. Only when the state restored to itself a monopoly of force—as it was to do in 1794—would the question go away. In this sense, at least, Robespierre would be the first successful counterrevolutionary. Mounier, who was most exercised by the threat of physical intimidation to the independence of the legislature, conveniently forgot that his own defiance of established authority in Grenoble two years earlier had been made possible by the Day of Tiles.

In the high summer of 1789 it was the murderously festive action of crowd violence—the evident satisfaction the crowd took from stringing up arbitrarily identified malefactors from the *réverbères* (street lamps) and from parading heads on pikes—that most disturbed "moderates" like Mounier. Clermont-Tonnerre was nervous enough to repeat a proposal which, when attributed to the King, had prompted suspicions of a royal coup d'état: the removal of the National Assembly from the vicinity of Paris. It was not just the spontaneous nature of popular retribution that alarmed them, but the verbal and journalistic violence that seemed to egg such demonstrations on. And there is no doubt that some of the most pungent and widely read of the many newspapers that began publication at this time discovered the shock appeal of abuse. Marat's *L'Ami du Peuple* (The Friend of the People), for example, routinely criminalized politicians of whom it disapproved as not just mistaken but as inhumanly vampirical—"blood-sucking" was a favorite term—and requiring speedy excision from the body politic.

More insidious, perhaps, was the tone taken by the most successful of all the new papers, Elysée Loustalot's *Révolutions de Paris.* Loustalot, who was to survive only into 1790, was a twenty-seven-year-old lawyer who had shown a natural genius for innovative journalism. He was able to cater to an entirely new readership with a brilliant blend of eyewitness reporting, vehement editorializing and, most important of all, for the first time, prints that illustrated current events and that were an intrinsic part of his newspaper. "The honorable calling of writing about the revolutions of the capital," he wrote in his paper in early August, "is not just to give an arid account of some facts . . . it is much more our duty to go to the source of the facts and discover the causes of changes, and to grasp the different nuances that every day take hold of the public mood according to the issues that excite general interest." It could have been the manifesto of modern popular journalism.

Loustalot understood what his readers wanted: less dreary recitation of institutional debates and more graphic reporting of events that would give readers in Paris and especially in the provinces a sense of immediate witness. So while he pretended to be shocked by much of the violence he described, his prose wallowed in it. The head of Foulon, hay stuffed in its mouth, stuck on a pike, its trunk dragged over the cobbles until it was shredded, "announced to tyrants the terrible vengeance of a justly angered people." Foulon was not just a pathetic, almost casually chosen sacrificial victim, but a monster whose malignity thus balanced his death: a "cruel and ambitious man who only existed to deserve the hatred of men and to make the unfortunate suffer."

Loustalot published, of course, in text and image, the moment on the twenty-second of July when Foulon's son-in-law, Bertier de Sauvigny, already arrested by the crowd, was confronted with his father-in-law's head before being strung up himself and mutilated. He had been led to the town hall, wrote Loustalot, in a procession with fifes and drums that proclaimed "the cruel joy of the people." When the waving head was thrust in his face, "Bertier shuddered and for the first time, perhaps his soul felt the twinges of remorse. Fear and terror seized him."

Even more sensational writing followed as Loustalot switched to the present tense for more immediate effect, describing a scene inside the town hall, where the electors had been unable to prevent the crowd from seizing their prisoner:

> Already, Bertier is no more; his head is nothing more than a mutilated stump separated from his body. A man, O gods, a man, a barbarian tears out his [Bertier's] heart from his palpitating viscera. How can I say this? He is avenging himself *on* a monster, the monster who had *killed* his father. His hands dripping with blood, he goes to offer the heart, still steaming, under the eyes of the men of peace assembled in this august tribunal of humanity. What a horrible scene! Tyrants, cast your eyes on this terrible and

revolting spectacle. Shudder and see how you and yours will be treated. This body, so delicate and so refined, bathed in perfumes, is horribly dragged in the mud and over the cobblestones. Despots and ministers, what terrible lessons! Would you have believed that the French could have such energy! No, no, your reign is over. Tremble, future ministers, if you are iniquitous. . . .

Frenchmen you exterminate tyrants! Your hatred is revolting, frightful . . . but you will, at last, be free. I know, my dear co-citizens, how these revolting scenes afflict your souls . . . but think how ignominious it is to live as slaves. Think what punishments should be meted out for the crime of *lèse-humanité*. Think, finally, what good, what satisfaction, what happiness await you and your children . . . when the august and holy temple of liberty will have set up its temple for you.

The assumption that there was a direct relationship between blood and freedom—indeed (as Loustalot implied elsewhere) between blood and bread—is usually thought of as the standard language of punitive Jacobinism, of the Terror. But it was the invention of 1789, not 1793. The Terror was merely 1789 with a higher body count. From the first year it was apparent that violence was not just an unfortunate side effect from which enlightened Patriots could selectively avert their eyes; it was the Revolution's source of collective energy. It was what made the Revolution revolutionary.

No one grasped this dismaying fact more immediately than Lafayette. As the darling of the crowd, he had been the figure to whom the votive gift of Bertier's *disjecta membra* had been offered. He had brushed it aside with the terse comment that he and the mayor were too busy to see any further "delegations." But the fact that the commandant of the National Guard had been impotent to prevent Bertier's summary execution was itself alarming evidence that something more than the lofty Declaration of the Rights of Man (on which Lafayette was still working with Jefferson) was needed if the Revolution in Paris was not to spiral rapidly downwards into bloody anarchy.

Sylvain Bailly must also have been affronted by the brutality he was forced to witness. It must have been jarring to his Enlightenment faith in the civility of man to be confronted by the results of man's beastlier aspects swinging from the *lanternes*. More immediately, Bailly faced the need to bring some measure of calm to the government of the capital, the possibility of which was jeopardized by the truculence of the district electoral assemblies. Just as the assembly of electors meeting at the Hôtel de Ville had remained in being, so had their constituents in the sixty "miniature republics" set up in the spring. They had converted themselves into regularly convened debating societies, examining, often quite critically, measures passed by Bailly's committee, especially concerning the two matters that would be at the center of Paris politics for the next five years: bread and police. The more articulate assemblies—none more so than the Cordeliers on the left bank—already saw themselves as reincarnations of Athenian democrats: the primary cells of freedom to which, ultimately, elected representatives had to defer. And it was precisely the freedom with which local journalists and café orators criticized decisions both in the Hôtel de Ville and at Versailles that made Sieyès want the National Assembly to repudiate the "imperative mandate." If deputies were forced to heed their constituents on every issue, then the National Assembly would be nothing more than a collection of glorified couriers, perpetually running to and from the districts. Bailly tried to arrest the drift towards a kind of Rousseauean primitive democracy by having each of the sixty elect two representatives to a body at the Hôtel de Ville to be known as the Commune. But once the wineshops found their voices and the street-corner presses their readers, and as long as suspicions persisted that men in office were conspiring to push up bread prices, it was hard to manage Paris politics from the center. At the height of the debate on the royal veto, for example, Loustalot seriously proposed that the National Assembly adjourn its sessions while every electoral *bailliage* in the kingdom was consulted on its views.

There were some measures that could be taken to prevent the complete collapse of organized authority. But even in the ostensibly liberal period of the Revolution its politicians rapidly discovered they had little room to maneuver between anarchy and coercion. Veering away from the complete breakdown of order, they were unable to avoid re-creating institutions of state power that, with little alteration, would become the instruments of the Terror. In the National Assembly, Volney and Adrien Duport established at the end of July two executive committees designed to centralize political decisions in two crucial areas. The first, the Comité des Rapports, had the authority, outside of the royal council, to approve or invalidate local appointments. Thus, as Ferrières pointed out with some alarm, its members could arbitrarily designate which of the countless municipal revolutions were legitimate and which were not. It had, in other words, the power to provoke civil war.

The second, the Comité des Recherches, was, in effect, the first organ of a revolutionary police state. It arrogated to itself all the powers which had been deemed so obnoxious under the old regime: opening letters, creating networks of informers and spies, searching houses without warrants, providing machinery for denunciation and encouraging Patriots to bring any of their suspicions to the attention of the authorities. This committee of twelve members (the same size as the future Committee of Public Safety) was even empowered to imprison suspects without trial for as long as they were deemed a danger to the *patrie*. Theoretically it was preferable to the caprices of a crowd that, on the strength of an article in Marat's newspaper, would identify individuals for proscription and summary justice. But it already had the potential to become what Ferrières called "the redoubtable tribunal before which everyone will tremble."

In Paris, the crucial dilemma of how to remain the master, rather than the helpless servant, of revolutionary force turned, in the last resort, on the Marquis de Lafayette. He was so commanding a figure in the summer and early autumn of 1789 that it comes as a shock to realize that he was still only thirty-two years old and a complete political novice. Nothing in his American experience had prepared him for the trial by fire in the Paris districts and *faubourgs*, for he had imagined the advent of liberty as an uncomplicated crusade with obviously identifiable heroes and villains. Frustrated by the conservative nobility of the Auvergne and obliged to obey their mandate in the Estates-General, he had still assumed that, at critical moments, a shared concern for the common good would bury differences in an outburst of fraternal concord.

Nothing like this happy scenario was unfolding in the streets of Paris on his watch. Instead he was confronted daily by desperately hungry, irrationally suspicious crowds that could turn within hours from anger to murder. Lafayette had to develop, very rapidly, skills as labor negotiator, arbitrator, militia commander and political diplomat. The wonder is not that his powers were eventually to fail him but that he managed to exert control in the capital for as long as he did.

His first concern was to see that supplies of grain, flour and bread reached designated markets and that their prices were held at levels that would not trigger riot. By the end of the first week in August, the price of the four-pound loaf had been reduced from fourteen and a half sous at its height to twelve sous. The prospect of a much better harvest in 1789 helped relax the sense of panic, but the weather was still playing cruel tricks on the Parisians. A drought had made the water mills inoperable once more, so that flour was often unavailable for the city bakers. The consequence was that the late summer and early autumn were punctuated by frequent riots around bakers' shops, robberies and seizures of loaves, many of the crowds led by women. Lafayette and Bailly had to do what they could to persuade the wage earners of the city that at least the municipal authorities were not actually conniving to *raise* prices and perpetuate the "famine plot."

116. P. L. Debucourt, Lafayette as commandant of the National Guard, 1789

Economic distress, then, remained a serious threat to the restoration of order. A succession of artisan groups demonstrated for higher wages to meet the inflated price of bread, and it was only after two rowdy meetings on the place de Louvre that the journeymen tailors succeeded in having their average daily rate raised from thirty to forty sous. Wigmakers, too, were incensed, both at the Revolution, for having made their skills redundant (undressed hair being *de rigueur* for many Patriots, Robespierre excepted), and at the "aristocrats," on whose fickle tastes they somehow blamed their plight. Most remarkable of all, there was a demonstration of four thousand Figaros and Suzannes—domestic servants—on the Champs Elysées demanding to have their disqualification (as dependents) from National Guard service rescinded.

Many of these demands were in fact typical of the angry parochialism of the revolutionary artisan. The domestic servants insisted that Savoyards be excluded from their profession and other artisan groups demanded the city close the public-relief works on the heights of Montmartre, on the strength of a pamphlet alleging that the indigents employed there were busy training guns on the city below. Lafayette thus had to face hostility from both sides—those who wanted these *ateliers de charité* shut and the indigent construction workers who were packed off to their native parishes outside the city as a result of the closure.

Further resentment arose from the need to see that sources of municipal revenues were protected without which the other *ateliers* that remained open would certainly have been discontinued. This involved the National Guard in patrolling some of the remaining customs posts where excises on items like tobacco were still being collected. But Lafayette managed, overall, to offset the obviously unpopular aspects of his police with occasions guaranteed to enhance his personal popularity, especially when given full coverage by his friend Brissot in his paper the *Patriote Français*. In one such affecting scene, the equivalent of what today would be described as a "photo opportunity," Lafayette visited houses in the faubourg Saint-Antoine where *vainqueurs de la Bastille*, wounded on the fourteenth of July, were languishing without food or elementary medical attention. In all these activities—and without any deliberate design on dictatorship—he was obviously moving into the space vacated by royal authority. For at least a few months Lafayette was the *père nourricier*, the father-provider of the city; its judge-arbitrator, the source of police protection and military authority. While his management of all these concerns was far from perfect, it is to his and Bailly's credit that they did succeed in establishing the credibility of revolutionary government.

None of this could have been done without the National Guard. And

Lafayette was required to exert enough control over the sixty companies attached to each district that they would not degenerate into the instruments of street-corner fiefdoms. This was brought home to him as early as July 16, when Georges Danton, the officer of the Cordeliers guards, frog-marched a miserable figure to the Hôtel de Ville. This was one Soulès, called "the second governor of the Bastille," who had refused to allow access to the militia without a specific permit. Soulès was in fact the elector whom the Hôtel de Ville had entrusted with the fortress as a kind of concierge pending the arrangements for its demolition, but it was only Lafayette's intervention that saved him from being badly dealt with.

The Guard had to wield a double-edged sword: against royalist conspiracy on one flank and against mob anarchy at the other. Lafayette saw to it—very much with Bailly and Necker's approval—that the force was made up exclusively from elements he judged to be dependable in both these respects. At its core were the forty-eight hundred salaried guardsmen, made up principally of former *gardes françaises,* deserters from line companies of the royal army and odd paramilitary units like the armed law students and clerks of the *basoche.* By mid-September this force was well armed with six thousand flintlock muskets and was established as the "center" of the National Guard. Lafayette avoided elitism by distributing its manpower throughout the sixty districts, so that each had one company of paid men to four of unpaid volunteers. The result, on paper at least, was a more effective police for Paris, some thirty thousand strong, than any that had been available to the old regime.

The integration of the various types of guardsmen was not completely smooth. There were disputes over distinctions of military dress. Should the former *gardes françaises* be allowed to preserve some outward form of separate identity? Were the saber-toting barristers of the *basoche* really entitled to parade around in their excessively glamorous scarlet-and-silver coats; who could wear epaulets and in what designs?

Lafayette tried to overcome this sartorial petulance by giving the Guard a uniform dyed in the colors of the *patrie*: blue coats with white lapels, facings, vests and leggings, and red trim. The fact that they had to pay for this splendid apparel as well as for their arms and ammunition ensured that the Guards were drawn exclusively from the propertied classes of the city. (Even Captain Danton in 1789 was a fairly substantial owner of property, albeit on the strength of his wife's credit.)

Lafayette also saw to it that, almost from the beginning, the Guard had a strong sense of its own *esprit de corps.* On Sunday the ninth of August, he had them appear for the first time wearing their new uniforms. Masses were sung in the company churches, the commander attending at Saint-

117. Plaster model of a National
Guardsman

Nicolas-des-Champs. In the streets outside, singers from the Opéra and marching military bands heralded the advent of a citizen corps. And in the afternoon, at the Palais-Royal, battalions from several districts paraded together "to the sound of drums and martial music." Each of the new battalions was commissioned to design its own flag; the flags were ceremonially blessed in the churches from which the districts took their names. Lafayette tried to attend as many of these ceremonies as he could and when that was impossible sent Bailly or, in the case of the *fête patriotique* at Sceaux at the beginning of September, the Duc and Duchesse d'Orléans with their children. On the twenty-seventh there was a general benediction at Notre Dame, preceded by a great parade of all the battalions, marching from their district quarters to the center of the city. At the cathedral the radical Abbé Claude Fauchet, deputy from Caen and preacher of "social religion," preached a sermon on the holiness of the armed freedom.

Lafayette had a genuine appreciation of the psychological power of emotive symbols. He knew that, at a time when the traditional bonds that

118. Le Sueur, gouache, the ceremony of the patriotic oath in the Paris districts. The *enfants de la patrie,* bottom right, emulate their elders.

had held men in deferential relations to one another had collapsed, it was vital to reincorporate them in a new patriotic community. For that to work, outward forms that could signify "friend," "brother," "citizen" were as crucial as—perhaps more crucial than—decrees coming from the National Assembly. So he invented the tricolor cockade as an obligatory badge of patriotic identity. Anxious to avoid any accusation that the Guard troops were the proprietary phalanx of the Duc d'Orléans, he added the Bourbon white to the red and blue that were coincidentally the colors of both Paris and the House of Orléans. It appeared everywhere: not only on the tricorn hats of the Guards but breaking out spontaneously in sashes worn against the pure white shifts favored by citizenesses, replacing silver buckles, attached to canes and used as fobs for watches. Into the bargain it created a huge boom for the manufacturers of dimity cotton. In the provinces it became, immediately, the badge of solidarity with Paris and the Assembly. In Brest on July 26, an actress, swathed in its colors, sang that it indicated white for purity, red for the King's love of his subjects and blue for the celestial happiness experienced by all Frenchmen in 1789. Mercier, who wrote an entire pamphlet titled *The National Cockade,* saw it as the emblem of the new breed of citizen-warriors. And Lafayette himself took up this theme of the empire of liberty when he prophesied that the cockade would "go around the world; an institution that is at one and the same time civil and military; which is bound to triumph over the old tactics of Europe and which will reduce arbitrary governments to the alternative of being conquered unless they imitate it."

There is no doubt that Lafayette relished playing the role of the new Father of the *Patrie,* but he also saw its usefulness as a rallying point. And he knew full well the value of family rhetoric in revolutions. His wife Adrienne and his daughter Anastasie accompanied him to many of the flag-blessing ceremonies, where they took up collections for the poor. At a special dinner given for them on September 22 by the Guards of Saint-Etienne-du-Mont, they were celebrated in songs and poems in which it was declared that Mme Lafayette was now with her family, since the family of the Marquis was, in truth, all of humanity. That made Adrienne the "universal mother." One day, it was predicted, her children would be honored throughout France as the offspring of the "father who had saved France." In the same spirit, when the Guards of the district of the Sorbonne wanted to make his ten-year-old son George Washington Lafayette their second lieutenant, the Marquis protested that the promotion was somewhat premature but that the boy would be honored to serve as a simple fusilier. (There were in fact children's companies of Guards that were a special feature of drill and parade days.) When the company persisted, the father yielded, assuming his most Roman manner: "Gentlemen, my son is no longer mine; he belongs to you and to the *patrie.*"

Through August and much of September, this combination of armed containment and patriotic charisma held the line in Paris against both counter-revolution and anarchy. On the thirtieth of August, for example, yet another radical aristocrat, the Marquis de Saint-Huruge (recently released from the insane asylum at Charenton, where he shared the exercise yard with the equally aristocratic de Sade), attempted to lead a popular demonstration from the Palais-Royal to Versailles. Saint-Huruge had drawn up a list of sixty partisans of the "absolute veto" whom he had proscribed in advance as "traitors" and whom he required to be expelled from the National Assembly. In addition he demanded the permanent return of the royal family to Paris. Lafayette was well prepared for the expedition, turning it back with strong detachments of the National Guard and arresting Saint-Huruge.

Although this threat was easily dealt with, Lafayette could not afford to be complacent. The mood near bakery shops frequently turned ugly, for despite efforts to control prices, supplies were short and lines long. Some bakers were threatened with the *lanterne*; Guards appeared on the bread-lines to keep order, and complaints were now becoming commonplace that city officials were complicit in a plot to starve the people. On September 3 a journeyman roof maker was arrested for blaming Lafayette himself for shortages and threatening to hang him.

This incident suggested that the hero of the hour, garlanded with flowers and looking imperturbable on his white horse, could very easily turn into tomorrow's villain or victim. Ultimately the ability of Lafayette and Bailly to keep the Paris crowd off the road to Versailles depended on the conduct of the National Assembly, of Necker's ministry and not least of Louis XVI himself. While the King's attitude to his impending transformation into a constitutional monarch remained unknown, Lafayette had the most earnest hopes of a happy outcome. Though the feeling was by no means recip-rocated, his attitude towards the King and Queen was, if anything, senti-mental. He hoped to make of Louis XVI in 1789 what he would make of Louis-Philippe in 1830: a citizen-king wrapped in the mantle of the tricolor.

There would shortly be another of those balcony appearances, featuring one of Lafayette's vintage performances. But it would be less of a patriotic coronation and more of a rescue act in which terror was but a hair's breadth away from applause.

iii THE QUARREL OF WOMEN
October 5–6

Marie-Antoinette was accustomed to receiving the market women of Paris at Versailles. Each feast day of Saint-Louis, August 25, they would be among the deputation of "honest folk" who would come to the château to offer their greetings and obeisances to the King and Queen. Attired in ceremonial white, suitably cleansed of the smells of the marketplace, they would present the Queen with bouquets of flowers as tokens of their loyalty and affection. Usually their little speeches would be written for them by a courtier working for the master of ceremonies, but occasionally a few lines might be jocularly offered in the true speech of the markets: *poissard*.

Its name deriving from the French word for "pitch" *(poix)*, the *genre poissard* was not so much a true patois as what its historian Alexander Parks Moore has characterized as a systematic assault on grammar. Using heavy elision, fractured grammar and syntax and forced rhyme, *poissard* was ideal for comic and abusive verse, rhymed insults and a kind of tough, threaten-ing talk in which jeering ridicule played an important part. Its songs and jokes had been kept alive spontaneously in the wineshops and street markets of Paris. But it had also been cultivated in the kind of literary slumming popular among the aristocracy at the end of the old regime. Those who roared with laughter at the foulmouthed, tobacco-stained abuse of the vaudeville Père Duchesne at the Saint-Germain fair were exactly those whose heads would be demanded by his political reincarnation in René Hébert's *enragé* newspaper. The Duc d'Orléans regularly performed *poissard* plays in his private theater, and in 1777 the Queen summoned a group of fishwives and market women to the Trianon to teach her amateur troupe how to pronounce *poissard* correctly.

In 1789 *poissard* suddenly stopped being amusing. The "Motion of the Herring Women of La Halle," an early revolutionary song, was all the more threatening because its last lines sarcastically mimicked the customary deference which market women had shown on their usual appearances at court.

> *Si les Grands troublent encore*
> *Que le Diable les confonde*
> *Et puisqu'ils aiment tant l'Or*
> *Que dans leur gueule on en fonde*
> *Voilà les sincères voeux*
> *Qu'les Harengères font pour eux*

> If the High-ups still make trouble
> Then the Devil confound them
> And since they love Gold so much
> May it melt in their traps
> That's the sincere wish
> Of the Women Who Sell Fish

There were still occasions during 1789 when the *poissardes*—fishwives and market women—conformed to their ceremonial role. At the *fête* of Saint-Louis they had led the procession of twelve hundred to Versailles, in the company of the National Guard, bearing bouquets wrapped in gauze and inscribed in gilt lettering: "Homage to Louis XVI, the Best of Kings." They also frequently participated in the many processions in honor of the *patronne* of Paris, Sainte-Geneviève, that took place in the late summer.

Out of their fancy dress, however, the working women of Paris increasingly turned to less polite activities. As those most immediately responsible for putting bread on the table, they were correspondingly most desperate and angry at the shortages which, following a good harvest, seemed to be all the more inexplicable. The October *terme* for rent and tradesmen's bills was fast approaching, and throughout September the tempo of assault on bakers' shops suspected of giving short weight or of hoarding speeded up. The women also became more adventurous in their expeditions to seek the grain that millers claimed was in short supply. At Chaillot, west of Paris, on September 16 they stopped five carts laden with grain and brought it to the Hôtel de Ville. On the seventeenth, after a demonstration against bakers, they stopped another wagon at the place des Trois Mairies and brought it to the local district headquarters.

There is no evidence that, faced with news of this hunger, Marie-Antoinette ever did say anything like "Let them eat cake." But the apocryphal fable is nonetheless eloquent testimony to the gathering suspicion and hatred directed at the court, which, along with officials in Paris, was held responsible for the plight of the common people. And as the subsistence crisis seemed to become worse in late September, so did the political crisis. In the popular mind both were connected.

On September 10, Mounier's *monarchiens* had been badly defeated in the vote over the first principles of the constitution. The National Assembly chose a one-chamber legislature over two chambers by 849 votes to 89, with 122 abstentions. The next day it opted for the Necker-Lafayette "suspensive" veto over an absolute veto by almost as impressive a margin, 673 to 325 with 11 abstentions.

Would the King, however, assent to his own constitutionalization? Ultimately, the orators of the Assembly believed that they had the power to institute the "fundamental laws" of the constitution over his opposition, should that become necessary. But they much preferred to have his assent. On September 19 the prospects of an amicable agreement seemed dim when the King's response to the Declaration of the Rights of Man and Citizen, and to the August decrees was read. Though he declared that he approved in general of the "spirit" in which they had been enacted, he qualified this with so many reservations concerning the redemption of such properties as tithes, seigneurial dues and hereditary offices that the statement read much more like a rejection than an acceptance. On the twenty-first, the King announced that he had ordered the *publication* of the decrees, a step which only made the withholding of their promulgation more glaring. Most imprudent of all was Louis' insistence that in the matter of feudal rights, special concern had to be paid to the rights of foreign, German princes who owned domains in Alsace. If he had wanted to invent reasons for journalists to accuse him of considering the rights of foreign dynasts over French patriots, he could hardly have done a better job.

In the cafés of the Palais-Royal, the political clubs and the pages of the polemical press, all this seemed, or was made to seem, tantamount to preparation for a new royalist coup d'état. The concept of a "veto" was in any case badly misunderstood. In the popular mind it was often thought to be some sort of new tax or a sinister weapon of the famine plot. Gorsas' *Courrier de Versailles* included an imaginary conversation between two peasants on the matter. The better informed asks his mate, "Do you know what the veto is?" and then replies, "I'll tell you. You have your bowl filled with soup and the King says to you: 'Upset your soup' and you've got to spill it. That's the veto." Given this degree of popular suspicion there was likely to be a responsive audience to Marat's calls in his *L'Ami du Peuple* to separate the villainous from the virtuous. "Open your eyes," he commanded his readers, "shake off your lethargy, purge your committees, preserve only the healthy members, sweep away the corrupt, the royal pensioners and the devious aristocrats, intriguers and false patriots. You have nothing to expect from them except servitude, poverty and desolation."

The worst of these suspicions were reinforced when, despite the defeat of his proposals, Mounier was nonetheless elected to the presidency of the Assembly, and when Saint-Priest, the Minister of War, decided to summon the Flanders Regiment to Versailles. In both numbers and deployment the move of the regiment could not possibly be compared with the offensive military campaign of July. The regiment had been mobilized as a precautionary measure to protect the government and the royal household at Versailles in the event of a new march. Needless to say, however, the summons provoked the very event it was designed to forestall.

All of these demons emerged in a spectacular way on October 2. On that day, Loustalot's paper reported a banquet given for the Flanders Regiment the previous evening by the royal bodyguard. Such banquets of welcome were a military convention, but this had been provided on a lavish scale in the enormous space of the Château Opéra. Tactless in itself, at a time of conspicuous want, the occasion turned into something of a demonstration of loyalty to the crown. Airs were played from Grétry's popular opera about the imprisonment of Richard Lionheart following the Crusade—among them, "*O Richard mon roi, l'univers t'abandonne*"—and the royal family were induced to make a brief appearance, which was unusual on such occasions, the Queen moving round the tables holding up the four-year-old Dauphin for the soldiers to admire. Toasts to their health were drunk and, after they had departed, with increasingly riotous frequency. And as the company became drunker and more uninhibited, court women began to hand out cockades—black for the colors of the Queen, white for the King.

On the following day, in Loustalot's paper, Marat's *L'Ami du Peuple* and in Desmoulins' *Les Révolutions de France et de Brabant*, this relatively innocuous celebration of loyalty turned into an "orgy," a term which, given the renewed crop of sexual libels circulating about the Queen, conjured up scenes of debauchery as well as gluttony and treason. The most infamous moment, however, was neither sexual nor gourmandizing. The patriotic cockade, it was said, had been trampled underfoot. This was an exaggeration of a genuine incident (carefully reported in Gorsas' *Courrier de Versailles*) that occurred when one officer exclaimed, "Down with the cockade of colors; may everyone take the black, that's the fine one." But the story had the predictable effect of provoking an immense uproar in Paris, where disrespect for the cockade amounted to a desecration of the Host. It had happened, it was said, with the Queen's approval, and when it was further learned that on receiving a deputation of the National Guard she had expressed her "enchantment" with the banquet it was assumed that she meant the deliberate insult given to the *patrie*.

Hunger and anger came together once more on the morning of October 5, and it was women who took the greatest offense. The previous day, women from the district of Saint-Eustache had dragged to the Hôtel de Ville a baker accused of giving short weight. There, he had only just been rescued from lynching. In a harangue to another crowd, one market woman blamed the Queen for their starvation and urged her listeners to march on Versailles to demand bread. Early on the fifth, the tocsin was rung from the Church of Sainte-Marguerite and, led by a woman beating a drum, a march formed, the crowd shouting the title of the latest pamphlet, *When Will We Have Bread?* As they marched, they recruited women from other districts, many of them carrying cudgels, sticks and knives. By the time they had converged on the Hôtel de Ville the crowd was some six or seven thousand strong.

As well as demanding bread they insisted that the insolent royal bodyguard be punished, since, following the banquet at Versailles, black and white cockades had appeared in numbers in the Paris streets, provoking brawls wherever they were seen. Before long the situation at the Hôtel de Ville threatened to get completely out of control. Unaccountably Lafayette had left less than a district battalion guarding the place de Grève. The crowd was confronted by Lafayette's deputy major Hermigny, but his men made it clear that they would not fire on the market women. A general ransacking took place that yielded some seven hundred rifles and muskets, to which were added two cannon intended for the defense of the Hôtel de Ville. Finally the crowd, now strengthened by some men from the neighboring districts, threatened to sack the building and burn all its papers and archives. They were only dissuaded from carrying this out by the intervention of the captain of a detachment of the Bastille Volunteers, Stanislas Maillard. Unlike his men, Maillard was actually one of the *vainqueurs,* and had become famous by claiming to have been the man who inched his way on the plank over the inner moat to take de Launay's note asking for a capitulation. (The man was more likely to have been the more modest Hulin.)

This local renown made Maillard a trusted figure among the women—as Lafayette was no longer, for there were several murmurs and some shouts that if the general refused their demands, he too should be strung up on the *lanterne.* Maillard cut down the unfortunate Abbé Lefèvre, who had been strung up, ready for lanternization, on account of his refusing the women guns, and promised to lead their march to Versailles. The extraordinary procession, coming this time not with bouquets but with cannon, pikes and muskets, set out in drenching rain for the royal palace. As they walked along the *quais* they shouted and sang that they were coming for "*le bon papa*" Louis. And it was in the nature of *poissard* that the line between affectionate and deadly abuse was never exactly clear.

The crowds had become so dense at the center of the city that it took Lafayette two hours to reach the Hôtel de Ville. By the time he did arrive—at about eleven o'clock—he learned that the women had already departed and that there was a serious movement afoot among the National Guard to make their own march to Versailles. One of the stated reasons was the wish of those who had been *gardes françaises* to resume their old duty of guarding the King, and the notorious banquet now seemed to them an additional reason to substitute themselves for the royal bodyguard. Lafayette immediately understood that a march of National Guards was a much more serious matter than that of the *poissardes,* for it could hardly help but be construed as an act of Paris's coercion against the King, his ministers and the National Assembly. He did his utmost to dissuade the grenadiers, but after many hours of fruitless argument and vain reminders of the oath of loyalty they had recently sworn in the battalion churches, it was evident that the rank and file were determined to go, if necessary without his consent. What was in the offing was a complete breakdown of discipline in the National Guard, shattering the image of orderly and responsible pacification that he had endeavored to build since July. Worse still, Lafayette was threatened by some of his own men. It was becoming apparent that if he did not grant their request, they would not only desert him, but in all likelihood murder him as well.

Whatever his many faults, Lafayette was not a coward. His own personal safety was less a consideration than the need to preserve at least a semblance

119. Anonymous drawing, "To Versailles, To Versailles"; the march of the
poissardes to the royal palace

of some order in the Guard. He also correctly assumed that only by going
with the march could he hope to ensure that his soldiers were acting for,
rather than against, the safety of the royal household and the Assembly.
Surrendering to the inevitable, he tried to give the march an appearance of
legality, requesting "permission" from the Paris city authorities, a leave that
was quickly given. To make sure that the Assembly and government were
alerted, Lafayette sent a fast rider to warn of the march. And at around four
in the afternoon, fifteen thousand of the Guard—an enormous brigade—set
off for the palace in soaking, windblown rain. Lafayette, on his white horse,
led the way—"the prisoner of his own troops," said one witness.

By the time the Guard reached the outskirts of Paris, the procession of
women, two of them riding astride the cannon, had already arrived at
Versailles. En route they had encountered some dragoons of the Flanders
Regiment, in whose honor the "orgy of the Guard" had been staged.
Expecting to be stopped, Maillard and the women were instead astonished
to hear shouts of "We are with you" and promises of fraternization. In
Versailles they were joined by more women, among them one extraordinary figure astride a jet-black horse. Sporting a plumed hat and a blood-red
riding coat and carrying pistols and a saber, this was Théroigne de Méricourt, whose appearance was obviously designed to attract attention and on

whom nineteenth-century writers developed a fixation as an "Amazon" of the Revolution, a woman sexually as well as politically liberated.

Though Théroigne was, by all reliable accounts, strikingly beautiful, she was important on the fifth of October only for her appearance as a symbol of the Revolution as an omnipotent woman: a prototype of "Marianne." Her future history, as we shall see, was eloquently emblematic of a particular kind of pathetic revolutionary career, and she would have the doubtful honor of being diagnosed by an Austrian prison doctor as suffering from that modern malignancy "revolutionary fever." But beneath the glamorous plumage was a banal history. "Théroigne the Amazon" was in reality Anne-Joseph Méricourt, whose well-to-do Liège family had fallen on hard times and had forced her to live by her wits and her body. In Paris she had been the mistress of the Marquis de Persan and the friend of the castrato opera singer Tenducci. From another liaison in Genoa she had returned to France and, like so many others, had changed personality in 1789. From being a twenty-seven-year-old courtesan she became an articulate—and to many male contemporaries—threatening political presence. The kept woman had become a free person. She also evidently enjoyed her dashing conspicuousness. At Versailles she was seen talking to the palace guard when the *poissardes,* who were later to be her downfall, marched into town, bedraggled, angry and famished after their six-hour journey.

A cordial reception, with speeches and wine, took the edge off their anger. They were greeted by the commander of the Versailles National Guard, and by representatives of the municipality and ministry. Only when they attempted to penetrate the grounds of the palace were they barred both by the locked iron grille and units of both the Flanders Regiment and the Swiss guards in front of and behind it. They had less trouble, however, at the National Assembly. Maillard was admitted by Mounier to explain the purpose of the march, which he did largely by citing *When Will We Have Bread?* "The aristocrats," he said, "want us to die of hunger." That very day he had been told that a miller had been bribed two hundred livres *not* to produce flour. "Name him," shouted the deputies, but before Maillard could bluster further, the Salle des Menus Plaisirs was invaded by hundreds of the women taking literally Rousseau's recommended right of "recalling" their deputies. Wet broadcloth, smelling of mud and rain, planted itself beside fastidious coats and breeches. Knives and clubs were set down on empty chairs, dripping onto papers printed with items of legislative debate. Some of the women, seeing the Archbishop of Paris, shouted the anticlerical slogans that had become popular in Paris and accused him of being a prime instigator of the "famine plot." In a misguided attempt to calm them, another deputy from the clergy made the mistake of trying to kiss the hand

120. Anonymous painting, Théroigne de Méricourt

of one of the women accusers. Shaking him off she replied, "I am not made to kiss the paw of a dog."

Mounier tried to reassure the women that the King and the government were doing everything they could to see that Paris was properly supplied, but it was evident that the women wanted to ask the King themselves. When news of the march had arrived at Versailles, Louis was out hunting at Meudon and rushed back to the palace just before its arrival. With some courage he agreed to see a small deputation of the women. Pierrette Chabry, a seventeen-year-old flower girl conspicuous for her polite turn of speech and virtuous appearance, was chosen as spokeswoman. At the crucial moment her nerves failed and she fainted at Louis' feet. No doubt sympathizing with someone who shared his own pain at public speech, the King brought her smelling salts and helped her to her feet. He then went on to explain that he had given explicit orders for any grain held up on the roads outside Paris to be delivered immediately. When the little delegation emerged, such were the suspicions against the court that Chabry was immediately accused of having been bribed by the King. But the aura of paternal majesty was not completely lost, for this direct encounter, combined with fatigue, did dispel much of the anger that had begun the march.

The danger, however, was by no means past. Lafayette's rider arrived to alert the Assembly to the march on Versailles of what amounted to a small army. Very few deputies greeted this news with enthusiasm, though some, like Barnave, who had already recommended that the King reside in Paris, felt vindicated in their prescience. Mirabeau, who delivered the bad news to Mounier, found him oddly jocular about the whole affair, as though he had already resigned himself to the end of his part in the Revolution.

At about six o'clock Louis agreed to accept without demur or qualification both the Declaration of the Rights of Man and the August decrees. He then took counsel from his ministers on the best course of action. Saint-Priest urged either flight or resistance; Necker opposed both, arguing that either course would give comfort to those who said that the King was making war on the Revolution rather than endorsing it. Louis was torn between concerns for the safety of his family and his distaste for appearing in any way to shirk his duty. He decided to stay put.

Not much before midnight, the National Guard trudged into Versailles, six abreast. Their numbers were so great that even marching at the double they took an hour to pass. While the idea had not really occurred to the market women until they reached Versailles, the guardsmen had already determined that they should return to Paris with the royal family and henceforth keep them there. Everything, then, was set for a violent tug-of-war between the royal bodyguard and the National Guard. Between them were the Versailles National Guard, who had been ordered to cooperate with their Paris counterpart. The bodyguard appreciated that they were about to be singled out for retribution and prepared to make a stand. At about nine o'clock there was some sporadic shooting but, concerned primarily with the safety of the King and Queen, the bodyguard withdrew to stations well within the courtyard perimeter and inside the palace itself.

At midnight Lafayette told the National Assembly that the expedition of the National Guard had no coercive purpose and all but confessed that he had had no choice but to bring it to Versailles. Calm could be restored if the King sent away the Flanders Regiment, if the *gardes françaises* replaced the bodyguard close to the King and if His Majesty could bring himself to make some sympathetic gesture with the national cockade. Though officers and men were reluctant to let Lafayette into the château unaccompanied, for fear that he would himself be trapped, it was the condition on which the King would see him. As he made his way to the royal apartments, he met with hostile glares and comments. Posted on the stairs was his own wife's father, the Duc d'Ayen, who, as a captain of the bodyguard, would doubtless have fired on his son-in-law at the royal command. As he proceeded, Lafayette heard one courtier remark behind his hand, "There goes Cromwell." "Cromwell," he snapped back, "would not have come unarmed."

Dramatically spattered with mud, the Hero of Two Worlds entered the royal presence with lines obviously rehearsed on the march: "I have come to die at the feet of Your Majesty." On the other hand, he said, lowering the dramatic tone, such extremes might be avoided if the King would allow the *gardes françaises* to "protect his sacred person," would guarantee food for Paris and consent to reside in the capital "in the palace of his ancestors at the Louvre." Louis acceded to the first requests and promised to consider the last, hinting that he would first have to consult his family. Lafayette reported this meeting to both the National Assembly and then his own officers and men. Though many subsequent histories complained that what followed happened because Lafayette fell asleep, he in fact stayed very much awake until around five in the morning, making sure that the threatened battle between the two sets of guards did not come to pass. The sun, which had not been seen all that day, finally rose in a clear sky before the Marquis collapsed on a couch at his grandfather's house.

He was to have a waking nightmare. At about five-thirty in the morning, an armed crowd found their way into the palace grounds. For some unknown reason—perhaps the imminent appearance of brigands—the commander of the royal bodyguard had sent a large detachment of his troops to the other end of the park around the Grand Trianon. This left the Cour des

Ministres itself relatively lightly patrolled. Probably introduced by one of the soldiers, the crowd broke into the Cour de Marbre and went up the stairs leading to the royal apartments. A guard later said that he heard one of the women shouting that it was necessary to "tear out the heart of the *coquine* [Marie-Antoinette], cut off her head, *fricasser* her liver and even then it would not be all over." A guard fired at the onrushing crowd; a man fell and the soldier was then killed on the spot. Miomandre de Sainte-Marie, a second guard posted outside the Queen's apartments, attempted to reason with them and, failing, shouted to those within that the Queen's life was in danger. He too was struck down, but his warning had come just in time. Terrified by the firing and yelling, Marie-Antoinette ran barefoot, holding her slippers and crying out loud, "My friends, my friends, save me and my children." A passageway took her to the King's quarters, but Louis had himself gone in search of the children. For more than ten minutes the Queen hammered desperately on the locked door while the crowd clattered through the Hall of Mirrors in enraged pursuit of the "Austrian whore" and the outnumbered bodyguards who retreated by stages through the enfiladed state rooms. Finally Marie-Antoinette's frantic cries and pounding were heard and the family was reunited in the Salon de l'Oeuil de Boeuf. The Dauphin and his sister were crying as their mother and father tried to comfort them as best they could. If Greuze had painted them there and then he would have been the lion of the Salon.

Before any harm could befall them, the first companies of National Guard, commanded by Lazare Hoche, later one of the Republic's most formidable generals, advanced against the crowd and delivered the royal family from danger. Outside, the heads of the two slaughtered bodyguards, stuck high on pikes, were being paraded around. Miomandre de Saint-Marie's head was waggled about by an artist's model named Nicolas, dressed in the pseudo-Roman robes he used for studio work. There was laughter, cheering and applause, and later in the day the trophies were taken back to the Palais-Royal, where they were exhibited in the garden like one of Citizen Curtius' waxworks.

Roused by the disaster Lafayette ran towards the château, not waiting for a horse to be saddled. Before he got there he confronted an armed mob falling on any bodyguards they could find and preparing to lynch them on the spot. Ordered to stop, one of the men turned on Lafayette and told the National Guards to kill him. In a rage Lafayette grabbed the man, attempting to arrest him. But he was distracted by the need to persuade his own guardsmen to release the bodyguards, declaring that he had promised the King they would come to no harm.

In the Salon de l'Oeil de Boeuf he found the royal family badly shaken by their ordeal. They knew they had come within a door's thickness of death. As the King recovered his composure he spoke quietly, but for once without awkward pauses, to the Paris guards—mostly *gardes françaises*— explaining that his bodyguard was innocent of the insults of which they had been accused. In response an unpredictable thing happened: the guards swore loyalty to him. Paradoxically, their desire to return to Versailles had nearly caused the end of the monarchy. Emboldened by this moment Louis then agreed to go onto the balcony with his family and tell the crowd in the Cour de Marbre that he would go to Paris, entrusting himself "to the love of my good and faithful subjects." After the burst of applause faded he then said that his bodyguard had been maligned. But it was Lafayette, with his innate genius for political theater, who crowned the moment by embracing a noncommissioned officer of the bodyguard and pinning a tricolor cockade on his hat. With that one gesture he had returned the King's guard to the Nation.

There was another "foreigner" to legitimate. This was the hardest moment of all. Lafayette asked the Queen to make an appearance on the balcony alone. Understandably, after what she had gone through, Marie-Antoinette had no illusions about her popularity and flinched from the request. "Haven't you seen the gestures they make at me?" she asked. "Yes, Madame," responded Lafayette. "*Venez*"—come. Bracing herself, she took her children with her, only to be met with a roar from the crowd below: "No children." The Greuze family had lost its power to charm. But Lafayette had not. She took her son and daughter inside and stepped out onto the balcony alone to face the crowd. Lafayette then joined her and, in what he later said was a moment of pure intuition, bowed low and kissed her hand.

The effect might have been catastrophic, ridiculous, confirming that he was nothing more than a court lackey pretending to be a Patriot. But it worked a miracle. Shouts of "*Vive la reine,*" which had not been heard since before the Diamond Necklace Affair, were mixed with acclamation for the commandant.

Three hours later an immense cortège, which Lafayette put at sixty thousand, moved off from Versailles. At front and rear were the National Guard; in their midst the royal carriage escorted by Lafayette, with ministers of Necker's government, deputies of the National Assembly and the remnant of the court of France following. Behind them was a train of wagons and carts filled with flour from the palace bins. Soldiers and women carried bread loaves on the ends of their pikes and bayonets and sang that they were bringing "the baker, the baker's wife and the baker's lad to Paris."

At the city gates, Bailly yet again presented Louis with the keys to the city, and the royal party went to the Hôtel de Ville, where a throne had

121. Anonymous, *The Triumphant Return of the Heroines from Versailles*, October 6, 1789. Women astride a cannon—a symbol of their potency—were henceforth given a special place in revolutionary ceremonies like the Festival of Unity in August 1793.

been set up to receive them. After more balcony appearances they finally reached their new residence in the Tuileries at eight in the evening. The Dauphin thought his new room very ugly, but the next day the Queen wrote to Mercy d'Argenteau, the Austrian Ambassador:

> Rest assured I am well. Forgetting where we are and how we got here we should be content with the mood of the people, especially this morning, if bread does not lack. . . . I talk to the people; to militiamen and to the market women, all of whom hold out their hands to me and I give them mine. Within the city I have been very well received. This morning the people asked us to stay. I told them that as far as the King and I were concerned, it depended on them whether we stayed, for we asked nothing better than that all hatred should stop, and that the slightest bloodshed would make us flee in horror.

For their part, the *poissardes* sang

> *A Versail' comme des fanfarons*
> *J'avions amené nos canons*

469

Falloit voir, quoi qu'j'étions qu'des femmes
Un courage qui n'faut pas qu'on blâme

Nous n'irons plus si loin, ma foi
Quand nous voudrons voir notre Roi
J'l'aimons d'une amour sans égale
Puisqu'il d'meur dans notre'Capitale

To Versailles like bragging lads
We brought with us all our guns
We had to show that though we were but women
A courage that no one can reproach us for

[Now] we won't have to go so far
When we want to see our King
We love him with a love without equal
Since he's come to live in our Capital

The same day, the National Assembly accepted Target's proposal that Louis' official constitutional title be *roi de Français,* instead of *roi de France et Navarre.* Never again should it be implied in any way that the realm was a kind of property. But to Target the new designation was also meant as an academic pun. Louis was to be the reincarnation of the medieval Rex Francorum, the territorial chief of the Franks whose very name proclaimed their freedom. It could not have escaped him, though, that the condition on which he would be hailed as the King of the Free was his own virtual imprisonment.

Twelve miles away, supervised by M. de La Tour du Pin, the great palace of Louis XIV was being boarded up. Massive iron locks were placed on its gates to discourage looters, and a few guards stood sentry over silent courtyards. Le Brun's Apollo king still rode his chariot against the upstart Dutch on the ceiling of the empty Hall of Mirrors, but the walls of the marble staircase were pockmarked with shot. Versailles had already become a museum.

JEAN JACOB.
Agé de 120 Ans.
Né à Sarsie au Mont Jura le 10 Novem.ᵇ 1669,
a eu l'honneur d'être présenté au Roi à la Famille Royale
le 11 Octob.ᵇ 1789 et le 23 à l'Assemblée Nationale.
Le Tableau Original de cette Gravure a été accepté par cette Auguste
Assemblée et déposé dans ses Archives le 3 Decemb.ᵇ suivant.

122. Anonymous engraving, Jean Jacob

CHAPTER TWELVE
Acts of Faith
October 1789–July 1790

i LIVING HISTORY

O<small>N</small> OCTOBER 23, 1789, the National Assembly met the oldest man in the world. His name was Jean Jacob and he was ushered into their presence clutching his baptismal certificate signed in the year 1669. That made him 120 years old. Specialists in improbability claimed that there was an even more ancient survivor: a Scottish crofter named John Melville who had been a baby when Charles I's head was struck off in 1649. But Jean Jacob's fleecy white locks and pale eyes were good enough witness to his honesty for the Assembly to declare him, officially, "the *doyen* of the human race." His face mapped by wrinkles, Jean Jacob seemed to belong to geological time. He had been born in the year the palace of Versailles was begun for the young Sun King and he had lived to see it become redundant, if not actually demolished. Isolated on a barren mountain in the Jura, his social existence had been preserved by the snowcaps, frozen in the norms of the old century's feudalism, so that the deputies could greet him as a living fossil—"The serf of the Jura mountains." Now, as he announced in a surprisingly audible grunt, he had come to Paris to offer thanks that he had lived to be a free man. Ancient as he was, like France itself, he had been given a second life by the Revolution. He had, in one of the key words of 1789, experienced the blessings of *régénération*. In return, the deputies each subscribed at least three livres in celebration of his continued vigor.

Other senior citizens, mere striplings beside Jean Jacob, also claimed to feel the Revolution as new blood coursing through old veins. The Comte de Luc, a real *noble-enragé*, swore that the Revolution had cured his rheumatism. The septuagenarian Chevalier de Callières had been so rejuvenated that he became a prolific composer of patriotic songs (including one which declared, unimpressively, that liberty was "a hundred times dearer to me than love"). De Callières' zeal moved him to form a special National Guard Battalion of Veterans which admitted no one under sixty and in which the wearing of beards was obligatory. (Some false pieces were discovered in fruitless attempts to secure admission.) Special places were reserved for venerable patriots in revolutionary festivities and ceremonies, often along-side children, symbolic expressions of the "Gothic" past from which France had been released and the innocent future into which it had been reborn. So when an eleven-year-old boy showed up at the Assembly with his silver buckles and christening cup as a "patriotic gift" and asked to be allowed to attend its debates, his request was granted, and he was given the compli-ment that his generosity showed he had profited from the fine citizen's education provided by his parents.

During its first year, the National Assembly entertained all kinds of demonstrations of patriotic devotion. For while it was, in the first instance, committed to the practical work of giving France new institutions of gov-ernment and representation, it also acted as a political theater: the place where oratory and gesture, even on some occasions poetry and music, would dramatize the principles for which the Revolution was said to stand. And since the Assembly had repudiated historicity and precedent, those legitimating principles had, necessarily, to claim universal validity. Some of the appearances before the tribune of the Constituent (as the Assembly now called itself) duly reflected that universality. In early July 1790, for example, two convicts from the Swiss canton of Fribourg who had been condemned to the galleys made a formal appearance. France had used its galleys not just for its own criminals but, on lucrative contracts, for those of other Euro-pean states needing somewhere to dump their undesirables. The Assembly had not yet taken the step of abolishing galley sentences for the native population (for one thing, there was a popular fear near the Mediterranean and Atlantic depots that *galériens* were about to be released). But it was eager to declare that it would no longer serve as the instrument of an ignoble "slavery" for European "despotisms." Cheered by the deputies and embraced by the President, the Swiss convicts, one of whom by a sublime stroke of luck was named Huguenot, were paraded as heroes and their chains hung from the rafters of the Eglise des Prémontrés as inspiration and warning. In their honor a play entitled *The Honest Criminal* was performed that night at the Théâtre-Français.

These spectacles were more than acts in a revolutionary circus. They sustained the deputies' self-belief and reassured them that their Nation did not, after all, stand alone in the world but was part of some bigger, indefi-nitely extended family of the "oppressed"—who might now look to France

473

for deliverance. On June 19, 1790, a delegation of representatives from the "oppressed nations of the universe," led by the self-designated "Orator of the Human Race," Anacharsis Cloots, appeared in appropriate national costumes—German, Dutch, Swiss, even Indian, Turkish and Persian, all of them encircled with the tricolor sash. They congratulated the Assembly for having "restored primitive equality among men" and promised that, "encouraged by the glorious example of the French, all the peoples of the universe sighing equally for liberty would soon break the yoke of the tyrants who oppress them." In response, the President, Menou, deftly told them to go away but in terms that would be taken as flattery rather than rejection. They should, he said, become the heralds of the new epoch. Returning to their native lands they should seek audiences with their respective rulers and instruct them to imitate the great and good example of the Restorer of Liberty, Louis XVI.

Skeptics found the whole thing risible. Ferrières wrote to his wife that the motley band of delegates had undoubtedly rented their costumes from the wardrobe of the Opéra. But as foolish as these occasions were, they corresponded to the equally sententious religion of universal brotherhood and amity being preached in speech and text, not least by Claude Fauchet. In his sermons, all printed in Nicolas de Bonneville's *Bouche de Fer*, Fauchet, a priest from Caen, preached a kind of Rousseauean Christian universalism that was the constitutive principle of his "Social Circle"—not a club, as he emphasized, but an association of Citizens scattered over the surface of the globe. Before the Revolution, the world had been ruled by laws of descent which sought to divide men from one another. Now men could cleave to the most basic of all Christian precepts, that of universal love, and find true freedom in fraternity. As Fauchet explained, the emblem of the circle had itself been chosen for its unifying power. The means by which this great "family pact" would be brought about was the moral regeneration of Truth in alliance with Reason. Other fashionable orators and writers like the ecumenical vegetarian Robert Pigott (who extended the message of fraternity into the animal kingdom) and the Quaker David Williams, both English pilgrims at the holy place of Liberty, echoed Fauchet's civic sentimentalism.

For the majority of deputies, though, Fauchet's millennial realm of love and brotherhood was just a utopian balloon, moved by its rhetorical hot air to drift over the revolutionary landscape. Their own work, they reckoned, was strictly down-to-earth. Yet the men who made up the committees of the Constituent—the real powerhouse of institutional change—were themselves guided by principles in many respects not much less abstract and optimistic. If they could not manage to subscribe to a universal religion that presented all men as brothers awaiting the fraternal embrace, they did presuppose that Frenchmen, at least, could be treated uniformly because they were moved by identical wants of material or mental satisfaction. Condorcet, for example, echoed Rousseau's basic axiom that all men were born equal and had only been separated from that natural equality by arbitrary socializing institutions that had been invested with illegitimate force. This late-Enlightenment view required them to strip away those "Gothic" accretions of history—arbitrary divisions of custom, habit and jurisdiction that were the products of ancient conquests. They would be replaced with rational, equalizing institutions that would put men into relations with one another as citizens, bound by the same laws and subject to the same sovereignty: their own.

The Declaration of the Rights of Man and Citizen had already expressed the essence of this view, especially in Talleyrand's sixth principle, setting out equality before the law and entitlement of all citizens to any office for which their talents qualified them. In practice it committed the Assembly to tear to shreds the crazy-quilt pattern of overlapping jurisdictions that characterized the old regime and cover France with a single mantle of uniform government. No one was more enthusiastic about this work than those two arch-rationalist men of the cloth, Sieyès and Talleyrand. It was the latter who first proposed uniformity of weights and measures, and Sieyès who was behind the startling proposal to substitute for the provinces of France a grid of eighty identical squares to be known as "departments."

Presented to the Assembly by the ex-Parlementaire from Rouen, Thouret, this uncompromising piece of political arithmetic had as its premise that the division of France into different, capriciously overlapping jurisdictions of taxation (the *Fermes*), church (dioceses), military command (the *généralités*) and justice (the *bailliages*) was incompatible with a "representative government." Instead France was to be rationalized; the "hexagon"— France's six-pointed shape—to be cubed. For the root 3 seems to have been an obsession of the revolutionary legislators, probably under the sway of Masonic axioms. In Thouret's plan there were to be eighty-*one* departments, each measuring 324 square leagues, the addition to the grid being made for Paris. Each would then be conveniently divided into nine districts and then by a further nine into communes. Each unit would have a local representative assembly from which the bodies of local government would be elected.

As radical as this measure was, it represented the culmination of many visionary plans drafted under the old regime. It had been d'Argenson, back in the reign of Louis XV, who had first coined the term *departements*, and the combination of strict uniformity together with governmental devolu-

France: Revolutionary Departments
and Their Capitals

0   100 Miles

0   100 Kilometers

tion had long been cherished by physiocrats like Du Pont de Nemours. Rationally treated, France would be governed at last by scientific practices instead of a nonsensical bundle of inherited "prejudices."

This vision of a standardized France chopped up into identical units did not, however, please everyone. Mirabeau, whose instincts were as much Romantic as rational, accused the drafting committee of excessive "geometrism" and "a priorism" and argued instead that a more sensible unit of measurement would be population rather than simple geographical extent. In this way it would be possible as well to take into account local topography, the rivers and mountains, valleys and forests that gave a particular area its identity. It was quickly apparent that the majority of deputies much preferred this manner of proceeding even though it embroiled them in countless local arguments about departmental boundaries that would have been obviated by the grid treatment. Besançon was typical in its dissatisfaction at being demoted from the seat of the sovereign Parlement of the Franche-Comté to a mere *chef-lieu* of the Department of the Doubs. The city sent to the Constituent the Abbé Millot and the lawyer Bouvenot as special delegates of protest to complain that while neighboring departments like the Haute-Saône had been allotted fertile lowlands, the Doubs was dominated by mountains and rocky uplands. Was Besançon now doomed to languish, as the equal of jumped-up burgs like Lons-le-Saunier, "its houses and buildings deserted and turning into miserable hovels; its streets and squares weedy with grass"?

These kinds of complaints were repeated all over France, but guided by the astronomer-cartographer the Comte de Cassini, and weathering many months of debate, each of France's eighty-*three* departments (a number happily indivisible by three) took shape, blessed by a name drawn from its native geography. From Normandy, Provence and Brittany, then, were cut Manche, Calvados and Bouches-du-Seine; Gard, Var and Bouches-du-Rhone; Morbihan and Finistère. The nomenclature was, and remains, a kind of bureaucratic poetry: rationalism reformed by sensibility.

There were other important symbolic exercises to plane down the outward differences that separated citizens. In October 1789 the deputies formally abolished the ceremonial costumes of their respective orders. And on June 19, 1790, they took the more dramatic step of eradicating all titles of hereditary nobility. When many forms of seigneurial labor dues had been swept away the previous August, it had still been widely assumed that forms of nobility would remain as honorific status. But now the Constituent declared these incompatible with the legal equality of citizenship. Expressly banned were all the insignia of social superiority: coats of arms on houses and carriages; livery for servants or jockeys (an important consideration for the late *ancien régime* elite); manorial pews and weathercocks. Henceforth no citizen was to bear a name that signified his domination or possession of a *place*. His sole inherited badge of identity was to be the family name of his father.

The most remarkable thing about these transformations was that they were, once again overwhelmingly, the work of aristocrats, *ci-devant* nobles. Though, numerically, aristocrats did not dominate the Assembly, the working committees that drafted the constitution and provided France with the shape of its new institutions were monopolized by a relatively small intellectual elite, many of whom had known each other before the Revolution and a striking number of whom had been officers of the old monarchy in either the army, judiciary, government or church. The one thing the Constituent Assembly was manifestly *not* was *bourgeois*.

Deputies of aristocratic origin could even be found among those who had been elected for the Third Estate—not just famous cases like Mirabeau, but Edmond Dubois-Crancé, the seigneur of Balans and army officer who sat for Vitry-le-François; Louis Laborde de Méréville, from a branch of the great financial dynasty, who had been elected for the Third of Etampes; Jean Mougins de Roquefort, elected for the Third of Draguignan in Provence; and Louis de Naurissart, the seigneur of Brignan who had been elected for the Third of Limoges. And there were no less than thirty-eight members of the Parlements among the deputies, including three presidents, all of whom were eager to give the deathblow to their former institutions. Army officers were also in the Assembly in striking numbers, many of course as deputies of the nobility. Overwhelmingly, the men who created the new France had been officials of the old regime.

It is evident, then, that the solidarity generated among these men by their dramatic experience at Versailles in the spring and summer of 1789 had superseded the importance of their social origins. They were now tied together by their shared recent history, but also perhaps by cultural habits. They had all read the same books even if they disagreed on the importance to be assigned to them. It was quite natural, for example, in debates over the powers to be given or denied to the monarchy, to cite Montesquieu, just as they had in the Parlement remonstrances. Their diverse manners of rhetoric—legal, theatrical, clerical and literary—all found receptive audiences. References to Plutarch or to Cicero were immediately understood. Their legislative interests read like the agenda of a provincial academy: the reform of justice; the selective dismantling of the corporate economy; sweeping schemes of education; a France governed by social utility rather than inherited prejudices. They were all devotees of Reason and votaries of Virtue. Above all, they all saw themselves as patriots. It might even be said that they constituted a new aristocracy, one whose sovereign credential was the possession of political language and whose most striking characteristic was a symbolic war on the very caste from which so many of them had come.

None of these affinities guaranteed political harmony. The second half of 1789 and 1790 in fact saw an increasingly sharp division between men of identical backgrounds and old friendships, now committed to opposing political positions. Adrien Duport, who had been a *conseiller* of the Parlement of Paris, and Michel Lepeletier (*ci-devant* "de Saint-Fargeau"), who had been one of its presidents, were both adamantly antimonarchical and described by Ferrières as "of the left"—the first use of the term in European history. They were joined by the impeccably aristocratic de Lameth brothers, who had served along with Lafayette in America but who had come to hold the deepest misgivings about his command of the citizen army.

That group, featuring Barnave as its most impressive and uncompromising orator, dominated the sessions of the Society of the Friends of the Constitution, which, following the removal of the Assembly to Paris, met in the old monastery of the Jacobins in the rue Saint-Honoré. But a number of their old colleagues from the Society of Thirty and its successor, the "Breton Club" at Versailles, separated themselves into a rival Club of 1789. Among them were Mirabeau, Sieyès and Talleyrand. While the Jacobins actively courted a public following and admitted nondeputies to their membership and tribune, the 1789-ers were by choice more exclusive, seeing their society as a continuation of the dinner debates and political breakfasts that, the previous winter, had created the sovereignty of the Third Estate. Now their concerns were more pragmatic, or rather more engaged in the problems of creating a viable state. While Barnave and the de Lameths saw the main danger to the Revolution coming from royalist conspiracy and the abridgment of democracy, Mirabeau and Talleyrand saw it as most seriously jeopardized by anarchy and bankruptcy. The Jacobin leadership suspected the 1789-ers of being elitist intriguers; their adversaries returned the compliment by portraying the de Lameths and Barnave as irresponsible, self-righteous windbags.

At stake was more than differences of political personalities, acutely important though these already were and would remain throughout the Revolution. (Overlooking these personality feuds as a serious issue in revolutionary politics has been one of the most glaring omissions of modern historiography.) What was at issue were the priorities of the Revolution, its reason for having happened. For the Jacobins of 1789 and 1790, everything turned on the securing of a free and accountable representation, the subordination of state to citizen. To their more moderate adversaries—

many of whom, like Du Pont de Nemours and Talleyrand, had been engaged in the reforming ministries of the monarchy—the point of the Revolution was the creation of a more powerful, dynamic France. Citizens would be gratified to the degree that the state in which they were represented was itself strengthened. Nothing that happened in the revolutionary years that lay ahead did anything to make that fundamental debate go away.

It was aggravated by the increasingly anomalous character of the official government. For all the hopes placed in him Necker had conspicuously failed to deliver the kind of constitutional authority that would resolve France's continuing financial crisis. The Declaration of the Rights of Man had not, by some political alchemy, made the threat of bankruptcy go away. In August, Necker had come to the Assembly needing a loan of eighty million to last the year and had secured the necessary authority. By late September, however, the situation remained perilous and he returned to the Constituent with a proposal to levy an exceptional tax amounting to one quarter of annual income. Citizens who earned less than four hundred livres a year were exempt; the tax was payable over four years and was to be regarded formally as a loan, repayable by the government as its fiscal circumstances gradually allowed.

Predictably, the proposal caused an uproar in the Assembly. Mirabeau, who continued to detest Necker, and, until the Constituent formally prohibited deputies from becoming ministers, hoped to replace him as the head of a Ministry of Talents, was happy to see the Genevan's evident discomfiture. He wrote to his constituents in Aix that the bankruptcy was being used as a threat to intimidate the Assembly into accepting a tax that would weigh heavily on the common citizens. "Since a bankruptcy would only fall on the big capitalists of Paris and other towns who are ruining the state with the excessive rates of interest that they exact, I don't see that it would be such a great evil."

Barely a few weeks later he had evidently changed his mind. Though he was still skeptical of Necker's plan, Mirabeau now represented bankruptcy as a frightful catastrophe that would fall alike on the defenseless widow and the honest tradesman. "What is bankruptcy if not the most cruel, the most iniquitous, the most unequal and the most disastrous of all taxes?" Arguing for means to avert it, and proposing an alternative scheme, namely a more selective forced loan on the greatest fortunes, Mirabeau brandished his most combative rhetoric to confront the Assembly with the shortcomings of its own collective naiveté. It was a phenomenal performance, boiling with vexation, rage and turbulent impatience. And though Mirabeau spoke of the sacrifice of money, not lives, his Roman manner of prosecution exactly anticipated a more sinister hyperbole to come. Robespierre was among those deputies who listened as the orator urged selective punishment and warned that those who flinched from it would themselves be held accountable:

> Choose! For surely it is necessary that a small number perish so that the mass of the people may be saved? . . . Strike, destroy without pity these sorry victims, hurl them into the abyss. . . . What, do you recoil with horror? Inconsequential men, pusillanimous men. . . .
>
> Stoic contemplators of the incalculable evils that this catastrophe will vomit up on France; impassive egoists who suppose that the convulsions of despair and misery will pass like so many others . . . are you so sure that so many men without bread will leave you in peace to savor the dishes of which you have reduced neither the number nor the delicacy? No, you will perish and in the universal conflagration that you have no fear to kindle, the loss of your "honor" will not save even one of your detestable pleasures.

If, he concluded, with their very first acts, the deputies "surpassed the turpitudes of the most corrupt governments," they would have no further claim on the people's trust, and all the promises of constitutional liberties would be shown to be built on sand.

The truth of much of Mirabeau's argument was compelling. Unless the needs of the state were met courageously and expeditiously, the new regime would remain a paper revolution. But the deputies of the Assembly did not care to be denounced as cowards and "egoists," a term of infamy drawn from the Rousseauean vocabulary that entered the currency of political prosecution and which would be used with deadly intent during the Terror. Besides, they suspected Mirabeau of pandering to public indignation to promote his personal popularity, while at the same time ingratiating himself with the court.

These suspicions were in fact well founded. As his opposition to a restricted veto and his support for royal control over decisions of war and peace attested, Mirabeau had remained a staunch monarchist. He saw no contradiction between this position and his embrace of the people's concerns, since it was exactly a type of "populist monarchy" that he thought best suited to France. In practice, though, it moved him to conduct that after his death would be exposed as Machiavellian hypocrisy. Early in October, through an intermediary, he put himself forward as the King's best hope of restoring royal authority. The means by which he would do this were shocking. Mirabeau recommended that the court abruptly take itself off to Rouen, where it would be beyond the reach of Parisian intimidation, and at the same time issue a general proclamation insisting that this was done not to sabotage but to reaffirm the Revolution.

It was a dangerous and chimerical fantasy. But it had been dreamt up not merely to promote Mirabeau's own career (important though that undoubtedly was) but to invest the executive side of the Revolution with some meaningful power. Otherwise, the orator knew, the entire event would drift, blown by gales of empty rhetoric, between anarchy and despotism.

ii APOSTASY

Who would help Mirabeau in his harebrained plan? Naturally he turned to his colleagues in the Club of 1789 to depose Necker and form an alternative government of national rescue. But his selections—Du Pont de Nemours, Ségur, Panchaud, Talleyrand—looked uncannily like a reunion of Calonne's junior brain trust. The one exception was Lafayette. The more the general became a popular cult figure, the less Mirabeau liked it, nicknaming him, sardonically, "Gilles César." But he was forced to recognize that Lafayette's active assent would be indispensable in legitimizing the "coup" he was planning. Most remarkable of all, on the face of it, was his choice of Talleyrand for minister of finance.

Perhaps only a chronic debtor like Mirabeau could have thought this a suitable post. Yet for all his expensive tastes, Talleyrand was no innocent where money was concerned. He had made his public reputation as a manager and accountant of church property and it was his firsthand knowledge of its locked-up capital that led to him to a daring solution to funding the Revolution. Like Mirabeau, Talleyrand fully recognized the need to empower a viable executive state if the new France was not to become a helpless creature of legislative whim. All his trained instincts were bureaucratic, rational and Voltairean. More than a nation of virtuous citizens linked together in fraternal embrace, he wanted a rejuvenated nation-state: an empire of reason where sense, rather than sensibility, was sovereign. But he also understood that the very powers that made Mirabeau remarkable often robbed him of common sense. As much as his friend, he liked a gamble, but as far as humanly possible Talleyrand wanted to bet on a sure thing. Where could it be found?

In the first week of October 1789, while Mirabeau was making up to the court, Talleyrand reflected on the fortune of the Church. He was still the Bishop of Autun but sartorially, at least, he had defrocked himself, allowing only the merest glimpse of an elegant pectoral cross beneath his coat to allude to his episcopal office. When his friends called him "The Bishop," it was usually with a grin on their faces as though enjoying an innocent joke. Though he was never as cynical as many of them liked to think, they treated him like Voltaire in a miter. As apostate aristocrats, they at any rate were not surprised when Talleyrand applied to the Church the principle of making war on one's own order.

On October 10, in the course of yet another debate on finance, Talleyrand declared that since the state was imperiled by financial disaster, "great dangers demanded equally drastic remedies." At hand was the answer, an immense resource lying unrealized in the property and estates of the Church. Recovered "for the nation" it might be used as collateral against a new loan or even sold off to meet the most pressing needs of the state. It was the insouciance with which this bombshell was dropped that particularly enraged his clerical colleagues. Affecting his most agreeable manner, Talleyrand claimed that the matter didn't even require lengthy discussion since "it is evident that the clergy is not a proprietor in the same sense that others are; since the property of which they have the use cannot be freely alienated and was given to them not for their personal benefit but for the exercise of an office or function."

Talleyrand's intervention was all the more telling because it did not depend on crude anticlericalism for its effect. Though he would be denounced in the pulpit as Judas, a minister of Satan, a beast of the Antichrist (among other things), he was not in fact an anticlerical bishop. His inclinations were pragmatic and utilitarian, and in that scheme of things the Church had a distinctive social role, ministering to the needs of the credulous, giving them spiritual succor and keeping them in orderly relation with the state. For this work, as he made clear in his speech on October 10, the state would guarantee clerics a decent living wage—substantially above the level usually enjoyed by a country curate. They were to become moral functionaries.

The air of sweet reasonableness by which Talleyrand seemed to be saying "Surely all men of goodwill and sound judgment must concur" was not as outrageous as his many enemies made it seem. His view of the Church was in keeping with a pronounced strain in the political thought of the late Enlightenment. For all his personal deism, Voltaire had always thought religion, stripped of its legally coercive power, indispensable for public morality. For Rousseau, veneration of the "Supreme Being" acknowledged the source of natural virtues and gave the state and its legislator their essential moral personality. For both writers, however, the sacerdotal mysteries and theological doctrines that set the institutionalized Church apart from citizens were dangerous frauds. Instead of an autonomous order claiming its own jurisdiction, they envisaged a church dissolved into the general purposes of the public realm: a useful, rather than an ineffable institution. The Abbé Raynal put it most succinctly: "The State, it seems to me, is not made for religion but religion made for the State."

At least one attempt to implement this vision of a practical Catholicism had been made outside France. During the 1780s, Marie-Antoinette's extraordinary brother, the Austrian Emperor Joseph II, had embarked on a systematic program to abolish the mendicant and contemplative monasteries and convents and turn their inmates into "useful citizens." Like Talleyrand he thought the clergy should be recruited into, but not control, a national system of elementary education that would supply literacy for the masses without theological indoctrination. And like Talleyrand he conceived of ecclesiastical property as a general fund, controlled by the state and disbursed for socially benevolent operations like poor relief, the training of orphans, hospitals and lunatic asylums. The salaried clergy might continue to administer these funds but on the strict condition that they acknowledged that they were public functionaries.

Needless to say, these policies resulted in an immediate collision with the papacy. But it was possible for the Emperor to use that conflict to emphasize the patriotic character of his reforms of the clergy. Similarly, in revolutionary France, those who wanted to integrate the clergy into the body politic represented their policy as a natural extension of national sovereignty. In August 1789, the National Assembly had already suppressed "annates"—the fees paid to the Pope in recognition of annual pilgrimages to Rome—as an infringement of that sovereignty. And by declaring the property of the Church to be at the disposal of the Nation, Talleyrand and Mirabeau (who placed a succinct resolution to that effect before the Assembly on October 13) hoped to appeal to the same kind of "Gallican" sentiment that had resulted in the expulsion of the Jesuits in 1765. They knew they had some allies within the Church: men like the Abbé Grégoire, who saw the reduction of ecclesiastical property not as plunder but as an opportunity to turn a corrupt establishment back to the purely evangelical purposes for which it had been established. And there was a considerable body of literature, some of it Jansenist, some of it "Richerist," arguing for a more austere Catholicism, cleansed of worldly impurities and even able to co-exist alongside other confessions. It was the kind of view expressed in prerevolutionary publications like *The Citizen-Priest* (L'Ecclésiastique-Citoyen) in 1787, which characterized the life of present-day monks as *une bonne vie bourgeoise,* an excellent table; all the pleasures allowed to men of the world; all the delicacies afforded by opulence . . . you frequent the best company; you receive a wide circle of friends [in] immense houses, superb apartments, fashionable dress even beneath your habits; fine books and paintings . . . hunting, gambling, every kind of luxury and entertainment and the pretended paupers of Christ are now only known as the darlings of wealth and fortune.

By contrast, the writer went on, the *curés'* poverty, solitude and weariness from their travail made them much more authentically the apostolic successors of the first Christians. It was by emphasizing the material gains for the rural clergy that Talleyrand hoped to recruit them as allies against the diocesan and monastic clergy, whom he knew would be his most serious enemies. One at least, Dominique Dillon, the *curé* of Vieux-Pouzanges who had been elected, however, for the Third of Poitiers, agreed that "if, in these difficult times, the sacrifice of the property of the clergy could prevent new taxes on the people," it should be done forthwith.

If Talleyrand really expected near-unanimous support from within the Church, he was to be gravely disappointed. Many of the rural curates who had been instrumental in accomplishing the victory of the Third Estate in June had been incensed by the casualness with which the Assembly had abolished the tithe on August 4, even though it had provided for its continued collection until other arrangements were made for financial support. In reality, as they knew all too well from their parishes, the mere news of the abolition of the tithe had made it uncollectable. But there was even more unpredictable opposition. The Abbé Sieyès, who for a long time had been even less ecclesiastically inclined than his old friend Talleyrand, spoke against Mirabeau's resolution on November 2, not on any grounds of piety but because he insisted it violated the Declaration of the Rights of Man's commitment to hold property as inviolable. "You have declared that property said to belong to the church now belongs to the nation but I only know that this is to declare something to be fact which is untrue. . . . I don't see how a simple declaration can change the nature of rights. . . . Why do you allow these petty hateful passions to lay siege to your soul and succeed in tainting with immorality and injustice the finest of all Revolutions? Why do you want to depart from the role of legislators and for what, to become anti-clerics?"

The unaccustomed note of passion that marked Sieyès' speech suggested the emotional turbulence that Talleyrand and Mirabeau's proposal had stirred. It was made worse, not better, by the fact that a considerable number of the parish clergy had been warm supporters of the Revolution and now for the most part felt betrayed and unjustly victimized. Their opposition to the Assembly's program was not merely the defense of vested interests, as the orators claimed. It arose from sincerely held convictions about the nature of their pastoral role and resentment at being demoted to some sort of department of state. While they readily acknowledged that their material position might be improved, the surrender of their autonomy to some sort of national superintendence seemed to be too high a price to pay. And they were even more anxious that the special position historically enjoyed by the Catholic Church would be jeopardized by the toleration of Protestantism. The months following the Assembly's acceptance of Mirabeau's resolution on November 2 by a margin of 510 votes to 346 saw a series of bitter disputes over the "nationalization" of the Church.

Figures like Boisgelin, the Archbishop of Aix, who had been among the warmest enthusiasts of the Revolution, now became at best tepid supporters. An initial tactic of resistance was to invoke the representative principle on behalf of the clergy, arguing that the decrees should be submitted to a specially convoked national synod. When that was rejected as an infringement of the sovereignty of the Nation embodied in the Assembly, Boisgelin became more impassioned. "You want to strike the ministers of the altar with the sword?" he said in a powerful speech to the Assembly on the fourteenth of April 1790. "We declare absolutely that we neither can, nor must, adhere to the decree which you will enact and that we reserve to ourselves the right to appeal to all the rights and prerogatives that belong to us by law, tradition and the establishment of the Gallican church." (Though the Archbishop was, in fact, to be one of those who would advise the King to sign the civil constitution.)

For their part, the reformers found themselves supported by exactly the kind of pugnacious Parisian anticlericalism they had hoped to avoid. On the day of the vote about "national property" ecclesiastical deputies known for their opposition were jeered and pelted outside the Assembly. Caricatures, songs and *poissard* poems drawing on an old and rich vein of satire against monks, popes and bishops took a new lease on life. One popular parody of the invocation O Filii ran:

> Notre Saint-Père est un dindon
> Le calotin est un fripon
> Notre Archevêque est un scélérat
> Alleluia

> Our Holy Father is a turkey
> The priest is a rogue
> Our Archbishop is a scoundrel
> Hallelujah

Another song suggested that these avaricious, sexually rapacious clerics were about to arm themselves and massacre citizens in a new St. Bartholomew's Eve, a much repeated theme and one which owed its currency to Marie-Joseph Chénier's immensely popular play *Charles IX*. In that drama cardinals and bishops were seen plotting and praying for the extermination of good citizens, and Chénier did his utmost to make the parallels with the Revolution quite explicit. The best actor in France, Talma, carried off a portrayal of the King as a kind of demonic halfwit in whom loathsome amorality and devious plotting were concentrated to an unusually abominable degree. A special deputation of clerical deputies and bishops petitioned the government and the King to close the play for its scurrilous quality and—an exception in 1789—the petition was granted. But even after the curtain was down, the identification in the Parisian popular mind of the priesthood with anticitizenship remained very strong.

As the partisans of the "national church" encountered stiff resistance from the clergy, they were tempted to use both high-minded and low-minded propaganda in their attempts to overcome it. On December 19 it was decided to auction off up to four hundred million livres' worth of ecclesiastical property through the agency of the municipality of Paris. This operation would allow the government to float a major new loan against the security of the proceeds and was, in effect, the beginning of the state's expropriation of the Church. Curates and bishops denounced the action from their pulpits, threatening to excommunicate buyers and warning that holy wealth might now fall into the hands of Protestants or even, Holy Mother forbid the thought, Jews. In response, pamphlets supporting the sale reminded the public that "aristocrats" of both clerical and lay kinds had been responsible for the shortage of coin. It was the bullion equivalent of the famine plot, the emigrants and the abbots either exporting or secreting vast caches of ingots and money to deplete the economy of its circulation.

The same sort of war of prayers against pamphlets broke out over the momentous decision taken by the Constituent on February 13, 1790, to withdraw recognition of monastic vows. At last, the reformers said, the armies of shiftless monks and nuns would be turned into useful citizens. The cloisters would be unlocked to allow their inmates to enter the public realm. The response of the two sexes to this sudden opportunity was, however, quite different. Very few nuns decided to depart other than those at the Convent of Sainte-Madeleine in Paris, where some of them organized a formal protest against the "despotism" of the abbess, an aristocratic Montmorency-Laval. A much more typical response was the declaration of the Carmelites of Paris, who protested that "if there be happiness on earth we enjoy it in the shelter of the sanctuary." Not all monks, either, were eager to escape. The Benedictines of Saint-Martin-des-Champs had voted in September 1789 to give up their property against allowances paid by the state but still decided in 1790 to retain their monastic vows. The most dramatic spectacle, though, occurred in the very heartland of the monastic renewal of the twelfth century: in the great Cistercian abbeys of Clairvaux, Cluny and Cîteaux. From the immense and beautiful Gothic refectories, libraries and dormitories, created to provide a self-supporting barrier *against* the corruptions of the world, issued a great exodus of tonsured citizens rejoining their fellow mortals.

The invasion of clerical autonomy by the state was felt everywhere in ecclesiastical life. Before the first property sales in December, commissioners had been sent into the diocesan chapter houses to inspect and seal title deeds against false disclosures or clandestine transfers to third parties. In March and April 1790 more men wearing tricolor sashes arrived at convents and monasteries to ensure that the decrees of the Assembly were being communicated and respected by abbots and mothers superior.

In February the pulpit itself had been conscripted into the Revolution. On the ninth, the Abbé Grégoire, the Lorraine curate and advocate of the emancipation of blacks and Jews, reported widespread rioting in the countryside of the rugged river country of the southwest. In the Quercy, the Rouergue and the Tarn peasants were committing acts of violence because they assumed the decrees of the fourth of August had abolished *all* dues and taxes payable to the landlord, rather than the all-important fine distinctions the Assembly had carefully drawn between personal services and what were now rental obligations. Much of this misunderstanding, Grégoire said, arose from ignorance of the French language in a region where local patois and varieties of the southern *langue d'oc* were spoken. But in the timbered Dordogne town of Sarlat, the Bishop had set a fine example by publishing a personal circular explaining the decrees and using the opportunity of his sermons to clarify misunderstandings—all in a pastoral way.

Grégoire's conclusion was, first, that one of the primary duties of the Revolution would be to unify the nation through an active campaign of instruction in the French tongue, supported by propaganda; one which he would lead. For the moment, however, the clergy needed to be recruited to help the people, especially in the countryside, to comprehend revolutionary legislation. On the following day Talleyrand said that this could best be done by having them read decrees from the pulpit and use the occasion to disabuse people of false rumors. The proposal was less shocking than it was made to seem since Louis XIV and many of his predecessors had often required royal decrees to be read by the clergy to their flock. Sunday Mass, after all, was one of the few times when one could be sure of gathering together peasants from widely scattered farms under the same roof. But occasional recourse to the Church to make known declarations of war or the stigmatization of heretics was not the same thing as turning the pulpit into a revolutionary bulletin board. And even the Sun King had conceded that he could not force the clergy to publish decrees.

By threatening them with removal of their parish and denial of their voting rights as "active citizens" the Revolution was going much further than the monarchy in annexing the Church as a department of public instruction. In effect, it was implementing the Abbé Raynal's demand that the state act as the final arbiter of public morality, determining whether the Church was acting in, or against, its interest. "The clergy only exists by virtue of the nation," declared Barnave, "so the nation [if it so chooses] can destroy it." And against this subaltern relationship and the acts of political intimidation to reinforce it, clerical publications mounted a spirited campaign of counter-propaganda. Journals like the Catholic-royalist *Acts of the Apostles* and the Abbé Barruel's *Ecclesiastical Journal* denied the right of the state to legislate on matters that concerned Christian teaching, ritual or liturgy. And in response to the official demand that the Church dissolve itself into the general purposes of the nation, they stubbornly reiterated the special, separate nature of its sacred authority.

Barruel's paper was particularly effective in that it not only printed the abbé's own eloquent tirades against the revolutionary legislation but letters from country curates, some of them at least bearing the stamp of authenticity, complaining bitterly of intimidation from the state. One wrote, "My house, Jesus Christ said, is a house of prayer, . . . our temples are not public places or town halls," and Barruel responded that "the disciples of Christ are not Caesar's men; if there are truths to publish in church they are the truths of the laws of Christ and the precepts of the gospel."

The dispute was, of course, only the latest round in an ancient cycle of hostilities between the Roman Catholic Church and the European states. Both in his pragmatic opportunism and his version of the obedience of the Church to lay statutes, Talleyrand was not much of an advance on Henry VIII's manager of the Reformation, Thomas Cromwell. Rousseau had replaced Luther as the alternative authority on the redundancy of priestly autonomy. In France, however, the situation was complicated by the evident reluctance, even among the majority of the Assembly, to abandon

Catholicism as a favored religion. It was only when they were pushed too far, as on April 10, when Dom Gerle insisted that the Assembly declare the Roman Church the only religion of state in France, that positions became dangerously polarized. But the legislators also expected the papacy itself to assume a passive if not a compliant role, especially since its territorial enclave at Avignon was under threat of "reunion" (that is, annexation) to France.

Instead, throughout the spring and summer of 1790, a growing sense of alienation from Paris and from the secular bullying of the Revolution began to make itself felt throughout the Church. The geography of disaffection was, as Timothy Tackett has charted it, quite distinctive. Resistance was most marked in the west and southwest and in eastern France from the Vosges through Alsace and Lorraine to Flanders and Picardy. The Rhone Valley and the Midi seem to have been marked both by anticlericalism and militant Catholicism, and the revolutionary settlement was most widely accepted in the Seine Valley, the Paris region and in the poorest regions of central France, where the attraction of a better stipend for curates may well have been a decisive factor. Even within specific areas, there were marked discrepancies of loyalty between country and town. In the Norman town of Bayeux, for example, Olwen Hufton found a high degree of rejection among the local clergy and noted that their colleagues in the neighboring countryside were likely to be more pragmatic.

Talleyrand's own chapter at Autun (which of course hadn't seen him since his ordination) was quite clear about their view and began to talk back to their bishop. They were particularly upset with him for proposing to the Assembly in January—along with that notorious sinner Mirabeau—the emancipation of the Spanish and Portuguese Jews. It all seemed to add up to a calculated act of betrayal, a bishop in league with Christ-killing usurers and other equally detestable capitalists to despoil the property of the Church and feather their own nests. Was this the way he fulfilled his sacred vow, sworn at the cathedral altar, "to defend with his life the estate of his bride, the church of Autun"? Letters to the local press called him a Judas, an apostate, a murderer of the evangel. Talleyrand pushed his pectoral cross a little deeper into his waistcoat.

In their turn, the legislators appreciated that the *curés-citoyens* on whom they had pinned their hopes—men of public goodwill who could reconcile their Christian vocation with their civic duty—were very rare birds indeed. Some could be identified—for example, one Pupunat, who, from his parish of Etables in the eastern department of the Ain near Nantua, wrote to the Assembly that local officials there refused to give him the text of decrees to read and that he had always felt it "his most religious duty to unite inseparably the teaching of the decrees of the august National Assembly with those of the dogma of Christian morality."

The growing realization that the Pupunats were few and far between dislodged the Assembly's convenient assumption that a dependable body of citizen-priests would spontaneously come into being. To fill the vacuum it moved in two directions. First, it decided to appoint *lecteurs*—readers—of decrees who would be the Assembly's official communicators and might, but not necessarily, make their announcements from the pulpit. Second, with the clergy excused from that duty, they would nonetheless be held to strict allegiance by the swearing of an oath of loyalty to the nation and its laws. This was nearly identical to the oath sworn by all public officials and soldiers whose loyalties might otherwise be called into question, but for the Church it represented the final subordination to profane authority. There are signs that when the Civil Constitution of the Clergy was presented to the Assembly in July 1790, it was seen by a majority of the legislators as no more than the final integration into the new revolutionary Nation of its salaried, certified and inspected personnel. Mirabeau had said, after all, that since "religion belonged to everyone," it followed that its ministers should be public servants like soldiers and magistrates. Henceforth, *curés* and bishops would be elected in the manner of the new justices of the peace and district tribunals, and dioceses would be identical with departmental boundaries.

The Abbé Montesquiou, who was well enough respected to serve as president of the Constituent, saw this not as reform but as annihilation. Was the constitution, he had asked in April, "now to be one of those pagan cults that demands human sacrifices?" Was it to sacrifice the holy clergy? Was "the exterminating angel to pass over the face of this Assembly?"

The Civil Constitution was not simply another piece of institutional legislation. It was the beginning of a holy war.

iii ACTING CITIZENS

All over France, during 1790, liberty trees sprouted on village greens or in public squares in front of town halls. Sometimes they were the real thing: *mais sauvages,* young trees or saplings, trimmed and transplanted. Too often, though, the leaves withered and boughs drooped, spoiling the intended effect of vernal rejuvenation. So they were replaced by stripped poles, more closely resembling the maypoles which were their immediate symbolic antecedent. Liberally festooned with tricolor ribbons, the poles

123. Etienne Béricourt, gouache, the planting of a liberty tree. The appearance of
the hat of liberty and the striped trousers worn by the flag bearers suggest the
drawing was done in 1791.

became the focal center of a village's allegiance to the Revolution, the
symbolic declaration that a place was no longer seigneurial property and
its people no longer dependents.

In special ceremonies the trees were dedicated to the cause of constitutional liberty: vows were sworn by the mayor and echoed by a local detachment of the National Guard; the trees were blessed by a local priest and
regaled with music and poems by schoolchildren and the local bard, who was
at least a corresponding member of the provincial academy of letters.
Around the civic mast would circle dances *en ronde:* a joining of hands of
different ranks and orders in the fraternal unity established by the new order.

The liberty trees celebrated the myth of harmony that revolutionary
politicians in Paris had decreed in their more Masonic manner. Devotion
to the *patrie* was supposed to be such that it collapsed all previous allegiances—to guild, province, social order or confession—within the new
indefinitely extended political family. But this militant inclusiveness by
definition required outsiders in order to define its limits and to give insiders
a sense of their own bonds. So all the images of incorporation presupposed
counter-images of denial: obstinate anticitizens who, refusing to sink their
differences within the revolutionary community, had to be extruded from

492

124. Detail from Jacques-Louis David, *The Tennis Court Oath*, 1791

125. Detail from Jacques-Louis David, *Brutus*, 1789

it. The painter Jacques-Louis David provided at least two such images: the deputy Martin d'Auch, who refused the Tennis Court Oath, sitting hunched up in dejection, his hands crossed miserably over his breast while every other was extended in the oath. More alarmingly there were the corpses of Brutus's sons, seen feet-first, executed by the writ of their own father for having turned their backs on republican Rome.

Increasingly such outsiders were identified by the treasonable epithet "aristocrats," even when their actual origin was from the commons or when their accuser was himself of noble birth. Conceivably, then, a *ci-devant* noble patriot could actually accuse a lowborn broker of being an "aristocrat" just because, say, he had once worked for the General Farm. Such social ironies produced bizarre confrontations. On April 27, 1790, the *Courrier de Versailles* reported a public brawl between two *ci-devants*, the notoriously militant Marquis de Saint-Huruge and the Chevalier de Ladavèse, near the rue Saint-Honoré. "*A l'aristocrate*," Saint-Huruge had shouted, sighting his adversary. "*Démagogue!*" yelled the Chevalier in response. Saint-Huruge, uniformed as a captain of the National Guard, drew his saber, the Chevalier his sword stick, and a fracas would have ensued had they not been pulled apart by yet a third *ci-devant*, the Comte de Luc, the septuagenarian whose rheumatics had been banished by a dose of Equality. It was wholly typical of the spirit of 1790 that the Comte was able to exert his authority over the two combatants by virtue of two heroic insignia—his uniform as a citizen-soldier of the district of the Oratoire and the cross of Saint-Louis, which he still wore beneath the tricolor sash.

Such encounters, in which each hostile camp tried to claim itself as representative of true revolutionary patriotism and its opponents as "aristocrats," reproduced themselves in all walks of life. Brothers—the Mirabeau brothers, for instance—accused each other either of fanaticism or treasonable irresolution. Personal scores became political causes. Jacques-Louis David, whose political zeal had been largely confined within the picture frame, now took the refusal of the Academy to grant his pupil Drouais posthumous honors not only as a personal affront but as a symptom of its aristocratic rottenness and obstinacy. Passing him over as director of the French School in Rome made things even worse. The Revolution gave David a vocabulary with which to articulate these grievances as public issues, so that henceforth his pictorial and verbal languages could complement each other. The artist, as well as the art, now became political.

The same process by which personal and professional affairs were swallowed up by political rhetoric reproduced itself in the career of David's friend the actor Talma. He had already shown himself to be an eager patriot in the springtime of the Estates-General by using the traditional *compliment*—a footlights speech delivered by one of the company of the Théâtre-Français at the beginning and end of their season—to preach the virtues of the Revolution in a fiery speech written by Marie-Joseph Chénier. "As my enemies," Talma perorated, "I have all those who owe their lives to prejudice and who regret the passing of servitude . . . as my friends I must have those who love the *patrie,* all true Frenchmen. . . . The remains of the feudal structure will soon collapse through the efforts of the august Assembly that represents you."

For Talma it was not just the officially instituted theaters that were now *ancien régime,* but the entire manner of their art: stilted, artificial, academic, preposterously elitist, dedicated to frivolity and remote from the powerful universal truths that could, and ought to, be communicated by the theater. No wonder Jean-Jacques had thought the theater incompatible with a virtuous society; no wonder that actors were still disqualified from the vote!

So Talma brought David's Roman history paintings onto the stage in a performance of Voltaire's *Brutus,* in which he had just seventeen lines as the tribune Proculus. Drawing on the coin and antiquities collection of David, he draped himself in a floor-length toga, cut his hair short and combed it forward in the manner of the Capitoline Brutus reproduced in his friend's painting. "Ugh, how ugly he is," commented his unreformed colleague, Mlle Contat (Beaumarchais' Suzanne), on seeing the Romanized

Talma; "he looks like an antique statue." Thus transformed, Talma took to the boards, deliberately embarrassing leading members of the company who continued to costume themselves in the style of the epoch of Racine and Corneille, bewigged and hosed in breeches. In startling contrast, Talma bound his feet in thongs and left his thighs naked.

His appearance caused exactly the sensation it was calculated to produce and exposed the senior members of the company as thespian aristocrats. In the autumn, the opportunity to perform Chénier's *Charles IX* deepened the rift in the company. In the climate of late 1789 no one in the troupe was eager to play the role of a murderous idiot-king. Offered the part when the first choice passed on it, Talma threw himself into the role in the high romantic manner of the British Shakespearean Kean, using makeup to alter completely his facial appearance. His Charles IX had thin pale lips and stretched, almost mongoloid, eyes. David was thrilled. He told Talma that he looked exactly like a Fouquet portrait in the Louvre. At the climax of the play, Talma made the King shrivel into himself with remorse like a dying insect:

> I have betrayed the *patrie* and the honor of the laws
> Heaven must make me an example to kings.

Though the bishops succeeded in suppressing the play after thirty-three packed performances, *Charles IX* made Talma a revolutionary celebrity in his own right. He now mingled among other leading lights of the political theater, in particular the consummate amateur actor Mirabeau. On the first anniversary of the fall of the Bastille he completed his political conversion by appearing in a play as the ghost of Jean-Jacques Rousseau, dressed precisely in the manner of memorial portraits. But it was a week later, on July 21, that theater and politics fused into one performance. That evening a *claque* of Provençals organized by Mirabeau shouted for the forbidden *Charles IX*. The principal of the company, Naudet, came to the footlights and said that that was impossible since the leading lady was ill and other crucial players were similarly indisposed. This reasoning was greeted by a rain of booing and shouting. At that point Talma emerged from the wings to announce that Mme Vestris' throat would allow her to act and that other parts could be read if necessary. The following night the play was duly performed to an audience of cheering National Guardsmen.

The drama was not yet over. In September 1790, despite his enormous popularity on and off the stage, Talma was suspended from the Théâtre de la Nation for indiscipline. But the deputy leader of the Patriot faction in the company, Dugazon, used the footlights once more to make a political

126. Marie-Joseph Chénier. The scene from *Charles IX* shown below features the Cardinal of Lorraine blessing the daggers that would commit the St. Bartholomew's Eve massacre—an inversion of the patriotic benedictions of 1789.

speech defending Talma as an exemplary citizen-player. The audience cheered, sang revolutionary songs as it smashed seats, climbed over them onto the stage and to the high-priced boxes. Dugazon and his wife joined Talma in a brief, heroic exile from the theater until they were forcibly reinstated by Mayor Bailly. On September 28 *Charles IX* was performed once again.

By mobilizing the audience as foot soldiers to help them fight their backstage battles, Talma and the Dugazons had broken the proscenium line that divided theater from politics. Just as David came to see his paintings as, in some sense, revolutionary participants, so Talma saw his rhetoric as an instrument to galvanize public virtues and dissolve the barriers separating leaders from the led. Henceforth, actors would be regular participants in revolutionary ceremonies and the streets would be the scene of political theater. When, for example, Dugazon wanted to demonstrate against the continuing privileges of the Comédie-Française, he dressed eight actors as Roman lictors, filled four great baskets with Talma's props—helmets, togas, cuirasses—and led this Roman army in a slow antique march to the Palais-Royal, where he fulminated against the patricians.

In Paris, at least, the limits of political participation were expanding fast, so that they pressed against not just the conventions of the old regime but those the new regime of 1789 had set for its own safety. The rhetoric of revolutionary leadership had encouraged this process. It had spoken in indefinitely inclusive terms—of the Nation, of the *patrie*, of citizenship—as if every French man and woman had a direct stake in that enlarged political family. Newspapers now repeated these universal nostrums not just in the language of the educated, but often in the street talk of the markets and *cabarets*. Popular expectations, then, were of multiple utopias springing up in city and countryside: farms without rents; churches without bishops and monks; an army without recruiting officers; a state without taxes. And the curiously transitional state of the country, in process of being constituted by the Assembly, heightened these unrealistic expectations.

Before long, the contradictions that lodged deep within the personality of the French Revolution would turn into open hostilities. For, while the expectations of a citizens' millennium proceeded from the antimodernist impulse that had mobilized crowds in the streets, those who had been the beneficiaries of their violence wanted something quite different for France. They wanted a modern, workable, powerful state: a constitutional monarchy with a Gallic accent, not a populist democracy.

To that end they introduced all kinds of limitations, distinctions and constraints on political participation that collided directly with the unifying myths they themselves had encouraged. The Declaration of the Rights of

Man and Citizen, for example, seemed to speak to all Frenchmen. And in 1791 the actress Olympe de Gouges would naturally extend that reasoning in a *Declaration of the Rights of Women and Citizenesses*, a document sneered at then and since, but which in fact makes a telling and moving case for the inclusion of women in the totalizing promises of the Revolution. Not only was the Constituent not, of course, prepared to contemplate women as part of the active political process, but it also rejected other supplicants for citizenship. Deputies from the French Antilles who freely invoked the principles of the Rights of Man to argue their liberation from colonial trade regulation fiercely denied the application of those same rights to black slaves. Albert de Beaumetz, who was one of the warmest supporters of full Protestant eligibility for office, made it clear on the twenty-fourth of December that the same rights could not possibly be extended to the Jews since they were "struck by a political and religious malediction."

The most glaring departure from a promise of *universal* rights was contained in the limits the Constituent placed on political participation. Having created an all-embracing concept of citizenship in the Declaration of the Rights of Man, the deputies subsequently decided that some were more equal than others. Only French males over twenty-five who had had an established domicile for over a year, who were not domestic servants or dependents of any kind and who paid the equivalent of three days' labor in taxes were entitled to vote in primary electoral assemblies. At higher levels of the electoral hierarchy these limits became even more restrictive. To be a member of an electoral assembly required a tax payment of the equivalent of ten days' labor, and to be eligible as a deputy in the legislature itself required the substantial sum of the silver mark, which was equivalent to fifty days' labor.

These limits disfranchised large sections of the population: all rural day laborers and hired hands, domestic servants, many journeymen artisans— all social constituencies which had been crucially engaged in the revolutionary agitations of 1788–89 and who had come to expect great things from their political deliverance. Even so, the electorate that was created numbered well over four million—much the broadest experiment with representative government attempted in European history. But to the advocates of a purer democracy—an eloquent minority in the Assembly—the restrictions were pusillanimous and hypocritical. They represented, said Maximilien Robespierre, a deputy from Artois, "the destruction of equality." Desmoulins repeated the charge in his paper *Les Révolutions de France et de Brabant:* "Who are truly the active citizens?" he asked rhetorically. "Those who have taken the Bastille, those who work the fields; while the *fainéants* of the court and the clergy, despite the immensity of their domains, are merely vegetables."

Desmoulins adopted the ingratiating Rousseauean manner of addressing his readers as though they were personal friends: *"mes chers souscripteurs."* And in his pages he tried to give them a sense of what the perfect revolutionary urban village could be like: the *incomparable* district of the Cordeliers, where, he claimed, he knew every citizen, the *terre de la liberté*, sometimes characterized as a "little Sparta," sometimes as a "little Rome," populated by untiring Patriots ready to debate public issues long into the night and spring to the defense of their friends and brothers against the machinations of the tyrants of the Hôtel de Ville. "I can never walk through its territory," he wrote in January 1790, "without a religious sentiment, thinking of the inviolability it has assured to honest men." The "honest men" he had in mind were of course journalists and, besides Desmoulins, the tight-packed community included Marat, Loustalot, Fréron and Hébert as well as the powerful printer-publisher Momoro and the playwright Fabre d'Eglantine. Its dominant personality, however, was the lawyer Georges Danton, who in January 1790 proposed a committee of five "Conservators of Liberty" (including himself) without whose counter-signature no arrest would be valid.

It was Marat, the vituperative physician-inventor turned journalist, who in his paper *L'Ami du Peuple* provided the test of the limits of free speech by repeatedly denouncing as "public enemies" Necker, Lafayette and Bailly. On the twenty-second of January an attempt was made to arrest him, enforced by two companies of hussars and hundreds more National Guardsmen who sealed off the streets near the Théâtre-Français where Marat lived and worked. Danton mobilized the district assembly and spoke of "our own territory" being "invaded," though he counseled nonviolent resistance. It was when he discovered that the warrant had been made out for the Châtelet, a jurisdiction in the process of being reformed out of existence, that he decided on an appeal to the National Assembly. By the time that appeal was heard and rejected, Marat had contrived to escape, though not before publishing an extraordinary pamphlet ridiculing the pains to which the city authorities had gone to catch him. Twenty thousand soldiers armed with eighty cannon and thirty mortars had come, it said, to seize the People's friend, shell the district assembly and post sappers on their roofs to puncture any balloon by which Marat (an enthusiast of flight) might attempt to fly the coop.

Much to Desmoulins' sorrow, the brief but spectacular career of the people's republic of the Cordeliers was brought to an end by the administrative reorganization of Paris from sixty districts to forty-eight sections. "O my dear Cordeliers," he mourned, "farewell to your bell; farewell to your speaker's chair, to the tribune resounding with the speech of so many illustrious orators." His grief, however, was premature, for while its "territory" was carved up among a number of sections, principally Théâtre-Français and Saint-André-des-Arts, the "Cordeliers" survived as the most important political club of the left bank. With a minimal subscription the Cordeliers went out of its way to recruit members from the working population who might give some credibility to its noisy claims to represent the People against the oppressors of the city government.

For all the talk of unity and indivisibility, the requirements of state-hood—like the sale of church property—bore fruit in division and conflict. The elective principle that had been introduced into municipal and departmental government made this still worse, since it provided opportunities for successive generations of local politicians to accuse incumbents of surrendering local interests to the greedy domination of the center. As long as representative institutions survived, the problem would never go away. At its most acute it degenerated into outright civil war between Paris and the most defiant of the provinces. Signs of dreadful things to come could already be seen in violent clashes in the south, where Protestants who had flocked to the National Guard were attacked by Catholic crowds urged on by priests and recalcitrant local administrations. In the worst of those clashes, at Montauban, five guardsmen were killed and more than fifty badly wounded.

And it was against this truculent localism that the solid citizens of the National Guard determined to link arms across the country in a show of fraternal allegiance. Wrapping themselves in the tricolor and binding each other in solemn oaths, they would constitute the invincible phalanx of patriotism.

iv SACRED SPACES

Revolutionary France could not be, at the same time, a rejuvenated great European power and a confederation of forty thousand elected communes. At some point its leaders would have to decide whether it should approximate more the model of imperial Britain, where constitutional devolution was stringently restricted in the interests of the power of the central state, or republican America, where the national government was supposed, in theory, to be no more than the agent of consenting provincial electors. In 1790, however, it seemed for a while as though it might be possible to preserve the happy fiction of a concord in which local and national concerns were innocently melted. The demonstrations of fraternity which climaxed in the great Paris Festival of Federation on the first anniversary

127. Anonymous painting on board, the Fête de la Fédération

of the fall of the Bastille all featured a coming together of individual wills into a fresh sense of community. Right arms extended in the same direction to a single center; thousands of voices harmonized in swearing oaths to the constitution; confessional differences dissolved in revolutionary mutuality. Just as the Orator of the Lodge of Perfect Union had recommended, the Revolution would become "a vast lodge in which all good Frenchmen will truly be brothers."

While the manifestations of the new revolutionary religion—the cult of Federation—were theatrical and necessarily ephemeral, they were no less important for being that. In the emotive climate of 1790 they arguably made *more* of an impact through arresting spectacle than any of the elaborate institutional alterations on which historians have, until quite recently, concentrated. And it would be quite mistaken to see them as so much orchestrated mummery, staged by defensive politicians to disguise the frailty of their legitimacy. Overwhelming evidence from many regions of France suggests not only that many of the "federations" of 1790 were spontaneous, but also that they engaged enormous numbers of people in their dramatizations of shared patriotic enthusiasm. Notwithstanding the fact that the organizing forces were always National Guardsmen who, at this time, were better-off "active citizens," the numbers of those involved both as participants and spectators make a better case for regarding the revolution of 1790 as more of a "popular revolution" than the coercive Jacobinism of 1793–94 to which the term has been more frequently applied.

The federation movement arose from the revolutionary obsession with oath swearing. The moment at which Louis XVI appeared to have finally turned into a citizen-king was on February 4, when he appeared before the National Assembly in a simple black suit to swear that he would "defend and maintain constitutional liberty, whose principles the general will, in accord with my own, has sanctioned." At the same time he promised to bring up the Dauphin as a "true constitutional monarch." Bailly responded to this pledge by promising the King that now "you will be Louis the Just, Louis the Good, Louis the Wise, you will truly be *Louis le Grand.*" Following the event Lafayette, who had presided over similar ritualized ceremonies the previous autumn, proposed renewals of patriotic oaths with guardsmen to defend the Law, the Nation, the King and Liberty.

However repetitive and redundant these ceremonies may have been, conscientious citizens never seemed to tire of imitating David's Horatii, their arms achingly outstretched, their individual identities fused into a single patriotic will. They took particular satisfaction from celebrating the union of allegiances which, it was said, the old regime had kept artificially divided. So on November 29, 1789, the first of the big ceremonies took place on the banks of the Rhone, with twelve thousand National Guardsmen from the Dauphiné and the Vivarais swearing "in the presence of Heaven, on their hearts and on their arms" that neither the river nor anything else would sunder them in their common aim to uphold constitutional freedom. Similar scenes of histrionic jollity took place the following spring in Marseille, Lyon, La Rochelle, and Troyes. On March 20, 1790, on the banks of the Loire, guardsmen from Anjou and Brittany embracing in "holy fraternity" vowed to abjure their old provincial rivalries, "being no longer Bretons or Angevins but French and citizens of the same empire."

In Strasbourg the Federation of the Rhine assembled fifty thousand guardsmen from all over eastern France, from the Haute-Marne to the Jura. Thousands more civilians were used as ceremonial extras, all heavily clad in the wardrobe of revolutionary religiosity. Four hundred adolescent girls dressed in virginal white bobbed up and down on the river Ill in a flotilla of tricolor-painted boats before proceeding to a huge "patriotic altar" erected on the Plaine des Bouchers. Two hundred small children were ritually adopted by National Guardsmen as the "future of the *patrie*"; fishermen dedicated the Rhine and its fish to the cause of freedom. Patriotic farmers were preceded in parade by plows pushed by intergenerational teams of children and old men all carrying sickles and scythes. Most important of all was the symbolism of confessional unity as two toddlers, one Protestant, one Catholic (in a city with a strong Reformation presence), were subjected to an ecumenical baptism with shared godparents of both faiths. Their new names were declared to be "Fédéré" and "Civique."

In Lyon the *mise en scène* for the federation was more elaborately neoclassical. On the left bank of the Rhone a temple of Concord was created with Doric columns eighty feet high. Above that a plaster mountain was piled another fifty feet into the air and the whole thing surmounted by a colossal statue of Liberty holding in one hand a pike and in the other the Phrygian bonnet presented to freed slaves in ancient Rome and faithfully copied from antique coins. The ceremony itself was held on May 30, but for two days the city filled up with fraternal delegations from other regions—Brittany, Lorraine, the Mâconnais and Provence—each wearing distinctive costumes but sporting their brotherhood with huge tricolor sashes. On the day itself, to the sound of cannon and music, fifty thousand people gathered on the riverbanks to watch more than four hundred flags of National Guard regiments saluting the Revolution and to join in mass chanting of the oath, which resounded through the streaming rain.

It is difficult, in the twentieth century, to sympathize with these mass demonstrations of fraternal togetherness. We have seen too much orchestrated banner waving—great fields of arms harvested in ecstatic solidarity—heard too much chanting in unison to avoid either cynicism or suspicion. But however jejune the experience, there is no question that it was intensely felt by participants as a way of turning inner fears into outward elation, of covering the dismaying sense of recklessness stirred by revolutionary newness with a great cloak of solidarity. How better to feel heartened than alongside thousands of strangers whom one could, at least for a wet morning, call brother?

It was a logical step to advance from the provincial days of federation to an even more ambitious Parisian event that would tie citizen-soldiers from all over France to the organizing powers of the Revolution. The suggestion for such a "general federation" seemed to come spontaneously from National Guard companies of the district of Saint-Eustache. Representatives of the Guards would swear an oath of allegiance in the presence of the legislators and the "best of kings." Sylvain Bailly, who was very partial to these large gestures, made the decision official and on June 7, Talleyrand reported on the proposed arrangements to the Constituent. Though he had lost none of his personal skepticism about such occasions, he also had the astuteness to recognize their psychological power. The proceedings, he reported, ought to be solemn, glorious but not ruinously expensive. (In the end they cost some three hundred thousand livres.)

The Champ de Mars, a large open space used for drill and parades by the cadets of the Ecole Militaire (and, exactly a year before, the site of de Broglie's encamped troops), was selected as the site for the ceremony. In keeping with the Roman fetishism of the Revolution, the space was to be made into a gigantic circus or amphitheater. It was to be tiered in thirty steps and at one end the entry point would be marked by a grandiose, triple-arched Arc de Triomphe. At the center would be the by now standard "Altar of the Fatherland" at which the sacred oath would be taken. Where to place the "best of kings" was harder to determine. He could not be positioned at the altar without seeming to give him too much importance, so a pavilion was decided on that would accommodate both the royal party (the executive) and deputies from the Assembly (the legislative) in symbolic association and interdependence.

These arrangements were not approved by the Constituent until June 21. Only three weeks were available, then, for the immense task of preparing the site. The vast space intended to accommodate no less than four hundred thousand people was full of rocks that needed to be removed before the heavy soil could be worked and made even. Most of the field was to be excavated to a depth of four feet so that the altar area at the center would be raised by that amount, but there were no drainage ditches, and heavy rains at the end of June had turned much of the amphitheater area, especially near the triumphal arches, into a quagmire. Huge amounts of sand and gravel were required to give the surface any firmness. There were other equally arduous preliminaries that had to be completed in great haste. The rue de Marigny and other streets had to be widened to a breadth of three carriages and the procession route for the *fédérés* liberally sanded.

It was a daunting assignment but one to which the febrile character of revolutionary enthusiasm could be usefully harnessed. In no time, the whole of central and western Paris was turned into a great pullulating ant heap of organized work. Contemporary accounts, both in text and image, all stressed the socially redemptive and egalitarian nature of the labor, with monks and women of quality, their hair tucked beneath large bonnets, working alongside artisans and soldiers. For Mercier, it was the *tableau* of a Paris altogether different from the muckheap of abominations he had so memorably anatomized. This was the pigsty become angelic, a great festival of mankind morally purified by their communal labor.

128. Anonymous engraving, preparation of the Champ de Mars for the Fête de la Fédération. At the bottom left, the King, leaning on a shovel, is being applauded for his contribution.

It was there [in the Champ de Mars] that I saw one hundred and fifty thousand citizens of all classes, ages and sexes making the most superb picture of concord, labor, movement and joy that has ever been witnessed. . . . What fine men and splendid citizens of Paris who could transform eight days of work into the most touching, unexpected and most novel festival that there has ever been. It is a type of spectacle so original that even the most *blasé* of men can hardly fail to be moved.

In this great army of patriotic workers, the mighty mingled with the modest. The Duchesse de Luynes allowed the special wheelbarrow she had had made in acajou to be wheeled by the flower girls who were her teammates. Amidst a group of toiling nuns and monks, Mercier saw the naval hero Kersaint "with the radiant physiognomy of liberty" pushing a wheelbarrow with the same gaiety that he showed on the *Belle-Poule* when he went to fight the enemies of the *patrie*. According to Mercier's ecstatic account, far from tiring those who participated in the shifts, the labor was so much one of love that it invigorated them to the extent that water carriers, peddlers and market porters competed with each other to see who could continue longest, and veterans proved "that their arms could be vigorous so long as their souls were courageous." Various trades displayed identifying attributes as they worked, the printers wearing on their hats cockades which read "Printing, first flag of liberty"; the butchers, more threateningly, "Tremble, aristocrats, here are the butchers' lads."

The work site was also represented as a family idyll. In one such scene a happy division of labor was accomplished with the father wielding the pickax, the mother filling the barrow and the four-year-old held in the arms of his ninety-three-year-old grandpa singing the "Ça Ira" to entertain the rest of the family. Social peace and exemplary altruism ruled to such an extent that amidst the enormous crowd, not one incident of violence or crime was reported. Mercier claims he saw one young man arrive for work, strip off his coat and throw his two watches on top. When someone reminded him he'd left them there, he responded with a piety straight out of Rousseau: "One does not mistrust one's brothers." When the portable *cabarets* came round with free wine or ale the casks bore the similarly optimistic slogan "Brothers, don't drink unless you're truly thirsty."

Even the royal family was affected by this epidemic of goodwill. A week before the Federation, Louis opened the royal library and the botanical gardens to the arriving guardsmen; coming to inspect the site himself, he was received by a guard of honor forming an arch with their pickaxes. At

129. The butchers' boys on the
Champ de Mars

a reception for provincial deputations the King said that he should have liked to have told all France that "the king is their father, their brother and their friend; that he can be made happy only by their welfare and sick by their ills." And he asked the *fédérés* to communicate this sentiment to the humblest "cottages and hovels."

The weather for the great day was not auspicious. Some citizens accused it of betraying aristocratic unhelpfulness. At dawn fifty thousand National Guards assembled on the boulevard du Temple together with the Paris electors of 1789, the present representatives of the Commune, a children's battalion bearing a sign declaring it to be "The Hope of the Patrie," the Chevalier de Callières' bearded veterans, companies of regular soldiers and sailors and finally the delegates from the departments, including guards from Lyon who had brought with them a Roman standard. The honor of carrying the departmental banner was given to the oldest guard in each regiment. Rain was descending steadily, and by eight, when they set off eight abreast in procession, it had turned into a drenching downpour. Undaunted by saturated uniforms and squelching boots, they marched westward through Paris along the rue Saint-Denis and then the rue Saint-Honoré to the sound of artillery salvos and military bands. Despite the miserable weather the crowds were huge and dropped flowers on the soldiers as they passed. Women and children ran to them with sweetmeats and pies and serenaded them with yet more choruses of "Ça Ira."

At the place Louis XV they were joined by deputies of the National Assembly, and the whole immensely long procession finally arrived at the Champ de Mars at around one. There the triple arch rose eighty feet above the amphitheater, surmounted by a viewing platform perilously crammed with spectators. The roars of four hundred thousand greeted their entry—a crescendo which can hardly have failed to send a thrill down the spine of country shopkeepers, attorneys or apothecaries soggily resplendent in their guardsmen's uniform of blue and white. At the center of the field was the "Altar of the Fatherland," finished in *faux marbre* and decorated with edifying symbols. On one side a woman represented the constitution; on the other warriors representing the *patrie* were shown with their arms outstretched in the approved revolutionary manner. A slogan announced

130. De Machy, the Fête de la Fédération in Paris, 1789

that "all mortals are equal; it is not by birth but only virtue that they are distinguished/In every state the Law must be universal and mortals whosoever they be are equal before it." On the opposite side the image of Fame proclaimed the decrees of the Assembly immortal and asked the people to think on the three "sacred words which guaranteed them":

> *The Nation, the Law, the King*
> *The Nation, that is you*
> *The Law, that is also you*
> *The King, he is the guardian of the Law*

At three thirty, Talleyrand began his ceremony of Mass and benediction. His responsibility was to provide a formula that combined piety and patriotism, and although it varied necessarily from the standard liturgical formulae, it was orthodox enough to make him nervous. As Bishop of Autun he had been notorious for botching the ritual. So the evening before, he had conducted a rehearsal at his friend de Sousseval's house, dressed in full episcopal fig, using the mantelpiece as an altar. With rather too much expert gusto for Talleyrand's liking, Mirabeau sang the parts of the choir and interrupted his friend whenever he made a mistake. An apocryphal story repeated long after has Talleyrand at the Champ de Mars imploring Lafayette, who joined him at the altar, not to make him laugh. But in fact there is every sign that both men took the occasion quite seriously. The Civil Constitution of the Clergy had been enacted by the National Assembly just two days before, on July 12; and as its major partisan Talleyrand was well aware of the need to provide some kind of inspirational revolutionary religion that could draw on the same emotive and even mystical passions on which the Catholic Church relied, to bind the faithful to the Revolution. And while Talleyrand was being put through his paces by his eminence Mirabeau, an extraordinary cantata, half sacred, half profane, called *The Taking of the Bastille* was being performed at Notre Dame. It featured actors from the Montansier troupe, singers from the Opéra and the Italiens and even *artistes* from the boulevard theaters of Nicolet and the Ambigu-Comique conscripted to play the part of belligerent patriots. Together with a full religious choir it used military orchestra, cannon and passages from the Book of Judith shouted above the din. It was the sort of thing Talleyrand thought good for general morale.

In the soaking wet, however, he was having difficulty preserving the dignity of the occasion. The wind kept putting out the incense and his saturated robes weighed a ton. From beneath a miter that dripped rain onto his elegant nose, the pontiff of the Federation grimly surveyed the endless

131. Anonymous, *The Oath of Lafayette*. Talleyrand is at the extreme right. The triple
arch, dangerously crowded with spectators, is in the background. On the steps
of the altar are the broken emblems of servitude, and at the extreme left one of the
officially recognized *vainqueurs* of the Bastille wears his pseudo-Roman helmet.

file of guards trooping into the arena. *"Ces bougres-là ne vont-ils pas arriver?"* (Those buggers, why don't they get a move on?), he remarked to his assistant, the Abbé Louis, later the self-defrocked Minister of Finance under the Empire and Restoration. Finally all was ready and Talleyrand proceeded with the Mass and the benediction of the banners, raising his arms benignly over the streaming flags. "Sing and weep tears of joy," he told his flock, "for on this day France has been made anew."

The rest of the day belonged to Lafayette. It was he, after all, to whom the country turned as the embodiment of the citizen-soldier, not only its commandant but its heroic exemplar. And as the impresario of a kind of conspicuous consensus, Lafayette was only too well aware that the viability of the constitutional monarchy required theatrical demonstrations of the patriotic will. In late October 1789 he had insisted on the rule of martial law in Paris to prevent injustices like the summary lynching of a baker who had been wrongly accused of giving short weight. But he had turned the occasion into a special ceremony, getting the King to stand as godfather to the orphaned children—a literal demonstration of his paternal benevolence. In April Lafayette had brought the hero of Corsican independence (wiped out by France in 1769), General Paoli, to Paris to show him that his countrymen had nothing to fear from their "brothers" in the new France. Together they visited the site of the Bastille and reviewed a parade of National Guards in a show of fraternity.

Not everyone endorsed Lafayette as the hero of the hour. Both Desmoulins' and Loustalot's papers suggested that the Fête de la Fédération had been planned as an exercise in self-glorification. But there was little sign that these criticisms had done much to dim Lafayette's great popularity with the provincial National Guard. At around five o'clock on July 14, 1790, he was the cynosure of all eyes. From the altar he mounted his white charger and rode through ranks of guardsmen that had parted to form an avenue toward the royal pavilion. There he dismounted and asked and received permission from the King to administer the oath to the assembled *fédérés*. Back at the altar, in his best Talma-esque manner, Lafayette stretched out both arms to heaven in a suitably priestly fashion, then touched his right hand carrying the sword to the altar in imitation of the ancient crusaders' vow. Since his voice was obviously inaudible to all but those closest at hand, deutero-Lafayettes read the oath as he was uttering it to their companies, and it finished with a thunderous chorus of *"Je le jure."* A volley of cannon sounded from one end of the field to the other. When it had died away, Louis used his new title for the first time, declaring that as "King of the French" he swore to "employ all the power delegated to me by the constitution to uphold the decrees of the National Assembly." The Queen, the ostrich plumes of her hat drooping with rain, held up the Dauphin, uniformed as a National Guard, to the cheers of the crowd.

A painting of the climactic moment, preserved at the Musée Carnavalet, hardly does justice to its power. But at least it captures not only the principals—Talleyrand in his oversized miter; Lafayette uniformed as the Commander; the *vainqueurs de la Bastille* at lower left in their officially designated Roman helmets and costumes—but also the mood of the scene. In keeping with the Romantic axiom that the elements were themselves political accompanists, the painter has the dark rain clouds pierced by a shaft of providential sunlight at the exact moment when Lafayette's sword touches the altar. It is the visual counterpart to a *poissard* song made popular following the Fête:

> Ça m'coule au dos, coule au dos, coule au dos
> En revenant du Champ de Mars . . .
> Que' qu ça m'fait à moi d'êt mouillé
> Quand c'est pour la liberté

> It runs down my back, runs down my back, runs down my back
> Returning from the Champ de Mars . . .
> What is it to me if I'm wet
> For the cause of liberty

The festivities continued for a week, with companies of National Guards only gradually wearing out their cordial reception in Paris, drinking too much and expecting a few too many free meals. On the evening of the fourteenth, many of them went to the great *bal de Bastille*, where Palloy had decked the site in lanterns and bunting and provided eighty-three trees, one for each department of France. Later that week they could hear more performances of Desaugiers' cantata *Prise de la Bastille* or go to the special ceremony on the place Dauphine honoring, for the umpteenth time, the friendly ghost of Henri IV. Finally, on the eighteenth there was a splendid water festival on the Seine, complete with musical barges and jousting. Its program was identical to those that, traditionally, had greeted the entry of visiting princes. Only now those princes were the people themselves.

Foreigners who had made their way to Paris to drink at the fountain of freedom were particularly convinced that they were witnessing the advent of the fraternal millennium. They had heard deputies in the Assembly announce a "Declaration of Peace to the World" and promise that France would never again be a military aggressor. "How can I describe all those joyous faces lit up with pride?" wrote the pedagogue Joachim Heinrich

Campe. "I wanted to fold in my arms the first persons I met . . . for we were no longer Brunswickers or Brandenburgers . . . all national differences had vanished, all prejudices disappeared." William Wordsworth, who landed at Calais on the day of the Fête, felt much the same way. Walking through triumphal arches bedecked with flowers, he sensed joy diffusing everywhere like the perfume of spring.

For the young Helen Maria Williams, looking down onto the wet streets as the guards marched through Paris, the fourteenth of July was the most "sublime spectacle" she ever hoped to behold. It was the true faith revealed at its most ecstatic. "Old men were seen kneeling in the streets blessing God that they had lived to witness that happy moment. People ran to the doors of their houses loaded with refreshments which they offered to the troops, crowds of women surrounded the soldiers and holding up their infants in their arms, promised to make their children imbibe from their earliest age, an inviolable attachment to the principles of the new constitution."

If this was silliness it was pardonable silliness, and other cultures at other times have been swept away by tidal waves of togetherness no less senti-mental than those of the Fête de la Fédération. But there were still hard heads about who understood the value of the occasion without ever being deceived by its power to create lasting unity from temporary warmth. Talleyrand, for example, who had contrived the business in the first place, was ever a man to hedge his bets. On the evening of the fourteenth he was finally able to peel off his sodden soutane. Dried out, he summoned a carriage to take him to the Vicomtesse de Laval's, where card games for high stakes were well under way. He coughed politely, took his seat and started to win. He carried on winning all evening, breaking the bank and "carrying off more money than my pockets or purses could hold." Perhaps it was a good omen: providence blessing the pope of the Federation with good fortune. But just in case all those blessings and oaths should turn out to be in vain, there was, at least, good solid gold to bite into. For Talleyrand never did put much faith in paper money.

CHAPTER THIRTEEN

Departures
August 1790–July 1791

i MAGNITUDES OF CHANGE

ON THE MORNING of September 30, 1790, a small, serious procession made its way to the Palais de Justice in Grenoble. At its head was the elected mayor of the city, M. Barral, who affixed to the great oak doors of the building iron padlocks from which hung officially pressed seals. A notice was then nailed to the door reproducing the decree of the Constituent abolishing the old sovereign courts of France and replacing them with elected judges and tribunals. The Parlement of Grenoble, which had been declared in indefinite recess, was now officially certified dead.

Surprisingly, the man who at least ceremonially delivered the coup de grâce had himself been a *conseiller de Parlement.* For plain citizen Barral was better known to the Grenoblois as the Marquis de Barral de Montferrat. He had become mayor when another colleague of his, the Marquis de Franquières, had declined the election on grounds of ill health. Not infrequently local notables pleaded indisposition when they wanted to extract themselves from revolutionary popularity, but in de Franquières' case the excuse was genuine, for he died a few months later. Barral then succeeded to the office and placed himself at the head of the local Patriots, who were determined to prevent Mounier, now returned to his native city, from establishing Grenoble as a center of opposition to the Constituent Assembly. Subsequently Barral was elected to both the administration of the department of the Isère and the presidency of the new district tribunal that took its seat in the same chambers where the Parlement had convened its senior court. On that tribunal with him, as judges, were four other ex-*avocats* of the Parlement: Duport *aîné,* Génissieu, Lemaître and Génevou.

The president of the administration of the department of the Isère was Aubert-Dubayet, another *ci-devant* army officer.

A revolutionary break with the institutional past, then, did not necessarily entail a complete sweep of personnel. While their collective existence was terminated by the Revolution, many individuals who had held office under the monarchy had no trouble in exchanging their corporate identity for that of citizen-servants of the *patrie*. Indeed many of them were among the most ardent prosecutors of their old colleagues. In the summer of 1792, it was the former Marquise de Montferrat, now Citizeness Barral, who made a passionate speech before the municipal council of Grenoble for the summary incarceration of Marié-Antoinette and the appointment of a "patriotic tutor" for the Dauphin.

Given this mixture of continuity and discontinuity, as well as the prominent part played by the nobility of the Dauphiné in hastening the end of the old regime, it is not surprising that the epitaph for the Parlement of Grenoble published by the local *Courrier Patriotique* blended official disdain with grudging respect.

> They are no more, those haughty bodies, those colossi whose incomprehensible existence served neither monarch nor subject and whose monstrous and bizarre organization could only have operated in a state where all principles [of government] were confused or misunderstood. I saw shut up the palace from where, like a fortress, they so many times braved the fury of kings; that palace where the liberty of Frenchmen . . . found an asylum.

The blending of old and new was repeated across France. On paper, the transformation could not have been more abrupt or more sweeping. As corporate bodies, the Parlements were simply replaced by the legislative *fiat* of the Constituent Assembly, and the old jurisdiction of the *bailliages* by those of elected *juges de paix* and the district and departmental tribunals. In the same way, the crazy-quilt nature of government, with overlapping and criss-crossing boundaries that differed from civil administration to military government to ecclesiastical diocese, was swallowed up in the catch-all unit of the department. Even more striking, the hierarchies of appointed royal officials—from municipal aldermen or "consuls" to *intendants* and *maîtres de requêtes*—were now moved aside for elected officials. Indeed the conscientious *citoyen actif* in 1790 was snowed under with elections, being asked to vote successively for his local mayor and councillors, officials of the district and departmental councils, justices of the peace and judges of tribunals; and, finally, at the turn of the year, for a constitutional bishop and the local curate.

The appearance of "new men"—doctors, engineers, lawyers in great numbers, the occasional merchant and tradesman—in the first wave of institutions created by the Revolution was certainly in part a function of the massive expansion of elected offices. In at least this response to the *cahiers'* appeals for more, rather than less, government, the revolutionary notables had more than amply fulfilled their duties. But, as in Grenoble, this sudden expansion of the demand for experienced officials meant that throughout the country many of those who came forward to fill positions had already been officials under the old regime. They did not often constitute a majority, but they were very frequently placed in the most influential offices, such as mayor or president of the departmental directory, and a striking number of them were in fact *ci-devant* nobles. The usual lists of occupations offered by historians in scanning the professions of the men of 1790 and 1791 often overlook this fact because "aristocrat" or "noble" had already become a synonym for "traitor" and many former *conseillers* of the Parlements now listed themselves simply as "lawyers," which indeed they were. In many cases, following the law abolishing hereditary titles, they had of course dropped their aristocratic nomenclatures, so that d'Eprémesnil was now simply M. Duval, and his adversary to the left Huguet de Sémonville was now simply M. (under Napoleon, Baron) Sémonville.

Closer inspection of the new regimes in many of France's provincial towns, large and small, reveals just how strategically placed many of these holdovers from the old regime were. In Toulouse, for example, the notoriously inflexible reputation of the local aristocracy—the *capitouls*—did not preclude some of them from rallying to the new regime. The elected official representing the King locally, the *procureur-général–syndic,* was Michel-Athanaze Malpel, who was not only an ex-*capitoul* but one of the richest, having acquired a fortune of over eighty thousand livres by his marriage. The new municipality which suceeded to the abolished *capitoulat* included another oligarch, Pierre Dupuy, and the president of the district tribunal was Etienne-François Arbanère, who had been a *procureur du Parlement.* At the other end of France, in the Channel port of Calais, Nicolas Blanquart des Salines and Pierre de Carpentier, two old hands as *procureurs du roi,* were elected, respectively, to the district tribunal and as mayor. When the latter was in his turn elected to the bench, he was succeeded in the mayor's office by the formidable Jacques-Gaspard Leveux, the son of a receiver-general in the Admiralty, one of the most lucrative posts the old regime had to offer. Leveux not only was elected over and again as mayor, he managed through a dogged concern for local interests to survive the Terror, the Directory, the Consulate and the Empire, dying in office as a Legionnaire of Honor in the reign of Louis XVIII.

These were not exceptional cases. In Paris, no less than 20 percent of the three hundred elected representatives of the municipality were ex-Parlementaires. In the district of the Filles de Saint-Thomas alone, the editor of the *Patriote Français,* Brissot, shared the delegation with *conseillers* Lacretelle and Sémonville, the financial official Mollien and Trudaine des Ormes, a high official of the General Farm. In Lyon, one liberal ex-noble, Palerne de Savy, replaced another, Imbert-Colombes, at the head of the city administration. They were both attacked by a third group of democrat Patriots led by Roland de La Platière, who came from a family of noble magistrates with domains near Amiens and who kept both a country estate at Thizy in the Beaujolais and a town house on one of the *quais* by the Rhone.

Socially, there was little to distinguish these men, especially in a great commercial center like Lyon, where the lines between nobility and vulgar wealth had long been indistinct. More important, though, they all belonged to a common cultural milieu: the world of the Academies and the Masonic lodges. They all subscribed to the optimistic late-Enlightenment project that saw the sciences as necessarily leading to greater prosperity and more perfect government. And in this respect, too, they represent a continuation of the cultural climate of the *ancien régime,* rather than a break with it. Roland, after all, had been a professional booster of the blessings of technology in his capacity as royal inspector-general of manufactures. His dependable enthusiasm for inventive processes even led him to promote the idea of manufacturing soap from the fat retained in human cadavers, without a twinge of morbid embarrassment. His colleagues, rivals and enemies in public life in Lyon included the deputy Pressavin, whose fame lay in weighty volumes devoted to venereal diseases; friend Lanthénas, who in 1784 had published a typical Enlightenment work, "Education [meaning the want of it] As the Proximate Cause of All Diseases"; and yet another physician, Dr. Vitet, who directed the city's midwifery school and who had helped promote Beaumarchais' breast-feeding fund in Lyon. Like Roland, Vitet was a more ardent revolutionary than Palerne de Savy, whom he replaced as mayor, but Palerne was also president of the Academy of Lyon, and Imbert-Colombes before him was also known best as a botanical scientist and rector of the Hôpital-Général for the poor.

This cultural fellowship did not, of course, preclude bitter political hostility. Indeed it may have added to it the venom peculiar to wars of *savants* (and academics). But it should be clear—since Lyon was far from atypical—

that the *sociétés de pensée,* academies and *musées* very often provided the apprenticeship through which members of different social backgrounds could challenge each other and make claims to belong to the same empire of reason. Moreover, the conspicuousness of the *savants* and provincial *philosophes* among the men of 1790 and 1791 testifies to their general conviction that the Revolution was in many respects continuing and consummating the modernizing enterprise that had been promoted—with uneven results—in the reign of Louis XVI. The representatives of the districts of Paris included among their number the architect and writer Quatremère de Quincy, and scientist-philosophers like Jussieu, Condorcet and the astronomer-cartographer who had been an important influence in determining the boundaries of the departments, the Comte de Cassini. And what more suitable deputy to the National Assembly from Calais than Pierre-Joseph des Androuins, the noble *amateur* of manned flight who had been the first to offer the hospitality of his château to the aeronauts Blanchard and Jeffries after their cross-Channel balloon flight?

I do not want to minimize the impact of the early Revolution on French life and institutions. There were important institutions—most notably the Church and the officer corps of the royal army—which were broken in two by its demands. But there is virtually no convincing evidence that the *criteria* by which officers, priests, former officials, or for that matter notaries and lawyers, made up their minds to support or oppose the Revolution, to become a Patriot or an émigré, were socially determined.

This is not least because the consequences of the Revolution from 1789 to the Terror were, for the most part, socially conservative. The effects of much of the legislation of this period played directly to the interests of groups who had done very well at the end of the old regime (though they may have been temporarily disadvantaged by the depression of 1787–89) and were now given further opportunities to do even better. It was those who had already been able to define their economic interests in terms of property and capital, rather than privilege, and the many more who became converted to that view, who found ample opportunity to prosper in the Revolution. This is not the same thing as saying that the Revolution was *necessary* for their prosperity, much less for the advancement of capitalism. But in its first two years—perhaps only in its first two years—it did little to impede or reverse the developments of the past decades.

Thus it was exactly those of whom rural *cahiers* complained so bitterly—acquisitive well-off peasant *coqs de village* and other proprietors (some of them noble)—who gobbled up the properties of the Church when they came on the market. The Constituent had seen to it that lots simply went to the highest bidder, ensuring that only when peasants could come together in a buying syndicate (as they did in some parts of the north) was it feasible for them to acquire land. At Pusieux-Pontoise in the Seine-et-Oise, for example, arable land was dominated by the estates of Rousseau's friend the Marquis de Girardin and the Abbey of Saint-Martin. When the latter came on the market it was Girardin's most aggressive tenant farmer, Thomassin, who could afford to snap up fifty-five hectares of the best land for the substantial sum of 69,500 livres. Other substantial lots were acquired by similarly well-endowed tenant farmers from neighboring villages and by a poultry merchant of Puiseux. Girardin himself, who, predictably, had become an ardent supporter of the Revolution, and whose son, Stanislas, was head of the departmental administration, picked up a fifteen-hectare property in partnership with another well-off *laboureur* farmer.

Nor was the abolition of the seigneurial regime quite so straightforward as it had seemed on the dizzy night of the fourth of August 1789. Once cooler heads prevailed, late-Enlightenment experts on feudal law, of whom there were legions, were summoned, to make telling legal distinctions between those rights (like *mainmorte*) deemed "personal" and abolished outright and those (by far the majority) deemed "contractual." Needless to say, the latter, being defined as a kind of legitimate property, could—if both parties agreed—be redeemed, often at twenty-five times their annual value, a rate which obviously precluded all but the most favorably endowed peasant cultivators from taking advantage of the law. All that had happened in these circumstances was that lords had completed their transformation into landlords, a process already well under way in the later part of the century.

Predictably too, the structure of power in the village changed very little. In the commune of Authieux-sur-le-Port-Saint-Ouen in Normandy, the local electoral meeting of forty villagers made their *curé* mayor, with a council shared between landed *laboureur* farmers and local tradesmen like the innkeeper and petty officials like the *procureur*.

The same pattern holds for the effects of the Revolution on urban France. Much of the legislation of the Constituent affecting urban France was designed to take up policies launched under Turgot and Calonne, pushing France further towards capitalist expansion. Turgot's thwarted reform of the guilds was now enacted as an outright abolition, early in 1791. But when the obvious delight which journeymen artisans took in being liberated from corporate restrictions turned into a series of strikes—notably by carpenters, farriers and hatters—the Assembly responded with the Le Chapelier law prohibiting altogether any kind of workers' coalition or assembly. As indicated by the relative absence of speeches and articles on the matter at the time, the Le Chapelier law was enacted less out of ideological fixation with free trade than out of a desire to protect citizens' common interests—as embodied in national institutions—against the particularism that strikes were held to represent.

Likewise, many of the uncertainties and divisions of opinion about the shortest route to economic modernization articulated during the closing decades of the old regime were simply reproduced in the Revolution. In the Constituent there was probably a consensus for preserving internal freedom for the grain trade but an equally strong determination to prevent any export from France. Textile towns in Normandy, which had taken a beating at the hands of British competition since the commercial treaty of 1786, lobbied hard for its repeal (indeed for prohibitions on *all* imported goods) while commercial entrepôts like Bordeaux, whose wine trade with England was flourishing, worked equally strenuously to retain it. When it came to colonial commerce, however, the merchants of Bordeaux, like those of Nantes and Rouen, suddenly stopped being free traders and argued (against the planters of the Antilles) for the preservation of the laws which forced colonial goods to be shipped exclusively through France. Needless to say, all of these parties resorted to the language of politics to justify their contradictory positions. But arguments for "liberty" or "patriotism" were but thin veneers cladding the tenacious defense of local interests.

With the momentous exception of the expropriation of the Church, between 1789 and 1792 the Revolution produced no significant transfer of social power. It merely accelerated trends that had been taking place over a longer period of time. The substitution of elected for appointed offices expanded the inclusiveness of government by bringing into the professions men who had been knocking at the door. But even before the Revolution that door was seldom the barred and bolted obstruction which subsequent rhetoric made it seem. As for the elite—both noble and ecclesiastical—it divided along lines of political conviction and regional solidarity, rather than social tiers. Those who clung to an anachronistic status that could only be preserved within a corporate society of orders were correspondingly penalized—stigmatized as uncitizens, forced into emigration or armed rebellion. Those, on the other hand, who were able to recast themselves as citizen-tribunes, servants of the state, and who were able to see their fortunes in terms of property rather than privilege, were able to make the crucial metamorphosis from nobles to notables. As landowners, state functionaries, departmental administrators and professional judges and doctors, bankers and manufacturers, they constituted a knot of influence and power that would effectively dominate French society for the next century.

i i THE INCONTINENCE
OF POLEMICS

This is not to imply, however, that *nothing* of consequence changed as a direct result of the first phase of the French Revolution. The liberties enshrined in the Declaration of the Rights of Man for the protection of free speech, publication and assembly had brought forth a political culture in which the liberation of disrespect literally knew no bounds. It was, by far, the most dramatic creation of the Revolution. For although its vituperative style and reigning conceptions had also been coined under the old regime by writers and journalists like Linguet and Mercier, the removal of censorship and prosecution made it possible for political argument to reach an unprecedentedly broad audience.

The result was a polemical incontinence that washed over the whole country. With news from Paris able to reach the eastern and southern limits of the country in three to four days, the Revolution nationalized information to the extent that one had to run very far indeed to escape the ubiquitous touch of politics. From army garrisons where soldiers demanded the right to fraternize with civilians and even attend meetings of clubs, to country churches where the doors were used for bulletin boards and the pulpit became a battleground of rival orthodoxies, to the balconies of boulevard theaters where crowds of journeymen artisans roared cheerful abuse and patriotic songs back at the actors, nothing outreached the long arm and booming voice of political harangue.

This degree of mobilization did not respect polite boundaries of privacy. Indeed privacy was itself suspect, being too close to the strategies of concealment that were said to be at the heart of aristocratic culture. So the tests of patriotic virtue did not stop at the bedroom door. Newspapers like Fréron's *Orateur du Peuple* enjoyed reporting (or inventing) stories of revolutionary Lysistratas who interrupted coition at critical moments to reprove their husbands for taking oaths of loyalty to Lafayette. "Stop, stop, *stop* right there," exclaimed one determined citizeness of the rue Saint-Martin in Paris; "nevermore shall you enjoy the tender caresses that I have so many times wasted on you until you abandon your infatuation with the Corrupter." By contrast, patriotic marriages were hailed as the rock on which a truly virtuous *patrie* would be built. In December 1790 Brissot ironically congratulated Camille Desmoulins on his marriage while expressing the hope that "in becoming happy their friend would be no less persistent as the defender of the public interest." One stage further on in the conjugal life cycle of patriots, prolific mothers were especially honored for their contribution to the *patrie*. One prodigy who claimed to have borne no less than twenty-five children was given the honor of carrying the national flag in a special ceremony in the Cathedral of Notre Dame at Rouen in May 1791.

Children were also conscripted into this world of relentless displays of public virtues. The Jacobins encouraged the formation of youth affiliates, the Young Friends of the Constitution, and occasionally allowed members to attend sessions of the "mother club" in Paris. Throughout France, "Battalions of Hope," consisting of boys between the ages of seven and twelve, were uniformed and taught to drill, recite passages from the Declaration of the Rights of Man and Citizen and parade before their doting citizen-parents in miniature versions of the uniform of the National Guard. In Lille, for example, a veteran soldier, the former Sieur de Boisragon, now just M. Chevallau, trained a group of eighty boys (as elsewhere, nicknamed, as a pun on the regiment of the Royal Bourbons, the "Royal Bon-Bons"). Together with his local *curé*, Chevallau organized a children's "*fédération*" complete with the benediction of the flag and the swearing of oaths. "We will live for our *patrie*," promised César Lachapelle, age eight, and Narcise Labussière, age nine, "and our last sighs will be for her." To the august deputies of the National Assembly they protested, "When our parents and teachers boast endlessly of the wisdom of your decrees and when from all parts of France we hear applause for your immortal work, when all of France showers blessings upon your heads, how can our hearts remain insensible. . . . No, Messieurs, recognition and respect know no age."

132. Le Sueur, gouache, oath of the children

A B O V E : 133. Plate representing the Bastille

B E L O W : 134. Sevres porcelain coffee cup and saucer
with children taking the patriotic oath

Nor was this kind of inspirational utterance confined to speeches, cere-monies and texts. It spilled over into the world of artifacts, covering ceramic dishes, coffee cups, pewter mugs with patriotic devices like the half-demolished Bastille surmounted by the Gallic cock greeting the dawn of freedom; the banners of the National Guard and the consecrated trinity of *"La Loi, le Roi et la Constitution."* Oberkampf's printed cotton manufacture at Jouy, which had first produced furnishing fabric with designs celebrating the American war, now turned to scenes from the epic days of 1789, so that the onslaught of political propaganda was as much a matter of graphics as of texts. The engravers of the rue Saint-Jacques who had turned out popular prints of saints, folk heroes and soldiers before the Revolution were now occupied almost full-time producing immense quantities of prints with overtly political subjects. The collections of the Bibliothèque Nationale contain literally tens of thousands of examples of these prints that not only documented for the illiterate the events of the Revolution and com-municated them to provincials far from Paris, but also established crucial stereotypes of heroes and villains. It is almost possible to calibrate the rise and fall of the prestige of figures like Necker, Lafayette and Mirabeau by the production rhythm and fluctuating tone of prints featuring those personalities.

Other forms of familiar illustrated literature were used in similar ways to inculcate the particular virtues advocated by competing revolutionary factions. Almanacs were a favorite medium. Sylvain Maréchal, for example, who had been imprisoned before the Revolution for producing his *Al-manach des Honnêtes Gens,* was now free to publish it, and his *Patriot's Portfolio* repeated his blend of practical information and utopian social egalitarianism. The playwright-actor Collot d'Herbois' *Almanach du Père Gérard* won a special prize from the Jacobins (awarded by a committee that included Condorcet and Grégoire) for being a work that combined the apostolic mission of political education with a deliberately simple manner meant to appeal to the peasants at whom it was ostensibly aimed. "Père Gérard" was a deputy to the Constituent from Rennes who had been celebrated for seating himself in the Estates-General in a plain brown fustian coat, apparently the very paragon of bucolic simplicity promoted in the Rousseauean code of social morality. And Collot had indeed managed a tone that dripped with rustic bonhomie, explaining the meaning of the term *constitution* by comparing it with the healthy body of a strapping peasant boy called Nicolas "whose healthy appetite, sane head and strong arms are the very picture of the Constitution."

The popular theater of the *vaudeville,* mixing song, dance, clowning and broad humor, was turned into yet another arm of patriotic propaganda.

Nicodemus in the Moon or the Pacific Revolution had a record-breaking first run of ninety performances at the Théâtre-Français, where it played to a genuinely mixed audience. It used the whole box of tricks from the boulevard du Temple and the Palais-Royal, exploiting the ballooning craze by sending its hero, the peasant Nicodemus—a peculiarly Gallic combination of simplicity and cunning à la Bourvil—aloft to the moon. There he discovered an amiable but forlorn king hectored by a difficult and devious wife. Nicodemus then paints a picture of an earthly paradise back in France, where his own sovereign freely accepted a revolution that had made the whole nation happy.

Even hairstyles were invested with political eloquence. Brissot's *Patriote Français,* for example, published a lengthy letter in October 1790 advocating short, straight, unpowdered hair as the appropriate patriotic coiffure. The reason given was that it had been the favored coiffure of the virtuous English Roundheads and, conversely, curled, lengthy tresses had been the outward sign of the vain, corrupt, aristocratic Cavaliers. As for the Romans, the writer assumed that decadent tyrants like Caesar and Antony fussed with their curling irons while Cassius and Marcus Brutus, "whose souls were proud and who struck terror into the heart of the dictator," cropped their locks short and combed their hair forward in the manner to be seen in Talma's stage roles. "This coiffure," the writer insisted, "is the only one which is suited to republicans: being simple, economical and requiring little time, it is care-free and so assures the independence of a person; it bears witness to a mind given to reflection, courageous enough to defy fashion."

Brissot's paper was not the only one to try to reinforce the news with editorializing, political preaching and exemplary anecdotes designed to create not just a curious but a morally alert readership. Of all the media through which a new political constituency was shaped, the press may have been the most powerful. The magnitude of its expansion after 1789 was itself astonishing. Before the Revolution there had been perhaps sixty newspapers in all of France—though as Jeremy Popkin has pointed out, the Francophone foreign gazettes were an important complement. By August 1792 there were close to five hundred in Paris alone. Not all of these, of course, were of consequence or could boast either a sustained life or more than a modest circulation. But the great successes, like Carra's *Annales Patriotiques,* certainly reached eight thousand, and the Abbé Cérutti's immensely popular *Feuille Villageoise,* meant to provide a political primer for the peasantry, reached far more. Jacques Godechot has even estimated that through extensive subscriptions taken by political clubs, Cérutti's paper may actually have reached a reading public of two hundred thousand—though this figure belongs to the realm of editorial optimization.

What was impressive about the explosion of the political press was not just its immensely expanded circulation but the huge range of styles, tones and formats adopted, embracing the tediously worthy reporting of the Constituent in Brissot's *Patriote Français* as well as the juicily scurrilous in the case of the much more readable *L'Orateur du Peuple.* Some papers, like Marat's, held the attention through the sheer relentless ferocity of their ranting and the waves of indignation and panic they could stir by pointing to hidden nests of traitors and conspirators—rather like political dowsers armed with accusatory divining rods. Others, still more experimental, like Hébert's *Père Duchesne,* and ephemeral publications like the apoplectic *Tailleur Patriotique* (Patriotic Tailor), contrived to reproduce the authentic voice of the *bon bougre*—the foulmouthed plain-talking man of the wine-shops and the markets, his head enveloped by the fumes of alcohol and tobacco and his tongue hot with expletives directed at the Autri-Chienne (the Austrian bitch, a.k.a the Queen). Their appeal was verbal violence, so that the *Patriotic Tailor,* for example, regularly described the clients who came to him to be measured for suits as *aristocrates à pendre* (aristocrats to hang).

The most successful of the papers were also meant as conversionary instruments, to stiffen the doubts of waverers, preach to the unenlightened and inform those who had difficulty understanding the decrees of the Assembly or the difference between "honest" and "feigned" patriots. Cérutti's *Feuille Villageoise* provided a primer for the Patriotic Peasant, offering advice on how to combat the equally pernicious blights of tree rot in the orchard and nonjuring priests in the pulpit. His paper also reproduced, with an ardent endorsement for general use, the text of Lequinio's Patriotic Prayer: "O God of Justice and Equality, since it has pleased you that our Good People has recovered all its rights, see that they are preserved despite the work of fools and fanatics and that brothers do not fight against brothers for fear they will all be vanquished by the Enemies of our Family." Cérutti also published accounts from far-flung missionaries of the revolutionary faith, hard at work spreading the gospel, often literally in their backyard. In one such letter, a schoolmaster reported that

> every Sunday in our village we gather in a little garden adjoining my house and there, seated on a mound, I read to our peasants, in a circle around me, the *Feuille Villageoise.* They listen so well that they make me repeat any word they do not understand. I explain to them everything that I know but often I realize that there are things I know little of or misunderstand.

According to Michael Kennedy's history of the Jacobins, *La Feuille Villageoise* was the subscription of choice in their clubs, especially in the provinces. And it was certainly in the popular societies that most Frenchmen—and some Frenchwomen—were initiated into the language of revolutionary politics. In its beginnings the Society of the Friends of the Constitution, which met at the convent of the Jacobins in the rue Saint-Honoré, was not so ambitious. It represented merely a continuation of the Breton Club of deputies at Versailles who had met to co-ordinate tactics that would ensure the victory of the Assembly against the machinations of the government. By expanding the society's membership to the public and lowering its annual subscription to twenty-four livres, payable monthly or quarterly, the Jacobins in Paris offered a place where citizens and their "mandatories" could debate public issues in an atmosphere of mutual reassurance. So even though it was not yet the hearth of militant egalitarianism it was to become after 1792, the society naturally generated criticism of governmental pragmatism or "moderatism," based on what it claimed to be the first principles of the Revolution.

In the spring of 1790, like-minded Patriots in provincial towns such as Dijon, Lille, Strasbourg, Grenoble and Marseille who wanted a rallying point from which they could denounce the intrigues of local recalcitrants (sometimes entrenched in local administrations) formed their own societies and wrote seeking affiliation with their "friends and brothers" in Paris. In turn, that "mother society" sent out activists to encourage the establishment of local cells in what one circular called "a holy coalition to maintain the Constitution," especially in towns where the society judged the true cause to be beleaguered. Sometimes the effort could go amiss, as when the actor Bordier was hanged at Rouen for inciting a popular insurrection; but more often the work was done peacefully and found a quick response in informal gatherings of zealots, be they lawyers, *savants,* officials or the inevitable local revolutionary *ci-devant* and patriotic curate.

By August 1790 the Paris Jacobins had twelve hundred members and a hundred and fifty affiliates in the provinces. A year later that number had risen to over four hundred. Such a phenomenal success can only be explained, as Kennedy has indicated, by the eighteenth-century addiction to clubby sociability, which suggests that the Jacobins inherited an emphasis on brotherly solidarity and equality from the equally popular Masonic lodges that had mushroomed around France in the later part of the century. They also took from Masonry the pleasure of ritual and arcane symbolism, grafting the messages of revolutionary politics onto Masonic emblems like the eye of surveillance and the stonemason's level (signifying equality) and the Masons' obsession with triangles. The high-minded professions of faith in the universal fraternity of well-disposed men were also reiterations of a familiar Masonic refrain. What was most strikingly different, however, was the Jacobins' abhorrence of secrecy and their proselytizing view of their clubs as schools of public morality.

Physically, too, the Jacobin clubs were a cross between a church and a school. Often they were located in disused (or, latterly, dispossessed) monasteries, sometimes in local government offices or even small theaters or taverns. Their layout almost invariably provided for a tribune for the speaker at the front of the room, raised on a low dais on which would also be chairs for the presiding officers of the society. Nonmembers might be admitted to meetings but were divided off from members by a low balustrade or cord strung across the width of the room. The Paris club, though, banked its seats along the wall-length of the old library, giving greater visibility to both speakers and audience. Decorating the walls were the obligatory signs of fraternity: plaster portrait busts of exemplary figures from antiquity like Junius Brutus and Cato, together with more contemporary heroes: Jean-Jacques Rousseau, Benjamin Franklin and (in those provincial clubs far from Paris, where he was more mistrusted than admired by the Jacobins) Mirabeau. Between these busts, framed copies of the

135. Anonymous engraving, interior of the Jacobin Club in Paris in early 1791.
Mirabeau is speaking from the tribune, at right; Charles de Lameth occupies the
presidency, at left.

Declaration of the Rights of Man often hung alongside engravings of the great revolutionary *journées*, usually taken from the series produced by the *Tableaux de la Révolution Française.*

But it was the sounds rather than the sights of the Jacobins that were their most compelling feature. The walls of their clubs echoed to endless speeches, arguments, critical readings of legislation—set-piece oratory in imitation of the virtuosi of the Paris club and the National Assembly. Every provincial club would have its local star emulating in expressions of patriotic indignation and Ciceronian rhetoric the alternative rhetorical styles of Mirabeau (hot), Barnave (crisp) and Robespierre (logical-sentimental). And it was in the large local clubs, at Bordeaux and Lyon, for example, that the next generation of revolutionary politicians who would go on to be the Ciceros and Catos of the Legislative Assembly—Lanthénas, Isnard, Vergniaud and Gensonné—had their apprenticeship.

Even during the early period, when their membership included many "moderates" (either declared or concealed monarchists), the Jacobins cast themselves in a role oppositional to the constituted authorities—local and national. They consciously set themselves up as the moral guardians of revolutionary principles who would unswervingly follow their patriotic duty even if it meant going against the majority of the Constituent or locally elected officials. Nonetheless their militancy was of a purely political rather than social kind. If they were democrats they were relatively well-heeled ones, comprising for the most part the same kind of people as those who were National Guard officers: professionals, writers and journalists, rather more tradesmen and merchants than would have been found in the local administrations and, perhaps 20 per cent of them, artisans, overwhelmingly independent master craftsmen.

That middling twenty-four-livre constituency left a space to the left of the Jacobins to be filled by political clubs catering specifically to the groups that had been excluded from the Revolution's first definition of citizenship. The most obvious of these were women and wage earners (though no society to my knowledge was founded for that very large group of the excluded—domestic servants). This was the stated aim of the revived Cordeliers, who dropped their admission fee to just one livre, four sous. Their meetings, according to an English observer, consisted of rowdies whose "dress was so filthy and unkempt that one would have taken them for a gathering of beggars." But dozens of smaller societies followed the example of the Cordeliers' policy of inclusiveness. The most notable were the Minimes, the Society of Indigents and especially the Fraternal Society for Patriots of Both Sexes, founded by the schoolteacher Claude Dansard. All of these clubs admitted women, and the Société Fraternelle in particu-

LA NATION LA LOI
LE ROI

UNION   LIBERTÉ   FORCE

136. Allegorical print celebrating the oath
to "The Nation, the Law and King"
taken in the Fraternal Society for Patriots
of Both Sexes. Minerva armed with the
pike and hat of liberty stretches her hand
over the flame of the constitution.

lar, women like Louise Robert (the daughter of the revolutionary Breton aristocrat Kéralio and the editor of the *Mercure Nationale*); Pauline Léon, the chocolate maker's daughter; Théroigne de Méricourt; and the remarkable Etta Palm d'Aelders (who was, simultaneously, a spy for the Dutch Stadholder's government and a committed feminist)—each of whom played a prominent part in the organization to which she belonged. It was from these clubs that proposals emanated to form companies of armed women—for example, to guard the royal family in the Tuileries in 1791 and as a frontier regiment in 1792—as well as reiterations of the demands first articulated by Olympe de Gouges and Etta Palm for female suffrage. They took particular exception to the typical Jacobin relegation of women to the hearth and home and comments like that of the brewer Santerre that "the men of this district prefer on coming home from work to find their household in order rather than to see their wives returning from an assembly where they do not always acquire a spirit of gentleness."

It was in the popular societies—attracting in Paris altogether no more than two to three thousand adherents in this period—that the ideals of social egalitarianism and democratic autonomy were pushed to their most extreme point. It was also there that the rhetoric of conspiracy and denunciation against traitors within and without the country was most shrill. While

Marat's and Fréron's papers were thought too coarse for the taste of Jacobins, they were read aloud to great approval in the Cordeliers. And just as the Jacobins' debates created the next wave of revolutionary politicians who would dominate the years of war and Terror, the popular societies produced still more militant figures who would in turn taunt them for their elitism and pusillanimity—extraordinary figures like the legless cripple Pepin-Dégrouhette, failed playwright, practicing lawyer and the advocate of the market porters of Paris.

It was also in these clubs that the dichotomy in the character of the French Revolution was most starkly exposed. The rage which bounced off the crossed daggers and production-line busts of Brutus, the table-pounding choruses of "Ça Ira" (*"tous les aristocrates on les pendra"* ["all the aristocrats will hang"]) corresponded exactly to the kind of anticapitalist, antimodernist fury embedded in the work of Linguet and Mercier that antedated the Revolution. The rhetoric was Rousseau with a hoarse voice and sharpened with bloody-minded impatience. The Revolution had led the members of the clubs to believe a world of economic and social justice was at hand, but as far as they could see they still had to pay taxes on their wine and tobacco, still had to implore bosses for work for which they were paid in paper money that depreciated through the depredations of speculators. The government and the Constituent were still filled with *les Grands,* "greedy financiers, gorged with the purest blood of the people, cynics, fools, men puffed up with pride" who had created barriers of eligibility that would have excluded even Jean-Jacques himself from sitting among them.

The antithesis of these "devourers of the substance of the people" was "Jacques Cordonnier" (Jack Shoemaker), a paragon invented by the *Révolutions de Paris* in December 1790, "a respectable artisan gathering his neighbors at his house and by the light of his lamp . . . reading the decrees of the national assembly, seasoning the reading with his own reflections and those of his attentive neighbors." It was the simple ardor of such *honnêtes hommes* that could make true democracy viable, if only those in political authority would have the courage to trust the people with their laws as Rousseau had (they claimed) recommended. One of the most extraordinary proposals in this direction came from none other than the *ci-devant* Marquis de Girardin, who in June 1791 argued that all laws enacted by the national legislature should be submitted to popular universal referenda. These plebiscites evidently embodied the meeting of history with theory, for, in his view, they would be both the descendant of the ancient Frankish horseback assemblies and the repository of Rousseau's omniscient General Will. Girardin's optimism about this level of popular commitment to civic duty was such that he even assumed that Sundays—devoted to praying or drinking or both—might be set aside for weekly votes!

Girardin's plebiscitary utopia and the *Révolutions de Paris'* invention of the ideal citizen-worker never stood any chance of being institutionalized in the French Revolution, not even at the height of popular influence on the National Convention. But their necessarily unsatisfied rhetoric and their chronic obsession with exploitation, conspiracy and public punishment were capable of mobilizing angry and powerful crowds that, at critical moments, decisively affected the course of events. Ultimately this perpetual oppositional pull was to make the Revolution completely unworkable, for it opposed impossible demands of political purity to the working needs of the French state. It opposed local, autonomous microdemocracies to the requirements of centralized power; the satisfaction of material needs through enforced intervention in the economy to the mobilization of capital for the state and the market; unlimited freedom of expression and assembly to the regularized transaction of public business; and summary, often spontaneous punishment to the orderly enforcement of the law.

The dilemma for successive generations of those politicians who graduated from oratory to administration was that they owed their own power to precisely the kind of rhetoric that made their subsequent governance impossible. The Revolution as insurrection would have been impossible without regular effusions of spleen and blood, but the Revolution as government was impossible unless they could be selectively managed.

It was the first time that a generation of revolutionary politicians had discovered the depressing dilemma that, in this sense, revolutionary liberty entailed revolutionary terror. But they would not be the last to fall apart over its consequences.

iii MIRABEAU PAYS HIS DEBTS

On July 3, 1790, Mirabeau kissed Marie-Antoinette's hand in a leafy corner of the park at Saint-Cloud and, like some badly dressed knight-valiant, promised: "Madame, the monarchy is saved." Though the Queen had once said that "our situation could never be so desperate as to have to resort to Mirabeau," she managed not to flinch as the pitted face bent over her arm. She had even rehearsed a suitable way of flattering the ogre. According to Mme Campan, she opened by remarking that "in the presence of an ordinary enemy who had sworn the destruction of the monarchy . . . I should be taking the most ill-advised step, but in the presence of a Mirabeau . . ."

For his part, Mirabeau was touched by the pallid woman with wispy gray hair, not exactly the Messalina of the pornographic satires circulating in Paris. He was also impressed by her fortitude and intelligence, especially when he compared it with the King's hapless irresolution. "The King has only one man" on whom he could depend, he remarked, "—his wife." Afterwards, in cool reflection, his impulsive gesture may have reminded him of Lafayette's tactical gallantry on the balcony of Versailles on the bloody morning of October 6. How embarrassing to have repeated the *beau geste* of someone Mirabeau so heartily despised as a self-important mediocrity; worse, a self-important *inarticulate* mediocrity! At least there had been no crowds on hand, though he worried that two grenadiers had recognized the two strollers in the park.

Saint-Cloud was a summer retreat where the royal family could escape the relentless daily scrutiny at the Tuileries, and the stinging abuse of the Paris press. For two months now Mirabeau had been taking the King's money. But he had been doing so with a clean conscience, never supposing he had been bought off, but rather that he was being paid for offering advice to the King on how to reestablish his authority. It was counsel that Mirabeau fervently believed was indispensable if the monarch was to be rescued from both counter-revolution and democratic nullity.

Not that the rewards for the "treaty" he had signed with the court in May were paltry. The ink was hardly dry when his debts, all 208,000 livres of them, were suddenly taken care of, effaced, gone. The two millstones of his life—his father and his creditors—were now both lifted from his neck. His father Victor, the apoplectic old tyrant, that self-designated "Friend of Mankind," had died two days before the fall of the Bastille, still jeering at his older son, whom he had imprisoned so many times and whom he now disinherited in favor of his younger son, the ultra-royalist. That fat dimwit was a constant thorn in Mirabeau's side, relishing his notoriety as a contributor to the counter-revolutionary journal *The Acts of the Apostles* the better to embarrass his elder brother. He was lampooned in the patriot press as "Mirabeau-Tonneau" (Mirabeau the Barrel), but somehow the nickname implicated Gabriel's own sobriquet "Mirabeau-Tonnerre" (Mirabeau the Thunderer) in its absurdity. His contribution to restoring order in the army had been to steal flags and tassels from his own regiment of Touraine quartered at Perpignan when he found that the rank and file were in revolt against their officers. Caught with the regimental standards in his trunk, he was arrested and only his elder brother's intervention on the grounds of the personal inviolability of a deputy to the Assembly secured his release. His gratitude took the form of emigration to the Rhineland, where he attempted to organize a brigade of "Death-Hussars" before impaling himself on the sword of another officer with whom he had picked a drunken quarrel.

With a monthly allowance of six thousand livres, Mirabeau *aîné* could at last afford to live in the manner which his own sense of magnificence had always required. He moved out of the apartment rented from Talma's actress friend Julie Carreau and into a handsome townhouse on the rue de la Chaussée d'Antin. He commanded a chef with whose culinary splendors he managed to take the edge off the wrath of even leading zealots like Camille Desmoulins. (Some thought the food overspiced. "I almost spat blood when I dined with Mirabeau," recalled one woman guest with a tender palate.) There was a valet who laid out those suits with the jeweled buttons that, to Mirabeau's delight, raised eyebrows at the Jacobins. Best of all he had a secretary, paid for by the court, with the perfect name (for an amanuensis) M. Comps, who dutifully transcribed an immense number of his memoranda and speeches. And he was damned if long-faced *bougres* like the Lameth brothers were going to rob him of innocent vanities like dressing his flunkies in livery and sporting the family arms on his shiny new carriage. Finally, he at last became a landowner, acquiring (though never paying for) a pretty seventeenth-century house and park once owned by the *philosophe* Helvétius, at Argenteuil.

The unlikely rapprochement between Mirabeau and the court had been brought about by his friend the Comte de La Marck, a Belgian aristocrat who had settled in France, bought land and been elected to the Estates-General. La Marck had insisted to the Austrian Ambassador Mercy d'Argenteau, the Queen's closest confidant, that Mirabeau was burning to be of service to the King, and in March 1790 the signal was sent from the other end to sound him out. By the end of May Mirabeau, duly signed up, fought his first battle in the Constituent, for the right to preserve some part for the monarchy in decisions of war and peace.

It was imprudent for Mirabeau to be on the monarchy's payroll at the precise moment when the publication of the *Livre Rouge* (Red Book), exposing the secret pensions of the old regime, was causing so much uproar. His suddenly improved life-style could hardly escape general attention, especially when it coincided suspiciously on May 21 with a passionate speech arguing for the retention of royal powers in declaring war. Soon after, a pamphlet written by Lacroix circulated in Paris claiming to have discovered his "Treason." Mirabeau's recklessness can only be explained by the fact that he believed his conduct to be quite pure—that he had received a fee for advice tendered disinterestedly and in complete accordance with the political principles he had always held.

At the core of those principles was the establishment of a constitutional monarchy that accepted the conquests of 1789 but without resigning itself to being a passive instrument of the will of a legislature. Mirabeau was, as he wrote to La Marck, in favor of "the establishment of order, not of the old order." The premise of his policy, then, was that the monarchy should eschew any flirtation with counter-revolution; should wave adieu to any thought of restoring a society of orders with corporate institutions like Parlements. Free, socially blind justice and a free press were also, in his view, irreversible. The crown should, moreover, embrace the Civil Constitution of the Clergy as the logical extension of Gallicanism and the absolutely indispensable means of avoiding bankruptcy. At the same time, however, it had to be a genuine executive, free to appoint ministers—and despite the Assembly's decree of November 7, 1789, Mirabeau still urged that they be accountable to and chosen from the legislature to avoid a constant battle between the two arms of the constitution. Unless the crown took urgent steps to recover some meaningful powers of government, he argued, the quasi-autonomous sovereignty of the legislature would become an accomplished fact. "The people would end by becoming accustomed to another type of government, and royalty, entirely null, steadily vilified but nonetheless very costly, would soon appear to be only a phantom."

These positions, as well as their immediate political and tactical implications, Mirabeau set out in two documents, one in October 1790 and the other in a much fuller memorandum for Montmorin, the Minister of Foreign Affairs, on December 23. The long "Aperçu" is an extraordinary work not for any great theoretical profundity but for its astonishingly modern understanding of the nature of revolutionary power. Before Lenin, Mirabeau was the most intelligent analyst of the machinery of tactics in revolutionary situations, able to see with the utmost clarity what lay below the rhetoric of which most revolutionary discourse was composed. When he came to discuss what he called the *irritabilité* of the National Assembly—its propensity to thwart decisive government in factious debate—he explained this as a natural outcome of posturing theatricality (to which, of course, he had himself unforgettably contributed). "It has its orators, its spectators, its theater and its *parterre*, its lobby and its galleries, it applauds talent when it serves its purposes and humiliates it if it contradicts it." He also appreciated the need for a successful government to have its own organs of press propaganda, cheaply priced and widely circulated so as to avoid surrendering the field to perpetual oppositions.

Mirabeau listed the other obstructions to the recovery of royal authority. He started with the King's own indecisiveness; the limitations placed on the Queen's action; the constant threat of physical intimidation in Paris and the demagoguery which incited it. To set the King on his own feet he needed able and determined ministers (like himself) and perhaps Talley-rand, Le Chapelier, Thouret. Necker, whom Mirabeau had never been able to abide, had finally resigned at the end of September, fatally lamed by his inability to deliver on his promises of fiscal magic or to live up to the Messiah-like publicity that had greeted his recall to office. But Neckerites like Saint-Priest and de La Tour du Pin were still in office, and Mirabeau urged a much cleaner break. Indeed, in a daring and canny move, Mirabeau recommended appointing ministers from among the zealots of the Jacobins, drawing the sting of their opposition. If they were in power, he guaranteed (with great prescience), the objective needs of the state were so compelling that they would neutralize their ideology. "Jacobins in the ministry," he commented, "would not be Jacobin ministers."

The other major figure from whom Louis had to be rescued was Mira-beau's arch-bugbear, the insufferable "Gilles César," Lafayette. It had been particularly galling to Mirabeau to see the Fédération stage-managed for the General's exclusive benefit and with the King deliberately reduced to an auxiliary role. Had Louis taken the oath at the altar—in the focal center of the proceedings—it might have set a perfect symbolic seal on his acceptance of the Revolution. Instead his part had been made shadowy and ambiguous and had not quieted the talk that the King was really still a grudging participant in the ceremonies. The National Guard, then, had to be reor-ganized and placed more firmly under government control if the King was not always to be a hostage to a Parisian army.

Since nothing at all could be done about the political effervescence of Paris, the best thing was to let it have its head. The more outrageous it became and the greater its appetite for anarchy and militancy, the wider would be the breach with the provinces which it presumed to govern in the name of "the Nation." As the conduct of government became paralyzed by threats from Parisian insurrections, the provinces would be persuaded that stronger public power was needed and would resent the monopoly of the capital. This turned out to be one of Mirabeau's most prescient forecasts, all the more impressive since it was made at a time when the sovereign fiction of a united nation had just been consummated on the Champ de Mars.

A similar solution to the truculence of the Assembly suggested itself. Let the Assembly be discredited by becoming hopelessly polarized between fatuous counter-revolutionaries on the one hand and impossible zealots on the other. When it had finally succeeded in making government impossible, the King might, in a bold move, call another election for a replacement legislature empowered to revise what for Mirabeau was a dangerously unworkable constitution. Here too he had a shrewd tactical move to recommend that would not be open to imputations of counter-revolution. Deputies to the new assembly, he argued, should only be eligible for the constituencies in which they currently resided, thus, he supposed, precluding the militants of the Paris clubs from standing as representatives of, say, Arras or Marseille. Pending its change of location, that second assembly should be provided with its own military force to release it from dependence on the Paris National Guard.

There was great wisdom and great craziness in Mirabeau's projects. On the one hand the notion of a Jacobin ministry proposing the replacement of the Constituent seems wholly fantastical. But on the other hand, Mirabeau saw with clear-eyed acumen the issues that would determine allegiance in a revolutionary era. Taxes, for example, would be one matter where "the veil will be torn asunder," for

> the people have been promised more than can be promised; they have been given hopes that it will be impossible to realize; they have been allowed to shake off a yoke which it will be impossible to restore and even if there should be fine retrenchments and economies . . . the expenses of the new regime will actually be heavier than the old, and in the last analysis the people will judge the revolution by this fact alone—does it take more or less money? Are they better off? Do they have more work? And is that work better paid?

The perspicacity of this judgment was all the more impressive coming from someone who was the acknowledged master of revolutionary rhetoric, but someone who evidently was not also bewitched by his own hyperbole. Mirabeau lent enormous passion to his defense of the mandatory use of the tricolor flag on naval vessels because he understood that what was at stake was not merely "a bagatelle" but (in another uncanny anticipation of twentieth-century concerns) what he called "the language of signs." That, he insisted, was everywhere the most potent symbolic code, denoting solidarity or conspiracy, loyalty or defiance. If naval officers were permitted to fly the white flag—that is to say, the color of counter-revolution—it would be a brazen announcement of their contempt for the Revolution. "Believe me, do not slumber in a dangerous sense of safety," he told the Assembly, "for your awakening will be terrible." Finally, Mirabeau foresaw that the imposition of a Parisian definition of revolutionary purity on the rest of the country would break open deep rifts that, unless managed by a solicitous government, would make civil war a certainty.

And even though his vision of a responsible monarchy, with ministers accountable to a legislature, seems hopelessly optimistic, given the nature of the historical players in 1791, it was not, of itself, an implausible scenario for France. With the periodic alternation of kings, emperors and presidents, most of French history in the two centuries that followed fully vindicated his vision.

In two matters alone—albeit ones of the utmost importance—Mirabeau's habitual shrewdness failed him. In the first place he flattered himself that by becoming a retainer of the court he was also becoming its political educator. He was not so naive as to suppose that Louis was ready to act on the lengthy and subtle instructions he was receiving. One wonders, in fact, if the King, who was steadily becoming more immobilized by helplessness and depression, actually read them. But in any event Mirabeau thought it his duty to articulate his plan for the salvation of the state and believed that the memoranda would have a cumulative effect in gradually showing Louis that there was an alternative to either capitulation or counter-revolution. The reality at court, however, was much less promising. The more Mirabeau deluded himself into believing he was the monarchy's tutor, the more the circle around the Queen rejoiced at having tethered a formidable opponent. The more he barked at the increasing number of his enemies to the left in the Jacobins, the better the court liked him for dividing its foes.

Even so, success at reeducating the King was not out of the question. Throughout 1790 Louis remained genuinely uncertain about his political direction and much less committed to counter-revolutionary intervention than the Queen was. What finally moved him to abandon any further thought of managing the Revolution along the lines recommended by Mirabeau was the religious question. In this all-important matter it is hard to know whether Mirabeau was obtusely incomprehending or actually ultra-Machiavellian. He had eagerly agreed to deliver the first salvo in the Assembly in November 1789 in support of Talleyrand's plan and, as the legislation to create a state church had become more detailed, had lent enthusiastic support at every stage. In Provence he saw the large Protestant population—well endowed, well disciplined and conspicuous for its civic and economic virtues—as a bulwark of the new regime. In the Jews of Bordeaux and Avignon he saw yet another commercial and erudite culture that made the dogma of Catholic monopoly a reprehensible absurdity. His own favorite banker in Paris, Panchaud, seemed to be half Protestant, half Jew.

And all other questions aside, the issue of the Civil Constitution was as much one of national integrity as social utility and philosophical humanity. The moral institutions of France should not, Mirabeau believed, be determined by dumb allegiance to a glorified Italian bishop who based his authority on the demonstrably risible claim of the succession to St. Peter. That issue of allegiance had become more serious when the Archbishop of Aix, Boisgelin, published his *Exposition* of the principles on which Pope Pius VI rejected all collaboration with the Constitution, and in effect threatened excommunication for all those who collaborated in the election of bishops and priests. Things became still more acute in November 1790, when the deputy Voidel described clerical resistance to the Civil Constitution as a kind of conspiracy involving priests urging troops to attack National Guardsmen and defy local authorities. (Indeed, revolutionary prints of the riots in the south commonly show priests holding up crosses to bless crowds attacking National Guardsmen in the manner of the Cardinal of Lorraine blessing the daggers in Chénier's *Charles IX*). To force the issue Voidel proposed that all clergy be made to swear an oath of undivided loyalty to the Constitution *within eight days.* In the debate of November 26 that deadline was extended to the end of the year, but it represented a brutal determination on the part of the state to test to the limit its enforceable sovereignty.

Mirabeau seemed to be single-minded on the matter. He denounced the episcopal deputies to the Assembly (forty out of forty-four of whom had rejected the Constitution) as hypocrites for claiming to want to prevent schism but urging their flocks to resist the laws of the state. To the Abbé Maury's insistence that bishops received their immediate authority from God through his vicar on earth, Mirabeau retorted that the division of the Church into units like dioceses was simply a matter of "ecclesiastical police" and administrative convenience with nothing sacred about it. For that matter papal authority was merely such a political jurisdiction writ large. The more withering his ridicule, the louder the applause, and his comments were entirely in keeping with his convictions and those of spiritual co-citizens like the Abbés Grégoire and Lamourette (who had written much of the speech). But, as Mirabeau noted in his private letters to La Marck, if the King was looking for an issue that would create disaffection from the Assembly out in the provinces, this was an ideal opportunity.

It was difficult, though, for Louis XVI to endorse Mirabeau's tactical cynicism. After much agonizing he had been persuaded by liberal bishops like Champion de Cicé of Bordeaux and the Archbishop of Vienne to sign the Civil Constitution. But the strictures from Rome increasingly troubled his conscience, especially since they were very eloquently defended not only inside the Assembly by Maury and Boisgelin but outside in newspapers and broadsides. He still liked to think of himself as the Rex Christianissimus anointed with the holy ampule at Reims: the sworn upholder of the apostolic faith. It was with the gravest misgivings, then, that he signed into law the Assembly's decree giving the traditional clergy of France—constituting perhaps half of the Assembly's own number and in certain regions like the west, southwest and Alsace-Lorraine an even greater proportion—a choice of being rebels or heretics, disfranchised or excommunicated.

It was surely this act which divided Louis' conduct into a public mask and a private confession. Encouraged by Marie-Antoinette, who regarded the ordination of constitutional bishops (by Talleyrand, who had already *resigned* his bishopric) as a blasphemous farce, Louis increasingly turned to private chaplains for confession. But in February 1791 the issue could no longer be kept from the public when his ancient aunts, Adélaide and Victoire, openly signified their dissent from the law by announcing their intention to go to Rome for Holy Week. Mirabeau strongly advised the King to forbid their journey since, he said, not only would it look as though he were condoning the infraction of his own laws but the trip would be taken as a rehearsal of his own emigration. Already journalists like Desmoulins and Fréron were insisting that the aunts renounce the million livres they enjoyed from the civil list if they wanted to consume it at Rome. The tocsins of the Paris sections were rung and meetings gathered to debate ways to prevent, if necessary with force, the departure of the *tantes*. The King, however, did nothing to prevent the journey and the two pious old ladies, sublimely indifferent to much of this agitation, set off with their usual modest retinue of twenty, accompanied by the commander of the Versailles National Guard, Berthier. Bellerive, their château, was overrun by crowds of angry *poissardes*, but it was at Arnay-le-duc that their carriages were stopped on the orders of a zealously patriotic mayor.

For Mirabeau, their departure was a matter of the greatest political imprudence, but he felt strongly that the Revolution had established as absolute the right of freedom of movement (something that had been frequently denied to him by his father's use of *lettres de cachet*). If the aunts had not actually violated any law there should be no reason to deny them that basic liberty, and he succeeded in persuading the Assembly to agree. On February 28 that issue became even more acute when the Assembly debated a law regulating the movement of suspected émigrés. The proposal was for a committee of three, appointed by the Assembly, to determine the right of anyone to exit and enter France, and to identify suspect absentees and to command their return on pain of being declared rebels.

Mirabeau understood intuitively that this was a moment of truth for the Revolution. His deepest conviction, expressed to the Assembly, was that such restrictions were irreconcilable with the liberty of movement guaranteed by the Declaration of Rights and the Constitution. But his debating tactics were maladroit. Trying to preempt discussion and even to avoid a reading of the proposal, he insisted on reading a letter he had written to the King of Prussia on the same matter declaring that men could not be forcibly tied to territory since they were not things—"fields or cattle." While he did not deny the validity of some sort of police, he was adamant in his insistence that its activities had to be conducted strictly through due process of law. Anything else would, he predicted, lead to dictatorship. As for the proposed law, it was "barbaric."

In a twentieth-century representative democracy it is impossible to read Mirabeau's speech (and the several further interruptions by which he tried to dominate the proceedings) without bearing witness to the irrefutable truth of his remarks and the moral nobility with which they were expressed. He was absolutely right. It was indeed *the* turning point of the French Revolution—the moment at which, less than two years after the opening of the Estates-General, it licensed itself as a police state. Mirabeau was not so naive as to close his eyes to genuine conspiracies and counter-revolutionary plots, especially thick on the ground in the Midi. That very same day, February 28, a group of army officers had been discovered in the King's apartments in the Tuileries with concealed swords and daggers, worn, they said, "to protect the King." But none of this, in Mirabeau's view, came remotely close to justifying the new regime appropriating powers for itself that might have shamed the old.

The debate degenerated into a procedural brawl between supporters of the original motion and Mirabeau, who wanted it replaced by a declaration on the unconstitutionality of any laws restricting freedom of movement. At one point he was accused of dictating to the Assembly, to which he responded rather self-righteously by proclaiming that "all my life I have fought despotism and I will continue to fight it all my life." When there was further murmuring on the left, he shouted like an irate schoolmaster, "Silence, the thirty voices!" The reproof was particularly mortifying to Barnave and the Lameths since it shrank their claims to represent the People into the head count of an unimpressive faction.

Mirabeau was not forgiven for this public dressing-down. That evening he was turned away from the house of the Duc d'Aiguillon, an old friend, with whom he had been bidden to dine. Later, Adrien Duport was astonished to see him calmly walk through the doors of the Jacobin club just as Duport was giving the society an account of the infamy of a fellow member. "The men most dangerous to liberty are not far from here," he announced, "indeed they are with us now, men in whom we have placed the greatest hopes." Fingers pointed at Mirabeau, shouts of "traitor" rained down on his head. "Yes, M. de Mirabeau," said Alexandre de Lameth, beside himself with rage, "we are not the thirty of this morning but a hundred and fifty that will never be divided." Mirabeau was accused of wanting to destroy the Jacobins over whom he had presided the previous November; of defaming and belittling his brother members; of betraying the Revolution itself.

Taken aback by the violence of the accusations, Mirabeau defended himself as best as he could, professing in the end devotion to the Jacobins as well as to the Revolution, his differences with them on this issue notwithstanding. Two years later that kind of publicly expressed difference (especially with Robespierre) would be literally fatal. But Mirabeau, apparently at the height of his powers, shrugged it off. His standing in the Assembly remained high. He had been an exemplary President in January, taking care to be impartial, and his intervention against the emigration law meant that he had real influence on the monarchist right. His latest Genevan scriptwriter-collaborator, Solomon Reybaz, was proving to be inspired, and Mirabeau was full of grand projects, none more important than an ambitious law on national education he had prepared with Talleyrand.

A month later he was dead.

On March 25 he had spent the night with two dancers from the Opéra, but whatever struck him with violent intestinal cramps two days later at Argenteuil was more than the penalties of sexual excess. He endured a journey to Paris to defend his friend La Marck's concession with the great Anzin coal mines in the Pas-de-Calais against the claim that the mineral rights belonged "to the nation." Reybaz had written an extraordinary panegyric to the intrepidity of the industrial entrepreneur, full of smoking mineshafts and heroic millions sunk into the greedy earth. Racked with pain and looking terrible, Mirabeau arrived at La Marck's house and promptly collapsed on the floor. You must not go, said his friend. I must and shall, said the tribune, and, fortified by a bottle of Esterhazy Tokay, managed to get to the Assembly and deliver the speech. His colleagues saw a phantom Mirabeau: white-faced, greasy with sweat, his frizzy hair gone lank and straight with sickness. The great baritone was now muted into a chesty growl. "Your case is won," he told La Marck afterwards, "and I am dead."

It was no exaggeration. A few days' rest at Argenteuil made him feel well enough to return to Paris, and he even tried an evening at the Italiéns to listen to the diva Morichelli. He left halfway through the performance, shivering, refusing to wait in a café until a carriage could be found, and staggering home. His friend and physician, Cabanis, found him prostrate, coughing blood. Just what was wrong with him was disputed then and has been since. Fréron, of course, and other enemy journalists implied he had finally been struck down by sexual disease. After an autopsy to investigate whether he had been poisoned, he was declared to have died of lymphatic pericarditis, complicated by inflammations of the liver, kidneys and stomach. But whatever the final cause, Mirabeau knew that he was dying and was determined to go in a style appropriate to his oversized life. Despondent crowds milled around his house as a stream of visitors passed through. One was Talleyrand, freshly excommunicated by the Pope and telling everyone delightedly about it. "A worthy confessor," said one wag. They talked for two hours with the elegant banter and intellectual purpose that had always formed the syntax of their peculiar friendship. "Conversation is supposed to be bad for the sick," said Mirabeau, "but one could live very well surrounded by friends and even die agreeably."

Talleyrand later commented, somewhat unkindly, that Mirabeau "had staged his own death." Perhaps he recalled his friend's remark on hearing the sound of cannon: "Have they already begun the funeral of Achilles?" But the deathbed was for the stoic neoclassicists of the late eighteenth century an exemplary art form, celebrated in David's great canvases of the deaths of Seneca and of Socrates. Mirabeau, too, wanted to depart with his affairs in order, surrounded by friends and acolytes, having made proper farewells. He urged La Marck to remove or burn any compromising papers and, though still more indebted than endowed, settled twenty-four thousand livres on his illegitimate son by Yet-Lie, Coco.

In the room below, his secretary, Comps, possessed by a fit of romantic melancholy, knifed himself in an attempt to follow his master. Oblivious to the melodrama, propped up against great puffy bolsters with the spring sunshine pouring in from his garden courtyard, Mirabeau announced to Cabanis on the morning of April 2 that he would like a shave, since, "My friend, I will die today. When one has come to that, all one can do is be perfumed, crowned with flowers, enveloped in music and wait comfortably for the sleep from which one will never awake."

iv RITES OF PASSAGE

Mirabeau's corpse was hardly cold before legends settled around the bier. At the autopsy ordered by the *procureur* of his Paris *section*, it was rumored, the defunct hero revealed an imposing erection. It was this evidence of "satyriasis" which led his son to characterize Mirabeau's notorious erotic appetite as "involuntary." His last words had actually been a request to Dr. Cabanis for opium, that he might be spared further pain. But the grief-stricken public needed something more edifying. So it was reported that he had provided his own oracular epitaph in the manner of the Stoics: "I

137. De Launay le Jeune (after Borel), *The Last Words of Mirabeau*, 1791

take with me the death of the monarchy. The factions will prey upon its remains." The words, or variations of them, appeared in many of the memorial prints that were hurriedly produced to assuage the stricken population of Paris. In one by Borel, Mirabeau's pessimism is transformed into a determination to "fight the factions wherever they may be," a sentiment engraved by his bed above copies of the Declaration of the Rights of Man and the Constitution. While Death approaches from behind a grieving France, Mirabeau points to a drape lifted by Truth, revealing in the right background a dismal scene of strife as "faction" reduces crown, clergy and people to a warring chaos.

When the news was brought to the Constituent Assembly, a crushing sense of loss immediately fell over the gathering, drawing into its shadow even those, like Barnave, who had been among Mirabeau's bitterest enemies. Sobbing broke out here and there as Bertrand Barère proposed that the entire Assembly, rather than just a deputation, attend the funeral. Talleyrand then stood as a last witness and communicant, the necessary Elisha. "I went yesterday to see M. de Mirabeau; there were many people in the house and I went with an even greater measure of sadness than that of the public sorrow. The sight of desolation filled one with the picture of death; it was everywhere save in the spirit of the one in most imminent danger. . . ." Mirabeau had given him his last speech, a gift snatched from the thief Death himself, the testimony of a public man.

What followed, alas, did not live up to this stunning piece of memorial stagecraft. Talleyrand read a lengthy and uncharacteristically dull discussion, written by Solomon Reybaz, of the laws of inheritance, the saving grace of which was that its subject was so obviously on Mirabeau's mind as he approached his end. The man who just before his death had argued so passionately for heroic materialism completed his career by commissioning an argument in the opposite vein: for the priority of fraternal justice (that is to say, inalienable equal inheritance) over the free disposition of legacies. Doubtless his own disinheritance had not been far from his mind.

On the following day the Assembly remained in session, which was unusual on a Sunday, purely to discuss the arrangements for Mirabeau's funeral. From the passions engaged, as well as the general sense of distress in the streets outside, and throughout France, it was apparent that the Revolution, which was committed to the enactment of abstract principles, also had the deepest cravings for heroes who embodied them. Modern historical writing (with some honorable exceptions) has been reluctant to acknowledge this, as though to do so were to acknowledge a nineteenth-century view of the Revolution as the product of Great Lives. The Revolution has instead been presented as the outcome of impersonal forces: of the friction of social structure and institutional dysfunction. For contemporaries, however, the confluence of the neo-Roman obsession with *exempla virtutes* and the Romantic infatuation with the Promethean will meant that no epochal event like the Revolution could be apprehended without its incarnation in cults of heroes and martyrs. That candidates for this exemplary role had paraded their imperfections was no obstacle, for had not Homer himself made much of such human frailty amongst the gods and heroes? So it was that Mirabeau, who in his forty-two years had exhibited every sign of common mortality, was the first to be elevated to the ranks of the modern Immortals.

In keeping with the cult of patriot-heroes that had been steadily growing since the Seven Years' War, it had already been determined that there should be a "Westminster Abbey for the French." The idea of a Panthéon predated the Revolution, and a number of projects of the 1770s listed the same worthies who had figured in the necrologies and medallic histories: Turenne, Colbert, Lamoignon. Such a monument to *"Grands Hommes"* would distinguish itself from a crypt of kings by celebrating virtue over lineage, self-invention over tradition. When the Marquis de Pastoret proposed a Panthéon, its first obvious candidate, Descartes, was represented as someone persecuted by kings, forced into the fugitive life of the independent philosopher. The imprisonment and exiles of Voltaire and Rousseau fitted conveniently into the same pattern.

Soufflot's handsome, still unfinished church of Sainte-Geneviève was thought suitable because its austere neoclassicism seemed to project the virtues associated with the philosophers and patriotic statesmen. The architect Quatremère de Quincy, to whom the commission was given, saw the building as ideal precisely because it was at the opposite extreme from the arbitrarily crowded Gothic crypt of kings at Saint-Denis. As Mona Ozouf has pointed out, the designated space was to be stripped of associations of death, since its function was to celebrate the immortality of heroes. Consequently it would be a triumphal, not a burial, space.

On the face of it, Mirabeau's candidacy as the first of the revolutionary heroes to be accommodated in the Panthéon raised all sorts of difficulties. The exemplary virtues of the *"Grands Hommes"* were supposed to be personal and familial as well as political or philosophical. But the great outpouring of lamentation that followed his death so drowned skepticism that even Robespierre and Barnave, to whom Mirabeau's vices had been all too apparent, voiced support for the proposal.

The funeral was thus designed as a great demonstration of patriotic reverence that would culminate in Mirabeau's arrival at the Panthéon. At around six o'clock on April 4, a long military procession left his house, led

by companies of the National Guard on horse and foot, the infantry showing their rifles reversed and drums muffled with black crepe. At the center
was a leaden urn containing Mirabeau's heart—the seat of what had been
decreed his sovereign virtues of candor, passion and sincerity. Behind the
pallbearers, also of the National Guard, followed battalions of veterans and
children (by now a standard feature of these occasions); representatives of
the municipality of Paris and the departmental administration on which
Mirabeau had served; virtually the entire Constituent Assembly; and even
more surprisingly, *en masse,* the Jacobins, who, notwithstanding his apostasy, had decreed a week of mourning for their ex-president and resolved
each year, on June 23, to read aloud Mirabeau's retort to the Marquis de
Dreux-Brézé. At the very end, the procession simply dissolved into a gigantic crowd of Parisians and those who had come to the city to be close to
the dead hero, a crowd, it was said, of three hundred thousand, an enormous
tide of humanity flowing through the streets bearing torches in the descending Paris night. "It seemed," wrote Nicolas Ruault to his brother,
"that we were travelling with him to the world of the dead."

At the black-draped Church of Saint-Eustache a halt was made so that

138. Tessier, bust of Mirabeau, 1790–91

the Abbé Cérutti could preach a eulogy to the dead man in a manner compatible with Mirabeau's not especially orthodox beliefs. The procession then resumed and plodded forward to the music of a requiem mass specially composed by Gossec and scored for unusual wind instruments that sounded keening notes amidst the conventional pomp. Near midnight the procession finally reached Sainte-Geneviève, where the heart of the orator was set on a catafalque beside the tomb of the philosopher.

Some accounts, in word and image, took the journey still further. An impromptu play, *Mirabeau's Arrival in the Elysian Fields,* acted out the content of an engraving by Moreau le Jeune that had the Count received by Rousseau, crowned by Franklin and fêted by Voltaire, Montesquieu and Fénelon. On another plane his virtues were celebrated by oratorical predecessors like Demosthenes and Cicero. Only Brissot in his paper objected to the incessant allusions to Mirabeau's *virtue.* He knew the dead man well enough to know that he would have struck the word from the testimonials, for his "tomb is not honored by a lie."

Mirabeau became the object of mass veneration not just in Paris but in the provinces. In Reims there was a requiem mass and in the Church of Notre Dame at Bordeaux a sarcophagus for the great man was raised on four columns, the exploits of the "heroic Hercules" engraved on its side. And in dramatic contrast to Mirabeau's unlikely beatification was the accelerated erosion of respect for the King. His connivance in the exit of the aunts was represented in the Patriot press as tolerance of, if not sympathy for, the position of the Pope, whose official denunciation of the Civil Constitution was announced in March, and whose effigy was burned on the streets of Paris. Pius VI had declared *ex cathedra* the ordination of constitutional bishops to be a sacrilege and required every priest who had taken the oath to recant within forty days on pain of suspension. Through all this Louis lay uncharacteristically sick, with high fevers and hacking bloody coughs. Brooding miserably on his assent to the law enforcing the oath, given on Christmas Eve 1790, he now repented himself of the apostasy. His chaplain, who had taken the oath, was replaced by a pious nonjuror, Père Hébert, and the King decided henceforth to avoid communion from a constitutional priest. With Holy Week approaching, the best solution seemed to be to travel to Saint-Cloud, where these devotions could take place away from the angry anticlericalism of the Parisians.

This was all the more necessary since the mood of the capital in the spring of 1791 was not benign. Angry crowds, often mobilized by the popular societies, protested lack of work and denounced counter-revolutionary traitors they claimed to have unmasked. There were repeated threats to close the public-relief works, which paid twenty sous a day to nearly thirty thousand men and women. On the same day as the "affair of the daggers" in the Tuileries, just such a crowd of workers from Santerre's brewery had attempted to march on the Château de Vincennes, which they said was being prepared as a new Bastille. A number were arrested and severely dealt with. But disorder continued with a wave of strikes called by the better-organized journeymen artisans—farriers, carpenters and hatters—against low wages.

All these moods—hunger, poverty, anticlerical rage and patriotic paranoia—converged on the Monday of Holy Week, April 18, when news spread in the *sections* that the King and Queen were about to depart for Saint-Cloud. On the previous day, the Cordeliers Club had published a resolution declaring that by flouting the Civil Constitution Louis had betrayed his own title of "the Restorer of French Liberty" and reminding him that as "first functionary of the state" he was also "the first subject of the Law." By his example, it was said, he had authorized rebellion and was "preparing for the French nation all the horrors of discord, and the scourge of civil war." And at the time of the King's illness, Fréron's paper had described the Assembly's official expression of concern as "twelve hundred legislators soiling their dignity as men and as representatives of the French nation by going into ecstasies for eight days over the state of the King's urine and his stools to the point of falling on their faces before his toilet as if it were the most resplendent throne."

When the King and Queen attempted to reach their carriage at the gates of the palace they found their way was blocked by a large and angry crowd. Marie-Antoinette then proposed they use a *berline* that could be harnessed inside the courtyard and escorted by National Guardsmen commanded by Lafayette. When, however, the General attempted to clear a path for its exit, his men refused to obey and began—as on the morning of October 5, 1789—to direct threats against him. Continued harangues were of no avail. For an hour and three quarters, the King and Queen sat inside the coach enduring ripe abuse. To the crowd and soldiers they were not much more than the hybrid monster of the print "The Two Make But One," which showed a horned (and cuckolded) goat-man at one end and a plumed hyena-woman at the other. When Louis tried to make a little speech, expressing surprise that "he who gave the French nation its freedom should now be denied his own," a grenadier of the Guard retorted, "Veto." Another told him that he was a fat pig whose appetite cost the people twenty-five millions a year. The Queen sat hunched against a carriage wall, tears of vexation and alarm streaming down her face. Terror at this ordeal gradually gave way to dejection and dejection to resignation. Lafayette realized that there was no way out but humiliation. The horses backed up and Louis and Marie-Antoinette returned to their apartments in the palace bitterly aware that, more than ever, they were captives. The next day the King reiterated his demand to the National Assembly that his legal entitlement to travel within a radius of twenty miles from the capital be honored. On the same day Brissot's paper appeared carrying a laudatory review of a work by one Louis La Vicomterie entitled *The Crimes of the Kings of France from Clovis to Louis XVI.*

It was this harrowing experience that, by his own account, led Louis to embrace a more drastic plan of escape. Mirabeau's death had removed the one figure whose persuasiveness and intelligence might have made a genuine constitutional monarchy possible. The King's troubled conscience over religion and his deepening anxiety over the physical safety of his family moved him further towards the secret plans for flight that had long been Marie-Antoinette's favored means of liberating the monarchy from its predicament. A succession of advisers had been urging this on her, most notably the ex-minister Breteuil, now safely ensconced in Switzerland. From his own exile in London, Calonne, who had assumed something like an active leadership of the counter-revolution, agreed that that would be the best strategy. And most important, Lafayette's cousin the Marquis de Bouillé, the army commander at Metz, indicated that troops at a frontier

139. Anonymous engraving, "The Two Make But One." Serpents uncoil from the Queen's hair.

garrison could be mustered in enough numbers to assure protection for the escapees. The previous August, Bouillé had responded with the utmost severity to a mutiny at the Nancy garrison of the Suisses de Châteauvieux— the last in a series of insurrections over wages and the right to fraternize. Since the soldiers were under special military jurisdiction, the sentences were draconian. One soldier had been broken on the wheel; twenty were hanged and forty-one sentenced to the galleys for life. To Marie-Antoinette this seemed assuring evidence that he would be dependable.

The selected garrison town was to be Montmédy, on the frontier of the Austrian Netherlands, where four German and two Swiss regiments of the royal army would provide adequate security for the King to plant his banner. It was the closest border from Paris, nearly two hundred miles— perhaps two days' hard drive. On the other side, the Queen's brother the Emperor Leopold might have enough military force to deter any attempt at recapture, or even to restore the King's authority in the same manner the Prussian grenadiers had restored Prince William V to The Hague in 1787. The co-ordinator of the plan of escape was Axel Fersen, an officer of the Swedish regiment of the French army who had become a passionate devo- tee of the Queen and increasingly anguished by the royal family's plight. Reams of paper have been wasted in an attempt to discover whether Fersen and Marie-Antoinette were or were not lovers, provoking prurience from her detractors and indignation from her defenders. Given the Queen's dramatically more somber manner and appearance during this period and her subjection to incessant surveillance, a sexual liaison seems wildly un- likely, but in any event it misses the point. In keeping with the culture of sentimental devotion, Fersen's passion was of a kind in which chivalric feeling overwhelmed erotic ambition. What he wanted was the freedom and dignity of the injured woman. "She is an angel and I try to console her as best I can," he wrote. One way, it seemed, was to buy her box after box of the softest Swedish calfskin gloves impregnated with attar of roses.

To secure the escape required careful planning and good fortune. In the event, however, the plans went awry and fortune looked the other way. Fersen had sensibly urged a light, fast coach for the journey, with the King and Queen traveling separately to divert suspicion. But the Queen insisted on a capacious *berline* that would carry the whole family, one which would only travel at about seven miles an hour. Since the Revolution was in the process of reducing them to common citizens, how fitting it would be to depart reversing roles with their servants. The royal governess, Mme de Tourzel, was to play a "Baronne Korff" in whose name passports would be supplied to Frankfurt; the Queen, looking persuasively prim in a plain black coat, was to be governess to the children (with the Dauphin dressed as a girl named, rather beautifully, Aglaé); Mme Elisabeth, the King's sister, was to be a bonneted nurse; and the King, in round hat, wig and plain coat, was to be the valet "Durand." At around midnight on June 20, he exited the palace past guards who mistook him for the Chevalier de Coigny, who for some weeks had carefully been dressed in the disguise costume and had been ostentatiously exercising his right to come and go as he pleased. Leaving soon after by an unlit and unguarded passage, Marie-Antoinette almost ran into Lafayette, who was doing his usual rounds of the palace security by carriage. She turned abruptly, pressing her face against the wall to avoid recognition. Her composure rattled, the Queen then got herself lost in the dark alleys around the Tuileries, taking half an hour before finding the carriage with its anxious passengers.

At two o'clock on a helpfully moonless night the coach passed through the Porte Saint-Martin going northeast. Beyond the *barrière* Fersen rode up with the *berline*, gradually moving alongside slowly and carefully enough that all the company could transfer from one carriage to the other without stopping. The first coach was left behind and six fast post-horses harnessed to its successor. Fersen took the coach the first stage of the journey and implored the King to allow him to continue, but Louis was at least aware that it would be unseemly for the King of the French to be conducted to the frontier by a foreign soldier. Fersen disappeared into the night promising a rendezvous in Brussels.

By dawn, the family was beginning to relax somewhat. Teams of horses came and went as planned. At Claye the Queen's maids joined her in a little cabriolet that followed behind. But there was nothing out of the ordinary in a fast-traveling heavily loaded black-and-green *berline* with yellow wheels, its baggage swaying, to arouse any suspicion. At Meaux, twenty-six miles from Paris, the party breakfasted on *boeuf à la mode* with *petits pois* and carrots snugly trapped in aspic while they, on the other hand, were beginning to feel free. "Once my bum is in the saddle again I'll be a new man," said the King, reverting to the kind of homely diction he was accustomed to use around Versailles. An even more obvious sign of his return to form was the obsessive way he plotted the journey on a specially prepared map. Cottages dotting the flat, prosperously uninteresting countryside of the Marne went by and at a posthouse near Châlons they were given *consommé* by the wife of a postmaster who recognized the King but registered nothing more than gratifyingly devoted silence.

Not long afterwards, cornering at speed (that is, around ten miles an hour) on a bridge, a wheel hit a stone post, breaking the traces and felling the horses. Another half hour was needed to right the carriage—which, added to earlier delays, meant that the *berline* was seriously behind schedule for its

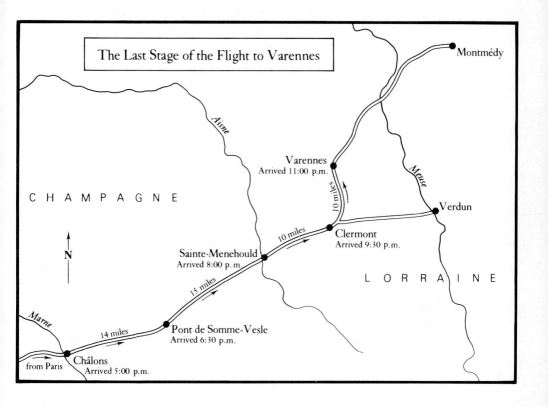

The Last Stage of the Flight to Varennes

Montmédy

Aisne

Varennes
Arrived 11:00 p.m.

Meuse

Verdun

C H A M P A G N E

10 miles

N

10 miles

Clermont
Arrived 9:30 p.m.

Sainte-Menehould
Arrived 8:00 p.m.

L O R R A I N E

15 miles

Marne

14 miles

Pont de Somme-Vesle
Arrived 6:30 p.m.

from Paris

Châlons
Arrived 5:00 p.m.

rendezvous with the military escorts planned to conduct it to Montmédy. Bouillé had instructed the young Duc de Choiseul to provide a military escort when the royal coach reached Pont de Somme-Vesle, the first in a series of escorts that would accompany the royal family until they arrived safely at Montmédy. But the unexpected arrival at Pont de Somme-Vesle of a troop of mounted soldiers had roused local fears that they had come to enforce tax collection, and groups of peasants and villagers were gathering in some force to resist. Waiting nervously for a coach that failed to arrive, Choiseul reassured the people that the guards were only needed to escort "treasure" to Sainte-Menehould farther along the road. By four thirty in the afternoon the royal party was two hours late for the rendezvous and Choiseul became gradually convinced that the plan had miscarried. Waiting with him was another figure, apparently indispensable to the Queen, her hairdresser Léonard, a veteran from the golden days of Mme Vigée-Lebrun and Rose Bertin. Departing in haste, Choiseul gave Léonard a note for the officers of the other relays indicating that something had gone wrong and that he would rejoin Bouillé. He waited another hour or so and then led his men into the forest of the Argonne, where they duly lost their way.

From this point, the crucial coordination of the journey unraveled. News of the King's escape from Paris had already beaten his coach to Sainte-Menehould and the local National Guard had forcibly disarmed a party of dragoons, suspecting them of abetting the fugitives. The postmaster, Drouet, had seen the Queen while serving in the cavalry, and with talk of the royal flight the main topic in the town, he needed little convincing of the passengers' identity. Checking the face of the large "valet" in the corner of the coach against the image of the King printed on a fifty-livre *assignat* removed all further doubts.

With none of the promised soldiers appearing, and the stares of village postmasters becoming interrogatory rather than sympathetic, Louis was growing acutely aware that June 21 was the longest day of the year, denying the travelers the anonymity of the night. But there were other troubles. At Varennes, just forty miles away from Montmédy, eighteen-year-old captain of the planned military escort, Rohring, faced with bored and baffled men, gave them permission to find quarters to sleep. Close to ten thirty he received orders to muster them again. But it proved impossible to extricate the soldiers from the taverns and houses where they had gone to seek sleeping quarters and other comforts.

By the time that Louis arrived at Varennes in search of fresh horses and the elusive escort, he had been overtaken on a back route by the postmaster, who, as an ex-dragoon, could ride hard and fast. A general alert had been raised and, with the mayor absent, the coach was stopped by the local *procureur*, M. Sauce. Papers which seemed to be in order were examined. It was only Drouet's insistence that they were indeed the King and Queen and that letting them through was tantamount to treason that changed Sauce's mind. The town was now wide awake, crowds with torches and local guardsmen with rifles at the ready filling the cobbled streets. Sauce had the party wait in his house, from which he sold candles and provisions. They were given an upstairs bedroom, in which the exhausted children were put to bed. At around midnight an elderly *juge de paix*, M. Destez, who had lived at Versailles, was led in. Looking aghast and overwhelmed by the King's presence, he instinctively fell on his knee. "*Eh bien,*" responded Louis, "I am indeed your King."

Was there something of a conditioned reflex about this? An emotionally overcome *subject*, rather than a citizen, crooking the knee and involuntarily eliciting the fatal words.

In Paris, consternation erupted on the discovery of the King and Queen's departure. "In twenty-four hours the kingdom could be in flames and the enemy could be at our door," exclaimed Charles de Lameth. Lafayette was the person immediately responsible for their safekeeping and, safe in his coach, Louis had gloated over his guardian's predicament. At the Jacobins both Danton and Robespierre used the occasion not only to hold the General accountable but to imply that he had been an accomplice in the escape. "You, M. Lafayette," threatened Robespierre, "will answer to the Assembly on the fate of the King with your head."

When the news was brought to the Assembly, the fiction of an *enlève-ment,* an abduction by ill-intentioned persons, was used to forestall an outburst of republicanism. But the Jacobin and Cordelier press, which for some days *before* the flight had pointed to unusual movements of troops and arms to the north and eastern frontiers, exploded in contemptuous indigna-tion. Fréron's paper was typical in seeing the event as the work of an infernal Austrian committee presided over by the Queen, with Lafayette as its accomplice and Louis the pathetic tool of its design.

> He has gone, this imbecile King, this perjured King, that scoundrel Queen who combines the lustfulness of Messalina with the bloodthirstiness of the Medicis. Execrable woman, *Furie* of France, it is you who were the soul of the conspiracy!

Enraged crowds went about the Paris streets defacing or smashing shop and inn signs bearing the King's name. Notaries whose profession was designated by boards bearing the fleur-de-lis hurriedly removed them. Someone posted a placard against the gates of the Tuileries palace reading *"Maison à louer"* (House to let). The more telling reaction, however, was among relatively moderate politicians whose faith in a viable *active* consti-tutional monarchy was irreversibly undermined. Condorcet, for example, was immediately converted to republicanism, hitherto the preserve of only the wilder zealots of the Cordeliers, and discussed with Brissot and Tom Paine plans to set up a journal actively campaigning for an end to the monarchy. Citizen Ferrières, no militant, writing to his wife, sounded for the first time like a revolutionary prosecutor distancing his own identity as Citizen Ferrières from the "aristocrats."

> So this, *ma bonne amie,* is where the intrigues and the little plots of those reckless and guilty Aristocrats have led. They have abused the weakness of the King to advise him to undertake so pernicious a deed; for their own selfish interests and the vengeance of their pride, they have not feared to expose the *patrie* to the horrors of the most murderous civil war, the King whom they say they love to the loss of his crown and all his family to the most

frightful consequences. They have been undone as they always
will be and their criminal efforts will come down on their heads.
I won't complain of that, they deserve their fate. But the King!
What humiliation! The Queen! That Queen whom, it seems, God
in his anger has given France!

Marie-Antoinette and her husband were indeed being forced to drink a
bitter cup to the lees. Confined in the upstairs room of the candlemaker-
procureur, they were confronted at dawn the next morning by two couriers
from the National Assembly requiring their return to Paris. The Queen
described the demand as insolence; Louis announced that "there is no
longer a king in France." They departed from Varennes surrounded by
six thousand armed citizens and National Guardsmen, enough to make the
King shrink from any suggestion that Bouillé's troops should be used to
secure his release by force. Only one pathetic attempt was ventured when
the Comte du Val de Dampierre, stricken by loyalist fervor, attempted to
ride to the coach and salute the King. Barely resisting, he was dragged away

140. The arrest of Louis Capet at Varennes: an almost wholly imaginative account
of the King apprehended at dinner

by the guard and hacked to death by a crowd comprised of peasants to whom he had been a notoriously callous *seigneur*.

Like the involuntary journeys to Paris of July and October 1789, the abject procession of 1791 signified the annihilation of the royal mystique. At Versailles, court hierarchy had been defined by strict conventions governing physical proximity to the persons of the King and Queen, enacted each day in the rituals of the *lever* and the *coucher*. At Epernay those taboos were casually tossed aside when two official representatives of the Assembly, Jérôme Pétion and Barnave, got into the coach and sat themselves, without asking permission, between the King and Queen. When they ate, the two men also ate; when Pétion needed to relieve himself, the coach stopped. Barnave had the Dauphin demonstrate what a good reader he was by repeating out loud the newly fashionable motto inscribed on his buttons: "*Vive Libre ou Mourir*" ("Live free or die"). Pétion, in his vanity, even imagined (or so his memoirs claimed) that Mme Elisabeth was so smitten with him that she pressed herself against him with meaningful insistence. On the other hand, the "air of simplicity and family feeling" that he found in the royal party surprised and pleased him.

Even as the coach trundled its way back to captivity, news of the flight was traveling around the country. Since it took three to four days for news to reach the farthest corners of the country, panics broke out, especially at the frontiers. At Bayonne there were reports of a Spanish invasion, to occur almost immediately; on the Breton coast, men were posted to watch for a British fleet of forty sail carrying an army of five thousand émigrés. Even when the news of the King's arrest was received at Metz, not far away, the Jacobins issued a proclamation calling all citizens to arms: "Defend your homes, count only on your brothers!" Many other rumors spread that Varennes had already been laid waste by Austrian soldiers as a reprisal for stopping the King.

Contempt lightened fear in the outpouring of satirical prints, many of them dwelling on the King's reputation for gluttony. A number showed him detained at dinner when enraged National Guards came to make the arrest. One primitive production in this vein, strongly reminiscent of English satires, has Louis attacking a roast as the decree for his arrest arrives. "Be damned with that," he replies, "let me eat in peace." Marie-Antoinette, admiring herself in the mirror, implores her husband, "My dear Louis, haven't you finished your two turkeys yet or drunk your six bottles of wine, for you know we must dine at Montmédy." The Dauphin is being congratulated for his efforts with the chamber pot, while on the walls a print of the fall of the Bastille is hung beside a royal proclamation turned upside down.

141. *Le Gourmand*, satirical print of Louis arrested while dining at Varennes

As the royal carriage approached Paris, the mood inside became fune-really somber. At Pantin, on the outskirts of the city, women shouted invective at the Queen. In Paris itself, unlike the arrivals of 1789, there was not even the faintest pretense of a royal entry. Instead of cheering, crowds had been instructed by the Assembly to show restrained disrespect. "Anyone who applauds the King will be beaten," read a widely posted sign; "anyone who insults him will be hanged." The Jacobins recommended that citizens keep their hats on their heads as the carriage passed to show displeasure. In the streets, National Guardsmen crossed their rifles in the air in attitudes of defiance. Even Lafayette was obliged (as much for his safety as the King's) to issue a reprimand by telling Louis that if he separated his cause from that of the people his own first loyalty would be to the latter. "It's true that you have followed your principles," Louis responded, and rather sheepishly confessed that only with this last penitential journey across France had he realized how widely those principles were shared.

With the royal family returned to Paris, the Assembly was in a quandary as to how to respond to the abortive flight. Having left behind him a long declaration, which had been read and published in all the newspapers in his absence, Louis himself had made it impossible to sustain the pretense that he had been "abducted." The document was a peculiar mixture of intelligence and tactlessness. The greater part of it was a lucidly reasoned critique of the constraints imposed on the monarchy by the decrees of the Assembly, largely echoing Mirabeau's own concerns, now shared by Barnave, Duport and the Lameths. In impressively argued paragraphs Louis raised the problematic nature of the place of the monarch in a system that purportedly gave him a constitutional role but in reality no power whatever to use it. How could magistrates be said to administer justice in the King's name when he had no part in either their nomination or confirmation and when the royal power to commute sentences and grant clemency had been stripped from him? How was it possible to pretend that France was represented abroad by his servants when he had a say neither in confirming ambassadors nor in negotiating and concluding treaties of peace? How could there be any discipline in the army if the clubs were allowed to purge or approve officers on some index of political orthodoxy—as the Jacobins were urging? How, in fact, was it at all possible to have a coherently governed state "of the size and populousness of France" with administrations hostage to the fickleness and hysteria of press and club opinion?

These were all perfectly legitimate and telling questions. As Louis himself noted, they had increasingly been on the mind of *"gens sages"* in the Assembly, but he had watched as those very men (like Mounier and later Sieyès) became discredited. Mirabeau's enemies, Duport, Barnave and the

142. The return from Varennes. The notice against applause or abuse is posted against the pedestal of the statue.

Lameths—and later even the Girondins—would follow in exactly the same path. Nothing vindicates the substance of what Louis argued in the declaration more than the fact that Robespierre and the Committee of Public Safety would come to exactly the same conclusion and resolve to reestablish state authority by crushing public opinion and club politics at the end of 1793.

Unfortunately, though, the King's declaration was also colored by characteristic petulance. He rehearsed the history of physical intimidation during 1789, which made it evident that all his professions of devotion to the people of Paris had only been made under duress and the need to safeguard the lives of his family. He complained that the twenty-five millions granted to him on the civil list was not enough to "sustain the honor of France" and that the accommodations at the Tuileries in October 1789 were far from what the royal household had a right to expect or to what they had been accustomed. He asked Frenchmen if they really wished the "anarchy and despotism of the clubs" to replace "a monarchical government under which France has prospered for fourteen hundred years," but he had made that anarchy more likely by forbidding his ministers to sign any kind of decrees in his absence.

More than anything in the text of the declaration, the manner in which it was issued by an absentee King traveling at speed to the frontier made it impossible to take seriously. It was not at all clear, however, to the majority of the Assembly what an appropriate response would be. The Cordeliers issued a characteristic statement on the twenty-second requiring their members to take a solemn vow of "tyrannicide" against threats to liberty from both without and within the country, "wherever they may be." Danton, who had previously declared that Lafayette must be either a traitor or an imbecile to have allowed the escape to happen, now applied the same descriptives to Louis himself. But he received very little support for his proposal to summarily replace the King with an executive council chosen by specially elected representatives. When Condorcet had the *Moniteur* publish a translation of a declaration written by Tom Paine arguing that the absence of "Louis Capet" had already in effect instituted a republic, it was refuted by a counter-argument by Sieyès reiterating that men were freer in a monarchy since "kings were necessary to save us from the peril of masters." Even Robespierre in the Jacobins fudged the issue by declaring that the constitution already gave France the best of both worlds, offering "a Republic with a monarch."

Even at this most discreditable moment in the King's career, then, most Frenchmen clung to the possibility that Louis' defection had been the work of an "Austrian Committee." When Bouillé, from beyond the frontiers, issued a proclamation threatening dire consequences should any harm befall Louis, it only seemed to confirm the conspiracy thesis. At any rate, as Marcel Reinhard has shown, demands for a republic in petitions to the Constituent from around the country were relatively rare.

What were the other options? Perhaps the King could be deposed in favor of the Dauphin and some sort of regency? Smelling an opportunity, "Monsieur Orléans," as he now liked to be called, had returned to Paris and, managed by the writer Choderlos de Laclos, even sought admission at the Jacobins as a testimony to his revolutionary ardor. But Orléanism had already had its day as a viable alternative to the Bourbons. There was also a growing anxiety that deposing Louis XVI might lead to a war with Austria, something the majority of the Assembly was still anxious to avoid. In mid-July the King's role in government was declared to be "suspended" until the Assembly had completed its work on the constitution. The entire constitutional project would then be presented to the monarch for a simple yes or no. As a living element in the body politic, however, Louis XVI had already become redundant. Condorcet, who detested the hypocrisy of preserving some sort of mummified convenience of the monarchy when its real raison d'être had gone, took this perception one stage further by publishing a mordant satire in which a mechanical robot-king was devised to go through all the necessary gesticulations of kingship—vetos and such like—leaving real power in the hands of those who switched the levers.

T H I S   J O U R N E Y   from sacerdotal absolutism to constitutional disposability was made more emphatic by a journey in the opposite direction that took place two weeks after the return of the royal family to Paris. In November 1790 yet another revolutionary marquis, Charles de La Villette, in whose house Voltaire had died, made a speech at the Jacobins urging that the philosopher's remains be given some sort of national recognition. The problem was acute, for the Abbey of Sellières, where he had been buried, was about to go on the auctioneer's block. "Will you permit this precious relic to become the property of an individual?" de La Villette asked rhetorically. "Will you allow it to be sold like so much 'national property'?" (*biens nationaux*—the euphemism Talleyrand had given to church property sold for the profit of the state).

De La Villette was, in any case, one of the prime movers of the Panthéon project, and the Constituent shared his appraisal of Voltaire—"the glorious Revolution has been the fruit of his works." Thus they agreed that Voltaire's remains should be brought back to Paris for interment in the monu-

143. Order of the cortège for the transfer of Voltaire's remains to the Panthéon

IL COMBATIT LES
ATHÉES ET LES FANATIQUES
IL INSPIRA LA TOLÉRANCE
IL RÉCLAMA LES DROITS
DE L'HOMME CONTRE LA SERVITUDE
DE LA FÉODALITÉ

ment to the *"Grands Hommes."* The moment was particularly timely. The spring of 1791 had seen something like a cult of Voltaire. Talma had been playing *Brutus* in the proper antique manner and had even added a scene which exactly replicated David's great history painting of 1789, with the actor sitting brooding in the shadow cast by "Mother" Roma while the bodies of his plotting monarchist sons, executed by his writ, are borne in on a litter. At the Cordeliers on the twenty-second of June, when the oath for tyrannicide was taken, speeches were made specifically referring to an earlier moment in the Brutus history, when news of the rape of Lucrèce by Tarquin's sons was brought to the consul and he swore "by the chaste dagger to exterminate the race of Tarquin." When the ignoble King attempted to return to Rome he had the gates of the city shut in his face. "What grandeur, what dignity," commented Fréron. "Frenchmen, why is there no Brutus among you?"

Voltaire's apotheosis on July 11 was deliberately stage-managed to stress his "Roman" virtues at the expense of the discredited monarchy. Fréron, whose father Voltaire had loathed and of whom he had memorably said "a snake bit Fréron; the snake died," allowed himself just one reference to the "irascible philosopher" but was thrilled by the elaborately antique nature of the memorial. The body had been transported from Romilly-sur-Seine in a simple wagon decorated with a blue cloth and had been received, at successive stages, by civic dignitaries and officials. At the outskirts of Paris it was escorted by National Guardsmen to the ruins of the Bastille, where the philosopher's smile might contemplate his victory over the fortress in which he had been twice incarcerated. He, the message ran, had endured while the stones had fallen! The coffin was then placed behind a barrier of poplars and cypresses and guarded by alternating shifts of National Guardsmen and girls dressed *à l'antique* in white robes.

For the procession to the Panthéon a monumental chariot, as high as a two-story house, was designed by a small committee that included Quatremère de Quincy and Jacques-Louis David. Its wheels were cast in bronze and according to Roman models. The sarcophagus was of imperial porphyry and was raised on three steps. At its top reposed Voltaire on an antique couch-bed in an attitude of sleep, his face settled into the benign expression made famous by replicas of Houdon's portrait busts. By his side was a broken lyre and behind the bolster the figure of Eternity placed a crown of stars on his head. At the corners of the catafalque figures representing Genius were seated in expressions of mourning, their torches reversed. Inscriptions from Voltaire's works were engraved on its four sides, including Brutus's "O gods, give us death rather than slavery." Four white horses caparisoned only with the tricolor drew the chariot.

The cortège included the usual cast of characters—Jacobins, deputies, representatives of the Commune, National Guardsmen—but was made much more interesting by the inclusion of representations from Voltaire's works and life. The twenty-third model of the Bastille to be made by Palloy from its stones was given prominence and a troupe of men dressed in Roman costume carried as trophies of glory editions of all Voltaire's works. Another group of actors from Talma's troupe represented the family of Jean Calas, the Protestant who had been executed for allegedly murdering his son and whose vindication became Voltaire's most famous *cause célèbre*. Citizens of the faubourg Saint-Antoine carried banners on which had been painted the faces of other comparable worthies: Franklin, Rousseau and Mirabeau.

As usual in a Paris July, it rained. But a hundred thousand turned out nonetheless to watch as the procession made its way in a series of "stations" to the Panthéon, stopping at the sites of Voltairean triumphs: the Opéra, where actresses sang a special hymn written by Gossec and Chénier; the Théâtre-Français, where the aria from *Samson* was sung urging "people to awake, break your chains, ascend to your greatness of old." It took from three in the afternoon until ten at night for Voltaire to finally arrive at the

144. Lagrenée, the arrival of Voltaire's remains at the Panthéon

Panthéon to become the third in the rather oddly assorted trinity. In many ways, however, the old Newtonian was a more suitable roommate for Mirabeau than for Descartes.

It was said that as the immense procession passed by the Pont-Royal, Louis XVI was watching furtively from an upstairs window. Everywhere, in the popular press and especially in printed images, the connection was made between the disgrace of the King and the apotheosis of the philosopher. In a typical example of the genre (fig. 145), the allegorical figure of Fame salutes Voltaire's pantheonization (seen in the background) in the customary way while providing an altogether different salvo for the toppling monarch. The invidious pairing is carried through all the details of the print, Voltaire's immortality being contrasted with the "Faux Pas" blundering mortality—a reference to the aborted flight to Varennes—reinforced by the motto, drawn from one of the philosopher's plays, that "A king is merely a man with an august title; first subject of the laws, he is forced to be just." At the foot of their respective pedestals are a lyre and a rank growth of weeds and thistles.

This unflattering comparison was not altogether the intention of those who organized the *fête de Voltaire.* If anything, they were more concerned with dulling the edge of the agitation for a republican democracy being waged in the popular societies than with sharpening it. On May 9 a decree had been enacted banning all petitions bearing "collective signatures." Together with the Le Chapelier law passed at the end of June proscribing worker "coalitions," it represented a concerted effort to place sharp limits on the disruptive capacity of popular politics. Accordingly, one of the inscriptions on Voltaire's sarcophagus made strong references to the favorite refrain of Lafayette and Bailly, now endorsed by Barnave and Duport: the necessity of obeying the law. And one of the heroes memorialized on banners in the procession was the soldier Desilles, who had been killed while attempting to separate royal and mutinous troops at Nancy and had become canonized as the martyr of the "moderates."

Most histories argue that these efforts to subsume republicanism in the fictions of revolutionary unity failed. On the sixteenth of July, François and Louise Robert's Central Committee of popular societies circulated a petition declaring that Louis XVI had "deserted his post" and that by this act and his "perjury" had, in effect, abdicated. Until the rest of the nation indicated a will contrary to the petition, the signatories declared, they would no longer recognize him as their King. A signing demonstration was called for at the Champ de Mars the following day on the "altar of the *patrie.*" On the morning of the seventeenth, two men who were found hiding under the altar were immediately suspected of evil intentions and

145. Satirical print on the two *journées* of June 21 and July 11

summarily hanged. Lafayette this time succeeded in persuading Bailly to declare martial law, so that around fifty thousand demonstrators, unarmed, and many of them from the poorer districts of the city, were confronted by the National Guard. Showered with stones, the guardsmen opened fire, killing a number put at thirteen by the authorities and fifty by one of the leaders of the demonstration.

In the chronology of revolutionary inevitability, this confrontation on the Champ de Mars is seen as not only anticipating but causing the popular republicanism of 1792 and 1793. But that is not at all how matters seemed to stand in August and September of 1791. On the contrary, the attempts of constitutionalists to arrest the drift of revolution towards what they called "anarchy" seemed to have succeeded. On April 18, when the King was prevented from leaving for Saint-Cloud, Lafayette had wanted Bailly to declare martial law and he had refused. In July he had concurred, and the repression was as severe as the General intended it should be. Robespierre had actually persuaded the Jacobins not to support the "abdication" petition, and while condemning the violent repression on the Champ de Mars, they refused to associate themselves with its cause. Despite this reticence, the club still broke in two over the crisis. By far the greater both in numbers and in influence were the newly baptized Feuillants led by

Barnave, Duport and the Lameths. Robespierre and Pétion found themselves in the rue Saint-Honoré talking to a small rump of a hundred or so members. Further repression against the Cordeliers and the other popular societies succeeded even more completely in wiping them out as effective centers of propaganda among the Paris artisans. Mme Roland wrote that Lafayette's guards went around seizing copies of Marat's newspaper from vendors and tearing them up with impunity.

On the other flank, the strategies of the traditional royalists—the *Noirs*—in the Assembly had been completely confounded by the fiasco of the King's escape. With Mirabeau gone, and Lafayette in bad odor after the Champ de Mars, the role of constitutional guardians fell to the "triumvirs": Barnave, Adrien Duport and Alexandre Lameth. All three were men who had come out of the judicial polemics of the old regime and had been converted to national, rather than popular, sovereignty. In September 1791 they had some reason for supposing that the chances of stabilizing the Revolution were better than they had been for some time. On the thirteenth the King accepted, without demur, the Constitution and the following day was officially installed in his political nullity as "King of the French."

Two days before, the biennial Salon had opened at the Louvre. At its

146. Laffitte, drawing, the massacre of citizens on the Champ de Mars: a powerfully romanticized account of the moment when the petitioners—one of whom, at extreme right, clutches a copy of the Declaration of the Rights of Man—are caught by the fire of the National Guard

center were three great canvases, all by Jacques-Louis David, which seemed to proclaim with an eloquence unmatched by any of the orators of the Assembly the reigning fictions of revolutionary patriotic unity. In the center was the brooding Brutus, loaned by Louis XVI, who was still its owner as well as principal victim. At left were the Horatii and immediately below them the deputies of the Estates-General echoing the gesture of the Roman brothers by raising their arms in the Tennis Court Oath. The latter, enormous work was still a drawing, but the austerity of the bistre monochrome seemed fitting for the devotional austerity of the mood and somehow reinforced the enormous compositional pull of the work towards its patriotic center, where light played on the head of Sylvain Bailly commanding the oath.

By this time, the harmonies the drawing celebrated were rapidly turning discordant. At the center of the work was the triangular concordance of faiths: the Protestant Rabaut Saint-Etienne, the Capuchin Dom Gerle (who was not even in the tennis court that day) and the Patriot Abbé Grégoire. But Dom Gerle had become an enemy of the Revolution since he had proposed on April 10, 1790 that Catholicism be declared the sole religion of state; Protestant guards and Catholic rebels were killing each other in the Midi and the Rhone Valley; and while Grégoire would go on to be a Conventionnel, Rabaut had already recoiled from the excesses of popular insurrection. Bailly, to whom all arms were raised, was rapidly losing control of government in Paris. Sieyès, seen at a desk as the ideologist of the national sovereignty, had been alienated by the Civil Constitution and had just produced a refutation of Tom Paine's republican manifesto. If Barnave (at right) was given prominence in the urgency of his gesture, he was at least counter-balanced by Maximilien Robespierre (who had been completely insignificant in June 1789), his arms crossed on his chest in the body language of Rousseauean sincerity and virtue.

Nowhere in the work, however, did David editorialize more optimistically on the Revolution than in the three corners where spectators are shown. It is there that the People, endlessly apostrophized by the politicians, make their appearance as audience, pupils and ideal citizens: patriotic in their muscularity but never threatening in their unruliness. For the most part they are emblems of Jacobin political aesthetics: the *sans-culotte* with the Phrygian hat is modeled like an antique statue and posed like a Michelangelo fresco. The group at top right (possibly drawn from David's own children) incorporates the inevitable sentimental alliance between the venerable and the juvenile: past suffering and future hope (figs. 148 and 149).

The clichés become forgivable as David throws into the composition the immense force of the revolutionary tempest, given literal visualization through the blown drapery. Old-regime conventions and traditional sover-

147. Jacques-Louis David, drawing: *The Tennis Court Oath*

148. Detail from Jacques-Louis David, *The Tennis Court Oath*

149. Detail from Jacques-Louis David, *The Tennis Court Oath*

eignty are turned inside out like the umbrella seen at top left. Even the expression given to its holder registers the exact, transforming moment, with a *coup de foudre* hitting the Royal Chapel. This great political gale surges into the empty space of the court to meet the straining, ecstatic collective gesture of the deputies, at the lit center of the orthogonal cross.

The figures, said one critic, "breathe with the love of the *patrie*, of virtue and liberty. Everywhere one sees Catos ready to die for them." The famous dissent of Martin d'Auch at bottom left only served to reinforce the feeling that this was a hymn to revolutionary unity. But David was never able to complete the work, precisely because in the course of the following year those unities were exposed as fictitious. On the revelation of his dealings with the court, Mirabeau, whom David had placed closer to the beholder than any other figure, fell into such deep disgrace that in 1793 his remains were disinterred from the Panthéon and thrown into a common burial pit. Bailly and Barnave would perish on the guillotine, Sieyès survive by great feats of agile pragmatism. David himself would sign warrants as a member of the Committee for General Security and surpass himself in public expressions of devotion to Robespierre and Marat.

Poets of Romantic weather-forecasting like André Chénier and William Wordsworth, who felt its drama, continued to describe the Revolution as a great cyclonic disturbance. But increasingly it was no longer the storm that invigorates and cleanses; rather, a dark and potent elemental rage, moving forward in indiscriminate destruction. Its breath was no longer sweet but foul. It was the wind of war.

CHAPTER FOURTEEN
"Marseillaise"
September 1791–August 1792

i FINISHED BUSINESS?

ON THE EIGHTEENTH of September 1791, a hot-air balloon, trailing tricolor ribbons, floated above the Champs Elysées to announce the formal acceptance of the constitution by the King. Though not without some misgivings, Louis had come to the Constituent four days earlier, to swear "to maintain it at home and defend it against attacks from abroad and to use all the means which it places in my power to execute it faithfully." The Queen had told him to indicate his acceptance with dignified terseness, and he made an effort to make it sound conditional on the Assembly's resolution "to re-establish order." But during the session he sat in an armchair conspicuously on the same level as that of the President of the Assembly, scandalizing the royalist right. No less than 150 of them declared they would never adhere to a document signed under duress by a "prisoner-king." At the same time, the left poured scorn on the notion that the fugitive of Varennes could possibly be acting in good faith.

That, however, still left a broad majority in the center. Ferrières, for one, believed the King had been chastened by his experience and clung to the constitution as a protection against both counter-revolution and anarchy. So for the moment, at any rate, innocent festivities drowned out the noise of dissent. A Te Deum was sung in Notre Dame; and when the King and Queen appeared at the Opéra for a suitably penitential performance of *Oedipus at Colonus,* they were greeted, for a change, with rousing cheers. Illuminations and fireworks lit the autumn night skies, and at public dances toasts were drunk to the constitution and the new era it announced.

The completion of what was declared to be the "Gospel" of the Revolution signified the end of the long travail of the Constituent Assembly.

Though altered by defections, withdrawals and a few substitutions, it was still, for the greatest part, the same body of men who had arrived as members of three separate orders in Versailles in May 1789. Now the product of their labors began with a preamble declaring:

> there is no longer any nobility nor peerage nor hereditary
> distinctions of orders nor feudal regime nor patrimonial justice
> nor any title, denomination or prerogative . . . there is no longer
> venality nor heredity in any public office and neither for any
> section of the nation nor for any individual can there be any
> exemption from the common law of the French.

It was one of the most astonishing collective personality changes in political history, this transformation from a realm based on ceremonially defined orders and corporations to that of the uniform entity of the sovereign nation. But the concept on which it was created was not, of course, invented in the two years since the calling of the Estates-General. In many respects the constitution was the realization of an Enlightenment project: of d'Argenson's dream of a "democratic monarchy" grounded on the political obliteration of the nobility.

Now that it was instituted and the long travail of the Assembly was coming to an end, there were increasingly frequent attempts to proclaim that the Revolution was finished. Adrien Duport had announced this in May; Le Chapelier made the same claim in proposing a law to restrict the freedom of clubs in September; and a majority in the Assembly endorsed a resolution proclaiming a *terme* to the Revolution. No one was more concerned than Barnave that France should emerge from a perpetual state of "becoming" to one of institutional arrival. Well before he had sat in the coach between Louis and Marie-Antoinette, making polite conversation and playing with the Dauphin, Barnave had been convinced of the need to strengthen the monarchy and defend the central organs of the French state against perpetual threats of popular insurrection. In fact his thoughts on these matters were very close to Mirabeau's. But ever since his sniping at the now officially designated *"Grand Homme"* in the National Assembly, Barnave had made a career out of outflanking Mirabeau on the left. With his old adversary dead he was free to adopt many of his cautionary ideas. Neither was Lafayette a stumbling block any longer. Even before the King's flight there had been a conspicuous warming between the General and the Lameths, and Lafayette's embarrassment in June meant that he was easier to co-opt into Barnave's plans to use force, if necessary, to terminate the insurrectionary phase of the Revolution.

With these two alternative centers of power effectively neutralized, Barnave assumed leadership of those who had an interest in making the constitutional monarchy operational. He was supported by those who had been his closest associates in the old Jacobins—Duport, Le Chapelier and the Lameths—and who now dominated the Feuillants. They all shared the general view that the "new" France would not survive repeated physical intimidation from the Paris sections, unrestrained polemics from the clubs and the press and most important of all, the democratization of discipline in the army and navy. At the same time, they believed it necessary to protect the state from any kind of counter-revolutionary plots or armed incursions. The wave of strikes and labor riots in the spring had also convinced them that the Turgot side of the modernization project of the Revolution—a liberal economic order—would also require protection against the social collectivism of revolutionary artisans and their advocates in the Cordeliers and Fauchet's Cercle Social.

Barnave's strategy in dealing with these challenges was carefully worked out. Having brushed off the threat of republicanism after Varennes, he negotiated secretly with the Queen, whom he expected to be sufficiently grateful to listen attentively to his advice. He counseled her to forswear, forever and in good faith, any kind of flirtation with armed counter-revolution; to make sure her brother the Emperor withdrew support from the émigrés; and to have the King persuade his brothers to return to France. In return for this he was prepared to work for the revision of the constitution so that it would strengthen the role of the royal executive. And throughout August and September, a lively and regular correspondence flew back and forth between Barnave and Marie-Antoinette. "The constitution," the Queen had written, "is a tissue of impracticable absurdities." "No no," he had protested, "it is *très monarchique,*" and if only the King and Queen would try to establish "confidence and make themselves loved," all France's troubles would be over; "no prince of Europe would be more solidly seated on his throne than the King of France."

Yet nothing very radical emerged from all Barnave's efforts in the Assembly to strengthen the executive. He failed to secure the bicameral parliament, with ministers chosen from the Assembly, that (he now agreed with Mirabeau) would be most likely to escape deadlock between the separate branches of the constitution. But his work was not completely fruitless either. Under the new provision, the King could choose his own ambassadors and was officially made commander in chief of the army; his ministers were permitted to defend policies before the Assembly. Even amendments which appeared to be more democratic—for example, the abolition of the silver mark (equivalent to fifty days' wages) as a fiscal criterion for eligibility to the legislature—were in fact a concentration of power. While the franchise was broadened for elections to local offices like justice of the peace, real estate ownership became the criterion for membership in the electoral college and eligibility as deputy. In practice this translated into a *narrower* electorate at the levels where it really counted—which was exactly the social strategy that reflected the boundaries of the cultural elite of the 1770s and 1780s and which created the long-lived "notabilities" of nineteenth-century France. In practice this meant that in a relatively poor department like the Aveyron, for example, this political power would lie in the hands of just two hundred–odd citizens who fulfilled the eligibility criteria.

This program did not go unchallenged. On September 29, the penultimate day of the Assembly's life, René Le Chapelier, speaking for the constitutional committee, tried to hurry through a law that would have the most profound consequences for French political life. It proposed an emasculation of political clubs by returning them to the status of private associations or organizations authorized to "instruct" citizens, in the tamest manner, on the content of decrees already passed by the legislature. Any kind of petitioning movement, any sort of critical examination of the conduct of the government and, most of all, any attacks on deputies of the Assembly would be construed as seditious and the malefactors deprived of their rights as citizens for a specified period of time. For the same reasons, affiliations between organizations would also be prohibited as conspiratorial threats to legally authorized institutions. It was, in other words, a crucial weapon (as was a similar law introduced by Duport to curb the press) in the Feuillant offensive against popular insurrection.

Le Chapelier justified the law with an eloquent analysis of the Revolution, praising the clubs for "rallying minds, forming centers of common opinion" in the "time of storms," but insisting that now that "the revolution is terminated" such "spontaneous institutions" had to give way before the crucial principle of the uncontested sovereignty of the people, vested in representatives. "The time of destructions is past," Le Chapelier proclaimed, "everyone has sworn to the Constitution; everyone calls for order and public peace; everyone *wishes* that the Revolution be over: these, now, are the unequivocal signs of patriotism." Only those "perverse or ambitious men" who wanted to manipulate the clubs for their own purposes and foment campaigns of libel against honest citizens could possibly object to the measure.

Le Chapelier's peroration was interrupted by a familiar high-pitched metallic voice coming from a slight bony man with immaculately curled and powdered hair and steel-rimmed spectacles. It was probably the aspersions cast by Le Chapelier on the supporters of political clubs that prompted an outburst from Maximilien Robespierre, who insisted that he be given the opportunity to respond, since a law had been proposed in direct conflict with principles of the constitution. But from the long speech that followed, it was evident that Robespierre had been carefully preparing for this confrontation. Since his own eloquence had persuaded the deputies to disqualify themselves from reelection to the new legislature, this would be the last occasion to impress on them, and the political nation beyond, his emphatic denial that the Revolution was indeed accomplished if not actually dead and buried.

It was the climax of his political career up to this point. In 1789 he had come to the Estates-General with two black suits, one wool, one velour; he was the fifth deputy of the Third for Arras, and a pure nonentity. Since then he had made more than a hundred and fifty speeches, sixty in the nine months of 1791 alone, and had survived brutal heckling in the Assembly and withering ridicule in the conservative press to become the manifest leader of the revolutionary left. He had done this largely by sheer consistency in a political world already notable for changes of mind and heart. The absolute conviction that he brought to his speeches, that only those of unimpeachable integrity could be made responsible for the public good, provoked mirth among the witty but as time went on the laughter became progressively more uncomfortable.

These lessons in moral earnestness he had learned from his lawyer father, from devotion to the precepts and life of Jean-Jacques Rousseau and from the passion for Latin history and oratory that earned him annual prizes at the Lycée Louis-le-Grand in Paris as well as the nickname "the Roman." Robespierre had been sent to this most famous of the Oratorian colleges on a scholarship, the protégé of his local bishop, yet another success story of the old regime's characteristic meritocracy. His years there formed a personality that would be exclusively committed to politics and, moreover, the intensely moral politics recommended by Rousseau: the reforming state must needs be a school of virtue, one capable of bringing about a great moral regeneration in individuals and in its collective life, or else it forfeited the right to allegiance. In his early trial cases in Arras, defending M. Vissery's lightning conductor and in 1788 an army officer who had been imprisoned by his own family under a *lettre de cachet*, Robespierre made his clients embodiments of general principles: victims in a Manichaean struggle between virtue and vice, freedom and tyranny. This kind of righteous indignation became his natural form of utterance, no less dramatic when spoken, as it often was, in tones of threatening and studious calm. And it found a responsive audience beyond the Assembly in a whole generation of likeminded young Ciceros and Catos waiting for the republic of virtues to be

150. Anonymous drawing, Robespierre at the tribune

inaugurated. As early as August 1789 Robespierre received an adoring letter from one such obscure devotee, Antoine Saint-Just:

> You who sustain the vacillating country against the torrent of despotism and intrigue, you whom I know as I know God by your miracles, I address myself to you, monsieur, to beg you to join with me in saving my poor region. I don't know you but you are a great man. You are not merely the deputy of a province, you are the representative of humanity and the republic.

Through the two years of the Constituent, Robespierre had done his best to live up to this weighty vocation by speaking out candidly on every topic that aroused his interest. The more his views placed him in a minority, the more eloquent he became—urging the emancipation of Jews and slaves, the abolition of the death penalty, the stripping from the monarch of any kind of veto whatsoever. During the crisis of 1791, with Danton in England and much of the radical press shut down, his own part in sustaining the confidence and above all in articulating the legitimacy of the militant revolution was crucial to its survival. The desertion of the Jacobins by the Feuillants only gave him an unopposed forum for his views, and he exploited the occasion to pin on his enemies the blame for the continuing schism, knowing that a majority of the thousand affiliated clubs in the provinces wanted nothing so much as a reunion.

It could hardly be said that he had a private life, since it was an article of faith that private and public were, for the true patriot, dissolved in a single existence of unselfish activism and moral regularity. But his domestic arrangements were well known and advertised as exemplary. From mid-1791 he lodged with the family of the Duplays in the rue Saint-Honoré. Duplay was a carpenter and cabinet maker but hardly a poverty-stricken son of toil, since besides his house he owned two other properties in Paris and employed a dozen journeymen. He was, in fact, exactly the kind of educated small tradesman glorified in Rousseau's panegyrics to craft and in Greuze's genre rhapsodies. Settled in a small room with writing desk and chair, Maximilien Robespierre emerged in the evenings to take a simple meal and read to the Duplay girls Corneille or Rousseau while peeling the oranges of which he was inordinately fond.

His other home was the Jacobins, where he felt safely among friends, as he did not in the Assembly. After the July split, his sense of moral proprietorship was even more marked, so that he would enter with studied informality, sit down at the very back of the vaulted room, cross his legs and wait for something of interest to strike him. Speakers at the tribune must have wilted on sighting the powdered hair and the thin, long nose cross the threshold.

Robespierre's speech refuting Le Chapelier was a typical example of the genre he had made his own. Its distinctive technique was the presentation of general principles as an account of his own personal life and standing. This oratory of the ego also attracted criticism from the ironically disposed but it corresponded brilliantly to the confessional manner invented by Rousseau. It also probed the emotions much more directly than the deliberately quiet, slightly fussy manner of speaking suggested. Passages, moreover, were invariably punctuated by professions of martyrdom, of invitations to death rather than the living ignominy of pragmatism, which heightened the dramatic pitch of the sentiment and made Robespierre sound exactly as though he were intoning lines from Corneille or Racine. He even adopted from the theater the mannerism of pausing lengthily after especially telling lines to let the full import sink in.

To Le Chapelier, and by extension to all the moderates, he retorted that what they sought was in direct and irrefutable conflict with the most important principles of the constitution: the right to assemble peacefully, to speak in freedom on matters of public concern and by writing or publishing to communicate with other like-minded citizens. Brushing aside Le

Chapelier's furious interruption—"M. Robespierre knows not a word of the Constitution"—he then returned to one of his favorite refrains, scored to melodies composed by Jean-Jacques: the "unmasking" of hypocrites. How dare Le Chapelier patronize the clubs by pretending to acknowledge their services when his real purpose was their destruction and for that matter the destruction of all constitutional freedoms? So the Revolution is finished, is it? "I don't quite understand what you could mean by this proposition," said Robespierre, affecting bewilderment, since to believe the Revolution to be truly finished presupposes the solid establishment of the constitution. And everywhere he looked he saw enemies, within and without, concerting to sabotage it. He then built up to a tremendous crescendo, using the phrase "I see" over and again as he surveyed the scene of perils to the *patrie*, not least from men "fighting less for the Revolution than for their own domination under the name of the monarch." Then came the usual offer of salutary martyrdom: patriotic paranoia at its most creative.

> If I am forced to use another kind of language, if I have to
> cease to speak against the projects of enemies of the *patrie;* if I
> must applaud the ruin of my country, well then order me to do
> what you will; let me perish myself before the death of liberty.

Finally, Robespierre turned himself into the implacable Roman tribune:

> I know that my candor has something harsh about it, but it
> is the only consolation that can remain to good citizens in the
> danger in which these men [contemptuous wave of the hand] have
> placed the public interest, to judge them in a severe manner.

Inside the Constituent, there was a war of the *claques,* but the Feuillants had enough votes to have their law enacted, even though it would never be enforced. Robespierre's speech, however, ensured him a public triumph. On the following day, when the Assembly finally ended its own existence, he was carried on the shoulders of a huge cheering crowd along with Jérôme Pétion, the hero of the working *faubourgs.* On a trip back to Artois the acclamation became something like an apotheosis, with his carriage mobbed wherever he went, flower petals raining down on his smartly coiffed hair. When he returned to Paris to establish a newspaper that would continue to project his views now that the parliamentary forum was denied him, its title, *La Défenseur de la Constitution,* did not seem absurdly grandiose.

ii CRUSADERS

The Legislative Assembly that replaced the Constituent is often seen as a kind of revolutionary interregnum, helplessly marking time between the constitutional monarchy and the Jacobin Terror. Compared with its predecessor, its personnel are thought of as nondescript, its utterances and decrees banal patriotic pieties lacking either the authentic conflicts of the Constituent or the feverish militancy of the Convention. Nothing could be further from the truth. A good case could be made that, in sheer political and intellectual talent, the Legislative was the most impressive of all the revolutionary assemblies. Its oratory was of an operatic intensity that made the speeches of its predecessor seem wan by comparison. And the war into which it led France was, arguably, the single most important event of the Revolution since the decision to call the Estates-General.

The Legislative came to Paris elected by a pathetically small proportion of the eligible voters: no more than 10 percent. Since the original elections to the Estates-General, in fact, it was a rule that the more radical the Revolution became, the narrower the electoral base on which it rested, for the Convention was to be produced from even fewer votes. Characteristically the Legislative's membership was provided by those politicians in the provinces who had made a reputation from opposing the incumbent notables who still dominated the mayoralties and departmental administrations. In the Constituent Assembly, of course, the new regime had seen off all the aristocrats and clergy who had hung grimly on to their status as deputies since the Estates-General. The Legislative Assembly did, however, include a number of revolutionary aristocrats like Condorcet, the Protestant Chevalier de Jaucourt, the Marquis de Rovère and the Comte de Kersaint as well as constitutional bishops like Lamourette of Lyon and Fauchet of Caen.

For the rest, there was nothing much to distinguish the new legislators from their predecessors, and historians have spent fruitless efforts trying to determine just *how* bourgeois either group was. For what it is worth, there were rather fewer merchants, industrialists and financiers in the Legislative than in the Constituent. But it makes no sense to anatomize the body in terms of occupational distribution, especially when categories like "lawyers" (who, nominally, again dominated the body) disguise huge differences of fortune and status. What linked the body together was a kind of cultural community, so that an army engineer like Lazare Carnot (like Robespierre, from Arras) could converse easily on technical matters with mathematicians like Monge and chemists like Guyton-Morveau who had written extensively on the military use of balloons. Other kinds of intellectuals were equally conspicuous: the arbiter of patriotic taste and designer of the Panthéon, Quatremère de Quincy; Patriote Palloy's learned friend from the department of inscriptions at the Louvre, Dusaulx; François de Neufchâteau, who had translated Richardson's most liquidly sentimental novels. Both deputies from Strasbourg were *savants* and, predictably, part of the intellectual circle around Dietrich: the mathematician-professor Arbogast and the historian Koch.

Politically, about half the Assembly declared its hand by the end of November. Just 136 were affiliated with the Jacobins, against 264 with the Feuillants. Though that gave Barnave the possibility of sustaining the kind of containment operation he and his friends had begun in the spring and summer, it was by no means a decisive majority. For it left 400-odd deputies determinedly uncommitted to either faction. That the Feuillants failed so signally to command their allegiance in the months that lay ahead was in large part due to the extraordinary influence exerted by a very small group gathered around the journalist Jacques-Pierre Brissot.

Brissot's paper the *Patriote Français* was one of the most successful in Paris (though, reading its rather arid formula, it is sometimes difficult to see why), and having been both a hack writer and a police spy in the 1780s, he

151. G-FM Gabriel, drawing, *J. P. Brissot*

had become something of an expert in manipulating public opinion. The son of a pastry cook in Chartres (where he had known Jérôme Pétion since their childhood), Brissot, unlike Robespierre, was familiar with grinding poverty and had been imprisoned for debt in London. Living hand-to-mouth off his writing, he had become something of a professional lobbyist for liberal causes like the liberation of black slaves in the West Indies, and had pamphleteered his way in and out of trouble in Belgium, Switzerland and Boston, where, in 1788, he thought he had at last discovered "the simplicity, goodness and dignity of men which is the possession of those who realize their liberty." Three years later, he had become a committed republican, and his professed aim was to thwart Barnave's moderatism at every turn by pressing on the Assembly issues that would force the King to reveal his true colors as an enemy of the *patrie*. By marginalizing the monarchy he would make it unworkable. While this strategy was implacably and successfully pursued, Brissot was certainly no more Machiavellian than Barnave, who was still secretly sending advice to the Queen on how best to respond to the offensive of the republicans.

Left to his own devices, Brissot would not have been sufficiently persuasive to command the votes necessary to enact the radical measures designed to embarrass the Feuillant ministers, who when they appeared before the Legislative sat, ridiculously, on little stools before the President's table. Supporting him, however, was a battery of orators the like of which had never before been heard together in one room and certainly not in France. They have passed into oblivion for a number of reasons, none of them good. They were first made the victims of the nineteenth-century poet-politician Lamartine's multivolume hagiography, the *History of the Girondins*. Their death on the guillotine at the hands of the Terror was invariably represented by anti-Jacobin historians as the fate of liberal republicans, doomed to perish at the hands of the unscrupulous. But to rob the Girondins (or "Brissotins," as they were first known) of their own unscrupulousness is actually to do them a disservice, for it also robs them of the political complexity they had in abundance. As the focus of revolutionary history later shifted from political to social analysis, the Girondins again seemed to make no sense, being socially indistinguishable from the Jacobins. They also disappointed analysts of "parties" in the Revolution, being not much more than a loose group of friends who sometimes all dined and wined together at Mme Dodun's in the place Vendôme, sometimes more amusingly chez Mme Roland at the Hôtel Brittanique. In 1792, however, an informal dining club or a like-minded group of friends, three of them from the same area of southwest France—hence the appellation of the Gironde—was a much *more* effective political unit than any kind of formally organized proto-"party." Moreover, Maximin Isnard (co-opted from the Provençal Department of the Var), Pierre Vergniaud, Marguerite-Elie Guadet and Armand Gensonné all recognized in each other the phenomenal power of their eloquence. While Robespierre deliberately worked alone, cultivating, Jean-Jacques-like, the austere isolation of the prophet, the Girondins played off each other like members of a string quartet, the cadence and tempo of their transcendent rhetoric rising and falling, swelling and fading with the effect they had on each other. More significantly, they were deliberately playing to an audience in the Manège, the former royal riding school next to the Tuileries that now housed the Assembly, both on the benches of the deputies and the public galleries that were packed for the big debates.

It is difficult to recover the music of that oratory, since its sound is lost to even the most imaginative history, though even reading it on the browning leaves of the *Archives Parlementaires* can be an electrifying experience. But all that needs to be acknowledged is a truism known to all the historians of revolutionary oratory at the turn of this century, Alphonse Aulard among them, that the cumulative effect of their speeches was decisive for the course of the Revolution. More than anything else—more than food riots or rising prices or Jacobin propaganda—they converted the deputies of the Legislative from politicians to crusaders. By the time that war was declared on the "King of Hungary and Bohemia" in April 1792, a substantial majority of the Assembly was convinced that at stake in what they themselves called their "crusade" was not just the future of France but that of humanity at large. And the first premise of Barnave's policy of stabilization—the preservation of peace—lay in ruins.

Well before that, however, it should have been obvious that the plan of Barnave and the other two "triumvirs," Duport and Alexandre Lameth, was in serious trouble. Though the rank and file of the Legislative were certainly not Jacobins, they did exhibit a kind of suspicious truculence towards the monarchy that, right from the start, made the position of the King and his government very difficult. In keeping with the whole history of the Revolution, matters of protocol assumed enormous symbolic importance, so that the first occasion on which Louis came to the Assembly was a kind of dethronement by gestures. Demands were made that he should not receive any special seating—and certainly not a throne. After gratuitous insults and threats from the Tuileries not to come at all, the King was provided on October 6 with a simple chair, painted with the fleur-de-lis, which was conspicuously positioned by the side of the President. When he arrived, he found the deputies already standing and, to his dismay, as he began to speak, they all sat down with studied discourtesy and replaced their hats, prompting the King to do the same. Seeing her husband, whose brow had been anointed with the sacred oil of Clovis at Reims, sitting down reading to the deputies like some glorified notary only served to sharpen Marie-Antoinette's already mortifying sense of indignity.

Though she replied attentively and politely to Barnave's letters, the Queen had no intention of heeding their instruction to take the constitution seriously. When Barnave assured her that political peace was in the offing if only she would sincerely support the status quo, Marie-Antoinette not unreasonably asked him what force was available to the monarchy should such ideal circumstances not prevail. He assumed the best; she assumed the worst. And it was the Queen's scenario that seemed more realistic when the Brissotins—who quickly dominated the crucial committees of the Assembly—promoted aggressive legislation designed to force the monarchy to make itself unpopular through the veto.

Two issues were of paramount significance and both were represented by the Brissotins as of demonstrably patriotic importance. The first concerned refractory priests, those who had still not taken the oath of loyalty demanded by the Civil Constitution. Recognizing the tragically disruptive potential of the religious schism then becoming steadily more bitter in large areas of France, Barnave had tried to relax the more punitive provisions of the Constituent's legislation. In response to continuing turmoil in southern and southeastern France, which were already in a condition of virtual civil war, and to the periodic establishment of armed camps of royalist Catholics, the Legislative made its religious policy more severe. Nonjuring priests were to have their stipends cut off forthwith; the legal clergy was to be allowed to marry; and on November 29 those who remained defiant against the laws of the nation were to be given just eight days to comply on pain of being declared in conspiracy against the *patrie*. Even Robespierre blanched at this measure, realizing that it would make inevitable the most intransigent kind of holy war. In his paper he declared that "time," after all, was needed to "mature the people" before they could face with equanimity the prospect of married priests. But it was Maximin Isnard from the embattled Department of the Var who set the inquisitorial tone of the session by declaring that "every corner of France is being soiled by the crimes of this caste . . . for when [a priest] ceases to be virtuous he becomes the most iniquitous of men." To punish such priests, he insisted, was not to persecute them, since one could only persecute holy saints and martyrs, whereas "most of the intriguers and hypocrites who preach religion do so only because they have lost their riches. To chastise such a class of men is at once to exercise a great act of justice and to avenge outraged humanity."

Needless to say, the King could not possibly sanction this criminalization of loyal Catholics. He had reluctantly assented, in September, to the "reunion" (for which read "annexation") of the papal enclave of Avignon with France. That had led to a murderous little war that culminated in the slaughter of moderate notables and aristocrats in the prisons of Avignon by an armed band led by "Coupe-tête" (Cut-head) Jourdan. Other cities like Arles were in the hands of equally implacable royalist Catholic powers who urged the people to spit on the Constitution and abuse the uniform of the National Guard. Louis was acutely averse to doing anything that seemed to further embitter this already tragic situation, even if this meant playing into the hands of his enemies. Barnave, who was doing his utmost to manage difficult decisions, had the refractory clergy of Paris petition the King on the grounds of the constitutional protection of liberty of conscience. Once this had happened, the royal veto was duly applied, setting off violent demonstrations in Paris and other centers of anticlericalism like Lyon and Marseille.

The second, but not unrelated, issue on which the Feuillant strategy would founder was the issue of the émigrés. Since the return of the King from Varennes, the pace of emigration had quickened markedly. Ferrières lamented to his wife that it had become an "epidemic" in the army; regiments had lost to the emigration a third of their entire complement of officers. For obvious reasons the numbers of émigré nobles and priests were most considerable at the frontiers—in Alsace and along the eastern border from the Vosges to the Ardennes; in the Pyrenees, the Roussillon and Provence in the southwest and east; and in Brittany in the west. But these were also exactly the regions of France where the nervousness about foreign invasion was most acute and also where the deputies to the Assembly were most militant, seeing themselves as beleaguered patriots in a sea of conspiracy and intrigue. Emigrants were held responsible for currency speculation that was driving down the paper *assignat* and fueling inflation—the latest version of the perennial "famine plot." From their bases first at Turin, and then at Coblenz, they were accused of planning invasions of France on the heels of absolutist armies that would put good patriots and their women and children to the sword and raze their cities. The Declaration of Pillnitz, which, as we shall see, was in fact a very guarded document issued by the Queen's brother the Emperor Leopold in August, was publicized in France as a direct threat to the nation's sovereignty and security.

On the thirty-first of October, the Assembly stated that all émigrés who, by the first of January 1792, had not dispersed from what were deemed to be armed camps would be declared guilty of conspiracy, and sentenced to the death penalty and the confiscation of their property. This draconian legislation was followed on the ninth of November by a summons to the

King's brother the Comte de Provence, to return within two months on pain of being deprived of the succession. Finally, on the twenty-ninth of November, the same day as the fiercest religious legislation, a law was adopted calling for the return of all the royal princes and making clear that confiscation of émigré property would include that owned by family members even if they had remained in France. Faced with this onslaught that affected not only the principles the King held but the fate of Louis' own family, Barnave not only advised but insisted on a veto. To do anything else, he wrote, would be tantamount to an admission of complete impotence, and would dishonor the King in the eyes of Europe. But the veto should be accompanied by a letter drawn up on his own initiative calling for the return of the princes and declaring that under no circumstances would he ever tolerate any kind of armed incursion on the territory of France on behalf of the émigrés.

This counsel was followed to the letter, and Louis even surprised the Assembly by appearing in person on December 14 to voice his own patriotic indignation at the possibility of any kind of military intervention on the part of European monarchs. While the Brissotins were (as Barnave had calculated) taken aback by the warmth of his ardor, Louis had his own reasons for sounding so determined. Guided by the one minister genuinely in his confidence, the ex-*intendant* Bertrand de Moleville, the King had come to appreciate that a war policy might actually be in his interest. Given his plight, he had hardly anything to lose (or so he imagined). Should such a war go well, it would surely be a means to concentrate power in his hands as commander in chief and might even give him the military force he needed to restore his authority at home. If it went badly, France could expect the foreign intervention that, in all likelihood, would also restore him to the throne. All this, of course, presupposed his abandoning the Feuillant peace strategy, and there is every sign that this indeed was his intention by December 1791, much applauded by the Queen and even more by his sister, Mme Elisabeth. The Queen had always detested the policy of compromise counseled by the Feuillants, and now that it was about to be wrecked she wrote a chuckling letter to Axel Fersen: "I do believe that we are about to declare war on the Electors [of Mainz and Trier]. The imbeciles! They cannot see that this will serve us well, for . . . if we begin it, all the Powers will become involved."

On December 7, the King appointed the Comte de Narbonne-Lara to the Ministry of War. Barnave had been urging the appointment for some time on the assumption that Narbonne would be an obedient Feuillant in office. But no sooner was he installed in his post than the new Minister realized, with his usual shrewdness, the true tenor of court policy. Instead of holding the line at peace, he began to prepare actively for war. It was, by common consent, to be a limited campaign against the minor German Prince-Bishop of Trier, on whose territory at Coblenz Artois and Condé had established their court. The size of the émigré army—no more than four thousand—precluded a serious campaign on its own. But it was large enough to act as a *casus belli* if the issue was pressed. Narbonne demanded a special subsidy from the Legislative of twenty million livres (in specie, not *assignats*) to spend on military preparations. And at the end of the year he established the prototype of a people's minister of war by going in person to the frontier to inspect fortifications and munitions and leading the patriotic salute in armed camps.

If this looked like stage conduct borrowed from Lafayette's promptbook, it was not accidental. The General had never really recovered his credibility after the flight to Varennes and had been humiliated in elections for the Paris mayoralty in October, when he had been soundly beaten by Jérôme Pétion. He had retired to his estates in the Auvergne and was actively lobbying for a military command that would restore his reputation. A patriotic war of limited extent against the Elector of Trier seemed a sure thing, and Narbonne was ready to oblige him. All that remained was to secure British neutrality in the event of hostilities, and in mid-January Talleyrand was sent to London on an unofficial mission to seek such an engagement.

Louis de Narbonne and Talleyrand had been good friends for some time and the warmth of their amity was not in the least compromised by the fact that the former had replaced the latter as the lover of Necker's remarkable daughter Germaine de Staël. Mme de Staël had been an unusual conquest for Talleyrand—articulate, generously emotional, but at times capable of irony that matched his own. Physically, she was a big-boned Junoesque woman much given to dressing in turbans and pseudo-oriental robes. For a while the shared pleasures of their merry intelligence and Germaine's genuinely affectionate nature made them happy lovers, but their relationship was deeper and more durable as friends. There seems to have been no romantic strategy in Narbonne recommending Talleyrand for the London mission, only an act of goodwill and a shrewd guess that the ex-bishop was better suited to diplomacy than episcopacy.

The first assignment in what was to be the most spectacular diplomatic career of the age was also Talleyrand's easiest, for William Pitt's administration had already determined that it would not be in Britain's interest to become embroiled in a European conflict. This, however, did not prevent Talleyrand's being subjected to the full withering force of British snobbery, which led many to turn their backs on the notorious Voltairean revolutionary scoundrel-bishop. Like Mirabeau, Talleyrand had long been convinced that Anglo-French understanding was the condition of French survival, but his enthusiasm for the project was sorely tried by his stinging rejection at the hands of polite British society. More humiliating still, his military friend Biron (once the Duc de Lauzun) was arrested while attempting to buy horses for the army and had to be bailed out. At least Grenville and even Pitt saw Talleyrand, the latter at the end of January 1792 for a wintry interview when Talleyrand's efforts to relax the tone by alluding to an encounter they had had ten years before at Reims failed to warm the bleak quality of the meeting. Since Talleyrand was not properly accredited he could expect nothing in the way of an engagement, or anything else for that matter, from His Majesty's government. That was all.

In the early months of 1792 the issue was in any case not so pressing since, for a while, the threat of war had temporarily receded. This was due more to the cautious attitude of the Emperor Leopold than any sudden turn towards peace on the part of French policy.

If the war party in both the court and the Legislative Assembly was looking for a helpfully bellicose adversary they could not have done worse than the Emperor. The younger of Maria Theresa's gifted sons, he had inherited from his brother Joseph an empire in a state of insurrection. Whole provinces, from the Netherlands to Hungary, were in outright revolt against the dramatically anti-aristocratic and utilitarian policies instituted by Joseph II in the extraordinary decade of his rule. On his deathbed many of the offending reforms like the land tax had been revoked, but Leopold had still needed exceptional qualities of tact and pragmatic intelligence to see the Habsburg Empire through the storm. Moreover, his major foreign-policy problems were in the east, not the west: in Poland, where Russia and Prussia were sharpening their knives for a further partition of that unfortunate kingdom, and in the Levant, where an unsuccessful war with Turkey was winding down.

For that matter, Leopold's own views on the world were in many respects closer to Condorcet's than to those of Artois, the émigré who was most aggressive in his advocacy of a war of restoration. As grand duke of Tuscany Leopold had been a model of enlightened absolutism, abolishing torture and the death penalty and beginning a legal codification on principles recommended by the great Milanese penal reformer Cesare Beccaria. He needed no lessons from the French on the costs and opportunities of creating a modern state.

Yet at the same time he could not altogether ignore the predicament of his sister and brother-in-law. He had not seen Marie-Antoinette for twenty-five years and in any event had always taken an even dimmer view of her fecklessness than had Joseph. But since the traumatic days of October 1789 he too had realized that the Queen and her family might, at any moment, be in physical danger. On the other hand, he thought that military action on his part would be more likely to increase that peril. So for two years he remained cautiously attentive, trying to comfort and calm his sister through Ambassador Mercy d'Argenteau while staying deaf to the repeated urging of Artois to commit the Empire to a counter-revolutionary campaign. Only when he was given the mistaken information that the royal flight from Paris had actually succeeded and the family was out of harm's way did he write breathlessly to the Queen: "Everything I have is yours, money, troops, everything."

When it became apparent that, far from the King and Queen recovering their freedom, their position was more helpless than ever, and that an "Austrian Committee" was being blamed by the Paris press for the flight, Leopold's attitude subsided again into prudence. But it was now an active, rather than a passive concern, guided by the principle that it was the duty of the powers of Europe to deter France from anything that might imperil the monarchy and lead to an irrevocable, bloody war. This was the purpose of the Padua circular in July and the rapprochement, later in the month, with the traditional enemy of the Habsburgs, Hohenzollern Prussia. When Leopold met King Frederick William at the spa of Pillnitz in Saxony at the end of August, they were joined by Artois, who arrived uninvited. But the common declaration that emerged was as much an expression of the two sovereigns' resistance to calls for a war of intervention as of their concern for the personal safety of the royal family.

The text of the Pillnitz Declaration stated that the fate of the French monarchy was of "common interest" to the powers and urged the restoration of its full liberty. Should warnings against harming the King and Queen go unheeded, it was implied, common action might have to be concerted. That the statement was meant as prophylactic rather than aggressive was plainly indicated by Leopold's emphasis on the indispensability of the collective agreement of *all* major powers before any action could be contemplated. Since it was known at the time that there was no question of British agreement to any such plan, the declaration could, at the same time, *sound* honorably firm, without committing Austria to anything at all. And without Austria, Prussia was very unlikely to act on its own. All the evidence indicates that the bellicose tone of the statement was meant to help the Feuillants within France to stabilize the position of the monarchy and to use the threat of a European war against the republicans. This was confirmed by the fact that both Leopold and his octogenarian adviser Kaunitz were prepared for the constitutional settlement as managed by

Barnave to have a chance of success. If it was viable, Kaunitz wrote, it would be "an act of terrible folly" to jeopardize it by an adventure along the lines proposed by the émigrés. If it was not viable, it was better that it should cave in on its own rather than be seen to be threatened by the shadowy hand of the "Austrian Committee."

In its serpentine rationality, this was a typical piece of eighteenth-century (or, for that matter, perennial) diplomacy. But its very calculation to do something other than what it seemed to say put the Declaration of Pillnitz at the opposite end of discursive expression from the world of revolutionary patriotism. While diplomatic language since the age of heralds had habitually used subterfuge, and presupposed distinctions between ostensible and actual intentions that would be read by those to whom its messages were addressed, the language of citizens was meant to be transparently sincere, direct and unmediated. Against the higher moral law of self-determination embraced by the Revolution, even the language of treaties between princes had no standing. How could the Pope claim to be sovereign of Avignon, or some German princes of the Empire claim property rights in Alsace, when the citizens of those places had never consented to the alienation of their territory? With these kinds of higher moral criteria in mind, nothing was easier than to represent the Declaration of Pillnitz as a direct affront to the sovereignty of the people, the first stage of a counter-revolutionary war. "A huge conspiracy against the liberty not only of France but of the whole human race" was being planned, said Hérault de Séchelles, ex-Parlementaire and eager Jacobin. But the brilliant light thrown by the Revolution would penetrate even the veil of obscurity which tyrants had thrown over their machinations.

The war crisis of 1791 and 1792 is often seen by modern historians (many of them not much interested in diplomatic history) as an aberration of the Revolution, something so obviously foolish as to be explicable only in terms of Brissotin tactics to capture power from the Feuillants. But this instrumentalist view of revolutionary war fails to see that patriotic war was, in fact, the logical culmination of almost everything the Revolution represented. It had begun, after all, as the consequence of patriotic exertion in America and had continued to define itself, through allusions to Rome, as the reinvigoration of national power through political transformation. From the very outset, there had been a strain of nervous defiance in revolutionary utterance which often translated itself at the popular level into paranoia. So in 1789 rumors abounded that the Austrians were already poised at the frontiers, that the British were sailing for Brittany and that Spanish cutthroats were about to pour into Roussillon. Worse, it was assumed the invaders had collaborators within France who placed their own selfish sectional interests above that of the *patrie*. Precisely because the new political world was defined as "the Nation" those who were deemed its enemies—aristocrats, nonjuring priests, the "Austrian" Queen—were stigmatized as foreigners, even when their credentials were as native as those of self-designated "Patriots."

Added to this was, paradoxically, a kind of philosophical universalism that made it even more difficult for the Revolution to act pragmatically. The Declaration of the Rights of Man and Citizen and the assertions of natural rights on which the constitution was based were, by definition, universally applicable. How could men be born to freedom in equality in one patch of the world but not another? So although the Constituent in 1790 had enacted a Declaration of Peace abjuring any war of conquest, even that statement had about it an air of sententious preaching to the unenlightened. "The trumpet which sounded the reveille of a great people has reached the four corners of the globe," claimed that specialist in international liberty, Anacharsis Cloots. For a while, this kind of messianic utterance could be dismissed as utopian raving. But once the international situation appeared to become threatening in the second half of 1791, the mood changed from amiable cosmopolitanism to crusading self-righteousness. "The French have become the foremost people of the universe," proclaimed Isnard, "so their conduct must now correspond to their new destiny. As slaves they were bold and great; are they to be timid and feeble now that they are free?"

Before the Revolution, Brissot had made a career out of linking arms with brothers-in-freedom in his Société Gallo-Américaine, so that a missionary approach to international liberation came naturally to him. Similarly his colleague and friend Etienne Clavière had been prominent among the Genevan democrats whose uprising against the patricians of that republic had been suppressed by Vergennes in 1782. There were already in Paris clubs of "free Allobrogians" (Swiss) and "Batavians" (Dutch) who saw themselves as part of an international league against "tyrants" and who were eager to send armed legions to fight alongside the French in the liberation of their respective homelands.

On October 14 Brissot, who effectively controlled the all-important Diplomatic Committee of the Legislative, rehearsed all these themes in a long and powerful speech. It was, in effect, an extended seminar on all the hurt suffered by French national interest at the hands of the absolutist powers and in particular Austria, France's ostensible ally since the Treaty of 1756. By the time that he had drawn his audience through a procession of wrongs and indignities, Brissot had sketched out the features of a vast conspiracy extending throughout Europe, designed to isolate and cripple French power forever. Posing a series of rhetorical questions, he put the pieces of the puzzle in place. Why had Russia suddenly made peace on its eastern frontier with Turkey if not to concentrate on something more sinister? Why had the King of Sweden, a known correspondent of the Queen's since his visit to France in the 1780s, mobilized his armies? Why indeed had those arch-enemies Austria and Prussia fallen into each other's arms at Pillnitz? The answer to all these questions was a dagger pointing directly at the heart of the only truly free nation of men in the Old World.

Brissot's speech had a dramatic effect on the Assembly not because it relied solely on new concepts of revolutionary polarity between the free and the "enslaved" nations, but rather because it appealed to conventional, even traditional, concepts of national interest, and especially the "honor" and even "glory" of France—terms more usually associated with Louis XIV. It was just because the "new" patriotism was in effect a Romantic reworking of much older themes of history—blood, honor and soil—that it was so irresistibly arousing. Thus when Brissot finished by exclaiming "I tell you that you must avenge your glory or condemn yourselves to eternal dishonor," he was greeted with thunderous applause not just from his own supporters but from the vast majority of uncommitted deputies in the center.

Now that he too was committed to a war policy (though for a reason the very opposite of the Brissotins'), Louis could respond actively to these attempts to replace the monarch by the People in Arms as the embodiment of French patriotism. That was the meaning of his appearance in the Assembly on December 14 to demand the dispersion of the émigré camp at Coblenz. And as if to oblige, the Elector of Trier speedily complied with the ultimatum. This was the signal, however, for a renewed campaign of patriotic exhortation in the press and the Assembly which would concentrate directly on the Austrian threat said to be mobilizing at the frontiers. The evidence of this was aggressive notes sent from Vienna on the subject of the Alsace princely properties and orders to the Austrian commander in the Netherlands (Belgium), General Bender, to assist the Elector of Trier should there be any French invasion of his territory. As T.C.W. Blanning has made clear in his perceptive work on the outbreak of the war, Kaunitz's more abrasive tone was based on a fateful misreading of French politics. Since the Austrians mistakenly congratulated themselves on having installed the Feuillants as a result of the Declaration of Pillnitz, another similarly minatory gesture was supposed to rescue the beleaguered government from the combined bellicosity of the Lafayette-Narbonne faction and the Brissotins. Needless to say, it had precisely the opposite effect.

The last week in 1791 and the first two of 1792 witnessed a succession of extraordinary rhetorical performances by the leading Brissotins, reiterated in Jacobin clubs and printed for distribution around the provinces. At the same time that they were contemptuous of General Bender, who was the butt of outrageous lampoons in popular caricatures, the speeches played on popular anxieties about retribution and called for an army of citizen-soldiers to show the world the invincibility of the free. On Christmas Day, Elie Guadet leapt from the President's chair to the tribune, unable to contain his passions as decorum required. "If the Revolution has already marked 1789 as the first year of French liberty, the date of the 1st of January 1792 will mark this year as the first year of universal liberty." Two days later Pierre Vergniaud, whose oratory could only be challenged by Mirabeau's as the most powerful and exhilarating of all the torrents of rhetoric produced during the Revolution, made the clinching speech. He painted a frightening picture of murderous émigrés, blessed by fanatical priests, gathering at the frontiers of the *patrie*.

The audacious satellites of despotism, carrying fifteen centuries of pride and barbarism in their feudal souls, are now demanding in every land and from every throne the gold and soldiers to reconquer the scepter of France. You have renounced conquests but you have not promised to suffer such insolent provocations. You have shaken off the yoke of your despots but this was surely not to crook the knee so ignominiously before some foreign

152. Anonymous engraving, Pierre
Vergniaud

tyrants and submit the whole system of your regeneration to the corrupt politics of their governments.

Vergniaud then used what would become a standard theme of revolutionary crusade: the pledge of patriotic self-immolation. "Yes, the representatives of free France, unshakably attached to the constitution, will be buried beneath the ruins of their own temple rather than propose to you [the people] a capitulation unworthy of them and of you." His coda was an almost hymnlike evocation of the nobility of French arms that anticipated Napoleon Bonaparte's much feebler campaign speeches. At its conclusion the entire Manège, including the public galleries, was on its feet waving hats, shouting oaths of loyalty, swept away in a great flood tide of patriotic rapture:

> So, led by the most sublime passions beneath the tricolor flag that you have gloriously planted on the ruins of the Bastille, what enemy would dare to attack you . . . follow the course of your great destiny that beckons you on to the punishment of tyrants who have placed arms in your hands. . . . *Union et courage!* Glory awaits you. Hitherto kings have aspired to the title of Roman citizens; it now depends on you to make them envy that of Citizens of France!

For the Brissotins, then, war would be what Mme Roland called "a school of virtue," much as it had been for the virile legions of Rome. In the Jacobins only one voice of any significance was raised against this truism: that of Maximilien Robespierre. He had originally approved of the martial rhetoric as a means of forcing the King's hand, but the apparent eagerness of Narbonne for war had made him reconsider. A war, he argued cogently, would play into the hands of the court or else it would create a military dictatorship. As for the supposed benefit to the rest of humanity awaiting the springtime of their liberation, "No one," he stated prophetically, "loves armed missionaries." Later, as the presiding figure in the most formidable machine for military mobilization seen in Europe, he would recant these views. In fact they remain some of the truest sentiments he ever articulated.

On January 25, 1792, Brissot's Diplomatic Committee persuaded the Legislative to send to Vienna what amounted virtually to an ultimatum. It required the Emperor to explain his conduct in respect of the émigrés and to desist not only from giving them aid and succor but to engage never to ally himself (under the terms of the Treaty of 1756) with an enemy of France. The response was equally sharp. Kaunitz mistakenly clung to the view that, in the last resort, the French were so ill prepared for war they would not dare to undertake it. There was some truth in the assumption that the army was not in a condition to mount a major campaign. But the Prussian intelligence on which Kaunitz relied had exaggerated the degree of disarray. On the first of January the émigré princes were declared traitors and their lands and titles forfeited. On the seventeenth a note from Vienna demanded not just the restoration of the German lands in Alsace and the liberation of the royal family but, for the first time, the return of Avignon and the Comtat to the Pope. A formal alliance was concluded between Austria and Prussia on February 7.

The deadline for the demand that Austria give France satisfaction over the Treaty of 1756 was March 1. (Indeed, the issue was set out virtually like a challenge to a duel, still a common practice even among revolutionaries who officially despised it as "superstition.") On that same day, Leopold died and was succeeded by his son Francis, a solemn lightweight who, much more than the late Emperor, was in the hands of advisers. They were much more disposed than the ancient Kaunitz to pick up the gauntlet thrown down by the Legislative, especially since Marie-Antoinette was sending them detailed plans of French military dispositions as soon as they were discussed in royal council. In the event, the decision was taken out of the Austrians' hands by a ministerial crisis in France. The Foreign Minister de Lessart had responded weakly to the latest sharp note from Vienna and on March 1 the humiliating exchange of correspondence was read to the Assembly, with the hapless Minister listening from one of the little stools in front of the President's desk. The Brissotin reaction was to launch a fierce attack on the incapacity of the Feuillants to stand up to Austria and Prussia, in effect accusing not only de Lessart but Bertrand de Moleville, the Minister of the Navy, of a form of disguised treason. When Narbonne actually joined in the onslaught, the King dismissed him on March 9. A week later Vergniaud moved for de Lessart's impeachment.

For a week or so Louis flailed around with increasing desperation to find an administration that could assuage the gathering hue and cry. Finally, perhaps recalling Mirabeau's advice to draw the sting from adversaries by co-opting them, he created a government wholly acceptable to Brissot and his friends: Clavière, the inventor of the *assignat,* was minister of finance; Roland, the ex-inspector of manufactures, minister of the interior; and Charles Dumouriez, the ex-commandant of Cherbourg, Louis XVI's pride and joy, had already been made minister of foreign affairs on March 1. Dumouriez was the odd man out here, more a Fayettiste than a Brissotin, but in his fifties someone with the military experience and the political grit to contain the crisis.

In Vienna the change of ministry was taken as a virtual declaration of war, all the more so since a special emissary from the Queen had recently arrived with bad news. This was the engineer Goguelat, who had been one of the miserable figures accompanying the Duc de Choiseul as he waited for the *berline* on the road to Montmédy. Before the imperial council he stated as a certainty the imminence of war, and Marie-Antoinette's own view that, in all probability, she would be put on trial. In the second week of April fifty thousand Austrian troops were moved to the Belgian frontier.

On April 20 Louis XVI came to the Assembly to hear Dumouriez' official account of the situation facing France. The House of Austria, the deputies were told, had "enslaved" France to its ambitions since 1756. The undoing of that treaty, Gensonné had already said, would be an act of joyous destruction akin to the demolition of the Bastille. War was demanded forthwith, with only a few deputies of Robespierre's mind opposing it. One, Becquet, from the Haute-Marne, warned that "we shall earn the reputation of being an aggressive and restless people who disturb the peace of Europe and disregard treaties and international law." These cautions were shoved aside by a great hallelujah of patriotic affirmation. Anacharsis Cloots was beside himself with messianic rapture:

> Here is the crisis of the universe. God disentangled the primitive chaos; the French will unravel the feudal chaos . . . for free men are Gods on earth. . . . [Kings] make impious war on us with slave soldiers and extorted money; we will make a holy war with free soldiers and patriotic contributions.

The commander in chief of what Brissot had called "a crusade for universal liberty" in which each soldier would say to his enemy, "Brother, I am not going to cut your throat . . . I am going to show you the way to happiness" was not himself visibly happy. In a flat, faltering voice Louis XVI then read the formal declaration of war as though it were a death sentence upon himself. Which indeed it was.

iii "MARSEILLAISE"

Five days after the declaration of war, the Strasbourg garrison was preparing for the "crusade for universal liberty" promised by Brissot. A public dinner was held in which officers—many of them, like de Broglie, d'Aiguillon and Kléber, from the liberal nobility—mingled with the local Patriot notables. none more important than the *ci-devant* Baron Dietrich, the mayor of the city. Toasts were drunk rehearsing the favorite themes of the war: death to despots; long live the *patrie* of Liberty. Someone asked the young army engineer Rouget de Lisle, who had made a minor reputation in Paris as a composer, if he could not produce a song that would send the armies off to the frontier with a patriotic march. The bouncing tempo of "Ça Ira," after all, was hardly suitable for a military step.

Rouget de Lisle had some experience in this work. The son of a Franche-Comté family of minor gentry, he had won a scholarship to the military engineering academy at Mézières, where he had met both Lazare Carnot and Prieur de la Côte d'Or. Though able enough as a sapper, he had taken time off from constructing bridges and artillery carriages to compose airs in the jaunty style that sold well in Paris. After five years of part-time composing he decided to try his luck in the capital, where he made friends with Grétry. His style became more serious; a "Hymn to Liberty" was produced, though it was the version of Strasbourg's local composer Ignaz Pleyel that was used in the grand *fête* for the acceptance of the constitution.

From this rather humdrum mix of talents, the musical engineer somehow came up with the "Chant de Guerre de l'Armée du Rhin" (Song of the Rhine Army). Energized by the sense of coming battle and fortified by champagne, Rouget de Lisle worked through the night of the fifteenth-sixteenth of April, flourishing the score before Dietrich in the morning. (The mayor somewhat boorishly performed it himself for the first time three days later.)

The song that, under the name "La Marseillaise," was to survive when all the works of Pleyel, Gossec, Méhul and Grétry combined were forgotten was an astonishing invention, the nearest thing to a speech of Pierre Vergniaud's set to rhyme and music, a tune and a rhythm to set the pulse racing and the blood coursing. When Dietrich's wife and Gossec had scored in the harmonics for a military band, it opened into a great swelling anthem of patriotic communion. Nothing like the "Marseillaise" has ever been written that comes so near to expressing the comradeship of citizens in arms and nothing ever will.

All the great emotive themes of the Revolution—family, blood, soil—were given their voice. The first verse is the family drama. The *patrie*—the Fatherland—calls its *children* to arms to defend its loved ones (*vos fils, vos compagnes*) against hordes of approaching mercenaries, bent on slaughter. Brilliantly the melody drops to a sinister murmur as the terror approaches, before being repelled by the great clarion call of "*Aux armes, citoyens,*" repeated as the chorus through all five verses. Throughout the song, images of blood and carnage are used to frighten and inspire. The *étendard sanglant* (the bloody banner) has been raised against the *enfants de la patrie;* so the *sang impur,* the tainted blood of tyrants, should *abreuve les sillons* (irrigate the soil) of the nation. Macabre though the images were, they exactly echoed contemporary feeling. Not long before, a young student had written to his father, justifying his decision to volunteer by declaring that "our liberty can only be assured if it will have for its bed a mattress of cadavers . . . I consent to become one of those cadavers."

The "Marseillaise" was not, then, a revolutionary song of the south. The patriotic anthem took its eventual name when a group of *fédéré* Guards from Montpellier brought it to Marseille en route to their encampment in Paris. Once in the capital local revolutionary militants who turned the five hundred–odd soldiers from Marseille into idealized heroes of the "second revolution" attached to them the new anthem. But in fact it was a true song of the eastern and northern frontier, something born not of Jacobin cocksureness, bragging threats to hang the aristocracy like those found in the "Ça Ira." Instead, it sprang from the nervous defiance shown against "tyrants" as the Revolution prepared, for the first time, to confront the armies of absolutist monarchy.

We do not know if those first soldiers marched out of Lille toward the Belgian city of Tournai with Rouget de Lisle's song on their lips. But if that was the case, then it certainly did them no good. For in embarrassing contrast not only to the invincible optimism of the anthem, but the equally expansive certainties of Brissotin rhetoric, the first campaign of the wars that would end twenty-three years and a million and a half dead Frenchmen later, began as a pathetic fiasco.

This was all the more shocking because the commanders appointed to the three major theaters of war were all famous veterans of France's last indisputably successful campaign in America. Lafayette was given the center front on the Marne, General Luckner the Alsace frontier and Rochambeau, the hero of Yorktown and Saratoga, the most immediately critical zone of the Belgian frontier in the north. Though Narbonne's touted tours of inspection had done their best to disguise the fact, Rochambeau was well aware that in respect both to the complement of troops and their battle-readiness and discipline, the French armies were far from prepared to face the Austrians. The breakdown of the regimental hierarchy that had been signaled by the Nancy mutiny in 1790 had not been arrested by the repression. Indeed, the increasing rate of emigration among officers after Varennes had if anything deepened suspicions among the rank and file that officers were not to be trusted and might be deliberately betraying the *patrie* in the guise of commanding it.

These suspicions were to have murderous consequences for Théobald

Dillon, the local commander of the force dispatched against Tournai. A cousin of Lucy de La Tour du Pin, Dillon was a typical product of the liberal nobility, patriotic and capable and certainly hostile to the émigrés. But like many of the career officers, he was most sympathetic to Lafayette and mistrustful of the Brissotin government. More specifically he had been enlisted by Dumouriez to activate the Belgian theater, which, the Minister believed, was just awaiting a sign from the French to begin a great anti-Austrian insurrection. Dillon's assignment was to carry out a modest expedition at Tournai, generally thought to be lightly defended. To do this he had a force of five thousand men, for the most part regular cavalry but complemented with a force of volunteer soldiers. Just because of this strength, success seemed guaranteed.

In the event, those expectations recoiled disastrously. At Baisieux the advance guard of the cavalry ran into artillery fire. Very quickly rumors of an Austrian advance spread through the French lines. A preplanned, tactical withdrawal speedily turned into an inglorious *sauve-qui-peut*, led not by the volunteers but by the regular horsemen. Caught up in the flight, Dillon took shelter in a peasant cottage and made the fatal mistake of taking off his uniform coat. Alerted by patriotic propaganda to the presence of spies and traitors, the farmer believed he had one in his house, sipping his broth, and alerted the garrison at Douai. The unfortunate general was taken under guard to Lille, where he was torn from his carriage by a crowd of townsmen, soldiers and National Guard, slashed in the face and finally bayoneted to death on the cobblestones. Dillon's body was then hanged from a *lanterne;* its left leg was severed as a trophy and paraded around town before the rest of the corpse was thrown on a bonfire.

The dismal impression given by the disaster before Tournai was made even worse when Biron's force failed to press an attack on Mons, though in this case the commander was preserved so that he might later perish on the guillotine. Since the Austrians failed to capitalize on the demoralization of the French troops, little was lost strategically. But the political consequences of the debacle were dramatically polarizing. On the right, many remaining senior officers of the line army now believed themselves to be risking Dillon's fate at the least setback. Some resigned, beginning with Rochambeau himself at the very apex of the northern command; others emigrated. Those who remained in service, like Lafayette himself, were now convinced that the precondition of military survival was the reestablishment of order both within the army and in Paris. Indeed he was now prepared to use military force to preempt the threat of insurrection in the capital. Early in May he wrote to the Austrian Ambassador Mercy d'Argenteau, proposing a suspension of hostilities while he dealt with the Paris militants.

153. Jean-Louis Prieur, engraving, the death of General Théobald Dillon in Lille, April 29, 1792. The center of the print shows his body being burned.

Lafayette's enemies, however, were not obtuse. Even the lull in fighting in May confirmed their suspicions that the commanders in the field were more interested in taking them on than the Austrians. This impression was not dispelled by the defection *en masse* of virtually the entire regiment of the Royal-Allemands, the cavalry that had charged the popular demonstration in the place Vendôme and the Tuileries on July 12, 1789. "I do not trust the generals," Robespierre said in the Jacobins; "most of them are nostalgic for the old order." This sense of deliberate sabotage by men who had maneuvered themselves into command was extended to economic and social grievances. The depreciation of the *assignats,* which fueled food price inflation, was blamed on systematic and politically motivated currency speculation. The harvest of 1791 had been average to mediocre but in some areas of France, especially the south and southeast, shortages were acute. The deregulation of the internal grain market that had been the physiocrats' legacy, the Revolution now used to pull supplies towards areas of shortage, but only after they had been kept back long enough to secure high prices. This is exactly what liberal economists had recommended as a way in which to ensure capital accumulation in agriculture. But fine theory invariably made for immediate misery, panic and riot. The tempo of attacks on wagons, barges and depots, which had been sluggish since 1789, now revived in earnest. With the additional gloss that the "famine plot" was part of a counter-revolutionary attempt to starve the people into capitulation, violent assaults on persons as well as property were more widespread and unrestrained. Finally, the black uprisings in the French West Indies had interrupted sugar supplies and had made other commodities to which the working population of the towns had become accustomed—coffee, for example—prohibitively expensive. The consequence was attacks on grocery stores in the spring of 1792.

The accumulation of these grievances gave the leaders and tutors of popular politics the opportunity to emerge from the subdued silence to which they had been confined since the repression of the previous summer. With Lafayette occupied at the front and the complaisant Pétion rather than the fretful Bailly as mayor, the militant press and the popular clubs quickly revived their following in the spring of 1792. Marat's *L'Ami du Peuple* and the Cordeliers Club were very much back in business, launching furious attacks not just against the court and the "Austrian Committee" deliberately sabotaging the war, but more generally against the rich, now expressly characterized as the "bourgeoisie," who had cut themselves off from the People and had forgotten how much they owed to them as the shock troops of Liberty. There were, moreover, some new and distinctively violent voices raised to weed out traitors and punish speculators. René Hébert's newspaper, the *Père Duchesne,* made free use of wineshop obscenities to rail against those in power. And Jacques Roux, the *curé* of Saint-Nicolas-des-Champs, in one of the very poorest quarters of Paris, filled with market porters and transient labor, also demanded summary punitive justice against those responsible for starving Patriots.

There was absolutely nothing new in these Christian-egalitarian polemics and it was precisely their familiarity which made them so popular. They harked back exactly to the anticapitalist, antimodernist rhetoric of Mercier, praising craft and detesting capital, which had been one of the most potent sources of revolutionary anger. The truly radical phase of the Revolution—its violent overthrow of the educated elite and notables who had dominated the Constituent and the reforming enterprises since the 1770s—was now at hand. And from the outset it was this aggressively illiberal, antipecuniary code of values that mobilized the population to take up arms. The designation *sans-culottes* (without breeches) was itself a kind of romanticization of the world of craft shops, since it insisted on the incompatibility of social virtue and silk hose and breeches (items that Robespierre himself invariably wore). In actual fact, the leaders of these breechless militants of 1792 and 1793 were often drawn not from the very poor but from the better-off strata of the artisanal trades and professions. Indeed some of their leaders, like the brewer Santerre, were not merely comfortable, but rich. Nonetheless they actively encouraged their constituents to demand things squarely at odds with economic individualism: the government regulation of grain and other food prices; enforced acceptance of the *assignat* at face value; and draconian punishments (including the death penalty) for anyone suspected of hoarding or speculation, a category notoriously hard to define in a liberalized economy. The republicanized paternalism of this program was summed up in a brochure produced in Lyon in June demanding the establishment of nationally established grain prices and titled, with disarming innocence, *Moyens Simples et Faciles de Fixer l'Abondance* (Simple and Easy Means to Establish Abundance).

What gave the sans-culottes' demands special force in 1792 was the added dimension of military patriotism. The enemies within were now not some abstractly defined class foe, but, as it were, Austrians in French dress. Indeed it was explicitly said that the sinister, ubiquitous "Austrian Committee" causing so much havoc and demoralization on the front was also deliberately fomenting calamity at home, causing food supplies to disappear. It was the perpetual craving to identify and punish the fifth-column patriot-hypocrites that fed the "unmasking" obsession (a good Rousseauean fixation) in the Jacobins and the Cordeliers. In the spring and summer of 1792 this need to distinguish between the true and the false patriot required the acceptance of visible badges of patriotic authenticity.

The most important was the red hat, the *bonnet rouge*. The French Revolution by no means invented liberty-hat symbolism. Drawn from Roman coins on which freed slaves were shown receiving the "Phrygian bonnet" at the moment of their emancipation, it had a history in graphic art, medals and inscriptions going back at least to the Dutch revolt of the sixteenth century. And it was in continuous use in both popular and polite culture for at least two centuries, usually in the form of a wide-brimmed round form with a flat crown. In a soft, bonnet variant it showed up frequently in such eighteenth-century English prints as Hogarth's unflattering image of the radical John Wilkes; in engravings celebrating American liberty in the 1770s; in the Dutch Patriot movement of the 1780s; and finally in much of the Fédération imagery of 1790, especially at Lyon. What was remarkable about the development in 1792 was the literalization of the symbol; people were now not only expected to recognize the emblem but actually wear it. Even in 1791, when David drew his idealized man of the people in the tennis court, the hat that man was wearing was an emblem rather than a real item of headgear. A year later that was no longer true.

Robespierre, of course, never deigned to don the bonnet over his powdered curls, but it began showing up in the Jacobins among both members and spectators, and in the more self-consciously popular societies and *section* assemblies it virtually became *de rigueur*. Even some army officers demanded the right to wear it instead of their military tricorn.

Not surprisingly, then, the ritual moment at which the man whom *Père Duchesne* now habitually called "Louis le Faux"—or sometimes just "le Faux-Pas," for the flight to Varennes—was unmasked as a non-king was on June 20, when a red bonnet was unceremoniously stuck on his head. Reduced to the ranks, stripped of the last remaining attributes of majesty (the Legislative had long debated whether they could continue to call him "sire"), Louis Capet was forced to drink the health of the true Sovereign People.

What made this possible was the transfer of armed power away from those whom the Jacobins deemed the fifth column and into the hands of "dependable" Patriots. The mayor, Pétion, ignored the restrictions on clubs, petitions and the press introduced by Duport and Le Chapelier in the last days of the Constituent and even encouraged the distribution of arms among the *section* assemblies, believing they might be needed to defend his allies the Brissotins against any attempt at a military coup d'état. To begin with, there was yet another literalization of a traditional emblem of liberty, the pike, which had almost as antique a pedigree as the hat. A *section* of Paris renamed itself "Les Piques" and Hébert told his readers, "To your pikes, good sans-culottes, sharpen them up to exterminate aristocrats." For all the hyperbole, the distribution of long, sharpened iron weapons was not an insignificant addition to the capacity for popular violence. By June, however, *section* assemblies were admitting "passive" citizens to their National Guard companies without seeking formal permission. And their equipment included altogether unsymbolic muskets, rifles and even, in some cases, cannon.

At the same time, formal demands were made to the King at the end of May to liquidate his own personal guard of six thousand, mostly stationed at the Tuileries. That corps had been part of Barnave's strategy of reassuring the court that a constitutional monarchy would have means to defend its authority against repeated insurrection, though he had to tell the Queen that the sky-blue uniforms she favored in contrast to the legitimate dark blue of the National Guard would immediately stigmatize the force as foreign mercenaries. Typically trading his strong cards for weak ones, Louis accepted this official disarmament, principally because he wanted to veto the enforcement of a decree enabling refractory priests to be summarily deported at the behest of no more than twenty active citizens.

Shortly after, he also vetoed a proposal from the Minister of War, Servan, to establish an armed camp of some twenty thousand *fédérés* from the provinces who would not only arrive for the festive purpose of celebrating the fourteenth of July, but who would also receive "training" (of indeterminate length) before being sent to the frontier.

Ironically, Robespierre also opposed the camp of the *fédérés*, seeing in it an attempt by the government to use provincial guards to cow their more politically radical Paris co-citizens. But in the Cordeliers, where once again the organization of insurrection was most intensively directed, the King's last feeble attempt at constitutional self-assertion met with a great chorus of abuse. His opposition to the *fédérés* was represented in the press as self-evident proof that he was himself planning an act of force from his "citadel" in the Tuileries. Mme Roland, who dictated a letter to her husband so that it should bear the official imprimatur of the Minister of the Interior, gave Louis XVI a severe reprimand for his audacity, and warned that "This is not time to retreat or to temporize. The revolution has been made in people's minds; it will be accomplished and cemented at the cost of bloodshed unless wisdom forestalls evils which it is still possible to avoid . . . I know that the austere language of truth is rarely welcomed near the throne but I also know that it is because it is so rarely heard that revolutions become necessary."

Not only did Louis not heed these warnings and withdraw his vetoes, but the lecture from the Rolands may have triggered him into dismissing the whole Brissotin ministry two days later. This sudden volte-face had been Dumouriez' idea, the better to establish his own domination of the government. Once that had been accomplished, he also asked the King to cancel his veto so as to minimize causes for popular disturbances in the *sections*. But this was exactly the kind of tactical deviation Louis was incapable of comprehending.

On June 20, a demonstration was mobilized in the *sections* by leaders of the popular societies, in particular Santerre; Danton's friend the butcher Legendre; another longtime publicist and militant republican, Fournier "the American"; the crazed *ci-devant* Marquis de Saint-Huruge; and Jean Varlet, like Santerre a well-to-do bourgeois (in his case a postal clerk) who had embraced the social egalitarianism of Jacques Roux. All of these figures were prominent in the resurrected Cordeliers; many of them had affiliations in other clubs like the Fraternal Society for Patriots of Both Sexes. Some of the leaders of the women's republican movement like Théroigne de Méricourt, the Dutch feminist (and spy) Etta Palm and the *chocolatier*'s daughter Pauline León were also involved in the mobilization of the crowd. They had already had some practice earlier in the spring when a festival involving mass participation had been organized by the Jacobins to celebrate the liberation of the soldiers who had been imprisoned in 1790 for their part in the mutiny of the Nancy garrison. (The right had promptly retaliated with a counter-festival honoring Simonneau, the mayor of Etampes killed by food rioters.)

But the festival of the Nancy prisoners was an orderly affair precisely because it had the blessing of the Jacobins and because the arrangements for the usual processions, music and speeches had to be so carefully programmed in advance. On June 20 things were quite different. The ostensible aim of the crowd coming from the artisan and poor *sections* (the two not being the same) was to plant a liberty tree in the grounds of the Tuileries. This would be both an act of protest against the removal of the Brissotins and a kind of ritualized flag of conquest in the last remaining royal redoubt. Since his colleagues had been summarily removed from government, Pétion was not particularly interested in restraining this protest, even though there was always a possibility it might imperil the safety of the royal family.

Two huge crowds formed, one at the place de la Bastille, the other at the Salpêtrière, and converged on the Tuileries; they were led by Santerre, already a kind of unofficial commander of the armed sans-culotte guardsmen. At around half past one in the afternoon they arrived at the Manège to ask admission to the Legislative to read their petition. The presentation of petitions backed by arms was precisely the kind of thing Le Chapelier's law had been meant to prohibit, but faced with the direct threat of intimidation—and with Girondins like Vergniaud still angry about the dismissal of the government—the deputies were disinclined to offer much resistance. While they were debating, the crowd planted a tall tree of liberty—a poplar—in the garden of the Capuchins and were finally admitted, singing the "Ça Ira," to the assembly hall.

But it was what followed this rowdy and intimidating parade that signified the beginning of the end of the reign of Louis XVI. The crowd massed in enormous numbers around the perimeter of the palace grounds themselves, with its leaders actually reluctant to press forward. But when the cannoneers of the Val-de-Grâce regiment, who had marched with the demonstrators that morning, now brought up cannon, the gates were opened as much to avoid a disastrous crush of people as with anything more sinister in mind. A huge crowd poured into the undefended palace, finding the King himself, with just a few unarmed guards and attendants, in the Salon de l'Oeil de Boeuf.

It was his worst moment and his best. He backed his big form into a window embrasure and, sometimes leaning against the seat, sometimes

154. J-B Mallet, engraving, Sulpice Huguenin,
one of the leaders of the crowd that entered
the Tuileries to protest the dismissal of the
Brissotin ministry, June 20, 1792

standing, faced the leaders of the crowd directly and with extraordinary composure. Pistols and naked sabers were brandished in his face. Some accounts claim that the heart of a calf, stuck on the end of a pike, was waved about to represent "the heart of an aristocrat." Louis had earlier used his own Rousseau-like heart language when, to show his grenadiers that he was not frightened of the crowd beating its way into the palace, he had taken one of their hands and placed it on his breast, remarking, "See, it does not palpitate." There is no doubt, though, that the afternoon was an appalling ordeal. Shouts of "Down with the veto; to the devil with the veto" were thrown at Louis as though the act and the man were one and the same. The sans-culotte butcher Legendre is said to have told him forthrightly, "Monsieur, you must hear us; you are a villain. You have always deceived us; you deceive us still. Your measure is full. The people are tired of this play-acting."

To each of these humiliations, Louis responded without seeming foolish. Presented with a red hat, he put it on his head and proposed the health of the people of Paris and the nation. Shocked royalists would recall the humiliation as Louis XVI's crown of thorns. But through the melee he remained adamant in his refusal either to withdraw the veto or to recall the

155. Louis XVI drinks to the health of the Nation, June 20, 1792. The inscription
"Aristocrats, do not concern yourself, the traitor Louis drinks like a Templar"
suggested that the print was produced after August 10.

Brissotin ministers. This combination of graciousness and dignity some-how defused the worst of the fury and certainly prevented violence. A whole afternoon was too long to sustain even the most murderous barrage of insults. At six in the evening Pétion, who had kept very much out of sight the whole day, now pushed his way through to the King's presence claim-ing, implausibly, to the King that he had just heard of the "situation you are in." "That is astonishing," replied Louis, "since this has been continu-ing for some hours." After prolonged harangues, Pétion managed to persuade the crowd to leave. At eight, Louis and Marie-Antoinette were reunited in a room where she had also been subjected to torrential abuse. Their exhaustion at the trauma was balanced only by the immense relief that somehow they and their children had physically survived. But it was equally clear that with the humiliation of June 20 the last vestiges of the royal aura had been stripped away. Unless something drastic was done, it would no longer be a question of the survival of the monarchy's authority, let alone its constitutional viability. All that would remain would be a brute trial of strength.

T H A T   T H I S   would in fact happen was not quite a foregone conclusion. The King and Queen still had their defenders. Once news of what had happened on the twentieth spread around France, loyal petitions from all over the country poured into the Assembly. Even some of the *section* assemblies repudiated the action. Pétion and Manuel the *procureur* were suspended from office by the departmental government for dereliction of duty. Some of Brissot's colleagues who had been more dismayed than exhilarated by the invasion of the palace now actively be-gan secret negotiations. At the height of a debate over the removal of the Dauphin from his family to ensure "a patriotic education," Guadet came to see the Queen. She showed him the Prince asleep behind a curtain in the adjoining room, and Elie Guadet, who was very much of his generation in being affected by the innocence of childhood, bent his immaculately curled head over the boy, brushed hair away from his face and kissed his brow. "If he is to survive," he warned the Queen, "you must bring him up to love liberty."

Offers of help from other quarters were less cordially received. On the twenty-eighth Lafayette made his last bid to command the political fate of France. He appeared before the Legislative to demand the enforcement of the classic Feuillant measures of closing the clubs, curbing the press and banning petitions. His listeners were unsympathetic since they correctly suspected this to be the preliminary announcement of a coup d'état. But Lafayette was no Bonaparte. He had not massed sufficient force in advance to make sure his words would be heeded. Indeed, attempts by him to mobilize the National Guard were a dismal failure. Challenged in the Assembly with leaving his troops without permission, he had no adequate answer. More surprisingly, the royal family—perhaps overconfident about its new Girondin connections—would have none of him. The Queen in particular had long hated Lafayette and had actually supported Pétion in the Paris mayoral election just for the pleasure of seeing him defeated. On this occasion she went to the length of alerting Pétion in advance of the review at which the General would try to rally the Guard.

Spurned by those he wanted to help, the butt of ridicule and hatred in the press, Lafayette returned to his military post in Alsace. After the fall of the monarchy on August 10, he made one last effort at a stand, summoning the mayor of Sedan and his officers to the ceremony at which he was most rehearsed: the swearing of a constitutional oath. But somehow he could not bring himself to take the next step of beginning a civil war. (It began in any case without him.) When the new authorities in Paris suspended him from his commission, he crossed the lines to the Austrian camp and spent the next five years in their prison at Olmütz. It was a wretched dénouement for the boy who had wandered into the woods to commune with the Hyena of Liberty. But it was not to be the end of Lafayette's career as the apostle of liberal revolution.

With the General out of the way, the last hope of arresting forces that were very rapidly becoming polarized lay in the Legislative Assembly itself. But the events of June 20, far from stiffening its resolve, had shaken it. Deputies nervous for their own safety began to drift away from the debates, so that at the height of the insurrection of August there were probably no more than one quarter of the eight hundred sitting. The Girondin leadership was divided over whether to throw their lot in with the *section* militants to avoid forfeiting all influence to the Robespierristes, or whether to defend the legal order by force. On July 5 a declaration that the *"patrie est en danger"* was proclaimed. But the emergency powers obtained by such a suspension of normal legal procedure were a dangerous means of legitimizing the government's policy. While they could justify, as Robespierre still feared, an attack on the clubs and *sections,* they could equally be used *by* those same elements to overthrow the government and the Assembly.

Despairing of any kind of pragmatic reconciliation, the constitutional Bishop of Lyon, Lamourette, tried instead to appeal to the deputies' sense of emotional theater. Appealing to all those who rejected, with equal vehemence, the demands of the right for a two-chamber parliament and those of the left for a republic, he asked for an "oath of eternal fraternity" and for it to be sealed by an embrace. For the last time, deputies stood, cheered, waved hats in the air, declared "The *patrie* is saved" and threw themselves into each other's arms, kissing and hugging in a great transport of collective rapture. It may have been this emotional abandon that led the Assembly naturally on to the next topic, which concerned allowing children to marry without their parents' consent. But it was brusquely interrupted by a furious delegation from the municipality who had learned that the authorities of the department had just suspended Pétion and Manuel for their responsibility in the events of the twentieth of June, and vowed to stand shoulder-to-shoulder with them.

Kissing gave way again to cursing. As the *fédérés* began to arrive in Paris, the *section* assemblies they attended began to demand the establishment of a republic. Marat's *L'Ami du Peuple* made explicit appeals to the poor, asking them why "the rich alone should harvest the fruits of the revolution while you have won from the revolution only the sad right to continue to pay heavy taxes and like Turks or Prussians be subject to conscription." Many of the *fédérés* National Guards came from areas of France where revolutionary Patriots were most embattled—Brittany, the Midi and the East—and responded eagerly to this kind of inflammatory rhetoric. Indeed, since many of them were sleeping on the premises of the Cordeliers or lodged out from there to Patriots of the most militant opinions, they were captive to the most uncompromising republican polemics. Some of them even heard the demands made by Théroigne de Méricourt and Pauline León for a women's regiment armed with pikes.

Steadily, ominously, Paris was turning into an armed camp. Every day companies of Guards paraded in public places, armed to the teeth and chanting the "Ça Ira." The climax, which had been carefully prepared by the radical Charles Barbaroux since the spring, was the arrival on July 30 of five hundred guards from Marseille singing Rouget de Lisle's anthem, which from then on bore their name. At the Jacobins, Robespierre, who finally seems to have been converted to the timeliness of insurrection, had established a bureau to concert their forces. Another central committee of insurrection was established at the municipal government of the Commune, comprising delegates commissioned from the *sections* and including Fournier, Santerre and the radical journalist Carra. Coordinating many of these efforts to create a cohesive popular military force capable of administering the coup de grâce was Danton, now at last in the official position he had long craved. Specifically he was in a senior legal post as the deputy *procureur* of the Commune, and so was in a vital strategic position to give or withhold commands as the situation required. When the *fédérés* (in particular the Marseillais) brawled with units of the loyal National Guard, nothing much was done to pursue the guilty parties, and the climate of chronic lawlessness in the city steadily escalated through the end of July.

On the last day of the month, the *section* Mauconseil published an address to the citizens of Paris declaring that "the most sacred duty and the most cherished law is to forget the law to save the *patrie.*" The enemy was approaching and very soon Louis XVI would deliver the nation's cities to the bloody fire of the despots of Europe. "For too long a despicable tyrant has played with our destinies. . . . Without amusing ourselves any longer by calculating his errors, his crimes and his perjuries, let us strike this colossus of despotism . . . let us all unite to declare the fall of this cruel king, let us say with one accord, Louis XVI is no longer king of the French." The General Will of the *section,* they said, would no longer recognize him as their sovereign.

This declaration created a moral and political vacuum from which, the *sections* claimed, an entire new order could be created. Three days later, another proclamation from a quite different source abruptly deepened the sinkhole by which the legitimacy of the constitutional monarchy was being swallowed. Earlier in the summer the Prussians had entered the war as allies of the Emperor and during July had advanced with ominous steadiness. Their declaration of intent was issued in the name of their commander, the Duke of Brunswick, but had been written by the émigré the Marquis de Limon. It asked the French people to rise against the "odious schemes of their oppressors" and threatened with unspecified "rigors of war" any who had the temerity to resist. In the event of any further assault on the Tuileries, Paris would be singled out for an "exemplary and unforgettable act of vengeance."

Needless to say, the proclamation resulted in precisely the consequence it was supposed to avert. It gave the organizers of the insurrection the opportunity they had been waiting for to raise the stakes of the political conflict into an all-out war. The Brunswick Manifesto in effect told the Parisians and their provincial supporters among the *fédérés* that they had already committed acts for which they would be unsparingly punished; they had nothing to lose by going the whole distance. All that counted was to keep those who threatened them at home from acts of betrayal. All calculations had come down to this final primitive determination: kill or be killed.

It was this perception of extremity that decisively altered the odds. Attempts had been made to mobilize the *sections* at the end of June, but they had all gone off at half cock. The Brunswick Manifesto speeded up a major alteration in the balance of military power in Paris. Local National Guards (who, in contrast to 1790, had not been especially happy to see their city overrun with the provincial *fédérés*) now began to desert their units. They were absorbed into a general command organized by the "Bureau of Correspondence" directed from the Jacobins and led by provincial officers, in particular the Alsatian François-Joseph Westermann.

Though Marat attempted to represent the rising of August 10 as a spontaneous outbreak of unstoppable popular anger, the truth was quite the opposite. Never had a revolution been more laboriously prepared or more hesitantly embarked on. The King's ministry was a straw government, bereft of any authority or power. Its master, the Legislative Assembly, was at a fraction of its strength and without any power to enforce its decrees or protect the constitution it had sworn (many, many times) to uphold. The National Guard was confused, divided and uncertainly led, concerned more with protecting its neighborhood of Paris from violence against property and persons than with the outcome of a political struggle. What, then, stood in the way of the insurgents? There was the opinion of most French men and women, who had been told endlessly that the constitution was sacrosanct and probably believed it, but who were now represented by armed, militant minorities acting in their name in the capital. More seriously, two thousand regular troops, of whom half belonged to the King's personal Swiss guard, were dug in at the Tuileries.

The outcome was never really in doubt. But as the tocsin rang through the night of the ninth-tenth of August, many of the men who made their way towards the Hôtel de Ville were apprehensive. After dinner Camille Desmoulins and his wife had gone to Danton's apartment to try to stiffen their morale but had found Danton's wife Gabrielle in floods of tears. Lucile, who remembered herself "laughing like a madwoman," took Danton's wife for some air in the street and found a great crowd in the apartment when they got back, everyone trying to outdo each other with grandiloquent utterances that seemed appropriate to their overwrought sense of historymaking. But beneath the oracular declarations, agitation and fear put everyone on edge. When Camille set off into the night, carrying a musket and promising his wife to stay with the reassuringly enormous figure of Danton, she too began to weep passionately.

At the Hôtel de Ville an "Insurrectionary Commune" had swept aside the authority of the sitting municipal council and was now giving orders to the National Guard. The Commune comprised three delegates, in principle sent via the "General Will" of each of the forty-eight *sections*. In fact, of course, it was a body made up exclusively from the militant sections of the east of the city and the central left-bank zone that had made up the old Cordeliers. It included Robespierre, the engraver Sergent, Billaud-Varenne and François Robert. Danton himself was obviously a crucial if not the commanding figure, though he actually returned home during the night while the first unsuccessful attempts were being made to mobilize the insurgent *sections*.

In the early morning of the tenth, the disposition made by the commander of the loyal National Guard, the Marquis de Mandat, to block the bridges across the Seine and prevent a juncture of armed *sectionnaires* from Saint-Marcel with those of the right bank, seemed to have worked. The King was confident enough to go down into the heavily fortified courtyard just after dawn and review his troops. The mixed reception he received— loyal applause from the Swiss guards, alarming shouts of *"Vive la Nation"* from the Paris National Guard—made him uneasy. Anticipating a headlong assault, the *procureur-général* of the department, Roederer, had been trying to persuade him to leave the château and place his own person in the trust of the Legislative Assembly. Though he had buckled on his sword, as Roederer informed him and the Queen that "all Paris" was on the march Louis' determination evaporated. He and his family walked across the courtyard with as much dignity as they could, listening to increasingly angry shouts of "No more veto." "The leaves are falling early this year," the King remarked to Roederer, suggesting either fatalistic remoteness or an uncharacteristic penchant for metaphor.

Once in the Manège, where a handful of deputies remained simply to preempt accusations that the Sovereign Nation was no longer constituted, the King was left waiting while a place was found for him and his family compatible with the prohibition on his presence during debates. Together with his sister Elisabeth, Marie-Antoinette and their children, they were finally ushered into the little caged space of the Logographie, assigned to reporters recording the proceedings. Inside this stuffy little hole, their faces shadowed by the cell-like grille, what was left of the French monarchy waited, helplessly, on its fate.

About two hours later, fighting began in earnest. From the beginning of the day it was apparent that blood would flow more freely than at any time since the beginning of the Revolution. The Marquis de Mandat had already been summoned by the new Commune to the Hôtel de Ville, ostensibly to explain his refusal to withdraw the defensive positions of the Guard. When Danton had finished shouting at him he was dragged off to detention and murdered en route, probably by Antoine Rossignol, another member of the Commune. With authority caving in at the center, no attempt was made to resist the insurgent troops moving across the Seine. When the brewer Santerre, leading the left-bank soldiers and those of the right bank with their commander, Alexandre, arrived at the Tuileries, they already outnumbered the defenders.

The slaughter that followed was largely produced by the impression, as on the fourteenth of July 1789, that a deliberate trap had been laid for the attackers. When the royal family left for the Assembly, word rapidly spread among the National Guard that there had been a capitulation. The Swiss were urged to fraternize, and some of them apparently discarded weapons. Encouraged by this the Guard went into the château, only to meet a raking volley of fire that pursued them in flight across the Cour Royale. When they regrouped, Westermann and Fournier led a furious counter-attack, with the Marseillais in the van shooting their way over the empty space towards the palace.

Eventually weight of numbers would have told. Perhaps Louis knew this and wanted to spare further loss of life by scribbling a note ordering the Swiss guards to lay down their arms. He might have remembered the fourteenth of July, when an aggrieved sense of betrayal assuaged itself in the murder of the single sacrificial victim of Governor de Launay.

Matters were resolved differently on the tenth of August. Obedient to the last hour of the monarchy, the Swiss were forming up to retreat to the palace when they were set on by the attackers and slaughtered brutally wherever they were found. Such was the hysteria of the moment that even the *fédérés* from Brest—among the most militant of the rebels—were killed because their red uniform fatally resembled that of the Swiss. Those soldiers who could see in time what was in store for them ran frantically, stripping off clothes, weapons, cartridge belts. Some threw themselves from high windows in the palace to the flagstones below to get a start on their pursuers.

But that noontime they were given neither shelter nor quarter. Hunted down, they were mercilessly butchered: stabbed, sabered, stoned and clubbed. Women stripped the bodies of clothes and whatever possessions they could find. Mutilators hacked off limbs and scissored out genitals and stuffed them in gaping mouths or fed them to the dogs. What was left was thrown on bonfires, one of which spread to the palace itself. Other bits and pieces of the six hundred soldiers who perished in the massacre were loaded haphazardly onto carts and taken to common lime pits. It was, thought Robespierre, "the most beautiful revolution that has ever honored humanity."

But the carnage of the tenth of August was not an incidental moment in the history of the Revolution. It was, in fact, its logical consummation. From 1789, perhaps even before that, it had been the willingness of politicians to exploit either the threat or the fact of violence that had given them the power to challenge constituted authority. Bloodshed was not the unfortunate by-product of revolution, it was the source of its energy. The

156. Anonymous engraving, August 10 at the Tuileries. At bottom left, National
Guards deliver the coup de grâce to a kneeling Swiss guard; others throw
themselves from windows. The sans-culotte pike carriers at right include a woman.

verses of the "Marseillaise" and the great speeches of the Girondins had spoken of the *patrie* in the absolute poetry of life and death. Perversely, only if it could be shown that blood did indeed flow in its defense could the virtues of the Revolution be shown to be worth dying for. Means had become ends.

CHAPTER FIFTEEN

Impure Blood

August 1792–January 1793

i A "HOLOCAUST FOR LIBERTY"

S OMETIME during the third week of August, a guillotine was set up on the place du Carrousel, in front of the Tuileries. The *"machine,"* as it was generally called, was not a complete novelty since it had been in sporadic use since April 1792 at the traditional site of public executions on the place de Grève. Forgers of *assignats* were a special target of popular hatred, so their decapitation was something of an event. But for crowds accustomed to the prolonged and emotionally rich ritual of penitential processions, loud public confessions, the climactic jump of the body on the gibbet, the exposure of the hanging remains, even in some rare cases the prolonged ordeal of breaking on the wheel, the *machine* was a distinct disappointment. It was too expeditious. A swish, a thud; sometimes not even a display of the head; the executioner reduced to a low-grade mechanic like some flunkey pulling a bell rope.

But this austere compression of the spectacle of punishment was exactly what the designers of the *machine* had in mind. In December 1789, Dr. Joseph-Ignace Guillotin, deputy of the National Assembly, had proposed a reform of capital punishment in keeping with the equal status accorded to all citizens by the Declaration of the Rights of Man. Instead of barbaric practices which degraded the spectators as much as the criminal, a method of surgical instantaneity was to be adopted. Not only would decapitation spare the prisoner gratuitous pain, it would offer to common criminals the dignified execution hitherto reserved for the privileged orders. The proposal also removed the stigma of guilt by association from the family of the condemned and, most importantly, protected their property from the confiscation required by traditional practice.

157. Dr. Guillotin's *machine*, 1789

A rather beautiful engraving made to illustrate the humanity of Guillotin's device suggests dignified serenity rather than macabre retribution. The setting is bucolic since the good doctor wanted the site of execution to be moved beyond town, away from what he thought was the primitive spectacle of the gutter mob. The action is stoical, perhaps even sentimental, since the executioner too has been transformed, from a brawny professional into a sensitive soul required to avert his eyes as he slashes the cord with his saber. The benevolent confessor is straight out of Rousseau's *Confessions de Foi d'un Vicaire Savoyard* and the few spectators are expressly kept from the *machine* by a barrier guarded by an impassive soldier.

Nothing could have been more in keeping with late-Enlightenment thinking on capital punishment. There were deputies to the Constituent, notably Robespierre, who would have preferred outright abolition as recommended by Beccaria (except in cases of regicide or treason). But if the death penalty was to be retained, better it should be swift, merciful and utilitarian. In 1777 Marat had recommended some sort of method that would combine deterrent grimness with painless efficiency, and the *machine* described to the Assembly by Dr. Guillotin seemed to meet those specifications perfectly. His description (as reported in the *Journal des Etats-Généraux*)—"The mechanism falls like thunder; the head flies off, blood spurts, the man is no more"—met less with somber appreciation than nervous laughter. And while the other items of his reform were adopted in 1790, it was not until two years later that the *machine* itself was set to work.

On the third of June 1791, the *ci-devant* Marquis Lepeletier de Saint-Fargeau, a militant Jacobin, proposed that every person condemned to death suffer the same penalty of having their head struck off. But there was as yet no indication that this equal treatment was to be mechanically applied. It was only the reservations expressed by the public executioner, Charles-Henri Sanson, that led the Feuillant government in the spring of 1792 to consider the *machine* once more. Sanson's worry (as a professional proud of his trade) was that decapitation offered far more possibilities for unfortunate mishaps than hanging, especially with a heavy caseload. The blades might dull; the executioners might not be sufficiently skilled; the riffraff who were to be decapitated might not show the seemly composure expected of gentlemen. This would all make his work terribly difficult.

As Daniel Arasse points out in his excellent study, Dr. Guillotin had abandoned the *machine,* perhaps stung by the failure of the Constituent to take it seriously. But Dr. Louis, the perpetual secretary of the Academy of Surgeons (and the author of the article on death in the *Encyclopédie*),

*Traîtres regardez et tremblez elle ne perdra son
activité, que quand vous aurés tous perdu la vie.*

158. The inscription below the
engraving reads, "Traitors, look at this
and tremble. It will still be active while
all of you have lost your lives."

rescued the project in a learned memorandum assuring the Legislative that
such a device would guarantee instantaneity by its radical severing of the
neck ligaments. In April a German piano maker, Tobias Schmidt, was
commissioned to build the prototype. He finished it in a week, and on the
seventeenth, in the Bicêtre prison courtyard, trial executions were performed on corpses. Though the results were satisfactory, at least one witness already felt that though justice demanded such a solution, humanity
could not witness it without "shuddering."

Dr. Guillotin seems always to have resented the fact that a device of such
mechanical impersonality should have been associated with his name—even
though in its early career it was also called a "louison" or a "louisette" after
its more recent promoter. His proposal, he insisted, had always been "philanthropic" and humanitarian. But it was certainly as the penal expression
of impartiality that it was introduced to behead the first criminal on the
twenty-fifth of April 1792, Nicolas Pelletier, who had committed robbery
with violence. Following the overthrow of the monarchy, the guillotine
seemed to the authorities competing to be its beneficiary an ideal way to

recover control of violent punishment. When it was used on August 21 for the beheading of Louis Collot d'Angremont, the secretary of the administration of the National Guard (accused of having taken part in the royal "conspiracy"), it had already returned to the exemplary and spectacular purposes which both Guillotin's "philanthropy" and Louis' surgical utilitarianism meant to preclude. The place du Carrousel was selected for the site of execution precisely because it was there that the criminal was said to have perpetrated his misdeed. The public were positively encouraged to bear witness to his atonement and the swift severity by which the justice of the Nation was accomplished.

All this was meant to be in deliberate contrast to, and if possible to correct, the atrocities of what was euphemized as "popular justice," or in other words, spontaneous and summary lynchings, and fatal beatings and stabbings. There was, of course, an element of disingenuousness about this official attitude. The very beginnings of the Revolution in 1789 had been not just marked but actually empowered by precisely these acts of spontaneous retribution and indiscriminate street murders. The willingness of politicians like Barnave to tolerate these acts, only to find themselves and their regime on the receiving end, perpetuated the notion that "popular justice" was part and parcel of the legitimate self-expression of the "sovereign people." At each successive phase of the Revolution, those in authority attempted to recover a monopoly on punitive violence for the state, only to find themselves outmaneuvered by opposing politicians who endorsed and even organized popular violence for their own ends. The fact that arms were now securely in the hands of unofficial gendarmes of the popular will meant that the only way to impose the authority of the state was through a military confrontation which itself seemed to justify yet further acts of violence on the streets. The core problem of revolutionary government, then, turned on the efforts to manage popular violence on behalf of, rather than against, the state. This was something even the Jacobins failed to secure without the most extreme forms of totalitarian control.

The problem posed itself immediately following the overthrow of the monarchy on August 10. The rump of the Legislative Assembly had reinstated in a "Provisional Executive Council" the Girondin ministers dismissed by the King—Roland, Clavière and Servan—and had added to them for good measure two Jacobins, the mathematician Monge and, at the Ministry of Justice, Danton. The latter had personally intervened to protect a group of Swiss guard prisoners from casual butchery on the streets on the eleventh but he appreciated that some sort of institutionalized accounting was crucial if the thirst for popular "vengeance" was to be brought under control. In the weeks following the uprising, the center of power was, in any event, not in the Assembly but in the "Insurrectionary Commune" at the Hôtel de Ville, which gave instructions to its officers, the mayor Pétion and the *procureur* Manuel, whom it had also reinstated. It was in the Commune that the demands were most vehement for some sort of extraordinary military tribunal to try the "criminals" of August 10 (the events of that day now being routinely described as a royal plot). On the seventeenth just such a tribunal was established, with members to be appointed by the new commander of the Paris National Guard, Santerre; its judgments and sentences would expressly preclude any kind of appeal.

Collot d'Angremont's death on the guillotine was the first such sentence of the special tribunal to be carried out. A royalist journalist, du Rozoi, and the *intendant* of the King's civil list, Arnaud de La Porte, followed. But from the point of view of militants in the Commune like Robespierre and Marat, there were disappointingly few other such cases. At least they had demanded, and had got from the Legislative, extensive police powers to detain, interrogate and incarcerate suspects without anything resembling due process of law. The organ to which this work was entrusted was a Comité de Surveillance (Committee of Vigilance) on which two of Danton's friends from the days of the district of the Cordeliers—the engraver Sergent and the lawyer Panis—were particularly important. Though it cannot be too much emphasized that it was in the mythical days of revolutionary liberty, in *1789,* that the Constituent set up executive committees that resumed much of the police and spy work and powers of arbitrary detention associated with the old regime, it was only in August 1792 that a true revolutionary police state came into being in Paris.

During the two weeks between the seventeenth of August and the prison massacres in early September, more than a thousand people were taken into custody on the flimsiest warrants. The vast majority of them were refractory priests taken from seminaries, colleges and churches—sometimes even from private houses where they had been hidden in lay dress. Other targets were any persons identified as having petitioned against the demonstrators of the twentieth of June or against the prosecution of Lafayette for abandoning his post. The whole of the royalist press was shut down overnight, its editors and printers arrested and their equipment staved in. Other less obviously threatening enemies of the "sovereign people" were also peremptorily seized, including virtually all the personal servants of the King and Queen, among them the governess Mme de Tourzel, who had played "Baronne Korff" on the unhappy excursion to Varennes. The biggest catch in this descent on the court, though, was Marie-Antoinette's old friend the Princesse de Lamballe.

Cold-shouldered by the Queen since the rise of the Polignac clique, Elisabeth had remained touchingly loyal. When the Polignac sisters had headed for the frontier along with Artois in 1789, she decided to remain with the Queen and became her mistress of the household. Though the repeated waves of pornography routinely depicted her as a lesbian whore, she could not have looked less the part. Her blond curls had lost their sheen and spring, but her face still possessed an extraordinary cherubic quality, as though permanently posing for one of Greuze's doe-eyed portraits. At the Temple prison, where the royal family had been taken after three days in the Logographie of the Manège, she continued to wait on the Queen. The guards who came for her and the other servants told them they were being taken only for interrogation, but both Elisabeth and Marie-Antoinette evidently feared they would not see each other again. They embraced with the kind of valedictory tenderness that the defamatory press inevitably reported as licentious.

At some point the arrests became absurdly indiscriminate. The Abbé Sicard, who was a popular hero among the artisans of Paris as the *père-instituteur* of deaf-mute children, was picked up and imprisoned in the Abbaye along with a large number of priests. On the thirtieth a deputation from the school came to the Assembly to plead for the release of their "instructor, their provider, their father, shut up as if he were a criminal. He is good, just and pure," they went on:

> and it is he who has taught us what we know; without him we would be like animals. Since he has been taken from us we are sad and sorrowful. Give him back to us and you will make us happy.

Moved by this demonstration, a deputy offered to take Sicard's place, but invoking the indivisibility of revolutionary justice, another member, Lequinio, insisted that there be no special exemptions, and the sad little delegation was sent away. The rejection very nearly cost Sicard his life.

Finally, the police action enabled some to settle old scores. Ever since they had crossed swords over the Kornmann Affair, in which Beaumarchais had defended the wife's reputation in a complicated suit and Marat had upheld the honor of the aggrieved husband, the two men had hated each other. The playwright's grand house in the faubourg Saint-Antoine had been threatened many times by popular riots but never seriously damaged. Now he was accused by the Commune of having bought a large cache of weapons for dubious purposes (much as he had purchased arms for the American war). Rumored to be a virtual arsenal, Beaumarchais' house was ransacked on the same day as the fall of the monarchy and on the twenty-third of the month he was arrested. At the *mairie* the charges were found to be without substance and Beaumarchais—told to call himself Citizen Caron henceforth—was on the point of being released when his old nemesis walked in and dispatched him to the Abbaye, where he too just escaped death by being released four days before the massacres began.

On the twenty-eighth of August, at the behest of Danton, what were politely called "domiciliary visits" were authorized, ostensibly in search of firearms with which to defend the beleaguered *patrie* but more often than not in search of suspects or incriminating documents. "Everything," said the proclamation, "belongs to the *patrie* when the *patrie* is in danger." Characteristically, the visits would be late at night or in the early hours of the morning, to catch all the occupants at home. Ten or even more men would batter on the door and fill the room with sabers, pikes and guns. While the experience was obviously terrifying for most people, at least some thought it a stirring demonstration of patriotic vigilance. Mme Jullien de La Drôme, for example, whose offer of her father's hunting gun was politely declined, wrote to her husband, "I approve of this measure and the surveillance of the People so strongly that I should have liked to have cried 'Bravo! *Vive la Nation.*'" Only those who were "dolts or criminals" could possibly be afraid of such visitations, she thought. Mme Jullien de La Drôme lived in the Montagne Sainte-Geneviève, one of the areas of Paris in which many arrests were made, and having watched seminarians shoved through the streets, jeered at by the crowd, pelted with mud or punched in the face and body, she enthused, "What an immense operation; how well the threatened public interest is defended!"

The roundups were so ambitious in their sweep that they finally provoked the rump of the Assembly into action against the Commune and its police committees. On the thirtieth of August a demand was made for its dissolution and replacement by a successor to be promptly elected. The effect of this move was unfortunate. For although a number of the less militant *sections* had also become disturbed by the arbitrary searches and arrests of the previous weeks, this outright challenge to the Commune resulted in their falling into line behind it. Robespierre, Marat and the radical Jacobins denounced the move as an attempt to reverse the revolution of the tenth of August and to protect criminals and traitors from the consequences of their misdeeds. Under this withering fire—and more particularly under threat of further physical intimidation by armed *sectionnaires*—the Assembly backed down two days later. A new Commune would come into being along with the new National Convention that was to be elected (much along the lines proposed by Robespierre on July 29) by universal male suffrage to create a new, presumably nonmonarchical constitution.

The need for emergency police powers might not have been accepted had there not also been at the same time a genuine and potentially catastrophic military crisis. Carrying out a strategy agreed upon by their ally the Austrian Emperor, the armies of the King of Prussia crossed the French frontier on August 19. Four days later the important defensive fortress of Longwy surrendered after little resistance to bombardment. On the thirtieth, the crucial stronghold of Verdun—for the first, but not the last, time in modern history—faced a Prussian siege. If it fell, and the forecasts were not cheerful, the road to Paris would lie open through the valley of the Marne.

In the circumstances, the capital became convulsed by a mixture of terror and martial exhilaration. The snail's pace of the Austrian campaign the previous spring had lulled Parisians into thinking of the "patriotic war" as something fought far away and mostly involving Belgian fields of flax and turnips. With shattering suddenness, the enemy seemed to be at their gates. Moreover, the revolution they had just consummated in deliberate defiance of the Brunswick Manifesto seemed to have exposed them to terrible retribution should the invasion succeed. Indeed, there were already stories of Teutonic abominations committed in the theater of war: peasant women raped and mutilated, children spiked and tossed on bonfires—the standard military nightmare. In response, the Provisional Executive Council ordered the immediate levy of a force of thirty thousand volunteers to be sent to the front and the creation of new reinforced *barrières* at the city walls.

With a proclamation by Hérault de Séchelles (now the President of the Legislative) once again officially declaring *"la patrie en danger,"* Paris became a scene of frantic activity. The streets echoed to the sounds of marching boots and drums beating *la générale.* Amid tearful parting scenes with loved ones, volunteers were inscribed on the Pont-Neuf in front of the statue of Henri IV. Paintings like Watteau de Lille's *Departure of the Volunteers* reversed the moral charge of Greuze's *Wicked Son* paintings by having a young man fulfill, rather than neglect, his duties by going off to war. In the 1792 version, the place of the sinister recruiting sergeant in the Greuze is taken by the trusty shakoed grenadier silhouetted against the doorway.

Orchestrating all this phenomenal effort was Danton. His own fearlessness and genuine belief that Paris and France would survive their trial by fire was extraordinarily infectious. And the proclamations he produced at the end of August for the Executive Council may well have made the

159. Watteau de Lille, *The Departure of the Volunteers.* Note
the portrait of the volunteer's father in military costume on
the back wall, urging the son on to patriotic duty.

difference between resolution and complete panic. He even managed to
turn the proximity of the enemy into an apparent asset for revolutionary
fortitude:

> Our enemies prepare to carry out the last blows of their fury.
> Masters of Longwy, threatening Thionville [on the Austrian-
> Belgian front], Metz and Verdun, they want to cut a way right up
> to Paris. . . . Citizens, no nation on earth has ever obtained liberty
> without a struggle. You have traitors in your bosom; well, without
> them the fight would have been soon over.

These last allusions to the "traitors within" were the most telling. It had always been a standard feature of revolutionary discourse to represent the enemies of liberty at home as armed foreigners, a fifth column working for the unholy coalition of international despotism. This was as true of the rhetoric of 1789 as it was of the rhetoric of the Brissotins in 1791. Now that war was actually at hand, the alliance between the "mercenary lackeys of tyranny," the émigrés who had gone to join them and the malevolent hidden saboteurs at large in the streets of Paris seemed even more danger-ous. Just as the "brigands" of 1789 were said to have been the cutthroat stooges of vengeful aristocrats, now another equally sinister threat was said to lurk in the prisons, where freshly arrived counter-revolutionaries—Swiss guards, refractory priests, royalist writers—could suborn common crimi-nals into being their accomplices.

To find a solution to this problem was particularly pressing, as it was commonly rumored that once volunteers had left for the front, a breakout from the prisons would occur. A defenseless city would be given over to the slaughter of Patriots' women and children, just as the Brunswick Mani-festo had promised. It may even have been the case that if members of the Commune did not actually credit such stories, they did believe that able-

160. Jean-Baptiste Greuze, drawing, *The Wicked Son*

bodied men might have been deterred from enlisting exactly because of apprehension.

What was to be done? Fréron's *Orateur du Peuple* was in no doubt.

The first battle we shall fight will be inside the walls of Paris, not outside. All the royal brigands clustering inside this unhappy town will perish in the same day. Citizens of all departments, you hold the families of émigrés [hostage]; at that time let them fall to the weight of popular vengeance; burn their châteaux, their palaces, sow desolation wherever traitors have fomented civil war . . . *the prisons are full of conspirators* . . . see them where they shall be judged.

A *jugement* in this kind of rhetoric was the standard euphemism for a summary execution. Marat left nothing in doubt when he urged "good citizens to go to the Abbaye, to seize priests, and especially the officers of the Swiss guards and their accomplices and run a sword through them" (*passer au fil de l'épée*). It has seriously been claimed that Marat was speaking metaphorically or with the kind of punitive hyperbole that he had made a speciality of his paper. But why his readers and devotees should have been expected to have distinguished between rhetorical figures of speech and literal instructions is hard to see. This is especially the case since he had, for the moment, ceased publishing the *Ami du Peuple* and was printing his comments in the form of *placards* posted around town in a manner that gave them the authority of semiofficial proclamations.

Or take another *placard*: the "*Compte Rendu au Peuple Souverain,*" unsigned though written by Danton's devoted friend the poet and playwright Fabre d'Eglantine. Nothing could have made the connection between a war to the death at the frontier and a preemptive strike in Paris more crystal clear:

Once more, citizens, to arms! May all France bristle with pikes, bayonets, cannon and daggers; so that everyone shall be a soldier; let us clear the ranks of these vile slaves of tyranny. In the towns let the blood of traitors be the first holocaust [literally, *le premier holocauste*] to Liberty, so that in advancing to meet the common enemy, we leave nothing behind to disquiet us.

News of the fall of Verdun arrived prematurely in Paris on September 2. By that time *section* assemblies, anticipating the worst, were already passing motions demanding, as did the Popincourt *section*, "the death of conspirators before the departure of citizens." Others, like Gobelins, where Santerre was the Jacobin leader, insisted on the internment of the families of émigrés and royalists to hold as hostages against Prussian violence.

What then followed has no equal in atrocities committed during the French Revolution by any party. Disturbed by its horror and poorly trained in their professional discourse to contemplate it, historians at this point tend to avert their eyes and dismiss the event as somehow incidental or "irrelevant" to any serious analysis of the dynamics of the Revolution. The Anglophone tradition in this century, which in almost every other respect has made a powerful and prolific contribution to revolutionary historiography, has a particularly egregious record of silent embarrassment, rather as though a dinner guest had met with an unfortunate but inexplicable accident in the college common room.

In France, until very recently, the literature on the September massacres was dominated either by counter-revolutionary martyrology or the massive volume by Pierre Caron, which self-consciously set out to purge the record of hagiographic myths. Caron's claim was that a careful sifting of contemporary sources would produce a more "objective" account of the episode, one cleansed of tendentious moralizing. The book that resulted, and which is still cited reverentially by historians, is a monument of intellectual cowardice and moral self-delusion. Purporting to evaluate eyewitness accounts against some scholarly index of reliability, Caron in fact privileges those which reflect the official revolutionary version while dismissing sources from the prisoners themselves (like the Abbé Sicard) as, by definition, "suspect." In a strenuous attempt to fit the event onto the procrustean bed of "objective historical explanation," Caron argued that the massacres were, somehow, no one's responsibility. Rather, they were the inevitable product of impersonal historical forces: mass fear and, he often implies, justifiable desire for revenge against the casualties of the tenth of August. The overall effect is meant to be comforting for the revolutionary historian: the scholarly normalization of evil.

Obviously, the killing of at least fourteen hundred people in cold blood *was* the consequence of some sort of phobic condition brought on by the military crisis and the apocalyptic rhetoric of prison conspiracy. There was also an element of armed sanitation about it, the logical consummation of Mercier's jeremiads against the cloacal filth of the metropolis. The trash to be disposed of comprised all his specified sources of contamination: gilded aristocrats, venal priests, diseased whores and court lackeys. But the work of eliminating all these human infections was not some generalized, indiscriminate mass mobilization, as suggested by Caron. On

the contrary, as François Bluche has argued in a courageous and perceptive account, the killings were the work of specific, identifiable human
agencies. And there is no shortage whatsoever of sources describing those
acts, which the historian can concentrate his attention on if he so chooses.
To those who insist that to prosecute is not the historian's job, one may
reply that neither is a selective forgetfulness practiced in the interest of
scholarly decorum.

To begin with, those who bore some responsibility for looking away and
not doing more to prevent the killings when they were incontrovertibly in
a position to have done so are not difficult to find. Chief among them were
Roland, the Minister of the Interior, and Danton. Roland did become
disturbed by the "excesses" with which the "children of liberty must not
soil themselves" but only *after* September 2; at the time, he maintained a
discreet silence. Danton's impassiveness is perhaps more damning since he
commanded such potent influence among the *sections* and with the police
committees. On the day that the killings began, he was, it is true, making
the speech of his life, in the belief that if resolution were not instilled into
the French, and more particularly the people of Paris, there would indeed
be a total disintegration. He may well have been right, especially since
Roland was all for moving the seat of government to Tours. At any rate,
the speech was, of its kind, a brilliantly muscular call to arms, at once a
flattering self-portrait of martial readiness and a reassuring manifesto of
victory:

> The *patrie* will be saved. . . . Everything is in motion, every-
> one burns to fight. . . . While one part of the people goes to the
> frontiers, another digs our defences and a third, armed with pikes,
> will defend our cities and towns. . . . Paris will go to second these
> efforts. . . . The tocsin that shall be sounded is not a signal of
> alarm but a summons to charge against the enemies of the *patrie.*
> To vanquish them, Messieurs, we need boldness, always boldness
> [*toujours l'audace*] and still more boldness and then France will
> be saved!

The effect of the oration, which was declaimed in what contemporaries
report as Danton's immense *vox humana* (not for nothing was he called
by his enemies "the Mirabeau of the *canaille*"), must have been electrifying. But at the same time, the Minister of Justice was turning a blind eye
to the violence he clearly knew was about to take place in Paris. When
the inspector of prisons, Grandpré, came to the Hôtel de Ville, where the
Minister was in a meeting with the Commune, to voice his concerns

about the prisoners' vulnerability, Danton brushed him off with a curt *"Je me fous bien des prisonniers; qu'ils deviennent ce qu'ils pourront!* ("I don't give a damn about the prisoners; let them fend for themselves.") On the third of September, as reported by Brissot, Danton claimed that the "executions were necessary to appease the people of Paris . . . an indispensable sacrifice. . . . *Vox populi, vox Dei* is the truest and most republican adage I know."

Even after it had become apparent that a massacre of appalling proportions was taking place, first at the Abbaye and then at the other prisons, on the afternoon of the second, the only move made by the authorities of the Commune was to appoint *commissaires* to investigate what was happening. But those same men were mandated less with a mission to stop the killings than to give the violence a gloss of judicial respectability. They included, most notoriously, Stanislas Maillard, the *soi-disant* hero of the Bastille moat on the fourteenth of July and the leader of the women on October 5, 1789. Maillard now liked to swagger around as the captain of a paramilitary troop of strong-arm men at the service of the most militant sans-culottes. He had been a zealous arresting officer in the roundups and was now commissioned to undertake the summary "trials" which passed as justification for the butchery.

The Abbaye was the site of the first mass killing. A party of twenty-four priests taken there under armed escort from the *mairie* only just escaped violent assault from the crowd at the rue de Buci. When they reached the prison, however, another crowd (possibly the same group that had attacked them earlier, swollen by reinforcements) demanded summary "judgment." A grotesquely perfunctory interrogation was followed by their being pushed down the steps and into the garden, where their killers waited armed with knives, axes, hatchets, sabers and, in the case of a butcher (by trade) called Godin, a carpenter's saw. In an hour and a half, nineteen of the group were hacked to pieces. The five who survived to bear witness to the atrocity included the Abbé Sicard, who had been spared only through the intervention of a grocer National Guardsman named Monnot. Later, in the Assembly, Monnot was decorated by Hérault de Séchelles, in an obscenely hypocritical act of condescension, for having saved "someone so valuable to the *patrie.*"

Later on the second, the sanguinary scene was repeated at the Carmelite convent used as a holding cell for another hundred and fifty priests. Assembled there by the ex-monk turned Jacobin Joachim Ceyrat, they were subjected to a roll call, each name being followed by the briefest questioning, a "sentence" and murder carried out with the usual assortment of weapons. The fortunate ones were shot. In a desperate attempt to escape from the convent garden, some climbed trees and threw themselves over the wall to the street below; others ran into the chapel, from which they were dragged, then bludgeoned and stabbed. In the midst of the carnage the *commissaire* of the Luxembourg *section*, Jean-Denis Violette, arrived, briefly halting the proceedings. A slightly more formal manner of judicial proceeding actually produced some "acquittals," but by the end of the day one hundred and fifteen persons had been subject to the *hache vengeresse* (the axe of vengeance), including the Archbishop of Arles, the bishops of Saintes and Beauvais and the royalist Charles de Valfons.

In the days that followed, return visits were made to the Abbaye, where the murderers subsequently referred to their *travail* (labor)—for which evidently they had been promised specific wage rates. According to the army officer Jourgniac de Saint-Méard, who somehow survived and whose story of what he called his "thirty-eight hours of agony" is one of the best accounts of the slaughter, the horror was compounded by the "profound and sombre silence" in which the executioners worked. About two thirds of the prisoners at the Abbaye were killed, including a valet of the King, Champlosse, the ex-minister Montmorin and two justices of the peace, Buob and Bosquillon, who had committed the "liberticide" crime of trying to prosecute those responsible for the invasion of the Tuileries on June 20. Among those who escaped was Martin de Marivaux, the Parlementaire advocate who, in 1771, had borrowed Rousseau's nostrums on popular sovereignty to attack the "despotism" of Chancellor Maupeou. By 1792 he had evidently had quite enough of the General Will.

At two thirty on the morning of the third of September, the General Council of the Commune was told by its secretary, Tallien (also one of the *commissaires*), that though safe-conducts had been issued to protect the prisoners, there were simply too many able-bodied citizens on military duty at the *barrières* to ensure their safety. This was a prime instance of the conspiracy of disingenuousness that enabled those few members of the Assembly still sitting to exercise a Pilatic impartiality while the massacre continued. Another *commissaire*, Guiraut, was even more self-exonerating when he claimed that "by exercising vengeance the people are also doing justice." To the Legislative Assembly he claimed there was a serious mutiny of prisoners under way at another of the prisons, Bicêtre, that had to be dealt with before it became a security threat to the whole city.

What was really taking place at Bicêtre was the systematic butchering of adolescent boys. While the inmates at the Abbaye, the Carmelites and another holding cell at the Monastery of Saint-Firmin, were nearly all priests and political prisoners rounded up over the previous two weeks, those at Bicêtre, La Force and La Salpêtrière, the scenes of similar slaughters, were common criminals, beggars and persons detained at the request of their own families under the conventions of the old regime. Forty-three of the one hundred and sixty-two persons killed at Bicêtre were under eighteen, including thirteen age fifteen, three age fourteen, two age thirteen and one twelve-year-old. It appears that the chief warden of the house, one Boyer, participated vigorously in killing his own inmates. At Saint-Bernard another seventy or so convicts waiting to be taken to the hulks were murdered; at La Salpêtrière over forty prostitutes were killed after being, in all likelihood, subjected to physical humiliation at the hands of their killers.

At La Force, the Princesse de Lamballe passed the time by reading devotional manuals and attempting to comfort the terrified ladies-in-waiting to the Queen. Confronted by another of the improvised courts that would be judge, jury and executioner, she was asked if she knew of the "plots of the tenth of August" and responded courageously that she was aware of no plots on that day. Required to swear an oath of loyalty to Liberty and Equality and one of hatred to the King, Queen and monarchy, she accepted the first but refused the latter. A door was opened off the interrogation room, where she saw men waiting with axes and pikes. Pushed into an alley she was hacked to death in minutes. Her clothes were stripped from her body to join the immense pile that would later be sold at public auction, and her head was struck off and stuck on a pike. Some accounts, including that of Mercier, insist on the obscene mutilation and display of her genitals, a story which Caron dismisses with the cloistered certainty of the archivist as intrinsically inconceivable. What is certain is that her head was carried in triumph through the streets of Paris to the Temple, where one of the crowd barged into the King's rooms to demand that the Queen show herself at the window to see her friend's head, "so you may know how the people avenge themselves on tyrants." Marie-Antoinette spared herself this torment by fainting on the spot, but the valet de chambre Cléry peered through his blinds to see the blond curls of the Princesse de Lamballe bobbing repellently in the air.

For Pierre Caron this kind of thing was no more than the regrettably inevitable "excesses" committed at such moments of mass hysteria. He describes the exhibition of the Lamballe head noncommittally as "the custom of those days," as though it were some picturesque folk pastime. And he goes to great lengths to dismiss stories of other atrocities as self-evident myths and items of royalist martyrology. Many of the stories—of the sexual molestation of the whores of La Salpêtrière; of the mutilation of the Princesse de Lamballe; of Mme de Sombreuil being forced to drink a glass of blood in order to save her father—may have been apocryphal. But Caron's dismissal was based partly on their not being recorded in the *revolutionary* sources to which he gives exclusive credence, and partly on his refusal to believe that human beings, especially those claiming to act in the name of the Sovereign People, could have perpetrated anything so obscene. He was writing, however, in 1935. Ten years later, European history was again disabused of the notion that modernity somehow confers exemption from bestiality.

Approximately one half of all the prisoners in Paris died in the September massacres. In some places like the Abbaye and the Carmelites, 80 per cent or more of the inmates perished. There were signs of remorse and even desperation among the helpless members of the Legislative and even among some in the Commune, like Manuel, who referred to scenes he had personally witnessed as "painful" *(douloureux)*. But the Commune never pursued the killers, and a number of its members actually praised the deeds as a useful purge of a fifth column. The signals sent to zealots in the provinces were clear, since in the two weeks that followed there

161. Anonymous, the head of the Princesse de Lamballe paraded before the Temple

were a number of similar summary judgments and executions there, almost all of priests and royalist suspects. A batch of forty-odd prisoners was being sent from Orléans to Paris, and the Legislative Assembly decided to divert the party to Saumur for its own safety. But one of the most militant of the Paris *sectionnaires*, Fournier "the American," actually set out with a company of armed men to ensure that the prisoners kept to the original plan. At Versailles the whole party, including the Feuillant Minister of Foreign Affairs de Lessart, were massacred in what looks remarkably like a premeditated plan.

For days the sites were carefully scrubbed down and doused with vinegar, though at some prisons, like La Force, some of the bloodstains were not expungeable. A drawing by Béricourt represents, all too graphically, the administrative banalization of mass murder. At bottom right an official, swathed in a tricolor sash, inspects the disposal of bodies while a figure beside him makes notes in a register. To their right stands a *vainqueur de la Bastille* recognizable from his helmet while another gazes unconcernedly at the severed head. On the cart the men are plainly enjoying their work.

In the last days of the Legislative and the first weeks of the National Convention which succeeded it, Girondin politicians, who had been far from blameless themselves, endeavored to use the deaths as a stick with which to attack their enemies among the Jacobins. Brissot, in particular, believed, not entirely without some justification, that he and his friends had also been earmarked for extermination and had only narrowly escaped.

Precisely because the massacres quickly became a feature of the partisan combats of the Convention, they have often been seen as just another episode in the polemics of faction. In this representation, or as a psychological aberration linked to the war panic, the event has been marginalized as somehow of interest only to sensationalist, anecdotal history and beneath the attention of serious analysis. But a good case, however, might be made for seeing the September massacres as the event which more than almost any other exposed a central truth of the French Revolution: its dependence on organized killing to accomplish political ends. For however virtuous the principles of the kingless France were supposed to be, their power to command allegiance depended, from the very beginning, on the spectacle of death.

One contemporary eyewitness, at least, acknowledged exactly the moral squalor of the revolutionary predicament. In a letter to a woman friend, unfinished and unsent, Claude Basire, a Jacobin deputy of unimpeachably Robespierriste militancy, expressed his relief that

162. Béricourt, gouache and pen drawing, burial of bodies following the September massacres

your beautiful eyes have not been soiled by the hideous sights that we have had before us these last days. . . . Mirabeau said that there is nothing more lamentable or revolting in its details than a revolution but nothing finer in its consequences for the regeneration of empires. That may well be, but courage is needed to be a statesman and keep a cool head in such upheavals and such terrible crises. You know my heart, judge the situation of my soul and the horror of my position. A feeling man [*homme sensible*] must simply cover his head in his cloak and hurry past the cadavers to shut himself up in the temple of the law [the legislature].

As Bluche points out, it is exactly when Basire is forced out of this shell of official self-protection that his account breaks off. Appointed by the Assembly as one of six commissioners sent to bring peace into the prisons, he walked to the Abbaye, "groaning inwardly at the slowness of our cortege." Before the building, where there was "a profound darkness lit only by the sepulchral light from some torches and candles," he halts and so,

638

abruptly, does his narrative. It is as if the reality within was too much for the *coeur sensible* to bear: the oracular utterance of the General Will expressed in an oblation of blood and bone.

ii GOETHE AT VALMY

What do cannonballs sound like? "The humming of tops, the gurgling of water, and the whistling of birds," according to Goethe. On the twentieth of September he made these experimental observations on the wooded hills of the Argonne, the same landscape through which a year earlier Louis XVI had botched his escape. Goethe's patron, Duke Karl-August of Weimar, had been given command of a regiment in the Prussian army. When it began its plodding advance into France in the late summer, his poet-philosopher followed, more out of a sense of scientific curiosity than political enthusiasm. He had as little use for Romantic egalitarianism as for archaic legitimacy, seeing both revolution and counter-revolution as brutal interruptions of the reign of reason. But a campaign of siege and march offered a fresh dramatic experience which Goethe found impossible to resist. He was deep in the reflections that would lead to his important work on the theory of color, the *Farbenlehre,* though Karl-August found it bizarre that during the bombardment of Verdun he should have been observing the scene to discover, if possible, what were the hues of war.

At Valmy, on a ridge looking down on the French artillery drawn up in an arc, he saw red. As balls burst around him, throwing up scorched dirt and smoking autumn leaves, "it appeared as if one was in an extremely hot place and at the same time penetrated by the heat of it so that one felt quite at one with the element in which one was. The eyes lose nothing of their strength or clarity but it is as if the world had a kind of brown-red tint which makes the situation as well as the surrounding objects more impressive. I was unable to perceive any agitation of the blood but everything seemed swallowed up in the glow."

At the end of the day, this "fever," as Goethe called it, cooled off within him and he rode back, unscathed, to the Prussian lines. There he found soldiers in a state of moral collapse. "That very morning they had thought of nothing short of spitting the whole of the French force and devouring them . . . but now everyone went about alone, nobody looking at his neighbor, or only to curse or swear." In fact, the Prussians had hardly been defeated, and on a strict accounting of casualties might even be said to have got the better of the day since they had suffered little more than a hundred killed or gravely wounded to about three times that number for the French. But the general recognition, from Brunswick's high command down to the rank and file, that the Prussian advance had received a fatal wound, was correct. The laborious pace of their army had been unable to prevent a junction of the forces of Dumouriez and Kellermann on the nineteenth. The French divisions then stood *behind* the Prussian army with their backs to the east. Hypothetically Brunswick could have tried to force an accelerated advance west towards Paris through the Marne, but he would have left himself vulnerable to being cut off in the rear by a large, well-positioned force. It was vital, then, to see that threat off before going further, especially since his army was already badly lamed by sickness, and the foul weather of September was slowing its progress to a muddy crawl.

For the French, a stand at what Dumouriez had already called their "Thermopylae" was all that stood between the Prussians and Paris. The General's strategy all along had been to arrest the Prussian advance by a counter-strike into the Austrian Netherlands, but this had been called off on the orders of the Executive Council in Paris until the immediate threat from Brunswick's army had been turned back. On the twentieth, Kellermann's troops, for the most part regulars rather than volunteers, took up position below a great windmill on the heights of Valmy. There they held their ground, first under intense bombardment, then returning heavy artillery fire at the Prussian soldiers. Marching steadily uphill in thin line order, Prussian style, the grenadiers heard, over the whistle and crash of the fire, the French singing the "Ça Ira" and shouting *"Vive la nation!"*

Unable to dislodge the French gunners, Brunswick called off the action rather than attempt a frontal charge. Both sides were suffering badly from sickness and food shortages, and each army lay athwart the other's lines of communication to the rear. Sensibly, Dumouriez had Kellermann withdraw further to Sainte-Menehould (where the King had been recognized by the postmaster) and gave orders for roads and fields to be wasted should the Prussians attempt a further breakthrough. But it never came. With his army halved by attrition, Brunswick decided on a protective retreat, thus completing the dissolution of its morale. It was, as Goethe immediately understood, a critical turning-point in both the war and the Revolution. Late at night, he sat with despondent soldiers in a circle, attempting to kindle a stubbornly damp fire, and was asked, as the resident Wise Man, what he thought of the day. "I had been in the habit of enlivening and amusing the troop with short sayings," he recalled in his journal of the campaign. But what he came up with, while irreproachably impartial, must have been cold comfort. "From this place and this time forth commences a new era in world history and you can all say that you were present at its birth."

In Paris, even before the outcome of Valmy was known, that new era was given an official designation. From September 20, the day of the opening session of the National Convention, all state documents were to bear the date "Year One of French Liberty." The Republic, which was formally declared on the twenty-first, was, then, a new beginning of historical time. With the King and his family imprisoned in the medieval citadel of the Temple, inanimate memories of royalty were being obliterated around Paris. The day after the seizure of the Tuileries, a great crowd of volunteers helped topple the statue of Louis XIV from his pedestal in the place des Victoires. Now, a month later, the Sovereign People had their own military prowess to celebrate. In fact, Valmy was overwhelmingly a victory of the old royal army, rebuilt by Guibert and Ségur, though strengthened by troops that had enlisted since the Revolution and with a sprinkling of volunteers. But as soon as stories of Kellermann's soldiers singing the "Marseillaise" and the "Ça Ira" circulated it was represented as the triumph of the citizen-in-arms over the armed flunkeys of despotism.

Dumouriez was far from being swept away by the rhetoric of invincibility. He was, in fact, pursuing a strategy of level-headed pragmatism. He had inherited two of Lafayette's tactical goals: the detachment of Prussia from the Coalition and the consolidation of military force to be used, if necessary, against insurrectionary Paris. Valmy was an opportunity to approach the Prussians when they were at their most vulnerable. Once news of the declaration of the Republic reached the front, however, King Frederick William stiffened his negotiating position, demanding the restoration of Louis XVI to the throne before the tenth of August as a precondition of any peace. In response, the French refused to consider further negotiations until the Prussians had completely evacuated the country. Discussions abruptly broke off, and followed rather than seriously harassed by the French, the Prussian army limped ingloriously back, first across the frontier, and then across the Rhine.

This left a group of little imperial states directly exposed to the advance of General Custine, who was Biron's field commander in the center. (Kellermann had been posted to Metz, while Dumouriez's army now swung north towards Belgium.) At the end of October, carriage trains bearing the persons and property of prince-bishops, electors, imperial knights and chancellors all departed from cities on the left bank of the Rhine like Speyer, Worms and Mainz. With them went chamberlains, judges, *Kapellmeisters*, postilions, masters of the hunt—the whole retinue that had sustained these pumpernickel principalities in the rococo style to which they had been indispensably accustomed.

In marched the French, cheered principally by the handfuls of intellectuals, journalists and professors who were promptly installed as the custodians of liberation. While proclamations went up promising the local population "liberty" from "despotism" or "slavery," what they invariably got was merciless requisitioning and steep indemnities imposed as the price of freedom. This was to be the pattern of French occupation for the next twenty years, but on the first encounter it was a brutal surprise. His compatriots would have been less cruelly deceived, the hitherto pro-French Mainz librarian Georg Forster complained to Custine, "if they had been told from the start 'We have come to take everything.'"

With French forces on the offensive, not just in Germany but in Savoy, where Chambéry and Nice had been "reunited" with *la Nation*, Dumouriez persuaded the Convention to advance against the Austrians in the Netherlands. There he fully expected to be supported by a resumption of the uprising against Habsburg rule which, in 1789, had briefly created an independent Belgian state. But the decisive factor was less indigenous enthusiasm for seeing the Austrians off (warm though that was) than the heavy preponderance of military force Dumouriez could bring to the engagement. In both men and artillery he outnumbered them almost two to one. On November 6 he attacked their high-ground position at Jemappes, just north of the city of Mons, by advancing on a broad front while sending another offensive wheeling round far to the right to cut off a retreat. Counter-attacked by the Austrian cavalry, especially where volunteers made the line unsteady, French positions themselves nearly caved in but each time managed a restorative rally. When the Austrians suddenly saw French troops in their rear, convoyed across the river in boats, Jemappes was evacuated, leaving about a third of the army, some four thousand men, dead or gravely wounded on the field. Mons opened its gates to the French on November 8 and a week later Dumouriez's victorious troops marched across the place Royale in Brussels.

In France, it was Jemappes, rather than Valmy, which transformed the war from an agitated defensive action into the "crusade for universal liberty" that Brissot had promised. In contrast to the rather subdued reaction of the printmakers to the first battle, a great outpouring of prints celebrated the victory over the Austrians. The Montansier troupe of actors, who under the old regime had regularly performed at Versailles, now specialized in patriotic drama, reenacting heroic scenes from the Revolution to bolster morale in Paris. After Jemappes, they took their tour right onto the battle-field to entertain the troops with a dramatic version of the engagement complete with cannon and suitably terrified white-uniformed Austrians fleeing from the scene. Having given the soldiers a sense of the historical significance of their action by framing it in dramatized rhetoric, they then returned to the capital to perform *The Battle of Jemappes* to cheering audiences in the capital.

The Convention was not immune to this heady atmosphere of invincibility. Though Robespierre had been against the war and was suspicious that Dumouriez wanted to use an independent Belgium as a base from which to march on Paris, he was unable to prevail against the great tide of martial enthusiasm washing over the deputies in the aftermath of Jemappes. Letters had been received from the little principality of Zweibrücken asking for French protection, and in response to this, on the nineteenth of November, the Convention made the dramatic gesture of promising assistance to "all those wishing to recover their liberty." Like all the utterances which issued from the Convention, this first so-called "propaganda decree" operated on two levels. Rhetorically, it was the first manifesto of revolutionary war in European history. But it should always be borne in mind that the French Revolution had in large part been caused by the wounds inflicted to national amour-propre and the need to reinvigorate the tradition of French patriotism. So that while the presence of *étrangers, amis de la révolution* like Etienne Clavière in the government might seem to signify a commitment to a proselytizing, ideological war, it was almost always outweighed by much more pragmatically defined interests of state. When Brissot, on November 26, warned, "We cannot be calm until all of Europe is in flames," what he had in mind was a strategic expansion that would create either allied satellites or frontier buffer zones behind which the Revolution could be adequately protected.

Was an independent Belgium to be such a zone? By late November, several deputies among the Convention were anxious lest it be turned into a military fief of Dumouriez, who, it was known, was conducting virtually his own foreign policy, promising, for example, to protect the property of the Catholic Church in return for a voluntary loan. To counteract this, the Convention passed on December 15 what seemed to European opinion to be a decree of much more radical significance since it required the French military authorities to execute the principal legislation of the Revolution— including the destruction of the feudal regime—in the occupied territories. Just as the "rights of man" were now deemed to be a universal possession grounded in nature, so a similar axiom of nature was to determine the territorial limits of the Revolution. Dumouriez and Danton both agreed that those limits were self-evidently provided by geographical barriers: the Pyrenees, the Alps, the Rhine, the Channel and the Mediterranean. This already meant that a policy of "liberation" was blurring into one of annexation, euphemistically known as *réunion,* in regions like Porrentruy on the Swiss border, which became the Department of Mont-Terrible, and Savoyard Nice.

The mere declaration of "natural frontiers," however, did not imply that

French arms would be confined within them. On the contrary, as long as they were threatened by coalitions of kings, or (as the propaganda decree now authorized) as long as they were summoned by peoples groaning under the yoke of despotism, the French would feel free to take the fight to the enemy, wherever he was. Nor did the means of this offensive have to remain orthodox. The *ci-devant* Marquis de Bry offered to found what was, in effect, the first organization of international terrorism, the Tyrannicides—twelve hundred committed freedom fighters despatched to assassinate kings and the commanders of foreign armies wherever they could be nailed down.

It was, indeed, as Goethe warned, a new moment in the history of the world.

iii "ONE CANNOT REIGN INNOCENTLY"

At least one revolutionary print shows the birth of the first French Republic with alarming clarity. From the capacious skirts of a formidable *sans-culotte* woman drops an infant—the embodiment, so the legend tells us, of a *citoyen né libre* (a free-born citizen). He is oversized, and from the beginning unmistakably combative. But at the outset of its history there were also instances of the metaphor of infancy being used to more benign effect. The Department of the Orne, for example, marked its election of deputies to the Convention on September 11 by a baptismal ceremony (as did the Department of the Meurthe). The entire assembly of electors was deemed to be godparent to the baby girl, the daughter of a young volunteer, though it was the Girondin retired army officer Dufriche-Valazé who did the honors at the baptism. Three hundred livres were collected and presented to the mother, Madeleine Chuquet, who in recognition of the honor named her child Aluise Hyacinthe Electeur.

The elections were supposed to represent a similar act of political innocence: the return to the People of their sovereignty so that they might reconstitute the forms in which it was vested. They were not a referendum on the suspension of the King (decreed on August 13), for although a few monarchists did in fact take part in the electoral assemblies, August 10 had wiped them out as a serious political force. Whatever reservations the Girondins had about the armed mobilization of the Parisian sans-culottes, they were not about to set themselves up as counter-revolutionaries by contesting the verdict of that insurrection. So it was a government domina-

Citoyens né libre.

163. Anonymous, *Citizens Born Free*

ted by Roland and his friends, cloaking itself in the legal forms of the Legislative, that sent out the elaborate instructions for the convening of primary and electoral assemblies based on manhood suffrage.

The results, however, were something less than democracy in action. While numbers are notoriously difficult to recover, it seems unlikely that more than 6 percent of the seven million entitled to vote actually did so. Once again, then, a more radical regime resulted from a diminished number of votes actually cast. There were, of course, good reasons for this electoral reluctance. In the north and east a military crisis was in full spate and two departmental assemblies actually had to hurriedly move their meeting places to avoid the theater of war. In major cities, the political atmosphere was so menacing that to participate was itself an act of considerable courage. In Paris, the electoral assembly convened at the Jacobins—not the most neutral site—on the second of September, the first day of the prison massacres. Voting in the capital, as in ten other departments, was, moreover, by public oral declaration, a method obviously open to intimidation. And even if, as has been argued, the proceedings there remained open enough for there to have been continuous uproar, it can hardly have been fortuitous that Paris returned a delegation of twenty-four of the most militant Jacobins on its slate, including Robespierre, Marat, Robert, Santerre, Danton, Fabre, Desmoulins and the actor Collot d'Herbois. Elsewhere in France attendance at the polls may have been kept down by the more banal pressures of the harvest calendar.

Whatever the reasons, it would be a mistake to assume that a low turnout meant a tacit rejection of August 10. The exhaustive study of the elections to the Convention produced by Alison Patrick showed that there was surprisingly little overt interference in the proceedings, either by noisy spectators or, still less, by armed crowds. Moreover, the elections were completed before much of the country had any knowledge of the Paris massacres or any real comprehension of their indiscriminate character. Essentially, the official version of August 10, in which an uprising of the people of Paris had thwarted a royalist military coup d'état, was generally accepted. It was only later in the year that the trial and execution of the King intensified the disaffection of whole regions of France to the point at which they moved close to outright revolt.

It might even be possible to interpret the elections as a vote for the continuity of the recent past, rather than a radical break. Of the seven hundred and forty-nine deputies to the Convention, no less than two hundred and five had been deputies to the Legislative Assembly, and a further eighty-three had sat in the Constituent. The reelection of the former in particular seems to indicate almost a predisposition to believe the version of legislators who had had immediate experience of the constitutional monarchy and who could thus vouch for its unviability in the hands of Louis XVI. The remainder were made up of men who had become conspicuous in local politics, usually in vocal opposition to incumbent administrations.

The Convention was a relatively young body of men. Its biggest generational cohort, about one quarter, were in their late thirties, but the stereotype of hot-blooded young republicans is not far from the mark, since it was at the younger end of the age spectrum that political engagement was most marked. Even more than its predecessors, the Convention was a gathering of lawyers. Fully 47 percent belonged to the profession at one level or another and this becomes of crucial significance when one considers that the founding deed of the Convention was to be a trial. Other conspicuously represented groups were fifty-five patriot clergy (including nine Protestants, among them Rabaut Saint-Etienne, and no less than sixteen constitutional bishops, including Fauchet and Grégoire). There were fifty-one civil servants, including postmaster Drouet, who had stopped the King at Varennes, and forty-six physicians. It also included at opposite extremes at least one poor peasant, Jacques Chevalier, and one former prince and landlord of the Palais-Royal, Philippe d'Orléans, now known as Philippe-Egalité.

This bald tabulation of age ranges, occupations and political experience hardly tells the whole story. Of much more significance than their numbers suggest was the injection into the legislative body of a group of journalists, writers and pamphleteers who already exercised enormous influence through their publications. Carra, for example, the Girondin editor of the *Annales Patriotiques,* received votes sufficient to elect him in no less than eight distinct departments (while Robespierre was elected in only two). Together with Fréron, Marat, Desmoulins and Brissot (whose fame of course had extended far beyond the readers of the *Patriote Français*), these writers transferred into the debating chamber the kind of histrionic, accusatory style they had perfected in their journalism. When set against the more luxuriant oratorical manner favored by Girondins like Vergniaud, it produced scenes of unpredictable drama and even verbal violence, Marat and Guadet shaking their fists at each other and screaming to be heard from opposite ends of the hall.

It was possible, then, for hostilities between a minority of the deputies to the Convention to lend, from the beginning, a tone of bitter intensity to its proceedings. It was among the ex-deputies of the Legislative, and to a lesser extent the Constituent, that enemy camps most decisively formed. The fact that these groups in no way resembled modern parliamentary parties ought not to disguise the real venom of their enmity, especially at the core of zealots around whom allegiances polarized. As in the Legislative, they gave expression to their combative relationship by sitting conspicuously far apart. Robespierre's allies took the benches high up against the wall, which, since the President's seat had been moved across the hall, were now, confusingly, on his right, but which gave the faction the name the Mountain. Initially the old seats of the Feuillants were avoided as if merely sitting there would somehow brand a deputy as royalist. But before long it became the area of the Manège where the principal Girondins gathered their forces. Lower down towards the debating floor sat the majority of independent deputies, known collectively as the Plain. Instead of voting in any coherent pattern, they would shift their individual allegiances according to the persuasiveness of cases made on individual issues. They were not, though, a faceless or a feckless group, including as they did men as experienced and intelligent as Sieyès and as eloquent as the lawyer Bertrand Barère, whose intervention was to have a decisive effect on the fate of the King.

Though there was nothing in social origins, occupational background or even political experience to distinguish Jacobins and Girondins, this does not mean that they were undifferentiated groups of men circulating loosely around a few recognizable core members like Robespierre and Brissot. There were crucial points at which their disagreement on the character of the Revolution was profound. A striking number of the Girondins came from maritime and port cities—not only Bordeaux but Brest and Marseille—and they were, by and large, antagonistic to the claims of Paris to dictate the course of the Revolution. Robespierre, in contrast, went out of his way, both in the Jacobins and in the Convention, to praise the Parisians as the indestructible source of revolutionary dynamism. But although at the summit of its leadership the Mountain was aggressively metropolitan, on its slopes and foothills were many Jacobins who came from widely dispersed areas of France. Very often, the more remote their department, the more beleaguered they had felt inside their little Jacobin affiliate in upholding what they took to be the pure revolutionary faith. Once in Paris they clung to the group with especial zeal and solidarity. They were likely, then, to take exception to the Girondins' attempt to represent themselves as the guardians of provincial liberties. This surfaced when the Girondins urged the formation of a special guard to protect the Convention against armed intimidation and when Barbaroux, the deputy from Marseille, tried to mobilize his co-citizens to the same end.

The Girondins also presented themselves, not altogether disingenuously, as the protectors of legality against the arbitrary brutalities of the mob. As the gruesome details of the massacres emerged, they used every possible opportunity to pin responsibility for them on the Commune and by extension on the Jacobins. Their domination of the presidency of the Convention and of its secretariat during its first three months allowed them to determine the order of speakers and even set the agenda for debates. But they manipulated this power so blatantly that instead of winning support from the unaligned Plain they began to alienate it. It was also apparent to many that while some of the Jacobin militants may indeed have played some part in the massacres, Girondins like Roland were not themselves blameless. Believing themselves to have barely escaped the assassin's knife, deputies like Vergniaud and Gensonné saw themselves as engaged in a life-and-death struggle with their enemies on the Mountain. But the vehemence with which they took the attack to the opposition often seemed to mark them out as obsessed with personal recrimination rather than the interests of the *patrie*.

This was notoriously apparent in the disastrous attack on Robespierre launched by the editor of *La Sentinelle*, Louvet, on October 29. Borrowing the form of Cicero's onslaught on the Catilines—a reference immediately understood by the hundreds of ex-schoolboy Latin debaters in the Convention—Louvet accused Robespierre of creating a personality cult, of placing himself above the people and aspiring to a dictatorship. On November 5 Robespierre counter-attacked with a speech which in many respects actually vindicated Louvet's reproach of self-obsession, but which by appealing to abstract political and philosophical principles managed to turn the Revolutionary "I" from a base vice to an unimpeachable virtue. Only a contemptible opportunist, scrabbling in the gutter of polemics, Robespierre implied, could possibly have confused his vanity with personal ambition. On the contrary, it was born of the humility associated with feeling oneself to be a mere repository of Historical Truth. (That this view met with respect rather than ironical laughter suggests just how far he had already won the crucial battle of tone.) Having exonerated himself, he then went on to defend the Revolution from charges of excessive violence. Did those who brought that charge not realize that from its very outset in 1789 the Revolution was, by conventional standards "illegal," and that its survival depended critically on the force that the People would bring to its support? To attempt to judge it by anachronistic standards of morality was already gratuitously apologetic. Worse, it was to rob the uprising of the people of its *natural* legitimacy. "Do you want," he asked the Convention rhetorically, "a Revolution without a revolution?"

The same contention surfaced again over the single issue that, following Valmy and Jemappes, exercised virtually the whole of the Convention's energies: the trial of the King. Self-evidently the status quo, with the King and his family imprisoned in the Temple, could not be indefinitely perpetuated. As long as he went unindicted, the action of August 10, not to mention the declaration of the Republic on September 21, was itself under reproach, or at least without adequate public legitimation. Yet the Girondins, some of whom had made overtures to the court just prior to the uprising, must have been unsettled by the prospect of a trial and did their best to put procedural roadblocks in its path. For the ranks of lawyers sitting in the Convention, it was, however, imperative that their repudiation of monarchy be legally justified by proof that the King had committed crimes and treasons so frightful as to warrant his elimination, in office and perhaps also in person.

Two preliminary commissions were set up. The first, presided over by Dufriche-Valazé, was set to examine the mountain of chests, boxes and flour sacks full of loose papers taken from the Tuileries to see if there was sufficient evidence for an indictment. The second, more expeditious committee, chaired by the Toulouse lawyer Mailhe, was to report on the prior procedural issue of whether or not the King, whose inviolability had been guaranteed by the constitution of 1791, could indeed be tried, and if so what the appropriate court would be. The difficulty arose from the fact that the constitution had also explicitly laid down the specific crimes (fostering armed rebellion, leaving the country with no intent of returning, etc.) for which the King could be removed. But it had also prescribed abdication as the only penalty. Since Louis had already been subject to a forced abdication, a strict legal interpretation might well hold (as his defense lawyers pointed out) that he could only be tried in his capacity as citizen for crimes *subsequent* to the abdication. Within the walls of the Temple there could hardly be any such crimes.

When the Mailhe commission came to the Convention on November 6 to present its report, it sidestepped these thorny issues with an appeal to general principles rather than juridical rectitude. The inviolability claimed under the constitution had been a quality granted by the Sovereign Nation and it could just as easily be withdrawn by the same hand. The King, then, could be tried, both as public officer and as citizen. By the same token the National Convention, as the current repository of that sovereignty, not only could but must be the appropriate court, since neither a regular court nor any special tribunal appointed by it could possibly have the necessary plenary authority to deal with a case of this magnitude. The verdict, moreover, should be indicated by the vote of each and every deputy as part of their responsibility as members of a sovereign body.

This awkward compromise between abstract principles on the one hand and judicial correctness on the other was painfully exposed a week later when the Convention began to debate the Mailhe commission report, with the ex-*conseiller du Parlement* Hérault de Séchelles presiding. A small minority of deputies, of whom much the most articulate was Morisson, insisted on inviolability. (He also took exception, as he said, to those who "brand others not of the same opinion as traitors.") A larger group, including some Girondins and many on the Plain, like Grégoire, believed, however, that "absolute inviolability would be a monstrosity, as it would provoke men to villainy knowing they had impunity for their crimes. To declare the king inviolable when he has violated everything," Grégoire went on, "and to charge him with observing the laws when he has broken them . . . is not only to outrage nature but also the constitution."

But the most devastating attack on the principle of a full trial came not from the right but the left, and was made in the most famous maiden speech of the French Revolution. The orator was Louis-Antoine Saint-Just, Robespierre's adoring correspondent in 1789 and at twenty-five the youngest deputy in the Convention. Saint-Just had come to Paris as the author of an interminable poem, "Organt," usually described (but only with the greatest generosity) as pornographic. Obviously influenced by Robespierre, he now carefully cultivated the manner of a young stoic whose concessions to dandyism only made the implacability of his intellect more disturbing. Tresses of black hair fell on his shoulders, a single golden earring hung from a lobe and Saint-Just's habitual expression was carefully arranged into a manner of unapproachable aloofness.

His remarks took to a chilling conclusion Robespierre's thesis about the objective morality of revolutionary conduct. To provide the King with a trial was to presuppose the possibility of his innocence. But in that case, the revolution of August 10 was itself open to question, something which the very existence of the Convention denied. What was at issue was not the guilt or innocence of a citizen, someone within the body politic, but the natural incompatibility of someone, by definition, outside of it. Just as Louis could not help but be a tyrant, since "one cannot reign innocently," so the Republic whose very existence was predicated on the destruction of tyranny could not help but eliminate him. All that was needed was a summary proscription, the surgical removal of this excrescence from the body of the Nation. A king had to die so a republic could live. It was as simple as that.

Though its conclusions were ultimately unpalatable to a majority of the deputies, Saint-Just's speech made a stunning impression both inside and outside the Convention. It undoubtedly put the Girondins on the defensive, since it made any further equivocation seem virtually a reproach against the Republic itself. They briefly toyed with just such a position, asking that the decree establishing the Republic be put to a popular referendum. But in the last weeks of November it became apparent that the only defensive position to which they could now possibly fall back was to accept a trial and try to affect its sentence, or mount a campaign to put both of those to a popular vote. That, at least, would avoid the Jacobin position, reiterated by Robespierre, that a judgment had already been rendered by the people on August 10. All that remained now was for the King to hear his indictment and be disposed of expeditiously. Anything else would, by definition, be a verdict *against* the Republic.

The uneasy backpedaling forced on the Girondins was accelerated by Roland's dramatic appearance before the Convention on November 20. With an air of self-congratulation that many deputies found infuriating, he told them that information from a locksmith appointed by the King had led to the discovery of an iron safe with a mass of documents that had direct bearing on their proceedings. Preserving an air of mystery, Roland managed to imply that the documents would somehow compromise members of the Mountain; thus many of its deputies, together with many from the Plain, became immediately incensed that he had taken it on himself to open the *armoire de fer* without witnesses from the Convention. Accusations flew that he might have suppressed or doctored the evidence. As the principal details became available, however, it was apparent that there was indeed seriously incriminating evidence in letters written by the King to Breteuil referring to the constitution as "absurd and detestable." They made plain that his ostensible acceptance of the document was no more than a disingenuous tactic extracted under duress. A popular print, however, showed that the real skeleton in the closet was that of Mirabeau, whose correspondence with Louis on how to restore his authority and the payments made for that counsel were now revealed. On December 5 Robespierre, whose natural talent for "unmasking" hypocrites rose to the occasion, demanded that Mirabeau's remains be removed from the Panthéon and the celebratory busts be smashed.

With this fresh and damning evidence of royal duplicity, the demands for an expedited trial became virtually irresistible. In the Paris *sections*, the King was even blamed for the economic crisis that was rapidly inflating the price of foodstuffs. It was said that he had deliberately stocked warehouses at Verdun and Longwy with bullion and grain to be taken by the Prussian advance. Deputations from the Commune led by Anaxagoras Chaumette appeared before the Convention, claiming that the failure to punish Louis for his crimes was directly responsible for high prices and the depreciation of the *assignat*. "It is time," said the *enragé* Jacques Roux in the poor section of Gravilliers, filled with market porters and street hawkers, "that the liberty of the people was consolidated by the shedding of impure blood."

Beside himself with rage at the revelations of the *armoire de fer* and the procrastination of the Girondins, Merlin de Thionville got up in the Convention on December 3 and said that he wished he had killed Louis himself on August 10, an outburst that provoked a censure attempt and general havoc in the hall. Two days later it was finally decided that a further committee would draw up an *acte énonciatif*—in effect, an indictment of accusation which would be communicated to the King—and at the same time determine the procedures for the trial.

T H E   O B J E C T   of all this infuriated attention was, in the meantime, existing in a state of almost meditative calm. Immured in the medieval keep of the Temple (which had formerly belonged to his brother Artois), and deprived of newspapers, Louis was largely protected from the festering hatred of the city outside. The family was lodged on two floors together with a catering staff of thirteen and a valet whom the Legislative Assembly had generously authorized. Books were brought in on request for the King: Roman histories, devotional manuals, Buffon's natural history, Tasso's poetry and Bossuet's sermons, and in addition Louis had access to the old library of the Order of the Knights of Malta kept in the tower.

These consolatory comforts were somewhat offset by the innumerable petty indignities which his guards were actually encouraged to inflict on Louis by way of reminding him that he was no longer anyone's majesty. Hats were ostentatiously kept on heads and bottoms planted on seats in his presence. He was forbidden to wear his decorations on his afternoon walk. Verbal abuse was commonplace, which predictably upset the Queen and Mme Elisabeth (who had asked voluntarily to be allowed to share the prison) more than the King. On one occasion a guard, who according to Cléry was a teacher of English, followed Louis to his reading table, sat down on the window seat beside him and refused to go away. Marie-Antoinette's sewing was confiscated on the grounds that she was embroidering some sort of secret code to smuggle out of prison. Anxious lest the King cheat the executioner, the Commune even took away his razor, insisting he be shaved only by their appointed man. To this act of petty spite Louis responded by cultivating a defiant growth of beard until he was permitted once more to shave himself, though only under watchful guard. Worse perhaps were the graffiti scrawled on the wall by the guards: grotesque images of a crowned stick figure hanging from a gibbet with the legend "Louis Taking a Bath in the Air" or a fat figure lying before a guillotine, *crachant dans le sac*—"spitting in the bag," as one of the many macabre jokes about the *machine* had it.

All these little humiliations were of no significance compared with the unreal air of bourgeois serenity that settled over the family, touchingly recorded by Cléry. Every morning they gathered for breakfast, having exchanged kisses and embraces, almost in celebratory gratitude for having survived another night. After the meal the King and Queen spent much of the morning giving lessons to their son and daughter respectively. The Dauphin, now to be known as the "Prince Royal," was given passages to read and recite from Racine and Corneille, but it was, of course, in geography lessons that father and son took the most enjoyment, coloring and tracing in (with striking political impartiality) the features of the eighty-three departments of the new France. Around midday they were allowed walks in the Temple garden, where Cléry bowled hoops and tossed balls with the children. At two they were served dinner while Santerre, the commander of the National Guard, came every day to search their rooms.

In the evenings, after games of battledore and shuttlecock and before

164. Popular print, "Louis Capet at dinner in the Temple with his family," published in Prudhomme's *Révolutions de Paris.* At left is the jailer; on the right, two representatives of the Paris Commune.

bedtime, Louis would sometimes read to the family from one of the Roman histories he had requested, often dwelling on passages which had striking and painful relevance to their own predicament. On the walls of the principal room in which they gathered was posted the Declaration of the Rights of Man and Citizen. But the grim lessons of recent history and the news of the latest demand for his head, shouted by a vendor at the tower window at seven o'clock, were softened and dulled by the regular exercises of piety that marked their daily routine. There were prayers first thing in the morning and last thing at night; every religious holiday was carefully observed by the King, who took responsibility for the spiritual well-being of his family in the absence of a priest. In his inward self, he remained as ever the Rex Christianissimus of his coronation title. But he was also more conscious than ever of fulfilling his duties as *père de famille*. At the moment of their most complete ostracism from the body politic, the royal family had finally become plain citizens.

iv TRIAL

On the eleventh of December Malesherbes wrote to the President of the Convention asking to serve as defense counsel for the King. He did this with a characteristic mixture of courage and self-effacement, as if apologizing for the immodesty of putting forward his name for Louis' consideration. Was there, however, a trace of irony in his observation that "I am far from supposing that so important a person as yourself [i.e., the President] should concern yourself with me, but I was twice called to the [royal] council of him who was my master at a time when that position was universally aspired to. I owe him the same service when it is an office that many people judge to be dangerous."

One of those people was the man who had had the reputation of being the greatest practitioner of legal eloquence in old-regime France: Target. Though his counter-attacking defense of de Rohan in the Diamond Necklace Affair had bloodied the nose of the monarchy, Target had since sat in the National Assembly as a loyal upholder of constitutional monarchy and had indeed devised the Rex Francorum (King of the French) formula that was supposed to signify peaceful transformation. He was Louis' first choice for the defense, but on being approached shrank from the service as if he had been offered a poisoned chalice. He pleaded age (though he was fourteen years Malesherbes' junior), infirmity, pressure of other affairs. He was sorry but he simply could not do it. A year later, though, during the Terror,

Target, the lion of the Parlement of Paris, was to be found acting as secretary to the *comité révolutionnaire* of his Paris *section*.

It was exactly this moral disintegration of intellectual comradeship that had most distressed Malesherbes during the Revolution. Throughout his long life he had believed in the ethically purifying power of reason. That was why he had been the most creatively complaisant of all *Directeurs de la Librairie*, not really comprehending on what possible basis of either morality or utility censorship could stand. In the spring of 1789, having withdrawn from the debacle of Brienne's ministry, he had completed a long memorandum on the freedom of the press which, in all innocence, he had sent to d'Hémery, one of the most assiduous cultural policemen of the old regime. What had since happened had not shaken his belief in the absolute importance on the freedom to publish, but rather in the morally base ways in which it could be abused. Worse still was the supine compromise with violence that had broken the back of the liberal coalitions of the 1780s.

What had happened to all that company of articulate friends supping together and disposing of the antiquated France with shafts of illumination and reams of legislation? Lafayette was in an Austrian prison, having committed treason; Mirabeau had been disgraced by the revelation of the court correspondence. Talleyrand was in London, ostensibly on diplomatic business for the Republic, but no one expected him to return. Both he and Du Pont de Nemours had narrowly missed death during the same week at the time of the prison massacres. La Rochefoucauld had not been so lucky. Identified as the signatory of a document drawn up by the department of Paris urging the King to veto the law deporting refractory priests, he had been brutally killed by a mob. Not altogether fairly, Malesherbes blamed Condorcet for La Rochefoucauld's terrible end, even attributing it to some intellectual squabble. Malesherbes' grandson-in-law de Tocqueville (the writer's father) heard him say that while he would shelter his enemies he would never give asylum to Condorcet (who very soon would be in desperate need of it), even if his life were in danger.

All that remained in this bottomless pit of sorrow and confusion was to pull together the threads of one's own integrity and expire with as much self-esteem as one could decently manage. Not that Malesherbes put himself forward in a spirit of fatalism. Though he was seventy-one, there was still a great determination and an energy set in his knobbly features that defied even Robespierre to dismiss them as aristocratic. Moreover, the years since 1789 had not been entirely fruitless and miserable. He had seen a granddaughter married into the Breton clan of the Chateaubriands. And he had spent many happy hours planning an expedition to the Northwest American Passage with the young writer François-René, who had seen rapture in the vision of the French navy at Brest. Together they pored over maps of the Bering Strait and the Hudson Bay and engravings of walrus and whales. "If only I were younger I would go with you," the old man confessed.

He had at least been able to do some Swiss botanizing. His daughter Françoise and her husband had emigrated to Switzerland and Malesherbes went to stay with them at Lausanne in the spring of 1791 while he collected samples of Alpine flora for his collection. Ironically it was this most innocent dalliance with the "émigrés Montbossier" that would be the pretext for bringing him before a revolutionary tribunal in the Terror. By midsummer he was back in Paris at his house in the rue des Martyrs. Though we have no idea what he thought of the flight to Varennes, he was sufficiently concerned about the King's plight to attend on him at the Sunday *levers* in the Tuileries despite "that cursed sword that gets in the way of my legs."

Malesherbes was not the only person to come forward and offer to defend Louis before the Convention. A much less probable volunteer was the feminist actress Olympe de Gouges, the author of the *Declaration of the Rights of Women and Citizenesses*, who, although an ardent revolutionary, felt Louis to be more victim than tyrant and evidently wanted to demonstrate that women were no less capable of "heroism and generosity" than men. The King passed up her offer but was glad to hear from his second choice after Target, François-Denis Tronchet, another ex-magistrate of the Parlement. In accepting, Tronchet grumbled about the interruption of his retirement, but he could not refuse to serve someone whose fate was "suspended beneath the blade of the law"—the current euphemism for the guillotine.

Louis needed all the help he could get. He had only been allowed lawyers after hearing the indictment against him, drawn up by Robert Lindet on behalf of the Commission of Twenty-one. The mayor of the Norman town of Bernay and an ex-deputy of the Legislative, Lindet usually echoed the views of the Mountain, although his sheltering of an officer in the Swiss guards on August 10 already spoke for his humanity. During the Terror he would be the only member of the Committee of Public Safety to refuse to put his signature on Danton's death warrant. His *acte énonciatif*, however, was a bleak document: a long history of the Revolution that represented the King's conduct, throughout, as a disingenuous rearguard action, full of deceit and intended violence. On many instances, now richly documented from the *armoire de fer*, Lindet could hardly be contradicted. The King had indeed resisted the calling of the Estates-General until threatened by complete fiscal subsidence; had prepared to use force against the union of the orders and the demonstrations against Necker's dismissal in Paris; had attempted flight; and had negotiated secretly to restore his authority in contravention of oaths he had publicly taken. It was a damning chronicle of subterfuge and bad faith. What was missing, of course, from the account was any sense of violence or intimidation from the other side; so that instead of the real trial of strength which had characterized the history of the Revolution, Lindet's indictment presented royal behavior as a series of indisputable crimes.

On the morning of the eleventh, the mayor of Paris, Chambon, came to fetch from the Temple the man he named "Louis Capet." "I am not Louis Capet," retorted the King indignantly; "My ancestors had that name but I have never been called that." It was one of the few moments of anger during a day when, however harried, he once again showed extraordinary self-possession. Wearing an olive-green silk coat, he stood before the Convention and galleries packed with spectators, until given permission by the President, Bertrand Barère, to be seated. Nothing, as the Convention was well aware, could have symbolized more exactly the inversion of the world of Versailles, where hierarchical precedence had been precisely indicated by conventions governing the possibility of sitting down in the royal presence.

Louis heard the full indictment and then responded to questions put by Barère, flatly denying that he had done anything illegal either before or after 1791, dismissing as absurd the accusation that the aborted journey to Saint-Cloud was an escape attempt. On laws that he had vetoed in 1791 he responded that the Constitution gave him the right to do so and rejected the characterization of his reinforcement of the Tuileries as preparation for "an attack on Paris." Throughout he showed the calmness of a man who actually believes he is irreproachably in the right. Only when Barère directly asserted that he was "responsible for shedding French blood" did Louis give way to an emotionally angry retort. Some witnesses saw a tear fall at this point, but determined not to allow his prosecutors to see any weakness Louis quickly put his hand to his cheek, following with a rubbing motion on his forehead as though the whole action was wiping away sweat that was anyway running freely in the stuffy Manège. The weakest part of his testimony was the almost careless way in which he failed to recognize his own hand on documents taken from the infamous *armoire de fer*.

Between the appointment of his lawyers and his full trial at the end of December, Louis' days were taken up preparing his defense. The Commune had decided to wound him further by refusing to allow him to see his children, a decree of gratuitous cruelty that the Convention somewhat softened by permitting occasional access. But the routine of the family group had been broken and was replaced by the comings and goings of the attorneys. Malesherbes, whose offer the King had accepted, and Tronchet had decided to ask for the assistance of a younger colleague with a reputation for the kind of powerful, sonorous eloquence in which the Bordeaux bar seemed to specialize: Romain de Sèze. As a group the King could hardly have asked for more formidable defenders, but they were not altogether united in their approach. Malesherbes, who, by one account, had discussed with the King as early as 1788 David Hume's treatment of the fall of Charles I, wanted Louis to challenge the credentials of the court to bring him to trial, and especially to attack the Convention's assumption of the roles of judge and jury, in contravention of the legal conventions set up by the revolutionary codes themselves. To have done this, of course, would have meant contesting the whole legality of the revolution of 1792—exactly as Robespierre had predicted—but, at least, Malesherbes thought the position would have great inner cogency and moral power.

The King, however, was stubbornly determined to play to his weakness, to insist on his constitutional inviolability, but then defend his conduct as a conscientious citizen-king, refuting the case point by point, much as he had already done on the eleventh. His belief that true justice would infallibly demonstrate his innocence even led him to suppress what he obviously regarded as the excessively rhetorical pleading contained in de Sèze's peroration.

On the morning following Christmas, Louis was brought once more to the bar of the Convention. Though he had not slept for four days, de Sèze was in brilliant form for his *plaidoyer,* reiterating the case that the position granted to the King precluded prosecution from what was, in effect, a coeval branch of the constitution. Nor could he be tried for actions for which he had already suffered abdication, still less by a body of men who had already determined and broadcast their views on his culpability. He then reviewed the narrative of Lindet's indictment from the other side, representing Louis' conduct not as calculated deception and conspiracy but as the response of legality against intimidation. This had been the King's consistent attitude, he claimed, right up until August 10. "Citizens," began his peroration,

> if at this very moment you were told that an excited and armed crowd were marching against you with no respect for your character as sacred legislators . . . what would you do? . . . You accuse him of shedding blood? Ah! he mourns the fatal catastrophe as much as you. It is the deepest wound inflicted on him, his most terrible despair. He knows very well that he has not been

the author of bloodshed though he has perhaps been the cause of it. He will never forgive himself because of this.

De Sèze finished by painting a portrait of a young king who had come to the throne as an honest reformer, benign in intentions and conscientious in government. It was, for the most part, a recognizable picture. The counsel made the serious mistake, however, of using one of Louis' favorite phrases, namely that he had "given" the French liberty—an account of 1789 not likely to have won sympathy among his audience. De Sèze's last words were, like almost all the great set-piece speeches of the Revolution, an appeal to History: "Think how it will judge your judgment."

It seems unlikely that being put in the dock of posterity by De Sèze did much to alter the conviction of the vast majority of deputies as to Louis' guilt. But this is not to say that his defense, both in his lawyers' impassioned and powerful presentation and in the silent dignity of his person, had no effect. It was apparent, not least from the strenuous efforts of the Mountain to get on with the business of the sentence, verdict and execution, that public opinion had been moved by both of Louis' appearances in court. Copies of the *plaidoyer* had been printed as an official act and were being distributed quite as widely as Lindet's accusatory act. There were even signs of popular disturbances on the King's behalf, for example at Rouen, where a riot broke out.

Sensing in this indeterminate movement of opinion a final opportunity to damage their opponents on the Mountain, a group of the Girondins made a dramatic move to shift the theater of judgment outside the Convention. An "appeal to the people" had been raised much earlier by deputies like Kersaint openly hostile to the trial itself, but now it was adopted by Vergniaud and Brissot in particular as a way of avoiding the otherwise inevitable death of the King. To demonstrate that in doing this they were not in any sense monarchist, another of their number, Buzot, renewed the attack he had launched on Philippe-Egalité, who sat with the Mountain. By demanding the death penalty for anyone proposing to restore the monarchy, he put the Jacobins, including Marat, in the distasteful position of having to defend the cousin of the King. And the Girondins showed a similarly subtle grasp of tactics in supporting the call for a popular vote on both verdict and sentence. Citing Rousseau, whose sacred texts were now routinely plundered for apposite supporting statements by both factions, Girondin orators like Vergniaud claimed that the Convention had no right to usurp authority that rightly still belonged to the people whose "mandatories" they remained. Logically, then, all forty-four thousand primary assemblies that had elected them ought to be reconvened to determine the King's fate. Only in this way could the Convention be sure that it was not acting in violation of the General Will. Characteristically, Brissot added a foreign dimension to the argument. All Europe was watching their conduct, he said, without much exaggeration. The enemies of France would be quick to accuse the Convention of being a plaything of isolated factions. How much more powerful would be the refutation if it could be shown through the vote of the people that they in fact acted in complete accord?

The most eloquent, and certainly the lengthiest, rebuttal came from Bertrand Barère on January 4, 1793. To the uncommitted deputies on the Plain it must have been all the more powerful because it echoed some of the standard views of the leading Jacobins without their partisan apoplectics. Barère brought the Convention back to a vivid understanding of its own position, which by definition was to make a final break with the monarchy. It should, he argued, accept that responsibility and not pass it off in a cowardly way to electors, especially since that would undeniably put them in the middle of appalling partisan conflict. The choice was between the Convention determining to act as the proper repository of sovereign power or abdicating liability, turning the country over to anarchy and civil war. His speech could not have been further from Marat's sanguinary hysterics, and to a body of men preoccupied with their own collective authority it had a deeply telling effect. By virtue of the fact that they were deputies at all, they had accepted republicanism. How could they shrink from taking the last logical step to sign and seal that identity?

None of this made Louis' fate a foregone conclusion. When the voting began under Vergniaud's presidency on January 4, there were three questions for decision: the guilt or innocence of the King, the sentence and the still unresolved question of a popular appeal. The order in which they were to be taken was immediately seen as critically important in that, once the King had been condemned and sentenced, the popular appeal would look like a desperate rescue act rather than an impartial consultation. The Girondins, however, split on the issue as they had over the appeal itself. Some members, among them Maximin Isnard, who had been very close to Vergniaud and Guadet, voted consistently with the Mountain on all these issues. After screaming matches and mutual denunciations thrown across the hall forced Vergniaud into suspending the session, a compromise was concocted by which the issue of the *appel* would follow that of the verdict, but precede that of the sentence.

On the morning of January 15 the voting began with the *appel nominal,* the oral vote, cast at the bar by each of the 749 deputies. This immensely laborious method of proceeding had been demanded by Marat as a way of exposing "traitors" in such a way that he could hardly be contradicted without proving his point. Required simply to answer yes or no to the questions, a few hardy souls—like the constitutional bishop of the Haute-Marne and the great scientist Lalande—refused to be put in the position of judges. No one, however, actively voted for Louis' innocence and 693 deputies (for some were absent) voted for guilt. As David Jordan points out in his fine book on the trial, when it came to the second vote on the appeal, its advocates realized there had been damaging attrition in their ranks since Barère's speech. Some even expressed their continued support for it in principle but voted against its likely consequences. In the end the issue was defeated 424 to 283.

The most dramatic of the three votes, of course, was that of the sentence, which began on January 16. As a preliminary, the Breton Lanjuinais, who had helped dig the grave of the old monarchy by leading the revolt of the Rennes magistrates against the Brienne edicts, now attempted to rescue its personification. Anything so important as the sentence of a king should be enacted only by a two-thirds majority. The proposal met with a crushing retort from Danton, recently returned from the army in Belgium, who said that since the Convention had not thought the abolition of the monarchy itself had required a two-thirds majority, it would be transparently specious to invent the rule now.

From eight in the evening until nine in the morning the deputies continued their procession to the tribune, watched, according to Mercier, by spectators drinking and consuming ices and oranges to sustain them through the long winter night. When Mailhe's turn came, he surprised the Convention by voting for death but then raising the issue of when the sentence should be carried out. He was, in effect, asking for a new vote on a reprieve and was followed in this by other deputies, including Vergniaud. That the Girondin, though, could answer the question of death in the affirmative had a shattering effect, not least on Malesherbes, who was devastated on hearing his vote. When the turn of the Paris delegation came, Robespierre spoke first as the deputy who had come at the top of the election poll. "I do not recognize a humanity," he said, "that massacres the people and pardons despots."

Last on the Paris list was Philippe-Egalité. The man who in the pecking order of court protocol had been permitted to hand the King his chemise at the daily *lever* now voted for his cousin's death on the grounds that "those who attack the sovereignty of the people" deserved it.

As dawn came up it was apparent that the death sentence would be passed. Of 721 present and voting, 361 had voted unconditionally for death and 319 for imprisonment to be followed by banishment after the war. There were two votes for life imprisonment in irons and two for execution after the war (presumably to preserve the King as a hostage). Twenty-three voted in the Mailhe manner for death but asked for a debate on a reprieve, and eight for death with the expulsion of all the Bourbons (including Egalité). The majority for death in one way or another, then, was not one but seventy-five.

After Vergniaud had pronounced the sentence, the King's lawyers were led in for a final address to the Convention. All three had been denied seats and had stood for thirteen hours during the voting. Tronchet first read a letter from Louis, who refused "to accept a judgment that accuses me of a crime for which I cannot reproach myself" and which asked for an appeal to the nation on the judgment of its representatives. Its tone was anything but that of a supplicant throwing himself on the mercy of his judges, and its defiance made it more difficult for Tronchet and de Sèze to reiterate the case that Louis' fate should be determined by the larger majority of two thirds.

Exhausted and despondent, Malesherbes then attempted to plead the compassionate case of common humanity. But he was too emotionally overcome to be coherent. Apologizing for not being able to improvise a speech, he stumbled over his words and fought back sobs: "Citizens, excuse my difficulties . . . I have observations to make to you . . . will I have the misfortune of losing them if you do not allow me to present them . . . tomorrow?"

Some of the deputies doubtless thought that the spectacle of the old man dissolved in misery for a client unworthy of him was pathetic. Many more were touched by the openness of his sorrow. Tears, after all, for this gathering of *coeurs sensibles* were supposed to be the milk of moral purity. But they let his syntax break down of its own accord into a distraught silence broken, predictably, by Robespierre. He could forgive Malesherbes for tears shed over the fate of the King, he generously conceded, but he rejected any further talk of an appeal to the people. And there was no more talk.

v TWO DEATHS

Malesherbes carried his grief with him to the Temple that same morning. Announcing the sentence of the Convention, which he said had been carried by a majority of just five votes, he broke down again, falling at the King's feet. Louis seemed more concerned with the old man's condition than his own, raising him gently to his feet and embracing him. Malesherbes

165. Royalist print, Louis XVI reading his will to
Malesherbes

then related the voting in detail, and it was only when he came to Orléans'
vote that the King seemed to betray any bitterness. That same evening was
the last time the King and the Minister saw each other. One account has
the King telling him, "We will be reunited in a better world. But I am sorry
to be leaving a friend such as you." It is probably apocryphal since, according to Cléry, Louis in fact expected to see Malesherbes again and became
increasingly upset at his absence in the days that followed. The old
man had, in fact, made several attempts to visit the King and on each had
been denied entrance on the express orders of the Commune and the
Convention.

It was another small cruelty. Well before his trial Louis had resigned
himself to expecting the worst. His principal concern was not to save his
own life so much as to vindicate himself from the accusations made against
him. And he was especially apprehensive (as well he might have been) for
the safety of his family. Being separated from them since December 11 only

made these fears more dramatic, and all these anxieties surfaced in the will he had dictated in Malesherbes' presence, surely not coincidentally, on Christmas Day. This was not in any sense a political document, though it insisted on his innocence and expressed forgiveness to his enemies as well as to "those whom I may have offended through inadvertence (for I do not recollect having ever willingly given offence to anyone)." Much of the testament was devotional, reaffirming his faith in the sacred creed and the authority of the Church and commending his soul to the forgiveness of the Almighty. But a good deal of it was directed to his family, begging forgiveness of Marie-Antoinette for any sorrows that his own troubles may have brought on her. As if responding with husbandly gallantry to the grotesque libels that continued to issue from the popular press, Louis expressly declared that "I have never doubted her maternal tenderness" and even asked her pardon "for whatever vexations I may have caused her in the course of our union."

Of his son Louis, the King wrote that, should he "have the misfortune to become King," he was "to reflect that he ought to devote himself entirely to the happiness of his fellow citizens; that he should forget all hatred and resentment and particularly in what relates to the misfortunes and vexations I have suffered; that he cannot promote the happiness of a nation but by reigning according to the laws; yet at the same time that a King cannot enforce those laws and do the good his heart prompts unless he be possessed of the necessary authority, for otherwise being fettered in his operations and inspiring no respect he is more harmful than useful."

It was, at last, a clear realization of the dilemma on which he had been impaled from the beginning to the end of his reign. How to do good without surrendering authority; how to make a people happy when they wanted to be free? Nothing the Revolution would do, and certainly not killing Louis Capet, would make the answer to that problem, perhaps the most deadly legacy left by Rousseau, any more obvious. Perhaps its intrinsic insolubility etched itself on the features of the King as he approached the end of his life, an expression of painful gravity caught in the half-profile drawn by Joseph Ducreux in the Temple.

In the Convention, from the eighteenth to the twentieth of January, last-ditch efforts were made to try to obtain a reprieve. Tom Paine, who had been elected a deputy on the strength of his reputation as the nemesis of Edmund Burke and who had come to Paris starry-eyed about the Revolution and speaking almost no French, now suggested through his interpreter, Bancal, that Louis be sent to the United States, where he might be rehabilitated as a decent citizen. Deputies on the Mountain who had been thrilled to see Paine arrive but had been suspicious about his friendship with

166. Joseph Ducreux, charcoal drawing with chalk
highlights, *Louis XVI*, 1793

Girondins (probably determined by the fact that they spoke better English), were now aghast at this intervention. Marat shouted that Paine was disqualified from expressing an opinion since he belonged to the sect of Quakers notorious for their opposition to the death penalty. But the proposal was taken no more seriously than Condorcet's long and densely reasoned Beccarian attack on capital punishment. Mailhe's amendment was pressed for the last time and lost, though again by a surprisingly close vote, 380 to 310.

It was, however, enough. On the evening of the twentieth, a deputation from the Convention, led by Grouvelle, came to the Temple to read Louis the final determination of the assembly. In response he asked for a three-day stay that he might better prepare for his execution; for a confessor of his

167. Hauer, *The Last Farewells of Louis XVI to His Family*. Cléry's account suggests a much more intimate scene than the operatic poses recorded in the painting.

own choice, naming the Irish priest Edgeworth de Firmont; and to be allowed to see his family. The first was denied and the last two granted. At about eight thirty that evening the family was reunited. No one had yet told them about the King's fate, and from behind a glass door Cléry could see the women and children rocking with misery as he gave them the news. For an hour and three quarters they remained together, weeping, kissing and consoling each other as best they could, the little boy clinging to his father's knees. When it was time to go, none of the family could bear the brutal weight of a final parting. Louis promised that he would see them all again at eight the next morning. "Why not seven?" said the Queen. "Of course, why not, seven." They were on their way out when the Princesse Royale, the King's daughter, suddenly threw herself at her father and collapsed in a dead faint. Bringing her round was the family's last embrace.

THE GUILLOTINE had been set up on the square renamed the place de la Révolution and is today the place de la Concorde. The great equestrian statue of Louis XV that had given the space its original name had been knocked down on the same day that Louis XIV had been struck from the place des Victoires. From his platform six feet above the crowd and the soldiers, Sanson could see the truncated pedestal still in place. Prepared to meet any kind of sympathetic demonstration, armed or otherwise, the Commune had turned Paris into an immense garrison. The city gates had been shut; a special escort of twelve hundred guards had been assigned to accompany Louis' coach to the scaffold, and the streets were lined four deep with soldiers. Santerre, who was in charge of all these operations, had even stationed cannon at strategic points along the route and elsewhere in the city.

Louis was woken in the wintry dark by Cléry and received communion from Edgeworth at around six. He dressed simply, but it was already apparent that he would not see his family again, since he asked the valet to give his wedding ring to the Queen along with a packet containing locks of hair from all the family. A royal seal, taken from his watch, was to be passed to his son as a sign of succession. When representatives from the Commune arrived, he asked them if Cléry might not cut his hair to spare him the indignity of being cropped on the scaffold. Needless to say, permission was denied. He was, for the purposes of the executioner, just another head. At around eight Santerre arrived and, after shuffling around somewhat, was put out of his misery by Louis' own command: "*Partons.*" The ride took two hours through Paris streets shrouded in damp fog. The sense of a blanket of quiet was strengthened by the closed shutters and windows which had been ordered by the Commune and the peculiar suspended animation of the crowds, who, on other occasions, had been vocal with both their cheers and their execration.

Not long into the drive a pathetic rescue attempt was made by the Baron de Batz and four followers shouting, "To me all those who want to save the King." They were immediately set on, as was one of the Queen's former secretaries, who tried to push his way through to the coach. At ten o'clock the procession arrived at the scaffold. Beneath the platform Sanson and his assistant prepared to undress the King and tie his hands, only to be told by the prisoner that he wanted to keep his coat on and have his hands free. He evidently felt so strongly about the last matter that it appeared for a moment he might even struggle, and it took a remark from Edgeworth comparing his ordeal to that of the Savior for Louis to resign himself to whatever further humiliations were to be heaped on him.

The steps to the scaffold were so steep that Louis had to lean on the priest for support as he mounted. His hair was cut with the professional briskness for which the Sanson family had become famous, and Louis attempted finally to address the great sea of twenty thousand faces packed into the square. "I die innocent of all the crimes of which I have been charged. I pardon those who have brought about my death and I pray that the blood you are about to shed may never be required of France . . ." At that moment Santerre ordered a roll of drums, drowning out whatever else the King might have had to say. Louis was strapped onto a plank which when pushed forward thrust his head into the enclosing brace. Sanson pulled on the cord and the twelve-inch blade fell, hissing through its grooves to its mark. In accordance with custom, the executioner pulled the head from the basket and showed it, dripping, to the people.

It was the relentless normality closing in around the spectacle that struck some witnesses as truly unbearable. Lucy de La Tour du Pin and her husband had heard the gates of Paris close earlier that morning and knew that hope had expired. They had strained their ears to listen for any sound of musket fire that might promise some kind of redemptive chaos. But there was nothing but silence in the murky fog. At ten thirty they heard the gates reopening "and the life of the city resumed its course, unchanged."

Mercier was also watching. One might have expected him to feel some sense of vindication since he had, so often and so vehemently, prophesied exactly the kind of king-destroying apocalypse that was presently overtaking France. But he felt nothing of the sort. For all his literary violence, he was becoming steadily more disgusted by the real thing. Though he had absolutely no illusions about the King's good faith during the Revolution, he had voted in the Convention against death, both for pity's sake and because he believed, again prophetically, that Louis' death would make a

European war of unprecedented scale inevitable. He was startled, then, to see the kind of brutal festivities that seemed to greet the execution, once the immediate shock had passed.

His blood flowed and cries of joy from eighty thousand armed men struck my ears. . . . I saw the schoolboys of the Quatre-Nations throw their hats in the air; his blood flowed and some dipped their fingers in it, or a pen or a piece of paper; one tasted it and said *Il est bougrement salé* [It is well-salted—alluding to the kind of livestock that was fattened on salt marshes *(pré-salé)*]. An executioner on the boards of the scaffold sold and distributed little packets of hair and the ribbon that bound them; each piece carried a little fragment of his clothes or some bloody vestige of that tragic scene. I saw people pass by, arm in arm, laughing, chatting familiarly as if they were at a fête.

Allowing for Mercier's own predilection for the bizarre, much of his account is likely to have been true. Sanson was entitled to sell items of clothing and mementoes from the execution as part of his perquisites. Less

168. Charles Monnet, engraving, *The Execution of Louis XVI.* Santerre is the figure on horseback; the empty pedestal of the statue of Louis XV is at right.

reliably documented, but in keeping with other sacrificial deaths that happened in moments of historical crisis, are accounts of spectators saturating their handkerchiefs in the royal blood. Was this, if indeed it happened, a kind of inverted baptismal rite, as Daniel Arasse has suggested? Or was it rather a craving to partake collectively in a kind of expiatory sacrifice: a death which once shared by all could not be laid at the feet of any individual?

It was not, however, the only death in Paris. The day before, as Louis was preparing for his end, one of the regicide deputies was fatally stabbed in a café in the Palais-Royal. Moreover, the victim, Michel Lepeletier, was not an anonymous face in the Convention. Far more than the sleazy opportunism of Philippe d'Orléans, his conversion to militant Jacobinism expressed just how far the *ancien régime* had been destroyed by its own beneficiaries. For Lepeletier had come from the cream of the judicial aristocracy and had himself been not just a *conseiller* but a *président* of the Parlement of Paris. A close friend of Hérault de Séchelles, he had been one of the most active reformers in the Constituent Assembly, especially prominent in the Committee for Public Instruction, which drafted an ambitious project for free compulsory elementary education. He had also lent his legal expertise to the reform of the penal code and had proposed a carefully graduated tariff of punishments, in the Beccarian manner, to match differentiated crimes. Reserving capital punishment for premeditated murders, for instance, was supposed to make it awesome enough to deter the villain.

169. Engraving after Jacques-Louis David,
Lepeletier Assassinated

170. Jacques-Louis David,
drawing of Lepeletier

Considerations of this kind did not weigh very heavily on the mind of Lepeletier's own assassin. A former member of the royal bodyguard named Pâris, he approached Lepeletier in the candlelit café amiably enough before pulling an enormous knife. Stabbing the deputy several times, he opened a gaping cavity in his chest.

The corpse of the martyr lay exposed for four days, laid out on a catafalque below which were written what were said to be his last words: "I die content that the tyrant is no more" (though it was unclear if, in fact, the King had predeceased him). Jacques-Louis David made a drawing, self-consciously based on a Renaissance pietà, that exposed Lepeletier's wound like a holy gash and suspended a knife over the torso. In the same representation his head, which was in reality memorably ugly, with a great hooked nose and exophthalmic eyes, was turned into a Roman bust of exemplary beauty. During the funeral, organized by David, the body was laid out on the empty pedestal in the place Vendôme from which a statue, of Louis XIV, had been removed. David had a great flight of steps constructed with a little platform on top, so that before the ceremonies patriotic mourners could ascend to the bier, past two great smoking urns, and behold

171. Exhibition of the body of Michel Lepeletier in the place des Piques (place Vendôme)

the Patriot on his Roman bed of death. At his feet, draped over a pike like a bloody flag, was the shirt in which he had been murdered, going brown-black in the January light. "I am satisfied to spill my blood for the country," announced an engraved plaque below, "[for] I hope that it will serve to consolidate liberty and equality. . . ."

After the eulogies, at which Robespierre was particularly sonorous, the body was lowered and borne through the streets, led by the holy chemise. With Lepeletier's brother Félix at the head of the procession, it made its way to the Convention and then to the Jacobins. There Lepeletier's daughter was declared to be "adopted by the nation," though she scarcely had the need, Mercier tells us, since her father's legacy came to some half-million livres. Later, this *fille de la nation* would become a passionate royalist. Tormented more by the memory of a regicide father than by his death, she concealed and possibly destroyed David's painting. She also mutilated the engraved plate made after that work. A single copy survives still bearing the coup de grâce the daughter inflicted on the image of her already wounded father.

While the Republic was beatifying its first martyr, the body of its king was being turned into nothingness. The theoretical immortality by which, when a king died, royalty lived—*Le roi est mort; vive le roi*—was now reversed. It was the Citizen who had become the heroic immortal; it was the death of the King that was made to kill kingship. The intention was to obliterate the remains of Louis Capet so thoroughly that nothing at all would survive except mortal dirt. Following the execution, the head was placed between his legs in a basket and taken to the cemetery of the Madeleine. From there it was placed in a plain wooden coffin of the kind used for the poorest burials and covered with quicklime. The grave into which it was lowered was said to be ten feet deep. Eight months later, fearing a trade in relics, the Commune issued a further order requiring any surviving items of clothing or any objects whatsoever taken from the Temple to be burned in a public immolation.

The Rex Christianissimus, incarnation of the Sun, had become, by turns, the Restorer of French Liberty, the King of the French, the Pig of Varennes, the tyrant Capet and finally a nullity dissolving in the Paris soil. Those who disposed of him intended an irreversible demystification, something that would make the act of king-killing almost prosaic. Before long this process had gone so far that Sèvres demitasses could be bought with Duplessis' design of Sanson holding up Louis' head rendered on the side in dainty gold paint. Good republicans could sip their coffee demonstrating at the same time their human normality and their political singularity.

It was indeed the case that, for all the attempts at restoration in the

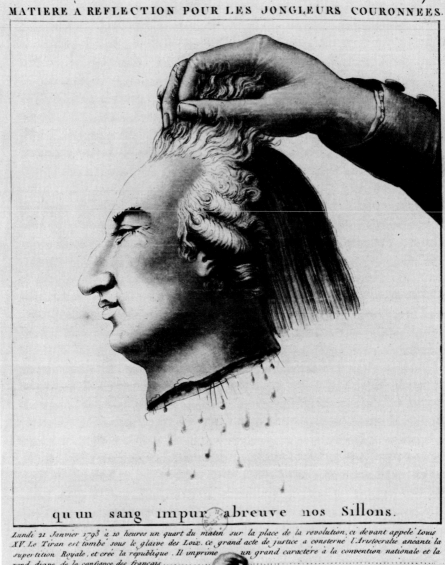

172. "Matter for reflection for the Crowned Jugglers of Europe." The inscription at the bottom is taken from Robespierre's letter to his constituents and declares that the execution has "imprinted a grand character on the National Convention and makes it worthy of the confidence of the French."

nineteenth century, kingship in France was killed along with the King. But the fundamental conflict that had led to this dénouement did not go away on January 21. For the designated successor to royal authority—the Sovereign People—was no more capable than Louis XVI of reconciling freedom with power.

Part Four

VIRTUE AND DEATH

CHAPTER SIXTEEN
Enemies of the People?
Winter–Spring 1793

i STRAITENED
CIRCUMSTANCES

HAT WAS IT about Talleyrand that moved people, especially the British, to compare him to lower forms of life? Hearing he had arrived in England in September 1792, old Horace Walpole, writing from Strawberry Hill, referred to him as "the viper who has cast his skin." When he learned that Talleyrand had been seen in the company of Mme de Genlis, he described the pair as "Eve and the serpent," though he trusted that "few would be disposed to taste their rotten apples."

Perhaps it was Talleyrand's sardonic self-possession that so provoked people. None of his British detractors would go as far as Napoleon, who, infuriated by his aplomb, would call him "a pile of shit in a silk stocking." But Talleyrand's notoriety as a clerical apostate, a political cynic and an amoral rake preceded him to the drawing rooms of polite British society. This was not at all the way he saw himself, either at that time or subsequently. The acts for which he was most reproached—his part in creating a constitutional monarchy—Talleyrand took to be the expression of consistent and genuinely held convictions. The misunderstanding of his politics was, he thought, all the more regrettable since, in the early autumn of 1792, he still hoped to be of service in preventing war between the two countries.

This was, at least, the pretext which led him to apply for a diplomatic passport to London after the revolution of August 10. He would, he told the Executive Council, renew his efforts, begun in the spring, to maintain British neutrality. Now that France was facing the hostility of Prussia as well as Austria, this seemed more than ever indispensable to its survival. Talleyrand's memoirs, however, make it clear that the violence of August 10 had persuaded him that the citizen-nobles associated with the constitutional revolution were not just politically redundant but in mortal danger.

In the days that followed the overthrow of the monarchy, many of Talleyrand's old friends had been turned into fugitives. Returning to find his home ransacked for a mythical cache of arms, Stanislas Clermont-Tonnerre was chased by a mob up to the fourth floor of Mme de Brissac's house. There he was shot and his body thrown from the window to the street. Louis de La Rochefoucauld, who was arrested at Forges-les-Eaux, was dragged from his carriage at Gisors, stoned in front of his wife and mother and cut to a gory mess with sabers and hatchets. His cousin, de La Rochefoucauld-Liancourt, who was commandant of the Rouen garrison, had attempted to rally his troops for the King. Faced with unsympathetic shouts of *"Vive la Nation,"* he escaped from Normandy by commandeering a small boat near Abbeville. Lying hidden with his servant beneath nets and bundles of wood, a pistol pressed to the side of the reluctant fisherman, Liancourt sailed off into the murky fog in the approximate direction of the English coast. At times they seemed so lost that his servant felt sure they were drifting back towards France. Landfall was made near Hastings, from where the two men walked to a tavern and asked for jugs of stout. Liancourt then passed out from the combination of heavy ale and exhaustion, awakening in a bleak room. For a moment, in a surge of panic, he feared that he was indeed back in France. Gradually reassured, he pieced his courage back together and ended up a few days later in East Anglia, where Arthur Young was repaying the Duc's hospitality by lecturing him on the irresponsibility that had led directly to his plight. Fanny Burney saw him as a fallen Romantic, "enveloped in clouds of sadness and moroseness," forcing himself from sheer politeness to entertain the aldermen of Bury St. Edmunds with the endlessly repeated story of his announcement to the King in July 1789 that Louis was indeed confronted with a revolution.

Characteristically, Talleyrand maintained his *sang-froid* while doing his best to ensure a safe and speedy exit. On August 31, Danton summoned him to the Ministry of Justice, in what was now called the place des Piques, to receive his passport. Barère found him there late at night, trying to look nonchalant dressed in hide breeches and boots, with his hair tied back in a pigtail as though prepared for a hard ride. But no passport was issued from Danton's office that night or during the nights that followed. Anxious lest some fool jokingly, or spitefully, hail him in public as "The Bishop," Talleyrand sweated out the week of the prison killings until, on the seventh, the precious document at last arrived. At the Channel ports he made his way through milling crowds of scared priests trying to get passages to England or Ireland. In that month alone seven hundred departed from Dieppe and Le Havre.

Though Talleyrand was safely established in Woodstock Street, Kensington, his official position remained precarious. The credentials of the French Embassy to the Court of St. James's had been damaged by virtue of the country's transformation into a republic, so that Talleyrand's reception from officials like Grenville, the Secretary of State, was even less cordial than it had been in the spring. Moreover, the pragmatic and defensive line he took in a memorandum to Paris written in early October was not in keeping with the increasingly messianic tone of the National Convention. "We have learned," he wrote optimistically, "that the only policy suited to free and enlightened men is to be sovereign over one's own affairs and not to have the ridiculous pretension of imposing it on others. The reign of illusions" (by which he meant the royal thirst for conquest) "is then over for France."

In fact, a new era of illusions, indistinguishable in their aggression from the old, was just beginning. To its clamorous rhetoric Talleyrand's pragmatic moderation was bound to seem suspect. On December 5, it was announced in the Convention that compromising documents linking him through the royal officer of the civil list, La Porte, had been discovered in the *armoire de fer*. Extremely courageously, his old assistant Desrenaudes, in a published memorandum, denied that Talleyrand had had any such communication with the court, and the evidence was, in fact, equivocal. But he was nonetheless placed on the list of proscribed émigrés. Arrest warrants were published including a description that asked citizens to be on the lookout for someone who limped "on either the left foot or the right."

Always an outsider, Talleyrand was now stateless but not friendless. Though shunned by conservative society in London, he radiated a kind of dangerous glamour that appealed to the radical wing of the Whigs, who clung tenaciously to their enthusiasm for the constitutional revolution. So he was much taken up by Charles James Fox and the playwright Sheridan as well as the partisans of the London Revolution Society (named for the celebration of 1688). At Fox's dinner table Talleyrand was paradoxically struck with the British orator's eloquence when he saw him conversing in sign language with his deaf illegitimate son.

It was an extraordinary time to have landed in England, for the country was in political uproar. In Scotland and Ireland, clubs and societies openly sympathetic to the Revolution had become defiant, calling for conventions. In provincial cities like Sheffield and Manchester, meetings were held each week to demand constitutional reform and to read the second part of Tom Paine's *Rights of Man,* with its astonishing demand for the introduction of a welfare state. The pamphlet's circulation may well have reached into the hundreds of thousands. In the capital, the London Corresponding Society had sent fraternal greetings to the bar of the Convention in Paris. And against this tide of dangerous disaffection, a loyalist Association for the Preservation of Liberty and Property was drilling volunteer militia in the counties.

Talleyrand is likely to have found both extremes of opinion just as unappetizing as they had been in France. His view of events was not far from that of the inspired caricaturist James Gillray, whose visual denunciations, both of British Jacobinophobia and French sans-culotte atrocities, were impartially savage. The *Zenith of French Liberty,* published at the time of Louis' execution, with its literally bare-assed *sans-culotte* sitting on a *lanterne* from which a priest was suspended, was not that far from Talleyrand's own increasingly bitter view of the fate of the Revolution. To his old friend Shelburne, now elevated as Marquess of Lansdowne and still the most friendly patron of the French citizen-nobles in exile, he wrote a damning account of recent events.

> At a time when everything has been disfigured and perverted, the men who remain true to liberty, despite the mask of blood and filth with which atrocities have covered it, are excessively few in number. Trapped for two years between terror and defiance, the French have become accustomed to slavery and say only what can be said without danger. The clubs and the pikes, deadening all free initiative, have accustomed people to dissimulation and baseness, and if the people are allowed to acquire these sorry habits they will have only the happiness of exchanging tyrants. Since the leaders of the Jacobins down to the most honest citizens defer to the head-cutters, there is to-day nothing but a chain of villainy and lies, of which the first link is lost in filth.

Chagrin was soothed only by *ennui.* In Woodstock Street, surrounded by the library that he had prudently sent ahead, and comforted by Adelaide de Flahaut, Talleyrand settled down to a humdrum routine. In the morning he would work on a biography of the Duc d'Orléans or, more enjoyably, his own memoirs. Adelaide had completed her novel *Cécile de Senange* and he helped her correct proofs. In the afternoons he might go to Half-Moon Street to visit Mme de Genlis and Orléans' sixteen-year-old daughter, also named Adelaide, who were living in such modesty that they were making straw hats, of the kind made fashionable by Elisabeth Vigée-Lebrun's portraits, to support themselves.

There was only one bright spot in this dreary exile. Periodically, Talleyrand would take a post coach out to the Worthing Road and travel south to the Surrey Downs. About five miles north of Dorking, near the village of Mickleham, Germaine de Staël had rented a Georgian house known as Juniper Hall as a gathering place for the remnant of the Club of 1789 and especially her inconstant lover Narbonne. Though she did not herself arrive in England until January 1793, the house was open for whomever among their old Paris friends wanted to stay there, and for many of them Juniper Hall became a blessed refuge from poverty and boredom. Among the regular guests were Lally-Tollendal; Mathieu de Montmorency; Beaumetz; Jaucourt and his mistress the striking Vicomtesse de Châtre; Stanislas Girardin (who naturally demanded to be shown the only site in the area associated with the memory of Rousseau); and Lafayette's second-in-command in 1789, General d'Arblay. Surrey society from Leatherhead to Reigate divided sharply between those who were scandalized and those who were fascinated. If there was muttering at Fetcham and West Humble, in Mickleham itself the Lockes of Norbury Park frequently entertained the French colony. There they met Mrs. Susanna Phillips, the daughter of the musicologist Dr. Charles Burney.

In November, Mrs. Phillips's forty-year-old sister Fanny, drawn irresistibly to a company of such social and cultural exoticism, paid her first visit. "There can be nothing imagined more charming, more fascinating than this colony," she wrote to her father, who was unnecessarily worried about the effect on her morals from exposure to French manners. Like almost everybody else outside the Lansdowne circle, she took an instant dislike to Talleyrand, but very soon fell under the spell of his considerable charm. "It is inconceivable what a convert M. de Talleyrand has made of me. I think him now one of the finest members and one of the most charming of this exquisite set. His powers of entertainment are astonishing both in information and raillery." She was most impressed by the group's obvious indifference to the horsey pleasures of the Surrey gentry and the unself-conscious liveliness with which they flung themselves into discussions of every kind: on history (especially their own), drama, poetry and philosophy.

Even more striking was the extent to which they all took their cue in these intellectual games from Germaine de Staël herself. They listened to her read passages from her *Apologie de Rousseau* and her dramatic essay in defense of suicide: *The Influence of the Passions on Happiness.* Typically, Talleyrand praised the piece but disparaged her manner of reading it in a singsong style as though, he said unkindly, it was verse. More trying for Fanny was Lally's rendition of his own historical drama *The Death of Strafford.* She noticed him at dinner mumbling the lines to himself so that he could recite them by heart afterwards. The reading was about to begin when d'Arblay's conspicuous absence was noticed. After more delay Germaine wanted to start but Talleyrand protested that *"cela lui fera de la peine"* (he would be upset by it) and limped off to find the absentee.

It was typical of Fanny's innocence in this company that she assumed Talleyrand was performing an act of kindness by subjecting d'Arblay (who had almost certainly concealed himself somewhere with a bottle of port) to Lally's performance. The "alternate howling and thundering of his voice . . . fatigued me excessively," she admitted, but it never occurred to her that Talleyrand was being mischievous in winkling the soldier out. She was too moved by the deep melancholy into which the company was thrown on learning of the execution of the King to notice the subtle strategies of their sexual politics. Jaucourt and the Vicomtesse de Châtre as well as Narbonne and Germaine were living together openly. Germaine at twenty-seven, though no classical beauty, had matured into a high-colored blossom whose personality poured out of her like some very strong scent. It seems to have been too much for Narbonne (whose son she had borne in Geneva the previous November), and he resented the moral blackmail by which she threatened to kill herself if he indulged his own tragic fantasy of going to Paris to testify in defense of the King. As he cooled towards Mme de Staël she began to cultivate Talleyrand once more, both to provoke Narbonne (unsuccessfully) and to liberate him from Adelaide de Flahaut, whom she evidently disliked.

It was, in Duff Cooper's memorable characterization (and he should have known), as if *Les Liaisons Dangereuses* had been transported to the landscape of *Sense and Sensibility*. For a long time, herself rather smitten with the gallant d'Arblay, Fanny was sublimely innocent of all these intrigues. To yet another wag of Dr. Burney's admonishing finger, she responded indignantly that "I think you could not spend a day with them and not see that their commerce is that of pure but exalted and most elegant friendship." When, finally, the truth dawned on her she rebuffed Germaine, who had taken her under her capacious wing, with shocked coldness. D'Arblay, however, was rescued from the den of iniquity by marriage to the virtuous Fanny and lived out his years as a charming curiosity among the English squirearchy.

Perhaps there were worse things than to be married to Fanny Burney. In March, Talleyrand's predicament became quickly more miserable. With his money gone, he was forced to surrender his library to the sale room, from which he made but a paltry £750. He left his little house in Woodstock Street and moved to smaller quarters in Kensington Square. On the thirteenth of the month he was officially proscribed in France, which meant that not only his but his family's property stood forfeit to the Republic.

Finally, in May, under the provision of the Aliens Bill which granted summary powers of deportation to the government, Talleyrand was told he must leave Britain as a political undesirable. Germaine had already gone back to Switzerland to reacquaint herself with her son Albert, whom she had left at the age of five weeks to be with Narbonne in Surrey. Though she was looking for somewhere for him to live nearby, Talleyrand was given to understand, both in Geneva and Florence, to which city he also thought of removing himself, that his presence would not be appreciated. Only America was left as a possibility. Armed with letters of introduction from Lansdowne to George Washington and Alexander Hamilton, he took ship on the *William Penn*. Hardly had he departed than the ship nearly foundered in a violent tempest in the Solent that had Talleyrand fearful he would be washed up on the French coast. But the vessel rode it out and, before resuming the journey, put into Falmouth harbor for repairs. There he fell into conversation with another fallen hero, with whom he could compare extensive notes on the ingratitude and misunderstanding of the ignorant world. Thus it was that the ex-general Benedict Arnold sent the ex-bishop Maurice de Talleyrand on his way to America.

I T S E E M S unlikely that Talleyrand thought his public career was over at the age of thirty-nine. He reassured Adelaide de Flahaut that he would be back and told Germaine to continue hunting for a house by Lake Geneva. But for the time being he was certainly a casualty of the war with Britain that he had always thought disastrous for French interests. His only hope had been that Dumouriez would inherit the Fayettist strategy of using military popularity at the front against the Jacobins in Paris. This was indeed the General's strategy but through the winter of 1792–93, its realization became more and more remote. His plan, following Jemappes, was to create an independent Belgian republic that would deny the southern Netherlands to the Austrians while not provoking the British into war. This meant supporting the more conservative of the two Belgian aspirant political groups, the "Statists," against the democratic republicans. This was a calculated decision to co-opt the Belgian elite who had led the revolt against the Austrians and avoid alienating the majority of the population by extending French anticlericalism to one of the most fervently pious Catholic populations in Europe.

It was, in fact, the only policy that had any chance of attaching Belgian loyalties to France, since, as Dumouriez understood, the rebellion against Austria had been fueled by the provinces' determination to *protect* traditional institutions against imperial reforms. But to the militants in the Convention, it looked suspiciously like a lingering Feuillant compromise with the counter-revolution. Dumouriez was accused of wanting to create his own military and political base by selling the "liberation" of Belgium short, repudiating the true indigenous revolutionaries and intriguing with local aristocrats, priests and army contractors. His proposed native Belgian army, for example, was to be financed by a loan from the clergy, produced on the understanding that they would not be subjected to French clerical legislation. To Dumouriez this seemed a sensible compromise; to Cambon and his critics in the Convention it was flagrant evidence of a Caesarist plot.

The decree of December 15 was expressly aimed at thwarting Dumouriez's autonomous policy by subjecting his authority to the Convention's representatives. The full force of revolutionary decrees, including those concerning the Church, was to be imposed on the Belgian provinces. At the end of March 1793, with his military and political strategy in ruins, Dumouriez complained bitterly to the Convention that it was its brutal disregard for local susceptibilities that had wrecked the Belgian campaign. The Belgian people were, he said, "subjected to every kind of vexation; what, in their view, were sacred rights of liberty were violated; and their religious feeling impudently insulted." The annexation of the province of Hainaut had been justified by a spurious "Convention" which in reality, Dumouriez said, was no more than twenty self-authorizing individuals in Brussels. Then its churches had been stripped of plate to pay for the "liberation." "From then on you regarded the Belgians as French but even if they had been, it would still have been necessary to wait until this silver would have been given as a voluntary sacrifice. Without that willingness its forcible seizure was in their eyes nothing but sacrilege."

Dumouriez's indictment of French policy in Belgium was not, of course, without its own self-interest. The Convention had sabotaged his plans to create a power base in the Netherlands, and military defeat had finished them off completely. For all his personal bias, however, his account of the beginning of French revolutionary imperialism was absolutely accurate.

It is certain, at any rate, that the new policy of annexations and aggressive revolutionary expansionism moved Britain decisively closer to war. The policy of strict neutrality sustained by both Pitt and Grenville had survived the overthrow of the French monarchy. Even in late October they saw no compelling reason to alter that basic position. But the French decision to open the river Scheldt to navigation on November 16, in defiance of the 1648 Treaty of Westphalia, confronted them with a much more provocative challenge. At the end of the long Dutch war for independence against Spain, the river had been closed in deference to Holland's concern about preventing either the economic or strategic revival of the port city of Antwerp. Since the Dutch and British had become allies against Louis XIV at the end of the seventeenth century, maintaining the closure had become an article of faith in their system of containing French expansionism in the Netherlands. The unilateral abrogation of the treaty (and the sending of a French gunboat downriver) seemed the clearest possible test of British commitment to an ally and to its determination to preserve the status quo. There were, moreover, other indications that "natural law" and "natural frontiers" would be allowed to override traditional diplomatic convention. On the twenty-seventh of November, Savoy, which had been occupied by Montesquiou's troops since mid-October, was formally annexed after a "Convention of the Allobroges" had voted to depose the King of Sardinia and to "reunite" the province with France. A day later, the President of the Convention, Grégoire, welcomed fraternal addresses from London with the announcement that "doubtless the moment is near when Frenchmen will bear congratulations to the National Convention of Great Britain."

On December 1 Pitt's government passed an act mobilizing the British militia, both to meet the challenge of domestic disorder and as a preliminary to hostilities. But its most urgent concern was less with revolution at home than in the Dutch Republic. For while the successful recruiting of a loyalist militia had given the government confidence it could contain the tide of revolutionary enthusiasm in England (it was less confident about Scotland and Ireland), it fretted that the Stadtholder's regime, restored by Prussian troops in 1787, was on the point of crumbling. A resurgence of Patriot politics in the Netherlands would provide the French with an irresistible target of opportunity. Either the "natural frontiers" would be extended north beyond the Meuse, or Dumouriez would succeed in reassembling the old seventeen-province Great Netherlands he had long been imagining. In either event the British treaty commitment to maintaining the Prince of Orange's government would be exposed as a feeble sham.

The British government moved towards war, then, not out of any desire to intervene in French politics, however distasteful the Republic might have been. On the eve of Jemappes, Grenville was, in fact, intelligently convinced that the worst thing opponents of republicanism could do would be to attempt some war of intervention that would infallibly be met by a further round of patriotic messianism. "I cannot but remain in the persuasion that the re-establishment of order in France, under any form, can be effected only by a long course of intestine struggles." It was, however, imperative for the balance of power and the stability of Europe that the explosive power of revolutionary disorder be contained well within France itself. Astonishingly, George III seemed to feel the same way, commenting to his secretary of state that "it is peace alone that can place the French Revolution on a permanent ground as then all the European States must acknowledge the new Republic." In December Grenville invited the Russian Empress Catherine to join in demanding "a withdrawing of their [French] arms within the limits of French territory, the abandoning of their conquests, the rescinding of any acts injurious to other nations and the giving in some public and unequivocal manner a pledge of their intention no longer to foment troubles and to excite disturbances against their own Governments." Should such assurances be given, he added, the powers "might engage to abandon measures or views of hostility against France."

A belligerent speech on January 1 by Kersaint, the naval hero of the American war, however, suggested that so far from the Convention accepting this kind of defensive pragmatism, it already regarded a conflict with the British Empire as both desirable and inevitable. Kersaint's address was full of fraternal wishful thinking, imagining not only the Scots and Irish but English "sans-culottes" on the verge of insurrection. Just as Brissot had insisted a year before that the rotting despotisms of Austria and Prussia would be easy prey, so Kersaint told the Convention that the apparent might of the British Empire rested on the fragile and unstable foundation of the national debt, and the collaboration of a handful of bankers. Britain was vulnerable in south India and in the Caribbean; its Parliament was captious, its chief minister wicked, and its king mad. A carefully planned invasion would undoubtedly meet with massive popular enthusiasm among the British citizenry, so that "over the ruins of the Tower of London [evidently seen as London's Bastille] . . . France will conclude with the liberated English people the Treaty which would guide the future development of the nations and establish the liberty of the world."

Even this kind of messianic reworking of traditional French Anglophobic patriotism was not a conclusive demonstration to the British government that there could be no reasonable negotiations with revolutionary France. But the execution of Louis XVI had a profoundly shocking effect in London. Pitt called it "the foulest and most atrocious act the world has ever seen," and Grenville wrote to the British Ambassador in The Hague, describing theater audiences demanding the curtain be lowered on hearing the news. Even more than the moral abhorrence felt by most of the British elite, it was the government's sense that it was now dealing with a phenomenon of uncontainable barbarism and irrationality that rendered all further discussions moot.

Only one final possibility remained, as Talleyrand pointed out to Grenville on January 28: that Dumouriez conduct his own foreign policy independently, if necessary, of the Convention. Indeed, Dumouriez seemed to have the ear of the Foreign Minister, Lebrun. The Ambassador in London, Chauvelin, was instructed to tell Grenville and Pitt that the promise of "liberation" contained in the Convention's decree of November 19 was not a blank check for insurrection. Rather it indicated that *once* freed by their own efforts, such "peoples" might reasonably expect France to come to their defense. But the apparently picayune matter of the Scheldt became a symbol of both sides' intransigence. The French justified its opening to free navigation as a nonnegotiable "right of nature"; the British, its closure as a matter of compliance with international treaties. What if the French were allowed to alter these as their caprice dictated, to make themselves the arbiter of what was, and what was not, permissible in the relations between states? When Hugues Maret arrived in London with proposals from Dumouriez for a negotiated pacification, Grenville thought it was just a delaying tactic. On February 1, before the envoy could explain the plan, the Convention declared war on Great Britain and the Dutch Republic.

It took very little time before it became apparent that this was a dreadful mistake. In the event of war Dumouriez had been anxious to avoid a complicated amphibious operation in Zeeland. But his preferred southern route through Dutch Brabant was almost equally laborious, since it necessarily involved besieging fortifications at Maastricht, Geetruidenberg and Breda before crossing the rivers to south Holland. More ominously, the French lines were already seriously overextended even before the Dutch invasion. In the aftermath of Jemappes, volunteers who had responded to the patriotic appeals of autumn 1792 had returned home, halving the army's effective strength. Exploiting the thinness of its forward positions, the Austrians and Prussians had succeeded in driving a wedge between the armies of the Moselle and Rhine in Germany and Dumouriez's main force in Belgium.

With Mainz under siege there were simply too many imponderables (and too many Austrians and Prussians) for a systematic advance into the Dutch Republic. While Dumouriez was planting a liberty tree in the main square of Breda on February 26 after a week's siege, General Miranda, to the south, was stuck in front of Maastricht, which had been heavily reinforced by the Prussians. On March 1 he heard that an army of forty thousand, nearly twice the size of his, had crossed the river Roer behind him. Hurriedly dropping back and abandoning Maastricht, he fought a disorganized action on the following day. His volunteers were cut to pieces by repeated Austrian cavalry charges. By the end of the day the French had lost over three thousand dead and wounded to the Austrians' forty.

Over the next week, Dumouriez tried to repair what he euphemistically described to the Convention as *un échec*. Leaving his expeditionary force in Holland, he concentrated on reinforcing Miranda's defensive position and taking dramatic action to reconcile the Belgians. Jacobin clubs were closed, revolutionary decrees revoked, a fulminating letter of complaint sent to the Convention. It was an exact rehearsal of Bonapartism, but it was too soon for France and too late for Belgium. Like Bonapartism, the politics of retrenchment meant nothing without military success. And on the eighteenth at Neerwinden, Dumouriez's army first failed to dislodge the Austrians, then buckled under their counter-assault. With the expeditionary force desperately trying to get out of Holland, the entire French position in the Netherlands, south and north, collapsed in a matter of days.

On the twenty-third Dumouriez opened negotiations with Coburg for evacuating Belgium on the condition that his army remain unmolested. The Austrian commander agreed to these terms because it was evident that Dumouriez meant to use his troops against the Convention itself. The following day, to the regret of few of the native population, the French marched out of Brussels, and by the last day of the month had recrossed the frontier. Worse was to follow. General Beurnonville, the Minister of War, who had been sent to the front to investigate Dumouriez's conduct, was himself arrested with his fellow commissioners and delivered to the Austrians. During the first days of April, Dumouriez attempted to persuade his own troops to go over to the Allies in a march on Paris. Much as many of the regulars mistrusted the Convention, their disaffection stopped well short of treason. So on April 5 Dumouriez, like Lafayette before him, rode to the Austrian lines, taking a handful of high officers, among them Philippe-Egalité's son the Duc de Chartres, the future Louis-Philippe.

When the news of this betrayal reached Paris, it seemed to vindicate the most exaggerated versions of the conspiracy theory. With hindsight, it seemed to the Jacobins in particular that the entire Dutch expedition had been a deliberate design by Dumouriez to hand over the army to Austria. Like the spurious white flag fluttering from the towers of the Bastille or the lull in firing from the château of the Tuileries, there had been a calculated attempt to lure Patriots to their doom. In a revolutionary culture where aristocracy was itself stigmatized by its addiction to stratagems and deceits, this latest betrayal seemed of a piece with the fifth-column saboteurs of the old regime.

To those skeptical of his patriotism, it came as no surprise to discover that it had been Dumouriez who had been responsible for the military

defense of western France. For in the same week that the tricolor fell in the
Flemish mud at Neerwinden, the Department of the Vendée had risen in
bloody insurrection against the Republic.

ii SACRED HEARTS:
THE RISING IN THE VENDÉE

The little grain-market town of Machecoul lay twelve miles from the
Atlantic. Just after dawn, on the eleventh of March 1793, seven-year-old
Germain Bethuis was woken by a dull, booming noise rather like the sound
of an angry sea. But to his young ears it seemed to come not from the west
but from the north, in the direction of the village of Saint-Philibert. The
sound grew louder and he became frightened. At the soirées of women and
children that helped pass the long winter evenings, some of the older
countrywomen had made alarming prophecies of battles and bloodletting
to be heralded by clouds bunched into sinister shapes and tinted with

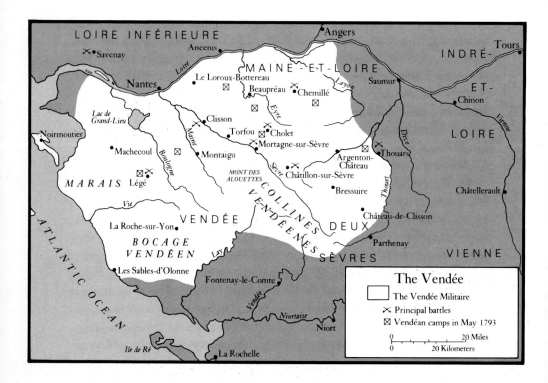

unnatural hues. As he peered into the thinning Vendéan morning mist, Germain thought he could make out just such an apparition, darker than the fog and moving slowly over the fields towards the town. His father, who was a thirty-two-year-old notary and member of the district administration, was still in bed when his son ran in to rouse him. "There's a black, noisy cloud, Papa, and it's coming to town," he told him. By now the sun had burnt off the mist to reveal a compact swarm of thousands of peasants, armed with pitchforks, skinning knives, billhooks, sickles, and more than a few hunting guns. As Germain remembered it, "Their wild cries alone were enough to spread terror."

His father hurried to join the handful of National Guards who had hastily assembled in the main street, and stood facing the crowd of perhaps three thousand peasants. The Guards were mostly older men and young boys, since Machecoul had produced its share of the military levy required under the Convention's plan, decreed on February 24, to raise an army of three hundred thousand. It had, in fact, been the descent of the recruiting officers on the villages of southern Anjou which had triggered spontaneous risings erupting throughout the region. At Machecoul it was left to the elderly president of the district administration and director of the local college, Dr. Gaschinard, to face down the alarming crowd. Summoning his best schoolmasterly manner, he made what Bethuis recalled as "a moving speech" (*"un discours pathétique"*) against violence. He would, he said, hand over, as the peasants demanded, the keys to the clock tower of the church if on their side they promised not to harm the inhabitants of the town.

Once the tocsin was ringing, however, this became a promise that was impossible to keep. The alarm brought to Machecoul peasants from all the surrounding villages, turning the swollen crowd into a rioting mob. Maupassant, the officer who had arrived in Machecoul to supervise the drawing of lots for the army, told the Guards to stand their ground, but most broke ranks and fled. Attempting to reason with the leaders of the mob, he was killed by a single pike thrust to the heart. At this point, the disorder became uncontrollable. The houses of anyone identified with the local administration were ransacked. Any men found inside were dragged to the street and badly beaten to the huntsmen's call of *hallali*, sounded when the quarry is at bay. The constitutional priest Le Tort was pulled from his church and stabbed in the face with a bayonet for ten minutes before he was finished off. More than forty men were killed on the street and another four hundred rounded up and marched to the Calvairienne convent as prisoners.

For a while, Bethuis *père* managed to evade the rampaging crowd by hiding in the house of a friend on the outskirts of town. Advised to flee, he refused to leave his family, and falling ill, not only returned to his own house, but took to his bed. Soon he had joined others in the improvised prison from which men were being regularly taken to summary judgment and execution. Chains of prisoners were formed by passing ropes under their arms in the infamous "rosaries" by which they were dragged to fields outside the town, made to dig ditches and then shot so that they fell neatly into their graves. The physician Musset was placed on the line twice and both times reprieved, before being executed on a final telling of the rosary. Growing desperate about his own fate, Bethuis threw himself from a second-story window, breaking his leg. His wife pleaded with the Vendéan commander Charette for her husband to see a doctor—perhaps Musset. But though Charette had come to Machecoul partly to impose some sort of order on the indiscriminate brutalities that were taking place, he told her that "a man destined to die in a few hours has no need of a doctor."

Bethuis perished along with more than five hundred citizens of

173. Anonymous print, "The Monster
Counter-revolution"

Machecoul in the bloodiest massacres perpetrated by the Vendéan rebels. The name of the town became a byword in republican rhetoric for the savagery and inhumanity of the rebels. And to this day, the history of the Vendée is capable of polarizing French historians and readers more implacably than almost any other event of the Revolution. What immediately strikes a non-French historian is how similar the gruesome events at Machecoul were to comparable acts of violent retribution committed by the republican side. Like the September massacres, the sanguinary acts began with an uncontrollable spontaneous need to visit public and brutal punishment on men who symbolized intolerable evils and immediate threats: foreigners inside the culture of hearth and home. Like the September massacres, the eruption of popular anger was quickly directed, controlled and even given some sort of spurious legal form. In Machecoul, the equivalent to Maillard was the *procureur* Souchu, who presided over the proceedings that condemned the prisoners to their death. Charette was in a similar position to Danton's—the warlord-judge ostensibly armed with authority to stop the murders but disinclined and ultimately impotent to do so.

The brutality of the Vendée rising, and of its repression, was a product of the Manichaean language of the revolutionary war. The "pathetic speech" of Dr. Gaschinard was an attempt to return both sides to a recognition of their common fraternity as Frenchmen. But they had each become so accustomed to damning stereotypes of monsters and incarnations of evil that reason collapsed back fatally to these mutual demonologies. A month before the uprising, the tapestry weaver Laparra, president of the local revolutionary club, the Société des Amis de la Liberté et Egalité at Fontenay-le-Comte, described the refractory priests and aristocrats as

> a monster with several heads which ravages France. The
> terrible blow that you have struck [the execution of the King]
> has removed its principal head but it is not yet dead, this mon-
> ster that devours the entire universe.

Urging on the convention to more exemplary executions, Laparra warmed to his subject: "Strike, strike great blows against these infamous heads which without any pity tear at the breast of their own mother [France] . . . let the avenging axe fall on them so that the death of these anthropophagi will give a terrible example to their imbecile accomplices . . . throw them, throw them from the heights of the Tarpeian rock." A good start might be made, he thought, by executing two of these eaters of men in the capital town of each department of the Republic.

In the same manner, rebels at the village of Doulon anathematized the republicans: "They have killed our king; chased away our priests; sold the goods of our church; eaten everything we have and now they want to take our bodies . . . no, they shall not have them."

In both the rhetorical dehumanization of the enemy and the extreme ferocity with which the war was waged, the Vendée anticipated a cycle of peasant uprisings. Wherever the armies and civilian commissioners of the Revolution confronted a pious peasantry led by locally familiar priests and powerful prelates, they met the same stubborn resistance. What began in western France in 1793 was repeated in the northern Italian "Viva Maria" riots, the Calabrian "Sanfedisti" and Belgian peasant revolts, all in 1799, as well as in Spain in 1808. In each case the authority of republican government was embodied in townsmen, often professionals, and in a minority of ardent politicians whose rhetoric was the more shrill for being isolated in regions largely unsympathetic to their doctrine.

In his classic work on the *pays des Mauges,* the subregion divided by the river Layon, Charles Tilly saw the river as a social as well as topographical frontier. To the north and east was the Val-Saumurois, a relatively densely settled and prosperous area where farmers and townsmen had a common interest in profiting from revolutionary legislation on the sale of church property. Literacy rates were higher, pious practices more moderate. Country and town were less abrasively juxtaposed. In sharp contrast, to the west and south, the Mauges presented a more silent, sparsely populated countryside with muddy runnels and cart tracks cutting a way between high hedgerows and dense woods. In the few towns of this region, like Cholet and Chemillé, textile entrepreneurs exploited the need of subsistence peasants for additional work by employing them as weavers at low wages and under harsh conditions. That population remained, in effect, urban peasants rather than townsmen. In contrast to the Val-Saumurois, then, the rural population of the Mauges perceived the town as exploiter and enemy.

Conversely, while in the more commercialized region farmers and bourgeois made common cause against nobles and the immensely rich Church, in the Mauges as well as in other subregions of the Vendée proper, like the wooded *bocage* and the Gâtiné, lines were drawn, as it were, vertically, rather than horizontally. They set off against each other an internally cohesive rural culture and an external urban world, invested by the Revolution with the powers of the state. In that rural world, the local nobility seems to have been more residential and less bitterly resented than in other parts of France. Violent riots had been few and far between in 1789. Because of the relative isolation of villages from each other, the Church and its curates exercised a disproportionately more influential role. They baptized, married and buried; gave education to the children; helped the infirm and destitute; and on Sundays provided the only place where inhabitants could recognize in each other their shared sense of community.

As Jean-Clément Martin has emphasized in the most recent and most balanced account of the revolt, there were other parts of France where the rejection of the Civil Constitution was just as vehement and widespread as in southern Anjou and the Vendée. But in none of those regions did the several components that made for a sudden and violent rising come together in quite the same way. In Flanders, Picardy and parts of Normandy, for example, nonjuring rates were very high. (In the eight districts of the Department of the Nord, for instance, there were only 190 jurors as against 1,057 nonjuring priests.) Paradoxically, rates of refusal were often higher in the towns than in the countryside, where the stipendiary *curés congrues* did better under the Revolution than during the old regime. The same was true for the Midi, where the rates of accepting the Civil Constitution ran around 80 percent in the villages of Provence, while entire towns like Arles remained royalist-Catholic and were only mastered by military force. In Alsace and Lorraine as well as Flanders and Picardy, hostility to the juring clergy also ran high, but these were war zones, studded with big garrison towns that could concentrate sufficient force quickly enough to prevent riots from turning into wholesale insurrections. Even in Brittany, where conditions were most similar to those in the Vendée, the royalist plot of the Marquis de La Rouërie could be nipped in the bud by picking off the principals and using enough punitive power to deter any popular demonstrations.

In the Vendée, by contrast, isolated urban representatives of the Republic, and of Jacobin patriotism, were cast adrift in a great ocean of fervent peasant piety. Moreover, as Dumouriez tried to tell the government throughout 1792, the region was dangerously undefended and would be vulnerable should a serious movement of protest occur. This complacency was all the more remarkable since the region had already given some earnest of its disaffection by serious disturbances at Challans and Cholet in 1791, and especially at Châtillon and Bressuire in August 1792. But there are signs that the authorities placed these events in the category of isolated incidents, no different from the many other rural riots that flared up in areas of France where the Revolution had disappointed the expectations of 1789. In the summer of 1792 there had been another wave of peasant *jacqueries* in upper Brittany; Quercy in the southwest of the Massif Central, and in the hinterland of Provence. In each of these regions discontent had been provoked by the inability of poorer peasants to profit from the sales of ecclesiastical property. In some areas fences enclosing the common land on which animals had been grazed were torn down, but in others demands were actually made for the partition of the common land among the most disadvantaged families of the village.

These grievances, however, were endemic to rural life in the *pays des petites cultures*. The drafting of the *cahiers* in 1789 had led the poorer cultivators, gathered in churches listening to their *curés,* to believe that their lives were about to be transformed by a magical act of social justice. What had in fact happened was that the Revolution had not only not reversed, but actually intensified, the differences between the relatively well-off and the impoverished populations of the countryside. The official response to mounting anger and violence in 1792 was a typical combination of symbolic legal concessions and selective repression. After the overthrow of the monarchy, in the last weeks of its existence the Legislative Assembly had swept aside the elaborate program of redemption payments for seigneurial dues set up in 1789 and had abolished them outright. But since the peasants had, in any case, stopped paying them, this had no effect on the higher rents with which property owners continued to compensate themselves. Companies of National Guards, together with small units of regular troops, were used to suppress further disorders wherever they flared up.

None threatened to develop into the kind of concerted insurrection that consumed the Vendée in the spring of 1793. That region, too, had its rural underclass, but historians like Marcel Faucheux have had to work very hard to make social grievances the determinant of the revolt's allegiance. (And Martin has pointed out that many of the exploited weavers of Cholet actually enlisted under republican rather than Vendéan colors.) One of the most striking features of the rebellion was the social *inclusiveness* and the ties which bound together people from widely separated economic groups. The Grand Royal and Catholic Army was made up not just of subsistence peasants but quite well-off livestock farmers and a strong concentration of just those village types—innkeepers, millers, carters, blacksmiths and the like—who were supposed to be the Revolution's representatives in the countryside. If there were representatives of those tied to local communities, like fishermen from the maritime villages near Paimboeuf, there were also boatmen and bargemen whose work took them traveling along the little rivers and canals of the Vendéan *marais*. Carters like the Vendéan General Cathelineau, itinerant merchants, commanded knowledge of different communities that gave them familiarity along predictable routes. The Mauges was famous not for its backwoods isolation but for its herds of fat cattle that were the prize stock of the Paris meat market at Sceaux and whose drovers were experts on the highways and byways of roads leading northeast to the Loire. There were, moreover, nobles on both sides of the war. While the noble commanders of the Vendéan army like d'Elbée and de La Rochejaquelein are better known, the commandant of the National Guard at Mortagne was the *ci-devant* Sieur Drouhet, who was a *chevalier* of Saint-Louis and had fought in America with Lafayette. At les Sables-d'Olonne the local military commander of the republican troops was Beaufranchet d'Ayat, a bastard son of Louis XV and Boucher's favorite nude, Mlle O'Murphy.

Instead of searching for a coherent pattern of social issues that would "explain" a religious revolt in terms of something else, it makes more sense to take at face value General Turreau's remark that "it is a true crusade." The clergy of Anjou and lower Brittany, who were at the eye of the storm, were, as recent research by Timothy Tackett and others has shown, one of the least impoverished of the French priesthoods. Both its salaried *curés congrues* and the tithed clergy were better off than their brethren in many other areas of France. A significant number had smallholdings of sufficient size to produce food for themselves and a modest income in addition. The secular clergy of the small towns often shared indirectly in the prosperous endowments which made the dioceses of the west at Luçon, Angers and Nantes some of the richest in France. And just because the region around La Rochelle had been one of the last strongholds of independent Protestant-ism in the seventeenth century, it had been the target of intensive Catholic preaching missions. The Missionaires du Saint-Esprit, for example, orga-nized by Louis Grignion de Montfort at the beginning of the eighteenth century, had apparently succeeded in implanting a genuinely popular and energetic ministry in the west. Not surprisingly, then, there was an unusual degree of solidarity extending through the church hierarchy and far fewer of the alienated country curates who, in the Midi and in the Norman countryside, provided natural candidates for the constitutional clergy.

It was also of the utmost significance that a very high proportion of the clergy in western France originated in the countryside. Given the Church's high status and well-endowed livings, a career in the Church was a natural ambition for a bright boy of peasant origins. Many of those who had become ordained after seminary education in the cathedral towns then returned to their native villages or at least to the locality in which they had been born. There they not only ministered to the spiritual needs of their flock but provided indispensable personnel for local schools and colleges and succor for the sick and poor. Thus, more than in many other areas, the priests of the Vendée could claim to be true sons of the *pays*. This made the constitutional clergy who replaced them seem all the more alien. They were universally described throughout the region as *intrus* or more col-loquially as *truts* or *trutons*—intruders. In their passion for the defense of hearth and home (as in so much else), the Vendéan rebels were mirror images of the sans-culottes who came to fight them. Only, the two sides had exactly opposing views of who the real foreigners were, whose extirpation was the precondition for peace and freedom.

The enforcement of the revolutionary legislation on the Church, then, was seen in southern Anjou, almost from the beginning, as an invasion. Large numbers of priests who, in obedience to the papal principles published by Boisgelin, refused to take the constitutional oath, wanted to abandon their curacies. Many did indeed follow their bishops by emigrating to Spain or sometimes farther afield to Ireland and England. Such was the rapid depletion of manpower in the region that some departmental authorities, in Maine-et-Loire for example, in July 1791, actually asked refractory priests to stay in their parishes if they could not be replaced. Pragmatic compromises of this kind, however, only infuriated local Jacobin militants all the more, and they sent petitions to the legislature in Paris denouncing clerical plots and demanding draconian measures against them. The 1792 decrees deporting stubborn refractories further aggravated the conflict. Priest hunts were authorized, with National Guards empowered to smash locks, break in doors and leave no stick of furniture unturned (or intact) in their searches. Houses where a capture was made would be forced to pay the wages and expenses of those performing the search. Needless to say, this had a dramatically alienating effect on an already incensed population. But despite these threats, many priests were hidden in barns, haylofts or sometimes in primitive huts and even caves in the thick of the wood, where they were brought food by loyal parishioners.

While efforts were made to shelter and conceal the refractory priests from the revolutionary authorities, at least as much effort was devoted to making the life of the *intrus* as miserable as possible. In some parishes the new curate would arrive at the church porch to find his refractory rival departing, fully dressed in the sacerdotal vestments, along with all of the church plate and the entire congregation following in procession. Not infrequently a local mayor of the commune led the resistance, when he was supposed to uphold the law. Many pretended to have lost the church keys when the new *curé* arrived. Altar cloths mysteriously disappeared, and the *curé* was unable to obtain clean ones unless he laundered them himself. If the clock broke (and sometimes the peasants ensured that it did) no one could be found to repair it. For his installation, the juring priest would often need a platoon of National Guards, who had to shove a way through crowds yelling *"Ne jurez pas, ne vous damnez pas"* (Don't take the oath, don't damn yourself).

After the Guards had gone, the *intru* was left alone to endure as best he could the constant harassment, not to mention embarrassingly empty churches. At Melay, the juring priest was one Thubert, who was the son of the republican mayor. He was hooted at, jeered and kicked whenever he made an appearance. To add insult to injury, his own sexton, as he complained, not only ostentatiously absented himself from Mass but on occasion had climbed to the belfry to pelt him with cobblestones. All of the resources of traditional village carnival rites, including hanging in effigy, were brought to bear on the hapless *truton.* In one such representation at Saint-Aubin, the curate was depicted with horns as the Devil's helper and also as the cuckold of the Church. Thubert's door was hammered on all night, and in other parishes the clattering cans and shrieking whistles of rough music ensured the priest's insomnia. Churches occupied by the intruders were often ritually defiled by bringing garbage inside or sometimes leaving excrement or even unattended corpses at the door. Alternatively, women might take the lead in ostentatious acts of cleansing the pollution. When, for example, the Parisian Peyre was installed as curate of Le May-sur-Evre, he was surprised to see women following him into the church wiping off traces of his footprints on the stone floor. In other villages, the fonts were aggressively emptied and refilled lest they become contaminated by the hands of the infidel.

Finally there was the strategy of refusal. The Revolution had made marriage a civil act but, as with baptism and burial, there were also religious forms which could supplement the registration. The refractory clergy had made it clear that none of these "civic" ceremonies had any standing in the true faith. Thus couples who submitted to a civic marriage and a ceremony blessed by a juring priest were deemed by the Church to be living in a state of sin. Similarly, the last rites performed by such men were declared invalid as a form of absolution. In these circumstances the refusal of parishioners to participate in these acts was not just a matter of ostracism but the salvation of their souls. The refractory priests often left them with elaborate instructions on how to cope in their absence. Burials were to be carried out in fields beyond the village, according to the proper forms. If the juring priests discovered the ceremony, they were physically barred from participation. Some priests even left instructions on how to continue their traditional Masses as if they were still present. For example, in his last sermon before leaving Saint-Hilaire-de-Mortagne, Mathieu Paunaud promised his flock that "wherever Providence shall lead me I will pray for you." In the event the congregation should be deprived of a "good priest," they should nonetheless assemble at ten o'clock as usual and say their responses in the knowledge that, at the same hour, he would be joining his worship with theirs. Finally, improvised chapels were created in which to say traditional Mass, either in the hiding places of the refractory priests or in remote farm cottages, their windows covered with cloth, to which the priests would be carefully escorted.

Obviously, with this history of tenacious resistance, it would not take much to tip the Vendée into more concerted violence. In January 1793, Biret, the *procureur-syndic* of les Sables-d'Olonne in the maritime district, wrote to the departmental administrators that "as for morals, I believe that by far the greater part of the people . . . is entirely corrupted by fanaticism and the efforts of domestic enemies . . . as for politics the same individuals are equally incapable of reasoning. The Revolution for them is just one long sequence of injustices of which they complain without really knowing why." The execution of the King evidently made things worse. At one gathering at les Sables, Biret reported, "Certain persons dared to call the legislators who had condemned Louis to death 'brigands' and 'scoundrels.' " Through February reports steadily accumulated of more brazen gestures: shouted slogans of "Long live the priests, religion, and the King [now, of course, the boy Louis XVII]; death to the Patriots."

The announcement of the recruiting levies turned all this pent-up anger and resentment into outright revolt. Interestingly, Reynald Sécher has discovered that the Vendée did in fact furnish at least its share of recruits from the small towns. It may well have been that those who were, by office or inclination, already committed to the Republic wished to make sure they were armed to defend themselves or, sensibly, to get themselves well out of the region. In any event, the symbolic force of the recruitment—which was not yet conscription but an appeal for volunteers to make up a levy, supplemented by a lottery in cases of shortfall—was enough in itself to provoke violence. And it was not helped by an order the previous day, on March 6, 1793, closing all churches where there was no juring priest in place.

The tenth to the twelfth of March saw the first stage in the uprising, when spontaneously assembled crowds in villages and *bourgs* attacked the offices and houses of mayors, *juges de paix, procureurs* and dangerously isolated units of the National Guard. The riot at Machecoul was repeated, with less murderous consequences, in Saint-Florent-le-Veil, Sainte-Pazanne, Saint-Hilaire-de-Chaléons and Clisson. The leaders who emerged from this first wave of violence were often, like the gamekeeper and ex-soldier Stofflet, men who had long been identified in their locality with resistance to the revolutionary authorities. Once they had evicted their enemies and taken their weapons, the crowds coalesced with each other, forming processions towards larger towns and snowballing in size as they traveled along the roads.

At this stage, the riots in the Vendée seemed no different from similar antirecruitment riots taking place in many other parts of France from the

Calvados in Normandy to the Côte d'Or in Burgundy and the Puy in the southern Massif Central. Some of the worst upheavals occurred north of the Loire in Brittany. But there the government had been so obsessed by the possibility of counter-revolutionary plots, it had in place sufficient force to take rapid and decisive action against the centers of resistance. The Vendée, in contrast, was dangerously depleted of troops. At Challans, for example, there were just two hundred Patriot Guards who had to face more than a thousand insurgents on the twelfth of March. By the time that reinforcements could be provided, the several riots had already fused into a general insurrection. Moreover, even of the fifty thousand republican soldiers who were eventually concentrated in the Vendée by the third week of March, only a tiny proportion—perhaps fewer than two thousand— were veterans of the "line"—the old royal army. The remainder were unseasoned volunteers, badly fed and equipped and, more critically for the situation they faced, extremely apprehensive about the rebels. None of the armies of France in the spring and summer of 1793 showed such propensity to take to panic and break ranks as the *bleus* of the Vendée. Perhaps they feared the fate of the republicans of Machecoul. As it was, many of them were dispersed in small units of fifty or some hundreds, numerous enough to provide a target for the infuriated rebels but not substantial enough to overawe them.

By the time that the Republic understood the gravity of the situation, the rebels had already taken many of the larger centers, in particular Cholet, Chemillé and Fontenay-le-Comte. On the fourteenth of March, Stofflet joined his forces with those attached to another gamekeeper, Tonnelet, and men following the wagoner-vendor Cathelineau. After failing to persuade the republican troops, commanded by the citizen-marquis de Beauveau, to lay down their arms, the rebels overwhelmed the *bleus* in a great barrage of fire, mortally wounding de Beauveau.

Despite this early success, it seemed important to recruit authority fig- ures from the local nobility, whose adhesion would itself help recruit more troops to the cause. This was not just a matter of status, since those ap- proached all had considerable military experience in the field that could be put to use as the theater of operations expanded. Deputations were sent to châteaux and manors, where they often had to overcome mixed feelings on the part of the local gentry on the prospects of the revolt. Indeed, what was striking about many of the gentry (the twenty-one-year-old Henri de La Rochejaquelein excepted) was not their royalist passion but their modera- tion. Those who had had experience of the emigration at Coblenz had returned disgusted by what they had seen. Others like d'Elbée, for example, had originally been partisans of the Revolution, had been deputed electors for the Third Estate at Beaupréau, had voted for the constitutional bishop

Pelletier and had only become alienated by the brutal legislation on deportation. Bonchamp, the other major noble commander, actually lectured the rebels on the seriousness of their conduct: "Cannot you feel the horror of our position? What are we doing? Making civil war. Against whom are we fighting? Against the nation of which we are a part." Without any question, what motivated the Vendéan gentry was a sense of local patriotism: the compression of the sentiments of the *pays* and the *patrie*. Both the émigrés and the *bleus* were stigmatized in their eyes as invaders. If France was ever to be redeemed, it had to be by local heroes, committed to protecting their own territory against despoilers. This gave a remarkably personal and parochial quality to their subsequent command. Often idolized by the troops, leaders like Charette, Sapinaud de La Verrie and d'Elbée were really romanticized patriarchalists, the eighteenth-century version of baronial warlords. Each drew his men from a specific region: Bonchamp from around Saint-Florent; Charette from around Machecoul and the *pays nantaise* to the north; d'Elbée from the country around Mortagne; La Rochejaquelein from Bressuire and Châtillon. They cultivated a clannish sentiment that made for great loyalty but worked against the cohesion needed if the Vendéan army was ever to be more than an ephemeral confederation of resistance bands.

Throughout the conflict, priests were not as much in evidence on the field of battle as historical tradition has supposed. There were exceptions to this surprising reticence. The force that took Cholet was controlled as much by the Abbé Barbotin as by Stofflet. Others—like the Abbé Bernier, Rousseau of Trémentines, Chamuau of La Jubaudière and Gruget of Saint-Florent—did become important figures in rallying the peasants to the Vendéan cause. And certainly the crusading nature of the struggle was publicly emphasized at every opportunity. After the capture of Chemillé, Barbotin became "Almoner of the Catholic Army" and gave mass absolution prior to battles. The Vendéans often sang hymns and canticles on the march, bore standards with the Virgin Mary at the head of their regiments and wore as their device the devotional emblem of the Sacred Heart surmounted by the cross. Before the end of March a counter-"Marseillaise" had been composed for the troops, which began

> *Allons armées catholiques, le jour de gloire est arrivé*
> *Contre nous de la République,*
> *L'étendard sanglant est levé . . .*
> *Aux armes poitevins, formez vos bataillons*
> *Marchez, marchez, le sang aux bleus,*
> *Rougira nos sillons*

It would be a mistake, though, to imagine the Vendéan army as a kind of primitive religious horde. Some of the early seizures of key centers like Cholet were indeed conducted without sophisticated tactics, large numbers of infantry moving in loose formation between columns of sharpshooters at each side, with a rudimentary cavalry and a cannon or two at the back. But by the end of the first week of hostilities, something like a serious army had come into being, with munitions taken from stores left behind by the fleeing republicans. Some of the larger cannon were given names, the most famous being the *Marie-Jeanne* (named for the two daughters of the cannoneer who trundled it along), an awesome piece whose effect on the enemy was exclusively a matter of the noise and smoke that issued from its occasional detonations. A cavalry of perhaps fifteen hundred to two thousand horsemen, often wearing clogs rather than boots, rode animals of all shapes and sizes.

The greatest asset of the Vendéans, however, was their mastery of home territory. Their tactics were impressively adapted to the particular terrain in which they fought. In the lower Loire, for example, they used armed boat patrols to intercept both munitions and food supplies going to republican garrisons. Windmills on the low hills of the *bocage* were used to relay messages to outlying units by operating the sails according to a code of communications. And throughout the region, noncombatants, often women and children, participated by keeping farms working and supplying food and clothing to their troops.

It was the kind of war with which we are now all too familiar but for which the army of the Republic, especially those troops who had been drawn from the battlefields of Belgium or the siege of Mainz, was completely unprepared. Uniformed troops in disciplined formation were tied down in isolated garrisons, able to control large towns on the perimeter of the war zone but helpless to patrol the interior, where every wood might conceal a murderous ambush, or to distinguish in villages between civilians and combatants. When the French generals who had fought in the Vendée discovered, to their dismay, similar conditions in the Peninsular War in Spain fifteen years later, they referred to it as *"la petite guerre,"* which in Spanish became rendered as *guerrilla.*

It was not, however, this kind of irregular combat which signaled to the Convention in Paris that it had a full-scale domestic war on its hands. The battles before Cholet and Fontenay-le-Comte had in fact been head-on confrontations in open country or fields in which the Vendéans had superiority of numbers and often of firepower. Through the night of the nineteenth and twentieth, a force of more than two thousand troops commanded by General Marcé fought a six-hour pitched battle on the banks of the Grand Lay north of Chantonnay. Hearing the strains of the "Marseillaise," Marcé thought he was being reinforced, when in fact it was a rebel column singing "Allons armées catholiques . . ." The struggle finally became unequal and disintegrated into a rout, with panic-stricken *bleus* fleeing south to Saint-Hermine and Saint-Hermand. The whole country of the southern plain and the Vendéan *marais* fell into the hands of the rebels, including the towns of Luçon, Fontenay and Niort. On the twenty-second, the disaster was repeated at the northern end of the region when at Chalonnes three hundred *bleus* faced almost twenty thousand Vendéans and fled, leaving most of their equipment and eighteen cannon to the rebels.

By early April, virtually the whole of the Vendée, with the exception of the northern maritime area, but including the island of Noirmoutier, was in rebel hands. At the urging of the officer of the royal bodyguard, Sapinaud de La Verrie, a unified command had been established, and elected parish committees set up to organize the collection of arms and victuals for the troops. *Assignats* were being printed with the image of the boy King Louis XVII, in whose name edicts and decrees were published by the Vendéan Grand Council. The rebels even boasted a primitive field-hospital service, complete with pharmacies and nursing sisters.

As with all irregular and spontaneously recruited armies, its most serious problem was maintaining cohesion, especially after the initial goal of ridding the Vendée of republican authority had been accomplished. The commanders recognized that this would be only a short-term victory unless their base was secured by the capture of major urban centers and, ultimately, by the overthrow of the Republic itself. However much their campaigns may have begun as a liberation of the home *pays*, once they were committed to civil war, there was no avoiding that much broader strategic goal. By the same token, though, the farther they moved from their base, the more likely they were to lose the special advantages it had given them. Initially, in mid-April, they suffered serious setbacks. But the forced capitulation of the garrison at Thouars in early May delivered an enormous quantity of provisions and munitions into their hands. Fontenay-le-Comte fell at the end of May and, most spectacularly, Saumur, on the ninth of June. But instead of striking further east, Charette concentrated on a fruitless siege of Nantes on the other side of the Loire.

In late May, though, the position of the rebels still looked formidable. They had decisively defeated the republican armies sent against them and had put into action the rudiments of a state within a state. Rather as though they were potentates addressing the minions of a foreign power, the Grand Council published an "Address to the French," written by the Abbé Bernier. It was, at the same time, a manifesto and an account of the Revolution that was remarkable both for its eloquence and the telling way in which it turned the revolutionary rhetoric of liberty against the Republic. More than any other document it succeeds in expressing the depth and simplicity of the convictions which fired the rebellion.

> Heaven has declared for the holiest and most just of causes. [Ours is] the sacred sign of the cross of Jesus Christ. We know the true wish of France, it is our own, namely to recover and preserve for ever our holy apostolic and Roman Catholic religion. It is to have a King who will serve as father within and protector without. . . .
>
> Patriots, our enemies, you accuse us of overturning our *patrie* by rebellion but it is you, who, subverting all the principles of the religious and political order, were the first to proclaim that insurrection is the most sacred of duties. You have introduced atheism in the place of religion, anarchy in the place of laws, men who are tyrants in place of the King who was our father. You reproach us with religious fanaticism, you whose pretensions to liberty have led to the most extreme penalties.

In the National Convention, amidst mounting rage and dismay, Bertrand Barère shrugged his shoulders at the conduct of what he called *"l'inexplicable Vendée."*

iii "PALTRY MERCHANDISE"
March–June

The second half of March brought a steady drumbeat of calamity to republican France. Within the same week, the Convention heard of the defeat at Neerwinden, a further military collapse near Louvain, Custine's abrupt retreat in the Rhineland and the Vendéan uprising. Report after report described Republican armies dissolving on contact with the enemy (especially in the Vendée); volunteers demoralized and disorderly, deserting or taking to their heels; the tricolor trampled in the mud. When Delacroix returned from the Belgian front, he brought with him a gloom as deep and as dark as the weeks before Valmy. French troops had fallen back on Valenciennes, but if that fortress fell, he warned, there was nothing between the Allied armies and Paris. To many deputies, and not just those of the Mountain, there could be only one explanation for this sorry trail of disasters: conspiracy. The commissioners with General Marcé's defeated army in the Vendée accused him of either "the most cowardly ineptness" or, worse, "the most cowardly treason." His son; his second-in-command, Verteuil; and another Verteuil presumed to be *his* son (but in fact a distant relative) were all arrested for being "in treasonable contact with the enemy." Barère, who saw the unmistakable signs of a vast counter-revolutionary plot, wanted Marcé tried by court-martial at La Rochelle. Lanjuinais, like Rabaut Saint-Etienne a survivor of the Estates-General who had turned republican, insisted that the aristocrats and refractories who were contaminating the *patrie* be mercilessly ferreted out.

Faced with this military landslide, the Convention, with very few exceptions, acknowledged that it had to strengthen the powers of the state. Without an effective executive and a coherent chain of command, centrifugal forces would pull France apart. For the first time since the beginning of the Revolution, the legislature set about creating strong organs of central authority authorized to do the Republic's work without endless reference to the "sovereign body." On March 6 it dispatched eighty of its own members (known, from April on, as "representatives on mission") to the departments to ensure compliance with the central government's will. They were, in effect, a revolutionary version of the old royal *intendants,* traveling embodiments of sovereignty. Much of their work was meant to concern itself with judicial and punitive matters. On March 11 a special Revolutionary Tribunal was established in Paris to try suspects accused of counter-revolutionary activities. On March 20, with the rebellions in the Vendée and Brittany in mind, the Convention adopted Cambacérès' proposal giving military courts jurisdiction over anyone who had been employed in public positions (including clergy and nobles) and who was found with the white royalist cockade or fomenting rebellion. If guilty, they were to be shot within twenty-four hours. A day later, every commune in the country was equipped with committees of surveillance and all citizens were encouraged to denounce anyone they suspected of uncertain loyalties. Predictably, the law rapidly became a charter for countless petty dramas of revenge.

Finally, on April 6, it was decided to replace the Committee of General Defense, set up in January as a body of twenty-five to coordinate the work of the several committees of the Convention. In its place was to be a much tighter committee of just nine members, to be known as the Committee of Public Safety. Though this was, of course, to be the key organ of the Terror, it was not a Jacobin but Isnard who proposed it, and many of the Girondins (though not Vergniaud, who compared it unfavorably with the Venetian Inquisition) accepted its indispensability. Initially, though, both the Committee and the Revolutionary Tribunal were suspected by Robespierre as bureaucratic tools in the hands of a Girondin offensive against the Mountain.

"Let us be terrible so that the people will not have to be," Danton told the Convention, defending the establishment of the Revolutionary Tribunal. With the memory of the September massacres still fresh, the argument was powerful. The Republic was seeking to achieve something that had eluded all previous regimes since Brienne failed to enforce his reforms: the recapture of the state's monopoly of authorized violence. To accomplish this it was necessary to do a number of things. First, as Danton recognized, it was essential that the state take into its own hands the kind of punitive powers needed to assuage the general thirst for symbols of conspiracy. It had to be prepared to use those powers, publicly and demonstratively, if the lynch mobs and the improvised murder gangs were to be denied their prey. Second, the endless factionalism which made it repeatedly possible for the government to be outflanked by a disaffected group appealing to the streets and the *sections,* had to be ended. On his return from the front in March, Danton was bold enough not only to defend Dumouriez from his growing number of detractors but to appeal to the Convention to avoid an internal war between Girondins and the Mountain that would inevitably result in its own loss of power.

This redirection of revolutionary energies was all the more urgent because, in addition to military reverses, the Republic faced in the late winter and early spring of 1793 another disruptive threat in the shape of an acute fiscal and economic crisis. This time it had not been brought by the weather. Instead, the Republic was confronted with a disturbing truth. The Revolution had started with a crisis of fiscal incapacity, but the new regime was no nearer to solving its problems than the old; perhaps, if anything, it was further away because of the seduction of the palliatives it had resorted to. Sale of church properties had started to become subject to the law of diminishing returns, all the more so since the issue of paper money it had made possible had now become as much a curse as a blessing. The real crisis of 1793 was a phenomenon for which a descriptive term had yet to be invented: inflation. The replacement of the monarchy's old direct taxes with a single tax on property, the *impôt foncier,* had resulted in massive losses to the Treasury. In addition, successive revolutionary governments had denied themselves the kind of dedicated pursuit of revenue that had made the Farmers-General so infamous. Nor did "patriotic contributions" ever seem likely to make good the shortfalls and arrears that were constantly being reported in public receipts.

The only way, then, in which it was possible to fund the war had been a dramatic expansion of the issues of *assignats.* Since military contractors and some regiments would only accept payment in metallic currency, the drain on hard reserves became acute, driving up the rate at which further paper was issued to cover the shortfall. That, in turn, had a seriously adverse effect on the domestic economy. For as the nominal value of the paper currency dropped, so suppliers of goods and services (such as farmers) were reluctant to part with their assets for depreciated money. Restricted supply then raised the price of goods further. By early 1793, soap bricks which had cost twelve sous in 1790 now sold for between twenty-three and twenty-eight sous. Not surprisingly, the Convention received a deputation of angry laundresses (a powerful constituency in Paris) on February 23, demanding that prices be officially pegged. Comestibles, candles and firewood were even more serious concerns. Unrefined sugar which had cost twelve sous a pound in 1790 now went for more than three times that figure; the price of coffee had risen from around thirty sous to forty. On February 25, there was a massive invasion of Paris grocery and chandlers' shops by angry crowds, beginning in some of the poorest *sections* like Gravilliers and Lombards but rapidly spreading to almost every part of the capital. In accordance with the traditional practices of these *taxations populaires,* the crowds did not loot the shops but imposed what they deemed to be just prices on the retailers: usually about 40 percent of current market value. But since they had had to pay inflated prices from wholesalers and shippers, it was the shopkeepers who were faced with the loss, as they eloquently reported to the Convention.

The grocery riots were roundly denounced by all parties in the Convention. Marat thought their concentration on what he described as "luxury goods"—coffee and sugar—was evidence of an aristocratic plot. Robespierre berated the rioters for debasing the sacred value of insurrection by directing it at "paltry merchandise." But even while some of its members, like Saint-Just, understood the inflationary causes of the disorders, the Convention seemed impotent to correct them. The Revolution changed much less in France than we often suppose, and one of the matters in which it did no better than the monarchy was the way in which short-term exigencies controlled longer-term fiscal rationality. The subsistence crisis obliged the government to fund all sorts of subsidies, from the price of bread in Paris (costing half a million francs a day by early 1793) to the public relief schemes inherited from the 1792 *camp des fédérés.* To cover these costs, the Caisse d'Escompte spuriously "lent" the government funds that were, in fact, the fruit of further issues of the paper currency, thereby contributing to the problem.

The sudden collapse of the war effort made all these problems even worse. In occupying Belgium and the Rhineland, the revolutionary government had at last stumbled onto the way to fund military policy: extortion. It was not terribly revolutionary and it conflicted somewhat with all the promises of abundant freedom and happiness brought to the slave nations by the People in Arms. On the other hand, it was argued, why should the liberated not pay for their own emancipation, achieved with French blood and arms? Massive "indemnities" were then levied on all conquered territories as the price of liberation, assented to by the "free" revolutionary governments installed after the occupation. By the beginning of 1793, this self-financing expansion—which was to be the rule over the next twenty years—seemed to offer a way out of the perennial constraints of French foreign policy. In fact it was the happy prospect of milking the notoriously superfatted Dutch economy that made Dumouriez's expedition into the northern Netherlands seem such a good idea. Robespierre—who had been suspicious of the adventure—actually priced an impending Dutch revolution at the nice round figure of a hundred million livres.

All these cheerful expectations rebounded disastrously when the expansion of the front went into reverse. Instead of accumulating assets, the Republic was suddenly faced, within the confines of its own frontiers, with a military emergency that could only be funded from domestic resources. The immediate answer, of course, was yet another massive issue of paper. Eight hundred million *assignats* were authorized, in addition to the four hundred million already printed since October. The circulation ceiling was extended upwards to thirty-one hundred million. This, of course, had the predictable effect of accelerating depreciation, so that by the time of the February riots, the *assignat* had lost 50 percent of its face value. Suppliers were even more reluctant to part with goods, and the inflationary spiral threatened to spin out of control.

That prospect presented clear dangers to the stability of the new Republic. Already there was serious disorder in the countryside among the disaffected poor who had not been among the beneficiaries of revolutionary legislation. Grain barges and wagons were being stopped in the Beauce and in Burgundy. Consumers in the cities were seeing dramatic rises in the prices of basic foodstuffs. Against the threat of unrest on a scale not seen since 1789, the Convention at the end of 1792 had debated the possibility of a return to monarchy's policies of short-term economic regulation. The doctrine of internal free trade in grain, some argued, might have to be modified to ensure reliable supply at prices that would not provoke riot. As minister of the interior, however, Roland was adamantly against any interference in the market, whatever the cost. He wanted instead to use the full repressive force of the government against anyone who dared to disrupt or control the markets by violence. In this he was supported not only by a succession of Girondin speakers but by Saint-Just, who on November 29 gave a speech of characteristic penetration on the relationship between the money supply and price rises. "Free trade," he reiterated, was the "mother of abundance," but he also warned that just as *misère* had given birth to the Revolution, *misère* could destroy it.

On this last point Saint-Just and Robespierre were in full accord, but they differed strikingly on what to do about the crisis. The young politician (whose utterances on the economy showed a much more impressive grasp of its mechanics than anything his mentor ever said) was concerned primarily with restraining the money supply. Robespierre, on the other hand, was more interested in committing the Republic to a form of social egalitarianism that would be the economic equivalent of the reign of virtue he wished to usher in, in politics. On December 2 he sketched the basis of a "right of subsistence" which would rapidly assume the status of a doctrine in Jacobin rhetoric. The rights of property were not, in this view, unlimited. In fact, only the surplus over and above the aggregate subsistence needed for the whole of society could be legitimately devoted to commerce. And those who abused this axiom by making money out of direct exploitation of subsistence were, in effect, committing a crime. "Why do the laws not arrest the homicidal hand of the monopolist as much as that of the ordinary assassin?" Robespierre asked rhetorically.

The Jacobins, however, were not yet prepared to make this punitive egalitarianism official doctrine. In this they were overbid for popular support in Paris by a loosely connected group of orators and politicians who became known as the *enragés,* a term that had originally simply connoted revolutionary zeal. Two figures in the group were of particular importance: Jacques Roux and Jean Varlet. Roux was vicar of the parish of Saint-Nicolas-des-Champs, one of the poorest in Paris, crowded with tenement lodging houses and garrets where, in the winter of 1793, poor market porters, water-carriers and unemployed building laborers attempted to survive in frozen hunger. In May 1792, Roux had published a sermon, "The Means to Save France and Liberty," in which a strong dose of social egalitarianism and attacks on the selfish rich were blended with fierce demands to punish traitors. Perhaps it was his zeal in the latter cause that led him, as the Commune's representative during Louis XVI's last days, to the rather un-Christian act of denying the fallen King a dentist to deal with a toothache, and to refuse to pass on his will to the family.

Suspect, even among the most militant figures of the Commune, like Chaumette and Hébert, as an ecclesiastical ranter, Roux delivered a message that was simplicity itself. The Revolution had been exploited by profiteers for their own selfish ends until the people were once again as famished as they had ever been under the old regime. The time had come to declare war on these economic traitors. Monopolists, hoarders and speculators should be punished by death, and if the government refused to institute those penalties, then the people should themselves launch a new round of massacres against the "blood-suckers." On the positive side the government should, as part of its routine activities, fulfill its obligation to provide both work and subsistence at prices the people could afford.

Much the same message was being articulated by Jean Varlet. As historians never tire of pointing out, this self-appointed friend of the poor was himself a well-off young man living largely on an inherited income. But political radicalism has seldom been determined by social origin. Most of the militants of the Paris *sections* in 1793 were not working artisans at all but professionals and, charitably stretching the term, intellectuals: lawyers, artists, printers, playwrights, actors and journalists. But the fact that they themselves were not needy in no way precludes (though it of course does not guarantee) the sincerity of their convictions. These were, especially for Varlet, wrathful. What they wanted was, essentially, blood and bread, the one supposed to guarantee the other, just as liberty in 1789 had been thought to improve the chances of not starving.

Denied both the Jacobins, where he was held in distaste, and the Convention as forums for his calls for insurrection against the rich, Varlet brought a portable tribune to the Terrasse des Feuillants, barely a stone's throw from the Convention. As prices in the shops rose, his audiences grew bigger, since he specialized in invidious contrasts between the "rich egoists," whose speculative profits allowed them to wallow in luxury, and the *bon sans-culotte* living by the sweat of his brow. In Jacques Roux's social gospel the sans-culotte took on an almost apostolic saintliness in which humility and compassion were allied to public-spiritedness and fortitude. While the *capitaliste* and the *gros négociant* were, by definition, always on the verge of treason if not actually guilty of it, the modest artisan was the epitome of selfless patriotism. In at least one anonymous print sanctifying the sans-culotte (indeed drawing on the iconic tradition of St. Jerome), the worker shares his frugal meal with his pets while his pike remains ready for action on the wall behind him. Other prints glorified the devotion of the sans-culotte to his family, showing the household in the harmony of the table or reading together some item of political edification, preferably by Rousseau.

Historians have often been quick to write off the *enragés* as lightweight ranters whose ideas only took on substance when they were finally adopted by the Jacobins in the summer of 1793. But though Roux and Varlet, and

174. *Le bon sans-culotte*

the rest of the *enragés,* can hardly qualify as deep political thinkers, much less as successful revolutionary tacticians, their *prejudices* did correspond closely to many of the reasons the common people had embraced the Revolution in the first place. They wanted paternalism rather than economic liberalism, the regulation of prices rather than a free market, and above all they wanted the public punishment of exploiters. On the eleventh of February a deputation of popular societies demanded a sentence of six years in irons for the first offense of anyone trying to sell a 240-pound sack of wheat for more than twenty-five francs and the death penalty for a second offense. That kind of draconian punishment for exploitation appealed enormously to the sans-culottes.

Nor were they prepared to stop at generalized accusations. On the contrary, they sponsored in the *section* clubs and assemblies a movement to incriminate the Girondins as specifically responsible for all the evils afflicting the Republic. Girondins were behind the conspiracies that had led to military defeat; were the patrons of Dumouriez, who was busily selling out the *patrie*; had obdurately refused to contemplate any measures of intervention like a price *maximum* that might alleviate the suffering of the poor. They had attempted to protect the traitor Capet to cover the tracks of their own rotten plots with him prior to August 10. Foiled in their hypocritical "appeal to the people" on the sentence, they were still conspiring to hand the Republic over to a confederacy of aristo generals. The first condition, then, for a true reign of the just and the virtuous was the excision of the Girondists from the body politic. And Varlet had a list, taken up by some of the more militant Paris *sections* like Gravilliers (in Roux's parish) and Mauconseil, of twenty-two members of the Convention whose arrest he declared to be a matter of the highest public emergency.

By themselves the *enragés* would have been impotent to do more than rail at their enemies. But by March 1793 they had succeeded in influencing the more militant *sectionnaires* who, independently, had been establishing a competing center of power with the Commune. The Revolution in Paris had shown a seemingly unstoppable capacity to generate these alternative centers of insurrectionary organization as soon as the previous one had been co-opted into the institutions of local government. So just as the Revolutionary Commune had been organized against the official authorities in the Hôtel de Ville in 1792, and had forcibly replaced it, so the popular societies and *section* leaders began meeting at the Archevêché—the former palace of the Archbishop of Paris, next to Notre Dame. From informal meetings these sessions turned into a regularized liaison of delegates from the most militant areas of Paris: Quinze-Vingts, Popincourt, Droits de l'Homme. As long as the economic crisis remained acute and the war went badly, the potential always remained for mobilizing enough armed men to dictate terms to the defenseless legislature.

It was first necessary, however, to persuade the shock troops that they needed another *journée,* that their vital interests were being threatened by conspirators. The reluctance of the Mountain to support any threat to the "national representation" had also to be overcome. Varlet and the committee at the Evêché were premature in believing both conditions to be realized by mid-March. On the ninth and tenth they attempted to stage an armed movement which fizzled out only after smashing the presses of the two most important Girondin newspapers: Brissot's *Patriote Français* and Carra's *Annales Patriotiques* (an alarming accomplishment in itself). It failed in two crucial goals: to impose a purge of the twenty-two *appelants* (those who had asked for the sentence on the King to be referred to a popular vote) and the liberation of prisoners who had been arrested for the February grocery riots. But it succeeded in at least one respect: polarizing the Convention so bitterly between the Girondins and the Mountain that Danton's appeals for unity in the face of common danger to the *patrie* were bound to go unheeded.

iv SATURN AND HIS CHILDREN

On the thirteenth of March, Pierre Vergniaud came to the tribune and delivered a speech which even by his standards was remarkable for its rhetorical power and political courage. After the routine denunciations of aristocratic machinations by which anarchy was doing the work of the counter-revolution, he deplored the fact that those convicted of violence in the February riots had been amnestied. When the laws were set aside out of fear of intimidation, "it is a great accomplishment for the enemies of the Republic thus to have perverted reason and set at naught all ideas of morality." He then proceeded to a famous and terrible prophecy. "So, citizens, it must be feared that the Revolution, like Saturn, successively devouring its children, will engender, finally, only despotism with the calamities that accompany it."

The Convention, he said, was brutally divided into two parties with conflicting visions for France. "One section of its members regarded the Revolution as finished the instant that France was constituted as a Republic. Henceforth it thought that the revolutionary movement should be stopped so as to give the people tranquillity and to make laws promptly that would make the Revolution endure. Other members, on the contrary, alarmed by the dangers with which the coalition of tyrants threaten us, believed that it was important for the energy of our defense to continue to sustain all the effervescence of the Revolution."

Vergniaud spoke for a while as if he could see the merits of both points of view, but he was merely building to a tremendous denunciation of *sectionnaire* violence and in particular of the vandalism of March 10. Continuing the Girondin theme of the dangers posed to the "national representation" by the unconstrained lawlessness of the Paris crowds, he characterized the devotees of the *sections* as "idlers, men without work, unknown, often indeed strangers to the *section* or even to the city itself . . . ignoramuses, great putters of motions" in love with the sound of their own voice, men easily corrupted for bad causes. As for the central revolutionary committee they had organized, "what revolution does it want to make now that despotism is no longer? . . . It wants to overturn the national representation itself." Vergniaud went so far as to name some individuals specifically: the Pole Lazowski, whose name he garbled to sound even more foreign, and Desfieux, whom he accused of being well known in his native city of Bordeaux for "all manner of crookery and bankruptcy."

In the course of his speech, interrupted many times by angry shouts of "calumny" from the Mountain, it became clear that what had really angered Vergniaud was the destruction of the Girondin news presses and the continuing attempt to gag opinion that dissented from the Jacobins or the popular societies. He compared the mob smashing printing presses to the Muslim fanatics who burned Philo's library at Alexandria, justifying their deed by commenting that the books were either the Koran or about some other matter. In the first instance they were redundant; in the second instance they were dangerous. The kind of liberty that was being imposed on the Republic was the tyranny of license, the freedom of brute force. As for the cries of equality, they reminded him, Vergniaud said, of the "tyrant of antiquity [Procrustes] on whose iron bed victims were mutilated if they were too long for its measurements." To a storm of boos and whistles he added that "this tyrant also loved equality and *voilà*, that is the equality of the scoundrels that would tear you apart with their fury."

"Citizens," he ended, "let us profit from the lessons of experience. We can overturn empires by victories but we can only make revolutions for other peoples by the spectacle of our own happiness. We want to upset thrones. Let us prove that we know how to be happy with a Republic."

I have quoted Vergniaud at length because his speech represents a rare attempt to stand back from the fray and survey the revolutionary landscape. Its purpose was, of course, partisan. Aware that he and his friends were being harried by the *section* militants, Vergniaud was trying to regain the polemical initiative. But the fact that he was nailing the colors of the Girondins to the mast so defiantly does not reduce the force of what was being said. Aside from any other considerations, he was attempting to defend the legislature against repeated attacks on its integrity and sovereignty.

It was also, transparently, an attempt to appeal to the Republic over the heads of the Parisians. Aware of the upheavals in provincial centers like Marseille and his own city of Bordeaux that were delivering power to the adversaries of the Jacobins, Vergniaud and the Gironde were playing to this budding federalism. They had already suggested that the Convention be protected by an armed guard drawn from the provinces and in May would resurrect Mirabeau's plan to move the assembly out of the capital to the cathedral city of Bourges should its safety not be guaranteed.

To the Mountain, all this sounded remarkably like a declaration of war on their own power base. Having held back for a long time from associating with the revolutionary committee at the Evêché, Robespierre and the leading Jacobins were pushed closer toward cooperation by the beginning of the Girondin offensive. Apart from anything else, their concern not to let the *enragés* or even the militants of the Commune like Hébert, Chaumette and Hanriot control the timing and magnitude of insurrection dictated a more activist policy. Nor is it impossible that the Jacobin leaders actually *believed* in the conspiracy theory that tied together the Girondins with military defeat, financial speculation and treasonable dalliance with the enemy. They were quite sure that, after Neerwinden, France had come close to a military coup mounted by Dumouriez and supported by the Gironde.

The first half of April, then, saw a series of statements, both at the Convention and at the Jacobins, in which the Mountain embraced social egalitarianism as a proper goal for the patriotic revolution. Danton (who had been rebuffed in private overtures to the Girondins) came out endorsing the principle of loans forced from the rich to subsidize the price of bread. Other items of the *enragé* program which now received favorable attention were a legally enforceable rate of exchange for the *assignat* and public works programs also to be funded from levies on the rich. On April 10 Robespierre signaled his conversion to the *enragé* axiom that the people were entitled to exercise direct democracy by "recalling faithless mandatories" whensoever the General Will beckoned.

By this time it was evident that a trial of strength was at hand in the Convention. The Girondins decided to test their power by attacking their most immoderate and relentless antagonist, Jean-Paul Marat, who had, moreover, just succeeded to the presidency of the Jacobins. He took every opportunity to abuse them from his eyrie seat high up on the Mountain, descending to trade insults and sometimes even physical blows at the bar of the tribune. "Croaking toad," shouted Guadet in one heated exchange; "Vile bird," yelled back Marat. Another deputy had demanded that the tribune be disinfected after every speech by the Friend of the People. Marat returned the compliment by characterizing his enemies as "Isnard the charlatan, Buzot the hypocrite, Lasource the maniac and Vergniaud the stool-pigeon."

Taking advantage of the absence of deputies *en mission* in the departments, the Girondins collected evidence from Marat's writings to show that he had violated the integrity of the Convention by calling for violent attacks on its membership. Given the general tenor of his journalism, this was not difficult to do. A nineteen-page indictment was drawn up for the Revolutionary Tribunal quoting passages from his *Journal de la République,* in

175. Boilly, *The Triumph of Marat*

which he enthused over a revolutionary dictatorship and regretted that a few hundred heads had been spared so as to preserve hundreds of thousands of innocents. He had repeatedly denounced those associated with Roland—who would include Clavière, Brissot, most of the Girondin leaders—as "statesmen" (a deeply insulting term in Marat's vocabulary), "criminal accomplices of royalty," "enemies to all liberty and equality," "charlatans," "atrocious men who every day seek to bury us further in anarchy and who try to kindle the flames of civil war." Using the individual *appel nominal*, which Marat himself had insisted on in the trial of the King, the Convention voted the indictment by 221 against 93, but with 128 on mission and 238 absentees.

What then followed turned into a dangerous fiasco for the Girondins. After eluding the police for three days, Marat finally turned himself in and was given a large room in the Conciergerie, where he received deputations of officials of the Commune and other citizens all eager to pledge their loyalty to the persecuted Friend of the People. On entering the courtroom on the twenty-fourth he was greeted with a storm of cheering from assembled spectators, which periodically burst out again, so that Marat had to ask his own supporters for quiet. He defended himself with great agility and conviction, claiming, not altogether disingenuously, that many of the apparently incriminating passages had been taken out of context; that he had never preached "murder and pillage" but had argued for energetic measures to avoid precisely those evils; that he had not called for the dissolution of the Convention but had said that the assembly would stand or fall by its own deeds and utterances. The judges, though approved by the Girondins in March, were plainly sympathetic to the accused, and the public prosecutor, a relative of Camille Desmoulins named Fouquier-Tinville, was less than zealous in his interrogation. They also concurred with Marat's argument that his denunciations had been righteous and patriotic and for that matter generalized in their targets.

When the acquittal came, it was transformed into a spectacular personal triumph. Laurel wreaths were thrown on Marat's head; his "large yellow face," as Michelet described it, grinned with pleasure as he was borne shoulder-high to the Convention. The roaring crowds paraded up and down the aisles of the assembly chanting and singing. On the twenty-sixth of April the Jacobins gave a special *fête* in his honor where so large a crowd gathered to celebrate their hero that one of the rows of benches collapsed under their pressing weight.

To say that the trial of Marat was a collective disaster for the Girondins would be to understate the case. They had selectively set aside the immunity of a deputy of the Convention, convinced that it could be shown he had himself abused its privilege. Indeed, from the many times Marat had fulminated that traitors existed "in the bosom of the Convention itself," they were confident the case could be proved. Now that it had failed, the withdrawal of immunity would be turned against them. Petitions and deputations from the more militant *sections* like Cité, Droits de l'Homme, where Varlet was president, and Bon-Conseil, demanding the exclusion of the "Twenty-two" (the number had virtually become a sans-culotte symbol of infamy) that had begun before the trial now began to knock more steadily on the Convention's door.

At the beginning of May the Girondins backed themselves further into a corner by arguing vigorously against the imposition of a *maximum* on grain prices. Charles Barbaroux, in particular, insisted that, however devised, the ceiling would have the effect of aggravating rather than easing supply. If it was set too high, no farmer would sell his goods below the stipulated ceiling; if it was set too low, he would not sell at all and consumers in all likelihood would simply rush to buy as much as they could, creating instant scarcity. How was the price mechanism to be set for different regions? If it was uniform throughout France, no producers would have any interest in shipping goods at their own expense; if it was variable, it would invite smuggling on a scale that would make the evasion of the old *gabelle* look like child's play. For that matter, how could such a system be enforced without recourse to the regiments of the Farmers-General? "Do you want to establish domiciliary visits in the town and country to uncover a *setier* of wheat as once was done with tobacco and salt? Do you want to arm the French against each other and have this group be the food victors over that group?"

Barbaroux's objections were an accurate prediction of exactly the problems the *maximum* would encounter. But its introduction had become a rallying cry among the sans-culottes. On May 1 a deputation arrived at the Convention from the faubourg Saint-Antoine demanding its imposition, as well as the immediate creation of a fund to assist the poor funded by a levy of half of all incomes over two thousand livres, and the conscription of anyone deemed "rich" into the army. The deputation backed its demands with threats of an immediate insurrection should they not be acceded to. On the very next day, the Convention voted in principle to regulate the grain trade and on the fourth enacted decrees which went straight back to old-regime paternalism. Ceilings were to be set by departmental authorities based on the mean average of prices fetched for the first four months of the year to date. Provincial printers started once again cranking out their old forms for requisitions, confiscations, market and milling licenses, which had not seen the light of day since the early 1780s. It was a classic instance of the French Revolution's yearning for security over freedom; for the values of paternalism over those of individualism.

In mid-May, the battle for survival between the Mountain and the Gironde was joined in deadly earnest. Moreover, since the disasters at the front had continued to accumulate, many of the uncommitted deputies of the Plain had begun to shift towards the Jacobins, much as they had done over the issue of the King's trial and sentence. Pressure from armed sans-culotte demonstrations, as well as their own sense that the Girondins were the aggressive party in sustaining the feud, led many of them to this conclusion. But until very late in May the balance of strength within the Convention seesawed this way and that. Isnard was elected president on the sixteenth, and two days later Guadet alleged that a plot to dissolve the Convention was under way. A new assembly should be convened at Bourges, the Commune dismantled, the leaders of the plot in the *sections* exposed and arrested. To deflect this kind of drastic action, a Committee of Twelve was instituted to investigate the threat to the national legislature posed by the popular societies and *section* committees. This rapidly turned into an organ of prosecution against leading *enragés* like Varlet and Claude-Emmanuel Dobsen. But by extending its writ against René Hébert (whose denunciations of the Girondins in the *Père Duchesne* made Marat's look quite temperate by comparison), the Girondins made allies, instead of rivals, of the Commune and the Evêché committee. To Hébert's horror, he was even forced to share a cell with the despicable gadfly Varlet. When the Commune protested to the Convention, Isnard thundered back in tones that made him sound like the Duke of Brunswick: "I tell you, in the name of the whole of France, that if these endless insurrections should cause harm to the parliament of the nation, Paris will be annihilated and men will search the banks of the Seine for signs of the city."

The liberation of this latest batch of "martyrs" then became a rallying cry in the general assemblies of the *sections*. As Richard Cobb memorably noted, historians of the sans-culottes were once much given to describing them as though they moved about in massive blocks and battalions, deployed here and there like marionette regiments of the workers. What we now know of the numbers of their activists suggests a much more modest participation. In all likelihood no more than 10 percent of the adult male population ever attended the "general assemblies" of the *sections*, and while there might have been between a hundred or two hundred at moments of crisis, attendance fell down to fifty or so immediately once the crisis was over. The whole sans-culotte "movement" at its height in Paris was made up of no more than two to three thousand committed revolutionary zealots. The same people came to the popular societies, drafted petitions, showed up with pikes at the doors of the Convention, "fraternized" with each other by showing up in force when fellow militants were threatened in their *section* by a hostile or "moderate" majority. Within Paris itself, moreover, they by no means dominated all forty-eight *sections*. The popular movement commanded dependable support only in twenty to thirty *sections* in a belt extending from Poissonnière and the faubourg Saint-Denis in the north, eastwards down through the ultramilitant Temple, Popincourt, Montreuil and Quinze-Vingts and down through the center of the city to the *sections* of Saint-Marcel in the south—Gobelins and Observatoire.

Its leaders, even outside the immediate circle of the *enragés*, were seldom artisans, much less wage earners. Claude-Emmanuel Dobsen, who would play a key role in the insurrection against the Girondins, was a lawyer, first judge of one of the Paris courts, ardent Mason, and officer in the National Guard since 1790. J-B Loys was a Marseillais lawyer and merchant who had denounced his own two brothers as royalists and who had been honorably wounded in the attack on the Tuileries. Two of those prominent among the militants were even of noble origins: Rousselin, who, like Varlet, had gone to Talleyrand's old school for young aristocrats, the Collège d'Harcourt, and Louis-Henri "Scipio" Duroure, who was a black-sheep Patriot turning to revolutionary politics after fathering a child by the family's English maid and continuing to live off an income of more than twenty thousand livres a year.

It would be a mistake, though, to imagine these men as playboy sans-culottes. They all lived in the neighborhoods they represented, often in lodgings indistinguishable from the artisans'. As a consequence, many of them were a great deal closer to the "people" than Robespierre, who so freely apostrophized them from the parlor of the Duplays. Though they were undoubtedly a minority in the relentlessness of their revolutionary convictions, the militants were capable, on days of crisis, of mobilizing armed crowds of tens of thousands. Success in creating an insurrection, however, required the assent, if not the participation, of figures higher in the revolutionary hierarchy. Summonses from leading figures in the Commune like Hébert, speeches from Danton or Robespierre and articles in Marat's paper were needed to recruit crowds from beyond the inner core of zealots.

What was also needed to trigger a decisive *journée* was a perceived sense of peril. After Isnard's threat to raise the departments against Paris, there was a rowdy sans-culotte invasion of the Convention on the twenty-seventh that succeeded in getting the deputies to abolish the inquisitory Committee of Twelve. On the following day, however, the decision was overturned when the Girondins demanded a new vote, claiming that spectators, mingling with the members, had voted illegally in the proceedings. Hébert and Varlet, however, had their liberation confirmed. Most important of all, Robespierre, who as late as the end of March had insisted on the inviolability of the Convention, now seemed to have given a green light for the uprising. At the Jacobins on the twenty-sixth he invited "the people to place themselves in insurrection against the corrupt deputies" and several more times that week spoke of the necessity for a "moral insurrection."

Just what distinguished a moral insurrection from any other kind was obscure, though evidently Robespierre wanted to avoid the kind of indiscriminate bloodshed of the previous autumn. Once initiated by Dobsen, Varlet and the central revolutionary committee at the Evêché, the event took on its own momentum. Under the direction of François Hanriot, a former customs clerk who had just been appointed commander of the National Guard in place of Santerre, then serving in the Vendée, armed sans-culotte guards accompanied the leaders of the Evêché committee to the Commune. Drummers and guardsmen entered the hall of the General Council to inform it that its mandate had been revoked by the "sovereign people." Once the General Council had accepted the essential points of the revolutionary program—a tax on the rich; the arrest of the Girondins and ex-ministers like Roland, Clavière and Lebrun; the creation of a sans-culotte army to enforce revolutionary laws, including the *maximum,* on the departments; and a payment of forty sous per diem to working citizens under arms—the Commune was reinstated.

These demands were then put to the Convention with the justification that the committee at the Evêché had discovered a conspiracy against liberty and equality that required a new uprising if the Revolution was to be saved. Though this was more or less exactly what Robespierre had himself signaled at the Jacobins, the Convention, and especially the deputies of the Plain, did not care to be dictated to in this manner. The leaders of the Gironde marked for expulsion and arrest had armed themselves in the early hours of the thirty-first on hearing the tocsin but could not bring themselves to accept Louvet's advice to leave Paris and raise the standard of anti-Jacobin revolt in the provinces. Not only did they not want to be responsible for all-out civil war, but it may well have been that with the experience of the failed uprising of March 10 behind them, they believed they could still prevail in the Convention itself. It was there, at any rate, that they chose to make their stand, attacking Hanriot for intimidation and asking for armed protection for the deputies. During the commotion, with sans-culotte soldiers standing about the aisles, waving pikes and rifles, cheering or scowling ominously, Vergniaud became curiously subdued. During Robespierre's long prosecutorial harangue he finally interrupted:

"Conclude then." "I will conclude," returned Robespierre, "and against you." In the end the demands were referred to the Committee of Public Safety.

Matters were obviously not going to rest there. Two days later, on June 2, a Sunday, when people of the *faubourgs* and the villages *hors des murs* crowded into the city, an immense throng surrounded the Convention. Most estimates place the numbers at eighty thousand, the majority of whom were carrying some sort of weapon. They had gathered to hear the report of the Committee of Public Safety and the response of the deputies, and made it plain that there would be a serious price to pay should their demands go unsatisfied. News of a rebellion in Lyon against the Jacobin municipality on the twenty-ninth had arrived in Paris, giving credence to the revolutionary committee's claim that they were confronting a counter-revolutionary conspiracy.

From the outset it was obvious that the Convention was willing, if not exactly eager, to do their bidding in order to avoid either a general massacre or the relinquishment of all effective power to the revolutionary committee. On behalf of the Committee of Public Safety, Delacroix conceded the formation of a revolutionary army paid forty sous a day, but Barère proposed that the offending Girondins be suspended rather than arrested and then only for a specified term.

This was unlikely to satisfy the sans-culottes, who were becoming angrier as the proceedings went on. Deputies were jostled and pushed about; Boissy d'Anglas' elegant scarf was torn from his neck; Grégoire was accompanied by four armed guards as he made his way to the privy. When Hanriot, commanding the guards outside the hall, was given a message from the President, Hérault de Séchelles, to end the intimidation, he replied, "Tell your fucking President that he and his Assembly can go fuck themselves, and if within one hour the Twenty-two are not delivered, we will blow them all up." Cannon were duly moved towards the doors of the Manège to suggest that he was not joking.

Desperate for some way to assert their authority or at least give the semblance of political free will, Barère suggested that the deputies as a body leave the debating hall and walk outside to mingle with the armed men. That would, he thought, defuse the dangerous polarization between soldiers and politicians. A hundred or so then trooped off behind Hérault de Séchelles like anxious schoolboys. Walking into the bright sunlight they found Hanriot on his horse, positioned before rank after rank of daunting, moustached guards obviously bristling with anger and waving their weapons. Hérault asked Hanriot to respect the obligation to free the entrance and exits of the Manège. The Commandant replied by assuring Hérault that the President himself was an approved patriot but asked for a promise "on your head" that the twenty-two villains would be delivered up within twenty-four hours. It was not an undertaking (especially with the price attached) that Hérault was prepared to give, so cannon were primed and pointed directly at the chamber. The pathetic column of deputies, under the glare of the soldiers, walked round the perimeter garden path outside the hall looking for some way out, but at each gate the exit was barred by yet more guardsmen. Finally they returned inside to find yet more *sectionnaires* sitting on the benches with the deputies of the Mountain.

A critical moment had come. A damp silence of guilt, fear and embarrassment settled on the Convention. It was broken by the cripple Georges Couthon, speaking from his wheelchair, who suggested that since, having mingled with the guards, the deputies knew that they were now "free" and that all the good people wanted was the removal of malefactors, they could surely proceed with their indictment. He then read the document of accusation against Clavière and Lebrun as well as twenty-nine deputies, ten of whom had sat on the Committee of Twelve. When the vote was finished, Vergniaud rose in sarcastic defiance to offer the Convention a glass of blood to gratify its thirst.

All this had happened while Hérault de Séchelles was in the President's chair. It is a measure of how far the Revolution had come to remember that this was the same young President of the Parlement of Paris who, in the 1780s, had been lionized as the paragon of legal eloquence. Like his dead friend Lepeletier, he had become a Jacobin able to turn out the standard denunciation of the malevolence of his own aristocratic class whenever required. None of this was in bad faith. There is every sign that Hérault had succeeded in replacing his aristocratic sense of elite status with that of the citizen's tribune. But what he abandoned on June 2, 1793, was the last scrap of pretense that the Revolution was founded on legality or indeed on representation—the issues on which, in 1789, he had asserted France must stand or fall.

Judgment of that day has perhaps been clouded by the partisan passions which in the centenary years of the Revolution divided historians between latter-day Girondins and Jacobins. The former were even unhistorically conscripted to stand as collective symbols for nineteenth- and twentieth-century concerns: liberals or social democrats. Romantic historians like Lamartine saw the Gironde as his political ancestors; he kindled his prose on the funeral pyre of their political extinction. Marxist historians of a later generation found that sentimentality typical of the bourgeois mawkishness of weak stomachs and flabby patriotism. The most recent, and excellent, account of the uprising even echoes the Marxist Albert Soboul's pastiche of Robespierriste denunciation, which says that the Girondins richly deserved to perish because "they had denounced the king but had recoiled before his condemnation; had sought the support of the people against the monarchy but refused to govern with it."

One does not have to subscribe to the "neo-liberal myth of the Gironde" to see through this appalling casuistry. Preference for a republic did not of itself necessarily entail enthusiasm for the King's execution; for that, not the conviction, is what was at issue. Still less did the creation of a new national representation require its deputies to accept what Morris Slavin calls, euphemistically, "participatory democracy" whenever it chose to exercise its rights in the form of heavy artillery. Even Robespierre, while undoubtedly happy with the results of the uprising, both in the removal of his enemies and in the avoidance of massacre and political chaos, was hostile to the chronic destabilization of government that would have resulted from the populace exercising its Rousseauean rights to "recall its mandatories" whenever the *sections* so chose.

It is also often said that such were the dire straits in which France found itself that some sort of purge was needed if the Revolution was to be preserved. The Republic could not have survived both reverses on the field of battle and endless contention within the Convention. That indeed had been Danton's point all along, even though he announced that he was "outraged" at the violation of the assembly on June 2. But what kind of revolution was it that merited preservation? One in which law had prostrated itself before the crudest form of bullying; one in which elected representatives of the nation could be humiliated by the armed minority of a portion of the people of Paris?

There was, however, a grim truth to this miserable episode of threat and surrender. The French Revolution had, from 1788 onward, been made possible by force of arms, by violence and riot. At each stage of its progress those who had profited from its force sought to disarm those who had put them in power. And at each successive stage they became, in turn, prisoners rather than beneficiaries. This would continue so long as the people of Paris were allowed to pursue their chaotic resort to arms. And it is probably not too much to say that from June 2 onward, the Jacobins were already planning to end this dangerous state of affairs. Unlike all their predecessors they would not hesitate to return to the revolutionary state the violence that had been liberated in 1789. Revolutionary democracy would be guillotined in the name of revolutionary government.

CHAPTER SEVENTEEN
"Terror Is the Order of the Day"
June 1793–Frimaire An II (December 1793)

i BLOOD OF THE MARTYR

OLLOWING their expulsion from the Convention, the Girondin leaders were placed under house arrest in Paris. Many chose to stay where they were, deliberately defying their ostracism from the body politic. Others, however, attempted flight. Two of their number, Jérôme Pétion and the Breton Kervélegan, succeeded in escaping their guards, the latter by throwing himself from the second-story window of his house. A larger group, already assuming the worst after the insurrection of May 31, had departed early from Paris, intending to make good their threat to raise the provinces against the capital.

In the first week of June 1793, it seemed as though they might succeed. For while a majority of the Parisian *sections* were militantly Montagnard, the reverse was true in some of the most important provincial cities. In Bordeaux, Lucy de La Tour du Pin saw a thousand young men drilling on the slopes of the Château Trompette. Encouraged by such deputies as Boyer-Fonfrède and Roger Ducos and paid by the Girondin municipality, they were supposed to form the nucleus of a "federalist" army mobilized to resist the dictatorship of Paris. Lucy worried that the noise they made with cannon and in the theaters in the evening was not a reassuring sign of their fortitude under fire. In Marseille too, the *sections* had staged a revolt in May against the militant Jacobin municipality. A new regime was installed, dominated by supporters of the leading Marseillais Girondins, Barbaroux and Rebecquy, many of whom came from the mercantile and commercial elite of the port city, as indeed was the case at Bordeaux. The Jacobin clubs were closed, their central committee dissolved and leading members imprisoned.

While the immediate causes of these urban revolts sprang from the intensity of local politics, the motivation of the insurgents was virtually the same in Bordeaux, Marseille, Toulon, Montbrison, and in Lyon, where much the most serious uprising occurred on May 29. In all these cases, men who considered themselves the "natural" political and cultural leaders of the city—lawyers, merchants, officials; the luminaries of the academies; the brothers of the Masonic lodge; the officers of the National Guard—had been ejected from the city government following the fall of the monarchy, often by blatantly manipulated or intimidated elections. Resisted by the departmental authorities but supported by representatives of the Convention "on mission," the local Jacobin regimes had then instituted little Terrors in the guise of house searches, forced loans on the rich, closure of opposing journals and societies, and selective arrests.

In Lyon, this militant offensive was directed by Joseph Chalier, whose histrionics were unsurpassed by any politician in the French Revolution. When he had brought one of the stones of the Bastille to the city, he organized a ceremony in which each of the devotees knelt to kiss the sacred stone. In a more sinister vein, Chalier threatened with the guillotine silk merchants who pleaded the depression as a reason for refusing their employees work. In early February he had convened a general assembly of the clubs, which began with a forced oath, on pain of death, to abide by the decisions the meeting was about to take. He then announced that there would be a revolutionary tribunal established in Lyon and that "nine hundred victims are needed for the *patrie en danger.* They would be executed on the Pont Morand and the bodies thrown into the Rhone."

Chalier's antics managed to alienate even those who had thought of themselves as orthodox Jacobins. Believing themselves to be on a potential list of proscribed "moderates," they made common cause with the broader opposition in the *sections,* including, crucially, National Guards whom the representatives on mission, Albitte and Dubois-Crancé, had attempted to disarm. On May 29 the moderate *sectionnaires* and Guards stormed the town hall, taking Chalier and the municipality prisoner. What was striking about the federalist uprising at Lyon, as elsewhere, was that while the commercial and professional elite of the town led it from their command posts in the *sections,* they could not have succeeded without the armed support of many humbler citizens, often the very artisans whom the Jacobins assumed were on their side. While journeymen silk weavers may have stood aside, many masters of small shops participated in the rebellion and went on to serve in the federalist army. In Marseille and Toulon dock workers and arsenal workers supported the revolt. It was not, then, the simple class war of Jacobin historiography. Paradoxically, the same rhetoric which in Paris blamed moderate governments for continuing economic crisis—unemployment, the depreciation of the *assignat,* food shortages and price rises—could in the provincial cities be turned against the Jacobin municipalities. In Toulon, for example, a man was arrested in July for having said that "we need a king because under the monarchy bread was two sous [a pound]." The arsenal workers in the same city petitioned the National Convention in the same tone, demanding "peace in our towns and bread for our families. A declining paper money and your terrible political squabbles suggest we will not obtain either."

The phenomenon of popular support for well-to-do moderates is only bewildering if one assumes that artisans and shopkeepers were really persuaded that the doctors, schoolteachers and hack writers who professed to be sans-culottes were somehow closer to their interests than the merchants and lawyers of the established elite. There is no reason to take at face value the Jacobin rhetoric that made this claim. But even had it been true, such imposed solidarity obviously would have been overriden by intense local loyalties and equally intense dislike of Parisian imperialism. Nothing was more damning to men like Chalier than to be stigmatized as "*étrangers,*" outsiders, especially when their power was propped up by representatives from the Convention. In this sense, the great centrifugal forces liberated by the revolution of 1789–91 could only be thrown into reverse by the application of military force.

The revolt in Lyon took place on the same day as the purge of the Girondins in Paris. In turn, news of that event fed the momentum of resistance to the Mountain and not just in southern France. Rennes, in Brittany, was an important center of disaffection, and it looked as though some of the major towns in Normandy would join the movement. On June 10, the most influential group of Girondin fugitives showed up in one of those towns, the cathedral city of Caen in the Department of the Calvados. They doubtless chose that place to make their stand for its relative proximity to Paris and perhaps because one of their company, Buzot, was himself a Norman. Mme Roland's lover, he arrived in the city with a bag full of her letters, locks of her hair, miniatures of her face—and his long-suffering wife. With him were other important figures such as Charles Barbaroux, Guadet, the journalists Gorsas and Louvet, the physician Salle, Lanjuinais and the two escapees Pétion and Kervélegan. Later in the week they were joined by a third group of deputies, and together they set up a political base in the Hôtel de l'Intendance in the center of Caen.

Their immediate aim was to raise a northern federalist force, commanded by General de Wimpffen, who had been one of the city's deputies in the Constituent. A march on Paris was to be coordinated with similar mobilizations in the other federalist centers that would withstand and ultimately reverse the Jacobin ascendancy. Though the federalists were explicitly nonroyalist, the inability of the republican armies to suppress the Vendéan rebellion was, they believed, an added distraction in their favor. The capital and its satellites would be borne down on from the disaffected perimeter of France in a circle that extended west from Normandy and Brittany through the Vendée to the Gironde and southern Provence, up the Rhone Valley and to Lyon and the Franche-Comté, where Besançon too was leaning to federalism. Gradually, they hoped, this ring would tighten like a noose around the necks of the beleaguered Mountain.

In Caen itself the prospects for such an ambitious anti-Jacobin crusade seemed good. On the fifteenth a manifesto had been drafted by the Girondins and the authorities of the department. It denounced "the conspiratorial commune [Paris], engorged with blood and gold, which holds our representatives captive. It is amidst bayonets that it dares to dictate its will. The national representation no longer exists. Frenchmen! The home of our liberty has been violated. The free men of Neustria [the Frankish name for Northern France] will not allow this outrage and either those brigands will be punished or else we shall all die." On the twenty-second a general assembly representing a substantial majority of the *sections* of Caen also adopted a motion against the continuation of "anarchy." Recalled by the Convention, de Wimpffen replied that he would come to Paris at the head of sixty thousand men to restore justice and liberty.

For the time being, though, his force was more modest. On the seventh of July, a military parade took place on the Grande Cour of Caen with not more than twenty-five hundred federalist troops: eight hundred from the Eure and Calvados; five hundred from the neighboring Department of Ille-et-Vilaine; eight hundred from the Breton departments of Finistère and Morbihan; and the remainder from the Manche and Mayenne. Striding along to the sound of military bands, it was enough for a good show in the summer afternoon, but it was not enough for a civil war. Though the Girondins had hoped the spectacle would produce a flood of spontaneous volunteers, the afternoon yielded the meager harvest of just a hundred and thirty to add to the ranks.

Watching the parade was a strikingly good-looking woman of twenty-five named Charlotte Corday d'Armont. The house in Caen where she lodged was just a few paces away from the Intendance, where the Girondins had made their headquarters. Since often, from the balcony, they exercised their oratory on sympathetic crowds, she had heard them many times and on the twentieth had managed to be introduced to the eloquent and dashing Provençal Charles Barbaroux. She needed no conversion, however, for Charlotte Corday was already consumed with an intense, almost feverish hatred for the Jacobins, whose conduct on May 31 and June 2, she believed, had brought the Republic to the lowest level of degradation.

It was a republic she wished to see flourish. For although Charlotte had been born in a timbered manor house to a family of minor Norman gentry, she was by no means a royalist. On the contrary, like Mme Roland (who much admired her abrupt intervention in the history of the Revolution), she had read deeply in Rousseau and the standard Roman histories and imagined the Revolution as dedicated to bringing about an exalted moral transformation. She became an assassin not to avenge Louis XVI— indeed, at her interrogation she explicitly repudiated any comparison with Pâris, the royal bodyguard who had murdered Lepeletier—but to help the Girondin and federalist cause. Her deed, she would write to Barbaroux from prison, had surely done more to help General de Wimpffen than any battle.

One event in particular violently alienated Charlotte from the Revolution. The Abbé Gombault, *curé* of Saint-Gilles in Caen, had given the last rites to Charlotte's mother in 1782, when she died in childbirth. As a refractory priest, he had been successively dispossessed of his living, threatened with deportation, and in April 1793 had gone into hiding in the woods of La Delivrande outside the city to avoid arrest. A search party of tracking dogs hunted him down and he was executed on the fifth of April in the place du Pilori, the first of those to be guillotined at Caen. Later that month the department of the Calvados addressed the first of many letters to the Convention complaining of the tyranny of a small clique of Jacobins. "Your divisions are the source of all our troubles. It is a Marat, a Robespierre, a Danton who preoccupy you and incite you and you forget that an entire people is suffering. . . ." These attacks on the Mountain were published and widely posted in Caen, and Charlotte is likely to have read them. One assault on the most notorious "sanguinary," Marat, by Pézénas, a deputy from the Hérault, circulating in Caen may have struck her as particularly compelling, not least for the way in which it turned against Marat his own obsession with the political economy of decapitation.

> Let Marat's head fall and the Republic is saved. . . . Purge
> France of this man of blood. . . . Marat sees the Public Safety only
> in a river of blood; well then his own must flow, for his head
> must fall to save two hundred thousand others.

Charlotte Corday came to the conclusion that this task was her vocation. A direct descendant of the classical dramatist Pierre Corneille, she seemed to cast herself in one of his tragic roles. She would take on herself the mission of patriotic martyr, a woman who would be prepared to die in the sacred deed of ridding the *patrie* of a monster. On the ninth of July, in sultry afternoon heat, she dispatched a letter to her father in Argentan, begging his pardon for leaving Caen without his permission, and boarded the *diligence* for Paris.

T H E   O B J E C T   of her attention was meanwhile lying sick at his house in the rue des Cordeliers. Never particularly healthy, Marat had lately developed a crippling dermatological disorder which, on periodic eruption, would turn his skin into a roasting mess of scaly flakes and sores. The only relief for this arthritic psoriasis was to lie in a cool bath. When the attacks came on him, Marat would retire to his tiled bathroom and continue his work on a small table improvised from an upturned wooden box that stood by the side of his shoe-shaped tub. The torrid midsummer heat may have made this condition worse, for Marat had absented himself from the Convention for an unusually long time. On the twelfth of July, a day after Charlotte Corday arrived in Paris, two deputies came to inquire after his health. One of them was the painter Jacques-Louis David, who found him "writing his thoughts for the safety of the *patrie*" in his tireless manner, the right arm slung out of the bath. On the walls of the room were a map of the departments of the Republic, emblems of the Revolution and a pair of crossed pistols below which was written the legend *"La Mort."* Perhaps struck by this alarming motto, David wished the Friend of the People a speedy recovery, to which he replied, "Ten years more or less in the duration of my life do not concern me in the least; my only desire is to be able to say with my last breath 'I am happy that the *patrie* is saved.'" Charlotte Corday could not have put it better.

Laid low as he was, Jean-Paul Marat was then at the acme of his powers and influence. Since the abortive effort by the Girondins to convict him in April, everything had gone his way. On the day of his acquittal by the Revolutionary Tribunal, a woman had placed a crown of roses on his brow. A month later victory became even more fragrant as he saw his bitterest enemies proscribed and hounded from the Convention. The institutional machinery for the revolutionary dictatorship he advocated was now set in place, so that the chaotic brutalities of the street mobs would be replaced by the systematic machinery of state punishment. The *enragés*, whom he disliked almost as much as he did the Girondins, had failed to profit from June 2, and Varlet himself had even been excluded from the Jacobins. Marat was listened to in the Convention, respected in the Commune, showered with flattering attention in the *sections*. He seemed to have become one with the persona he had devised: Friend of the People; oracle of the Republic; unmasker of conspiracies; mortifier of hypocrites.

He had certainly come a long way from the itinerant medical and scientific man of letters who had traveled throughout Europe in search of recognition for his theories on optics, aeronautics and electrical therapy. Like Jacques-Louis David's, his political life was the fruit of a bitter personal rejection. In David's case the refusal of the Academy to exhibit the works of his favorite (and prodigiously gifted) student, Drouais, had persuaded him that it was in the grip of an aristocratic clique. From there it was but a short step to espousing its destruction as incompatible with revolutionary freedom, and a political engagement that had made the painter a deputy to the Convention and a member of the Comitee of General Security. Marat's failure to secure recognition from the Royal Academy of Science for his theories on the igneous fluids that he took to be the essential property of electricity was much more alienating since, unlike David's dispute, it damaged his career. Before this crisis in 1780 he had been, at least nominally, physician to Artois and had a thriving practice in electrotherapy. Afterwards his clientele shrunk under the imputation that he was a quack, a disaster for which a prize conferred by the Academy of Rouen only inadequately compensated him.

Smarting from this affront, Marat recast his identity. Instead of ingratiating himself with the fashionable aristocracy, he turned to snapping at its heels. Instead of hunting for publicity, he created his own by living in the area of the Cordeliers where he had easy access to printers. In England the career of John Wilkes had shown him how a mocking, combative journalism probing the limits of conventional decorum could actually create a new political public. But what Marat put together from other elements of metropolitan culture was distinctively French. From Linguet and Mercier he took an apocalyptic tone and the verbally violent polemics that tore into the vices of political fashion. In retrospect one can see that Marat's peculiar family origins, combining Sardinian Jesuitry with Genevan Calvinism (the latter on his mother's side), were a perfect training for this kind of hectoring messianism. From Rousseau he took the polemics of paranoia. This both concentrated his attack against liberal self-congratulation and ensured that when the counter-attacks came (from Lafayette, for example) he could turn that "persecution" into a political asset. Goading into action adversaries whom he depicted as traitors, conspirators, tyrants or poltroons, he could then pose as the champion of the freedom of the press. "The liberty of saying anything," he once memora-

176. Joseph Boze, Marat

bly remarked, "has enemies only among those who want to reserve for themselves the right to do anything."

His chosen role, then, was that of an outcast—the man who abjured wit, elegance, the fashionable obsession with beauty for the imperatives of truth and virtue. Reason was itself suspect, for, as he wrote in June 1793, the Revolution had been nearly aborted by men who wanted *philosophie* rather than the passions to be its guide. Polite manners were, as Rousseau had seen, merely a form of corruption practiced by "charlatans." "To pretend to please everyone is mad," he wrote in 1793, "but to pretend to please everyone in a time of revolution is treason." Displeasing as many people as possible, by the same token, was projected as a sign of his integrity. Marat made an art form of this kind of confrontational ugliness, for which his personal appearance was ideally suited. His eyes were not quite aligned but they glittered blackly from out of a broad, flattened face. Contemporaries who were much taken with zoomorphic analogies divided on which kind of bird Marat most resembled. His friends and admirers compared him with an eagle; his enemies with a scavenging crow. For his self-presentation Marat discarded the perfectly conventional attire he had worn for an appearance of ostentatious simplicity: bare-throated; unkempt black hair; an old ermine scarf sometimes thrown over his shoulders. It was not at all the attire of a true sans-culotte, but it was a suitably theatrical costume for a Friend of the People. He gloried in rudeness. Hunting Paris in October 1792 for Dumouriez, whom he wanted to confront, Marat burst in on a dinner party given by the actor Talma to harangue the General at table. He would seek out the truth; nothing was to evade him. His eyes were the eyes of surveillance; his voice lifted to wake the people from their deadly slumber.

Essential to Marat's adoption of the personality of the revolutionary Jeremiah—dreamer, prophet, bringer of doom—was the challenge of martyrdom. Like Robespierre and many other Jacobins, he was constantly offering to die rather than compromise his principles; to sacrifice his own person to the vengeance of the "liberticides." The fact that Marat often took to his heels when danger actually closed in did not seem to tarnish this image of proffered self-immolation. He habitually carried a pistol to the Convention—less, one suspects, to defend himself than as a stage prop. When the Girondins were working on his indictment, he pressed the pistol to his temples during a speech, declaring that "if, in the fury that has been shown towards me, the decree of accusation is carried, I will blow out my brains." On other occasions he declared that he, the "voice of the people," was being "smothered," "strangled" or (still more frequently) "assassinated."

At eight o'clock on the morning of July 13, Charlotte Corday walked from her lodgings near the rue des Victoires to the Palais-Royal. It was a Saturday and the gardens and galleries were more crowded than usual with people from outlying villages who had come to join the celebrations for Paris's adhesion to the new constitution: a ceremony deliberately planned for July 14. Charlotte moved between columns decorated with tricolor ribbon and emblems of the new republic: the carpenter's level signifying equality; the ubiquitous liberty bonnet. Under a brilliant sky, men and women were sipping lemonade to fortify themselves against the stifling heat that seemed to have stalled itself over the city. From a vendor she bought a newspaper that reported Léonard Bourdon's demand in the Convention for the death sentence to be brought against the Girondins. At a shop in one of the arcades she stopped to replace her white *Caennaise* bonnet with a more sporty black hat decorated with green ribbons. After the deed, all the witnesses would remember that green headgear. Had she chosen it as the color of 1789, Camille Desmoulins' token of freedom? Charlotte Corday would make it the color of counter-revolution, prohibited, to the ruin of drapers and haberdashers, from any public dress. At a cutler's shop near the Café Février, she bought a wooden-handled kitchen knife with a five-inch blade, which she slipped beneath her dress.

Charlotte had been disappointed to learn of Marat's sickness, since she had planned to kill him in the midst of the Convention itself in full view of the "representatives of the Nation." But the Friend of the People was reputed to open his doors to anyone who needed his help or could suggest a denunciation, so she decided to do the deed in his own home. She must have wandered the streets for a while before taking a carriage, since by the time that she arrived outside Marat's house in the rue des Cordeliers, it was nearly eleven thirty. At the foot of the stairs leading to his apartment, Catherine Evrard, the sister of his fiancée Simonne, turned her away, saying that Marat was too ill to see anyone and she should wait until he was properly recovered. Frustrated, Charlotte wrote him a letter calculated to arouse his curiosity, suggesting she could inform him of the plots being hatched at Caen by the escaped Girondins. She asked for a response but in her nervousness forgot to add her address.

At seven o'clock in the evening she returned to Marat's house, armed not just with the knife but with another letter imploring him to see her. Her arrival coincided with the delivery of fresh bread and the day's newspapers, so that she was already up the stairs when she was stopped by Simonne herself, who was suspicious of Charlotte's determination to see Marat. As they argued, Charlotte deliberately raised her voice to let Marat know that she wanted to give him special information about the traitors in Normandy.

"Let her in," came the voice from the bath. She found him soaking, with the habitual wet cloth tied about his brow, an arm slung over the side of the tub. For fifteen minutes they talked about the situation at Caen, with Simonne in attendance. Then Marat asked Simonne to fetch some more kaolin solution for the water. To demonstrate her impeccable Jacobinism, Charlotte, in response to his request to name the plotters, recited a comprehensive list. "Good," replied Marat, "in a few days I will have them all guillotined."

Her chair was directly by the side of the bath. All she had to do was to rise, lean over the man, pull the knife out from the top of her dress, and lunge down hard and quickly. There was time for but one strike, beneath the clavicle on the right side. Marat shouted *"A moi, ma chère amie"* before sinking back into the water. As Simonne Evrard ran into the room, crying

177. Duplessis-Bertaux, Charlotte Corday. The panel shows her calmly seated while awaiting her arrest.

"My God, he has been assassinated," a jet of blood gushed from the wound where the carotid artery had been opened. *"Malheureuse,* what have you done?" was all she could say to the murderess. Laurent Bas, who worked for Marat distributing his newspaper, ran into the room, throwing a chair at Charlotte, missing and finally pinning her down, as he told the court, "by holding on to her breasts."

The evening was hot and windows were open. Marat's scream had carried across the streets. On hearing it and the cries that followed, Clair Delafonde, a dentist who lived opposite, dropped his work and rushed through the little courtyard and up the stairs. Lifting Marat from the tub, he attempted to stanch the bleeding with cloths and sheets. In a few minutes he was joined by Philippe Pelletan, an army surgeon also living nearby. But nothing the two men did could stop the blood flowing through the improvised bandages. Sanguinary imagery had featured prominently in Marat's polemical vocabulary. "We must cement liberty in the blood of the despot," he had often said. Now his own announced the beginning, not of freedom, but of Terror. When the local *commissaire de police,* Guellard, arrived, he followed the trail of blood to the bathroom and then to an adjoining bedchamber where Pelletan was standing by the body. The Friend of the People, he was told, was no more.

The deed done, Charlotte waited impassively for her own fate to unfold. Caught virtually in the act itself, she had no desire to evade its consequences, only to explain clearly and coolly her motives. She had her wish. To Guellard she calmly explained that "having seen that civil war was on the point of exploding throughout France and persuaded that Marat was the principal author of this disaster, she had wished to sacrifice her life for her country." A committee of six further officials, including Drouet, the postmaster who had recognized Louis XVI at Saint-Menehould, continued the examination in Marat's apartment while they sipped refreshments. To this group Charlotte Corday admitted having come to Paris from Caen with the premeditated design of killing Marat but insisted (to the obvious disappointment of the investigators) that the design was hers alone.

As news spread quickly through the faubourg Saint-Germain, enraged and anguished crowds gathered, wanting to tear the murderess to pieces. One woman even said that she would like to dismember the monster and eat her filthy body, piece by piece. Drouet could only dissuade them by reminding the crowd that they would lose "the links in the plot" if they killed the principal miscreant on the spot.

In the Abbaye prison—the site of the first of the September massacres—Charlotte was taken to a small cell that had previously housed both Brissot and Mme Roland. She sat on a straw mattress, stroked a black cat and wrote a letter to the Committee of General Security (the police committee of the Convention). As if she were anxious not to be robbed of sole responsibility, she protested against the rumored arrest of Claude Fauchet, the Girondin deputy and constitutional bishop of Caen, as an accomplice. Not only had they not concerted the plan, she insisted, but she neither esteemed nor respected the man, whom she had always thought a frivolous fanatic with no "firmness of character." In contrast, at many points in her investigation, Charlotte stressed her own resolve and believed that the common delusion that women were incapable of such acts had played to her advantage. It was evidently a point of honor with her—and in deliberate repudiation of the revolutionary stereotypes of gender—to affirm that her sex was both physically and morally more than strong enough to commit acts of patriotic violence.

This emerged strikingly from her three cross-examinations, two by the president of the Revolutionary Tribunal, Montané, and one by the court's chief prosecutor, Fouquier-Tinville. They all did their best to draw from her information that would prove the existence of an extensive Girondin plot to kill Marat. There was a recognizable undertow of sexual fear of the avenging gray-eyed fury, so apparently self-possessed. Surely she must have been put up to it by some controlling, masculine hand? "It has been mathematically demonstrated," claimed Georges Couthon in the Jacobins, "that this monster to whom nature has given the form of a woman is an envoy of Buzot, Barbaroux, Salle and all the other conspirators of Caen." Every line of questioning met with the same stubborn denials that had, after all, the consistency of being true. In a final exchange with Montané on the seventeenth she at least admitted to reading Girondin newspapers but took the opportunity of turning that acknowledgment into another statement of righteous indignation.

MONTANÉ: Was it from *those* newspapers that you learned that Marat was an anarchist?
CORDAY: Yes. I knew that he was perverting France. I have killed one man to save a hundred thousand. Besides he was a hoarder; at Caen they have arrested a man who bought goods for him. I was a republican well before the Revolution and I have never lacked energy.
MONTANÉ: What do you mean by "energy"?
CORDAY: Those who put their own interests to one side and know how to sacrifice themselves for the *patrie*.
MONTANÉ: Didn't you practice in advance, before striking the blow at Marat?

CORDAY: Oh! The monster [i.e., Montané], he takes me for a murderer! (Here, [says the court record] the witness appeared violently moved.)

MONTANÉ: Nonetheless it was proven in the medical report that if you had struck the blow in this manner (demonstrating with a long motion) you would not have killed him.

CORDAY: I struck him just as you found. It was luck.

MONTANÉ: Who were the persons who counselled you to commit this murder?

CORDAY: I would never have committed such an attack on the advice of others. I alone conceived the plan and executed it.

MONTANÉ: But how are we supposed to believe you were not advised to do this when you tell us that you regard Marat as the cause of all the evils in France, he who never ceased to unmask traitors and conspirators?

CORDAY: It's only in Paris that people have eyes for Marat. In the other departments, he is regarded as a monster.

MONTANÉ: How could you look on Marat as a monster when he only allowed you access to him through an act of humanity because you had written to him that you were persecuted?

CORDAY: What difference does it make that he showed himself human towards me if he was a monster towards others?

MONTANÉ: Do you think you have killed all the Marats?

CORDAY: With this one dead, the others, perhaps, will be afraid.

Duly convicted and condemned to a prompt death, Charlotte awaited execution in the Conciergerie, to which she had been transferred from the Abbaye. In both prisons she had been allowed to write letters, probably in the hope that they might incriminate others in the "Girondin plot" the authorities were sure had directed the murder. The day before her trial, she had written two letters, each in a different manner. To her father she reverted to the conventional role of obedient daughter, imploring his forgiveness for "having disposed of my existence without your permission." There was no dishonor in what she had done, for "I have avenged many innocent victims and [more naively] I have prevented many other disasters. . . . Adieu, my dear father, I beg you to forget me or rather to rejoice at my fate. The cause is good." She concluded by presenting herself as one of their ancestor Corneille's tragic heroines, dying in virtue. But the line she cited for her epitaph was, alas, not from the great tragedian Pierre but his second-rate brother Thomas:

Le crime fait la honte et non pas l'échafaud (It is not the scaffold but the crime which makes the shame)

The other letter was to Charles Barbaroux. She had begun it in the Abbaye, representing herself as an unrepentant Norman Judith, but blessed with her due share of *sensibilité.* "I have never hated a single being . . . and I pray that those who regret my passing to consider that one day they will rejoice to see me enjoy the repose of the Elysian Fields with Brutus and the ancients. For the moderns, there are so few patriots who know how to die for their country; everything is egoism; what a sorry people to found a Republic." At her trial the next morning she would show the judges and jury "the value of the people of the Calvados since [they will see that] even the women of that country are capable of firmness."

In a final extraordinary gesture of self-dramatization, Charlotte asked the court whether she might have her portrait painted before her execution. During the hearing she had noticed a National Guard officer sketching her likeness. As a citizen in good standing with the *section* (Théâtre-Français), the officer, Hauer, was allowed to return to the Conciergerie with her to

178. Anonymous drawing, Charlotte Corday on her way to her execution

turn the sketch into a painting. It took two hours, during which she made suggestions to him for alterations here and there. When they were finally interrupted by Sanson the executioner, she took the scissors from him, cut off a lock of her hair, and presented it to the painter as "a souvenir of a poor dying woman."

It was early evening when she got into the tumbril that would take her to the guillotine. Refusing both the services of a juring priest and a seat, she stood upright, steadying herself over the cobbles by leaning her knees on the back of the cart. A large crowd, curious to see the virago who could have perpetrated such a crime, pressed into the rue Saint-Honoré to see her pass. Pierre Notelet's house gave on to the street and he noted, as she passed, that the skies suddenly darkened and a summer storm shook heavy drops of rain into the dust. In seconds she was soaked, the scarlet shirt worn by assassins of the "representatives of the people" clinging to her body. "Her beautiful face was so calm," he wrote, "that one would have said she was a statue. Behind her, young girls held each other's hands as they danced. For eight days I was in love with Charlotte Corday."

INFATUATION with the assassin could be dangerous. A German Patriot who had fled the debacle at Mainz, Adam Lux, was bold enough to publish a poem comparing Charlotte Corday with Brutus. After some debate as to whether he was mad, Lux went to the guillotine in November. Marat, on the other hand, became the immediate object of a cult of veneration. After Charlotte had been taken away to the Abbaye, a notice was posted on the door of his house declaring, in tragic meter, what had happened:

> People, Marat is dead: the lover of the *patrie*
> Your friend, your succour, the hope of the afflicted
> Has fallen beneath the blows of the withered horde [the Girondins]
> Weep but remember that he must be avenged

Every so often a sans-culotte holding a pike would read the declaration to crowds in his most grandiloquent manner.

The morning following Marat's death, in the Convention, the stoic drama became even more worked up. After the President, Jeanbon Saint-André, had made the announcement of Marat's death, a representative of the *section* Contrat-Social, Guiraut, turned the moment into a theatrical performance:

> Where is he? A parricide hand has wrenched him from us.
> People! Marat is no more.

Turning to the portrait of Lepeletier that hung in the hall, Guiraut then exclaimed, "David, where are you; take up your brush, there remains one more painting for you to make."

David, of course, rose to the occasion. Not only was he prepared to create an enduring image of the revolutionary martyr, but he set about designing the death rites as a great demonstration of patriotic devotion. Following the precedent of Lepeletier, the body would be embalmed and exhibited to the public for three days, after which there would be a solemn and elaborate funeral procession. The challenge for the artist was somehow to clean up Marat's corpse enough to represent the idealized, sanctified figure he had in mind, but to leave enough evidence of violence to suggest the blood the hero had shed for the Revolution. We shall see that he was to achieve this simultaneous invocation of mortality and immortality in his painting by formal devices of brilliant inventiveness. But the immediate rites presented some serious technical problems. Lepeletier's body had been displayed in mid-January, when the weather helped extend its period of natural preservation. Marat's cadaver, on the other hand, almost immediately began to putrefy in the fierce midsummer heat.

For 7,500 livres (materials included) David hired Louis Deschamps, by general consent the genius of his art, to do the embalming. With his five assistants he worked quickly, but his task was complicated by David's exacting specifications. The painter had a particular inspirational scene in mind: the martyr shown in repose on a Roman bed, his face displayed in an attitude of sublime peace. The upper part of his torso would be exposed to display the wound and his right arm would be extended, holding the iron pen that symbolized his tireless devotion to the people. It was a powerful concept but an embalmer's nightmare. Marat's alarming skin condition had to be carefully disguised cosmetically and the wound itself, which had begun to gape, sewn so that it provided just the right degree of shock. Since his head was propped up on a pillow, the ligature of the tongue had to be cut to avoid it lolling in a way unbecoming to martyrs. Worst of all, there had been some serious dislocation of the arm. The *ci-devant* Marquis de Créqui (not a sympathetic observer of the scene) claimed that to solve this problem, an arm from a different cadaver had been attached, but that one night, to the consternation of devotees, it had separated itself from the body and dropped to the floor still gripping the pen.

179. Anonymous painting, the exposure of Marat's body at the church of the Cordeliers

An anonymous painting suggests how successful the exhibition in the church of the Cordeliers was. The bed was set against tricolor draperies designed and provided by Patriot Palloy, who also supplied two stones from the Bastille engraved, respectively, with Marat's name and *"Ami du Peuple."* A crown of oak leaves, symbol of Marat's immortal genius, was placed on his brow and flowers were thrown on his bier. Far below (for the platform on which he rested was much higher than suggested in the painting) were gathered the attributes of his martyrdom: the porphyry bath, the bloody robe, the box desk with its inkwell and paper. Displayed about the chapel were Marat's writings.

So many people crowded into the church on the fifteenth and the morning of the sixteenth of July that the viewing might have continued for many days. But the process of putrefaction was accelerating inexorably. Vinegar and perfume were periodically sprinkled on the body in attempts to disguise the increasingly pungent odor. In the circumstances there was nothing for it but to advance the funeral to the evening of the sixteenth. Possibly because of the haste with which the occasion was organized, there was a conspicuous absence of formal representation from the Convention and its committees. Instead, the funeral was very much an affair of the Cordeliers

Club and the other popular societies and the *sections*. In a torchlight procession, to music and songs by Gluck, four women carried the bath; another, the bloodied shirt on the end of a pike. As the body passed through the streets, more women threw flowers on Marat's heavily whitened face, but the prize relic was an agate urn containing the heart of the hero. Separately embalmed by Deschamps, it had been declared the "natural property of the Cordeliers" and was suspended from the vault of their meeting hall, forever swinging over the heads of the tribunes. The body was to have its repose in a rocky grotto, swiftly improvised by the architect Martin in the garden of the club.

As Jean Guilhaumou has emphasized, the funeral was orchestrated around the imperishability of the martyr. The immortality of his words and principles guaranteed that as long as the Republic lived, so would Marat. His copiously shed blood would not simply drain away from the *patrie* but actually nourish its vitality—the stuff of life rather than death. "May the blood of Marat become the seed of intrepid republicans," proclaimed one orator, sprinkling an unidentified liquid from a chalice. This denial of death could not have been more categorically stated than by Jacques Roux (one of the claimants to Marat's mantle) in his paper the *Publiciste de la République Française*. "*MARAT N'EST POINT MORT,*" he insisted in capital letters. "His soul, released from its earthly casing, glides around all parts of the Republic all the more capable of introducing itself into the councils of federalists and tyrants." Marat the eagle, then, had been set free to soar above the beleaguered territory of France, swooping and diving to harass its enemies or spy, invisibly, on their machinations. Oddly enough, this airborne version of the omniscient Patriot harked back to many of the themes Marat had himself anticipated in his visions of the politics of ballooning.

Thus ascending from the tomb, Marat naturally reminded hagiographers of another resurrection. Prostrating himself before the agate urn, the Cordelier Morel intoned:

O heart of Jesus, O heart of Marat . . . you have the same right to our homage. O heart of Marat, *sacré coeur* . . . can the works and benevolence of the son of Mary be compared with those of the Friend of the People and his apostles to the Jacobins of our holy Mountain? . . . Their Jesus was but a false prophet but Marat is a god. Long live the heart of Marat. . . . Like Jesus, Marat loved the people ardently. . . . Like Jesus, Marat detested nobles, priests, the rich, the scoundrels. Like Jesus, he led a poor and frugal life. . . .

180. Copia (after David), the dead Marat

While this was an extreme example, the sacralization of Marat became a powerful tool of revolutionary propaganda. Indeed, Marat dead was perhaps more useful to the Jacobins than the unpredictable, choleric live politician. In his name Simonne Evrard was mobilized to attack the *enragés* when the time came for their political elimination. To defend Paris and France against the "plots" that had destroyed him, the revolutionary dictatorship he had recommended had to be implemented in earnest. To identify with Marat rapidly became a testimony of revolutionary purity. Place names were altered so that Montmartre became Mont-Marat; the rue des Cordeliers, the rue Marat; and over thirty communes throughout the Republic incorporated the martyr in their new name. A bust of the great man replaced the statue of the Virgin on the rue aux Ours and a new restaurant opened in the rue Saint-Honoré called the Grand Marat. Songs like "La Mort du Patriote Marat" became instantly popular and at the Théâtre de la Cité, a play dramatizing his death was an immediate success. In September two married priests baptized an infant "in the name of the Most High Liberty" Brutus-Marat-Lepeletier. Even the young soldier Joachim Murat, who was to be the most flamboyant of Napoleon's marshals and King of Naples, signed on as an adept of the cult by substituting an *a* for the *u* in his name.

Though prints of the hero and the way in which he met his end circulated in enormous numbers through France, many of them distributed by Jacobin clubs, they were all overshadowed by David's masterpiece, completed in October. The public was admitted to David's studio; a great feast was given in celebration by the *section* du Muséum and the painting, rather alarmingly, was carried in triumph, along with David's Lepeletier, through the streets and to the Louvre, where it had pride of place in the first Salon of the Republic.

Every generation has seen the painting as a transfiguration; at once a startlingly realistic account of the murder and a revolutionary *pietà*. The blood of the martyr is there in abundance, rendered with shocking clarity. Marat bathes in it. Everywhere deep red and dead white are set together: blood staining the purity of the sheet; smeared on Corday's letter; coating the knife, the handle of which David has altered from wood to ivory, the better to sustain the contrast. Near Marat's hand are set the unanswerable documents of his saintliness. They are juxtaposed in glaring moral contrast. The murderess's hypocritical letter implores, "It is enough that I am unhappy to have the right to your benevolence," while papers on Marat's desk reveal him to be the true Friend of the People. Beside an *assignat* David has a note in Marat's hand bearing instructions for it to be given to a widow with five children whose "husband has died for the *patrie.*" At the moral heart of the painting, then, is a death within a death, lit by the cold steady light of immolation.

ii "TERROR IS THE ORDER OF THE DAY"

As the August sun came up over the site of the Bastille, a chorus of girls dressed in white greeted it with Gossec's *Hymn to Nature.* The space had been landscaped so that trees and shrubs testified to the victory of benign Nature over the dead stones of despotism (the latter, of course, supplied by Palloy). In this renamed Champ de Réunion an enormous crowd witnessed the rites of revolutionary druidism. When the cantata based on Rousseau's ecstatic pantheism in the *Profession du Foi d'un Vicaire Savoyard* had faded away, the President of the Convention, Hérault de Séchelles, slowly climbed a flight of white steps. Seated at its top was a statue in the Egyptian manner, enthroned between lions. Its hands cupped breasts from which water poured into a small tank below. Greeting both the statue and the crowd, the orator addressed it as the incarnation of Nature, whose fecundity was blessing the Revolution, and this day in particular—"the most beautiful that the Sun has ever lit since the first time it was suspended in the immensity of space."

181. Jacques-Louis David, *Marat Assassinated*

182. Detail from Jacques-Louis David, *Marat Assassinated*

Aiming carefully, he held out an antique chalice to catch this miraculous fluid, then poured it onto the ground, rebaptizing the soil in the name of Liberty. Draining a second cup, he was followed in this ritual by eighty-six old men, each representing a department of France. As each stepped forward there were drum rolls and brass fanfares, silence while the cup was emptied, followed by cannon and the fraternal kiss.

This extraordinary ceremony had been devised by David, together with a team of collaborators that included Gossec and Marie-Joseph Chénier, to consummate the formal acceptance of the new constitution. It was designed to rehearse the history of the Revolution in an allegorical pageant, moving a large crowd from site to site and culminating on the Champ de Mars, where the "tablets" of the constitution were set up on the altar of the *patrie*. This Festival of Unity and Indivisibility, taking place on August 10, the first anniversary of the overthrow of the monarchy, was a supremely Parisian occasion. As if reaffirming that Paris *was* the Revolution, it used the topography of the city as a series of theatrical settings, each of which referred to some point in the recent past, the transforming present and the indeterminate but benign future.

It was also—as Mona Ozouf, the historian of revolutionary festivals, has pointed out—a carefully planned alternative to the spontaneous disorders and acts of violence which the Jacobin leadership found increasingly distasteful even when they profited from them. The chaotic people were to be overawed (and so defanged) by colossal statues representing, among other things, The People; by expansive music scored for enormous choirs

183. Anonymous print, The Fountain of
Regeneration at the *Fête de l'Unité*

184. Liberty with the debris of monarchy
at her feet

(Gossec wrote five cantatas for the day); by imposing oratory and visual
pyrotechnics. Jacques-Louis David would honor them with their own
self-importance safely imprisoned in the calm, adamantine universe of
symbols.

Accordingly, the second "station" of the ceremonies was a triumphal
arch erected on the boulevard des Italiens. In deliberate repudiation of
Caesaro-monarchist victories, the celebrated warriors were the women of
October 5, 1789, who had brought the King from Versailles to Paris. But
the disturbingly potent image of belligerent *poissardes* astride their cannon
had been carefully neutralized in conformity with standard Rousseauean-
Jacobin doctrine on the wife-mother role for women patriots. The authentic women of October were replaced by prettified actresses whose brows
were crowned with laurel and who were told "O women! Liberty attacked
by the tyrants has need of heroes to defend it. It is for you to breed them.
Let all the martial and the generous virtues flow together in your maternal
milk and in the heart of the nursing women of France."

The most spectacular moment of the day occurred on the next "station,"
on the place de la Révolution. The pedestal which had once borne the statue
of Louis XV was now occupied by the figure of enthroned Liberty. At its
feet were dumped a collection of the attributes of royalty: scepters, crowns,
orbs—even busts, including one resembling the young Louis XIV. Like the
pseudo-*poissardes*, most were not the real thing, but had come from the prop
rooms of the Paris theaters and had been carried on an immense coffin from

the Bastille to the statue. At a given signal, a torch was put to the pile, and as the flames began to jump from the smoke, a great cloud of three thousand white doves was released into the sky. The doves were a stunning *coup de théâtre*, signifying the liberation of France from monarchy, rising, as the emblems of Christian peace and republican freedom, into a dazzling blue sky.

The entire day was, of course, an elaborately constructed, operatically executed fantasy. Even skeptical witnesses who thought the whole business foolish, such as the artist Georges Wille, confessed to being moved and elated by the proceedings, and there seems little doubt that the same was true of the crowds. But for all the bravura of the occasion there was something slightly desperate and defensive about it, built as it was on the systematic denial of revolutionary realities. The constitution, which had been rewritten by Hérault de Séchelles from the discredited Condorcet's February draft, offered universal male suffrage, direct elections and even the commitment of the state to a "right of subsistence." But the million who had ratified it paled into insignificance beside the six million who had abstained, either from bewilderment or prudence. And from the moment of its acceptance it was made meaningless, first by the Convention itself, which had been charged to dissolve itself on completion of the document, then by the construction of the working institutions of the Terror, which effectively superseded all its provisions.

Perhaps the most defiantly optimistic of all David's monuments was sited on the Invalides, where he had built a gigantic Hercules representing the French people crushing federalism. The hero was already familiar as one of the standard attributes of the Renaissance princes and under Henri IV had been appropriated as the "Gallic Hercules." In David's version, one arm prepared to smite the monster federalism that writhed at his feet, while the other was placed about the Roman lictor's bound sticks, or *fasces*, representing the unity of the departments of France.

In the midsummer of 1793, however, this happy outcome of an omnipotent and united People vanquishing its enemies was by no means assured. There was some good news to enjoy. On July 13 the modest Norman "army" commanded by de Puisaye encountered a republican force at Pacy-sur-Eure. Both sides had run away on hearing the first cannon shots, but the federalists had run faster and further and so were more decisively demoralized. Since significant parts of Normandy had failed to rally to their cause, it was, in effect, the end of the attempt to create a federalist arc from the Pas-de-Calais to upper Brittany. In the south, on July 27, General Carteaux had retaken Avignon from the little expeditionary force from Marseille and so precluded any junction between the federalists of the Midi and those of Lyon.

185. The French people crushing federalism

186. Anonymous, painted board, the Unity of the Republic

751

187. L. David, drawing, Georges Danton

Those crucial victories were, however, offset by a more alarming string of disasters. During the last two weeks of July, the frontier fortresses of Condé and Valenciennes fell to Coburg's Austrian army, which then began to besiege Maubeuge. If that last stronghold fell, the valley of the Marne would lie open for an advance on Paris. On the Rhine, General Custine decided to evacuate Mainz and leave it to the Prussians (and was promptly declared a traitor in Paris). In the northeast, the Duke of York's army in the Netherlands was advancing on Dunkirk; and in the southwest, the Spanish were threatening Perpignan. In the Vendée, small successes had not compensated for major defeats at Châtillon and Vihiers. Sans-culotte generals such as Ronsin and Rossignol bickered with such *ci-devants* as Lafayette's old comrade-in-arms Biron, while Barère compared the republican army to the baggage train of the King of Persia: dragging 120 wagons behind it while the "brigands" marched with a crust of black bread in their bags. Finally, though the federalist cities had been separated, they had not been defeated. Marseille and Toulon were known to be negotiating with the British fleet for food supplies and the Lyonnais had responded to the Convention's formal proscription of their rebellion by executing Chalier on the same day that Charlotte Corday went to the guillotine.

What made this alarming situation worse were the bitter divisions (notwithstanding the cult of unity) within the various revolutionary authorities and factions over how best to confront the crisis. Until July 10 the dominant presence on the Committee of Public Safety had been Danton. He was now faced with the same dilemma that had sabotaged the governments of the Girondins, the Feuillants and the King: How to create a viable state amid political turmoil? His answer, like those of all of his predecessors, the King excepted, was pragmatic rather than dogmatic. But he was astute enough to disguise his pragmatism in rhetorical vehemence. At the tribune, Danton could brush off criticism by the sheer power of his aggressive personality. Unlike Robespierre, whose rhetorical delivery was relatively flat and academic, and who depended for persuasion on carefully crafted arguments and confessions of personal integrity, Danton had developed a style that was improvised, and unpredictable. Like Mirabeau (whom he much resembled) he used his big, solid head, often compared by contemporaries to that of a bull, to maximum effect, growling at enemies, bringing the voice up to its full, resonant volume to shake the Convention into assent.

In the summer of 1793, Danton's was the counsel of restraint and skepticism. Using the bludgeon of his ridicule, he attacked Anacharsis Cloots in particular for his revolutionary messianism, which would take the revolution in arms ever further from France's frontiers until a universal republic had been established. Had not Cloots even claimed that he would not rest until there was a republic on the moon? For the present, Danton reminded his listeners, it was enough to try to save France. To do this he was prepared to undertake initiatives he had violently condemned a year before when the Republic was facing a similar situation. Like Dumouriez he hoped to detach the Prussians from the coalition. Though the Austrian Emperor was unlikely to negotiate, especially since his military position seemed powerful, Danton believed that the security of Marie-Antoinette might be used as a diplomatic card and so resisted demands from the Commune for her trial.

At the same time, he offered relatively magnanimous terms to the Isère and other departments which had been leaning towards federalism but which had prudently stopped short of military commitment. He even approached Montpellier with a view to deflecting the federalists' troops away from Paris and towards Lyon. In the Vendée, Biron had been appointed to see if there was any possibility of a political settlement. And another of Danton's allies, Westermann, was endeavoring to impose the discipline of the old professional army of the line on the sans-culotte generals. Finally, in Paris itself, Danton opposed the proposals for the economic Terror—extensive price controls, poor relief funded by draconian forced loans and taxes on the rich—that were emanating from the *enragés* and the Commune.

A startling appearance by Jacques Roux in the Convention on the evening of June 25 seemed to play into the hands of this pragmatism. He was accompanied by a group of sans-culottes and asked to read an address that had been adopted by the *sections* of Gravilliers and Bonnes-Nouvelles and the Cordeliers' Club. It was, in fact, a diatribe against its audience. "Legislators," he shouted at them, "you have done nothing for the happiness of the people. For four years only the rich have profited from the Revolution." The "commercial aristocracy, even more terrible than the nobility, has played a cruel game with . . . the treasure of the Republic." And what has been done to exterminate these "vampires"? Nothing. Has the death penalty against hoarding been enacted? Have the people been protected against brutal price rises created by speculators?

Roux was greeted with irritated fidgeting, organized coughing, forced sighs and rolling of the eyeballs to the ceiling. This was the kind of thing, Barère felt, they had to sit through in the name of humoring the sans-culottes. Five minutes into the speech, though, one particular remark of the orator-priest had them sitting bolt upright or standing indignantly, shouting back, waving papers at his audacity. It was, he had said, "the shame of the eighteenth century . . . that the representatives of the people had declared war on external tyrants but had been too cowardly to crush those within France [the rich]. *Under the old regime it would never have been permitted for basic commodities to be sold at three times their value*" (my emphasis). The new constitution would do nothing to remedy these miseries and the Convention continued to commit *lèse-nation* by allowing the *assignat* to fall and prepare the way for bankruptcy.

The imputation that the Republic was actually harsher toward the common people than the old monarchy had been was so shocking that it moved some of Roux's enemies (of whom there were many on virtually all sides of the Convention) to suggest that he had been put up to his attack by counter-revolutionaries. The offense was enough to get him arrested and for the Committee of General Security to run an aggressive campaign in Gravilliers that forced the *section* authorities to disown him. But in his disheveled sincerity Roux had in fact hit on an essential truth. Many of those whose violence in 1788 and 1789 had made Paris ungovernable, and thus allowed the Revolution to succeed, had never been much enamored of economic liberalism or individualism. Much of their anger had been a reaction against the unpredictable and impersonal operation of the market. They had clung to the traditional mind-set which saw in price rises and shortages the operation of a "famine plot" and, so far from wanting the state to dismantle all customary protection, wanted a *more* interventionist policy. They were not only indifferent, then, but actually hostile to much of the modernizing and reformist enterprise embarked on, first by the monarchy and then by successive revolutionary inheritor regimes.

This had put them at odds with the revolutionary elite, including most of the Jacobin leadership. As recently as February 1793, the grocery riots had provoked denunciations against popular price-fixing by the threat or reality of violence. By the summer, however, bread was being sold for six sous a pound and much of the *enragé* program—the death penalty for hoarders and speculators; price ceilings and enforced acceptance of the *assignat*—had become articles of faith, not just in the Cordeliers but in the Commune as well. Robespierre's speech the previous autumn, suggesting that property rights were not absolute but limited by a responsibility not to hurt the subsistence of others, opened the way for a serious change of heart among a section of the Jacobins themselves. Attacks on *"riches égoïstes"* and "bloodsuckers," and proposals for progressive taxes and forced levies on the rich to subsidize public-relief works and the price ceilings became commonplace.

Mid-July was a crucial turning point. Undercut by a succession of reverses and accumulating chaos, the Dantonist position crumbled. Westermann was recalled, possibly to face the Revolutionary Tribunal. The position was not helped by Danton's own casualness about defending himself and his allies in the Jacobins. When on July 10, in new elections, the Convention dropped him and his close colleague Lacroix from the membership of the Committee of Public Safety, he seemed not much put out. Indeed he showed visible relief at recovering his freedom of action outside the government. He may well have calculated that the position the Republic found itself in was so serious that no revolutionary government could survive without some further great upheaval.

Those calculations turned out to be seriously misplaced. Following the death of Marat, the stripped-down and rebuilt Committee of Public Safety rapidly turned itself into the most concentrated state machine France had ever experienced. It grasped the nettle of revolutionary government with a determination that had eluded all its predecessors. For the first time since Brienne, or indeed Chancellor Maupeou, the interests of the warrior state were given absolute priority over those of political expression. The Terror thus represented the liquidation of the initial dream of the Revolution: that liberty and patriotic power were not only reconcilable but mutually dependent. Accordingly, what had seemed the most irrepressible feature of the French Revolution—its political effervescence—was trapped inside the bottle of a national dictatorship. Politics had to end so that patriotism might conquer: that would be the founding creed of Bonapartism.

There were to be four elements to this new revolutionary state: a return to traditional economic regulation; the massive mobilization of military resources; the reabsorption into the state of the powers of punitive violence; and the replacement of spontaneous politics by a program of official ideology. (It is sobering to realize how all the items on this list could equally describe the France of Louis XIV.) The men who set themselves these tasks were, for once, ideally equipped for the work. Robespierre, Saint-Just and Georges Couthon were the ideologues, eloquent at representing the Committee to the Convention, carefully orchestrating the timing and intensity of judicial offensives designed to preempt flanking movements against the Committee, either from Danton's supporters to the right or Hébert's on the left. While Robespierre and Saint-Just provided high-flown incriminating rhetoric against "foreign plots," Bertrand Barère and Hérault de Séchelles organized the deputies of the Plain, without whose assent the dictatorship could not have been sustained. Another group in the Committee saw themselves as war bureaucrats: managers of logistics. Lazare Carnot and Prieur de La Côte d'Or were both engineers who devoted themselves to supplying the army, while Jeanbon Saint-André attended to the navy. Robert Lindet, the ex-priest, became the head of the Commission des Subsistances, moving huge supplies of food to the army and major centers of population. A year later, these two different visions of a France steeled in the fire of war would pull the Committee of Public Safety apart. To the bureaucrats and engineers—the inheritors of the monarchy's passion for technological government—Robespierre's Rousseauean concept of the Republic as an immense enterprise in moral instruction would seem not just farfetched, but actually subversive. For the next nine months, however, as the Republic steadily beat back its enemies, the division of labor among those who ran the Terror worked with surprisingly little friction.

A first priority was to neutralize centers of opposition. The highly democratic electoral provisions of the new constitution had the potential to decentralize power even further. So on August 11, a day after the festival celebrating its acceptance, a proposal to dissolve the Convention and hold new elections was indignantly brushed aside. And since successive revolutionary governments had fallen to disaffected groups prepared to sponsor or legitimate popular insurrections, the current contenders—Hébert's supporters in the Commune—had to be cut adrift from their rank and file in the *sections*. Just as Hébert and Chaumette had taken over *enragé* doctrine minus the *enragés*, so the Jacobins were now prepared to preempt the Hébertistes. This was not just a matter of political tactics. A decisive number on the Committee and in the Convention were convinced, by late July, that the kind of measures they had long resisted now were actually indispensable for the survival of the Republic.

On the twenty-sixth of July, for example, the Convention finally adopted Collot d'Herbois' proposal to institute the death penalty for hoarders. The same law itemized a long list of "goods of the first necessity" that included not just bread, salt and wine but butter, meat, vegetables, soap, sugar, hemp, wool, oil and vinegar. Anyone possessing stocks of this market basket was required to make a formal declaration to the authorities within eight days. With this information on hand municipalities could oblige wholesalers or retailers to put their wares on the market at any time on pain of being declared a "hoarder." On the ninth of August another giant step backwards to pre–Louis XVI practice was made when, on the urging of Léonard Bourdon (deputy for Gravilliers and thus especially concerned with preempting Jacques Roux), *"greniers d'abondance"* (grain storage silos) were instituted throughout the country. In times and places of good harvests, surplus grain was to be stored against years of shortage, when it could be released onto the market, helping to lower prices. This "revolutionary" act was more or less identical with one of the standard regulating institutions of the old regime. The only difference was that under the monarchy the provinces had had more authority to act on their own initiative than was now granted by the more paternalist economic Terror.

These measures presupposed, of course, a great network of information about crops and harvests that in turn implied an unprecedented intrusion into the rural economy by the bureaucratic state. Even the Terror had inadequate resources for this enormous exercise in snooping, and very often it degenerated into the sans-culotte *armées révolutionnaires,* sent to enforce the economic Terror, ransacking villages for concealed sacks of wheat or guarding fields, lest the peasants cut the crop while it was still green rather than surrender it at dictated prices.

Along the same lines, Cambon's answer to the depreciation of the *assignat* was to demonetize it, detaching it entirely from nominal values set by the old royal hard currency. In part this action was taken in deference to objections against money still bearing the King's likeness. But it was somehow hoped that by this crude sleight of hand producers would stop treating the *assignat* as a fraction of "real" money and so refrain from the inevitable upward adjustment of their prices. It was in keeping with this naive exercise in financial ideology that the Bourse was closed, officially putting out of work the "vile speculators" who infested the money market and unofficially creating an instant black market in hard money. At the same time, the state decided to restore secrecy surrounding decisions concerning the issue of money.

When the next revolutionary *journée* duly occurred on September 4–5, the orators of the Commune who demanded economic protection and aggressive punishment of malefactors found themselves knocking on an open door. Indeed, an important group of the Jacobins had actually spurred on the "insurrection" by holding a mass demonstration before the Convention on August 23, demanding a purge of nobles in the army, a more inclusive policy towards suspects, and a sans-culotte "revolutionary army" to enforce revolutionary laws in the departments. On the twenty-eighth, the Jacobins went so far as to "invite" the Paris *sections* to petition the Convention for those demands. All the evidence, then, points not to some anonymous and spontaneous movement bubbling up from the militant and the poor, but a carefully cultivated strategy. Though on the second of September Hébert made a specific appeal for the *sections* to join the Commune in petitioning the Convention, he seems to have been surprised two days later, when crowds of unemployed workers, mostly from the northeast *section* Temple, forced their way into the Hôtel de Ville.

The Commune's leaders did, however, turn the opportunity to their advantage. Chaumette got on a table in the General Council to declare that "we now have open war between the rich and the poor" and urged the immediate mobilization of the *armée révolutionnaire* to go into the countryside, uncover the machinations of the *malveillants* and the *riches égoïstes*, liberate food from their clutches and deliver them to republican punishment. For good measure Hébert added that each battalion should be accompanied by a mobile guillotine. This demand, he said, should be taken to the Convention the following day.

Since the Commune had also ordered the closure of workshops, it guaranteed that a large turnout would, as on May 31, surround the Convention. And while Robespierre in particular did not care to share his bench with the "People" he rhetorically embraced from the tribune, the day should not be read as the imposition of sans-culottism on a reluctant and frightened Convention. In fact the occasion was dominated not by the economic crisis but by the shattering news that Toulon had opened its harbor and city to the British fleet commanded by Admiral Hood. This created the atmosphere of patriotic emergency in which Danton and Barère thrived. It was no hard thing, then, to decree that "terror will be the order of the day," since the Convention and the Committee of Public Safety had a shrewd idea that they would be its executors.

As enacted, on September 5, the *armée révolutionnaire* was also a long way from being the mass squadrons of republican vengeance. Instead of the great sans-culotte army of a hundred thousand envisaged in the earliest petitions, or the thirty thousand demanded by the Commune, the Convention authorized a force of just six thousand infantrymen and twelve hundred cavalry to operate in the Paris region. (By the end of the year, however, the creation of departmental armies had raised the total number of troops to forty thousand, spread around the country.) It was also deprived of the kind of summary punitive powers Hébert had anticipated. For the Jacobins it was less a matter of launching a republican mission than exporting some of the most troublesome militants to the countryside and applying force to the crucial issue of food supply for the capital, thus disburdening themselves of two of their most intractable problems at the same time.

Following the same tactical route, Danton was particularly inspired in coming up with a scheme that appeared to be surrendering to the militants while it was actually taking the first decisive step to undermine their power base. He understood, perhaps from his own days in the "republic of the Cordeliers," that those who called themselves sans-culottes and purported to be of the common clay were not, by and large, the wage-earning poor. Indeed many of the leading *sectionnaires*—never more than 10 percent of the adult male population of their neighborhoods—were not even master artisans. They were predominantly petty-professionals, tradesmen, hack intellectuals and journalists, and they had achieved their ascendancy in the *sections* by sheer relentless assiduousness in the popular societies and the *section* assemblies as well as by staffing such local institutions as the revolutionary committees of surveillance. Turning their own populist rhetoric against them, Danton proposed ending the "permanence" of the *section* assemblies and instead limiting meetings to twice a week, when sans-culottes would be paid forty sous a day for attendance. Dressed up in patriotic imperatives this looked like a way to subsidize the participation of the common people in democratic politics. But what the Jacobins had in mind was exactly the opposite: the cultivation of a poor constituency that would be *less,* not more, susceptible to the Commune's control. They knew what they were doing. More money for less politics echoed precisely what the hard-pressed wage earner wanted to hear. And if he was slipped a little bonus here and there for spying for the Committee for General Security, or disrupting *sections* where the Hébertistes were strong, so much the better. All this could be reinforced by the decision (taken in the name of containing "anarchy") to replace the elected local revolutionary committees with appointed bodies, accountable to the executive committees of the Convention.

Far from being the high-water mark of popular democracy, September 5 was the beginning of the end of revolutionary insurrection in Paris. It was also the end of revolutionary innocence. Instead of being continually surprised by the contingencies and unforeseen consequences of their actions, the Jacobin elite had learned enough to manipulate the language and tactics of popular mobilization for the reinforcement, rather than the subversion, of state power. It was a Faustian moment.

With September 5 behind them, the Committee of Public Safety and the Convention could safely ignore some of the more extreme demands of the Commune. There would be no purge of all aristocratic army officers; the *armée révolutionnaire* would not have summary powers of surveillance, judgment and punishment, but would be restricted to enforcing the laws of the Convention. A *maximum* was applied to grain on September 11, and on the twenty-ninth the prices of forty grocery and household items were fixed at no more than one third above their level in 1790. But at the same time, the government equally reserved the right to set a *maximum* on wages. Predictably, the immediate results of this ambitious regulation were disastrous. As soon as the statutory prices were announced, thousands descended on the shops, picking them clean and thus creating an immediate shortage. Once inventories were exhausted, producers refused to supply new stock, and at least some hungry workers were employed as *vérificateurs* to make searches of shops, cellars and attics for hidden bars of soap or sacks of sugar.

Ultimately, such institutions as the *maximum*, the forty-sou subsidy and the *armée révolutionnaire* should be seen as improvised ways by which the Committee of Public Safety contained the political consequences of hunger. None of them, however, addressed the critical issue of military mobilization. The Revolution, after all, had begun as a patriotic argument about the inadequacies of the French state, and its latest custodians would stand or fall by the verdict of battle. Though later generations would flatter themselves into imagining that the French created a great "empire of laws" in the Europe they dominated for the next two decades, the nineteenth-century historian Gabriel Hanotaux was more accurate in describing it as "an empire of recruitment." For good or ill, it was as a military banner that the tricolor made its appearance from Lisbon to Cairo.

Of all the innovations of 1793, then, the *levée en masse*—the creation of a national conscript army—was by far the most important. Its success would determine the ability of the Republic to retake Lyon and the Vendée and to prevent the French rebels from linking up with foreign armies. It also provides another instance of an institution created in a fit of Romantic enthusiasm evolving into a professionally organized and highly disciplined arm of the state. The *levée* was born in desperation: an attempt to mobilize the population of areas immediately threatened with being overrun by the invader. At Lille in July, for example, a general conscription was proposed so that citizen-soldiers would "fall *en masse* like the Gauls on the brigand hordes." In August the *représentant-en-mission* and career soldier Milhaud, memorably painted by David, had the tocsin sounded in the area of Wissembourg in the Moselle. Peasants were given rudimentary drill and armed

188. Jacques-Louis David, General Milhaud as *représentant-en-mission*

(sometimes with nothing more than their pitchforks and hunting knives) to fall on the Austrians. "One alone killed seventeen Austrians," it was reported after the skirmish, "and women threw themselves into the battle with rifles."

In its original incarnation, then, the *levée* was meant to be a spontaneous explosion of martial enthusiasm involving large numbers of men, loosely organized and separated from the professional army. It need hardly be said that this version of anarchic belligerence did not recommend itself to the engineers and technologists of the Committee of Public Safety. But it was a nonmember, namely Danton, who in the third week of August tried to put the concept of a conscript army back on the rails by making its expansion strictly proportionate to the amount of munitions, clothing and food with which it could be supplied. The inspiring rhetoric of the Convention's decree on August 23 was less a prescription for an uncoordinated call to arms than a vision of a militarized commonwealth with every lever and pulley working in perfect mechanical articulation. The language drew heavily on Roman history but the vision was that of Guibert's total war.

> From this moment on, until the enemies have been chased from
> the territory of the Republic, all Frenchmen are in permanent
> requisition for the service of the armies. The young men will go
> to combat; married men will forge weapons and transport food;
> women will make tents and uniforms and will serve in the
> hospitals; children will make bandages from old linen; old men
> will present themselves at public places to excite the courage of
> the warriors, to preach hatred of kings and the unity of the
> Republic.

All bachelors and childless widowers between eighteen and twenty-five were conscripted in this call. There were no restrictions on height, though serious disabilities and sicknesses would disqualify a recruit from service. (The decree naturally provoked an immediate epidemic of mutilations.) No substitutes were officially permitted, although in practice brothers or friends over twenty-five were often allowed to serve in place of a recruit needed to work the farm. The most popular musical of the Paris theater in the year II (and indeed throughout the Revolution) was *Au Retour*, a melodrama. Even though the hero, Justin, will be twenty-five in three days—and so, overage for the draft—he refuses to wait. "It is *today* I must obey," he tells his tear-stained but admiring fiancée, Lucette. He even declines the offer of a young lad, not quite eighteen, to stand in for him, and goes off to war, exchanging cockades with Lucette as keepsakes. "Day and night we will keep it on our hearts," they warble. At the tear-jerking climax, a screen was lowered from the wings during the verses of the hit song and the whole audience stood to bid the conscript farewell with a chorus of "Au Retour." Notwithstanding this commendable selflessness, the exemption of married men produced a mass rush into conjugality in many departments. Local authorities had to rule on whether marriage *after* the decree would be allowed to stand as exemption. Usually it did, and so did marriage to a pregnant fiancée, even if the conception had postdated the decree. In keeping with Rousseauean doctrine on the sacred nature of the family, "It is not the legal condition but the act of paternity which constitutes marriage."

The vast majority of the recruits were, of course, peasants, and it was with this in mind that the Convention, in July, finally abolished, without compensation, the last vestiges of the seigneurial regime. Official propaganda tried to sweeten the serious loss of manpower to family farms that conscription represented by explaining that the armies of the Republic were defending the peasants' own interest. Should they lose the war, they could expect to see the return of the seigneurial regime, the priestly tithe and all manner of taxes which had been abolished by the Revolution, not to mention those parasites the bailiffs and stewards who had tabulated their services and evicted the delinquents. Worse still the "anthropophagi" (a favorite term in the year II for counter-revolutionaries) would exact a terrible revenge, seizing the peasants' property, enslaving or abducting their wives and daughters, cutting off the hands of anyone who had planted a liberty tree, ripping apart pregnant women.

This rather bleak picture of the penalties of defeat must have impressed many of the rural population to whom it was addressed. For while there were anticonscription riots in the Finistère, the Vosges, the Tarn, and the Ariège, none of them threatened to develop into "little Vendées." Though the most recent historian of the *levée*, J-P Berthaud, cautions about the difficulty of even guessing desertion and no-show rates, he estimates that these first waves of conscription probably raised some three hundred thousand men for the Republic. That was considerably less than the half million required by the Committee of Public Safety, but it was an extraordinary accomplishment nonetheless. During the autumn of 1793 villages and small towns throughout France witnessed the same sad ceremonies of departure. Two or three days after the Convention's proclamation had been publicly read and posted, a local commission would publish a list of men of draft age who were called and of those exempted. Weapons would be requisitioned and hastily adapted to take bayonets, and the little troop would move off under a temporarily appointed officer to the sound of drums, the crying of women, and the singing of the "Marseillaise." Small children would run alongside the line of un-uniformed men, waving little tricolor flags until the men disappeared over a hill towards the town where they would join other detachments bound for the brigades.

Once in camp, they would be subject to the competing influences of the professional *amalgame,* designed to integrate them with the regular troops of the line, and sans-culotte officers who wanted to keep them politically pure. The latter goal was helped by the fact that the Ministry of War remained an Hébertiste fief until quite late in 1793 and even took upon itself the spending of over a hundred thousand livres to distribute copies of the *Père Duchesne* gratis to the soldiers. Some units, in particular those serving in the Vendée, where the Hébertiste commanders were powerful, were even subjected to political lectures or given time off to attend meetings of the local Jacobin club, events from which many undoubtedly slipped away towards the nearest hostelry. Some commanders, among them General Houchard, insisted on wearing their liberty hats during councils of war (a gesture that did not spare Houchard from the guillotine), and for a while there was a movement to have officers elected for a specific term and then rotated amongst other men of the ranks. Should citizen-soldiers wish to write to their senior officers, they could begin their letter "*Salut et fraternité,* from your equal in rights."

This could not last. The *amalgame,* which combined forty conscript companies with twenty companies of the line in a single half-brigade, gradually came to exert its influence in professionalizing the recruits. Increasingly too, military discipline was restored by the intervention of *représentants-en-mission* and such members of the Committee of Public Safety as Prieur de La Marne and Carnot, who in their own right showed a remarkable grasp of the elements of strategy. The young Saint-Just, who made several trips to the Belgian front, was capable of draconian acts of punishment if he discovered looting or other acts of military disorder on which his excessively tidy mind frowned. More than once he had delinquent officers cashiered and shot in front of their own troops, *pour encourager les autres.*

All these efforts would have been in vain had not the government, at the same time, managed to supply its massively increased manpower with arms, food and clothing. Despite Danton's sensible warnings, it seems plain that recruitment did in fact run ahead of supplies; in the Vendée, in particular, the *bleus* were often much less well-equipped than their enemies, who had come off the farms and lacked the most basic necessities—especially, and most crucially, decent shoes (not to mention boots). By midautumn, however, the revolutionary state had committed itself to an all-out mobilization

189. Le Sueur, gouache drawing, the manufacture of arms in the year II

of resources that would not be seen again in Europe until the twentieth century. Advisory committees were formed from the chemists, engineers, and mathematicians who like Monge, Berthollet and Chaptal were ardent revolutionaries. The great metallurgical factories of Le Creusot and others at Charleville in the Vosges were effectively transformed into state enterprises turning out cannon, rifle, ball and shot to government specifications and contracts. Church bells from all over France were removed and taken to the foundries, some of them arriving at the open-air forges that had been set up in public parks in Paris, at the Invalides and the gardens of the Tuileries and the Luxembourg. By the spring of 1794 three thousand workers were producing seven hundred guns a day and, according to Bertrand Barère, six thousand workshops were busy making gunpowder.

Finally, Robert Lindet's provisioning agency, the Commission des Subsistances, working with what by the standards of the time was an enormous staff of over five hundred, used whatever authority or force was necessary to feed the armies. Inspirational propaganda was in order here too, with part of the Tuileries dug up and turned over to potatoes. In theory, at least, the soldiers of the Republic were entitled to a ration consisting of a pound and three quarters of bread, together with a few ounces of meat, beans or some other dried vegetable and wine or ale. If they were lucky they might get an onion and a slab of cheese, and where there was no brandy, gin or tobacco to start the day, the officers could expect trouble.

By the autumn of 1793 this enormous but still disjointed military machine had begun to make its force felt on several fronts. General Carteaux defeated the Marseillais army on August 25 and entered the city; those federalist leaders who could escape in time fled to Toulon. The siege of Lyon had begun early in August but it took two months before the military noose tightened enough to force the capitulation of the starving city on October 9. On the northern fronts the British advance was halted at Hondschoote on September 8 and the Austrians at Wattignies on October 16. Perhaps most important of all, the Vendéan armies had suffered their most serious defeat at Cholet on October 17.

This recovery was substantial enough to persuade the Convention and its committees that the Republic had come through its baptism of fire. Some of the Jacobins, notably Danton and Desmoulins, now saw no reason not to relax somewhat the institutional coercion of the Terror. Through journalism and oratory they created an *"Indulgent"* policy that was designed to resist show trials of Marie-Antoinette and the Girondins and work for a new elected legislature and a negotiated peace, based on the frontiers of 1792, with the Coalition powers.

After some initial success they were overwhelmed by a solid phalanx of opponents. Their most implacable adversaries were Hébert, Chaumette, Hanriot and the leaders of the Commune together with their supporters in the popular societies of the *sections*. Within the Committee of Public Safety, the *"Indulgent"* policy was opposed not only by its two most fanatically punitive members—Collot d'Herbois and Billaud-Varennes, who had been co-opted on September 5—but also by more bureaucratically minded members such as Carnot and the Prieurs, who thought it dangerously imprudent to loosen the Terror just at the point at which it seemed to have rescued the Republic from disaster.

On October 10 Saint-Just came before the Convention to issue a report in the name of the Committee of Public Safety on the "troubles affecting the state." He took the righteously self-scrutinizing line of declaring that the people had only one enemy, namely the government itself, infected as it was with all sorts of spineless, corrupt and compromised creatures of the old regime. The remedy was unremitting austerity of purpose, implacable punishment for the backsliders and the hypocrites. The charter of the Terror—the Law of Suspects, enacted on September 17, which gave the Committee and its representatives sweeping powers of arrest and punishment over extraordinarily broad categories of people defined as harboring counter-revolutionary designs—should be applied with the utmost rigor. "Between the people and their enemies there can be nothing in common but the sword; we must govern by iron those who cannot be governed by justice; we must oppress the tyrant. . . . It is impossible for revolutionary laws to be executed unless the government itself is truly revolutionary."

A new Sparta was needed. Citizens must be ever vigilant; the representatives on mission must be the "fathers and friends of the soldier," sleeping in the same tent, sharing their food, frugal and inflexible. The Republic had to be terrible if it was to prevail, and those who governed must never, ever relax their guard. "Those who would make revolutions in the world," said Saint-Just, the very clay from which Leninism was to be shaped, "those who want to do good in this world must sleep only in the tomb."

iii OBLITERATIONS

The Jacobin Republic wore two expressions: the bullying scowl of the *Terroriste* and the serene countenance of its official icons. In the parts of France touched by federalism, or reluctant to yield up their grain to the cities, the Terror arrived as a disruptive and brutal presence. A *représentant-en-mission* such as Claude Javogues, who operated in the Loire, was capable of sudden acts of violence, punching people in the face whom he suspected or simply disliked. Riled up, drunk, or both, he could use his unchallenged powers in the department to stage elaborate humiliations or subject local officials to torrents of abuse. A petition from some farmers that incurred his displeasure was torn to shreds and then trampled underfoot by his horse, after which Javogues set about the farmers with the flat of his saber. Having kept a line of prisoners from Montbrison (renamed, after its conquest by the Republic, Montbrisé—Broken Mountain) waiting two hours in the snow, he told the judge of the Revolutionary Tribunal, "How I will relish the pleasure of having all these buggers guillotined." In the town itself, he said, "One day blood will flow like water in the streets after a great downpour."

At Saint-Etienne, Javogues presided over a public session of the municipality, convened to impose "revolutionary taxes" on the better-off citizens, while mauling pretty girls placed next to him and emptying thirty bottles of beer and wine. When one of the public made a comment on the arbitrary nature of the taxes, Javogues shouted to the officer of the guard, "*Sacré mille foutre!* Arrest that bugger over there so that I can have him shot." At a woman, described in the shocked report as "*une vieille fille*" and who protested that she had been assessed at more than her whole fortune, he launched into an obscene tirade. "You're a bitch [*garce*], a whore, you've screwed more priests than I have hairs on my head; your cunt's so big I could get all of myself in there," and more in this vein.

Javogues' behavior was extreme, even by the standards of the anarchic period of the Terror between September and December 1793. To the more prim Jacobins who would eventually bring him down, it may have seemed especially scandalous, since he was hardly someone who had grown up in the gutter. His father had been a lawyer and a *conseiller du roi* at Montbrison, where he had a house in one of the richest quarters of town. Like so many given sudden power in the autumn of the year II, Javogues obviously enjoyed playing the role of hometown avenging angel, throwing dirt in the faces of the local *bourgeois* and peasants. Others from backgrounds of real hardship used their new position to exact specific revenge from those who they felt had been the authors of their misery under the old regime. Nicolas Guénot, for example, who had been employed in the terrible work of floating logs down the Yonne to the wharves and sawmills of Paris, became an agent for the police organ of the Convention, the Committee for General Security. In that capacity he sent a number of well-to-do merchants he discovered from his old neighborhood in Paris to the tribunal, before he himself was arrested.

Often the bark of these men was a good deal worse than their bite. But the mercurial, arbitrary manner in which they exercised their jurisdiction still seemed outrageous to politicians in Paris whose image of the Jacobin Republic was intensely moral. To such puritans as Robespierre and Saint-Just, the drunken rampages of such men as Javogues disgraced revolutionary authority so badly that they supposed that the latter must be working for the counter-revolution. The situation was particularly galling since, while Javogues had his hands inside the shirts of citizenesses (sometimes in public), the custodians of official Jacobinism were trying to make an icon out of the republican breast: fecund, innocent and generous. Boizot's *La France Républicaine,* for example, is a secular reworking of traditional images of the Virgin Mary in which the exposure of the breast signified her intercession before Christ on behalf of the sinful. In the Jacobin version, the exhibition is an emblem of egalitarian inclusiveness. The equality of "all Frenchmen" regenerated by the nurturing breasts of the Republic is symbolized by the strategically hung carpenter's level, while the dawn of freedom is represented by another traditional Gallic emblem, the rooster.

Jacobin iconography was a reprise of all the standard themes of prerevolutionary *sensibilité*: domesticity, the purity of rustic labor, the mutual benevolence of liberty and prosperity. In a typical version of this idyll, an idealized sans-culotte family, the plow by their side, stand before two incarnations of France. Beneath the benign light of the ubiquitous eye of surveillance, industry, symbolized by the beehive, is represented as the source of the horn of plenty, spilling its fruits on the ground while the

190. A. Clément (after Boizot), *La France Républicaine*

191. Anonymous, "The Virtues of the Republic"

Republic holds the standard devices of liberty and equality along with the Rights of Man.

As trite and repetitious as these images were, they represented a systematic attempt by the propagandists of Jacobin culture to build a new, purified public morality. The nation would not be truly secure until those whom it comprised internalized the values on which it had been reconstructed. Inheriting from Rousseau (albeit in garbled form) the doctrine that government was a form of educational trust, the guardians of the Revolution meant to use every means possible to restore to a nation corrupted by the modern world the redemptive innocence of the presocial child. On the ruins of monarchy, aristocracy and Roman Catholicism would sprout a new natural religion: civic, domestic and patriotic. Songs and public festivals, necessarily held out of doors, would bring together citizens in communities of harmony. Theater would become more participatory, drawing audiences into its inspirational histories. But it was to images, in their broadest sense, that the Jacobin evangelicals paid special attention. Fabre d'Eglantine, for example, Danton's poet friend (and accomplice in peculation), used sense-impression theory from the Enlightenment to convince the Convention that "we conceive nothing except by images: even the most abstract analysis or the most metaphysical formulations can only take effect through images."

There was, then, an organized endeavor to replace the visual reference points of the old France with a whole new world of morally cleansed images. The public Salon of 1793, for example, featured, along with David's two martyrologies, innumerable paintings in which domestic and patriotic virtues were fused. The "Woman of the Vendée," for instance, in many versions, blows up herself and her family rather than surrender powder to the "brigands." Child-heroes became important, among them the "young Darruder," who picked up his father's weapon on the field of battle and charged the enemy with it. At the level of popular art, tradesmen were encouraged to exhibit their patriotism by displaying "civic boards" outside their shops in place of the traditional signs. Even playing cards were subjected to this *épuration,* the queen of hearts being transformed into "Liberty of the Arts" while the king was a sans-culotte general.

The most serious attempt to create a new "empire of images," in Fabre's arrestingly modern term, was the invention of the revolutionary calendar. This was also an attempt to reconstruct time through a republican cosmology. The special commission appointed to make recommendations was a peculiar mixture of literary men such as Fabre Romme and Marie-Joseph Chénier and serious scientists such as Monge and Fourcroy. Together they saw the reform as an opportunity to detach republicans from the superstitions they thought embodied in the Gregorian calendar. Their efforts were directed especially at the rural world, to which the vast majority of Frenchmen still belonged. In keeping with the cult of nature, the twelve months were to be named not just after the changing weather (as experienced in northern and central France) but in poetic evocations of the agricultural year. The first month (which necessarily began with the founding of the Republic in late September) was the time of the *vendange,* the wine harvest, and thus was called *Vendémiaire.* The voluptuous incarnations of Salvatore Tresca's calendar illustrations would, they calculated, make a happy change from St. Mark, the patron of the vineyard. Fabre was explicit about detaching the cultivator from the superstitions by which he sought the blessing of priests for his crops and livestock. There would be no more of the nonsense by which the Church said, "It is through us your granaries are full; believe us, obey and you will be rich. Disobey, and frost, hail and thunder will blacken your crops." The frontispiece to Millin's *Annuaire Républicain* (fig. 195) made explicit the vanquishing of the old Gregorian tyrannies by the simplicity of rural husbandry.

Fabre and the commission were not content just to provide a new nomenclature. Each of the twelve months—for example, *Brumaire,* the misty month; *Frimaire,* the cold month—was divided into three ten-day units, the *décadis,* and each of those days was also renamed. In place of the

192. Anonymous, "The Woman of the Vendée"

193. Playing cards of the year II

194. Salvatore Tresca (after Laffitte), *Vendémiaire* from the republican calendar

daily associations of the old sacred calendar, Millin's almanac provided objects of bucolic virtue for daily contemplation. These consisted of crops, vegetables, fruit and flowers on weekly days, an agricultural implement on the tenth-day *décadi* and an agricultural animal every fifth day. For the third *décade* of Fructidor—the transition between summer and autumn—the calendar, for example, prescribed:

> eglantine rose
> hazelnut
> hops
> sorghum
> CRAYFISH (fifth day)
> Seville orange
> goldenrod
> maize
> chestnut
> BASKET

Each object listed in this calendrical veneration of nature was, Fabre said, "more precious in the eyes of reason than some skeletons found in the catacombs of Rome."

After twelve months, each of thirty days, there would be five remaining days left in the year, named by Fabre *sans-culottides*, and, lest he seem too deferential to the *section* militants, he provided an implausibly erudite justification. Ancient Gaul, he claimed, had been divided into *Gallia braccata*—the breeched half, which was (of course) the region around Lyon; and unbreeched Gaul, which was the rest of ancient France. So that, as historical good fortune would have it, the free Franks were already in some sense sans-culottes. The five days would be devoted to festivals, respectively, of talent *(génie)*, industry, heroic deeds and ideas *(opinions)*. This restructuring of republican time was to be completed every four years by a great occasion of patriotic games and athletics, held on the "day of the Revolution" (presumably, August 10).

Though it seems unlikely that the peasants appreciated the replacement of Sunday and "Saint Monday" by the single *décadi*, coming as it did once every ten days, rather than every seven, the revolutionary calendar was one of the more enduring elements of republican culture, surviving by twelve years the fall of the Jacobins. But although it became accepted as a rather innocuous element of the new France, its introduction was an integral part of a much more aggressive program of iconoclasm. Three days after the calendar had been voted in the Convention, Thuriot told the Jacobins, "It

195. The republican calendar vanquishing the Gregorian calendar

196. J-G Wille, *Les Moustaches Républicaines ou les Bons Patriotes.* Soldiers in the *armées revolutionnaires* lovingly cultivated their whiskers as part of the appurtenances of Terror—or so it seemed to the peasants among whom they were billeted.

is time, since we have arrived at the summit of the principles of a great revolution, to reveal the truth about all types of religions. All religions are but conventions. Legislators make them to suit the people they govern. . . . It is the moral order of the Republic, of the Revolution, that we must preach now, that will make us a people of brothers, a people of *philosophes.*"

In practice, however, dechristianization owed less to these high-flown principles and more to the anticlericalism, especially violent in Paris and the Midi, that had played a crucial role in radicalizing the politics of the Revolution. It was carried to the departments by the agents of the Terror who fanned out in the autumn of the year II to bring orthodoxy to disaffected regions of France. They were supported by local Jacobin militants who had either been harassed during the federalist ascendancy or who simply enjoyed showing off their anticlerical zeal. The *armées révolution-naires* were, predictably, the agents of the most chaotic and brutal attack on clerical culture. Their Parisian headquarters on the rue Choiseul was dominated by theater people: such actors as Grammont and such playwrights as Ronsin, who brought virtually all of the Montansier troupe into the staff with them. They had a long tradition of loathing the Church, which had constantly interfered with the stage and which they had enjoyed pillorying since 1789.

But the most unruly demonstrations of dechristianizing zeal probably happened more or less spontaneously. When a regiment of the army, two thousand strong, arrived at Auxerre en route to Lyon, for example, the cannoneers smashed in church doors and mutilated images and statues of saints. A crucifix was taken from the chapel of Mary and paraded about upside down for citizens to spit on. When a local quarryman refused to do this, one of the soldiers cut off a part of his nose with his saber. On arriving at Clermont-Ferrand, a gang of soldiers, many of them ironworkers from the *section* du Luxembourg, whose officer called them his "Vulcans," went directly to the cathedral and

> there with terrible vigorous blows they swooped on St. Peter, smashed Saints Paul, Luke and Matthew . . . all the angels and the archangel Raphael himself, the winged fowl of the celestial band, the beautiful Mary, who bore three children while remaining a virgin . . .

More orderly forms of dechristianization were provided by such *représentants-en-mission* as the ex-Oratorian priest Fouché, who undertook a particularly enthusiastic campaign in the Nièvre, where he stripped cemeteries of all religious symbols and posted on the gates his famous dictum "Death is but an eternal sleep." Such campaigns often began with formal resignations of the constitutional clergy, accompanied by public declarations of their "fraud" and folly. In the Hérault, for example, Jean Radier, the *curé* of Lansargue, announced that since he now knew that "the occupation of priest is contrary to the happiness of the people, retards the progress of knowledge, and impedes the march of the Revolution, I hereby abdicate and throw myself into the arms of society." Along with these formal renunciations there were often marriage ceremonies for ex-priests (sometimes involuntary) and, especially in the Midi and the Rhone Valley, burlesque charivaris in which donkeys were dressed in a bishop's robes and miter and led through the streets. Sometimes mannequins of the Pope would be burned after a similar ceremony of ridicule. Like much else in the violent popular politics of the Revolution, these inversion rites were not fresh inventions but traditional practices crudely modernized for the purposes of the day.

The churches themselves were often stripped of all sacerdotal objects. There were, in any case, urgent practical reasons for this despoliation. Church bells were needed for the arms foundries, gold and silver for the Republic's treasury, though a great deal of the latter certainly found its way into the pockets of the dechristianizers. But there was also pure vandalism on a massive scale. Altarpieces were slashed, stained-glass windows broken.

In Amplepuis, in the Haute-Beaujolais, a liberty tree replaced the crucifix in the crossing of the church. In many other places devotional manuals and hymnals were burned in great bonfires, together with the plaster and wood saints found on every road crossing, crackling and melting in the flames like inanimate victims of an auto-da-fé.

The climax of this extraordinary onslaught on Christian practice occurred in the second week of November. A delegation including Anacharsis Cloots and Léonard Bourdon went to see Gobel, the constitutional Bishop of Paris, got him out of bed and obliged him to abdicate in the Convention the following day (November 7). Letters were read, including one from the *curé* of Boissise-la-Bétrand in the Seine-et-Marne that began, "I am a priest, a *curé*, that is to say a *charlatan*; up to now a *charlatan* in good faith, for I have deceived no-one but myself." Gobel then announced that "there should be no other public cult than liberty and holy equality" and duly resigned, followed by Julien, a Protestant pastor from Toulouse, who declared that "the same destiny awaited every virtuous man whether he adores the God of Geneva, Rome, Mahomet or Confucius."

Three days later a festival was held in Notre Dame, *débaptisée* the Temple of Reason. In the interior a gimcrack Greco-Roman structure had been erected beneath the Gothic vaulting. A mountain made of painted linen and papier-mâché was built at the end of the nave where Liberty (played by a singer from the Opéra), dressed in white, wearing the Phrygian bonnet and holding a pike, bowed to the flame of Reason and seated herself on a bank of flowers and plants. Mercier went to see similar ceremonies organized by the Commune, in Saint-Gervais, where the church "smelled of herring," and Saint-Eustache, where actresses trod on creaking planks beneath stage scenery of woodland cottages and rocky escarpments. Around the choir he was horrified to see "bottles, sausages, *andouilles*, pâtés and other meats."

In Paris, the Jacobins were divided over dechristianization. Hébert's supporters were enthusiasts, none more so than the self-styled "printer of liberty" Momoro. Danton had complained about rhetorical excesses but had then asked the Convention at the end of October to grant him leave to retire to his home in Arcis. But some of his allies, such as Thuriot, were conspicuous dechristianizers, possibly to fight accusations that they were going soft on the Revolution. Robespierre, on the other hand, was deeply shocked by what he took to be the immorality of an assault that pretended to pass itself off as a "philosophy." The festivals of Reason, he thought, were "ridiculous farces," staged by "men without honor or religion." To Fouché's cemetery notice he retorted that death was not just "eternal sleep" but "the beginning of immortality." It was probably his influence that prevented the Convention from accepting the invitation to go en masse to Notre Dame.

In Lyon, on the other hand, Fouché's authority to conduct dechristianizing ceremonies went unchecked. As one of the *représentants-en-mission* in the city reconquered from the federalists at the beginning of October, he was given virtually dictatorial powers. He began by removing all traces of Christian iconography from the medieval clock tower of Saint-Cyr and replacing them with the revolutionary calendar. On the tenth of November, Chalier's remains were borne in triumph through the streets (his head was later dispatched to Paris to receive the honors of the Panthéon, as had Marat). An ass, dressed in the robes and miter of Lamourette, the constitutional bishop (he who had orchestrated the "fraternal kiss" in the Legislative in 1792), and with a Bible and a missal tied to its tail, was followed by cartloads of church vessels that, at the end of the procession, were solemnly smashed over Chalier's tomb. Drinking from an enormous chalice, Grandmaison, one of the most uncontrollable of the Jacobin exterminating angels, parodied the communion liturgy: "Verily I say to you, my brothers, this is the blood of kings, the true substance of republican communion, take and drink this precious substance."

Three weeks later a *fête de Raison* was held in the Cathedral of Saint-Jean, at which republican officials bowed before a statue of Liberty and sang an antihymn to words by Fouché celebrating "Reason as the Supreme Being."

Lyon, however, had lost more than its church. After a long siege during which outlying satellite towns such as Saint-Etienne were evacuated, the famished, shell-shocked city capitulated on October 9 to the republican armies that encircled it. The *muscadins* of Lyon, like their counterparts at Marseille and Toulon, had not declared, as had the Vendéan rebels, for the old monarchy, but for the constitution of 1791. At one point, in fact, their commander, de Précy, had told the federalist municipality that he wanted to support a "Republic, one and indivisible." His reputation in Paris, though, was of an aristocrat who had fought on the wrong side in the battle for the Tuileries on the tenth of August 1792. As a result, the city was subjected to something akin to a colonial occupation. To suggestions that the city might be treated as leniently as Bordeaux, Robespierre fulminated, "No, their memory [of Chalier and those who had been arrested with him] must be avenged and these monsters unmasked and exterminated," adding, as usual, "Otherwise I myself will perish."

It was Robespierre's friend and loyal supporter the crippled Georges Couthon who, with two other colleagues, Châteauneuf-Randon and Delaporte, was first responsible for re-Jacobinizing the rebel city. On October

779

13 he wrote to Saint-Just that a wholesale regeneration was called for. People needed to be taught their "alphabet" all over again, but this would not be easy because the local population "are stupid by temperament since the mists of the Rhone and Saône carry into the atmosphere a fog which enshrouds clear ideas." They should be given strong republican medicine: "a purge; a vomit and an enema."

He wasted no time in applying this treatment. After reinstating the municipality removed on May 29 and reopening the popular clubs, Couthon, in his first decree, on October 12, announced the Convention's policy of wiping Lyon off the map of the Republic. Henceforth it would be known as "Ville-Affranchie" (Liberated Town). The houses of the rich and anyone associated with the crime of rebellion would be demolished, leaving only those of the poor. On their ruins a column would be erected bearing the legend

Lyon fit la guerre à la liberté	Lyon made war on liberty
Lyon n'est plus	Lyon is no more

On the twenty-sixth of October, Couthon was carried in his invalid's chair, on the shoulders of four sans-culottes, to the place Bellecour, the most famous and elegant parade of eighteenth-century townhouses built at the beginning of Louis XVI's reign. In a surprisingly powerful voice that belied his disability, Couthon declared to the crowd that the houses had been condemned to death "as habitations of crime where royal magnificence affronts the misery of the people and the simplicity of republican manners. May this terrible example strike fear into future generations and teach the universe that just as the French nation, always great and just, knows how to reward virtue, so it also knows how to abhor crime and punish rebellion." With that, he raised a silver mallet, custom-made for the occasion, and struck a wall three times, pausing solemnly between each blow, like the great raps on the floor that announced the beginning of a play in French theaters. Hundreds of workers, including women and children, many of them from the depressed silk industry, ran forward with sledge-hammers and pickaxes to inaugurate the demolition. Fifteen thousand people would be employed on this work before it was completed, paid by a six-million-livre tax on the rich. Sixteen hundred houses were demolished, including many in the Bourgneuf quartier, through which a new road to Paris was being built. Most important of all for the Republic, the fortifications that had served the federalists so well were razed, including the old Roman-medieval citadel of Pierre-Scize.

When the demolitions were reported to the Convention, not all deputies were happy with the policy. Most of the members of the Mountain had a deep respect for property, and one of them, the silk merchant Cusset, who had been born in Lyon, asked rhetorically, "Is it republican to tear down houses?" It was not houses, after all, he pointed out, but men who had fought against the Republic. How much better to follow the precedent of the Romans, who, on entering conquered cities, did not complete their destruction but on the contrary restored them to new grandeur and prosperity.

The mood in Paris, however, was not much disposed towards magnanimity. At the end of October, Couthon was recalled and Fouché and Collot d'Herbois, who replaced him, substituted for his surrogate violence against property rather than people, much more direct forms of retribution. For Collot, the actor, stage manager and author of *Lucie, or the Imprudent Relatives,* it was a return to a scene of mixed notices. In 1782 he had been welcomed to the Théâtre des Terraux (which looked onto the square where the guillotine had been set up) by the *intendant* de Flesselles. But his relations with the theater management, the local critics and the audience had not been warm. A good portion of them were about to learn the penalties of tepid applause. Collot's general view of republican justice was ominously summarized in his remark, "The rights of man are made, not for counter-revolutionaries but only for sans-culottes."

Together with Fouché, Collot decided that Couthon's approach had been too fastidious. A mere twenty to thirty executions, most of them confined to officers in the federalist army and the most prominent members of the municipality, had taken place in October. This was to change dramatically. A Temporary Commission was set up to reinforce the local agents of revolutionary justice who were suspect for their leniency. Its leading figure was Mathieu Parein, a lawyer (and son of a master saddler), a friend of Ronsin's and like him promoted with improbable swiftness to the rank of brigadier general in the *armée révolutionnaire.* He came to Lyon from the Vendée, where he had presided over a Revolutionary Tribunal at Angers, and the declaration published by the Commission bears the mark of his steely temperament as well as that of Fouché, with whom he predictably got along very well. It announced a regime of swift and massive punishment, encouraged denunciation (partly by a tariff of rewards with special bonuses for aristocrats and priests), and made a direct and unsparing attack on the rich, instituted through forced levies. Those, for example, whose income amounted to thirty thousand livres or more were required to pay a capital sum of thirty thousand livres immediately. All vestiges of organized religion would be obliterated, since "the republican has no other dignity than his *patrie.*"

The Terror went into action with impressive bureaucratic efficiency. House searches, usually made at night, were extensive and unsparing. All

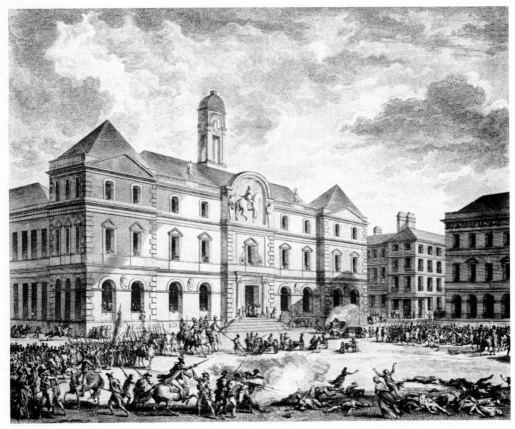

197. Duplessis-Bertaux has unhistorically set the scene of the *mitraillades* in the center of Lyon instead of the Plaine des Brotteaux, but note the cannon in the center of the engraving.

citizens were required to attach to their front doors a notice indicating all residents who lived inside. Entertaining anyone not on that list, even for a single night, was a serious crime. Denunciations poured into the Commission. People were accused of defaming Chalier, of attacking the liberty tree, secreting priests or émigrés, making speculative fortunes and—one of the standard crimes of the year II—writing or uttering *"merde à la république."* From early December the guillotine went into action at a much greater tempo. As in Paris, pride was taken in its mechanical efficiency. On the eleventh of Nivôse, according to the scrupulous accounts kept, thirty-two heads were severed in twenty-five minutes; a week later, twelve heads in just five minutes.

For the most eager Terrorists, though, this was still a messy and inconvenient way of disposing of the political garbage. Citizens in the streets around the place des Terreaux, on the rue Lafont, for example, were complaining about the blood overflowing the drainage ditch that led from beneath the scaffold. A number of the condemned, then, were executed in mass shootings on the Plaine des Brotteaux—the field beside the Rhone where Montgolfier had made his ascent. Yet another ex-actor, Dorfeuille, presided over some of these *mitraillades,* in which as many as sixty prisoners were tied in a line by ropes and shot at with cannon. Those who were not killed outright by the fire were finished off with sabers, bayonets and rifles. On the fourth of December, Dorfeuille wrote to the President of the Convention that a hundred and thirteen inhabitants of "this new Sodom" had been executed on that single day and in those that followed he hoped another four to five hundred would "expiate their crimes with fire and shot." Three days later, the barber-surgeon Achard wrote delightedly to his brother in Paris: "Still more heads and every day more heads fall! What pleasure you would have experienced if, the day before yesterday, you had seen national justice meted out to two hundred and nine villains. What majesty! What imposing tone! How completely edifying. How many of those grand fellows have that day bitten the dust [literally: *mordu la poussière*] in the arena of Brotteaux. What cement for the Republic." "PS," he added jovially, "say hello to Robespierre, Duplay and Nicolas."

By the time that the killings in "Ville-Affranchie" had finished, one thousand nine hundred and five people had met their end. They included, of course, many of the Lyonnais notability—among them the seventy-five-year-old Albanette de Cessieux; Laurent Basset, the lieutenant of the old royal *Sénéchaussée* de Lyon; and Charles Clermont-Tonnerre. Aristocratic army officers, members of the rebel department of Rhone-et-Loire, federalist magistrates and priests were all high on the list, as was anyone who could be associated with the capacious category "the rich," with "merchants" or with any tradesmen or manufacturers accused by sansculottes of economic crimes. That still, however, left a vast number of the condemned who were quite ordinary types, presumably the *sectionnaires* who had supported the Girondins against Chalier, but who came from backgrounds identical to their Jacobin counterparts' in Paris. (While the well-off were disproportionately represented in the death roll, the notion that the rich were being executed by the poor in Lyon seems to be pure myth.) If there were many silk manufacturers among the condemned, there were also no fewer than forty journeymen weavers. Trades that provided pro-Jacobin militants in Paris, such as those of hatters, cabinet makers, tailors and grocers, supplied the anti-Jacobin rank and file in Lyon. Other occupations represented were locksmiths, cobblers, coopers, innkeepers, café owners, waiters, brewers (in some numbers); vinegar makers, lemon-

198. Anonymous, Collot d'Herbois and the
republican triumph in Lyon

ade vendors, bookkeepers, architects; chocolate makers; butchers, bakers
and candle makers; doctors, the director of the bureau of wet nurses;
coachmen, domestic servants; dyers, hosiers; muslin workers; two drummers, two other "musicians"; three actors (who, one hopes, had not crossed
Collot in the green room); wigmakers, haberdashers, seamstresses; painters,
two women's hairdressers; a herbalist; a boatman, printers, a twenty-year-
old mathematics student; a coal miner; the fishwife Pierrette Butin; a pastry
cook, a public scribe, notaries; lawyers, a number of young men listed as
"unemployed" and the forty-five-year-old Jacqueline Chataignier, who
went down classified simply, but for the purposes of the tribunal, adequately, as "*fanatique.*" Among the last batch to be guillotined were the
executioner Jean Ripet and his assistant, whose hard work over the months
did not succeed in sparing them. A colleague from Clermont-Ferrand was
specially summoned for the job.

Since many Lyonnais had also died under the saturation bombardment
of the siege, an entire microcosm of Lyon society had been annihilated. The
trauma left scars that took several generations to heal and that, even today,

make its citizens less than radiantly warm on the subject of Paris and the Parisians. But because of the long-term importance of the great silk *fabrique* and the enormous expansion of markets created by the Napoleonic Empire, Lyon managed a partial recovery of its economic vitality. In some ways, the economic fate of the federalist port cities of Marseille, Bordeaux and Toulon, though they mercifully escaped mass executions on the scale of Lyon, was more permanently crippling.

In Ville-Sans-Nom (Town Without Name), as Marseille was now called, the *représentants-en-mission* Barras and Fréron seemed just as bent on a wholesale purge as Fouché and Collot. "Marseille," they wrote, "is the original and primordial cause of nearly all the evils that have afflicted the *patrie.*" And like Couthon they borrowed from Montesquieu a geographical theory to account for its recalcitrance. "By its very nature," Marseille regarded itself as apart: "The mountains, the rivers which separate it from the rest of France, its own language all feed federalism; . . . they want laws for themselves; they see only Marseille; Marseille is their country; France is nothing." And their conclusion was the same as Couthon's. The stubborn localism was to be uprooted by ripping out the commercial elite who were at the core of the city's prosperity and pride. The Revolutionary Tribunal that performed this work was, however, a good deal more attentive to legal forms than the one in Lyon. Of the 975 prisoners who appeared before it, almost half were acquitted. Among the 412 who were condemned to death was the cream of local society: men whose status and fortunes straddled the nobility and the bourgeoisie in precisely the manner so characteristic of *ancien régime* capitalism. They included, for example, Joseph-Marie Rostan, who was noble by birth but who described himself as a *commerçant,* who lived in the elegant rue Solon and who owned soap factories, warehouses, dwellings, and stock in Black Sea wool, colonial sugar and coffee. "I do not know if I am a noble," he told the tribunal. "I have gloried in being a merchant." His bewilderment at being socially stigmatized is an eloquent testimony to the anticapitalism of the Jacobin revolution. Rostan assumed that by professing himself to be a merchant, he would dilute the accusation of nobility, when in the eyes of his prosecutors his profession actually compounded it. Many others like him, including Antoine Chegarry, Jean-Joachim Dragon and Honoré-Philippe Magnon, the magistrates of the old tribunal of commerce, fell to the same condemnation.

Not all of France suffered in this way. Thirty-five years ago Donald Greer showed that 90 percent of all the executions during the Terror took place in only twenty of the eighty-six departments. All of those areas, excepting Paris, which had a special status in the matter, were war zones: either the theater of combat against the Coalition, the federalist strongholds of the Midi or the Rhone Valley and the western insurrection with its core in the Vendée. In thirty departments there were fewer than ten executions. During the hell of the Terror in Lyon and Nantes, there were major cities of France such as Grenoble and Besançon that, through the careful pragmatism of their public guardians and the simple good fortune of being out of the way of a war zone, were spared much of the domestic violence of the year II. There were other, smaller towns in the federalist orbit which remained conspicuously obedient to the Republic—not least because their relationship to Lyon or Bordeaux was as envenomed as the sentiment the big cities had towards Paris. The immediate threat to their food supplies came not from Paris or the armies but from their big neighbor. So on the principle that their enemy's enemy was their friend, such towns as Clermont-Ferrand and Le Puy were fertile recruiting ground for the *bleus* who descended on Lyon.

In countless other places the Terror barely lived up to its name. The proceedings of the Revolutionary Tribunal in the Meurthe, for example, which according to Greer recorded ten to fifty executions, does not make for sensational reading. Though Saint-Just and his colleague *en mission* Lebas had set up a special commission to levy forced loans on the rich, in the department outside the *chef-lieu*, Nancy, the Terror petered out in inconsequentiality. A twenty-year-old ex-postilion serving with the hussars is court-martialed for kissing the fleur-de-lis on his old uniform. Three peasants are accused of making off with a cartload of oats they were supposed to deliver to the army and spoiling another load by mixing it with straw and manure, but are acquitted for lack of decisive evidence. A fisherman is tried in December 1793 for shouting "*Vive* Louis XVI" but since he also shouted "To the devil with the Catholic religion, bring Mohamedanism to France" it was concluded that he was drunk, mad or both. In January a twenty-two-year-old soldier named Vattel declared in public, "When I served the King I had money, now I serve the Nation and I am never paid and am miserable," but spoiled this undeniable if dangerous truth by adding, "So I shit on the Nation. . . . I am not a citizen and will die for my king," an ambition he was duly permitted to fulfill. For every Vattel, though, there was an equal number of his opposite in these village dramas—for instance, Nicolas Tronquart, a schoolmaster at Lunéville who was arrested not for royalism but utopianism (specifically, for preaching the *loi agraire,* the division of all agricultural land among the peasantry).

The Terror, then, was highly selective in its geography. The harshness of its impact critically turned on the assiduousness or laxity of the *représentants-en-mission;* the seriousness with which the local revolutionary committees took their duties; the militancy of the popular societies;

whether or not a town was on the route of the *armées révolutionnaires*, and for that matter how long the *armées* stayed in a particular region. Yet if it is important not to generalize from the experience of Lyon and Marseille, it is just as important not to relativize the Terror so that it becomes merely a set of lurid anecdotes, marginal to the history of some notionally "average" town. For if it operated with crushing effect on areas that were indeed the centers of war or revolt, those same areas happened to be exactly on the economically dynamic periphery of France. Though the Jacobins, as every history relentlessly points out, were great respecters of property, their war was a war against commercial capitalism. They may not have intended it that way at the beginning, but their incessant rhetoric against "rich egoists" and the incrimination of the commercial and financial elites in federalism meant that, in practice, mercantile and industrial enterprise—unless it had been pulled into the service of the military—was itself attacked. Not surprisingly, then, it was the great growth areas of eighteenth-century France—the Atlantic and Mediterranean ports, the textile towns of the north and the east, the great metropolis of Lyon—which were the major casualties of the Revolution. The "bourgeoisie" which Marxist history long believed to be the essential beneficiaries of the Revolution was, in fact, its principal victim.

The scholarly view of a limited Terror, moreover, hardly survives a scrutiny of the most dreadful enormity of the year II: the wholesale destruction of an entire region of France. Nowhere as much as in the area of the Vendée—including the neighboring departments of Loire-Inférieure and Maine-et-Loire—did the Terror fulfill Saint-Just's dictum that the "republic consists in the extermination of everything that opposes it."

The tide had turned in the war with Charette's inability to take Nantes. By the end of the summer, the republican armies had been reinforced by the regiments that had been released from the defense of Mainz, and by the first major draft of the *levée en masse*. At Cholet, on October 17, the rebels lost a decisive battle, but they also lost a coherent military leadership. Charette's army became detached from the main Grand Army, which on the death of Cathelineau before Nantes had fallen to the young La Rochejaquelein. Probably hoping to link up with a British disembarkation on the coast (which never came), the Grand Army crossed the Loire on October 19. Together with a huge train of women, children, priests and other noncombatants, possibly as many as twenty thousand, this nomadic army wandered around Brittany and Normandy for three months, harassed by the inexorably growing republican armies and occasionally fighting actions in which they did little more than stand their ground. At Angers they lost another major battle, and at Savenay on December 23, what was

199. Gabriel, drawing, Carrier of Nantes

left of their army was routed, leaving La Rochejaquelein to take to the woods dressed as a peasant. Westermann, who had thus rehabilitated himself, wrote to the Committee of Public Safety, "There is no more Vendée, citizens, it has perished under our free sword along with its women and children. I have just buried it in the marshes and mud of Savenay. Following the orders that you gave me I have crushed children under the feet of horses, massacred women who at least . . . will engender no more brigands. I have no prisoners with which to reproach myself."

In the true Terrorist style, Westermann may have exaggerated in order to show his zeal. But a policy of extermination, if not already embarked on, would shortly become an all too exacting reality in the Vendée. It had been announced much earlier in the summer when General Beyssier had decided that since the Republic had to fight a war of brigands it had better do it with brigandlike ruthlessness. In the urban centers, during December, this meant a Terrorism of exceptional brutality. Two hundred prisoners were executed at Angers in December alone, two thousand at Saint-Florent. Others were brought from the crowded prisons at Nantes and Angers to places like Pont-de-Cé and Avrillé, where three to four thousand were shot in one long, relentless slaughter.

The most notorious massacres were at Nantes, where the *représentant-en-mission,* Jean-Baptiste Carrier, supplemented the guillotine with what he called "vertical deportations" in the river Loire. Holes were punched in the sides of flat-bottomed barges below the waterline, over which wooden planks were nailed to keep the boats temporarily afloat. Prisoners were put in with their hands and feet tied and the boats pushed into the center of the river to catch the current. The executioner-boatmen then broke or removed the planks and made haste to jump into boats that were alongside, while their victims helplessly watched the water rise about them. Anyone attempting to survive by jumping in was sabered in the water. At first these drownings were confined to priests and took place, almost guiltily, by night. But what the sans-culotte "Marat company" conspicuous in the repression humorously called "the republican baptisms" or the "national bath" became routinized and were executed in broad daylight, where some witnesses survived to describe them. In some cases, prisoners were stripped of their clothes and belongings (always an important source of perquisites for the soldiers), giving rise to accounts of "republican marriages": young men and women tied naked together in the boats. Estimates of those who perished in this manner vary greatly, but there were certainly no fewer than two thousand and quite possibly as many as forty-eight hundred.

What unfolded in the Vendée itself in the first two months of 1794 was no more charitable. The basic republican strategy for reconquest had been set the previous summer, and it marked a radical departure from prevailing conventions of the "rules of war." Since the Vendéans' greatest asset was the strength of their home base, their opponents determined to destroy it. As well as the usual military targets of encampments, garrisons and arsenals, the entire social and economic infrastructure of the region was to be torn apart until those concealed within it were exposed to fire. Crops were to be burned, farm animals slaughtered or seized, barns and cottages razed, woods set on fire. More ominous still, distinctions between combatant and noncombatant sections of the population were to be blurred. Women and children were known to give support to the rebels, sometimes even fight with them. Very well, then, they too would fall under the injunction of "extermination." Any town or hamlet known to have received rebel troops would automatically be wiped out. Ronsin, the senior militant commander in the Vendée, even proposed systematic depopulation, with the "brigands" deported and dispersed throughout France or sent to Madagascar. In their place legions of "pure" French colonists would settle the country and breed families untainted by their crime. There were still more sinister anticipations of the technological killings of the twentieth century. Carrier had suggested putting arsenic in the wells. Westermann thought a cask of poisoned brandy might be sent to the Vendéans (though he was worried

200. Anonymous, Thermidorian engraving of the
"republican marriages" on the Loire. As is typical in
these anti-Jacobin prints the sans-culotte soldier is seen
making off with the victims' clothes and property.

lest his own soldiers drink it by mistake). Rossignol even asked the distinguished chemist Fourcroy to study the possibility of using "mines, gassings
[*fumigations*] or other means to be able to destroy, put to sleep or asphyxiate
the enemy."

The mass production of death through the marriage of technology and
bureaucracy would have to wait another century and a half. But what
happened in February and March was bad enough. With the military
rebellion more or less extinguished, the republican armies embarked on a
march of "pacification" through the region. General Turreau's twelve "infernal columns" were encouraged (if they were not given direct orders) to
massacre virtually every living person who stood in their path. This indis-

criminate slaughter inevitably included some on the wrong side. The family of Honoré Plantin, a well-off farmer and impeccable republican patriot living near Machecoul, survived the Vendéan massacre in that town only to succumb to the infernal columns. On their first visitation three of his sons and a son-in-law were killed and when they returned, the last son, his wife and their fifteen-year-old daughter were all massacred. Every atrocity the time could imagine was meted out to the defenseless population. Women were routinely raped, children killed, both mutilated. To save powder General Cordellier ordered his men to do their work with the saber rather than the gun. At Gonnord on January 23, General Crouzat's column forced two hundred old people, along with mothers and children, to kneel in front of a large pit they had dug; they were then shot so as to tumble into their own grave. Some who attempted to flee were struck down by the hammer of a local Patriot mason. Thirty children and two women were buried alive when earth was shoveled onto the pit.

As in all places where these horrors were perpetrated, there were those on the republican side whose stomachs were turned by what they witnessed and who were haunted by the massacres for many years afterwards. Beaudesson, a chief agent of military provisioning, wrote that he "found fathers, mothers, children of all ages and both sexes swimming in their own blood, naked and in positions that the most ferocious soul could not imagine without shuddering."

By mid-April 1794, the military pacification of the Vendée was more or less complete. The only surviving commanders of the once imposing Grand Royal and Catholic Army were Stofflet and Charette, both of whom took to a *petite guerre* of harassment, ambush and surprise raids, avoiding pitched battles and eluding capture. But their homeland was, as the republican generals had promised, a desert, its farmland incinerated, its great herds of fat cattle slaughtered, its villages razed and depopulated. Like the other centers of insurrection it had lost its very name, to be known henceforth as Vengé (Avenged).

It has been customary for scholars to be skeptical of the claims of pro-Vendéan historians' estimates of massive population loss, and Donald Greer's figure of forty thousand deaths for the whole period of the Terror in all departments has been accepted as plausible. It is not necessary, though, to accept Reynald Sécher's characterization of the massacres as "genocide" to see that a human catastrophe of colossal proportions occurred in the Vendée in the year II that demands a substantial upward revision of these fatalities. Jean-Clément Martin, whose book on the same subject is a model of reasoned research, gives a total loss for the Vendée, Loire-Inférieure and Maine-et-Loire of just under a quarter of a million, or one third of the entire population of the region. This figure, moreover, does not include the tens of thousands of republican soldiers who lost their lives in the war.

Confronted with evidence of an apocalypse, it does historians no credit to look aside in the name of scholarly objectivity. True, events in the Vendée were in the nature of a war (though the butchery was at its worst after the battles were over); true, the Vendéan rebels themselves committed their share of massacres in the early stages of the rising. But whatever claims on political virtue the French Revolution may make on the historian's sympathy, none can be so strong as to justify, to any degree, the unconscionable slaughters of the winter of the year II. Still less does it seem right to shunt off the history of the Vendée into a special category of works set aside from the rest of the history of the Revolution, as though it were some sort of aberration. The exterminations practiced there were, in fact, the logical outcome of an ideology that progressively dehumanized its adversaries and that had become incapable of seeing any middle ground between total triumph and utter eclipse. Commenting on the revolution of the tenth of August, Robespierre had rejoiced that "a river of blood would now divide France from its enemies." That river was now swelling its banks; the current was flowing fast but it remained obscure, except to the intimates of the Incorruptible, where it was taking the Republic.

CHAPTER EIGHTEEN

The Politics of
Turpitude

i SHE-WOLVES AND OTHER DANGERS

I KNOW NOTHING so cruel as to wake up in a prison cell, in a place where the most horrible dream is less horrible than reality." From his eminence as a minister of the Napoleonic Empire, Jacques-Claude Beugnot, looked back with horror and loathing on his months spent in the Conciergerie at the end of 1793. In retrospect he was also amazed that he had survived, when so many hundreds of others, arrested on the flimsiest of pretexts, had exited by tumbril for their appointment with the guillotine.

More than fifty places of detention operated in Paris during the Terror. The September 17 Law of Suspects had made the criteria for arrest so elastic that it had swollen the prison population to around seven thousand by early December. Even allowing for serious overcrowding, the number of prisoners so exceeded the available space that major new sites were found to specialize in political detainees. Some of them, like the old headquarters of the Farmers-General (a batch of whom would be guillotined in the spring) and the splendid Palais de Luxembourg, might have been requisitioned with poetic justice in mind. Available room, however, was the major consideration; barracks, convents, schools and the famous Jansenist seminary and library of Port-Royal (renamed Port-Libre) were all converted to places of incarceration.

Of all these prisons, the Conciergerie, on the Ile de la Cité, had the most sinister reputation (though the dank unhealthy Sainte-Pélagie ran it a close second). Beugnot called it "a vast antechamber of death," since it not only acted as a holding center before arraignment and a place of confinement for common criminals, but was also the temporary lodging of those awaiting their execution after sentence. Beugnot often lay awake at nights listening

793

to sobbing and moaning, indistinguishably coming from the sick and the terrified, while the prison's many dogs barked at the gloomy clock-tower bells chiming the hours.

Even by the standards of the time, the Conciergerie was a wretched hole, a place which managed to engender phenomenal squalor within imposing architectural precincts (for it too was a former princely residence). As another of its inmates who survived to tell his story, the journalist Claude-François Beaulieu, reported, many of the prisoners compared it to one of the lower circles of Dante's Inferno, a house of vermin, smelling of sickness and ordure. On admission, Beugnot shared his fifteen-foot-square cell (one of the larger rooms) with a forty-year-old man who was accused of murdering his mother and whom Beugnot suspected of being a lunatic, and a more amiable young forger "from the aristocracy of crime." Not everyone was so badly off. Wealthier prisoners (like Marie-Antoinette) were accommodated *à la pistole*, which is to say they could afford a bed at the rate of twenty-seven livres, twelve sous for the first month. Since this sum was payable in advance, the increasingly brisk turnover supplied by the Revolutionary Tribunal made it a major source of income for the prisons. At Sainte-Pélagie, the first question put to incoming prisoners was "*As-tu de la sonnette?*" (Have you the chinking stuff?). Those who did not (the vast majority) slept *à la paille*, on straw, in tiny *cachots*, deprived of air and water, with no place to relieve themselves except the floor. After a while prisoners ceased to care, sleeping by and in their own excrement, covered with lice and open sores. To vary the routine they could walk together under the ogival vaults of the long, somber corridor known as the "rue de Paris," watch the scuttle of rats and exchange gossip about the latest admissions.

There was, however, one moment during the day to which all the male prisoners looked forward. Around noon, the women came down from the quarters *à la pistole* on the second floor to an open courtyard where, as best they could, they washed their clothes and themselves. Through a grille the men were able to exchange conversation, admire the women's desperately kept-up appearances and even flirt a little. At the meal that followed, the men sat on benches placed directly beside those of the women, with only the barred partition separating them, so that at least for a short time they had the illusion of companionability. It was at one of these times that Beugnot discovered "Eglé." She was busy berating the sixty-six-year-old Duc de Châtelet, the ex-commander of the *gardes françaises*, for losing his composure, telling him in no uncertain terms that carrying on so was unworthy of a duke. Her disapproval of his collapse of dignity suggested to Beugnot that she must have been a woman of quality.

In fact, Eglé was a prostitute, who had lived for the past two years on the rue Fromenteaux. Her trade may have suffered from the Revolution: on the streets she worked, she took every opportunity of announcing her dislike for the new order. As the result of these tirades she had been denounced, arrested with a friend in the same line of trade and brought to the Conciergerie. Her primitive royalism was so passionate and so pithily expressed that, according to Beugnot, Chaumette had had the inspired notion of bringing the two girls to trial at the same time as Marie-Antoinette. To the *procureur* of the Commune, the spectacle of three whores sharing the same tumbril would provide an eloquent symbolic statement of the sans-culotte view of the ex-queen. The idea was, of course, too outrageous for the Revolutionary Tribunal. But though the Queen and the street whore did not share the same cart, their fates remained entangled since, three months after Marie-Antoinette's beheading, when Eglé's indictment was read, it was found to contain an article accusing her of "conspiratorial relations" with the Queen. Eglé cheerfully confessed to her unrepentant royalism but, Beugnot reported, when the interrogator came to her "plot," she shrugged her shoulders and replied ironically, "That's just fine, and *ma foi* you certainly show some wit, but me, accomplice of the person you call widow Capet and who was very much the Queen, me who earned my living on street corners and would never have even made the humblest maid in her kitchen; that's really worthy of a bunch of crooks and imbeciles like you." Strangely enough, the audacity of this outburst led one of the jury to declare that she must be drunk. Her friend seized her only real chance for clemency by confessing herself pregnant (and therefore protected from the guillotine). Eglé, on the other hand, insisted that not only was she neither drunk nor pregnant but meant every word she said, and was duly condemned to death—but not before accusing of being a thief the judge who ordered the confiscation of her property. When the time came, "she leapt on to the tumbril," says Beugnot with gallant romanticism, "like a bird." She may have been "the prostitute Catherine Albourg" mentioned in the official list of the condemned as being guillotined on December 12.

There is no way of substantiating Beugnot's account of Chaumette's scheme. But given the violence of feeling against the Queen in Paris, it does not seem all that farfetched. Since the Dantoniste Committee of Public Safety had shown some reluctance in bringing her to trial in the spring and summer, Hébert was using the issue as a stick with which to beat them for *"modérantisme,"* the latest sin in the revolutionary catechism. With the change in policy and personnel in July, a process of systematic degradation and dehumanization got under way. Reports were leaking out of Marie-Antoinette's tenderness as a mother to her son and daughter, both of whom were frequently sick and whom she tended with great devotion. The corrective was to separate her from the seven-year-old Louis-Charles, who was henceforth to be a ward of the Republic. After an hour of desperate weeping and pleading, he was taken down to a room immediately below the Queen's where she could hear him sobbing for days on end. His education, over which, following Louis' example, she had taken the greatest pains, was now given to a semiliterate shoemaker named Simon, who was himself later guillotined. Already sickly and possibly suffering, like his elder brother before him, from tuberculosis, the boy, after his mother and aunt's death, would be treated like a caged animal, living in darkness and filth and dying sometime in 1795.

To preempt possibilities of escape as well as to sustain the intensity of her humiliation, Marie-Antoinette was then parted from what was left of her family. She was awoken in the middle of the night of August 2 and taken from the Temple to the Conciergerie, where she occupied a room about eleven feet by six feet off the main ground-floor corridor and directly next to the two gendarmes who were responsible for guarding her at all times. At the end of the month a halfhearted attempt at rescue was made but was aborted when one of the guards panicked and led her back to the cell. On the twelfth of October, thin and wasted, she was taken to the nearby Tribunal for interrogation. Hébert had prepared public opinion by stepping up his invective in the *Père Duchesne*. Thus she was commonly referred to as a ravening beast—the "Austrian she-wolf" or the "arch-tigress," a "monster who needed to slake her thirst on the blood of the French . . . [who] wanted to roast alive all the poor Parisians . . . who caused the massacre at Nancy of the first soldiers for liberty" and so on. Even if she had not committed all these atrocities, Hébert wrote (echoing Saint-Just's remark, "One cannot reign innocently"), merely having been queen was enough to condemn her, for those who reign are the most deadly enemies of humanity. Since such creatures are by their very nature biologically dangerous, "it is the duty of every free man to kill a king or those who are destined to be kings or those who have shared the crimes of kingship." In this he was only parroting the general *ultra* view, expressed, for example, in Sylvain Maréchal's apocalyptic drama *Le Dernier Jugement des Rois* (The Last Judgment of the Kings), where the "crowned monsters" (a standard euphemism), in the persons of Catherine the Great, the Emperor Francis II, the Pope, "George Dandin" of Britain and their brethren from Spain, Naples, Sardinia and Prussia were all taken by sans-culottes to a volcanic island, where in the last act they were satisfyingly consumed in a boiling eruption.

Maréchal's play placed great emphasis not just on the despotism but on the moral corruption of the princes. "Has there ever existed a nation that,

201. De Brehen, Marie-Antoinette (considerably idealized) in mourning dress in the Temple Prison

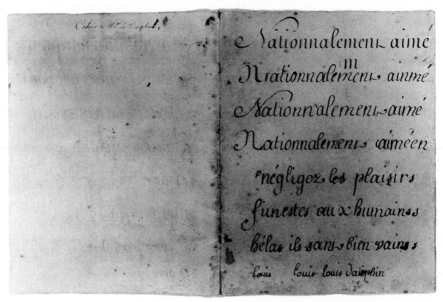

202. Line from the Dauphin's prison notebook: "Nationally beloved; forgo pleasures harmful to humans, alas they are indeed vain."

at the same time, could have a King and morals?" asks his sans-culotte rhetorically. Before the explosion, the monarchs lose their semblance of pride and fall to their characteristic vices, fighting each other with scepters and crosses, the libidinous Catherine inviting anyone interested to follow her into a cave. This was in direct contrast to the sans-culotte, who, it is explained to an old man who has been exiled to the island, "is a free man, a patriot *par excellence* . . . they are *pure* citizens . . . who eat their bread by the sweat of their brow; who love work, who are good sons, good fathers, good husbands, good relatives, good friends, and good neighbors. . . ."

The case against Marie-Antoinette (and in fact virtually all of those who followed her to the guillotine during the Terror) was much the same. She was, essentially, impure in body, thought and deed. Her conspiracies thus followed axiomatically from this moral turpitude. In the initial interrogation by Tribunal president Herman, she was represented as an ungovernable wife, forcing Louis, for example, to issue the veto against anticlerical legislation and organizing the flight to Varennes. Like all uncontrollable women she was simultaneously greedy for money and prodigal with it, "passing the gold of patriots out of the country." The infamous "orgy" of the Swiss guards at Versailles in 1789 was another instance of her lust for domination. One of the forty-one witnesses called against the Queen reported having seen bottles under her bed, which, he said, led him to believe she was intent on making the soldiers drunk.

The testimony on her immoral character culminated in Hébert's own notorious intervention, and the statement he had induced Louis-Charles to sign, confessing that his mother and aunt had taught him to masturbate and had forced him to commit incest. Some of these exertions had actually injured him, and it was only since he had been removed from their tainting presence, Hébert claimed (in direct contradiction of the truth), that his health had taken a turn for the better. There were other ways in which she had forfeited the right to be considered a good mother. Instead of bringing up her son as a virtuous republican, she had attempted to indoctrinate him with royalism. Proof of that was the damning fact that he was served first at meals, by virtue of his sovereign rights as "Louis XVII." A Sacred Heart, pierced by an arrow (a gift from Mme Elisabeth, the Queen said—alas for her sister-in-law), the well-known totem of the Vendéan brigands, had been found among the boy's possessions, indicating that he was being groomed by her to be the mascot of that barbarous horde. Not content with destroying one of the male Capets, she was now determined to do her worst with another. This was all conclusive proof of her "unnatural" character, "*féconde*" (the word was surely not casually chosen) only in intrigues.

More to the point than all of this were the letters, produced by Fouquier-Tinville, the prosecutor, showing the Queen in treasonable correspondence with the Austrian court at about the time the two countries were preparing for war. But this actually damning piece of evidence was somehow swallowed up in the more generalized character assassination. The jury was told, in effect, that the shrunken, white-haired woman they had before them was a *furie*, someone who had bitten open the cartridges for the Swiss guards on the tenth of August so they need waste no time in murdering as many patriots as possible. Such animals required swift extermination.

After the inevitable sentence, Marie-Antoinette was taken back to the Conciergerie, where she wept, wrote a last letter to her sister-in-law, confiding the children to her, and changed into a white dress, a plain bonnet and the plum shoes with raised heels that she had managed to keep with her in prison. Prepared for death with her hair cut, she flinched on seeing the open cart, for she had been expecting, or at least hoping for, the same closed carriage that had carried Louis to the place de la Révolution, sparing her the obloquy of the crowd. Sitting erect and gaunt as she was driven through the streets, she was sketched by Jacques-Louis David as an object of curiosity, and only at the very last minute on the scaffold itself did she begin to tremble. This was not enough for the Père Duchesne, who would have liked to have seen much more terror on her face—the kind that would, in fact, be exhibited by Hébert when his turn came to follow her. "The bitch was audacious and insolent right to the very end. However, her legs failed her at the moment of being tipped over to shake the hot hand" *(jouer la main chaude)*—Hébert's current favorite nickname for the guillotine. It was, all the same, as his front page announced, "the greatest of all the joys of the Père Duchesne, having with his own eyes seen the head of the female veto separated from her fucking tart's neck."

Marie-Antoinette was not the only woman at about this time to be incriminated for conspiring against the Jacobin ideology of obedient wife-mother. The wretched Mme Du Barry, Louis XV's last mistress, had in fact been absurdly imprudent in trips to London, where she made elaborate arrangements with, among others, the ex-minister Bertrand de Moleville to smuggle her jewelry out of France. But it seems likely that even had she been more careful in these matters, her reputation would have caught up with her. When she was interrogated, it was the spurious Countess of Pidanzat de Mairobert's *Mémoires du Du Barry* that the court had in mind, squandering the country's money on jewels, houses and favorites and in cahoots with the notorious Abbé Terray of unlamented memory. One especially poisonous polemic called her "this barrel of infection; this drain of iniquity; this impure cloaca who not content with devouring the finances of France nourished herself on human flesh on the model of the anthropophagi."

Mme Roland was not subjected to quite this degree of sexual patho-phobia, but nonetheless, after testifying at the trial of the Girondins, she returned to Sainte-Pélagie smarting at "questions which outraged her honor." Since her admirer Buzot had been one of the ringleaders of the attempt to raise a federalist rebellion in the Calvados, it seems quite likely that she was questioned about her relations with him. At her own trial on November 8, Fouquier-Tinville had the easy job of simply connecting her to the Girondins, who had already been convicted and executed ten days before. But there was some effort to depict her too as an unnatural wife, someone who had turned her home—a place which by the lights of Jacobin orthodoxy should have been the seat of patriotic domesticity—into a nest of conspiracy. It smacked too much of the salon, an institution with a flavor of aristocratic patronage and ingratiation about it.

In fact, the precise period of these trials marks the stormiest phase of sexual politics in the Revolution. Fights had broken out between the femi-nist Society of Republican Women and the *poissardes* over the propriety of women wearing the cockade and the *bonnet rouge*. Claire Lacombe and other militants believed that women not only should be permitted but

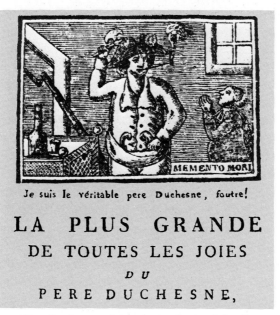

203. Père Duchesne rejoices at the death of the Queen.

204. Ceramic plate bearing legend: "Madame Veto has promised/to have all Paris slaughtered/But now thanks to our cannoneers/It's her neck that's missing,/Dance the Carmagnole."

ought to be obligated to do this and even sought entry to the National Guard. In late September the Convention had acceded to some of the radical demands about dress, but on October 28 there was a violent encounter between the two groups that ended in ferocious beatings inflicted on the feminists. The Convention then reversed itself and on November 5 ordered the closure of all women's revolutionary clubs in Paris. The decree came three days before Mme Roland's trial and execution and two days after that of the actress Olympe de Gouges. The latter had already had the temerity to present herself as a defender of Louis XVI and had compounded that sin by openly advocating federalist solutions and calling for popular referenda to determine the form of government. Even after her arrest on the twentieth of July, she attempted to publicize her direct attacks on Robespierre and Fouquier-Tinville by having friends post them in public places throughout Paris.

Given the efforts expended to represent these women as dangerous deviants from the prescribed norms of domestic life, it is striking how virtually all of them (Jeanne Du Barry excepted) in their parting letters showed themselves models of tender and conscientious motherhood. In her passionate defense of the Queen, Germaine de Staël emphasized her selfless devotion to her sick children and appealed to the women of France in the name of "sacrificed motherhood" to demand that she be reunited with her son. Olympe de Gouges wrote to her son serving in the army, telling him to pass on her own sense of the unjust perversion of the Revolution. And in her touching letter to her twelve-year-old daughter Eudora, Manon Roland reminded her of the deepest bonds that tied them together:

> I do not know, my little friend, if it will be given to me to see you or to write you again. Remember your mother. These few words contain all that I can best tell you. . . . Be worthy of your parents, they leave you great examples and if you profit from them your existence will not be without value. *Adieu* beloved child, you whom I have nourished with my milk and whom I would like to penetrate with all my sentiments. A time will come when you will be able to judge the effort that I make at this time not to weaken [at the thought of] your sweet face. I press you to my breast. Adieu my Eudora.

Husbands, even ones whose wives had taken a lover, were equally capable of dramatic demonstrations of *sensibilité*. At the time of the Girondin flight north from Paris, Roland de La Platière had gone not to Caen but to Rouen, and had stayed there as a fugitive throughout the summer and autumn. When he heard, first of the execution of the Girondins and then on the tenth of November of his wife's death, he decided on suicide. A few miles outside Rouen on the Paris road, sitting on the ground against a tree, he leaned hard into his swordstick. The passerby who found him the next day thought he was asleep, until he found a note by Roland's side which ended with the words "I left my refuge as soon as I heard my wife had been murdered. I no longer desire to remain in a world covered with crime."

His allies, the Girondins, had suffered through a long and particularly distorted judicial process that had culminated in a notorious effort by Fouquier-Tinville to cut short proceedings. Whenever his smoothly organized prosecutions seemed to be slowing down unduly, or the defense beginning to sway the jury, he had the right to ask them if they "had heard enough to be illuminated" as to the facts of the case and to be in a position to give a verdict. This was all the more urgent in the case of the Girondins, since Brissot and Vergniaud in particular had given a powerful account of their own conduct, refuting point by point the initial indictment contained in a report to the Convention by Saint-Just and later expanded by Amar, for one of the leading members of the Committee of General Security. Its principal thrust was that the group, whatever its outward professions, had always been devoted to royalism and had done their utmost to preserve it.

The key figure in this determination was Brissot, so every effort was made to reveal his own character in as unsavory a light as possible. He was exposed as having been a police spy, something he denied but which in fact had been the case before the Revolution. He was also described as a common forger, having gone to Switzerland at some point to obtain a false passport. From this evidence of a double life in the 1780s it was possible to build a case in which his entire revolutionary career had been a lie, a stratagem for self-promotion; so that while he professed to be, in the title of his journal, the *Patriote Français*, the reality, according to the act of accusation, was that he had, all along, been an enemy agent. Indeed, at the very moment he had claimed to have been an ardent republican, he had actually conspired to put the Duke of York on the throne of France. Even if he was at times unaware of it, Brissot had been, throughout, the devoted creature of William Pitt's strategy. "Pitt wanted to vilify and dissolve the convention, they [the 'Brissotins,' as they were called throughout the trial] have worked to dissolve the convention; Pitt wanted to assassinate the faithful representatives of the people, they have assassinated Marat and Lepeletier." Even Brissot's passionate advocacy of a war was interpreted through the revolutionary obsession with the *guêt-apens*—the ambush—as a way of drawing France prematurely and gratuitously into conflict with the Coalition, the better to destroy French unity. The British eyed the

French empire, Brissot gave them the opportunity to seize it; Pitt wanted to destroy Paris, "they did what they could to destroy Paris."

The mentality of Jacobin prosecution (like that of all other revolutionary dictatorships) was necessarily holistic. Accidents, contingencies, changes of heart and plans were by definition impossible, ruses presented to distract the inquisitor from understanding the true coherence, the necessary interconnectedness of his enemy's thoughts and deeds. Just as the pure revolutionary was all of a piece, his moral direction established early in life and unwaveringly pursued, so the counter-revolutionary, however he might attempt to represent his conduct as sometimes haphazard or unplanned, was also all of a piece. All that needed to be exposed, like flipping open the back of a timepiece, was the essential motion of the machine. In the case of the Brissotins this was easy: their motive was shared self-interest. Their stigmatization as a "faction" suggested that all of their revolutionary conduct could be explained as an appropriation of personal power. The selfish immorality of such careers was the precise opposite of true patriotism, defined as selflessness. And the means by which they pursued wealth, vanity and power were, first, the creation of a puppet dynasty and, when that had been ruled out, the dismemberment of France itself into baronial fiefs.

Once the Brissotins' defense had been cut short by Fouquier's suggestion to the jury that they might have heard enough, the verdict and sentence were not in question. Nonetheless, the jury's formal announcement created a moment of extraordinary drama. Brissot's head fell sadly onto his chest and, according to one of the jurors, Camille Desmoulins started and shouted, "My God I am sorry for this." While Boileau continued to protest his innocence, Dufriche-Valazé suddenly fell backward off his bench. One of his friends thought he too had been emotionally overcome, but in seconds it was seen that he had stabbed himself with a knife concealed in his papers. He was dead a few minutes later, as blood poured onto the courtroom floor. Miffed at being denied an execution, Fouquier-Tinville demanded that the cadaver be guillotined anyway, along with the rest of the prisoners, and so it was.

Though there was something like an epidemic of suicides among the fallen revolutionaries, the Girondins seem to have been especially susceptible to the poetry of self-destruction. Clavière also took his life and, later, Condorcet, as we shall see, may have taken poison to avoid the humiliation of the Revolutionary Tribunal. Vergniaud had also secreted poison but decided, according to Riouffe, who saw him in the Conciergerie the last night of his life, to share the fate of his friends. The next morning, October 31, they mounted the steps of their cart defiantly singing the "Marseillaise." It was their own last gesture of *fraternité*. On the scaffold, Sanson took just thirty-six minutes to cut twenty-two heads, and was remarkably pleased at this further evidence of the efficiency of the *rasoir national.*

i i T H E E N D O F I N D U L G E N C E

This process of republican housecleaning through judicial murder was continued by selecting other key figures who represented the impure past. Sadly for the Revolutionary Tribunal, a number of the most obvious candidates for expiatory retribution were beyond their reach: Dumouriez in exile, Lafayette in an Austrian prison, Mirabeau in the Panthéon (though not for long). Barnave and Bailly would have to do instead, and duly paid for their respective attempts at revolutionary containment. On November 7, Philippe-Egalité, the Duc d'Orléans, also went to his death, in the company of a locksmith condemned for insulting the republican colors. Reportedly he made a public statement of regret for his responsibility for shedding the blood of an innocent, presumably his cousin.

Purity became a political fetish. Following a proposal by Merlin de Thionville, the Jacobins initiated a laborious self-scrutiny in which each member answered the questions "How much were you worth in 1789; how much are you worth now and if you are worth more how did you come by it?" In late November, when this *scrutin épuratoire* got under way, it seemed that the chief beneficiaries of this relentless process of self-reduction would be Hébert and his allies. He himself served on the purging committee of the club. Bouchotte and Vincent commanded enormous resources of patronage at the Ministry of War; Ronsin was firmly entrenched as the commander in chief of the *armées révolutionnaires.* In Paris, the partnership of Hanriot, the commandant of the National Guard; Chaumette, the *procureur* of the Commune; and Paché, the mayor (who had gone, successively, from Girondin to Montagnard to Hébertiste) seemed to provide, for this group, the possibility of turning popular violence on and off as they chose.

"Hébertisme," then, had men, money and authority at its disposal and was beginning to use them to powerful effect. As minister of war, Bouchotte had appropriated large sums to distribute the *Père Duchesne* gratis throughout the army. Just what these men stood for beyond a brutal accusatory style was less certain, since they defined themselves more in terms of what and whom they were against than what they were for. They were against the "fanatics" of Christianity; against any mercy for the defeated "brigands" and "monsters" of federalism and counter-revolution; against the rich and the *beaux esprits*—the intellectuals who presumed to talk down to the People. Insofar as they were for anything, it was an anarchic notion of popular government, always armed to impose the will of the people on its mandatories. They also favored the extension of state power into the economy. In number 273 of the *Père Duchesne*, Hébert had argued that "the earth has been made for all living creatures, and from the ant to the haughty insect called man, each of them must find his subsistence from the production of this common mother . . . the merchant must live from his industry, to be sure, but he must not fatten himself on the blood of the poor. Property is [simply] existence and one must eat, at whatever price." In keeping with this concept of the state as a protector of minimum subsistence (a view more or less shared by Robespierre and Saint-Just), Hébert wanted a more aggressive policy of requisitions to meet local crises. To ensure adequate supply and low prices, as a temporary expedient the entire product of wine and cereal harvests should be compulsorily bought up by the state (while compensating the producers). In a speech to the Commune on October 14 Chaumette even proposed that the state repossess workshops and manufactures closed or deserted by émigré entrepreneurs (a scheme that would be taken seriously eighty years later by the Paris Commune of 1871).

Above all, though, the Hébertistes were for unrelenting surveillance, denunciation, indictment, humiliation and death. *Père Duchesne*'s image of the Republic was of a kind of locker-room egalitarianism, where *bons bougres* would have nothing to hide from each other and would embrace in muscular fraternity. The "*homme pur,*" Hébert was much given to saying, "always says frankly what he thinks, and calls a cat a cat, he never manipulates people, and if in his anger he strikes some brave bugger by mistake, then he asks his pardon and redresses the wrong by taking him off to the nearest wine-shop to knock back a few." (The French is much better: "to smother half a dozen choirboys"—*étouffer une demi-douzaine d'enfants de choeur.*)

The Hébertiste ascendancy did not, however, go unresisted. For all the appearance of capitulation to popular intervention, the Jacobin control of the *journée* of September 5 implied a determination by the Mountain not to be at the mercy of the Commune. Hence a majority of the Committee of Public Safety, especially after Saint-Just's declaration on October 10 that the government was to be "revolutionary [that is, dictatorial] until the peace," were determined to use state power to neutralize the threat of insurrection. Through November and December, however, the Mountain was itself divided. A number of important figures, including Robespierre and Couthon, were hostile to dechristianization and were ready to listen to complaints about punitive excesses committed by such militant *représentants-en-mission* as Javogues, Carrier and Fouché. On the other hand, they remained obsessed by the holy grail of republican purity. Since it would, by definition, remain forever out of reach, its paladins would constantly see themselves confronted by impure soldiers of darkness and crime who stood between them and their prize and who had to be cut down if the Reign of Virtue were ever to be realized.

The major challenge to the Hébertistes, then, had to come from a different group of Jacobins who were more concerned with the pragmatic stabilization of France than with its devotion to the Ideal Republic. Danton was the all-important figure in this group. Joseph Garat, who had been his successor at the Ministry of Justice and, until August, minister of the interior, later wrote that towards the end of 1793 Danton had sounded him out in several private conversations. Garat was himself under suspicion of being too closely linked to the Girondins, so it was natural for Danton to confess to him his chagrin: by rebuffing his offers of a truce, Brissot and his friends had left the Republic at the mercy of Hébert and the most fanatical Terrorists. Ironically, it had been Danton himself who had coined the ringing slogan "Terror is the order of the day" on September 5 when pulling the Convention's irons from the fire. But revolutionary government in his mind was contingent on military desperation, and the victories of Hondschoote and Wattignies had removed those Terrorist imperatives. He confided to Garat a strategy to correct the course. A press campaign would be mounted for clemency and against the Hébertiste Commune. Robespierre, whose trust he still had, and Barère, whom he judged also to be, at heart, a pragmatist, would be courted inside the Committee, the result being the isolation of militants like Collot and Billaud-Varennes and, eventually, a wholesale change in personnel. The economic Terror would be dismantled

205. Jacques-Louis David, drawing, Danton, 1793

and France would open negotiations for a peace with the Coalition while remaining fully mobilized lest diplomacy fail.

The plan was but another attempt to return the revolutionary genie to the bottle of state power. Intrinsic to its realization was the cynical use of conspiracy paranoia against those who were its habitual practitioners. It seems likely that Danton approved of Fabre d'Eglantine's revelation of a "foreign plot" in mid-October, in which friends and supporters of Hébert were said to be implicated in a scheme to suborn the Convention and overthrow the committees. In other words, those who purported to be most truculently patriotic were in fact foreign agents. For a while the tactic seemed to pay off. Stanislas Maillard, Anacharsis Cloots (to whose "Prussian" birth the Dantonistes repeatedly drew attention) and the Belgian van den Ijver were indeed arrested. To beat the patriotic drum Fabre went even further, demanding that any British subjects remaining in France be arrested and their property confiscated. He extended the net of the "foreign network" to two more of Hébert's colleagues, Desfieux and Dubuisson, to the ex-*capucin* Chabot, who had married into a family of Moravian Jewish bankers, the Belgian democrats Proly and Walckiers, and even to Hérault de Séchelles, who was accused of somehow protecting foreign banking interests in the Committee of Public Safety.

The denunciation was crazy enough to be credible to Robespierre, especially because it linked together men on the right (relatively speaking) like Hérault, whose aristocratic birth and intellectual manner rendered him suspect, with lunatics and thugs on the left like Maillard and Cloots, whom he found simply disgusting. As in a conspiratorial circle, *les extrêmes se touchent.* It all made sense. On October 16 Saint-Just denounced not only the corrupt but "men impatient for offices," a remark obviously directed at the Commune, and Robespierre, in one of his university lectures pretending to be a political speech, offered a new geography of counter-revolutionary intrigue. There was, apparently, the "Anglo-Prussian" branch associated with Brissot's yearnings to put either the Duke of York or the Duke of Brunswick on the throne. And then there was the "Austrian" branch, which extended from the Vienna government (one of the accused, Proly, was said to be a bastard son of Chancellor Kaunitz) to the Belgian bankers and war contractors with whom Dumouriez had been thick, and to their minions and agents at large in Paris and even within the Convention itself.

So far, so good. But in mid-November, a disaster suddenly loomed. On the tenth of that month Chabot and his friend Claude Basire, very much under suspicion, had argued in the Convention for the limitation of the committees' powers of arresting deputies. Before any deputy could be sent before the Revolutionary Tribunal, the accused should be given a right of defense before the whole body of the Convention. This echoed the kind of *"Indulgent"* position taken by Danton himself. And predictably the measure, though passed into law, was opposed by militant Terrorists both in the Convention and on the Committee of Public Safety, among them Billaud-Varennes, who insisted, "No, we will not step backward, our zeal will only be smothered in the tomb; either the revolution will triumph or we will all die." Barère was even more critical on the grounds that such a law made invidious distinctions between deputies and other citizens. The law, enacted just a day before, was overturned.

This, however, was not the root of the matter. As the sponsors of the measure, Chabot and Basire were not exactly disinterested. They had been abusing their position as the appointed liquidators of the colonial trading monopoly, the Company of the Indies, to speculate outrageously in its stock, secretly extorted from its directors as the price of official leniency. This squalid exercise in asset-stripping had meant large-scale bribery and the falsification of accounts and of the official decree of liquidation. It was all the more scandalous since Chabot and Basire, together with two other colleagues in the Convention, Delaunay and Julien de Toulouse, had posed in the summer as the most implacable scourges of corrupt capitalism. By denouncing banks, speculators on the Bourse, and the merchant monopolists, they had secured for themselves the perfect strategic positions from which to maximize their plunder while remaining safe from official investigations.

None of this would have necessarily imperiled Danton's offensive against Hébert had it not been for the entanglement of Fabre d'Eglantine. While Fabre had not been the instigator of the fraud, he had been handsomely bribed to collude in it, and it was his own signature that was on the crooked act of liquidation. This, however, had not stopped him from including Chabot in his "foreign plot" so as to throw Robespierre and the Jacobins off his own track. Besides, Chabot's marriage to Léopoldine Frey, the daughter and sister of a family that had also called itself, successively, Dobruška and von Schönfeld, was perfect material for the "foreign plot" designed to show him off as a super-patriot. Chabot could hardly issue a counter-denunciation without incriminating himself.

All this, however, began to unravel in mid-November. It brought Danton hurrying back to Paris from his little estate at Arcis-sur-Aube where, for a month, he had been happily playing country gentleman and enjoying domestic pleasures with his second wife. Following the defeat of their measure, Chabot and Basire had been relentlessly hounded by the *Père Duchesne* and zealots in the Jacobins and the Cordeliers. Believing he was about to be exposed, Chabot tried to cut his losses by a preemptive denunciation. He went to Robespierre on the morning of November 14 and got him out of bed to enlighten him concerning a shocking plot, evidently the work of the counter-revolution, to pillage the Nation of its sorely needed funds. He named Delaunay and Julien but assured Robespierre that while he himself had gone along with some of the conspiracy, it had been in the nature of a patriotic infiltration, the better to catch all the criminals involved. He had with him, he said, material evidence in the shape of a hundred-thousand-livre bribe, which he would give to the Committee of General Security along with the names of the conspirators, provided he could have some assurance that he would not himself be implicated. Taken aback by the news, Robespierre encouraged him to proceed on that basis. But within a few days the arrests were made, of both the denouncer and the denounced.

Somehow Fabre himself had escaped scrutiny and actually succeeded in putting further distance between himself and the peculators by more denunciations of Chabot. Betrayal begat betrayal. Just as Chabot had fingered Delaunay and Julien to save his neck, Fabre now sold Chabot to save his. For a while this tactic worked. Robespierre seemed to have enough faith in Fabre to give him a part in the official investigation, in which, of course, he managed to "cook" more evidence and attempt to implicate leading Hébertistes, including Chaumette.

Danton, however, was no fool, and he was no virgin himself when it came to imaginatively acquired money. Fabre was an old friend from the Cordeliers of 1789, his protégé in the club and the district assembly. Danton liked his wit and he pretended to like his plays, but he was under no illusions about Fabre's virtue. In any case, Danton disliked the moral self-righteousness of the Mountain and the posturing of the Hébertistes and thought the whole issue of corruption much less urgent than virtually every other problem facing the Republic. He himself had on occasion been known to dip his fingers into the sticky pot, almost certainly agreeing with Mirabeau that sweeteners were routinely necessary to make government work. His philosophy in this respect might best be characterized as "late Ottoman." Given the Jacobin obsession with probity, and Robespierre's own addiction to spotless, indeed transparent politics, the unthreading of the plot threatened to backfire disastrously on Danton's campaign to end the Terror.

The best defense, then, was a spirited offense. Fabre had made a start by throwing suspicion on precisely those people positioning themselves to pounce: the Hébertistes. But the real attack was to be launched by someone who had Robespierre's affection and who had been completely uncompromised: Camille Desmoulins. When Desmoulins launched the *Vieux Corde-*

lier at the beginning of December, Danton could not possibly have known what an extraordinary effect it would have, nor indeed how Desmoulins would rise so brilliantly to meet the crisis. The title of the paper, which appeared every five days, should have given him some clue, for it was a deliberate attempt to distinguish the "veterans" of freedom, the men who had been democrats in 1789, from *arriviste* demagogues like Hébert.

In every conceivable way, Desmoulins' paper turned the tables on the *Père Duchesne*. It had become habitual, in the militant press, to review the history of the Revolution as evolving ever forward from impurity and tainted compromise towards higher stages of purity and popular democracy. Desmoulins had the courage to break that prescribed momentum, by romanticizing the virtues of the *founding* revolution, at least as it was fought in the streets and districts in 1789. He liked to review (many times) his own famous part in triggering the Parisian insurrection of July 12 and contrasted it invidiously with Hébert's career at that time as a ticket taker at the Variétés Theater. The "new Cordeliers" were thus attacked for usurping a title that had been precious to the old revolutionary hands, without whom they would have had no career and no liberty to print their filthy calumnies. (He took care to remind people of the heroic role of Loustalot in creating a truly popular journalism.) Desmoulins also poured withering scorn on Hébert's pretensions to be "of the people." His choice of language for this counter-attack was deliberate. He reverted to a lucid, elegant, ironic manner, without Marat's rant, the better to contrast the integrity of his own personality with Hébert's imposture as one of the lads. The way I write is truly the way I am, his style implied. Hébert gives you the "language of the charnel house," as if the virtue and candor of his prose could be measured by the number of *foutres* and *bougres* in a single paragraph. To Hébert's accusation that he, Camille, had married a rich girl, he responded with an act of candor designed to win Robespierre's applause, declaring that this "fortune" his wife brought him consisted precisely of four thousand livres. His enemy, who pretended poverty, had in fact used his connection with Bouchotte and Vincent to secure 120,000 livres for the distribution of his own rag, as if it were the official journal of the army! Desmoulins even appended his version of Hébert's bill of accounting, claiming to show how much old Père Duchesne had pocketed for himself.

Hébert, however, was not Desmoulins' only target. He was concerned with warding off attacks on Danton from the Terrorists who felt themselves threatened by the *Indulgent* program. And in fact he did a better job of defending his hero than Danton himself had on December 1 at the Jacobins. Desmoulins went directly for the jugular by celebrating the attack on Danton as William Pitt's finest hour ("O Pitt, I render homage to your genius!"), thus feeding Robespierre's own conviction that the *ultras* were really a branch of the counter-revolution. In subsequent numbers Desmoulins went on to attack another favorite bugbear of both Danton and Robespierre: the dechristianizers. "Liberty," Desmoulins reminded his readers, "is not a nymph from the Opéra, it is not a *bonnet rouge,* or a dirty shirt . . . liberty is happiness, reason and equality." From this he went on to confront the institutions of the Terror itself, starting with the law of suspects. If the government asked that he spill his blood for liberty, it should honor its commitment to that principle by opening the prisons and liberating two hundred thousand people "that you *call* suspects, since in the Declaration of the Rights there are no 'houses of suspicion.'" Such a measure would be "the most revolutionary one that you have ever taken." What, after all, was the alternative?

> Do you want to exterminate all your enemies by the guillotine?
> But this would be the greatest folly. Can you destroy even one on
> the scaffold without making ten enemies from among his family
> and friends? Do you really believe that it is women, old men, the
> feeble, the "egoists" who are dangerous? Of your true enemies
> only the cowards and the sick are left,

and those, like the *rentiers* and shopkeepers currently filling the prisons, are hardly worth all the anger spent on them.

In number 4, Desmoulins suggested an immediate specific reform: a "committee of clemency" operating independently of the Committees of General Security and Public Safety, one that could review cases of questionable accusation or conviction. It would be, of course, a direct challenge to the Commune-dominated Revolutionary Tribunal. It could act as a safeguard against malicious denunciation and correct such glaring travesties of justice as the arrest of a friend of Desmoulins who had been accused of having given dinner to someone later deemed to be a political undesirable. In a revolution one had to be careful, wrote Desmoulins, not fearing to quote Mirabeau (though in terms less earthy than the orator): "Liberty is a bitch who likes to be bedded on a mattress of cadavers."

The *Vieux Cordelier* was a sensation, much the most powerful weapon in the armory of the *Indulgents.* Its calculated tone meant that it was deliberately addressed to the revolutionary elite, not just those in the Convention but those in the western and central sections of Paris who were tired of being bullied by the Commune and who applauded Desmoulins' rhetorical question: "Is there anything more disgusting and more execrable *(ordurier)* than the *Père Duchesne*?" And even more specifically it was aimed at the one person on whom, as Danton and Desmoulins knew, the success or failure of their campaign turned: Maximilien Robespierre. In number 4 Desmoulins had even invoked the fact of their having been schoolfellows together at the Lycée Louis-le-Grand, in an explicit appeal for Robespierre to consider the virtues of humanity as consistent with patriotism.

Robespierre was, in fact, extremely receptive to the appeal. He had had quite enough of the dechristianizers, who on November 11 had gone so far as to bring cartloads of sacerdotal objects to the Convention and dump them unceremoniously on the assembly floor. Engravings show sans-culotte guards wearing bishops' mitres and cassocks. He had also intervened personally to prevent the arrest of the seventy-three members of the Convention who in June had signed a petition against the expulsion of the Girondins. More surprisingly, in view of what was to unfold three months later, he was still firmly devoted to Danton and defended him fiercely against critics in the Jacobins on December 3. He even implied that merely to impugn Danton's patriotism was to do the dirty work of William Pitt, who would like nothing better than to set good patriots at each other's throats.

With Robespierre apparently leaning towards the *Indulgents*, they pressed home their attack. Another of Danton's allies in the Convention, Philippeaux, delivered a scathing report on the brutality and corruption he said had been perpetrated by Ronsin and the *armées révolutionnaires* in Lyon. As a result, Ronsin and Vincent were both arrested and Desmoulins' proposed clemency committee was actually established. It looked for a moment as though the Terror might begin to be dismantled. Even the famous law of 14 Frimaire (December 4), often misleadingly called "the constitution of the Terror," was in fact aimed *against* all those who had exacted the most brutal retribution in the name of republican orthodoxy. While it subordinated "all constituted authorities" to the Committee of Public Safety, it ended the anarchic process by which zealots could take the law into their own hands. Local revolutionary committees were now required to make a report every ten days to the district administration; no public official (including the *représentants-en-mission*) was permitted to expand or augment laws enacted by the Convention or impose forced loans or improvised taxes. Much, of course, turned on the temper of the Committee of Public Safety itself. But when news came of both the recapture of Toulon on December 15 (thanks to General Bonaparte) and, a week later, the final decisive battle at Savenay against the Vendéans, there was reason for the *Indulgents* to hope that a brighter military outlook would reinforce the case for a more relaxed government.

They were to be sharply disabused. On December 21 Collot d'Herbois, freshly returned from Lyon, made an appearance at the Jacobins. There he attacked those (especially Fabre) responsible for Ronsin's imprisonment and upbraided the members for their creeping pusillanimity. Speaking with the spurious authority of a man who has been fighting at the front and has returned to find the home guard gone soft, Collot declared, "Two months ago when I left you, you were burning with the thirst for vengeance against the infamous conspirators of the city of Lyon. Today I hardly recognise public opinion; if I had arrived two days later I would perhaps have been put under indictment myself." He concluded rhetorically by asking, "Who are these men who reserve their *sensibilité* for counter-revolutionaries, who evoke so mournfully the shades of the assassins of our own brothers, who have so many tears to shed over the cadavers of the enemies of liberty while the heart of the *Patrie* is ripped apart. . . ?"

It was one of the best performances of Collot the actor, and it marked the exact point at which the *Indulgent* campaign started to go on the defensive. To Collot's question, Hébert was only too happy to supply names—Desmoulins, Fabre, Philippeaux, Bourdon de L'Oise. Though the secret of his collusion in the Company of the Indies fraud was not yet out in the open, Fabre was the object of increasingly pointed attacks, not least in a petition to the Convention from the Cordeliers Club. The decisive shift occurred, however, in the Committee of Public Safety itself. Collot had a dependable ally in Billaud-Varennes, and Saint-Just, still on mission, could probably be counted on in a crisis. The Committee of General Security was even less warmly disposed towards the *Indulgents*. One of its most enthusiastic Terrorists, Vadier, had commented that he meant to "gut that fat turbot Danton," to which Danton is said to have crisply responded that if he dared to lay a finger on him, he would eat Vadier's brains and shit in his skull.

For Robespierre, it was the "orderly" institution of revolutionary government as set out in the law of 14 Frimaire which was at stake. The cohesion of the Committee of Public Safety could not afford a serious schism, pulled apart by competing influences from the Dantonistes and Hébertistes. It was essential for its executive authority that it be seen to rise above "faction," indeed be seen to strike impartially at it. Moreover, at some point in late January, or perhaps in early February, he had clear and shattering evidence of Fabre's criminality: perhaps the signature itself. There was nothing Robespierre hated more than crime disguised as patriotism. Nor did he much like being made to look like an idiot. He was already being twitted by Billaud-Varennes for having agreed to the committee of clemency and had to protest rather feebly that he had had no part in its membership. Now it was glaringly obvious that Fabre had led him by the nose to the point, even, of permitting Fabre to investigate a fraud to which

Fabre himself had been a party! In this light, Robespierre was inclined to write off the entire *Indulgent* campaign as an appalling exercise in hypocrisy designed merely to cover the tracks of criminals and of Fabre in particular. He believed and still wanted to believe that Danton himself was not implicated and, learning of his wife's death in early February, wrote a touching letter to him in the warmest terms, appealing to their old friendship. What he was asking of Danton, in fact, was that he desert his corrupt friends and adhere to the fiat of the Committee. In practice, of course, this meant that at some point Danton would be asked to incriminate Fabre and perhaps even Desmoulins, and this he steadfastly refused to do. Perhaps it was this unconscionable devotion to friends even when they had been exposed as crooks, rather than to the "objective" sacrifices needed to be made for the *patrie*, that in the last analysis Robespierre found so unforgivable. If Danton could not act Brutus, then he deserved to perish like Brutus' sons.

On the other hand, Robespierre also had no intention of allowing the prosecution of the *Indulgents* to become a victory for the *ultras*. He still had not forgiven Hébert for dechristianization, even though the latter had tactically decided to soft-pedal the cause for a while. The last thing Robespierre wanted was a renewal of the Commune's insurrectionary politics against the committees, and the release of Ronsin and Vincent amidst scenes of sans-culotte jubilation seemed to make that more likely. Acknowledging that the economic Terror had generated more hardship and inflation rather than less (exactly as Barbaroux had predicted), the Committee was also considering modifying the *maximum* to allow for transport costs, thus at least giving some sort of incentive for producers to move their goods from the place of origin. To preempt the inevitable protests that this was once again to overlook the government's duty to the poor, Saint-Just came forward with the radical decrees of Ventôse (February 26 and March 3). These provided for the distribution to the needy of property confiscated from émigrés. But it also presupposed that the needy would declare themselves to be such at a time when others in the Convention were proposing to transport vagrants to Madagascar. In any event, the decrees remained a dead letter partly because so few of the Committee seem to have been party to them (Robespierre having been ill since early February) and partly because much more urgent political decisions intervened.

A day after the presentation of Saint-Just's second decree, Hébert and Carrier (back from drowning priests at Nantes) veiled the bust of Liberty at the Cordeliers: the ritual which signified a call for insurrection. But as they fatally discovered, the machinery of popular mobilization had been effectively sabotaged by government control since 14 Frimaire. The revolutionary committees were riddled with government spies who knew the movement of the "insurrection" better than its leaders did. The Commune, now more anxious to please the committees than Hébert, refused to call out its troops and the rising fizzled out. Five days later Saint-Just delivered a blistering attack on faction as an "enemy of sovereignty" and thus a tool of the counter-revolution, and in the days that followed virtually all of Hébert's principal supporters were arrested, including those originally named by Fabre in the "foreign plot." Among them was the bizarre Anacharsis Cloots, the self-designated "Orator of the Human Race," who had tried to exonerate himself by confessing in print, pathetically, that "if I have sinned it is by too much candor and naiveté. Marat used to tell me 'Cloots, tu es une foutue bête.' " There, at least, the Friend of the People had not erred.

On the twenty-fourth of March, Hébert and nineteen of his friends went to "hold the hot hand"; "look through the republican window"; be "shaved by the national razor" (among other comical euphemisms favored by *Père Duchesne*). There was a strong emotion of *Schadenfreude* among the crowd, who plainly enjoyed seeing the man who had so celebrated the guillotine quail visibly at the prospect of his own destruction. Huge, noisy crowds, cheering and jeering, greeted the progress of the Hébertistes to the place de la Révolution. "They died like cowards without balls," said one man overheard by a government agent. "We thought that Hébert would have more courage but he died like a *Jean-Foutre*," said another, suggesting a keen sense of poetic justice.

A week later Danton and some of his closest friends, including Desmoulins, Lacroix, Philippeaux and, on a different day, Hérault de Séchelles, were arrested in their turn. The killing of the Hébertistes had always, of course, implied the end of the *Indulgents*, since to have attacked the one without the other would have been to fatally alienate the hard-core Terrorists on both committees. On the twenty-ninth of March there had been one last meeting between the two giants. Danton tried to persuade Robespierre that their friendship had been deliberately broken by Collot and Billaud, who had sown discord between them to exonerate themselves from Terrorist excesses. But Robespierre was not listening. He in his turn demanded that Danton sacrifice the self-evidently corrupt as the price of his own self-preservation. It was a dialogue of the deaf. A persuasive version of the night of the arrest has Marat's sister, Albertine, actually warning Danton and urging him to go directly to the Convention to denounce the Committee. At first he was reluctant to consider this, as it meant calling for the proscription of Robespierre, but persuaded he had no alternative he eventually went. On entering the assembly, Danton saw Maximilien in such apparently friendly conversation with Camille Desmoulins that he relaxed his guard and went home. He was picked up later that night.

Everyone concerned in the hunt knew that closing for the kill would not be easy. In Hébert they had slain a weasel (albeit one with sharp teeth). In Danton they had a wounded lion to dispatch and one whose belligerent roars could resound around Paris. On the evening of the thirty-first of March, the two committees had met in joint session to consider tactics. Saint-Just brought along the indictment, of which he was unjustifiably proud, and said he would read it in the Convention the following day, after which they could arrest Danton and his friends. Vadier and Amar looked at him as though he were off his head. First, they insisted, arrest Danton, then denounce all you like. Any other way would invite disaster. At this slight to his persuasive powers, not to say his manhood set against Danton's, Saint-Just became uncharacteristically angry. But the policemen from General Security had their way.

The indictment against Danton, corrected in its final form by Robespierre, was, even by the standards of the Revolutionary Tribunal, an incredibly feeble document. The charges against Hérault de Séchelles were even more specious. Accused of being an aristocrat, he invoked the memory of his best friend, Michel Lepeletier, a *ci-devant* of even more illustrious breeding. Danton, however, was accused of every kind of perfidy, from plotting to put the Duc d'Orléans on the throne to rescuing people, including Brissot, from the September massacres, to laughing whenever the word *vertu* was mentioned. He was, in short, a bad lot. Obviously the Committee hoped that by surrounding Danton and Desmoulins with the crooks of the Company of the Indies fraud, including a whole variety act of assorted foreigners—the brothers Frey, the Spaniard Guzmán, the Dane Friedrichsen, the Belgian Simon—the blame for the swindle would rub off on their major adversary, even though they had no evidence to show he was in any way connected.

An enormous crowd crammed into the courtroom on April 2, for Danton's following was still formidable. Fouquier-Tinville had tried to contain popular interest as much as possible by waiting until the last minute before announcing the trial, but he was still in danger of being swamped by a rowdy court. This deeply offended his sense of orderly procedure. Even the number of the accused seemed to go awry when, during the course of the proceedings, Danton's old comrade Westermann insisted on being indicted with his friend. When the president of the Tribunal assured him that that was "only a formality," Danton commented, "Our whole presence here is just a formality." Disruption followed disruption, revealing Danton's frighteningly accomplished sense of public theater. Failing to cut short one of Danton's booming tirades, the president, Herman, asked, "Didn't you hear the bell?" Danton replied, "The voice of a man who has to defend both his life and honor must vanquish the sound of your little bell." He was, in fact, fully determined to exploit the advantage in volume he had over his judges, knowing that a great, deep voice not only made its interrogators sound ridiculous but seemed to testify to resources of virile power that republican culture associated with virtue. To thunder was to be patriotic. The next day, at the beginning of the defense, addressing the public rather than the judges or the jury, he declared, "People, you will judge me when you have heard me; my voice will not only be heard by you but throughout all of France."

That, indeed, was just what the Tribunal was afraid of. They had no intention of allowing Danton to run the trial his own way and scorned as outrageous his demand to call a long list of witnesses, including such members of the Committee of Public Safety as Robespierre himself and Robert Lindet, who alone among Danton's colleagues had refused to sign the arrest warrant. Though no complete record of the proceedings survives, it nonetheless seems that Danton spoke nearly the whole day and with stupendous effect, brushing off the charges against him like insects crawling up his clothes. "Will the cowards who are slandering me dare to attack me to my face?" he demanded, and in a more stoical-Romantic vein, "My domicile will soon be in oblivion and my name in the Panthéon. . . . Here is my head to answer for everything." At the end Danton seemed to want to lift the moral squalor of the occasion up to the level of tragic rhetoric, making of his own end something as weighty and as memorable as that of a Homeric hero, a patriot from the annals of Rome.

> During the past two days the court has got to know Danton. Tomorrow he hopes to sleep in the bosom of glory. He has never asked for pardon and you will see him fly to the scaffold with his usual serenity and the calm of a clear conscience.

During their detention and trial the Dantonistes were incarcerated in the Luxembourg. It was perhaps the least wretched of all the prisons of the Terror, and those who saw them there remember Danton and Philippeaux affecting a kind of forced gaiety. Danton, in particular, seemed resigned to parting from his second wife, Louise, a girl of just sixteen. Camille Desmoulins, however, was uncharacteristically thrown into the deepest dejection at having to separate from Lucile, with whom he remained passionately in love, was very much alive and, whenever she could, came to see him, standing at the permitted distance, something that gave her husband both

206. J-B Wille, drawing, Danton—his hands tied—on the way to the guillotine

intense pleasure and dreadful emotional torment. In his last letter written before his execution, he told his wife that at the sight of her and her mother he had thrown himself against the bars in grief. The letter is astonishing, the outpouring of a man completely undone by sorrow and regret, thrown into the depths of a kind of Romantic phantasmagoria, someone who wants to renounce his whole public life for the possibility of private peace.

> My Lucile, *ma poule*, despite my torment I believe there is a God, my blood will efface my faults, I will see you again one day O my Lucile . . . is the death which will deliver me from the spectacle of so many crimes such a misfortune? Adieu Loulou, adieu my life, my soul, my divinity on earth . . . I feel the river banks of life receding before me, I see you again Lucile, I see my arms locked about you, my tied hands embracing you, my severed head resting on you. I am going to die. . . .

Still fighting, Danton continued to demand the right to call witnesses. His insistence was so adamant and the public so supportive that, fearing the entire process might collapse, Saint-Just went to the Convention and told them that the prisoners were fomenting insurrection against the court and that Desmoulins' wife was involved in a plot to murder members of the Committee of Public Safety. Preposterous as all this was, it gave the Committee enough authority to return to the court and have Fouquier proceed to his usual shortcut of "asking" the jury if they had been sufficiently "enlightened." They had. Knowing he had lost in a final court of appeal, Danton became resigned. In prison, according to Riouffe, who said he heard him through the walls, he voiced regret that he was leaving the Republic in such miserable condition, run by men who had no clue about government. "If only I could leave my balls to Robespierre and my legs to Couthon the Committee might live a little longer."

On the fifth of April, Danton, Hérault, Desmoulins and the rest went to their death. Watched by a vast and mostly silent crowd, they conducted themselves with great dignity and composure. Danton was determined to show affection and friendship. He and Hérault de Séchelles, the prodigy of the Parlement turned regicide Jacobin, tried to embrace but were roughly separated by the executioner Sanson. "They will not prevent our heads from meeting in the basket," Danton is reported to have said. But his last remark was better still. As he stood before the plank, his shirt splattered with the blood of his best friends, Danton told Sanson, "Don't forget to show my head to the people. It is well worth the trouble."

207. Hubert Robert, drawing of Camille Desmoulins in prison

CHAPTER NINETEEN

Chiliasm

April–July 1794

i DEATH OF A FAMILY

T WAS NOT himself Malesherbes was anxious for, but his family. At a dangerous moment during the King's trial, one of the deputies of the Convention had asked, "And what makes you so bold?" to which he had retorted, "Contempt for life." It was true. The Terror had no power to frighten an old man of seventy-two. Since the committees seemed bent on rewriting French history by exterminating those who had helped shape it, he supposed that sooner or later his turn would come. After all, the mere fact of his survival into old age was a piece of effrontery, since he carried with him the possibility of transmitting a history of the reform that had begun before the Revolution. That he was still popularly known as "the Virtuous Malesherbes" made things even worse. It meant that the Terror would see him as a challenge to the axiom that anyone whose career stretched back two reigns must necessarily be imprinted with the corruption and tyranny associated with the "Capets."

In any event, there was nothing to be done but wait and see how events unfolded. After the execution of the King, he had returned to the château at Malesherbes, near Pithiviers in the Department of the Loiret, and gathered his family around him as if they might draw strength and reassurance from their union. His younger daughter, Françoise-Pauline, living in London with her husband Montboissier and writing frightened, concerned letters, was the only missing loved one. They were especially poignant since she was an émigré twice over, having left for Switzerland in 1789, returned to France in the spring of 1792 and then, following the September massacres, having decided to go to England in the great wave of departures of October. Malesherbes disapproved of emigration in principle but, feeling sure her life would be in danger, urged her to go. Now his feelings were torn once more. The virtual certainty that he would never see her again was made bearable only by the relief that at least one branch of the family was out of harm's way.

His older daughter, Marguerite, had brought all of her children to the château. Now thirty-eight, she was married to a *ci-devant* president of the Parlement of Paris, Lepeletier de Rosanbo. This in itself made him a marked man, and his remote kinship to the Lepeletier who was now hallowed as the first martyr of the Republic was unlikely to count in his favor. Two of their three daughters, moreover, had married into the same kind of distinguished clans of the legal nobility: Aline-Thérèse to the older Chateaubriand boy, Jean-Baptiste, and Guillemette to a Lepeletier d'Aulnay. There was a last wedding at Malesherbes on March 12, 1793, when the youngest of the girls, Louise, was married to Hervé Clérel de Tocqueville, from an old Norman military family.

In early September, Malesherbes volunteered to defend Marie-Antoinette, as he had the King. The offer was declined, but the fact that it was made at all suggests how unconcerned he was for his own safety. In fact, it was Rosanbo who was in most danger. In 1790 he had served as the president of the Chambre des Vacations of the Parlement of Paris, which continued its judicial functions when the full court was suspended. In that capacity, and like his counterparts in many of the other sovereign courts, he had written a formal protest against the Constituent's decree abolishing the Parlements. This left him vulnerable to the usual charge of "conspiring against the liberty and sovereignty of the French people." And on December 16, 1793, a family dinner was interrupted by a group of National Guards bearing a warrant from the revolutionary committee of the *section* de Bondy, where Rosanbo's town house was located. A search had been made which turned up a copy of the incriminating document. The following morning, the library was ransacked in front of Rosanbo and Marguerite, and the many letters written to her from her sister in London were found.

The next day the husband was taken away to Paris and held in the new prison of Port-Libre. On the nineteenth the family tried to decide what to do for the best. Guillemette's husband had already departed (and would be arrested in the Nièvre in May). It was Aline's husband, Chateaubriand, who seemed to be in most peril, as he was a returned émigré. Malesherbes advised him to flee, but after hiding himself for a short time in a local farm, he decided he could not leave his wife and two small children, just five and three, and returned to the château to be with them. Though a search through Malesherbes' own papers had turned up nothing incriminating, it is clear that the decision had already been taken to add his name and those of his children to the original decree of Rosanbo's arrest. Bagging entire *ancien régime* families was coming to be a matter of honor for the revolutionary committees and tribunals, as if the future of the Republic depended on extirpating any capacity the old ruling class had of reproducing itself. When, for example, Loménie de Brienne had been arrested, four other de Briennes of various generations had been taken with him and were duly executed; the same would be true for the du Plessis and indeed those of the Gouvernet de La Tour du Pin who could be found. On December 20, two carriages with an armed escort came to take the Malesherbes-Rosanbo family to Paris.

Once in the capital they were sent to different prisons: Mme de Rosanbo to the Couvent des Anglaises; her two sons-in-law, de Tocqueville and Chateaubriand, to La Force; Malesherbes and his sixteen-year-old grandson Louis to the Madelonettes; and the three girls to another convent, not yet converted into a prison, in the Marais. After a few days, the Committee of General Security responded favorably to the sons-in-law's request that the family be reunited, and they were brought together in Port-Libre.

For prisoners of the Terror, there were far worse places to be. Though the Jansenists had been famous for their austerity, there was at least light and air in quantities that seemed luxurious to anyone coming from Sainte-Pélagie or La Force. Conspicuous among the six hundred inmates were groups of *ancien régime* officials and *financiers*, scooped up in batches by the revolutionary committees and kept together as if they were exhibits in a short-term museum of the corporate society. Immured in Port-Libre then were twenty-seven Farmers-General, including Lavoisier, another large group of Receivers-General, former ministers and *intendants*—among them Saint-Priest—and several Parlementaires who, in common with Rosanbo, were soon transferred to the Madelonettes to await trial. With so many luminaries of the old world of Paris culture gathered together, it was inevitable that they should fashion a kind of prison salon; in the evenings, they listened to Vigée (the painter's brother) recite his latest poems or to such actors as Fleury and Devienne declaim lines they knew by heart, or heard Witterbach's viola d'amore drift sad, deep tones through the vaulted cells.

In this kind of company a strong sense of honor was bound to prevail. They were horrified to learn that it was an elegant young man, apparently of a good family named Duviviers, who had stolen a watch from Mme Debar. He had smuggled it out in a pile of dirty laundry carried by his mistress, an actress at the Opéra with orders to sell it for as much as she could get. But a prospective buyer would only part with five hundred livres on receipt of a written declaration of ownership. The girl then admitted that the piece was not hers and wrote a letter to her boyfriend complaining about the difficulty of the assignment. It was intercepted by one of the jailors and the thief confessed to the crime. Before his transfer to a different and less comfortable prison, he was ostracized by the rest of the prisoners as though he were a source of infection.

In March, they were joined by a number of those who had been their most relentless persecutors: the Hébertistes. Few of the *ci-devants* bothered to hide their pleasure at seeing their archenemies brought low and especially enjoyed Hébert's obvious terror at his impending fate. The wife of the printer Momoro, who was said to have played "Reason" in the dechristianizing *fête* in Notre Dame, was given a particularly hard time. Another officer from the Parisian *armée révolutionnaire,* Bertaux the engraver, though sporting the obligatory moustaches and looking fierce, was despised for "crying like a baby." (In fact, he seems to have been imprisoned for a *lack* of militancy, and a record of supporting Lafayette.) His commander Ronsin, on the other hand, got high marks for affecting at least the appearance of insouciance in the best aristocratic manner.

Universally treated with respect and deference, Malesherbes liked holding forth occasionally on his own political history and that of the monarchy. To Hué, the ex-valet of the Dauphin, he confessed that he had learned that "to make good ministers, knowledge and probity are not enough. Turgot and I were proof of that; all our science was in books and we had no understanding of men." He constantly reverted, though, to the pathetic tragedy of the King himself and his trial: a man bewildered by the position he found himself in and who, in Malesherbes' view, paid with his own blood for being unwilling to shed that of others.

On the eighteenth of April there was suddenly an acceleration of their case. Rosanbo was taken to the Conciergerie to await his trial, and while he was there, Malesherbes decided to try reasoned argument one last time. He dictated a memorandum about his son-in-law for Fouquier-Tinville, and appended a letter imploring him to read it, so that the case would have proper consideration. With considerable cunning Malesherbes actually invoked Saint-Just to the effect that, as he had said in the proceedings against Danton, there had been in 1790 an Orléanist conspiracy against the constitutional monarchy. By supporting the throne so vigorously, he said, Rosanbo was actually being a good patriot. Moreover, in those days it was customary for such petitions and protests to be drafted without any sense of conspiracy. He concluded by depicting Rosanbo (much as he himself had been certified by his local municipality at Malesherbes) as a true and virtuous citizen *avant la lettre.*

No-one, according to all those who have known him, could have been more scrupulous or more disinterested in the administration of justice; more solicitous in his manners or more of an *honnête homme* in his proceedings. From well before the revolution he already practised those private virtues, the love of humanity, the regard for his fellow-men, that rare and precious fraternity with his co-citizens which is one of the greatest benefits of our regeneration.

A copy of the memorandum (which, needless to say, cut no ice at all with the prosecutor) was sent to Rosanbo. To it were attached a few lines from his sixteen-year-old son, who after a brave beginning had started to weep a lot at night, and a last letter from his wife. It was typical of such parting messages, colored by all the domestic tenderness which, according to the official Jacobin canon, aristocrats were incapable of feeling.

> You know that to live beside you, to care for your health and to surround ourselves with our children and to care for the old age of my father has always been my only preoccupation . . . we will soon be together, *oui mon bon ami,* I hope so. *Adieu* good and tender friend, think of a being who lives only for you and who loves you with all her heart. My father, aunt and children who are here about me share these sentiments. . . .

On the first of Floréal, the day of the oak, according to Fabre's new calendar, Rosanbo was guillotined. The next evening Malesherbes was himself brought for his interrogation. He denied both charges of "conspiring against the liberty of the French people" and saying that "he would use every means to bring down the Republic." His daughter was accused of having entered into treasonable correspondence with "the internal and external enemies of the Republic." The only evidence against Malesherbes was from someone who had reported to a revolutionary committee that when Malesherbes' sister the Comtesse de Senozan had told him the vines on her estate were frozen, he had replied it was a good thing, as that would deny wine to the peasants, and had it not been for their being drunk there would have been no revolution. The self-evidently ludicrous nature of the evidence did not for a moment prevent Fouquier-Tinville from claiming that "Lamoignon-Malesherbes presents all the characteristics of a counter-revolutionary." His writings dwelt constantly on the old order of things; he was the center of an entire group of conspirators, many of whom had already been judged by "the blade of the law." His offer to defend the King had to be read in the light of his continuing connection to a notorious émigré son-in-law, making it obvious that Pitt had put him up to it. As for his daughter, she, like her husband, had always been an enemy of the Revolution . . . and so on.

That night, Louis and his three sisters dissolved into tears. Their mother, who had kept up her fortitude, seemed distracted and lost. The next morning, she seemed to have collected herself and remarked to Mlle de Sombreuil (the daughter of the old commandant of the Invalides, reputed to have drunk the notorious cup of blood to spare her father during the September massacres) that "you had the honor of saving your father; at least I will be able to die with mine." Sharing their tumbril were the Princesse de Lubomirski, the Duchesses de Châtelet and de Grammont as well as three ex-deputies of the Constituent: Huel; Thouret, the mastermind with Mirabeau of the new map of the departments; and Jean-Jacques d'Eprémesnil. That last and most famous figure had, of course, been the greatest thorn in Brienne's side when Malesherbes had been one of his ministers. But in the spring of 1794 it was entirely commonplace for veterans of wholly different and even hostile politics to share the same scaffold. The bureaucratic economy of the guillotine was quite indifferent to such niceties.

Last of his family to be beheaded, the old man had to watch as his daughter, a granddaughter and her husband Chateaubriand were executed before him. The other grandchildren were imprisoned and were released after Thermidor, but Fouquier-Tinville was not satisfied until he had guillotined Malesherbes' seventy-six-year-old sister and his two secretaries, one of whom was damned by the fact that a bust of Henri IV (the idol of 1789) was found among his belongings.

Of all the cruelties visited on the old man, the most painful was the likely reflection that by not heeding his younger daughter's advice to emigrate he had somehow attracted the attention of the Tribunal and destroyed his family. And did he ponder whether, if Louis had listened to his counsel and had abandoned the Estates-General altogether in favor of an entirely new constitution that might have avoided the polarization of the orders, the worst calamities of the Revolution might have been averted? He knew, at any rate, that his penchant for reason would not have gotten him very far once blood had started to flow and heads were spinning with patriotic rhetoric. Writing to another old Parlementaire, Rolland, in 1790, he had remarked that "in times of violent passions, one must surely keep from speaking reason. [Otherwise] one may even harm reason, for enthusiasts will excite people against the same truths that, in another time, would be received with general approbation."

ii THE SCHOOL OF VIRTUE

Robespierre's teachers at the Lycée Louis-le-Grand must have been important to his political education since, in the end, he saw himself as a messianic schoolmaster, wielding a very big stick to inculcate virtue. He came to conceive of the Revolution itself as a school, but one in which knowledge would always be augmented by morality. Both, moreover, depended on discipline. Terror and virtue, he was fond of saying, were part of the same exercise in self-improvement, "virtue without which terror is harmful and terror without which virtue is impotent." Once the criminal element, morally and politically speaking—the libertines, the atheists, the prodigals—had been eliminated, it would be possible to begin this vast exercise of enrolling an entire nation in the school of virtue.

In some respects, then, for Robespierre the most important committee of the Convention was neither that of public safety nor that of general security (which he came to see as the fief of low-life policemen like Vadier and Amar) but that of public instruction. It was, moreover, an institution that had accompanied the Revolution from its very beginnings, when Talleyrand and Sieyès had been important members, right through to the Terror, producing enormously long and ambitious plans that covered education from the elementary level through the new technical colleges that would produce an elite of enlightened engineers. At his death, Michel Lepeletier, of sainted memory, was working on just such a plan to create "houses of national education" at the elementary level, and it was this grandiose plan that Robespierre expanded. Its essence was to bring together those two pillars of the moralized republic: the school and the family. Perhaps it could have only been created by aristocratic schoolboys like Lepeletier whose parents had habitually surrendered them at tender ages to the mercies of gloomy Jesuits, since its principal object was to bring mothers and fathers back into the "house of instruction." The size of each school was to be determined not by an arbitrary decision but by a specification for the ideal number of families it comprised. This was set at fifty, deliberately corresponding to the number of décades in the revolutionary calendar. For one décade during the year, each mother and father would come to live at the school as the children's residential parents, dispensing fatherly severities and motherly tenderness as the children might require. In this way, the acquisition of knowledge would be reinforced by domestic virtue. There would be Spartan games, speeches from the Romans and a great deal of botany.

Needless to say, nothing came of such schemes, not least because, as the post-Jacobin committees of public instruction discovered, by decimating the clergy the Terror had destroyed the only reliable (and cheap) source of teaching personnel available for elementary education. But the passion for Improvement which fired Robespierre in the last months of the Terror flowed into all his policies and speeches until, in the end, politics itself seemed a rather squalid pastime compared with the transcendent calling of the Missionary of Virtue.

For those Jacobins who shared Robespierre's vision, there were two necessary stages to this enterprise of moral regeneration. First, the appalling cultural anarchy unleashed by the dechristianizers and the Hébertistes had to be stopped in its tracks; second, it had to give way to an imposing and orderly program of republican edification. That program would leave no part of a citizen's life untouched. It would use music, open-air pageants and theater; colossal public monuments; libraries, exhibitions, even sports competitions, to stimulate the great republican virtues: patriotism and fraternity. The exaltation of the collective life would be in the strongest possible contrast to the acts of indiscriminate destruction characteristic of the extreme phase of the Terror.

One of the most enthusiastic devotees of this Rousseauean cultural revolution, Henri Grégoire, the ex–constitutional Bishop of Blois, had coined the term *vandalism* when denouncing the most wanton assaults on statues, paintings and buildings condemned as part of the ecclesiastical, feudal and royal past. One of the most glaring instances of this had been the wholesale destruction of the royal tombs in the Saint-Denis chapel. Though Thermidorian stories of sans-culottes playing skittles with the bones of the Valois and the Bourbons were probably apocryphal, a painting by Hubert Robert, that connoisseur of ruins, certainly shows coffins being lifted from their graves and stones being overturned and removed. Grégoire had to be careful in his criticism, since the ransacking of Saint-Denis had been authorized by a decree of the Convention of August 1, 1793, and he was, in any case, anxious not to repudiate the official attack on totems of the past. No Jacobin even in this "instructional" phase of the Terror would have dared suggest restoring the statues of Louis XIV and Louis XV to their pedestals in Paris. But from Germinal onwards, Grégoire pressed on the Committee of Public Instruction an activist program which would turn back the vandal hordes from the gates of the new Rome and begin to "make the walls speak" the dignified language of republicanism.

On 20 Germinal, Grégoire turned his attention to another group of vandals as dangerous as the iconoclasts: *bibliophages*, the eaters of books. These were men who, in the name of misguided republicanism, wanted to burn down libraries, destroying in its entirety the wisdom accumulated before the Revolution, with perhaps a few honored exceptions, such as the work of the English regicide Algernon Sidney and Jean-Jacques Rousseau. Such barbarians were, said Grégoire, doing the work of the enemies of France by stripping it of its cultural patrimony and, in all likelihood, like the worst Hébertistes, they were actually foreign agents. What Grégoire proposed by way of a counter-attack was a great national bibliography—the *bibliographie française*—that would compile a record of the entire holdings of private libraries, which could then be made available to the Nation. It could be extended to include related objects of interest: medals and portraits, collections of scientific instruments and, most important, maps. In the Versailles ministries alone, he reported to the Convention, there were twelve *thousand* maps waiting to be catalogued. The department of Paris was even more "engorged" with these patriotic assets: some 1,800,000 volumes, which constituted the founding inventory of a *bibliothèque nationale*. Properly organized for the promotion of republican virtue, libraries and museums would be, he said, "workshops of the human mind," designed especially to lead the young away from the customary frivolities of their age, to places where they could "commune with the great men of every country and every age."

The other major figure in this program of republican instruction was Jacques-Louis David. He had already taken charge of the commissions to create permanent monuments from some of the statues used in the Fête de l'Unité: a colossal Hercules representing the French People, for example, was to be erected on the Pont-Neuf. Together with his brother-in-law the architect Hubert, he was producing a plan to relandscape the Champs Elysées as a huge Jardin National, with an enormous domed amphitheater at its center crowned by a statue of Liberty, suitable for the mass spectacles and patriotic games favored by Robespierre. (Albert Speer was not, then, the first to plan an architectural ideology around this kind of colossal collectivism.) At the same time, David was also busy designing "national costumes" that would express the proper dignity of true republicans—and which were clearly meant as a correction to the aggressive display of *bonnets rouges* and striped trousers that had been the hallmark of the militant sans-culotte. As if all this was not enough, David produced one of his most grandiose designs for the curtain of a composite production at the Opéra called *The Inauguration of the French Republic*, in which the usual woodenly didactic drama was enlivened with songs, speeches, poems, military marches and the occasional cannon designed to wake up those of the audience stunned into slumber by this relentless onslaught of republican virtue.

As a specimen of the juggernaut approach to Jacobin culture, David's curtain was rather impressive. Clearly inspired by antique reliefs, it lines up in profile a procession of republican paragons, at the center of which is a triumphal car whose wheels are rolling over the debris of royalty and episcopacy. In front of the chariot, muscled patriots are about to plunge their swords into hapless fallen monarchs, all viewed by the impassive giant Hercules, on whose lap rest the miniaturized female figures of Liberty and

Equality. By the side of and behind the car are ranged exemplars of the virtues: Cornelia and the Gracchi (dropped from David's final design); Brutus; William Tell (rapidly becoming a cult hero in Paris) and a group of martyrs, including Marat bearing his stigmata; Lepeletier; and, the latest additions to the pantheon, two patriots hanged by the British at Toulon.

All of these cultural techniques were brought together by David and Robespierre in their most ambitious political production: the Festival of the Supreme Being, held on the eighth of June (20 Prairial). Robespierre had announced the creed a month earlier, on May 7 (18 Floréal), in a painfully crafted speech on "the relations between moral and religious ideas with republican principles." "The true priest of the Supreme Being," Robespierre declared to the baffled and the bemused, "is Nature itself; its temple is the universe; its religion virtue; its festivals the joy of a great people assembled under its eyes to tie the sweet knot of universal fraternity and to present before it [Nature] the homage of pure and feeling [*sensible*] hearts." At the end of his deist sermon, the Convention decreed that "the French people recognize the existence of the Supreme Being [for which, presumably, he was to be duly thankful] and the immortality of the soul."

It hardly needed spelling out that the decree on the Supreme Being was a frontal attack on the dechristianizers, many of whom, like Fouché, were still important deputies of the Convention. The festival, announced at the same time as the decree, was to be the occasion when the Supreme Being's moral and political ascendancy over the infidels was to become irreversible. This time there would be no Hérault de Séchelles (a notorious unbeliever) to steal his thunder. Robespierre was elected president four days before the festival to ensure that he would play, ex officio, a central role.

Perhaps the weather on June 8—the day of Pentecost on the old Gregorian calendar—convinced skeptics that there was, after all, a Supreme Being and Robespierre was his prophet. A radiant sun shone down on the Tuileries, where thousands of Parisians gathered for the morning ceremonies. Looking down from a window on the banks of roses that David's team of florists had gathered and on the regiments of girls in white lawn dresses who carried baskets of fruit, Robespierre remarked to his companion Vilate, as if in rehearsal for his speech: "Behold the most interesting portion of humanity assembled here." Working with his usual music-lyrics team of Gossec and Marie-Joseph Chénier, David had conceived of the event as a vast revolutionary oratorio. One huge choral group was formed by twenty-four hundred delegates from the *sections* of Paris, each divided into human groups of old men, mothers, young girls, boys and small children (there seems, as usual, to have been no place for old *women* in the universe of Jacobin culture). At various moments each of these groups were to sing choruses

208. Jacques-Louis David, design for opera curtain, "The Triumph of the French People"

appropriate to their role in the new France and would then be echoed by their counterparts among the mass audience listening. At the moments of maximum drama—like the first and last verses of the "Marseillaise" and the new "Hymn of the Supreme Being"—the entire twenty-four hundred would sing out together, their voices dissolving into an immense chant of the people, which echoed throughout the amphitheater Hubert had constructed for the occasion. For Robespierre the new hymn was to be the anthem of his republican religion, and when Chénier's draft verses displeased him, he fired him angrily from the production team, replacing him with the poet Théodor Désorgues. Gossec and David had fretted about the audience's unfamiliarity with the hymn so much that in the weeks before the festival they had sent out teams of music teachers from the Institut National to instruct patriots in the *sections* on the melody and words.

As the last strains of the hymn faded, Robespierre appeared for his morning speech. He was dressed exquisitely in a blue coat, a tricolor sash and plumed hat, though in his nervousness he had forgotten the huge bouquet that one of the Duplay girls had specially made for him. (Each of the deputies of the Convention was carrying wheat sheaves and bouquets of flowers, though it seems incredible that Barras, for example, would have done so with a straight face.) "French Republicans," Robespierre declaimed, as if he were announcing the return of the Ovidian Golden Age, "it is for you to purify the earth that has been soiled and to recall to the earth Justice which has been banished from it. Liberty and virtue spring together from the breast of the divinity—neither one can live without the other." At the conclusion of the oration he took a flaming torch and, in one of David's visual metamorphoses, burned the effigy of Atheism from which (some said, in pure whiteness; others said, looking slightly sooty) the statue of Wisdom emerged. "He has returned to nothingness," intoned the Incorruptible, "this monster that the genius of Kings has vomited up on France."

In the afternoon, the crowds of people formed a long procession to the Champ de Mars. At the parade's center was a triumphal car (similar in design to that featured on the Opéra curtain) drawn by eight oxen, with their horns painted gold and bearing in the wagon a printing press and a plow, symbols of different kinds of officially approved labor. Further ahead a cart of blind children sang a "Hymn to Divinity" and were followed by columns of mothers bearing roses, and fathers leading their sons, who were armed with swords in the manner of David's Horatii. At the center of what had been renamed the Champ de Réunion, where the altar of the *patrie* had stood since 1790, David had built, at astonishing speed, an enormous plaster-and-cardboard mountain (modeled in fact on the one used at Lyon for the Fête de la Fédération). On its summit, standing on a fifty-foot column, was a colossal Hercules with the ever-diminishing figure (now virtually a figurine) of Liberty in his hand. Liberty had not been altogether banished from the world of the Supreme Being, since it was represented, also at the top of the mountain, by an enormous tree. Its presence was a response to another disquisition of Grégoire's, in which he sought to revive the liberty-tree cult of 1791–92 and even declared that the most appropriate species to celebrate the resurrection of primitive freedom was the oak, "the most beautiful of all the vegetables of Europe." It was, he said, the genealogical tree of the Great Family of the Free which, one day, would people the universe. Since it would endure for so many generations, children who were small at its planting would be able to gather *their* offspring beneath its branches and recount to them the heroic days of the founding of freedom.

For the afternoon music the fruited and floreated deputies of the Con-

209. Naudet, drawing, the Festival of the Supreme Being

vention climbed to the summit and looked down to the twenty-four hundred deployed along the paths, slopes and terraces that had been cut into the mountain. At a crucial moment, when the singing and blaring of martial brass had been silenced, Robespierre descended from the mountain like some Jacobinical Moses, parting the waves of tricolored patriots, and graciously received the burst of orchestrated applause that broke over his head. Even hearing, unmistakably, the sounds of cackling disrespect or outright hostility from some quarters could not spoil the apotheosis. "Oh day forever blessed," Robespierre would exclaim to the Convention on July 26 (8 Thermidor), "Being of Beings! Did the day of Creation itself—the day the world issued from thy all-powerful hands—shine with a light more agreeable in thy sight than that day on which, bursting the yoke of crime and error, this nation appeared in thy sight in an attitude worthy of thy regard and its destinies?" The question was, of course, strictly rhetorical.

iii THERMIDOR

While banks of roses perfumed the air at one end of Paris, puddles of blood contaminated it at the other end. The guillotine had no place in the visual *mise en scène* of the Supreme Being, so Robespierre banished it from the place de la Révolution to the open space at the end of the rue Saint-Antoine that would become the place de la Bastille. There it continued its busy operation, up and down, for three days, until local residents complained so angrily of the overflow of the blood, the dangerously "mephitic odors" from bodies going off in the June heat, that it was trundled off again, ever eastwards, to the barrière du Trône, now of course called the place du trône *renversé*.

There its productivity would be pushed by Fouquier-Tinville and the Sansons to industrial levels. Two days after the Festival of the Supreme Being, the Convention passed a decree which remains the founding charter of totalitarian justice. It was enacted in the wake of abortive assassination attempts, one on Collot d'Herbois on May 23 and one on Robespierre on the twenty-fifth. In the latter case a girl named Cécile Renault had been caught trying to gain access to Robespierre armed with two small knives, curious to know "what a tyrant looks like." She did not try very hard, but no one needed reminding of the example of Charlotte Corday. Introducing the decree of 22 Prairial, Couthon argued that ·political crimes were far worse than common crimes because, in the former case, "only individuals are wounded," whereas in the latter "the existence of free society is threatened." (This sort of argument anticipated Robespierre's remark on the eighth of Thermidor that atheism was far worse than famine because while "we" could stand hunger no one could stand "crime.")

In these circumstances, Couthon went on, as the Republic is threatened with conspiracies, "indulgence is an atrocity . . . clemency is parricide." Some adjustments would have to be made in both the criteria defining conspirators and the manner with which they were dealt. Henceforth anyone denounced for "slandering patriotism," "seeking to inspire discouragement," "spreading false news" or even "depraving morals, corrupting the public conscience and impairing the purity and energy of the revolutionary government" could be brought before the Revolutionary Tribunal. That court could issue only one of two sentences: acquittal or death. To expedite the march of revolutionary justice, no witnesses would be allowed to be called nor could the accused have a defense counsel. Were not the jurymen, after all, good citizens, capable of coming to a fair and unbiased verdict on their own judgment?

Not everyone in the Convention was delighted with this measure. The deputy Rouamps requested a delay in the vote by threatening to blow out his brains in the Convention if his motion was not granted. Robespierre, of course, managed to insinuate that anyone with any objections to the bill could only have something to hide and submitted that "there is no-one here who is not capable of deciding about this law as easily as he decided about so many others of greater importance. . . ." He insisted that it be debated point by point and then voted on, a motion which was adopted in an atmosphere of nervous resignation.

The law of Prairial had an immediate effect on the tempo of executions, which in weeks before had already been accelerated. With the closure of provincial revolutionary tribunals, except a southern branch at Orange that dealt brutally with the culprits of Toulon, suspects from the departments were now brought to Paris for trial. The grim results were as follows:

	Executions	*Acquittals*
Germinal	155	59
Floréal	354	159
Prairial	509	164
Messidor	796	208
Thermidor 1–9	342	84

From an average of five executions a day in Germinal, the rate then went to seventeen in Prairial and twenty-six in Messidor.

210. Anonymous print, "It is dreadful but necessary" ("*C'est affreux mais nécessaire*"),
from the *Journal d'Autre Monde*, 1794

This intensification of what came to be called the Grande Terreur was all the more emphatic because it took place at a time when French military fortunes were markedly improving. The *levée en masse* had brought more than three quarters of a million men under arms and the *amalgame* had survived the most chaotic period of integrating volunteers with troops of the line. Through the prodigious logistic and strategic efforts of Carnot, Prieur de La Côte d'Or and Jeanbon Saint-André, the Comte de Guibert's rather frightening prophecy of total war was about to be fulfilled. Thirty thousand pounds of gunpowder a day were being manufactured at the Grenelle works alone and much of it was about to explode in the face of the surprised Coalition. On June 25, at Fleurus, General Jourdan, at one point going aloft in a hot-air balloon for a bird's-eye view of the battle, decisively defeated Coburg's main Austrian army. Eight thousand enemy dead were left on the field, including some British grenadiers much exulted over by the Jacobin poets. In no time Valenciennes and Condé, taken with such pain by the Allies, were recaptured by the French, who advanced through Belgium to Brussels and Antwerp. Holland seemed open once again.

Since the military crisis had receded so dramatically, it was hard especially for the two engineers on the Committee of Public Safety, Carnot and Prieur de La Côte d'Or, to see what Robespierre was going on about when he referred to the ubiquitous monster conspiracy. Cécile Renault, surely, did not present a threat sufficient to warrant passage of the Law of Prairial, and they worried particularly about the complete surrender of immunity for members of the Convention. In his bluff way Carnot hated the self-righteous posturing of the cult of the Supreme Being and told Robespierre so in no uncertain terms.

There were other rifts opening in the Jacobin elite. In April Robespierre and Saint-Just had created a special police *bureau de surveillance* that reported directly to the Committee of Public Safety and so infringed on the jurisdiction of its sister-committee of general security. The most powerful men in that institution were Vadier and Amar, who, as enthusiastic Terrorists and dechristianizers, felt themselves the main targets of Robespierre's pieties. They had allies, moreover, on the Committee of Public Safety itself—men whose growing opposition to the Dictatorship of Virtue was not fed by the milk of human charity but by an acute sense of self-preservation. Collot d'Herbois and Billaud-Varennes, after all, had always been somewhat apart on the Committee—promoted essentially as a sop to the sectional insurrection of September 5, 1793—a threat which had now largely evaporated. Collot had had to defend his conduct as a *représentant-en-mission* at Lyon, and recently there had been other colleagues who felt themselves unfairly put on the defensive for enforcing policies that had been Jacobin orthodoxy but a few months before. Javogues, for example, was put through a particularly difficult *scrutin épuratoire* at the Jacobins, and on July 11 (23 Messidor) Robespierre made a violent attack on Fouché, whom he wanted expelled from the club. (Very sensibly Fouché declined to answer Robespierre's command that he appear at the club to defend his action and lay low for a while, avoiding his house and carrying pistols.)

This was, in fact, one of Robespierre's increasingly rare appearances at the Jacobins. He was even more seldom seen in the Convention and completely absent from the Committee of Public Safety. He had evidently decided, after a bitter and bizarre joint meeting with the Committee of General Security at the end of June, that he had had enough of the institution as presently constituted. Vadier had discovered a wonderfully eccentric old lady named Catherine Théot, living in the rue Contrescarpe, who claimed to be the mother of an impending new Messiah and proclaimed Robespierre to be the herald of the Last Days, the prophet of the New Dawn. When the police arrived at her lodging, they also found Dom Gerle, the Carthusian monk who had been a deputy in the Constituent. Embarrassingly for David, who currently sat on the Committee of General Security, Gerle featured very prominently in the sacred triangle of patriotic clerics in the *Tennis Court Oath*. (Of the other two, Rabaut Saint-Etienne had been guillotined and Grégoire was still very much alive and well.) Vadier seized the case as a precious opportunity to ridicule Robespierre's messianic pretensions, and his adversary saw that the unmasking of the "conspiracy" was a pretext for a Voltairean attack on the Supreme Being. After a furious and venomous argument, he succeeded in quashing the proceedings, but not before the solidarity of the committees had been irreparably damaged.

Gradually, over the last weeks of July, the pieces of an anti-Robespierre coalition began to fall into place. Those who, like Fouché, had been publicly threatened as "criminals," and those like Collot and Billaud who felt their turn was not long in coming, began to be apprehensive of a new insurrection. The partial dismantling of economic controls, coupled with the liquidation of the *armées révolutionnaires,* had resulted in a new erosion of the *assignat,* which had sunk once again, to about 36 percent of its face value. Food shortages and rising bread prices had generated both serious unrest among artisans and wage earners and a wave of strikes in late June and July. Should this discontent be skillfully mobilized, a very dangerous situation could quickly arise. As the author of the Ventôse decrees, Saint-Just had a reputation as a champion of social equality. Were he to ally with Hanriot, still the commander of the National Guard, and bring out the troops from the militant *sections,* then the committees and the Convention could be put under siege until they were forced to purge themselves as they had the previous June. But this time it would be Jacobins who would be the victims.

Barère was especially anxious for this not to happen. Dogmatically aligned with neither Robespierre's group nor their opponents, he correctly foresaw that once the unity of the revolutionary government was broken it would be the prelude to its end. On the twenty-second of July (4 Thermidor) he attempted to patch together a compromise which would preserve the solidarity of the governing committees and, more important, announce that cohesion to the Convention. The plan was to court Saint-Just and Robespierre with an enforcement of the Ventôse decrees in return for abandoning any plans for a purge. Initially the scheme seemed to work, since both Saint-Just and Couthon gave it guarded approval. But it fell apart the following day when Robespierre made his first appearance in three weeks at another joint meeting of the committees. He set much less store than Saint-Just did by the kind of social engineering implied in the Ventôse decrees and his young friend's *Institutions Républicaines.* As usual, virtue and terror were uppermost in his mind, and so far from going along with the compromise, he made perfectly plain his unrelenting pursuit of villains in both committees.

Robespierre appeared to be isolated since Barère persuaded Saint-Just, despite Robespierre's intractability, to deliver a report to the Convention advertising the government's unity and saying little or nothing about the Supreme Being. Saint-Just also—perhaps fatally for him—signed an order dispatching artillery units out of Paris to the Army of the North. But although Robespierre's own allies seemed to be dividing, he prepared one of his great Manichaean appeals distinguishing between the forces of light and darkness. In the last resort, he believed it was inconceivable that Saint-Just would desert the man he had written to so adoringly in 1789.

Just such an oration, two hours long, was brought to the Convention on July 26 (8 Thermidor). Robespierre started innocuously enough by declaring that "the French Revolution is the first that will have been founded on the rights of humanity and the principles of justice. Other revolutions required only ambition; ours requires virtue." But he then went on, at first opaquely and then transparently, to warn the assembly that a conspiracy was brewing that threatened the Republic with ruin. Defending himself against charges of dictatorship and tyranny, he gradually let the deputies piece together a picture of those he had in mind by alluding to "monsters" who had "plunged patriots into dungeons and carried terror into all ranks and conditions." They were the true oppressors and tyrants. Resting on the basic doctrines of revolutionary *sensibilité*, he declared, "I know only two parties, that of good citizens and that of bad citizens. I believe patriotism not to be a matter of party but of the heart." By the end of the speech, though no names had been named except, oddly enough, Cambon, the head of the Finance Committee, allusions to the inheritors of Chabot, Chaumette and Fabre made it obvious to everyone just who the authors of the "volcanic" conspiracy were.

The speech appeared to be warmly received, but to Robespierre's evident amazement there then ensued a fierce debate over whether or not it should be printed, as was the custom of the house whenever a major oration had been made. As the argument became more heated, Vadier attacked Robespierre for ridiculing the importance of the Théot "conspiracy" and Cambon defended himself, only to hear his enemy describe his remarks as "as unintelligible as they are extraordinary." Pressed by another deputy to name those he accused, Robespierre refused to do so, whereupon Amar attacked him for indicting members of the Committee en bloc without letting them have a hearing. Seeing the session disintegrate into bitter hostilities, Barère attempted to wind up the debate, which he said "can only benefit Pitt and the Duke of York." (If he had ever read the proceedings of the Convention, the Duke would have been astonished to discover what a major part he played in its debates.)

That evening Robespierre delivered the same speech at the Jacobins, where he received a tremendous ovation. Collot d'Herbois, who was then in the president's chair, and Billaud-Varennes both tried to defend themselves and turn the attack, but found themselves isolated and drowned out with cries for their expulsion and, more ominously, "*à la guillotine.*" They were, however, far from finished. During the course of his speech Robespierre had included his usual rhetorical tactic of offering his personal sacrifice for the good of the *patrie.* This time they would take him up on the offer.

The following morning, July 27 (9 Thermidor), Saint-Just, as agreed, began a speech which was to have been on the political situation facing the government. But in the time that had passed since Barère suggested he do that, the political climate had abruptly changed, and seeing him working through the night on the speech in the offices of the Committee, Billaud and Carnot knew that, far from an anodyne statement on unity, they could expect a tirade of dangerous denunciation. Saint-Just had hardly reached his first obligatory reference to the Tarpeian rocks when he was, by previous agreement, interrupted by Tallien condemning Robespierre for having departed from the collective leadership to make a speech "in his own name." Billaud-Varennes followed with a more

211. Anonymous, Robespierre

pointed denunciation of a threat by Robespierre against members of the committees and the Convention. Astonishingly, instead of Saint-Just launching one of the counter-attacks for which he was much feared, his eloquence seemed to dissolve. He sat wanly in his seat while the accusations mounted. Seeing his defense falling apart, Robespierre attempted to secure the tribune for himself but was shouted down. The moment of complete collapse was perhaps not when his arrest was called for by an obscure deputy but when Vadier held up the standard devices of his rhetoric to ridicule. "To hear Robespierre, he is the only defender of liberty; he is giving it up for lost; he is a man of rare modesty and he has a perpetual refrain 'I am oppressed; they won't give me the floor' and he is the only one with anything useful to say, for his will is always done. He says 'so and so conspires against me, I who am the best friend of the Republic.' That is news." The one weapon against which Robespierre was helpless then struck him down: laughter. When words failed him, a deputy shouted, "The blood of Danton chokes him!"

The day was not yet won, however. Prudently, the Thermidorians had decided to arrest not just Robespierre, Couthon, Saint-Just and Le Bas but Hanriot, the commandant of the Guard, as well. But once the Commune heard of the proceedings, it refused to open any of its prisons to take the men and began, rather tardily, to mobilize the machinery of popular insurrection. The difficulty with this was that the Terror had damaged that machinery by executing its major operatives and filling the *sections* with spies and trusties, and it no longer really worked. Of the forty-eight *sections*, only twenty-four actually asked the Commune for instructions and only thirteen sent troops as the tocsin rang. They were enough, however, to liberate the five men and for General Coffinhal to march a substantial number against the Convention itself. For a while, some of the deputies believed themselves to be lost and prepared to be fired on. But the unity of the anti-Robespierristes held, almost certainly because, for the first time, they knew they could mobilize a counter-force from the central and western *sections against* the Commune. They appointed Barras commander of their own force and declared Robespierre and his associates *hors de la loi*—outlaw. This meant that they could be taken on mere verification of identity and summarily executed within twenty-four hours.

It proved to be the turning point of the day. Disturbed by having to confront a united Convention and clearly intimidated by the frightening outlawry, the troops at the Convention became restive. No orders came from the Commune, so Hanriot decided to withdraw what was left of his force to a station in front of the Hôtel de Ville. When that force in turn melted away at two in the morning, the troops under Barras' orders took their place and advanced to seize the proscribed deputies, who had taken shelter inside the building. As they did so, a body fell from a window at the feet of the officers. It was Augustin Robespierre, Maximilien's younger brother. Inside, they found the crippled Couthon lying helplessly on the staircase, having fallen down the steps. Inside the hall of the General Council, Le Bas had shot himself and Robespierre's face and body were covered in blood, his jaw shattered, presumably from a botched attempt at suicide. Saint-Just rose, standing quietly and almost nonchalantly to greet his captors.

The next morning Parisians awoke to discover that the guillotine had been moved back to the place de la Révolution. After summary identification by the Tribunal, seventeen of the Robespierristes were guillotined. Eighty-three members of the Commune and the *mairie* followed in the next two days, making it clear that the victorious party for the moment concurred with Couthon's claim that "clemency is parricide." The end of the

212. Berthaut (after Duplessis-Bertaux), Robespierre laid on the table of the Committee of Public Safety, morning of 10 Thermidor

architects of the Grande Terreur was particularly gruesome, like some mad exorcism of horror. The cripple Couthon was strapped to the plank in appalling pain, his bent limbs smashed from the fall. Saint-Just went to his death every bit the Roman stoic, in which role he had evidently cast himself. Robespierre had spent the night helpless on the table of the Committee of Public Safety, where he had presided in icy discipline so many times. The fastidious prophet of Virtue was thrust onto the plank by Sanson, blood smeared over his coat and blotching his nankeen breeches. To give the blade of the guillotine an unobstructed fall, the executioner tore away the paper bandage that had been holding his jaw together. Animal screams of pain escaped, silenced only by the falling blade.

T H E D A Y S and weeks that followed saw two-way traffic in the prisons of Paris. Jacques-Louis David, as he saw Robespierre attacked on the eighth of Thermidor, had insisted on life imitating art (specifically *his* art) and had borrowed from his *Death of Socrates* the line "Robespierre, if you drink the hemlock I shall follow you." He did nothing of the sort, of course, and lay low for a while until inevitably he was imprisoned in the Luxembourg. He could count himself fortunate that the numerous artists whose arrest warrants he had signed, including Hubert Robert and Joseph Boze, bore so little grudge. In prison he would paint a tormented, bewildered self-portrait and a lyrical therapeutic landscape of the park seen from his cell window.

On October 24, Hervé de Tocqueville emerged from the Madelonettes. He was just twenty-two years old and his hair had turned snow-white. Reunited with Malesherbes' granddaughter Louise, he found her undone by the destruction of their family. She would never properly recover but fall into fits of dejection and melancholy. Back at Malesherbes, Hervé managed to find his two little Chateaubriand nephews, Christian and Louis. They were now orphans at the ages of five and three and Hervé took them in as his own; eleven years later they would be joined by an infant cousin, Alexis.

There was at least one survivor of the Terror who remained gratefully behind bars. At the Jardin des Plantes, barely alive there, lay an old lion. He had been moved to Paris when the Revolution had broken up the royal menagerie at Versailles and when his keeper, aptly named Leroy, had died in 1789. During the height of the Revolution he had had to endure being poked at, laughed at, even spat on for having been not just a "creature of royalty" but the "King of Beasts." Now he was scruffy and lank; his coat had suffered from mange, and open sores and blisters had appeared on the exposed flesh. But he was at least alive and about to enjoy the fruits of Grégoire's trumpeted rehabilitation of knowledge, including zoology, as, after all, patriotic. In the meantime, he looked at the English spy who wrote about him (and perhaps sympathized with his fallen heraldic royalty) with a yellow, knowing eye.

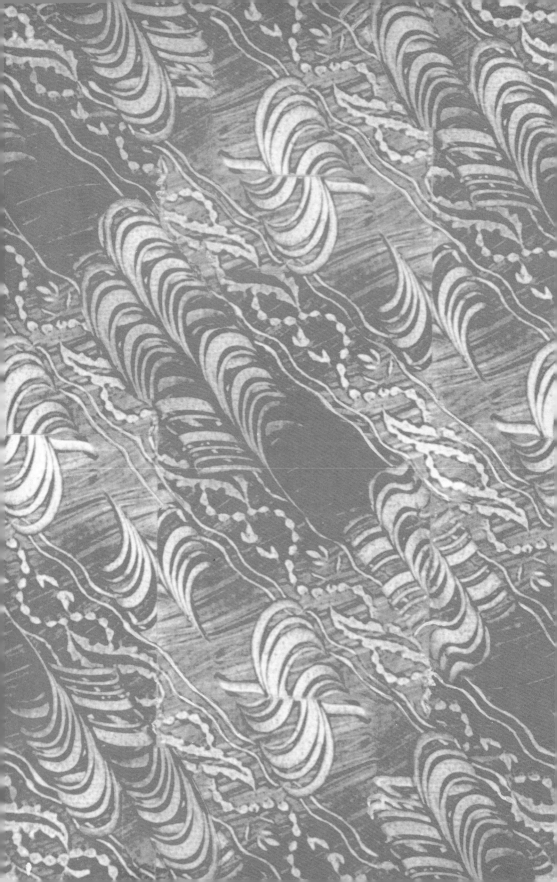

EPILOGUE

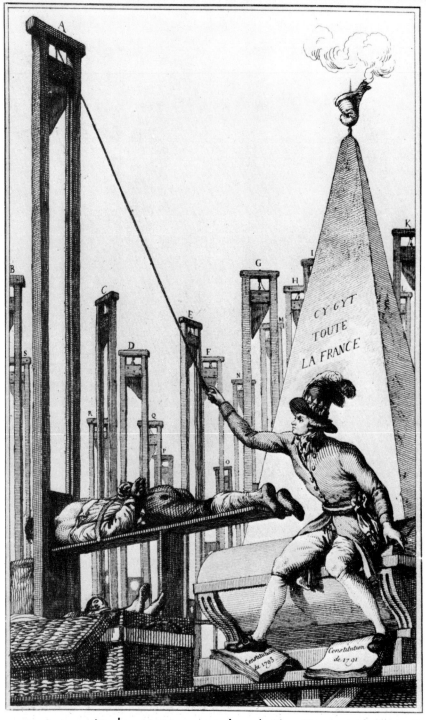

ROBESPIERRE, guillotinant le boureau après avoir fait guillot.^r tous les Francais

213. Anonymous, Robespierre guillotining the executioner

HO CAN BLAME the Thermidorians for depicting France as a hecatomb? It was, of course, in their interest to represent the atrocities of the Terror as the special responsibility of Robespierre and his confederates, since the hands of men like Collot d'Herbois, Tallien and Fouché were by no means unstained. Their most useful scapegoat was the prosecutor of the Revolutionary Tribunal, Fouquier-Tinville. Four days after Robespierre's execution, Fréron (who had been an enthusiast of the Law of Prairial) demanded in the Convention that Fouquier "expiate in hell the blood he has spilled." After his arrest he was taken to the Conciergerie, where, on learning the identity of the new prisoner, even hardened Jacobins began to bang the walls and shout invective at the "monster." On trial, Fouquier disappointed those expecting to see the incarnation of evil dissolve in shame and fear before his judges. But twentieth-century readers will recognize an ideal instrument of mass killing in the mild-mannered family man who pleaded that he had always obeyed the law and done his duty. He went to his execution in May 1795 worrying that the wife and children on whose behalf he had worked such long hours would now be threatened with poverty and ostracism. His last letter replicated exactly those of many of his prisoners: "Tell the children their father died unhappy but innocent."

Even allowing for a good deal of cynicism and hypocrisy on the part of the Thermidorians who encouraged their production, there is no doubt that the outpouring of anti-Terror prints was a genuine expression of relief. In one of the most alarming of these images, Robespierre, dressed as he had appeared at the Festival of the Supreme Being, guillotines the executioner, "having guillotined all of France." Each of the guillotines that extend behind him like some monstrous forest is labeled for a category of his victims: "L: Hébertistes; O: Old Men, Women and Children; P: Soldiers and Generals"; and so on. At the top of the obelisk bearing the legend "Here Lies All France," an inverted liberty bonnet has been spiked through and turned into a chimney of cremation.

Epilogue

It is a horrifying and haunting image, and there were many more: of pyramids of skulls surmounted by Robespierre's own death mask grimacing at the beholder; Marat dancing in hell, surrounded by writhing serpents; a *danse macabre* performed by a blindfolded France teased by the capering skeleton of Death. They all share a powerful sense of having drawn back from the edge of apocalypse.

The violence did not stop, however, with the Terror. Richard Cobb has written eloquently of the waves of the Counter-Terror, especially brutal in the Midi and the Rhone Valley; of anarchic murder gangs picking off selected targets implicated in Jacobinism. Republican officials; army officers; members of departmental administrations; conspicuous militants of the popular societies; and, in the south, Protestant farmers and merchants— all became prey for the *sabreurs* of the year III. Corpses were dumped in front of cafés and inns in the Midi or thrown into the Rhone or Saône. In many areas, the Counter-Terrorists would gather together at an inn as if for a day's hunting, and go off in search of their quarry.

The winter of 1794–95 was almost as murderous, pushing into destitution those already hit by a drought-withered harvest and high prices. With the destruction of the Church, and the slow recovery of its pastoral functions, many of the traditional resources for succoring the needy had also disappeared. At the most bitter point of the cold, in Nivôse year III, the government finally did away with what was left of the *maximum* and the regulatory controls. The result was desperation and abnormally high mortality, not just in the poorest regions of France but even in coastal areas of Normandy, where frozen harbors precluded the import of emergency grain. In the starving cities, fights again broke out for bread and firewood. Coal became a great luxury and men stood in long lines for a number entitling a family to a ration. In Paris, gangs of men, women and children trudged off to hack at trees in the Bois de Boulogne or the forests of Vincennes and Meudon for their firewood. With all municipal water fountains frozen, the carriers had to go further for their supply and, on reentering Paris, pay steep tolls which they tried to pass on to their customers. The hunger and cold were so extreme that foraging animals—foxes and even wolves—began to appear on the perimeters of cities, looking for sustenance. No wonder that in the winter of "*nonante-cinq,*" artisans began, once more, to look nostalgically back to the Terror, "when blood flowed and there was bread," in the words of one of the rioters of Germinal year III.

These were short-term miseries. But the damage inflicted by the Revolution went much deeper. Considerable areas of the country—the Midi and Rhone Valley, Brittany and western Normandy—remained in a virtual state of civil war, though the violence now proceeded in a haphazard, hit-and-run fashion rather than by organized insurrection. The great engines of capitalist prosperity in late eighteenth-century France, the Atlantic and Mediterranean ports, had been broken by antifederalist repression and British naval blockade. When Samuel Romilly returned to Bordeaux during the peace of 1802, he was dismayed to find the docks silent and ghostly and grass growing tall between the flagstones of the quai des Chartrons. Marseille and Lyon only recovered as the Revolution receded and the reorientation of the Bonapartist state towards Italy offered new markets and trade routes.

In such textile towns as Lille, many trades went into steep decline. For obvious reasons, all those employed in the *métiers de luxe*—wigmakers, tailors, dancing masters, teachers, musicians and watchmakers—saw their clientele disappear. But Cobb's research also showed more popular occupations, like shoemaking, suffering as badly, with the exception of the fortunate few who could land local contracts to supply the Armée du Nord. In the textile industries, manufacturers had been ruined by the *maximum*, which had forced them to sell at prices well below what they had paid for raw material before the controls were imposed. And given the dependence of weavers on piecework put out to them, the economic hurt would have extended right through the industry. What good was the freedom of the labor market, ostensibly available to them after the abolition of the guilds, if demand had collapsed? It is, in any event, far from certain that all artisans were universally thrilled with their new freedom, since it came with the stringent prohibition against any kind of labor organization in restraint of competition. Here too, at least in some industries, there was a tendency to fall back on the patterns of collective solidarity and organization of the old *compagnonnages* even when they were legally prohibited. In the heavy industries, such as iron-making, the spectacular opportunities generated by the ever-extending war again only accelerated and reinforced the concentrations of capital and labor and the technologically driven economies of scale that had already been apparent before the Revolution. De Wendel and the other great barons of metallurgy, it cannot be said too often, were by-products of the old monarchy, not the new revolution.

What had the Revolution accomplished to balance these penalties? Its two great social alterations—the end of the seigneurial regime and the abolition of the guilds—both promised more than they delivered. Though many artisans were undoubtedly happy to be free of the hierarchy of the corporations that constrained their labor and reward, they were, if anything, even more nakedly exposed to the economic inequities that persisted between masters and journeymen. Likewise the abolition of feudalism was more in the way of a legal than a social change and merely completed the evolution from lords to landlords that had been well under way in the old regime. There is no question that peasants were thankful for the end of seigneurial exactions that had imposed a crushing burden of payments on static rural incomes. Equally certainly, they were determined at all costs to oppose their reimposition. But it is hard to say whether the mass of the rural population were measurably better off in 1799 than they had been in 1789. Though the redemption tariff for feudal dues had been abolished outright in 1793, landlords often compensated themselves by various rent strategies that deepened the indebtedness of share-cropping *métayers*. Moreover, the taxes demanded by the Republic—among them the single land tax, the *impot fôncier*—were certainly no lighter than those exacted by the King. Before long the Consulate and Empire would revert to indirect taxes on at least as onerous a scale as under the old regime. All that they were spared, fiscally, were extraordinary poll taxes, including the old *capitation* and the *vingtième*, but this relief was only a consequence of the ever-expanding military frontier. Taxes lifted from the shoulders of the French were now dropped on those of the Italians, Germans and Dutch. When that frontier suddenly retreated in 1814, back to the old limits of the hexagonal *patrie*, the French were stuck with the bill, which, just as in 1789, they adamantly refused to pay, thus sealing the Empire's fate.

Was the world of the village in 1799 so very different from what it had been ten years before? In particular regions of France where there had been heavy emigration and repression, rural life had indeed been emptied of noble dominance. But this obvious rupture disguises a continuity of some importance. It was exactly those sections of the population who had been gaining economically under the old regime that profited most from the sale of noble and church lands. Those sales were declared irreversible, so there was indeed a substantial transfer of wealth. But much of that transfer was *within* the landed classes—extending from well-to-do farmers up to "patriot" nobles who had managed to stay put and actually benefited from the confiscations. Fat cats got fatter. In Puiseux-Pontoise in the Seine-et-Oise, the Marquis de Girardin's biggest tenant and neighbor, Charles-Antoine Thomassin, was well positioned to snap up available lots and did so well that he competed with his former landlord for any remaining parcels. There were, to be sure, many regions of France where the nobility as a group lost a considerable part of their fortune. But there were also others—in the west, the center and the south—where, as Jean Tulard has shown, lands that remained unsold could be recovered by families who returned in substantial numbers after 1796. Thus, while many of the leading figures in this history ended their lives on the guillotine, many others stayed put and reemerged as the leading notables of their department. The callow young *maître de cérémonies* who wilted before Mirabeau's wrath on June 23, 1789, the Marquis de Dreux-Brezé, was still the fourth richest man in the department of the Sarthe during the Consulate and Empire. Barral de Montferrat, the ex-president of the Parlement of the Dauphiné who became mayor of Grenoble during the Revolution, remained one of the great powers of the Isère well into the nineteenth century. In the Eure-et-Loir the Noailles family remained the great landed dynasty; in the Oise, the Rochefoucauld-Liancourts were still among the greatest proprietors, notwithstanding the disasters that had befallen the citizen-nobles of the clan.

By contrast, the rural poor gained very little at all from the Revolution. Saint-Just's Ventôse laws remained a dead letter and it became harder than ever to pasture animals on common land or gather fuel from the open woods. In all these respects the Revolution was just an interlude in the inexorable modernization of property rights that had been well under way before 1789. No government—that of the Jacobins any more than that of the King—had really answered the cries for help that echoed through the rural *cahiers de doléances* in 1789.

Likewise, the brutal rupture of religious continuities under the Terror was only a passing phenomenon—though never forgotten in the villages. Liberty hats that had replaced crosses on spires and towers were abruptly removed and destroyed in the year III. The cult of the Supreme Being gradually gave way to open profession of the old faith, often pressed by women, who, in many parts of France, embarked on an angry campaign of reconsecration, forcing juring priests to scrape clean the tongue of anyone who had been polluted by a constitutional communion. Bells began to chime again over the fields and cottages and traditional festivals were restored, even if they had to be celebrated in Nivôse and Germinal rather than December and April.

Had the Revolution, at least, created state institutions which resolved the problems that brought down the monarchy? Here, too, as de Tocqueville emphasized, it is easier to discern continuities, especially of centralization, than any overwhelming change. In public finance, the creation of a paper currency came to be recognized as a catastrophe beside which the insolvencies of the old regime looked almost picayune. Eventually the Bonapartist Consulate (whose finances were administered overwhelmingly by surviving bureaucrats of the old regime) returned to a metallic system based on Calonne's important monetary reform of 1785 fixing the ratio of silver to gold. Fiscally, too, post-Jacobin France slid inexorably back to the former mixture of loans and indirect as well as direct taxes. The Republic and Empire did no better funding a large army and navy from these domestic sources than had the monarchy and depended crucially on instutionalized extortion from occupied countries to keep the military pump primed.

The Napoleonic prefects have always been recognized as the heirs of the royal *intendants* (and the revolutionary *représentants-en-mission*), brokering administration between central government priorities and the interest of the local notability. Without any question that notability had suffered a violent shock during the height of the Jacobin Terror, especially in the great provincial cities, where, after the federalist revolt, they were virtually exterminated. The constitution of the year III, however, with its reintroduction of tax qualifications for the electoral assemblies, returned authority to those who had, in many places, exercised it continuously between the mid-1780s and 1792. As we have seen, in some small towns, such as Calais, where adroit mayors paid lip service to passing regimes, there was unbroken continuity of office from 1789 through to the Restoration. Looking at the department of the Orne, Louis Bergeron has found an extraordinary degree of continuity in the notability, whether measured by income, status or office. Goupil de Prefeln, for example, had been a *conseiller du Parlement* at Rouen and deputy to the Constituent, and became *procureur-général* of the Napoleonic court at Caen in 1812. Descorches de Sainte-Croix, who had been *maréchal de camp* in the old royal army, was now a prefect and baron of the Empire. For these men and countless others like them, the Revolution had been but a brutal though mercifully ephemeral interruption of their social and institutional power.

The Dictatorship of Virtue had also threatened the growing orthodoxy in the reign of Louis XVI according to which public officials ought to have a modicum of professional expertise, and at high levels should make full use of the "modern" professions: engineering, chemistry, mathematics. The great exponent of a state in which science and virtue would be mutually reinforcing, the Marquis de Condorcet, died in abject defeat, escaping from house arrest in Paris in May 1794 and walking all the way to Clamart only to arouse suspicion at an inn when he ordered an omelette. "How many eggs?" asked the *patronne*. "Twelve," replied Condorcet, suggesting a damaging unfamiliarity with the cuisine of the common man. He was locked up for the Revolutionary Tribunal but was found dead in his cell before he could be transported to Paris. A choice of legends is available to explain the disaster: exhausted starvation or the more glamorous end of poison taken from a ring. If the latter is true, it would have been in keeping with the rage for suicide that swept through the Girondins after their proscription.

Though the author of the *Esquisse du Progrès Humain* (The Sketch of Human Progress) had perished, the intellectual elite of the academies continued the colonization of government they had begun in the reign of Louis

XVI. The great reforms of higher education that embodied the thought of the late Enlightenment took place under the Directory with the creation of the *écoles centrales*. And the world of the *musées* and academies in both Paris and the provinces resumed its intellectual energy free from political intimidation (though not from infighting, since that is in the nature of the beasts) during the 1790s. The councils of state and ministries under the Consulate and Empire were filled with the intellectual eminences of the 1780s. Some had been, en route, ardent revolutionaries; some had not. Chaptal, the royal inspector of mines and professor of chemistry, ennobled by Louis XVI in 1788 on the usual meritocratic ladder, became a Napoleonic minister of the interior. Charles Gaudin, the Minister of Finance, was the son of a Parlementaire lawyer who had worked for the administration of the *vingtième* tax before 1789. Two ministers of justice, Abrial and Regnier, had both likewise been Parlementaires before the Revolution, had public careers early in the Revolution, survived the Terror and sailed on to power and status in the Directory and Consulate.

What killed the monarchy was its inability to create representative institutions through which the state could execute its program of reform. Had the Revolution done any better? On one level, the succession of elected legislatures, from the Estates-General to the National Convention, was one of the most impressive innovations of the Revolution. They took the intensive debate on the shape of governing institutions in France, which had been going on for at least half a century, into the arena of representation itself and articulated its principles with unparalleled eloquence. But for all their virtues as theaters of debate, none of the legislatures ever managed to solve the issue that had bedeviled the old regime: how to create a viable working partnership between the executive and the legislature? Once the Constituent had rejected Mounier and Mirabeau's "British" proposal of drawing ministers from the assembly, it regarded the executive not as the administration of the country, working in good faith, but as a fifth column bent on subverting national sovereignty. With this doomed beginning, the executive and legislative branches of the constitution of 1791 simply intensified the war with each other until their mutual destruction in 1792. The Terror effectively reversed matters by putting the Convention under the thrall of the committees, but still made it impossible to change governments except by violence.

The framers of the constitution of the year III (1795) obviously learned something from this unhappy experience. A two-chamber legislature was introduced, elected indirectly from colleges in which property was the criterion for membership. A governing council was in theory accountable to the legislature (as indeed the committees had been). In practice, however, the experiment remained darkened by the long shadow of the Revolution itself, so that factions inevitably crystallized, not around specific issues of government but plans for the overthrow of the state, hatched either by royalists or neo-Jacobins. With the separate organs of the constitution in paralyzing conflict with each other, violence continued to determine the political direction of the state far more than did elections.

But the violence was, after the year III, no longer coming from the streets and *sections* but from the uniformed army. If one had to look for one indisputable story of transformation in the French Revolution, it would be the creation of the juridical entity of the citizen. But no sooner had this hypothetically free person been invented than his liberties were circumscribed by the police power of the state. This was always done in the name of republican patriotism, but the constraints were no less oppressive for that. Just as Mirabeau—and the Robespierre of 1791—had feared, liberties were held hostage to the authority of the warrior state. Though this conclusion might be depressing, it should not really be all that surprising. The Revolution, after all, had begun as a response to a patriotism wounded by the humiliations of the Seven Years' War. It was Vergennes' decision to promote, at the same time, maritime imperialism and continental military power which generated the sense of fiscal panic that overcame the monarchy in its last days. A crucial element—perhaps, indeed, *the* crucial element—in the claim of the revolutionaries of 1789 was that they could better regenerate the *patrie* than could the appointees of the King. From the outset, then, the great continuing strand of militancy was patriotic. Militarized nationalism was not, in some accidental way, the unintended consequence of the French Revolution: it was its heart and soul. It was wholly logical that the multimillionaire inheritors of revolutionary power—the true "new class" of this period of French history—were not some *bourgeoisie conquérante* but *real* conquerors: the Napoleonic marshals, whose fortunes made even those of the surviving dynasts of the nobility look paltry by comparison.

For better or worse, the "modern men" who seemed poised to capture government under Louis XVI—engineers, noble industrialists, scientists, bureaucrats and generals—resumed their march to power once the irritations of revolutionary politics were brushed aside. "*La tragédie, maintenant, c'est la politique,*" claimed Napoleon, who, after the coup d'état that brought him to power in 1799, added his claim to that which had been made by so many optimistic governments before him, that "the Revolution is completed."

At other times, though, he was not so sure. For if he understood that one last achievement of the Revolution had been the creation of a military-technocratic state of immense power and emotional solidarity, he also realized that its *other* principal invention had been a political culture that perennially and directly challenged it. What occurred between 1789 and 1793 was an unprecedented explosion of politics—in speech, print, image and even music—that broke all the barriers that had traditionally circumscribed it. Initially, this had been the monarchy's own doing. For it was in the tens of thousands of little meetings convened to draft *cahiers* and elect deputies to the Estates-General that French men (and occasionally women) found their voice. In so doing, they became part of a process that tied the satisfaction of their immediate wants into the process of redefining sovereignty.

That was both the opportunity and the problem. Suddenly, subjects were told they had become Citizens; an aggregate of subjects held in place by injustice and intimidation had become a Nation. From this new thing, this Nation of Citizens, justice, freedom and plenty could be not only expected but required. By the same token, should it not materialize, only those who had spurned their citizenship, or who were by their birth or unrepentant beliefs incapable of exercising it, could be held responsible. Before the promise of 1789 could be realized, then, it was necessary to root out Uncitizens.

Thus began the cycle of violence which ended in the smoking obelisk and the forest of guillotines. However much the historian, in a year of celebration, may be tempted to see that violence as an unpleasant "aspect" of the Revolution which ought not to distract from its accomplishments, it would be jejune to do so. From the very beginning—from the summer of 1789—violence was the motor of the Revolution. The journalist Loustalot's knowing exploitation of the punitive murder and mutilation of Foulon and Bertier de Sauvigny conceded nothing in its calculated ferocity to the most extreme harangues of Marat and Hébert. "*Il faut du sang pour cimenter la révolution*" (There must be blood to cement revolution), said Mme Roland, who would herself perish by the logical application of her enthusiasm. While it would be grotesque to implicate the generation of 1789 in the kind of hideous atrocities perpetrated under the Terror, it would be equally naive not to recognize that the former made the latter possible. All the newspapers, the revolutionary festivals, the painted plates; the songs and street theater; the regiments of little boys waving their right arms in the air swearing patriotic oaths in piping voices—all these features of what historians have come to designate the "political culture of the Revolution"—were the products of the same morbid preoccupation with the just massacre and the heroic death.

Historians are also much given to distinguishing between "verbal" violence and the real thing. The assumption seems to be that such men as Javogues and Marat, who were given to screaming at people, calling for death, gloating at the spectacle of heads on pikes or processions of men with their hands tied behind their backs climbing the steps to the *rasoir national* were indulging only in brutal rhetoric. The screamers were not to be compared with such quiet bureaucrats of death as Fouquier-Tinville who did their jobs with stolid, silent efficiency. But the history of "Ville-Affranchie," of the Vendée-Vengé, or of the September massacres suggests in fact a direct connection between all that orchestrated or spontaneous screaming for blood and its copious shedding. It contributed greatly to the complete dehumanization of those who became victims. As "brigands" or the "Austrian whore" or "fanatics" they became nonentities in the Nation of Citizens and not only could but had to be eliminated if it was to survive. Humiliation and abuse, then, were not just Jacobin fun and games; they were the prologues to killing.

Why was the French Revolution like this? Why, from the beginning, was it powered by brutality? The question might seem to be circular since if, in fact, reform had been all that had been required, there would have been no Revolution in the first place. The question nonetheless remains important if we are ever to understand why successive generations of those who tried to stabilize its course—Mirabeau, Barnave, Danton—met with such failure. Was it just that French popular culture was already brutalized before the Revolution and responded to the spectacle of terrifying public punishments handed out by royal justice with its own forms of spontaneous sanguinary retribution? That all naive revolutionaries would do, would be to give the people the chance to exact such retribution and make it part of the regular conduct of politics? This may be part of the explanation, but even a cursory look beyond French borders, and especially over the Channel to Britain, makes it difficult to see France as uniquely damaged, either by a more dangerous distance between rich and poor or indeed by higher rates of crime and popular violence, than places which avoided violent revolution.

Popular revolutionary violence was not some sort of boiling subterranean lava that finally forced its way onto the surface of French politics and then proceeded to scald all those who stepped in its way. Perhaps it would be better to think of the revolutionary elite as rash geologists, themselves gouging open great holes in the crust of polite discourse and then feeding the angry matter through the pipes of their rhetoric out into the open. Volcanoes and steam holes do not seem inappropriate metaphors here, because contemporaries were themselves constantly invoking them. Many of those who were to sponsor or become caught up in violent change were fascinated by seismic violence, by the great primordial eruptions which geologists now said were not part of a single Creation, but which happened periodically in geological time. These events were, to borrow from Burke, both sublime and terrible. And it was perhaps Romanticism, with its addiction to the Absolute and the Ideal; its fondness for the vertiginous and the macabre; its concept of political energy as, above all, electrical; its obsession with the heart; its preference for passion over reason, for virtue over peace, that supplied a crucial ingredient in the mentality of the revolutionary elite: its association of liberty with wildness. What began with Lafayette's infatuation with the hyena of the Gévaudan surely ended in the ceremonies of the pike-stuck heads.

There was another obsession which converged with this Romanticization of violence: the neoclassical fixation with the patriotic death. The annals of Rome (and occasionally the doomed battles of Athens and Sparta) were the mirrors into which revolutionaries constantly gazed in search of self-recognition. Their France would be Rome reborn, but purified by the benison of the feeling heart. It thus followed, surely, that for such a Nation to be born, many would necessarily die. And both the birth and death would be simultaneously beautiful.

REUNIONS

On a crisp late September day in 1794, in the Hudson Valley, a young woman sat outside her log house boning a leg of lamb. Above her, the leaves of the oaks and maples had turned to brilliant scarlets and golds, hues of an intensity she could never have seen in France. Though she had been in America for less than a year, she already looked the part of a modest farmer's wife, her hair cut short and pushed into a white bonnet, her skirts covered with an apron. It was the kind of dress which French girls, cultivated in rustic *sensibilité,* had labored to reproduce in the 1780s. Now it came, as Jean-Jacques would have said, naturally. The lamb trimmed and boned, she made ready to stick it on the open-air spit, where it would roast for the hour or two that, in the French manner (to the shock of her Dutch neighbors), would guarantee that it was done. As she pushed it onto the iron, a big voice startled her from behind: *"On ne peut embrocher un gigot avec plus de majesté"* (One could hardly spit a leg of lamb with greater majesty). Lucy de La Tour du Pin looked up to see the famous smile of M. de Talleyrand beaming at her and at his own wit, which seemed not to have been much damaged by the displacement to the New World.

Like so many others—Fanny Burney, for example—she wanted to dislike Talleyrand. Indeed, she felt public decency demanded that she despise him, but she couldn't. He had known her since she was a child and "talked to me with an almost paternal kindness which was delightful. One might," she confessed, "in one's inmost mind regret having so many reasons for not holding him in respect, but memories of his wrongdoings were always dispelled by an hour of his conversation." Seeing him standing over her in the American autumn, with his friend Beaumetz, was not a complete shock since he had written to her from Philadelphia inquiring where he could find her after one of his expeditions into the interior in search of land to sell to French émigrés. But Lucy had not expected him to look so intact. His elaborate concern not to trespass on her demureness (or at least to offer smiling apologies when he did) was almost an exaggerated version of the elegant politeness she remembered at home, as if in insistence that America could not, in what he called his "old age" (forty), remake Talleyrand. Moreover, the compliment about the *gigot* betrayed a certain hungry sincerity, so she asked him to return the following day for dinner with her husband.

He was staying in Albany for just two days with an English friend named Thomas Law who had been something in British India and with whom Talleyrand was concocting a trading venture between Calcutta and Philadelphia. If he needs must travel, then why not think globally? Her mentor, General Schuyler in Albany, had told him where to find her and had commissioned Talleyrand to ask the de La Tours du Pin back to dine with him the next day. Since he had agreed to return and Lucy, for all her misgivings, was still obviously greedy for his company, they decided to travel back to Albany together, leaving the children with the maid. Talleyrand and Beaumetz had come from Niagara. Though he notoriously affected indifference to the brutish splendors of the American landscape, in his memoirs Talleyrand would own up to being emotionally stirred by the virgin wilderness; but on the road back to Albany what he and Lucy wanted to talk about was France and the intertwining of their personal and public histories.

They were stories worth telling, full of peril and sadness. Lucy and her husband had found themselves trapped in Bordeaux in September 1793 and had witnessed the antifederalist Terror there. Though it was not nearly as grim as the events in Lyon or even Marseille, the guillotine on the place Dauphiné was still busy and, since both husband and wife were members of families of the military nobility, they had every reason to be frightened. Long lines for bread and meat rations were endured while they watched serving boys take the best cuts and loaves to the *représentants-en-mission*. Lucy faithfully posted on the door the names of the residents of her house, writing, like everyone else, as illegibly as possible and hoping for rain. Since he was the son of the Minister of War in 1790, de La Tour du Pin's name was too well known and the revolutionary authorities began to drop ominous hints. Nearing the term of her pregnancy, Lucy found shelter at Canole in the house of her doctor, M. Brouquens, while her husband went into hiding. He was first concealed in a tiny room, barely bigger than a closet, belonging to a locksmith relative of one of their servants. When the man understandably panicked at the fate awaiting those caught hiding wanted men, de La Tour du Pin left and climbed through a back window of his own country house at Tesson, which had been locked and bolted. When a troop of soldiers and revolutionary officers arrived to make an inventory of the property, he was nearly discovered.

They were saved by a combination of gallantry and corruption. One of the two *représentants* in Bordeaux was Tallien; the other, the more austere and sinister ex-*capucin* Ysabeau. Tallien's mistress was Theresa Cabarrus, already famous as a spectacular beauty, who divorced as soon as the revolutionary laws allowed and had considerable influence over her twenty-six-year-old paramour. She had met the de La Tours du Pin only once, at the theater, but was concerned about their fate to the extent that she persuaded Tallien to grant a safe-conduct to the family on the pretext of their visiting their estates in Martinique. (This was only days before Tallien was himself summoned back to Paris to answer Ysabeau's complaints about unseemly leniency.)

After a nerve-racking departure by river from his hiding place, de La Tour du Pin was reunited with his wife at the house of a Dutch merchant and commercial consul named Meyer. The next day Theresa Cabarrus saw them off from a jetty of the quai des Chartrons, "her beautiful face wet with tears."

> When the Captain seated himself at the tiller and shouted "Off," an inexpressible happiness flowed through me. Seated opposite my husband whose life I was saving, with my two children on my knee, nothing seemed impossible. Poverty, work, misery, nothing was difficult beside me. There is no doubt that the heave of the oar with which the sailor pushed us off from the shore was the happiest moment of my life.

Bound for Boston aboard the *Diana,* which avoided French warships with the help of fog, she performed her own revolution. One day, dressing her hair, it seemed to her absurd to go through the elaborate rigmarole of pomades and curls. She took scissors to herself and cut it, "anticipating as it happened the 'Titus' fashion. My husband was very angry. I dropped the hair overboard and with it went all the frivolous ideas which my pretty fair curls had encouraged." The rites of passage continued with her sitting in a half-covered galley boiling haricot beans with the ship's cook while she tried to learn from him the nature of the land she was going to.

From the moment she laid eyes on it, America was a blessed shelter from the dark storm of the Revolution. Her four-year-old son Humbert understood enough of what had been happening in France to know that the family was running away because men in red hats wanted to kill his father. On board the ship he cried a good deal, "but when from the narrow creek through which we were passing [in Boston harbor] he saw the green fields, the flowering trees and all the beauty of a luxuriant vegetation his joy was beyond words." For Lucy, New England and New York were more than just asylum. In the affability and simplicity of people she encountered, she saw all the virtues she had been taught to admire: candor, artlessness, thrift and industry. It was as if, in a revolution on one side of the Atlantic, the culture of *sensibilité* had been forced into a grotesque caricature of the gentle morals it was supposed to embody, while on the other it had been miraculously preserved. Without affecting it, America still had the innocence and spontaneous freshness that had to be legislated in France. To her grateful eyes, the country was a procession of idylls which even her real material hardship could not spoil. At Wrentham, Massachusetts, she stayed at the house of a West Indian planter, where "there were lakes strewn with small forested islands that looked like floating gardens." At a farmhouse near Albany they dined with three generations of a family that evidently should have posed for Greuze: a white-haired grandfather, a husband and wife, "both remarkable for their strength and beauty," and children who were the nearest things on this earth to creations by Raphael and Rubens. After lunch the patriarch rose, took off his cap and announced that the company "will drink to the health of our beloved President."

The inevitable news of her father's execution only made Mme de La Tour du Pin the more determined to have her own family survive. While they were waiting, first to buy a small farm and then to be able to move into it, she threw herself into the routine of a countrywoman, rising at dawn to feed animals or milk the cows, attend to the cooking or read to the children. Settled in, she transformed a dirty and broken-down house into a hive of activity and was proud of the team of eight cows that produced butter "that was much in demand" in the locality. Once a seigneurial family, the de La Tours du Pin now paid rent, in bushels of corn, to the Dutch *patroon* Rensselaer. Lucy went about in the blue-and-black-striped woollen skirts and calico bodices of the Hudson Dutch farmwives, shocking La Rochefoucauld-Liancourt when he arrived to pay his respects, though when she had changed to go into town she, in her turn, fretted about his much-mended nankeen breeches.

Every so often, packages would arrive from Talleyrand tracking the route of his peregrinations: some from Maine; some from Pennsylvania; some from New York. They were all godsends: a fat, sweating, Stilton cheese to impress the neighbors; a spectacular lady's saddle and saddlecloth; a box of quinine when he heard through some roundabout route on the émigré gossip circuit that she was laid low again with tertian fever; and, most precious of all, timely information that her husband's American banker was about to go bankrupt. A prompt visit from Talleyrand, armed with an expression indicating serious business (not to mention the threat of publicity), extracted from the defaulter the Dutch bills of exchange that constituted the savings of the de La Tours du Pin. When her husband went to Philadelphia to settle the business, she went with him as far as New York, where they joined Talleyrand again at the house of his Anglo-Indian friend Law.

There she met up with Alexander Hamilton, whom she had already encountered in Albany. He had just resigned from the Treasury to repair the family fortunes in a private law practice. Talleyrand was aghast at the idea that government office anywhere in the world should actually make men poorer, but was immediately sparked by Hamilton's darting inquisitorial intelligence into long discussions of the vices and virtues of the two revolutions. Tea was served on the veranda and Lucy sat with the group of men—Law, Talleyrand, Beaumetz and others who came by, among them Emmery, another ex-deputy of the Constituent—talking politics and history, the caprices of fortune and the follies of men, until the stars came out in the June Manhattan sky.

The enchantment disappeared from America with cruel abruptness when her two-year-old daughter Séraphine, born in Bordeaux at the height of the Terror, died of an intestinal fever. Lucy and her husband attempted to distract themselves with new farm projects, such as harvesting their big orchard for apple cider, pressed and drawn into old Médoc casks. News of political changes in France began to open the possibility of return. Many of her refugee friends, including Talleyrand, had already decided to go, but she had mixed feelings about a return. "France had left me only memories of horror. It was there that I had lost my youth, crushed from my being by numberless, unforgettable terrors." But she felt she could not stand in the way of her husband's obvious wish to go back. To arm herself against what she feared would be a new chapter of anxieties, Lucy decided on a public deed: an act of liberation that had no hint of revolutionary terror about it. In a public ceremony she freed her four black servants, much to the displeasure of the *patroon*'s steward. In May 1796 the family embarked for France and Mme de La Tour du Pin watched New York harbor slip away, feeling pangs of regret and longing for her small patch of freedom in the Hudson Valley.

TALLEYRAND, on the other hand, was eager to get back. Germaine de Staël had, as usual, fixed things miraculously. By sheer relentless persuasion she had managed to get Boissy d'Anglas to make a speech in the Legislative Corps insisting that Talleyrand had been unjustly proscribed since he had not emigrated in 1792 but had actually been dispatched on an official mission. Fugitives from the September massacres, in any case, were now to be properly distinguished from craven lackeys of the old monarchy who had fled, tails between their legs, to Coblenz or Turin in 1789. That dependable old hack Marie-Joseph Chénier had used what was left of his stagecraft to make an even more impassioned appeal for the wronged patriot, and the long and short of it was that France awaited Talleyrand: "*Citoyen, La France t'ouvre ses bras.*" He was never one to spurn a proffered embrace.

For Talleyrand, in any case, America had been primarily a matter of real estate. He appreciated its shelter and had even grown fond of the way in which perfect strangers behaved with disturbing cordiality, as though they had known him all his life. Occasionally he felt they must have been brought up by the tutor of *Emile.* Unlike Lucy de La Tour du Pin, he had never rated candor, artlessness and simplicity high on his scale of qualities that made life worthwhile. So he affected great boredom on reaching Philadelphia. "I arrived, full of indifference to the novelties which generally interested travellers." He also was depressed by the grandees of local society turning their back on the sacrilegious rake, just as they had done in London. Worse, Washington, whom he had been eager to meet, would not see him. The French Ambassador of the Terror, Fauchet, had in effect made him persona non grata. As for the Philadelphia Quakers of William Penn's city, he could see they were, well, honorable, in the way in which *Bonhomme Richard* was honorable, but behind *that* mask of virtue there was Benjamin Franklin, which was more, alas, than one could say for many of his fellow citizens. So Talleyrand enjoyed outraging them, parading down Market Street with his limping gait, his black mistress on his arm and his little dog at his heel. His mistress was more to him, however, than someone to shock the burghers. Her house on North Third Street was one of the two places in his American exile he could call home.

The other was a bookshop on First Street, owned by his old friend from the Society of Thirty and the Constituent, Moreau de Saint-Méry. From its back room, Moreau put out a modest publication for the émigré community called *Le Courrier de la France et des Colonies,* which acted as a journalistic postal service, letting the community know where each of its wanderers had washed up and what the prospects were for return, and allowing them to rejoice at the news of their enemies' eclipse, especially after the ninth of Thermidor. Chez Moreau, Talleyrand met up with a number of his companions: Noailles, who almost alone of the veterans of the American war had managed to return; Omer Talon, the constitutional Bishop of Chartres; the Marquis de Blacon; and the ubiquitous La Rochefoucauld-Liancourt. At such gatherings they could escape the cramping gait of their awkward English and fly into the garrulous, bubbling French of the salons. Drink and noisy talk would continue deep into the night until Moreau's wife complained that while it was all very well for them to carouse and bellow until God knows what hour, some people had to be up early in the morning. Often, Talleyrand slept over, surrounded by Moreau's books and the smell of the printing press, as happy as he could be in exile.

There were, in any case, some aspects of America which appealed to him immediately, not least its potential for making a great fortune at high speed. In the New World he was constantly struck by the great store society set by sheer wealth, and though money for him was merely the means to be liberated from humiliating dependence or to enjoy the pleasures of generosity, these were reasons enough to set about realizing his own American fortune. Not that Talleyrand, again unlike his little farmer Lucy de La Tour du Pin, cared for the approved route of industry and perseverance. The equally authentic American way of speculative adventure was more to his taste. "One of the special characteristics of the revolutions of this century, whether for or against liberty," he wrote, "is to hold capital captive." From Panchaud in Paris he had learned the importance of its liberation, and one of the aspects of Jacobinism he most detested was its irrational hatred of the money market. It was typical, he thought, of their utopianism, their hopeless antimodernism, their dogmatic simplicities; and he was not surprised to learn that Cambon's prescription for arresting inflation had been to close the Bourse.

He, by contrast, would liberate risk capital, making it work for both himself and the interests of his new country (to which he had sworn allegiance in a Philadelphia magistrate's courtroom). In the first instance, he attempted to float American bank and government securities on the London market. But despite his friend Hamilton's best efforts, financial conditions in the New World were not yet secure enough to attract a sufficient number of buyers in the Old to make the venture worthwhile.

Then he tried buying grain in the primitive futures market, almost as if deliberately defying the ordained economic moralities of the Terror. The land market seemed more promising then either of these enterprises, for northern New England and New York had thousands of acres that might attract investment capital for development. Talleyrand would take a commission on purchases from big vendors—among them General Knox, the Secretary of War, who had large holdings in Maine—or make profits from speculative transfers conducted through such businesses as the Holland Land Company, based in Amsterdam but operating in America through a Philadelphia office. Through Thomas Law he even dreamed up the original idea of selling American lands in *India* to the great moneyed plunderers of the British East India Company, who would acquire attractive investments while bypassing all the scrutiny (and taxes) they incurred when remitting payments to London.

The historian in search of French capitalism need no look further than Talleyrand in 1794–95. Educated by a Swiss banker in the 1780s; frustrated by what he took to be the Revolution's reactionary dogma of economic regulation; liberated in America to play with bonds, futures, land, urban real estate—whatever came his way—Talleyrand the noble, the bishop, the constitutionalist, the diplomat, was also Talleyrand the capitalist: the herald of the modern world.

By an irony which he keenly appreciated, realizing this dream of easy money meant turning himself into a backwoodsman. In the fall of 1794, before the snows set in, he embarked with his servant, Courtiade, and Beaumetz on two journeys of survey and exploration. One took him up the coast of Maine, past Portland as far as Champlain's Ile des Monts Déserts. The extensive notes he took are largely confined to careful explanations of economic opportunities for agriculture, descriptions of the excellence of the natural harbors to be found at the mouth of the Kennebec, and a damning account of the fishermen whom he chided for their lack of enterprise in seldom going beyond a couple of miles offshore and "dangling an arm over the side of their boat." Instead of clusters of poor, windswept cottages clinging to the rocks, Talleyrand envisaged a great agricultural hinterland, rich in pasture and arable crops, feeding both itself and the more densely settled regions of Massachusetts.

Bald rock and dense forest provoked in Talleyrand a rationalist, not a Romantic, response. Where the revolutionary sensibility might have swooned at being enveloped in the wilderness, or meditated darkly on the origins of liberty rising from the primeval woods, or gazed in rapture on the crashing waterfalls, the modern entrepreneur in him brooded on what might be *done* with all this real estate. Even when, as on one instance, he allowed himself to surrender to the beauties of landscape, his thoughts were never far from projects to domesticate it. "There were forests as old as the world itself; green and luxuriant grass decking the banks of rivers; large natural meadows; strange and delicate flowers quite new to me . . . in the face of these immense solitudes we gave vent to our imagination. Our minds built cities, villages and hamlets. . . ."

At some points, however, the civilization that Talleyrand carried around in his head, and to which he always yearned to return, seemed to be almost swallowed up by American savagery. But every time he was faced with the ghost of Jean-Jacques, he fought it off with the counter-shade of Voltaire. Once he completely lost sight of his servant in the darkness of the forest and had to shout out, "Courtiade, are you there?" Back came the reply: "Alas, *oui* Monseigneur, I am." That he should be ceremoniously addressed with his full ecclesiastical title struck both men as so richly comic that their laughter cut through the arboreal thickness like Talleyrand's civilizing hatchet.

A year later he was ready to go back to Paris. In May 1795 much of his personal property had been auctioned off to keep him going in Philadelphia. Violet soutanes, lace cuffs, spectacular furniture, paintings and drawings all went on the block for niggardly sums which Talleyrand, as an accomplished speculator, bitterly resented. The item which seemed to confirm his reputation was an enormous wardrobe full of exquisite women's clothing—silks, taffetas, muslins, gowns, hats, even stockings. Had they belonged to Adelaide de Flahaut? Or were they simply an expression of Talleyrand's excessive sense of hospitality? The sense of personal loss he may have felt over the disappearance of his possessions may have been more acute since he had, by the sheerest luck, been able to return a precious treasure to Lucy de La Tour du Pin. A woman he knew in Philadelphia had shown him a cameo of Marie-Antoinette, curious to know if it was a good likeness. On seeing the piece, he started, recognizing it immediately as belonging to his friend. It had been "entrusted" by the family's Dutch agents to a young American diplomat for safekeeping and instead the man had kept it for himself. Talleyrand snatched the piece and sent it directly back to its grateful owner.

Perhaps it was this haunting coincidence that made him even keener to return home. On receiving the news of his exoneration, Talleyrand wrote a letter of heartfelt thanks to Germaine de Staël and prepared, somewhat unhurriedly, to leave by a spring sailing. Before his departure, in June 1796, he walked along the Battery ramparts of Manhattan with his old friend Beaumetz, trying to soften the blow of his departure, of his sabotaging their carefully laid plans to make a fortune in India. With his companion relapsed into a strange Romantic silence, Talleyrand had the sudden presentiment that Beaumetz was about to do something violent, something revolutionary: to kill him, to commit suicide or both. He confronted him with this and the miserable Beaumetz collapsed in tears in his arms.

It was pathetic, but these passions could not hold up serious business. His Danish ship, *Den Ny Proeve,* waited. Its rather forbidding name meant "The New Ordeal." But Talleyrand embarked feeling confident that he had already weathered more than his fair share of ordeals. What terrors could the Atlantic Ocean hold when he had survived the September massacres?

H I L E Talleyrand tasted American freedom, the Frenchman most honored by the New World was languishing in an Austrian prison. The generation of 1776 had fared disastrously at the hands of the Terror. Kersaint and d'Estaing, the idols of the new navy of Louis XVI, had both been guillotined. Rochambeau had been due to mount the tumbril immediately after Malesherbes but somehow had been overlooked and spent the rest of the Terror in prison, from which Thermidor released him. Biron, Lafayette's companion-in-arms (the former Duc de Lauzun), had fallen to the Hébertiste offensive against noble generals in the Vendée and he too had lost his head on the place de la Révolution.

While Lafayette was still alive—as were friends of his who went with him to the Austrian lines in 1792, among them the *constitutionnels* Bureau de Pusy and Mirabeau's old nemesis, Alexandre de Lameth—their ordeal was nonetheless serious enough. Characteristically it was made worse by Lafayette's self-righteousness. Unlike Talleyrand the pragmatist, Lafayette invariably believed everything he did to be in strict conformity with particular principles. Even when he had deserted his own army, he told himself that it was not France, but the cutthroats who had made off with it, that he was escaping. This made him a patriot, not a traitor. So when the Austrians and Prussians asked him, first, whether he had brought the "treasure" with him, he laughed in disbelief that they, too, had fallen for the caricature of the émigré according to which everyone who left France had to have done so for the most dishonorable reasons. Then they asked him if he would let them have details of French military strategy, a suggestion he received with indignation.

Since Lafayette seemed determined to behave like a republican, the Austrians thought they might as well treat him like one. An official declaration proclaimed that "the existence of Lafayette is incompatible with the security of the governments of Europe." The Prussians took charge of him first, taking him to Magdeburg prison, where he was given a damp and airless cell of five and half paces square. He remained intractable, even refusing personal requests from King Frederick William of Prussia, and so was moved in January 1794 to the fortress of Neisse, where for a few months the French prisoners were allowed the luxury of seeing each other and even receiving an occasional letter.

Some time towards the end of that year, however, Lafayette was handed back to the Austrians like a parcel no one really wanted, for his plight was generating hostile criticism both in America and among Whig circles in Britain. He was taken to Olmütz Castle, a grim moated citadel. There all pretensions of special treatment were abandoned. His possessions were removed, except for a watch and one change of clothing. He was forbidden to see anyone, to communicate with the outside world or his fellow prisoners or to receive any kind of official news on the progress of the Revolution or the war, much less personal news of his family, trapped in France. The jailors were even forbidden to use his name. He was to be a Nonperson, entombed alive in just the way Linguet had written of the Bastille.

At some point, almost certainly in response to hostile publicity relayed by the American Ambassador in Vienna, John Jay, his routine changed. He was now allowed daily walks in the woods and fields, under armed escort. And it was from this small relaxation of his confinement that an attempt at escape was made. Its author was a young German physician, Justus Bollmann, who had been a visitor to Juniper Hall and had been swept off his feet by Germaine de Staël, Talleyrand, Narbonne and the rest. Determined to rescue Lafayette, he befriended the prison doctor and managed to smuggle in letters, to which the Marquis replied either with paper pricked with toothpicks or an invisible ink made with lemon juice, water and soot. At the pre-assigned day, Bollmann had horses waiting just beyond Lafayette's walking route, but when the prisoner pretended to admire his guard's saber and asked if he might see it, the soldier became suspicious. A struggle ensued in which Lafayette got away, but only after the guard, evidently an unsporting fellow, had bitten off part of his finger. In pain and panic, he heard Bollmann shout "Hoff," which he assumed meant, in the broken English they shared, "Get off" or "Go away." In fact, it meant the village of Hoff, where fresh horses and help had been stationed. Lafayette took the wrong road, and twenty miles away, at the hamlet of Sternberg, he was caught and returned to Olmütz.

There now began the most desperate part of his imprisonment: solitary confinement, barely enough rations to keep him alive, no books. He fell sick constantly, lost much of his hair and grew thin and wasted. The darkness seemed to be closing around his life.

One morning in October 1795, without any warning, the double doors of his cell were opened. In the light that suddenly shone on the cell, he beheld his wife, Adrienne, with their two daughters, Virginie and Anastasie. It was not a trick of his imprisoned imagination. Fantastically, they stood before him, the joy of reunion shattered by his spectral appearance, a ragged skeleton barely alive, gripped by a hacking cough. Adrienne's determination to go to Austria to find her husband surpassed in its courage and devotion anything that could have been conjured up by the novelists of *sensibilité.* First she had had to survive the Terror and in fact had been for some time imprisoned in Paris, before Thermidor rescued her from the guillotine. But it was not until January 1795 that, with the help of the American Ambassador in Paris, James Monroe, she was released. She moved into his house and, using his kind offices again, managed to get a visa for herself and her daughters; she had gone to Vienna and secured an interview with the Emperor Francis II. It was thus by imperial writ that she had secured the right to share her husband's imprisonment.

A bizarre life, at once wretched and consoling, then unfolded for nearly a year and a half. Adrienne and Gilbert shared one wretched cell; the girls, thirteen and eighteen years old, another. The only missing member of the family was their brother, George Washington Lafayette, who was safe in Mount Vernon, being taken care of by his illustrious godfather. It was virtually impossible to re-create in Olmütz the domestic idyll—that obsession of the eighteenth-century citizen-nobility—but the three women tried their utmost. The family ate their horrible meals together from unwashed wooden bowls, but even these little rituals were brutally interrupted by guards who sent the girls away after only ten minutes or so. As Lafayette got somewhat better, Adrienne's health began to deteriorate badly. Finally, in May 1796, George Washington, who had been restrained by the need to preserve American neutrality, wrote a personal letter directly to the Emperor:

> Permit me only to submit to your Majesty's consideration
> whether [Lafayette's] long imprisonment and the confiscation of
> his Estate and the Indigence and dispersion of his family—and the
> painful anxieties incident to all these circumstances, do not form
> an assemblage of sufferings, which recommend him to the
> mediation of Humanity?

Might he not be allowed to come to America?

Appeals to the humane conscience, however, had little effect on Reason of State. It was only the following spring, when the Austrian armies in Italy were so decisively demolished by Napoleon Bonaparte that they needed to sue for peace, that Lafayette's condition became a matter for negotiation. By 1797 Talleyrand was back in France; indeed, in the thick of politics. Sieyès and other men of 1789 were once again in positions of power and influence, and Lafayette's name was no longer an abomination. The French governing the Directory, however, beleaguered by royalists on one side and neo-Jacobins on the other, was not sure it wanted to risk having him back home. His release, along with that of Latour-Marbourg and Bureau de Pusy, was demanded on the assumption he would go to America and on condition he did not travel to France. The Austrian Chancellor, Thugut, at first refused, and it was only because of Bonaparte's insistence that the release was eventually secured.

On the very brink of freedom, though, as the nervous French consul at Hamburg (where the Lafayettes had arrived) wrote to the new Foreign Minister Talleyrand, the Marquis had raised an issue of principle. The Austrians had consented to his liberation on condition that he sign a document promising never again to set foot in the domains of the Emperor. This Lafayette refused to do, since there was only one country that had "sacred rights" over him, and in the future he would have to go wherever it might decide to send him. In spite of this last adamant silliness, the arrangements for the release went on without him. To Lafayette this was of no concern. He had remained constant to his only abiding faith: patriotism and freedom. To these principles he was resolved to be constant, even when France betrayed them. Indeed, however many times she would betray them, in revolution or reaction, she would find Lafayette still loyal to the spirit of 1790: the man on the white horse with the tricolor wrapped about his body.

F o r Lafayette, throughout his life, revolutionary memories were a liberation; for Théroigne de Méricourt they were imprisonment.

In the spring of 1793, while speechifying on the Terrasse des Feuillants for the Société des Femmes Républicaines, she had been violently attacked by market-women supporters of the Mountain. They were tired of being lectured to on the duties of citizenesses and detested her attempts to defend the Girondins. Stripped and beaten senseless, she was rescued, some claimed by Marat. Whether or not the stories were true, Théroigne recovered her consciousness but not her sanity. She was taken to a hospital for the poor and the deranged in the faubourg Saint-Marceau. She would stay locked up for the remainder of her life, another twenty-three years, moved from one gloomy hospital to the next, ending up in La Salpêtrière, more a prison than an asylum, where she died in 1817.

Théroigne had been in prison before. In an imprudent journey back to her native Liège in 1791, she had been arrested by the Austrians and treated as though she were a great and important spy. After interrogation in Belgium, she was transported to Kufstein Castle in the Tyrol (where, two years later, the balloonist Blanchard was confined after crash-landing in the mountains, also on the assumption that he was a spy). After more intensive interrogation, the Austrians could get nothing out of her and had to be satisfied with a diagnosis from the prison doctor that she was suffering from "revolutionary fever."

After her skull had been staved in, that fever returned with all the force of an unstoppable delirium. She sat in a cell, her hair cropped, glaring at the walls. Periodically the black silence that descended on her would be interrupted by a torrent of denunciation in half-intelligible revolutionary phrases: *"comité de salut public," "liberté," "coquins."* In the fiercest paroxysms of her dementia she would rage against "moderates." In a period of relative lucidity around 1808, someone who remembered the *belle liègeoise* of 1789 asked to see her and was immediately accused by Théroigne of "betraying the cause of the people." He left not knowing how mad she really was.

To some, Théroigne became a source of amusement; to others, a quaint kind of living museum of half-forgotten and embarrassing slogans. Periodically, well-meaning officials attempted to trace her family and wrote to the prefect of the department of the Ourthe for information. The physician and specialist in the insane Esquirol, who was writing a treatise, *Les Maladies Mentales,* classified her as *lypémanique* or suffering from a form of manic depression. The autopsy he performed after her death convinced him its cause lay in the irregular alignment of her colon.

By 1810 she had disappeared from the land of the living in all but biological fact. Clothes had become abhorrent to her, so she sat naked in her cell, angrily refusing even the simplest wool dressing gown offered to protect her from the winter cold. On the rare occasions when she emerged for air or to drink from the filthy puddles that formed in the courtyard, she consented, sometimes, to wear a light chemise but nothing more. Every day she would throw cold water on the straw of her bed, sometimes breaking the ice in the yard to get at it, as if only glacial saturation could cool the heat of her dementia. Periodically she was heard, still, to mutter imprecations against those who had betrayed the Revolution.

Oblivious of all visitors, concerned or callous, who saw her, Théroigne, it seems, now lived entirely inside the Revolution and the Revolution inside her. Sympathy seems out of place here, for in some sense the madness of Théroigne de Méricourt was a logical destination for the compulsions of revolutionary Idealism. Discovering, at last, a person of almost sublime transparency and presocial innocence, someone naked and purified with dousings of ice water, the Revolution could fill her up like a vessel. In her little cell at La Salpêtrière, there was at least somewhere where revolutionary memory could persist, quite undisturbed by the quotidian mess of the human condition.

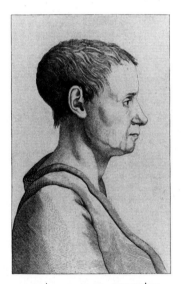

214. Anonymous, engraving,
Théroigne de Méricourt at
La Salpêtrière, circa 1810

SOURCES AND
BIBLIOGRAPHY

INDEX

SOURCES AND BIBLIOGRAPHY

PROLOGUE:
POWERS OF RECALL — FORTY YEARS LATER

The history of the elephant of the Bastille may be found in Marie Biver, *Le Paris de Napoléon* (Paris 1963). For Talleyrand in 1830, Georges Lacour-Gayet, *Talleyrand* (vol. 3, Paris 1931); also the appropriately sardonic modern biography by Jean Orieux, *Talleyrand ou le Sphinx Incompris* (Paris 1970, 737 –44). Talleyrand's own *Mémoires* (vols. 3 and 4, ed. Duc de Broglie, Paris 1892) are, even by his standards, excessively laconic on his part in the Revolution of 1830. M. Colmache, *Revelations of the Life of Prince Talleyrand* (London 1850), is much more forthcoming and has the ring of authenticity. The self-consciousness of Lafayette's memory of 1830 is all too obvious from a reading of his own *Mémoires, Correspondances et Manuscrits* (Paris 1837–38, vol. 6, 386–415) as well as from the account of his secretary in this period, B. Sarrans, *Memoirs of General Lafayette and of the French Revolution of 1830* (2 vols., London 1830). By far the best account of the events of July 1830 in Paris is David Pinkney. *The French Revolution of 1830* (Princeton 1972) is a splendid history of Lafayette's triumphal progress in the United States in 1825. A startlingly public report of Charles Delacroix's *tumeur monstrueuse* and its surgical excision can be found in the *Moniteur* for 24 Germinal, an VI (April 13, 1798).

CHAPTER ONE
NEW MEN

i FATHERS AND SONS

For Talleyrand's visit to Voltaire, see Colmache (82 –86). Voltaire's last months in Paris are vividly recorded in No. 276 of Pidanzat de Mairobert's wonderfully gossipy *L'Espion Anglais ou Correspondance Secrète entre Milord All Eye et Milord All Ear*, published in London but widely available in Paris. Lafayette's expedition to America is treated in detail in the first two volumes of Louis Gottschalk's monumental biography, *Lafayette Comes to America* (Chicago 1935) and *Lafayette Joins the American Army* (Chicago 1937). Citations from the letters to his wife are from this second volume. Stanley J. Idzerda, in an extremely persuasive and important article, "When and Why Lafayette Became a Revolutionary," in Morris Slavin and Agnes M. Smith (eds.), *Bourgeois, Sans-culottes and Other Frenchmen: Essays on the French Revolution in Honor of John Hall Stewart* (Waterloo, Ontario, 1981, 7 – 24), has attacked Gottschalk's emphasis on callow adventurism and expediency and has reasserted the ideological and psychological roots of Lafayette's commitment. The letter to Vergennes on page 25 is cited in Gilbert Bodinier, *Les Officiers de l'Armée Royale Combat-*

tants de la Guerre d'Indépendance des Etats-Unis de Yorktown à l'An II (Vincennes 1983, 285). Lafayette's devotion to Washington is probably best read in their correspondence, edited by Louis Gottschalk, *The Letters of Lafayette to George Washington 1777–1799* (New York 1944). For further insight into the companionship of the young liberal nobility, see *Lettres Inédites du Général Lafayette au Vicomte de Noailles 1780–81* (Paris 1924).

ii HEROES FOR THE TIMES

The history of French patriotism before the Revolution remains a seriously underinvestigated topic. For outline sketches, see Jean Lestocquoy, *Histoire du Patriotisme en France* (Paris 1968); and Marie-Madeleine Martin, *Histoire de l'Unité Française: L'Idée de la Patrie en France des Origines à Nos Jours* (Paris 1949). A more specific study that documents the rise of a more aggressive patriotism after the Seven Years' War is Frances Acomb, *Anglophobia in France 1763–1789* (Durham, N.C., 1950). A key contemporary work is J. Rossel, *Histoire du Patriotisme Français* (Paris 1769). For another powerfully Romantic discourse on the passion for the *patrie*, see "Discours sur les Evénements de l'Année 1776," in *Le Courrier d'Avignon* (1777: 6). Gilbert Chinard has provided a helpful introduction to his edition of Billardon de Sauvigny's *Vashington* (Princeton 1941) that also describes the theater history of his *Hirza ou les Illinois*. The performance history of de Belloy's *Siège de Calais* may be found in the 1787 edition of the same play; see also Acomb, *Anglophobia* (58–59), and John Lough, *Paris Theatre Audiences in the 17th and 18th Centuries* (Oxford 1957). The best account of du Couëdic's battle and his cult is in Georges Lacour-Gayet, *La Marine Militaire de la France sous le Règne de Louis XVI* (Paris 1901, 297–98), and for the decision to exhibit paintings of the battle in the naval academies, ibid. (575). For the similar cult of the "Belle-Poule," see *L'Espion Anglais* (1778, vol. 9, 146–47). See also *Brest et l'Indépendance Américaine* (Brest, 1976); Lee Kennett, *The French Forces in America 1780–1783* (Westport, Conn., and London 1977); and Jonathan R. Dull, *The French Navy and American Independence* (Princeton 1975). On representations of American themes in French travel literature, decorative art and engraving, see the exhibition catalogue by Betty Bright P. Low, *France Views America* (Eleutherian Mills Historical Library, Wilmington, Del.) and *Les Français dans la Guerre d'Indépendance Américaine* (Musée de Rennes 1976). Durand Echeverria's *Mirage in the West: A History of the French Image of American Society to 1815* (Princeton 1956) was a pioneering study in this field. For Lafayette's reception in France and the cult of Franklin at court, see Madame de Campan, *Mémoires sur la vie de Marie-Antoinette* (Paris 1899, 177–79). There is a large literature on Franklinomania in France. See, in particular, the fascinating article by James Leith, "Le Culte de Franklin avant et pendant la Révolution Française," in *Annales Historiques de la Révolution Française* (1976, 543–72); the exhibition catalogue by Louise Todd Ambler, *Benjamin Franklin: A Perspective* (Fogg Museum of Art, Cambridge, Mass., 1975); Gilbert Chinard, "The Apotheosis of Benjamin Franklin," in *Proceedings of the American Academy of Arts and Sciences* (1955); Jonathan R. Dull, "Franklin in France: A Reappraisal," in *Proceedings of the Annual Meeting of the Western Society for French History* (no. 4, 1976); and Kenneth M. McKee, "The Popularity of the 'American' on the French Stage in the French Revolution," in *Proceedings of the American Philosophical Society* (vol. 83, no. 3, 1940). Much of this material is brought together by Philip Katz, *The Image of Benjamin Franklin in the Politics of the French Revolution 1776–1794* (Harvard University Program for Social Studies Dissertation, 1986). The account of the "13" celebrations at Marseille is in *L'Espion Anglais* (1778, vol. 9, 75–76). The Abbé Robin's comments on Americans are cited by Gilbert Bodinier, *Les Officiers de l'Armée Royale Combattants de la Guerre d'Indépendance des Etats-Unis de Yorktown á l'An II* (Vincennes 1983, 345). For Vergennes' American policy, see Orville T. Murphy, *Charles Gravier, Comte de Vergennes: French Diplomacy in the Age of Revolution 1719 – 1787* (Albany 1982); his comparison of Genevan and American policy is on p. 400.

CHAPTER TWO
BLUE HORIZONS, RED INK

i "*LES BEAUX JOURS*"

On the coronation of Louis XVI, see H. Weber, "Le Sacre de Louis XVI," in Actes du Colloque International de Sorèze, *Le Règne de Louis XVI* (1976, 11 –22); idem, "Das Sacre Ludwigs XVI vom 11 Juin 1775 und die Krise des Ancien Régime," in Ernst Hinrichs, E. Schmitt and R. Vierhaus (eds.), *Vom Ancien Régime zur Französischen Revolution: Forschungen und Perspektiven* (Göttingen 1978); also the superb essay (virtually a small book in itself) by Jacques Le Goff, "Reims, Ville du Sacre," in Pierre Nora (ed.), *Les Lieux de Mémoire*, vol. 2, *La Nation* (Paris 1986, part 1, 161-65). Turgot's complaints about the expenses of the coronation as well as details of the decorations were reported by Pidanzat de Mairobert in *L'Espion Anglais* (1775, 320 –27).

Louis XVI's upbringing is described in P. Girault de Coursac, *L'Education d'un Roi: Louis XVI* (Paris 1972); much of his diary was published by L. Nicolardot, *Journal de Louis XVI* (1873). For the royal visit to Cherbourg in June 1786, see *Histoire Sommaire de Cherbourg avec le Journal de Tout Ce Qui s'est Passé au Mois de Juin 1786* (Cherbourg 1786); *Voyage de Louis XVI dans la Province de Normandie* ("Philadelphie" [Paris] 1786); *Gazette de France* (July 4, 1786); J.-M. Gaudillot, *Le Voyage de Louis XVI en Normandie* (Caen 1967); and Georges Lacour-Gayet, "Voyage de Louis XVI à Cherbourg," in *Revue des Etudes Historiques* (1906). For the King's familiarity with nautical culture, see Louis-Petit de Bachaumont, *Mémoires Secrets pour Servir á l'Histoire de la République des Lettres* (36 vols., London 1781 –89, July 2, 3, and 9, 1786).

For Louis' passion for the hunt (and for the best general survey of the reign), see François Bluche, *La Vie Quotidienne au Temps de Louis XVI* (Paris 1980).

ii OCEANS OF DEBT

The passage from Chateaubriand is from *Mémoires d'Outre-Tombe* (Paris 1849, vol. 1, 91). Figures for the cost of the French navy are taken from Dull, *French Navy and American Independence*; naval construction is also helpfully tabulated in T. Le Goff and J. Meyer, "Les Constructions Navales en France," in *Annales: Economies, Sociétés, Civilisations* (1971, 173ff.)

The two articles which, taken together, make an overwhelming case for revising traditional assumptions about the incidence and burden of French taxation are Peter Mathias and Patrick O'Brien, "Taxation in Britain and France 1715 – 1810," in *Journal of European Economic History* (1976, 601 –50); and Michel Morineau, "Budgets de l'Etat et Gestion des Finances Royales au 18e Siècle," in *Revue Historique* (1980, 289 –336). Other important studies on finance are J. F. Bosher, *French Government Finance 1770 –1795* (Cambridge, England, 1970), and C.B.A. Behrens, *Society, Government and Enlightenment: The Experience of Eighteenth-Century France and Prussia* (New York 1985, especially chapter 3). The emphasis in these works on the structural and institutional blocks to solvency is, however, seriously put into question by an exceptionally powerful if rather technical work of James Riley, *The Seven Years' War and the Old Regime in France: The Economic and Financial*

Toll (Princeton 1986). François Hincker, *Les Français Devant l'Impôt sous l'Ancien Régime* (Paris 1971), is a clear and helpful survey of the problem. The standard institutional history, now somewhat dated, is Marcel Marion, *Histoire Financière de la France Depuis 1715* (Paris 1921). On venality as a source of revenue before the Revolution, see the important contribution by David D. Bien, "Offices, Corps, and a System of State Credit: The Uses of Privilege under the Ancien Régime," in Keith Michael Baker (ed.), *The Political Culture of the Old Regime* (Oxford 1987, 89 – 114).

iii MONEY FARMS AND SALT WARS

For the Farmers-General, see George Matthews, *The Royal General Farms in 18th-Century France* (New York 1958), and Yves Durand, *Les Fermiers Généraux au XVIIIe Siècle* (Paris 1971); also Jean Pasquier, *L'Impôt des Gabelles en France aux XVII et XVIIIe Siècles* (Paris 1905). On the salt smugglers, see the superbly evocative account in Olwen Hufton, *The Poor of Eighteenth-Century France* (Oxford 1974). On the stereotypes of the *"financiers,"* see H. Thirion, *La Vie Privée des Financiers au XVIIIe Siècle* (Paris 1895), and Jean-Baptiste Darigrand, *L'Anti-Financier* (Amsterdam 1763).

iv LAST BEST HOPES: THE COACHMAN

There are two excellent accounts of Turgot's career: Douglas Dakin, *Turgot and the Ancien Régime in France* (London 1939), and Edgar Fauré *La Disgrâce de Turgot* (Paris 1961). For a much more hostile approach (which is quite persuasive in places), see Lucien Langier, *Turgot ou la Mythe des Réformes* (Paris 1979). Some of Langier's prosecution is borne out by R. P. Shepherd, *Turgot and the Six Edicts* (New York 1903). For the effects of physiocratic reform on the grain trade, see S. L. Kaplan, *Bread, Politics and Political Economy in the Reign of Louis XV* (2 vols., The Hague 1976). On physiocratic theory, see G. Weulersse, *Le Mouvement Physiocratique en France 1756 – 1770* (2 vols., Paris 1910) and the important intellectual history by Elizabeth Fox-Genovese, *The Origins of Physiocracy* (Ithaca, N.Y., 1976), Ronald L. Meek (ed.), *Turgot on Progress, Sociology and Economics* (Cambridge, England, 1973).

v LAST BEST HOPES: THE BANKER

Two works have contributed to a major reassessment of Necker's administration: Jean Egret, *Necker: Ministre de Louis XVI* (Paris 1975), and R. D. Harris, *Necker, Reform States-man of the Old Regime* (Berkeley 1979), the latter based on new documentary research at Coppet bearing out many of the claims made in the *Compte Rendu*. See also H. Grange, *Les Idées de Necker* (Paris 1974), and Edouard Chapuisat, *Necker 1732 – 1804* (Paris 1938).

CHAPTER THREE
ABSOLUTISM ATTACKED

i THE ADVENTURES OF M. GUILLAUME

The standard life of Malesherbes remains the excellent work by Pierre Grosclaude, *Malesherbes, Témoin et Interprète de son Temps* (Paris 1961). On his developing political ideology, see the excellent anthology and critical introduction by Elizabeth Badinter, *Les Rémonstrances de Malesherbes 1771 – 1775* (Paris 1985). At least two other works are worth consulting: J. M. Allison, *Malesherbes* (New Haven 1938), and his first biographer, Boissy d'Anglas, *Essai sur la Vie, les Ecrits et les Opinions de M. de Malesherbes* (Paris 1819).

ii SOVEREIGNTY REDEFINED:
THE CHALLENGE OF THE PARLEMENTS

A number of essays in the important work edited by Keith Michael Baker, *The Political Culture of the Old Regime* (Oxford 1987), address this theme, in particular those by Dale van Kley and William Doyle. Baker has also published an important essay on the mutation of opposition ideology, "French Political Thought at the Accession of Louis XVI," in *Journal of Modern History* (June 1978, 279–303). The axioms of royal absolutism as restated by Louis XV are examined in the essay by Michel Antoine, "La Monarchie Absolue," in the same volume. The fundamental discussion on the development of oppositional vocabulary and ideology in Parlementaire discourse remains a remarkable work, much ahead of its time: E. Carcassonne, *Montesquieu et le Débat sur la Constitution Française* (Paris 1927). For the diffusion and popularization of Montesquieuan ideas, see Franco Venturi, *Utopia and Reform in the Enlightenment* (Cambridge, England, 1971). Carcassonne's one important omission is the contribution of Jansenist rhetoric at the time of the attack on the Jesuits, a subject covered by the remarkable work of Dale van Kley, *The Jansenists and the Expulsion of the Jesuits from France 1757–1765* (New Haven and London 1975). See also the same author's *The Damiens Affair and the Unravelling of the Ancien Régime 1750–1770* (Princeton 1984). J. Flammermont published the full texts of the *Rémontrances du Parlement de Paris au XVIIIe Siècle* (3 vols., Paris 1888–89). The same author's work on the Maupeou crisis has now been superseded by Durand Echeverria, *The Maupeou Revolution: A Study in the History of Libertarianism: France 1770–1774* (Baton Rouge, La., 1985). See also Jean Egret, *Louis XV et l'Opposition Parlementaire* (Paris 1970), and William Doyle, "The Parlements of France and the Breakdown of the Old Regime 1771–1788," in *French Historical Studies* (1970, 429). For the royal case in the crisis, see David Hudson, "In Defence of Reform," in *French Historical Studies* (1973, 51–76). Accounts of the ceremonies for the return of the Parlements at Metz and Pau may be found in Pidanzat de Mairobert, *L'Espion Anglais*, (1775, vol. 2, 200); see also H. Carré, "Les Fêtes d'une Réaction Parlementaire," in *La Révolution Française* (1892).

There is now an abundance of fine studies that treat the Parlements as a social as well as a political institution. The pioneers in this area were Franklin Ford, *Robe and Sword: The Regrouping of the French Aristocracy after Louis XIV* (Cambridge, Mass., 1953), and François Bluche, *Les Magistrats du Parlement de Paris 1715–1771* (Paris 1960), which remains one of the masterpieces in this genre but covers, alas, only the period to the Maupeou crisis. Bailey Stone's excellent *The Parlement of Paris 1774–1789* (Chapel Hill, N.C., 1981) continues the story through to the Revolution and shows exactly how the judicial nobility divided over how far, in both tone and substance, to press their redefinition of sovereignty. William Doyle's superb *The Parlement of Bordeaux and the End of the Old Regime 1771–1790* (New York 1974) studies one of the most eloquent of the sovereign courts, but also shows the hesitation of its personnel during the Maupeou crisis. The most important and far-reaching tract produced by a Bordeaux magistrate was Joseph Saige's *Catéchisme du Citoyen* (Bordeaux 1775, reprinted 1788). Other important local studies are M. Cubells, *La Provence des Lumières: Les Parlementaires d'Aix au XVIIIe Siècle* (Paris 1984), and A. Colombet, *Les Parlementaires Bourguignons à la Fin du XVIIIe Siècle* (Dijon 1937), now supplemented by Brian Dooley, *Noble Causes: Philanthropy Among the Parlementaires in 18th-Century Dijon* (Harvard University Dissertation, 1987).

Sources and Bibliography

iii NOBLESSE OBLIGE?

There is no good modern study of d'Argenson, but this extraordinary figure is, in any case, best studied through his own writing, especially the *Considérations sur la Gouvernement de la France*, published thirty years after they were written (Amsterdam 1764).

There is now a large literature on questions of social mobility and privilege. Two starting points must be Colin Lucas, "Nobles, Bourgeois and the Origins of the French Revolution" in *Past and Present* (60, August 1973, 84 – 126), and the important revisionist work of Guy Chaussinand-Nogaret, *The French Nobility in the Eighteenth Century: From Feudalism to Enlightenment* (trans. William Doyle, Cambridge, England, 1985), whose position on the *noblesse commerçante* I follow very closely. The Kress Library of the Harvard Business School possesses contracts for trading and industrial syndicates at the end of the eighteenth century which make the active participation of the nobility dramatically evident. See, in this connection, the Abbé Coyer, *Développement et Défense du Système de la Noblesse Commerçante* (Amsterdam 1757). Patrice Higonnet's important *Class Ideology and the Rights of Nobles During the French Revolution* (Oxford 1981) begins with a discussion of the degree of separation and fusion of bourgeoisie and nobility and challenges some of the revisionist assumptions. Other important studies are: David Bien, "La Réaction Aristocratique avant 1789," in *Annales: Economies, Sociétés, Civilisations* (1974); Alfred Cobban, *The Social Interpretation of the French Revolution* (Cambridge, England, 1964); R. Forster, *The Nobility of Toulouse in the 18th Century* (Baltimore 1960); idem, *The House of Saulx-Tavannes, Versailles and Burgundy 1700 – 1830* (Baltimore and London 1971); idem, "The Provincial Nobles: A Reappraisal," in *American Historical Review* (1963); J. Meyer, *La Noblesse Bretonne au XVIIIe Siècle* (Paris 1972); and G. V. Taylor, "Non-Capitalist Wealth and the Origins of the French Revolution," in *American Historical Review* (1967). Gail Bossenga has extended David Bien's methods to create a fresh and exceptionally illuminating approach to the social and political history of institutions in this period. See, in particular, "From Corps to Citizenship: The *Bureaux des Finances* Before the French Revolution," in *Journal of Modern History* (September 1986, 610 – 42), where she shows the privileged holders of office, paradoxically, developing theories of solidarity and citizenship with which to defend the reforming encroachments of the crown on their corporation.

Grouvelle's attack on Montesquieu is cited by Carcassone, *Montesquieu et le Débat*, 620.

CHAPTER FOUR
THE CULTURAL CONSTRUCTION OF A CITIZEN

i COLLECTING AN AUDIENCE

Robert Darnton first drew attention to the balloon as one of the scientific novelties provoking a kind of generalized social hyperbole, in *Mesmerism and the End of the Enlightenment* (Cambridge, Mass., 1968). For the Versailles balloon ascent, see *L'Art de Voyager dans l'Air* (Paris 1784, 68ff.), and [Rivarol], *Lettre à M. le Président de xxx sur le Globe Airostatique* (London 1783); more ironic comments appear in François Métra, *Correspondance Secrète Politique et Litteraire...* (London, February 15, 1784); the heroic description of Montgolfier appears in B. Pingeron, *L'Art de Faire Soi-Même les Ballons* (Paris 1784, 15). One of the many ecstatic odes in praise of Montgolfier, Le Roy's *Le Globe-Montgolfier* (1784), compares him with an eagle:

Sources and Bibliography

Quel volume! Quel poids! Quel vol majestueux
Quel pompeux appareil dans les airs se deploie
Paris, j'entends ses cris de surpris & de joie....

The ironic remarks on social chaos brought about by ballooning were Rivarol's in *Lettre* (12 – 13). On Pilâtre de Rozier, see *Vie et Mémoires de Pilâtre de Rozier* (Paris 1786); also Léon Babinet, "Notice sur Pilâtre de Rozier," in *Mémoires de l'Académie de Metz* (1865). The daily *Journal de Paris* (1782) gives notices of the lectures by Pilâtre de Rozier on *Electricité et Aimant* at the *musée* as well as other lectures on physics and chemistry; the number of February 11, 1782, offers demonstrations of his waterproof robe. The reaction of the public to the ascent at Saint-Cloud is described by Linguet in his *Annales Politiques* (London, vol. 11, 296 – 303). The Lyon ascent is vividly described in the *supplément* to the second edition of *L'Art de Voyager dans l'Air;* the flight of Blanchard in Normandy in *Journal de Paris* (July 18, 1784, 893 –96); see also the elaborate engraving in the same journal (July 28, 1784, 968). Pilâtre's death is described in [J.-P. Marat], *Lettres de l'Observateur Bons-Sens* [sic] (London 1785). The instructions on home-made balloons appear in Pingeron.

Pidanzat de Mairobert's description of the Salon appears in *L'Espion Anglais* (vol. 7, 72). Thomas Crow's *Painters and Public Life in Eighteenth-Century Paris* (New Haven 1986) is the most important discussion of the Salon's public and critics. The public of the boulevard theaters is brilliantly treated in Robert M. Isherwood, *Farce and Fantasy: Popular Entertainment in Eighteenth-Century Paris* (New York and Oxford 1986), as well as in another excellent study, Michele Root-Bernstein, *Boulevard Theater and Revolution in 18th-Century Paris* (Ann Arbor 1984), which deals with some of the same material as Isherwood but is more ambitious in giving it political implications. The author also provides (80) a splendid sense of the physical milieu of the little theaters on the boulevard du Temple. Linguet's *Annales Politiques* for 1779 (236) contains a eulogy of Audinot's L'Ambigu Comique theater and especially the use of child actors and mimes "which bring tears to the eyes, excite terror, admiration and produce all the effects that are so often missing from the grand theaters and in the best plays...." (Linguet also urged a *révolution* in the ballet in which dancers would become true actors and their dances narratives rather than "a succession of ridiculous pirouettes without object or design."

On the theatrical background of Ronsin and Grammont, see Richard Cobb, *The People's Armies (Les Armées Révolutionnaires)* (trans. Marianne Elliott, New Haven and London 1987, 68 –69). On the public of the Palais-Royal, see François-Marie Mayeur de Saint-Paul, *Tableau du Nouveau Palais-Royal* (2 vols., Paris 1788). See also Isherwood, *Farce and Fantasy* (248 –50), and Louis-Sebastien Mercier, *Le Tableau de Paris* (12 vols., Paris 1782 –88, vol. 10, 242). Marmontel's remark on audiences is cited in the useful work by John Lough, *Paris Theater Audiences in the 17th and 18th Centuries* (Oxford 1957, 211). The account of the dispute in the Comédie-Française is taken from Bailey Stone, *The Parlement of Paris* (102ff.); Mme de Campan's *Mémoires* (201 –04) give an account of the reading of *Figaro* to the King; the *Mémoires de la Baronne d'Oberkirch* (new edition, Paris 1970, 303 –04), give a vivid account of the atmosphere surrounding the performance of *Figaro* and her response to it.

ii CASTING ROLES: CHILDREN OF NATURE

On Beaumarchais' maternal nursing scheme, see Nancy Senior, *Eighteenth-Century Studies* (1983, 367 –88). The standard tract on this subject was Marie-Angélique Rebours, *Avis aux Mères qui Veulent Nourrir...* (Paris 1767). Rousseau's influence on breast-feeding habits and the moral philosophy of nature is discussed in Carol Blum's outstanding work, *Jean-Jacques Rousseau and the Republic of Virtue* (Ithaca, N.Y., 1986); also Joel Schwartz, *The Sexual Politics of Jean-Jacques Rousseau* (Chicago 1984). See also Susan Okin, *Women in Western Political Thought* (Princeton 1979, 99 – 196), for Rousseau's treatment of women. Moissy's play *La Vraie Mère* is cited in Anita Brookner, *Greuze, the Rise and Fall of an Eighteenth-Century Phenomenon* (Greenwich, Conn., 1972), which also gives an excellent account of the cult of "*sensibilité.*" Edgar Munhall's exhibition catalogue, *Jean-Baptiste Greuze* 1782 – 1805 (Wadsworth Atheneum, Hartford, Conn., 1977), has excellent entries on, among other paintings, *Girl Weeping* and *The Marriage Contract;* see the same author's "Greuze and the Protestant Spirit," in *Art Quarterly* (Spring 1964, 1 – 21). Charles Mathon de La Cour's comments on Greuze's weeping girl are in his *Lettres à Monsieur xxx sur les Peintures et les Sculptures et les Gravures Exposées dans le sallon* [sic] *du Louvre en 1765* (Paris 1765, 51 –2). Michael Fried, *Theatricality and Absorption: Painting and Beholder in the Age of Diderot* (Chicago 1980), is an important discussion of the formal techniques of moral and dramatic absorption in Greuze's work. Mercier's remark on the virtuous heart is in *Notions Claires sur les Gouvernements* (Paris 1787) and is cited by Norman Hampson, *Will and Circumstance: Montesquieu, Rousseau and the French Revolution* (London 1983, 77). Diderot's famous comment on the *Mère Bien-Aimée* can be found in J. Seznec, *The Salons of Denis Diderot* (Oxford 1975, vol. 2, 155). Guides to the "moralized landscape" were given not only in Girardin's own *Promenade* of 1788 but, in a potted version, in Luc-Vincent Thiéry's important *Almanach des Voyageurs* (1785) and the *Guide des Amateurs* (1788). The posthumous tributes to Rousseau, his plays and memoirs are described in P.-P. Plan, *Jean-Jacques Rousseau Raconté par les Gazettes de Son Temps* (Paris 1912). Robert Darnton, "Readers Respond to Rousseau," in *The Great Cat Massacre*, gives a powerful sense of the personal identification felt by readers with the author. D. G. Charlton, *New Images of the Natural in France* (Cambridge, England, 1984), is an excellent discussion of many of the implications of the Romantic cult of nature, including those of gender and child-rearing. Other useful works on related themes are D. Mornet, *Le Sentiment de la Nature en France de J.-J. Rousseau à Bernardin de Saint-Pierre* (Paris 1907); and Paul van Tighem, *Le Sentiment de la Nature dans le pré-Romantisme Européen* (Brussels 1912).

iii PROJECTING THE VOICE: THE ECHO OF ANTIQUITY

The report on Hérault de Séchelles' speech appears in the *Journal de Paris* of August 7, 1785 (897); for details of his career and early works, including the account of the journey to meet Buffon, see Hubert Juin (ed.), *Oeuvres Littéraires et Politiques de Jean-Marie Hérault de Séchelles* (Edmonton, Alberta, 1976); see also Hérault de Séchelles, *Oeuvres Littéraires* (ed. Emile Dard, Paris 1907). Jean Starobinski has recently published two important articles, "Eloquence Antique, Eloquence Future: Aspects d'un Lieu Commun d'Ancien Régime," in Baker (ed.), *Political Culture* (311 –27), and, at greater length, "La Chaire, la Tribune, le Barreau," in Pierre Nora (ed.), *Les Lieux de Mémoire*, vol. 2, *La Nation* (Paris 1986, part 3, 425 –85). For the continuing humanist tradition of eloquence, see the splendid work by Marc Fumaroli, *L'Age de l'Eloquence: Rhétorique et Res Literaria de la Renaissance au Seuil de l'Epoque Classique* (Paris 1980). (I am most grateful to Natasha Staller for drawing my attention to this important work.) The standard work for prerevolutionary legal eloquence is P.-L. Gin, *De l'Eloquence du Barreau* (Paris 1768). On revolutionary eloquence and rhetoric, see Hans Ulrich Gumbrecht, *Funktionen der Parlamentarischen Rhetorik in der Französischen Revolution* (Munich 1978); Simon Schama, "The Self-Consciousness of Revolutionary Elites," in *Consortium on Revolutionary Europe* (Charleston, S.C., 1978); Lynn Hunt, "The Rhetoric of Revolution," in her *Politics, Culture and*

Class in the French Revolution (Berkeley and Los Angeles 1984). The standard anthology of revolutionary eloquence is still François-Alphonse Aulard, *Les Orateurs de la Révolution Française* (2 vols., Paris 1905, 1906–07). François Furet and Ran Halevi are currently preparing collections of revolutionary oratory, the first volume of which is to appear in May 1989. On Linguet's turbulent career at the bar, see Darline Gay Levy's excellent biography, *The Ideas and Career of Simon-Nicholas-Henri Linguet* (Urbana, Ill., 1980); his ideas on the relationship between antique virtue and oratory appear on pp. 17–21. On the Academy speeches and *éloges*, see the *Recueil des Harangues Prononcées par les Messieurs de l'Académie Française* (1760–89).

For education in Latin oratory and the reading of Sallust, and the imitation of Cicero, see Harold T. Parker, *The Cult of Antiquity and the French Revolution* (Chicago 1937), a book well ahead of its time. For the neoclassical program of exemplary virtues in the arts, see Robert Rosenblum, *Transformations in Late Eighteenth-Century Art* (Princeton 1967) and Hugh Honour, *Neo-Classicism* (London and New York 1977). On the oath of the Horatii in particular, see Crow, *Painters*, and also Norman Bryson, *Word and Image: French Painting of the Ancien Régime* (Cambridge, England, 1981). The report in the *Journal de Paris* on the *Horaces* appears September 17, 1785 (1092). On the reform program of the Comte d'Angiviller, see the unpublished dissertation of Barthélemy Jobert, Ecole des Hautes Etudes en Sciences Sociales (Paris). Further discussion of David's crucial reinterpretation of Roman virtues may be found in Robert Herbert, *David, Voltaire, Brutus and the French Revolution* (New York 1973) and in the forthcoming work on David and the Revolution by Warren Roberts (Chapel Hill, N.C., 1989).

iv SPREADING THE WORD

Robert Darnton's work has transformed the ways in which historians understand censorship, the commerce in banned books and the crucial area of "impolite" reading. See, in particular, *The Literary Underground of the Old Regime* (Cambridge, Mass., 1982); for his extraordinary account of the production and diffusion of the quarto edition of the *Encyclopédie*, see *The Business of the Enlightenment: A Publishing History of the Encyclopédie, 1775–1800* (Cambridge, Mass., 1979). On prohibited books there are still some important details to be gleaned from J.-P. Belin, *Le Commerce des Livres Prohibés à Paris de 1750–1789* (Paris 1912). On the Dutch gazettes, see Jeremy Popkin, "The *Gazette de Leyde* in the Reign of Louis XVI," in Jack Censer and Jeremy Popkin (eds.), *The Press and Politics in Pre-Revolutionary France* (Berkeley 1987); see also, especially for Linguet, idem, "The Prerevolutionary Origins of Popular Journalism," in Baker (ed.), *Political Culture*. For Panckoucke's all-important contribution see Suzanne Tucoo-Chala, *Charles-Joseph Panckoucke* (Pau 1977). For literacy rates, see Daniel Roche, *Le Peuple de Paris* (Paris 1981, 208–09 and, more generally, chapter 7); for the provincial academies, see the same author's classic work *Le Siècle des Lumières en Province* (2 vols., Paris 1978). The provincial diffusion of culture may also be understood from Daniel Mornet's classic study, based on libraries, *Les Origines Intellectuelles de la Révolution Française* (Paris 1910).

CHAPTER FIVE
THE COSTS OF MODERNITY

Fernand Braudel, *L'Identité de la France*, vol. 2, *Les Hommes et les Choses* (Paris 1986, especially 267–306), emphasizes the importance of prerevolutionary industrial growth in France, as well as (238–39) the rapid growth of market possibilities through the transformation of communications between the 1760s and the 1780s. For further detail on commercial and industrial change in the old regime, see Ernest Labrousse et al., *Histoire Economique et Sociale de la France* (vol. 2, 1660 –1789), especially the contributions of Pierre Léon, "L'Elan Industriel et Commercial" (499 –528). For French Atlantic trades, see Paul Butel, "Le Commerce Atlantique Français sous le Régne de Louis XVI," in *Le Régne de Louis XVI* (Actes de Colloque International de Sorèze 1976, 63 –84). On the application of science to industry, see the essay by D. J. Sturdy in the same volume. On other aspects, see C. Ballot, *L'Introduction du Machinisme et l'Industrie Française 1780 –1815* (Paris 1923); G. Chaussinand-Nogaret, "Capitalisme et Structure Sociale," in *Annales: ESC* (1970); and R. Sedillot, *Les de Wendel et l'Industrie Lorraine* (1958). For evidence of the entrepreneurial ethos in prerevolutionary France and a specific appeal for a commercial nobility, see, for example, [L.H. Dudevant], *L'Apologie du Commerce* (1777); also the elaborate and fascinating account of coal and ore mines in *Exposition des Mines* (1772), many of which, including the Anzin coal mines, were noble-owned. The most spectacular document of elite interest in industrial technology (as well as in the mechanization of older craft and luxury trades) is the multivolume *Description des Arts et Métiers* (Académie Royale des Sciences, Paris 1761 –88)—for example, *L'Art du Fabricant de Velours de Coton*, commissioned from the Academy of Science in 1779 specifically with British competition in mind and to exploit French West Indian raw cotton supplies from Guadeloupe, Saint-Domingue and Cayenne.

On the *intendants*, see Vivian Gruder, *The Royal Provincial Intendants* (Ithaca, N.Y., 1968); and for the practical details of their administration, see the superb collection of documents and correspondence published by R. Ardascheff as *Pièces Justificatives*, volume 3 of his monumental work, *Les Intendants de Province sous Louis XVI* (Paris 1900 –07), from which I drew material on Saint-Sauveur in the Roussillon.

On the blind school, see Valentin Haüy, *Essai sur l'Education des Aveugles* (Paris 1786), which includes a description of the royal visit on December 26.

The emblematic depiction of eighteenth-century France in L. S. Mercier's *L'An 2440* (3 vols., 1786 ed.) is in volume 2, p. 68ff. See also Henry Majewski, *The Pre-Romantic Imagination of Louis-Sebastien Mercier* (New York 1971). Mercier is also interestingly discussed by Norman Hampson, *Will and Circumstance*. Linguet's more optimistic writing on economic change is in his *Mémoires sur un Objet Intéressant pour la Province de Picardie* (The Hague 1764), and his apocalyptic comments on industrialization are cited in Levy, *Ideas and Career* (86 –87). His *Annales Politiques* for 1777 (83 –84) has a wonderfully evocative account of the extremes of wealth and poverty in France's economic acceleration.

CHAPTER SIX
BODY POLITICS

i UTERINE FURIES AND DYNASTIC OBSTRUCTIONS

The smutty joke about the *rivière* diamonds appears in [Pierre Jean-Baptiste Nougaret], *Spectacle et Tableau Mouvant de Paris* (vol. 3, 1787, 77). This publication is a wonderful source of miscellaneous information, gossip and scandal on Paris at the end of the old regime. My account of the Diamond Necklace Affair is reconstructed from the printed primary sources, especially the justificatory memoirs bound together as the *Recueil des Mémoires sur l'Affaire du Collier* (Paris 1787). Serious research on the pornographic libels against the Queen is only just getting under way, though see Hector Fleischmann, *Les Pamphlets Libertins Contre Marie-Antoinette* (Paris 1908). Robert Darnton's "The High Enlightenment and the Low Life of Literature," in *Literary Underground*, discusses the political importance of the *libelles*. The important essay by Chantal Thomas, "L'Héroïne du Crime: Marie-Antoinette dans les Pamphlets," in J.-C. Bonnet et al. (eds.), *La Carmagnole des Muses* (Paris 1988), appeared too late, alas, for me to take into account its discussion of much of the same evidence. The principal items considered here are the many editions of the *Essai Historique sur la Vie de Marie-Antoinette, Reine de France. La Vie d'Antoinette; Les Amusements d'Antoinette; Les Passe-temps d'Antoinette* were all slight variations on the *Essai*. The *Memoirs of Antonina Queen d'Abo* (London 1791) was an English version of yet another variation that appeared shortly before the Revolution. Other items in the canon were the spurious history *Les Amours d'Anne d'Autriche* ("A Cologne," 1783); *Anandria* (possibly by Pidanzat de Mairobert, 1788); *Les Amours de Charlot et Toinette* (1789); *Le Bordel Royal, Suivi d'Entretien Secret entre la Reine et le Cardinal de Rohan* (1789); *Le Cadran des Plaisirs de la Cour ou les Aventures du Petit Page Chérubin* (1789). Information about the new editions of Bienville's *La Nymphomanie ou Traité sur la Fureur Uterine* (Amsterdam 1778) comes from the printed catalogue of the bookseller Théophile Barrois le Jeune, who sold from a shop on the quai des Augustins and who evidently specialized in sexual and obstetric works, since he also advertised Tissot's tract against masturbation, *Onanie;* Angélique Rebours' work on breastfeeding; Vacher's treatise on tumors of the breast; and innumerable books on venereal disease. The record of the Queen's trial before the Revolutionary Tribunal was published as *Acte d'Accusation et Interrogatoire Complet et Jugement de Marie-Antoinette* (Paris 1793).

Elisabeth Vigée-Lebrun's own *Mémoires*, while not without interest, are, alas, a model of tact and discretion. The best source on the artist's career is an outstanding exhibition catalogue by Joseph Baillio, *Elisabeth Vigée-Lebrun* (Kimball Museum, Fort Worth, 1982), from which I take the comment on her in the *Mémoires Secretes*. See also Anne Passez, *Adelaide Labille-Guiard* (Paris 1971). There is, however, a great deal of research still to be done on women artists of the 1780s and 1790s. Marie-Antoinette's correspondence with her mother and brother has been translated and published by Olivier Bernier as *The Secrets of Marie-Antoinette* (New York 1985).

ii CALONNE'S PORTRAIT

On Talleyrand's work as agent-general of the clergy, see Louis S. Greenbaum, *Talleyrand, Statesman-Priest: The Agent-General of the Clergy and the Church at the End of the Old Regime* (Washington, D.C., 1970). The best modern biography of Calonne is Robert Lacour-Gayet, *Calonne* (Paris 1963), but the much older work of G. Susane, *La Politique Financière de Calonne* (Paris 1901), is still an important study of his administration. Wilma J. Pugh, "Calonne's New Deal," *Journal of Modern History* (1939, 289–312), offers a generous view of his reforms. The opposite view of Calonne's responsibility for the financial crisis is presented in R. D. Harris, "French Finances and the American War 1777–1783," in *Journal of Modern History* (June 1976). James Riley's important article "Life Annuity Based Loans on the Amsterdam Capital Market Toward the End of the Eighteenth Century," in *Economisch-en-Sociaal Historisch Jaarboek* (vol. 36, 102–30), is the best account of French efforts to raise annuity funds on the Dutch money market and the manner in which Calonne short-circuited the enterprise in 1786–87. My own conclusions derive in part from a remarkable series of handwritten *tableaux* of the ordinary revenues and expenditures of the kingdom, from 1786 to 1789, the first of which appears to come from Calonne's office of the Contrôle and may well have been prepared for the Assembly of the Notables. These documents are now preserved at the Kress Library of Harvard Business School.

iii NOTABLE EXCEPTIONS

Much the most important study on the Assembly of the Notables is Vivian Gruder, "Class and Politics in the Pre-Revolution: The Assembly of Notables of 1787," in Ernst Hinrichs et al., *Vom Ancien Régime*. See also A. Goodwin, "Calonne, the Assembly of French Notables of 1787 and the Origins of the *Révolte Nobiliaire*," in *English Historical Review* (1946). See also Jean Egret, *The French Pre-Revolution* (trans. W. D. Camp, Chicago 1977, chapters 1 and 2). P. Chevallier (ed.) has published the *Journal de l'Assemblée des Notables* (Paris 1960) kept by the Briennes.

CHAPTER SEVEN
SUICIDES

i THE REVOLUTION NEXT DOOR

For the Dutch Patriot Revolution of 1783 –87, see Simon Schama, *Patriots and Liberators: Revolution in the Netherlands 1780 – 1813* (London and New York 1977, chapter 4). See also idem, "The Past and the Future in Patriot Rhetoric"; Jeremy Popkin, "Print Culture in the Netherlands on the Eve of Revolution"; and Nicolaas C. F. van Sas, "The Patriot Revolution: New Perspectives," all in Margaret Jacob (ed.), *Enlightenment and Decline: The Dutch Republic in the Eighteenth Century* (forthcoming).

ii THE LAST GOVERNMENT OF THE OLD REGIME

The most comprehensive and balanced account of the Brienne administration is Egret, *Pre-Revolution*. Guibert is probably best studied from his own *Essai sur la Tactique* (Paris 1774). See also Guibert, *Ecrits Militaires 1772 – 1790* (ed. L. Menard, Paris 1977), and for a discussion of their implications, Geoffrey Best, *War and Revolutionary Europe 1770 – 1870* (London 1982, 56 – 58). On Malesherbes and the emancipation of the Protestants, see Grosclaude, *Malesherbes* (559 – 602).

iii THE SWAN SONG OF THE PARLEMENTS

See Egret, *Pre-Revolution*, for the political conflict. For the pamphlet literature, see Boyd C. Shafer, "Bourgeois Nationalism in Pamphlets on the Eve of the French Revolution," in *Journal of Modern History* (1938, 31 – 50). The Pasquier and d'Eprémesnil citations are from Stone, *Parlement of Paris* (158 and 171). De La Galaizière's address and the remarks by Bertier de Sauvigny and Cordier de Launay are all published in Ardascheff, *Intendants* (vol. 3, 187ff.) For the Lamoignon speech, see Egret, *Pre-Revolution* (168). The anti-Brienne pamphlet is *Dialogue entre M. l'Archevêque de Sens et M. le Garde des Sceaux* (1788). For another violent attack on Lamoignon's reforms, see H.M.N. Duveyner, *La Cour Plénière* (1788), a pamphlet that was lacerated and burned by the public executioner. The story of the bleeding statue is from Oscar Browning (ed.), *Despatches from Paris 1784 – 1790* (London 1909 – 10, vol. 2, 72).

iv THE DAY OF TILES

Stendhal's account is given in *The Life of Henry Brulard* (trans. B.C.J.G. Knight, London 1958, 76). See also Charles Dufayard, "La Journée des Tuiles," in *Revue Historique* (vol. 38, 305 –45). For Grenoble in this period, see Vital Chomel (ed.) *Histoire de Grenoble* (Grenoble 1976); Paul Dreyfus, *Grenoble de César à l'Olympe* (Grenoble 1967). Kathryn Norberg, *Rich and Poor in Grenoble 1600 –1814* (Berkeley 1985) is an important social history of the town. The politics are covered in Egret, *Pre-Revolution*, and Mounier's part in Egret, *La Révolution des Notables: Mounier et les Monarchiens* (Paris 1950). See also F. Vermale, "Les Années de Jeunesse de Mounier 1758 –1787" in *Annales Historiques de la Révolution Française* (January–February 1939). On the assembly at Vizille, see Charles Bellet, *Les Evénements de 1788 en Dauphiné;* Champollion-Figéac, *Chroniques Dauphinoises.*

CHAPTER EIGHT

GRIEVANCES

ii THE GREAT DIVIDE

The evening with Malesherbes is described in Samuel Romilly, *Memoirs* (London 1841, vol. 1, 71 –72); for Malesherbes' memorandum, see Grosclaude, *Malesherbes* (655 –663). On radical pamphlet literature in the autumn of 1788, see especially Carcassonne, *Montesquieu et le Débat;* the excellent and underused study by Mitchell B. Garrett, *The Estates-General of 1789* (New York and London, 1935); Shafer, "Bourgeois Nationalism"; and a number of important studies in Baker (ed.), *Political Culture*, especially those by Keith Baker, François Furet, Ran Halevi and Lynn Hunt, all of which bear on the crucial issue of representation. For d'Antraigues, see Carcassonne, *Montesquieu et le Débat* (614 –15), and his important *Mémoire sur les Etats-Généraux* (1788). On the background of double representation, see George Gordon Andrews, "Double Representation and Vote by Head Before the French Revolution," in *South Atlantic Quarterly* (vol. 26, October 1927, 374 –91). Mirabeau *père*'s memorandum on doubling in provincial assemblies was published as *Précis de l'Organisation ou Mémoire sur les Etats Provinciaux* (1758). Condorcet's comment on Lafayette is given in Louis Gottschalk, *Lafayette Between the American and the French Revolutions* (Chicago 1950, 416). On noble opposition, see Daniel Wick, "The Court Nobility and the French Revolution: The Example of the Society of Thirty," in *Eighteenth-Century Studies* (1980, 263 –84); also Elizabeth Eisenstein, "Who Intervened in 1788?" in *American Historical Review* (1965, 77 –103). Arthur Young's description of the atmosphere in Nantes at the end of 1788 is in his *Travels in France in the Years 1788 and 1789* (ed. Constantia Maxwell, Cambridge, England, 1929, 117). The Volney comment is cited in Garrett, *Estates-General* (127); Lanjuinais in ibid. (139). The text of the *arrêt* of the Parlement of Paris on December 5 is given in J. M. Roberts (ed.), *French Revolution Documents* (Oxford 1966, vol. 1, 39 –42), and that of the Memorandum of the Princes of the Blood in ibid. (46 –49). On Sieyès, *Qu'est-ce que le Tiers Etat?* see Paul Bastid, *Sieyès et sa Pensée* (Paris 1970, 344 –49), and more recently the discussion by Roberto Zapperi in his edition (Geneva 1970). See also Lynn Hunt, "The National Assembly," and Pierre Rosenvallon, "L'Utilitarisme Français et les Ambiguités de la Culture Politique Prerévolutionnaire," who argues Sieyès' debt to Helvétius for a theory of representation based on social utility; both essays are in Baker (ed.), *Political Culture*. For Necker's policy toward the elections, see R. D. Harris's biography. For a rapidly developing polemic against the "uselessness" of the nobility, see, for example, the play *Triomphe du Tiers Etat ou les Ridicules de la Noblesse* (n.d., but probably early 1789), in which the views of the noble who had described the "*Peuple*" as "insects swarming at our feet" are refuted by the village schoolmaster, who insists that "we are all equal because we are all brothers..." and who concludes his speech by declaring (21) that "I was born free and rational [*raisonnable*], there are my prerogatives." The Guillotin petition is discussed in C.-L. Chassin, *Les Elections et les Cahiers de Paris en 1789* (Paris 1888, vol. 1, 37).

iii HUNGER AND ANGER

For Mirabeau's journey to Provence in winter 1789 and for his career at this time, see the excellent biography by Guy Chaussinand-Nogaret, *Mirabeau* (Paris 1982). Arthur Young, *Travels*, has vivid accounts of the distress endured as a result of the poor harvest and terrible winter of 1788–89. The standard introduction to the twenty-five thousand *cahiers de doléances* is Beatrice Hyslop, *Guide to the General Cahiers of 1789* (New York 1936), though both the categories of her classification and the gloss she puts on them give a specific bias to her analysis. A helpful and fairly representative small sample may be studied in Roberts, *Documents* (55–95). During the centenary year of 1888–89, commissions throughout the departments of France embarked on the huge enterprise of publishing all the *cahiers* of the three estates. I have relied on those records for my own readings, and in particular those edited by Camille Bloch for Orléans, the Loiret and the Beauce; D. F. Lesueur and A. Cauchie for Blois and the Loir-et-Cher (Blois 1907); Émile Bridrey for the Manche and Cotentin; E. Le Parquier for Le Havre (Le Havre 1929); V. Malrieu for Montauban; E. Martin for the *bailliage* of Mirecourt in Lorraine (Epinal 1928); D. Ligou on Rivière-Verdun in the Tarn-et-Garonne (Gap 1961); V. Fourastié on the Quercy (Cahors, 1908); Brian Dooley's unpublished Harvard University Ph.D. dissertation on the Côte d'Or; and especially the spectacular archival work of C.-L. Chassin on Paris and the countryside *hors des murs*. The citation from Ducastelier is published in Chassin (vol. 4, 31); for the d'Argis pamphlet, see *Cahier d'un Magistrat sur les Justices Seigneuriales* (1789).

iv DEAD RABBITS, TORN WALLPAPER

On the riots of the spring of 1789, see Jean Egret, "The Pre-Revolution in Provence," in J. Kaplow (ed.), *New Perspectives on the French Revolution* (New York 1965); also "Les Origines de la Révolution en Bretagne" (1788–89) in *Revue Historique* (1955, 213). For the game riots, see Georges Lefebvre, *The Great Fear of 1789: Rural Panic in Revolutionary France* (trans. Joan White, Princeton 1973, chapter 4, and especially 44ff.); see also the same author's *Paysans du Nord Pendant la Révolution Française* (Paris and Lille 1924). The Reveillon riots are best followed in the documents published by Chassin (vol. 4, especially 579–86). On Orléanist politics in the spring of 1789, see G. A. Kelly, "The Machine of the Duc d'Orléans and the New Politics," in *Journal of Modern History* (1979, 667–84).

CHAPTER NINE
IMPROVISING A NATION

The passages from Ferrières are taken from Henri Carré (ed.), *Correspondance Inédite, 1789, 1790, 1791* (Paris 1932). For details of Mirabeau's role in the Estates-General, see

Chaussinand-Nogaret, *Mirabeau*, and for the Provence riots of 1789 see Egret, "Pre-Revolution in Provence," in Kaplow (ed.), *New Perspectives*. The popular biography by Antonia Vallentin (trans. E. W. Dickes), *Mirabeau* (London 1948), is still a valid and entertaining account of his life and politics. On the nobility in the Estates-General, see J. Murphy and P. Higonnet, "Les Deputés de la Noblesse aux Etats-Généraux de 1789," in *Revue d'Histoire Moderne et Contemporaine* (1973). On the clergy, see R. F. Necheles, "The Curés in the Estates General of 1789," in *Journal of Modern History* (1974); M. G. Hutt, "The Curés and the Third Estate: The Ideas of Reform in the Period 1787–89," in *Journal of Ecclesiastical History* (1955 and 1957); Pierre Pierrard, *Histoire des Curés de Campagne de 1789 à Nos Jours* (Paris 1986, especially 15–30); and especially the outstanding work of Timothy Tackett, *Priest and Parish in Eighteenth-Century France: A Social and Political Study of the Curés in a Diocese of Dauphiné 1750–91* (Princeton 1977). See also C. Langlois and T. Tackett, "Ecclesiastical Structures and Clerical Geography on the Eve of the French Revolution," in *French Historical Studies* (1980, 352–70).

For the atmosphere in Paris during May and June, see Young, *Travels in France*. Robert D. Harris's *Necker and the Revolution of 1789* (Lanham, Md., New York and London 1986) gives careful consideration to Necker's role in these months and corrects the conventional wisdom concerning his alleged passivity. Harris's superbly detailed study also makes a powerful case against the inevitability (and the desirability) of Third Estate sovereignty. The book is indispensable reading for any balanced judgment of the politics of 1789. For the full text of the royal speech of June 23, see Roberts, *Documents* (vol. 1, 115–23).

CHAPTER TEN

BASTILLE

i TWO KINDS OF PALACE (THE PROBLEMS OF ORDER IN PARIS)

For the history of the Palais-Royal, see Isherwood, *Farce and Fantasy* (chapter 8); also W. Chabrol, *Histoire et Description du Palais-Royal et du Théâtre Français* (Paris 1883).

Jacques Godechot's *The Taking of the Bastille* (trans. Jean Stewart, London 1970) is a superb narrative account of that event with a number of contemporary eyewitness accounts appended. On the military security of the capital, two works are essential: Samuel F. Scott, *The Response of the Royal Army to the French Revolution: The Role and Development of the Line Army* (Oxford 1978, especially 46–70); and the definitive monograph by Jean Chagniot, *Paris et l'Armée au XVIIIe Siècle* (Paris 1985), which, among other things, completely revises many of the conventional clichés about the *gardes françaises*. On other problems of order, see Alan Williams, *The Police of Paris 1718–1789* (Baton Rouge, La., and London 1979). For the revolutionary crowd, see George Rudé, *The Crowd in the French Revolution 1789–1794* (Oxford 1959); see also the very interesting work by R. B. Rose, *The Making of the Sans-culottes: Democratic Ideas and Institutions in Paris 1789–92* (Manchester 1983). See also Jeffrey Kaplow, *The Names of Kings: The Parisian Laboring Poor in the Eighteenth Century* (New York 1972, especially chapter 7). The best work on the social anatomy of the most revolutionary *faubourg* is Raymonde Monnier, *Le Faubourg Saint-Antoine 1789–1815* (Paris 1981), which is also important for understanding the Réveillon riots.

Sources and Bibliography

ii SPECTACLES: THE BATTLE FOR PARIS

For Curtius, see Mayeur de Saint-Paul, *Le Désoeuvré ou l'Espion du Boulevard du Temple* (London 1781); also *Tableau du Nouveau Palais-Royal* (1788). On Desmoulins, see R. Farge, "Camille Desmoulins au Jardin du Palais-Royal," in *Annales Révolutionnaires* (1914, 446–74).

iii BURIED ALIVE? MYTHS AND REALITIES IN THE BASTILLE

I have taken my accounts of the histories of Linguet and Latude from the texts of their memoirs, reprinted by J.-F. Barrière, *Mémoires de Linguet et de Latude* (Paris 1886); Latude's memoirs were originally published as *Le Despotisme Dévoilé ou Mémoires de Henri Masers de Latude*. Though historians have been understandably skeptical of F. Funck-Brentano's excessively optimistic claims about conditions in the Bastille, the meticulous research of Monique Cottret, *La Bastille à Prendre* (Paris 1986), confirms the view that the prison was rapidly becoming redundant under Louis XVI, and that conditions for most of the inmates were a great deal better than at other places of incarceration. Cottret also has an important discussion of the various elements of Bastille mythology. See also H.-J. Lüsebrink, "La Bastille dans l'Imaginaire Social de la France à la Fin du XVIIIe Siècle (1774-1799)," in *Revue d'Histoire Moderne et Contemporaine* (1983). On the importance of Linguet's *Mémoires*, see Levy, *Ideas and Career*.

For the events of the fourteenth I have largely followed Godechot, *The Taking of the Bastille;* see also Jean Dussaulx, *De l'Insurrection Parisienne et de la Prise de la Bastille* (Paris 1790).

vi THE AFTERLIFE OF THE BASTILLE: PATRIOTE PALLOY AND THE NEW GOSPEL

For Palloy, see H. Lemoine, *Le Démolisseur de la Bastille* (Paris 1929); V. Fournel, *Le Patriote Palloy et l'Exploitation de la Bastille* (Paris 1892); and Romi, *Le Livre de Raison du Patriote Palloy* (Paris 1956), which is a fascinating and underused document.

Popular songs celebrating the fall of the Bastille are collected and analyzed in Cornwell P. Rogers' immensely valuable *The Spirit of Revolution in 1789* (Princeton 1949).

CHAPTER ELEVEN
REASON AND UNREASON

George Lefebvre's *The Great Fear of 1789* remains a masterpiece, the finest of his books. (The episode at Rochechouart is on p. 148). It can be supplemented by his work *Les Paysans du Nord Pendant la Révolution Française* (Paris and Lille 1924, vol. 1, 356–74). For the cultural and psychological roots of the fear of "brigands" and the slipperiness of official classification of the vagrant poor, see Olwen Hufton, *The Poor of Eighteenth-Century France* (220–44), and Michel Vovelle, "From Beggary to Brigandage," in Kaplow (ed.), *New Perspectives*. Madame de La Tour du Pin's experiences are described in her *Memoirs* (ed. and trans. F. Harcourt, from *Journal d'une Femme de Cinquante Ans*, London and Toronto 1969, 111–14). On the destruction of châteaux in Burgundy, see Joachim Durandeau, *Les Châteaux Brulés* (Dijon 1895).

I have taken my account of the night of August 4 principally from the *Archives Parle-*

mentaires and contemporary press reports, in particular the *Point du Jour* (1789, 231ff.). For the night of August 4, see P. Kessell, *La Nuit du 4 Août* (Paris 1969). On the debates over the constitution in the autumn of 1789, see Jean Egret, *La Révolution des Notables: Mounier et les Monarchiens* (Paris 1950), and Paul Bastid, *Sieyès et sa Pensée*. An extremely useful source for the politics of the Constituent are the "bulletins" written by the deputy Poncet-Delpech to his constituents in the Quercy; see Daniel Ligou, *La Première Année de la Révolution Vue par un Témoin* (Paris 1961). For Mirabeau's conduct during this period, see E. Dumont, *Souvenirs sur Mirabeau et sur les Deux Premières Assemblées Legislatives* (ed. M. Duval, Paris 1832).

On Lafayette, the problems of violence and the National Guard, see Louis Gottschalk and Margaret Maddox, *Lafayette in the French Revolution Through the October Days* (Chicago and London 1969, chapters 8–12). On the flag-blessing ceremonies, see J. Tiersot, *Les Fêtes et les Chants de la Révolution Française* (Paris 1908, 14–16); also Rogers, *Spirit of Revolution* (134–59). For another eloquently expressed view about the problem of violence and legitimacy, see Abbé Morellet, *Mémoires* (Paris 1822, 362). Loustalot's extraordinary journalism and his exploitation of violence must be studied in the original. In the number August 2–8, for example, he reports that Paris authorities received a chest packed with six heads from various parts of France: Provence, Flanders, etc. The passage quoted at length is from the same number (27–29). See also Jack Censer, *Prelude to Power: The Parisian Radical Press 1789–1791*, for an important analysis of these influential publications.

For the October days, see Albert Mathiez, "Etude Critique sur les Journées des 5 et 6 Octobre 1789," in *Revue Historique* (1898, 241–81); vol. 67 (1899, 258–94) and vol. 69 (1899, 41–66) of the *Revue* are still important. See also Gottschalk and Maddox, *Lafayette in the French Revolution* (chapters 14 and 15); Henri Leclerq, *Les Journées d'Octobre et la Fin de l'Année 1789* (Paris 1924); Harris, *Necker and the Revolution of 1789* (chapter 18); and Rudé, *The Crowd* (chapter 5). On the role of women in October 1789, see Jeanne Bouvier, *Les Femmes Pendant la Révolution de 1789* (Paris 1931); Olwen Hufton, "Women and Revolution," Douglas Johnson (ed.), *French Society and the Revolution* (New York and Cambridge, England, 1976, 148–66); Adrien Lasserre, *La Participation Collective des Femmes à la Révolution Française: Les Antécédents du Féminisme* (Paris 1906); and most recently Dominique Godineau, *Citoyennes Tricoteuses: Les Femmes du Peuple à Paris Pendant la Révolution Française* (Aix-en-Provence 1988).

CHAPTER TWELVE
ACTS OF FAITH

On Jean Jacob, see, for example, the report in Desmoulins' *Révolutions de France et de Brabant* (December 12, 1789), in which engraved portraits were advertised for 30 sous (3 livres if hand-colored). On the background and consequences of the Civil Constitution of the Clergy, see J. McManners, *The French Revolution and the Church* (London 1969). Timothy Tackett, *Religion, Revolution and Regional Culture in Eighteenth-Century France: The Ecclesiastical Oath of 1791* (Princeton 1986), is an outstanding study which places great emphasis on a clearly defined religious geography in France; Albert Mathiez's neglected *La Révolution et l'Eglise* (Paris 1910) has an interesting essay on the campaign to politicize the pulpit. For an example of prerevolutionary Jansenist and "reformist" clerical ideology, see *L'Ecclésiastique Citoyen* (1787) and Ruth Necheles, *The Abbé Grégoire 1787–1831: The Odyssey of an Egalitarian* (Westport, Conn., 1971). For anticlerical songs in Paris, see Rogers, *Spirit of Revolution* (200ff.).

For Talma, see F. H. Collins, *Talma: Biography of an Actor* (London 1964). The most detailed and interesting account of *Charles IX* is A. Liéby, *Etude dans le Théâtre de Marie-Joseph Chénier* (Paris 1901). On politics in the Cordeliers, see Norman Hampson, *Danton* (London 1978, chapter 2); and R. B. Rose, *The Making of the Sans-culottes*. For the Fête de la Fédération, see Mona Ozouf, *Festivals and the French Revolution* (trans. Alan Sheridan, Cambridge, Mass., 1988); Tiersot, *Les Fêtes et les Chants* (17–46); and Marie-Louise Biver, *Fêtes Révolutionnaires à Paris* (Paris 1979). On the Strasbourg *fête*, see Eugène Seinguerlet, *L'Alsace Française: Strasbourg Pendant la Révolution* (Paris 1881). See also Albert Mathiez, *Les Origines des Cultes Révolutionnaires 1789–1792* (Paris and Caen 1904).

CHAPTER THIRTEEN
DEPARTURES

For accounts of the personnel changes (or lack of them) in the municipal revolutions of 1789–90, some of the older local histories are very helpful. See, in particular, A. Prudhomme, *Histoire de Grenoble* (Grenoble 1888); and Victor Dérode, *Histoire de Lille* (Lille 1868). For the epitaph to the Parlement, see the *Courrier Patriotique du Grenoble* (October 2, 1790). By far the most important modern comparative history is Lynn Hunt, *Revolution and Politics in Provincial France: Troyes and Reims 1786–1790* (Stanford 1978); see also idem, *Politics, Culture and Class* (chapter 5), though the author draws clearer lines between the old and new political classes than seem to me to be everywhere evident in the earlier stages of the Revolution. Other important local studies on which I have drawn are J. Sentou, *Fortunes et Groupes Sociaux à Toulouse sous la Révolution* (Toulouse 1969); Louis Trénard, *Lyon de l'Encyclopédie au Préromantisme* (Paris 1958, vol. 2, 229ff.); the more aggressively anti-Parisian Albert Champdor, *Lyon Pendant la Révolution* (Lyon 1983); and Claude Fohlen, *Histoire de Besançon* (Besançon 1967, 229ff.). For Strasbourg, Seinguerlet, *Strasbourg Pendant la Révolution* (352ff.), and Gabriel G. Ramon, *Frédéric de Dietrich, Premier Maire de Strasbourg sous la Révolution* (Paris and Strasbourg 1919). On the village history of Puiseux-Pontoise, see the extremely interesting essay by Albert Soboul in his *Problèmes Paysans de la Révolution Française* (Paris 1976, 254). Patrice Higonnet, in *Pont-de-Montvert: Social Structure and Politics in a French Village* (Cambridge, Mass., 1971), found the same combination of high-minded revolutionism and predictable opportunism in the acquisition of *biens nationaux*.

On the press, see Censer, *Prelude to Power*. The report from *L'Orateur du Peuple* on conjugal politics is from 1791 (481). Brissot's sardonic congratulation of Desmoulins is in the *Patriote Français* for December 30, 1790. The Lille "Battalions of Hope" are mentioned in Dérode, *Histoire de Lille* (47). On almanacs, see Henri Welschinger, *Les Almanachs de la Révolution* (Paris 1884), and G. Gobel and A. Soboul, "Almanachs," in *Annales Historiques de la Révolution Française* (October–December 1978). On the Jacobin competition of 1791, see Gobel and Soboul (615ff.). For the correspondence on the "coiffure Brutus," see *Patriote Français* (October 31, 1791). Lequinio's prayer was published in the *Feuille Villageoise* (November 17, 1791, 184), as was the schoolmaster's letter (September 1791, 51).

For the foundation of the Jacobins, Michael L. Kennedy, *The Jacobin Clubs in the French Revolution: The First Years* (Princeton 1982), is an extremely important work. On the popular societies of Paris, see R. B. Rose, *The Making of the Sans-culottes* (chapter 6); Santerre's remark is cited in ibid. (114). Rose also gives the text (104) of the petition of the Société Fraternelle. See, in addition, the older work of Isabelle Bourdin, *Les Sociétés Populaires à Paris Pendant la Révolution Française* (Paris 1937). Girardin's plebiscitary utopia is set out in his *Discours sur la Ratification de la Loi par la Voix Générale* (Paris 1791). For the background to the labor unrest of 1791, see Michael Sonenscher, "Journeymen, Courts and French Trades, 1781–1791," *Past and Present* (Feb. 1987, 77–107).

Mirabeau's correspondence with the court and his strategy for reinvigorating the constitutional monarchy is set out in full in Guy Chaussinand-Nogaret (ed.), *Mirabeau entre le Roi et la Révolution* (Paris 1986). His last days are described in the same author's *Mirabeau*. For the funeral procession and especially for Gossec's music composed for the occasion, see Tiersot, *Les Fêtes et les Chants* (51ff.). Ruault's comment is quoted in Biver, *Fêtes Révolutionnaires* (35). On the foundation of the Panthéon, see Mona Ozouf, "Le Panthéon," in Nora (ed.), *Les Lieux de Mémoire*, vol. 1, *La République* (Paris 1984, 151). Brissot's cool response was given in the *Patriote Français* (April 5, 1791).

The Cordeliers petition against the court's attempted journey to Saint-Cloud for Holy Week 1791 is given in Roberts, *Documents* (vol. 1, 292–93). Fréron's scorn for the Constituent's expression of concern over the health of the King is in *L'Orateur* (1791, 215). The best account of the impact of the flight to Varennes in in part 1 of Marcel Reinhard's superlative history of 1791 and 1792, *La Chute de la Royauté* (Paris 1969), and see the set of documentary appendices on both the period of the flight and the Cordeliers campaign that led to the massacre on the Champ de Mars. For the Jacobin reaction, see Kennedy, *The Jacobin Clubs* (chapter 14). Fréron's denunciation of the King is in *L'Orateur* (1791, 370). Ferrières' letter to his wife on the flight is in Carré (ed.), *Correspondance* (vol. 1, 363, June 23, 1791). On the cults of Voltaire and Brutus, see Robert Herbert, *David, Voltaire, Brutus*; also the excellent forthcoming study by Warren Roberts on Jacques-Louis David. For the Fête de Voltaire, see Nicolas Ruault, *Gazette d'un Parisien sous la Révolution* (July 15, 1791); and Biver, *Fêtes Révolutionnaires* (38–42).

For the massacre on the Champ de Mars, see Rudé, *The Crowd* (80–94) and G. A. Kelly, "Bailly and the Champ de Mars Massacre," in *Journal of Modern History* (1980). The full history of David's *Tennis Court Oath* is given in a fine monograph, Philippe Bordes, *Le Serment du Jeu de Paume de Jacques-Louis David* (Paris 1983).

CHAPTER FOURTEEN
"MARSEILLAISE"

The principal elements of the constitution of 1791 are published in Roberts, *Documents* (vol. 1, 347–66), and the debate on political clubs in the Constituent, with Robespierre's speech, ibid. (366–76). For the Feuillant attempt to stabilize the constitutional monarchy, see Marcel Reinhard, *10 Août 1792: La Chute de la Royauté* (Paris 1969, chapter 8).

Robespierre has, of course, been the subject of countless biographies. Among the more recent studies are Norman Hampson's *The Life and Opinions of Maximilien Robespierre* (London 1974), an interesting attempt to write the biography in the form of a historical discussion by different participants (pro and con), each of whom tries to sustain his point of view—along with a token "undecided." George Rudé is more orthodox and sympathetic in *Robespierre: Portrait of a Revolutionary Democrat* (New York 1985). David Jordan's *The Revolutionary Career of Maximilien Robespierre* (New York 1985) comes closest to exposing his political psychology and intense historical self-consciousness, but it should be read in conjunction with Carol Blum's fine study on Rousseau and revolutionary language, *Jean-Jacques Rousseau and the Republic of Virtue*. Alfred Cobban, *Aspects of the French Revolution* (London 1968), also includes an excellent essay on Robespierre's application of Rousseauean ideals and language. The enormous edition of Robespierre's *Oeuvres Complètes*, ed. Eugène Déprez et al. (10 vols., Paris 1910–1968) was completed in 1968.

For a good instance of the sharpening of the Revolution's war against the traditional Church, see Y.-G. Paillard, "Fanatiques et Patriotes dans le Puy-de-Dôme," in *Annales Historiques de la Révolution Française* (April–June 1970). On the timing and geography of the waves of emigration, see Donald Greer, *The Incidence of the Emigration During the French Revolution* (Cambridge, Mass., 1951). For violence in the Midi, see, most recently, Hubert Johnson, *The Midi in Revolution: A Study of Regional Political Diversity 1789–1793* (Princeton 1986); also the first chapters of Gwynne Lewis, *The Second Vendée: The Continuity of Counterrevolution in the Department of the Gard 1789–1815* (Oxford 1978), and a stimulating and important article by Colin Lucas, "The Problem of the Midi in the French Revolution," in *Transactions of the Royal Historical Society* (1978, 1–25).

The origins of the war of 1792 are discussed in the outstanding book by T.C.W. Blanning, *The Origins of the French Revolutionary Wars* (London 1986). On the foreign clubs and legions, see Albert Mathiez, *La Révolution Française et les Etrangers* (Paris 1919); Jacques Godechot, *La Grande Nation: L'Expansion Révolutionnaire de la France dans le Monde 1789–1799* (Paris 1956, vol. 1); and Schama, *Patriots and Liberators* (introduction and chapter 4). For Brissot's early career, see Robert Darnton, "A Spy in Grub Street," in *Literary Underground* (41–70), which settles the issue of his prerevolutionary double allegiance but perhaps underrates the power of his patriotic rhetoric in the crucial winter of 1791–92. See also Eloise Ellery, *Brissot de Warville: A Study in the History of the French Revolution* (Boston and New York 1915). On Vergniaud, see Claude Bowers, *Pierre Vergniaud: Voice of the French Revolution* (New York 1950).

The best way to study the extraordinary patriotic oratory of this period is to read it, uncut, in the *Archives Parlementaires* or the *Moniteur*, where it springs to life with startling vigor and resonance. Historians have just rediscovered the importance of rhetoric in the Revolution, but a much earlier generation was well aware of it. See, for example, the classic work of Alphonse Aulard, *L'Eloquence Parlementaire Pendant la Révolution Française*, vol. 1, *Les Orateurs de l'Assemblée Constituante* (Paris 1882), and for the great speakers of the Legislative Assembly, vol. 2, *Les Orateurs de la Législatif et de la Convention* (Paris 1886). There is a helpful introduction in the excellent collection of speeches published by H. Morse Stephens, *The Principal Speeches of the Statesmen and Orators of the French Revolution 1789–1795* (2 vols., Oxford 1892). For more recent treatments, see Lynn Hunt, "The Rhetoric of Revolution," in *Politics, Culture and Class* (19–51); Gumbrecht, *Funktionen der Parliamentarischen Rhetorik*; Schama, "The Self-Consciousness of Revolutionary Elites," in *Consortium on the French Revolution*; and Starobinski, "La Chaire, la Tribune, le Barreau," in Nora (ed.), *Les Lieux de Mémoire*, vol. 2, *La Nation*. Pierre Trahard, in an unduly neglected introductory work, *La Sensibilité Révolutionnaire* (Paris 1936), also had much of interest to say on this same topic.

On the history of the "Marseillaise," see the splendid essay by Michel Vovelle, "La Marseillaise: La Guerre ou la Paix," in Nora (ed.), *Les Lieux de Mémoire*, vol. 1, *La République* (85–136); also Julien Tiersot, *Rouget de Lisle* (Paris 1916). On the effect of politics on the army at the beginning of the war, see Scott, *The Response of the Royal Army* (chapters 3–5).

For the economic crisis of spring and summer 1792, the exceptionally clear and helpful book of Florin Aftalion, *L'Economie de la Révolution Française* (Paris 1987, chapters 4–6), is an indispensable guide. It also demonstrates the disastrously inflationary consequences of the monetary policy of the Constituent and Legislative Assemblies. See also S. E. Harris, *The Assignats* (Cambridge, Mass., 1930). On the development of sans-culotte consciousness, see R. B. Rose, *The Making of the Sans-culottes* (chapters 8 and 9); on the cult of the *bonnet rouge*, see Jennifer Harris, "The Red Cap of Liberty: A Study of Dress Worn by French Revolutionary Partisans 1789–1794," in *Eighteenth-Century Studies* (1981, 283–312).

Reinhard is especially good on the preparation of the revolution of August 10 and on the details of the day itself. The major, gigantically detailed work on the organization of the insurrectionary Commune (though not on the events of the day itself) remains Fritz Braesch, *La Commune de Dix Août, 1792: Etude sur l'Histoire de Paris de 20 Juin au 2 Décembre 1792* (Paris 1911). Morris Slavin has questioned Braesch's classification of the political complexion of the Paris *sections*: see his "Section Roi-de-Sicile and the Fall of the Monarchy," in Slavin and Smith (eds.), *Bourgeois, Sans-culottes and Other Frenchmen* (59–74). For another of Slavin's fascinating micro-studies see his *The French Revolution in Miniature: Section Droits de l'Homme 1789–1795* (Princeton 1984).

CHAPTER FIFTEEN
IMPURE BLOOD

On the invention and politicization of the guillotine, see the brilliant work by Daniel Arasse, *La Guillotine et L'Imaginaire de la Terreur* (Paris 1987). For the Commune's campaign of repression and its combative relations with the Legislative Assembly, see Braesch (334–61).

The standard work for the last fifty years on the prison killings has been Pierre Caron, *Les Massacres de Septembre* (Paris 1935). Though its reading of the evidence seems to me to be, in the last analysis, tendentious, it is still useful for its massive archival research. I follow much of Frédéric Bluche's criticism in *Septembre 1792: Logiques d'un Massacre* (Paris 1986). Though Braesch does not make the prison massacres a central part of his story, he is more forthright in tracing responsibility among the *section* leadership (464ff.) and concludes that there was "*complicité d'une grande partie de la population parisienne avec les massacreurs*" (490). For Danton's period as minister of justice see Hampson (67–84).

Alison Patrick, *The Men of the First French Republic* (Baltimore 1972), remains the standard analysis of the personnel of the Convention and is especially valuable for not collapsing political beliefs into occupational origins. It is also a corrective to M. J. Sydenham's excessively skeptical *The Girondins* (London 1961), which argued, peculiarly, that since the Girondins could not be shown to be a cohesive "party" in the modern sense, their grouping in the Convention was essentially a matter of random associations and personal affinities. Friendships and personal affinities could, of course, exercise the strongest allegiances for a Romantic generation in which the cult of *amitié* was an index of ideological purity. The looseness of the group and the tendency of some of its members (such as Isnard) to go their own ways on votes did not, however, mean it had no sense of its own solidarity vis-à-vis the Mountain. It may be that Albert Soboul (ed.), *Actes du Colloque "Girondins et Montagnards"* (Paris 1980), went too far in the opposite direction in attempting to pin the Girondins down to a distinctive class ethos, but the volume contains interesting contributions by Alan Forrest on the Bordeaux federalists and by Marcel Dorigny on the economic ideas of some of the Girondins' leading members.

For the trial of Louis XVI, much the best account is David Jordan, *The King's Trial* (Berkeley and Los Angeles 1979). Michael Walzer's edition of some of the major speeches, *Regicide and Revolution* (Cambridge, England, 1974), is useful for its documentation, but offers a troubling defense of the trial and execution as "nothing other than the acting out in legal form of the overthrow of divine right monarchy." This seems to overlook the glaring issue that the King was in fact on trial for offenses committed as a *constitutional* monarch and that the trial did not in fact at all turn on the naked mutual exclusivity of popular sovereignty and divine-right theories of sovereignty. Patrick, *The*

Men of the First Republic, is extremely good on the politics of the trial. For the King's captivity and last days, see J.-B. Cléry, *A Journal of the Terror* (ed. Sidney Scott, London 1955); and Gaston de Beaucourt, *Captivité et Derniers Moments de Louis XVI: Récits Originaux et Documents Officiels* (Paris 1892), especially vol. 2, which has the official statements and proceedings of the Commune as well as accounts by the Abbé Edgeworth and the text of Louis' last will and testament. For Malesherbes' defense, see Grosclaude, *Malesherbes* (703–16).

CHAPTER SIXTEEN
ENEMIES OF THE PEOPLE?

For Talleyrand in London, see Orieux, *Talleyrand* (192 –209); Fanny Burney's encounter with Mme de Staël and the "Juniperians" is in Joyce Hemlow (ed.), *The Journals and Letters of Fanny Burney* (vol. 3, Oxford 1972). For the climate of British politics in late 1792 and early 1793, see Albert Goodwin, *The Friends of Liberty: The English Democratic Movement in the Age of the French Revolution* (London 1979, especially chapter 7). The background and buildup to the war with England, Spain and the Netherlands are discussed in T.C.W. Blanning, *Origins*. For Kersaint's speech, see *Moniteur* (January 3, 1793). See also J. Holland Rose, *William Pitt and the Great War* (London 1911). Documents on the Scheldt and the defense of the Netherlands are given in H. T. Colenbrander, *Gedenkstukken der Algemeene Geschiedenis van Nederland van 1789 tot 1840* (Gravenhage 1905, vol. 1, 285 for Grenville to Auckland and 291 for Talleyrand to Grenville). See also Schama, *Patriots and Liberators* (153 –63), on the Dumouriez campaign. The full text of Dumouriez's letter to the Convention appears in the Paris newspaper *Le Batave* for March 25, 1793.

There is an enormous literature on both the origins and the course of the Vendée rebellion. Yet another masterpiece of late nineteenth-century archival editing and research by the apparently inexhaustible C.-L. Chassin, *La Préparation de la Guerre de Vendée 1789 –1793* (3 vols., Paris 1892), is the place to begin to understand fully the collision between republicanism and the Church in this region. Bethuis' account of his childhood experience of the Machecoul massacre is from Chassin (vol. 3, 337ff.). The Laparra harangue at Fontenay is in ibid. (220), as are the Biret reports (213 –78). Chassin's other great documentary compilation on this subject is *La Vendée Patriote 1793 –1800* (4 vols., Paris 1893–95). Though Charles Tilly's *The Vendée* (Cambridge, Mass., 1964)—as French historians are quick to point out—treats not the whole of the Vendée *militaire* but just the region divided by the Layon, it is still of great importance and value in describing the social geography of allegiance. The other major work, in something of the same style but with extraordinary descriptive richness, is Paul Bois, *Les Paysans de l'Ouest* (Paris 1960). Two recent works, however, have transformed the historiography, albeit in very different styles. Jean-Clément Martin, *La Vendée et la France* (Paris 1987), mostly based on printed sources from Chassin, is a model of empathy and historical sensitivity. Its endeavor to try to see both sides of the conflict makes its terrible conclusions all the more chilling and should put an end, once and for all, to skepticism about the scale of the population loss and destruction of the region. Reynald Sécher's *Le Génocide Franco-Français: La Vendée-Vengé* (Paris 1986) is more avowedly polemical but, deeply researched in departmental and national archives, is nonetheless persuasive to a great degree. Its arguments are imbued with a tragic intensity that makes academic appeals for "dispassion" seem comically amoral. At the opposite extreme of historical temperament, the stolidly sociological Marcel Faucheux, *L'Insurrection Vendéenne de 1793* (Paris 1964), does its best to explain everything in terms of socio-economic structures and mostly fails. On the course of the war itself, P. Doré-Graslin, *Itinéraire de la Vendée Militaire* (Angers 1979), is a haunting evocation, in contemporary documents and maps as well as modern photographs, of the sites of battle and destruction. Jean-Clément Martin has also contributed a wonderful essay on the subsequent echo of the Vendée war in later periods, "La Vendée, Région-Mémoire, Bleus et Blancs," in Nora (ed.), *Les Lieux de Mémoire*, vol. 1, *La République* (595 –617). For a related but distinct revolt in Brittany, see Donald Sutherland, *The Chouans: The Social Origins of Popular Counter-Revolution in Upper Brittany 1770 –1796* (Oxford 1982); also T.J.A. Le Goff and D.M.G. Sutherland, "The Social Origins of Counter-revolution in Western France," *Past and Present* (1983).

For the economic crisis of 1793 and the conversion of the Jacobins to economic regulation, see Aftalion, *L'Economie de la Révolution* (chapters 7 and 8). For the *enragé* principles, see R. B. Rose, *The Enragés: Socialists of the French Revolution?* (Melbourne 1965). See also Walter Markov (ed.), *Jacques Roux: Scripta et Acta* (Berlin, DDR, 1969). On the food riots of February, see George Rudé, "Les Emeutes des 25, 26 Février 1793," in *Annales Historiques de la Révolution Française* (1953, 33 –57); and Albert Mathiez, *La Vie Chère et Mouvement Social sous la Terreur* (2 vols., Paris 1927). On the social base and organization of the sans-culottes, see Albert Soboul, *The Parisian Sans-culottes and the French Revolution* (Oxford 1964), and Gwynn Williams's excellent comparative study with English labor, *Artisans and Sans-culottes* (London 1968). Soboul's classic position of a social cleavage between "bourgeois" Jacobins and artisanal sans-culottes has not stood up well to closer inspection on the level of individual *sections*, where "sans-culottes" are often found to be composed of exactly the same social groups—tradesmen, wineshop intellectuals, lawyers, officials and professionals, and occasional wage earners—as the Jacobin rank and file. For a still valid analysis of Jacobin personnel, see the outstanding work by Crane Brinton, *The Jacobins* (New York 1930). The most powerful attack on the whole concept of a sans-culotte "movement" came in Richard Cobb's great tour de force, *The Police and the People: French Popular Protest 1789 –1820* (Oxford 1970), and was renewed in his *Reactions to the French Revolution* (Oxford 1972). Michel Vovelle tries to answer the question "What was a sans-culotte?" in *La Mentalité Révolutionnaire: Société et Mentalités sous la Révolution Française* (Paris 1985, 109 –23). For a very original and important perspective, see R. M. Andrews, "The Justices of the Peace of Revolutionary Paris, September 1792– November 1794," in Douglas Johnson, *French Society and the Revolution*, 167–216. On the anti-Girondin riots of March 10, see A. M. Boursier, "L'Emeute Parisienne du 10 Mars 1793," in *Annales Historiques de la Révolution Française* (April–June 1972). On Marat's battle with the Girondins, trial and acquittal, see the strangely bloodless biography by Louis Gottschalk, *Marat* (New York 1927, 139 –68). For the expulsion of the Girondins and the Jacobin politics leading to it, see the readable, detailed narrative by Morris Slavin, *The Making of an Insurrection: Parisian Sections and the Gironde* (Cambridge, Mass., 1986).

CHAPTER SEVENTEEN
"TERROR IS THE ORDER OF THE DAY"

On the Girondins in Normandy, see Albert Goodwin, "The Federalist Movement in Caen During the French Revolution," in *Bulletin of the John Rylands Library* (1959 –60, 313 –44). For other (and more important) centers of federalist resistance, see Alan Forrest, *Society and Politics in Revolutionary Bordeaux* (Oxford 1975); W. H. Scott, *Terror and Repression in Revolutionary Marseilles* (London 1973); Hubert Johnson, *The Midi in Revolu-*

tion (chapter 7); M. Crook, "Federalism and the French Revolution: The Revolt of Toulon in 1793," *History* (1980, 383 –97); D. Stone, "La Révolte Fédéraliste à Rennes," *Annales Historiques de la Révolution Française* (July–September 1971); and, most important of all, in Lyon, C. Riffaterre, *Le Mouvement Anti-Jacobin et Anti-Parisien de Lyon et dans le Rhône-et-Loire en 1793* (2 vols., Lyon 1912 –28). For a discussion of the regional strength of federalism in the Loire and its urban bases, see Colin Lucas, *The Structure of the Terror: The Case of Javogues and the Loire* (Oxford 1973, 35 –60).

Marat's assassination, funeral and cult are the subject of a fascinating collection of essays, edited by Jean-Claude Bonnet, *La Mort de Marat* (Paris 1986). See in particular the contributions of J. Guilhaumou, J. C. Bonnet (on Marat's journalism) and Chantal Thomas on the image of Charlotte Corday. Rather surprisingly, perhaps, modern interest in the cult of Marat, the exploitation of blood imagery and David's invention of a republican martyrology was anticipated in the excellent work by Eugène Defrance, *Charlotte Corday et le Mort de Marat* (Paris 1909), from which I take many of the more extreme examples of Maratology. See also F. P. Bowman, "Le Sacré Coeur de Marat," *Annales Historiques de la Révolution Française* (July–September 1975). Charlotte Corday's journey, deed and trial can be followed in exhaustive detail in the somewhat hagiographic (but still rivetingly interesting) Jean Epois, *L'Affaire Corday-Marat: Prélude à la Terreur* (Les Sables-d'Olonne 1980).

For the Fête de l'Unité and revolutionary festivals generally, the crucial work is Ozouf, *Festivals and the French Revolution*. Ozouf is particularly eloquent on the official attempts to reshape citizens' sense of space and time through the festivals. For the Hercules image, as well as other important issues concerning the symbolic practices of revolutionary discourse, see Hunt, *Politics, Culture and Class*. A number of other works deal with David's role in orchestrating the great festivals, in particular D. L. Dowd, *Pageant-Master of the Republic: Jacques-Louis David and the French Revolution* (Lincoln, Neb., 1948); see also idem, "Jacobinism and the Fine Arts," in *Art Quarterly* (1953, no. 3). On David, see also Anita Brookner, *David* (New York 1980), and the excellent forthcoming study on the artist by Warren Roberts. A vivid description of the *fête* of August 10, 1793, was left by the artist Georges Wille, *Mémoires et Journal* (ed. G. Duplessis, Paris 1857).

On the early phase of the Committee of Public Safety and Danton's role in it, see Hampson, *Danton* (117 –36). For Jacques Roux's crucial if personally disastrous intervention of June 25, see Markov, *Jacques Roux* (480 –86ff.). For the foundations and operation of the economic Terror, see Aftalion, *L'Economie de la Révolution*; also H. Calvet, *L'Accaparement à Paris sous la Terreur: Essai sur l'Application de la Loi de 26 Juillet 1793* (Paris 1933). For what the enforcement of the *maximum* meant at the level of the village, see Richard Cobb, *The Police and the People*, and his classic work, *The People's Armies*.

For the *levée en masse*, the work that supersedes every other is J.-P. Berthaud, *La Révolution Armée: Les Soldats-Citoyens et la Révolution Française* (Paris 1979). I draw heavily on this superb book for my own account of the mobilization. R. R. Palmer, *Twelve Who Ruled: The Year of the Terror in the French Revolution* (Princeton 1941), is still an exceptionally readable, if somewhat idealized, account of the revolutionary government.

On the mentality, institutions and practices of the Terror, Colin Lucas's *The Structure of the Terror* is a brilliant monograph, both persuasive in its account of the controlling complications of local allegiances and alarmingly vivid in its portrait of Javogues. See also Lucas, "La Brève Carrière du Terroriste Jean-Marie Lapalus," in *Annales Historiques de la Révolution Française* (October–December 1968). There are a number of other excellent local studies, in particular Martyn Lyons, "The Jacobin Elite of Toulouse," in *European Studies Review* (1977). See also Richard Cobb's account of the career of Nicolas Guénot and other Terrorists in his *Reactions to the French Revolution*. The most brilliant characterization of the "revolutionary mentality" shared by both Terrorists and sans-culottes is Cobb's essay "Quelques Aspects de la Mentalité Révolutionnaire Avril 1793–Thermidor An II," in his *Terreur et Subsistances 1793–95* (Paris 1964), a shortened version of which also appeared in his *A Second Identity* (Oxford 1972). For the legal structure of repression, see John Black Sirich, *The Revolutionary Committees in the Departments of France 1793–94* (New York 1971). At a Harvard University Center of European Studies Colloquium, "Republican Patriotism and the French Revolution," Richard Andrews read an extraordinarily important and provocative paper which demonstrated that the legal basis for the Revolution's definition of political crimes was laid not in 1793 by the Law of Suspects (which did, however, broaden it) but by the Penal Code of 1791. Finally, an important work, whose essential findings correlating the Terror with civil war departments of France have not been much shaken by criticism of the author's use of statistics, is D. Greer, *The Incidence of the Terror During the French Revolution: A Statistical Interpretation* (Cambridge, Mass., 1935).

On the federalist repressions, see, for Lyon, Edouard Herriot, *Lyon n'est Plus* (4 vols., Lyon 1937–40). Baron Raverat, *Lyon sous la Révolution* (Lyon 1883) is predictably (and with good reason) hostile to the Jacobins but contains much interesting material. See also M. Sève, "Sur la Pratique Jacobine: La Mission de Couthon à Lyon," in *Annales Historiques de la Révolution Française* (April–July 1983); Richard Cobb, "La Commission Temporaire de Commune Affranchie," in *Terreur et Subsistances* (55–94); and William Scott's excellent book, *Terror and Repression in Revolutionary Marseilles* (London 1973). For the "infernal columns" and the devastation of the Vendée, and the *noyades* at Nantes, see Sécher, J.-C. Martin and Gaston Martin, *Carrier et sa Mission à Nantes* (Paris 1924).

On dechristianization the essential work is now Michel Vovelle, *Réligion et Révolution, la Déchristianisation de l'An II* (Paris 1976). On the revolutionary calendar, see Bronislaw Baczko, "Le Calendrier Républicain," in Nora (ed.), *Les Lieux de Mémoire*, vol. 1, *La République* (38–82); see also James Friguglietti, *The Social and Religious Consequences of the French Revolutionary Calendar* (Harvard University Ph.D. Dissertation, 1966), and Louis Jacob, *Fabre d'Eglantine: Chef des Fripons* (Paris 1946).

CHAPTER EIGHTEEN
THE POLITICS OF TURPITUDE

Beugnot's account of his stay in the Conciergerie and his encounter with "Eglé" can be found in C. A. Dauban, *Les Prisons de Paris sous la Révolution* (Paris 1870), which also has a wealth of other information about the prisons of the Terror, including Riouffe's splendid *"Mémoires d'un Détenu,"* originally published under the Thermidorian regime of the year III, a date which I do not automatically take to disqualify it from serious attention. Olivier Blanc, *La Dernière Lettre: Prisons et Condamnés 1793–94* (Paris 1984), also provides a guide to conditions in the various prisons and reproduces a dossier of some of the most moving and distressing letters written by the condemned. See also A. de Maricourt, *Prisonniers et Prisons de Paris Pendant la Terreur* (Paris 1927), and part 1 of Cobb, *The Police and the People*.

For the imprisonment and trial of Marie-Antoinette the reader has to choose between hagiography and demonology. G. Lenôtre, *La Captivité et la Mort de Marie-Antoinette* (Paris 1897), and E. Campardon, *Marie-Antoinette à la Conciergerie* (Paris 1863), are both sympathetic; Gerard Walter, *Marie-Antoinette* (Paris 1948), hostile. The trial proceedings, such as they were, were published in the *Acte d'Accusation* and the *Bulletin* of the *Tribunal Révolutionnaire*. The period following Louis XVI's death saw a renewed burst of violent pornography, elaborating on such earlier items as *L'Autrichienne en Goguettes ou l'Orgie Royale* or purporting to be new works, such as *La Journée Amoureuse ou les Derniers Plaisirs de Marie-Antoinette*, in which Lamballe supplies every kind of sexual pleasure for the Queen while she masturbates an enfeebled Louis. These pornographic pieces in turn stimulated a genre of hate literature of which the *Père Duchesne* was by no means the most vitriolic. For some choice items, see *J'Attends le Procès de Marie-Antoinette*, in which the guillotine itself gloats over the Queen's fate: "You are already in a cell; come one step more and I await you; a pretty head like yours makes a fine ornament for my machine." The *Grande Motion des Citoyennes de Divers Marchés* is another chorus for death to the "*bougresse*" but advocated that she be flogged and burned before decapitation.

For the other notable women victims, see Guy Chaussinand-Nogaret, *Madame Roland* (Paris 1985), and Olivier Blanc, *Olympe de Gouges* (Paris 1981). Darline Gay Levy, Harriet Branson Applewhite and Mary Durham Johnson, in *Women in Revolutionary Paris* (Urbana, Ill., 1979), deal with the Jacobins' attitude to the women's political clubs and societies and their response. See also Dominique Godineau, *Citoyennes Tricoteuses*.

On the use of the guillotine as political theater and the mechanization of killing, see Arasse, *La Guillotine et l'Imaginaire* (97 –164). On Fouquier-Tinville and the routine of the Tribunal, see Albert Croquez and Georges Loubie, *Fouquier-Tinville: L'Accusateur Public* (Paris 1945).

For the immensely complicated swindle of the "Pourris," see Norman Hampson, "François Chabot and His Plot," in *Transactions of the Royal Historical Society* (1976, 1 –14); see also Louis Jacob, *Fabre d'Eglantine* (168 –274). Albert Mathiez published a great number of articles attacking Danton for corruption, and just as heatedly Alphonse Aulard defended him. Much of this literature is reviewed in an essay, essentially sympathetic to Mathiez's case, but more open to argument, by George Lefebvre, "Sur Danton," reprinted in his *Etudes sur la Révolution Française* (Paris 1963). For a more balanced treatments of the close of Danton's career, see Norman Hampson's excellent biography and the vivid and engaging portrait by Frédéric Bluche, *Danton* (Paris 1968). Desmoulins still needs a new modern biography. See J. Claretie, *Camille Desmoulins, Lucile Desmoulins, Etude sur les Dantonistes* (Paris 1875). The brilliance of the journalistic strategy of the *Vieux Cordelier* has at last been recognized in an important article by Georges Benrekassa, "Camille Desmoulins, Ecrivain Révolutionnaire: 'Le Vieux Cordelier,'" in Bonnet et al. (eds.), *La Carmagnole des Muses* (223 –41). The seven numbers of the journal were prepared in a critical edition by Henri Calvet (Paris 1936), though ideally they should be experienced *without* any critical mediation.

CHAPTER NINETEEN

CHILIASM

For the destruction of Malesherbes' family, see Grosclaude, *Malesherbes* (chapters 16 and 17). See also the *Mémoires* of Hervé de Tocqueville, utilized by André Jardin, *Tocqueville: A Biography* (trans. Lydia Davis and Robert Hemenway, New York 1988); and R. R. Palmer (ed.), *The Two Tocquevilles, Father and Son: Hervé and Alexis de Tocqueville on the Coming of the French Revolution* (Princeton 1987).

For the attack on "vandalism," see the excellent essay by Anthony Vidler, "Grégoire, Lenoir et les 'Monuments Parlants,'" in Bonnet et al. (eds.), *La Carmagnole des Muses* (131 – 51). On the Feast of the Supreme Being, see Ozouf, *Festivals*; Biver, *Fêtes*; and especially Julien Tiersot, *Les Fêtes*, 122 –68, who explains more fully than other accounts the essentially musical conception of both the morning and afternoon assemblies. For David's part, see Dowd, *Pageant-Master of the Republic*, and Warren Roberts' forthcoming study. On the abrupt promotion of Désorgues, see Michel Vovelle, *Théodore Désorgues ou la Désorganisation, Aix-Paris 1763 – 1808* (Paris 1985).

Figures of executions during the Grande Terreur are given in Greer, *The Incidence of the Terror.* Richard T. Bienvenu, *The Ninth of Thermidor: The Fall of Robespierre* (New York, London and Toronto 1968), is a helpful anthology of edited documents with a detailed critical guide to events. They may also be followed in the recent biographies, notably Jordan's and Hampson's. One of the liveliest accounts is in the older biography by J. M. Thompson, *Robespierre* (2 vols., Oxford 1935). For an orthodox Jacobin view, see Gerard Walter, *La Conjuration du Neuf Thermidor* (Paris 1974).

The leonine survivor of the royal menagerie is described by Raoul Hesdin in *The Journal of a Spy in Paris During the Reign of Terror* (New York 1896, 201 –02).

E P I L O G U E

I have not attempted any kind of general survey of the consequences of the Revolution but have tried instead to summarize the fate of some of the principal enterprises narrated in the book, in particular the doomed attempt to reconcile political liberty with a patriot state. There are, however, a number of important works dealing with the period between Thermidor and Brumaire, which was, in its own right, an important chapter of the French Revolution. See in particular, Martyn Lyons, *France under the Directory* (London 1975); M. J. Sydenham, *The First French Republic 1792 – 1804* (London 1974); and Denis Woronoff, *The Thermidorean Regime and the Directory 1794 – 1799* (London 1984). For the fate of revolutionary politics in this period, see Isser Woloch, *Jacobin Legacy: The Democratic Movement under the Directory* (Princeton 1970), and R. B. Rose, *Gracchus Babeuf: The First Revolutionary Communist* (London 1978).

Overshadowing all these, however, is the remarkable synthesis by D.M.G. Sutherland, *France 1789 – 1815: Revolution and Counterrevolution* (London 1985). (See below.)

On the social results of the Jacobin revolution, see Richard Cobb, "Quelques Conséquences Sociales de la Révolution dans un Milieu Urbain," in his *Terreur et Subsistances*, in which he concludes that for the majority of the Lillois, the year II was not a happy experience. Cobb has also written movingly in the same work, in *The Police and the People* and in *Reactions to the French Revolution*, of the problems of dearth that affected many parts of France in the year III, as well as the Counter-Terror in Lyon and the Midi. See also Colin Lucas's essay "Themes in Southern Violence after 9 Thermidor," in Lucas and Gwynn Lewis, *Beyond the Terror: Essays in French Regional and Social History* (Cambridge, England, 1983).

Robert Forster argued strongly that the nobility was radically destroyed as the result of the Revolution, in "The Survival of the French Nobility During the French Revolution" in *Past and Present* (1967). I incline to the more nuanced and conservative view—of this as of other aspects of the attempted restructuring of social relations—offered in Louis Bergeron's excellent work *France under Napoleon* (trans. R. R. Palmer, Princeton 1981).

For Talleyrand in America, see Michel Poniatowski, *Talleyrand aux Etats-Unis 1794 – 1796* (Paris 1967), and Hans Huth and Wilma J. Pugh, *Talleyrand in America as a Financial Promoter: Unpublished Letters and Memoirs* (Washington, D.C., 1942). For Lafayette in prison, see Peter Buckman, *Lafayette: A Biography* (New York and London 1977, 217 – 34). Mme de La Tour du Pin's stay in America is movingly described in her *Journal.* For the madness of Théroigne de Méricourt, see J.-F. Esquirol, *Les Maladies Mentales* (2 vols., Paris 1838, vol. 1, 445–51).

There are several general works to be strongly recommended to any student of the French Revolution. For the collapse of the monarchy, William Doyle's *Origins of the French Revolution* (Oxford 1980) is a brilliant analysis and succinct narrative of events leading to 1789. It has an excellent introduction on the historiographical debates (which for the most part I have deliberately avoided). Another excellent account of conflicting interpretations may be found in J. M. Roberts, *The French Revolution* (Oxford 1978).

D.M.G. Sutherland's *France 1789–1815: Revolution and Counterrevolution* is one of the most remarkable histories to have appeared in a long time, for the subtlety of much of its argument, the richness of its detail and its extended chronological scope (perhaps 1774 to 1815 was too much to ask for). It is, overwhelmingly, a social rather than a political or cultural history, and thus offers an implicit interpretation of where the significance of the Revolution lies. It will be apparent that my own emphasis is in the opposite direction and in many respects follows the path first tracked by Alfred Cobban, whose essay "Myth of the French Revolution" was once thought so scandalous and whose *Social Interpretation of the French Revolution* (Cambridge, England, 1964) has since become a classic of historical reinterpretation. Much of the extraordinary writing of Richard Cobb reconstructed the lives of many who survived and endured the Revolution, rather than being placed on center stage by it. By claiming the "irrelevance" of the Revolution to those enduring rhythms of abundance and want, crime and desperation, he necessarily raised the question, "If the Revolution was *not* a social transformation, what was it at all?"

Increasingly the answer has been found in the realm of political culture, and François Furet's *Penser la Révolution* (Paris 1978), translated as *Interpreting the French Revolution*, was of fundamental importance in redirecting revolutionary history back towards politics. The books of Lynn Hunt and Mona Ozouf sustained this imaginative insistence on the power of cultural phenomena—images and icons, speeches, festivals (and one might add, newspapers and songs)—to remodel allegiance. Ultimately, the Revolution gave birth to a new kind of political community sustained more by rhetorical adrenaline than organized institutions. It was, therefore, doomed to self-destruct from overinflated expectations. Rousseau, after all, had warned (more or less) that to expect a Republic of Virtue to become instituted in a Great State was to ask for pie in the sky.

INDEX

Ripet, Jean, 785
Rivarol, Antoine, 124, 126
Robert, *illus. 129*, 130
Robert, François, 566, 613, 646
Robert, Hubert, 389, *illus. 390, 821*, 829, 846
Robert, Louise, 530, 566
Robespierre, Augustin, 845
Robespierre, Maximilien de, xvi, 153, 445, 451, 480, 542, 560, 569, 577–80, *illus. 578*, 583, 584, 602, 604, 610, 734, 753, 779–80, 792, 806–16, *illus. 843, 850*, 851–2, 858; and "abdication" petition, 567–8; arrest of, 844–5, *illus. 845*; assassination attempt on, 836; on capital punishment, 621; on clergy, 585; and Committee of Public Safety, 707; in Constituent Assembly, 498; in Convention, 646–9, 722, 723, 725; and Danton's arrest and trial, 816–18, 820; David and, 572; and dechristianization, 778–9; and economic crisis, 709, 710; education of, 170, 380; in Estates-General, 354; execution of, 846, 851; on execution of Louis XVI, *illus. 674*; fall of, 839–42; *fédérés* and, 605; and flight of royal family, 555, 560; Girondins and, 716; de Gouges' attacks on, 802; *Indulgents* and, 813–16; and insurrection, 611, 613, 615; in Insurrectionary Commune, 624, 626; and law of Prairial, 837; Le Chapelier refuted by, 577, 579–80; at Lepeletier's funeral, 673; Malesherbes and, 656; Mirabeau and, 546; oratory of, 168, 529; on property rights, 755; and public instruction, 827–31, 834, 836; Saint-Just and, 578, 651; Terror and, 756, 758, 768; and trial of Louis XVI, 652, 659, 662, 663; during war, 601, 643, 708; war opposed by, 595, 597
Robin, Abbé, 48
Rochambeau, Jean-Baptiste Donatien de Vimeur, Comte de, 599, 600, 870
Roche, Daniel, 180
Roederer, Pierre Louis, Comte de, 614
Rohan, Louis, Cardinal de, *illus. 204*, 205–10, 655
Rohring, Captain Léonard, 554
Roland, Eudora, 802

Roland, Manon Philipon, 153, 159–60, 171, 568, 583, 595, 605, 728, 729, 737, 800, 802, 859
Roland de La Platière, Jean-Marie, 192, 517, 596, 605, 623, 632, 646, 649, 652, 709, 718, 722, 802–3
Rolland, 827
Romainville, Antoine de, 120
Roman Republic, 32, 169–74, 861
Romanticism, 46, 60, 354, 398; ballooning and, 128; of Guibert, 257; hatred of New in, 209; heroes and martyrs and, 546; history and, xiii, 5, 7; and hostility toward *financiers*, 72; identity and, 394; Lafayette and, 26; and *levée en masse*, 760; of Mercier, 198; Mirabeau and, 341; oratory and, 168; in poetry, 572; of Robert, 389; in theater, 495; war and, 593; *see also sensibilité*
Romilly, Samuel, 295–6, 354, 853
Roncours, Prudent de, 179
Ronsin, Charles Philippe Henri, 168, 776, 789, 805, 813–15, 825
Roosevelt, Franklin, 283
Root-Bernstein, Michele, 133
Rosanbo, Lepeletier de, 823–6
Rosanbo, Louis de, 826
Rosanbo, Marguerite de, 823, 824, 826–7
Rossel, C. A., 32
Rossignol, Jean Antoine, 614, 790–1
Rostan, Joseph-Marie, 785
Rothschild family, 288
Rouen: ballooning at, 128; book smuggling in, 179, 181; *cahier* of, 311; clergy in, 350; crops destroyed in, 305; industrialization in, 193–4; lead mills in, 83; Parlement of, 32, 104, 117, 272, 856; prolific mothers honored in, 522; riots in, 419, 527; Roland de La Platière's suicide in, 802–3; trade through, 520; transport to, 189; unemployment in, 307
Rouget de Lisle, Claude Joseph, 598, 599, 611
Rousseau, Jean-Jacques, 8, 44, 48, 89, 139, 164, 175, 180, 181, 197, 291, 322, 506, 565, 621, 665, 829, 861, 869; d'Antraigues and, 300; d'Argenson and, 113; ballooning and, 129, 131;

PHOTOGRAPHIC CREDITS
(by figure numbers)

C. N. Ledoux, *L'Architecture*, Princeton University Press, New Jersey: 23.

Author's collection: 71.

Bibliothèque Nationale, Paris, France: 8, 13, 14, 15, 19, 20, 21, 27, 28, 30, 36, 53, 54, 55, 56, 64, 65, 66, 69, 70, 74, 78, 79, 80, 83, 84, 85, 87, 90, 91, 92, 122, 126, 128, 129, 135, 136, 137, 138, 139, 140, 141, 142, 143, 144, 145, 150, 153, 154, 155, 156, 157, 158, 161, 162, 164, 171, 172, 173, 174, 177, 183, 186, 190, 191, 193, 194, 197, 200, 212, 214.

Collection, Comte de Castellane, Paris, France (Photo Giraudon): 6.

Collection, Célébrités Français, Paris, France (Photo Giraudon): 35.

Collection, Château de Valençay, France: 4.

Collection, Château de Versailles, France: 17 (Photo Giraudon).

Cincinnati Art Museum, Ohio: 33 (Bequest of Herbert Greer French, 1943).

Sterling and Francine Clark Art Institute, Williamstown, Massachusetts: 60 (1785).

J. Paul Getty Museum, Malibu, California: 32 (circa 1818 – 1819, glass enameled metal, gilt-bronze, 4'3" x 3'2").

Journal d'Autre Monde, Paris, France: 210 (1794).

By permission of the Houghton Library, Harvard University, Cambridge, Massachusetts: 2, 10, 11, 18, 22, 29, 31, 38, 41, 45, 46, 47, 48, 68, 195, 203 (The Charles Motley Clark Memorial).

Kimball Art Museum, Fort Worth, Texas: 58 (circa 1781).

Kress Library, Harvard University, Cambridge, Massachusetts: 12, 50, 51, 52.

Metropolitan Museum of Art, New York: 16 (Bequest of William H. Huntington, 1883), 24 (Purchase, Mr. and Mrs. Charles Wrightsman Gift, 1977), 61 (Bequest of Edward S. Harkness, 1940).

Musée des Beaux Arts, Lille, France: 9 (1781), 42, 160 (Photos Giraudon), 175.

Collection, Musée Dauphinois, Grenoble, France: 76 (1889).

Musée Lambinet, Versailles, France: 178.

Musée du Louvre, Paris, France: 5, 37, 44, 49, 88, 124, 125, 147, 148, 149, 169, 188 (Photos Lauros-Giraudon).

Musée Municipale de Limoges, France: 25.

Cliché des Musées Nationaux, Paris, France: 3, 63.

Musée Nissim de Camondo, Paris, France: 26 (Photo Laurent Sully Jaulmes).

Musée de la Ville de Paris, France: 1, 75, 81, 82, 86, 89 (20 June 1789), 93, 94, 95 (12 July 1789), 96, 97, 98, 99 (Photo M. Toumazet), 100, 101, 102, 103 (Photo Andreani), 104 (23 July 1789), 105 (14 July 1789), 106, 107, 108, 109, 110 (Photo Berthier), 111, 112, 113, 114, 115, 116, 117, 118, 119, 120, 121, 123, 127, 130, 131, 132, 133, 134, 146, 151, 152, 159, 163, 165, 166, 167, 168, 170, 176, 179, 180, 184, 185, 189, 192, 196, 198, 199, 201, 202, 204, 205, 206, 208, 209, 211 (Photo Giraudon), 213.

Courtesy Museum of Fine Arts, Boston, Massachusetts: 39 (circa 1780, Purchase, Jessie H. Wilkinson, Grant Walker, Seth K. Sweetser Residuary, and Abbott Lawrence Funds, 1976).

National Gallery of Art, Washington, D.C.: 7 (Rosenwald Collection, Bocher 1882), 34 (Widener Collection, 1787).

National Galleries of Scotland, Edinburgh: 40.

The National Trust, Waddesdon Manor, Aylesbury, England: 59 (1783, Collection, Baron Ferdinand de Rothschild).

Overijssel Provincial Museum, Netherlands: 73.

Private collection: 77 (1792), 207.

Rijksmuseum voor Volkskunde, Arnhem, Netherlands: 72.

The Royal Collection, London: 67.

Royal Museum of Fine Arts, Brussels, Belgium: 181, 182.

Virginia Museum of Fine Arts, Richmond, Virginia: 57 (1784, Gift of Mrs. A. D. Williams, 1949).

Collection, Princesse von Hessen und bei Rhein, Darmstadt, West Germany: 62 (Photo Giraudon).

Witt Library, Courtauld Institute of Art, University of London, England: 43 (Collection, Marquis de Laborde, Paris).

A NOTE ON THE TYPE

This book was set in a digitized version of Janson. The hot-metal version of Janson was a recutting made direct from type cast from matrices long thought to have been made by the Dutchman Anton Janson, who was a practicing type founder in Leipzig during the years 1668 – 1687. However, it has been conclusively demonstrated that these types are actually the work of Nicholas Kis (1650 – 1702), a Hungarian, who most probably learned his trade from the master Dutch type founder Dirk Voskens. The type is an excellent example of the influential and sturdy Dutch types that prevailed in England up to the time William Caslon (1692 – 1766) developed his own incomparable designs from them.

Composed by The Haddon Craftsmen, Inc.,
Scranton, Pennsylvania

Printed and bound by Halliday Lithographers,
West Hanover, Massachusetts

Designed by Iris Weinstein